D1212545

T. M. Healy

T. M. Healy

FRANK CALLANAN

CORK UNIVERSITY PRESS

. . . but hunt me the journeyon, iteritinerant, the kal his course, amid the seminary of Somnionia. Even unto Heliotropolis, the castellated, the enchanting.

James Joyce, *Finnegans Wake*

In memory of
Richard Callanan and Margaret McGuinness
Francis Magan and Sybil Stanton
Ellen Macken

First published in 1996 by
Cork University Press
University College
Cork
Ireland

British Library Cataloguing in Publication Data
A CIP catalogue record for this book is available from the British Library.

ISBN 1 85918 009 4

Typeset by Tower Books of Ballincollig, Co. Cork
Printed by ColourBooks, Baldoyle, Co. Dublin

Contents

Acknowledgements

I am greatly indebted to Conor and Maire Cruise O'Brien for encouragement and inspiration over a considerable number of years. As a friend, and authority on Irish nationalism and unionism, Dr. Margaret O'Callaghan has been an unfailing source of support. If there is a tendency to write with a single critical reader in mind, it was Margaret in this instance.

Patrick Healy has by his scholarship, wit and friendship sustained me in writing this work, on the proofs of which he has perceptively commented. Dr. Deirdre McMahon has enlarged my understanding of the treaty negotiations and the establishment of the Irish Free State. I acknowledge my debt to Dr. George A. Colburn, whose pioneering 1971 doctoral thesis at Michigan State University on T. M. Healy and the Home Rule Movement was of considerable assistance. I thank Gerard Torsney for his advice, and the benefit of reading his 1980 M.A. thesis for University College Dublin on the Monarchy in the Irish Free State, 1922–32.

Patrick MacEntee has given polite but firm encouragement. Peter Kenneally has valiantly striven to keep me abreast of contemporary political theory, as well as commenting on my progress with Waughesque asperity. Ivan Kelly has provided a Catalan perspective.

I am grateful to Michael Foot, Lord Jenkins of Hillhead, and Robert Kee for the benefit of discussing Parnell and Healy with them. I thank Jonathan Armstrong, Dr. B. S. Benedikz, Seamus Helferty, Paul Dunne and David

Sheehy for their assistance. James Dillon, Sean MacBride and Thomas V. Murphy, all now deceased, kindly spoke to me in relation to the subject matter of this book.

Dr. T. M. Healy has been throughout helpful, and has observed an enlightened neutrality in relation to my treatment of the subject for which I cannot adequately thank him. Independent Newspapers have provided a number of the photographs of T. M. Healy which are here reproduced.

I am obliged also to Eileen Battersby; Prof. Terence Brown; Julian Deale; Robert Dore; T. A. Finlay; Prof. Tom Garvin; Oliver St. John Gogarty SC; Jerry Healy SC; Michael Holroyd; Roddy Horan; Charles Lysaght; Prof. Patrick Lynch; Proinsias Mac Aonghusa; Prof. Donal Macartney; Prof. W. J. Mc Cormack; Brian Murphy; Rex Mackey SC; Fiona Reddington; Seamus Sorahan SC; Ralph Sutton SC.

My friends have gracefully borne an extended vicarious acquaintanceship with T. M. Healy. I thank in particular Maurice Biggar, Daniel Brown, Laurence Browne, Una Clarke, Kyran FitzGerald, Peter Flood, Eugene Gleeson, Gerry Harrison, Anne Marie Johnston, Cecily Kelleher, Vaughan Kinghan, James McGeachie, Diarmuid McGuinness, Eamon O'Flaherty, and Sally O'Sullivan. I remember Dr. Vibeke Sørensen. I thank my family.

For permission to make use of and to quote from various collections of papers I am grateful to the following: the Director and Trustees of the National Library, Dublin; the Director of the National Archive, Dublin; University College, Dublin; the Board of Trinity College Dublin; the Council of the Bar of Ireland; the Honourable Society of Grays Inn; the Honourable Society of the Kings Inns; the Historical Library of the Religious Society of Friends in Ireland; His Grace the Archbishop of Dublin; the Trustees of the National Library of Scotland; the British Library; the Record Office of the House of Lords, and the Trustees of the Beaverbrook Foundation; Dr. T. M. Healy; Mrs. Dorothy Walker; Mrs. Nuala Jordan; Sir William Gladstone and Sir John Moberley. I thank the staff of the National Library for their unfailing civility.

Eileen Francis and my publishers have by their skill made possible the astonishingly rapid publication of this book, after years of malingering research and writing on the part of its author.

T. M. Healy can no longer carry out the threat he levelled at Liam O'Flaherty, to write his biographer's life. However, as I have invested a very considerable amount of time over close on two decades to his life and rhetoric, there is at least a certain balance of jeopardy.

Frank Callanan
Dublin, 1 September 1996

List of Abbreviations

I Writings and Correspondence of T. M. Healy

Healy, 'Rise and Fall'	T. M. Healy, 'The Rise and Fall of Mr. Parnell, *New Review*, vol. IV (Mar. 1891), pp. 194–203
Healy, 'A Great Man's Fancies'	T. M. Healy, 'A Great Man's Fancies, Some Reminiscences of Charles Stewart Parnell', *Westminster Gazette*, 2–3 Nov. 1893
Healy, *Why Ireland is Not Free*	T. M. Healy, *Why Ireland Is Not Free, A Study of Twenty Years in Politics* (Dublin, 1898)
Letters and Leaders	*T. M. Healy, Letters and Leaders of My Day* (2 vols., London, 1928)
Letters and Leaders, Proofs	Galley Proofs for *Letters and Leaders*, Beaverbrook Papers c/167, House of Lords Records Office
Healy typescripts	Typescripts of letters of T. M. Healy to Maurice Healy 1892–1923, Healy–Sullivan Papers, UCD P6/E/2

II Other Works and Sources

Arnstein, *Bradlaugh*	Walter L. Arnstein, *The Bradlaugh Case, Atheism, Sex and Politics Among the Late Victorians* (Columbia, 1983)
Beaverbrook, *Decline and Fall of Lloyd George*	Beaverbrook, *The Decline and Fall of Lloyd George* (London, 1963)
Bew, *Parnell,*	Paul Bew, *C. S. Parnell* (Dublin, 1980)

Byrne, *Parnell*	Edward Byrne, *Parnell, A Memoir,* ed. Frank Callanan (Dublin, 1981)
Callanan, *Parnell Split*	Frank Callanan, *The Parnell Split, 1890–1* (Cork, 1992)
Chamberlain, *Political Memoir*	*Joseph Chamberlain, A Political Memoir 1880–92*, ed. C. D. H. Howard (London, 1953)
Chisholm and Davie, *Beaverbrook*	Anne Chisholm and Michael Davie, *Beaverbrook, A Life* (London, 1992)
Cooke and Vincent, *Governing Passion*	A. B. Cooke and John Vincent, *The Governing Passion* (Sussex, 1974)
Dangerfield, *Damnable Question*	George Dangerfield, *The Damnable Question, A Study in Anglo-Irish Relations* (London, 1976)
Davitt, *Fall of Feudalism*	Michael Davitt, *The Fall of Feudalism in Feudalism Ireland* (London and New York, 1974)
Devoy, *Post Bag*	John Devoy, *Devoy's Post Bag*, ed. William O'Brien and Desmond Ryan (2 vols., Dublin, 1948 and 1953)
Foster, *Parnell*	R. F. Foster, *Charles Stewart Parnell, The Man and his Family* (2nd ed., London, 1979)
Frederic, 'The Ireland of Today'	'The Ireland of Today', by 'X', in *Fortnightly Review*, no. 323 (1 Nov. 1893), pp. 686—706
Frederic, 'The Rhetoricians of Ireland'	'The Rhetoricians of Ireland', by 'X', in *Fortnightly Review*, no. 324 (1 Dec. 1893), pp. 713—27
Frederic, 'The Ireland of Tomorrow'	'The Ireland of Tomorrow', by 'X', in *Fortnightly Review*, no. 325 (1 Jan. 1894), pp. 1—18
Gwynn, *Redmond*	Denis Gwynn, *The Life of John Redmond* (London, 1932)
Hamilton diary	E. W. Hamilton diaries, 1880—1906, BM Add. MS 48630—48683.
Hamilton, *Diary*	E. W. Hamilton, *The Diary of Sir Edward Walter Hamilton 1880–5*, ed. Dudley W. R. Bahlman (2 vols., Cambridge, 1972); E. W. Hamilton, *The Diary of Sir Edward Walter Hamilton 1885–1906*, ed. Dudley W. R. Bahlman (Hull, 1993). The 1993 volume is here referred to as volume iii.
Hammond, *Gladstone*	J. L. Hammond, *Gladstone and the Irish Nation* (London, 1938)
Harrison, *Parnell, Chamberlain, Garvin*	Henry Harrison, *Parnell, Joseph Chamberlain, and Mr. Garvin* (Dublin and London, 1938)
Harrison, *Parnell Vindicated*	Henry Harrison, *Parnell Vindicated, The Lifting of the Veil* (London, 1931)
M. Healy, *Munster Circuit*	Maurice Healy, *The Old Munster Circuit* (London and Dublin, 1939)
Heyck, *Radicalism*	Thomas William Heyck, *The Dimensions of British Radicalism, The Case of Ireland, 1874–95* (Illinois, 1974)
Hind, *Labouchere*	R. J. Hind, *Henry Labouchere and the Empire 1880–1905* (London, 1972)
Irish Party Minutes	Minutes of the Irish Parliamentary Party: (1) 7 Apr. 1880—5 May 1885, TCD MS 9223; (2) 11 Jan. 1886

	to 4 Dec. 1890, Dillon Papers TCD MS 6500; (2) 11 Dec. 1890 to 24 June 1895, Dillon Papers, TCD MS 6501.
Jenkins, *Gladstone*	Roy Jenkins, *Gladstone* (London, 1995)
Jones, *Whitehall Diary*	*Thomas Jones, Whitehall Diary*, ed. Keith Middlemas (London, 1971), iii. Ireland 1918–25
James Joyce, *Finnegans Wake*	James Joyce, *Finnegans Wake* (London, 1939; Faber ed., 1975)
James Joyce, *Ulysses*	James Joyce, *Ulysses* (Paris, 1922; Bodley Head ed., corrected text ed. H. W. Gabler, London, 1986)
Kee, *Laurel and the Ivy*	Robert Kee, *The Laurel and the Ivy, The Story of Charles Stewart Parnell and Irish Nationalism* (London, 1993)
Kettle, *Material for Victory*	Andrew J. Kettle, *Material for Victory*, ed. L. J. Kettle (Dublin, 1958)
Laffan, *Partition*	Michael Laffan, *The Partition of Ireland 1911–1925* (Dublin, 1987)
Larkin, *Fall*	Emmet Larkin, *The Roman Catholic Church in Ireland and the Fall of Parnell 1889* (Liverpool, 1979)
Larkin, *James Larkin*	Emmet Larkin, *James Larkin, Irish Labour Leader 1876–1947* (London, 1989)
Leamy, *Parnell's Faithful Few*	Margaret Leamy, *Parnell's Faithful Few* (New York, 1936)
Lee, *Ireland*	J. J. Lee, *Ireland 1912–1985, Politics and Society* (Cambridge, 1989)
'The Liffey at Ebb Tide'	United Irish League, *'The Liffey at Ebb Tide' Mr. William O'Brien's opinion of Mr. T. M. Healy M.P. and Mr. T. M. Healy's opinion of Mr. William O'Brien M.P.* (Dublin, 1910)
Lucy, *Balfourian Parliament*	H. W. Lucy, *The Balfourian Parliament 1900-1905* (London, 1906)
Lucy, *Home Rule Parliament*	H. W. Lucy, *A Diary of the Home Rule Parliament, 1892-1895* (London, 1896)
Lucy, *Salisbury*	H. W. Lucy, *A Diary of the Salisbury Parliament 1886–92* (London, 1892)
Lucy, *Unionist Parliament*	H. W. Lucy, *A Diary of the Unionist Parliament 1895-1900* (London, 1901)
Lyons, *Dillon*	F. S. L. Lyons, *John Dillon, A Biography* (London, 1968)
Lyons, 'Economic Ideas of Parnell'	F. S. L. Lyons, 'The Economic Ideas of Ideas of Parnell' *Historical Studies* ii. ed. Michael Roberts (London, 1959), pp. 60–78
Lyons, *Fall*	F. S. L. Lyons, *The Fall of Parnell* (London, 1960)
Lyons, *Irish Parliamentary Party*	F. S. L. Lyons, *The Irish Parliamentary Party 1890–1910* (London, 1951)
Lyons, *Parnell*	F. S. L. Lyons, *Charles Stewart Parnell* (London, 1978)

Lyons, 'Political Ideas of Parnell'	F. S. L. Lyons, 'The Political Ideas of Parnell', *Historical Journal*, xvi. 4 (1973), pp. 749–75
Macardle, *Irish Republic*	Dorothy Macardle, *The Irish Republic* (London, 1937; 4th ed., Dublin, 1951)
McCarthy and Praed, *Book of Memories*	Justin McCarthy and Mrs. Campbell Praed, *Our Book of Memories* (London, 1912)
McCarthy and Praed, *Book of Memories* Draft	Draft of *Our Book of Memories* including Book of original of many typescript letters, NLI MS 24958
MacDonagh, *Home Rule Movement*	Michael MacDonagh, *The Home Rule Movement* (Dublin, 1920)
McDonald, *Daily News Diary*	John McDonald, *Diary of the Parnell Diary Commission,* revised from the *Daily News* (London, 1890)
Mansergh, *Unresolved Question*	Nicholas Mansergh, *The Unresolved Question, The Anglo--Irish Settlement and its Undoing 1912–72* (New Haven and London, 1991)
Moody, *Davitt*	T. W. Moody, *Davitt and Irish Revolution 1846–82* (Oxford, 1981)
Morley, *Gladstone*	John Morley, *The Life of William Ewart Gladstone* (3 vols., London, 1903)
J. V. O'Brien, *William O'Brien*	J. V. O'Brien *William O'Brien and the Case of Irish Politics 1889–1918* (Berkeley, Los Angeles, 1976)
C. C. O'Brien, *Parnell and his Party*	Conor Cruise O'Brien, *Parnell and his Party* (Oxford, 1957)
C. C. O'Brien, 'Timothy Healy'	Conor Cruise O'Brien, 'Timothy Michael Healy' in Conor Cruise O'Brien (ed.), *The Shaping of Modern Ireland* (London, 1970), pp. 164–73; reprinted in Conor Cruise O'Brien, *Writers and Politics* (London, 1965), pp. 128–36
R. B. O'Brien, *Parnell*	R. Barry O'Brien, *The Life of Charles Parnell 1846–91* (2 vols., London, 1898)
Sophie O'Brien, 'Recollections'	Sophie O'Brien, 'Recollections of a Long Life', unpublished typescript, O'Brien Papers, NLI MS 14218
W. O'Brien, *Evening Memories*	William O'Brien, *Evening Memories* (Dublin and London, 1920).
W. O'Brien, *Irish Revolution*	William O'Brien, *The Irish Revolution and how it came about* (London, 1923)
W. O'Brien, *Olive Branch in Ireland*	William O'Brien, *An Olive Branch in Ireland and its History* (London, 1910)
W. O'Brien, *Parnell*	William O'Brien, *The Parnell of Real Life* (London, 1926)
W O'Brien, *Recollections*	William O'Brien, *Recollections* (London, 1905)
W. O'Brien, 'Secret History'	William O'Brien, 'The Irish Free State: Secret History of its Foundation', unpublished manuscript in the hand of Sophie O'Brien, with an introduction by her, O'Brien Papers, NLI MS 4210

O'Casey, *Autobiographies*	Sean O'Casey, *Autobiographies, I (I Knock at the Door; Pictures in the Hallway; Drums under the Window), 2 (Inisfallen, Fare Thee Well; Rose and Crown; Sunset and Evening Star)* (repr. London, 1992)
O'Connor, *Memoirs*	T. P. O'Connor, *Memoirs of an Old Parliamentarian* (2 vols., London, 1928)
O'Connor, *Parnell*	T. P. O'Connor, *Charles Stewart Parnell, A Memory* (London, 1891)
O'Connor, *Parnell*	T. P. O'Connor, *The Parnell Movement* (2nd ed., London, 1886)
F. H. O'Donnell, *The Irish Party*	F. H. O'Donnell, *A History of the Irish Parliamentary Party* (2 vols., London, 1910)
F. H. O'Donnell, *The Lost Hat*	F. H. O'Donnell, *The Lost Hat, The Clergy, the Collection, the Hidden Life* (Dublin, n.d.)
O'Hegarty, *Ireland Under the Union*	P. S. O'Hegarty, *A History of Ireland Under the Union* (London, 1952)
O'Shea, *Parnell*	Katharine O'Shea (Parnell), *Charles Stewart Parnell, His Love Story and Political Life* (2 vols., London, 1914)
Packenham, *Peace by Ordeal*	Frank Pakenham (Lord Longford), *Peace by Ordeal The Negotiation of the Anglo-Irish Treaty, 1921* (London, 1935, re-issued 1992)
J. H. Parnell, *Parnell*	John Howard Parnell, *Charles Stewart Parnell, A Memoir* (London, 1916)
Plunket Barton, *Healy*	Sir Dunbar Plunket Barton, *Timothy Healy, Memories and Anecdotes* (Dublin, 1933)
Robbins, *Parnell*	Alfred Robbins, *Parnell, The Last Five Years* (London, 1926)
Sexton, *Governor-Generalship*	Brendan Sexton, *Ireland and the Crown, 1922–36, The Governor-Generalship of the Irish Free State* (Dublin, 1989)
Special Commission Brief	Special Commission Act 1888. Brief on behalf of Mr. C. S. Parnell M.P. and other Irish M.P.s against whom charges and allegations may be made. Lewis and Lewis Solicitors (including instructions, witnesses, proofs, etc.) NLI ILB 348, p. 8
S.C.P.	*Special Commission Act, 1888: Reprint of the Shorthand Note of the Speeches, Proceedings, and Evidence taken before the Commissioners appointed under the above named Act* (12 vols., London, 1890)
Donal Sullivan, *Room 15*	Donal Sullivan, *The Story of Room 15* (Dublin, 1891)
Maev Sullivan, *No Man's Man*	Maev Sullivan, *No Man's Man* (Dublin, 1943)
Maev Sullivan 'Tim Healy'	Maev Sullivan, Notes and Scripts for a second part of Healy's life (*c.* 1950–60, never completed), Healy–Sullivan Papers, UCD MS P6/E/5
T. D. Sullivan,	T. D. Sullivan, *Recollections of Times in Irish Politics* (Dublin, 1905)

Taylor, *Beaverbrook*	A. J. P. Taylor, *Beaverbrook* (London, 1972)
Thornley, *Butt*,	David Thornley, *Isaac Butt and Home Rule* (London, 1964)
Thorold, *Labouchere*	Algar Labouchere Thorold, *The Life of Henry Labouchere* (London, 1913)
Tynan, *Memories*	Katharine Tynan, *Memories* (London, 1924)
Tynan, *Twenty-Five Years*	Katharine Tynan, *Twenty-Five Years: Reminiscences* (London, 1913)
Under Which Flag?	*Under Which Flag? Or is Mr. Parnell to be the Leader of the Irish People?* by 'A Gutter Sparrow' (Dublin, n.d.)
Words of the Dead Chief	*Words of the Dead Chief, being extracts from the public speeches and other pronouncements of Charles Stewart Parnell, from the beginning to the close of his memorable life*, compiled by Jennie Wyse Power, with an introduction by Anna Parnell (Dublin, 1892)

III Newspaper Abbreviations

B.D.P.	*Birmingham Daily Post*
C.A.	*Cork Accent*
C.F.P.	*Cork Free Press*
D.C.	*Daily Chronicle*
D.E.	*Daily Express*
D.N.	*Daily News*
D. Nat.	*Daily Nation*
D.T.	*Daily Telegraph*
F.J.	*Freeman's Journal*
I.C.	*Irish Catholic*
I.I.	*Irish Independent*
I.N.	*Irish News*
I.T.	*Irish Times*
I.W.I.	*Irish Weekly Independent*
K.M.	*Kilkenny Moderator*
L.W.	*Labour World*
M.G.	*Manchester Guardian*
N.P.	*National Press*
N.Y.T.	*New York Times*
P.M.G.	*Pall Mall Gazette*
T.L.S.	*Times Literary Supplement*
U.I.	*United Ireland*
W.F.J.	*Weekly Freeman's Journal*
W.I.T.	*Weekly Irish Times*
W.N.	*Weekly Nation*
W.N.P.	*Weekly National Press*

IV Other Abbreviations

BM	British Museum
DDA	Dublin Diocesan Archive
NA	National Archives, Dublin
HC	House of Commons
NF	Irish National Federation
NL	Irish National League
NLI	National Library of Ireland
NLS	National Library of Scotland
RIC	Royal Irish Constabulary
TCD	Trinity College Dublin
UCD	University College Dublin

List of Illustrations

Between pp. 404 and 405:

Preface

On Saturday 6 December 1890 the Irish parliamentary party met in Committee Room 15 of the House of Commons, to decide the question of the chairmanship of the Irish party to which Parnell had been elected on the opening of parliament on 25 November. There had followed the publication by W. E. Gladstone of his letter to John Morley warning that Parnell's retention of the Irish leadership in the wake of the O'Shea divorce case would render his own leadership of the Liberal party 'almost a nullity'. Parnell had retaliated by an inflammatory manifesto to the people of Ireland. The existence of a clear majority against Parnell was already apparent from the Tuesday evening. The refusal the previous day of the Liberal leadership to give assurances in relation to the issues of land and police under home rule, which Parnell had put in issue in his manifesto, had removed whatever limited prospect there had been for Parnell's voluntary withdrawal.

Tempers were frayed, and the party was within hours of dissolution. There already had been an outbreak of bitter recrimination when Parnell called on his supporter John O'Connor, over the anti-Parnellite William Abraham. In the ensuing uproar, Parnell furiously snatched from Justin McCarthy Abraham's resolution terminating his chairmanship of the party, and thrust it crumpled into his pocket. Eventually order was restored, and John O'Connor spoke. Parnell was sitting sideways in the chair, tensely holding the *Freeman's Journal* open before him.

> *John O'Connor*: . . . Sir, you are leader of the Irish people, and when I say to some of my friends that they are acting wrongly in trying to depose you from that leadership, they say: 'We will have no one-man power – it is Mr. Parnell against the country. I deny that proposition' (*applause*). They say 'we will submit to no one-man power', and still every act of theirs goes to show that while rejecting you as their chief they place themselves unreservedly under the leadership of Mr. Gladstone (*cries of 'certainly not'*). They say 'no', but read Sir William Harcourt's letter; he says 'treat with Mr. Gladstone'.
>
> *Arthur O'Connor:* He is not a member of the party.
>
> *John Redmond:* The master of the party (*cheers and counter cheers*).
>
> *T. M. Healy:* Who is to be mistress of the party? (*cries of 'shame', noise, several members calling out remarks which could not be distinguished in the uproar*).
>
> *William Redmond:* They must be very badly off when they go to arguments like that.
>
> *A Voice:* It is true.
>
> *Arthur O'Connor:* I appeal to my friends (*noise*).
>
> *C. S. Parnell:* Better appeal to your own friends. Better appeal to that cowardly little scoundrel there (*noise*), that in an assembly of Irishmen dares to insult a woman (*loud cheers and counter cheers*).[1]

It was as Michael McDonagh later wrote 'magnificently said', and had a profound effect. Parnell had risen and appeared ready to strike Healy, his right arm fully extended and his clenched fist close to his face. Healy sat impassively 'with folded arms, unmoved either by Parnell's rhetoric or threat, or the hostile roar that hurtled about his head'.[2]

Healy lives in popular historical memory in Ireland largely for this interjection, taken as emblematic of his want of civility, his genius for provocation, and his abrogation of all restraint.

The career of T. M. Healy traces a great tracking movement. He was in the thick of Irish politics from the last years of Isaac Butt until shortly after the entry into the Dáil of Eamon de Valera's Fianna Fáil party in August 1927. In terms of British politics, his political involvement commenced in the era of Disraeli and Gladstone, and reached into that of Lloyd George, Bonar Law, and Stanley Baldwin. He confronted Lord Randolph Churchill and (rather less affectionately) Winston Churchill; Austen as well as Joseph Chamberlain. Drawn in the mid-1880s by the glittering cynicism of Henry Labouchere and Harold Frederic, he was two decades later the intimate of Lord Beaverbrook and the friend of F. E. Smith. Of those who opposed home rule, only Arthur Balfour and Edward Carson rivalled him in political longevity.

In Irish politics he pitted himself successively against Isaac Butt, Charles

Stewart Parnell, John Redmond, John Dillon, and Eamon de Valera. The only nationalist with a comparable period of active political involvement was John Devoy, who remained sequestered in New York. In continental politics, the span of his career matched that of Georges Clemenceau.[3]

Healy witnessed the dissolution of Irish parliamentarianism, which coincided with that of Irish unionism in its conventional form. He was the only member of Parnell's party to play an active, if largely ceremonial, role in the politics of the independent Irish state. Of the fractured rhythm of Healy's career, Conor Cruise O'Brien has noted that its peculiarity lay in the fact that 'its most positive period came before the death of Parnell and to a lesser extent after the rising of 1916 . . . In the three decades between – the years which would normally be those of the maturity and fulfilment of a public life – he is as active as ever, but squalidly in a sort of wilderness within a wilderness'.[4] Across that acrimonious quarter-century, Healy became, by a remarkable irony, the connecting figure between Parnell's Irish party and Sinn Féin. An improbable Talleyrand, whose survival owed rather more to chance than foresight, his career mediates the sharp narrative discontinuities of 1916–18.

One of the key figures in parliamentary nationalism, Healy remains the most elusive and neglected. He was widely discounted as an embittered maverick. His opposition to Parnell in the split became for Parnellites a fable of personal betrayal, his rhetoric a study in exhilarated vengeance. With Parnell's death, this became something on which Parnellites and moderate anti-Parnellites could comfortably agree. Healy as scoundrel became, as he had anticipated, to some extent a convenient scapegoat for the split itself.

Healy's attack on Parnell in 1890–1 was of unbridled vehemence, and charged with bitter personal animus, but he made of it the stuff of nationalist politics. Determined that the rejection of Parnell should become an enduring act of nationalist self-definition, he not merely assailed Parnell's Anglo-Irish provenance, but proclaimed a post-heroic nationalist era. He was nothing if not thoroughgoing. After Parnell's death he rapidly resumed his onslaughts, now directed at his successors. His estrangement was progressive. He came to question the idea of a dynamic, disciplined nationalist movement on the Parnellian model, which he proclaimed to be neither achievable nor especially desirable. He did much to deepen the disillusion of the years after the death of Parnell.

Healy's career has to be set against, as well as his contemporary rivals of the Parnell era, the ideologues of nationalism in the next generation, most notably D. P. Moran and Patrick Pearse. Healy did much to invent the idiom of modern nationalism. If Parnell was the soaring eminence who embodied the most austere conception of Irish statehood, the rhetoric of nationalism owed palpably more to Healy's influence.

Francis Cruise O'Brien's characterisation of Healy 'in a formulaic way as an Anarchist'[5] does not fully capture Healy's significance within Irish nationalism. He was a brilliant nay-sayer who exploited from the right the oppositional possibilities within nationalist politics. With extraordinary persistence, he insinuated into his attacks on his nationalist and Liberal adversaries, at their most seemingly wanton, the postulates of a conservative Catholic nationalism. His dissidence was that of a politician cunningly aligned to a nascent Catholic proprietorial order. He articulated a deep-seated resistance to the centralising ambitions of secular governance, whether British or Irish. Some of that recalcitrance is implicit in his punning conception of the Irish as 'a resolutionary race'.

Healy is remembered chiefly for the violence of his attack on Parnell, 1890–1. If his savagery of utterance was the most conspicuous feature of his language in the split and in the years that immediately followed (C. P. Curran referred to his 'blasts of unique vituperation')[6] it was not his only rhetorical mode. Whether in excoriation or pathos, he was an orator of surpassing fluency and verve. A barrister with a parodist's ear for the cadences of ideology, he was able brilliantly to rehearse the arguments of his opponents by a brief and cynical feat of imagination. He was moreover capable of a haunting lyricism: even his astonishing virulence had a strangely poetic vein.

Speaking in 1897, W. B. Yeats favoured the humour of insult over that of servility: 'the humour of insult has given us Swift, Mitchel, Tim Healy . . . Tim Healy is only divided from Swift by an abyss of genius'.[7] The poised qualification left the comparison intact. The Parnellite themes of Yeats' poetry enact an argument with Healy's proclamation of a post-heroic nationalism as much as a lament for the dead leader. From his lost first published poem, 'Et tu, Healy',[8] to *Finnegans Wake* Healy pervades Joyce's disconsolate aftermath of Parnell, exuding a sanctimonious villainy.

Healy has received little biographical attention. A rambling and inconsequential *Life of Tim Healy*, of which Liam O'Flaherty was the avowed author, was published by Jonathan Cape in 1927. Healy's daughter Maev Sullivan published her *No Man's Man* in 1943: its title, taken from Healy's declaration in his speech in the Leinster Hall on 20 November 1890 ('Servile to Parnell! Who is servile to him? I am no man's man but Ireland's!'), proclaimed its apologetic purpose.[9] Dealing with Healy's career up to the split, it contains some family information of interest, and conveys something of the embattled sense of allegiance of the Healy–Sullivan families. By far the most substantial source of biographical information was Healy's own memoirs, *Letters and Leaders of My Day* published in two volumes in 1928. Even though the correspondence of which they were comprised was evidently edited, they remained in the phrase of John Redmond's biographer 'disarmingly frank'.[10] Healy's was by far the most substantial political memoir of an Irish politician of his epoch.

The neglect of Healy in modern historiography owes much to the perception that there was no substantial body of private papers. There is a certain amount of Healy's correspondence in the Healy–Sullivan papers deposited in the archives of University College Dublin in 1992. It does not include the originals of the letters Healy wrote in shorthand to his brother Maurice, on which his memoirs were largely based (the correspondnce was one-sided: Healy had not preserved Maurice's letters to him).

It is however possible to reconstitute to a considerable extent Healy's letters. The early proofs of Healy's memoirs in the Beaverbrook papers in the House of Lords contain some material deleted from the published correspondence. These are substantially supplemented by typescripts of his letters in the Healy–Sullivan papers, commencing with Healy's letter of 12 January 1892 and ending with his last letter to Maurice of 2 November 1923 (the last letter published in the memoirs is that of 30 November 1922). These were prepared, evidently from the shorthand originals (which must therefore have been extant for some considerable time after Healy's death), at the direction of Maev Sullivan, who intended to complete a sequel on a more ambitious scale to *No Man's Man*.[11]

I have drawn extensively on the Healy typescripts in the third section of this book. While the correspondence relates to the period after Parnell's death, in its rotation it intermittently illuminates the hinterland of the earlier period. Alternating between defensiveness and self-congratulation, always caustic, and frequently witty, it affords the most detailed record of Healy's private thinking, especially in the critical years 1912–33. He was the privileged recipient of political intelligence which was frequently excellent, and was never less than revealing of contemporary perceptions. His letters provide a uniquely vivid chronicle of the decline of the Irish party, and chart the accommodation of a parliamentarian of the old order to the ascendancy of Sinn Féin.

I have generally chosen extracts from Healy's correspondence not pubished, or significantly abridged or edited, in *Letters and Leaders of My Day*. As with his speeches and journalism, I have frequently quoted extensively from his letters rather than paraphrased them, so as better to convey Healy's pungency of style, and his political temper. I have not duplicated the narrative of the split itself, nor the assessment of Parnell's campaign, contained in *The Parnell Split*.

Even though Healy outlived him by forty years, his biography remains in large measure the obverse of Parnell's. Almost from its inception, Healy was, at first secretively, the most incisive critic of the Parnell myth, which he turned with devastating effect against Parnell himself in the split. In all his controversies after Parnell's death, there was an inclement sub-text in which he bitterly disparaged Parnell's character and achievement. C. P. Curran commented of Healy's memoirs:

> Unlike Mme de Sevigné, he remembers not with tact but with design. His memory is not the peaceful gathering place of many harvests; it is an armoury where an old fighter moves about restlessly, picking up and polishing his old weapons, many of them still shining, some of them rusty and stained, and best forgotten. He kills his enemies again not without a certain anxiety that even yet they are not securely slain. Ghosts are hard to lay: they are impervious to the weapons of their first undoing.[12]

Above all, Healy never ceased to rehearse the controversy of the Parnell split, 1890-1.

Notes and References

1 *F.J.*, 8 Dec. 1890.
2 McDonagh, *Home Rule Movement*, pp. 220-1.
3 William O'Brien's wife Sophie considered that Healy and Clemenceau had marked temperamental affinities: Sophie O'Brien, *My Irish Friends* (Dublin and London, *c.* 1937), pp. 66-7.
4 C. C. O'Brien, 'Timothy Michael Healy', p. 165.
5 *Leader*, 9 Apr. 1910.
6 *Irish Statesman*, 23 Feb. 1929. Curran added in parenthesis: 'one of his former colleagues, now, perhaps, censorious, said that in this respect he leaves Joyce standing'.
7 *Lady Gregory's Diaries 1892-1902*, ed. James Pethica (Gerrard's Cross 1996), p. 287; Lady Gregory, *Seventy Years*, ed. Colin Smythe (Gerrard's Cross, 1974), p. 355; see also Stephen Gwynn, *Experiences of a Literary Man* (London, 1926), p. 108. Healy's purchase from the auction of his friend Larky Waldron in 1924 of 'a fine bust' of the Dean, a replica of the original in Trinity College, reflects Healy's own sense of affinity (Healy to Annie Healy, 21 Nov. 1924, Healy-Sullivan Papers, UCD P6/A/108).
8 Stanislaus Joyce, *My Brother's Keeper* (London, 1958), pp. 64-5; Richard Ellmann, *James Joyce* (2nd ed. with corrections, Oxford University Press, New York, 1983), p. 33.
9 Maev Sullivan, *No Man's Man*, p. 60. Conor Cruise O'Brien in the *Irish Times* unkindly observed that the book 'resembles less a piece of historical writing than a legal brief, prepared with such laborious rancour that it arrives half a century too late for the hearing of the action' (Conor O'Brien, 'Parnell and Tim Healy', *I.T.*, 8 Jan. 1944).
10 Gwynn, *Redmond*, p. 171.

11 There was in some degree an effort not to duplicate material in *Letters and Leaders* (see typist's note to the transcription of Healy's letter of 13 Jan. 1903, Healy typescripts). By way of random example, Healy's letter to Maurice of 23 Apr. 1923, which appears in the galley proofs, does not appear in either the published memoirs nor the typescripts; his letter of 5 Dec. 1915, which does not appear in the published memoirs, is in the proofs and the typescripts.

The typescripts therefore do not contain the entirety of the correspondence from 1892, and the deletion of some material from individual letters is indicated. The typescripts are however much fuller than the correspondence published in *Letters and Leaders.* In relation to the post-1915 period, it is noteworthy that while Healy in his correspondence with William O'Brien refers routinely to the 'Shins', the typescripts refer, with orthographic correctness and less disrespect, to 'Sinn Feiners', or occasionally 'Sinns'.

The fact that Maev Sullivan did not make use of the original correspondence to which she had access in *No Man's Man*, which relied chiefly on contemporary newspaper reports of speeches, suggests she was in two minds at that time in relation to the public opening of what could have proved from her point of view a Pandora's box.

At the time of writing *The Parnell Split* I was under the misapprehension that the typescripts were in fact those used by Healy in preparing his memoirs. I erred also in stating that the typing-up of the shorthand correspondence for the memoirs was undertaken by Healy's sister Lizzie rather than his daughter Liz (*Parnell Split*, pp. 308–9).

12 *Irish Statesman*, 23 Feb. 1929, C. P. Curran, 'The Reminiscences of Mr. Healy'.

— Part I —

T. M. Healy
and the
Rise of Parnell

1

Childhood and Exile

And well we hope the world may see,
    Ere many years have passed away,
The sons of patriot ancestry
    Again hold sway by Bantry Bay.
        T. D. Sullivan, 'Bantry Bay'[1]

Timothy Michael Healy was born in the town of Bantry, west Cork, on 17 May 1855, the second son of Maurice Healy and Eliza Sullivan. His father was a clerk of the Bantry Poor Law Union. His grandfather, Thomas Healy, formerly of Donoughmore, had settled in Bantry as a teacher of classics, following the profession of his father before him.

Tim Healy had what he described as 'a Spartan upbringing', presided over by a father of formidable austerity. Maurice Healy later admitted that in his youth, like many of his generation in Ireland, he had had Jansenistic tendencies. Rebuked by his confessor, he had sought to correct them.

Tim Healy's mother, Eliza, died when he was four, after giving birth to twins. One of them survived, Maurice, from whom Healy was to be inseparable. Healy's daughter wrote that Healy 'remembered a rainy day with pools of water on the ground where he was playing when he was called indoors and told his mother was dead', and recalled the coffins borne from the house in rain. He attributed the deafness in his right ear to falling asleep during a long drive with the rain beating down on his face, remarking that if he had had a mother's care this would not have befallen him.[2]

Wishing to quit after the death of his wife, Healy's father took up the clerkship of the Poor Law Union in Lismore, County Waterford in 1862. At the insistence of his mother-in-law, who nominated the bride, he remarried. In 1869, at the age of thirteen, after a meagre formal education with the Christian Brothers in Fermoy, Tim Healy, a boy endowed with a voracious power of assimilation and an enemy for life of the rules of grammar and the phonetic system, left Lismore. He went first to stay with his aunt and her husband T. D. Sullivan in Dublin, and then into exile in Newcastle-upon-Tyne. His childhood was prematurely at an end.[3]

Healy's upbringing was austere, although there is nothing to suggest it was unhappy. His was however a highly politicised childhood. He would later emotively praise Gladstone's first home rule bill as assuaging

> the intense feelings of bitterness that have been stored up as it were in a reservoir in this country for so many centuries and generations of men, and in their minds, bitterness I know myself is taught even the little children from their cradles . . .[4]

The historical remembrance of dispossession and famine cast a shadow upon Healy's childhood that darkened his persona and his political convictions.

The extended Healy family had originally held large tracts of land in East Muskerry centred on Donoughmore. Dispossessed after the forfeiture of the lands of Jacobite Earl of Clancarty after 1690, as Catholics under the penal laws they were ineligible to hold land other than on the precarious footing of tenants at will. One line of the Healys had prevailed in adversity by conforming to Protestantism. Of that line, Francis Healy married the daughter of a man who had acquired other parts of the former Healy lands. Their grandson Richard Hely-Hutchinson, created Earl of Donoughmore, was a prominent supporter of the Act of Union. A complex and shifting sequence hardened the genealogical lore of the Healy family into an enduring sense of sectarian dispossession. Healy's grandfather taught his sons that the family had been despoiled under the penal laws by a relative who turned Protestant to obtain their property. Healy's daughter described him as a descendant of 'the Catholic cousin who kept his faith and lost his lands'. Their kinsmen the Sullivans also bewailed the loss of ancestral lands.[5]

Healy's daughter was told that her grandfather had retained a trunk containing parchments relating to the Donoughmore lands. In Healy's childhood, deciding they were 'a source of pride and perhaps of rebellion or resentful feelings', he had burnt them. The incident is not recorded by Healy, who shared some of his father's reticence on the subject. As his daughter wrote, 'long descent where there is nothing to show for it is almost in bad taste, and although T. M. H. had a private pride in it, he felt that the less said about it the better'. She shrewdly surmised that 'this marriage of proud memories with present poverty was responsible for many of the contradictions in T.M.H's character', as well as of his 'fierce ardour in the cause of the Irish peasant'.[6]

The influence of a rancorous sense of ancestral dispossession, felt almost as a personal trauma, was to suffuse Healy's political rhetoric. Even at its most vehement, his agrarian rhetoric was deceptively conservative. His was an insistently restorationist idiom. The family's deeply felt sense of despoliation inspired in Healy an abiding preoccupation with the theme of dispossession. He wrote in 1881:

> The earliest records of Ireland, as well as of all other countries, relate to disputes concerning *land* . . . All the great invasions of history . . . had as a motive not merely a lust for conquest or the desire for extended sovereignty — their direct and principal object was to gain possession of the land of the conquered country. This is peculiarly the case with Ireland.[7]

His abiding fixation with dispossession drove him, when a busy King's Counsel, to embark on extensive research to write his *Stolen Waters*, published in 1913, which chronicled the deprivation of the fishermen of Lough Neagh of their fishing rights by legal chicanery, perpetrated through 'the parchments of bygone rascaldom'.[8]

Moreover the sense of dispossession shaped his fascinated subversion of legal forms as a parliamentarian and barrister. Healy became the most assured legal ironist of his time. In 1887, denouncing 'the force of legal superstition' which excluded leaseholders from the benefits of the Land Acts, he memorably parodied the English perception of the Irish leaseholder:

> Most of them are so rude and barbarous in their ideas that they are unable to realise the added element of sanctity and holiness which is given to contract by means of sealing-wax and sheepskin. That is the more remarkable when it is remembered that all other savages respect some fetish, and that these leaseholders, being generally Popish, are naturally of an idolatrous turn of mind . . .[9]

The remembrance of the famine also lay heavily on Healy's childhood. The famine smote Bantry and its hinterland with terrible severity. Both Healy's father and A. M. Sullivan, as administrators of the poor law, witnessed the devastation it wrought. If, as Healy's first biographer surmised, his 'childhood dreams were visited by ghouls', they were those of Ardnavaher, where two pits containing the graves of unnumbered victims of the famine lay alongside an abbey graveyard. T. P. O'Connor wrote in 1886 that 'Mr. Healy will tell you with a strange blaze in his eyes that even today the Earl of Bantry, the lord of the soil, will not allow these few yards to be taken into the churchyard, preferring that they should be trodden by his cattle'.[10] The remembrance of Ardnavaher remained with Healy, prompting his denunciation in 1889 of

> this hateful and rotten system, built upon sand, which had its foundation in rottenness, aye, and under that rottenness lie the bones of the victims of this system, the whitening skulls of the poor naked and hungry beings – this abominable system which was responsible for so many horrors would go down in the whirlwind of indignation that its infamies produced from one end of Ireland to the other.[11]

Significantly, this attack was detonated by the prosecution of a priest. Where nationalism and Catholicism touched, Healy's rhetoric had carried a supplement of vehemence.

The fact that Healy's background and circumstances were the reverse of those of the man whose destiny was to be most closely intertwined with his own was to have far-reaching and tragic consequences. Charles Stewart Parnell was born nine years before Healy on his family's estate at Avondale, County Wicklow, some four thousand acres in extent. He belonged to the seventh generation of a family which had emigrated from Chester in the later seventeenth century and acquired lands in Ireland.[12] The same historical forces which had dispossessed Healy's forbears were those which had endowed Parnell's family with its lands.

Healy's furious sense of despoliation not merely informed his agrarian rhetoric, but provided the ideological rationalisation for his resentment of Parnell. Land was the medium through which their conflict was to be articulated. The language of nationalism was the rhetoric of provenance. In the split of 1890–1 Healy proclaimed himself to be sprung from a dispossessed people, and assailed Parnell as the descendant and archetype of the expropriating Anglo-Irish class. The psychology of dispossession was formative. Healy came to conceive of the political qualities for which Parnell was lauded – of command, froideur, self-control – as the characteristic attributes of an aristocracy founded on the expropriation of native Irish Catholics. In his relentless attack on those attributes in the split there was a jealous intimation which he could never quite suppress that his own fractured and inconstant temperament was the product of a relatively austere upbringing, and of a childhood interrupted by displacement and exile, from which Parnell had been spared by his superior circumstances.

The contrast which Healy drew between Parnell as a member of a leisured caste and himself as a representative of the oppressed peasantry was not without irony. Healy, reared in towns, in contrast to Parnell had no experience of agriculture. T. P. O'Connor recalled an improbable tutorial:

> Mr. Parnell had been a practical farmer during a portion of his life, and could talk learnedly about the rearing of pigs, the calving of cows, and the top-dressing of land. Tim, reared in town and offices, was, like most of the other leaders of the agrarian movement, unable to tell the difference between a horse and a cow, or between a field of potatoes and of oats. Parnell quite gravely answered all the questions that Tim put to him, explaining all these mysteries in very simple and intelligible language.[13]

Healy, with that mimetic fluency which was so characteristic of him, quickly learnt to dissemble his town origins, and to articulate a skilfully contrived rhetoric of peasantry.

The self-image Healy promulgated of a self-made man of the people (in contrast to Parnell as the scion of landlord family) was not an altogether accurate reflection of the reality. If Healy's immediate family were of restricted means, the wider family was well-connected in nationalist politics. His uncle by marriage, T. D. Sullivan, was one of the five sons of Daniel Sullivan, formerly of Bantry. The most talented of the brothers was Alexander Martin Sullivan, journalist and orator, parliamentarian, and belatedly a barrister. The object of virulent Fenian hatred, Sullivan as editor of the *Nation* espoused a scrupulously moderate parliamentary nationalism, and was credited with first coining the term 'Home Rule' in 1860.[14]

His brother T. D. Sullivan, whose nationalism was rather more flexibly 'advanced', was his coadjutor and successor as editor of the *Nation*. An inveterate composer of patriotic verses and ballads (one of which, 'God Save Ireland', became the anthem of late-nineteenth-century nationalist Ireland), T. D. Sullivan was to be one of Healy's closest parliamentary allies. Donal Sullivan, another brother, was to sit for Westmeath South from 1885 until his death in 1907. Denis Baylor Sullivan was a journalist on the *Nation*'s sister paper until he went to the bar where he acquired a considerable practice: he was characterised as 'the last remaining representative of the fervid, picturesque school of Irish forensic oratory'.[15]

William Martin Murphy was born in Bantry in 1844. While not a kinsman of the Sullivans, he was a loyal disciple of A. M. Sullivan, who died at Murphy's residence in Dartry in October 1884. Murphy's father had moved from Castletown Berehaven to Bantry in 1846 where he became a successful building contractor. On the father's death, Murphy inherited a substantial business. In 1870 he married the only daughter of James F. Lombard, who had amassed a fortune in the drapery business and was one of the first promoters of tramways in Dublin. Murphy's own wealth was to owe much to the construction of tramways and light railways. He would be a close collaborator of Healy.[16]

Tim Healy, Maurice Healy, T. D. Sullivan and Donal Sullivan along with William Martin Murphy later provided the core of the 'Bantry Band', or the 'Bantry Gang', which came to be the largely pejorative designation of the Healy—Sullivan connection in Irish politics.[17]

The Sullivans were a minor though not an insignificant dynasty in Irish politics. They were fiercely proud and possessive of their contribution to parliamentary nationalism, whose seemingly guttering flame in the 1860s and 1870s they had done much to keep alive. With marked reservations in the case of A. M. Sullivan, they assisted the rise of Parnell. The sentimental nationalism of the Sullivans could not hold its own against Parnellite *Realpolitik*, and their standing was to be eclipsed by the ascendancy of Parnell. While Healy fiercely supported the emergence and early ascendancy of Parnell, in his later career he gravitated back to a nationalism closer to that of the Sullivans.

The jealous kinsmanship of the Healy—Sullivan clan was further heightened by intermarriage. On 29 August 1882 Healy married his first cousin, Erina Catherine Mary Sullivan, the daughter of T. D. Sullivan, against the opposition of her parents. Healy's brother Maurice five years later married Annie Sullivan, the daughter of A. M. Sullivan.[18] These were neither the first nor the last intermarriages within a dense and intricate family connection.

A highly politicised family, their politics were in turn familial. The closeness of the family relationship which underpinned the Healy—Sullivan connexion was extremely important for Healy. The exaggerated sense of intimacy, and of shared and embattled adversity against those outside the circle of his family and close friends, did much to insulate Healy from any sense of remorse for his implacable violence in public controversy. It conferred a moral privilege which permitted an exculpatory dissociation of his public persona and his private self.

His character united private grace with public ferocity, familial *tendresse* with the capacity for vicious aggression towards enemies, or still more, estranged allies. A politician capable of the most atrocious vituperation, Healy revelled in the company of children. John J. Horgan recalled that one of his earliest amusements at his father's table was a game he invented 'in which Tim Healy, playing the part of an angry bear, crawled about the floor emitting ferocious growls whilst I simulated an innocent sheep about to be devoured'.[19] 'Concealed within this strange personality by his public ferocity are the heart and the temperament of a warm-hearted child', wrote Lord Birkenhead in 1924. T. P. O'Connor had early noted the irony that so fierce a politician retained immense affection and charm for children. Harold Frederic observed that he was 'the idol of clever children'.[20]

Healy's exaggerated sense of family and childhood cast some light on the paradox of a sceptical, even cynical politician, who engaged in political combat with the cheerful ferociousness and moral certitude of a warrior-saint.

Healy's political initiation was provided by his stay in Dublin. He haunted the *Nation* office. He watched Isaac Butt, the leading parliamentary advocate of home rule, and George Henry Moore address an amnesty meeting in Cabra in October 1869. He ferried volumes of the *Nation* to the home of Butt, who was endeavouring to arbitrate a dispute between A. M. Sullivan and his bitter enemy Richard Pigott, proprietor of the *Nation*'s rival, the *Irishman*. He witnessed the Dickensian spectacle of Butt lurking in T. D. Sullivan's home to avoid imprisonment for debt in advance of the Limerick election of September 1871. In March 1872, two months short of his seventeenth birthday, Healy left for England.[21]

Healy was employed as a shorthand clerk in the office of the superintendent of the North-Eastern Railway. His older brother, Thomas, of whom, even though he sat for North Wexford 1892–1900, little is known, preceded him there, and he was later joined by Maurice.[22]

Healy first stayed in Manchester with John Barry, a distant relative. Born in County Wexford in 1845, Barry was the paramount figure in Irish *émigré* politics in England. The organising force behind the establishment in Manchester in February 1873 of the Home Rule Confederation of Great Britain, he was a member of the Supreme Council of the Irish Republican Brotherhood until the enforced resignation of its home rule activists in 1877. Barry's shrewd judgement was not confined to politics. The firm of which he became a partner, Barry Ostlere and Company, manufacturers of linoleum, became the largest of its kind and was to be a significant source of future financial support for Healy.[23]

Healy was very active in Irish political and cultural circles in Newcastle, and became known as 'an ardent, self-sacrificing man of culture, who, even as a boy, was the life and soul of the National movement' in the town. By October 1873 he was the joint secretary of the Newcastle Home Rule Branch, a post he held repeatedly thereafter, and was for a considerable time secretary to the Irish Literary Institute.[24]

The general election of February 1874 had returned a large body of Irish members who had declared in favour of home rule. In many cases their commitment to home rule was nominal. Insofar as it was possible to speak of a home rule party it was divided, ineffectual, and friendless at Westminster. Isaac Butt, the home rule leader, was forced to practise a supplicatory politics. On 30 June 1874 Healy made his first visit to the Commons, in the company of John Barry, and witnessed the humiliating defeat of Butt's resolution for an inquiry into the demand for home rule. Barry was to play a central role in the emergent opposition to Butt's leadership, for which the initiative came from the *émigré* Irish in England rather than Ireland itself.[25]

Tyneside was the region of urban England where the prejudice against the *émigré* Irish was least, due in large part to the solidarity which existed between the Irish and the radicals of Newcastle.[26] Healy felt deeply the prejudice he observed. Actively involved in local politics, he celebrated the defeat of a candidate in municipal elections whose firm had refused to employ Irishmen. Those who knew what it was to go from house to house in England to be met by the refrain of 'no Irish' would rejoice that for once 'a stand has been made on behalf of those who feel the curse of Swift'.[27]

Like other nationalist *émigrés,* Healy looked impatiently back to an Ireland still sunk in political torpor, chafing at its inactivity. The eighteen-year-old Healy wrote to the *Nation* in February 1875 protesting at the imprisonment of two nationalists in Meath, and lamenting the lack of response in Ireland: 'In their person the whole nation has been insulted, and by their unwarrantable arrest every Irishman who feels his nationality with any degree of keenness should resent it as if it were personal to himself'.[28]

In the split of 1890—1, Parnell, in a blistering attack on Healy, charged that he had joined the Fenians in Newcastle and had betrayed the Fenian oath to enter parliament. There is nothing to substantiate this suggestion, and it is most doubtful that Parnell himself believed it.[29] The allegation was part of the rhetorical litany of betrayal Parnell alleged against Healy. It was not apparently the first occasion on which Parnell had made use of the suggestion. If a note of an interview taken by F. H. O'Donnell's solicitor, R. A. Biale, in 1888, published in O'Donnell's memoirs, is to be believed, Parnell counselled against calling ex-Fenian members of the Irish party as witnesses in O'Donnell's action against the *Times*, and among the ex-Fenians he numbered Healy.[30] If Parnell thus designated Healy as a former Fenian, it is readily explicable in terms of a desire to exclude Healy, whom he had by that time come to mistrust, from any role in the proceedings.

The influence of his father's morbidly strict Catholicism, and the longstanding acrimony between the Sullivans and the Fenians, acted in some degree as deterrents to Healy joining the Fenians. More importantly, Healy subscribed to a newer political dispensation, committed to ruthlessly efficient electoral organisation, and temperamentally impatient with quixotic notions of armed insurrection against English power in Ireland. It was unnecessary for Healy to attest to the strength of his convictions by taking the Fenian oath. In the melting pot of Newcastle *émigré* politics, the line of demarcation between Fenians and home rulers was not rigidly drawn. Historically Fenianism had struck deep roots in the north of

England: as one authority has written, 'in Lancashire and the north of England in the 1860s Fenianism *became* the politics and political life of the immigrant Irish'.[31]

Healy in Newcastle encountered both active and former Fenians. He wrote somewhat guardedly in his memoirs that when he met Edmund O'Donovan in 1872, 'I inferred that he was the organiser of the IRB for the North of England'. He added that Arthur Forrester, the IRB organiser for southern England, often called at Barry's home. He was nominated to a committee charged with organising the funeral of the old Fenian John O'Mahony.[32] One of Healy's local nationalist adversaries wrote of 'the veritable Tim Healy who many times to my certain knowledge declared his diffidence to the efficacy of the Home Rule movement, and avowed his confidence in principles much more advanced'.[33] The writer was a partisan of P. J. Smyth M.P., a bitter adversary of the home rule movement, and the letter reflects the factionalism of nationalist politics in Newcastle. The thrusting incursions of the youthful Healy had made enemies as well as winning admirers. As he prepared to leave Newcastle he wrote to his father that 'my departure is sure to delight a lot of them'.[34]

In Newcastle, Healy fused a familial tradition of learning with a late-nineteenth-century pursuit of self-betterment. He attended night-classes in physics, and learned French and a little German at the Mechanics Institute. (He also, in the hope of correcting a stoop, joined the 3rd Northumberland Artillery Volunteers.) He displayed that capacity for rapid assimilation which would characterise him as a politician and reflect itself not least in the mimetic fluency and aptitude for devastating parody. T. P. O'Connor wrote in 1886 of Healy that 'the "rude barbarian" of the imagination of English journalists is keenly alive to the most delicate beauties of Alfred de Musset or Heinrich Heine, and could give his critics lessons in what constitutes literary merit and literary grace'. G. K. Chesterton later observed that Healy quoted Shakespeare like part of his ordinary table talk.[35]

Healy also became proficient in Isaac Pitman's recently developed shorthand, which he first learnt from Isaac's brother Henry in Manchester in 1872. This was to render possible his remarkable prolificity as a newspaper-writer, barrister, letter-writer and politician. Less positively, it permitted him to realise in script the fast and savage fluency of his verbal expression.[36]

Healy was not unhappy in Newcastle, a city to which he acknowledged he and his brother owed much. He remained acutely sensitive to anti-Irish prejudice, and to the rigours of the English class system. (When in the United States in 1882 he met a man from Mayo who having started as a navvy became manager of a Texas railway, he was prompted to observe '. . . so far as my experience goes he would be a navvy of commanding genius who could work his way, say, upon the North Eastern Railway, to the position of manager or secretary in a few years'.[37]) England was good to Healy. Yet he cannot have failed to feel the separation from his family. He wrote from Newcastle in November 1875 to his sister Mary, one year his junior, on her nineteenth birthday which was to be her last, sending her *The Mill on the Floss*.[38]

Healy's involvement in Irish *émigré* politics in England brought him into close contact with Irish parliamentarians and with leading members of the Home Rule Confederation of Great Britain who espoused more aggressive tactics than Butt's. In April 1875, the young Charles Stewart Parnell, who had failed in his first bid to enter parliament in the Dublin county by-election the previous year, was returned for Meath at the age of twenty-eight. Nine years older than Healy, he had become actively involved in nationalist politics at the same political moment. The first sighting of Parnell to which Healy refers in his memoirs was at a convention in Leeds later in 1875. In September 1877 he induced Parnell, along with F. H. O'Donnell and John O'Connor Power, to attend a meeting in Newcastle. Before the meeting started, the supporters of Isaac Butt mustered: 'Parnell kept nudging me to say nothing and the scene ended'.[39]

Of the political relationships formed by the young Healy, the most emotionally close was with Joseph Gillis Biggar. He was already friendly with Biggar, then forty-nine, by late 1877. A Belfast Presbyterian and a pork butcher by trade, Bigger had become a nationalist and converted to Catholicism. Of the small band of Irish members who engaged in obstruction, none did so with quite the same relish as Biggar. Healy wrote to his brother in May 1877 that 'the idea of Biggar up all night after having a good breakfast "feeling equal to any amount of legislation" is delightful'. Healy affectionately lauded him as 'the upright and downright member for Cavan' (Biggar was a hunchback, and notoriously plain-speaking).[40]

In November 1877, Healy broke ranks with local nationalists to support the municipal candidacy of Biggar's uncle, a Tory magistrate at Gateshead, swayed by the consideration that 'Joe told me he was the only one of his relatives who had "stood up" for him when he turned Catholic'.[41] Healy was enchanted by Biggar's double-conversion: 'By what strange channels did his stark Presbyterian soul drink in the fertilising dews of the traditions of Irish Nationality?' He made the curious observation that the sole regret occasioned by the acquaintanceship with Biggar was that 'you did not know him as a young man so that you might grow old with him in harness together'.[42] Biggar was to be Healy's friend and mentor in the years that followed. His death in February 1890 left Healy inconsolable, and removed from the scene shortly before the split the only person capable of exercising a stabilising and restraining influence on Healy.

In early 1878 T. D. Sullivan invited Healy to move to London to contribute a weekly letter to the *Nation* at £1 a week. During the session the letter would be almost exclusively concerned with parliamentary affairs 'with special reference to Irish business and "our men". You would have to drop into the house nearly every night and keep relations with Parnell, Power, etc., and see A. M. S[ullivan] and get his views now and again'.

It represented for Healy a decisive break which permitted him to quit Newcastle, brought him into closer contact with the Irish parliamentarians, and put him in a position to enter politics in due course. Healy wrote to his father in the stifled accents of youthful ambition:

> I must have eaten lotus with my cabbage, as I don't care one way or another what I do. I lack push to waddle about the streets of London looking for a job, and there is too much good nature about the offer of a pound a week for what I could write to make it acceptable to 'noble independence' . . . It is generous of him to give me a chance, but that is what I object to.

Healy's pound a week was supplemented by work as a confidential clerk in John Barry's linoleum business.[43]

T. P. O'Connor wrote of Healy that 'probably he himself, if he were to trace the mental history of his political progress, would declare that in his case, as in that of so many other Irishmen, it was an English atmosphere that first gave form and intention to his political convictions'.[44] Lauding Healy at a banquet after he had left office as Governor-General, Lord Birkenhead observed that while Carson, Glenavy and Oscar Wilde were at Trinity College, Dublin, Healy was 'writing shorthand at 18s. a week at a railway station in Newcastle. Not for him were the brilliant academical opportunities, not for him the stimulus of competitive intellectual debate . . .'[45] Yet Healy's dialectical aptitude did not notably suffer for want of a university education. Allied to his own devouring precocity, the political academy of *émigré* nationalism served him well.

If his achievement could be regarded as that of an Irish nationalist in England prevailing over what were somewhat disadvantageous circumstances, as he himself tended to view his early career, it was perhaps more a classic study in the late-nineteenth-century *carrière ouverte aux talents*. On leaving Newcastle, Healy was presented with a writing desk at a meeting of the Irish Literary Society, a poignant tribute from Irish workingmen to a clever and ambitious young man. Reported to be 'very much affected', Healy declared that 'whatever little service he had rendered to the national cause was only his duty'.[46] Irish nationality, as he declared fifteen years later in what was perhaps his closest approximation to an expression of solidarity, was 'a cause dependent on the shillings of the poor and the brains of the poor man's son'.[47] His first *Nation* letter appeared on 23 March 1878.

2

Journalism and Politics

The choice of Healy to write the *Nation*'s parliamentary letter proved inspired. The parliamentary obstructives now had a formidable journalistic champion whose despatches from the parliamentary front helped to rally opinion in Ireland in their favour, and to counteract the hostility of Edmund Dwyer Gray's *Freeman's Journal.* His writing inaugurated the journalistic revolution of Parnellism. 'It was Healy that first helped to get access through journalism to the mind of Ireland', T. P. O'Connor later wrote: 'the *Nation* was Parnell's first organ and Tim Healy his first spokesman in the press'.[1]

Healy became the chronicler and connoisseur of obstructionism, which he chronicled collusively from the visitors gallery. He was dependent on Irish parliamentarians to get him access; prior to 1881 only the London press had access to the gallery, excluding the provincial and Irish press.[2] Arriving in the evenings, he stayed till midnight or the early morning if there was anything to cover: 'Sitting in the Strangers' Gallery when there is no fun on would shatter the British Constitution, and mine was built in more fragile lines'.[3] Otherwise he went to the City News Rooms.[4]

Healy broke with the more staid forms of parliamentary correspondence. He despatched a vivid, perceptive and openly partisan account of the activities of the obstructives at Westminster. His style, as T. P. O'Connor noted, was founded palpably on that of John Mitchel, by whom Healy was greatly influenced.[5]

As the *Nation* correspondent Healy charted the final year of Isaac Butt's leadership of the Irish party, as the trial of strength between the ailing moderate and the handful of parliamentary obstructives came to a head. The principal obstructives were Charles Stewart Parnell, Joseph Biggar, Frank Hugh O'Donnell and John O'Connor Power. Healy's *Nation* letter did much to undermine Butt's standing in Ireland.

That Butt's predicament was ineluctable was evidenced by the fact that his anti-nationalist adversaries were unable to resist the temptation to deride his weakness, to Parnell's advantage. Thus the historian and anti-nationalist publicist Richard Bagwell wrote:

> The nominal leader of the so-called Irish party — and he has become very nominal indeed — is essentially a man of compromise. According to his view the true Irish policy is to take Grattan's advice and keep knocking at the Union; but with gentle and persuasive taps. The door has often proved too strong for blows, but it may be possible to humbug the porter. This lawyer-like mode of proceeding does not suit the Left, or even the Left Centre, of his party. They decline to roar like sucking doves.[6]

Healy had already privately concluded that Butt was 'no man to lead. He is too soft and easily gammoned. He is clever, plausible, statesmanlike and eloquent, but he is not a leader of men'.[7] He wrote to his brother in May 1878 of the difficulties in replacing Butt:

> If Butt were to persist in retiring (which I don't believe) I hardly like the idea of putting the leadership 'in commission'. It's like an admission that no-one could be got to take his place — the fact being that better men could easily be got, only that the useless fellows who make up the Party are too eaten up with jealousy of each other to permit anyone else to lead them.

The reference to 'better men' in the plural signified that Healy was not yet wholly committed — nor altogether reconciled — to Parnell's hegemony. He observed however that if Butt were to hold on a little longer Parnell would prevail.[8] While apprehensive that the government's Irish University Bill of the following year might 'clip Parnell's wings', Healy was confident the initiative would remain with the obstructives: ' . . . the Moderates will in the meantime keep going to pieces, and the others will be gaining in courage and audacity'.[9]

In his *Nation* letter, Healy deprecated Butt's belief that 'great principles are settled in Parliament less upon their merits than upon the prevailing tone of the House'. He attributed the government's introduction of the Intermediate Education Bill to the actions of the advanced party rather than to Butt's 'confiding trust in official honesty'. With cold derision, he described Butt's attempt to arrogate to himself the credit for the bill: '. . . he got up and shook hands with himself for his performance and

Mr. Parnell kept watching the Government bench with a meaningful smile. No sign was made by its occupants to justify Mr. Butt's self-congratulations except that the Chancellor buried himself deeper in his hat'.[10]

The obstructionist opposition to Butt hardened in response to Butt's support of the policy of the Conservative government on the eastern question. At the executive of the Home Rule Confederation of Great Britain, Healy proposed a resolution condemning Butt's support of the government's policy as 'contrary to the principle of independent opposition'. He subsequently proposed a resolution to convene a conference of the Confederation in Dublin against the declared wish of Butt, who believed it would do 'great mischief'.[11]

In his *Nation* letter, declaring that 'it almost looks as though Mr. Butt is going to be the chief difficulty of the Home Rule movement in the future', Healy pronounced an epitaph for a patriot: 'How rapturously the Tories cheered his speech! And how delighted he was by their cheers! Poor stuff it was, though, and poor indeed compared with the eloquence of the same Isaac Butt pleading for the Irish cause . . . Can it be the Tories who have changed, or Mr. Butt?'[12]

At the end of November parliament was recalled to debate the war in Afghanistan. Butt refused to call a meeting of the party, and publicly discountenanced the strategy urged by the obstructives of threatening to block supply unless the government was prepared to make concessions to their demands. Butt's imperialism infuriated the obstructives, and removed the last inhibitions on the expression of their contempt for his submissive political course.[13]

Healy wrote a fierce attack in the *Nation*. In an ugly allusion to Butt's support of the policy of Disraeli's government, Healy wrote 'the mantle of O'Connell is in pawn to the Jews!' Butt had, gradually but thoroughly, 'separated himself from general patriotic thought' and gone over to the enemy. Deprecating 'these absurd apostrophes in the mouth of an Irish leader about Crown and constitution', Healy woundingly continued: 'There is something positively senile in the notion that the insignia of domination could be made to spell a charm with in Ireland, not to speak of other outrages on Irish feeling'. Butt, he shrewdly concluded, had 'gone too far even for his Tory friends'.[14]

John O'Connor Power came under attack from Butt's supporters for referring to him as 'a traitor to the Home Rule cause and to the Irish party'. Healy, who had himself written that 'treason has done its worst', came to the defence of O'Connor Power. It was small wonder that 'earnest men, impatient at artificially-created helplessness, speak of "treachery" and "treason"'. Of O'Connor Power's expression of regret at being obliged to condemn Butt, Healy wrote: 'And who *could* be glad to attack this old man whom we trusted'.[15] Ridiculing a circular got up in support of Butt as an endeavour 'to bolster up the great Humpty Dumpty', he noted that prominent Irish members who occupied the middle ground had 'declined to give a scrape of their pen to Ireland's quondam leader'.[16]

Butt's health and political fortunes continued to deteriorate. Within the Irish party, the anomalous 'demand for energetic action . . . coupled with a desire to retain the existing leader'[17] ceded to a steady drift of support in Parnell's favour. Butt's death on 5 May 1879 obviated the need for a final assault on his leadership. Healy's obituary of the dead leader concluded: 'Every quality almost that a leader should possess, he had, save one, though the want was fatal. Patience, pains, experience, tact, a winning way and eloquence — all these were his. But of the hard-set grit of resolution none he had'.[18] Six years later Healy wrote that Butt 'a veteran constitutional lawyer, lacked altogether that Rapparee touch which alone keeps an enemy at bay', and that his followers were 'almost wholly unpurposeful . . . and speedily would have justified the Fenian dogma that Parliamentary spouting never did any good and never would gain much for Ireland'.[19] It is difficult to disagree with Healy's assessment of the ineffectuality of Butt's policy. Yet the gratuitous excesses of wounding derision so characteristic of Healy were already discernible in his attacks on the failing Irish leader.[20] He had already, by twenty-three, shown himself an accomplished propagandist and a dangerous adversary.

The obstructives were far in advance of nationalist opinion in the country, which remained divided and demoralised. The ultimate purpose of obstructionism was to elicit a response in Ireland. Healy wrote in May 1878 that in Ireland itself 'some are faint-hearted and amiably lack gall to make oppression bitter; and others in spite of many bitter teachings, persist in affecting to despise any means of asserting Irish rights milder than powder and shot'. He conceded that most people in Ireland 'have had in times past good reason for dissatisfaction with the way in which "constitutional agitations" have been occasionally conducted'. Healy propounded, as a departure from the feeble constitutional agitations of the past, a doctrine of 'constitutional insurrection':

> It is evident from the actions of a few brave men that the House of Commons is the weak spot in the British Empire, and we now have it 'on the raw'. By reinforcing the active members of the Home Rule party, and seizing every opportunity to encourage and sustain them, Ireland would soon have at her disposal a force which, for all purposes offensive and defensive, would render her more formidable to England than she has been at any time in this century.[21]

He bitterly decried the readiness of the anti-obstructionist Irish members to defer to the 'tone' of the House of Commons: 'Is it supposed that every

Irish question and grievance is to wait discussion until some definite time when those skilled in the tone-ometer decide that it registers favourable?'[22] He defended the obstructives against their critics in the Irish party:

> . . . the gentlemen who now lift up their hands against 'disunion' have done their best to provoke it themselves by bitter speeches and denunciations of their more active colleagues who until now have rarely attempted to retort. No-one can have any conception of the treatment which men like Messrs. Parnell and Biggar received in private at the beginning of their efforts and all up to the present has been borne studiously without complaint.[23]

There was a marked class difference between the Home Rule League in Dublin and the Home Rule Confederation of Great Britain. While the composition of the League was distinctly middle class, and included many Protestants, the Confederation was as Butt described it, 'an association of working men'.[24] Healy felt the hostility of the old guard of the home rule party, mixed as it was with a complacent disdain for the Irish in England. Until Parnell had established his ascendancy, the *émigré* supporters of the advanced section in England were pariahs of Irish as well as of English political life. As the Home Rule Confederation of Great Britain prepared to meet in Dublin in 1878, Healy observed that their support for an active parliamentary policy 'has brought them into very bad odour with the sweet do-nothings of the party. To them they are "strangers", "intruders" and "dictators" in their own country, and persons whom it is by no means desirable to see return with a vengeance'. At their conference 'the raiders of the Confederation, denounced as Saxon invaders and dictators', had taught their countrymen 'lessons of boldness and prudence'.[25]

While Healy looked to a purge of 'pledge-swallowing placehunters', he was aware of the need for tactical accommodation in the shorter term. Of Edmund Dwyer Gray he wrote 'there is plenty of room in the national ranks for politicians of all shades'. The benefit of his tolerance extended to such mavericks as James Delahunty, the member for County Waterford, who campaigned against the pound note in which he discerned a conspiracy against Ireland.[26] He estimated that a third of the existing home rule party were 'thin-veneered Liberals', and warned of the destructive effects of Liberal propaganda and Gladstone's rhetoric — 'artful speeches, primed with well-directed allusions and gauzy promises' — on the cohesion of an unreconstructed party. The Ennis election had exploded a plot for 'a general Whig descent on the constituencies for the next election . . . an electioneering New Departure'.[27] Healy wrote his father: 'If we can increase the strength of the "active party" at the next election I know not how far the cause may not be pushed during the life-time of the next Parliament'.[28] The oratory of five sessions 'has not produced one single convert':

> The notion that eloquence influences divisions, and that concessions are obtainable by the politics of sweetness and light is dead. The bottom is out of the thing. On the other hand, the application of pressure, whether on members of the House or embryos at the hostings has had noteworthy results. The history of concessions to Ireland is the history of pressure.[29]

Healy was a consummate publicist of the doctrine of obstructionism, which he justified as a parliamentary retaliation for British intervention in Irish affairs. He commended 'Mr. Parnell's policy of reciprocity in intermeddlesomeness', defined by Biggar as 'the policy of industry and threat'.[30] Healy wrote that 'the Act of Union has made the House of Commons ours as well as theirs, but that portion of its members of English nationality have hitherto exercised therein a monopoly of obstruction'.[31] In July 1879 he mused on the possibility of obstructing the Army Discipline Bill: 'An attempt by Irish members to abolish the British army would not be an altogether unappreciated enterprise in Ireland'.[32] He adroitly coined the term 'conciliatives' as the antonym of 'obstructives'. The latter would be able to point to legislative achievements, 'while the conciliatives are without any programme that I ever could hear of except a trust in the ultimate operation of grace upon the British sinner'.[33]

Healy articulated an implacable nationalism. When, during the war in Natal, Parnell frustrated a measure to enable reserves to volunteer for active service, Healy exulted:

> Their robber army will continue to rot in Zululand, and Irishmen will have the gratification of knowing that the Parliament of the English is becoming as useless to them as it is us and that our arm is long enough to work hurt and harm on the enemy in at least some parts of the world. Remembering the persistent contempt with which England treats the demand of weaker countries for justice it is impossible not to feel the liveliest satisfaction in watching the development of this African business, so barren of everything but disgrace for our masters.[34]

Healy's vehemence also enabled him to distinguish his position from that of British radical opponents of imperialism. Unlike some of his nationalist contemporaries, such as John Dillon and T. P. O'Connor, Healy declined to regard nationalism and radicalism as doctrinally convergent.

The government sought to thwart obstructionism by new procedural rules. This necessitated a more sophisticated approach by the obstructives. Healy charted the refinement of obstructionism in its second phase. By June 1879 he was writing that 'such brutalities as the constant motions for progress or adjournment known in the rude practise of the early days' had ceded to the 'cat-like tenacity and close attention to detail of the scientific period'. He commended ironically Biggar's ability to interject 'hear, hear' at the critical moment: 'When a debate is flagging a well-directed fillip will often set it going half the night, and the art of sitting patiently in the House by the hour, in order modestly to administer the stimulant, is one of the most difficult in the profession of the obstructive'.[35] He endorsed the practice of an economy of obstruction. Parnell had been 'the earliest to discover the difference between obstruction and obstruction', and was sufficiently astute to avoid a futile pitched battle when the same end could be achieved over a more extended period.[36]

Healy watched with satisfaction the process by which the House of Commons was being 'slowly revolutionised', a fact which even 'dull Tory wit' was beginning to realise: 'The more stupid Tories as yet do not understand the object of the Irish members. Certain things go on under their eyes but the "natural perversity of the Celtic character" will for them be a sufficient explanation of any unusual action that takes place'.[37] He amusingly epitomised the spirit of obstruction by a Swiftian device in describing the turbulent reaction of the English members when O'Connor Power moved the adjournment of the House on 26 June 1879: 'these people are unable to control themselves, their leaders and chief men lose their heads on the smallest occasion, and it is beginning to be seriously doubted whether, after all, they can be considered fit for Parliamentary Government'.[38]

Healy's chief function was to explain, justify, and dramatise the policy of obstruction with the intention of arousing public opinion in Ireland from its listlessness. He depicted heroically the struggle of the obstructives in parliament, as in his vivid triptych of St Patrick's Day 1879:

> Still quietly sitting between his friends, Mr. Biggar is the picture of repose, and, now the tuft of magic greenery which adorns his vesture lends the calm an almost sylvan air. Close by him Mr. Parnell looks heated with the constant strife of one bearing the brunt of battle; and at times flinging back some taunt the face of Mr. O'Donnell glows angrily.[39]

While Healy's *Nation* letter ranged widely over the personnel in the Irish representation, the most striking and closely observed descriptions were of Parnell. Through his journalism Healy sought to convey a collusive intimacy, and to achieve a rapport in irony, with Parnell.

Of Parnell's blatant obstructionism, he wrote 'the member for Meath cannot give up his habit of annotating his Parliamentary papers, but the unused notes serve only as a monument to his unstinting concern for the wellbeing of the British taxpayer'. He suggested that the 'guardian genius of the British taxpayer', if rendered visible, 'would surely have been discovered bending over Mr. Parnell in an attitude of benediction, weeping tears of gratitude'.[40] He commented that 'it is supposed that because Mr. Parnell looks so serious over such business that he does not enjoy the fun. This I believe to be a mistake. How he represses himself cannot be discovered, but I think he smiles inwardly. It is an excellent play'.[41] He described Biggar, Parnell and O'Donnell in the House in May 1879 in a rare moment of repose as 'looking as if they never did anything, and watching the progress of business with the interested curiosity of novices'.[42] Of late, he wrote in June 1879 'the member for Meath has brought the satirical method of address to refined perfection'.[43] He depicted Parnell replying to the young Lord Randolph Churchill 'with the smile of an angel'.[44]

The obstructives were themselves divided. Drawn to Parnell, Healy retained an instinctive sympathy with the obstructives eclipsed by his inexorable rise. He maintained relations with Frank Hugh O'Donnell and John O'Connor Power, and in his political dealings and his journalism sought unavailingly to mitigate the angry clash of vanities. Healy went so far as to offer a condonation of the imperialistic views expressed by O'Donnell.[45] He sought to shield O'Connor Power from the wrath of Parnell and the Fenians alike. He watched powerlessly as the bitter and painful rift between Parnell and O'Connor Power widened. Revealingly he believed that greater allowance should have been made for O'Connor Power's humble origins: in his memoirs he described O'Connor Power as 'an able and eloquent man, reeking of the common clay, at which Parnell's aristocratic sensitiveness recoiled'.[46]

With Parnell's election as leader, it was no longer possible to maintain sentimental affections for his erstwhile rivals for hegemony among the obstructives. Healy wrote to Maurice on 18 July 1880: 'Biggar still clings to O'Donnell, as I did for a long time, on account of his past services. I fear that his conduct is dictated by annoyance over Parnell's election to the Chair, and the same may be said of O'Connor Power'.[47] O'Donnell's pride and eccentricity proved ungovernable: Healy later denounced him as 'Crank' Hugh O'Donnell.[48] When O'Connor Power later joined the Liberals Healy denounced him as a traitor to the Irish cause, and dubbed him 'Judas O'Carey Power' (Carey was the betrayer of the 'Invincibles').[49]

In his letters to his brother, Healy gave vent to his frustration, which arose from his anger at the political lethargy of the Irish at home, and from the impatience of his own ambition. He was quick to perceive in the endemic localism of Irish politics a threat to the creation of an effective nationalist party. As early as 1877 he wrote to Maurice:

> The talk about local men 'sits urgent' in the grey fallacy of the British system of representation. There should be no 'local' representation: there should only be 'country'; and if the representation has to be subdivided,

> it should only be for the purpose of convenience, counting votes etc., and then care should be taken that the constituency was large enough to swamp local influence.[50]

Privately Healy berated Maurice, who had evidently complained about the representation of Waterford, for his failure to take 'a single step to move things up out of the muck'. His impatience owed much to repressed ambition:

> Somebody must incur the charge of 'officiousness' or 'meddling', and the issue at stake is worth incurring unjust charges for. I will take credit to myself and say I played the dictator when I thought it right, regardless of claptrap. A man may as well be called a schemer as a fool.[51]

Healy wrote a similar letter to Maurice two months later, assailing what he called 'your do-nothingness' in Waterford:

> It is very fine to ask: what is the Home Rule League doing? What the devil could the Home Rule League do with such a lot of fellows as you? Do you want it to take you by the throat and run you into mass-meetings? . . . You are a lot of noughts. When I found a Utopia I shall abolish representative institutions as a humbug, seeing that they were established for the protection of the liberty of imbeciles, who could not take care of themselves, it passes me that there should be imbeciles whose imbecility is so enormous that they would not employ the things got upon purpose to bulwark their native defenceless.[52]

He wrote again in February 1879 in the same tones of thwarted activism:

> If you mean to be an honest politician in this country you cannot be a *moderate* one. It is impossible for a man of strong convictions to be moderate, for any notions that are worth holding are worth holding strongly. It is the same in religion. The lukewarm, who are neither 'hot nor cold' will be spewed out. I could find it in my mouth to do some spewing! Moderation is a curse in Irish politics, but unfortunately it is not the moderate men who are held accursed.[53]

Of the Irish leadership of the Home Rule League, he wrote 'I am sick of the knot of fatuists who sit at ease in Dublin with no other policy than to wait for "something to turn up"'.[54] Healy mused later that year on the preconditions of political success: 'Many have laid down that the two things necessary to win a constituency are money and cheek'. He concluded that 'all unpleasant thick-skinned people are successful, and the probability of a man's chances may be measured by the density of his epidermis'.[55]

When Healy wrote in the *Nation* in mid-1880 that 'nothing but organised determination protracted if necessary over years, will have any effect on the net result'[56] he was even then not altogether clear what form this was to take. It was Parnell who gave direction to Healy's furious organising energies.

Ennis

On the death of the sitting member for Ennis, Parnell had publicly committed himself to a trial of strength on the adverse terrain of a borough with a highly restricted franchise, against William O'Brien Q.C., a 'nominal' home ruler with strong local support.[57] He had moreover neglected to provide himself with a candidate. Parnell and O'Connor Power first proposed that Healy contest the seat. That plan was abandoned on receipt of a cable from T. D. Sullivan. On the basis of information from a Parnellite priest in Ennis, Sullivan warned of the adverse prospects, and specifically against running the unknown Healy as the candidate. Healy wrote his father that 'Parnell said T.D.S. was a timid man, but I was glad of the excuse for gracefully retiring'.

T. D. Sullivan wanted to see Healy returned to parliament, but thought Ennis was not the right constituency. He wrote to Healy explicating his wire to Parnell:

> If Parnell is still in London you can let him see this. First as to recent telegrams – mine to him was not intended as a throwing up of the sponge in Ennis, but was a true account of matters according to my information. I had received a letter from a priest of the town who is a good Parnellite, giving a discouraging account of the condition of the borough. Under these circumstances I could not see that a young and unknown man such as you would have any chance. My reference to O'Brien Q.C. was not meant as commendation of that gentleman, but merely a statement of fact for Parnell's information and yours. I am quite in favour of fighting the borough against him. We must not allow the constituencies to be seized by a new relay of do-nothings and shams, if we can help it. Yet I cannot think that to start you for Ennis would have been a wise move. Not that the idea of your being sent into parliament is at all new to me. I suggested that a good while ago, as John Ferguson can tell you; and a correspondence has gone from this office to some leading men in Wexford on the subject. I take it that you will be run for some place at the General Election; but it must be for some 'advanced' constituency – a county probably, not a borough. The frieze coats of the counties are a more reliable class of voters than the small traders of the towns; the former expect no money to be spent among them; with the latter, in many cases, it is the reverse.[58]

On receipt of Sullivan's cable in the small hours of the morning, Healy had brought Parnell to his lodgings at No. 15 Doughty Street. There he finished his *Nation* letter, and then fetched James Lysaght Finegan, a London Irish barrister and journalist who was pressed into service as the candidate for Ennis. They scrambled together an election address, which they cabled at dawn to the *Freeman's Journal*.[59]

Edmund Dwyer Gray, the 'Whiggish' proprietor of the *Freeman's Journal* and member for Tipperary, was engaged in a desperate struggle to thwart Parnell's rise. Healy wrote to Maurice that after Finegan had been nominated

> Parnell would almost have withdrawn him next day, through Gray's strong pressure, had it not been for my vigilance and persistent coaching. The House adjourned at seven till nine; and during the most part of that time Gray kept pegging into Parnell. I remained in the lobby, waiting until he had said his say. I then got him to wire to Finegan to stand firm, and that he would be with him on Sunday without fail. This was the Friday night, and he would have to leave London next morning at 7.15 by the mail to accomplish this. To enable him to be at Euston in time he proposed to make the House sit all night on Report of the Army Discipline Bill, but things change so quickly that I didn't think he would do this, and I told him I would undertake to get him called if he would come home with me. After 4 a.m. he decided to allow the Bill to pass, and we went to my place. With an effort I succeeded in getting him up a couple of hours afterwards, and off to the train, rather in a despondent frame of mind. I wired T.D.S. to go down with him.[60]

When Parnell reached Ennis his despondency appeared justified. Finegan's candidacy was almost abandoned, and ten years later in the split Parnell charged Sullivan, 'shivering and shaking as he is now', of having wavered in the face of clerical opposition. In the event Finegan's extremely narrow victory was achieved only through the intervention of a Conservative candidate. The result, as Healy later wrote, was regarded by the Irish people 'as a proclamation that in Mr. Parnell a new leader had arisen'. On his return to London Parnell thanked Healy and credited him with the result, which four years later he asserted had ensured his perseverance in Irish public life.[61]

Healy in his *Nation* letter denounced Gray's opposition to Finegan's candidacy and his exploitation of the opposition of the local clergy: 'This continued exploitation of the feeling and traditions of a Catholic nation by interested politicians is heartless and demoralising . . . perhaps after what has occurred it will probably be some time before he again meddles so furiously with matters which apparently he as yet scarcely understands'.[62] Gray was not quite finished. Immediately after Ennis, the *Freeman's Journal*, in what was to prove Gray's last and decisive joust with Parnell, alleged that after a meeting of the party, Parnell had referred to a number of his colleagues, who opposed his proposal to defer the Queen's College's estimate until the University Education Bill was adjudged satisfactory, as 'a cowardly set of papist rats', and had made highly contemptuous remarks of leading members opposed to him on the platform at Limerick junction.[63] Healy wrote Maurice:

> At the next meeting of the Party Parnell will state what occurred, which was that when these fellows, after the meeting was over, were telling him he was wrong to propose such a resolution, a discussion occurred amongst them before leaving the room, and he told them that they were 'a set of cowards'. Finegan told me that he said to Parnell on the stairs, though in an undertone, as they were lingeringly leaving the room, 'Come along, Parnell, they are a lot of wretches!' But such a phrase as 'a cowardly set of papist rats' remained for the malignant minting of Eddy Gray. When Parnell told Gray in the lobby that he was 'a damned coward', as it was Gray who really prevented Parnell's resolution from being passed, Gray afterwards complained of it to O'Donnell – at whose request Parnell later on went to Gray and withdrew the expression, apologising for having used it.[64]

The *Freeman*'s sectarian embellishment of Parnell's remarks was cunningly plausible, and potentially devastating for Parnell's pretensions as a Protestant to leadership. It was the last and potentially the most dangerous hitch in his rise to power in Ireland. T. D. Sullivan wrote to Healy that 'if Parnell has flung the word "papist" in the teeth of Irish Catholics the people will resent it. I never fancied Parnell *could* use that Orange epithet'. (He admitted he had been somewhat taken aback at Parnell in Ennis incautiously referring in the presence of a waiter to the clergy as 'those fellows'.) Of the remarks attributed to Parnell at Limerick Junction, Donal Sullivan wrote: 'All that he said was true but if Parnell is ever to be leader he must show more sagacity and more control over himself than late episodes prove him to be possessed of'. He added that 'Eddy Gray is a serpent'.[65]

Prominent among the Irish members who supported Parnell were T. D. Sullivan and A. M. Sullivan, both of whose credentials as Catholic parliamentarians were unimpeachable. Healy drafted a letter from leading members of the party, taking care to send it to the *Freeman* at so late an hour that, as he told Maurice, 'they would be unable to make any comments on it – on which point you will have seen their snarling remark'. He also prevailed on Parnell not to despatch an inflammatory letter drafted by O'Donnell:

> O'Donnell was disgusted, after we had with much labour and doubt agreed to a form of words, to find that when he went away to vote in some division, I retained Parnell in the tea-room and got him to refuse to send his document. For your amusement I enclose bits of the intended

> replies. It astonishes me how unassumingly Parnell accepts the advice of other people, and places himself in their hands.[66]

In his *Nation* letter, Healy's indignant reply to the *Freeman*'s allegations was revealingly expressed as a defence of Parnell's honour as a gentleman: 'With unexampled impudence an Irish gentleman has been asked to take up a string of accusations of which no proof has ever been furnished, and deny them one by one'.[67] In relation to the Ennis election and the 'papist rats' episode, he had rendered Parnell considerable service as an adviser and aide, and as a journalist. He wrote almost woundedly in his memoirs 'I was then Parnell's closest counsellor, and never did an assailed man so need friends'.[68]

Healy was already under a misapprehension which contained the seeds of their future estrangement. He was tormented by what he took to be Parnell's susceptibility to passing influence, the seeming off-handedness of his mode of taking soundings. His attitude towards Parnell was untenably possessive: there was an inherent tension between his deprecation of Parnell's impressionability and his vaunting of his own influence. Healy had failed to recognise Parnell's political technique, his habitual waiting on forces and events, and his shrewd sifting of the diverse counsel he received. What appeared to Healy as suggestibility was a considered forbearance, a capacity for assimilating the range of options open to him from which he would choose unerringly, and strike at the right moment with irresistible force. Rapidly disillusioned, Healy came to see only remorseless self-advancement and a calculated exploitation of the good-will of others. Others did not make the mistake of misinterpreting Parnell's tentativeness in council. Describing Parnell as 'a man of commanding intellect', Justin McCarthy wrote of him immediately after his death:

> He took in new ideas slowly, but when once they had got into his mind they spread and germinated and became fertile there. He had a very quick and keen observation, and a remarkable judgement as to character and nature. He could look across a whole field of politics, and take in the complete situation. He had above all the instinct and genius of the commander-in-chief. In the council-room he was often slow, uncertain, undecided; sat silently listening to the opinions of others, put off his own judgement to the last, sometimes gave no opinion of his own, but suddenly adopted the opinion of another man. In whatever course he decided on taking he was almost sure to prove himself right in the result. But it was not in council that he showed himself at his best. It was in a crisis that his genius came suddenly out.[69]

Wilfully oblivious to the evidence which Parnell had already provided to the contrary, Healy persisted in his view of Parnell as a sterile and derivative politician. When T. P. O'Connor commented that Parnell was fond of seeking counsel, Healy uncomprehendingly agreed and commented that Parnell did not object to having his thinking done for him. Healy systematically misunderstood and underrated Parnell. Thomas Sexton more perceptively remarked of Parnell that there was a little dust on top which one might brush as one pleased, 'and then you come to granite'.[70]

The New Departure

Healy's own perspective was narrowly parliamentary, limited to the prosecution of obstruction, and electoral organisation in Ireland to swell the ranks of the obstructives in parliament, and in England to put *émigré* nationalists in a position to affect the outcome of the general election. Just as Healy was the most articulate advocate of the policy of obstruction, he was also paradoxically the most parliamentary of Parnell's early lieutenants and collaborators. Healy sought publicly to goad Parnell into campaigning more actively. In his *Nation* letter in September 1878, he wrote that kind, enquiries were being made for Parnell, '"the ablest of the Home Rulers"'

> and it is desired to know whether his silence is ominous, or if he will have the goodness to rise and explain. That is exactly what a good many people — friend and foe — want to know. Will he make an effort this year, as he did last, to rally Irish opinion upon the question of parliamentary action, or will the months of the recess be left to pass unemployed.

The following month, at the conference in Dublin of the Home Rule League, Healy proposed a resolution commending Parnell for his offer to tour boroughs in England.[71]

In his correspondence with his brother, Healy disclosed in mid-1878 his growing admiration for Parnell. Then came a series of criticisms, which revealed a systematic belittling of Parnell's ability and purpose, side-by-side with a somewhat Iago-like commentary on his own gathering influence over him. The first criticisms were of Parnell's organisational abilities outside parliament. Looking to the general election he believed Parnell would make a 'bad electioneering tactician'. Parnell did not understand 'the necessities of agitation', as O'Connor Power did.[72] It was a pity he wrote Maurice in April 1879 that Parnell 'has no head for organisation work outside the House of Commons. He is a child in some respects'. In October he described Parnell as 'unmethodic'.[73]

Yet Parnell's strategy was to prove far more ambitious than Healy realised, and extended beyond the parliamentary arena. When Healy in his *Nation* letter of 30 November 1878 asked '"And what will Ireland do?" says the

Shan Van Vocht. Parliament meets in a week "and what *should* old Ireland do?"'[74] he had himself no very precise idea. It was the supposedly unimaginative and impractical Parnell who suddenly and decisively widened the political arena beyond the narrow parliamentary sphere within which Healy's thinking was confined.

Healy wrote to his brother in February 1879 outlining the thinking of T. D. Sullivan. Even so moderate a nationalist as T. D. Sullivan was driven to countenance a mass defiance of the government, even though his ideas about how to bring this about were unsure and archaic. He was inhibited equally by fear of a denunciation by Butt and a Fenian anti-home rule takeover:

> TDS was telling me when I was home that some were talking of a Convention to 'smash the Convention Act', and by means of a defiance of the Government and imprisonment to revive the drooping interest of the public. He would be for working this, but was afraid Butt would come out with a denunciation, saying that he had pointed out that Obstruction was only an initiation of evil courses, which would land them in revolution, and here was the beginning of an illegal policy.
>
> He feared, too, that the Fenians might come in and pass anti-Home Rule resolutions, or swamp the Convention so as to render it unmanageable by the Constitutionalists.[75]

Sullivan's views disclose the combination of unimaginativeness and near-desperation of conventional nationalist thinking. It was from this impasse that Parnell was to release the home rule movement.

It was not a narrowly nationalist but an agrarian issue, and not the eastern capital but the farms of the west, that transformed the prospects for Irish nationalism. In spite of the fact that he was at this time close to O'Connor Power, who with Michael Davitt attended the meeting at Irishtown, County Mayo, on 20 April 1879 which marked the commencement of the agrarian agitation, Healy had no involvement. Parnell shared a platform with Davitt at a land meeting in Westport on 8 June 1879. Healy was still slow to grasp the significance of what was occurring. He was indeed somewhat surprised at Parnell's involvement, writing to Maurice some five weeks before the establishment in October 1879 of the National Land League that 'I think this is the first outside work in which Parnell has taken a personal initiative'.[76] Healy had badly underestimated Parnell. He was unaware of the extent to which Parnell was in communion with extremely diverse nationalist forces, delicately brokering their conflicting interests.

Healy's private criticism of Parnell actually intensified. On 9 November Healy wrote Maurice that he had not made up his mind about Parnell's character 'and have felt inclined recently to assume a critical attitude towards his doings. As a parliamentary leader he is unequalled, but for action out of doors he would require guidance from abler men'.[77] Healy's adjustment to the impact of agrarian events continued to be notably sluggish. Five weeks after the foundation of the Land League on 17 October, Healy wrote to Maurice that the land agitation was 'touch and go'. He feared that the government would proclaim the Land League, and evinced his disdain for the professional agitators of the Land League and his anxiety to conserve Parnell for the purposes of parliamentary action:

> What will 'the force of opinion' avail against soldiers and prison bars? It's all right for Davitt, Daly, Louden and the rest to talk sedition. It is their *métier*, but I can't help regarding it as unfortunate that a man so useful as Parnell (while he remains outside jail walls) should be placed in a position of jeopardy when the elections may occur at any hour . . .

Of the meeting at Balla on 22 November, which followed the arrest of Davitt and two other Land League leaders, Healy wrote:

> Had there been bloodshed at the Balla meeting the Central News and the Press Association were prepared to say that it was rumoured in Nationalist circles that in the event of Parnell's arrest 'reprisals' were possible. If the Government took an extreme step I would regard it as a declaration of war, and put up with any necessary consequences. It will take much to convince me of the wisdom of a policy which might have the effect of driving people into warlike courses.

The inception of the Land League had precipitated the final breach between Parnell and O'Connor Power.

> Have you heard if Parnell expressed any view on Power's refusal to attend the Balla meeting? Finegan dragged me out of bed at 3 a.m. to furnish the wherewithal for the journey, and to go down to Power's through the snow to argufy the matter with him. I told Finegan I felt sure Power would refuse, and that I could not urge him to go. Had I done so strongly Power might have been moved. The telegram Finegan dictated to me was not bad as a model of composition (at that hour of the morning, and in his nightshirt), but Power didn't say that he was going, which caused Parnell to make me waste fifteen pence afterwards on a reply to his question 'Did Power leave?' These two men hate each other and they have fair reason.[78]

There was little in Healy's cavilling to forewarn of his outburst against Parnell in his letter to his brother of 4 December 1879. He first asserted his privileged position as a close observer of Parnell: 'I speak as one of the few persons . . . who understand (I was going to say "see through") what manner of man is Charles Parnell'. His point of departure was his professed surprise 'that any person could, while granting to Parnell all the public virtues he so shiningly possesses, endow him with private and personal qualities of head and heart – of which they have had not the slenderest evidence'.

> I regard it as almost a calamity that our political interests compel us to idolize this man in public, so insecure do I feel as to the possible protrusion of those 'feet of clay' at any instant before the crowd of worshippers, whom it would drive into irreverent and unriskable derision.[79]

In his memoirs Healy leaves largely unedited the early criticisms of Parnell in his correspondence, evidently in the belief that they reveal the prescience of his reservations. Yet the correspondence rather discloses Healy's marked failure to anticipate Parnell's political course and his tardiness in appreciating its significance. He had acute difficulty then and later in acknowledging Parnell's decisive contribution in bringing together the agrarian movement and parliamentary nationalism in 1879. Casting a backward glance on the eve of the 1885 election, he wrote interrogatively:

> It is not clear whether, when he set out on his work, he proposed any definite policy to himself, but simply acted in revolt against a system which allowed the enemy to escape all inconvenience, while the most terrible losses were being inflicted upon Ireland. Slowly, but with certainty, his work evoked an echo in the country.[80]

The culmination of Healy's rhythm of disinfatuation occurred at the moment when Parnell's momentum towards perceived greatness sensibly gathered force, and when Parnell showed a political imagination and strength of judgement which defied Healy's criticisms. Healy had from the outset misunderstood Parnell. His initial underestimation of the Irish leader in some degree predetermined his personal estrangement. While Healy put aside his reservations in the hectic period which followed, at least until the spring of 1881, the tragic course of their relations was already set.

Healy was tortured by proximity, compelled to watch at close quarters the making of a leader. If he was unclear as to Parnell's precise means of ascent, he had a clear intimation, not far removed from dread, of the stature he would attain. A uniquely privileged observer of Parnell's rise, he was among the first to experience his allure, to feel the force of what was a disarmingly plain and unpretentious charisma. Healy was at the outset, and thereafter fitfully and incompletely, susceptible to Parnell's appeal: for the most part he fought against it, with a stubborn irascibility which suggested he did so against the grain. In spite of his private denigration of

Parnell, he knew all too well the strange force of his character. While to many contemporary observers Parnell's transition from agitator to statesman appeared an astonishing transformation, for Healy it had a terrible inevitability.

What was particularly disorienting for Healy was the speed of Parnell's rise which carried him in five years to national leadership at the age of thirty-four. During that period the formation of the public man was unnervingly rapid. Justin McCarthy described the initial impression created by Parnell as a parliamentarian:

> His peculiar quietness of manner, combined with his indomitable perseverance and dauntless courage, filled me with respect and admiration. It seemed nothing to him, a raw young man just come from Cambridge, to stand up night after night and every night, and face the whole hostile House of Commons. He was a bad speaker at first — he was not anything of an orator even at the last — words came to him with difficulty — his range of ideas seemed curiously narrow; in short, according to all the recognised rules and traditions of Parliamentary criticism he ought to have been a dead failure in the House of Commons. Yet there was the hard fact staring any impartial observer in the face — he was not a dead failure.[81]

Healy was gripped by the presentiment that Ireland would present — quite how he was unsure — the arena of Parnell's greatness. He realised the possibilities which awaited a strong home rule party which could hope to hold a balance of power at Westminster, and was aware that — even apart from the New Departure — the prevailing political listlessness in the country could not long endure. Parnell's good fortune appeared not to be limited to his social circumstances. Healy was afflicted by an envy he had necessarily to repress, for he knew he could never hope directly to rival Parnell. He was still in his early twenties and out of parliament. Though possessed of remarkable political talents, he could not match Parnell as a leader of men. As his presentiment was translated into reality, he came to resent Parnell's hegemony as an act of usurpation, almost of plagiarism.[82]

It is significant that Healy's private denigration of Parnell was expressed as a critique of the process of political heroicisation. Unprepared to acknowledge Parnell's qualities as more than superficial, he embarked on an obsessive deconstruction, a pseudo-rational critique, of Parnell's attributes as a leader. Already he was the morbid connoisseur of the Parnell myth; to some extent his precocious revisionism actually anticipated the myth itself.

With Parnell in America

In December 1879 Parnell, accompanied by John Dillon, embarked on a tour of the United States to raise funds for the relief of distress in Ireland. The organisation of the tour proved hopelessly deficient. As Parnell observed on his return, 'we found that the work we had to do would take ten times as many as the two who went out'. Healy was sent for. He reached New York on 24 February 1880 and caught up with Parnell at Iowa.[83]

Healy quickly made himself indispensable. He corresponded on Parnell's behalf, and even gave interviews in his name. It was Healy who drew up the resolutions to establish the Irish National Land League in America (Parnell told the meeting: 'I have asked Mr. Healy to draw up certain resolutions which will be submitted to you, but of course I do not wish to bind the League down to my ideas').[84]

On the American trip, Healy witnessed what was the final stage in the shaping of Parnell as a public man. In the view of one astute Irish-American observer, Alexander Sullivan, it was in the United States that Parnell achieved his oratorical maturity. He watched Parnell at Indianapolis

> When he first spoke in my hearing in public his voice was unsteady, his address without evidence of previous mental plan, his ideas, each sharp and substantive, without cohesiveness, his feeling towards his audience timid and ineffectual. He stood erect as a young pine, his handsome face winning admiration and his pose arousing trust; but his defective articulation, his feeble monotone, and excessive shyness proved seriously disappointing to great gatherings eager to have another O'Connell bring their hearts into their mouths and fill the air with their shouts of slumbering passion and reawakened hope.

In a few weeks Parnell was transformed. 'The man faltered at Indianapolis was the calm, cold, clear, convincing speaker at Chicago':

> Every sentence he uttered was clear-cut, incisive, apt, and telling; his speech as a whole, while not ostentatious was one of a series which made a profound impression upon the American people. I never heard any human being, whether uncouth or cultivated, doubt his sincerity, or hesitate, after seeing and hearing, to trust and follow him.[85]

In America Healy was thrown into the close company of Parnell and his family. In his letter to Maurice of 25 February, written on his arrival in the United States, he referred to Parnell for the first time as 'Charles', the name by which Parnell was known to his family. In doing so, he put the name in inverted commas. Writing to Maurice on 20 March, on board ship on his way back to Ireland, he referred three times to Parnell as

'Charles', omitting the quotation marks.[86] This was perhaps the high point of their relations. Healy never again referred to Parnell in this manner.

In the course of the 1880 general election, Parnell described Healy as 'my friend and companion in America', and repudiated a reference in the *Freeman's Journal* to Healy as his 'paid secretary', stating that 'the services of Mr. Healy who came out to America at my request, so far from being "paid", are given at some sacrifice to himself and are entirely honorary'.[87] Healy told Maurice that 'Parnell's instructions to me were to spend the money I had, and that when it was used up he would give me more; although our hasty departure prevented my putting this magnificent system to a practical test'.[88]

The most serious oversight of the tour related to fundraising. To the chagrin of Healy, and of Parnell's American supporters, no part of the monies collected had been designated for political purposes in Ireland. Too late, Parnell published a letter to Patrick Egan, the treasurer of the Land League, which Healy had drafted:

> I feel confident that, in addition to a very large amount for the charitable objects of my visit, such a sum will be entrusted to me for the purposes of our political organisation as will, if suitably invested, secure for the Land League a permanent income upon the capital, and thus enable it constantly and energetically to direct attention to the evils of the present land system until its destruction becomes inevitable. By this means we shall have done something to prevent these recurring famines, and thus save our countrymen from future misery, while we shall be spared the shame of seeing Ireland presented as a mendicant to the nations of the earth.[89]

The administrative arrangements remained chaotic. Healy wrote to Maurice:

> We took charge of no money at the meetings, leaving the proceeds to be forwarded by the local men, and at one or two places they sent the cash collected to the Bishops, much to Charles's indignation! He is 'dead nuts' on some Western priests for the way, he says, they tried to divert it from the Movement to religious objects. I know of nothing to confirm this.[90]

Another incident further revealed Parnell's sceptical assessment of the political capacity of Catholic clerics.

> Archbishop Lynch had written warning Parnell not to go to Toronto on account of the Orangemen, but Parnell took no notice of his letter until I arrived. Then I wrote His Grace a polite note saying that it was impossible for Parnell to break his engagement. Parnell commented on the letter much in the spirit of the landlord who said people could not intimidate *him* by shooting his agent. We feared, however, that there would be a riot in Toronto, but fortunately all was still.

Parnell 'with an enigmatical smile' commented to Healy, 'perhaps the Orangemen do not wish to attack a Protestant'.[91]

They went on from Toronto to a triumphant reception in a snowbound Montreal.

> Here we were met by the most extraordinary procession I ever saw. We were invested in enormous fur-caps and coats, and put into sleighs (the cold being intense, and snow two or three feet deep), and escorted, as an enthusiastic admirer told Parnell, by ten thousand torches, fourteen bands, and countless horsemen. We drove through illuminations to the hotel.

It was the biggest meeting of the tour. 'The enthusiasm was tremendous', Healy told Parnell's biographer. 'Parnell sat like a sphinx the whole time. He seemed not to be a bit touched by the demonstration. The whole town went mad about him. Everyone was affected but himself'.[92] Speaking for the first time on the tour, Healy wound up the second Montreal meeting by referring to Parnell as 'the uncrowned king of Ireland', the appellation formerly applied to Daniel O'Connell. Healy claimed the credit for the first use of a phrase which, passed into circulation through the correspondent of the *New York Herald*, became Parnell's definitive synonym.[93]

In Montreal, they received a telegram from Biggar announcing the dissolution of parliament:

> . . . we did all sorts of telegraphing and breaking of engagements and were very sad! Parnell remarked that it would be awfully flat work going back to Ireland for contested elections. We were to have gone to Quebec and Ottawa, had we been permitted by the dissolution.[94]

Later, as Healy wrote, 'at a brilliant little supper given in his honour, the cold and impassive agitator electrified his hosts by a most touching and tender-worded speech, in which he proposed the toast of "Michael Davitt"'.[95]

On the voyage back to Ireland, Parnell took Healy into his confidence to a greater extent than before. Healy relayed to his brother Parnell's attitude to the partisans of physical force nationalism in the United States:

> He says that since the initiation of the Land Movement he has lost some interest in Parliamentary work, believing that they can obtain a settlement of the Land Question best by outside effort. We heard a rumour that the 'Skirmishing Fund' fellows have been urged to expend it in sending over picked men with Winchester repeating rifles to make a Ballycohey of every eviction, and take their risks of hanging — the idea being to cow the police everywhere. Except for John Devoy, however,

> I don't think there is much in them, and, according to Parnell, everything that Clan-na-Gael took in hand they spoiled, and it was only by freeing himself from their control that he made any success.[96]

The close proximity of the American trip excited conflicting responses on Healy's part, of renewed affection for Parnell and of fascinated suspicion of his public mask.

When they boarded ship in New York for the return journey, Healy headed for his cabin to shelter from the driving snow. 'Parnell stood on the bridge the whole time until the tender left with head uncovered; and it was a fine sight to see the 69th salute as we sailed off, and Parnell wave his hand in response, looking like a king'.[97]

When at the journey's end they reached Queenstown, Parnell at dawn waited impatiently for the tender bearing the welcoming party. He irritably asked of Healy if his colleagues did not think it worthwhile to meet him. This Healy later wrote was 'a revelation, and unveiled the true character of one who was outwardly a man of bronze. In an instant he bared his soul and let me know that his ordinary reserve was merely a mask'. When the tender eventually reached the ship, with Biggar, Davitt, T. D. Sullivan and others on board, Parnell 'hardened into steel . . . he banished all traces of emotion and became the superman once more. . . . As he stepped into the tender no one would have dreamt that his chagrin of a few minutes before had been transformed into gratification. His acting was superb'.

Healy's account is consistent with the pointed rebuke Parnell delivered at a banquet in Cork later that day, contrasting the welcome accorded him in New York and the homecoming: 'our reception committee this morning was not able to come out to meet us until eight o'clock, although it was composed of many good men'. The *Cork Examiner* explained almost apologetically that the ship had not been sighted by his supporters due to the prevailing haze.[98]

Parnell would have left Healy to work on with Dillon in America, or to remain in New York organising as Fanny and Anna Parnell wished, 'only he thought I could be more useful with him going around Ireland during the elections. He wants me to stand for somewhere also, but "somewhere" is so vague and other people having had a fortnight's start at all likely places, I don't think there is much chance of my achieving celebrity in that way at present'. Parnell had the further idea that Healy should be engaged as an organising secretary by the Land League, as well as entering parliament.[99]

There is nothing to substantiate the later assertion of T. P. O'Connor, angrily denied by Healy in his memoirs, that Parnell's rift with Healy originated with an unspecified incident in the United States that 'produced some disagreeable impression in Parnell's mind'.[100] The American trip, though regarded by Parnell as a nightmare,[101] rather marked the zenith of their cordiality.

Years later Parnell's widow informed the young Henry Harrison that Parnell had told her that Healy had been suitor of one of his sisters, and had taken mortal offence when Parnell had dismissed the idea on account of Healy's social origins. Conor Cruise O'Brien considers this probably a fantasy, although revealing in its emphasis on class. Yet it remains distinctly possible that Healy in America conceived a romantic interest for the sister whom Parnell told him was his favourite, Fanny, who was six years Healy's senior.[102]

Fanny Parnell died suddenly two years later at her mother's home in Bordenstown, New Jersey, at the age of thirty-three. Immediately after the break-up of the Irish party in December 1890 Healy gave to the *Pall Mall Gazette* what was otherwise a highly poised interview. It was in referring to the death of Fanny Parnell that Healy faltered:

> [Parnell] was a gentleman and a landlord; and one of the main things that influenced Ireland was the disinterestedness of his sisters – one of whom, Miss Anna Parnell, is one of the most remarkable women who ever lived, the other of whom, Miss Fanny Parnell, is dead, but whose name I can hardly mention without emotion. My chief regret these last bitter days has been to think of the extraordinary poem she wrote, beginning 'Shall mine eyes behold thy glory, O my country?' . . . Parnell himself is a man, no doubt, very difficult to gauge, but taking his sisters, his mother, and his entire family, no man can deny the extraordinary embodiment of Celtic popular feeling expressed in the heart of this family of Protestants and landlords. And when the English people chide us for not hurriedly cashiering Parnell there was in our minds a feeling which Parnell himself never, I believe, recognized – namely, the thought of his mother and of his sisters, and of his ancestry, all of whom had worked for Ireland and had done yeoman service in the Irish cause. We did not wish to desert them. This lady, Fanny Parnell was dead, and his ancestors were dead too, but the memory of them lingered on.[103]

Healy was not an especial admirer of Parnell's ancestry, as his speeches in the split were about to make plain. He had only a passing acquaintance with Parnell's operatic mother, and he and Anna Parnell had had their differences over the Ladies' Land League. The invocation of Parnell's family provided a cover for a reference to the dead Fanny. Its emotionalism, and fractured coherence, may well reflect the remembrance of an unrequited passion. There is nothing to bear out Katharine Parnell's suggestion that Parnell had intervened or discountenanced Healy's interest; although it is evident that if Healy did form an attachment to his sister, Parnell was aware of the fact.

Unhappily, if Healy was attracted to Fanny, she appeared more drawn by the melancholy handsomeness of John Dillon, Healy's future rival, of whom she wrote:

> I heard thee speak, and dreamed of Galahad
> the chaste,
> Of Launcelot the brave, and Arthur's
> kingly glory;
> Mailed shadows on thy form the
> helm and hauberk placed
> And bade thee forth to take up knighthood's
> broken story.[104]

The Parnellite campaign of 1880 was an exercise in desperate improvisation. By the time they reached Ireland, Healy wrote, 'there were comparatively few places where without scandal thoroughgoing candidates could be started'. The Parnellites were moreover under severe financial constraints. The campaign was chaotic and exhausting. In the small hours of 27 March, Healy wrote his brother from Dublin 'don't inflict moral hysterics on me, as my brain is almost burnt for want of sleep and want of everything else, especially good candidates and money for them'.[105]

Healy in the election displayed tireless vigour, and an instinctive mastery of the arts of Irish politics. As Parnell's amanuensis, he dealt with a dispute with Thomas Quinn, returned for Leitrim against Parnell's wishes, who charged that Parnell had threatened to descend on the constituency 'to pick holes in his coat'.[106] He wrote at Parnell's request to deny a remark attributed to Parnell as to the notorious venality of the voters of Mallow: 'He certainly did not intend to convey that any more than a small minority of the electors were corrupt'.[107]

The first campaign in which Healy played an active role was that of Andrew Kettle in County Cork. He proved an adept campaigner, putting the habitual vituperation of Irish elections at the service of the new political dispensation. Kettle's opponent, the nominal home ruler Lieutenant Colonel David La Touche Colthurst, he denounced variously as 'reared and brought up and imbued with landlord prejudice', 'a man who had been serving in the ranks of the sabering assassins', who 'had the flogging instinct in him'.[108] Speaking alongside Parnell after the declaration of the poll, Healy blamed Kettle's defeat in large measure on the clergy, regretting that 'at most of the booths yesterday the celebrants of the altar had become the touts of the polling booth'.[109] Ironically Andrew Kettle was to be the Parnellite candidate in Parnell's last election, at Carlow in July 1891, when Healy's was the foremost voice against him.

Healy was exasperated by the fact that circumstances had not permitted a clean electoral sweep, and infuriated by the Land League's embargo on the expenditure of its funds for electoral purposes. Its funds stood at about £40,000, 'but as I tell Parnell, it is the greatest farce for him to have exhausted himself in collecting this in order that it may be pieced away by a little knot of nobodies in Dublin':

> I would be anxious for Parnell to go again to America to raise a purely election fund, so as to fight every seat, and make our candidates a terror. We should smash the local bosses, and the knowledge that there were funds behind us would make them sing dumb .... We should 'go for' every Irish M.P. sitting on the Government side except Pat Martin or Colonel Nolan .... if we have audacity enough we should soon control the country.[110]

Among the English adversaries of Irish nationalism, Parnell's rise engendered alarm, tempered by a repressed fascination with the character of the Irish leader. The *Spectator* in July 1880 lamented that Parnell was 'at bottom a fanatic of the logical French type':

> What Ireland wants is a rival to Mr. Parnell, of wider and more generous sympathies, whose motive should be hearty love for the Irish, and not bilious jealousy of the English – with a temperament and a mind to charm Ireland, which Mr. Parnell has never had, and a mind apt to convince England, to which Mr. Parnell does not so much as aspire.[111]

Parnell's severe hegemony had already rendered nostalgic this appeal for a loveable Irish leader. A. M. Sullivan commented with rueful admiration the following year of Parnell's unyielding attitude to English politicians: 'He distrusts the whole lot of them, and is always on the watch. They have got their match in him, and serve them right. It is not poor Isaac Butt that they have to deal with, or even O'Connell. Parnell is their master as well as ours'.[112] By the end of 1880, *The World* referred succinctly to 'Parnell Imperator'.[113]

3

Parliament

The Member for Wexford

Immediately after the general election a vacancy arose in Meath as a result of Parnell's decision to sit for Cork City, for which he had also been elected. A. M. Sullivan had been returned as one of the two members for Louth, but furious at being out-polled by the disreputable Philip Callan had refused to take his seat. A meeting of the clergy of Meath, under the chairmanship of Bishop Thomas Nulty, which Parnell attended, recommended that A. M. Sullivan be nominated to fill the vacancy 'provided he feels able to co-operate cordially as a fellow-labourer with Mr. Parnell'. At a public meeting afterwards, Parnell delivered a less than ringing endorsement of Sullivan. After some words of highly conventional praise, he added that 'he did not say Mr. Sullivan was perfect, or on many occasions he and Mr. Sullivan had not differed', but declared it would also be a loss to the country were Sullivan not returned.[1]

If Parnell was not flatly opposed to Sullivan's candidacy, neither was he especially enthusiastic about it. He was mistrustful of Sullivan's moralistic conception of politics, and aware that Sullivan's refusal to compromise his independence was inimical to the creation of a highly disciplined Irish party at Westminster. There had been a discernible coldness between the two men from the outset. Parnell was aware that Sullivan had initially opposed his nomination as the home rule candidate for County Dublin in 1874. Sullivan had nevertheless loyally supported his candidacy thereafter, and at a meeting of the Home Rule League in the Rotunda on 10 March 1874 delivered the first panegyric of Parnell, albeit by reference to his illustrious patriotic ancestry rather than his own merits:

> . . . we see these men rising once more, impelled by the example of their forefathers, and quickened with the spirit that animated the Grattans and Charlemonts and Floods and Parnells of '82. . . . More honoured is the grandson of that man when he sits on this platform as Charles Stewart Parnell, High Sheriff of the County Wicklow, than if he took his place amidst the titled enemies of Ireland; and it will be found when the polling day comes round that his place in the esteem and in the hearts of his countrymen will be all the higher because he wears no coronet stained with treason to his native land.[2]

In 1877 Sullivan denounced 'the sham and humbug imposture which surrounds the alleged "policy of obstruction"' of Parnell and Biggar, adding the patronising observation which cannot have failed to infuriate Parnell, that he thought Parnell and Biggar had 'much to learn yet in a cause they embraced so recently, though so honestly'. Yet Sullivan declined to support any move to censure Parnell or Biggar. He helped draw Butt back from an open breach with Parnell, whom he defended in the Commons.[3] This did not suffice to allay Parnell's innate mistrust of Sullivan, whom he believed had inspired an attack upon him by H. W. Lucy in 1877 – a belief sedulously exploited by Sullivan's bitter enemy Richard Pigott.[4] Healy's own relations with Sullivan were distinctly cool. After he began to attend at the Commons for his *Nation* letter he reported to Maurice that he 'spoke to Parnell, Power and O'Donnell, *nodded* to A. M. Sullivan'.[5]

Sullivan declined the Meath nomination on the terms proffered, insisting that his independence could not be circumscribed. Endorsed by the *Nation*, Healy declared his candidacy for Meath on 12 May in an address issued 'at the request of many influential electors and with the approval of Mr. Parnell'.

On 7 May, Sullivan, whose response to the invitation of the Meath clergy had been in the nature of a well-judged opening gambit, despatched a letter of considerable astuteness which did not reach the Bishop of Meath until the eve of the reconvened conference of the clergy on 17 May. He interpreted the proviso as 'an expression of fealty and approval projected towards the future of the great-hearted leader who you were parting with such reluctance'. He was prepared to cooperate with Parnell 'as a fellow-labourer' as he had in the past. Parnell knew that that cooperation 'had its chief value in the circumstances of my well-known and unfettered independence' and was not 'the price or bargain for my place in parliament or out of it'. Healy persisted in his candidacy, but was overwhelmingly defeated by thirty-five to nine votes of the clergy present. Sullivan was returned unopposed as the nationalist member for Meath.[6]

Healy had needed little prompting to go forward. Driven by ambition, and his zeal to root out from the Irish parliamentary ranks all except committed nationalist activists, he persevered in his challenge to the end. If Sullivan had emerged as the member for Meath, Parnell had the grim consolation that he had divided the Sullivan connection, and bound Healy more tightly to him. Healy never again referred to his attempt to win the Meath nomination against his kinsman, but a bitter sense of the lengths to which he – and the Sullivans – had been prepared to go in supporting Parnell informed the vehemence of his attacks on Parnell in the split.

On the same day that Healy's ambitions were thwarted in Navan, Parnell was elected chairman of the Irish party in Dublin. Healy, whose presence at a caucus for members of parliament favourable to Parnell on the eve of the party meeting attested to his standing, had advocated Parnell's candidacy 'with infectious vehemence'. At the party meeting the O'Gorman Mahon proposed Parnell as chairman. Biggar seconded the nomination with his habitual forthrightness: ' . . . there is no member of the party who can compete with Parnell at all. Mr. Parnell first, and all the rest are nowhere (*laughter*). That is a bona fide fact, and no one can controvert it'. Parnell's restrained acknowledgement of his election reflected the slender margin by which it was achieved:

> The functions of Chairman were strictly defined and limited by the resolutions adopted some years since unanimously by the party. They do not imply in any sense leadership of the party, and I do not wish it to be supposed by the country that the Irish party in conferring the high and honourable position of Chairman upon me have in any sense entrusted me with leadership of the party (*hear, hear*).

To attest to the modesty of his ambition, Parnell stated that he had himself suggested Justin McCarthy as a suitable chairman. In singling out the worthy but uninspiring fifty-year-old McCarthy, Parnell had unerringly selected the perfect foil to his own harsh charisma.[7]

Healy resumed his *Nation* letter, and his role as Parnell's aide:

> I give Parnell a little help occasionally, and drew up any questions that he puts in the House. You will see four, for instance, tomorrow. I wrote that letter he addressed to the Land League some weeks ago, and was very glad to be afforded the opportunity for what I do, but apart from the pleasure I take in work of this character, I should expect political recognition.[8]

While as he indignantly insisted in his memoirs Healy 'was never "employed" by Parnell, nor got a shilling from him', he was paid for work on behalf of the Land League. In June 1880 he received £140, out of which he appears to have paid his subscription to Gray's Inn; in October he received a further £150, he assumed on Parnell's initiative.[9]

Healy returned to a parliament 'transformed by the alchemy of elections'.[10] The election of a Liberal government under W. E. Gladstone required more discriminating parliamentary tactics. Healy patiently sought to explain to his readers the constraints under which Parnell was now working. Obstruction was all very well while the Conservatives were in office, but faced with a Liberal administration 'the exhibition of an impatient temper, instead of quickening their action this year might mar the statesmanship of the next'.[11]

While Parnell's election had thrown 'an unreal air of earnestness over the entire of his following', the truth was that Parnell presided over 'to phrase it gently a composite party', with only a precarious majority in favour of an active policy.[12] Its operating strength was lower than was generally perceived. In the *Nation* Healy wrote that between twenty and twenty-five members were willing to engage in some form of obstruction, of which twelve could be relied on to do so effectively. Privately he estimated that only eight or nine 'first rate men' had been returned.[13]

Parnell was accordingly constrained to proceed with caution: 'it becometh not the Chief continually to go down with the footmen'. Of the narrow balance in the party, Healy lamented that

> the result of his election will be that instead of their dragged up to his level he will probably be pulled back in line with them . . . thus the Obstructive disappears in the leader. Wilkes at one time was able to assure King George that *he* had never been a Wilkite, and if the present state of things continues Mr. Parnell will be able to plead that he at least could not be a Parnellite.[14]

Healy described an incident in the debate on the Compensation for Disturbances Bill which conveyed the tightened direction of the party under Parnell's leadership. While some Irish members were moving the inclusion of their constituencies within the scheduled area, Parnell insisted on brevity, and on his followers not forcing divisions. Healy evoked with comic pathos Biggar's conflicting emotions:

> Now it came to the turn of Cavan. The domain of Mr. Biggar had not been treated courteously in this bill, and its watchful representative determined that at least a foreign legislature should pay it a tribute of obeisance by a march through the lobbies. But sternly came the whispered mandate of the chief, 'Withdraw, Biggar!', admitting of no parley. Never had a devoted follower been called upon for such a sacrifice as this. Withdraw his amendment, he, J. G. Biggar, who had taken more divisions and

> worried more Ministers than any man since Hampden, and that too upon occasions of lighter purpose than the present! Is it now, indeed, that he must yield, when there is a question of his own cherished Cavan? It was a terrible moment. Revolt, with all its promptings, surged for one instant through his mind, and then as loyalty reasserted itself, a shock of despair passed down his spinal marrow. 'Parnell, Parnell!', he tried to gasp, 'I don't like to withdraw'. In good truth he did not. But perish self in times like this and the command 'Withdraw, Biggar!' fell once more – a leaden message – upon his ears. The fiery pride of Cavan was quenched. Droningly the chairman put the question without challenge, and then more monotonously still the craven words, 'amendment by leave withdrawn', were pronounced in careless official tones that told no story of a valiant soul in agony, somewhere upon the benches below the gangway on the Opposition side of the Commons House of Parliament this Monday night.[15]

Healy's description of an incident in the debate on the second reading of O'Connor Power's land bill further attested to the affection in which he held Biggar:

> Condescendingly Mr. Gladstone bends forward to hear what message there might be from Cavan, and cranes his neck as if absorbed in the orator. 'All this talk about law and ordher', said Mr. Biggar 'law and ordher – is getting rather stale!' In that hour the Premier was settled. A kink seized him, and falling back on his seat, he laughed for five minutes, leaving the wise to recognise that to the influence of Mr. Biggar his subsequent surrender must largely be attributed.[16]

Parnell's success had brought about a temporary resurgence of Healy's early admiration. He wrote his brother in July that he had 'come to be a believer in Parnell's capacity and all-round cleverness'. The following month his criticism of Parnell was unwontedly mild, and almost proprietorial: 'I am glad you think Parnell has been doing well. For myself, I have been rather dissatisfied, and have told him so'.[17]

Healy's polemical ire was now directed against a Liberal government, and most of all at the Chief Secretary, W. E. Forster. While he initially observed that 'Mr. Forster's tone and bearing is certainly kindly enough', it did not take long for what he described as 'the anti-Irish temper of the Liberals' to discover itself.[18] He predicted Forster's failure as Chief Secretary: 'this sort of "bluff Englishman" style turns awfully rough on Irish stomachs'. In Forster he mockingly discerned 'the slouch and shagginess of conscious greatness'.[19] The following year he described him as 'a poor, vulgar, obstinate English *bourgeois*, possessed of some cunning and considerable patience'.[20]

From the outset Healy exempted the Prime Minister from his strictures on the government: 'Poor Gladstone! He is the best of his crowd'. In spite of his majority, Gladstone was 'practically powerless to deal with the question which his statesmanlike mind feels to be really the most important – Ireland'. Elected on an anti-Beaconsfield platform, he had not 'worked up the mind of England by months of agitation to his own level'.[21] Healy showed an early susceptibility to Gladstone's 'perennial fluency' (which he irreverently compared to 'the gush of a Vartry main'), and a fixation with what he termed 'the swatching mazes of Gladstonian rhetoric'.[22]

In the wake of the rejection by the House of Lords of the government's Compensation for Disturbance Bill on 3 August, Parnell needed to sound a note of considered defiance. On 19 September he went from his home in Avondale to Ennis, where he made his celebrated speech advocating the shunning of tenants who took land from those who had been evicted. He urged his audience to mark the transgression of 'your unwritten code of laws' by any such tenant, 'by leaving him severely alone, by putting him into a sort of moral Coventry, by isolating him from the rest of his kind as if he were a leper of old'.[23]

Healy's last parliamentary letter appeared in the *Nation* of 18 September. He went to Ireland to organise Wexford at Parnell's request. From there he returned to Bantry for the first time since he had left as a child in 1862.[24] He was determined to prove his mettle as an agrarian agitator. An attempt to murder a Cork land agent had resulted instead in the death of his driver. Healy responded with a deliberately inflammatory rhetoric. While his argument was predictable it was prefaced by an unexpected and revealing question: 'how long should this go on; how long should they have this crimson stain upon them?' The responsibility lay with the relentlessness of the land agent: 'The result was now seen in the stiffened corpse that lay in the police barrack at Aghaveel and Mr. Hutchins might thank God that it was not himself that lay there'. Hutchins was attacked at a fair shortly after, and the state of west Cork was sufficiently troubled to prompt the government to despatch a gunboat to Castletown Berehaven where Healy was to address a meeting. There he again denounced Hutchins and asserted that one murder hardly equalled 2,470 evictions which were 'sentences of death'.[25]

Evicted from his holding at Kealkill near Bantry, Michael McGrath had taken refuge with his family under an upturned boat on the seashore. Healy and another Land Leaguer visited Cornelius Manning, who had taken the McGrath farm and thereby attained the reviled status of a 'landgrabber' in the language of the Land League. According to Healy, they merely conveyed 'the polite request of the Land League to surrender the farm'. Healy and his Land League colleague were promptly prosecuted for intimidation under the provisions of 1 & 2 of William IV, one of the hated 'Whiteboy' acts.[26] McGrath died four years later of fever.[27] Healy in 1907 referred in parliament to the case of the McGraths: 'He remembered the state in which the husband was buried, the corpse taken out of the boat, the rain pouring down as the priest said the last absolution, and that was a decent, substantial tenant before his cruel eviction'.[28]

Healy was arrested at Roche's Hotel, Glengariff, where the proprietor engagingly congratulated him, and told him his fortune was made. His arrest, at a time when concerted government action against the Land League was widely anticipated, brought him for the first time to national prominence. The *Nation* headlined 'The First Arrest: Mr. T. M. Healy'. It coincided with a parliamentary vacancy in Wexford. Supported by Parnell, Healy was preferred by the Wexford Home Rule Club over John Redmond, the son of the late member, who reluctantly stood aside with the promise of a later seat. 'I can back him', T. P. O'Connor told the voters of the borough, 'to be the most troublesome customer the House ever saw'. Healy was returned unopposed on 24 October 1880. On 15 December he was acquitted at the Cork Winter Assizes.[29]

Healy had an unprecedented parliamentary debut. He immediately embarked on a series of fierce attacks on Gladstone's government, exhibiting a precocity in virulence for which the previous five years of obstruction had not altogether prepared the House of Commons. Against precedent, he spoke on his first day in the House, 11 January 1881, and delivered a vehement reply to Marquis of Hartington, then Secretary of State for India and the pre-eminent Whig parliamentarian. William O'Brien wrote:

> A quarter of an hour after he took his seat as member for Wexford he started up to make his maiden speech — tiny of frame, sad of visage, his hands in his breeches pockets, as coolly insolent as a Parisian *gamin* roaming through the Tuileries Palace at the heels of Louis-Philippe . . . as entirely detestable as a small Diogenes peering out over the rims of his pince-nez, as from his tub, through bilious eyes . . . and horrified the House of Commons with the following exordium: 'Mr. Speaker, if the noble Marquis thinks he is going to bully us with his high and mighty Cavendish ways, all I can tell him is he will find himself knocked into a cocked hat in a jiffey, and we will have to put him to the necessity of wiping the blood of all the Cavendishes from his noble nose a good many times before he disposes of us'.[30]

O'Brien's account, though heroically exaggerated, conveys the provocativeness of the twenty-five-year-old member for Wexford. While the *Freeman's Journal* charitably asserted that Hartington 'clearly winced' under Healy's attack, T. P. O'Connor considered that the speech was 'delivered in a hard dogged style, and gave evidence rather of fierce conviction than of debating power'.[31] Within days, the *Pall Mall Gazette* was referring wearily to 'the new but already familiar member for Wexford'.[32]

On 23 January 1881 the jury disagreed in the long drawn-out prosecution of Parnell and others in Dublin for conspiring to prevent the payment of rents. The collapse of the case served only to increase the zeal with which the Liberal government veered towards repression. The following day W. E. Forster introduced the first of two promised 'coercion' bills, the Protection of Person and Property (Ireland) Bill, which provided for the suspension of habeas corpus in 'proclaimed' districts. Healy participated in the protracted and acrimonious resistance to the bill. After the House had been kept in continuous session by the nationalists on a radical amendment for forty-one hours, the Speaker on 2 February broke with precedent to put the question. The nationalists withdrew to confer. Parnell, who had left to get some sleep at the Westminster Palace Hotel, was roused by Healy. Unperturbed and placidly smiling, he arrived to confer with his agitated colleagues. After a heated discussion, O'Connor Power's rash proposal that the Irish members retire from the House to consult their constituents was defeated.[33]

The government proceeded to suspend the ticket of leave on which Michael Davitt had been released from Dartmouth in 1877. In the Commons, Liberal cheers greeted the Home Secretary's announcement of Davitt's arrest in Dublin. Dillon then refused to cede to the Prime Minister, whom the Speaker had called. He was suspended. Parnell then rose and was in turn suspended, followed by the remainder of his supporters, each waiting to be touched on the shoulder by the Sergeant-at-Arms to signify his forcible removal.

While Parnell had appeared fleetingly to favour a policy of leading a withdrawal of the Irish party from parliament on the passage of the bill to regroup in their constituencies, following which he would announce that the first arrest under the new law would be the signal for a general withholding of rent, this was a temporising feint. Parnell cheated the expectation of his left wing that he would lead a withdrawal. At his direction, the party held back and urged a policy of self-restraint on the Irish people. The final decision as to Parnell's course of action was left to the next meeting of the executive of the Land League, which was to be held in Paris.[34]

Paris

This was a time of uncertainty and dread. It was feared that Parnell would be arrested, with potentially devastating consequences. Parnell disappeared. There was feverish speculation as to his whereabouts. He was lost from public view between 5 February (when he was in London) and 12 February when the Press Association caught up with him and Andrew Kettle at Calais. The agency published what was evidently the authorised version of the Irish leader's itinerary, which extended from Paris to Frankfurt (to seek better terms for the investment of Land League funds) back to Paris, then to Boulogne (where he visited his sister, 'a lady associated with banking interests in that town'), and thence to Calais en route back to Paris for the meeting of the Land League executive. This odyssey was less than convincing. Moreover it is inconsistent with Kettle's (much later) recollection of crossing with Parnell on a crowded packet from Dover. Parnell remained highly defensive on the subject of his movements. The London correspondent of the *Freeman's Journal* reported that Parnell on his return had 'every reason to complain of the malignant and underhand aspersions which have been cast on his movements in Paris'. Parnell was clearly anxious to avoid any suggestion that he had lingered in England.[35]

Though not a member of the Land League executive, Healy had gone to Paris at Parnell's request. In his memoirs he describes the members of the executive waiting a week in Paris for Parnell's arrival. This is incorrect. A number of members crossed the weekend of the meeting itself, although Healy was apparently there a longer time, as was Patrick Egan, and perhaps also James O'Kelly.[36] It appears that there was an agreement to regroup in Paris, and that contrary to Healy's account no specific date had been fixed initially. Andrew Kettle recalled learning after some days, getting a letter in Dublin telling him his fellow members of the executive were in Paris.[37]

Parnell's unexplained disappearance caused panic among those present in Paris. Healy's is the only account of what occurred. The members of the executive learnt from him that he had brought unopened letters addressed to Parnell in a woman's hand which could afford a clue as to his whereabouts. On being asked to furnish one of the letters, Healy insisted on a resolution of the executive. Having stipulated that the contents of the letter should be known only to Dillon and Egan, Healy handed over one of the letters which they opened and read. It was decided that Biggar and Healy should leave the next morning to seek out Parnell at the address disclosed in the letter.[38] It is a considerable irony that one of the reasons for convening the meeting in Paris in the first place was, in Healy's phrase, 'the suppression of liberty and prying into private correspondence at home'.[39]

According to Healy's account, on the following morning, that of Sunday 13 March, he and Biggar set out for the Gare du Nord. As their carriage left the courtyard of the Hotel Brighton on the Rue de Rivoli, a carriage bearing Parnell pulled in. Healy ran up the stairs of the hotel after him and knocked at his door. Parnell half-opened the door and then, according to Healy, shut it in his face: 'It was his only act of rudeness in all our relations'. Later that day, without apology or explanation Parnell presided over the meeting of the executive, which Healy as a non-member did not attend.[40]

At the meeting, Dillon conveyed to Parnell the resolution of the Central Branch of the Land League which recited 'our conviction that the Irish people have very little to expect from Parliamentary action during the present session' and requested that Parnell go to America. Parnell rejected the resolution, which was intended to remove his restraining influence from Ireland and from parliament. He would return to the Commons.[41] Parnell published an open letter to the Land League in which he staked out his own position. In response to the suggestion that he go to America he underlined the primacy of the struggle in Ireland: '. . . if there is the slightest flinching or reaction in Ireland it will produce the most disastrous result in America'. He rejected the premise of the Land League resolution that little could be expected from parliament in the near future, and pointed out that the Irish members expelled from the Commons had 'almost unanimously' agreed to remain in place, a decision with which he fully concurred. He posited a loaded choice. The first option was that 'the Irish members should retire in a body from the House of Commons, and announce to their constituents that the weapon of Parliamentary representation had been snatched from their hands', and that nothing remained but 'sullen acquiescence or an appeal to force in opposition to that force which had been used against us'. This course he stated he had dismissed from consideration. The alternative Parnell presented in a shrewd radical pitch was 'deepening the lines and widening the area of our agitation', holding out the prospect of 'a junction between English democracy and Irish nationalism'.[42]

The lines laid down were, classically, Parnell's. It is likely that Healy provided some of its rhetoric. A phrase such as 'appealing, I say, against the territorialism and shopocracy which dominate in Parliament, to the workingmen and agricultural labourers of Britain, who verily have no interest in the misgovernment and persecution of Ireland', was certainly not composed by Parnell himself. Healy's role in the drafting of the letter represents his last act as Parnell's secretary.[43]

In the abstract, the episode afforded a classic study of Parnell's political technique. He had allowed a sufficient period of time to elapse for tempers to cool, and for a realisation of the risks inherent in radical departures to take hold. Then, as the vista of agrarian violence in a political void could be glimpsed, Parnell — whose absence could only have served to sharpen the intimation of chaos — re-appeared at the last moment to re-assert his control of the direction of the movement, and to rescue the headstrong advocates of a withdrawal from parliament from the predicament in which they had almost entrapped themselves.

Parnell's absences, other than those occasioned by ill-health, were more calculated than Healy at first believed (he later came to believe that Parnell was both cultivating, and succumbing to, a myth of elusive solitude). Parnell was alert to the dangers of taking action where events were evolving too rapidly to permit of rational evaluation. He instinctively avoided ceaseless and indeterminate discussions which a change of events were almost certain to render nugatory, and which served at most to fortify a sense of embattled collegiate solidarity. He was acutely alive to the need not to appear hesitant or irresolute, and to ensure that his interventions were perfectly timed and decisive. In that sense at least, he was properly jealous of what was becoming his own myth.

It cannot be doubted that Parnell spent much of the week of his disappearance with Katharine O'Shea, with whom he had begun an affair in September or October of the previous year. He disdained to acknowledge any possible conflict between his public and private lives. What was more serious was his refusal to recognise the dangers of the perception of such a conflict taking hold among his colleagues. He appeared to believe that he could regulate his public appearances to achieve the maximum political impact and to conform to the requirements of his personal life. In this respect his own easy, even ironic, professionalism brought him close to hubris. He was confident that his success would affirm the allegiance of his loyalists and cow the more critically disposed members of the party.

Parnell's haughty disregard of the alarm his delayed arrival in Paris generated among his lieutenants was ominous. The wracking anxiety left a residual unease which the sureness he demonstrated in dealing with the issue in hand could not altogether dispel. Parnell's enigmatic disappearances were to recur through his career. Even though they owed much to his policy of holding back, and to his later ill-health, it was inevitable that his bereft colleagues should attribute his absence chiefly to his affair with Katharine O'Shea.

In his memoirs Healy was at pains to underplay the significance of the handing over of the letter in Paris for his relations with Parnell. However on their return to London, he told Parnell he could no longer continue to act as his secretary, using as an excuse his need for time to pursue his legal studies. He proposed as his replacement Henry Campbell, to whom he had taught shorthand in Newcastle. Campell, who was in 1885 returned for Fermanagh South, was to prove a secretary of positively conspiratorial fidelity.[44] T. P. O'Connor wrote of Campbell: 'Like the faithful partisan he was, and being of a nature almost as suspicious as Parnell's own, he had a certain tendency to watch with a rather jaundiced eye the doings of Parnell's lieutenants . . . I have an impression that, quite innocently, Campbell may have helped to widen the gulf between Parnell and the few men in Parnell's party who were personally hostile to him'.[45]

The day after the meeting of the executive, Healy and Biggar returned on the mailboat to participate in the committee stage of the 'coercion' bill.[46] Parnell remained for some days in Paris. According to the *Freeman's Journal* he was welcomed by most of the parties other than adherents of Léon Gambetta, at the time President of the Chamber, whose opposition Parnell attributed to a desire to ingratiate himself with the Prince of Wales.[47]

Parnell met with Georges Clemenceau.[48] At the instigation of James O'Kelly he met the former *Communard* Henri Rochefort, then an outspoken radical, who would later become a rabidly chauvinistic French nationalist. Rochefort proclaimed himself as deeply moved as he had been on embracing Garibaldi some months previously to shake the hand of the Irish leader (who was evidently less ready to be embraced).[49] Accompanied by Rochefort, Parnell and O'Kelly dined at the home of Victor Hugo on the Place de Vosges.[50]

Rochefort assured Parnell and O'Kelly that he would get Hugo to issue a declaration in their support. According to Rochefort's *L'Intransigeant*, it was agreed at the dinner that Parnell would send to Hugo a letter on the condition of Ireland, to which Hugo would respond with a manifesto calling on all the countries of Europe to support the cause of the martyred nation.[51] Parnell on his return to Paris from London the following week despatched a letter to Hugo describing the prostrate state of Ireland and concluding:

> Quant à vous, honoré Monsieur, qui avez si bien su éveiller la sympathie du genre humain pour 'les Misérables', nous sentons que notre appel vous ira droit au coeur, et nous sommes surs que vous éleverez la voix en faveur d'une brave mais infortunée nation.[52]

However Hugo never responded with the promised manifesto. A French biographer of Parnell, L. Nemours Godré, later wrote that it had not been possible to obtain from him the slightest statement, in prose or verse, of support for the nationalist cause. According to the Catholic and Hibernophile Nemours Godré, Hugo had looked into the matter but declined to intervene:

> Il y avait trops de 'curés' dans l'affaire. L'immense poète qui profitait de chaque crime politique pour addresser aux souverains d'Europe des dithyrambes humanitaires et de pompeux appels à la clémence en faveur d'assassins, se garda bien d'écrire un mot en faveur de l'Irlande affamée et opprimée.

He attributed Hugo's decision to the influence of an English friend of the editor of the journal *Le Rappel*, Frederick Augustus Maxse, 'radical en Angleterre, revolutionnaire en France'. Maxse argued that home rule entailed the betrayal of the principles of the French revolution and would give Ireland over to the horrors of a medieval clericalism.[53]

There was a somewhat farcical sequel to Parnell's relations with Hugo. Parnell was invited to become a member of the *comité d'honneur* organising the celebrations to mark Hugo's eightieth birthday on 26 February. When the posters appeared with Parnell's name on the walls of Paris, the President of the Republic and the President of the Council demanded that Parnell's name, or in the alternative those of the Presidents of the Senate and the Chamber of Deputies, be deleted. The Parisian police also intervened. The organisers decided rather than deleting Parnell's name to cease circulating the poster. Parnell's name was however mysteriously struck out of the official programme at the printer's. *L'Intransigeant* fulminated against the obsequiousness of the French government towards its British counterpart.[54]

There was unfounded press speculation that Parnell would meet the exiled Fenian diehard James Stephens. Stephens told the *Freeman's Journal* that he had never met Parnell, and that 'so long as he advised Constitutional action I have no desire to meet him in that sense'.[55] Parnell did meet the Clan na Gael extremist William Mackey Lomasney, who three years later while endeavouring to dynamite London Bridge succeeded only in blowing himself up.[56]

When he learnt from James O'Kelly, with whom he shared lodgings, of Parnell's intention to return to Paris, Healy objected that Parnell's place was in the Commons rather than on the boulevards. He renewed this plea in vain when O'Kelly woke him before dawn to say goodbye before leaving for Paris: 'as I heard O'Kelly's footfalls clatter down the stairs I thought they thudded defeat on the Irish cause'. Healy later saw Parnell's second Paris trip as merely a cover, abetted by the *Freeman's Journal*, which permitted him, after giving 'racy interviews' to the French press, to slip away from O'Kelly and visit Katharine O'Shea on his way back to London. Certainly, while Parnell met the Archbishop of Paris and Marshal MacMahon among others, his return visit to Paris at a time of parliamentary crisis was devoid of any immediately obvious political benefit.[57]

Parnell's public courtship of French left-wing republican figures permitted him to cut a radical dash. It served his purpose as a gesture to his own restive left wing, cheated of the radical agrarian courses it had espoused in the crisis over the coercion bills. As Conor Cruise O'Brien has written, his actions were those of a master of constitutional politics 'adept at the cape-work of the pseudo-revolutionary gesture'.[58]

Parnell's conduct however risked alienating the church and excited deep unease among conservative nationalists of the old dispensation. The (anti-nationalist) Catholic Archbishop of Dublin vociferously denounced his first Parisian visit. Responding to a public letter of A. H. Bellingham, the member for Louth, A. M. Sullivan agreed that 'the deep seated sentiments of the Irish people would be *outraged* by any attempt to ally or associate the Irish cause with French Communism or European Revolution'. The Irish nationalist movement was 'an eminently conservative movement, in the best and highest sense of that word'. Asserting that the national cause had enjoyed the support of the Irish clergy 'from generation to generation', Sullivan added the patronising (and faintly sectarian) observation that 'it would hardly be fair to expect Mr. Parnell to appreciate as we might do the feelings that underlay our aversion to continental parties known to us as "anarchists and communists" but to him only as democrats'. The Irish people would 'recoil in horror from any allegiance or association with the party and principles represented by MM. Rochefort and Clemenceau'. Parnell responded by denying that there was any question of an alliance between Rochefort and the Land League.[59]

From as early as the 1880 general election, before Parnell had met Katharine O'Shea, Healy suspected that Parnell, whom he believed to be of an amoral and promiscuous disposition, was prepared to subordinate political responsibilities to romantic pursuits. In his memoirs he claimed that Parnell had wished to adopt as a candidate at the 1880 election the disreputable Edward St John Brenon, whose wife was, Healy wrote insinuatingly, 'so dainty that Parnell often went to Kingstown to dine with her while the election was in progress'. St John Brenon was shortly afterwards expelled from membership of the Land League on the motion of Patrick Egan, on the grounds of his authorship of an article published in *Mayfair*, a London society magazine, which 'foully and scandalously libelled the character of the ladies of the city of Dublin'.[60] Healy in his memoirs congratulated himself on the prescience of his observation to his brother in a letter of August 1880, prior to his knowledge of the affair with Katharine O'Shea, that 'there must be a lady in the case, else he would not be in such a hurry to leave the House as he has been, two or three times this week!'[61]

In his memoirs as published Healy claimed that the letter he handed over in Paris came from a girl in Holloway, to whom he referred as 'Lizzie from Blankshire', a Manchester barmaid. The account in the proofs of his memoirs is more detailed, in that it identified the hotel where she worked, and her employers:

> He started for Manchester as soon as the elections were over, and there another drama was being staged. The Wellington Hotel, Manchester, kept by Mr. and Mrs. John Barker, was an Irish centre. Mrs. Barker was an

> Irishwoman, and her husband was an English Catholic. For everyone connected with the Home Rule Movement, it was a rallying point. Parnell often stayed there. The barmaid, whom I shall call 'Lizzie from Shropshire' was a gracious and amiable girl. Her connection with politics seems remote, but was real.

In the published version Healy added the comment, 'Parnell often stayed at that hotel'.[62]

Healy claimed that Parnell had passed some days in her company after the general election and immediately before the opening of the parliamentary session, when his presence was urgently required in Dublin: 'dallying at Manchester during these important days, Parnell forgot ambition'. J. A. Shaw was elected leader of the Irish party, and this was only undone when Shaw agreed to the convening of another meeting. Healy's crude linkage of sexual cause and political effect was, as so often, highly suspect. Parnell was absent from the first party meeting, but not in the haphazard circumstances described by Healy. When Shaw's supporters on 17 April convened the meeting of the party for 27 April in Dublin, Parnell objected on a variety of grounds, including the fact that many of the party had left for London 'and it would be unfair to compel these needlessly to return for a premature meeting in the City Hall'. The issue quickly developed into a contest of will between Parnell and Shaw. The *Nation* and A. M. Sullivan among others supported the objections of Parnell, who wrote to Shaw's ally C. H. Meldon warning that 'a large number of men have written disapproving of the day you have selected and giving their reasons. They represent a body of opinion it would not be wise to overlook'. The council of the Home Rule League proposed a conference between Shaw and Parnell to settle the matter, and Parnell wrote coolly to Shaw on 25 April that any conference should take place immediately 'as I am obliged to leave for England tomorrow morning and cannot return before Thursday [29 April]'. The meeting proceeded, but Parnell's actions had deprived Shaw's election of any political legitimacy. Parnell narrowly defeated Shaw at the reconvened meeting of the party on 17 May.[63]

Healy states in his memoirs that he subsequently learnt that Biggar, with the intention of avoiding a scandal, had sent a friend to the address disclosed in the letter. Biggar's emissary reportedly found the woman with a baby in a sparsely furnished garret, where a newspaper engraving of Parnell was pinned to the counterpane. 'Though in want, she was staunch to the father of her child, and never let fall a complaint'. Her immediate needs were provided for, and she was told where she might apply for further assistance.[64]

There is one further reference to the story of the Manchester barmaid. On 17 December 1890, after the schism in the Irish party and just before the North Kilkenny poll, the radical Henry Labouchere, who had for long been an intimate of Healy, wrote to Herbert Gladstone, the son of the Liberal leader:

> They [the anti-Parnellites] are thinking of making the following story public. In 1878 Parnell seduced and took away from the Wellington Hotel Manchester a barmaid. He lived with her in London and had a child by her. In '82 he was missing. It was decided that his letters should be opened by Biggar, Barry and Healy. There were several letters from her imploring Parnell to come to her, or to send her the means to exist. Barry went to see the girl in Camden town. She was absolutely without means, and appeared a very quiet respectable girl, and she was dying. Barry advanced money to her. But Parnell, having taken up with Mrs. O'Shea would do nothing for her. She died.[65]

Labouchere's account to Herbert Gladstone differs from the Healy version in two material respects. The first is that John Barry does not feature in Healy's account. The second is more troubling: the lurid suggestion that the girl later died was not made by Healy. As Healy is unlikely to have drawn a veil over the fact – or rumour – of her death, one must assume that the suggestion that the woman died represented a characteristically sensationalist garbling by Labouchere of what he had been told (it is possible that Labouchere had been apprised of the details of Healy's allegation at the height of their political intimacy, in 1885–6, and that they were not fresh in his mind at the time of writing to Gladstone five years later).

The first public reference to the opening of the letter came in T. P. O'Connor's *Parnell* published some ten days after his death.[66] On the fourth anniversary of Parnell's death, J. J. O'Kelly charged that Healy, 'this contemptible mountebank', had opened a private letter of Parnell's in Paris and circulated its contents 'among those he thought most likely to use the information to injure Parnell'.[67] O'Connor took it for granted that the letter was from Katharine O'Shea, and O'Kelly was evidently of the same belief. Healy's claim that the letter opened in Paris came from the Manchester barmaid has long been disputed. While accepting that the issue of her existence remains an enigma, Parnell's leading modern biographer F. S. L. Lyons accepts – on balance – the assumption of Davitt and T. P. O'Connor that the letter was from Katharine O'Shea, a belief she herself shared. His argument incorporates – though it does not rest upon – one error of fact. Assuming that the letter was written to Parnell's Paris hotel, he observes that the address was far more likely to have been known to Katharine O'Shea than to the Manchester barmaid, if she existed. However it is clear from Healy's account that the letter came from a batch of unopened correspondence 'in a woman's hand' he had brought with him to

Paris for Parnell, and which presumably had been addressed to Parnell at the House of Commons. This reverses the inference that might be drawn: it is in any event unlikely that Katharine O'Shea, who had a better knowledge of Parnell's whereabouts than anyone else, would have written a compromising letter to him at the House of Commons.[68]

One can readily subscribe to Lyons's distaste for accepting the veracity of an allegation pertaining to Parnell's personal life for which Healy was the sole authority. Yet why Healy should have fabricated so intricate an allegation remains to be explained, and the greater detail contained in the proofs of his memoirs, coupled with the Labouchere letter, increases somewhat the weight to be attached to his assertion. James Dillon's recollection of being told by his father that the address was in Holloway, while it hardly constitutes reliable evidence, is more consistent with Healy's account than with the suggestion that the letter was from Katharine O'Shea.[69]

The matter of the Manchester barmaid remains a persisting riddle. Healy's belief that Parnell had such an affair deepened his disenchantment with the public myth of Parnell, and fed his obstinate conviction that Parnell's relationship with Katharine O'Shea was merely the latest, and as it transpired the last, in a promiscuous sequence.

The Land Law (Ireland) Act 1881

The Irish land bill introduced by Gladstone's government on 7 April 1881 was of a political significance which far surpassed its restrictive conceptual framework. It substantially conceded the traditional demand for the three 'Fs' (freedom of tenure, fair rent, and free sale). It made only very modest provision for land purchase, and was in this respect rapidly overtaken by the Purchase of Land (Ireland) Act of 1885 and the succession of land purchase acts which followed. The act set in train a revolution in expectations among the Irish tenantry, after more than a decade of abortive attempts by Irish parliamentarians to win a substantial measure of land reform.[70] Under a thin fiction of finality, it marked a decisive shift of social power in Ireland.

Healy displayed restless energy and high legislative acumen in the debates on the bill. He coupled vociferous denunciation of the bill's restricted scope with the relentless pursuit of ameliorating amendments. He warned that 'freedom of sale' derogated from the other two 'Fs'. He attacked Gladstone's stress on freedom of contract in relation to the exclusion of future tenancies, declaring that the bill was 'about to commit a wrong for the sake of a theory which existed only in the inner consciousness of the Prime Minister'. Freedom of contract was the '*bête noire* of this Bill'.[71]

Healy's mastery of the bill was achieved with the assistance of memoranda and drafts furnished by his brother Maurice, then a twenty-two-year-old solicitor's apprentice of exceptional ability. To Maurice he wrote in April 'I don't quite understand yet the bill, as I have only read it twice. Criticisms will be valuable for Committee, where I shall be sitting listening to the clauses, and shall have acquired bit by bit the knowledge necessary to avail of your suggestions'. They continued to exchange views by letter through the debates. He wrote in July 'your amendments have been conceived with so much skill that I am looked upon as having a perfect mastery of the Bill!'[72]

At the outset of the debates on the land bill, Healy wrote to Maurice that 'the prejudice in which I am regarded makes every suggestion, on account of its proposer, have a slender chance. However, that will wear off if I can show that I understand what I am talking about'.[73] In the course of the debates Healy sloughed off the disrepute in which he was held at Westminster.

The dramatic change the debates wrought in Healy's standing was reflected in the fact that twice in the course of July the Prime Minister openly approached him on the floor of the Commons. Of the first encounter Healy wrote to Maurice:

> Gladstone came up to me last night on the floor of the House after our division against the Irish Board of Works, to make a little joke.
>
> I had never spoken to him, and was astonished to see him sailing up the floor towards me, with a twinkle in his eye. I had been pitching into Colonel McKerley of the Board of Works, and said he was an old man, and should be pensioned off and new blood thrown into the place.
>
> During the division when we re-entered the House from opposite doors, Gladstone opened out on me with a smiling broadside: 'I quite see the force of your arguments, Mr. Healy, as to pensioning off the old man! Yes, pension off the old man'.
>
> I protested, but he rather 'had' me in a playful way.
>
> The House was in amaze to see the Prime Minister communing openly with one of its greatest horrors.[74]

Of reported conferences between Healy and Gladstone the *Daily Express* commented: 'tell it not in Land League circles'.[75]

On 27 July, Healy's efforts were rewarded by his greatest legislative prize. T. P. O'Connor described Healy 'in mild and careless tones' proposing an amendment which provided that no increase in judicial rent could be allowed in respect of improvements effected by a tenant. The government agreed to adopt the import of the amendment but proposed to substitute its own wording. O'Connor wrote:

> Apparently nothing very particular had occurred: the whole business had passed over in unbroken tranquillity and overflowing amicability. But the prime mover in the business knew well what he had done. With a face of sphinx-like severity Mr. Healy whispered to the friend at his side: 'These words will put millions in the pockets of the tenants'.[76]

The government's draft of what became universally known as the 'Healy clause' passed into law as section 8(9) of the act. Its effect was to be significantly curtailed by the Irish Court of Appeal in the case of *Adams v Dunseath* in 1882.[77] Yet it conferred a significant benefit on the Irish tenants which did much to address their long-standing grievance at being compelled to pay increased rent as a result of their own improvements to their holdings. It marked Healy out as the leading parliamentary champion of the interests of the Irish tenant farmer.

Healy wrote to Maurice of E. P. Marum, who sat for Kilkenny: 'Marum is mad about the "Healy clause" and claims it as his. *Hansard* leaves no doubt as to where its initiation lay'. The amendment could not have passed without the support of Hugh Law, the Attorney-General for Ireland, who had accepted the thrust of his amendment. He later asserted that the good in the act was due to Law whom the tenants should thank, 'and any evil is due to Mr. Gladstone the Prime Minister'.[78]

Healy's parliamentary role excited the deep mistrust of the radicals of the Land League, which he fully reciprocated. William O'Brien wrote in his *Recollections* of 1905 that Healy's 'own mastery of the Bill, and the perfectly voluptuous delight with which he revelled in its details, had so far deadened him to all broader considerations of National policy that his scorn for its opponents knew no bounds'. He accused Healy of 'incipient rebellion against his colleagues', alleging that he had persevered in his attempts to amend the bill long after Parnell and the majority of his colleagues had resolved to withdraw.[79]

The latter allegation was unfounded. Healy fully supported the decision of the party to leave the House of Commons in a body on the division of the second reading.[80] Indeed at the party meeting he proposed the counter-motion to that proposed by Edmund Dwyer Gray and seconded by A. M. Sullivan seeking to have the debate adjourned to enable the party to consider further its action on the second reading. Parnell was navigating a difficult course between those on the left who were opposed to the land bill outright, and those on the Catholic right who favoured the party giving it open support. Writing to his brother, Healy defended the action of the party in abstaining:

> I can understand the action of our Party on the Bill in abstaining caused a 'sensation', and why wouldn't it, from the way the news was printed. The newsmen now see, after all their talk about 'Splits' the demonstration of unity, which brought out thirty-five men, practically the entire of our number. John Daly and O'Connor Power were the only ones sitting with us who voted for the Bill.[81]

Yet O'Brien was correct in discerning a divergence between Healy and Parnell which was to deepen over the ensuing decade. While skilfully dissembling his purpose in the vehemence of his rhetoric, Healy was of all the Parnellites the most eager to ensure the passage into law of the government's land bill in the most comprehensive form possible. He was disconcerted by Parnell's lack of enthusiasm for a sustained effort to amend the bill, and dissented from Parnell's observation to him that 'we were only wasting our time trying to amend the bill'. He on the contrary believed that 'the Government are behaving fairly, taking into account difficulties with the Whigs, the Tories and the Lords'. In his memoirs he characteristically attributed Parnell's conduct — in an obvious allusion to his affair with Katharine O'Shea — to the fact that his mind was 'far away'. His earlier assessment that 'the influence of the so-called extremists deterred Parnell from personally devoting himself to amending the Bill' acknowledged the considerations of policy by which he was constrained.[82]

Occasionally the difference of approach between Healy and Parnell emerged into the open. In one instance, following a temporising and equivocal statement by Gladstone in response to an amendment of Healy's, Parnell intervened to urge Healy to withdraw the amendment, as he did. Healy later ventured that Parnell had been a little too hasty in acceding to the suggestion that the amendment should be withdrawn, as it was of wider scope than he seemed to think: 'it was one of the amendments which the Irish hierarchy had stated to be of vital importance, and was one upon which the acceptance of the Bill by the Irish members depended'.[83]

In 1881, Healy and Parnell were pursuing convergent strategies. Parnell's aloofness complemented Healy's extraction of practical gains. As Healy later boasted to Labouchere, 'the beauty of the measure was that it was supposed to be disapproved of by the nationalists'.[84] In the domestic political aspect, Healy subscribed fully to Parnell's purpose of putting down his agrarian left wing.

Healy's success led him to acquire a taste for *haute politique*, for which he altogether lacked aptitude. Anticipating an attempt by Salisbury, the pre-eminent Conservative leader, to eviscerate the bill in the Lords, Healy wrote to his brother that he would advise Parnell to learn from Salisbury what he was going to do with the bill, 'and direct our course on the third reading accordingly. My present impression is that we should vote for it then so we may be able to resist Whig assaults at the Dissolution'.[85]

At the convention of the Land League held after the bill's third reading, Parnell adroitly negotiated a middle course between rejection and overt acceptance of the bill when enacted, by urging on tenants a policy of holding back until after a series of test cases had been brought under Land League auspices. Healy was charged with the supervision of the legal strategy. While Parnell addressed a series of meetings in Ireland and conferred with local leaders, Healy sifted the test cases and directed the local attorneys concerned.[86]

Healy duly selected cases which affirmed the Land League's version of Irish social reality. What he sought were holdings with high rentals and where extensive improvements had been carried out by the tenant. Parnell's strategy was precarious. An *Evening Standard* journalist who accompanied Healy in Fermoy and Mitchelstown quickly concluded that the leaders of the Land League would find that they had carried the doctrine of testing the act too far. 'Time after time I have seen a sharp farmer's face cloud over doubtfully when he has been told that he should abstain from going into Court until test cases, not affecting in any way the principle upon which his own must be decided, have been heard'.[87]

The virtuosity of Healy's rhetorical denunciations of landlordism provided his ideological cover. His speeches and writings under the guise of a hostile critique of the act's limitations imparted information intended to enable the tenants to exploit to the maximum the act's provisions. Healy's *Tenant's Key to the Land Law Act 1881* was itself highly deviant in Land League terms.[88] For the agrarian radicals its publication was the culmination of an insidious propaganda, and led both Dillon and Patrick Egan to oppose Healy's election to the executive of the Land League.[89] Conversely the *Tenant's Key* commended itself to the *Irish Times*. Even W. E. Forster advised Gladstone that it was 'not bad and will tempt the tenants into court. The man's intellect has got for a time the better of his vice'.[90]

The Land League radicals' mistrust of Healy was well founded. In doctrinal terms he was a formidable and elusive adversary who, working for the present under the protection of Parnell's hegemony, exploited to the full the ambivalence and indefiniteness of agrarian nationalist rhetoric. As a parliamentarian he had emerged transformed from the debates on the land act. What was less immediately obvious was that he had acquired his enduring role in Irish politics as the ideologue and jurist of a proprietorial solution to the Irish land question.

United Ireland

At the 1880 election, the Parnellites had suffered from the lack of a daily newspaper.[91] As Healy wrote to his brother, 'we cabled from Montreal to know if the *Nation* could be brought out as a daily paper during the elections (the Land League guaranteeing risk), but I suppose this was impossible'. Parnell was driven to conclude that Land League funds should be expended on starting a daily newspaper. A. M. Sullivan had once hoped to start the *Nation* as a daily paper, but was outmanoeuvred by Edmund Dwyer Gray 'and the Sullivan's never succeeded in capturing the profitable part of Nationalist journalism'.[92]

However, after Parnell's election to the chair, Dwyer Gray, already bruised by the 'papist rats' episode, took care never again to defy him. Parnell's mind then turned to the establishment of a weekly newspaper. Apart from enforcing the armed truce with Gray, this had other attractions. A weekly paper would marginalise T. D. Sullivan's *Nation*. An independently controlled weekly, even if favourably disposed, was no substitute for a paper instituted and controlled by Parnell through his lieutenants. The fact that the *Nation* had initially failed to support Parnell's policy on the land bill sealed its fate.

There was moreover the attraction of countering the influence of Davitt and the Land League radicals. By creating William O'Brien, on whose complete loyalty he could depend, editor of a popular nationalist and agrarian weekly, Parnell could institutionalise a 'soft left' within the movement he led. He could rely on O'Brien to articulate an agrarian nationalism which deferred to his leadership, upheld parliamentary methods, and accepted the primacy of home rule over land reform. The so-called 'Kilmainham party', constituted of imprisoned Land League activists, were for good reason strenuously opposed to Parnell's newspaper project.[93]

When to these considerations was added the possibility — delusive though it was to prove — of ridding nationalist politics of Richard Pigott, Parnell acted. The sale of Pigott's stable of waning newspapers, the *Irishman*, the *Flag of Ireland* and the *Shamrock*, had been mooted as far back as 1875. As one veteran nationalist later recalled, the papers 'always seemed to be in the market, whether to the Government or Nationalists after-events showed to be a matter of perfect indifference to him'.[94] In May 1881 Pigott made a fresh overture to Parnell and Patrick Egan, arguing that Parnell and the Land League 'cannot well do without an organ'. The entire press had favoured the land bill; renewing his old vendetta with the Sullivans, he added 'even the *Nation* is opposed to its rejection'. Using Land League funds Parnell and Egan purchased the papers from Pigott for the very considerable sum of £3,000.[95]

Given Pigott's reputation – Egan described him as 'for many years past the *bête noire* of Irish politics' – the purchase of his papers excited widespread distaste. Egan sought to justify the purchase of the papers from Pigott at a price in excess of their commercial value 'in order to purify National politics of his presence'. Parnell likewise, in urging O'Brien to accept the editorship of *United Ireland*, expressed his fear that the *Irishman* would have been maintained by secret service monies as an ultra-nationalist organ opposed to the Parnellite movement. Pigott had blithely sought an increase in the price which had been agreed in the event that the purchasers did not retain his services. Parnell commented to O'Brien 'that is pretty cool, considering that we paid nine-tenths of the purchase money to get rid of him'.[96]

There was some slight benefit from Parnell's point of view in acquiring a newspaper which had under Pigott's editorship struck a pose of high-minded Fenian opposition to parliamentary nationalism. The indulgence of what O'Brien described as 'the old Fenian public, less numerous, perhaps, than worthy of respect', was carried too far in permitting the *Irishman* to continue to appear without strict Parnellite editorial supervision. The content of the paper was later to provide the *Times* with considerable assistance at the Special Commission. Parnell told the Commission that his first instinct had been to stop the publication of the *Irishman*, but that he had come to agree with O'Brien, who had urged that he 'should not be a party to depriving the Extreme Nationalists of what they might regard as their organ', and that it would be preferable to allow the paper to expire commercially rather than to suppress it. Characteristically, O'Brien was too squeamish to deprive its editor James O'Connor of his livelihood.

If Parnell and O'Brien had at the outset made a conscious decision to defer to the *Irishman*'s diehard Fenian constituency by not suppressing the paper, they had thereafter little if any familiarity with the contents of what was a politically marginal paper with a tiny circulation. The difficulty was that to an English audience this state of affairs understandably seemed odd, if not highly improbable. O'Brien, who admittedly was seeking to shield Parnell as much as possible, told the Special Commission that Parnell, on learning in early 1882 that the *Irishman* was still extant, told him 'for goodness sake drop it', but again relented and agreed to permit it to die a natural death. Parnell described the *Irishman* as 'a sort of *damnosa haereditas* which we had received from Mr. Pigott, which we carried on for a time for the purpose of giving this employment to James O'Connor'. Both O'Brien and Parnell lamely professed astonishment when it was put to them that the paper had lingered on until February 1885.[97]

The acquisition of Pigott's papers with a view to the publication of what was in effect an authorised Parnellite rival to the *Nation* was a bitter blow to T. D. Sullivan. Parnell responded stonily to the remonstrances of T. D. Sullivan when they met in the Commons on 15 July. Sullivan recorded: '. . . I stigmatised in strong terms the course that had been taken . . . I said it was absolute treachery towards myself, ungrateful towards a national journal which had stood by the Irish cause in all weathers, and which had helped to make the Land League, and to defend it and its leaders when they needed help very much'. Parnell replied that the matter had given him some trouble as being hardly fair to the *Nation*. As Parnell told the Special Commission, Sullivan 'had every reason to feel annoyed that the funds of the Land League should be used for setting up what was undoubtedly an opposition paper to his, and which eventually ruined his paper'.[98]

On 21 July, Healy informed his brother 'Parnell tells me T.D.S. is sore about the *Irishman* purchase from Pigott, and half-hinted at the formation of a *Nation* Party'.[99] Pigott boasted to the Chief Secretary: 'I think we are not far from that apparently inevitable concomitant of every Irish movement, a split'.[100] Whether or not Sullivan gave such a 'half-hint', which is much to be doubted, Parnell's purpose in stating this to Healy was to remind him that his primary allegiance was owed to his leader rather than to his kinsman. He was posing a test of commitment which Healy could not afford to fail.

The first issue of *United Ireland* appeared on 13 August 1881. Parnell had, for the first time, an organ absolutely loyal to his leadership, while remaining protected by William O'Brien's editorship from responsibility for its contents. He could calmly assure the Special Commission that 'paragraphs and articles have often appeared of a stronger character than I could have approved, from time to time, and they appear to this day'. He considered that 'the people of Ireland everywhere understand that Mr. O'Brien's opinions are considerably in advance of mine'.[101]

Healy was unconstrained by sentimental allegiance to Sullivan or to the *Nation*, a paper which the rise of Parnellism had already made to appear archaic. Woundingly he wrote for *United Ireland* the parliamentary letter that he had formerly contributed to the *Nation*. For an extensive period prior to the Galway election of 1886 he virtually co-wrote the paper with William O'Brien.[102] Parnell had thus driven a further wedge deep into the Sullivan connection.

Kilmainham

Unnerved, the government obtusely misinterpreted the ostensible vehemence of Parnell's speeches in Ireland, through which he sought to impose the substantively moderate policy of testing the land act. Gladstone at Leeds on 7 October delivered an ill-tempered speech in which he memorably warned, in an obvious threat to imprison Parnell, that 'the resources of civilization are not yet exhausted'. Parnell responded at a meeting in Healy's constituency two days later by attacking Gladstone as 'this masquerading knight-errant'. Speaking after Parnell, Healy strove unavailingly to strike the same note of high defiance:

> They had heard how Mr. Parnell had dealt with the babbling of this old man, Gladstone (*cheers*), who had charged him with being the leader of a party of public plunder . . . What mattered it to them? They cared not for their sayings. They were not Englishmen, they were Paddies evermore.

The next day Parnell, having been presented with the freedom of the borough, passed through the thronged streets of Wexford. He whispered to Healy sitting beside him in the carriage, 'Healy, we have pressed this movement as far as it can constitutionally go!'[103]

On 12 October the government resolved on the imprisonment of Parnell. He was arrested in Dublin at Morrison's Hotel on Dawson Street and taken to Kilmainham. He responded in his severest mode. He insisted on posting his correspondence before entering the jail.

> Some dozen or twenty hawkers, labourers and car-drivers recognised him here, and seeing that he was under arrest pressed forward to touch and speak to him. He drew back, and would give his hand to no one as he passed into the courtyard of the prison. With no less *hauteur* he entered the prison itself, and standing erect in the outer hall scarcely condescended to recognise those of his acquaintances among the suspects who advanced respectfully to greet him.[104]

Parnell was held at Kilmainham from 13 October 1881 to 2 May 1882. The depth of his anger and resentment at this incarceration, concealed at this time beneath his studied impassiveness, did not become apparent until the split.[105] *United Ireland* characterised the incarceration of 'our chief, our guide' in almost biblical terms: 'Let them wring their hearts; let them manacle the body of our beloved chief. His spirit is abroad in a million Irish hearts. His work is done; his lesson taught. It has sunk into our souls . . .'[106] O'Brien himself was soon to be arrested.

Healy in London was having lunch when he heard the newsboys on the Strand crying the news of Parnell's arrest, and immediately set out for Ireland. At Holyhead on the ship's gangway he was met by an official of the Land League, who gave him a letter from Thomas Sexton conveying the unanimous wish of the Land League that he should remain in England until the executive had considered the position. Thus excluded from what he described as 'the Land League Academy' of Kilmainham jail, he returned to London.[107] He would have been gratified to learn of Sir William Harcourt's commentary on events: '. . . Forster goes on bagging his Leaguers, and Dillon and Sexton are now in the mouse trap. I am sorry he has missed Healy who is the most dangerous . . . of them all.'[108]

In a press interview Healy observed that the government had damaged the prospects for its own land legislation: 'if I were a farmer in some country district in Ireland, I would not care to be the man who would now apply to the courts under its provisions with Parnell in gaol'. He anticipated a general refusal to pay rent, rates and taxes while Parnell was imprisoned.[109] He wrote anxiously to Maurice:

> Write me the feelings of the people over the situation. What do they think, and what will they do? Are they intimidated? Will the priests act? I suppose the next move will be to suppress *United Ireland*.[110]

Healy was instructed to go to Paris. There Patrick Egan devised a plan to send Healy and the firebrand Father Eugene Sheehy to the United States. Healy complied, although he would certainly have preferred to remain in London. Healy and Sheehy arrived in the United States on 8 November, joining T. P. O'Connor who had been there for the previous month. Healy remained in the United States until 14 February 1882, maintaining a gruelling series of speaking engagements. The least-known of the Irish delegates, he was assigned mainly to the southern and mid-western states, and attracted significantly less press attention than either O'Connor or the wrathful ecclesiastic. He was not in his rhetorical element. He confided to his father that he was wretched at the art of the fundraising declamation. On his return he wrote: 'The Americans . . . are a great people for going to hear lectures — and a lecture, not a speech, is what is expected from a speaker on the Irish question'.[111]

Healy's speeches in the United States were characterised by a somewhat contrived vehemence. At Boston he declared: 'As the Master said unto the tempter when he offered him the kingdoms of the earth, "Begone Satan", so we will say unto them, "Begone Saxon"'. This was necessary not least to allay Irish-American reservations as to the political legitimacy in nationalist terms of the land movement. He asserted that he was in America not merely in the interest of the Irish farmer, 'but as an Irish Nationalist, and I believe that the destruction of Irish landlordism involves the creation of an Irish nationality'.[112]

All three delegates were present at the Chicago convention which was subsequently described by John Bright as 'a convention of traitors'. While only Sheehy spoke at the convention, Healy and O'Connor addressed a meeting after the convention proper. Their attendance was to bulk large in the *Times* case at the Special Commission. Baulked of Healy's appearance as a witness, counsel for the *Times* cross-examined T. P. O'Connor in relation to Healy's words: 'For what is the business of the Convention assembled? It is the purpose of revenge as I take it; revenge upon the enemy which drove you and your fathers forth from your own land'.[113]

Healy's fierceness was deceptive. He was profoundly impressed by the conservatism and sagacity of most of the Irish Americans, an impression he sought to convey in a series of articles published in the *Newcastle Daily Chronicle* on his return, under the title 'The Irish and the Land League in America'. He dismissed the predominant English depiction of the Irish American as a sanguinary *émigré* ('the swashbuckling Irish American has become one of the most effective pieces of stage property of Sir William Harcourt in his heavier roles'), and argued on the contrary that

> it may truly be said that a more cautious conservative and thoughtful body of men does not exist. The Irishmen who conduct the land movement in America may almost be called cold-blooded in their methodical determination by no official act to commit the people at home to any imprudence.

This moderation he explained as a response to the failure of Fenianism: 'Ten or fifteen years ago the Fenian movement permeated them to an extent little understood here – certainly never before by me'. He had been surprised at the widespread deprecation of Jeremiah O'Donovan Rossa. While Healy praised John Devoy's 'considerable coolness of blood', he was struck by other more moderate figures: '. . . it is doubtful whether any three members could be picked out of the present Irish Parliamentary representation equal all round in oratory and *tactique* to three of the men sent as delegates to the Chicago Convention – Collins of Boston, and Hynes and Finerty of Chicago'.

On this occasion, the United States left a lasting impression on Healy. He wrote admiringly 'American air sharpens Irish wits, and today the sons of the hodman and of the navvy throng every avenue of progress in the Republic'. It seemed as if 'the chief evil of emigration were to divorce Ireland from her intellect'.[114] Healy observed the United States with an eye sharpened by ambition rather than moist with sentiment. His tour affirmed his vision of a property-owning nationalist society. He told the Commons that contrary to the prevalent perception, 'dealing with the American-Irish as a whole, he found them the most Conservative body of men he had ever met. Every Irishman in America had some little property, and there was nothing made a man so Conservative as the possession of property'.[115] As he wrote to Maurice, 'it makes a change to be cut loose for four months from Ireland, and to have lived among a free people'.[116]

On his return Healy began contributing an influential letter to the Boston *Republic* in which he explained and defended Parnell's policy from the Kilmainham treaty onwards. Flatly opposed to Davitt's espousal of the land nationalisation doctrines of Henry George (the 'California communist'), the *Republic* was appreciative of Healy's anti-radicalism: 'Mr. Healy's letters have been copied by every Irish-American paper and the press generally throughout the land, and have done much to counteract the dangerous tendencies in certain quarters, in the direction of socialism, communism and other pernicious doctrines'.[117]

The Kilmainham Treaty

Healy returned to a political impasse. The no-rent manifesto which Parnell had authorised on his arrest had, as he probably anticipated, fallen on deaf ears. 'The Irish leaders were ahead of the people', Healy wrote in the Boston *Republic*, and 'the Irish cottiers are not a phalanx of heroes'.[118] What was more significant was that the government's policy had likewise demonstrably failed. The expectation that the imprisonment of Parnell and the leaders of the Land League would bring to an end agrarian disturbances had, predictably, not been borne out. Gladstone was increasingly trapped within the confines of his own policy: Parnell's imprisonment precluded a change of direction towards constructive engagement with the Irish nationalists. Those within the government who had never been entirely at ease with the decision to arrest Parnell began to cast around for a way forward, while Parnell chafed at the protraction of his confinement.

On his return to London, Healy had evident difficulty recovering his political bearings. There was in place an intact chain of command from which he was excluded. He was unaware of how far advanced Parnell's strategy already was, and could not entirely accommodate himself to a situation in which nationalist policy was being directed from Kilmainham rather than Westminster. He wrote to Maurice on 25 February:

> Have you done anything about the Bill to amend the Land Act? Biggar was telling me today the Party had given notice of one, but that it is not yet drafted, and that it will probably fall on me to do it! This is charming. If you will let me know whether you have any ideas on the subject I will get from the Party on Monday the notions they themselves have . . .
>
> There seems to be unlimited communication with the men in jail, as Parnell directs lots of things here. The Government are in the devil's mess . . .
>
> Have you ever had to meet any of those Lady Land Leaguers? Tell me about them. I am curious. What about Parnell's mother?[119]

In fact it was Maurice who had been entrusted with the responsibility for the drafting of the amending land bill. Parnell told the Special Commission that he had asked permission for a private interview with Maurice Healy, still at that time a solicitor's apprentice, and had several extended interviews in which he gave him the necessary instructions to draft the bill, providing among other matters for tenants who were in arrears.[120]

While in the bitterness of the split, Parnell sought to deny Maurice the credit, he was at the time appreciative of his work on the bill, whose felicitous drafting Gladstone had praised. In what Alfred Robbins described as 'a wonderful tribute from so customarily reticent a man', Parnell told him in the spring of 1890 that Maurice Healy knew more about the Irish land question than any man living, and that his services in the drafting of the bill had been invaluable.[121] Maurice Healy's indentures of apprenticeship were subsequentiy transferred to MacGough, the Land League solicitor in Dublin. Later in the year Healy wrote to Maurice that Parnell had spoken to him 'about the desirability of having you in Dublin, and from what I could gather he desires to get rid of poor MacGough', whom he later described as 'hopeless'.[122] Maurice, who had settled in Cork, did not displace MacGough, but became for a period in effect parliamentary draftsman to the Irish National League. Healy in a letter in early 1883 referred to Maurice having drafted three bills, and written what he called 'the Land pamphlet', for the League.[123] Maurice also wrote for the National League a *Summary of the Law Relating to the Parliamentary Franchise in Irish Counties* (Dublin, 1883). This in turn shaped his legal practice. He told the Special Commission that 'ever since I have been in the law business my business has largely lain in the landlord and tenant department, as I may call it'.[124]

On the amending bill, the divergence of approach which had emerged between Healy and Parnell on the act itself sensibly widened. Parnell sought a narrow and concise bill. Healy wanted it to be as comprehensive as possible. He wrote to Maurice on 16 March that 'with regard to the amending Land Bill I don't agree with Parnell as to "small details" not being provided for . . . Nor do I agree with Parnell that Ministers will not read a long Bill. Assure him that there will be the greatest anxiety to see our Bill, for high interest is felt in it'. His political thinking was already driven by the anticipation of a large Conservative measure of land purchase:

> The Tories are determined to dish the Whigs on the Land question, and have a scheme by which tenants can become proprietors on paying the present rents for forty years. Well, if we have not every detail inserted in our new Bill we cannot hope to amend the Government Bill by proposing further details when it comes on, as the Government will say, 'Oh, you had a bill of your own recently and it contained no such proposals'.

He wrote shortly afterwards reiterating his conviction that 'it is a mistake not to insert *every* amendment, no matter how small, to the Act of 1881'. By November he was writing 'Parnell doesn't understand law points'.[125]

On 1 April, awaiting the proof of the land bill, Healy wrote to Maurice: 'What about the labourers? Wouldn't this be the time for Parnell to show his sympathy towards them? Where are his projects for their emancipation?' The fact the bill had been drafted, the interrogative form, and Healy's own failure to make proposals for the 'emancipation' of the Irish labourers suggest the shallowness of his professed concern. The conspicuously aspirational nature of his concerns for the Irish agricultural labourer was by no means unrepresentative.

Having evidently made some indiscreet allusion to Maurice's consultations with Parnell, Healy sought to defend himself. His response evoked the strained and unnatural conditions under which the government was obliged to deal with Irish affairs during Parnell's imprisonment:

> I am surprised at what you tell me about the Government not knowing your business with Parnell in Kilmainham Jail. I thought they understood, as I could not suppose that they would allow you in, day after day, without knowing that it was not upon private matters you conferred. I imagine they know very well, and wink at it, as they are very sensitive about comments in the House.
>
> Gladstone would not like (while he would not admit Parnell's right to conduct affairs) to stop him in the exercise of his functions as director of policy. Although it cannot be clearly seen, yet our sarcasms are keenly felt, and they would not needlessly run amok with us.
>
> I may be excused for not knowing that your visits were not known to be on public business, seeing that I could not imagine on what other basis the Government allow them to take place. If anything happens to Dillon in jail Forster will go mad. Sometimes I pity him.[126]

Healy was impatient at Parnell's absence from Westminster, and had difficulty concealing his contempt for the Land League radicals with whom he was incarcerated in Kilmainham. His attitude was implicit in the terms in which he urged Parnell's release in the Commons:

> They claimed that when Dick, Tom, and Harry had been released on parole to sow their potatoes or attend their shops, Charles Stewart Parnell, the Leader of the Irish race, and his Colleagues, ought at least to be allowed to attend the House of Commons to record their votes on so vital a question.[127]

Three weeks later he turned an attack on the counterproductiveness of the government's coercion policy into a striking disavowal of the Land

League. The government's mistake arose from 'the fancied connection' between the Irish party and those responsible for agrarian violence in Ireland:

> In the Land League there was a large number of men who viewed Parliamentary action with the greatest jealousy; they were men who believed Parliamentary action to be entirely useless; and, therefore, when the Government attempted to fix upon the Irish Parliamentary Party, who were but very small agents in the matter, any responsibility, they were doing them a great injustice, and exhibiting the ignorance and misconception of Irish affairs which so charmingly distinguished Englishmen in general . . .
>
> For his part, he had never any connection with the Executive of the Land League, or with the apportionment of its funds. If he had an offer of the kind, he should decline with thanks, for the gentlemen of the Land League were well able to conduct their own affairs. The connection between the Land League and the Irish Party simply amounted to this. The latter were engaged as the champions of a particular scheme of agrarian reform which was similar to that advocated by the Land League; but there the connection ended. He himself could say faithfully that he had as little to do with the political working of the Land League as any Gentleman of the Treasury Bench ('*Oh*'). That was absolutely a fact. He challenged anyone to deny it.[128]

The contrast with Parnell's strategy could not have been more marked. Parnell avoided any open breach with the Land League executive, and instead turned its radicalism to useful purpose within the complex and shifting coalition over which he presided. He moreover was never so careless as to leave open the inference that the Land League had any responsibility for agrarian violence. The timing of Healy's speech was significant. He publicly dissociated himself from the Land League at a time when the momentum towards a political settlement which would marginalise the League was becoming irresistible. It was a deliberate, and characteristic, essay in polarisation, positing a choice between allegiance to Parnell and to the Land League. He was staking out a distinctive position within the protective shade of Parnell's authority.

On 22 April the cabinet authorised Joseph Chamberlain to communicate on his own behalf with members of the Irish party, including Healy, but did not empower him to negotiate. Chamberlain's purpose was to ascertain whether an accommodation with the Irish party which would permit the release of the 'suspects' was possible on the basis of the government's agreement to a legislative remission of arrears of rent. Chamberlain's initiative was characteristically predicated on the existence of distinct wings (if not of a line of schism) within the Irish party. His memorandum to the government advocated an approach to 'some of the leaders of the extreme party, especially Mr. Healy and Mr. Sexton, who I think recently have shown a desire to come back to a more moderate policy', as well as to those considered better disposed to the Liberal government. Significantly he referred throughout to the Irish party's amending bill as 'Healy's bill', even though it was in fact introduced by John Redmond and had not been drafted by Healy. Chamberlain wrote of the bill: 'Speaking generally its proposals are not unreasonable and afford a basis for agreement, and if they were in principle adopted, Mr. Healy and all who follow him would be of necessity committed to the Land Act in the successful operation of which they would have a joint interest in future with the government'.[129]

According to Healy, he was asked by Captain O'Shea to speak to Chamberlain, which he agreed to do in the belief that Parnell wished it. Chamberlain however claimed that O'Shea had told him that Healy had requested the interview. On the evening of 24 April, O'Shea introduced Healy to Chamberlain in a downstairs room of the House of Commons, where Healy and Chamberlain had a meeting of some length. Healy was at a disadvantage. In Chamberlain's later account 'I did not refer to the information I had received on Mr. Parnell's opinions or to my previous conversation with Captain O'Shea, but sought to gather Mr. Healy's individual opinions on the questions at issue'. Healy was in effect being invited to volunteer his own views as to how an arrangement might be come to between the government and Parnell.[130]

Healy had permitted himself to be placed in a false position. He was unaware of Parnell's thinking, or of the extent to which Parnell's efforts to come to an accord with the government were already advanced. Parnell left Kilmainham on parole on 10 April to attend the funeral in Paris of his nephew, and returned to Kilmainham on 24 April, the day of Healy's meeting with Chamberlain. By that time O'Shea had already outlined to Chamberlain the basis on which Parnell was prepared to come to an accommodation with the government, while Parnell moved to open a second and more reliable channel of communication with Chamberlain through Justin McCarthy.[131]

Healy had always regarded O'Shea with a contempt which verged on loathing. He was completely ignorant of Parnell's dealings with O'Shea. On 16 March he had written to his brother in Dublin urging him to ask Parnell to write to the O'Gorman Mahon who had indicated he would vote with the government on the cloture. He added: 'if he writes to O'Shea also it may be useful. They are both humbugs'.[132]

Parnell's letter to O'Shea of 28 April, which O'Shea forwarded to the Chief Secretary, provided the protocols of what became known as the 'Kilmainham treaty'. Parnell sought the resolution of the arrears question, and the admission of the leaseholders to the 1881 act, and looked to an extension of the land purchase provisions of the act. Such a programme would he believed permit the restoration of order, and dispense with the necessity for a renewal of coercion at the end of the session. Parnell added the astonishing and gratuitous statement that such a programme 'would enable us to co-operate cordially for the future with the Liberal party in forwarding Liberal principles and measures of general reform'.[133]

On 3 May, the release of Parnell, Dillon and O'Kelly from Kilmainham was announced, along with the resignation of W. E. Forster in protest. That evening, the day before Parnell reached London, a meeting took place in the lower smoking room of the Commons between Chamberlain and leading members of the Irish party including Healy. The meeting, held on Chamberlain's initiative, proceeded on the erroneous assumption shared by everyone present that Chamberlain would succeed Forster as Chief Secretary.

In McCarthy's account, Chamberlain 'got together a few of the leading men of the Irish Parliamentary Party and consulted with them and asked for their opinions. This was the first time we were ever consulted by a Minister. This took place in the lower smoking room, there were about a half a dozen of us there'. In his later memoir Chamberlain made no reference to the meeting. He did acknowledge receiving a warning he considered 'kindly' from Healy, whom he met in the lobby. Healy expressed the hope that for Chamberlain's sake he was not appointed Chief Secretary: 'He said he would personally do what he could to help me but that the situation was impossible. Sooner or later I should find myself unable to satisfy Irish demands and then they would no more spare me than anyone else'.[134]

It is inconceivable that O'Shea omitted to advise Parnell that Healy had met Chamberlain on 24 April. O'Shea rarely passed up an opportunity to discredit Healy. (On 8 May, two days after the Phoenix Park murders, he wrote Gladstone seeking to arrange a meeting to discuss matters he could not explain by letter: 'They range from a "cave" which is being formed by Mr. Healy, to a warning of intended assassinations'.[135]) It is certain that Parnell would have been immediately apprised of the meeting of 3 May by the other Irish party participants.

O'Shea's sedulous fanning of Parnell's suspicions of Healy was hardly necessary. The knowledge that Healy had met alone with Chamberlain sufficed to harden Parnell's attitude towards Healy, as his habitual watchfulness turned to mistrust. An encounter between two men who were in different ways potential adversaries could not have failed to arouse his darkest suspicions. In the split he would furiously charge that while he was in Kilmainham Healy had sought to conclude a treaty with Chamberlain 'behind my back and the backs of his party, and sell the cause of Ireland for nothing'.[136]

Davitt was unreconciled to the accommodation reached between Parnell and the government. The Irish promotion of what became the government's arrears bill he later described as 'a huge tactical blunder' calculated to kill the agrarian agitation and quieten the country. Of Healy's characterisation of the Kilmainham treaty, quoted in R. B. O'Brien's biography of Parnell, as 'one of the most sagacious arrangements that ever enabled a hard pressed general secure terms for his forces', Davitt noted acidly, 'Tim's view (or one of them) of the Kilmainham Treaty'.[137]

Criticism of the Kilmainham treaty was not confined to the nationalist left wing. There was an unease among conservative and moderate nationalists which owed much to the conspicuous involvement of the reviled W. H. O'Shea. Following a defiant speech at Manchester on 21 May insisting that the Land League was not dead, Davitt received a letter of support from A. M. Sullivan, an unlikely source: 'Much depends on *you* just now. Would to God we had never heard of "Captain O'Shea M.P." and his negotiations and intrigues'.[138]

The Phoenix Park Murders

> Horror, in this case, is due to Mr. Parnell: he sits before posterity silent, Mr. Forster's appeal echoing down the ages.
>
> Robert Louis Stevenson and Fanny Van de Grift Stevenson, *The Dynamiter*[139]

On the evening of 6 May, the new Chief Secretary Sir Frederick Cavendish and his Under-Secretary T. H. Burke were stabbed to death in the Phoenix Park, within sight of the Vice-regal Lodge, by members of a secret society which called itself the Invincibles. Rarely has so brutal an atrocity been perpetrated in a political situation of such delicacy. The assassinations struck at the root of Parnell's parliamentary policy. Aghast, he immediately conveyed to Gladstone an offer to resign his seat if Gladstone judged it necessary for the furtherance of their common purpose. He met Davitt, Dillon and O'Kelly at the Westminster Palace Hotel. There they were joined by Healy and other nationalist leaders as Davitt drafted a manifesto condemning the murders. Those present were utterly downcast. Healy proposed they should all resign their seats, and Parnell appeared to lean to this course. In McCarthy's account

> Mr. Parnell seemed determined to resign public life, he said this crime would be the ruin of Ireland for another generation and it was no use trying to do any good when we were exposed to the commission of a crime like this behind our backs. Some misfortune seemed to hang over everything done for Ireland. The act of some criminal might thus destroy

> the hopes of a generation. For a long time he remained earnest in his desire that we should all go out of Parliament. He said that the public mind of England would regard us with a kind of repulsion not because they thought we had sanctioned these outrages, but because in some way they sprang out of the Irish movement.

For Parnell to argue through his position in this way suggested rather that he was already resolved to persevere. The sense of the meeting was against resignation. After Parnell, his severe taste intact, had struck out the maudlin extravagances from Davitt's draft, he along with Davitt and Dillon signed the manifesto on behalf of the executive of the Land League. Parnell and McCarthy left to confer with first Sir Charles Dilke, and then Joseph Chamberlain.[140]

The sentiments expressed by Parnell to the Press Association bear out those recalled by McCarthy: 'It seems to be as if there were some unhappy destiny presiding over Ireland which always at the moment when there seemed a probability of some chance for our country, comes in suddenly to destroy the hopes of her best friends'.[141] Parnell's position was fraught with peril, poised between the disillusionment of nationalist radicals and extremists at the Kilmainham treaty, and the bitter hatred of many English parliamentarians who held him directly or indirectly responsible for the Phoenix Park murders: for them Parnell, if he was not an accomplice, was at the very least a politician who had practised a murderous duplicity. All of his skill and resolve were required to contain the destabilisation of his policy brought about by the assassinations following so swiftly upon his accommodation with the government. Healy wrote in *United Ireland*:

> Of all living Irishmen, Mr. Parnell is the most to be pitied. The whole public burden of a deed which wrecks his prospects, and is abhorrent to his soul, falls upon his shoulders, and now must he address himself to the task of facing a Coercion Bill which his Party have done nothing to provoke, but which he must meet with proper spirit, despite the odious and clamorous cries of reawakened British ferocity.[142]

In the Boston *Republic*, Healy wrote that Parnell in Kilmainham had been oppressed by the murders committed in Ireland during his imprisonment, knowing that his efforts were liable to be negated by 'the acts of a few hare-brained fanatics'.[143]

In the Commons, Parnell rose after Gladstone and Sir Stafford Northcote. Florence Arnold Forster described him as 'dressed in mourning and looking deadly pale. The few words he said were not distasteful to the House and were quietly received in all parts'. Her account did not convey the depth of the barely muted hatred for Parnell in some quarters of the House.[144]

In the debate a week later on the Kilmainham treaty, its English critics had the satisfaction of witnessing the discomfiture of Parnell, who read out a transcription of his letter to Captain O'Shea which omitted the last paragraph about cooperating in the future with the Liberal party. This gave Forster the opportunity to make a devastating intervention to compel O'Shea to read out the complete text. It was the most deficient performance of Parnell's parliamentary career. He bitterly blamed O'Shea not just for the omission from the transcription but for the reading of the letter in the first place. The memory long rankled. Two days before the resignation of the Salisbury government in January 1886 Katharine O'Shea wrote to Gladstone to open a channel of communication between him and Parnell. She attributed Parnell's reading of the letter in the Commons, 'for which I have always rather reproached myself', to the fact that Captain O'Shea, dining at Eltham, had said that Gladstone desired that O'Shea should read out the letter. Parnell thought it better that he should read it himself. 'Since that episode Parnell has declined to confide his political views to anyone except myself'. She reiterated in the conclusion of her letter: 'Mr. Parnell has long wished you to understand that it was only a threat of its being used against him that decided him to read that letter in the House'.[145]

The assassinations rendered at least a show of further repression inevitable. The Prevention of Crime (Ireland) Bill, introduced on 11 May, was however of unexpected harshness. The opposition offered by Parnell was studiously temperate, so much so that Davitt later commented that 'Parnell really favoured the Coercion Act which followed the Phoenix Park tragedy. But *we all lost our heads*'.[146]

Healy was encumbered neither by the mantle of leadership, nor involvement in the negotiations leading to the Kilmainham treaty. He furiously denounced the bill. Rather than a measure for the preservation of the law and order in Ireland 'it would be much better described as a measure for the better preservation in office of the Liberal Party'. Moreover he disloyally and opportunistically linked his repudiation of the bill with a sparsely veiled attack on Parnell's accord with the government:

> Personally, he was not sorry that this Bill had been introduced, and that it was as stringent and as dramatic as it was. His reason was that it would destroy for ever the last vestige of that absurd idea that there could ever be peace between Ireland and England. It would destroy the rubbish people talked about compacts and compromises – as if any one man had power to make compacts or compromises behind the backs of his Party, or as if that party would tolerate them.[147]

While Healy's conscious purpose was presumably to condemn the pretensions of W. H. O'Shea rather than to undermine Parnell's position, his vehemence carried him into what sounded ominously like a repudiation of the Kilmainham treaty itself.

Healy's provocativeness threatened the prospects for a tacit understanding between Parnell and the government on the bill. It also afforded Captain O'Shea an opportunity to vaunt his influence, which he was quick to seize. He wrote to Gladstone: 'The outrageous speech in which Mr. Healy tried to damage Mr. Parnell as much as the government, I have already turned to some purpose. My object now is to induce Mr. Parnell to retire from interference for the present, urging those whom he can influence to do the same, so as to defeat attempts to obstruct'. Parnell hardly needed O'Shea's prompting to reprove Healy for his speech. (Healy ascribed Parnell's censure to the influence of Edmund Dwyer Gray.) O'Shea complacently wrote to Gladstone the next day that the bill was 'safe from obstruction'.[148]

Healy's opposition persisted in more temperate form, not without tactical advantage to Parnell. On 15 June O'Shea wrote to Chamberlain that 'it is only fair to let you know that he told Healy he would walk out if that member forced a division on a previous amendment'.[149] On 23 June O'Shea wrote, and presumably despatched to Parnell, a characteristically pompous remonstrance:

> A very considerable period of debate has now elapsed since at your request I informed the Prime Minister that there would be no obstruction to the Bill.
>
> I have therefore a special right to beg of you to carry out the engagement in its spirit as well as letter.[150]

Nothing so powerfully attests to the strength of Parnell's attachment to Katharine O'Shea as the fortitude with which he endured her husband's remorseless self-aggrandisement.

By this stage a second channel of communication with the government had been opened up through the radical M.P. Henry Labouchere. While he had an insatiable appetite for intrigue, Labouchere at least lacked O'Shea's exasperating combination of petulance and conceit. On 16 May Labouchere forwarded to Chamberlain the bill with the amendments sought by Healy. He had gone through the bill thus amended with Parnell, who 'agrees with them in the main but would like the opinion of a lawyer with regard to them'. Parnell said that if the government would meet him and his party in the conciliatory spirit of the amendments, he would promise that the opposition to the bill would be conducted on honest parliamentary lines. Labouchere met Parnell and Healy separately on several occasions thereafter, and conveyed their views to Chamberlain. On 10 June he even referred to having 'appealed' to Healy successfully on a point which Parnell was not prepared to concede. 'He said that they were bound not to insist on more than had been submitted to you, as this would not be honourable, and therefore all trouble on this head is avoided.'[151]

Parnell was playing a masterful hand, unashamedly exploiting his own vulnerability in Ireland. Chamberlain forwarded to Gladstone a letter from Labouchere stating that Parnell wished Gladstone to understand his position, that he had laid an embargo on the funds of the Land League and was at daggers drawn with Egan, and that if he had nothing to show from a conciliatory policy, 'he will have to retire from all present connection with his party and will probably be shot'. A list of concessions sought by Parnell followed. Labouchere advised that Parnell 'still is most anxious for the arrangement of some kind, which will enable him to throw in his lot with the Liberals, but he begs that the great difficulties of his position may be fairly weighed'.[152]

In his dealings with the government, Parnell also exploited to the full the need to contain opposition within the party itself. Chamberlain reported to Gladstone on 7 June that Parnell, whom he had met in the lobby the day before, was anxious to know if there were to be any concessions made on the report stage. He had advised that if all his proposals were rejected 'he cannot keep his party from bitterest opposition'.[153] Parnell's tactics were not ineffective. On 24 May Gladstone's secretary E. W. Hamilton noted that a series of divisions that morning

> ended in disclosing serious differences of opinion between Mr. Parnell and some of his followers; and Mr. G. is fearful whether Parnell will be able to maintain his position and guide his party. His fall now would, in Mr. G.'s opinion, be anything but a public advantage . . . I should not be surprised if Parnell by slow degrees is supplanted and replaced.[154]

The debates on the coercion bill culminated in a set piece confrontation on 1 July in which seventeen members of the party, including Parnell and Healy, were suspended.[155] This served to strengthen Parnell's position in Ireland, where he still had to contain the backwash from the Kilmainham treaty. Davitt, en route to Glengariff, complained to Dillon: 'The belief is abroad that we are "burst up" . . . Fancy my feelings upon hearing that the people in a neighbouring village were reported to be "*waking the Land League*" because they heard it was dead'.[156]

Parnell asked Healy to criticise the expenditure of the Ladies Land League. He did not require much prompting, and duly wrote in the Boston *Republic* of the 'enormous strain' placed on the funds of the Land League by their activities. When an irate Anna Parnell called to his lodgings to remonstrate, Healy refrained from disclosing the inspiration of the article.[157] Parnell's request to Healy was a prelude to his suppression of the Ladies Land League by the cutting off of its funds. *United Ireland* pronounced a cloying *nunc dimittis*: 'They cease their work where others take it up, and return to brighten and sweeten their own Irish hearths again'.[158]

The Land League was, in spite of Davitt's endeavours, effectively defunct, and Parnell was not in any hurry to replace it. Electorally there was an obvious need for a national organisation, but Parnell shrewdly held back. After an interval of some months after the Kilmainham treaty, Parnell, at a meeting in Avondale in September, acceded to the urgings of Davitt and Dillon to establish a new national organisation. His agreement was subject to strict conditions. As Davitt told the lawyers appearing for him at the Special Commission: 'Before Mr. Parnell consented to call such a convention he insisted that he should draft the programme or constitution in order that it should be more strictly constitutional than the Land League and that he should have the task of defining what the policy of the new organisation would be upon the land question'.[159]

Healy wrote to his brother on 5 October:

> There is little less than a split between Davitt and Parnell. The *Irish World* this week is packed with mischievous stuff – notably a letter from Henry George. Davitt had some 'constitution' prepared, and Parnell remarked yesterday that he had one ready himself, and would not have Davitt's. If the Conference passes off safely it will be a relief. I think Davitt feels that he has no one behind him. There was some intention of proposing a 'Board of Trustees' for the old Land League Fund, but Parnell says he will not surrender his position unless to a regularly elected Convention, so that there is no use discussing that point, unless they desire to bring about an *esclandre*.[160]

Under Parnell's supervision, Healy drew up the constitution for the new body.[161]

At the conference to establish the Irish National League in Dublin on 17 October 1882, Healy opposed the proposal from Davitt's supporters that each county should elect a representative to the executive council. He referred to the disparity in political activism and calibre between the different counties and added that 'the distinction of counties is not an Irish idea, and it is nothing more than the English shireground'. Parnell observed that 'if you take a county as the electoral unit you will have a very uneven unit'. For the original proposal Davitt substituted a proposal that the executive council should consist of thirty-two members elected by the organisation, with no nominees of the Irish party; T. P. O'Connor promptly charged that this raised a question of confidence in the Irish party, Davitt withdrew the amendment. The outcome was a council of forty-eight members, of whom thirty-two were to be elected by county conventions and sixteen nominated by the Irish party. This was entirely academic, as the council never met. What was significant was the rout of Davitt and his supporters.[162]

Healy was to be the greatest beneficiary of the establishment of the National League. The agrarian organisation had been disbanded and replaced by what was effectively an electoral machine. The executive of the Land League, which had been profoundly suspicious of Healy, no longer existed to deprive him of access to the direction of the movement in Ireland. He was to wield great influence in the informally constituted organising committee of the Irish party which controlled the National League during elections. Moreover, the superseding of the Land League removed the last inhibition on Healy's championship of a proprietorial nationalist society. It was not then apparent that the dissolution of the institutional power of the movement's left wing would in time render Parnell's own position very much more vulnerable.

4

Parnell Ascendant

> Not long after Parnell had been formally elected leader of the Irish National Party, my daughter who was then but a young girl, had hung up in our dining room a photograph published by some Irish photographer, which contained a small portrait of Parnell in the centre, and the portraits of several of the more conspicuous Irish Nationalist Members surrounding it. She had written on the margin of the engraving the line from Matthew Arnold's poem, 'The leader is fairest, but all are divine'. Parnell happened to be in our house shortly after the setting up of this group of portraits, and he looked at it and read the line which served as its motto. 'It is not for me to complain', he said to her, 'but do you think that the word "divine" describes quite correctly the appearance of our friend' – and he mentioned the name of the Irish Member whose warmest admirer would not claim for him the divine charm of personal beauty.
>
> Justin McCarthy[1]

The Parliamentarian

In his rhetoric in the Commons, Healy was as much concerned to destroy the mystique of British authority in Ireland as to compel British parliamentarians to come to terms with the nationalist demand. In his first speech, in January 1881, he dramatised the spectacle of an embattled minority locked in conflict with a hostile House of Commons, 'the magnificent English Thermopylae of five hundred against fifty'.[2]

In a debate on the Irish magistracy the following month, he declared:

> What had occurred tonight would be read in every village in Ireland . . . Honourable Members received the speeches of Irish Members with their usual jeers and scoffs; but the people of Ireland would read what had been said . . . Honourable Members knew how sluggish were the ordinary channels of information in Ireland – how in some places, the people were fifty or sixty miles away from a railway, and consequently did not get a newspaper, perhaps, more than once a week – but in time they would read accounts of what had taken place tonight, they would see how the conduct of the magistrates had been brought before the highest Assembly in the United Kingdom, and how the magistrates had been mentioned by name. They would learn at length that Mr. So-and-so was not the highest individual on earth and entitled to the highest consideration and reverence, and they would take heart.[3]

The Commons was an arena of ritualised combat, of simulated revolt. At the Parnell banquet in December 1883 Healy defined the histrionic role of the party at Westminster:

> The Irish people are not able to throw ourselves into a struggle such as animated our fathers in former years, but at least we can try to bring some faint echo of the clash of spears and combat upon the hills which moved our fathers' clans into the struggle which we carry on in an alien Parliament (*applause*) – can give the Government of England back blow for blow, hate for hate, and so I trust we will pursue our course, patient, relentless, and untiring.[4]

In the wake of the Kilmainham treaty, seeking to deny any conflict between home rule and land purchase, Healy came perilously close to conceding that an aggressive parliamentary policy was a substitute for nationalist protest in Ireland rather than its reflection:

> . . . as for coercion, the quietness of the country is much more to be attributed to the high price of cattle and the Arrears Act. But although the island being no longer desperate wears the appearance of calm, quiescence in Ireland does not mean inaction in the House of Commons. The agrarian question and the national questions are different things. If every farmer in Ireland were the owner of his holding tomorrow, it would rather intensify than weaken that national feeling which sends Parnellites to Parliament.[5]

Paradoxically, Healy's acute awareness of the effect of parliamentary demonstrations on Irish opinion, as much as his parliamentary skills, rendered him among the most Westminster-orientated members of the Irish party. His studied ferocity, and cultivated disrespect for the rules and conventions of the Commons, belied the extent of his preoccupation with the parliamentary arena. The shrewder English members were quick to discern that his vehemence was something of a mask, part of the armour of an exceptionally talented and ambitious Irish parliamentarian.

For domestic purposes, it was necessary to emphasise the status of the nationalist parliamentarians as outsiders, as pariahs of Westminster. Striking a pseudo-radical note, Healy declared in Dublin in late 1883:

> The Irish members represented a class of person whom he might describe as people who would be intruders at that banquet – the masses of the people, the democracy, the proletariat, whose instincts were unknown to the Parliament before which the Irish members had to plead.[6]

It was likewise important that the Irish parliamentarians were not seen to become implicated in the social rituals of Westminster:

> During the last day or two of the sessions he was amused by some comments in the *Pall Mall Gazette*, which speaking of his humble self, said 'Mr. Healy is a gentleman who would do very well if only he would civilize himself, (*laughter*). If he possessed the confidence of the men whom he represented, and if he was entitled to any credit from the borough, it was that he always refused and would refuse to 'civilize himself' (*hear, hear*). They were threatened by Mr. Gladstone with 'the forces of civilization'. If he was allowed to put his interpretation on the forces of civilization he would say that so far as the House of Commons was concerned the first great force of civilization was the dinner napkin (*laughter*) . . . He had . . . no respect for this fetish dignity.[7]

Recalling this speech, the *Freeman's Journal* would in the split accuse Healy of having succumbed to 'the dinner napkin'.[8] Healy likewise assured his prospective constituents in Monaghan that 'I have never taken pride in making myself acceptable to the House of Commons. I have never been glad of being bowed to or shaking hands with the Prime Minister or members of the Government'.[9]

When first elected, Healy was regarded in parliament and in the British press with political hatred and social disdain. His former employment as a clerk with the North-Eastern Railway led to his being derided in hostile newspapers as a 'ticket-nipper' and the like. This snobbery was compounded by Healy's ferocity of manner. The Dublin *Daily Express* opined that his 'bearing was even more repugnant than his principles'.[10] The witty and urbane Baron Dowse shrewdly captured the element of cultivated uncouthness in Healy's early political style. At dinner with the Lord

Lieutenant, he observed that Healy could not have been such a blackguard by nature and must have taken 'great pains' with himself to become what he was.[11]

It did not take long for Healy's remarkable aptitude to be recognised. His parliamentary standing was rapidly transformed as a result of the precocious ability he had demonstrated in the debates on the land bill, and the fearless *élan* of his attacks on the ministry. H. W. Lucy, the doyen of parliamentary sketch-writers, noted Healy's metamorphosis as early as July 1881. Healy had embarked on his parliamentary career as 'an ill-dressed man with a sullen manner, who audibly gnashed his teeth at the Mace, and did not think it necessary to take his hands out of his pocket when addressing the Speaker'. This was a state of affairs he had 'sufficient intelligence to discover, and sufficient good sense to mend'. In March 1882 he wrote that from inauspicious beginnings Healy had 'taken on some of the polish which the company of gentlemen bestows on the most unpromising material'.[12]

Healy was adept at the oblique exploitation of the idiom of extreme nationalism, as if in crude parody at the level of rhetoric of Parnell's high strategy. One early passage of arms in the Commons is of particular significance. In a speech on the land bill of 1881, he declared with arch provocativeness:

> Mr. John Mitchel had advised those who were evicted by their landlord to shoot him like a dog (*'Oh!') – stay, he had not finished; and if they could not catch the landlord, they should shoot the agent, and if they could not catch the agent, they should shoot the bailiff, and if they could, they should shoot all three. He referred to that statement merely to show how eviction was regarded by some persons in Ireland, because what the Government called 'resumption' would be looked upon as 'eviction' in Ireland.*

Healy's remarks, more disingenuous than truly inflammatory, precipitated the parliamentary incident he intended, along with what the Irish Times described as a 'remarkable falling-out' with A. M. Sullivan.

Gladstone rebuked Healy, though in notably temperate terms. Sullivan's disavowal was more trenchant. While 'in times past Irish Members had been too fond of "dissociating" themselves from one another, and perhaps, were still so', Sullivan felt himself compelled to state he had heard Healy's speech 'with grief and, indeed, with intense pain':

> He had the pleasure of knowing personally Mr. John Mitchel, and he knew, as many others knew who were acquainted with him, that he had

> a North of Ireland Presbyterian bitterness of expression – but while he should say nothing that would cast a reflection upon the name of John Mitchel, he should, in justice to his own principles and character, say that if any Irishman in his hearing in Ireland now uttered such exhortations to shoot landlords, and if they could not shoot landlords, to shoot their agents or bailiffs, he should heartily regret that he voted in the House for the abolition of capital punishment.

Healy in reply professed his indifference to English opinion. His views enjoyed the support of his constituents, and it was not for Sullivan to disavow them. To Sullivan's principled condemnation of violence, he responded with ugly derision.

> They knew that the hon. and learned Member for Meath was not a man of blood. For his own part, like the fop described by Hotspur, he might regret that villainous saltpetre, which had laid many a fellow low, had ever been digged out of the bowels of the innocent earth; but he had never been an advocate of the 'single drop of blood theory'.

The veiled taunt of cowardice was mixed with a proclamation of the redundancy of Sullivan's rigid moralism under the new Parnellite dispensation. Sullivan rejoined with dignity and moderation.[13]

Herbert Gladstone, the Prime Minister's son, reproved Healy in a speech to his Leeds constituents. His strictures were judiciously mixed with flattery. He deplored Healy's speech

> because everyone who had sat in the House of Commons this session had recognised that Mr. Healy was a man of remarkable ability. Not only Mr. Healy, but Mr. Parnell and his other colleagues had in their power, even yet, to earn the respect of the English nation.[14]

Healy immediately despatched an elaborate self-justification to Herbert Gladstone. Gladstone had omitted to state that

> on the occasion of my bloodthirstiness I was combating the insertion of the gentle euphemism 'resumption' which the Government introduced into the Land Bill, that I pointed out the fact that the said 'resumption' was but naked English for 'eviction' and that if the Government wanted to know what was thought of eviction in Ireland, they must remember the words of John Mitchel which I then quoted.[15]

A. M. Sullivan also wrote to Herbert Gladstone, but almost six months later, the day after he had ceased to be a member of parliament, to correct Gladstone's statement at Leeds that Healy had spoken without protest from the nationalist side. Sullivan's repudiation of Healy extended beyond the immediate issue: 'Not only was that short speech, as it now happens, my last or nearly my last parliamentary utterance, but it had, for non-public reasons unnecessary to state, no little importance for me as a signal of my position, though to the outer world a trivial and paltry incident'. He had been ill at the time of the Leeds speech,

> but I meant some day to remind you of an error particularly unfair to me. *I never yet held my tongue*, no matter what the penalty for protesting might be, whenever the taint of assassination doctrines were brought to touch the cause of Ireland.[16]

In declining to concede any distinction between Healy's opportunistic vehemence and physical force nationalism, Sullivan's swan-song was both a protest against what he considered to be the debased ethos of Parnellism, and a pointed repudiation of his younger kinsman.

Prison

After the end of the session, Healy embarked on a series of speeches in Ireland calculated to purge himself from the taint of moderation on the land question, and to re-establish his credentials as an agrarian agitator.

At Miltown Malbay, County Clare, Healy declared that as the land act was passed to pacify the country and did not do so 'it was a failure and a fraud and a farce, and these were the only three Fs which were on the whole of it'. In Wexford two weeks later with Davitt, Healy declared 'at least they could use that Land Act as a shelter trench from behind which they could pour out fresh volleys upon the citadel of landlordism'. At Mullins, County Carlow on 26 November, Healy put himself at the head of what he described as the 'landless resolutes' of the nationalist movement in denouncing the government of the country as 'simply an organisation of so many pirates and brigands'.[17] Healy's fiery rhetoric belied the substantive moderation of his views. Yet it permitted him to surpass Davitt in vehemence on Irish platforms.

Following his Mullins speech, an application was brought to have Healy required to provide sufficient sureties 'to be of good behaviour towards her Majesty the Queen and towards all her Majesty's subjects', and in default that he be committed to prison. Similar proceedings were instituted against Michael Davitt and P. J. Quinn, a former secretary of the Land League.[18]

Appearing in person against the Attorney-General, Healy skilfully turned his defence into an attack on the government and the Liberal party. He cited observations of W. E. Gladstone, Herbert Gladstone, Chamberlain and Cobden — 'these gentlemen whom I have quoted were the gods of the Liberal party – the gods whom the Attorney-General falls down and worships on every occasion'. The remarks for which he was being prosecuted went no further than theirs. Of Gladstone's celebrated observation as to the effects of Fenian violence, Healy declared:

> Who said that the blowing down of Clerkenwell prison brought the disestablishment of the Irish Church 'within the range of practical politics'? – a very velvety phrase when used by the Prime Minister on a public platform, but if it were used by me we should hear the Attorney-General describing how it burned in the minds of persons who read the seditious literature of this country in the low tap-rooms of Dublin.[19]

On 24 January 1883 the Lord Chief Justice, who referred throughout a long judgement to Healy as 'Thomas Healy', found his language 'clearly and grossly seditious'. The other judges agreed. Healy and Davitt were ordered to enter into recognizances of £1,000 each and to prove sureties in the same sum, the condition of the recognizances that they be of good behaviour for twelve months. In default, they were to be imprisoned for six months.[20]

Although widely urged to enter into the recognizances, Healy and Davitt declined to do so. This was hardly an article of nationalist faith: Dillon had no compunction about entering into recognizances under the same act in 1886. Two leading nationalists thereby took themselves out of the fray at a critical time. Parnell may have regarded Healy's somewhat contrived act of martyrdom with some suspicion. The comment of the *Times*, ever ready to discern a split in the Irish ranks, that Parnell's Fabian tactics had 'encouraged ambitious or fanatical members of the Irish party, not for the first time, to supplant a leader more feared than loved', if it went too far, was not altogether impercipient.[21]

On 8 February Healy, who was having breakfast with his wife at his residence at 20 Harrington Street, Dublin, was arrested and taken to Kilmainham. There he was briefly imprisoned in the rooms which had formerly been occupied by Parnell, Dillon and O'Kelly, before being transferred to the Richmond Bridewell. Davitt was arrested the same day.[22] While enjoying the relatively privileged status of a first-class misdemeanant, Healy took imprisonment badly, much more so than the practised Davitt. At the end of the first month Davitt believed Healy in better health: 'He appears to take his retirement philosophically – but he could be of far more use to his party if he exchanged Richmond Jail for the House of Commons'. Though prey to episodes of lassitude, Healy released his hyperactivity drafting and scrutinising bills (of which his County Councils Bill was the most important), reading the newspapers and learning Irish from Davitt. 'Though we don't mind being in jail', Healy wrote Maurice, 'I chafe at seeing points missed in the House.'[23]

The prisoners were thus not entirely cut off from the outside. Healy even succeeded in contributing an article to *United Ireland*. For smuggling out contributions to the Parnell testimonial, which had been initiated during their confinement, the prisoners lost their privileges for a week. Healy continued to maintain a shrewd eye on national politics. He complained to Maurice about the lax editorial control of *United Ireland* after O'Brien's election to parliament:

> The happy-go-lucky style in which that paper is conducted while O'Brien is in London would amaze any person who realised that the Government is watching every chance to strike.
>
> William sends nothing but his London Letter, T. P. Gill, the sub-editor has left for America, so there is practically no one but James O'Connor to attend to it.

Healy's concerns were well-founded. The contents of *United Ireland* over this period were to provide the *Times* with a rich seam of damaging material at the Special Commission.[24]

Healy's custodial *rapprochement* with Davitt afforded him a glimpse of a wider political world than that with which he was familiar as a parliamentarian. His last prison letter to his brother fleetingly illumines the dark and choppy waters which still lapped the periphery of Irish politics:

> They are hunting all the young fellows out of the country under the pretext that they are to be arrested. The fear of informers makes everyone who was connected with the Nationalists afraid of the charge of 'conspiracy to murder'. This is the Government game, and they will try to clear Ireland of everybody formidable to the landlords. I expect to hear that Nally, 'Scrab's' brother, who broke up our Land League meeting in Bolton last year, and whom O'Connor Power got Forster to allow back to Ireland (there was a warrant out for him), will come into the limelight. Yet they have arrested a lot of our enemies in Mayo – Power's backers – to whom, with secret service money, he supplied revolvers.[25]

Healy and Davitt were released after four months. Healy was described by the *Freeman's Journal* as looking 'a little careworn and delicate' on his emergence. More ominously *United Ireland* referred to him as 'peculiarly gay and festive', in spite of 'the torments of a maddening fit of neuralgia'. Healy left for London the next day.[26] From Westminster he went to Cork, and spoke at Bandon in support of the Parnell testimonial, which was being raised to avert the necessity for Parnell to sell his estates.

> They met there to endeavour to give strength and sustenance to Charles Stewart Parnell, the leader of the Irish people. If he [Parnell] was one of

> themselves, or if he were, as he [Healy] himself was, sprung from the peasant class, a man of the people born with the people, educated amongst them, and of the religion of the people, then they might say of him that it would be kind for him to have struggled in aid of the oppressed people of this country. But was that the case? (*No, no*) Nothing of the kind. He was a man, he might say, of English connections, of English education; a man connected with the English aristocracy in the realm; not a tenant or a democrat, but an aristocrat, or a landlord, and that man had toiled so hard, and had so endeavoured for the people's cause that he had been brought to the very pinch of poverty, and he was obliged to mortgage his property in order to enable him to carry on still further the struggle for popular rights (*applause*).[27]

The emphasis on Parnell's landlord origins (presented as 'English' rather than Anglo-Irish) was excessive, and he lingered rather too long on what he inaccurately described as his own roots in 'the peasant class'. This was the polarity on which his rhetoric against Parnell in the split was to be predicated.

Still unwell, Healy planned to go abroad. However at Glengariff he received a telegram from Parnell asking him to contest the pending Monaghan by-election.[28] He was adopted as the nationalist candidate at a convention in the chapel at Castleblayney, which might be thought an unpromising venue for the commencement of what was heralded as a non-sectarian campaign. Parnell campaigned vigorously, playing hard on the Healy clause and his connoisseurship of the land act: 'Mr. Healy's knowledge of that act is admitted even by his enemies to be unrivalled. It is admitted that to him belongs the credit of the clause that bears his name, and that is the only part of the act which is worth a thraneen'.[29]

Before the count, Parnell believed Healy's candidacy lost. (Healy attributed this to his superstitious horror at the fact that Healy had occupied room number thirteen in the hotel at Castleblayney on the eve of poll.) Healy was returned by a narrow margin in a result marked by the collapse of the Liberal vote. Parnell compared the victory to O'Connell's at the Clare election. He noted that Butt had failed in 1871 to carry the county and hailed the result as a tribute to 'the power and terror of the magic name of Parnell'.[30]

The Monaghan result was a significant *coup*, but had unanticipated repercussions. Far from presaging a thaw in Ulster politics, Healy's election precipitated a hardening of its glacial formations. It prompted the beginning of concerted unionist resistance to what was characterised in the territorial idiom of Ulster politics as the nationalist 'invasion' of the province. Intensified nationalist campaigning in the northern counties, theretofore largely ignored by the Parnellites, was met by unionist counter-demonstrations under the aegis of local landed magnates. Healy's own career, as member of parliament successively for Monaghan and South Derry, was caught up in the unfolding unionist response.

Spencer and Trevelyan: The Liberals in Ireland

Healy's initial involvement with *United Ireland* was limited to his parliamentary letter. The high period of his collaboration with the editor William O'Brien, during which they together co-wrote the paper, dates from Healy's release in June 1883 until the Galway election of February 1886, when he ceased writing for *United Ireland*.[31]

Standing in their room in the office of *United Ireland*, Healy announced to Justin McCarthy: 'Here we compose our little salads. O'Brien supplies the oils and I pour in the vinegar'. As O'Brien nostalgically recalled, on the day the paper went to press, 'we would fall to work — Mr. Healy at one side of the *escritoire* and myself at the other — and divide up our subjects, and exchange stimulating suggestions, and pursue one another page after page in a sort of steeple-chase'. Finished in the small hours, they repaired to the back bar of the Imperial Hotel. There Healy's wit often sustained them until dawn, when the cries of the newspaper boys broke on Sackville Street, and they could read the paper wet from the press.[32]

Healy was aware of the difference of their rhetorical modes. Years later he wrote to O'Brien that 'though I dislike the "Davis to Duffy" style I think I ought to say how much I liked your speech'.[33] Yet their styles were oddly complementary, and their confluence was responsible for the distinctive tone, and the remarkable vigour, of *United Ireland* at the period when its influence was at its greatest.

There was perhaps an inherent tendency for Healy's acerbic vehemence to predominate over O'Brien's grandiloquent ardour. The paper was fiercely loyal to Parnell. While he did not share O'Brien's intense personal fealty to the Irish leader, Healy was absolutely committed to ensuring that Parnell prevailed over his domestic rivals and adversaries, and to the entrenchment of the Parnellite organisation. In terms of editorial policy, Healy's influence was most clearly discernible in *United Ireland*'s unsparing advocacy of land purchase. If Healy was responsible as much as O'Brien for the success of *United Ireland*, his contribution was not exclusively positive. His penchant for highly personalised attacks was in 1883–4 to expose the paper, and O'Brien as its editor, to potential catastrophe.

In the Commons in August 1883 Healy launched an attack on a sub-inspector of the Royal Irish Constabulary called Cameron, who had directed the suppression of a riot in Wexford. In the course of his speech he twice stated that Cameron had lived with his wife before they were married. The Chief Secretary the next day refused to answer a parliamentary question from Healy relating to the Royal Irish Constabulary, until Healy withdrew the imputation he had made against the honour of a woman under cover of parliamentary privilege. The *Times* wrote that 'that unwritten code of good breeding and good feeling which all once obeyed sits loosely on a certain section'. Defiantly impenitent in parliament, Healy was privately depressed. He gratefully accepted T. P. O'Connor's suggestion of a consolatory drink: 'when I left to him the choice of drink we should take . . . he mentioned Lachrymae Christi as a wine he had often heard of but never drunk; and we had our bottle of Lachrymae Christi'.[34]

Healy took fierce umbrage, as he would again in the Parnell split, at the proposition that questions on matters of private morality lay outside the sphere of legitimate political attack. He dismissed the pretended incivility of public allusion to personal matters as the self-protective device of a privileged caste, shielding the ruling class in Ireland from the exposure of their larger political depravity. It was an issue that touched a curious edge of rabid class resentment among conservative Catholic nationalists.

Healy's attack on Cameron marked the first in a series of fractious interventions. The next day he supported Biggar in opposition to the Tramways Bill. Biggar under pressure from Parnell withdrew in the face of nationalist appeals not to put the issue to a division. The *Daily Express* wrote of Healy 'this hon. member now denounces everything'.[35] The following day he launched an especially virulent attack on the Chief Secretary, for which he was reproved by Gladstone.[36]

It is possible that Healy had still not recovered from the ill-health he was suffering on his release from prison, and that the punishing pace of his political life was taking its toll of his equanimity and political judgement. As in the split of 1890, there was a marked correlation between Healy's ferocity and the degree of stress he was under. A rebuke from the *Freeman's Journal* infuriated Healy. *United Ireland* carried a response which he wrote. It asserted there had been no attacks on private characters 'except those which affect the public position of Castle officials', and concluded:

> If the House of Commons wants to make rules to stop such questions as Mr. Healy's, it is open to it to devote its valuable time to the attempt, but it will not do so until the life and adventures of what is called the 'private character' of various Crown employees in Ireland, from Corry Connellan, to Detective Director and County Inspector James Ellis French are fully laid bare to the universe.[37]

Healy had thereby plunged *United Ireland* into what was the first of a cascading series of libel actions taken by three of the most senior officials of the crown in Ireland. Healy's allusion to French was prompted by information confidentially provided by R.I.C. District Inspector Thomas Murphy, then of Monaghan, to the effect that French was sexually involved with young police officers. Constrained to sue, French's nerve did not hold. He stalled for a time on grounds of ill-health, but his action was struck out for delay in June of the following year.[38] In exposing the man whom Arthur Griffith later described as 'the bestial ruffian, Ellis French, chief spy and agent-provocateur to English Government in Ireland', which had shielded his 'loathsome immoralities', [39] *United Ireland* had won what was to be only the first round. In the Commons, Healy taunted that it seemed to him that Joe Brady, the executed Phoenix Park murderer, had had one great misfortune, that 'he could not get three good doctors to certify to his general debility'. Had he been able to do so, 'he would not at the present moment by lying calcined in a cell in Kilmainham Prison'.[40]

French was not however the only victim. The career of Thomas Murphy in the Royal Irish Constabulary was ruined. First transferred from Monaghan to Charleville, and thence to Nenagh, he was dismissed shortly thereafter. He blamed Healy, and to greater extent O'Brien, for permitting him to become identified as the source of the information pertaining to French, leading to his dismissal and penury. Understandably embittered, and insensed by Healy and O'Brien's later *rapprochement* with Spencer, he denounced them at length as opportunistic 'lickspittles' in a privately published pamphlet in 1894.

In attacking the procrastination in French's proceedings, *United Ireland* libelled Gustavus C. Cornwall, Secretary of the General Post Office, a prominent figure in Castle society. The administration, as O'Brien wrote, now had 'a champion more doughty than the grovelling Detective Inspector. Cornwall was an aristocrat of quite ducal presence and with nerves of steel'. Cornwall pressed on with his action. The position of *United Ireland*, and of O'Brien as its editor, was extremely vulnerable. The prosecution for criminal libel of those responsible for the publication of *United Ireland* was widely rumoured. At the trial in July 1884, *United Ireland* led evidence implicating Cornwall in a homosexual ring in Dublin Castle. He lost his action. *United Ireland* celebrated the consignment of 'the foul beasts' to eternal infamy.[41]

The third libel action was brought by George Bolton, the Treasury Crown Solicitor. A *United Ireland* sub-editor had inserted the heading 'A Precious Trio' over a piece referring to French, Cornwall and Bolton. Bolton had directed the prosecutions arising from the Phoenix Park murders, and was the object of nationalist execration. He was moreover not of especially estimable character: he was denounced by Healy in the Commons as a 'self-convicted thief, fraudulent bankrupt, wife-cheater, and heartless debauchee', and by *United Ireland* as a 'forger, adulterer and wife-swindler'. Bolton's action succeeded. But he was by then a broken man, and the damages awarded were never recovered.[42]

In his *Evening Memories*, published in 1920, William O'Brien claimed that the failure of Cornwall's action 'broke the neck of the Coercion Act of 1882–5'. This was a considerable overstatement. *United Ireland* had in the event succeeded in discrediting high personages in Dublin Castle, two of whom were closely involved in the administration of justice in Ireland. In doing so, it had assumed appalling risks which extended beyond *United Ireland* itself. Parnell had remonstrated with O'Brien, 'but said he knew I was quite right as to the facts, that the thing had to be fought out now that it was forced on me'.[43] O'Brien's account, written at a time when he was reconciled with Healy, suppressed the views he had expressed on the subject in 1900 in the course of their long mid-career estrangement. In a public letter in February 1900 he had bitterly blamed Healy for the 'eighteen months of agony' he had endured, and complained that Healy had done nothing to assist him to escape from the 'hell of litigation' into which he had plunged him.[44]

Healy was not possessed by implacable moral prejudices, nor was he personally especially intolerant. The company of incorrigible cynics such as Henry Labouchere and Harold Frederic of the *New York Times* was to complete his sentimental education. He was immune to the moral shock in the face of metropolitan decadence which Harold Frederic derisively imputed to less sophisticated members of the Irish party in London ('droll stories . . . are told of the horror with which they discovered, when they came to this great Babylon, that all the finely dressed ladies they saw in the street were not virtuous and valuable members of society').[45]

As Joseph Hone was to point out, Healy was untroubled by the behaviour of his mentor Joseph Biggar, 'whose philanderings were indiscriminate and notorious'. In the course of his engagingly blunt defence of a breach of promise action tried before the Lord Chief Justice of England in 1883, Biggar was cross-examined as follows:

> You have told me, Mr. Biggar, of two children?: 'Yes'.
> Is their mother still living?: 'The mother of one is living. In fact, I think both mothers are living' (*laughter*) . . .

The plaintiff lost her action. In his memoirs, T. P. O'Connor sought ungallantly to revenge himself on Biggar, commenting archly that 'in his last, as in all the other hours of his life, he was not without female companionship'.[46]

In his memoirs, Healy relates an exchange with Biggar during the time of the libel actions against *United Ireland:*

> Biggar, one night, as we were going home from the House of Commons, queried, 'Have you noticed that almost all those blackguards were musical?' To be 'musical' was almost a capital offence with Joe. I answered with the quote that those 'who have no music in their souls are fit for treasons, stratagems and spoils', but Biggar did not agree with Shakespeare.[47]

'Musical' was society code for homosexual. The anecdote is admittedly recounted by an older, studiedly mellow, Healy. Yet it still suggests that Healy was less in the grip of primitive moral prejudices than ready to exploit to the maximum any weakness he could discern in an adversary.[48] His moralism was highly politicised. Where political enmity and moral vulnerability touched, Healy was capable of unremitting ferocity, attended by a lurch into excess and a loss of self-mastery which argued an instability of temperament.

Healy's attacks on French, Cornwall and Bolton were part of a systematic campaign against the administration of Earl Spencer, the Lord Lieutenant, and G. O. Trevelyan, his Chief Secretary. In the aftermath of the mishandling of the Maamtrasna murders, and the execution of Myles Joyce who died protesting his innocence, public opinion was already inflamed against 'the Castle'. Healy was determined to fix Spencer and Trevelyan with a personal complicity in miscarriages of justice in Ireland which went beyond conventional ministerial responsibility.

Healy denounced a visit by the Prince of Wales 'in order to use him as a species of whitewash brush for the dirty reeking walls of Dublin Castle'. Referring to 'the filthy sceptre which has been wielded by his Excellency in Dublin Castle', he described Spencer as 'the hangman of Myles Joyce, the executioner of Francey Hynes . . . the screener of French and Cornwall, the sustainer of George Bolton and knighter of Samuel Lee Anderson'.[49] Following a visit to the scene of the Maamtrasna murders he denounced Spencer: 'no man in his opinion since the time of Cromwell would leave so odious a memory in this country as the gentleman at present presiding over its destinies'.[50]

Healy was the author of the virulent attacks on Spencer and Trevelyan which appeared in *United Ireland*. Of these the most notorious was the jibe that Spencer, having 'shielded criminals, rewarded scoundrels, and hung innocent men', should be raised a step in the peerage 'with the appropriate title of the Duke of Sodom and Gomorrah'.[51] William O'Brien told the Special Commission that he had not written the controversial attacks on Spencer and Trevelyan charging them with personal responsibility for the perversion of the course of justice in Ireland.[52]

By that stage, in the aftermath of Gladstone's endorsement of home rule, which was staunchly supported by Spencer, O'Brien was personally mortified by the attacks on Spencer and Trevelyan. He came to blame Healy for the violence of the attacks he had written in *United Ireland.* He charged in 1900 that Healy 'never dreamt of owning his share of the responsibility, but went on gaily hobnobbing with the statesmen whom he was anonymously attacking'.[53] Still discomfited thirty-five years later, O'Brien in his *Evening Memories* sought to make characteristically extravagant atonement: 'Earl Spencer, as it turned out, had the probity of a Stoic and the greatness of a Statesman; his Chief Secretary, Mr. Trevelyan, had the charm of a cultured gentleman'.[54]

The unfolding of Healy's relations with Gladstone belied his pseudo-revolutionary violence of utterance. On 28 January 1881, very shortly after his election, Healy had interrupted the Prime Minister and won a notably temperate rebuke. Gladstone flatteringly described him as one who 'after a few weeks in this House has already given indications which promise him a considerable prominence', and advised him to show tolerance in permitting others free expression of their opinion. Healy interjected 'we have got none'. Gladstone retorted: 'If he will take a little friendly recommendation from me, I will say that his demeanour is not the best way to get it'.[55] This exchange was the seemingly unpromising point of departure for what was to be a sustained mutual courtship.

Seven months later Healy wrote to thank the Prime Minister for a contribution to a nationalist charitable cause. The tone of his letter afforded a marked contrast to his implacable parliamentary demeanour. He wrote that 'I cannot refrain from noting my sense of the constant anxiety displayed – so far as official ties will allow – by yourself to endeavour to meet Irish feelings, and my sole regret is that your many cares and occupations prevent us from being able at all times to appeal personally to the Head of the Government'.[56] This did more than indicate Healy's personal amenability to Gladstone: implicit within it was his purpose of seeking to divide Gladstone from the administration in Ireland.

Henry Labouchere was among the first to discern Healy's excessive susceptibility to Gladstone's allure. He wrote to Chamberlain in May 1882 that Healy 'says that the P.M. paid him a compliment in the House and evidently since that date he has become his ardent admirer'.[57] Gladstone in turn, undeceived by Healy's grimace of ferocity, was intrigued and impressed. His daughter recorded a discussion in November 1882 in which he expressed his preference for Healy over Thomas Sexton.[58] When the Queen called Gladstone to account for his failure to repudiate a speech by Healy on the marriage grant to Prince Leopold, in the course of which he had, treasonably in her view, quoted a Jacobite song, the Prime Minister was constrained to reply that he would respond to any return to the subject by Healy 'a man of singular and apparently mixed character with a strong ruffianly element'.[59] He could hardly in the circumstances have said less.

Healy's fierce attacks on Spencer and Trevelyan, combined with the studied politeness he displayed towards Gladstone in their private communications, was intended to play on the Prime Minister's unease at the drift back towards confrontation in Ireland. In February 1883 Healy wrote appealingly directly to him over the head of the Lord Lieutenant. He had laid the ground for this intervention by observing to Herbert Gladstone that he supposed correspondence with his father would be unavailing as it would only be referred to Spencer. He complained that the regime in Ireland did nothing to check the crimes of violence by 'Orangemen', while nationalist districts in which crimes had occurred were without investigation levied with heavy local charges to cover the cost of additional policing. He concluded with an overt attempt to divide Gladstone from Spencer:

> What is operating on his mind is evident to all of us, viz. that the Orange are the loyal class and he won't disaffect them to do us justice. We cannot hope therefore to influence his judgement by argument. As a last resource I address you, fully persuaded that you have not lost faith in the ultimate efficacy of justice. I am sure if you knew the way things are managed in Ireland your heart would be a great deal hotter than ours against the oppression of the poor people. Even if Lord Spencer's views about the necessity of maintaining the garrison faction in Ireland were the true one, England could do it much cheaper and content the bulk of the inhabitants much better, by doubling her standing army there and paying it a fourth of the sum which the 'loyalists' now levy off the people, as the price of their attachment to the Crown. Soldiers are much less costly to keep than landlords, and you can hire a regiment for what it now takes to preserve the allegiance of a single rentcharger. Begging that my presumption may be excused . . .[60]

Healy's strategy took its toll on the morale of the Spencer–Trevelyan administration. In February 1884, the beleaguered Chief Secretary complained to Spencer of Gladstone's responsiveness to the Irish, and his indulgent treatment of Healy in particular.[61]

Healy in his platform rhetoric expressly exempted Gladstone from his strictures on the Liberal party ('the general bodies of Liberals in England were the worst enemies of Ireland. You could see the hatred and rage depicted in their countenance; you could feel the venom, you could see the rage in their eyes as they glared at you').[62]

Gladstone was by the same token expected to live up to nationalist expectations. In September 1884, Healy responded to a speech by the Prime Minister in Edinburgh, which he treated as a profession of ignorance of conditions in Ireland. It was remarkable 'that he — who could go so far afield over sea and mountain to rake up the woes of the Bulgarians, the

Greeks, the Italians and the Poles – knew absolutely nothing about what was transpiring in Ireland'. If 'the greatest intellect, the most gifted intellect, and I believe the most generous mind amongst the English people in relation to Ireland' was so obtuse, what were the Irish to expect from the bulk of English politicians? If Gladstone was to be believed, he had been first induced to pay attention to Irish demands by agrarian outrages. This position Healy proceeded to assail:

> You may argue, you may demonstrate, you may speechify, you may assemble in your thousands, you may send your representatives to Parliament, but until the rattle of slugs are heard upon the roadside the Prime Minister of England will not even take the trouble of investigating the ordinary facts in connection with the commonest grievance of our native land (applause). I must say I regard this as a painful and melancholy confession.

Of Spencer's declaration that there would be no further concessions on land legislation, he declared

> We have been familiar with these *non-possumus* declarations of British statesmen from time out of mind, and we heard them upon every subject upon which this country was agitated, and the Irish people have triumphed in spite of them . . . And if declarations such as that of Earl Spencer were accepted by the people it would be a bad day for what is called law and order; because if the Irish people believed that they can get no further concessions by peaceful agitation, they would resort to the old weapons which won so much for them in the past (*hear, hear*). Shake the confidence of the people in their legitimate leaders, and the people will go back to illegitimate leaders . . .[63]

The speech, an exercise in polemical ingratiation characteristic of his treatment of Gladstone, was shrewdly pitched, intuiting as it did the direction of Gladstone's own thinking.

The Parnellite Organisation

Healy's zeal in establishing and maintaining Parnell's authority was undeviating. Realising that the establishment of a strong parliamentary party at Westminster exercising unquestioned authority in Ireland depended upon Parnell's leadership, and cognisant that his own power was derivative of Parnell's, he subordinated his private reservations. He was the most vehement exponent of the idea of a tightly disciplined political machine. While he eschewed gratuitous praise in Parnell, he did not hesitate to laud him extravagantly when he judged it necessary to call in aid the mystique of the Irish leader to crush dissentient nationalists.

Healy relentlessly championed a centralised nationalism against the claims of local organisations and favourite sons. At the inaugural conference of the National League in October 1882, Healy had opposed Davitt's proposal for a central council comprised of county delegates which would have inhibited the power of the Irish party and its leader. In October 1885 he proclaimed that the electoral aim of nationalists, at least until they got an Irish parliament, was 'to efface and blot out every local distinction and recognise only the interests of the country at large.'[64]

Healy constituted himself the scourge of 'Whiggish' or 'nominal' home rulers. In October 1881 he compiled a pamphlet entitled *A Record of Coercion – Votes of Irish Members for the Enlightenment of Irish Electors* setting out the voting records of each of the Irish members on each of the divisions on the 'Coercion' acts of 1881. At a meeting of the party he proposed a resolution calling on the Irish constituencies to denounce those members who failed to vote with the party in the division on the cloture of March 1882.[65]

Healy dedicated himself to purging the Irish party of the old 'Whig' nationalists, and of the maverick former pretenders to national leadership displaced by Parnell. Frustrated by the paucity of capable and committed members of the party, Healy wrote to Maurice 'it is hard to say which is worse, Whig fraudulence or the bumptious and hollow pretence of advertising nationalists'.[66]

His fiercest onslaught was reserved for John O'Connor Power, the member for Mayo, whom he had once sought to protect from Parnell's ire. O'Connor Power's speech in the debate on an amendment proposed by Parnell to the Queen's speech in February 1884 marked his repudiation of the Irish party. It fell to Healy to retaliate. In 1874, the year he was first returned to parliament, O'Connor Power had delivered a celebrated attack on The O'Donoghue, who sat for Tralee, by quoting against him his own words: 'it is melancholy to observe how a patriot falls; there are few to remind him of his duty, and the power of the seducer is great'. Retorting the words of The O'Donoghue upon O'Connor Power, Healy interposed 'I trust the Prime Minister will pardon that expression. It is not my expression'. Healy proceeded to flay his former colleagues:

> When he condemns the course of conduct adopted by Members of our Party, whom he states are influenced in their action in Ireland by a desire to oust the Leader of the Party from his position, I would remind the hon. Member for Mayo of what his own course in this House has been. Who was the first man in the whole Irish Party to denounce the late Mr. Isaac Butt as a traitor? The hon. Member for Mayo. Who was the first

> man to leave the existing Party of the hon. Gentleman the Member for the City of Cork (Mr. Parnell)? The hon. Member for Mayo. And, in fact, I may say that not merely his personal but his political life are strewn with the wreck of broken friendships. The hon. Gentleman the Member for Mayo has taunted me with the fact that in my address to the electors of Monaghan there was not a word about Irish Nationality. If so, I can say, at least, I did not hoodwink the electors with false pleas about Irish Nationality, and then run away from the Party with which I was associated, and endeavoured by skilful artifice in this House to curry the favour of English Ministers. I have not attacked in Ireland what I have not attacked here. I have not referred in Ireland to 'the pirate flag of England', and then come to this House with some paltry reference about a 'local assembly' and 'as much self-government as is compatible with the safety of Parliament and the integrity of the Empire' . . . Then we are told that we deprived the hon. Member for Mayo of the right of free speech. When did we deprive the hon. Member of free speech? Does he not know the way to the railway station at the Broadstone? Does he not know where the Midland Railway leads to? Does he not know it will take him today to the town of Ballina, or Claremorris, or Irishtown, as of yore? And when did we ever stand between him and his constituents in those places?[67]

O'Connor Power was by then an easy target. A former Fenian who had once vied with Parnell for the hegemony of the advanced party, he stood unsuccessfully as a Liberal for a London constituency at the general election the following year.[68]

Healy determinedly sustained Parnell against Davitt and the agrarian left of nationalism. In a final attempt to constrain Parnell's hegemony, and to arrest the rightward drift of the movement, Davitt sought to shift the balance of power within the party by seeking the return of radical nationalists at the general election. He advocated the nomination of those who had been detained as 'suspects' in 1881–2. There were 'scattered through the length and breadth of the country something like eight hundred or nine hundred men who were thrust into prison without trial'. These were the (agrarian radical) 'Irish representatives racy of the soil' whom Davitt wished to see elected.[69]

Seeking to pre-empt Parnell, Davitt advocated the early holding of conventions, to prevent the country at the general election being 'overrun by carpet-baggers from England' professing to be fervent Parnellites. T. C. Harrington, the acting secretary of the National League who was unswervingly loyal to Parnell, responded that the National League organisation was still not sufficiently established and that there was no justification for 'pledging the constituencies now to candidates who are themselves unpledged'. Davitt denied that 'the test of a candidate's fitness for a constituency is to insist in his willingness to pledge himself to some policy or programme which is not yet before the country'.[70] Heading off Davitt's challenge, Parnell warned against 'final action' in the selection of candidates, and urged consultation with the party: 'This has been done at every election since 1880, and with the best results'.[71]

This was Davitt's last serious bid to wrest the initiative back from Parnell, at least prior to the split. Its failure marked a turning point in the history of Parnellite nationalism. In espousing the power of the constituencies, Davitt was seeking to reconstitute the power of the former Land League cadres through the country. This was premised on the belief that the party leadership under Parnell had moved to the right of the constituencies. By the end of the decade this pretence could no longer be sustained. Healy, on the right of the Irish party, emerged as the champion of the power of the constituencies. In the split he successfully appealed to rural Ireland to repudiate Parnell's leadership. Thereafter, particularly in the later 1890s, he looked to the rural constituencies, where a firm expectation of land purchase had taken hold, as bulwarks of social conservatism and resistance to the centralising pretensions and metropolitan Liberal leanings of the Irish party leadership. Healy's supplanting of Davitt as the champion of constituency power reflected a decisive political and socio-economic shift within the nationalist polity.

Healy was determined to ensure the return of a disciplined party of effective parliamentarians. He complained to Maurice that 'it is enough to drive people to despair to see the possibilities which parliament offers for an effective and capable Party, and to think that we cannot get twenty useful members returned'.[72] There was however a paucity of suitable candidates. William O'Brien later wrote that in 1882–5 and for some time afterwards 'Parnell had rather to beg for recruits than to force them on the constituencies'. Healy complained in November 1882:

> The Irish middle class (if there is such a thing) does not largely recruit the ranks of popular members of Parliament. Most of its talent drains away to America, or is absorbed into the priesthood, the medical, or legal professions, all three being callings which entirely preclude a six months' residence in London.

The following year he deplored 'the great dearth, the national bankruptcy for want of public men'. *United Ireland* protested in January 1883:

> We receive suggestions from time to time that Mr. Parnell and his friends should have a list in preparation. Do such advisers imagine that he is acquainted with all the talent and patriotism of the island, and that candidates will start up, Minerva-like, equipped at all points with means, leisure, and genius, when nomination arises.[73]

The problem was addressed, if to a very limited extent, by the payment from nationalist funds of members who lacked the means to finance their parliamentary attendance. Long espoused by *United Ireland*, the establishment of a fund for the payment of members was adopted by Parnell in March 1884, and put into effect after the 1885 general election.[74] The payment of members from party funds was a revolutionary innovation, both in terms of Irish politics and the organisation of parties at Westminster. English critics discerned a further extension of Parnell's sinister dictatorship.

Even for some supporters of Parnellite nationalism, the idea was hard to stomach. Archbishop Croke of Cashel opposed the payment of members from a central fund. Their needs should rather be met by their constituents. He urged the adoption of local candidates. Once they conformed to the criteria he had set, local men 'should in almost every instance be preferred to strangers'.[75] *United Ireland* took issue with the Archbishop. The experience of the last few years had shown 'that a National party cannot be elected on parish cries . . . Mischief-making factionists will, of course, go about developing the parish pride of particular districts, counselling local men to resist "dictation"', but they would not prevail: 'The enemies of the Nationalist Party will do their best to fan the baleful blaze of localism as against the National interest, while self-seeking individuals, no doubt, will swell the cry of the parishmakers'.[76] The designation of the parish as the seat of recalcitrant localism was plainly intended to convey that the parochial clergy were not exempt from the rule of Parnellism.

United Ireland insisted that Parnell's authority had to be upheld in the selection of candidates. 'Should disaster occur once the new party is formed, as it is upon the head of Charles Stewart Parnell the blame of failure will be, so also in his discretion should rest the responsibility of anterior arrangements.' If the party did not succeed 'the leader alone should face unfriended a disappointed nation'.[77]

Of all of Parnell's lieutenants, Healy was the fiercest exponent of a disciplined party machine. Against the idea that a nationalist candidate was mere 'slave' or 'nominee' of Parnell's, Healy retorted that 'for that matter the twelve apostles were nominees, and Parnell's followers were selected by a great chief to preach the gospel of Irish nationality before the world'.[78]

In the *Pall Mall Gazette*, Healy defended Parnell's role in the nomination of nationalist candidates, before the convention system was put in place against widespread English taunts of 'dictatorship': there were Irish constituencies which would take 'the peasant from the plough-tail — yea the scavenger from the streets' as parliamentary representatives in preference to 'faithless aristocrats, as to their sorrow they have done for eight fruitless years'. Dropping his tone, he asked: 'What is it to them whom Mr. Parnell nominates for country or town, so long as the work they want done is performed?'[79] Michael Davitt was outraged. Privately he characterised Healy's argument as 'simply disgusting': 'What does it matter to Ireland who Mr. Parnell nominates for its constituencies!!! Nice doctrine for a democrat! If only Parnell knew what local country leaders are *thinking* and *saying* he would pray to be saved from his worshippers'.[80]

Healy went so far as to assert that the fabled discipline of the Irish party under Parnell's leadership was too lax: 'Mr. Parnell has been accused of being a dictator, but he was sorry to say that Mr. Parnell was not being sufficiently dictatorial. There was no party in which there was so much individual liberty'. He defiantly characterised Parnell as 'the most kindly-hearted and mildest of leaders'.[81]

Healy subsequently claimed credit for the invention of the Irish party pledge. This was a characteristic exaggeration. In an interview in the *Freeman's Journal* in March 1884, Parnell had anticipated that candidates would be required to subscribe to 'a pledge to sit, act and vote with the Irish party, and to resign one's seat if it should become impossible to carry out such an undertaking'. Healy subsequently drafted a pledge in these plain terms (with the refinement that the member would resign if the party determined that he had not abided by the terms of the pledge), and presided at the Dungarvan convention of August 1884 where it was first used.[82]

Explaining the effect of the pledge to his constituents on his nomination at the 1885 election, Healy's imagery slid revealingly from the martial to the ecclesiastic:

> I say that for every member of our party to put forward an individual view of his own against the opinion of the majority of the party formally and duly expressed and carefully registered would in my opinion be treason to the Irish cause . . . Some persons think that it is a slavish and servile thing that a man should, as it is called, surrender his own independence, forsooth! The soldier who goes into the field of battle must be prepared to surrender his own independence . . . The priest when he enters his sacred ministry – the highest ministry – when he accepts the tonsure, and the sacred oils are poured upon his forehead, knows that as far as his religious duties are concerned he surrenders his independence for the good of the united Church – the Church militant.[83]

He lauded the Parnellite convention system as a modernising reform, eliminating the wasteful expenditure of Irish elections, and the turmoil of the hustings: 'they had begun through these Conventions what was in reality a revolution'.[84]

In laying the foundations of Parnell's electoral hegemony there was one matter to be addressed which was not within the power of the party itself: the extension of the franchise. The third of the great reform bills of the nineteenth century, the government's franchise bill of 1884, would extend household franchise from the towns to the counties. When enacted it trebled the Irish electorate to just under three-quarters of a million voters. On the enlarged franchise, Parnell was to sweep the country the following year.[85]

The Irish party's strategy was exceedingly sophisticated. While they naturally wished to ensure that the bill passed into law, in their public pronouncements and their dealings with the government the Parnellites engaged in an elaborate feint of indifference. The reasons for this were various. To ensure the bill's passage it was important to defuse opposition in Ulster and to avoid provoking a veto in the House of Lords. Most of all, the Irish party had to avoid any linkage of the bill to a reduction in the Irish representation at Westminster. Quite apart from such parliamentary considerations, Parnell did not wish to appear indebted to the Liberals. There was moreover a domestic political purpose: in quietly facilitating the extension of the franchise which Davitt vociferously advocated, Parnell could outflank him and divest the measure of its radical *éclat*.

The operation of Parnell's strategy can be seen in a letter from E. W. Hamilton to Gladstone in January 1884. Lord Richard Grosvenor, the government whip, had learnt that Parnell, although unable to resist the extension of the franchise,

> is in his heart of hearts not favourably disposed to such extension, as he believes he will be unable to command as many votes at a general election with the franchise lowered and equalised, as he would have been able to command, had the Registration (Ireland) Bill of the last session been passed, and were he to appeal to the country of the present franchise system. This point might have some weight with Lord Hartington.[86]

Healy was one of the chief architects of the party's strategy, and conferred closely with the responsible minister, Sir Charles Dilke. In the course of their discussions Dilke was surprised to be told by Healy that it was his private opinion that the land act had quieted Ireland.[87] When the bill was enacted Healy asserted that 'he was not one of those who attached enormous importance to the extension of the franchise in Ireland'. While he favoured the measure 'undoubtedly the intention of the Liberals was to reduce the number of seats allocated to Ireland'.[88] He boasted to his constituents shortly before the 1885 election of the cunning of the Irish party's strategy. Parliamentary movements had sometimes to pursue in 'devious and hidden — perhaps unintelligible — ways':

> It is perfectly true that we pretended that we did not want it. It is perfectly true that we assumed a negligent and independent and callous and perhaps icy attitude towards the granting of this great measure which we prize

> so much . . . The Parliamentary Party has got only its discipline, and we cannot wear our hearts upon our sleeves for daws to peck at. We are obliged to keep our own counsels, and sometimes perhaps to undergo the risk of misrepresentation. We are obliged, perhaps, though we never say what Swift calls 'the thing that is not', we are sometimes obliged to let go unsaid the thing that really is . . .[89]

With the electoral machinery of Parnellism in place, and the party poised for triumph on the enlarged franchise, Healy responded to a toast to the party at the Lord Mayor's banquet in Dublin in September 1885. Bidding farewell to the old Irish party, he looked to the unimpeachable legitimacy of its successor as the voice of nationalist Ireland:

> . . . we have taken a very narrow and limited view of our functions in the past. We have never forgotten that we were elected by a minority of the votes of the Irish people . . . Under these circumstances, I say, I am glad that for the last time we have drunk its health (*hear, hear*). I am glad we shall be able to toast the Irish party of the future . . . But sir, we who are shortly to pass away have never in any sense regarded ourselves – owing to the character of the franchise given to the Irish people – as other than, if I may employ a legal term, life tenants. We were not tenants in fee simple of this Irish movement.[90]

Healy continued to be derided as a professional Parnellite apparatchik. *Vanity Fair* in 1886 wrote that Healy had taken up 'the only industry that flourishes in Ireland, by appointing himself an Irish Patriot . . . He has also been called to the Irish Bar, and has scraped together a little practice; but his profession is still that of an Irish Patriot'.[91] The taunt, if condescending, was neither altogether inapt nor devoid of wit (Parnell was described as Healy's 'original inventor and leader'). It was however sociologically inexact.

Healy had received testimonials from his constituents – £600 from his former Wexford constituents in 1883, and £1,000 from his Monaghan constituents in 1885[92] – but by 1886 he had already done much to provide himself with means of support independent of his involvement in Irish politics. Prior to his election to parliament in November 1880, Healy had commenced reading for the bar. Following the prescribed route to the Irish bar, he was admitted a member of Gray's Inn on 7 June 1880, and the following year as a student to the King's Inns in Dublin. He was called to the Irish bar on 10 November 1884, listed eighth of the fourteen on his call.[93] Healy quickly came to prominence as a barrister.[94] If the rapid development of his practice was unquestionably assisted and shaped by his status as 'an Irish patriot', it was thereafter sustained by his demonstrated ability.

John Barry's firm of Barry Ostlere and Company Limited, of Kirkcaldy, which had a significant share in the market for linoleum, provided Healy with a further substantial source of income from 1878 onwards. By 1888, according to figures which Chamberlain had prepared on the income and capital of Irish members, Healy had £2,000 invested in Scottish securities, presumably those of Barry's firm. In December 1888, Healy was sufficiently well-off to respond with a show of reluctance to an invitation to become a director of Barry's company at a salary of £150 per annum, explaining to his father that he had enough to do even though his legal business that term was 'dull'.[95]

While their political collaboration endured, the estrangement of Parnell and Healy pre-dated its public consummation in the Galway election of early 1886. Healy's relationship with Parnell was inherently unstable. T. P. O'Connor, in the life of Parnell he published very shortly after the death of the Irish leader, wrote of the early period that

> Tim, who was a hero-worshipper, was entranced by Parnell's fascinating personality. Curious as it may seem, Parnell retained his fascination for Healy to a certain extent even unto the end. Months after the quarrel had broken out, I heard him speak with something like awe of the hypnotic influence which Parnell could exercise over people – himself included.

Healy's adulation always had a treacherous undertow. O'Connor, at the time sympathetic to Healy, wrote that 'though Healy loved Parnell, Parnell never cared for Healy; and was always unjust and childishly inaccurate in his judgement of him'. He surmised indulgently that while Healy would have been constrained to oppose Parnell in the split in any event, 'he would have remained always the affectionate, if not worshipping friend of Parnell to the end, if Parnell had only let him'.[96] O'Connor discerned in Parnell a 'natural suspiciousness of character': once he 'formed a prejudice and got a suspicion of a man, he was never able to feel towards that man the same way again'.[97]

Parnell had never taken Healy into his confidence. William O'Brien wrote that Parnell's reservations 'began at an astonishingly early period'. T. P. O'Connor was of the same view, although there is nothing to substantiate his ascription of Parnell's 'silent but unconquerable aversion' to Healy to the American trip of 1880.[98] Parnell intuited Healy's unassuageable resentment perhaps before Healy had himself come fully to terms with it. Parnell's need for absolute loyalty, and his suspiciousness, increased with the commencement of his relationship with Katharine O'Shea in late 1880. His attitude towards Healy hardened from watchfulness into mistrust, quickened by his belief that during his imprisonment in Kilmainham Healy had disloyally intrigued with Chamberlain.

Healy grew apprehensive as to Parnell's attitude towards him. He wrote to Maurice in March 1884 complaining of the *Cork Examiner*'s 'mischievous' carrying of an account of a parliamentary sitting by the anti-nationalist Central News agency 'saying that I "took the leadership out of Parnell's hands", and that he disapproved of our conduct — both false. Some protection should be afforded against newspaper lying'.[99] His unease was justified. Exasperated by the discipline of the Irish party under Parnell's leadership, the English press were ever eager to discern potential lines of schism within the Irish party. Parnell and Healy could readily be depicted as anti-types by the contrast which Healy's restless energy afforded with Parnell's remoteness.

Healy had achieved a considerable prominence, to the point of prompting suggestions in the anti-nationalist press that he was usurping Parnell's position. *The World* wrote in exasperated tribute:

> The position occupied by Mr. Healy in the ranks of the Irish party, if less authoritative than that of Mr. Parnell, is just now more conspicuous and significant. Ostensibly a loyal follower of his titular leader, he is resolved to miss no chance of putting himself in evidence . . . Mr. Parnell is at present enjoying a repose, suitable to the season, in his beautiful Vale of Avoca. He nominates candidates for constituencies; he is possibly elaborating the plan of a coming campaign. But he ascends no platform, he makes no speeches . . . Mr. Healy, on the other hand, is aggressively on the alert. He is the most industrious, indefatigable, unscrupulous, and gifted of Irishmen . . . If he is inferior to several of his colleagues in the gift of oratory, he is their superior in the art of debate, and he enjoys an almost unrivalled capacity of exasperating the Prime Minister, and making the life of the Irish Secretaries almost unendurable. His own extraordinary powers of will and application have enabled him to acquire two European languages, and to write English so pungent and vigorous that it at once secures him a livelihood from his pen, and makes him a power as a publicist . . . Mr. Healy is the most ambitious and capable type of a class of politician with whom we are destined in the future to make an extensively increased acquaintance.[100]

Parnell had taken a close interest in the choice of candidates to contest the by-elections which arose during the parliament of 1880–5. A highly centralised system of nomination evolved as he strengthened his grip. He had to ensure that those nominated would be amenable to tight political discipline and could not afford to leave the nomination of candidates to the vagaries of local preference. Parnell chose a minimalist personal role. His method was to reserve a veto on candidates he judged unsuitable rather than to impose his own nominees.

A letter from Parnell to T. C. Harrington, written from Rathdrum, in August 1884 in relation to the selection of the candidate for a pending vacancy in County Tipperary gives some idea of his *modus operandi*. He explained that he was unable to attend a meeting of the Central Branch of the National League 'as I am in the midst of my harvest etc.' He instructed Harrington to consult the people in the constituency, and to show his letter to Healy and O'Brien. He had asked John O'Connor to stand, but he preferred to await the general election. He would not object to Doherty standing but he would have to be bound by a pledge to sit, act and vote with the party. 'Allingham should not be tolerated as he took the chair at [Henry] George's disruption meeting, and in any case little is known of him and his record is very new'. The choice was between Doherty and O'Connor, 'almost too good a man to give to such a safe constituency'.[101] In the event O'Connor was returned in January 1885.

At the 1885 general election there were a large number of candidates to be nominated. While he was assailed by his English critics of nationalism as a dictator, Parnell did not seek to impose a slate of personal nominees. His absences from Ireland in any event lessened his ability to select candidates personally even had he wished to do so. An informal committee of the party met in Morrison's Hotel on Dawson Street in Dublin to approve the selection of candidates before the election. T. P. O'Connor noted that Parnell rarely intervened.[102]

As the general election approached tensions within the party grew, and Healy's relations with Parnell became for the first time openly strained. Healy attended the meetings in Morrison's Hotel.[103] There were a couple of fractious incidents. A dispute flared between Healy and Harrington as to the form the pledge should take. Writing much later, T. P. O'Connor recalled that 'it was not pleasant but it was not devastating'. Parnell was unsettled and explained to O'Connor that such scenes made him nervous. He told O'Connor that Healy was 'a selfish man'. When O'Connor shook his head in dissent, Parnell, quietly 'but almost angrily', asked if he would form or express opinions of men without reason.[104]

There was also a serious altercation between Healy and Henry Campbell, his successor as Parnell's secretary. Seizing eagerly on the rumours which reached him through W. H. O'Shea, Joseph Chamberlain wrote to Gladstone of 'internecine conflicts in the nationalist ranks' and alleged that Healy and Campbell 'actually came to blows at a recent convention'. He commented that 'if we have a good majority it may be possible to divide them and to secure some support for our proposals'.[105]

Some of Parnell's closest supporters, notably Henry Campbell, grew uneasy at Healy's success in securing the nomination of candidates proposed by him. O'Connor was summoned from London by Campbell on one or two occasions in an effort to thwart Healy.[106]

O'Brien and Healy failed to persuade Parnell to agree to the candidacy of Thomas Murphy, the District Inspector who had been dismissed from the Royal Irish Constabulary after providing information in relation to James Ellis French to Healy and *United Ireland*. Healy had also pressed the claims of his friend P. A. Chance. Writing in 1900, the zenith of his estrangement from Healy, O'Brien extravagantly proclaimed that Parnell's opposition to Murphy and Chance was for Healy, 'another drop added to the bitterness of the implacable personal feud against his leader, which has since exercised so sinister an influence upon the fate of Ireland'.[107] Chance was in fact returned for South Kilkenny.

Healy was especially concerned to procure the election of his brother Maurice. His original preference was for Maurice to contest his own old seat in Monaghan: to that end Maurice had addressed a meeting in the constituency. The alternative was for Maurice to stand in Cork, where he lived and practised as a solicitor. Healy had misgivings, as this would involve his brother sharing the representation of the city with Parnell, 'who begins to take opportunities of snarling at me, and these strained relations will increase, instead of diminish, as I am not a man to make any overtures or explanations'. While he had not spoken to Parnell on the subject. Healy wrote Maurice that 'he will only have you as a colleague when he fails, as fail he will, to get anybody suitable whom the Cork people would adopt'. At a meeting of the election committee the next day in Dublin, Campbell read a memorandum from Parnell (who had gone to Liverpool to campaign for W. H. O'Shea) stating that either Joe Horgan or Maurice Healy was to be the candidate, and that he had no preference between them. On discussing the matter with Harrington, Healy 'came to be of the opinion, that, little as I desire your being Member for Cork, it is preferable to your being put forward for Monaghan, as it would look as if you could not get any other constituency. I think Parnell has acted the reverse of well towards you, but that can't be helped'. He added:

> I may be wrong about Parnell, and therefore don't let any feeling of constraint on my part affect you. It in no way affects my regard for him, and if you go forward your course should be to act just as if he were not your colleague, and do your work in your own way. Probably the whole thing may wear away after these frightful personal questions are settled, and we get back into the true political current once more.[108]

On 27 November Maurice Healy was returned for Cork city, close behind Parnell, in an exact and disciplined division of the nationalist vote.

A formidable complement of Healy's friends and relatives were returned in addition to his brother, notably Donal Sullivan, Daniel Crilly, P. A. Chance and William Martin Murphy. T. D. Sullivan, who had formerly sat for Westmeath, was returned for Dublin (College Green). Healy himself defeated Sir John Leslie in North Monaghan. He was also returned with a slender majority in the highly marginal constituency of South Derry, for which he opted to sit. Together they formed in the words of a hostile observer 'a kind of party within the party'.[109]

The election of his kinsmen and allies did not inhibit Healy in the split from assailing Parnell for having packed the party with his creatures. In 1900 Healy went so far as to make the astonishing assertion that in relation to the personnel of the party 'my responsibility at any time in twenty years . . . was limited to recommending one candidate – viz. Mr. Thomas Sexton'.[110]

Land and Nationalism: An Agrarianism of the Right

> In that single word 'rent' was bound up a volume stained with blood and watered with tears – a volume of emigration, of extirpation. In that word was bound up the fate and fortunes of the Irish nation.
>
> T. M. Healy, June 1883[111]

W. E. H. Lecky in his *Leaders of Public Opinion in Ireland* sought to account for the violence of Daniel O'Connell's rhetoric: 'The spectacle of a Roman Catholic fearlessly assailing the highest in the land with the fiercest invective and the most unceremonious ridicule, was eminently calculated to invigorate a cowering people. A tone of extreme violence was the best corrective for a spirit of extreme servility'.[112] While his choice of language owed more to John Mitchel, Healy was the successor to this rhetorical tradition. However even by the early 1880s the morale of Catholic nationalists had been to a considerable extent restored. The transformation wrought by Parnellism diminished the necessity and the justification for inspiriting ferocity, which Parnell himself habitually avoided. Healy's virulence was unabated.

Healy's rhetoric was charged with the gathering impetus towards peasant proprietorship, and sounded a note of Catholic nationalist supremacism which was not reducible merely to a strategic threat. What was distinctive was his pursuit of proprietorship through the medium of a chauvinistic, pseudo-revolutionary idiom. While his rhetoric was directed in the longer term to the re-definition of nationalism, his immediate concern was to dispel any residual deference towards the landlord class, and to re-adjust the balance of social power in Ireland by driving down the price at which tenants could expect to purchase their holdings. His purpose was crudely proclaimed in a speech at Mullingar in June 1884

> The landlords now found themselves unable to pay the Jews their mortgages and their loans, and as the Jews, having no mercy, were now pressing them as the landlords used to oppress their tenants, the landlords were crying out for mercy. What mercy would they show them? The mercy they showed their unfortunate tenants when they flung them out upon the road unless they could pay the last farthing . . . If instead of the Jews, it was the devil himself that was on their heels, the Irish people would only be delighted the more (*cheers and laughter*).

In the same speech, Healy proclaimed the new realism which had superseded older modes of romantic nationalism, as well as the Land League itself:

> This movement had been represented as a selfish movement. It had been discredited because there had not been much poetry about it. There had not been much about Brian Boroimhe and the Battle of Clontarf. The green flag had not been so often on the horizon, and for that reason some critics classed the Land League movement as a selfish one. He believed the error that the leaders of previous movements committed was in attempting to crown the edifice of Irish Liberty before the foundations had been dug. No movement could ever succeed that had only beggars at the back of it, for beggars must always be slaves. So long as Ireland was under the heel of landlordism they had a nation partly of slaves and partly of beggars . . . The passionate effervescence of the Land League movement might have passed away, but it had at least left a good deal that was practical to follow (*applause*).[113]

Healy's position was astutely judged. His agrarian rhetoric pursued a proprietorial solution to the land question with a vehemence which surpassed that of the agrarian left. Thus he could declare that the convention of September 1881 to consider the land act 'declared not for peace, but for war to the knife with landlordism'.[114] After the convention he had written:

> We hear tell of a fair rent. A thing so called is about to be fixed and determined by men learned in the law. But have we yet arrived at the epoch where a fair rent can be settled? Have we taught the pundits the real standard of measurement or has there been time to educate our people up to the proper standard of legitimate expectation? Does the worn and haggard cottier, paying wearily his £50 a year, whose bleared eye looks back on a vista of forty rent days, and whose back is bowed with the anxious striving and misery which each recurring gale-struggle has brought him, does such a creature comprehend that though it is sweet to have the rent-load lightened by a score of annual pounds, yet that his due and right may be the almost entire abolition of a bitter tribute? Much is to be doubted that he can. His burden has been too heavy, his rights too few, and the tradition of his servitude too deep and rooted.[115]

Healy was the nationalist politician most acutely – and least inhibitedly – aware that the nationalist movement functioned in one aspect as a tenants' cartel. The political economy of the Irish question was the arithmetic of social power. There was a seamless continuity in Healy's argument as to what was a fair rent and what was a just price for the purpose of land purchase. The calculus of proprietorship was central to a rhetoric which, confirming the worst fears of high Fenians of the old school, promiscuously merged the agrarian and nationalist causes.

On the land question, Healy's espousal of the state-aided land purchase by tenants of their individual holdings was the diametrical opposite of the land nationalisation advocated by Davitt. 'The general question of land nationalisation', he declared at the end of 1884, 'is no more within the sphere of practical politics than the emigration of the Chinese. Some time in the twentieth century will be time enough to consider it'.[116] It is hard to dissent from this assessment. Land nationalisation was never a practical policy. By the mid-1880s the drive towards proprietorship had already rendered it largely academic.

With the passage of the Purchase of Land (Ireland) Act of 1885 (the Ashbourne act), Healy was in a position to complete his rhetorical outflanking of the agrarian radicals. An editorial in *United Ireland* of August 1885 perfectly conveyed Healy's position. Defending this first significant measure of land purchase against radical nationalist attack, *United Ireland* argued that 'if what the critics desire is that nothing should be passed to enable the tenants to buy, then we are firmly opposed to them; but if they simply advocate that only a low price should be given, we are entirely of their opinion'. Land purchase was the *fait accompli* of the New Departure:

> In a few months, we believe, people will look back with amazement at the controversy that has been started by those who wish to mix up the question of principle with the question of price . . . We put it to the country . . . whether the Land League principle of making the tiller the owner of the soil was a sound or an unsound one, and if sound whether, now that its propriety has been legislatively admitted, there is room for any other dispute amongst Land Leaguers except as to the price at which the transfer is to take place.[117]

In early 1885, Sir Charles Gavan Duffy, decidedly *démodé* if vaguely venerable, appealed to the Irish landlords and to the Conservative party to restore Ireland's legislative independence. *United Ireland* dissented, contrasting his attitude with that of Healy, who in the *Fortnightly Review* had urged the Conservatives to break their link with the Irish landlords. *United Ireland* asserted that 'the way to deal with native Tories is not to bargain with them, but to wipe them out'. Contrary to Gavan Duffy's archaic and sentimental hopes, there could be 'no restoration of Grattan's Senate except over the corpse of Irish landlordism . . . The hope of winning over the landlords was a purely '48 idea, which is now out of date . . .' Parnell's dictum that the landlords had to be bought out or fought out was true so long as they continued to enjoy imperial backing, 'but what will most probably happen is that England before long will utterly desert them . . . and they will then be carved up at leisure by their enemies at home'.[118] The views expressed were Healy's. That they overbore those of O'Brien, which retained a distinctly 'Young Ireland' hue, reflects the extent to which Healy defined the editorial policy of *United Ireland* in the two and half year period prior to the Galway election of 1886.[119]

In 1886 Healy sought to bring Gladstone's espousal of home rule to bear on the balance of social power in Ireland. He asserted a strict linkage between the acceptance by nationalists of the land purchase bill which accompanied the home rule bill, which he described as 'a raft of safety to the landlords', and the acceptance by Irish unionists of home rule. Of Gladstone's provision for purchase at the 'extravagant rate' of twenty years, rent, Healy restated the fundamental axiom of his agrarian politics:

> It must be remembered now that not merely morally, but by the demands and the wills of the people of these kingdoms, the tenant's interest in the soil is the dominant interest; that the landlord's interest is a precarious interest; that the interest of the tenant is the substantial, dominant, permanent, and enduring interest.[120]

Before the 1885 election Healy repudiated 'with indignation the taunt of religious intolerance'. When home rule was won, there would be 'no bitter memories in our hearts, no recollections of revenge, no thoughts of retaliation'. To every honest Protestant they would say 'let us shake hands across the bloody gulf of centuries'.[121]

In an interview in December, he disdained 'to offer any guarantees other than those which the friendly attitude of the great mass of the population in the three southern provinces every day towards the Protestant minority affords to any impartial observer'.[122] Unionists were invited to trust to nationalist magnanimity, which if his own speeches were any indication was hardly likely to be overflowing.

Healy's attitude to the position of the Protestant minority in Ireland contrasted starkly with Parnell's fastidious pursuit of a political equilibrium:

> I say it will be time enough for them to cry out when they are hurt; it will be time enough for them when an Irish Parliament begins to oppress them to cry out for protection from England; and I believe the strong hand of England will always be sufficient under the Irish constitution to afford them every protection.[123]

Healy was looking to the residual external framework of English power to guarantee rights of unionists. This was in stark contrast to the more sophisticated design of Parnell, who sought to entrench the position of the minority by the internal disposition of power within a home rule state. Healy certainly conceived his rejection of the necessity to offer guarantees as a negotiating position (and then perhaps more in relation to land purchase than home rule): he took no exception to any of the safeguards provided for in Gladstone's scheme of home rule. Yet the crudity of his argument was hardly calculated to allay Irish unionist fears, and reflected an attitude of complacent dismissiveness towards the opposition within Ireland to home rule which was to prove seriously misconceived.

Unionism was reducible to the politics of self-interest. 'Loyalty and disloyalty in the present century mean nothing more than satisfaction and dissatisfaction' Healy wrote in November 1883.[124] Speaking in Fermanagh in October 1883, he declared: 'When the landlords were crying out about the Queen, it was not of the Queen but of their pockets they were thinking. It was not about the sovereign on the throne but about the sovereigns in the bank'. The Protestant tenants of Ulster were undeceived, and would not 'be roused by the bloody shrouds of Aughrim and the Boyne'.[125]

Healy unremittingly assailed Orange and Conservative violence and bigotry in Ulster. Reversing the taunt of lawlessness, he proclaimed that 'the party of disorder in Ireland is the Tory party', and mocked 'the invincibilism of the Orange Lodges'.[126] In an influential pamphlet called *Loyalty Plus Murder* Healy published an anthology of 'the writings, speeches and placards of the Orangemen – unsurpassed in political literature'.[127]

Writing immediately prior the 1885 general election, Healy prophesied the success of what he incautiously and revealingly called 'the Parnellite *razzia* [raid, plunder] in the North'. He looked to an excess of nationalist over anti-nationalist seats at the election (which was duly achieved): British admirers of 'the Ulster of geography . . . will have to rectify its frontiers, and declare that Ulster really consists of one whole county and some scraps of three others'.

Healy with metropolitan disdain declined to take seriously opposition to home rule in Ulster. He wrote in the *Contemporary Review*, anticipating a nationalist victory in Ulster:

> Of course there will remain for the present a considerable minority in Ulster opposed to Home Rule because of religious fears; but the very cause of their antagonism demonstrates the intellectual calibre of such a party. To my mind the ignorant opposition of uneducated Orangemen is far less worthy of being taken into account by Englishmen than the Platonic resistance to Home Rule offered by the cultured minority about Dublin, whom nobody considers . . . The bigots who are fools enough

> to suppose that the Ministers of an Irish Parliament would dine off roast Protestant must be left to the care of the National schoolmaster.[128]

Healy's brusque refusal to seriously take account of Irish unionist opposition to home rule is most clearly evinced in a remarkable letter to Henry Labouchere in October 1885, written to persuade Labouchere (and through him W. E. Gladstone) that unionist opposition in Ireland to home rule would be easily over-ridden:

> As for the minority, the Protestants would be the worst enemies England would have. They would soon be the Separatist party here, just as now they are the Unionist, because the moment they realised they were safe with the Catholics (and they would be the pets of our people) they would be most anxious to revenge themselves upon the English. If the Catholics made a bargain with you they'd be always troubled about their 'consciences', but the Protestants would not have the smallest scruple in breaking any arrangement they agreed to, if they found it in their interest and could do it safely. They hate and curse England now — only they don't show it lest it would gratify us, but if those who call themselves 'loyalists' could hear them privately they would open their eyes. Let there be by all means every guarantee for their protection. In fact I would have no objection, and it would be the worst humiliation that could be inflicted on them, to an enactment that the whole of Antrim and a bit of Down, Derry and Armagh be excluded from the jurisdiction of the Irish assembly and in about twelve months they'd be howling to come in. It would be hard on the Nationalists there, but they would not have long to wait.[129]

At once bigoted and cloying, Healy's brutally whimsical argument was conducted in terms of absurd stereotypes: caricatural (of Irish Protestants) and self-regarding (of Irish Catholics). His facetiously professed readiness to countenance partition — later publicly dismissed by him as 'the pseudo-Radical cry for a *cordon sanitaire* around the Belfast district'[130] — attested to the superficiality of his assessment. The contrast between Healy's coarse and bumptious Catholic nationalism and Parnell's restrained statecraft could hardly have been more sharply rendered. Two months later Labouchere blithely relayed to Herbert Gladstone Healy's trivialisation of the strength of northern unionist resistance to home rule: 'By the way Healy says there is not the slightest fear of the Orangemen of Ulster breaking out into rebellion. There are not a thousand of them who would risk their skins. Their strength has been that they have had, up to lately, the Government and the Magistrates on their side'.[131]

The deep-seated policy differences between Healy and Parnell tend to be overshadowed by the drama of the split, where Healy was pitted against his former leader. Yet parallel to their deepening personal estrangement ran a political conflict which went to the roots of nationalism. Parnell and Healy stood alone in the acuity of their political realism, remote from O'Brien's effervescent romanticism, Davitt's doctrinaire radicalism, and Dillon's austere distaste for the politics of proprietorship. They harboured irreconcilable conceptions of the nationalist polity which the combined impact of land purchase and home rule would create. The striking divergence of their views is obscured in the equation implicit in the conventional classification, meaningless without further refinement, of both as conservative in their socio-economic views.

By taking fuller account of Healy's position it is possible to redraw the cartography of Parnellism. Parnell's fragile and ambitious endeavour was predicated upon the containment of an assertively Catholic agrarian nationalism. Parnell's authority was directed to the containment of precisely the forces which Healy sought to exploit through a rhetoric of proprietorial nationalism, and which had potentially devastating implications for Parnellism in the longer term, even had the split not intervened. Yet during Parnell's hegemony the chief threat to his position was not perceived as emanating from the Catholic agrarian right. Conventionally the left-wing agrarianism which the Land League had represented, and the opposition of hardline Fenians to constitutional action, continued to be considered as the principal constraints on Parnell's leadership long after they had ceased to be so. Parnell himself rather encouraged this obsolete paradigm which well served his immediate purposes. It was to contribute to a dangerous underestimation of the strength of Healy's challenge in the split, and an almost complete lack of readiness to confront it.

5

Nationalists and Radicals:
Healy and Henry Labouchere

I wonder what passed in that most intricate and Jesuitical mind [W. E. Gladstone's] in the months between June and December 1885. I am surprised that nothing has come out of the negotiations with Mrs. O'Shea for I suppose there were negotiations although I knew nothing of them at the time.

But I have proof that at the very time when Mr. Gladstone wrote to me that he had no communication with Parnell, there was an active correspondence going on between Herbert Gladstone at Hawarden, Labouchere and Healey [*sic*].

Joseph Chamberlain to Sir Charles Dilke,
29 September 1891[1]

To the Irish Nationalist, concerned for his own country, it is a toss-up which side he supports. The Celtic husbandman grubbing out his living on some hillside recks not of *haute politique*.

T. M. Healy, November 1883[2]

They saw a lack of unity among the Liberal party because it had been disorganised by Mr. Parnell (*loud applause*).

T. M. Healy, August 1885[3]

Relations between the Parnellites and the radicals, the two avowedly progressive blocs at Westminster, were highly fraught. From the era of obstruction through the Liberal schism on home rule in 1886 to the split in the Irish party four years later, the interaction of radical and nationalist sentiment did more to sharpen rancour than engender solidarity. The prevalent perception that radicals and nationalists were naturally allied served to increase the tension between them. Adhering to conflicting philosophies, each was determined not to be defined by reference to the other. There were moreover marked temperamental sensitivities. On either side the figures who stood out in ambition and fractious pride were Joseph Chamberlain and T. M. Healy.

Many radicals, while suspicious of costly imperial adventures, were in British terms staunchly nationalistic, and disdainful of the combination of near-treason and mendicancy which they considered to characterise the Irish party. The thinly repressed mistrust was reciprocated. If nationalism had a specific ideological content apart from the furtherance of the claim to statehood and Irish land, it lay in its hostility to the ideology of liberal capitalism, which provided the credo of radicalism. That hostility, deriving from Thomas Davis and Young Ireland, was deepened by considerations of class and religion. Nationalists affected to despise the rootedness of radicalism in the industrial middle class. 'The Philosophical Radicals', complained *United Ireland*, 'are merely rich *bourgeois* with a grudge against the aristocratic society from which their vulgarity excludes them'.[4]

Conor Cruise O'Brien has discerned 'a curious type of mimetic snobbery' at work in the hostility towards the radicals of many nationalists, particularly Healy, noting 'the assumption, by middle-class professional people, who were themselves often of peasant origin, of the aristocratic contempt for persons "in trade"'. The pro-Toryism of which Davitt accused Healy was, he suggests, 'primarily a social attitude rather than a political outlook'.[5]

This phenomenon accounts for much of the furious edge of social rancour which frequently arose in nationalist dealings with the radicals. Catholic nationalist suspicions of radicalism nevertheless ran deeper. Healy's observation in a short story written for *Young Ireland* when he had just turned twenty-one that 'we cannot be everlastingly permitting the Juggernaut of utility to tear down upon and crush all the "useless" gaiety out of our lives'[6] discloses an incipient mistrust of utilitarianism and radical political thinking.

In his *Nation* letter, Healy gave further indications of a strikingly anti-radical disposition. On imperial matters on which nationalist and radical views generally coincided, Healy distinguished his position from that of the radicals by arguing from deliberately crude and provocative nationalist premises.[7] While other nationalists – most notably T. P. O'Connor, seven years Healy's senior, who had been returned for Galway in 1880 – were highly sympathetic to the radicals, Healy was instinctively opposed to the identification of the Irish party with British radicals. He was determined to ensure that the Irish nationalist demand (which in any event by no means commanded the united assent of British radicalism) was not reduced to a subordinate item in an otherwise largely uncongenial radical agenda. Thus in September 1880 he had commended Parnell's refusal to a government invitation to move a vote of censure on the House of Lords for its rejection of Irish bills. It was not the concern of the Irish party 'to make the running for the English Radicals . . . let the English put their own house in order. We want no knight-errantry for their sweet sakes'.[8]

Healy was acutely sensitive to the tension between Liberal – and in particular radical – ideology and Catholic teaching. He wrote in 1878 that those in England with vested interests, including the Church of England, were 'not blind to the ultimate tendings of Liberalism':[9] he was fully aware that the same 'ultimate tendings' were inimical to institutional Catholicism. He observed that 'the whole tendency of English political Catholicism is towards the Conservative party'. While in Ireland the Catholic priesthood frequently favoured the Liberals

> here on the contrary the word [Liberalism] seems to be already acquiring a tinge of its continental meaning and ecclesiastical politicians seem naturally to gravitate towards Toryism. Mainly no doubt, this is immediately caused by the secular progress of the Radicals upon the education question, but alongside of this a remote cause must exist in the consciousness that English liberalism must at some future time have developments against which the Church will be obliged to range itself officially.[10]

Healy's evangel at this time was emphatically more Parnellite than Catholic, and he was fiercely critical of the resistance of many Catholic churchmen in Ireland to the rise of Parnellism. Yet, already displaying that acute sensitivity to the thought-processes of Irish Catholic ecclesiastics which was to characterise his later career, he discerned the secularising proclivities of Liberalism as a fault-line in any Liberal–nationalist entente: on this issue at least, Irish nationalists had more in common with the Conservative party.

The issue of the admission to parliament of the declared atheist Charles Bradlaugh, first returned for Northampton in 1880, which was to engender bitter controversy until he was finally permitted to take his seat in 1886, heightened Healy's divergence from the radicals. In the *Nation* he deplored the parliamentary preoccupation with Bradlaugh at the expense of Irish affairs:

> Bradlaugh, Bradlaugh, Bradlaugh, week after week for a couple of months . . . Doubt not the benevolence of your rulers, however, poor people of

> Connaught! The survivors will be attended to when there is time, but just now Mr. Bradlaugh is waiting and cannot brook delay, whereas a little starvation more or less in the west is simply an affair of coffins. If necessary afterwards, provision can be made to supply suitable sound deal to workhouses at low rates, and the land question will be settled forever in the graveyards with unquestioned fixity of tenure.[11]

Healy did not then profess opposition to Bradlaugh's admission on religious grounds, and his views were constrained by the line of schism which ran through the Irish party. Parnell and his closest supporters were initially sympathetic to Bradlaugh, but came later to oppose the Liberal government's attempts to procure his admission, partly out of deference to Catholic sentiment in Ireland. F. H. O'Donnell allied himself with the more conservative wing of the Irish party in fiercely opposing from the outset Bradlaugh's admission. Ever eager to posture as a high-spirited Catholic gentleman, and seeking to turn the Bradlaugh issue against Parnell, O'Donnell protested against 'the honourable weapons of the Active Policy being degraded by use to protect, not Irish national interests, but the interests of "Atheism and Filth"', and commended 'the merited imprisonment of the foul-mouthed insulter of Christ'. Healy rallied to Parnell's defence, condemning the 'most venomous' letter of O'Donnell, whom he derided as 'our peerless Roland'.[12]

When elected, Healy was himself to the fore in opposing Bradlaugh's admission. He did not profess to do so on religious grounds but used the issue to harry the Liberal government, and in particular its radical supporters. He treated the time the government devoted to the Bradlaugh case as an index of its indifference to Irish affairs. Following the arrest of John Dillon in May 1881, Healy protested at the devoting of a morning to the Bradlaugh issue, while Dillon 'who had not blasphemed God, but who had blasphemed the Government in Ireland, had not been allowed a minute's time for the discussion of his arrest'.[13]

During the nine-month period of his temporary admission to parliament in 1881–2, Bradlaugh came to be unfairly pilloried by nationalists as a supporter of the 'coercion' regime of W. E. Forster as Chief Secretary. Bradlaugh especially resented the manner in which his voting record was presented in Healy's *A Record of Coercion,* a collation of how members had voted in the debates on the two acts of 1881 which drew no distinction between votes on procedural questions and votes on the substantive legislation. In his *National Reformer* Bradlaugh published a damaging and not altogether implausible account of a meeting with Healy on the *Arizona en route* back from the United States: 'On board that vessel he pretended to be extremely friendly to me, but said that his opinions on religious questions did not differ much from mine, but that he represented a priest-ridden constituency, and was obliged to attack me'. Bradlaugh insisted on the veracity of this account in the face of Healy's furious denial.[14]

Liberal exasperation at what latterly became the Parnellites' opposition to the admission of Bradlaugh was provokingly exacerbated by Healy. Speaking in Ireland with cheerful cynicism in January 1884, he suggested to laughter that the Irish party, 'having last year used Bradlaugh as a battering ram for knocking down the Whigs', might that session use him 'as a battering ram for knocking down the Tories'.[15] Healy continued to play a prominent role in the opposition to Bradlaugh.[16]

On 6 July 1885, Bradlaugh made his penultimate attempt to be admitted to the House of Commons as a member. The votes of thirty-five Parnellites (nine of whom returned from Ireland to vote for the purpose) decided the issue against him. Bradlaugh, a little shocked at the 'exhibition of Irish ferocity', professed surprise that Parnell had supported Healy on the issue. Bradlaugh finally prevailed on 13 January 1886, when the new Speaker permitted him to take the oath.[17]

Healy made occasional perfunctory references to the radical leaders Joseph Chamberlain and Sir Charles Dilke. As early as 1878, he looked to concessions from Chamberlain 'once the Birmingham citadel is pierced by Irish power'.[18] He referred to Chamberlain in September 1883 as a future Prime Minister, but this compliment was part of the strategy of bidding up Gladstone's support for home rule; moreover he discounted the prospects of Dilke, 'a gentleman who, because he was intended to be the Premier would never be that or anything else'.[19]

From 1884, relations between the nationalists and the radicals grew increasingly strained. The Parnellites were affronted by the readiness of the radicals to acquiesce in renewed coercion by the Liberal government, and increasingly made common cause with the Conservatives in attacking the government. This in turn alienated the radicals. In an article, 'The Irish and the Government', in November 1884 Healy sought to explain the Irish position to bewildered and aggrieved Liberals.[20]

At the end of 1884 Joseph Chamberlain revived the idea of a solution to the Irish question by way of an ambitious scheme of administrative devolution of powers to an Irish 'central board'. While he was willing to devolve significant legislative powers on matters such as land and education, Chamberlain's purpose was to repair relations between Liberals and nationalists without conceding an Irish parliament. He proceeded on two fronts. The first was to approach Parnell through the medium of W. H. O'Shea. While Parnell had a clear interest in seeing how far Chamberlain could be drawn, he emphasised to O'Shea that administrative reforms, however far-reaching, could not be confused with or substituted for home rule. That fundamental distinction was imperfectly conveyed, if not actively suppressed, by O'Shea in his dealings with Chamberlain.[21]

Chamberlain also unveiled his proposals in a letter to W. H. Duignan, a Walsall solicitor of Irish extraction and connections, whom he authorised to show the letter to leading nationalists. Healy was a particular target of this stratagem. Chamberlain had shrewdly intuited both his underlying conservatism and his restiveness under Parnell's leadership. He further believed that Healy was predisposed to the kind of scheme he had in mind. This was in large part attributable to an erroneous inference he drew from Healy's role in drafting a bill for elective councils in Ireland, completed in March 1883. The text published in the *Freeman's Journal* included provision for a central council with the powers of private legislation then vested in select committees of the House of Commons. The clause providing for a central council was later struck out when a proof of the bill was submitted to the party, on the grounds that it eroded the distinction between local government and the demand for home rule.[22]

Healy's response to the Chamberlain letter was blunt. He declined to comment on the details of Chamberlain's plan. Individual Englishmen might wish to act nobly, but they were restricted by 'the hogs who mostly composed the House of Commons'. Englishmen would never give anything unless compelled to, and the Irish were holding out for a parliament. Chamberlain decided to suspend the project. He wrote to Duignan 'we know generally how such a proposal would be regarded and it is evident from Healy's letter that the simplest action may be misconstrued'.[23]

Chamberlain and Dilke resigned from the Liberal government shortly before its fall in June 1885 in protest at its failure to adopt Chamberlain's policy. They ill-advisedly announced a plan to visit Ireland. Chamberlain failed to recognise that his scheme fell critically short of nationalist requirements. Moreover he was regarded by nationalists with wary respect rather than warmth. For them he appeared an unsympathetic champion of Irish interest, authoritarian and imaginatively frugal. Even as he embarked on what he considered to be a bold step into the future, he appeared increasingly redundant in the nationalist scheme of things: Irish hopes were directed toward Gladstone and home rule rather than to Chamberlain's central council. His projected trip to Ireland presented itself to nationalists as a regressive voyage into condescension.[24]

United Ireland maintained a series of withering attacks on Chamberlain and Dilke following their resignation. It advised Chamberlain, 'with his bastard out-of-date sympathy', and Dilke to stay at home.[25] While not inspired by him, the *United Ireland* attacks on Chamberlain and Dilke furthered Parnell's immediate purpose: they assisted his extrication from his negotiations with Chamberlain, and averted an Irish expedition which he can only have regarded with suspicion as a presumptuous incursion into his own political terrain. Chamberlain complained to Dilke: 'I cannot altogether acquit Parnell of duplicity'. Labouchere conveyed to Chamberlain Parnell's assurance 'that he regrets greatly the articles in *United Ireland* about your visit, and says that he had nothing to do with them. This may or may not be true, probably the latter'.[26]

Parnell rightly judged that the attacks went somewhat too far. He remonstrated mildly with O'Brien:

> Mr. Parnell said we were injudiciously hard on him. He said, of course, he was a man who could not be relied on, and that we were quite right that he should not be allowed to exploit the Irish Cause and make his own of it, but he said he was a man who could be a dangerous enemy and that he was willing to go as far as he wanted, and in fact a great deal farther than we want. In consequence of that representation I did moderate our tone as to Mr. Chamberlain, but the visit to Ireland never came off.[27]

The first person plural refers to O'Brien and Healy. Parnell — almost certainly correctly — held Healy chiefly responsible for the virulence of the *United Ireland* attacks on Chamberlain and Dilke.[28]

Parnell came to impute to Healy responsibility for driving Chamberlain into opposition to home rule, having first (as he falsely believed) intrigued with him, and then with opportunistic inconstancy assailed him in gratuitously offensive terms.[29] Parnell himself had some responsibility for the alienation of Chamberlain, having shamelessly used him to bid up Liberal support for home rule, and by dealing with him through so inept and wilful an intermediary as W. H. O'Shea. Yet neither his nor Healy's role could be considered to have exercised a decisive influence. The estrangement of the radical pretender to the Liberal leadership was an inevitable incident of the nationalist drive to home rule, and Gladstone's willingness to engage with it.

When the newly installed Conservative government conceded an inquiry into the Maamtrasna convictions, Healy took the opportunity to deride the absent Chamberlain and Dilke with peculiar provocativeness:

> Were the Irish people to understand that in this even-keeled vessel of the Liberal Party, when in full sail, Gentlemen like the rt. hon. Member for Birmingham (Mr. Chamberlain) and the rt. hon. Member for Chelsea (Sir Chas. W. Dilke), whenever any dirty work was to be done, could send the noble Marquess (Hartington) and the rt. hon. Gentleman the member for Derby (Sir William Harcourt) to swab the decks, whilst they retired to the cabin with the sublime serenity of men in the possession of a first-class passage?

Earlier, when Harcourt had asserted that the colleagues of Spencer supported his actions, Healy interjected: 'Where is Dilke and Chamberlain? (*Cries of 'Order'*)'.[30] Writing in September 1885 Healy looked to the '"white plume" of Midlothian': 'there is no man in the Liberal party to compete with Mr. Gladstone for breadth of view, be the professions of his Radical lieutenants what they may'.[31]

On 8 June the Parnellites and Tories combined to inflict a narrow budgetary defeat on the government, on the issue of the duty on whisky. Healy had been summoned from Dublin the previous day by a telegram from Parnell. He wrote in his memoirs of the government's unanticipated fall: 'The Western Question had entered unannounced, and the East vanished in mist . . . So finished in fever a night begun in fog. Lord Spencer's Irish "policy" perished in a whisky ambuscade'.[32] It was central to Parnell's strategy that the Irish party showed itself prepared to vote out a Liberal government. He had changed the rules of the game, and the politics of Ireland and Britain would never be quite the same again. The Conservatives took office under Salisbury on 15 June.

On 1 August 1885, Parnell met secretly with Lord Carnarvon, the newly appointed Lord Lieutenant, to whom he outlined his demand for an Irish parliament. Carnarvon was alone in the government in his readiness to consider home rule, and the significance of their meeting in terms of policy was negligible. Justin McCarthy, who had already himself met Carnarvon, later wrote: 'Mr. Parnell . . . expressed grave doubts as to whether Lord Carnarvon was strong enough to carry his party with him. Mr. Parnell, in fact, attached but little importance to the entire negotiation'.[33] It was however of the greatest consequence in breathing life into the strategic fiction of Parnellism that it was possible to play the Conservatives off against the Liberals in the quest for home rule. Parnell also met Randolph Churchill, of whom he observed to W. S. Blunt the following year: 'We never believed in him — at least, I never did. And we got more out of him last year than ever he got out of us'.[34]

'Labby'

Harold Frederic recalled the parliamentary ghetto in which, on coming to London in 1884 as the correspondent of the *New York Times*, he found the Parnellites.

> I remember the time when not all the forty of Mr. Parnell's followers, collectively, had a speaking acquaintance with more than fifteen English members. There used to be in those days some furtive whispering in the lobby or on the terrace with intriguers like Chamberlain or Lord Randolph

> Churchill; an open friendship with a few Radicals like Henry Labouchere, Thorold Rogers, Sir Charles Dilke, and Mr. Story, of Sunderland, and a nodding acquaintance with a few of the Radicals of lesser importance.[35]

H. W. Lucy likewise wrote:

> The camaraderie which is one of the most attractive characteristics of the House of Commons, placing dukes' sons and cooks' sons on a footing of equality, did not in the 'Seventies and 'Eighties extend to the Irish Member. No British representative walked or talked with him in the Lobby, the corridors, the Terrace, or other quarters of social intercourse. As for asking him to dine at their houses, they could as readily have distributed cards of invitation among a colony of lepers.[36]

The widespread holding back from relations with the Irish members was undermined by Parnell's effectiveness in constituting the Irish party a third force at Westminster, and crumbled as the Conservatives and Parnellites increasingly made common cause in opposition to Gladstone's administration.[37]

Henry du Pré Labouchere (1831–1912) was among the few who had maintained good relations with the Irish members from the outset. The radical member for Northampton, of French ancestry, owed his considerable wealth to his family's banking interests. Rejecting his father's puritanism, Labouchere developed a predilection for gambling and a taste for the Bohemian life: W. S. Blunt found him in 1861 'entirely in the society of whores and croupiers'. He was part-owner of the *Daily News*, the leading Liberal morning paper. He established and personally conducted the tendentious and entertaining *Truth* from 1877.[38]

Labouchere was a wit, gossip and compulsive schemer, of whom it was observed that 'his scepticism and realism were of the French rather than the English cast'.[39] In pursuit of his entertainment and advancement (he could never wholly bring himself to acknowledge their incompatibility) he assiduously cultivated the leading Parnellites. Initially he hoped to promote a Chamberlain-led Liberal government with Parnellite support. Caught up in his own intrigue, he evolved from an ally of Chamberlain into a disciple of Gladstone.

Labouchere's accessibility and readiness to espouse home rule led Healy to overlook his previously expressed strictures on 'champagne-swilling radicals'.[40] There was an affinity of purpose and temperament between the two men. Bonded in sardony and self-interest, they collaborated closely in the mid-1880s. Their relationship attested to Healy's predisposition for roguishly cynical male company, manifested also in his relations with Harold Frederic, and much later with Lord Beaverbrook.

Labouchere was baffled by Healy's occasional displays of Catholic nationalist sentimentality. He reported to the Earl of Rosebery in December 1885 of 'one beautiful touch' in a conversation with Healy, which had amused him greatly. He had characteristically enquired of Healy as to the potency of nationalist sentiment, and whether it had merely been invented. Healy had replied by citing the case of a devoutly Catholic constituent:

> 'He was dying and could not leave his bed. His last words were to tell his son to personate him for me, which the son – a pious Catholic – did.' Healy did not the least see the joke of this, but told it me with almost tears in his eyes to think that his country should have such dead and living citizens.[41]

The combination was in some respects incongruous.

In 1885–6, in the prelude to and the aftermath of the 1885 election, Healy and Labouchere conspired to out-flank Parnell and to bring into being a Liberal–nationalist home rule alliance on their preconceived terms. Herbert Gladstone provided the conduit for their intrigue. Then thirty-one years old, Herbert Gladstone was the youngest son of the Liberal leader, and the member for Leeds, where the previous year he had declared in favour of home rule.[42] Joseph Chamberlain dubbed him less than affectionately 'the junior G.O.M.'[43] He was his father's confidant and often acted as his secretary. He was privy to the unfolding of his father's thinking on home rule, and relayed to him the intelligence he received from Labouchere.

A veil was later drawn over the communications between Healy, Labouchere and Herbert Gladstone. The correspondence between Labouchere and Herbert Gladstone was omitted, and the passages in other letters which disclosed Labouchere's role in conveying Healy's views to Herbert Gladstone deleted, in Algar Labouchere Thorold's *Life of Henry Labouchere*, published in 1913, when Healy was still an active parliamentarian. Thorold skilfully edited the correspondence between Labouchere and Chamberlain, and the sparser correspondence Labouchere received from Healy, so as to suggest that Labouchere's predominant purpose was the conversion of Chamberlain to home rule ('the angel wrestles with Jacob and knows it is in vain').

In his own memoirs, published in 1928, Healy coupled gross disingenuousness with a revealing error in writing that before the 1885 election Labouchere had sent him letters from W. E. Gladstone 'evidencing the old man's trend towards Home Rule'. These he coolly claimed to have withheld from Parnell on the grounds that the latter 'preferred to trust the Viceroy, Lord Carnarvon, as the agent of Lord Salisbury, and considered himself bound to the Tories'. Herbert, by then Viscount, Gladstone, in his memoirs, *After Forty Years*, published the same year as Healy's, omitted all reference to Healy's role in the curt statement that Labouchere 'in active relation with Parnell and Chamberlain, wrote me scores of letters before and after Parnell's manifesto'.[44]

The purpose of Healy's clandestine parleys with Labouchere was to lay the foundations of a home rule alliance which Parnell would be compelled to accept as a *fait accompli*. The assertion by A. B. Cooke and John Vincent in their influential *Governing Passion* that 'it is reasonably clear that Gladstone was not in consultation with the Irish' requires some qualification in the light of the correspondence.[45]

The course of the Healy–Labouchere parleys can be reconstructed from the papers of Herbert Gladstone, supplemented by the Chamberlain and Rosebery papers, together with the letters published in Thorold's *Labouchere*. The latter is an essential source, as Labouchere's papers have not survived. The reliability of the correspondence published by Thorold is best assessed by a comparison of transcriptions taken by Herbert Gladstone of the four *original* letters from Healy which Labouchere furnished to him, and which he returned to Labouchere. The published texts are substantially accurate, but delete material damaging to Healy, and in particular suppress all reference to the involvement of Herbert Gladstone.[46] The reliability of what purport to be transcriptions of letters received by Labouchere from Healy forwarded to Herbert Gladstone is more uncertain. As a rapporteur Labouchere was thoroughly unreliable and self-serving, as well as excitably and imaginatively indiscreet. It can hardly be doubted that Labouchere's transcriptions were edited to delete material which did not further his design, and perhaps supplemented by unctuous insertions. The views which Labouchere imputed to Healy in conversation require to be read with great circumspection. Labouchere was perfectly capable of putting his own views in the mouths of others: a letter to Herbert Gladstone in December 1885 attributes views to Justin McCarthy which were most uncharacteristic of McCarthy, but were vintage Labouchere.[47]

If Healy was aware that Labouchere was passing on what he wrote in correspondence, he did not suspect that Labouchere was also furnishing what purported to be accounts which contained arrestingly vivid deprecations of Parnell attributed solely to Healy. In this respect Healy was the victim of his own intrigue. Labouchere was Healy's Captain O'Shea.

The Labouchere–Herbert Gladstone correspondence does reflect a common purpose on the part of Healy and Labouchere. They shared a personal dislike of Parnell and a belief that he was an overrated figurehead, an attitude which owed much to Parnell's reluctance to confide in either of them. While the vicious portrayal of Parnell in the correspondence is a composite Healy–Labouchere characterisation, it owes more to Labouchere than to Healy. The denigratory themes of the correspondence imperfectly match the criticisms made by Healy of Parnell in his letters to his brother, and in his later attacks on Parnell in 1890–1. This is most clear from the depiction of Parnell as a coward. Physical cowardice was perhaps the one personal failing of which Healy never accused Parnell, while Labouchere was entranced by Parnell's supposed terror of assassination, which had its origins in the immediate aftermath of the Phoenix Park murders and Parnell's adroit playing on his own vulnerability thereafter. Furthermore it is evident that Labouchere's accounts of his conversations with Healy were highly selective. The views which Healy expressed were likely to have been very much more tentative and shifting than Labouchere's rendition of them, and to have fallen short of the fixed and obsessional loathing of Parnell imputed to him.

Healy was estopped from denying the compulsive boastfulness as to his own influence attributed to him in the correspondence, given that the entire intrigue was predicated on the notion of Healy's great, even decisive influence in the counsels of the party. Healy was covertly usurping Parnell's position in seeking to conduct negotiations by indirection with W. E. Gladstone, on the unwarranted basis that Parnell, paralysed by a cynical cautiousness and possessed by a personal resentment of the Liberal leader, was disabled from reaching an accommodation with the Liberals.

Within six months of Parnell's election as leader of the Irish party, Labouchere was already persuaded that he was a grossly overrated titular leader presiding over a divided party. He wrote to Chamberlain in December 1880 that Parnell was menaced by a revolt among his followers. He was 'practically only the figurehead of the ultra-Fenians' to whom he had capitulated, and entirely in the hands of Davitt, 'a far abler man than Parnell'.[48] In November 1881, Labouchere wrote in *Truth*: 'At various times I have had a good many conversations with Mr. Parnell . . . I always found him practical and reasonable, although I confess that I never thought he understood the details of the Land Question like some of his followers'.[49] With variations these were to be Labouchere's refrains in his dealings with the Irish parties over the ensuing decade.

Parnell himself made deliberate and shrewd use of Labouchere to flutter the Liberal dovecote. Thus on 2 March 1885 Labouchere wrote to inform Herbert Gladstone that Parnell had told him that he would propose to the Conservatives that they let home rule sleep for a time on condition they took action on land purchase, and granted money for public works in Ireland. On this basis the Irish party would vote with the Conservatives for three years.[50]

Labouchere's radical enterprise was threatened by the deepening rift opening up between Chamberlain and the Irish, and ultimately between

Chamberlain and Gladstone. On 17 July, some days before Parnell's motion for an inquiry into the administration of the Crimes Act in Ireland, he wrote urging Chamberlain to seize the opportunity to create a popular radical–nationalist alliance. Parnell had 'come to some sort of understanding with Churchill, but nothing definite, it is based upon the Tories agreeing to spend money in Ireland, and arranging facilities to buy the landlords out'. Parnell had told him a few days previously that he would prefer a settlement of the home rule question over the arrangement with the Conservatives. His demand was for a separate parliament. Parnell envisaged a fixed Irish contribution to imperial expenditure, with the Irish parliament having the right to levy taxes in Ireland. The Irish members would sit at Westminster only when imperial questions were under consideration.

Parnell had enquired of Labouchere '"supposing that I did come to an arrangement with Chamberlain, how could I be sure that he would stick by it? He might either get out on the grounds that he was beaten by his colleagues, or that his Government was beaten in the House of Lords."' Labouchere parried by asking whether Parnell would accept an assurance from Chamberlain and Dilke that they would leave any cabinet which for one reason or another was unable to carry out such a home rule programme, 'and he seemed to think this a reasonable assurance'. With that almost frivolous cynicism which was his dominant characteristic, Labouchere urged Chamberlain to throw himself into a great radical initiative: 'Do pray, therefore, be revolutionary. Get the Irish, no matter what it costs. Get the agricultural labourers, no matter what you promise them. We look to you as our political leader. Lead us'. Chamberlain was unmoved, and responded that 'the Irish members must "stew in their juice" with the Tories until they find out their mistake'.[51]

Labouchere at the same time sought to constitute himself the architect of an entente between the Liberals and the Irish party. Three months later, writing to Chamberlain, he claimed that towards the end of the session Herbert Gladstone had come to him and asked that he endeavour to arrange some sort of *modus vivendi* with the Irish. The suggestion that Herbert Gladstone entrusted Labouchere with such a mission is patently absurd, and it was exceedingly mischievous of Labouchere so to inform Chamberlain. At most Labouchere may have been asked to ascertain the thinking of the Irish party, and to keep open his lines of communication to its leading members. He had told Gladstone that he was convinced that Parnell for various reasons did not want any arrangement with the Liberals, 'and that he would prefer to remain an irreconcilable, but that it might be possible to influence him through Healy and others. So I sent to Healy, who came over to England'.[52]

On 22 July Labouchere saw Healy for three hours. In the account sent to Chamberlain, he exaggerated Healy's receptiveness to radicalism in general and to Chamberlain's central council proposals in particular. What was most striking was the virulent trivialisation of Parnell ascribed to Healy, which was to become familiar in Labouchere's correspondence with both Chamberlain and Herbert Gladstone:

> Healy said that Parnell in his heart cared nothing for the Irish – particularly since a mob ill-treated him in 1880. He regretted to be obliged to admit, that personal feeling actuated his leader. He felt his dignity offended by his arrest, and his present feeling was revenge on Gladstone and Forster.
>
> I suggested a rebellion. But he said that this was impossible, because the present mania of all Irishmen was hanging together, for they attributed all their troubles to divided councils.
>
> He said that Parnell was very cunning. He generally finds out which way the feeling is amongst his followers, before he suggests anything, but in one or two cases, he has put his foot down, when he has obtained his way.

Healy disclosed to Labouchere the nationalist plan to put out a manifesto calling on the Irish in England to vote for the Conservatives. If the Liberals embraced home rule, he would propose that no manifesto was issued, leaving the Irish in England to vote as they pleased. Following his habitual practice of lauding the merits of his *interlocuteur valable* of the moment, Labouchere pronounced Healy 'by far the most honest and the ablest of the Irishmen', and added the tasteless observation that 'it is a pity that some Fenian does not "remove" our friend Parnell'. Healy was leaving London the following day for the Cork assizes, where he expected to make £50. Labouchere crassly commented: 'I thought first of offering to lend him this, had he felt inclined to remain here, but I did not know how he would take it'.[53]

Chamberlain was unyielding in his refusal to accede to Labouchere's urgings to constitute a radical–nationalist alliance. Indeed Labouchere's crude invitation to bid against Gladstone for Irish support can only have served to stiffen his resistance to home rule. Labouchere was driven to rely solely on the Gladstonian track. Acting through Healy and Herbert Gladstone, he endeavoured to mediate between the Liberal leader and the Parnellites.

The main corpus of the obliquely trilateral Healy–Labouchere–Herbert Gladstone correspondence dates from October 1885. Healy's views – filtered through Labouchere – were reaching W. E. Gladstone as early as August. On 4 August in conversation with Herbert, Gladstone said that Parnell's offer to withdraw after the Phoenix Park murders, and his general moderation in the House, entitled him to some confidence in his intentions and courage. Herbert Gladstone's dissent bore the impress of Labouchere's lobbying:

> I did not take this view and told father that I had heard from Labouchere that Healy thinks Parnell is now playing a wholly personal and selfish game – that he is vindictive and will never forgive his imprisonment; that he is afraid of the responsibility which a settlement of the administrative and local Government questions would throw on him; and that he is therefore against coming to terms. He is for waiting upon events and looking to the Tories at least as much as to the L[iberal]s. As the feeling so far as I can learn among Parnell's colleagues is for settlement, the line he has taken in avoiding an understanding which separates him from them, bears out Healy's views of him. At this time he is so strong that an open split now is not possible, though it may come before long.[54]

On 7 October 1885 Healy wrote to Labouchere from his residence in Great Charles Street, Dublin. He was to see Parnell that day, 'but don't think I could open up the G.O.M. question'. He was in favour of joining the Liberals if they could give 'any guarantee about muzzling the Lords'. In what was almost certainly an insertion at Labouchere's suggestion (a characteristic device), Healy lauded Gladstone: 'I am convinced and always have held that Gladstone is the best Minister for Ireland that ever lived and that if he were Dictator of England we might safely trust him, but that he has many bad and base admirers to whom he is more or less linked'. Dissociating himself from Parnell's espousal of protectionism at Arklow in late August, Healy plaintively enquired: 'Could we not learn exactly what Gladstone would give us, and then make up a compromise? If we go on as we are going we shall simply be running amuck with you at the elections, for want of an understanding'. Parnell, he added, kept his own counsel. They hardly ever discussed policy with him, 'but he has done everything so well, I would rely more on his instinct than on the judgement of many others'.[55]

Forwarding this letter to Herbert Gladstone, Labouchere wrote that Parnell's three lieutenants were Healy, T. P. O'Connor, and Sexton: 'The latter is a fool. The second is "on the make" and can easily be influenced'. What was required was some general basis for an Irish settlement. In a postscript, he wrote that 'for some reason best known to themselves, the Parnell gang have conceived a violent dislike of Chamberlain – probably because of his intended visit to Ireland'. Parnell regarded him as a rival. Most of the Irish would be much more inclined to meet Gladstone's father half-way than to accept any scheme of Chamberlain's. Labouchere archly added 'a few words saying "my father says" sent privately to Healy would,

I am sure, work wonders'.[56]

Labouchere's elaborately orchestrated correspondence failed to break the deadlock. In reply Herbert Gladstone stated that his father did not disapprove of the attempt by the Irish to secure agreement from the Conservatives: 'I have often heard him say that unless the Irish wish permanently and unconditionally to sink or swim with the Tories, they had better bring the matter to a very speedy upshot'. He did not believe that the Liberal leader would consider gratuitously launching an Irish initiative.[57]

By the time Healy wrote again to Labouchere, on 15 October, he had seen Parnell, who appeared confident that whether the Liberals or the Tories won the election, home rule would be achieved. Labouchere forwarded Healy's letter to Herbert Gladstone, accompanied by his usual denigratory gloss ('the fact is that I never knew anyone with less constructive skill than Parnell, and his utter ignorance is perfectly astounding').

By his reply, Herbert Gladstone sought again to ensure that relations between the nationalists and the Conservatives were brought to a crisis before the election. If not, the Conservatives 'might escape from settling, and might be kept in office by a secession of Liberals partly exasperated with the Irish, partly unwilling to concede to them'. While an opposition comprised of Liberals and nationalists might work, 'a Liberal Government could not stand on that basis to procure a settlement. This I gather is fundamental. Nothing but a clear majority in Parliament could enable Liberals in Government to carry a plan and it is my opinion that my father could not entertain any other idea'. This was the real point of difference with Parnell. The Liberal leader was asserting the necessity for what Parnell was determined to deny him – an overall Liberal majority.

Herbert Gladstone had already conveyed his father's opinion that the Irish would be quite right to deal with the Tories, but warned that 'unless they are tackled on the subject they will avoid aye or no and keep the thing dangling. And if this is tolerated it is likely to spoil all hope of a settlement'. In a superbly conceived proposition, which bore the stamp – as did the rest of the letter – of Gladstone *pére*, he contrived to avoid a clear commitment which would have carried the correspondence into the forbidden domain of 'negotiations'. One thing seemed plain to him – 'that if we do come in by a majority whether large or small, either we shall deal effectively with the question of the Irish Government, or the Party will break up'. Any attempt to settle the Irish question at the beginning of the next parliament would require the frank cooperation of the Irish members, 'and it is desirable to know as speedily as possible exactly how we stand in order to carry the Party with us on the question should a workable plan be arrived at'. Labouchere replied that he would again press Herbert Gladstone's views on the Irish members. The difficulty lay in the fact that 'Parnell is a natural trickster, and is afraid of losing his position, if he agrees to any compromise'.[58]

Labouchere wrote to Healy asking to secure the Irish vote for Shaw Lefevre in Reading. Healy explained in reply on 10 November: 'It would I think be indesirable if not impossible for us to adopt a piecemeal policy, altho' it certainly is the intention to issue instructions that in regard to half a dozen Liberals they can be supported at all hazards, but as far as I can gather up to the present from the cautious working of Parnell's mind it is not certain that he will go against your party bald-headed if at all'. He went on to assert 'if we cd. have an understanding with the leaders of your party it wd. settle this & every other question'. He responded sceptically to the suggestion that the Irish define their demand. Healy attacked Trevelyan: 'Little Trevelyan shd. catch lockjaw on Irish matters. He's a very small man. Spencer & Forster were hit a thousand times worse than he, & yet they never went puling about, spilling gall as he has done. One would think the Irish were not human beings'. Healy lauded Gladstone as 'the father of them all', and expressed the hope that he would develop the lines of his recent speech. He went on to add, in what an amused Labouchere described to Chamberlain as 'a puff of the G.O.M.'s article against Darwin': 'Even things such as his article on the Dawn of Creation & Worship create a great feeling for him amongst educated Catholics in this country. It had some very noble passages'. Labouchere forwarded the letter to Rosebery to reach Gladstone *pére et fils* who were in Scotland.[59]

W. E. Gladstone's unease was mounting. Writing to Chamberlain on 10 November Labouchere stated that Herbert Gladstone had written some days earlier suggesting that Labouchere and Healy should 'by chance' come to Chester, and that he would drop in from Hawarden. Labouchere had replied that this was impossible, as it would be reported 'and there would be an outcry about his father negotiating'.[60] Healy likewise could not have risked such an assignation. Any disclosure of his role would have provoked Parnell's wrath, and brought his career in nationalist politics to a sudden close.

On 16 November, days before Parnell's manifesto, Herbert Gladstone launched a last, despairing, initiative. He proposed a 'kind of Conference' between the Irish representatives and the Liberals, to be convened after the election to discuss the question of Irish government on the basis of heads which conformed closely to the Parnellite scheme of home rule. This proposal he extolled, in terms which the progress of Parnellism had already rendered patronising and archaic, as 'a splendid departure . . . from the old practice of ascertaining through Dublin Castle the wishes of the minority in order to coerce the majority'. He added that should the outcome of the election permit, 'my father would be for entering into early communication with those who would represent the Irish nation'. It was his own belief 'that in view of the gravity of the position, and of the inherent right of the Irish nation to make a constitutional demand to be allowed to manage their own affairs in their own way, he is prepared to stand or fall by a satisfactory settlement of the question'.[61] This was too veiled and too late.

Labouchere misconstrued an adroitly evasive letter from T. P. O'Connor as indicating that the Irish had not made up their minds as to how they would direct the Irish vote in England, and wrote unpleasantly to Herbert Gladstone of O'Connor, whose influence over Parnell he exaggerated: 'I am afraid that the ingenious T. P. has been bought by the enemy. Considering his influence, and the belief of Parnell that he (T. P.) understood English politics, it is almost a pity that we did not buy him, for I fancy that he is not dear'.[62]

Labouchere grew increasingly nervous. On 19 November he despatched to Rosebery an assessment of the situation. This contained his habitual characterisation of Parnell. Of the supposed triad of his most influential lieutenants, only Healy escaped denigration.

> Parnell, being a moral coward, and not liking responsibility would personally prefer no arrangement which would throw any administrative responsibility upon him. He is quite satisfied with being the 'uncrowned' King of Ireland . . . He is without any constructive ability himself, and his ignorance is phenomenal. He would, I think, knock under to Healy and T. P. O'Connor, while Sexton, the third of the trio who constitute his lieutenants, has no option of his own upon any matter and drinks heavily. My impression is that O'Connor has received a little money from the Conservatives.[63]

On 21 November Parnell's axe fell with the publication of the manifesto directing the Irish vote in England against the Liberals. Humiliatingly in the light of the pretensions displayed in his dealings with Labouchere, Healy, whose name was appended as a signatory, was not consulted, and first learnt of the manifesto from a Dublin evening paper.[64]

The following day he returned Herbert Gladstone's letters to Labouchere: he had burnt Labouchere's letters to himself. He wrote that the manifesto had been issued before he could show Parnell the last letter, that is Herbert Gladstone's of 16 November, which it is possible he had intended to show to Parnell. The abashed negotiator concluded: 'It is no use now saying anything further. *Fin ist Fin*'.[65] For Labouchere also, it was a damaging rebuff. Writing to Rosebery, he complained of Parnell's duplicity, citing also the experience of the Tories at Parnell's hands, as told by Randolph Churchill:

> The difficulty of negotiating with Parnell is that he is not to be trusted. I do not mean that he would reveal anything private, but he would dodge and trick. Churchill has formed the same estimate of him. He confided to me that the bargain with the Cons. was that on condition of their vote, and no Coercion Bill, the Irish were to support the Cons. until the end of the Session. Churchill bitterly complains of Parnell having sprung the Maamtrasna business upon them without notice, and, as he considers, in defiance of the agreement.
>
> There was a general sort of understanding that Parnell would support them in the next Parliament, provided something was done in the way of loans to buy out the landlords, and money spent on public works. Parnell told me this himself. But no sooner were the Cons. in, than he came to the conclusion that this would not be enough, and that he must have Home Rule. This is the state of things at present. The Irish have gone Tory without any bargain, and merely in order – if possible – to hold the balance. Healy insists that Parnell is actuated by two motives in this course:– 1. he is very vindictive, has not forgiven his arrest, and wants to be revenged; 2. he is a moral coward and is afraid of the responsibility of governing Ireland were Home Rule to be granted. If however, he sees that his Lieutenants, who are greedy for office, are ready to make terms he will capitulate, for he has already been beaten once or twice in his own party, or rather what have been known to be his views, have been beaten, as when he sees that he cannot carry a thing, he relapses into a sort of Constitutional King.[66]

If Healy was momentarily chastened, he rapidly resumed his intrigue. The Healy–Labouchere axis endured. Just prior to the poll, Labouchere wrote to Healy telling him, according to what he later told Herbert Gladstone, 'to go to Parnell and reason with him that the Tories were tricking him and that the only man who could carry Home Rule was Mr. Gladstone'.[67]

Herbert Gladstone wrote a carefully couched letter to Labouchere enquiring as to Irish intentions: 'do they know that the Government will give them an absolute *non possumus* on Home Rule?' Sounding a truly Gladstonian note, he warned against any Conservative–nationalist alignment arrived at on the basis of the expenditure of public monies in Ireland: 'The government may try to buy the Irish support by hard cash; but they will not find it an easy matter. I am confident that my father will deal generously so far as he is concerned with Irish members in regard to their government; but he will, I am equally sure, resolutely oppose any proposal to stave off the main question at the taxpayer's expense'.[68]

Polling in the election, held on the new franchise, stretched between 23 November and 19 December. As the smoke of battle cleared, the outgoing Conservatives were left with 249 seats, the Liberals 335, and the Irish party 86. Parnell, by the narrowest margin possible, held the balance of power.

As the outcome unfolded, Labouchere launched a new phase of his diplomacy. He wrote to Herbert Gladstone on 8 December that Healy and O'Brien were doing their best to induce Parnell to be reasonable, and forwarded telegrams from Healy which have not survived. His disparaging of Parnell continued unabated (' . . . the main difficulty is that he wants no arrangement, for he is afraid of losing his commanding position. He can only be forced into one by his Lieutenants'). He wanted W. E. Gladstone to advise the Irish of the extent to which he was prepared to go to meet their demands. Herbert Gladstone replied that the responsibility continued to rest with the government, which had not yet definitely thrown over the Irish.[69]

Labouchere on 9 December wrote to Herbert Gladstone enclosing what purported to be a transcribed extract of a letter from Healy of 7 December. Healy did not see what alternative Parnell had other than to put out the Conservative government, and he proposed tactics on the address. The text Labouchere forwarded to Gladstone contains a passage which does not appear in that published in Thorold's *Labouchere.* After urging him to see Parnell immediately, Healy, according to the text furnished to Gladstone, continued: 'You know him personally very well, and you know his peculiarities. He is still rancorous about his arrest, as I have told you, and he is without constructive skill. You should be able to show him something in black and white. That is how to deal with him'. Healy and others would seek to influence Parnell. This was subject to the rather abject proviso that 'if he is not won over we will support him for the sake of unity'. Forwarding the letter to Herbert Gladstone, Labouchere added: 'What Healy says about Parnell is perfectly true, he keeps to the vague, because he is incapable of being definite . . . If anything is to be done, I must show him a definite programme, otherwise he will maunder about Grattan's Parliament, respecting which he knows nothing'.[70]

Herbert Gladstone replied to Labouchere on 10 December. While stressing his father's anxiety to achieve an Irish settlement, he reiterated that the responsibility rested in the first instance with the government. Healy wrote to Labouchere the same day urging him to convey to Parnell the view of the Liberal leadership. With admirable off-handedness, he added 'there is no necessity to refer him to the correspondence that has taken place'.

Labouchere wrote immediately to Herbert Gladstone. To cover Healy's tracks, he asked Gladstone to rewrite his letter of 10 December omitting reference to Healy, so as to put Labouchere in a position to read the letter to Parnell, 'who is of a jealous disposition'. In the context of Healy's engaging in independent communications with the Liberals, this last remark must be considered a heroic understatement. The usual disparagement of the Irish leader followed:

> He is one of the most difficult persons in the world to bring to book — to a certain extent because he, even within his own party, will never show his hand until the last moment, and to a certain extent because if he thought it safe with his followers, he would prefer to remain an 'uncrowned king' to assuming any responsibility.

In a characteristic flourish, Labouchere added: 'That Parnell will attempt to trick you in an argument, I think very probable: but you may absolutely trust him in secrecy as to negotiations. To be regarded as more of a gentleman than his following is his weakness'.[71]

Labouchere wrote also to Justin McCarthy: 'If you can influence Parnell's mind so as to lead him to assent to Home Rule on your lines, the matter is settled and the feud between the Liberal and the Irish party is bridged over'. He urged him to speak to Parnell at once, without mentioning the letter. He warned that the present opportunity, if lost, might never recur: 'The G.O.M. is simply mad to get in'.[72]

The Liberal leader was beginning to chafe somewhat at the constraints imposed by his own position, as enunciated through his son. In a letter which he intended Herbert to forward to Rosebery, he restated his reasons for leaving the onus of dealing with home rule to rest with the government, but added: 'If the moment ever came when a plan had to be considered with a view to production on behalf of the Liberal party, I do not at present see how such a position could be dissociated from another vital question, namely who are to be the government. For a government alone can carry a measure; though some outline of essentials might be put out in a motion or resolution'.

Forwarding to Rosebery this letter from his father, together with Labouchere's letter of 9 December, and Labouchere's transcription of the extract from Healy's letter of 7 December, Herbert Gladstone conveyed his father's suggestion that Rosebery, who was privy to his thinking, should arrange to see Labouchere, who was then at Brighton, as soon as convenient. His father's letter expressed 'his exact opinion on the *present* situation. But he thinks you might use your discretion as to greater explicitness with L. — only that if you touch in general terms on the plan itself you would speak as expressing your opinion of what might be expected from my father'.[73]

Labouchere on 14 December met Justin McCarthy, who had like himself been unable to locate Parnell. He did garner some useful intelligence from McCarthy who had dined the previous day with Carnarvon. Labouchere reported to Herbert Gladstone: 'Lord C. said that personally he was in favour of a large measure of Home Rule, but that he despaired of winning his party and some of his colleagues. He asked McCarthy whether he thought that Parnell 'would accept an "Inquiry", during which the Conservatives might be educated. McCarthy said that this would not do . . .'[74]

Labouchere reported to Rosebery that Parnell 'had disappeared with an Egeria of some kind'. With his usual facility for putting words in the mouths of his interlocutors, he reported improbably of his conversation with McCarthy:

> I asked him whether there was any scheme in this. He replied 'no, probably a woman, he is always doing it, and it is one of our greatest troubles' . . . Parnell, he says, is desirous of solving the question and then retiring on his laurels, so far as he can make out. He abused his revered leader for half an hour, as frivolous, ignorant, and many other things – he never listens to discussion, seldom arrives at conclusions by reflection, but suddenly jumps to one. Was there ever such a faction in politics before with 87 [sic] slaves?[75]

Labouchere found the tensions within Gladstone's strategy of reserve increasingly wearing, and wrote exasperatedly on 16 December to Rosebery:

> Strictly between you and me, the GOM's mind is so large a one, that he absorbs two ideas, one to tackle Parnell at once, the other to wait. Yesterday H.G. came up, gave me long explanations etc., and when I said that it was well not to appear in a hurry with P., said yes, but that it was very essential not to lose time.

Parnell had disappeared 'like the Mahdi from his followers'. Healy however had written that he had entirely won over William O'Brien, who now displaced Sexton in Labouchere's promiscuously shifting triad of Parnell's key lieutenants:

> I have to get the three lieutenants of P. breast high for an arrangement – McCarthy, Healy & O'Brien – this I always felt was the only way to go to work, for the man himself likes his position as an uncrowned King, striding into Parliament occasionally, dreaming *post coitum* too much to abdicate it, and to assume any responsibilities'.

Even Labouchere by now appeared confused by the intricacies of Gladstonian diplomacy, and lost his bearings somewhat. He concluded to Rosebery:

> Don't tell the GOM that I have heard from you about what he writes to you respecting not seeing Parnell, because it will only lead to lengthy

> explanations. I suppose that he is getting ready to swear that he had nothing to do about any negotiations, beyond expressing his views in the bosom of his family.[76]

Unknown to Labouchere, the appearance the following day of Herbert Gladstone's 'Hawarden kite' was about to transform the situation.

On 13 December Thomas Wemyss Reid, the editor of the *Leeds Mercury*, wrote to warn Herbert Gladstone at Hawarden that he had learnt on very high authority that it was the intention of Chamberlain and Dilke (together, most improbably, with Morley) to thwart the formation of a Gladstone government: 'They *allege* . . . that Mr. Gladstone has come to an agreement with Parnell, and that it is to prevent his carrying out a scheme which Mr. Parnell accepts that they were determined to thwart his plans'. Wemyss Reid's concern was to prevent the non-aligned Liberal press being drawn into declarations of opposition to home rule, and he looked to Herbert Gladstone for guidance:

> Now, you know pretty well my views about the Irish question. But I have the greatest faith in your father and believe I am absolutely loyal to him as my leader. I am determined to support him as loyally as I can against any Birmingham intrigues — especially against intrigues in which I have a strong suspicion Randolph Churchill has a share. I am quite prepared to yield my own judgement to his on the Irish question. The present crisis is one of extreme gravity, and the forces which Chamberlain can command in Parliament and the press are formidable . . . Can you give me any help in this matter? . . . I do not wish to commit your father in any way whatever, but I certainly think that you might be of great use both to him and to the Liberal party just now, if you would give all the assistance you could to those who are anxious to sustain Mr. Gladstone in this crisis . . . .[77]

Reid's allegations were not altogether convincing. However similar rumours reached Herbert Gladstone from Sir Lyon Playfair, and the threat of a pre-emptive radical declaration against home rule, which could have finished his father's career, could not lightly be dismissed. He was concerned that his father, sequestered at Hawarden 'engrossed in his Irish studies', was cut off from his usual channels of information. Parnell's stance, and the prospect held out independently by Healy, to which he made no reference in his memoirs, greatly added to his sense of urgency.[78]

Herbert Gladstone replied the following day from Hawarden. He conveyed to Wemyss Reid, with the evident sanction of his father, the position he had previously communicated to Labouchere:

> I say then this to you, in full conviction that I faithfully represent to you my father's exact view: that if the Tories can conscientiously deal with

the question of the Irish government in a satisfactory manner on a fair and lasting basis, they would have my father's support fully and loyally, as they have had his support in their recent right attitude on the Afghan and Bulgarian questions. But it is his view that the Irish question is of the utmost importance, and that it must be dealt with before anything else.

If however the Tory government refused to deal with the task, 'they become 250 men in the House out of 670, and the leaders of the Liberal party must decide at once whether they are prepared to take office to deal with the Irish question'. As leader of the opposition, Gladstone could not formulate a plan.

Were he to do so, he would play into the enemy's hand, and moreover it probably could not be done without entering into direct communications with Parnell, and thereby committing the party to something which might appear to be or which might virtually be a bargain.

My father has laid down in public the principles on which he is prepared to take up the question, and has indicated the *spirit* in which it ought to be dealt with and solved. But it is now for the Government to speak, or for Parnell. It matters not which. Suffice it to say that nothing could extort a scheme or plan from my father, privately or publicly, until he is called upon by the failure or collapse of the Government to deal with the question as to the responsible head of the executive Government. No action which C[hamberlain] and D[ilke] think fit to take as independent members of the party can drive him from his position, or prevent him from going forward with the policy which seems to him just and right, if he is supported by the party at large.

I observe that attempts are now being made to justify C. and D. by the statement that *now* my father is in direct communication with Parnell in order to turn out the Government and to carry a scheme for the disruption of the Empire. This is a lie.

He opined that 'it is most fortunate for us that the Irish opposed us tooth and nail at the elections. We are quite independent of them. They may support us if they like, but my father's position relatively to the Government of the day is precisely that which he would occupy if there were no Parnellites . . .' This assertion would have prompted Parnell's sardonic amusement.

It is hard to resist the impression that Gladstone *pére et fils* were in some degree beguiled by the schematic elegance of their stated position, by what was almost its aesthetic perfection. The possibility on which it was premised, a Conservative espousal of home rule, was so thin as to risk its collapse into an endorsement of home rule by the Liberal leader. This was implicit, if unstated, in Herbert Gladstone's consideration of the alternative scenario:

> Now I suppose the Tories to refuse to deal with Ireland, and the Nationalists to refuse to deal with them. My father will not lead on the terms of C. and D. Either the Irish question must be at once taken up or the Party must choose a new leader, or break up. Dilke's proposal is impossible. We cannot calmly proceed to look on a Tory Government dealing with local government, and to ignore the 86 Irish and their action. There are two alternatives, conciliation or coercion. I have reason to know that the state of Ireland is most ominous, and that, in consequence of the Irish policy of the Government, coercion, even if possible at Westminster, would plunge Ireland into fearful disorder. The only hope is by doing justice on a liberal scale, with adequate precautions and limitations, to hold the elements of disorder by making responsible under the crown those who for good or ill have secured the support of the masses in Ireland.[79]

Herbert Gladstone left Hawarden that day for London, where he gave interviews over the following two days to Wemyss Reid and to representatives of the National Press Agency. Unsurprisingly his attempts to observe the intricate obliquity of the contrived distinction between his own views and those of his father, which had been so fastidiously maintained in the correspondence with Labouchere, broke down. It was almost inevitable that what had been conceived as a carefully circumscribed briefing of sympathetic newspapermen should have miscarried into a disclosure of the Liberal leader's larger intentions. The press on 17 December reported his definite embrace of home rule. 'Fat all in the fire', Herbert Gladstone wrote in his diary. W. E. Gladstone responded with paternal indulgence ('Father quite *compos*') to the consternation created by the so-called 'Hawarden kite'. His equanimity was due in part to his consciousness of his own involvement, and in part to a realisation that the hoisting in some form of the standard of a home rule administration under his premiership could not have been deferred for very much longer.[80]

On the afternoon of 19 December, Healy 'turned up' at Labouchere's residence at Queen Anne's Gate, St. James Park, and stayed six hours. Labouchere showed him a letter he had received the previous day from Parnell stating that he was out of town and that his present impression was that it would be better to await events. Labouchere sent to Herbert Gladstone an account of their meeting, which ran to considerable length. In the form of a dialogue, it was a highly dramatised account of their conversation as Labouchere wished to present it, no doubt liberally supplemented by Healy's observations in their exchanges over the previous months as Labouchere chose to recall them.

Labouchere quoted Healy as saying, as if emboldened by the belief that the coast was clear, that it was quite as well that Parnell should keep away. He was in a position to agree everything. He had seen McCarthy,

Harrington, Dillon and O'Brien and they were prepared to accept Gladstone's views, provided they could agree the details. This was to say the very least an exceedingly liberal paraphrase on Labouchere's part. However self-aggrandising the premises of Healy's role, it is inconceivable that he would have so explicitly invoked the authority of Dillon and Harrington in particular. Labouchere's account continued:

> 'But, Parnell —', I said.
> 'Parnell is half-mad – to tell you the truth we settle everything almost always, and he accepts it'.

The Irish were putting in place a 'Cabinet'. The effect of this bravado was undercut by the caveat that it could never be revealed that he had made any proposals, 'as it would ruin me with my party'. Healy proceeded to outline a comprehensive home rule scheme of his own devising. He envisaged a close alliance of parties: 'We would regard ourselves as member of the Liberal Party, we would vote fairly and squarely with the Liberals on any test question against the Conservatives'.

Healy firmly rejected the veto of the imperial parliament on Irish legislation, but was prepared to accept the nomination for two parliaments or five years of a quarter of the members of an Irish assembly. There was no objection to the Protestant churches electing these members. Healy was quoted as stating that they did not object to the nominated members 'because they would be of use to us. It would enable us to hold our own against any combination of Orangemen and Fenians. You people *will* not realise that we are moderate now'. (This was intended to meet concerns expressed to Labouchere by Herbert Gladstone on 15 December in relation to the representation of the Protestant minority, although these were not referred to to avoid carrying the correspondence into the forbidden domain of 'negotiations'.) Landlords who wished to leave the country would have the right to have their land valued by the land judges, with allowance being made for improvements effected by the tenants. 'This proposal would meet with great opposition from Davitt and Co., but this we could hold against.' In relation to matters of contract a right of appeal to the judicial committee of the House of Lords would be acceptable, once the Irish could nominate a Law Lord. They did not wish to be 'eternally deprived' of dealing with the land question. 'We have no more notion of confiscation than you. Our ideas are not more radical than those of Chamberlain, but we must do something.'

Ireland would pay her quota of taxation, 'to be raised as she pleases. Say nothing about Protection. The only man in Ireland who wants it is Parnell, and I cannot understand why he raised the point'. There would be no objection to 'a member of the Royal Family being Governor, or coming to Ireland to hold court. Why not the son of the Prince of Wales?

This would probably be a great sop to the "Loyalists"'.

Healy held out the promise of a sternly right-wing home rule state, committed to containing internal dissent and resisting external destabilisation. In what Labouchere headed as 'a curious proposal', he quoted Healy as saying: 'We should like to be able to turn any alien out of the country. We shall otherwise be overrun by Americans and Fenians, who would give us much trouble in the future'. Healy denied that the separatist movement was of any importance. 'It is kept up by the Fenians, and as we have to look to America for our money, we cannot well denounce it. If you gave us Home Rule, we would deal with it, and should.' As Labouchere later wrote to Rosebery: 'Do realise that these Irish are by no means radicals. If they got their home rule, and could settle the land questions, they would astound us by their conservatism'.

To Herbert Gladstone, Labouchere hailed his interview as a triumphant vindication of what he called 'my plan of turning the difficulties in the character of Parnell by getting up a sort of revolt amongst his lieutenants'.

> Parnell, as I told you, is a dreamy figurehead. He will be obliged to yield — or rather he will — as he always has done — endorse everything, but he must not know what steps have been taken to 'corner' him; indeed one great guarantee of secrecy is that his devoted followers have no intention ever to let him know them.

Healy told him that Parnell always said that W. E. Gladstone was too clever, and that whilst he would bind the Irish, they would get nothing in black and white from him. Healy was to see Labouchere again before returning to Ireland, and if Gladstone sent a letter to be forwarded to Healy, 'don't forget that he is an Irishman, and is not averse to being praised. He particularly values this, when he thinks it emanates from Mr. Gladstone'.[81]

Labouchere wrote a much shorter *résumé* of his conversation with Healy to Rosebery, emphasising that Irish opposition to the veto of the imperial parliament was immovable: 'Healy says that if they were to agree they would all be driven out of the country as traitors — in fact they could not take on themselves the responsibility of maintaining order'. He reassured Rosebery that 'I do not think there is any fear of them letting the cat out of the bag. They are born conspirators, and as Healy said: "the only time anything came out it was the fault of Forster and O'Shea"'.[82] The ultimate guarantee of Healy's absolute discretion lay in the necessity to avoid any knowledge of his actions coming to the knowledge of his leader.

By the time Healy saw Labouchere the next day, he had become deeply apprehensive. As Labouchere informed Herbert Gladstone, Healy had met Parnell, and formed the impression that he was in negotiation with W. E. Gladstone. Herbert Gladstone denied that what he underlined as '*negotiations*' (a term with an exceedingly narrow and exacting definition in the Gladstonian lexicon) were taking place between Parnell and his father. The Liberal leader would not be a party to any negotiations until the government had declared its policy: 'At present in the face of the world the alliance between the T[orie]s and the N[ationalist]s exists and will exist until it visibly dies'. W. E. Gladstone was however much interested in Healy's views on the subject 'for he has not forgotten H's mastery of the Irish Land Bill': these were the words of praise the insertion of which Labouchere had advised.[83]

Labouchere was by now thoroughly irritated by Gladstone's strategy, which he considered hypocritical and sanctimonious. On the issue of whether or not Gladstone had approached Parnell, Labouchere wrote in exasperation to Rosebery: 'Who are we to believe . . . Can our great leader be so silly as to try and humbug the Irish? He is capable of it. We ought all to sit at the feet of this unscrupulous Gamaliel; he will stick at nothing. How pleasant it must be to have such a conscience!' While they had to choose 'between serving God and the Irish', Gladstone 'does both with infinite satisfaction to the inner monitor'.[84]

Healy's mounting suspicion that negotiations were in progress between Parnell and Gladstone threatened Labouchere's enterprise. On 27 December Labouchere wrote to Herbert Gladstone that what he now described as the 'secret committee' of the Irish party had been won over. But he warned that 'Healy and his friends . . . are just now disgusted with the idea that there is something going on between you and Parnell. They are curious people – at one moment sensible and practical, at another childish, but always intensely suspicious'.

Labouchere's self-congratulation was equalled only by his dread that the temperamental deficiencies he discerned in the Irish party and its leader would combine to deprive him of the prize of the credit for putting in place a Liberal–nationalist alliance under Gladstone:

> We are so very near getting these Irish fast and tight, that it will really send me to my grave if we don't definitely hook them. And I think that we may regard it as a triumph to have cornered Parnell in his own party. But they are so impulsive, and so suspicious, that the least thing may lead them to fly off, and Parnell, let him say what he will, will be glad of an excuse. The others have – and have had – a great admiration of Mr. G. He is spiteful on account of his imprisonment, afraid of responsibility, and without being a Fenian – an Irish-American – terribly afraid of his ultra allies turning on him, and perhaps shooting him.[85]

Herbert Gladstone's reply of 28 December rang down the curtain on this second phase of Labouchere's intrigues. It was a magisterial restatement of his father's reserve, now coupled with the clear hint that when the time came for negotiations, they would be with Parnell. There was no reason for Healy's uneasiness. In what was an implicit rebuke to Healy as well as to Labouchere, he continued:

> Given the fact that the question must be taken up and thoroughly dealt with, and that the Irish party wish to settle it honourably and fairly, no sane man would wish to do anything to break up or weaken that party whose unity would be essential to the working out of a lasting settlement. So far as we are concerned there has not been nor will there be any manoeuvre or negotiations. And if communications have to take place with the Irish party, and I hope they will soon, only one channel will be recognised.

In an addendum the following day, Herbert Gladstone wrote that Chamberlain failed to appreciate that it was impossible for his father to temporise:

> If the Liberal [party] chooses to break upon an Irish parliament, it can't be helped. But to think only of temporary cohesion of men not strong enough to take decisive action on the one essential question of the day, such cohesion to be kept until the Irish difficulty once more grows sufficiently urgent to compel attention, seems to me a poor as well as a disastrous line to take.
>
> My father cannot express an opinion now as to what amendment should be moved [to the address]. He is utterly ignorant of the relations now existing between Parnell and the Tories, and until he knows what they mean to do it would be rash generalship on his part to commit himself to the appropriateness of any particular course. I entirely share your view of the desirability of acting in harmony with the Irish. I don't however think there is a chance of bringing the party up to scratch before Parliament meets. Men will go on talking of the Union and so forth, and will not reason the position until they see the eighty-six members in the flesh.[86]

There was little Labouchere could do in the face of Herbert Gladstone's reiteration of the constraints which inhibited his father from playing out the role assigned to him in Labouchere's elaborate choreography. He replied that he understood the difficulties and would do his best to keep Healy and his friends quiet. 'The dangers on the other side are that they are very impulsive — and Parnell himself would, I think, prefer to do nothing beyond the old mysterious Mahdi business, and those who can coerce him require time to do so.'[87]

The Labouchere–Healy intrigue was proving barren. Its only public fruit was a letter from Labouchere in the *Times* of 28 December 1885 setting out his estimate of what the *Irish Times* would accept. As he confidentially advised Herbert Gladstone, a considerable portion of it had been written by Healy.[88] Labouchere wrote to Rosebery that the letter contained the Irish minimum: 'It has been looked over and indeed partially written by our Irish friends. They want to bring their moderation before the English public, and yet if necessary to be able to say that they have not stated any terms. So we hit upon this way. If Mr. G. would say that the scheme meets with his approval they would be with him'.[89]

Healy and Labouchere now busied themselves to devise a basis for Liberal–nationalist collaboration in the debate on the Queen's speech. Their endeavours were jeopardised by Liberal suspicions that Healy was concurrently intriguing with Churchill. These suspicions had been sown by Lord Richard Grosvenor, who alleged that Churchill had been twice in contact with Healy in the course of his habitual Christmas sojourn with Gerald Fitzgibbon in Howth.[90] Grosvenor had heard that Parnell would definitely move a home rule amendment to the address, and that when this was defeated would lead a withdrawal *en bloc* of the Parnellites. He added the almost hysterical aside that 'in consequence of his having made this arrangement with the Fenians he is getting any quantity of money now'. He had heard also that Churchill and Healy had come to a definite arrangement, but what it was he did not know.[91]

Properly loath to put his faith in whips, Gladstone in reply pointed out that Grosvenor's information comprised two contradictory scenarios. Of the first, 'the Parnell initiative', he wrote that he would regard a nationalist withdrawal from parliament 'as by far the most formidable thing that can happen. It will be followed by an assembly in Dublin, which will bring in view very violent alternatives'. He added that if Parnell was wise 'he will keep to the game he has been upon heretofore, viz. the ejecting of governments'. It may be doubted that Gladstone attached any great credence to this possibility. What he described as 'the Randolph–Healy concordat' caused him more immediate concern, and prompted his comment that 'I am not quite certain how long we ought to persist in the system of making no spontaneous communication to Parnell'.[92]

Healy enjoyed reasonably familiar relations with Churchill, for whom he shared the preference over other Conservative leaders common among nationalist parliamentarians. In August 1885 he hailed him as 'the most distinguished, able, and promising of Tory leaders . . . the game little bantam of Woodstock'. Even after Churchill had played the 'Orange card', Healy's attitude towards him was markedly indulgent.[93] In his turn Churchill in the Commons in January 1886 referred to his pleasure at listening to 'the not ungenial or ill-natured, though sometimes bitter, humour of the hon. Member for South Derry'.[94]

The suspicion engendered by Grosvenor that Healy and Churchill were endeavouring to put in place a Conservative–nationalist alliance was unwarranted. However, their encounters had been provocatively conspicuous, and attracted widespread comment and speculation, rendering Healy vulnerable to Grosvenor's unfounded allegations. The Liberals remained abidingly suspicious of the role of Healy and Churchill in the downfall of Gladstone's government in 1885.[95]

Healy wrote in wounded tones from Dublin to Labouchere on 15 January. He protested that Herbert Gladstone was 'totally wrong about me'. He had had no communication with Churchill or any member of the government since the House had risen, reinforcing Churchill's own denial that he had met Healy in Ireland.[96]

From Dublin on 17 January, Healy wrote again to Labouchere. In the absence of a move by Gladstone, the nationalists would probably let matters drift, or else settle on some sort of amendment to the address. He now claimed that he would have preferred all along not to have been the repository of the views of the Liberal leadership (an observation which Labouchere took care to delete from the version of the letter communicated to Herbert Gladstone), and unnecessarily added that any proposal should be communicated to Parnell 'otherwise than through me'.[97]

Healy's new-found spirit of chastened fealty lasted all of three days. After a meeting of the Irish party on 20 January he repaired to Labouchere's residence to advise him of what had transpired, and to relaunch their intrigue. According to Labouchere, Healy now declared that he could carry the party in support of Gladstone, if only Gladstone moved on the Queen's speech. Healy recommended an amendment condemning coercion. 'Parnell, he says, so far as he can make out what he thinks, is inclined to let a Coercion Act be brought in, and do all he can to make the confusion worse confounded, as the only way to convince the English that there must be home rule.' Labouchere asked Herbert Gladstone to come to the House at one o'clock – an hour before the Queen's speech was circulated – to say whether his father was agreeable to moving an amendment 'on the clear understanding that the Irish would vote for it', which Labouchere could convey to Healy before the 'private Council' of the Irish party met. He added that Healy 'begs you not to mention that he has seen me or any of his suggestions to anyone, as some of his party might think – if it were to come out – that he was taking a great deal on himself, to reveal their plans etc.'[98]

This was a considerable understatement. Healy had by now abrogated every principle of Parnellite political action. Of all the Healy–Labouchere initiatives, this last frantic intervention was perhaps the most jejune. Herbert Gladstone had already conveyed his father's disinclination to raise the Irish question on the address. To do so would have risked a precipitate polarisation on the issue of home rule which could have jeopardised the formation of a Gladstone government.

Labouchere also wrote to Justin McCarthy seeking to track down Parnell: 'Where is the errant chief?' Oblivious to the existence of other channels to the Irish leader, he wrote very shortly afterwards that 'H.G. came up from Papa to find out what is doing & explain. The G.O.M. will certainly go mad if we can't get hold of P.' He sought to constitute a troika of McCarthy, Healy and himself to settle the details of a home rule scheme which could be put to Gladstone. One of the difficulties, he asserted, referring to Parnell, 'with our friend is his singular ignorance of details. I am afraid he will take refuge in Grattan's parliament'.[99]

Healy and Labouchere had badly underestimated the Irish leader, who was pursuing a masterly strategy. What his manifesto had signalled was his repudiation of the role traditionally assigned to the Irish party of the passive and grateful beneficiary of Liberal concessions, rather than the resentment of Gladstone, and aversion to taking responsibility for a home rule settlement, they had so readily imputed to him. Parnell's reserve was complemented by that of Gladstone. The Liberal leader, under the watchful gaze of Joseph Chamberlain who had written in late October that he had 'the senile passion of an old man for a girl to come again into office', awaited the correct alignment of political forces.[100]

Prior to the election, Parnell had opened a largely one-way line of communication with Gladstone through Katharine O'Shea. On 30 October she had sent Gladstone a 'proposed constitution for Ireland'. Parnell resumed these communications after the election. Katharine O'Shea in a series of letters politely sought to ascertain what course of action Gladstone proposed to take. Gladstone declined to address her enquiries, insisting that it was for the government to declare its intentions.[101] With the exhaustion of the possibility of the Conservatives taking up the issue of self-government for Ireland – always exceedingly remote, but of a strategic significance both recognised – Gladstone and Parnell, having staked out their respective positions, gravitated towards political alliance. On 29 December, Katharine O'Shea wrote unavailingly seeking assurances from Gladstone on the issue of 'coercion'; on 7 January she outlined Parnell's proposals for a resolution of the land question along with home rule.[102]

On 22 January Labouchere read to Parnell the contents of a document from Chamberlain urging him to agree to the deferral of home rule, and to turn out the government in return for a promise of a Liberal land purchase bill. (A similar proposal was conveyed through the medium of

Captain O'Shea.) Parnell dismissed Chamberlain's proposal out of hand. Labouchere predictably wrote conflicting accounts of Parnell's stated intentions to Herbert Gladstone and Chamberlain. To Herbert Gladstone (from whom he had less to dissemble) he wrote that Parnell had indicated a readiness to assist his father to form a government, and to leave to the Liberal leader the judgement as to when and how the Conservative government was to be brought down. Parnell however made clear his preference for a Conservative regime over a Whig administration under Hartington, supported by Chamberlain.[103]

The following day Katharine O'Shea wrote to W. E. Gladstone that she was authorised by Parnell to state that the Irish members would vote against the government on the amendment to the address of the radical Jesse Collings, 'if Mr. Parnell could have a reasonable assurance that firstly, you will be sent for by the Queen, and secondly that you will form a ministry'. She reiterated that the Irish party would prefer to support the government if the only consequence of its defeat was to be the formation of a ministry by Hartington in alliance with Chamberlain.

> Mr. Parnell has already been invited by Mr. C. to help in this latter course but has declined to do so – in fact they, the Irish party, would prefer to pin their faith on you for doing the best for their country – and if not *you* they would prefer to support the present Government and not in any case accept Mr. C's invitation. I am sure they will not vote for Mr. Jesse Collings' amendment, which is really Mr. C's I suppose, unless they *fully* understand that *you* wish them to do so, and on the security of your forming a Ministry.

She believed it would be 'advisable for Mr. Parnell to understand your opinion on these subjects, but of course you know best, as I believe, on all things'. In his reply on 26 January Gladstone merely indicated that he would speak and vote for the Collings amendment that evening. In the small hours of the following morning, the government was defeated by the combined votes of the Liberals and nationalists, and resigned the following day.[104]

After three months of unremitting tenacity, Parnell led his party into the division lobbies to bring down the Conservative government without preconditions. In terms of the antecedent adversity of Gladstone and Parnell it was a finely wrought anti-climax. The grace of the final gesture showed Parnell at his most unconventional and most assured. He had allowed all the alternatives to pass through Gladstone's mind. He had demonstrated how resourceful an adversary, and how stalwart an ally, he could be.

One further matter required Parnell's immediate attention. He profoundly distrusted Labouchere, on account both of his association with Chamberlain, and of his want of reticence. He had already had Katharine O'Shea advise Gladstone: 'I doubt Mr. Parnell's confiding in Mr. Labouchere who talks too much and is working hard for a treaty'. After the fall of the government Parnell moved swiftly to put an end to Labouchere's relentless intermeddling. On 30 January Katharine O'Shea wrote to Gladstone. Labouchere had told Parnell that he was requested by Herbert Gladstone on behalf of his father to ask whether Parnell would have objection to '"open communications" of the nature of those which took place with Lord Salisbury on the Redistribution Bill, if they should become necessary bye and bye'. Parnell had put him off by saying he would think about it. If Gladstone had any message to convey to him in future, Parnell 'thought it would be more prudent that they should be sent through myself or Lord Grosvenor as Mr. Parnell has not a high opinion of Mr. Labouchere's discretion'. Grosvenor replied stating that Herbert Gladstone had had no such communication with Labouchere. While some time would elapse before it was necessary to have further communication with Parnell, 'when that time does arise it will not be difficult to find some better mode of communication than Mr. Labouchere'.[105]

Labouchere, whose cynicism was closely allied to *naïveté*, blithely persevered. On 2 February, he advised Herbert Gladstone: 'Don't whatever you do put forward Chamberlain on Irish matters. To a certain extent Parnell is a lunatic, and like lunatics, he has antipathies . . . Whenever I see him he drifts into abuse of Chamberlain, and silly unreasoning abuse'. On 11 February he complained of Parnell:

> He asked me the day before the Division whether I would give him my word of honour that Mr. G. would assent to an Irish Parliament. I said that this was impossible, and that he must judge this himself. He had again, like the Mahdi, disappeared from his followers when the O'Shea incident occurred, and he turned up in Dublin. I am sure that he is mad.[106]

As late as 17 February, in the wake of the Galway election, he wrote to Herbert Gladstone suggesting that he should be given some quasi-official status or appointment to permit him to negotiate with the Irish. 'From a knowledge of the Irish party', he tendered the following advice:

> Never try to bargain with Parnell, before having, without his knowing it, got hold of Healy and O'Brien – and if possible T. P. O'Connor. I am convinced that he, in his heart, does not want a settlement, and he can only be forced into one by his lieutenants. At present this is all the more essential owing to a split about O'Shea. All the lieutenants were against him in this matter, and only knocked under in order to avoid a split. The result of this is that both Parnell and his lieutenants will be

> watching each other, and either can 'corner' the other by howling the louder for Irish rights. Parnell recently told them that if things were settled he should go abroad for a couple of years. Personally he would, for he is a terrible coward, but what is certain is, that he prefers being what he is to going abroad.[107]

This marked the close of Labouchere's intrigue. It afforded a startling study in disloyalty on Healy's part, a badly misconceived venture in usurpation in which he represented himself as free to treat, albeit tentatively and secretly, on behalf of a collegiate leadership of which he was avowedly the directing intelligence. In the event Healy and Labouchere's roguish confederacy, their trafficking in the sentimental grievances of Ireland, was a parody of Victorian high politics which scarcely impinged on the formation of the home rule alliance.

That the practical consequences of their collaboration were negligible was due to Gladstone's faultless response. Having extracted what advantage he could from the Healy- Labouchere nexus, he resolutely refused to engage with it, or to resort to the traditional device of seeking to split the Irish party. As Gladstone told Hartington, 'I have never looked much in Irish matters at negotiation or the conciliation of leaders'.[108]

It was an appropriate coda to the collaboration of Healy and Labouchere in 1885–6 that it was Healy who in 1892, at the request of John Morley, broke to Labouchere the news of his exclusion from Gladstone's last government, on the grounds of the Queen's opposition.[109]

Healy's collaboration with Labouchere revealed, in addition to his (still publicly veiled) antipathy to Parnell, a profound divergence on the issue of the relationship of the Irish party and the Liberals. Parnell resolutely refused to concede the inevitability of an alliance with the Liberals, and sought to exorcise the debilitating dependence on the Liberal party which had been the endemic weakness of parliamentary nationalism. For Parnell it was imperative that the Irish party stood clear of the Liberals, in a position to treat from a position of independent strength. For Healy, 'independent opposition' was a short-term tactic, necessary only to secure a Liberal commitment to home rule: thereafter the comity of purpose between Liberals and nationalists in the face of a mutual unionist adversary would suffice to ensure that the Liberal commitment to home rule was made good.

As Parnell brought Irish constitutional politics to levels of sophistication and modernity never previously attained, Healy was conforming to an older political type. His combination of public ferocity and exaggerated private amenability contrasted sharply with Parnell's reserve. To those who knew of them, Healy's parleys with Gladstone affirmed the traditional hostile stereotype of the Irish parliamentarian at Westminster as inconstant, incapable of disciplined allegiance, and easily flattered. Few

English parliamentarians subscribed so unquestioningly to this stereotype as the professedly Hibernophile Henry Labouchere.

As in 1878–80, Parnell had demonstrated sureness of judgement and strength of action in the face of Healy's virulent doubting of his capacity. In the outcome Healy stood rebuked. His dealings with Labouchere had issued in his galling humiliation before his Liberal interlocutors. Parnell's career now moved swiftly towards what was to be its parliamentary culmination. Healy was obliged to watch Parnell moving ever closer to appropriating the historic credit for an Irish settlement. His betrayal of Parnell had been furtively consummated, in advance of the Galway election and the withdrawal of Healy's brief to appear before the Special Commission, the milestones by which the public history of their estrangement was to be charted. For a man of Healy's temperament there could be no turning back. He had shifted ineluctably closer to open opposition to Parnell.

It is difficult to read the Labouchere–Herbert Gladstone correspondence without a sense of the cold wrath, tinged by grim amusement, which it would have elicited from Parnell. The Irish leader was the only major actor in the home rule drama who did not know of the Healy–Labouchere nexus. Harcourt told Edward Hamilton that what he revealingly characterised as the correspondence between Herbert Gladstone and Healy had become 'common property'. He was prompted to warn W. E. Gladstone that Labouchere was 'specially dangerous and unreliable', and that of all advisers '*rebus in arduis*' he was the 'most untrustworthy'.[110] Joseph Chamberlain had been kept apprised by Labouchere of the general course of his dealings with Healy. While he was protected by conventions of confidentiality, Healy's peace of mind cannot have been enhanced by the awareness that Chamberlain was in possession of information concerning his secret negotiations, the disclosure of which would have gone far to destroy his career in nationalist politics.

Ironically Healy was to some extent protected by Parnell's suspicions that he was intriguing with Chamberlain. If rumours of communications between Healy and Labouchere had reached Parnell, he is likely to have concluded that Labouchere was acting on behalf of Chamberlain whose ally he had long been. In January 1886 Chamberlain asked Healy to dine with him, and Healy agreed. Parnell, alerted by Morley, vetoed the assignation.[111] Harcourt recorded in his diary:

> Chamberlain said he had asked Healy to dine with him the other night but the day before he was to come Healy came to him in the H. of C. and said 'It's got out'. Chamberlain asked 'What?' Healy replied 'That

> I was going to dine with you and I have been told by those whom I cannot resist that I am not to do so'. This is Parnell who was afraid that Healy might be 'squared' and would not let him go. It is wonderful to see the personal power he has over his followers even in small matters.[112]

Alfred Robbins wrote that Parnell 'during the indirect parliamentary negotiations with Mr. Gladstone on the scheme for Home Rule, believed that Healy was intriguing with Chamberlain'. Parnell likewise told Davitt in 1887 that he had caught Healy intriguing with Chamberlain, but did not give any details. Parnell according to Robbins also resented what he considered to be Healy's lukewarm support for his efforts to arrange a satisfactory home rule bill with Gladstone in 1886, which he may have misconstrued as a further indication of an involvement on Healy's part with Chamberlain.[113]

Healy's supposed involvement with Chamberlain became part of the legend of the fall of Parnell. Katharine Tynan's friend Rosa Mulholland met Chamberlain's ally Sir Charles Dilke (who in fact broke with him to support the home rule bill) in London in 1886: 'I detested him, sitting there in a chair and looking like a malevolent monkey as he rubbed his hands together saying that Mr. Parnell was nothing at all and that Healy was the man'.[114]

6

The First Home Rule Bill

Captain O'Shea

At the 1885 election Parnell had the unpleasant and delicate task of finding a seat for Katharine O'Shea's husband, the outgoing member for county Clare. The constituency had been split in two. While W. H. O'Shea probably realised he was unelectable for either division, his opening gambit was to insist that Parnell secure his return for West Clare. An undated draft or copy letter to Parnell conveys his temper and tactics in the prelude to the 1885 election:

> As you are aware I have for some time been telling several friends of mine of your promises to secure my re-election for Clare. As it may possibly be that you will deny them I think it right to leave you no excuse in the way of forgetfulness.

These pledges, he alleged, had been given on the narrow division on the Egyptian question, and later on other occasions. On one such occasion, at Eltham, 'you asked me to think over the matter well and let you know which division of the county I wished to represent and you would arrange the matter. It is not very long since I wrote from London, choosing the Western division'.[1]

O'Shea went so far as to induce his adopted mentor Joseph Chamberlain to write one of the most curious letters of his career, commending him to George Mulqueeny, a shady Fenian contact of O'Shea's.[2] Parnell's diffident soundings as to the possibility of O'Shea running for either of the Clare constituencies confirmed what he already knew: that even had O'Shea been prepared to take the parliamentary pledge he could not be returned in Clare.[3] O'Shea now began to call in his obligations in earnest.

Parnell tried to induce him to contest mid-Armagh as a Liberal with nationalist support, as part of a complicated arrangement involving other Ulster seats which he put to Lord Richard Grosvenor, the Liberal chief whip. The plan miscarried. Ill and holed-up in the Shelbourne Hotel in Dublin, O'Shea wrote a pompous and menacing letter to the Irish leader. He complained that in urging him to contest the Armagh seat Parnell had misstated the proportion of Catholic to Protestant voters. He refused to go forward. Of Parnell's failure to support him in Clare, he wrote that 'you were aware all along that I would take no such pledge as you have formulated, consequentially the adoption of it by yourself and your friends has nothing to do with me':

> Several very important personages who have had the best opportunity of appreciating what I have done for you are of opinion that, as a gentleman, you are under the clearest obligation to declare to your friends that you insist on my being returned to Parliament *quand même*, and that if the necessary steps are not taken for this purpose you will resign the leadership of your party.[4]

The main arbiter of honour whom O'Shea had in contemplation was Joseph Chamberlain. Generally aware of Healy's parleys with Labouchere (to which he made no reference), Chamberlain alluded to an intrigue between Parnell and Gladstone:

> I am quite unable to make head or tail of the mystery. It is evident that something has been going on of which we are ignorant. I do not believe that the plot – if plot there be – will be successful . . . Meanwhile you have been shamefully used and have much greater reason for complaint than myself, although I am not by any means satisfied with the way a pledged word has been kept.[5]

O'Shea's object was to increase the pressure on Parnell to secure his election. However his widespread dissemination of his political grievance against Parnell raises the issue of whether he was ignorant of his wife's relations with Parnell, or was ostentatiously feigning his innocence of any knowledge of the affair. If the question does not admit of a definite answer, the cynical interpretation is the more plausible.

O'Shea also approached Henry Labouchere who wrote that 'it will never do for you not to get into Parliament. I suspect that Parnell did his best, but that the "boys" were too much for him'. The 'boys' were chiefly Healy and Biggar, the members of the Irish party most implacably opposed to O'Shea. Even before Parnell's involvement with Katharine O'Shea, Healy in his *Nation* letter had singled out 'the gallant captain' for attack in July 1880. The animosity was fully reciprocated by O'Shea, who repeatedly congratulated himself on having through his influence with Parnell thwarted Healy. Labouchere went on to observe that 'the pity is that the matter was not settled in time for you to stand for an English constituency with an Irish contingent'.[6]

Parnell now belatedly resolved to run O'Shea for just such a constituency, the Exchange division of Liverpool. After some bullying from Katharine O'Shea, Lord Richard Grosvenor obtained Gladstone's endorsement for her husband and went to Liverpool in his support. O'Shea's candidacy entailed disposing of the existing Liberal pretender. Chamberlain, who presided in Birmingham over the most efficient electoral machine in England, wrote condescendingly that 'I am surprised at nothing from Liverpool politics but they seem on this occasion to have exceeded their usual imbecility'. He enquired 'what is the good of a whip if he can't get rid of a fellow like Stephens?'[7]

As a feint, Parnell declared his own candidacy but withdrew in favour of O'Shea. Parnell's strenuous attempt to ensure O'Shea's return consumed most of his energies in the 1885 election: his only incursion into the campaign in Ireland was in North Louth, to oust Phil Callan, who had unwisely bruited about the fact that Parnell was having an affair with Katharine O'Shea.[8] It was all in vain. Parnell irritably blamed O'Shea's narrow defeat on the local Liberal organisation: on this at least he was in agreement with Joseph Chamberlain.[9]

In early November Labouchere wrote informing Chamberlain that he had received a long missive from O'Shea asking him to denounce Parnell for his failure to back O'Shea:

> These are the real facts. Parnell is — or is supposed to be — the lover of his wife. He told me several times that he would do all that he could for him, but that it was very difficult. I found out from the 'boys' that the difficulty was in their knowledge of the love affair, and in their not seeing why on account of it he was to be treated better than others who had given half support to Parnell. Of course it is impossible to explain this to him, as we must assume that he knew nothing of the domestic detail.[10]

The presupposition that Chamberlain did not already know of the affair (of which it is likely that he was aware from May 1882[11]) is a little surprising. Labouchere may of course have been deliberately circumspect in his mentioning of the matter; it is also possible that he was succumbing to the gossip's habit of conveying stale intelligence with breathless ardour. What was certain was that O'Shea's insistent demand for a seat, and Parnell's endeavours to comply with it, were drawing increasing attention to the matter of Parnell's relations with his wife.

Labouchere wrote to Rosebery, 'if you wish to know the cause of Parnell's erratic movements at Liverpool, *cherchez la femme'*. The account Labouchere gave Rosebery is notable chiefly for its mention of Cardinal Manning, the Catholic Archbishop of Westminster:

> Parnell is on *very* friendly terms with Mrs. O'Shea – the latter [W. H. O'Shea] probably knows this, but pretends not to. Parnell had promised him to bring him in for Clare County. The party were indignant, and said that it was monstrous that an exception should be made for him. So he, notwithstanding Parnell's assertions, was ruled out. On this there was a row. O'Shea appealed to Cardinal Manning of all people, and, with the Cardinal to back him, called upon Parnell to tell his followers that he must keep faith or resign the leadership. To get out of this mess, and to continue in the good graces of the lady, Parnell gave up standing in the Liverpool district, where he had announced his candidature, and put up O'Shea, who very nearly got in. Parnell lost his temper at the Conservatives not realising his position, and withdrawing their candidate, so that O'S. might walk in. Had Parnell stood himself – on some plea or other, this would have been managed.[12]

Parnell's promotion of O'Shea's candidacy – even for an English constituency – excited deep resentment within the Irish party. Fresh from a lengthy interview with Healy, Labouchere wrote to Herbert Gladstone on 19 December:

> There seems to be a good deal of ill-feeling between Parnell and his followers. In general terms, they profess that he has done so much for the country that they would die for him – but in their hearts they rather despise him. Healy gave me the particulars about O'Shea. There was quite a row in the party about Parnell's having, as they said, sacrificed a seat in Liverpool for him, and having tried to sacrifice a seat in Ulster. One said to Parnell: 'We are not all under Kitty O'Shea'. They understand that Parnell has broken with her, and that there is a new Venus in the ascendant. Some of them believe that he is secretly married this time.[13]

It is almost inconceivable that such a remark was addressed to Parnell – even in private by Biggar at his most blunt.[14] Healy is the likely source of the suggestion that Parnell and Katharine O'Shea had ceased to be lovers: he continued at least up to the split to believe that Parnell's relations with

Katharine O'Shea were transiently promiscuous, and even then had evident difficulty in accepting the sincerity of Parnell's attachment to her. This is of some significance in relation to the Galway election. If Healy continued to hold the belief that O'Shea's candidacy represented the squaring of the husband of a discarded mistress, it may have led him to underestimate the extent to which Parnell was prepared to go to sustain it.

Parnell on 17 December 1885 sent Healy a somewhat chilling letter of congratulation on his election for South Derry. He expressed his belief that Healy would also have won North Tyrone — which he had evidently suggested he should contest — and 'that a less strong man could have won the three-cornered fight in South Derry'. The letter went on to discuss the need for public moderation, and ended: 'Show this to O'Brien and consult him'. It was not an impolite letter, but it clearly indicated that he was putting their relations on a formal footing.[15]

The Galway Election

Parnell had exhausted the expedients which would have spared him what he most dreaded, the necessity of running O'Shea for a nationalist constituency in Ireland. T. P. O'Connor, who had been returned for the Scotland division of Liverpool and for Galway, chose to sit for Liverpool. O'Shea had already cast his eye on the Galway seat in early December. Parnell temporised, but when he acted he did so with a speed calculated to disorient the opposition. On 5 February he informed a startled O'Connor that he was running O'Shea for Galway. O'Connor and Biggar immediately cabled to Healy in Dublin, and crossed to Ireland to oppose O'Shea's candidacy. In a second cable, O'Connor urged Healy to see Edmund Dwyer Gray of the *Freeman's Journal* as 'an article tomorrow would kill the whole thing'. He badly underestimated Parnell's desperate resolve.

While opposed to O'Shea, Healy had no wish to embark upon an open challenge to Parnell's authority. In the considered attack on O'Shea's candidacy which he despatched to the *Freeman's Journal*, he chose his ground carefully, leaving open a line of retreat in the event of Parnell forcing the issue. He expressed his regret that 'the unexpectedness of the intelligence should have created an emergency, which necessitates the public ventilation of the matter before time permitted of a consultation with Parnell and the Party, whose decision, of course, would be final'. The most revealing part of the letter was its concluding sentence: 'I understand that Mr. T. P. O'Connor, accompanied by Mr. Biggar, left London tonight on their way to Galway where, if necessary, I shall be happy also to attend'. Healy thereby made clear his anxiety to avoid the election acquiring the aspect of a confrontation between Parnell and himself.

In the small hours of 6 February, Gray received a telegram announcing Parnell's support of O'Shea's candidacy, and refused to publish Healy's letter. T. P. O'Connor was by now having second thoughts. To Healy's undying fury, he declined to oppose Parnell. Healy and Biggar went on together. While O'Connor later asserted that it was Healy who insisted on recovering, Healy's assertion that he went to Galway in response to an appeal from Biggar is to be preferred.[16]

The Galway election was a tense study in brinkmanship. Each side sought frantically to avoid a confrontation by inducing the other to back off. Healy and Biggar came under intense pressure from their parliamentary colleagues to withdraw. John Deasy, one of the whips, conveyed the threat that Parnell would resign if O'Shea was not returned in deference to Chamberlain's wishes. This, an attempt by Parnell to avoid a personal descent on Galway, was discounted by Biggar. Cabling to Gray, Healy defensively couched his position in terms of fealty to his friend: 'I will stand by Biggar in the right rather than Parnell in the wrong'.[17]

The next morning, before addressing the first meeting in support of O'Shea's local rival, Michael Lynch, Healy wrote to Col. J. P. Nolan, O'Shea's campaign manager, in an attempt to procure bloodlessly the withdrawal of his candidature. If he persisted in his candidacy, O'Shea was doomed to defeat, and 'you, who are on the spot as his friend, will be responsible for not advising him against such a course'. If on the other hand O'Shea withdrew, 'the public will know next to nothing of his adventures, as we shall make no speeches, nor allow any to be made, and the entire situation will have been saved'. Of the telegrams they had received that morning, Healy wrote:

> We replied to them that the threats with which our action has been met would render it necessary for us, if Captain O'Shea compels us to hold a meeting today, to place the issues clearly on record. If I were the only speaker this would not be so serious, but I fear even if Parnell's threat [of resignation] were not bluff, Biggar will say things which will make it a reality.[18]

Healy did not for a moment believe that Biggar would risk the destruction of Parnell's leadership by an explicit public reference to Parnell's relations with Katharine O'Shea. He was aware of Biggar's pledge to Gray the previous day that 'in speaking tomorrow we will be studiously temperate and give no cause for offence' and indeed it is most unlikely that he had not himself elicited from Biggar a similar commitment. He hoped however that the fear of Biggar running amok would force O'Shea's withdrawal.

After the break-up of the party in 1890, Healy protested that 'the truth is that I was constantly moderating him and repressing his allusions to the

O'Shea scandal'. Contrary to the later suggestions of the absent O'Connor, Biggar did not make public reference to Parnell's affair with Katharine O'Shea.[19] According to the account of John Muldoon, present as a reporter, Biggar in conversation with local nationalists referred to Captain O'Shea as the husband of Parnell's mistress, and Healy spoke to Michael Lynch in similar terms.[20] This was the extent of the disclosure made.

On brakes stationed beside the Railway Hotel on Eyre Square later that day, Healy and Biggar addressed their first meeting in support of Lynch. Denouncing O'Shea as 'this chameleon *militaire*', Healy declared that had the Irish party been consulted, and had he found himself in the minority, he would have bowed to the decision, 'but the Irish party could not be found to ratify the betrayal'. Slipping into a suggestive idiom of dishonour, he declared he would allow no Whig 'to capture, aye, and to defile the honour of an Irish constituency'. In a veiled reference to Kilmainham, Healy asserted:

> Ireland needs no carpet knights; we need no negotiators and no diplomatists. If we wanted diplomatists there is no abler, no more skilled, more cautious, and experienced diplomatist than our great leader himself (*loud cheers*). He is not only first in the field, but he is also prudent at the council board.

In the account of John Muldoon, Healy made his most overt threat when, fixing his gaze on the figure of O'Shea seated in a window of Mack's Hotel opposite, he declared that 'we may yet have to raise other issues in this election and we shall not fear to do so before we allow the honour of Galway to be besmirched'.[21]

The next day, Monday 8 February, both O'Shea and Lynch were nominated. The reciprocal bluff had failed, and in the stand-off which ensued both sides were braced for conflict. Healy and Biggar addressed their second meeting in support of Michael Lynch. Healy now apprehensively alluded to the possibility of Parnell coming to Galway. Of O'Shea he asked, 'even if by some political legerdemain or sleight of hand he could by some political miracle secure here the presence upon his side of his illustrious chief, knowing as he does his own defeat is an absolute certainty', what would be the value of the friendship of a man who would thus expose Parnell to humiliation. He professed not the smallest doubt that if 'any illegitimate influence of this kind' were brought to bear, Parnell himself 'would be the first man who would declare Ireland first, and O'Shea to the devil'. He wondered 'when this political caterpillar, this Whig grub, is going by-and-by to change into a gaudy-hued Nationalist butterfly'.[22] In mounting desperation O'Shea despatched no less than five telegrams to Parnell, the texts of which mysteriously came to Healy's knowledge, and are set forth in the proofs of his memoirs.[23]

A pencilled note in the papers of T. P. Gill sets forth the text of Parnell's telegram announcing his departure:

> Missed train last night by a few seconds coming tonight without fail. Arrange editorial article in Freeman's Journal tomorrow.
>
> Calling country and constituency to support my authority at this juncture. Why I hold an Irish parliament in my hand. If I be weakened now no other man in our time will ever get so near success and advise all friends of my decision and that the only course now open failing serious injury and possible fatal loss to the Irish cause is to withdraw Lynch. O'Shea has given most satisfactory pledges and he will not sit in opposition.

The *Freeman's Journal* editorial of 9 February echoed the phrases of the telegram, which were to recur in Parnell's own first speech in Galway.[24]

On the morning of 9 February Parnell arrived at Kingstown, and went on to Broadstone station. There he was joined for his descent on Galway by a contingent of Irish members. He told T. P. O'Connor: 'I'm rather hard to start, but when I do, I keep on'. He held Healy rather than Biggar responsible for the Galway revolt. He expressed no animosity to Biggar, but when urged *en route* to treat Healy considerately, ominously replied that he would use '"all the resources of civilisation"' – the famous phrase of Gladstone which had heralded his arrest – to achieve an accord with Healy. He added that Healy had been trying to stab him in the back for years, and that he was now doing so in the belief that the opportune moment had come.[25]

Parnell's train reached Galway station in the early afternoon to a hostile and turbulent reception. The ten or so parliamentarians in Galway closeted themselves in a room in the Railway Hotel. According to O'Connor's 1891 account, Healy stated his case 'with profound emotion'; in the later account in O'Connor's memoirs, Healy wept before a gathering which listened in hostile silence as he, broken-voiced, repudiated the charge that he was motivated by personal hostility towards the Irish leader. Outside, Michael Lynch could be heard declaring to the crowd from the steps of the hotel that just as the people had made Parnell, so they could unmake him. Parnell tranquilly asserted that he had not wanted the position of Irish leader, but that since he held it he was bound to Ireland to retain it: 'I have no intention of abandoning it. I would not do so if the people of Galway today were to kick me through the streets of Galway'. Healy capitulated. Biggar held out to the last in a speech interrupted by Healy, who jumped up to restrain him in the mistaken belief that he was about to make reference to Katharine O'Shea.[26]

The electors of Galway had still to be faced. Parnell, in O'Connor's account, instinctively recognising 'the fact that this small meeting, fierce, untutored, in a little hall in a remote town — that this meeting held for the moment his fate and that of Ireland in its hands', rose to the occasion in a speech in which he mortgaged his stature as the Irish leader. He warned that if he were defeated 'there will rise a shout from all the enemies of Ireland 'Parnell is beaten; Ireland no longer has a leader'. Lynch in the event withdrew.[27]

Following the vote on the home rule bill in June 1886, O'Shea claimed in a characteristically indignant reply to a letter from James O'Kelly that statements made subsequently in the course of the election that he would act with the party were made without his authority. On learning of them, he professed to have been anxious to resign his seat forthwith. The day after the poll he had called on the bishop who discouraged him from resigning, advice confirmed by 'one of the highest political authorities', almost certainly Joseph Chamberlain, with whom he had discussed the matter.[28]

The Galway election precipitated a deep rift in the Irish party which prefigured the split five years later. Apart from John Dillon, all those who declined to subscribe to a public declaration endorsing Parnell's position belonged to the Healy—Sullivan connection. Maurice Healy, T. D. Sullivan, and William Martin Murphy, along with P. A. Chance, refused to sign. The *Nation* in an editorial written by T. D. Sullivan referred to the candidature of O'Shea as 'a deplorable mistake'.[29] The day after O'Shea's election Biggar writing to T. D. Sullivan ventured the prophecy that 'the Parnell—O'Shea connexion is a disgusting one, and unless the former ends it, the ruin and that of his leadership will follow. I wish the party to be ruled by Mr. Parnell but not by Mrs. O'Shea'.[30] The Galway election prompted in turn a rallying of the diehard Parnellite and Fenian opposition to the Healy—Sullivan faction of the Irish party. A handbill urged the working men of Dublin to boycott a banquet being held under the auspices of T. D. Sullivan as Lord Mayor. In fusing the long-standing Fenian antagonism to the Sullivans with fervent support for Parnell, it foreshadowed the Parnellite attacks on Healy and Sullivan in 1890—1. Sullivan was denounced as 'Father-in-Law to the traitor Tim Healy, who at the most vital time in the history of our country attempted to parlize [*sic*] the action of our Leader'. Just as 'this Sullivan Brood of ill omen' had in the past pitted itself against Fenian initiatives in the 1850s and 1860s, ' . . . now in 1885 . . . we have those Ishmaels of Irish politics endeavouring to cripple the power and lessen the prestige of Charles Stewart Parnell'.[31]

The speculation about Parnell's leadership was such as to prompt the usually diffident Justin McCarthy to boast coyly to his literary collaborator:

> By the way isn't it a curious comment on Labouchere's saying that the extreme men of the Irish party had no confidence in me, that at this

> moment the strongest men among them talk seriously of dethroning Parnell, if needs be, and setting me up as leader. Of course this won't come to pass, but I feel a pardonable vanity in calling your attention to the fact. But you did not want to be told – perhaps for that very reason I am pleased that you should know – what indeed I am sure you do know – that I am not a weakling . . . but am considered by my political colleagues to be a pretty strong man, to be trusted in a case of difficulty and danger.[32]

Labouchere wrote to Herbert Gladstone:

> Healy has been an ass in the O'Shea business. Harrington, O'Brien and O'Connor and the others were with him, but they knocked under to avoid a split. They now console themselves by saying that the Captain must have letters of Parnell about Mrs. O'Shea, and thus can make him do what he likes. I doubt this. When once Parnell gets an idea into his head, he sticks to it with the tenacity of a lunatic.[33]

To Rosebery he wrote (erroneously) that 'it really is a fact that Parnell had to threaten his resignation to force O'Shea on his party. What a difference between the two husbands'.[34]

The anti-nationalist press hailed the emergence of the long-foretold rift within the ranks of the Irish party. The *Times* derided Parnell's self-elevation into the position of 'Grand Elector', while the Tory *Saturday Review* wrote provokingly of Parnell having quelled the Galway mutiny 'with an almost Cromwellian promptitude'. The unionist *Galway Express* shrewdly commented that Parnell had emerged victorious, 'but the victory has cost him much – another such victory will cost him the leadership of the Irish party, if there is an Irish party to lead'.[35]

Unionist commentaries on the Galway election sought to exacerbate the rift between Parnell and Healy. A Catholic unionist present at Galway strikingly characterised the outcome in terms of social and racial archetypes, and conveyed Parnell's mastery through the image of the huntsman:

> Parnell comes of the conquering race in Ireland and, he never forgets it, or lets his subordinates forget it. I was in Galway when he came over there to quell the revolt organised by Healy. The rebels were at white-heat before he came but he strode in among them like a huntsman among the hounds – marched Healy off into a little room, and brought him out again in ten minutes, cowed and submissive, but filled, as anybody could see, ever since, with a dull smouldering hate which will break out one of these days, if a good and safe opportunity offers.[36]

In an editorial in *United Ireland* William O'Brien sought to salve Healy's wounded pride:

> Those who counted on defections from Mr. Parnell's side have been rudely undeceived. The shallow cockney journals who expected Mr. Healy to break into mutiny against the chief whom he had served from the first dawn of his power with the fidelity of a Crusader and the courage of a lion, have been taught how little they know of the depths of a nature whose ferocity is reserved for the enemies of Ireland, and whose key note is a tenderness of heart as fascinating as the fiery play of his intellect.[37]

The schism between Healy and Parnell could no longer be mediated through O'Brien's sentimental blandishment.

The Galway election had an intriguing sequel. Three months later O'Shea re-opened the controversy with a characteristically provocative and inept speech in Galway. He boasted that his election 'had struck a heavy blow against political blackguardism', and that Michael Lynch was now 'as warm a supporter of his as there was in the borough'. This elicited immediate denials from Healy and Lynch. In his rejoinder O'Shea sought to twist the knife by asserting that 'for some years I have known Mr. Parnell very well indeed, and when Mr. Healy styles himself his trusted follower I can answer for it that Mr. Healy is nothing of the kind', and promised further revelations on the subject if required. O'Shea had alleged that Healy had sought a reconciliation with him. In the controversy which ensued he sent a telegram to the Lord Chief Justice to whom he looked to support this improbable claim. Lord Justice O'Brien despatched a stinging rebuke from the Four Courts:

> Healy never expressed to me in any way whatever a desire to be reconciled with you nor did I ever tell you that he did. I write quite astonished at your telegram. I did not say anything at O'Shaughnessy's as to overtures from Healy to you or anything of the kind. Healy always spoke of you in most contumelious manner. Do not introduce my name into this matter.

Compelled to withdraw the allegation against Healy, O'Shea ill-advisedly shifted his attack to Lynch, whom he accused of having sought patronage for his relatives. In his reply Lynch proved an uninhibited and effective controversialist. O'Shea, he wrote, had led him to believe in a smoking room of the House of Commons that he was at one time involved in the Fenian organisation. He had moreover 'talked glibly and in a light-hearted manner of a certain rumour concerning himself, which, if he were possessed of a particle of fine feeling he would have left unsaid'. The unmistakable allusion to Parnell's affair with O'Shea's wife terminated the correspondence.[38]

The Home Rule Bill

Remote from the drama of the Galway election, Gladstone was, in the phrase of E. W. Hamilton, 'gradually delivering himself of his huge plan'. Parnell was kept generally apprised of the later stages of the drafting process at meetings with John Morley, to which Gladstone referred as 'the communications westwards'.[39] On 25 March, the day before Gladstone presented to the cabinet the draft of the home rule bill, which precipitated the resignations of Chamberlain and G. O. Trevelyan, Katharine O'Shea wrote to Gladstone. Seizing on a vague statement of Morley to Parnell that he thought Gladstone might wish to see him, she sought to arrange a meeting between the Liberal and nationalist leaders, suggesting Morley's rooms in the Commons as a discreet venue.[40]

W. H. O'Shea chose the same day to make what was, even by his standards, a spectacularly inept intervention. He sent by hand to Gladstone a letter which purported to be from Katharine O'Shea at O'Shea's Albert Mansions apartment conveying the contents of a memorandum from him. The avowed purpose of O'Shea's memorandum was to head off a split in the Liberal ranks. He proclaimed a compromise still possible, though not, he self-importantly added, on the basis of any scheme previously discussed. He condemned the 'mischief-makers' who claimed that Chamberlain was not prepared to compromise. Chamberlain was 'not wedded to mere words' and could be brought to support a scheme 'so long as the integrity of the Empire and the supremacy of the Imperial Parliament were safeguarded'.

The next morning the Prime Minister received a telegram from an irate Katharine O'Shea: 'I understand that a communication was sent to you yesterday from Albert Mansions in my name. I do not know anything whatever about it and have not seen it. I have not been in London for some days'. O'Shea noted ruefully alongside the copy of the letter retained by him that 'I was surprised afterwards that Mrs. O'Shea would have expressed herself annoyed at the note having been sent. She had even telegraphed that she would come at any moment for the purpose of comm[unicating] with Gl[adstone]'. The obliquity and gaucheness of O'Shea's intervention owed much to his secondary purpose of impressing upon Gladstone the felicity of his domestic relations: his memorandum addressed Katharine as 'dearest'.[41]

The same day that O'Shea despatched his memorandum to Gladstone, Parnell made clear to Labouchere his opposition to any modification of the scheme of home rule to accommodate Chamberlain's objections. Labouchere reported to Herbert Gladstone that Parnell had 'said that — with every desire to be as conciliatory as possible — he was anxious that it should be known that it would be impossible for him to agree to

Mr. G's scheme being modified to meet the wishes of Chamberlain, if these modifications were in the sense of his utterances'.[42]

The last outstanding issue to be resolved between Gladstone and Parnell was that of control over customs and excise. At a meeting with Gladstone on 5 April Parnell was eminently realistic. He was prepared to concede control of customs and excise in return for which he looked for a reduction of Ireland's contribution to imperial expenditures. Hamilton spoke to Gladstone early the following morning:

> . . . after commenting on the astuteness and reasonableness of Parnell, Mr. G. announced that Parnell being convinced that he had no chance of getting the power to set up Protection, was willing to give up the Customs and Excise duties, and to give them up without any direct representation of Ireland at Westminster, provided he could secure somewhat more favourable financial terms, that is rather a larger balance to the good. This evidently admits of being attained without great alteration. . . . It is impossible to overrate the importance of the effect which this change may have on the measure. It has ensured the unanimity in the cabinet, and for the first time for many weeks I see a chance of Mr. G.'s carrying the measure in the House of Commons. It will disarm much opposition and quiet many alarms.

Parnell had unavailingly argued for an Irish contribution of the order of one-twentieth rather than one-fifteenth. As he told William O'Brien, 'the old gentleman, when it comes to be a question of cash, is as hard as a moneylender'. He did succeed in having the contribution expressed as a fixed sum for thirty years rather than as a proportion of imperial expenditure.[43] This was the last accommodation. Parnell thenceforth rigidly upheld, and sought to enforce, the compact. In particular he set his face against any concession designed to placate Chamberlain.

On 7 April 1886, the eve of the introduction of the home rule bill, the Irish party met, in the absence of Parnell and Healy. The members resolved to take their seats early, to occupy their own benches in a body, and 'not to interrupt in a violent way any member who may speak against the Home Rule measure'. Chamberlain was the person principally contemplated by the latter part of the resolution.[44] The same day, Parnell assembled the senior members of the party, including Healy, to advise them of the contents of Gladstone's bill. While sharing their disappointment with the financial provisions, in inviting them to assume responsibility for its rejection, he made clear he was insisting on support for the bill. (When, later in the debates, O'Connor in a speech suggested that the bill might be regarded as a draft measure, Parnell said with emphasis to O'Connor after he had sat down, '*this* is the bill we want'.) At a meeting of the Irish party immediately after Gladstone's speech, 'general dissatisfaction' was expressed on four points, mainly financial and fiscal, and it was agreed that Parnell would raise those points in his speech later that day.[45]

Healy spoke on the second day of the debate on the introduction of the bill, immediately after Chamberlain, on whom his speech was a sustained attack conducted in terms of an extended contrast with Gladstone. Almost thirty-five years later William O'Brien recalled Parnell listening to the debate, preoccupied among other things with 'how shrewdly "Tim" was galling, perhaps over-galling, the Lucifer of the Unauthorised Programme'. Healy's characterisation of the attack Chamberlain had just delivered on the Prime Minister was most unfortunate:

> I do not know if ever I shall rise to the dignity of being a Minister under an Irish Parliament under this new Bill. But if I should happen to have such a position of the kind under my hon. Friend the Member for the City of Cork, and if I should want, when I am leaving him to give him a very deadly stab, I will take right good care to imitate as closely as possible the action of the rt. hon Member for Birmingham, and turn up the pages of *Hansard* to see how it was done.

While Healy denied that he had ever 'used the language of adulation to any man in this House', his speech was a panegyric to Gladstone, 'the greatest man his country ever produced', to whom by implication he accorded the entire credit for the introduction of the bill. He concluded extravagantly with the words of Isaiah: 'How beautiful upon the mountains are the feet of him that bringeth good tidings, that publisheth peace'. (Healy's friend and admirer Harold Frederic later observed: 'Probably any other man in the House might have used the quotation effectively. Upon Mr. Healy's lips it irresistibly suggested a comic cartoon of the Premier traversing rocky crags with feet of exaggerated dimensions'.[46])

Labouchere wrote proprietorially to Herbert Gladstone: 'I begged Healy to avoid in his speech all further wrangling with the Orangemen, and I think he did this capitally. His speech was an extinguisher to Chamberlain. Parnell will make his men talk or not as desired. I should think that as they are the parties concerned and their votes are safe that they will do well to hold their tongues. I can get as many Radicals to speak as may be wanted'.[47]

Healy's unprepared speech on the second reading, made at Parnell's request, in reply to Trevelyan, was much more effective. He again lauded Gladstone: for the first time in English history a statesman had brought forward a great measure for Ireland, without being under the compulsion of armed threat, 'which recommends the scheme of the Prime Minister to the Irish people, and has produced a softness of heart towards him'. He concluded with a moving peroration in the course of which he asked: 'Are we Irishmen, I might almost say, as was asked of the Jew, not men like yourselves? . . . I believe, Sir, in the alchemy of justice, in its efficacy and permanent effects . . .'[48]

It quickly became apparent that the revolt of the radicals and Whigs against the bill was more formidable than had been allowed for. One of the most delicate issues was the exclusion of Irish members from Westminster. Parnell on 8 May gave Morley, who was seeking to find areas of compromise, the impression that his opposition to retention had stiffened. This was to some degree a feint to ensure that there would be no compromise on any issues which he considered central. Two days later he told Labouchere that he would raise no difficulties and assent to Irish representation 'in other Imperial matters', and proposed a scheme he thought might be workable.[49] Even Labouchere's zeal for intrigue was not equal to the task of bringing round the radical malcontents: 'Chamberlain in his present state of mind will do his best to make an arrangement impossible . . . At the present moment, the Bill is lost. Only *les grand moyens* can save it'.[50]

When Chamberlain on 1 June declared, of his proposals for a national council, that he had 'irrefutable and incontrovertible evidence that those proposals at the time they were made received the approval and support of distinguished members of the Nationalist Party', Healy interjected 'O'Shea'. While Healy correctly calculated that Chamberlain was not in a position to venture into his dealings with Parnell and O'Shea, it was a reckless intervention which could only have served to deepen the mistrust in which Parnell had come to hold him.[51]

Shortly before the vote on the second reading, Parnell claimed that had the Conservatives won a majority, they would have granted to Ireland a statutory legislature. He declined however to name Lord Carnarvon, the minister on whose authority he purported to rely for the assertion. According to Healy, as he rose to wind up the debate, Gladstone sent his chief whip Arnold Morley to him with a message that if Parnell was agreeable, he proposed to ask Parnell for further information on the subject. Parnell refused. In the event three days later, after the bill's defeat, Carnarvon himself made a statement in the Lords. In his memoirs Healy argued unconvincingly that, had Parnell acceded to Gladstone's request, it would have averted the bill's defeat. Healy did not repeat in his memoirs the allegation made by him in June 1892 that his first difference with Parnell occurred when he refused to disclose in the Commons his own conversations with Tory ministers, when urged by Parnell to do so after his own oblique allusion to his meeting with Carnarvon.[52]

Parnell fastidiously respected political confidences. Some on the government side regarded the discretion of the Irish party with an astonishment tinged with scepticism. E. W. Hamilton dined with Morley in early May:

> It is certainly most remarkable, as M. observed, how the communications with him have been kept dark. Nothing has been breached about them; nor was any disclosure made, though the draft was shown to some others besides P. himself, all more or less connected with the Press. Does this mark honourable conduct or is it merely characteristic of the attitude of conspirators?[53]

On 8 June the home rule bill was defeated. When Gladstone moved the adjournment of the House, Healy interjected: 'I would ask the rt. hon. Gentleman the Prime Minister (*Cries of "Order!"*) to remember the words of Frederic Douglas, the Negro orator — "God and one make a majority" (*Cries of "Order!"*)'.[54]

Out of Parliament

The general election which followed the defeat of the home rule bill returned a unionist government. Healy narrowly lost the South Derry seat he had won in 1885. He was to be out of parliament for six months. His defeat did not suspend his political activities. Labouchere once more interposed, this time to avert the *rapprochement* he erroneously feared between Parnell and the unionists, and to re-instate himself as the Hermes of the home rule alliance.

Healy wrote on 22 July stating that he considered 'we owe such a debt to Mr. Gladstone that for my part I would deplore anything that would not help his immediate return to power'. He did not know what were the views of Parnell, whom he had not seen since the defeat of the home rule bill, 'but having said there were no gentlemen except Carnarvon in the Tory cabinet and called Chamberlain "a guttersparrow" I fancy he won't be anxious to have much dealings with them'. Besides, Healy surmised that as the facts of the Kilmainham treaty had come out 'they would probably not care to come to such close quarters again'. He favoured a 'strict alliance offensive and defensive' with the Liberals.[55]

Labouchere told Herbert Gladstone that he had begged Justin McCarthy to find out Parnell's views: 'as you know it is impossible to get hold of that wary person, who never adopts a course without first finding out what his lieutenants will think of it'. McCarthy told Labouchere that 'Mr. G. may be assured that our party will never desert him'. McCarthy favoured a division on the Irish question in the debate on the address, as against forbearance in the hope of conciliating the Liberal unionists: 'Personally I am altogether for throwing over the secessionists, or at least the worst of them. Let us have, as Carlyle would put it, "the forlorn hope of God's battle clear of them at all events"'. Forwarding McCarthy's letter to Herbert Gladstone, Labouchere endorsed its argument. He proposed 'never to lose an opportunity of accentuating the difference between Whigs and Radicals'. Conceding that the government could not be defeated, he argued 'a division on the Irish question will do no harm, and will blood the Irish. Your father has created an Irish Home Rule party, and it will fall to pieces if the principle of Home Rule is not maintained'.[56]

The person most carried away by this redundant plotting was predictably its chief author. Labouchere wrote to Herbert Gladstone on 7 August

> I wrote to Healy and told him the only chance for the Irish was to accept the views of your father and to possibly join the Liberals. I suggested to him that he should previously consult you and get your maximum, and then adopt it in his article in the *Contemporary*.[57]

Labouchere had 'preached the same doctrine' to T. P. O'Connor, 'without of course saying anything about Healy'.[58]

Herbert Gladstone remained somewhat uneasy about Healy. He wrote to Labouchere in November reviving his old concern: 'I can't help feeling that Healy and Randolph Churchill have some conditional understanding between them, for Healy appears less keen for an arrangement with us. . . . He is in my opinion wrong in believing that my F[ather] will be obliged to minimise although it is natural that he should fear this'.[59]

In the debate on the address in the new parliament, Parnell in the course of an attack upon Chamberlain, made a cutting allusion to the absent Healy:

> It will be very interesting for the rt. hon. Gentleman to go over to Ireland and complete the inquiry, which was shortened by the ill-advised threat of Mr. Healy that he might duck him in a horse pond. He will have an opportunity now of going over under different auspices, and under the protection of the Royal Irish Constabulary, and he will not have the slightest risk of any fate such as that foreshadowed by Mr. Healy under the changed circumstances.

Chamberlain replied that while Parnell 'had the good taste to say that I was deterred from that visit because Mr. Healy threatened to duck me in a horse-pond', he did not believe Healy had made any such 'course and vulgar threat'.[60] Coming from so notoriously laconic and deliberate a politician, this first public intimation of Parnell's mistrust of Healy was distinctly ominous. The attack was evidently predicated on Parnell's belief that Healy had intrigued with Chamberlain against him.

Maurice Healy wrote to commiserate with his brother: 'it was a mean proceeding, and I was glad to hear Chamberlain's allusion to it, though, of course he did not speak through any friendliness to you'. Healy's ally P. A. Chance complained to Dillon. Alive to the dangers of schism, Dillon took Chance aside and warned him against speaking too openly, as Maurice reported to Healy:

> Chance says that Dillon agreed as to the offensiveness of Parnell's action, and that the view Dillon took was, that perhaps you had been talking too freely, and that someone had repeated to Parnell something you said. Dillon thought it would be a great danger if the idea got abroad that there was any quarrel between Parnell and you, for Parnell might make the thing a personal matter. So far as I could gather, what Dillon said appeared to be speculation. Parnell has not spoken to me since, except in a casual way, to ask me to speak in the debate.

Healy's disingenuous assessment of what he described in the draft of his memoirs as 'Parnell's sneer' as a riposte for Galway belied the depth of the rift that had opened between them.[61]

The Irish party passed a resolution urging Healy and William O'Brien (who had lost his South Tyrone seat) to allow themselves to be placed in nomination, and requesting Parnell to make the necessary arrangements. If the resolution appeared unexceptionable, it is likely to have owed something to the alarm on the part of Parnell's lieutenants that the estrangement between Parnell and Healy was moving out of control.[62] As the first set of by-elections in nationalist seats approached early the following year, nothing had been done, and Healy felt obliged to take the initiative to ensure his own return. He declared his candidacy for the South Donegal vacancy, and wrote to Parnell. Parnell replied with a letter of intimidating formality. He had understood from Biggar that Healy was willing to contest North Longford. He expressed his 'very strong opinion that it would be politic for us to give the only existing *Ulster* vacancy to a Protestant nationalist'. He explained optimistically that 'the love of tolerance on the part of the Catholics thus exhibited at the doors of Ulster Liberal Protestants would have the best possible effect, and could not fail to win over many of them at the next general election . . .' He looked forward to hearing that Biggar had not been mistaken in supposing Healy would contest the Longford seat 'as we cannot spare you from Parliament next session, when there will be constant occasion and necessity for your great talent and experience'.[63]

In a letter to the press dated 22 January 1887, Parnell announced that 'after consultation with my principal colleagues', it had been decided that in furtherance of his policy of putting forwards Protestants for Ulster seats, Swift McNeill would stand for South Donegal. Healy would contest North Longford so that the party would not be deprived of Healy's 'great energy and fighting power, which was so missed during the last session'.[64] On 5 February, Healy was duly returned for North Longford.

The Union of Hearts

Labouchere wrote to McCarthy on 31 July 1886 that he had heard from W. E. Gladstone 'in a great state about the idea of the Irish perhaps deserting him after all etc.' Labouchere subsequently forwarded to McCarthy the text of a letter he had received from Herbert Gladstone on 1 August stating that nothing had been settled about the address, and continuing:

> If Parnell does accept crumbs which is likely and not unnatural, we ought I think to fall in with it, unless it is at the British tax-payer's expense. But any local government reform which he can accept must strengthen his hands in Ireland. But he most certainly ought to back us in nailing up the Home Rule flag. Of course my father has already done this: & if Parnell accepts a plan on the Hartington & Chamberlain lines, there can be no reason whatever for my father to continue in active politics.[65]

Justin McCarthy met Parnell after the latter's meeting with John Morley on 18 August. Parnell saw no purpose in pressing the home rule issue in a hostile Commons, and favoured the Irish party confining itself to the land question. On home rule in the longer term he was confident: 'he seemed, as he usually is, quite serene and well satisfied as to the condition of things. He looked the defeat straight in the face and was not in the least inclined to shirk it. But he looked through it and over it and beyond it and seemed well content'.[66] Likewise, Parnell was disinclined to give the Tories and Liberal unionists the opportunity to unite and demonstrate their large combined majority on Irish questions. As McCarthy observed 'Let them alone – let them come into collisions among themselves – and let us stand by ready to strike at the right moment – that is *his* policy'.[67]

Within the Liberal–nationalist alliance Parnell courteously but adamantly upheld the primacy of home rule. Through late 1886 and 1887, he came under pressure to facilitate Liberal re-union – and in particular Chamberlain's return to the Liberal fold – by acquiescing in intermediate measures of devolution. The pressure was far from overwhelming, and easily shrugged off by Parnell, who was absolutely determined to permit neither a dilution nor a deferral of the Liberal commitment to home rule.

The subject was first broached by Morley, at his meeting with Parnell on 7 December 1886, after they had disposed of the pressing issue of the Plan of Campaign. Morley reported to Gladstone:

> I then opened the question whether it might not be worth his while, if the chance came, to give at least a provisional acquiescence to intermediate projects of self-government, good in themselves, though not in his view adequate, or in ours either. I told him that I knew this was a possibility in your mind. He said at once, with his usual tranquillity, but with emphasis, that he could not do anything of the kind; that it would be the signal for revolt in his own army; that no truce of this sort would be condoned by the active men of his party.
>
> I then said – 'supposing that Mr. Gladstone, despairing of carrying public opinion beyond one of these intermediate projects, were to retire from the fight – where would you be?' 'O, then, I should have nothing for it, but to go the whole length of my tether, and beyond'.

While Parnell was at the same time 'perfectly willing to accept great modification of detail', Morley added, 'I am bound to say, however, that his language on this head was very uncompromising'.[68]

Gladstone in reply anxiously enquired as to whether Parnell had understood the idea of 'intermediate measures', 'namely not that we were to disown our own aim or dispense [with] our sentiments, but only that we were to abstain from open and violent warfare against some measure *ex hypothesi* good in itself'. Gladstone believed any such measures could only increase the means at the disposal of the Irish people for pressing home rule forward: 'I can hardly think that Parnell would take an extreme view of this. It is, however, a matter for much deliberation'. Morley replied confirming that Parnell comprehended clearly what was involved.[69]

Morley resumed his discussions with Parnell and four days later reported to Gladstone:

> He would, of course, accept for what it was worth any measure expressly limited to reform of local government – for elective county boards for instance. But it must be a measure that could not be mistaken for even a partial settlement of the larger question. He would have nothing to say to anything in the nature of a Central Council; because that would be an attempted substitute for a parliament, and he would be attacked for having swallowed a sham. He had at one time been inclined to believe that it might be possible to separate administration from legislative business in a Central Council, and in that belief he had not opposed the constitution of such a Council for administration. But further reflection had convinced him that the body would become legislative – and as a pseudo-legislative system, he could have nothing to do with it.
>
> Hence he would assent to a scheme for county boards, but could not acquiesce in intermediate measures, even if good so far as they went, if they advanced towards the ground filled by our Home Rule Bill.

Parnell thus skilfully dissociated himself on grounds of first principles from the kind of devolutionary 'national council' favoured by Chamberlain as a substitute for home rule. Morley enquired whether it might not be desirable to bring in a measure for county government to force the hand of the Liberal unionists. Parnell agreed, but — very possibly with a view to ensuring that nothing came of the proposal — said that if it was thought advisable he would himself introduce such a scheme.[70] Parnell and Gladstone were in perfect accord. Parnell's response to Morley's mild probings conformed exactly to Gladstone's purpose of adhering absolutely to their joint home rule schema without appearing to thwart Liberal re-union.

Morley assured Parnell in January 1887 that Gladstone would hold himself aloof from the so-called 'Round Table' conference with the dissenting Liberals, and that even if Gladstone's friends 'were capable of giving up essentials', the 'final action' would be Gladstone's and not theirs. Parnell was, he reported, 'very sensible and made no stand'.[71] Parnell in the event was not pressed further, as the 'Round Table' conference collapsed from its own inner tensions.[72]

In mid-September 1887, Parnell again met Morley. He played adroitly on the agrarian situation in Ireland, sought to achieve a relaxation of the stringent finances of the home rule bill, and for good measure referred to a nebulous scheme of evolutionary home rule which he suggested might be forthcoming from the government. Morley reported to Gladstone

> He is much afraid that outrages will begin again, and that the violent men both in Ireland and America will insist on revenge. He was rather melancholy on this head — thinking that it might put back the present goodwill of the English Liberals to Ireland.
>
> He declared himself to have come round to our view that the Land Question must be dealt with concurrently with Home Rule. Dwelt on the sovereign importance of a favourable financial arrangement; the terms of the Bill of 1886 too hard; would not leave them any margin for works etc.; I reminded him that I had already informed him of your later views as to the financial terms.
>
> He said that about a fortnight ago a communication had been made to him from the other side, as to the possibility of a moderate, gradual, and probationary attempt at H[ome] Rule. Lord Carnarvon's scheme had been of this kind. Ireland was to have the powers of an American state, but not all at once . . .[73]

Parnell's suggestion of a Conservative home role solution was canvassed with conspicuous mildness, and owed more to a mischievous urge to alarm the ever-apprehensive Morley than to remind Gladstone of the Irish party's independence of action. The strategies of the Liberal and Irish leaders in upholding the home rule alliance remained finely intermeshed.

The Plan of Campaign

The defeat of the home rule bill, and the return of a Conservative government, created a delicate and unstable situation in Ireland which it required all of Parnell's skill to contain. Labouchere wrote with his customary cynical frivolity to Herbert Gladstone at the end of July 1886:

> I very much doubt whether Parnell will be able to prevent a little playfulness in Ireland, if nothing be done before winter, and I see no reason to regret if there is a little playfulness. Revolutions are not made with rose-water. This would force the Tories into coercion, which would be advantageous to us.[74]

If Labouchere's feckless candour was unique, his underlying view was shared by an influential fringe of the Liberal party which believed that a degree of agrarian resistance in Ireland would assist in returning the party to office. This was to provide one of the more complicated sub-themes in the course of the Liberal–nationalist alliance over the ensuing five years.

Alive to the threat which agrarian distress and agitation in Ireland posed to his parliamentary strategy, Parnell in the Commons on 3 September declared his intention of introducing a tenants' relief bill to empower the courts to reduce judicial rents, to stay ejectments on the payment of a proportion of the arrears, and to admit leaseholders to the benefits of the land acts. His egregiously moderate speech revealed how sharply his thinking diverged from that of the authors of the Plan of Campaign which would be launched the following month. In a classically Parnellian gesture, he looked at once to disavow and to exploit any recrudescence of agrarian agitation in Ireland.

> The Irish members have no control, neither have the government control, over the events in Ireland in the coming winter. The rt. hon. Gentleman [Balfour] need not suppose, by my allusion to the events of 1880, that I am going to head any such agitation as then took place. I do not believe there will be such an agitation: but I do believe that the situation of the tenantry will be so desperate, so much more terrible, desperate, and critical, than it was in those days, that there will be a spontaneous movement among them which neither the Irish members nor the Government, nor anyone else will be able to control, and which will excite irritation, passion, and indignation in this country against the Irish people, so that politicians and statesmen will lose their balance.

He professed his belief that when the moderate nature of the bill was revealed, it would be supported by both sides of the House. Churchill, for the government, pledged a special sitting to discuss Parnell's measure when drafted.[75]

This was a graver Parnell, embarked on the deceptively hazardous fourth phase of his career, striving to maintain the momentum and the constitutional legitimacy of the home rule alliance during a period when the Liberals were out of office. Writing to Gladstone, John Morley's reaction was grudging, reflecting the alarm with which Liberals viewed any possible *rapprochement* between Parnell and the government. He supposed that Parnell 'counts on a troubled winter, and that he wishes to be able to say that this bill would have prevented the mischief', and moreover 'relished the prospect of putting the Liberal Unionists in a fix'.[76]

Parnell's Tenants' Relief (Ireland) Bill, drafted in consultation with Sexton, Dillon, T. P. O'Connor and Arthur O'Connor, and evidently without reference to either Healy, was as Morley later observed 'not brilliantly framed'.[77] After discussions with the Liberals, the bill was published on 14 September. Parnell's gracefully professed hopes of cross-party support were disappointed, and the bill was lost.[78] Its introduction had served Parnell's purpose. He could thenceforth fairly claim to have done everything he could to pre-empt a renewal of agrarian agitation in Ireland.

The initiative thus reverted to Parnell's restive lieutenants in Ireland. The 'Plan of Campaign' originated with an article which appeared in *United Ireland* on 23 October 1886. The Plan contemplated the collective proffering by the tenants on particular estates of reduced rents; if the rent tendered was refused, the monies were to be applied to the sustainment of tenants ejected for the non-payment of rent.[79]

Bereft of historical imagination and political judgement, the Plan was a misconceived attempt to re-enact the heroic phase of the land struggle, 1878–82, in altered social conditions. Notionally spontaneous and decentralised, it was in fact conducted under the direction of John Dillon and William O'Brien. Riven by contradictions, it strove uneasily to marry the concept of an agrarian cartel with a stylised nationalist struggle against 'coercion'. William Martin Murphy declared of the Plan: 'Their policy was to form a gigantic Trade Union, the same as the existing Trade Unions, to get from under the control of capital, and if the tenant farmers can only stick together they can accomplish a similar object'.[80] That an adversary of trades unionism such as Murphy felt able to commend the Plan in these terms attested to its deep-seated incoherence.

The idea was not novel. Healy later claimed it originated from a suggestion of Parnell. Angered by the failure of the 'no-rent' manifesto, he had told Healy on his release from Kilmainham that he would never head another agrarian movement unless the tenants lodged 75 per cent of their rents in a common fund.[81] Healy had advanced a concept very close to that of the Plan of Campaign as early as June 1883, and again in August and October 1885, on the last occasion suggesting a centralised national policy rather than one decentralised to individual estates.[82]

Healy's position differed from that of Dillon and O'Brien. He had little interest in the attempted mobilisation of Irish tenant farmers to radicalise and re-energise the nationalist movement. His overriding objective was to create the political and economic conditions favourable to land purchase on the most advantageous terms possible. His position was that expressed in a *United Ireland* leading article of 15 August 1885 entitled 'Are the Farmers Fools?', which asserted that tenants, 'by a little combination and forethought, could regulate the price of land'.[83]

Parnell would repeatedly insist that he was not consulted about the Plan. This was substantially correct. William O'Brien claimed to have discussed it with him, but evidently only generally in terms of a strategy of agrarian resistance in the event of the defeat of Parnell's Tenants' Relief Bill. (Labouchere wrote to Gladstone in January 1887 after meeting Healy, Dillon and O'Brien that 'they said it was not exactly correct that Parnell had known nothing of the "plan of campaign" because O'Brien had come over to consult him before it was inaugurated'.) Sexton warned Healy not to support the Plan, on the grounds that Parnell had not been consulted, and would resent his doing so.[84]

The Liberal leadership sought urgently to make contact with Parnell. Morley wrote to Gladstone on 15 November that 'P. has gone completely underground'. When Morley eventually met Parnell on 7 December, their encounter revealed with what care Parnell had chosen his ground. Morley reported to Gladstone:

> He had been very ill and in the hands of his surgeons, and he has taken no part in the direction of the campaign: he is therefore entirely free and uncommitted. He was anxious to have it fully understood that the fixed point in his tactics is to maintain the alliance with the English Liberals.

When Morley criticised a recent speech of Dillon's, Parnell had made 'some remarks on Dillon's impetuosity when on his feet', then fell back on a narrow construction of the offending remarks, and finally agreed to urge Dillon to explain away what he had said.

> As to the 'plan of campaign' generally, I told him that the dishonest character of the operation (viewed apart from its true nature as an act of war) offended our people almost more deeply than outrages themselves. He could not help that: they must break the power of the landlords, as the class that stood between them and self-government; that the tenants had first not very willingly looked at the plan of campaign; that when

> the Government struck at Dillon, then the young men were roused and made the elders go for it, and at this moment there was every sign that it might become a very dangerous movement indeed.

It was a classic essay in Parnell's political technique. He agreed to send for 'a certain of his lieutenants', and press for an immediate cessation of the inflammatory speeches, and a modification of the tone of *United Ireland.*

> Of course, he referred with most justifiable bitterness to the fact that when Ireland seemed to be quiet some short time back, the Government at once began to draw away from all their promises of remedial legislation. If now, rents were paid, meetings abandoned, and newspapers moderated, the same would happen. However he would do almost anything to prevent weak men in the English camp from having an excuse for deserting.[85]

Parnell duly summoned William O'Brien to meet him behind the Greenwich observatory. The spectral apparition of Parnell, emerging from the chill early morning fog clad like some bizarre huntsman, is mythically limned in O'Brien's memoirs. The account given by O'Brien in the proof of his intended evidence to the Special Commission does not differ substantially from the later account in his memoirs, but makes explicit that an outright repudiation of the Plan by Parnell would have risked precipitating his and Dillon's resignation:

> He told me he had had a dangerous attack of illness, and looked so ill that he terrified me. He looked so fagged and ill that I had not the heart to argue with him. I simply told him that the tenants were coming imploring advice, and that there was a most frightful danger of their relapsing into crime and into secret societies, and that having nobody to consult with a few of us had, at our own risk, hit upon this as a plan that would at once give confidence to the tenants and keep them from crime . . .
>
> The Government had at that time struck at us publicly, and I told him that we had now our backs to the wall and must fight it out to the death; that the only possible alternative to Mr. Dillon and myself was a withdrawal from public life, and this we would of course most cheerfully do, and in the friendliest possible manner, for we would rather cut off our right arms than do the smallest mischief consciously, to the movement, or to his leadership. He said that withdrawal would be fatal, and that he, of course, recognised that we were bound to fight out the struggles on which the tenants had already entered, but he insisted that we should not ourselves induce any new body of tenants to join the Plan, and this I at once agreed to.[86]

According to O'Brien's *Evening Memories*, published in 1920, Parnell was relieved to learn of the moderate spirit in which the Plan of Campaign had been commenced, 'and in particular to find that, of the two members of the Party of whom he was beginning to entertain a settled distrust, one [Dillon] was potential chiefly by the multiplicity of his speeches, and the other [Healy] had, to my own deep regret ceased to interfere at all'. O'Brien had characterised Healy's role to Parnell as that of 'a friendly outsider'.[87]

Parnell reported to Morley on 12 December that he had conveyed his disapproval of the violence of the language recently used and of the Plan itself. When Morley said Gladstone could not countenance illegality, Parnell replied that he understood 'but was anxious that there should be as little in the way of public disavowal as might be. He is fully alive to the mischief that the affair has done to opinion in this country'.[88]

Healy remained circumspect, holding back from an endorsement of the Plan of Campaign. In a letter to Labouchere in early November, which was subsequently shown to Morley, Healy explained that he had refrained from addressing agrarian meetings

> though Dillon and O'Brien have gone on the war-path, because it is not clear to me yet what is the best line to take, and besides I think Parnell should give the note, so that nobody may get above concert pitch. What Parnell's views are I don't know, and he is the man on the horse.

Morley conveyed to Gladstone the contents of a further letter from Healy to Labouchere in early December. Healy professed to believe the Plan, which he claimed as his own invention, would spread, and be used against good landlords as well as bad, giving rise to the prospect of a widespread breakdown in the payment of rent, and to a crash when landlords found themselves unable to meet encumbrances.[89]

Healy told a National League meeting in Dublin on 30 November that 'the duty at the present time before the Irish people was to walk wisely and cautiously in the path before them', to avoid giving the government excuses for coercion, and to be sensitive to the constraints of the Liberal alliance. This was a matter for the judgement of 'the men who were more hotly engaged in the struggle than himself'.[90]

On 7 December, the day of his interview with Parnell, Morley wrote to Gladstone that 'Healy is complained of for standing aloof'. That evening in Dublin, Healy defended the Plan while elaborately eschewing personal responsibility for the fate of participating tenants:

> The tenants of Ireland have now, in my opinion, the means of winning, but this League has in no way forced the tenants of Ireland into any plan or scheme of any kind. If tenants like, or if their circumstances lead them to pay their full rents without abatements that is their own affair . . . But where men of resolution, of courage, adopt a different course they will have the blessing of every honest man in the country.[91]

If Healy's endorsement of the Plan was notably tentative, his agrarian rhetoric was of unbridled vehemence:

> If men allow themselves to be evicted out of their property by means of bad seasons, I say by reason of the circumstances over which they have no control – if they allow themselves to be hunted out like vermin and like rats and dogs, then they deserve the fate of rats and dogs (*applause*). But if they stand up and resist, then what will happen to them is what has always happened in Ireland, the law will be changed to suit them (*applause*) . . . the whole history of this country is and of its success is the history of defiance in the law (*applause*).[92]

The Irish people, he declared the following month, would take 'a moderate course if they can, and a desperate course if they must'.[93]

Healy's laxly opportunistic stance on the Plan of Campaign was to serve him well. His rhetoric in defence of the Plan, and his appearances as counsel on behalf of Dillon and O'Brien in the prosecutions which ensued, were coupled with a careful avoidance of involvement in its direction. The split would reveal just how astutely calculated Healy's position was in permitting him, notwithstanding the equivocality of his own role, mercilessly to assail Parnell for standing aloof from the Plan, and for indifference to the fate of the evicted tenants in its course.

While Dillon and O'Brien were aggrieved by Healy's lack of participation in the Plan, their relations with him remained amicable up to the split. What they most dreaded was an open rift between Healy and Parnell. Writing on Christmas Eve to allay Healy's concern that he and Dillon were acting without reference to him, William O'Brien added presciently:

> The only possible ground of estrangement between us (and it is with the utmost sorrow that we ever saw its shadow come between us) is as to Parnell – as to whom there is nothing more unalterably fixed in my mind than that he is the corner-stone of our cause, and that the moment I would feel bound to renounce a frank allegiance to him would be my last in public life.[94]

Parnell's aloofness from the Plan of Campaign continued to exasperate its chief promoters in Ireland. Their resentment was constrained, in O'Brien's case by his personal attachment to Parnell, and by the awed admiration in which Dillon held his tactical acumen. Dillon proffered a somewhat crude assessment of Parnell's policy to John Morley at the end of November 1887. Morley relayed to Gladstone Dillon's professed view that the Fenian section were coming to the fore, and

> that the only man who can put down the Fenian section is Parnell; that Parnell has been absolutely invisible since the end of the session and will

> doubtless remain so; that in this Parnell is taking a very astute line, as he will be able to point to any trouble which the Fenians give as evidence of the inability of the Government to keep the country quiet, and of the mischief done by the refusal of his policy.[95]

Parnell bided his time. By May 1888 he was in a position boldly to vaunt his reservations regarding the Plan of Campaign, and, balancing with superb assurance the English and Irish theatres of policy, to re-assert his supremacy. Speaking at the Liberal Eighty Club in London, he gave the Plan only the most grudging *ex post facto* support, on express conditions. He claimed that he had been ill at the time of its inception. By early 1887, when he was better, the imprisonment of Dillon and O'Brien had precluded disavowal of the Plan on his part.[96]

Parnell remained careful to avoid an actual repudiation of the Plan which could have precipitated the resignation of Dillon and O'Brien, and exposed him to an out-flanking movement on the nationalist left. He looked to strengthen his own role, in Ireland and at Westminster, as a restraining force. His approach reflected a cruelly prescient contempt for the judgement of the promoters of the Plan. He awaited the out-turn of events, bleakly confident that the failure of his lieutenants' initiative would render them dependent on him to extricate them from their difficulty. While his judgement of the Plan was penetratingly accurate, the apparent coldness of his reserve was to tell heavily against him in the split.

Parnell's speech produced a crisis in his relations with O'Brien and Dillon.[97] In July, O'Brien wrote to Dillon, who was in prison in Dundalk, that 'relations between Parnell and myself are still strained to the point of frigidity'. O'Brien was concerned to ensure that at any one time either he or Dillon should be at large: 'I think Healy will do us an occasionally good turn, but the more I think of it the less I like the prospect of our being in together, so I shall do nothing foolish'.[98] Parnell's confidence in the strength of O'Brien's allegiance to him was not misplaced. In the next missive, after the *Times* allegations against Parnell had been revived, he wrote: 'Late troubles have thrown the Chief and myself very intimately together again. I think he recognises now his mistake in attempting to crush us'. Parnell however would not agree to the creation of a special American fund for the Plan of Campaign.[99] He next reported 'Parnell and myself getting on famously'. Parnell had 'no objection that a good many of our men should be run in this winter. Many of them are fit for nothing else'.[100]

Parnell's Absences

From the end of 1886 Parnell suffered intermittent bouts of serious illness. With that economy of manner which was an aspect of his hubris, he did not scruple to avail politically of the cover his illness provided. However he was genuinely ill, and his initial concern was to suppress any reference to his physical condition. Morley wrote to Gladstone after seeing Parnell in December 1886 that he was 'anxious not a word should come out as to his health just now'.[101]

Parnell did little to allay the unease of the members of his party caused by his absences and rumoured illness. E. W. Hamilton wrote to Gladstone on 19 December 1886, referring to the Irish party, 'I hear there is a good deal of dissatisfaction in those quarters at the total disappearance of Parnell'.[102] Labouchere seized on the private grumblings of the Irish as verification of his *idée fixe* that Parnell's leadership of the Irish party was essentially titular. After meeting Dillon, O'Brien and Healy in early January 1887 he wrote to Gladstone:

> They complain a good deal, between ourselves, of Parnell keeping in the background, and they say that they go on as though he does not exist, for they know that he will accept anything they may do. He is in fact, becoming more and more a King Log every day, and becoming more and more touchy, if they suggest that he should take more active interest in what is going on.[103]

Labouchere continued to play upon the anxieties created by Parnell's absences for his own ends. He reported to Herbert Gladstone on 21 June that 'in the Irish party, there is the most angry feeling respecting Parnell, on account of his almost entirely absenting himself, and not leaving any directions'. He claimed that Parnell 'has developed a great jealousy of his authority, and he is especially jealous of Dillon', whose moving of the adjournment in the House some days previously he had deprecated.[104]

Parnell's absences, as well as giving rise to concern among the members of his party, created difficulties for the Liberals. Morley wrote to Gladstone on 5 October 1887 that he would do his best to find out where Parnell was and if possible to meet him 'even at the cost of sea-voyage'.[105] Parnell was at this time seriously ill. McCarthy monitored the intermittent appearances of the Irish leader at Westminster. On 18 May 1887, he was horrified by Parnell's appearance:

> Only one impression was produced among all who saw him – the ghastly face, the wasted form, the glassy eyes gleaming, looking like the terrible corpse-candles of Welsh superstition. If ever death shone in a face it shone in that. I came on John Morley a moment after. We could both only say in one breath 'Good God! have you seen Parnell?'

The following month he still looked deathly. By July he was somewhat improved. Later that month he took the chair at the first meeting of the party he had attended for some time. 'But fancy, on such a burning day as this, he wore a thick outside coat and soft felt hat — and he shivered so often.'[106] H. W. Lucy in *Punch* described Parnell turning up in the Commons 'looking like a ghost'.[107]

The strength and subtlety of Parnell's political strategy after the defeat of the home rule bill and the return of a unionist government have been underrated then and since. His biographer R. B. O'Brien wrote:

> Throughout the years 1887, 1888, and 1889 Parnell remained comparatively inactive, as he had remained throughout the years 1883, 1884, and part of 1885, and for the same reasons — public policy, health and Mrs. O'Shea. His health seems to have been in a precarious state all the time. He appeared to me during the latter years to be morbidly nervous.

In giving primacy to the political, Barry O'Brien's argument was astute as well as apologetical. He added that 'when we speak of Parnell's comparative inactivity, we must never forget that — rightly or wrongly — Parnell was at this period in favour of an inactive policy'.[108] Yet to describe it as 'inactive' is not an altogether adequate characterisation of Parnell's policy.

In terms of home rule, it was a period of enforced passivity. Parnell was determined to ensure that the prospects for home rule were not compromised by nationalist impatience or miscalculation. Although blocked from making progress on this front, his strategy was not quiescent. He strove to entrench the Liberal–nationalist alliance, while maintaining the maximum freedom of action within it. He sought to counteract the deepening polarisation of British and Irish politics on the home rule issue, chiefly by the ostentatiously moderate tenor of his leadership and his policy on land purchase. In championing a limited measure of land purchase he sought to play off the Liberals against the Conservative government, and to allay Irish unionist fears by ensuring the retention, albeit on a reduced scale, of a viable class of residential landlords. Within nationalism he sought to contain the Plan of Campaign, and sought to thwart those such as Healy who looked to the wholesale displacement of the landlords.

Parnell's conflating of his ill-health and his political tactics, which owed much to the exigencies of his affair with Katharine O'Shea, was to prove perhaps the greatest single miscalculation of his career. In the split Healy was relentlessly to indict Parnell on the charge of abdicating his political responsibilities to pursue his affair with Katharine O'Shea on the pretext of ill-health. It was a charge that Parnell, cast in the role of a leader seeking desperately to throw into reverse a process of withdrawal from active leadership over the previous years, struggled unavailingly to rebut.

Healy had severed his connexion with *United Ireland* after the Galway election. For a few months in 1887 he resumed contributing a parliamentary letter to the *Nation*. Even though he took care to express no criticisms of Parnell – rather the reverse – he knew that Parnell would regard with suspicion the resumption of his involvement with the *Nation*, as a step in the direction of the formation of a '*Nation* party' to which he had so pointedly alluded in conversation with Healy immediately after the acquisition of Pigott's newspapers in 1881.

Healy assailed Balfour's coercion legislation, and the changes in parliamentary procedure which facilitated its enactment. In his *Nation* letter, in what was in one of its aspects a sentimental reversion to their old relationship of leader and sketch-writer, he lauded Parnell's return to spirited leadership of the Irish resistance as reminiscent of the heroic days of obstruction. In March he wrote 'Is it 1887 to 1878? . . . Never since his earlier struggles has Mr. Parnell developed more energy or watchfulness than he is showing now, throwing himself into a discussion of every technicality as if he were as friendless and unsupported as in the days when everything depended on his single arm'. Two weeks later he wrote 'there has been nothing more skilful in Parnell's parliamentary career than his tactics and speeches in these Cloture debates'.[109] Healy was to some extent overstating Parnell's return to a vigorous parliamentary role to allay mounting unease as to his physical condition. Morley wrote of the same debates 'Parnell was in bad health and took little part but he made more than one pulverising attack in that measured and frigid style which . . . may be so much more awkward for a minister than more florid onslaughts'.[110]

In the opposition to Balfour, the solidarity of the Liberal—nationalist alliance was sealed. Healy wrote of the Liberals: ' . . . whereas a year ago the Gladstonian Home Rulers were hesitatingly doubting, unsure-footed travellers upon a path carved out for them by a veteran pioneer, they are now a convinced and compact army who know every foot of the ground themselves. . . . Home Rule has now mastered their intellect and their hearts'.[111] In his description of the scene on the first application of the cloture to the coercion bill, Healy's encomium to Gladstone was positively embarrassing ('the old veteran is got up like a bride, his evening dress creaseless and lustrous, orchid in buttonhole, without a crumple in his historic collar, and his tie set as square as if it had been arranged in his wife's looking glass'). His heroic rendering of Gladstone's leading the Liberal party out of the Commons after the government had carried its cloture resolution ('the destruction of Grattan's Parliament is being revenged') revealed his excessive susceptibility to the Liberal leader's allure.[112]

At Westminster, Parnell's absence created practical difficulties. At a meeting on 5 May, Harrington prudently dissuaded the party from carrying in Parnell's absence a resolution to constitute a legal committee of the party to draw up amendments to the coercion bill, in which Parnell would certainly have discerned a challenge to his authority.[113] The party inevitably was compelled to look to the Liberals for guidance. Morley wrote Gladstone on 30 May that Healy had sent him a communication 'to the effect that they would do in respect of amendments whatever we wished – and in fact seeking a lead from our bench'.[114]

By this time the subject of Parnell's health, carefully played down in the nationalist press in Ireland, was the subject of much comment and speculation in British newspapers. In the *Nation* Healy wrote that the Irish party had suffered keenly from Parnell's absence: '"There is na luck aboot the House when our gudeman's awa"'. A brief resumption of attendance by Parnell in June prompted from Healy an extended and melancholy panegyric, which, in the explicitness with which it addressed the subject of Parnell's health, and its disquieting mawkishness of tone, can only have alarmed his readers in Ireland:

> Mr. Parnell's return to the House in restored health is a bitter disappointment to the enemies of Ireland. Those who see only friendly Irish papers can form no notion of the brood of malignant stories as to the physical condition of the Irish leader circulated by Tory manipulators in the English and foreign press. Not only was he suffering from a hopeless and deadly malady, but even were there any chance of his recovery his return to political life was all but impossible. He was 'dispirited' and 'disgusted', and already for his garments they cast lots. His following was reduced to chaos, and the time-honoured 'split' had not only taken place but was become a chasm, and the great Irish party which had stood inflexibly through twenty-seven sessions would never trouble its enemies more . . . Mr. Parnell, however, with his usual bad taste has indecently got well again . . . That Mr. Parnell was at all vitally affected none of his friends ever believed, knowing the toughness of a magnificent physique that has defied many a strain; nevertheless, as his absence grew prolonged they could scarefuly remain unaffected by the exhalation from festering rumours engendered daily in a hundred broadsheets. The pale and wasted aspect of their leader on his first visit to the House, on returning from Avondale three weeks ago, therefore, gave rise to gloomy concern in the hearts of men who, year in year out, for many a night outwatched the stars, or bore captivity side by side or cell by cell with him. The mind went back to many a stormy time when the tide of battle was turned by that valorous and undaunted heart whose craft had knit together the sundered units of the sea-divided Gael, with mournful questionings of the future if indeed that heart were stilled; for differ with Mr. Parnell how men may, both friends and enemies alike discern that though he might be succeeded, he could never be replaced.[115]

Healy's commentary was a strange palimpsest: the private graffiti of disenchantment was still legible through the calligraphy of public tribute.

On a strict Parnellite reading, betrayal was implicit in every line. It is difficult not to read back into this passage Healy's brutally physical idiom in the split, and his avowed determination to allow Parnell no quarter on the subject of his alleged abnegation of his responsibilities as leader, remorselessly ascribed to the frailties of the flesh in their moral rather than physical aspect.

The passage was not cynically conceived, nor without a certain poignancy. In a psychologically complex movement, Healy was endeavouring to resuscitate some of his old affection for Parnell by the contemplation of his physical condition, and of the iniquity of the Tory enemy they had in common. He sought to whip himself into a sentimental enthusiasm by evoking the heroic early years of obstruction, engaging in a strenuous *recherche du temps perdu* which elided the souring reservations he held even then. It was an elegy for allegiance: in the willed nostalgia was inscribed an intimation of the ineluctability of schism.

Crossing to London in mid-June for the debates on Balfour's Criminal Law Amendment Bill, Healy was injured in a train collision in Euston Station. Compelled to rest, he departed on a tour of Germany and Switzerland, having entrusted his draft amendments to the bill to P. A. Chance. On his travels he kept up a fretful commentary on parliamentary affairs in his letters to Maurice. His views were a *reprise* of those expressed in his correspondence of 1878–80: criticism of what he saw as Parnell's complacency and inertia, and a restless demand for an indeterminate policy of parliamentary activity.

In Constance he wrote 'let me know how Parnell is, and if he is working again!' From Zurich he despatched a sustained critique of the inactivity of Parnell and the Liberal leadership in the face of the application of the cloture to the bill. He supposed the Liberal party dispirited by the split in its ranks, and the Irish party 'completely demoralised by Parnell's absence'. Unless the Liberals re-asserted themselves,

> our Party will make a fatal mistake unless it is aggressively led. There is no development to be expected from within, and the Party contains some worthless elements. There is all the more necessity therefore for tactical skill and alertness on the part of its Chief . . . Unless something is done within a few sessions a feeling of numbness may creep over our people at home and abroad, and the unity of the party may suffer – which it never could do, even with failure only to point to, if Parnell would not rest on his oars.[116]

From Interlaken he wrote on 5 July:

> The Spalding election is first rate, and goes far to justify the attitude of the Liberals. Still, I cannot get out of my head that the Kingdom of Heaven

> is 'taken by violence'. Except Gladstone, there is no effective helper of Ireland on the Opposition benches. Harcourt, if his heart were in the work would be magnificent, but he has not enough conscience in the business, and Morley is no parliamentarian.

He added ambivalently 'if Parnell's health would have allowed him, I think it was deplorable he did not say something against Smith's closure motion'.[117]

On his return, Healy, still not perhaps entirely recovered, was in fractious form. In a debate on the Irish Land Law Bill on 28 July he permitted himself to be provoked by the interruptions of an English member, De Lisle, who sat for Mid- Leicestershire. He called out De Lisle 'if you are a man', and threatened to break his neck if he interrupted him again. Justin McCarthy wrote:

> We had a stormy scene there yesterday. Healy lost his temper and his head because of some interruption from an English Catholic called De Lisle and he used insufferable language to De Lisle: and in spite of all Parnell could urge, he would not apologise and was suspended. We did not vote against the suspension: we let it go without even challenging a division. Parnell and most of us felt that we could not in any way seem to defend Healy's conduct. For the first time in the history of the party an Irish member was suspended without any protest or intervention on the part of his colleagues. The newspapers I have seen don't appear to understand this, or even to take notice of it; and they describe the scene as if we were supporting Healy. And this though Parnell sent for the clerk of the House and told him to tell the Speaker that we did not intend to oppose the motion or challenge a division. It was all very painful. I like Healy so much: but we could not support him.

Healy knew his position was untenable. He begged that none of his friends voted against the motion for his suspension, and walked out of the chamber.[118]

He renewed his private criticisms of Parnell. On 27 August he wrote to his brother that Parnell had arrived in the Commons 'but didn't seem to take the least interest in what was going on'.[119] While Healy in the split would assail Parnell for culpable neglect of his responsibilities, which he attributed to his affair with Katharine O'Shea, he was well aware of what Parnell's strategy was intended to achieve. In his 1898 polemic against Dillon he wrote that 'the policy recommended for the management of the Irish movement by Mr. Parnell was to allow the situation quietly to ripen, and await the play of English strife . . . In this situation he gave for the guidance of the Irish Movement the simple command "Mark Time"'.[120]

7

The Special Commission:
Parnellism and Crime

On 7 March 1887 the *Times* commenced publication of a series of articles under the title of 'Parnellism and Crime' which charged Parnell, and other members of the Irish party and leaders of the Land League, with direct complicity in political crime in Ireland. It culminated with the publication on 18 April of a facsimile of a letter purportedly from Parnell which implicated him in the Phoenix Park murders. A clumsy and improbable forgery, it commanded widespread credence.

Among Parnell's unionist adversaries there was a persisting conviction that his apparent transcendence of the sordid and criminal intrigues to which they believed the nationalist movement was reducible was a deftly contrived but fragile illusion. Even among Gladstonian Liberals there was an uneasy apprehension that Parnell's unnatural perfection as a constitutional nationalist leader could not survive sustained scrutiny.

Three days before the publication of the forged letter, the Ulster unionist Col. Edward Saunderson had charged in the Commons that Parnell and his associates had consorted with those they knew to be murderers. Healy called him a liar, and refusing to withdraw the statement was suspended. He left bowing to the chair amid cheers from the Irish members who rose and waved their hats.[1]

Immediately on the publication of the Parnell letter, Healy correctly concluded that it had been forged by Richard Pigott, and so advised Labouchere. In the *Nation* he dismissed as 'simply grotesque' the idea that

Parnell would write such a letter: 'if instead of the authority of the *Times* for its authenticity, this was deposed to by a seraph before a Commissioner of Affidavits, it would not carry conviction to my mind'. Yet he went on to develop a disquieting distinction between the enduring nature of the nationalist demand and the transience of its exponents.

> If, instead of being charged with murder, a dozen Parnellites were hanged for being murderers, the vacancies created would simply be supplied by fresh elections, and the Irish problem would still confront the English people, and call even more clamantly for action. The notion that a cause seven centuries old, depends merely on the character of its ephemeral spokesmen springs from foolish brains. If the *Times*, instead of conniving at the moral assassination of Mr. Parnell, employed its hirelings to actually slay him, and with him all his party, would the government of Ireland be simplified or the rental of Ireland become more collectable?

In taking out a nationalist policy of insurance against the destruction of Parnell, Healy's concerns went beyond the Pigott forgeries. While Parnell might survive the immediate crisis, the greater peril of the disclosure of his relations with Katharine O'Shea lay beyond.[2]

Parnell declined to pick up the gauntlet flung down by the *Times*, and wisely refused to be provoked into a libel action at that time. He confined himself to a repudiation of the letter as a forgery in the Commons. His denial, which dwelt excessively on the idiosyncrasies of his own handwriting, fell somewhat flat.[3]

The crisis ebbed temporarily. Healy the following week permitted himself a jab at the eponymous W. H. Smith, then the Leader of the House of Commons, whose business sold cheap reprints of the *Times* articles, as 'an unimaginative old bookseller'. Three months later, with the practised eye of a master-polemicist, he suggested the Tories had miscalculated the tempo of their attack:

> 'Parnellism and Crime' was very well for two or three weeks, but like other strong medicines whose dose had to be increased, that purgative had ceased to work. The *Times* should have begun by charges of minor offences against the decalogue, and then worked up gradually according to electoral exigencies, whereas now the repetition of its stale charges of the most hideous crime fail to create any effect.[4]

It was a false lull. Parnell's former rival for ascendancy among the obstructionists, F. H. O'Donnell, whose unimportance was surpassed only by his self-regard, instituted libel proceedings against the *Times* arising out of the 'Parnellism and Crime' articles in which he had been peripherally mentioned. The proceedings were curiously – some thought suspiciously

– misconceived, as well as badly conducted. Not merely did O'Donnell lose, but the Attorney-General, Sir Richard Webster, who appeared for the *Times* in the course of his successful application for a non-suit at the end of O'Donnell's case introduced new allegations, including further incriminating letters, against Parnell and other Land League leaders.[5]

Following the failure of the action, Parnell was quick to dissociate himself from O'Donnell. He said that he had no communication with O'Donnell on that or any other matter. 'I have kept Mr. O'Donnell consistently at arm's length – I may say at pole's length – and have declined to meet him or write to him.' He added that he had returned proofs of evidence forwarded by O'Donnell. This was misleading. While Parnell had had no part in O'Donnell's decision to institute the proceedings, he had met with O'Donnell's solicitor R. A. Biale. Biale replied to Parnell's statement by citing a letter from Michael Davitt on Parnell's behalf offering assistance in the case, and asserting that thereafter 'every step and proceeding in the course of the recent action against the *Times* were communicated to Mr. Parnell personally in this office or his representative Mr. Davitt'. Parnell moreover was in court for part of the case. Although he had intimated to O'Donnell's solicitor that he preferred not to be called, he later told the Commons that he had been present in court in the expectation of being called as a witness to answer on oath the charges made, but 'the unexpected turn which the case took deprived me of that opportunity'.[6]

The *Times* exulted: 'We have never written one word to suggest that Mr. O'Donnell, distinguished while a member of the House of Commons for his vanity, his garrulity, his inconsequence, but certainly for nothing worse, was of the stuff of which conspirators of that sort are made'.[7] Well-informed contemporaries were at a loss to account for O'Donnell's decision to sue the *Times*. E. W. Hamilton wrote:

> What on earth induced him to bring this action one cannot say. There are all kinds of stories put forward. It may have been an attempt to clear his former colleagues; or it may equally have been an attempt, with or without the connivance of the *Times* itself, to make it hot for those from whom he had separated himself by compelling a disclosure of the evidence on which the *Times* had rested its case. He may have been merely activated by motives of personal vanity.[8]

Many nationalists were inclined to believe that something more sinister than vanity lay behind O'Donnell's action. In his memoirs Healy noted that O'Donnell lacked the resources to mount an action against the *Times*, and left open the question as to 'whether, in provoking this bogus trial under the pretence that he had been attacked, O'Donnell was merely spiteful or an agent for (or in collusion with) an undisclosed principal'. Such suspicions were widely canvassed at the time, prompting Davitt to intervene within days of the collapse of the action to categorise allegations of collusion on O'Donnell's part with the *Times* as 'a most unjust aspersion'.[9]

The *Times* the following month reported that O'Donnell had written from Italy to his solicitor instructing him to institute proceedings for libel against Parnell. However, the paper reported that counsel had advised against an action, and that O'Donnell's further instructions were awaited. This most unusual disclosure of professional advices could only have emanated from O'Donnell or Biale. The *Freeman's Journal* subsequently published a short paragraph summarising a letter from O'Donnell to the effect that Parnell had denied that he had ever suggested there was any collusion between O'Donnell and the *Times*.[10]

The disreputable Philip ('Phil') Callan, whose defeat in North Louth Parnell had procured in 1885, was O'Donnell's foremost collaborator in his proceedings against the *Times* and made a perhaps decisive contribution to their institution. Alfred Robbins wrote in the *Birmingham Daily Post* that O'Donnell 'is known to have brought the action out of no love for Mr. Parnell, seeing that he has nursed a bitter dislike towards his old leader for some years, and that his chief adviser throughout has been Mr. Callan, the ex-member for Louth, who likewise considers himself to have received harsh treatment at Mr. Parnell's hands'. This was almost certainly written with Parnell's direct authority: indeed Callan subsequently approached Robbins to threaten libel proceedings unless Robbins told him whether Parnell had inspired the report.[11] There was indeed a matrix of collusion underpinning the proceedings. The villain of the piece is likely however to have been Callan rather than O'Donnell, even if the latter's preposterous self-regard rendered him a uniquely avid dupe.

Wemyss Reid of the *Leeds Mercury* informed Labouchere that Callan had shown the Parnell letters to Herbert Gladstone some days before their publication. At the request of Parnell's solicitor, George Lewis, Labouchere wrote to Gladstone seeking confirmation of this, 'and also whether Callan told you anything which might lead to how he got hold of them'. Labouchere wrote the same day to W. E. Gladstone:

> The matter has a certain importance. Callan is now employed by the *Times*. It may be that he was consulted about the authenticity of the letter, or that Houston spoke to him about it. It may also be that he was mixed up with Pigott in the forgeries. This Pigott denies, but of course, no great dependence can be placed on what he says.[12]

The *Times* was desperately anxious to elicit evidence damaging to Parnell from former members of the Irish party estranged from him. Healy wrote in his memoirs that John O'Connor Power, whom he considered a renegade, 'rejected overtures from the *Times* to "form" against former colleagues at the Forgery Commission', and added that another ex-M.P. 'privately gave information to little purpose'.[13]

Some light is shed on the stratagems to which the *Times* resorted in the remarkable narrative contained in the proof of evidence prepared for the Special Commission of Thomas Quinn, who had been elected for Kilkenny in July 1886.[14]

While a member of the party of negligible stature, Quinn was a natural target for the *Times*. If the paper's allegations were upheld, he was vulnerable on circumstantial grounds. He had been treasurer of the Land League in England when it had as its secretary Frank Byrne, who was an accessory to the Phoenix Park murders. Byrne's brother — who was also suspected of involvement — had served his time as a bricklayer to Quinn, and been employed by him. Around Christmas 1882, pleading illness, Byrne went to France. From Cannes he wrote to Quinn on 10 February 1883 remitting some Land League funds. (Two days previously Byrne had written to the executive of the Land League in England acknowledging receipt of £100 from Parnell on the day he left London, a letter to which the *Times* attached great weight as evidence that Parnell had financed Byrne's flight from justice.) An attempt to extradite Byrne from France failed, and he prepared to leave for the United States. The day before he left Quinn went to see him in Le Havre to collect an accounts book and to check accounts. Apart from his dealings with Byrne, the *Times* is likely to have considered Quinn susceptible by reason of the parlous state of his personal finances.[15]

Three weeks before O'Donnell's action came on for hearing, his solicitor R. A. Biale asked to see Quinn. On the assurance that Parnell was taking a part in the proceedings, Quinn gave Biale two letters from Byrne, one of which was the Cannes letter of 10 February. On 3 July 1888, cross-examining a journalist called on behalf of O'Donnell, Sir Henry James for the *Times* put to him the names of various nationalists to ascertain whether they fell into the category of Parnellite leaders. The names included, improbably, that of Thomas Quinn.[16] Quinn had good reason to feel alarmed. The next day in court he met Callan who asked him, 'what about those letters of yours that you gave Biale?' The *Times* had learnt of the letters he had entrusted to O'Donnell's solicitors.

The former nationalist member for Ennis, the barrister Lysaght Finegan, pestered Quinn that day and the next. On 6 July he caught up with Quinn on a train. In his proof of evidence, Quinn stated that he tried to shake Finegan off: 'I had the idea for some time that Finegan had a softening of the brain, and was a little bit off his head. That was one of the reasons I did not want to continue talking to him'. He agreed to meet him later, but first went with a solicitor to see R. A. Biale to find out how Byrne's letter had come to the knowledge of the *Times*. On entering Biale's office, he found O'Donnell and Finegan discussing the breakdown of the case the previous day. Biale provided an extraordinary explanation as to how the *Times* had the letter, claiming that 'Callan got into his office one morning, in his absence, and took copies of certain documents, and that there was no doubt about it that this was how the *Times* came into possession of the contents of the documents'.

That afternoon in the Commons, Finegan again sought Quinn out. Finegan insisted it was important for Quinn to accompany him to see a barrister who had something extremely important to tell him. Quinn reluctantly agreed. After a cab ride to Lincoln's Inn Fields he was ushered into the office of Joseph Soames, the solicitor to the *Times*, to whom Finegan introduced him. Soames, according to Quinn, asked him whether he was aware that the government were going to prosecute the Irish members for treason, and that Quinn was bound to get fifteen years imprisonment. In an attempt to get Quinn to provide information, Soames referred to his meeting with Frank Byrne at Le Havre, and accused him of providing money to Byrne to get out of the country. When Quinn referred to the Parnell letters as forgeries, he was taken aback when Soames produced the original of Byrne's letter to the Land League in England of 8 February. Soames and Finegan urged him to make a clean breast of it. Quinn declined as he had nothing to admit to. As he got up to leave, Soames asked him how his business was getting on. He threw out a hint that money might be forthcoming, and referred to a property which Quinn had at one time discussed selling to a company of which John Walter, the proprietor of the *Times*, and the Prime Minister Lord Salisbury, were directors. Quinn stated that he went to the Commons to seek out Parnell or T. P. O'Connor 'but did not wish to have it published, and for one thing I wanted to keep Lysaght Finegan's name out of it'.[17]

While Quinn did not give evidence at the Special Commission and his account is uncorroborated, there is no obvious reason to doubt the general veracity of what he told Parnell's solicitors, Lewis and Lewis. His account suggests how far the *Times* was prepared to go in the use of the most dubious means, and the creation of a climate of fear. The paper's desperate endeavours reflected an intimation that all was lost if it could not, in the immediate aftermath of the publication of the Parnell letters, succeed in generating independent verification of the allegations against him.

Parnell's dilemma after the failure of O'Donnell's action was unenviable. Even Liberal observers in England were markedly uncertain of the degree of innocence which he could demonstrate, and unsure of the course he should adopt. E. W. Hamilton wrote in his diary:

> Parnell and company have had a terrible indictment brought against them and unless they take the challenge up, the inference will be that they don't dare face inquiry. That they will not proceed against the *Times* is certain. Among other considerations which may deter them is the doubt whether they would get a fair trial by an English jury. Indeed, I hear that Herschell [the former Liberal Lord Chancellor] has said that on this account alone it would be 'madness' for them to take proceedings. Another deterrent is said to be, as regards Parnell himself, that the evidence would be certain to involve the endangering of the character of a woman.

Two days later, Hamilton reflected coldly on Parnell's repudiation in the Commons of the new matter introduced by the Attorney-General in the O'Donnell case: 'Until better proof is forthcoming, I shall believe Parnell's word, though I daresay he has been connected with some very fishy transactions . . . meanwhile society of course has made up its mind that Parnell is a liar and a funker . . . why does he not sue?'[18]

Parnell now resolved to confront his adversaries. In the teeth of Liberal advice, he demanded the appointment of a Commons select committee to investigate the allegations. Determined to destroy Parnell and discredit the Liberal—nationalist alliance, the government responded with a bill to establish a judicial commission, whose remit extended beyond the issue of the authenticity of the letters to encompass the entirety of the *Times* charge of Parnellite responsibility for agrarian crime in Ireland. Whatever the odds against his being able to demonstrate conclusively that the letters were forgeries, it was difficult to see how Parnell could hope to rebut a series of newspaper editorials on the troubled condition of Ireland over the preceding years.

As what was devised as the government's trap snapped shut about him Parnell responded with cold and unflinching resolve. He was determined that the inquiry, however constituted and whatever its terms, should proceed. To the unnerved Morley he observed with studied insouciance: 'Of course, I am not sure that we shall come off with flying colours. But I think we shall. I am never sure of anything'.[19]

Parnell was under no illusions as to the risks involved. Labouchere wrote to Gladstone:

> Parnell himself thinks that the general inquiry will reveal lamentable indiscretions of subordinates, and that therefore it is all the more desirable that discredit should be thrown upon the whole action of the *Times* by proving to the hilt that the letters are forgeries. Matt Harris is the worst case. Parnell has kept so clearly out of everything, that he does not know what may be proved against the others.[20]

In his speech on the second reading of the government's bill, Healy made a scathing denunciation of the conduct of the defence of the O'Donnell action by the Attorney-General as epitomising the collusion between the government and the *Times*. The retaliation of an Irish junior counsel against an English Attorney-General, it affords a fine example of Healy's mordant ire:

> Of all the forensic indiscretions of the hon. and learned Gentleman — I should be out of Order if I referred to the hon. and learned Gentleman's conduct as acts of indecency — therefore, I say of all the acts of indiscretion of the hon. and learned Gentleman, his late action is the worst. Of course, he acted without pay — disdaining the vulgar lucre of the *Times*, scratching out with his pen the very large number of noughts that followed the first figure in the amount and tearing up the cheque, and for two days first thundering with his cannonade and then his big gun, at one time charged with the bullets of Patrick Ford and another with the dynamite of Dr. Gallagher. After 18 hours — 'Oh, lame and impotent conclusion!' — he appealed to the Judge, saying — 'Does your Lordship think we need go into our case?' Mr. Speaker, I am a very poor man. I have never probably earned as many guineas in my life as the hon. and learned Gentleman has in the *Times* case. But if I were instructed to make a series of the most abominable charges — including murder, hypocrisy, villainy, assassination — every combination that a man could cram into 18 hours of declamation — and then, at the conclusion of my oratory, I had to ask the Judge 'Need I go into my case?', all I can say is, I would tear the stuff gown off my back before I would do it. And then what does he do? Reference has been made to Dr. Jekyll and Mr. Hyde. The hon. and learned Attorney-General, having acted his part as Mr. Hyde in the Royal Courts of Justice, came down to the House of Commons as Dr. Jekyll, and with a sanctimonious smile of primitive virtue, began to draft the Bill, from which, however, he had the modesty to exclude his name.[21]

The effect of this searing onslaught was marred by Healy's concluding peroration, in which he again distinguished the cause of Ireland from the fate of its transient representatives:

> Your good opinion or your bad opinion does not weigh in our opinions a feather's weight, but as it may affect the minds of the electors of this country. On that ground, and on that ground alone, if it were necessary to clear our characters as members of the first Home Rule ministry, I have no objection to an inquiry. But it seems to me that if this is proposed in order to brand the first Home Rule ministry as a gang of murderers, a much simpler way would be to insert a provision into the first Home Rule Bill that Charles Stewart Parnell, Justin McCarthy, your humble servant, and the Lord Mayor of Dublin shall take no part in the future

> administration of Ireland. Put that in your bill, and if that is your objection to Home Rule, I, for one, will gladly accept it. The Irish cause is a permanent and a living cause . . . The sacred cause of Ireland has embalmed within it the principle of Nationality which Englishmen in all times and in all ages have worshipped, aye, and have died for. We, for the moment, it is true are the Representatives of that cause, and shall perish and pass away; but there will come those after us who, whatever happens to us, will carry that cause forward. Do you think you can put a big gravestone on the cause of Ireland by proving the truth of the libels in *Parnellism and Crime*? I defy you. The spirit of Ireland which has risen superior to the million calumnies with which you have poisoned the ear of the world, rises defiant and resplendent against all your attacks. In the name of the Irish people, we, on their behalf, bid you defiance, and we tell you to do your best and your worst against the spirit of Irish Nationality.[22]

The argument was more subtle than that in his earlier *Nation* letter. Yet in the coupling of a modest avowal of his own dispensability with a suggestion of Parnell's there was a discernible undertow of unease.

Speaking of the vagueness of the charges against the Irish members, Healy superbly taunted that 'the Government has lain like Moonlighters behind a hedge with their faces blackened'. He denounced the inversion of the obvious mode of proceeding, in not permitting the Irish members first to deal with the forgeries, and attacked the partial nature of the inquiry:

> If agrarian crime was to be gone into, there must be inquiry into causes as well as effects; into rack-renting, and evictions, pauperism and emigration, and into the treatment and deaths of prisoners. If they were to go into *Parnellism and Crime*, why should they not have *Balfourism and Crime*, *Landlordism and Crime*, or *Orangeism and Crime*.

He tellingly and provocatively equated the terms of reference of the inquiry with a situation in which Lord Hartington had been charged with having had one of his jockeys pull a horse, and had demanded an inquiry into the allegation, to which the government had instead proposed 'a general inquiry into this system by which the public are swindled and defrauded'.[23]

Healy threatened to absent himself from the hearings of the Commission unless his objections were met. He reminded the government that 'however much they might think that they had the Irish Members trapped, yet the hon. Member for the city of Cork would only have to lift up his little finger and they would not be able to get a man in Ireland nor a single one of the eighty-six members of the Irish Parliamentary Party to go before the Commission'. He attacked the constitution of the

Commission: 'He neither trusted the trinity nor the unity . . . he would not trust any tribunal selected by a Tory Lord Chancellor from Tory judges'.[24]

The *Daily Express* wrote on 2 August that 'Healy reduced the whole day's proceedings to an absurdity and a farce by a broad caricature of the bill'. Its parliamentary correspondent observed Gladstone in close conference with Healy 'with whom, by the way, he walked arm in arm into the lobby last night'.[25] Healy's trenchant opposition to the bill, his touches of hilarity, and his threat of abstention were at odds with Parnell's strategy. Parnell was less unsettled than the Liberals by the government's raising of the stakes. He resolved to meet them. He was determined to participate in the proceedings of the Special Commission, and to render them the theatre of his solemn vindication.

Parnell indicated to Morley that it was his intention that each of the Irish members should institute proceedings against the *Times*. Morley was subsequently advised — erroneously — by Sir Charles Russell that writs had been issued on behalf of Parnell and other Irish party leaders. Morley informed Gladstone that Russell was of the opinion that the institution of proceedings was inadvisable, in that it would allow the *Times* to plead that the specific matters with which the Commission was charged with investigating were *sub judice*: 'It will, in other words, tend to withdraw exactly the most specific allegations from the Commission, and leave merely the vague, general fishing allegations which are exactly the most objectionable'. The belief that Parnell had directed the institution proceedings in disregard of the advice of the Liberals and of Russell was the last straw for the pusillanimous Morley. He wrote to Gladstone: 'So far, then, as Parnell goes, I think we are at liberty to take what line we please at the Commission'. He urged that after Lord Herschell's speech in the House of Lords that day, 'we should do best to leave the Commission pretty much alone, and to try to get the public mind back to the Irish question properly so called'. He concluded grimly: 'If Parnell persists in actions now, then supposing Russell's anticipations to be right, Parnell will have made the worst of all his blunders'.[26]

Gladstone, just as he had been more sympathetic to Parnell's approach to the establishment of the Special Commission than his lieutenants, was less faint-hearted. He replied to Morley that he agreed that the Liberals should not intermeddle in the proceedings of the Commission (it is difficult to see how they could have done so), though he felt they should have someone monitor its proceeding 'which is so unjust to Parnell and so disgraceful to the Government and to Parliament'. He disagreed with Morley in relation to the institution of libel proceedings: 'I think the actions *may*, and I hope they will, reduce the Commission to impotence and inanity'. George Lewis took the same view at a consultation the following day attended by Morley, from which Parnell was absent. Morley reported that it was now anticipated the writs would be served the following week 'but this ought not yet to be whispered, as they may change their minds'.[27]

Morley opposed a Liberal contribution to Parnell's defence fund. He argued that the defence was adequately funded: 'Parnell is not in want of money, for Russell warned him in my presence that he ought to be well provided for; and P. said £20,000 would not frighten him'. A subscription would not enjoy general support among Liberals 'many of whom will prefer to wait until they are more completely satisfied that Parnell's hands are clean'. Parnell had no claim on the Liberals, having 'brought on the whole of this most evil business, by his steady disregard of our advice. Therefore, I am strongly of the opinion that the movement for a fund from the Liberal party is premature, and that for any of us to give it public countenance would be downright mischievous'. If such hostility to Parnell's course of action on the part of the most pro-home rule of Gladstone's lieutenants was disquieting, the political advice could hardly be faulted. Rosebery at Dalmeny expressed similar views to Hamilton. Gladstone was 'too squeezable. The Irishmen were fully aware of this and took every advantage of it. He can come forward later and help Parnell, if Parnell is able to clear himself'.[28]

It is against these reservations, as much as against the ferocity of the attack on Parnell mounted by the *Times* and the government, that the scale of Parnell's ultimate vindication in the matter of the forgeries has to be measured. When Pigott was exposed, Reginald Brett, later Viscount Esher, wrote to W. T. Stead: 'I hope that J. Morley and the others, under whom I have groaned for months, will eat their prophecies of evil. Parnell has a genuine triumph over them all. Heaven knows they abused him enough for insisting upon clearing his reputation'.[29]

Healy was the pre-eminent jurist of the Irish party. In his contribution to the debates on the bill to set up the Special Commission he was rehearsing the prominent role he naturally expected to play in the proceedings of the Special Commission itself. On 4 September, George Lewis wrote at Parnell's request to offer him a brief, which he accepted. His retainer was publicly announced. Four weeks later the brief was abruptly withdrawn. Lewis wrote to Healy that Parnell 'considers that the case, so far as it affects him, has taken such a turn that it is desirable that you should appear only as counsel for yourself, and in that capacity it is Mr. Parnell's wish that I should deliver you a brief upon the usual professional terms'. It is difficult to conceive of a more wounding blow to a parliamentarian and advocate of Healy's standing, aggravated by the preposterous suggestion that he should be retained to appear for himself.[30]

From Lewis, Healy could establish only that the terms of the letter were effectively dictated by Parnell, who had offered no fuller explanation. T. C. Harrington told Healy on 18 October that he had been unable to draw Parnell on the issue. He wrote to Healy later the same day, after seeing Parnell at the offices of Lewis and Lewis. Parnell had insisted he was in no way to blame, and said to Harrington 'in the most earnest manner':

> I can assure you, Harrington, when I explain the circumstances to Healy no man will more readily recognise that I have taken the proper course than Healy himself. You know that, both because of his usefulness in this case, and especially because of another incident which you are aware of, he is the first man I would offer a brief to if there were not grave reasons, which will be quite apparent when the case is developed.

Parnell was gambling heavily on Harrington's fidelity, and on his credulousness. When Harrington suggested that he should give up his own brief, Parnell replied 'in very strong terms, "I assure you, you are quite wrong in thinking that I have acted from any motive but prudence, and the development of the case will show that"'. This was Parnell at his most disingenuous and ruthless: he was never to explain the 'circumstances' to Healy or anyone else.

Harrington was duly persuaded that Parnell had some good reason for his action. He surmised, 'judging by some hints he threw out to me afterwards when we were alone, and talking on another matter', that letters supposedly written by Healy and Biggar had been sold to the *Times* and subsequently discovered to be forged. Healy wrote to his father that Harrington 'is a truthful and loyal colleague, but there are others who are neither, and since hearing tonight of the backing away from the promise to explain matters to myself, I think he has been imposed on'.[31]

On 22 October Biggar and John Barry both wrote letters of support to Healy. Biggar had written to Lewis refusing to permit him to act on his behalf. Parnell met Biggar at the National Liberal Club to persuade him to relent. Biggar accused Parnell of acting shamefully towards Healy. Parnell sought to assure him he was not motivated by any personal feeling. But when Biggar said that he would reconsider his position if Healy was advised of the reasons and expressed himself satisfied, Parnell 'replied he was not in a position to tell you'. Parnell in Biggar's phrase was now 'shuffling', resiling even from his earlier commitment to explain his reasons to Healy if requested to do so.[32]

Healy wrote his father that Biggar and Barry both urged him to appear for them 'and it is likely that I will go tomorrow as an independent counsel. It is a most unpleasant business, but fathom it I can't'.[33] Healy wisely thought better of appearing for Biggar and Barry, which would have been construed by Parnell as an act of open revolt. Labouchere wrote to W. E. Gladstone on 30 October:

> There is just now a little trouble in the camp. Healy received a brief. Parnell directed Lewis to withdraw it. Healy was very indignant, and wrote to me to ask Parnell his reasons. Parnell replied he would only state them, if Healy wrote to ask him. This Healy declines to do, and several of the party side with him. Today Healy appeared in Court, and says he is there to conduct his own case. Fortunately all this has been left out of the newspapers.[34]

Healy was taken aback to find the consummation of his own antagonism towards Parnell so brutally pre-empted. To his father he wrote, somewhat embarrassedly, that in the light of Parnell's refusal to offer an explanation he had reverted to the view that it was a speech he had made in Wicklow backing Dillon and O'Brien on the Plan of Campaign 'that has got me chucked'. Writing to Maurice, 'wavering often as to this extraordinary man', he advanced the same unconvincing hypothesis. What was clear was that he was now confronted by Parnell's implacable hostility towards him, and the near-certainty of his exclusion from the centre of affairs for so long as Parnell was leader of the Irish party. To Maurice he wrote ominously that Parnell's refusal to advise him of the grounds for the withdrawal of the brief 'creates a change in my obligations towards him'.[35]

The termination of Healy's retainer was a violent gesture. Parnell had decided that in meeting the *Times* case at the Special Commission he did not wish to be inhibited by the presence as a barrister of the man he most distrusted in the Irish party. With the terrible and often false lucidity of a man turning to confront his external adversaries, his glare fell first within his own camp. Parnell had decided that he could afford to risk alienating Healy. When O'Brien warned Parnell that it was unwise to make an enemy of Healy by excluding him from the Special Commission counsel, Parnell replied, 'Oh, Tim is all right so long as he is afraid of you'.[36] Parnell's judgement of Healy was essentially correct. He divined Healy's hostility towards him, and instinctively realised – more clearly than Healy himself did – that it could not be assuaged. He accordingly resolved under no circumstances to seek to placate him.

The withdrawal of the brief signalled to close observers that Healy did not enjoy Parnell's confidence. He correctly judged that Healy could not afford to make a public issue out of the withdrawal of his brief, while it might at a later stage provoke him into a public dissent in which his temperament was likely to betray him (in this respect at least, he underestimated Healy). If the further alienation of Healy was not of itself a mistake, the withdrawal of the brief deepened the Galway rift which the rest of the party had wished to see close over, and revealed an implacability on Parnell's part which cannot have enhanced the affection in which he was held by other members of the party. It may ultimately have contributed to the tolerance with which Healy's savage attacks on Parnell in the split were regarded by many even of the more moderate anti-Parnellites.

Parnell's decision to exclude Healy was not dictated exclusively by personal hostility. He knew that Healy, by reason of his independence of temperament, his idiosyncratic forensic style and his penchant for improvisation, and the fact that he was a politician in his own right as well as a barrister, would have precluded himself from being a conventionally submissive junior counsel in the Parnellite legal representation. Moreover his open hostility to the establishment of the Special Commission was at odds with Parnell's own strategy. Healy's contributions to the debates on the bill suggested that he would treat the Commissioners with no more respect than he accorded Irish magistrates. His cross-examination of William Irwin, a police shorthand reporter, was not a triumph of advocacy. Sir Alfred Robbins later observed that while Healy appeared to believe that he could have done better at some points than Sir Charles Russell, 'the present writer, who sat the Commission right through, recalls the fate of Healy's parliamentary colleague and fellow-barrister from the Four Courts, Timothy Harrington, who tried Irish methods on a witness with devastating results to himself'.[37]

Parnell had already to deal with the divergent approaches members of the party would take in their testimony. Robbins wrote: 'While the Special Commission was sitting, Mr. Parnell more than once talked very freely as to the progress of the enquiry. He did not sympathise with the line taken in the witness box by some of his colleagues, but slightly shrugging his shoulders, he observed, "you see they have their methods, and I have mine"'.[38]

Parnell determinedly centralised the direction of the Special Commission case, and was more than usually taciturn. As Harrington wrote in an attempt to console Healy, 'Parnell is taking his own course in all this case, both with respect to his confidences with Lewis and with Russell'. He was not especially communicative even to them. Lewis observed that Parnell was the most remarkable man he had ever come across, 'dreadfully secretive, and the more you tried to draw him the more he closed up'. Parnell was unremittingly assiduous in meeting the *Times* case, although his application attracted less attention than his absences from parliament. Lewis had not previously known Parnell and knew little of Irish politics, but (having perhaps taken advice) had agreed to act on one condition, 'that he gave me his word of honour that he would come to me, at all times, when I wanted him. He gave me his word, and faithfully kept it'.[39]

Parnell took the *Times* attack to be directed overwhelmingly at himself. Moreover it raised issues of the deepest personal concern to him. As Davitt wrote: 'Mr. Parnell believed in one source, and one only, as to the origin of the forgery and of the deadly blow which was aimed at him by its publication. Captain O'Shea was the object of this suspicion'. No amount of argument could persuade him otherwise. Parnell's conviction on this subject was so deeply rooted that it appears to have persisted even after the incrimination and suicide of Pigott. Labouchere asserted that Parnell went to his grave the sole man who did not believe that Pigott had forged the *Times* letters.[40]

It is not without significance that O'Shea was fully aware of Parnell's belief that he was instrumental in procuring the forged letters. He complained in his evidence to the Special Commission about the 'slanders which had been circulated about me by Parnell and his friends with regard to these letters'.[41] Chamberlain, in response to what was evidently an enquiry from O'Shea, wrote on 31 December that 'Morley said nothing to me about Callan – but he did tell me that Parnell believed that you had been at the bottom of the letters – forged them I presume. I told him that I was certain you had neither done nor said anything at that time to help the *Times*'.[42]

Parnell's belief in O'Shea's complicity was fortified by his knowledge of O'Shea's Fenian contacts. The captain was in the habit of seeking in Pigott-like fashion to ingratiate himself with Parnell's ultra-nationalist adversaries. He cultivated relations with Fenians (whom he dubbed 'the real boys', in contrast to 'the boys' of the Irish party) in Clare and London. In particular he maintained contact with a maverick Fenian in London called George Mulqueeny.[43] O'Shea under cross-examination at the Special Commission accepted that he had once stated on Mulqueeny's authority that someone knew of a payment of money by Parnell to Frank Byrne to enable him to escape arrest on a charge of complicity in the Phoenix Park murders, but denied that he had attached credence to this. As this had preceded his candidacy in Galway, he could hardly have said otherwise. Asked whether he had told anyone in the winter of 1885–6 that there were American Fenians hostile to Parnell in London, who held letters compromising him, O'Shea accepted that Mulqueeny had told him of the presence in London of the American Fenians, but stated that to the best of his belief he had not known of the existence of compromising documents prior to seeing the facsimile of the Byrne letter in the *Times*. O'Shea had in his evidence-in-chief stated that he believed that the signature on the main letter published in facsimile by the *Times* was genuine, but on cross-examination stated that he did not believe the text of the letter to be genuine.[44]

Parnell was preoccupied with O'Shea's testimony. Labouchere reported to W. E. Gladstone of a conversation with Parnell: 'he is in a somewhat agitated state of mind about O'Shea as a witness, for there are reasons why it is difficult to reply to O'Shea. He says, however, that he will not spare him, and if he holds to this, it can be proved that O'Shea was an actual thief in money matters'.[45] Labouchere's conversation with Parnell had taken place on 26 October. Neither Parnell nor his lawyers had the slightest idea that O'Shea would take the stand five days later.

The Commission hearings had commenced on 22 October 1888. Parnell arrived just before the judges emerged on to the bench. Oscar Wilde's brother William, who covered the Special Commission for the *Daily Chronicle*, wrote: 'The uncrowned king looked ill and anxious. His hair was almost as disturbed as his air when, taking off his hat, he saluted his solicitor, by whom he sat. His nervous nostrils were dilated, and his eye roved over the court, as though it half-expected to be confronted by a face it did not desire to see'.[46]

Biggar appeared for himself. Wilde reported that 'he makes no secret of his dislike and contempt for the employment of English counsel, who, in his view, are nothing but candidates for Gladstonian offices'.[47] On 30 October, Healy dispensed with the services of R. T. Reid Q.C. who was assigned to represent him, and advised the Commission that he would thenceforth appear for himself. He unsuccessfully raised a plea of *autrefois acquit*. As the Commission had not dealt with the disputed letters as the principal issue, he asked to be advised when matters affecting him were being put in evidence: 'For my part I have business to attend to elsewhere. I have no desire whatever to be present here while the criminality of Mr. O'Donovan Rossa or Mr. Scrab Nally is being referred to'. Healy was sitting second, next to Parnell, 'but I took no notice of him although he addressed some words to me while I was making some remarks to the court – by way of giving assistance, I think. I didn't however hear what he said, and I made no sign'.[48] William Wilde, noting that Healy's reference to O'Donovan Rossa and Scrab Nally was made 'very scornfully' wrote that 'his court manner is an improvement on his Parliamentary style, for it enables him to say most insolent things in a way at which it is difficult to take offence'.[49]

In what could without excessive cynicism be construed as an attempt to catch Parnell off guard, O'Shea was suddenly and without warning interposed as a witness on 31 October, the second day of the evidence, on the grounds that he was going abroad. Sir Charles Russell on Parnell's behalf protested strenuously but unavailingly. He argued that it was not possible for him to embark on a satisfactory cross-examination of O'Shea at that stage of the case. He was over-ruled and proceeded under protest. After O'Shea was sworn, Parnell in William Wilde's description 'fixed his gaze on the witness with an expression that was nothing less than anxious, and kept it so fixed for the greater part of the day'.

The cross-examination of O'Shea included the following tense and perilous exchange:

> Russell: 'Have you ever said you would be revenged on Mr. Parnell?'
>
> O'Shea: 'I never remember using the expression . . .'
>
> Russell: 'Have you ever said that you have a shell which would blow him up charged with dynamite?'
>
> O'Shea: 'I should think not; it is most unlikely that I should use such an expression'.[50]

What Russell could not disclose was that this phrase came from a letter from O'Shea to his wife of 2 November 1885. Furious at the setbacks he was encountering in obtaining a parliamentary seat, O'Shea had written: 'I have been treated in a blackguard fashion and I mean to hit back a stunner. I have everything ready . . . I packed my shell with dynamite. It cannot hurt my friend [Chamberlain], and it will send a blackguard's reputation with his deluded countrymen into smithereens'.[51]

After Russell finished his cross-examination, O'Shea left the box. However Healy had risen and O'Shea was recalled. Parnell apprehensively enquired of Healy what he was going to say. Healy replied that he would ask nothing sensational, and would confine himself to showing that he and Biggar had opposed O'Shea at Galway:

> I just wish to ask you one question. You were opposed at Galway I think by some members of the Irish party? – Yes.
>
> You went down there on the Saturday – Yes.
>
> Do you remember beginning operations in the *Freeman's Journal* announcing yourself as a candidate there? – Yes.
>
> And by the next train you were followed down by certain members? – Yes.
>
> Who were they? – You and Mr. Biggar, if I remember right.
>
> We immediately addressed meetings against you? – Yes.
>
> Several? – Yes.
>
> And attacked and denounced you in every way in our power? – Yes.
>
> That is all I wish to ask.

As William Wilde wrote, 'Mr. Healy, having thus established the fact that he was his own leader on occasion, subsided smiling, and Captain O'Shea with radiant visage retired, being doubtless well satisfied that his ideal was over'.[52] Healy's cross-examination of O'Shea, though mercifully short and narrow in scope from Parnell's point of view, marks a decisive moment in their mutual estrangement. Healy had retaliated, for Galway and for the withdrawal of his Commission brief. Their adversity was now engaged.

After the opening days, Healy was conspicuous by his absence from the Commission. He reappeared on 26 February 1889 for what should have been the fourth day of Pigott's evidence, when the witness failed to appear, and the day after when he sat with Labouchere at the end of the solicitors' bench.[53]

The Special Commission inevitably prompted further comment among the politically initiated on Parnell's relations with Katharine O'Shea. Starved of definite information, Labouchere wrote to Herbert Gladstone after O'Shea's testimony describing him as a 'thorough-paced rascal'. Katharine O'Shea had been to see Lewis, 'but Parnell is so touchy on the subject that it is impossible to enter upon it with him. The wife seems to have separated from her husband'. He went on to suggest that, while O'Shea had said at the Commission that he had destroyed a number of papers relating to the Kilmainham negotiations, 'I believe that, if the truth was known, it would be found that he had not destroyed a single paper, but that he could not find them, owing to a domiciliary visit of Mrs. O'Shea to his room when he was not there'. Labouchere made the unfounded suggestion that while O'Shea had referred to '*his* home at Eltham and *his* chambers at Victoria Street, it would be found that Parnell paid the rent of both', and added: 'When he spoke of his connection with his friend, Montagu, M.P., it would be found that his friend and other Directors had to turn him out as manager, for certain vague views in respect of *meum et tuum*, which if pushed to its ultimate consequences would have landed him in the dock'. Labouchere concluded with a graphic comparison of the elusive Irish leader to Jack the Ripper:

> Parnell insists to Lewis that he never sees Mrs. O'Shea now. Neither Lewis, nor his secretary Campbell have any notion where he lives. I left him a few days ago at about 12 at night. He had on a filthy flannel shirt, a still more filthy white coat with the collar turned up, and a pot hat. In his hand, he carried a shiney leather bag. I could not help thinking as he vanished into space, that he ran the risk of being arrested as the Whitechapel murderer. However he takes a great interest in the case, and shirks no work in connection with it.[54]

On the second day of his cross-examination by Charles Russell, Friday 22 February, Richard Pigott began to fall apart. His erstwhile collaborator James O'Connor later wrote that those who knew him anticipated that

> in the witness-box he would flounder and fumble into all sorts of contradictions and admissions. They hardly expected that he would make such a shocking exhibition of himself. What they counted upon was, that after fencing and stumbling for a time, he would blurt out the whole truth, and throw himself upon the mercy of the court. This would have been in keeping with his character, as it was understood years ago. It was not imagined or believed that for a day and a quarter he would have stood the raking fire of a terrible cross-examination. Had Pigott the faintest notion of the crucial ordeal before him, all the money in the coffers of the *Times* – unscrupulous as he was – would not have induced him to go back into the box. He had no conception of what was before him, much less had he any suspicion of the crushing evidence in Sir Charles Russell's hands.[55]

The cross-examination was broken by the weekend. Pigott's last hapless days were now played out. On the Saturday he made an unsolicited visit to the home of Henry Labouchere and, in the presence of George Augustus Sala, signed a confession that he had uttered the forged letters. He subsequently met a Dublin solicitor who was working with Soames, the solicitor for the *Times*, whom he advised that he had forged only some of the letters, not including the letter which implicated Parnell in the Phoenix Park murders, and swore an affidavit to that effect on Monday 25 February, when he pressed for further monies from the *Times*.

Pigott fled first to Paris and thence to Madrid. He was dogged to the end, and ultimately trapped, by his chronic impecuniosity. Before leaving London, he picked up a cheque from Sotheby's for the sale of some books, to provide for his immediate needs. When he reached the Hotel Embajadores in Madrid, it was a telegram to the Dublin solicitor sent under the name of Roland Ponsonby, looking for a payment which he claimed was promised to him, that betrayed his whereabouts to the English police. The next day there was no reply, and he grew fretful: 'He moved about in an aimless, restless kind of way, and his evident anxiety began at length to attract attention, which is a bad thing for a stranger in Spain'. At a Madrid bank he presented a cheque for a considerable sum, again in the name of Roland Ponsonby, drawn on the Dublin branch of the Ulster Bank. The Spanish bank, displaying better judgement than the *Times* and the Irish Loyal and Patriotic Union, declined to cash it. In the late afternoon of the same day, Pigott shot himself as an English police inspector entered his hotel room. 'Dismal and ghastly has been the end of this most miserable wretch', the *Daily Telegraph* observed with its habitual charity, 'it is impossible to overlook the feebly humorous side of his character'.[56]

When Pigott failed to appear at the Special Commission on 26 February, Russell rose and 'betraying great excitement by the twitching muscles of his face, said he deliberately charged that behind Mr. Houston and Mr. Pigott, there was a foul conspiracy, by whom he did not declare'.[57] The President of the Special Commission subsequently ruled that by reason of the limited nature of the inquiry it would 'not be part of our duty to make any report on the suggestion of foul conspiracy on the part of anybody behind Pigott'.[58] Russell was in any event somewhat constrained in his development of the charge of 'foul conspiracy' by reason of the central role ascribed by his client to W. H. O'Shea in the conspiracy.

Parnell stood now at his zenith. As he proceeded to Bow Street to procure the issue of a warrant for Pigott's arrest, he was followed by a cheering crowd. In the Strand 'a little street urchin vending newspapers, who, with the sharpness of the London boy, was already well informed of what had taken place, danced in front of the Irish statesman and bowing with mock gravity said "Charlie, you've done it nice"'.[59] The tumult outside the court posed something of a threat to civil order. When someone claimed to have spotted Pigott, 'in an instant a crowd of over a hundred and more was blocking the approach to the refreshment bar, nearly opposite the corner of Holywell Street, and peering at somebody not at all unlike Pigott, a stoutish, grey-whiskered gentleman harmlessly consuming his bun'.[60]

Vindicated, Parnell conformed to his myth. Of his brief formal evidence to the Commission denying the authorship of the letters, the correspondent of the Liberal *Daily News* wrote, 'of feeling of triumph there was, in his pale countenance and pale gaze, not a trace'.[61] Harcourt urged McCarthy to prevail on Parnell to speak in the Commons on the evening of 1 March, where he would 'get such a reception as no man ever got before in the House of Commons'. McCarthy wrote to Mrs. Campbell Praed that he would seek to persuade Parnell, 'but I shan't tell him anything about the intended demonstration, as if I did it might only make him shrink from appearing'.[62] Parnell attended and impassively endured a tumultuous ovation. His short, conciliatory speech avoided the mildest hint of exultation. In 1891, admittedly a time when it was in the immediate interest of the Conservative party to resuscitate the menace of the beleaguered Parnell, Sir Edward Clarke said, addressing a meeting in Plymouth:

> Sir, it was an incident which might have disturbed the balance of mind of a smaller man. I saw Mr. Parnell standing erect among the whole standing crowd. He took no notice of it whatever. He had not asked them to get up. When they had finished standing up they sat down, and he took no notice of their rising or their sitting down; and when they had resumed their places he proceeded to make a perfectly calm and quiet speech, in which he made not the smallest reference, direct or indirect, to the incident, extraordinary as it was, which had just happened. I thought, as I looked at him that night, that that man was a born leader

> of men — calm, self-confident and powerful; and depend upon it, that so long as Mr. Parnell lives, he is a living force with whom the Gladstonians will have to reckon if they want to enter into alliances for the sake of Home Rule.

The scene was re-enacted at the Liberal Eighty Club a week later.[63]

The sudden enthusiasm for Parnell, and the deep impression created by his restraint, were too much for Labouchere:

> Mr. Parnell, no doubt, has a very proper sense of personal dignity, yet I must confess that I can't help being amused by the extravagant eulogies which are now heaped upon him on this score. It seems to have been expected that, a genuine British cheer would have been too much for him, and that upon first hearing it he would have burst into wild whoops of delight, and danced breakdowns to show how pleased he was.[64]

Parnell was now acclaimed by a Liberal party which had always doubted his ability to achieve so complete a deliverance. Even Harcourt's reservations were momentarily suspended. He wrote to Gladstone that 'there need now be no further difficulty in public recognition of our *solidarité* with Parnell in the interest of Home Rule . . . in future they will fling the taunt of "Parnellite" against us in vain'.[65]

The collapse of public interest in London in the further proceedings of the Special Commission had been almost immediately apparent. No longer was the court the focus of lively social curiosity. The correspondent of the *Daily Telegraph* wrote:

> With the exodus of Pigott and the complete exposure of the forgeries, the glory of the Commission has departed. There were places to spare all over the court yesterday, and no ladies, eager and excited, occupied the narrow seats between the jury-box and their lordships; neither did any unoccupied judge pay the illustrious trio a visit. Eminent 'specials', representing both home and foreign journals, and many of the artists disappeared altogether after the luncheon hour, and in the afternoon, during the protracted legal argument, not a pencil moved on a note-book, and the judges laid down their pens and put their hands in their pockets.[66]

Healy sought to intervene, rising to cross-examine Joseph Soames, the solicitor for the *Times*. He came under immediate attack from the President of the Commission on the grounds that the only question they were at that time considering was the authenticity of the letters and that this did not affect Healy. After endeavouring to argue that as he was accused of being a co-conspirator, he should be entitled to proceed with his cross-examination, he did not press the matter further.[67]

Parnell had reached a fork in the road. Healy in his memoirs wrote that every friend of Parnell's 'save his London advisers' had counselled withdrawal from the Commission after the triumphant exposure of the forged letters. According to William O'Brien, Parnell favoured an early withdrawal, but was opposed by Sir Charles Russell and Michael Davitt, both of whom were set on delivering the perorations they had prepared. Frank Lockwood Q.C. told Edward Hamilton that the time to withdraw was after the collapse of Pigott, 'but that Charles Russell wanted to make his speech and it would have been difficult to have done him out of that'. From the contemporary comments of Lockwood and Reid, both of whom appeared for the Irish, to Edward Hamilton, it is clear that they took insufficient account of the risk of the Commission throwing into the scales, against the forgeries, adverse findings on the role of Parnellism in agrarian violence, and in particular reposed exaggerated faith in the presiding Commissioner, Sir James Hannen.[68]

Yet it would be incorrect to suppose that Parnell's judgement was overborne by professional advice. His strategy of confronting his adversaries however adverse the terrain had already achieved the *éclat* of the exposure of the letters as forgeries. He resolved to persevere in his original determination to avail of the Special Commission to achieve the vindication of his constitutional purpose. As a secondary consideration, he hoped also to be able to establish the precise provenance of the forgeries. This second throw of the dice was a rare misjudgement on his part.

Belying his opening assertion that 'the utter, absolute collapse of the forged letters has taken out of this inquiry its pith and marrow', Russell proceeded to deliver over eight days an epic Victorian set-piece oration on the ills of Ireland. Although deeply affected by Russell's address, Parnell admitted to Robbins that 'all the life of the inquiry went out with the forged letters: it's now perfectly flat'.[69]

The proceedings dragged on, remarkable chiefly for a notably weak performance by Parnell as a witness over eight days, culminating in an unhappy lapse into candour. Pressed upon the assertion he had made in 1881 in opposing the coercion bill that there were no secret conspiracies in Ireland, he replied, 'it is possible I was endeavouring to mislead the House on the occasion'. Regarding this 'so-called "startling admission"', Morley reported to Gladstone that two informants who were present told him that Parnell was utterly exhausted, 'and had the air of a man who hardly knew what he was saying'. Gladstone's daughter Mary, who had described Parnell the previous day as 'so done he sometimes looked like fainting', wrote that he seemed 'utterly weary and almost ready to fall into any trap that was set for him'.[70]

Belatedly, Parnell decided to withdraw. His counsel applied for an order for the inspection of the books of the Irish Loyal and Patriotic Union, to ascertain the circumstances in which the forged letters were procured. When Sir James Hannen on 12 July refused to grant the inspection, Parnell immediately passed a note to Russell, who advised the Commission he would have to consider his position. H. H. Asquith, Russell's junior, told Hamilton that Parnell attached great importance to the documents, believing they would prove the last link of the conspiracy. He said Parnell was very determined, 'though he might defer to the advice of his Counsel. They had not made up their minds as to what advice to tender'. Asquith underestimated Parnell's resolve. On 16 July Russell announced that he was under written instructions no longer to appear, and in succession the counsel for the other respondents advised the Commission in like terms.[71]

It was by now abundantly clear that Parnell had erred in failing to withdraw after the exposure of the forgeries. The Special Commission, when it finally reported on 13 February 1890, found that the respondents had entered into a conspiracy to promote an agitation for the non-payment of rent, and that the allegations as to links with extreme nationalists were merely 'not proven'. The government thereby recouped some at least of the heavy political losses it had sustained from the setting up of the Commission.[72]

Parnell's application to the Commission for an order for the inspection of the books of the Irish Loyal and Patriotic Union was not the end of his attempts by legal process to identify those who had procured the forged letters. He brought an application in the libel proceedings he had instituted against the *Times* for liberty to administer interrogatories on the subject of the source of the forgeries. The application was refused in the Queen's Bench Division of the High Court on 11 January 1890, on the grounds that the origins of the allegations were irrelevant as the *Times* had in its defence admitted liability.[73]

The failure of this application deprived Parnell's proceedings against the *Times* of much of their political purpose. The following month his action against the *Times* was settled for £5,000. While this was a very substantial sum, the libel on Parnell was of unparalleled gravity. Lewis considered it a very good settlement 'regard being had to the probable chariness of the estimate which a British jury would form of the damage to Parnell's character'.[74]

In the Commons, two days before the publication of the report, Harcourt moved a motion that the publication by the *Times* of the main Parnell forgery was 'a false and scandalous libel, and a breach of the Privileges of the House'. He was strongly supported by Gladstone. The government countered with a negativing amendment. Parnell angrily protested. He demanded and obtained the insertion of the word 'forged' in the government motion. E. W. Hamilton wrote in his diary:

> Both attack and defence were poor. Had I been Parnell, I should have insisted on J. Walter's the proprietor of the *Times* being brought to the bar of the House to apologise; and, if the leader of any other party had been falsely charged in such a manner, this would no doubt have been done. But there is one law for the British statesman, and another for the Irish politician.[75]

Parnell now reverted to an idea which, according to Robbins, he had first entertained after the Special Commission refused to embark on the inquiry he had demanded into the origins of the forged letters. He wanted a select committee to inquire into the history of the letters. Robbins initially reported – erroneously – that the Liberals were favourable to this course.[76] Their priority was rather to put the Special Commission and its report behind them. The immediate issue was the debate on the report of the Special Commission. Labouchere came to Morley with the suggestion that Parnell should merely second the government motion on the report as a matter of course. Morley reported to Gladstone:

> He thinks that in any debate we should be damaged by the hostile matters in the body of the Report.
>
> I should think it very doubtful whether Parnell could afford to take this course – especially in view of the peculiarly unfavourable line of the Report as to Dillon and Davitt.
>
> I confess I do not see how we are to avoid a debate. I wish that we could.[77]

After the debate on the report it was again stated authoritatively by Robbins that Parnell intended seeking the appointment of a select committee on the origin and purchase of the letters. However on 24 March he reported that 'a curious hitch' had arisen:

> The Gladstonians do not desire to move in the matter; if Mr. Parnell likes to do so, they will support him; but they evidently lack enthusiasm on the subject, which they would prefer to raise in some other form, and at a later date. It is not improbable that this feeling has been stimulated by an inkling they have got that the Government might possibly grant Mr. Parnell's request in substance without debate.[78]

The Liberals had no desire to rake over the ashes of the Parnell forgeries which they feared would expose the Liberal–nationalist alliance to attack on the basis of the other matter in the Special Commission's report.

Parnell's own position was by no means straightforward. It was open to him to move for the appointment of a select committee, but he had chosen instead to prime Robbins to disclose his intention to do so. Parnell conceived the threat to be one of the weapons in his armoury against W. H. O'Shea, who had by then instituted divorce proceedings against his wife in which he was named as co-respondent.

Healy was the only nationalist openly to criticise Parnell's decision to embark on a defence before the Commission. Speaking in Dublin on 22 April 1889, after Russell's opening speech but before Parnell's evidence, Healy revealed that dangerous capacity for colouring issues of high strategy in the lurid hues of popular clamour which was to make him so dangerous an adversary of Parnell. Denouncing the Commission as an 'absolutely unconstitutional' tribunal ('it is constituted by our enemies, it is composed of judges who are our enemies, and it was originated in the interest of our enemies'), Healy dissociated himself from the proposal to enter into any defence as 'lending only respectability to the case of the other side'.[79] Under the cover of an ultra-patriotic protest, Healy for the first time publicly dissented from a decision of Parnell on a matter of policy.

On the subject at issue, Healy was isolated within the party. His close associates and kinsmen continued to attend and participate in the hearings of the Special Commission until Parnell resolved on withdrawal. Biggar addressed the Commission, while Maurice Healy, T. D. Sullivan and Donal Sullivan all gave evidence.[80] Yet his stance was well-judged. With this speech, the political prelude to the split was engaged. In the ensuing months his friends and relatives drew closer about him to constitute a loose but increasingly identifiable cabal within the Irish party.

On the eve of the withdrawal of counsel for the Parnellites from the Special Commission, Healy at the National League in Dublin hailed the decision as a belated vindication of his own view:

> Speaking for myself, I have found it extremely difficult during many months past to refrain from expressing the disgust which I felt at the continued association of our party with these proceedings; but even now at the eleventh hour the fact that the retirement has been decided upon will restore something of our national pride that such a stand has at last been taken (*loud applause*). For my own part I regard the incidents connected with this Commission and the submission of the Irish leaders to the jurisdiction and authority of that tribunal – a tribunal of penance to which they were bound forsooth to resort for full confession and absolution – as one of the most lamentable incidents in the history of the present movement.

Healy asserted that, after Salisbury had expressed the view even after the flight of Pigott that the forgeries might still be genuine, he had counselled his colleagues to withdraw: 'However, the proceedings were continued, and for five months we have been butchered to make a London holiday'.[81]

What was most striking was Healy's reference to 'the Irish leaders' in terms which implicitly excluded himself. He was signalling that, having been shut out by Parnell from any effective role in the direction of the policy of the Irish party, he was no longer constrained by the implicit allegiance to Parnell's decisions which passed for collective responsibility among his lieutenants. While remaining one of the most prominent members of the party, he was openly holding himself at one remove from Parnell's leadership. His position was shrewdly judged. Healy had the acumen to turn the nationalist predicament, of politics without power, to his advantage. He had discovered the knack of criticising aspects of nationalist policy while appearing merely to bid up the nationalist demand. He knew how to make dissent seem a surfeit of patriotic ardour. Through what seemed a series of commendable flourishes of nationalistic bellicosity, Healy had embarked on a determined endeavour to constrain, though not to challenge openly, Parnell's leadership. The split was to reveal the care with which he had chosen his ground.

8

Before the Split

'Healy', said an old Fenian to Parnell, 'seems to have the best political head of all these people'. 'He has the only political head among them', rejoined Parnell.[1]

In an extended article in the *New York Times* in 1887 Harold Frederic sketched a group portrait of the Irish party. Its centrepiece was his evocation of his friend Healy. Frederic's physical description of Healy was finely drawn.

> He is now in his thirty-third year, in stature just realizing what is called medium height, and of slender build, with a longish neck and narrow, sloping shoulders. He wears a thin black full beard and gold-rimmed eyeglasses. His face is a notable one — but as variable in expression, and even in contour, as an April sky. In repose, the rounded profile is of exquisite delicacy — the high forehead, the pencilled brow, the aquiline nose, the curved lips, all carved as in ivory by some deft mediaeval Florentine hand. But I have seen this same profile, in the heat of debate over a dinner table, drawn into one straight terrible line, like the face of a Greek Fury, and I have seen it again, relaxed over some droll fairy tale to which the children were listening, when it was the embodiment of feminine softness and lightness of heart. In pleasant moments — and these are all the moments when he is not thinking of the Liberal Unionists — there is a pale rose flush on his cheeks; this vanishes on the instant of excitement,

> leaving the smooth skin one uniform ivory pallor. His eyes are a deep brown black – large, fine eyes, which can light the merriest laughter, but which one shrinks from when they blaze.[2]

T. P. O'Connor later recalled Healy confronting the government, standing 'with bent shoulders with very bright eyes gleaming through the spectacles he had always to wear, and with the most foreboding expression he could give to his face, from the scowling brow to the small, beautifully shaped, but venomous-looking lips'. The long-estranged Katharine Tynan wrote of the Healy of the 1880s, 'I remember when his face, with its light brown eyes, its odd whiteness of skin and blackness of hair and beard, was a very pleasant thing in my sight'.[3]

Frederic wrote of Healy's character:

> The man himself is a strange compound of poet, guerilla, and practical politician – of Italian dreamer, Gaelic chief and modern Irish party manager . . . He has that universal quality of strength which overshadows, wipes out all traces of beginnings . . . He is of an almost painfully acute and alert temperament. He notes everything, comprehends everything, remembers everything, anticipates everything.

Aside from his remarkable legislative acumen, Healy's savage effectiveness as a parliamentary speaker was unrivalled. Frederic wrote:

> The Healy whom the English know might be of another world. Of all the fierce, bitter, ferocious assailants who have lifted their voices in St Stephens against British rule these last dozen years, Healy is the one whose knout lash tongue has raised the biggest and reddest welts. To see him in his place below the gangway, standing with pale, set face boldly uplifted against the tiers of seated Tories opposite; to hear the terrific tongue lashing which he alone can lay upon them – the scorn, invective, biting sarcasm, burning wrath – is to have an experience not to be matched in another Parliament House in Europe. In the use of jeering satire, which amid laughter cuts to the bone, he has no rival save Sir William Harcourt, and no equal in him.[4]

Writing at the end of 1888, the doyen of the parliamentary sketch-writers, H. W. Lucy, recorded the completeness of Healy's parliamentary transformation. From a starting position of 'consummate contempt and hatred' for the House he had matured into one of its most acceptable and influential debaters. Lucy asserted that, conservatively, half the practical work accomplished by Irish members in the preceding five years had been achieved by Healy.

> The Member for North Longford, like some other of his compatriots, has gained in polish at the expense of a long suffering House. . . . he is a very different person from the one whom, eight years ago, Wexford Borough sent to Parliament . . . When addressing the Speaker he would not even take the trouble to remove his hands from his trousers pockets. With both hands hidden away, with neck bent forward in slouching attitude, a scowl on his face, and rasping notes of hatred in his voice, he scolded at large. All that is changed. Mr. Healy is now 'the hon. and learned gentleman', one of the leaders in debate, in open counsel, even in colleagueship, with right hon. gentlemen on the Front Opposition Bench.[5]

Healy had already given evidence of what T. P. O'Connor later described as 'these tremendous upheavals of contradictory sentiments in this curious nature', which prompted him to liken Healy to 'a wife in bedlam, who when she received a visit from her husband, might either kiss him or stab him, or both'. The fact that Healy could be moved to tears unexpectedly in public O'Connor, who by then was an implacably hostile witness, attributed not to hypocrisy but to 'his strange and ill-balanced temperament'.[6] Harold Frederic observed that Healy was 'not yet master of himself'.[7] For so long as Parnell's unchallenged hegemony endured, his defects of temperament were kept for the most part in check.

In the latter part of the 1880s, Healy's national standing lagged behind that of Parnell, and of Dillon, O'Brien and Davitt, who made up the next tier of the nationalist hierarchy. Writing in January 1886, the astute and well-informed R. Barry O'Brien listed Healy along with Parnell, Davitt and Archbishops Croke and Walsh as 'the five most influential men in Ireland'. Surprisingly he omitted Dillon and O'Brien, the latter of whom Katharine Tynan described as 'the best-loved man of the Irish people'. Barry O'Brien however discounted Healy's independent standing. He rightly considered Healy important 'mainly through Mr. Parnell', although he had won a distinct position by the ability he had displayed in the debates on the 1881 land act. Unlike Davitt, he had 'no political following apart from Mr. Parnell'. He speculated that if the bishops were to support Davitt 'then his opposition would be very serious, although in the end Mr. Parnell would probably bear it down'. He did not consider the prospects of an alliance between Healy and the bishops.[8]

Barry O'Brien's assessment is representative of contemporary opinion, and owes much to the prevalent perception (which had been encouraged by Parnell for his own purposes) that if Parnell was vulnerable, it was from the agrarian left (represented by this time by the Plan of Campaign, rather than by Michael Davitt). Though regarded with deep suspicion and mistrust by Parnell's partisans in Ireland, Healy was not considered capable of mounting a serious challenge to Parnell.

Healy had commenced to distinguish his position from Parnell's on a number of key issues, of which the most important was land purchase. He still could not think in terms of open criticism of Parnell's leadership. At the fortnightly meetings of the National League's central branch in Dublin, and on platforms in rural Ireland, he delivered populistic improvisations on issues of the day, engaging in a kind of free association of Catholic nationalist themes and ideas. What was not immediately obvious was that he was developing an alternative version of nationalism to Parnell's. The astonishing vigour and comprehensiveness of Healy's assault on Parnell in the split reflected much more than the inventiveness of an inspired rhetorician. His critique of Parnell – politically as well as personally – had evolved over the preceding decade, and had begun to take coherent form from 1886. It was the combination of the acerbity of the moment with long-nurtured disenchantment which gave his attack its furious *élan*.

Healy's platform oratory in the late 1880s was uninhibited. His was the rhetoric of the agrarian nation triumphant, unchecked by the transient rigours of Balfourian 'coercion'. It was a paean to Catholic nationalist tenurial strength, and a celebration of the waning of unionist power in Ireland. Healy's vehement supremacism was at odds with Parnell's temperate reserve. It was calculated not merely to heighten the contest between landlord and tenant in Ireland, but to shift the balance of power within nationalism itself adversely to Parnell.

Healy championed the aspiration towards proprietorship and a Catholic nationalist social order with unprecedented explicitness. Many other leading nationalists tended to regard the compromising of political nationalism by its linkage to the pursuit of land purchase with grave, if rarely expressed, misgivings. Healy did not recognise any conflict between nationalism and land purchase. He rather sought to define each in terms of the other. He was not prepared to countenance fastidious distinctions between ends and means, between first and second order objectives. Home rule and the politics of proprietorship became indistinguishable in his speeches and writings. His rhetoric of the late 1880s marks the emergence of a stridently Catholic nationalism, and constitutes the first essay in conservative Irish nationalism in a recognisably modern form.

In fusing the pursuit of home rule and land purchase, Healy devised a powerful demotic idiom. What rendered his position so formidable was that it was coupled with unswerving support for Gladstone and the home rule alliance. Even if the Conservatives were more sympathetically disposed to a generous measure of land purchase than the Liberals, the frugal terms on offer from a reviled Chief Secretary held few attractions for Healy. His combination of an ultra-Liberal stance with the aggressive pursuit of peasant proprietorship, while ideologically contradictory, was to permit him to inflict incalculable damage on Parnell in the split.

Healy proclaimed the progression from the reform of tenure to land purchase to be inexorable. Writing in 1887, he celebrated the revolution in expectations wrought by the 1881 land act:

> . . . the clearest justification of the tenant's position is the rights which the Land Acts recognise him to have in his farm. Since 1881 the word 'landlord' is indeed a misnomer, and, scientifically speaking, should be no longer employed, as the tenant's interest is the superior of the two. Rent was declared by the Act of 1881 to be no longer chargeable on the tenant's improvements, and though unfortunately that proviso has been nullified in the Law Courts, its effect on the popular mind can never be rooted out . . . Since 1881 the tenant's interest has become the dominant and genuine interest in the land.[9]

Warning against the premature purchase of individual holdings on disadvantageous terms, he urged the tenants to hold out. He sought to align the pursuit of land purchase with the progress towards home rule. He declared that 'until a great treaty of peace had been made between England and Ireland, no Irish farmer ought to make a treaty of peace on his own account, and the man who purchased under Ashbourne's Act was making a treaty of peace behind the backs of the nation as a whole'. At Granard in April 1889, proclaiming home rule to be inevitable, he made a revealing comparison: 'They were not going to accept a bad settlement, they were not going to rush in like a farmer to buy his land at too big a price. They would wait until Home Rule was ripe, and then it would drop into their mouths (*laughter*)'.[10]

Healy had an aptitude approaching genius for the rhetoric of affront. This he directed against Irish unionists and landlords to banish any vestigial deference towards them. Campaigning against Sir Edward Sullivan in the St Stephen's Green division of Dublin at the 1886 election, he declared: 'These gentlemen think it is a very hard thing that a little plain language should be used about them. These scented and powdered gentlemen do not like at all the touch of a rotten egg upon their alabaster faces'.[11]

He vividly charted the economic decline of the Irish landlord:

> And I say to myself when I think of the homes and the cabins of the people that were tumbled that the time won't be far distant when you will see as many vacant houses of the landlords and the landladies as there are ruins of the peasants (*cheers*). And when I see the big houses empty and untenanted and rotting I say to myself 'Glory be to God that I have lived to see this day' (*loud cheering*).[12]

The admission in 1887 of leaseholders to the benefit of the land acts would be 'the last blister on the landlords' back', and it would be a bad year for them. In a parodic inversion of the famine, he celebrated the immiseration of the landlords. If they would live in peasant conditions on peasant rations, the National League would pay for them: 'There is money enough in the National League to buy Indian meal for the landlords of Ireland'.[13]

Healy at the same time was insistent that nationalism was untainted by materialism. He asserted, albeit somewhat perfunctorily, the pristine purity of nationalism: 'The ideal of the Irish people has not been founded upon material greatness or for material objects. It has been founded upon noble motives — those impulses which move the soul. They have been the ideas wrought from the works and sacrifices of the martyrs of past generations'.[14] He asserted the ancient continuity of the land struggle. The Plan of Campaign was 'no "new movement". This Irish movement, this Irish land struggle is as old as the hills . . .'[15]

However a hard-headed approach was more characteristic. He emphasised the commercial logic of agrarian solidarity: 'No one who has invested a shilling in his Land League card will deny that he has made interest at one hundred per cent upon it . . . Now I say that for the farmers of Ireland this movement has been a good security'.[16] The Plan of Campaign he characterised as 'an eviction insurance company', and a 'mutual system of guarantee'.[17] The idioms of commerce and nationalist sentimentality fused: 'The Irish tenant . . . has banked his heart in the affection of his countrymen, and he has banked his money in the war chest'.[18] What Healy termed 'the iron code of discipline'[19] sustained an agrarian cartel.

The appointment of Arthur Balfour as Chief Secretary in March 1887 introduced a formidable adversary. Healy joined in the chorus of nationalist hilarity which greeted his appointment. While initially dismissing Balfour as 'a pitiable incompetent in Irish affairs', characterised by 'his ladylike ineptitude', Healy was soon compelled to change his tone.[20] He charged that the unionists 'thought the Irish question was settled when the Irish Secretary dropped a little vitriol on some sensitive Irish heart'.[21] With greater rhetorical aplomb, to laughter at the National League, he coined the term 'Balferocity' in substitution for 'Balfourism'.[22]

Healy was admitted as a student of Gray's Inn, London, on 7 June 1880. In Trinity term 1881 he was admitted to King's Inn, Dublin, and was called to the Irish bar on 10 November 1884.[23] That Healy's increasing neglect of his parliamentary responsibilities in the late 1880s attracted very much less attention than did Parnell's parliamentary absences was largely due to the prominent role he played in highly publicised political prosecutions in Ireland. In his professional capacity, Healy was the pre-eminent nationalist jurist of 'coercion'. In a series of cases, defending or challenging prosecutions under Balfour's Criminal Law and Procedure (Ireland) Act of 1887, Healy, frequently pitted against the fast-rising Edward Carson for the crown, profitably combined his political and forensic roles.

His political advocacy constitutes in itself a striking essay in the interrelationship of law and power in late-nineteenth-century Ireland. In a seminal chapter in Irish jurisprudence, Healy as an advocate played a central role in eliciting from the Irish Court of Exchequer a series of judgments of enduring legal significance by which the court tempered the rigour of Balfour's 'coercion' regime. The ambit of conspiracy was narrowed by judicial codification of its evidentiary constituents. The aggrandisement of the jurisdiction to review judicially the decisions of magistrates furthered Healy's long-espoused ulterior purpose of checking the powers of the magistrature, which he considered the spine of unionist power in Ireland.[24] 'Nothing', he declared, 'has succeeded in Ireland, nothing will ever succeed in Ireland against the landlords which could not be brought within the range of the sentence of two resident magistrates.'[25]

Healy's courtroom rhetoric drew on the long and honourable traditions of invective by disaffected Catholic members of the outer bar. Rather than engage in forensic persuasion (which he reserved for the superior courts), he habitually practised a comedy of provocation calculated to reduce the proceedings to politically charged farce. Prior to the prosecution of William O'Brien at Mitchelstown in 1887, he announced publicly that his client was 'to go before this brace of gibbeting Castle hacks, who would settle everything beforehand'.[26] The prosecutions were replete with picaresque legal incident. At Loughrea in 1887, Healy and McDonnell Bodkin conducted an elaborately filibustering defence of O'Brien. They had a lot of suspense as to which of them could cross-examine the crown witnesses at the greater length. Healy and Bodkin took the witnesses in turn, their watches openly in front of them as the coin passed back and forth.[27] Healy defended O'Brien again in Carrick-on-Suir in January 1889. When the magistrates ordered that the court be cleared, Healy on the spur of the moment declared 'we won't be convicted here in camera', and left the court as did the defendant, leaving the magistrates in the words of the *Freeman's Journal* 'looking as if they had been struck by lightning'.[28] Defending O'Brien again in Tralee, Healy's opening submission was that Cecil Roche, one of the magistrates presiding, was not a proper person to hear the case since he had previously convicted a man for cheering the defendant. Edward Carson for the crown responded that a bolder or more insulting application had never been heard in a court of justice. Healy then referred to a divisional magistrate as 'a sneak', and, declining to withdraw the remark, was himself expelled.[29]

In one highly controversial instance, however, Healy's dual roles as a nationalist politician and a barrister came into sharp conflict. At Gweedore, County Donegal, in February 1889 an R.I.C. district inspector, while incautiously attempting to arrest the parish priest who was on his way to celebrate mass, was set upon and killed. Healy was junior counsel for the defence in the prosecutions which followed. When the trial came on for hearing at Maryborough, a plea bargain was offered by the crown, which the defence, given that some of the defendants faced the capital charge of murder, could not lightly refuse. Healy was initially opposed to any compromise. When his leader, the McDermott, asked him what his objections were, Healy replied to the effect that the defendants were soldiers in the fight and should accept whatever fate might befall them. McDermott made clear he would not permit political considerations to prevail, and Healy relented. However when his case came to be discussed, the parish priest, McFadden, refused at first to plead guilty to any charge. Healy declared that if he were McFadden he would rather cut off his hand than plead guilty. Healy's instructing solicitor then made what Healy later described as 'a very proper observation . . . though I felt it at the time: "Do you give that advice as a counsellor or a politician?"' When McFadden decided to plead guilty to the minor charge of obstructing the police on the day preceding the killing, Healy told him that he was right as a priest, but wrong as a politician.[30]

The *Freeman's Journal*, in what was intended primarily as a cut at Healy, declared that 'a great mistake was made by the counsel for the defence in withdrawing from the uncompromising position which the public expected and hoped they would maintain throughout the whole proceedings'.[31] It was an ugly and misconceived slur: if Healy was to be faulted, it was rather in permitting his political views to colour his professional advice. The charge entered popular mythology. The venomous M. J. Kenny wrote to an acquaintance that 'The Prince of Coolavin [McDermott] and Tim Healy rank in the popular imagination with Corydon and Carey . . . a worse-assorted team could not be found and the fate of the Martyrs of Maryboro will be kept fresh in the memory of the Irish public as long as Tim Healy has an enemy who wants to keep him out of position'.[32] Healy at the time publicly defended his position as much as the duty of professional confidentiality permitted, insisting that his professional obligations had to take precedence over his political allegiances, and defended McFadden for a decision 'taken with absolute reluctance'.[33]

Throughout the split, Healy was harried by the Parnellite charge that he had received additional fees from the crown arising from the pleas –

in effect that he had accepted a crown bribe. The taunt of 'remember Maryborough' rang in his ears. Healy successfully sued the *Freeman's Journal* for libel in an action which came on for hearing in July 1891 and eventually recovered damages in the very substantial sum of £700. He was thus belatedly exonerated of what he categorised as Parnellite allegations against their opponents of 'foul crimes . . . in their professional capacity, which, if committed, would almost justify their assassination in the street'.[34]

In the split, Healy would devastatingly charge Parnell with pursuing a sinister *rapprochement* with the Conservatives on the land question. Parnell's policy on land purchase is central to an understanding of his statecraft, and of its undoing. While he did not fully unveil his policy until 1890, his thinking on the subject had crystallised at least as early as 1886.

On 7 January of that year, Katharine O'Shea had forwarded to Gladstone a letter from Parnell outlining a measure for the resolution of the Irish land question. Remarkably, it was avowedly based on proposals remitted to Parnell by 'the representatives of one of the chief landlord political associations in Ireland'. Parnell looked to the compulsory expropriation of all land in the occupation of agricultural tenants (a term which under the 1881 land act excluded the tenants of large pasture holdings); a scheme of compensation skewed in favour of smaller residential landlords; and the reduction of encumbrances on estates by 20 per cent. This would reduce opposition to home rule, he argued disingenuously but not without intelligence of purpose, as 'the Protestants, other than the owners of the land, are not really opposed to such a concession'.[35] Parnell, in his egregiously moderate speech in the debate on the address later that month, alluded to the possibility of land purchase proceeding on the lines indicated by Sir Robert Giffen, the eminent statistician. Once again he asserted that 'this is a limited question', by reference to the value of the holdings of agricultural tenants as statutorily defined.[36]

To this proposal Parnell was to revert in the split. Supporting an amendment to Balfour's land purchase bill of 1891 which discriminated in favour of holdings in excess of £30 valuation, he asserted that such a measure, which would resolve the main part of the land question, was a reform he had long had in mind: 'it is one the principle of which I placed before Mr. Gladstone in a written memorandum so far back as the beginning of '86, when I pointed out to him that it was possible to materially limit the area of the land purchase question'.[37]

What Parnell sought was a settlement of the land question which would permit the purchase by small tenants of the holdings on which they were actually resident, which fined down the rent on the remaining holdings, and which gave preferential treatment to the smaller residential landlords over the absentee owners of large estates. In seeking to conserve a residential landlord class in Ireland, Parnell's purpose was to maintain a residual grid of unionist socio-economic power capable of redressing the disequilibrium to which Catholic nationalist predominance in a home rule state would otherwise give rise.

Parnell's policy, in placing limits to the extent of land purchase and in seeking to discriminate between tenants on the basis of the size of their holdings, was in nationalist terms profoundly heterodox. It constituted his most ambitious attempt to mould the socio-economic framework of a home rule polity. While he could perhaps have succeeded in imposing such a settlement in the Ireland of 1886, his policy became more difficult to sustain with every year that passed. Parnell's boast of consistency in the split was all too accurate. On the land question, he evinced not so much his fabled resolve as a curious, almost pedantic inflexibility. He clung to his views after they had been superseded, and in the split was engulfed in the rising tide of nationalist expectations of an untrammelled measure of land purchase.

Healy was instinctively suspicious of Parnell's attitude to the land question. In mid-1887, on the basis of a conversation with the Attorney-General for Ireland, Healy formed the (erroneous) view that the government did not greatly care whether Balfour's first land bill was carried or not. He reported to Maurice:

> I was speaking to Parnell about this, saying we should only let the first clause, that which admitted leaseholders to the benefits of the Land Acts pass, and he quietly said 'don't you think it would be a pity to allow these fellows to deal with the leaseholders' question?', or words to that effect.[38]

The thinking of the two men could hardly have been more starkly opposed. For Healy the pursuit of the amelioration of the position of the tenants was an end in itself, the use of which as a subordinate instrument of policy he was not prepared to countenance. Moreover as a barrister and parliamentary expert on land law, he prized the winning of legislative concessions. Parnell's attitude he considered neglectful and cynical, and in the split went so far as to accuse him of manifesting a predominant allegiance to his own social caste in his approach to the land question.

Parnell publicly signalled his position in proposing an amendment to the land purchase bill of 1888 to restrict tenants from purchasing more than one holding where the rateable value of the holding exceeded £20. He sought thereby to limit the ambit of land purchase, avowedly on the basis that this represented the most effective application available of the public monies:

> He had always held that the necessary dimensions of the purchase question waiting solution by Parliament were not nearly so large as was generally considered. He considered that beyond providing the tenant with the holding upon which his house stood, it was not requisite that the State should interfere . . . If they would look at the question of land purchase from the point of view he invited them to look at it, it became narrowed down to the necessity of securing that the holding on which the tenant lived should be his, and there was no claim and no argument in favour of extending the principle of purchase beyond the limit suggested by reasons of state.

Although Healy supported the amendment, the views expressed by Parnell were diametrically opposed to his own.[39]

The main Irish business of the 1890 parliament was Balfour's Purchase of Land and Congested Districts (Ireland) Bill. Balfour intended the measure as the culminating achievement of his Chief Secretaryship, and revelled in the intricacies of a measure whose excessive complexity did much to ensure its failure in practice.[40]

Balfour's bill threatened to expose deep contradictions within the Liberal–nationalist alliance. Radicals in the Liberal ranks looked on land purchase with profound suspicion. Their ideological distaste was compounded by the conviction that Gladstone's parliamentary defeat in 1886 was the result of the land purchase measure that accompanied the home rule bill. Not altogether in jest, Labouchere epitomised the radical antagonism to land purchase: 'the policy adopted in the last few years in Ireland has been a policy of kicks and ha'pence. I have been opposed to the kicks; I am equally opposed to the ha'pence. The ha'pence are, perhaps, more demoralising, and would more lower the patriotic fibre of Irishmen than the kicks'.[41] The unease was not confined to the radicals. In less overtly doctrinaire form it suffused the Liberal party, and was deepened by the dread of an entente between Parnell and the government. Parnell in the event allayed Liberal fears. Morley met Parnell, apparently in Ireland, in mid-April, and was able to assure Gladstone that Parnell had 'willingly' agreed to move the rejection of the bill, 'so that's now all in order'.[42]

The accord was however deceptive. Morley later wrote that Parnell in 1890 was much exercised on land purchase: 'He once asked me to speak with him, having devised a very complex and impractical set of notions of his own, which he slowly expounded to me. I asked would his people like it? He did not care whether they did or not, he had thought it over for ten years'.[43] These were the proposals with which Parnell startled his own followers and the Liberal leadership by unveiling in the course of his unexpectedly moderate — and unwontedly lengthy — speech in moving the rejection of the bill on 21 April.

He first stated that he favoured a 20 per cent reduction in judicial rents, 'at all events as a preliminary to land purchase', and proceeded to condemn the bill as a measure not to settle the Irish land question, but to enable 'about one-ninth or one-tenth of the larger and absentee owners to get out of the country at an exorbitant price, leaving their smaller resident brethren in the lurch'. The bill was unfair to resident Irish landowners. Parnell then advanced his own proposals. He had thought for many years over the question, and proposed a solution which had first suggested itself on the introduction of the 1881 land bill. His essential point was that 'this land question is not so large a question as many will suppose'. He argued that the larger class of tenants, over £50 valuation, could be 'fairly protected' under the provisions of the 1881 Land Act as amended, standing as they did on a more equal footing with their landlords, 'and it is not, in my judgement, necessary for the sake of settling the Irish land question that it should include the class of tenants above £50 valuation in any Purchase Bill'.

He spoke of the desire of nationalists to see resident landlords 'taking the part for which they are so well fitted in the future social regeneration of the country'. Parnell went on to divest this assertion of any smack of platitude by asserting that the distinguishing feature of the bill was 'the utter unscrupulousness with which it throws overboard the Irish resident landowners, and leaves their future to be utterly destroyed and ruined'.[44]

Parnell's speech sowed consternation in the ranks of Liberals and nationalists alike. Gladstone falteringly pronounced his proposals 'chivalrous'. His confession that 'I am not certain that in all its details I have a perfect comprehension of it' was greeted by laughter from the government benches. Morley later described the speech as 'slow, interesting, serious, but horribly obscure'. At midnight he was approached by Parnell's 'most important lieutenant' (whom he does not identify), and asked could he explain what Parnell meant by the speech, which had completely mystified the Irish party. Gladstone jested that 'it is difficult enough for him to be absent and inaccessible, but if besides that, when he does appear – to plunge into unexplained politics, that is indeed too bad!' A member of the cabinet was said to have observed that it would be well in future if Parnell pinned his notes together. Radical unease was increased by the Chancellor of the Exchequer's statement that the government would consider Parnell's scheme at the committee stage.[45] Parnell's subsequent claim that his proposals constituted an integral alternative to Balfour's scheme rather than a set of proposals which could be incorporated piecemeal into Balfour's bill was the minimum necessary to allay Liberal fears of a widening rift within the home rule alliance.[46]

E. W. Hamilton, a uniquely privileged observer in that he had assisted

Balfour in settling the provisions of the bill while remaining a confidant of Gladstone, observed of Parnell that 'he certainly is a most extraordinary fellow. He had never consulted even his principal followers, or given Mr. Gl[adstone] a hint of the line he was going to take'. While he was generally on the right track on Ireland, 'one can't help feeling that on this occasion he has embarked on the wrong tack. The scheme seems to be replete with objections, and utterly impractical'. He rightly noted that 'the most statesmanlike part of his speech was the *conserving* spirit which he displayed towards Irish landlords', but erred in believing this to represent a sudden change on Parnell's part: 'The fact is, the nearer becomes the approach of Home Rule, the more he must feel the responsibility of his position and the more conscious he must be to retain a portion of the natural governing class of the country'.[47]

In the debate which followed Parnell's speech, the only critical nationalist voice was Dillon's. His dissent was tentative, and he explicitly deferred to the authority of his leader, whose speech 'if it errs at all, errs in the direction of being too moderate from my point of view'. It had been widely noted that nationalist members did not cheer Parnell's proposal: 'That is perfectly true. They have not received it with enthusiasm, because its character is not one which excites enthusiasm among those who are a party of war'. He disagreed with the proposal to draw the line at a valuation of £50, but declared that Parnell was the only man who could settle the Irish land question on the lines he had indicated: 'The hon. Member for Cork could settle the Irish land question on the fining down proposal; but in a year it may be impossible and it is for the Irish landlords to say whether they are acting wisely'. The prophecy proved ironic. The tide was by then running against the Irish leader more than the landlords.[48]

Chamberlain, whom Parnell's proposals were intended to discomfit, retaliated. He described the proposals as very unexpected, sarcastically adding 'at all events very unexpected to those of us who are not in his confidence'. He pointed out that as the Parnellites had always alleged that rents were extortionate, it was strange that Parnell should propose that landlords should be compensated for reducing them: 'Is Saul also among the prophets? Has the hon. Member for Cork joined the Landlords' Convention?'[49] Having insouciantly unleashed his thunderbolt, Parnell did not attend to hear the speeches of Chamberlain and Balfour, and confined himself to slipping into the division lobbies to oppose the bill on its second reading.[50]

In the vote on the Chief Secretary's office in July, Parnell again distanced himself from the Plan of Campaign ('I do not, and never have, concealed my views with regard to the Plan of Campaign'). He restated his position on the land purchase bill, but asserted that he had advanced his proposal for the fining down of rents merely in the context of the limited finance available under the bill: 'But, of course, I shall prefer a solution by occupying ownership, and I do not advance the principle of fining down the rents as a better and more perfect way'. He left it to be inferred that he still looked to a discrimination in land purchase in favour of the smaller tenants.[51] Robbins reported that Parnell's speech

> has caused some irritation among advanced Gladstonian Liberals, who frankly describe him as 'a Tory on the land question'. From some points of view it is strange that they have not discovered this before; but there is a possible explanation of the Irish leader's attitude at this moment beyond that of his innate Conservatism on agrarian matters. The fact is that he is thoroughly weary of the session and is longing for rest. Immediately Parliament rises, he intends going to Avondale for the shooting season . . . Those who have carefully followed his utterances on the land question will, of course, remember that he has never expressly countenanced the extremer views of some of his political associates, and particularly as regards the 'plan of campaign'; but they will not build upon this fact, or upon his present weariness of futile discussions, any lively hope of his giving assistance to the passage of the Land Purchase Bill.[52]

Parnell elaborated on his views in an interview with Robbins the next day. Throughout the agrarian agitation Parnell had expressed himself in favour of occupying ownership, 'using that phrase because he felt that the more commonly used phrase "peasant proprietary" did not quite fit the condition he wished to create'.[53] Parnell's chosen terminology was significant: the concept of peasant proprietorship was too narrow to encompass the retention of a residential landlord class. In relation to the Liberals, Robbins reported that if they could show they had 'the overwhelming support of the British people in antagonism to an advance of money under any circumstances to solve the Irish agrarian problem, it will have serious weight with Parnell and the party he leads'.[54]

In Morley's last interview with Parnell before the divorce crisis, at Brighton on 10 November 1890, the main legislative business under discussion was the Balfour land purchase bill, which was to be re-introduced the following session. When Morley accepted that the government's figure of £33 million represented the maximum finance available, Parnell said 'then we must see that it is used as wisely as possible'. To that end he advocated pressing for a limit on the size of holdings eligible for purchase, as well as vesting of a right of veto in democratically elected Irish local authorities. 'He feels as strongly as I do', wrote Morley, 'the danger of H[ome] R[ule] with the land question left open.'[55]

To Healy, Parnell's stance on Balfour's bill was deeply objectionable, and afforded for the first time proof positive of what he had long suspected, that Parnell was determined to retain a residential landlord class, primarily at the expense of the larger tenant farmers. Speaking in Dublin on 25 March 1890, before Parnell's speech on the second reading, Healy staked out the position from which he was to assail Parnell in the split. He condemned the bill as incompatible with both the achievement of land purchase and the furtherance of the Liberal alliance. He now espoused the fixed policy of Joseph Biggar — which he had previously declined to follow — of opposing all proposals from a hostile government. The bill emanated from a tainted source — 'a government charged and corrupted by landlord prejudices and principles'.[56]

The *New York Times* of 13 July carried a fierce attack on Parnell's speech on the Chief Secretary's vote written by its London correspondent, Healy's friend and confidant Harold Frederic. Frederic accused Parnell of betraying the Irish party and the Plan of Campaign in collaborating with Balfour to remodel the land purchase bill. He predicted a protest by the party, and even Parnell's retirement from his post as leader 'which latterly he has only used to insult and affront his colleagues':

> There has all along been the difficulty of seeing how he could maintain this post once the O'Shea case had come to trial, and last night a number of Irish members were disposed to fear that brooding upon this trouble had brought on the mental disturbance to which he is hereditarily predisposed. It is the only way in which they are able to account for his astonishing and contemptuous act of treachery to them.[57]

Healy fell under immediate suspicion, as the inspiration if not the source for Frederic's article. To many it appeared as if his public mask of loyalty to Parnell had slipped. He protested that the attack was published before he had read Parnell's speech: 'it would be intolerable in a member of any party to inspire attacks which he was afraid to make himself, and I would scorn, directly or indirectly, to suggest or inspire others to make such criticism'. He nonetheless conspicuously failed to dissociate himself from the sentiments expressed, which corresponded to his private criticisms of Parnell. In the face of disavowals from Dillon and O'Brien, Frederic maintained his position, insisting that his statement that Irish members bitterly resented Parnell's 'studied insolence' was 'absolutely and literally true'. In the split, Parnell would angrily charge that Healy had cabled to America 'to consign me to a lunatic asylum'.[58]

When in April 1888 the papal rescript condemning the Plan of Campaign was published, Healy, along with T. D. Sullivan, was a member of the committee which drafted the resolution of Catholic nationalist members of the

Irish party declining to recognise the right of the papacy to intervene in Irish affairs.[59]

Healy had for some time feared an intervention by the Vatican. In his pessimistic assessment of the political prospect written to Maurice from Zurich on 3 July 1887 he wrote that 'if the Pope means to interfere with friendly priests, as seems probable, it would be hard enough to maintain an effective struggle under Coercion'.[60] Publicly, he struck a note of calculated defiance: '. . . insofar as I have given my approval, my intellectual adhesion, to the manifestations known as the Plan of Campaign and boycotting, I remain, with regard to these two matters in face of the Roman circular, a wholly unregenerated and unrepentant sinner'.[61]

The papal rescript elicited the last great rallying of nationalists within a united Irish movement to Parnell. Healy's defence of Parnell served his own purposes. In his attacks on the rescript he sought to solder an overt alliance of church and nation. His assured idiom of Catholic nationalism prefigured his rhetoric in the split. As Parnell reached his zenith in Ireland, Healy's inchoate challenge acquired its most dangerous form. He struck a gallican stance. He argued not for the subordination of church to state, but for the rights of the Catholic church in Ireland against Rome. In an almost feudal formulation, by which he accorded to the Catholic church in Ireland the status of an estate of the nation, Healy declared that 'an impudent assault had been made upon the rights of the bishops and upon the liberties of the clergy'.[62] Healy drew an equation rare in Irish politics between political Catholicism in Ireland and on the continent, placing the Irish parliamentary party in the ranks of European Catholic parties, notably those in Belgium and in Germany. He made a comparison between the papal rescript and Bismarck's invocation of papal intervention against Windthorst in the course of the *Kulturkampf*.[63] Healy's grounds for opposing the papal rescript diverged sharply from the liberal nationalism of John Dillon, who argued that Irish Protestants were entitled to expect that Catholic nationalists did not take their orders from Rome.[64]

What was striking was Healy's coupling of an aggressive political Catholicism with his championship of the Liberal alliance. Like the *Irish Catholic*, Healy had no difficulty repudiating Balfour's briefly espoused and swiftly retracted Catholic university project, declaring 'come weal, come woe, their fate was inextricably bound up with that of the Liberal party'.[65]

Healy broadened his attack on the rescript to denounce Conservative intermeddling at the Vatican in Irish Catholic affairs. He attacked 'the hope and the policy in the breasts of the Government of controlling and divorcing the Catholic ecclesiastics of Ireland from the movement of the people, and by these means reducing, as they expect, this movement and this country to subjection'. He went on to condemn rumoured Conservative intrigues with the Vatican in relation to the appointment of a bishop to the diocese of Kerry, and what he alleged to be a plot to appoint the anti-nationalist Bishop of Clonfert to the vacant see of Waterford.[66]

Healy maintained his attack on the endeavours of the government to enlist the support of the Vatican in a searing speech in the Commons, which contained a rare, and somewhat anomalous, invocation of the memory of Daniel O'Connell:

> God rest the honest soul of Daniel O'Connell, and if Catholics, ay and Nonconformists and Jews, have now religious liberty, they owe it to that great heart which is enshrined in its proper place almost under the shadow of the Vatican . . . Our forefathers won our rights and liberties in face of most abominable persecution, and O'Connell, by those appeals which the *Times* said were condensed of 'Irish bog', won those rights for the cowering Norfolks and others who now seek to defame his race.[67]

The twenty-seven-year-old David Lloyd George, who had been elected for Caernarvon Boroughs the previous April, wrote delightedly to his wife of Healy's speech:

> He was frightfully biting . . . He broke the rules of propriety which are so stringent in the House but it was very amusing. There is a psalm-singing Wesleyan on the Tory side – the only Wesleyan on that side – a fellow who is always at Church & missionary meetings. Healy called him 'the honourable & *pious* member for Boston'. The Chairman very angrily pulled him up but the House roared with delight at this impudent sally. He referred to the Under-Secretary, a sanctimonious-looking Scotch Protestant as 'sleeping with Foxe's Book of Martyrs under his pillow'. A more impudent, audacious speech has hardly been delivered ever with impunity within these walls. The Celts are having their revenge upon the brutal Saxon.[68]

Healy's increasing estrangement from Parnell in the late 1880s coincided with the emergence of an explicitly Catholic strain of nationalism. With the establishment in May 1888 of the *Irish Catholic*, Catholic nationalism had for the first time in the history of the Parnellite movement a distinctive voice. The paper was the successor to the Sullivans' *Weekly News*, established in 1860 as 'the organ of the artisan and tenant farmer', discontinued in favour of 'a new journal more exclusively devoted to the religious interests of the Irish people'.[69] It was a suggestive shift of constituency.

The establishment of the paper closely preceded the withdrawal of the Sullivans from ownership and editorial control of the *Nation*, its sister paper which had encountered increasing financial difficulties. In April 1890, T. D. Sullivan relinquished the ownership and editorship of the *Nation* to associates.[70] Too traditional in its ways to sound the authentic Parnellite note, it had long been driven from the high political terrain. Sullivan's abandonment of a cherished historical association with Young Ireland attested to the isolated and atrophied condition of the Healy–Sullivan connection in Irish politics, before the divorce crisis revolutionised its political fortunes.

The declared role of the *Irish Catholic* was as 'an organ of Irish Catholic opinion', conceived in opposition to the Toryism of the *Tablet*.[71] Its editor and part-proprietor was William F. Dennehy (1853–1918), the eldest of the seven children of Alderman Cornelius Dennehy J.P., a Dublin merchant, who through the encumbered estates court became the proprietor of an estate in Longford.[72] Formerly a minor pedant who wrote on nationalist historical and antiquarian subjects, W. Dennehy became in the split Parnell's most pietistically vituperative assailant.

Under Dennehy's editorship, the *Irish Catholic* combined a strident defence of Catholic interests with support for the Liberal–nationalist alliance. A primer of illiberal and anti-modernist values, it addressed with disconcerting starkness themes inimical to the maintenance in the longer term of Parnellite consensus, even had the divorce crisis not arisen. Although Healy in a later phase of his career was to assert that he was 'just as much responsible for the Pekin Gazette', the paper was from the outset closely associated with 'the brilliant member for North Longford'.[73]

The appearance of the *Irish Catholic* was of consequence for the Catholic church in Ireland as well as for nationalism. The irruption of vehement laical zealotry was subversive of the more subtle episcopal *haute politique* practised by Archbishops Croke and Walsh through the 1880s. The paper's unctuous assertion in its obituary of Dennehy in 1918 that 'he always bore in mind that the proper place of the Catholic lay journalist is one of the most docile subordination to the official authorities' did not quite capture his genius for fractious provocation. In 1894 an enraged Walsh was prompted to despatch his administrator to advise Dennehy that as bishop of the diocese he was satisfied that 'the publication of the paper *as a Catholic paper*, was seriously injurious to religious interests, and that if it were not at once divested of all appearance of being a Catholic organ, it would be publicly condemned by me'.[74]

The *Irish Catholic* vociferously championed the establishment of a Catholic proprietorial class, to the extent of supporting, contrary to the declared policy of the Irish party, Balfour's land purchase bill. The bill would sweep away a large number of landlords 'and establish in their stead an absolutely independent Irish yeomanry class. Now, we know that the members of this new class in the social organisation of their country will be, whatever faults and defects may be theirs, at any rate Irish, Catholic and Nationalist'.[75] The paper's condemnation of Balfour's brief espousal of a Catholic university was in the same vein: 'Any University establishment must not be one which will turn out Catholic Mahaffys, men contemning their native land, but honest, devout, manly young Irishmen, loving their own country'.[76]

The paper denounced discrimination against Catholics in commercial and professional life and in the government services, and urged the organisation of Catholics for the purpose of 'the securing of fair play for Catholics *as* Catholics in every walk of life, commercial, professional and official'.[77] It obsessively denounced Protestant proselytism, the *bête noire* of extreme Catholic nationalism.[78]

Predictably, organisation among the working classes elicited a less enthusiastic response. Professing not to condemn socialism as such ('there are of course Socialists and Socialists'), the paper championed the labour programme of the Archbishop of Dublin and warned 'we do not want in Dublin or Ireland associations even remotely resembling the Socialist clubs of London, Berlin, or Paris'.[79] This was the religious and social context of Dennehy's resolute deprecation of Fenianism: 'between believing Christians and secret conspirators there can be no truce, no union'.[80]

On 11 February 1890, Joseph Biggar moved the re-election of Parnell as sessional chairman of the Irish party in what was described in the minutes as 'a very feeling and sympathetic speech', to which Parnell replied in somewhat perfunctory tones.[81] In the small hours of 19 February Biggar acted as a teller on the vote on Parnell's amendment to the address. He died later the same morning.[82] At the funeral in Clapham on a foul day, Justin McCarthy had a presentiment of catastrophe: 'The service was solemn, intensely gloomy and I sat through it with darkening mind'.[83]

Healy was bereft and inconsolable. For him, the death of Biggar marked a traumatic rupture. Biggar's position as what *United Ireland* called the father of the Irish party had in Healy's case a psychological reality. Healy wrote to his father that Biggar's death was the 'greatest blow I have ever received. After yourself he was the best man I ever met'.[84] Significantly ten years later it was from the death of Biggar that Healy dated the disintegration of his political world. After Maurice's defeat in Cork at the 1900 election Healy wrote to his father in anguished retrospect: 'Poor Biggar's death was the first wrench, then the Split, then Gladstone's disappearance, then the Bounder-*Freeman* racket, and now comes this squalid army of frauds and parasites fed on the thirty pieces of silver. Poor Ireland!'[85] Healy's *Great Fraud of Ulster* (1917) was dedicated to Biggar 'the most unselfish, fearless, and straightforward public man that I have known'.

Twenty-seven years his senior, he had been to Healy a mentor and a stabilising influence. Engagingly blunt and thick-skinned, Biggar's heart was unlacerated by the envies and insecurities to which Healy was prey. He was endowed with common sense so robust as to approach intellectual originality. Had he lived, it can hardly be doubted that he would have opposed Parnell in the split. Yet his presence would have mitigated Healy's loss of control and direction, and curtailed the sterile offensiveness of his rhetoric against Parnell, whom Biggar had loved. His death was a personal tragedy for Healy, and a calamity for the Irish party.[86]

Relations between radicals and Parnellites grew increasingly strained in the years 1889–90. The matter of the royal grants in July 1889 raised an issue of exceptional sensitivity for Gladstone. The Liberal leader sought to persuade Parnell that it would be wise if the nationalists did not alienate the Prince of Wales (the future Edward VII) who was far less prejudiced in relation to Ireland than the Queen. Parnell was said to have admitted the force of Gladstone's argument, and looked to the day when the Prince of Wales would inaugurate a parliament in Dublin. Gladstone believed he could carry Parnell.[87] While Parnell's stance was not popular with all of his parliamentary colleagues, they followed him into the division lobby in support of the royal grants to Conservative cheers. Labouchere said irritably to Justin McCarthy who was sitting beside him: 'Go in and get your cheer; it will probably be the last Tory cheer you will ever get'.[88]

Parnell's action was not taken out of deference to Gladstone, but as part of his own larger strategy. Two months previously, in conversation with George Lewis, he had counselled against a proposed visit to Ireland by the Prince of Wales, on the grounds that while he would have nothing to complain of in the reception he would receive, it was better if he did not go, as he could not avoid being associated to some degree with the policy of the Conservative government. Parnell was diplomatically understating the risks of demonstrations of hostility in Ireland. He advanced the view that the way to enhance loyalty in Ireland would be for the Prince to reserve himself for the opening of an Irish parliament, when he would be accorded a reception such as he had not encountered elsewhere.[89]

Tensions between Parnellites and radicals were further exacerbated by Balfour's railway legislation of 1889–90. The provision of public funds to finance the construction of railways by private promoters, which at least provided employment in disadvantaged areas, was viewed with marked disfavour by radicals, and elicited conflicting responses among nationalist parliamentarians. Healy had supported Biggar in opposing the emigration clauses of the Tramways Bill of 1883, but they withdrew their opposition, according to Healy, under pressure from Parnell.[90] Biggar continued thereafter to oppose railway legislation, his antagonism towards railway promoters sharpened by the belief that Captain W. H. O'Shea had assisted 'a swindling syndicate'.[91] He received intermittent and somewhat tentative backing from Healy.

Healy did not join Biggar in opposing the Light Railways (Ireland) Bill of 1889. When the bill was discussed at a party meeting, Parnell, personally sympathetic, expressed no view. Biggar spoke against, William Martin Murphy for. Confronted by a division among his allies, Healy 'deprecated any division in the party over the measure'. Parnell pointedly asked if there was a resolution before the meeting. As there was not, the meeting dissolved without the party taking a formal position for or against. The support of the measure by most of the Irish members offended the radicals. Healy condemned radical attempts 'to prevent us from getting this miserable little benefit that the Government are willing to give us'. Alfred Robbins discerned 'a distinct soreness between the Radicals and the Nationalists which even dinners at Mr. Labouchere's cannot allay'. In the split, Parnell extravagantly but revealingly attributed the intrigues of the radicals Philip Stanhope and Henry Labouchere against his leadership to resentment at his support for the 1889 bill.[92]

In August 1890, Balfour's Railways (Ireland) Bill provoked an open rift within the Irish party. At the end of the session, when parliamentary time was severely restricted, Healy and W. M. Murphy led a tiny contingent of Irish members in opposing the passage of the bill in an all-night sitting. Healy was thereby able to assert himself at the end of a session when he had been conspicuous chiefly by his absence. The majority of the party supported the measure, and Sexton, in Parnell's absence, had agreed with Balfour and the Attorney-General for Ireland that it should pass.

The Healy–Murphy opposition was in the event somewhat lamely withdrawn in the face of overwhelming nationalist opposition, leaving the radicals alone in voting against the bill. Their opposition was ill-judged, and the divergence within the Irish party ominous. The sitting, Robbins concluded, 'strikingly exemplified the jealousies in the Nationalist ranks. Whenever Mr. Parnell is out of the way there is an almost open struggle for the deputy leadership; and as Mr. Dillon and Mr. William O'Brien are now absent, the contest during the past week has lain between Mr. Sexton and Mr. Healy'. Within three months the contest would extend to the leadership of the party.[93]

Stung by criticism of his action in the nationalist press, Healy's response was disquietingly emotional. Embattled, he identified himself with the dead Biggar: he had supported the Light Railways Act of 1889 'against the advice and action of one of the greatest and noblest Irishmen that ever lived

— their lamented friend Mr. Biggar, whose name would be held in eternal honour by everyone who studied his noble and massive character'. Still more alarmingly, Healy situated his opposition to the Railways Bill in a litany of dissent, which pointedly included one of the very rare public references by a nationalist to the Galway election at a time when the shadow of Captain O'Shea had once again fallen across the path of the Irish party:

> Having formed one of several minorities within the Irish Party — the minority protesting against the ghastly loopline needlessly erected so as to destroy Dublin's finest view, the minority which resisted the exclusion of Ireland from the extended municipal franchise accorded to Belfast, the minority which opposed the selection of a discredited candidate for Galway — I believe that though in deference to the majority of our colleagues the Railway Bill has been allowed to become law unamended, events will justify the resistance of those who would have insisted on one day of the holidays of the Ministers being sacrificed to the threatened distress of the Irish people.[94]

In his last two speeches prior to the divorce crisis, in Dublin in late August and late September 1890, Healy's agrarian rhetoric became ever more strident. He effectively advocated the withholding of rent in the distressed areas of the west of Ireland. He asserted that if, after the precedent of the famine, 'tenants again hand over to the landlords the property, the money, and the substance, which are necessary for those men to keep themselves alive during the coming winter, I say the world is well rid of such a spiritless race'.[95]

Healy's rhetoric in the latter half of the 1880s attests to the excessive susceptibility of contemporary nationalists to Gladstone's charisma. The Liberal–nationalist alliance was sealed as much by the defeat of Gladstone's home rule bill as by its introduction. For nationalists such as Healy, the *éclat* of Gladstone's embrace of home rule was perpetuated through a sentimental solidarity in defeat. A sense of unrequited moral purpose suffused what had been a parliamentary alliance to achieve a defined end. When Davitt in 1888 denounced the cry of 'Gloria Gladstone in Excelsis', he had Healy in contemplation as one of the principal choristers.[96]

Healy's panegyrics to Gladstone frequently proceeded, in the manner of chauvinistic nationalism, by means of an extended contrast between Gladstone's enlightened attitude to Ireland and the anti-Irish comments of sections of the English press. (Parnell, possessed of better judgement and taste, steadfastly ignored such provocations.) In his speech on the introduction of the home rule bill, in which he lauded Gladstone, Healy responded to a reference by Trevelyan to the 'assassination literature' of extreme American nationalism: 'Does he ever read the assassination literature of England? Do men think that our blood is so cold and our bodies so clay-like that we should not feel the deadly stings and stabs of the poignard press of England?' He protested at the Irish being daily degraded in the English press 'and represented in your so-called comic journals as half-thug, half-chimpanzee'.[97]

He hailed Gladstone for having raised his voice in protest 'against the whole system of exaggeration and caricature directed in England towards the Irish character'. He had 'pierced the crusts of bigotry that shut out from the minds of the English people the real facts of the Irish cause'. He credited Gladstone with having transformed English attitudes towards Ireland: 'their minds now are as sensitive to the light as the sensitized paper of the photographer'. Gladstone had 'rolled away the stone'.[98] In a characteristic sacrificial image, Healy asserted that Gladstone had 'placed his whole reputation — his fifty years of statesmanship — in pawn in order to make himself the scapegoat for the sins and crimes of centuries'.[99] Gladstone appeared to unite in his person a timeless integrity with modern enlightenment. He was, Healy declared, 'the greatest intellect of the age'.[100]

Healy pressed his allegiance to Gladstone to heterodox extremes. Speaking in Dublin in December 1886, Healy, in asserting the existence of a dual leadership of the Liberal–nationalist alliance, acknowledged a divided allegiance:

> He would not express any opinion as to whether they could get on better if they were not spancilled, so to speak with the English party; but he would say that in addition to their own great leader they had another great commander (*applause*) whose actions towards them had given him just claims upon their consideration, and he was willing to consider the claims the Liberal leaders and the Liberal party had upon the Irish people generally.[101]

Healy was not alone in his adulatory attitude towards Gladstone. In April 1887 the *Nation* proposed the erection of a statue of Gladstone in Dublin close by the old parliament house on College Green: 'Why should we make another day's delay before commencing a movement for the erection on Irish soil of a monument of our nation's gratitude to William Ewart Gladstone? . . . Why wait until the Home Rule victory has been won? Won it will be, and with God's blessing before long'. This ineptly conceived project violated every axiom of Parnellite nationalism, and was rapidly quashed. The following week's *Nation* announced that it had been suggested that 'a short postponement of the movement would be desirable', and that the Lord Mayor (T. D. Sullivan) had deferred a meeting he had called at the Mansion House 'in approval of which he had received letters from several of the Irish Bishops, from members of the Parliamentary party, and others'.[102]

The Liberal leader was more alive to the delicacy of the situation than his fervent Irish admirers. When John Dillon proposed a meeting in Dublin at which Parnell and Gladstone would share the platform, Morley discountenanced the proposals: 'I was at Hawarden a few days ago, and something was said of a project of Mr. Gladstone receiving a portrait of himself at the Mansion House in Dublin. "No", he said, "I feel the less direct dealings I have with the Irish people, the more useful I shall be to them". The same sort of consideration rather applies in this case'.[103]

By 1888 Healy's relations with Gladstone were exceptionally cordial. In the late summer, Gladstone extended to Healy an invitation to visit him at Hawarden, which the *Times* unkindly observed 'has become to the faithful a kind of Mecca or Lourdes'. In a shrewd letter of apology, written after he had received a reminder from Gladstone, Healy, having evidently reconsidered his position, politely discouraged the idea. He had not in the event had occasion to cross to London from Dublin, and had gone down to Butlerstown, County Waterford, from where he was writing. He had thought to 'make up a little party from Dublin in a week or two'. However, he had since realised that 'such a visit would look more formal than one undertaken by way of a break of journey, returning to Ireland, and therefore perhaps objectionable as invested with a character which it otherwise would not have worn in the case of it becoming a matter of press comment afterwards'. Having thus signified his view of the inadvisability of the visit, Healy shifted the responsibility to Gladstone: 'should you however think we might still avail of your too kind suggestion, we could on any day that you fix be delighted to go over, and for myself, I will say that I have known no such honour in my life'. The point was not lost in the flattery, and Gladstone took the hint, writing that a trip from Dublin 'would not be worth your while', and leaving open the possibility, which had been rendered academic, of a visit in November.[104] Healy thus wisely averted a visit to Hawarden which would have been regarded by Parnell as an open act of usurpation.

Gladstone had originally contemplated a visit by the collective leadership of the Irish party, rather than a meeting with the Irish leader alone. In December 1888, shortly after the suggested visit by Healy had miscarried, Gladstone wrote to Justin McCarthy resuscitating the idea of which he had talked for some sessions past of a visit to Hawarden by Parnell, McCarthy, and others (McCarthy thought Healy and Sexton). The proposal, McCarthy wrote, 'has not come to anything so far. I don't think Parnell has yet quite seen his way'.[105] Parnell was determined to ensure that if he went to Hawarden, he would go alone. His visit to Hawarden in late December 1889, was a triumphant public affirmation of the Liberal–nationalist alliance.[106]

Healy dined with Gladstone and G. O. Trevelyan in London shortly after the abandonment of the projected Hawarden visit. Writing to inform his father he added that 'Trevelyan invited me to his place in the country but we really must draw the line somewhere'.[107] Healy again dined with Gladstone, in the company of Lord Acton and E. W. Hamilton, on 17 June 1890. He had been brought back by Gladstone, who was delighted by an attack he had made on Balfour's land purchase proposals. Hamilton's patronising entry in his diary on balance says rather more about enduring prejudices against Irish nationalist parliamentarians than it reveals about Healy:

> I had never met Healy before, and I certainly was not favourably disposed towards him. I looked upon him as a somewhat unscrupulous legal adventurer, clever, and out of touch with ordinary humanity. I was agreeably surprised with the man – there was no trace of vulgarity in him. He was modest and respectful; and apparently gratified by being asked to dinner. I am sure it would be a good thing if a little more attention were shown to such men as Healy, so that they might be civilised and better understood.[108]

Parnell's participation in divisions in the Commons was very much better than hostile commentaries suggested.[109] However, the system in the pattern of his attendance was altogether lost on his parliamentary colleagues, left leaderless and prey to wild rumours. His appearance was unpredictable. When absent, he was severely *incommunicado*.

Edward Byrne of the *Freeman's Journal*, in London in November 1889, was unable to make contact with either Parnell or his secretary Henry Campbell. Campbell would not reply to his notes. 'As for the Chief, so far as I can make out he holds communication with nobody. He won't see or write to anybody.' The Irish members Byrne met had not had better luck. T. P. O'Connor had met Parnell, but only by chance in a railway station. 'And Campbell, why Campbell affects the same mystery as his principal has really invested himself with.'[110]

Parnell was about to re-assert his leadership, by his visit to Gladstone at Hawarden, and by the speeches he made before and after at Nottingham and at the Liverpool Reform Club respectively where Byrne accompanied him. Byrne was startled by Parnell's eloquence (' . . . for he was not a fluent man. His talent lay rather in terseness and crispness. But at Nottingham he literally let himself out . . .').

As to the political enigma of Parnell's physical condition, the reports despatched by Byrne at the time provide an intriguing text. He described Parnell arriving at Nottingham 'looking very pale, but quite vigorous'. Parnell's health was steadily improving. He had 'caught a chill similar to the chill which he caught two years ago, and from the effects of which he suffered so much'. The next day he reported that Parnell desired him to say 'that he is growing daily in strength. All who heard him in Albert Hall, at Nottingham, last night, were delighted at the vigour he displayed'.[111] As astute propagandist as well as a loyal adherent of Parnell, Byrne was at once talking up and talking down Parnell's illness. In tentatively asserting Parnell's gradual return to health, he was seeking to allay the concerns of the nationalist public while doing nothing to deprive Parnell of the alibi his fragile health afforded.

The uneasy sense of abandonment of members of the Irish party engendered by Parnell's elusiveness was exacerbated by the absence from Westminster of his leading lieutenants. Dillon and O'Brien were in and out of prison, their energies absorbed in the prosecution of the Plan of Campaign. Healy's attendance was inconstant. Almost certainly prompted by Parnell, Robbins in the *Birmingham Daily Post* in May 1890 denied the improbable rumour that a round robin would be despatched to Parnell remonstrating with him on his neglect of his parliamentary duties. Parnell had been 'in more constant attendance at the House this session than any even of his chief followers, save Mr. Sexton; for, from various causes, Mr. William O'Brien, Mr. Dillon, and Mr. Healy have so far been seen but little at Westminster this year'. Parnell 'as is his known habit' did not sit through long debates because of the state of his health, and was 'husbanding his strength for the prolonged struggle that is promised on Committee on the Land Purchase Bill'. Following on the Archbishop of Dublin's attack on Irish party attendances, Robbins reported Parnell's return after a chill: 'The Nationalist leader since his illness of three years ago, has had to be specially careful in cases of cold, owing to the liability of certain bronchial tubes to become affected', but was otherwise in good health.[112]

Quite apart from the issue of his own attendances, Parnell was held responsible for the absenteeism of members of the party. Conscious of the existence of a large government majority, and alive to the difficulties which attendances presented for many Irish members, Parnell, while repeatedly drawing the party's attention to the need for a strong Irish presence at Westminster, did not seek to enforce an unrealistic level of zeal. In 1888 he pointed out to the Commons that 'the return journey of some of his colleagues covered 1,200 miles'. He summoned meetings of the party in June 1888 and August 1889 to discuss unsatisfactory attendances, and wrote at the start of each session stressing the need for high attendance. On 30

January 1890 he wrote to the *Freeman's Journal* urging 'constant and unremitting attention to their parliamentary duties' on the part of the Irish members.[113]

In a division on the Local Taxation (Customs) Bill on 13 June 1890, Parnell was pleased to have reduced the government majority to a third of its normal size. The *Freeman's Journal* however attacked lax Irish attendance, on the basis that the government's majority could have been pared to a mere seventeen votes. Parnell, infuriated, defended 'the party as a whole whose zeal and assiduity leaves nothing to be desired'. Parnell believed that the attack was inspired by Archbishop Walsh and complained to Robbins: 'Why don't these priests leave politics alone? They never interfere but to make mischief'.[114] The *Freeman's Journal*'s attack prompted Parnell to arrange with Labouchere a snap division a week later to coincide with the Gold Cup at Ascot. The government's majority was cut to four. This had the reverse of the intended effect in eliciting from Walsh an open condemnation of Irish party attendances, as eighteen of the Irish party were absent.[115]

What was to render Parnell peculiarly vulnerable in the split was the combination of his absences from Westminster and from Ireland. He incautiously admitted at Edinburgh in July 1889 that he had not spoken in Ireland 'for years and years'.[116] He did not address a meeting in Ireland between the Galway election of February 1886 and the Rotunda meeting of 10 December 1890, after the split in the party. His presence in Ireland was confined to his habitual sojourns in Avondale after parliament had risen.

Healy wrote later that Parnell's 'remissness in attendance at Westminster had become such a scandal within the Party that it contributed enormously to his downfall'. He was absent for the debates on the estimates for two months towards the end of the 1890 session when the Irish estimates were debated. 'When all was over he came up, and remarked to Mr. Sexton, who had been slaving away in his absence: "I have never known such a perfunctory discussion on Irish Estimates as this session". Absurdities of this kind from a man for years inattentive to his own duty sapped the allegiance of friends whose confidence had already disappeared.'[117]

Healy did not have the responsibilities which the leadership of the Irish party imposed on Parnell. Yet the infrequency of his own attendances render his later attacks on Parnell's absenteeism somewhat hypocritical. The remunerativeness of the bar was exercising an ever more insistent tug on Healy. In the latter half of the decade, he was spending an increasing amount of time away from parliament in what he later described as 'the dusty, but not unprofitable, Four Courts'.[118] Out of parliament in 1886, he wrote Labouchere that returning would entail 'a heavy monetary loss to me'. In September 1887 he complained to Maurice as he set off to defend

Harrington in a prosecution 'which I would give twice my fee (if I get one) to be out of, as it is most injurious to me to be out of town'.[119]

Healy's absence did not pass unremarked. H. W. Lucy wrote in early February 1888 that Healy was in Ireland and 'likely to remain there for some time, being engaged in the lucrative business of the Bar'. Later the same month he wrote again of Healy that 'the harp that once through Westminster's halls used to ring forth angry and angering questions is now mute, or at best capable only of a spasmodic twang'.[120] The London correspondent of the Dublin *Daily Express* noted in August 1890 that very little had been heard that session of Healy, Redmond and other formerly active nationalist parliamentarians.[121]

Parnell maintained his policy of reserve towards the Plan of Campaign, making only minimal gestures, grudgingly and belatedly, towards its sustainment. In response to the formation of a landlords' syndicate to resist the Plan of Campaign, he agreed in July 1889 to the establishment of a tenants defence league. O'Brien's hopes of drawing Parnell into support of the Plan were again frustrated. When O'Brien protested, and informed him that he and Dillon would have to consider whether they could remain in so intolerable a situation, Parnell retorted 'with the most brutal frankness that we could not get out of it – that we had got ourselves into it, adding "you forced me to say that"'.[122]

A letter from J. J. Clancy to Joseph Kenny of 3 September 1889 gives a striking illustration of Parnell's flint-like determination to stand aloof. Clancy had met Parnell that day 'by the merest accident', and told him that a deputation of those involved in the Plan of Campaign in Tipperary had come over expressly to wait on him. When Parnell learnt what they wanted to see him about, 'He replied that there was no use in his seeing them as he could not undertake the responsibility of advising tenants to give up their interests in their holdings'. He did however discuss the support of the evicted tenants: 'He said there should be no difficulty in raising £30,000 in Ireland for the purpose. I said there would be unless he himself took the initiative. He then referred to the holding of Conventions throughout the country with Sexton as speaker'. Clancy added that he had not told the deputation he had seen Parnell, 'for he did not wish it to be known he was in London'.[123]

O'Brien's hopes that Parnell would inaugurate a series of conventions in support of the Plan of Campaign, culminating in 'a great National Banquet in Dublin in Parnell's honour', were remarkably obtuse given Parnell's declared attitude. Parnell did not attend the inauguration of the Tenants' Defence Association in Tipperary on 15 October 1889, sending Sexton in his stead.[124]

Healy's support of the beleaguered Plan of Campaign was limited to platform rhetoric and court appearances. O'Brien complained to Dillon in March 1890 that Healy, Sexton and Redmond could not be induced to speak at meetings in England, 'where the real work (except in Ireland) is to be done'.[125] Healy's withholding of active support of the Plan did not inhibit him from striking vehement postures in public. At the National League on 16 July 1889, Healy against the grain of Parnell's policy discountenanced compromise on the part of the evicted tenants: 'in my opinion negotiations and arrangements and settlements – the very name of them is pestilent'. At Tipperary in September he denounced 'backstairs arrangements'. Quoting Disraeli's celebrated phrase, he expressed himself vaguely in favour of 'peace with honour' while repudiating 'any disgraceful peace'.[126]

Healy's opportunistic agrarianism, his sinuous interweaving of the politics of home rule and land purchase, sharply diverged from the severity of Parnell's strategy. In the split, Healy would pillory Parnell for cynical indifference to the plight of the evicted tenants of the Plan of Campaign (as a manifestation of Anglo-Irish cold-bloodedness, and of his economic interests as a landlord) and for neglecting the struggle in Ireland to pursue his affair with Katharine O'Shea in the south of England.

Parnell no longer concealed his hostility to Healy. John Barry informed Healy that Parnell had asked Arthur O'Connor to go to America in September 1887. 'P. A. Collins wrote twice to Parnell asking that I should be sent, but he never replied to his letters, whereat Collins was mad.'[127] Discussing possible emissaries to raise funds in the United States in the autumn of 1890, O'Brien wrote to T. P. Gill that he thought Healy would agree to go 'if he could have Parnell's cordial sanction, but there's the rub'.[128] Morley reported to Gladstone of his interview with Parnell in Brighton, just before the divorce crisis broke, that after the policy business had been disposed of 'we had much general talk about his colleagues etc. – curiously shrewd, very benignant (save as to Healy), and hitting on the exact word most apt for each, with singular precision'. The very mention of Healy's name had made Parnell angry.[129]

John Dillon and William O'Brien found themselves increasingly constrained in financing the Plan of Campaign, and faced government prosecution. They resolved to break bail and leave for France, en route to America to raise funds. In early October 1890 they made a midnight departure from Dalkey harbour. Healy provided them with whiskey for the journey, and sat up late into the nights that followed with Joseph Kenny speculating uneasily on their crossing. Days passed before a wire from Cherbourg confirmed their safe arrival.[130]

None of those involved could have realised how fraught with consequence the leave-taking would prove. The departure of Dillon and O'Brien led to their absence in the United States when the divorce crisis broke and the first stages of the split were engaged. Their breaking of bail resulted (by their submission to arrest) in their incarceration in Galway Jail from February to July 1891. It was not merely their allegiance to Parnell which was to be unalterably changed. The amicable relations which then united the triad of Dillon, O'Brien and Healy, Parnell's most formidable lieutenants, would never again subsist between all three of them at any one time in the three fractious decades of Irish parliamentary politics to follow.

Parnell's policy was increasingly abstractly conceived, as he pursued from Westminster, Eltham, and latterly Brighton the most ambitious political strategy of the late-nineteenth-century United Kingdom, a combined exercise in *haute politique* and in the redirection of what had been a semi-revolutionary movement. He was exaggeratedly rationalistic, remaining out of Ireland, holding back and waiting on events to take what he judged to be their ordained course. His own myth had become disembodied, a piece on the chessboard of his strategy. In this, rather than in any narcissistic self-regard, lay his hubris.

Like other contemporary politicians and commentators, Parnell evidently discounted Healy's ability to mount a challenge to his leadership, and was oblivious to the threat which the gathering strength of Catholic proprietorial nationalism posed to his hegemony. While his policy in the longer term was directed towards the containment of the predominance of the nationalist farmer class, he did not perceive this as a constituency which could be mobilised against his leadership in advance of the achievement of home rule. He situated this contest of strength in the remoter reaches of post-home-rule politics.

With what came to appear fatal presumption, Parnell was moving boldly to address the phase of policy which would follow the winning of home rule. As the prime minister of a home rule government in waiting, he sought to create a socio-economic equilibrium in Ireland which could enable him to procure Conservative acquiescence in a Liberal-enacted measure of home rule.

In the split Parnell fought fiercely to reverse the effects of his neglect of the Irish terrain. Straining to re-assert his supremacy, he had to double up the roles of agitator and statesman. His campaign, as he sought to bring together in his person the politics of the New Departure, the Liberal alliance, and of the wresting and governance of a future home rule state, was necessarily awkward. In terms of his strategy, politics in Ireland had moved disastrously out of phase. Caught off balance, he displayed much of his old mastery, but in the last eleven months of his life never quite recovered his former poise.

9

Divorce

> I once said to David Plunket, 'I knew I was throwing a bombshell into the Irish camp, but I did not know it would do quite so much mischief'. 'Ah', said he, 'you didn't know that when it burst they would pick up the pieces and cut each other's throats with them.
>
> Sir Edward Clarke K.C.[1]

The news that Captain W. H. O'Shea had on 24 December 1889 filed a petition for divorce, naming Parnell as co-respondent, was first disclosed in the Tory *Evening News and Post* of 28 December. Interviewed at his rooms in London, O'Shea expressed surprise that the fact of the institution of proceedings had become known.

Parnell responded immediately. In an interview in the *Freeman's Journal* of the following day, he asserted that O'Shea had threatened such proceedings for years past, in fact since 1886 when O'Shea had broken politically with him. He asserted that O'Shea had always been aware that he was constantly at his wife's residence in Eltham in O'Shea's absence during the period from the end of 1880 to 1886, and since 1886 had known that he had constantly resided there over that period. This was to be the only occasion on which Parnell made specific assertions of fact in his own defence. He was subsequently precluded from doing so by his decision not to defend the proceedings at the initial hearing, and thereafter to permit

O'Shea the decree nisi of divorce made absolute.

Stopping (only just) short of admitting his relations with Katharine O'Shea, the implicit suggestion of connivance on O'Shea's part was subsumed in a larger political defence. He charged that O'Shea had been incited to institute the proceedings 'in the interests of the *Times*', by E. C. Houston, the secretary of the Irish Loyal and Patriotic Union, who had been instrumental in the publication by the *Times* of the Pigott forgeries. The immediate purpose, Parnell claimed, was to limit the damages in the libel action he was bringing against the paper arising out of the forgeries. Houston and O'Shea both denied the allegation, the latter describing it as 'too fantastic to deserve remark'.[2]

Parnell maintained his posture of defiance the following day. The London correspondent of the *Freeman's Journal* asserted that the elapse of a week without the service of a citation on Parnell or Katharine O'Shea indicated that the proceedings were not seriously intended. Parnell had instructed his solicitors, Lewis and Lewis, to ascertain whether a petition had in fact been filed, and if so to communicate with O'Shea's solicitors to make the earliest possible appointment for the service of the citation, as he was determined to frustrate any procrastination by the *Times* in his libel proceedings.[3]

The *Freeman's Journal* of 4 January announced 'on the highest authority' that 'the connection between O'Shea, Houston and the *Times* will be proved as clearly, if the conspirators stand their ground, as was the forgeries conspiracy of the suicide Pigott'. As if to underscore the parallel, the paper looked forward to Sir Charles Russell 'taking in hand' Captain O'Shea, 'if he steps into the witness stand'. J. M. Tuohy, the London correspondent, added that Parnell had in fact retained Russell. Parnell, he reported, believed that the plan had been to reveal the fact that the petition had been presented on the eve of his libel action against the *Times* (which was settled a month later), but that 'the friends of Captain O'Shea thought it desirable, for reasons best known to themselves, to burn the Captain's boats', by the premature disclosure of the institution of the proceedings to the *Evening News*.[4]

The evocation of his triumphant vindication in the matter of the forgeries was of course intended to allay the concerns of the nationalist public. Yet this was probably more than a propaganda exercise. Given Parnell's conviction that O'Shea had been involved in the Pigott forgeries, it is quite likely that he believed that O'Shea in instituting divorce proceedings was acting in concert with Chamberlain and the *Times* (the most likely candidates for the appellation of 'friends of Captain O'Shea'). The positing of a conflict of interest between the conspirators in the timing of the announcement rather weakened the thrust of the accusation of conspiracy. The threat, as addressed to O'Shea, was to expose what Parnell believed to be his complicity with the *Times* in the publication of the Pigott forgeries, rather than in the institution of the divorce proceedings. Even if O'Shea was, as Parnell believed, implicated in the Pigott forgeries, the threat to expose him was hardly coercive, given that he had not previously succeeded in doing so. Moreover there was something self-deceiving in appearing to promise a deliverance in the divorce proceedings as complete as that achieved in the matter of the forgeries.

Thus the public silence concerning what was an open secret in political society in London and Dublin was at last broken. Edward Hamilton described Parnell's relations with Katharine O'Shea as 'a notorious and recognized fact'. Herbert Gladstone later said that gossip on the subject in the lobbies and smoking rooms of the Commons had reached its high point as early as 1885.[5] It was Healy's friend and confidant Harold Frederic who had made the most explicit public reference to Parnell's affair. In the *New York Times* of 26 October 1888 he characterised W. H. O'Shea as 'the despicable creature for whom Mr. Parnell in his ruinous infatuation created that ruinous split in the Irish party at Galway three years ago'.

Few of the Irish party members were as naïve as the gentle Quaker Alfred Webb, elected for Waterford West in February 1890, who bitterly complained that he thought Parnell's absences were due to his love of chemistry: 'when he heard about all the experiments he was carrying on in a scientific way he was fool enough to believe it'. The Irish members overwhelmingly maintained a discreet silence, reflecting the depth of their apprehensions. One exception was M. J. Kenny, the member for Mid-Tyrone who was to be one of Parnell's most foul-mouthed opponents in the split. He wrote to a correspondent in November 1889 that 'Parnell thinks fornication in Hastings [*sic*] preferable to a little effort in politics in Ireland'.[6] Others in Dublin political circles learnt of the affair. A member of the Ladies Land League referred jestingly to it to Anna Parnell, in the presence of Katharine Tynan, who recalled 'Miss Parnell's pale Sibylline smile'. The same lady persisted in her indiscreet comments, and received a letter from Parnell some years later which Tynan described as 'a masterpiece of icy and stinging rebuke', at which the recipient laughed 'a little unsteadily'.[7]

Some Irish members favoured an immediate demonstration of support for Parnell. Wiser counsels prevailed. William O'Brien, writing to John Dillon, felt the institution of the proceedings as 'a horrible blow'. Like most contemporary observers in both countries he erroneously believed that the moral backlash against Parnell would be confined to Britain, and complacently misread the likely response among Irish nationalists:

> Here in Ireland, of course, there is no danger of evil results, whatever happens. I confess I have horrible misgivings as to what might be the

> result in England if the evidence is in any way damaging . . . if anything is proved which could give British Pharisaism an excuse for one of its virtuous fits, a declaration binding us as a party to brazen the thing out *per fas aut nefas* would be seized upon as a grizzly immoral act and a wanton affront to honest feeling.

He therefore shrank from any concerted response by the Irish party, and favoured 'waiting at all events until we can feel the pulse of English opinion upon the question'.[8]

Parnell wrote to O'Brien on 14 January 1890 that if the case was ever fully gone into, 'a matter which is exceedingly doubtful', he could rest assured that it will be shown 'that the dishonour and discredit have not been upon my side'. O'Brien wrote to T. P. Gill that the note was very touching, and that Parnell was 'bold as a lion'. He commented over-sanguinely that the Tories 'seem desperately nervous about touching the business', but added that 'it is slow after-effects we would have most to dread'.[9]

Parnell's personal assurance that he would emerge without a stain on his name or reputation was taken by Michael Davitt with almost wilful *naïveté* to mean that he could disprove the allegation of an affair with Katharine O'Shea. Davitt disseminated this interpretation of Parnell's assurance widely among English home rulers. Informing W. T. Stead, he added that Parnell has 'never deceived me in his life'. Davitt's vanity was thus engaged. The claim that he had been cynically misled by the leader whom he had trusted implicitly figured prominently in his rationalisation of his opposition to Parnell in the split.[10]

The nationalist press rallied to Parnell with panegyrical evocations of his vindication in the case of the Pigott forgeries. The epithets of the myth were deployed in defensive formation. In an inapt angelic metaphor, the *Freeman's Journal* declared that Parnell 'rose calmly' above the means resorted to against him, 'and trampled them underfoot, as an Archangel might stamp upon a many-headed dragon'. *United Ireland* observed that there was something 'almost fiendish' in the manner in which Parnell's adversaries pursued him, but that 'his armour of quiet scorn shields the Irish leader from their poisoned weapons'.[11] After the initial spate of fervent endorsements of Parnell in the nationalist press, and by some municipal bodies, an almost complete public silence settled on the divorce proceedings in Ireland until they came on for hearing in mid-November.[12]

Justin McCarthy wrote in January of the eerie lull: 'People now seem to think or doubt whether the O'Shea case will ever come on. Some think it was a mere attempt to frighten Parnell, but who on earth could believe in frightening Parnell? I think myself much more seriously of the affair'.[13] Remarkably a few days later McCarthy began, in what was a testament both to his own innocence and to the mystique of Parnell's invincibility,

1. T. M. Healy with his father Maurice and his eldest brother Thomas (Oct. 1865)

2. T. M. Healy with his father and T. D. Sullivan (May 1902)

3. Fête champêtre: Healy is on the right, John Barry on the left (Kirkaldy, August 1886)

4. Maurice Healy

5. Joseph Biggar

6. A. M. Sullivan

7. T. D. Sullivan

8. T. C. Harrington

9. Henry Labouchere

10. T. P. O'Connor

11. Richard Piggot

12. Charles Stewart Parnell

Mr. Parnell.—"Pat, you are crushing the wrong men. Here are your enemies."
Pat.—"Where Mr. Parnell? Is it Gladstone and Croke? Arrah tell us another!"
Landlord.—"Now is my time to strike."

13. Parnell seeks to persuade 'Pat' to attack Gladstone and Archbishop Croke, rather than Balfour and his landlord. Cartoon from the anti-Parnellite *Nation* (March 1891)

14. His candidate defeated in the Carlow election of July 1891, 'Mr. Fox' is hunted back to Brighton (cartoon from the *Weekly National Press*)

15. 'Humpty Dumpty': Parnell's leading supporters in the split – clockwise from upper left, John Redmond, T. C. Harrington, Patrick O'Brien and Joseph Kenny – seek to restore a broken Parnell to the Irish leadership. The cartoon appeared in the *Weekly National Press,* ten days before Parnell's death.

16. Lying in state: Parnell's coffin in the City Hall, Dublin (11 Oct. 1891)

guardedly to entertain the possibility that Parnell had held back from consummating his relationship with Katharine O'Shea:

> It is beginning to be believed I don't know how or why that he will be able to come out of the whole affair triumphantly. I hope so with all my heart and soul. I had not thought that could be so. But he is a strange man quite capable of imposing on himself a powerful restraining law and not allowing a temptation to draw him too far. The West End drawing-room does not believe in such men . . .[14]

The Liberals looked on uneasily. E. W. Hamilton dined in the company among others of Morley, the Prince of Wales and George Lewis. In an egregious breach of professional confidence, Lewis discussed Parnell's libel action against the *Times* and the divorce proceedings. He was satisfied with the settlement of the libel action shortly before; but in relation to the divorce, Hamilton recorded: 'I could see that Lewis is much more anxious. He should put it off as long as he could. He evidently thinks that Parnell will damage himself by it not only in the eyes of the strait-laced and the Nonconformists in this country, but also of his fellow-countrymen in Ireland, where scandals are regarded with a holy horror'. Morley wrote to Harcourt that John Walter, the proprietor of the *Times*, 'will have his five thousand pounds worth of revenge': 'it will be a horrid exposure, and must, I think, lead to the disappearance of our friend'.[15]

On the morning of 21 March, E. W. Hamilton called on Gladstone at his residence in St James Square. The Liberal leader was waiting for Parnell (Hamilton offered two to one he would not turn up). He was in sombre mood:

> Mr. G. is afraid that, from his not having asserted himself much lately, Parnell feels that matters may go so badly for him in the impending divorce case that he may have to withdraw from public life and that he had better commence to prepare for this. His withdrawal would, in Mr. G's opinion, be a public calamity; it would be a great blow to this country as well as to Ireland; and in Ireland would be left leaderless: there being no one at all marked out to be Parnell's successor. Mr. G. thought that possibly it would be best for the Irishmen to take Davitt.[16]

Gladstone was evidently in two minds, on the one hand hoping that Parnell might brave the storm, and on the other elliptically reconciling himself to the inevitability of his departure. Gladstone's assessment of Parnell's likely response to the divorce crisis was heavily influenced by his offer of withdrawal in the wake of the Phoenix Park murders. It was a false parallel. He had no conception of the placid fury of Parnell's resolve to maintain his leadership.

In June 1890 the last social gatherings of the united Irish party took place. On 11 June William O'Brien married Sophie Raffalovich in London. The wedding was attended by almost all the members of the Irish party. Parnell, relaxed and happy, made a short speech. Archbishop Croke blessed the couple. T. P. Gill wrote that 'it was the peak of the happy time, the last of "glad confident morning" for us all'. Wilfred Scawen Blunt was deeply affected and wrote: 'It is all very well to scoff at the age in which we live, but the Catholic Irish are a standing miracle of God's grace. I should say there has never been — certainly not in the last hundred years — a political party so pure in its purposes'. Blunt's diary entry unwittingly disclosed the extent of Parnell's predicament.[17]

Later in the month, seventy members of the party — among whom Healy was not numbered — attended a banquet in London to mark Parnell's forty-fourth birthday. William Martin Murphy was present, as was T. D. Sullivan to perform his balladic party pieces, 'Three Brave Blacksmiths' and 'Murty Hynes', as Parnell with heroic fortitude submitted to an evening of Hibernian revelry. John Barry sang 'The Felons of our Land', and Sullivan led the singing of 'God Save Ireland'. 'Mr. Parnell and his colleagues', declared the *Nation*, 'are now plainly entered upon the last stages of the fight'.[18]

Parnell took no steps to shore up his position in advance of the hearing of the divorce petition. This apparent insouciance was attributable to his hopes that an accommodation could be reached with Captain O'Shea, and to an exaggerated belief in the strength of his position in Ireland. He was also aware of how a sudden change in the tempo of his leadership was likely to be interpreted. For once his habitual practice of waiting on events was to betray him.

Morley went to Ireland in mid-September. His hopes of meeting Parnell to discuss the land purchase bill were disappointed. He wrote to Gladstone from Dublin on 23 September that Parnell 'has agreed to come down from the queer Olympus of his, and preside over a meeting of the party on the first Monday in October'. When the Irish party met in Dublin on the ill-omened date of 6 October, Parnell telegraphed regretting his inability to attend. Crossing to Ireland the previous day to preside in his leader's stead, the long-suffering Justin McCarthy wrote to his literary collaborator, 'I have been called on to preside scores of times on a moment's notice in Parnell's sudden absence'.[19]

Morley eventually succeeded in setting up a meeting with Parnell for 10 November, to discuss the business of the forthcoming session. Parnell arrived at the Brighton Metropole 'only two hours late', as Morley informed Gladstone. At the end of dinner, after the legislative business was disposed of, Morley with due apology enquired whether there was any chance of certain legal proceedings resulting in his disappearance, temporary or permanent, from the political stage. 'He took it graciously enough, though he showed no inclination to discuss the subject.' Parnell smiled, and said that so far as he was concerned nothing in the least leading to his disappearance would come out of the proceedings. The other side did not know 'what a broken-kneed horse they are riding'. The Irish, he explained, were very slow to give a man their confidence, and still more slow to withdraw it. Morley concluded that Parnell meant there would be no adverse decree. Evidently concerned at Parnell's parliamentary absences, which Gladstone feared were a prelude to his withdrawal from public life, Morley urged Parnell, if there was nothing pointing to his disappearance, intrepidly to attend the Commons and to participate in its business. '"That", he replied, "is just what you may depend on my doing. I assure you there will be nothing to prevent it".' Of Parnell, composed and judicious in their discussion on political business, Morley wrote to Gladstone 'on the whole, I liked him very much better than I usually do, and felt all the force of his sense, penetration and sagacity'.[20]

While many contemporaries were persuaded that Katharine O'Shea prevailed on Parnell to ensure that a decree of divorce would be granted, whether at her suit or her husband's, there is little to sustain their view. More convincingly Henry Harrison accepted the account of events which Katharine Parnell gave him in the period after Parnell's death — that from the moment she was publicly named Parnell himself insisted that there should be a divorce. On this she was unwaveringly consistent. Parnell's course of action may have been ordained by the terms of their relationship. That is not to say it was dictated by Katharine O'Shea. There is nothing to suggest that Parnell was troubled by the formal illicitness of their relations; on the contrary his appellatives of 'Wifie' and 'Queenie' evince an imperturbably settled domesticity. However once the issue was publicly joined, he insisted on a divorce, one way or another.[21]

Contemporary surmise to the contrary was to prevail in the split, and to compound the damage which the divorce wrought to Parnell's political mystique. T. P. O'Connor's obituary of Katharine Parnell thirty years later reflects the prevalent perception. He asserted that the chief cause of the divorce proceedings was that they were strongly desired by her, suggesting vaguely and unconvincingly that Parnell, mindful of the political peril, 'probably had other views . . . But nothing is more remarkable in this tragic love story than the complete subjection in which this man of iron and of ice stood to this woman. He seemed to have his will paralysed in her presence'.[22]

The widespread belief among Liberals and Irish nationalist parliamentarians that Parnell's own wishes had been overborne by Katharine O'Shea owed a good deal to the perceptions — and professional indiscretion —

of George Lewis, the solicitor initially consulted by Parnell in the divorce proceedings, who judged Katharine 'very charming, but . . . impossible'.[23] Thus Reginald Brett recorded on 23 January 1890 that 'Stead came today — very low — from an interview with George Lewis. Mrs. O'Shea *wishes* to be divorced and to marry Mr. Parnell. Mr. Parnell, whether he wishes it or not, agreed'.[24]

Lewis's belief that Katharine O'Shea was instrumental in convincing Parnell to ensure that a divorce decree was granted was an erroneous inference drawn from the prominent role she played in giving instructions in relation to the conduct of the case. With fateful complacency Parnell delegated the direction of the case to her. It is in this limited sense that the issue of Katharine's 'dominance' arises: around this grain Lewis's influential myth accreted.

T. P. O'Connor cited rumours which, while of manifestly weak evidentiary strength have a plausible ring, and again bear the impress of George Lewis:

> . . . there are legends of strange interviews between Parnell, Mrs. O'Shea and Sir George Lewis, in his old-fashioned office in Ely Place . . . In these interviews Mrs. O'Shea insisted on stating her views; her opinions are said to have been erroneous; but Lewis had to sit and listen patiently, with Parnell standing by, silently, and, if not approvingly, at least submissively; the mouth of the solicitor was closed.

The replacement of Lewis by another solicitor was O'Connor surmised, probably correctly, at her instigation.[25] The termination of his retainer was an exercise in self-indulgence Parnell and Katharine O'Shea could ill afford. The most esteemed solicitor of late-nineteenth-century England, and respected by Parnell, he had some prospect of exercising a restraining influence.[26] In the event Katharine O'Shea was not represented by either the solicitor or counsel who had appeared for Parnell before the Special Commission. Two weeks before the divorce case Morley wrote gloomily to Gladstone: 'C. Russell is *not* going to take the brief'.[27]

Katharine O'Shea was neither qualified nor temperamentally well-suited for the role with which she was entrusted in the direction of the defence of the divorce proceedings. Henry Harrison considered her clever, formidable, and immensely self-confident, but a legal amateur, 'and — an even greater handicap — she was high-tempered, and, as is inevitable with such a combination, prone to let temperament supplant reason in the determination of both opinion and action'. Moreover the divorce proceedings were complicated by the initiation of proceedings by her relatives (including her husband) challenging the enormous bequest left to her under the will of her aunt, Mrs. Benjamin Wood. It was her aunt's death on 19 May 1889 which left W. H. O'Shea at liberty to institute proceedings for divorce without jeopardising his wife's inheritance (his subsequent participation in the probate action was presumably intended to increase his leverage, and to enable him profess innocence of any venal intent). A complex double-game of litigation was thereby engaged. Katharine O'Shea and Parnell found the bequest, to which they looked to fund an arrangement with her husband in the divorce proceedings, frozen as a result of the probate action.[28]

Over the eleven months between the presentation of the petition and the hearing, Parnell and Katharine O'Shea pursued an uncertain course, fluctuating between the denials and counter-allegations raised in her defence, and the pursuit of a settlement with her husband which, even if it were achievable in principle, they were unable immediately or definitely to finance. Parnell's defence consisted of a simple denial. Katharine O'Shea coupled a denial with counter-allegations of connivance (which of course were inconsistent with the denial), adultery, cruelty, and desertion on the part of her husband. Particulars of these allegations were furnished on 3 June, 25 July (when the improbable allegation of Captain O'Shea's adultery with Katharine O'Shea's sister Anna Steele was added), and 4 November.[29]

Parnell and Katharine O'Shea persevered in the attempt to achieve an arrangement with her husband. Katharine told Henry Harrison shortly after Parnell's death that had she been able to find the immense sum of £20,000 (which her aunt's legacy could alone have provided), the matter could have been resolved by the grant of a divorce at her suit. That such a figure was at least mooted to Captain O'Shea is corroborated by Sir Edward Clarke in his memoirs.[30]

It is highly questionable that an arrangement along these lines was ever achievable. Quite apart from the inability of Katharine O'Shea and Parnell to fund such a settlement, it remains doubtful that it would have been acceptable to her husband, among whose unattractive characteristics pride probably enjoyed a narrow ascendancy over avarice. O'Shea's unsolicited and elaborately contrived assertions of innocence in his communications with Chamberlain and Cardinal Manning attest to his preoccupation with his reputation, however risible this might have seemed in the circumstances. For O'Shea to have acquiesced in a divorce at his wife's suit in the proceedings, against the background of her inheritance, would have attracted political obloquy and social derision of a kind he would have found exceedingly difficult to endure.

It is possible that one of the options considered by O'Shea was an arrangement under which he would obtain an unopposed decree of divorce on the basis of his agreement not to have gratuitously damaging evidence against Parnell led on his behalf. According to John Morley's intelligence, such an arrangement was proposed (although without financial inducement) by Parnell and Katharine O'Shea as one of their last desperate expedients in the immediate prelude to the hearing. Morley wrote to Gladstone on 3 November:

> I understand – this is for yourself *exclusively* – that O'Shea was formally asked recently whether, if no defence were made, he would still insist on casting mud at Parnell. He replied, No, but he must be guided by his counsel. His counsel is Clarke, and I fear Clarke will be likely to do his best to get as many nasty things out as possible. I fear there is plenty of them.[31]

Quite apart from Morley's fear of the partisanship of Sir Edward Clarke, the unionist Solicitor-General, it would have been difficult to ensure that satisfactory effect could have been given to such an arrangement under an adversarial system of law, particularly given the involvement of a jury and the public policy of thwarting collusive proceedings for divorce. Moreover from O'Shea's point of view, there could be no guarantee that obtaining a divorce under such circumstances would not have deepened the suspicion of connivance on his part which he was so anxious, however unrealistically, to dispel.

On 13 November, two days before the petition was listed for hearing, Frank Lockwood Q.C. on behalf of Katharine O'Shea applied for an adjournment, on the grounds that an order made two days previously giving Anna Steele liberty to intervene was the subject of an appeal which it was hoped would be heard the following week. When the presiding judge, Mr. Justice Butt, asked how her intervention prejudiced the respondent, Lockwood haplessly replied that 'the papers relating to the matter have only been placed in my hands within the last few minutes', and fell back upon a point of law he wished to argue. Clarke opposed the application on the ground that the suit had been ready for trial as early as 12 May, and had only been impeded by Katharine O'Shea's delay in making discovery. The adjournment was unsurprisingly refused.[32]

What subsequently transpired between Parnell and Frank Lockwood became the subject of much controversy. As Sir Edward Clarke, still bewildered almost thirty years later, wrote, 'the whole business was full of puzzles'. A neglected account in the memoirs of A. E. (later Sir Alfred) Pease, a Liberal who sat with Lockwood for York, of a conversation with Lockwood shortly after the divorce case provides some elucidation.

Pease dined with Lockwood on the evening parliament reconvened. Lockwood was furious with Parnell, whom he called 'a "damned scoundrel", for having said to him that "his people would never believe him guilty and that his divorce case would *only injure* us"'. Parnell's perhaps intentionally provocative assertion of his invulnerability in Ireland was intended to impress upon Lockwood, a prominent Liberal advocate and parliamentarian, who was to be in Rosebery's Solicitor-General in 1894–5, the divergence between Parnell's interests and those of the Liberal leadership in the proceedings. Specifically, while the Liberals wanted to avoid or at least to minimise the damage to Parnell's political standing, Parnell's overriding purpose was to ensure that a decree of divorce was granted. Speaking to Pease more than a week later, Lockwood still felt Parnell's needle.

Lockwood also complained that Parnell and Katharine O'Shea had not let him know until eleven o'clock on the night before the hearing that they would not give evidence: 'They wanted him to cross-examine O'Shea, but he declined to go on a foraging exhibition and to throw dirt unless they would go into the box to prove an issue'.[33]

Parnell had settled upon what was, in the abstract, a strategy of considerable ingenuity. He sought to adumbrate through Lockwood's cross-examination of O'Shea a vindication of Katharine O'Shea's and his own honour, without actually jeopardising the grant of the divorce (in the absence of testimony from Katharine O'Shea or Parnell, the weight of the evidence would have been such as to compel the jury to find for Captain O'Shea). It was a course of action which commended itself to Parnell in achieving a partial reconciliation of the impossibly conflicting personal and political constraints which bound him. In the hard collision between the politician and the barrister which ensued, Lockwood insisted that his view of his own responsibilities as an advocate did not permit him to accept such instructions. In professional terms, Lockwood's objection could not be faulted. Had he agreed to do as he was asked, he would have encountered adamant judicial resistance, and provoked a searing denunciation of Parnell and Katharine O'Shea for making allegations against O'Shea through her counsel which they were not prepared to stand over in the witness-box.

Thus Parnell at the eleventh hour found his elaborately devised fall-back position closed off. He and Katharine O'Shea were compelled to adopt an entirely passive stance in the proceedings. He was caught off balance — a balance he would never quite regain. With a sang-froid which was perhaps for the first and only time in his career contrived and self-deceiving, Parnell persevered in his determination to ensure that Katharine O'Shea's marriage was dissolved.

In her memoirs, Katharine O'Shea unsurprisingly made no mention of a confrontation between Parnell and Lockwood, but her account of the consultation on the eve of the hearing in other respects bears out that given by Lockwood to Pease. Lockwood had begged her to get Parnell to let him fight the case. She tried to persuade Parnell, but to no avail. They left Lockwood with a promise to telegraph him by eight o'clock the following morning if they were willing to give evidence. Either late that evening, or early the following morning, Parnell sent a telegram confirming they would not do so.[34]

Part of the confusion which later came to surround the conduct of Katharine O'Shea's defence is attributable to the fact that Parnell had a further — and even more acrimonious — falling-out with Lockwood. When the court had risen at the end of the first day's extremely damaging evidence, Parnell called on Lockwood in a highly agitated state: Lockwood thought his manner so wild and peculiar as to show signs of madness. He bitterly reproached Lockwood for failing to make an agreement with Clarke for the custody of the children, and accused him of betraying himself and Katharine. When Lockwood rose angrily, Parnell suggested that Lockwood, the bigger and stronger man, was about to throw him out the window. Lockwood replied that he had been thinking of doing so. The tension thus dispelled, Parnell immediately calmed down. It has been suggested that on this occasion Parnell briefly considered giving evidence for the purpose of securing custody of the children for Katharine O'Shea, but as Henry Harrison has pointed out, he would have been advised by Lockwood that such evidence would have been likely to have prevented the granting of the divorce decree.[35]

The confusion and controversy surrounding what had transpired can be traced back to Parnell himself. In a letter to the *Cork Free Press* in 1913 (which was to provide the ostensible pretext for the publication of Katharine O'Shea's memoirs), William O'Brien wrote that Parnell had told him at Boulogne that the outcome of the case would have been different had he given evidence, that he had pressed upon Lockwood in the strongest terms that he should have been called, and that on one occasion he and Lockwood almost came to blows on the question. By conflating his two contretemps with Lockwood, Parnell had contrived to give O'Brien an entirely misleading impression as to what had occurred. O'Brien's account of what Parnell had told him was to enter Parnellite mythology.[36]

Parnell's deft misleading of O'Brien reveals the terrible constraints under which he was working. After the grant of the divorce decree nisi, he had to seize any political opportunity he could to emphasise that his side of the case had not been put, without however provoking the intervention of the Queen's Proctor to set aside the decree. Moreover, pride and considerations of policy alike forbade him justifying his actions to O'Brien in terms of his determination to wed Katharine O'Shea.

At the time of the letter's publication, Healy observed to his brother 'the conception of Parnell as a liar seems not to have occurred to William O'Brien', and that the notion 'spread by Parnell' that Lockwood prevented him giving evidence was false. Healy's own somewhat garbled accounts of what he had been told by Lockwood also merged the two distinct disputes which had taken place between Parnell and Lockwood. 'Frank Lockwood told me it was Parnell himself who refused to give evidence, and insisted on allowing the case go by default. Yet the two fought over it.' Lockwood had according to Healy told him that he threatened to throw Parnell out of the window at a consultation when he said he would let the case go by default.[37]

The action of O'Shea versus O'Shea and Parnell (Steele intervening) came on for hearing before Mr. Justice Butt on 15 November 1890. Their defence in disarray, the respondent and co-respondent found themselves constrained, by their overriding wish to see the divorce go through, to adopt an entirely passive stance. After the pleadings had been opened, Frank Lockwood (who appeared for Katharine O'Shea, Parnell being unrepresented), rose to declare he would not cross-examine the petitioner's witnesses nor would he call witnesses or take part in the proceedings. Edward Clarke, guessing what was to come had refused to hear anything privately from Lockwood earlier that morning, and had thus put himself in a position to declare that Lockwood's announcement 'was just as much news to him as it was to the Court'. While it materially altered the nature of the case, the mere abandonment at the last moment of the respondent's counter-allegations 'could not be any satisfaction to the husband who, having been originally gravely injured, had been subsequently grossly insulted by such pleadings being put on record'.

There followed two days of extremely damaging evidence. O'Shea's case was directed towards proving not merely adultery but that he had been systematically deceived. After an address by the judge in the prescribed tones of strangled outrage, the jury almost immediately found the adultery proven, and dismissed the defence of connivance. The circumstances in which Captain O'Shea obtained his conditional decree of divorce were for Parnell quite the most damaging conceivable.[38]

Parnell was never to regain his equilibrium in the ruthless struggle for ascendancy which ensued. On 25 November the Irish party re-elected Parnell as its leader: some, perhaps many, of its members were naive enough to believe that Parnell would thereupon resign. Gladstone immediately published his letter to Morley in which he stated that Parnell's leadership of the Irish party would render his own leadership of the Liberal party 'almost a nullity'. Parnell retaliated with his 'Manifesto to the Irish People'. Healy, who had endorsed Parnell at a meeting in the Leinster Hall in Dublin on 20 November, crossed to London to rally the opposition to him. After a week of acrimonious debates in Committee Room 15 of the houses of parliament, the party split asunder. Parnell retained the allegiance only of a minority. He returned to Ireland where his candidate lost the first by-election of the split, in North Kilkenny. Negotiations between Parnell, William O'Brien and John Dillon at Boulogne to reach an accommodation broke down in February. On 7 March the *National Press*, the anti-Parnellite daily newspaper controlled by Healy, was launched. The following month Parnell lost the second by-election of the split, in North Sligo. On 25 June, just before the third by-election, Parnell married Katharine O'Shea. His candidate was heavily defeated in the Carlow election. Released from prison, Dillon and O'Brien lent their weight to the campaign against Parnell, and sought to wrest from Healy control of the direction of the opposition to Parnell.

Parnell fought on with his habitual tenacity, awaiting a reversal of political fortune. He died at Walsingham Terrace, Brighton, on 6 October, aged forty-five.[39]

— Part II —

T. M. Healy and the Fall of Parnell

10

Healy's Rhetorical Strategy in the Split

> There is no epithet in the English language strong enough to apply to Charles Stewart Parnell. Such terms as liar, coward, traitor, adulterer, etc. are all too milk and watery. We want one vast, stupendous, comprehensive word which will express all his latter-day history, and there is not a language, ancient or modern, which will supply it.
>
> *Waterford Citizen*, 4 July 1891

> Anyhow (the matter is a troublous and a peniloose) have they not called him at many's their mock indignation meeting, vehmen's vengeance vective volleying, inwader and uitlander, the notables, crashing libels in their sullivan's mounted beards about him, their right renownsable patriarch?
>
> James Joyce, *Finnegans Wake*[1]

Healy's rhetoric in the split, an exercise in polemical revisionism, sketches a great and vehement popular biography of Parnell. He seized the opportunity which the split presented to inaugurate a new mode of nationalist rhetoric. He defined Parnellism and nationalism as antonyms, and recast the case against Parnell, in nationalist, even ethnic, terms, remote from the exigencies of the Liberal alliance. It was a rhetoric destined to outlast the immediate issue of the split.

Parnell had sought to use his embodiment of the nationalist cause to contain its excesses. Healy devastatingly seized on the latent opposition inherent in Parnellism, which set Parnell's myth against the concept of a supremacist Catholic nation, to consummate Parnell's political destruction. Healy's was a skilled and subtle deconstructing of the Parnell myth, which redirected the attributes of the myth against Parnell himself. Brilliantly reversing the logic of the mythic process, Healy retorted the myth upon the leader.

Healy's attack on Parnell was of remarkable comprehensiveness, as if exhausting the expressive possibilities of opposition to Parnell. His rhetoric constitutes arguably the single most remarkable corpus of rhetoric in the history of nationalism, and one of the most significant texts of the Irish nationalist sensibility. Healy minted the coin of modern chauvinistic nationalism. He proved himself a masterly epigrammatist of derision. Concentrated in the attack on Parnell, his rhetoric surpassed the flaccidity of its premises to attain a striking astringency. His attacks achieved the lucidity of disdain, even a cruel elegance. The pervasiveness of his rhetoric can hardly be overstated. Disseminated through an efficient anti-Parnellite press, it was calculated to pass directly into popular usage, as well as to provide primers for parish orators, lay and clerical; provincial papers readily adopted his arguments and political idiom.

Healy availed of Parnell's manifesto and his refusal to resign to maintain a tactically advantageous defensive posture in the split, even when he had passed on to the offensive. In the deceptive dialectic of the split, it was Healy who seized the initiative, and embarked on a massive and vehement conservative nationalist counter-offensive, in the face of which Parnell by the time of his death had been unable to regroup his support.

Healy's ostentatious claim to humility – he asserted that he had made himself 'the humble instrument of carrying out the wishes of my fellow-countrymen'[2] – belied his role in stamping the electoral repudiation of Parnell with his peculiar implacability, and in recasting the values of Irish nationalism. His rhetoric not merely mediated but transfigured popular opposition to Parnell. The 'popular rage, *hysterica passio*' dramatised by Yeats owed much to Healy's inspired ventriloquy. His was a brilliant populist rhetoric. In clever mimesis, Healy in the practised accents of peasantry insinuated into his rhetoric the peculiar intimacies of Irish life. In a studied subversion of the formality of political discourse, he asserted the naturalness of his own idiom over what he derided as Parnell's stilted and condescending artificiality.

He contrived to achieve a deepened complicity on the part of anti-Parnellite voters. While for many nationalists the rejection of Parnell was contingent and pragmatic, even tentative in character, he sought to invest their choice with a vehement finality. It was essential for him to constitute the repudiation of Parnell a definitive and irreversible act of national will. This strategy of implication is central to an understanding of his rhetoric in the split, and helps account for the confused remorse which the death of Parnell elicited.

Healy's attack on Parnell plied brilliantly between the pragmatic and the absolute. He at once urged the overthrow of Parnell in terms of the exigencies of the Liberal alliance, and denounced him as a pariah of a nationalist moral order. That order was heavily coloured by proprietorial aspirations. Pragmatism and proprietorship merged in an avowedly transcendental nationalist rhetoric.

Healy cast the split as at once a personal engagement and a great nationalist controversy: 'this question cuts deep tracks down to the very roots of public action'.[3] What was professedly a high argument addressed to the political nation was couched in terms peculiarly designed to goad the fallen leader. His determination to wound Parnell in almost intimate personal encounter, and at the same time to address larger themes of nationalism were inextricably fused. Healy no less than Parnell ensured that the split's bitter dialectic endowed the controversy with the character of a classic, even definitive schism. The rhetoric of the split set the themes of modern Irish nationalism.

11

T. M. Healy: Artificer and Revisionist of the Parnell Myth

> And I say this for Mr. Parnell that so little did we know him, that if the greatest master of the human heart, if Shakespeare himself had been acquainted with that man for the twelve years that he worked along with him, he could never have constructed out of the wealth of his imagination the Parnell that we have known subsequent to the Divorce Court . . . We had known Parnell, I may say, all the years of his political life, and not one man of us conceived that he was the soul of fraud and falsehood and folly that he has since proved himself to be.
>
> T. M. Healy, 30 September 1891[1]

> His former character must not be judged by the wild frenzy of the last few months. Let us carry our minds back to the Parnell of the old day, the practical patriot, the cool, the fearless, the indomitable, before the cancer of a guilty passion forbidden by the laws of God and man ate into his heart . . . Characters, it has been well said, are not cut in marble . . . Evil influences slowly ate out manhood and patriotism, truth and courage, from the heart of a man whom Ireland once regarded as her greatest.
>
> *Evening Press*, 7 October 1891[2]

Healy had the unique privilege as one of the chief artificers of the Parnell myth of consummating its destruction. The most articulate exponent of the Parnell myth, he became its most incisive critic.

> I had a long record of old comradeship, much friendship, much intimacy. Why I might even say it was the 'Bantry gang' who created Mr. Parnell (*laughter and applause*). It was Mr. T. D. Sullivan who put him forward; it was T. D. Sullivan in the *Nation* newspaper when every journal and individual who is now supporting him had nothing for him but insults, when the *Freeman* said he had called Irish members 'Papist rats'; it was Mr. T. D. Sullivan who backed him up, and when he wanted a pen to explain his policy and his position in the country, mine was the hand that he selected (*applause*). I have written out his speeches for him (*loud applause*); I have given interviews in his name (*applause and laughter*); his public letters were often of my composition, and now having done everything that one man could do in the interests of unity to keep our country solid, because we gave a vote wrung from us by the terrible necessities of the case, we are described as ingrates, scum, gutter sparrows, men he took out of the sewers.[3]

Healy exaggerated his own contribution and that of the Sullivans to the rise of Parnell. Yet what is most striking is the degree to which his attack on Parnell in the split was implicit in his earlier paeans to the Irish leader.

It had been a commonplace English criticism that Parnell was the dictator of a servile nation, and master of a preternaturally docile party. Healy's friend Harold Frederic likewise wrote of Parnell in the *New York Times* in August 1887 that 'the deference which is paid to him by his followers has no close parallel anywhere within my knowledge', while the Irish members 'have little personal feeling towards their chief one way or the other'. Contemporary comments on Parnell's authority within the nationalist movement were almost invariably couched in terms of racial or religious stereotypes, and Frederic's consideration of the Parnell myth was no exception:

> Most nearly he rules them as an emotionless Archbishop might rule the priests of a province. He is the embodiment of authority . . . who . . . must be at once approachable and solitary. It is really the Catholic training and instincts of the Irish members, I fancy, which have developed this curious hierarchical relation, and it is not made the less interesting by the fact that their Primate is a Protestant.[4]

Some fervent Parnellite apologists defiantly embraced the taunt of subservience. Katharine Tynan wrote: 'I think most of us are proud rather than otherwise of our one-man-rule and one-man-allegiance . . . We Irish are no democrats . . . We cling to old faiths and old sentiments'.[5] Such fierceness of allegiance inspired J. L. Garvin's observation that 'the only political institution of the Celt is the Chief'.[6]

The suggestion that the Irish were obsequiously loyal to Parnell rankled deeply with Healy. Healy was morbidly conscious of the prominent role taken by Protestant nationalists in the Irish patriotic tradition, which had prompted W. E. H. Lecky's wounding comment of Irish Catholics before O'Connell that 'the iron of the penal laws had entered into their souls, and they had always thrown themselves helplessly on Protestant leaders'.[7] Reverting to this theme years later in a review of R. B. O'Brien's biography of Parnell, Lecky asserted that 'it has been truly said that when Irishmen wish to throw themselves into democratic revolution their first instinct is to look for some one of good family to lead them, and the fact that Parnell belonged to a different social level from most of his followers was never forgotten either by himself or by them, or by the great masses who supported him'.[8] Underlying the derisive characterisation of nationalist social deference, and the imputation of arrogance to Parnell, was the accurate perception that his social class was a defining attribute in the nationalist myth of Parnell.

Healy responded to the accusation of subservience in an article published in the *Pall Mall Gazette* in 1883 entitled 'The Secret of Mr. Parnell's Power'. It was a rationalisation of Parnell's hegemony in terms of the disadvantaged circumstances of Irish nationalist politics, rather than an enthusiastic commendation of the Irish leader.[9] His tributes to Parnell were cold and restrained, and within his occasional and perfunctory panegyrics lurked an implied reservation. Healy's preferred role was rather as an ostensibly rational exegete of the cult of Parnell against its English critics than as a eulogist.

He argued that the Parnell myth was shaped and defined by English hostility. His defence of Parnell in 1883, in sustainment of the Parnell testimonial, was expressly couched in response to the attack on the nationalist cause which the English assault upon Parnell necessarily entailed.[10] His ironic reservations were manifest in a speech he made in response to a suggestion of Parnell's secretary, Henry Campbell, that he deflect by praise Parnell's hostility: at Killucan in County Westmeath, in public tribute and private irony Healy applied to Parnell the lines from Thomas Davis's 'Lament for Eoghan Roe' – 'Sure we never won a battle – 'twas Eoghan won them all'.[11]

Yet these reservations did not inhibit Healy from trenchantly asserting Parnell's supremacy against challenges from within nationalism. In this respect, Healy had been the most unsparing Parnellite *apparatchik*, determined to brook no challenge to Parnell's ascendancy, either from Davitt, or from reactionary local champions of constituency rights. Addressing Liverpool nationalists in the prelude to the 1885 election, he declared:

> There was no dissension and disunion amongst them, for from the humblest to the highest they were determined to follow the leader of genius who God had sent to them like another Moses (*applause*). He said 'Woe to the man who in the great crisis of Ireland's fortune lifted up his puny

> cackle against the united advice of an experienced party and a determined nation (*renewed applause*). It had been the misfortune of the Irish race in past times to have too many great men, and too many people who could do things better than anybody else. What they wanted for 200 years was an honest dictator, and they had at last got one in the person of Mr. Parnell (*applause*). Their cause would win if it were united, but it might be lost by cranks who set themselves out as rulers and judges of men, and with their tinpot intelligence attempted to chime a discordant note against the great nationalist tocsin which Mr. Parnell was clanging to the national ear (*applause*).[12]

The seeming extravagance of the panegyric to Parnell was rigorously subordinated to Healy's purpose of sustaining the Parnellite edifice to crush its Irish adversaries. His argument was unstable, deploying a sentimental rhetoric to a functional purpose. In the split, Healy would carry the economy of heroics for which he argued to its logical extreme, and consign the 'honest dictator' to the ranks of the 'too many great men' of which he spoke.

The commonplace nationalist emphasis on Parnell's landlord origins and his Protestantism, to underscore his aristocratic qualities and the avowedly non-confessional character of Irish nationalism, was given unusual prominence in Healy's rhetoric. He pressed and twisted the argument so as almost to foreshadow his rhetoric in the split. He highlighted the English rather than Anglo-Irish aspect of Parnell's background: 'Of English extraction, and of the Protestant faith, he was "more Irish than the Irish themselves"'.[13] He thus recast the concept of *hibernior hibernis ipsis* to characterise Parnell's avowal of nationalist views, rather than the assimilation of his stock into a unitary Irish nation.

Healy described Parnell as 'an unselfish Protestant gentleman'.[14] Drawing the contrast between his own origins and those of Parnell which he would savagely turn against Parnell in the course of the split, he declared:

> They met there to endeavour to give strength and sustenance to Charles Stewart Parnell the leader of the Irish people. If he were one of themselves, or if he were, as he (Mr. Healy) was, sprung from the peasant class, a man of the people, born with the people, educated amongst them, and of the religion of the people, then they might say of him that it would be kind of him to have struggled in aid of the oppressed people of this country. But was this the case? Nothing of the kind. He was a man, he might say, of English connections, of English education; a man connected with the English aristocracy in the realm; not a tenant or a democrat, but an aristocrat and a landlord, and that man had toiled so hard, and had so endeavoured for the people's cause that he had been brought to the very pinch of poverty, and he was obliged to mortgage his

> property in order to enable him to carry on still further the struggle for popular rights.[15]

The submerged text, of Parnellism as the politics of condescension, would break to the surface in Healy's rhetoric in the split.

These speeches were in sustainment of the Parnell National Tribute of 1883, when a sum of almost £39,000 was raised by public subscription to permit Parnell to avoid selling his heavily encumbered Wicklow estate.[16] By a profound irony Parnell became a landlord by public subscription, as if through a ritual process of surrender and regrant by the nationalist population. If the testimonial was a sustained act of acclaim of Parnell, it was also a reminder of the anomalousness of his position. This did not escape Richard Pigott, who noted that, while the extirpation of landlordism was the object of the nationalist agitation, its leader was a landlord who himself 'has been presented with £40,000, which was mainly subscribed by Irish tenants'.[17]

A troubling sectarian rancour underlay Healy's ostensibly pluralistic treatment of the issue of Parnell's Protestantism. In a parliamentary debate on the composition of the magistracy in April 1884, Healy paid tribute to the tradition of Protestant leadership in Ireland. He did so however in terms of a bitter reflection on the deficient nationalist sentiment of Irish Catholics. Healy declared his belief that the people of Ireland were 'the greatest serfs that ever existed in any country' in permitting the British government to tyrannise them, and continued in response to the government's boast that it had increased the number of Catholic magistrates:

> . . . he regretted to say that some of the greatest villains in Ireland had been Roman Catholics. He preferred the honest Protestants of Ireland, who stood aloof from the religion to which they belonged, to the unfortunate Catholic serfs. In the whole course of history the leaders of the Irish people had been Protestants. If the people of Ireland had to erect monuments to their great men, there would be a long roll of Protestants to come.[18]

Healy declared of Parnell in January 1885: 'They were fortunate, fiery and impetuous Celts as they were, in being guided by his coolness, aye, by his calculation'.[19] In the split Healy would maintain the contrast, but reduce Parnell's impeturbability to callous Anglo-Irish self-regard. In February 1888, Healy invoked Parnell's Protestantism to celebrate the non-sectarian character of nationalism, or rather the innate magnanimousness of Irish Catholics.

> The Irish Catholic had no exclusive heritage of Irish nationality. They had received from the mouths of their forefathers and others the lessons

> of respect for public worship and public conscience, and they had received it from the tongues of their priests and leaders – not merely from McHale and O'Connell, but also from Dean Swift and Edward Fitzgerald (*cheers*) . . . It was their Protestant fellow-countrymen who had given them Swift, Emmet, Mitchel, Butt and Parnell (*great cheering*) . . . They would plant a new shamrock in the soil of Ireland, a shamrock on whose leaves should be written Catholic, Protestant, and Presbyterian (*loud cheers*).[20]

What is most arresting in Healy's rhetoric in the split is the success with which he fashioned out of his personal antagonisms the stuff of nationalist politics. The most disturbing feature of his rhetoric was its invidious coupling of proclaimed public purpose and private animus. In this he brilliantly exploited the malleable and subjective character of nationalist rhetoric. He legitimated his own resentment of Parnell by enrooting it in the historic antagonism of the tenantry to the Anglo-Irish landlord caste: his own course of estrangement from Parnell became a stylised personal dramaturgy of the nationalist repudiation of Parnell's class. What was disquieting was the quest for an ideological correlative of personal resentment, the illiberal soldering of nationalist values to the pursuit of personal vengeance.

Healy early in the split declared he had steeled himself against remorse. Having done their best for Parnell in vain, they were now compelled 'to set their face against him like flint'.[21] He appreciated the 'terrible wrench' of the Irish people in breaking with Parnell: 'For myself, though I have gone into this movement in a determined and thorough manner, I have done so with a heavy heart, because it involved the tearing up by the roots of the association of the last ten years – the association of a large character since the beginning of my political life'. The validating scheme of his rhetoric predicated an ineluctable sacrificial dilemma between Parnell and Ireland:

> We treated Mr. Parnell with the tenderness of loving sons for a father (*A voice: God knows you did*). We bore him, we sustained him, and it was only when it became a choice between Ireland and Mr. Parnell that we said: Down with the man in order that the nation may live.[22]

He denied that he bore any animus against Parnell: 'I can say from my heart I have no ill-feeling against Mr. Parnell, no personal ill-feeling'.[23] He later declared: 'I was very sorry I had to vote against Mr. Parnell. It was the most bitter occasion in the course of my entire life'.[24] He asserted the severe impersonality of his stance in the split:

> Yet, I can safely say to myself that, strongly as I condemn him, fiercely as I fight against him (*hear hear*), determined as I am to fight against him (*applause*), I never attack him without a pang, without thinking of his past

> services to his country, without regretting that he should have acted in the atrocious way he has done. But having so acted I regard him as a worse enemy of Ireland than the most bigoted Orangeman that ever sat in an Orange Lodge.[25]

Strikingly, Healy invoked the course of his own former allegiance to present himself as an authority on the Parnellite sensibility: 'I can sympathise with the Parnellite as he is breaking my head. There is not a stage in Parnellite feeling I have not gone through'.[26] He even jocosely boasted that his own Leinster Hall speech defending Parnell immediately after the divorce decree represented the definitive statement of the Parnellite case:

> I really think if I may be guilty of the egotism that I put the case better for Mr. Parnell than it has ever been put since (*cheers*) — at least I judge so from the frequent quotations which are made from it. Nobody ever quotes Mr. Redmond's speech at Leinster Hall though he is the most eminent and intellectual of all the Parnellites.[27]

If these calculated remarks tend rather to exclude any hint of ambivalence or regret, Parnell in decline retained for Healy a persistent fascination. He wrote to his father in May 1891: 'Parnell is a monomaniac. I pity the poor devil often enough . . . Sometimes he looks awfully haggard, but other times he looks like cast-iron'.[28] A revealing deletion in the published version of a letter from Healy to his father during the Kilkenny election of the two words italicised below discloses Healy's later determination to suppress any trace of the residual admiration he felt for Parnell in the split:

> We were never engaged in a worthier cause and I never felt so certain that we are right. I am sorry to attack Parnell as I have done and will do, but it is a necessary evil to bring the truth home to the common mind, where his name is ensanctuaried. If he was treated tenderly a la O'Brien, he would know no bounds in audacity *and courage*, so that it was only by the terror of plain truths that he could be reduced to some appreciation of his position.[29]

In the split, Healy's fractious temperament was moving out of control. The sundering of the nationalist movement removed the externally imposed order of Healy's career. Bereft of the restraining discipline of Parnell's leadership, his political course lost much of its former direction and purpose.

In attacking Parnell, he was a politician with little to lose. As the withdrawal of his brief in the Special Commission signified, he had good reason to fear a permanent exclusion from substantial influence under a home rule administration led by Parnell. Moreover, even at his political zenith in 1890–1, Healy did not rank as a serious contender for the nationalist leadership in his own right. The anti-Parnellites looked rather to John Dillon: even Croke, who praised Healy as 'that eminently caustic and clear-headed man', appeared to endorse Dillon.[30] Healy was thus liberated from rational constraints, from the disciplines and responsibilities which a realistic ambition for leadership would have entailed: his career was a study in the void of politics without the prospect of power.

He was in the mischievous position of wielding enormous influence under conditions where he knew that leadership would elude him. A majoritarian anarch, he strove recklessly to maximise his influence and to dictate the course of nationalist politics. That entailed deepening the polarisation of the split, which he pressed to the point of almost destabilising the nationalist democracy.

He was determined to maintain the tautness of the split's controversy. His avowed pursuit of the extirpation of Parnellism became more intense in triumph. This reflects an obsessive resolve not merely to efface the emotional residues of Parnellism but to frustrate any moderate re-alignment of nationalist politics after Parnell. The calculated offensiveness of his rhetoric in the split's latter phase was directed less towards Parnell than Dillon and O'Brien. He articulated a political position which he knew would be highly objectionable to them but which they would be unable to disavow. He was determined to ensure that his formative influence on anti-Parnellite nationalism would endure, and that if Dillon and O'Brien were to assume control of the anti-Parnellite party and organisation, they would do so on his terms.

The repercussions of Healy's stance far outlasted his campaign against Parnell. Not merely did Dillon and O'Brien have to address the poisonous legacy of his campaign against Parnell, but successive leaders of the Irish party would find themselves trammelled by the recalcitrant Catholic proprietorial nationalism which Healy had brought into play. If Dillon and his partisans were correct in imputing to Healy a spoiling role in Irish politics, they erred in assessing this exclusively in terms of his temperamental idiosyncrasies. His was a shrewder ideological purpose than they could ever bring themselves to concede.

There was a bitter edge to Healy's awareness of the transience of his ascendancy in the split. He knew that as 'the man in the gap', in assuming the chief responsibility for Parnell's overthrow, he was taking upon himself, at least metaphorically, the role of regicide. He would be lastingly the object of Parnellite execration, and the scapegoat of anti-Parnellite remorse. He was at once executioner and martyr. The equation of his own fate with Parnell's — the assertion of a sacrificial parity between them — was integral to his scheme of self-justification in the split. He professed the belief that the leading protagonists of the split would be effaced from Irish politics, in the striking image of a mortal fosse: '. . . the split will not be patched up. It will rather be filled in with the remains of the combatants, and a re-united party will be organised to continue the struggle'.[31]

Healy's forebodings aggravated his loathing for John Dillon. Harold Frederic in a vicious attack on Dillon in 1893, which drew heavily on information provided by Healy, alleged that when a member of the party had spoken to Dillon prior to the divorce crisis of the dangers created by Parnell's absences, Dillon assented: '"Something ought to be done", he admitted; "only", he added, "bear this in mind – the man who pulls Parnell down will be damned in Ireland"'. Healy came to believe that Dillon, having cunningly flinched from assuming responsibility for Parnell's overthrow, became its principal beneficiary.[32]

Healy's belief that he would be victimised for his role in bringing about Parnell's fall reflected a deep and prescient fear that the resilience of the Parnell myth would prove too much for him, that the belief in Parnell's greatness would re-assert itself after the acrid débâcle of the split. With Parnell's death, what Healy believed to be his own martyrdom was sealed. The association with the fall and death of Parnell would continue to haunt him in public life.

From the outset of the split, he pitted himself against the idea of Parnell's greatness. Concurrently with his polemics against Parnell in Ireland, Healy, as if intuiting he was working against the grain of history, articulated an assured and ostensibly dispassionate critique of Parnell's career on the plane of historical judgement. Surveying the antecedent decade with the practised eye of the propagandist, he presented a partisan retrospect which impugned the entirety of Parnell's personal achievement.

Parnell's career was re-cast as a sham and a fraud, conducted under the cover of a fabulous myth wrought for him by ingenious publicists, notably Healy himself: a myth as extravagant and as deceptive as the ornate breastplate of an indolent and shrinking prince. Parnell's feats were not his own. His career was a parasitic growth on the manifest destiny of Irish nationalism, derivative of the endeavours of his clever lieutenants, who self-effacingly wrought for him his myth and provided the substantive achievements to sustain it.

On the day after the party broke apart, Healy sought to disloign himself from the acrimony of the Committee Room and to shift the campaign against Parnell to a more sophisticated altitude. In an archly poised interview to the Liberal *Pall Mall Gazette* he initiated his high revisionist critique of Parnell's leadership.[33] In addressing himself to what the paper called 'the genesis of the Parnell legend', Healy deployed the Parnell myth against Parnell in an attempt to sever the man and the achievement:

> Mr. Parnell is one of the most extraordinary men that ever lived. We created Parnell, and Parnell created us – the Irish party. We seized very early in the movement the idea of the man, with his superb silences, his historic name, his self-control, his aloofness – we seized that as the canvas of a great national hero. But, upon the other hand, with what I believe to be an entire absence of introspectiveness, Parnell placed himself in the hands of his friends . . . Mr. Parnell is, in my judgement, an abler man in respect of reticence, determination, and unscrupulousness than any member of his party. We were conscious of these qualities, of which, perhaps, he was at first not wholly appreciative; and worked him for all he was worth.

A decade of parliamentary success was brought about not by Parnell, but through the subjective instrumentality of his myth. Parnell's character was itself defined by the mythic process, as he became corrupted by the allure of the myth and the unionist counter-myth.

> He has been largely created not only by himself and his colleagues, but by his enemies. He has been moulded too in a sort of English matrix. When he did not appear in the House of Commons, and the Tory press got out stories of his mysterious disappearances, and referred to him as the one solitary man wrapping his cloak around him like Napoleon at St. Helena, or as the one strong man defying and despising everybody else, he, of course, read these things, and as Oscar Wilde put it, lived up to the level of his blue china.

In succumbing to its excesses, Parnell was fixed with responsibility for the myth. He was attacked not merely for his aristocratic origins, but for what his nationalist critics now fastidiously discerned as the vulgarity of his cult. Parnell was the usurper of nationalist historical providence, a vain and shallow figure who sought to arrogate to himself credit for the achievements of his colleagues, and the vindication ineluctably due to Ireland. He was a plagiarist even of his own myth, in Healy's image a nationalist Frankenstein. In response to the criticism that he had for so long acquiesced in and supported Parnell's leadership, Healy insouciantly asserted that he did his best to keep him in position 'knowing well that he was acting of late years as a good figurehead'.[34]

Healy reverted to his ostensibly elevated critique in an article in the *New Review* for March 1891, entitled 'The Rise and Fall of Mr. Parnell'. It was a stylised political obituary: 'Mr. Parnell has got a good grip on the public imagination, and his character in process of *detritus* will be well worth study'. He analysed the course of Parnell's career in terms of the corruption wrought by power. Out of political necessity, plenary power had been entrusted to Parnell, but the chief defect of this arrangement proved to be 'the deterioration which unchecked power seems to produce in the mind of its possessor'. The degeneration arose from what Healy discerned as a paranoid strain in Parnell's character, deepened by the secretiveness which the circumstances of his personal life dictated: 'His besetting sin was over-caution, which finally bred in him mistrust and untruth and silent jealousy. Weighted by enormous responsibilities, and surrounded by powerful enemies, he felt the importance of keeping himself uncommitted — and the secret habits of his life fitted in with his train of thought, the one reacting on the other'.

Healy's allegation of 'over-caution' was the first public expression of the charge levelled privately against Parnell by Labouchere in the virulent characterisation of Parnell in Labouchere's correspondence with Herbert Gladstone in 1885–6, in which Parnell's strategic refusal to treat with or ally himself with Gladstone in advance of the 1885 election was attributed to a pusillanimous evasion of political responsibilities, and specifically to a fear of Fenian revenge.

On Parnell's death the *National Press* blamed the calamity of the split on Parnell's arrogance, fed by the sycophancy of supporters who knew his course of action was 'madness': 'no intellect, however great, can be proof against the assaults of floods of endless flattery'. The paper made the extremely questionable assertion that had Parnell accepted the invitation conveyed by Sexton in Committee Room 15 on behalf of the majority to resign the leadership with the possibility of a later return, he would 'now be awaiting if not unremembered retirement that generous recall which those mindful of his past would gladly have spoken at the earliest moment. Suspicion, however, at the sterner counsels of the upright grew rank in a mind accustomed only to parasitic incense'.[35]

Healy returned to the issue of the myth two years after Parnell's death. In two articles in the *Westminster Gazette* in November 1893, entitled 'A Great Man's Fancies', he sought to align the myth with the enigma by emphasising the superstitious element in Parnell's 'great but simple intellect': 'like a vein in marble, a mystic strain seemed to thread its way through Mr. Parnell's mind'.[36] He rehearsed his argument that Parnell had succumbed to the allure of his legend:

> Hostile journalists who pursued Mr. Parnell at the outset of his Parliamentary career as a bore, a blunderer, and a petulant, wheeled round later on to invest his successes with unfathomable accompaniments of surprise and mystery. It is true that the conditions under which he came to live after some time lent themselves to such treatment — lurid or mystic — according to the bias of the daily purveyor of spiced condiments for the public palate. It is equally true that in the end it came to suit the harassed politician to don as his permanent raiment the 'cloak of darkness' and 'shoes of swiftness' which sensationalists cheaply presented him with.

This much – Parnell trapped within the confines of his own myth, a superficial figure whose character was moulded by the impress of his political image – was familiar. Healy proceeded to postulate a deep rapport between Parnell's myth and his superstitiousness:

> Some of the strangeness, however, that tantalised the inquisitive came rather by 'suggestion' and 'transference' from the ready writers of the day, whose colourings the keenly-watched statesman adopted and even intensified to 'make up' for the part of the Unaccountable which the critics willed that he must play. Still, there underlay these wrappages a foundation which gave body and substance to the descriptions the public received. In those strange eyes there lay at times something of 'the light that never shone on land or sea', and then they shot a power that easily affected the susceptible. Occasionally from Mr. Parnell's lips would fall in some snatchy way traces of a belief in portents and signs which awed the unsuspecting listener.

In the manner of other contemporary commentators and memoirists seeking to solve the Parnell 'enigma' by biographical anecdote, Healy set down selective reminiscences of Parnell through all of which ran 'the mystic vein', manifested in his horror of funerals and omens of death.

A suggestion of mystical abstractedness as accounting for Parnell's 'enigma' was commonplace in the reminiscences of his contemporaries. To Healy's comment that 'in those strange eyes there lay at times something of "the light that never shone on land or sea", and then they shot a power that easily affected the susceptible', corresponded T. P. O'Connor's observation in an obituary to Parnell: 'he was curiously unconscious sometimes of surroundings, and used to sit with those strange, red-brown eyes of his, as though, like the raven, he had fallen into a sleepless and unending dream'.[37] Parnell's superstitions were widely attested to, but no treatment of Parnell's superstitiousness was remotely as thoroughgoing or bibliographically deliberate as that in Healy's *Westminster Gazette* articles, with the possible exception of the obituary of Parnell written by Harold Frederic for the *New York Times*, which characterised Parnell as 'the most strange, weird, and tragic figure of his time':

> Even before the beginning of this terrible last act in his life drama last November, there was an uncanny element in the fascination he exerted over the popular fancy. His unusual personal appearance, with his shaggy hair and beard and his bright, eager eyes, his habitual reticence and his mysterious disappearances, his unaccountable patience under false charges and the almost demonic completeness of his final triumph over his accusers – all this invested his personality with a fantastic interest . . . How deeply the events of the past eleven months would strengthen such an

> impression hardly needs to be pointed out. His behaviour throughout, even when it was most clearly dictated by unscrupulous craft, always had an eerie side.[38]

Healy wrote that Parnell sometimes hinted that his religious leanings were towards the Plymouth Brethren, 'but his thoughts, as outwardly expressed, were not often cast in a speculative direction'. Healy elsewhere noted Parnell's ignorance of religious distinctions: he wrote to his daughter in 1928 that Parnell had unsuccessfully run Harold Rylett, a unitarian minister, as a candidate for Tyrone in 1881 'as Parnell didn't know that Presbyterians hated Unitarians!'[39]

Healy's articles concluded with the incident which occurred when Parnell, overcoming his lifelong aversion to funerals, attended in June 1891 the funeral of the O'Gorman Mahon at Glasnevin:

> After the interment, as he passed through the gate to leave the cemetery, a ghastly and awful cheer went up from his followers, startling the abode of the dead . . . A chill must have pierced that stoical but bodeful heart as his creed of fate bore in upon him . . . Within four months Parnell himself was laid in Glasnevin amidst the wailing of the corpse whose hosannas had resounded through its tombs in his acclaim . . .
>
> Only nine months before he had electrified his party in the stormy leadership debates of Room 15 by announcing with a vehemence which thrilled every man who heard it, 'I don't intend to die'. The declaration was made with a certainty which seemed almost inspired, and if ever conviction on such a matter could be imparted to mortals, tone, gesture, and force combined alike to overwhelm opponents and inspire partisans. If genius is sometimes 'fey' does it not also draw from its own mysterious lights a compelling power to affect and awe the minds of men?

Healy's *Westminster Gazette* portrait of Parnell was an essay in his remorseless reductionism of Parnell's persona and political career. As well as achieving a subtle self-exculpation, it was a considered discounting of Parnell's greatness by reference to his 'fancies': his stature was reduced to a subjective phenomenon, an interaction of his own superstitiousness with the susceptibility of those who succumbed to the myth, so as to elide the substance of his achievement.

It was moreover a portrait of Parnell in lurid sectarian hue reflecting Healy's fascinated disdain for Parnell as a nominal Protestant, the void of whose religious convictions he believed to be filled by bizarre doctrines of fate. He observed and exaggerated Parnell's superstitiousness with an enthralled horror, refracted through a sensibility characterised by a fusion of Irish Catholic values with a Victorian sense of the macabre. Healy had used his sense of Parnell's superstitiousness to try to unnerve him psychologically in the split. Now the theme, treated with sepulchral mellowness, rendered in biographic form the taunts of callous egotism, of the lack of a moral faculty, and of insensitivity to religious values which Healy levelled against Parnell in the split.

Healy's subtly plausible critique of Parnell in terms of his myth reflects an acute, even morbid, sensitivity to the political mechanics of greatness and its mythology. He had a shrewd grasp both of the myth of the hero in Irish history and politics, and of the nineteenth-century concept of the great man – in particular the debased Hegelianism of late Victorian politics of which the perception of Gladstone as the demiurge of a sentimental providence was a manifestation.

Healy's skilful and relentless belittling of Parnell's achievement was of a piece with his earliest enthralled but resentful perceptions as a young man of Parnell, compelled as if in exquisite penance for his own ambition to watch his rise, aware from the outset that Parnell would achieve greatness, and initiating a bitter private critique, a distorted and obsessive measuring of Parnell's political stature against his human frailty.

Healy's table talk in later years tacitly conceded that his celebrity owed much to his assault on Parnell in the split. The second Earl of Birkenhead, writing of dinners in Gray's Inn, recalled Healy's 'describing, under much pressure, how he broke Parnell'.[40] Healy similarly regaled Lady Lavery with ugly jibes about Katharine O'Shea.[41]

Neither age nor time was to diminish Healy's denigration of Parnell, as his later comments in his private correspondence, often suppressed in his published memoirs, attest. Even as expurgated, the memoirs are unrepentant and unforgiving. Of them, C. P. Curran wrote perceptively: 'Towards his English adversaries Mr. Healy shows himself uniformly, studiously, benign; towards his Irish one-time colleagues he turns the unblunted cutting edge of memory'.[42]

12

The Heroic Predicament: The Structure of the Parnell Myth

And then, like Gambetta in France, he had a legend.

T. P. O'Connor[1]

. . . we cannot remember when the myth which has so fatally damaged Mr. Parnell, in utter misconception of his essential character, has ever gathered round an Irish leader before.

The Spectator[2]

. . . a born leader of men which undoubtedly he was and a commanding figure, a six footer or at any rate five feet ten or eleven in his stockinged feet . . . It certainly pointed a moral, the idol with feet of clay, and then seventy two of his trusty henchmen rounding on him with mutual mudslinging . . . a magnificent specimen of manhood he was truly augmented obviously by gifts of a high order, as compared with the other military supernumerary that is . . .

James Joyce, *Ulysses*[3]

A pedestal may be a very unreal thing. A pillory is a terrific reality.

Oscar Wilde, *De Profundis*[4]

'It is true', wrote the *Spectator* on Parnell's death, 'that he fell almost in a moment, like an idol shattered by a shell — that two-thirds of the people he had ruled deserted him at once, and that they did this on grounds – for the divorce business was a feeble pretext – which showed that he had not won their completest loyalty.'[5] While the *Spectator* was habitually concerned to suggest the volatility – if not the treacherousness – of Irish nationalist allegiance, the comment raised the fundamental question of the degree of actual support enjoyed by a leader conventionally considered invincible.

The split is an essay in the dissolution of the Parnell myth. It disclosed the underlying fragility of a hegemony which the triumph and acclaim of a decade of nationalist parliamentary achievement had served to obscure. The unassailability of his position was systematically exaggerated by the Irish myth of his invincibility and the complementary English perception of Parnell as the dictator of the Irish nation. The tightening objective limitations on his power derived from the changing configuration of Irish society; subjectively the Parnell myth was disquietingly double-edged, and particularly vulnerable to the successive shocks of the divorce court, the schism with Gladstone, and defeat in Ireland.

The very epithets of the myth – impassive, coldly proud, regal – suggest the latent frailty of Parnell's position. The dissociation of Parnell from the people he led was integral to his myth. The split revealed how susceptible it was to deployment against him. Its attributes proved unexpectedly reversible. Healy devastatingly exploited this inherent tension. Parnell's legendary reserve was re-interpreted as arrogance and heartlessness. His landlord origins no longer were considered to reflect his selflessness, but rather a cynicism bred of caste.

The campaign against Parnell in the split was a bizarre *ricorso.* It was grimly ironic that Parnell, who had been attacked by unionist publicists for over ten years, was now more comprehensively and virulently assailed in remarkably similar terms, this time from within the nationalist camp. The attributes imputed to Parnell as the villain of nationalism corresponded with those of unionist polemic: renegade, aristocrat, Fenian fellow-traveller, dictator and opportunist. In the bleak language of unionist tracts, Parnellism and crime were again equated, the crime now being an offence against nationalism itself. Parnellism was 'unmasked', or 'unveiled' *de novo.*[6]

Parnell's stature depended on the confident deployment of an unquestioned supremacy, which belied the delicacy of his political undertaking. On Parnell's death, J. M. Tuohy of the *Freeman's Journal* recounted a classic instance of Parnell's exercise of his authority in Ireland as he approached his zenith, displaying 'his capacity for over-mastering the will of a body even of the most determined men'. A substantial number of the delegates at the Cork convention of 1885 were resolved to oppose one of the approved candidates. Parnell decided to disregard their objection and to persevere with the candidacy. As chairman he put the nomination in the usual way. When the recalcitrant delegates gave a voluble 'no', Parnell turned his face 'and fixing his eyes with a stare of stern surprise upon the malcontents he again in measured tones put the question'. He put the question seven times, until eventually the diminishing minority fell silent 'and Mr. Parnell, with a slight inflection of scorn in his voice, asked "What is the meaning then of this pretence that this convention is not unanimous?"' It was, Tuohy observed, 'a magnificent display of concentrated power'.[7] Once Parnell's unquestioned supremacy cracked, its disintegration was unexpectedly rapid.

One of Parnell's strengths was his unassimilability to stereotypes, which throughout his career enabled him to exasperate and fascinate public opinion in Ireland. He conformed to the type neither of the Anglo-Irish landlord nor of the nationalist parliamentarian (he departed yet more egregiously from the paradigm of the continental European nationalist or revolutionary). It was central to his myth and power that he was perceived to stand in opposition to the stereotype of the Irish character. Ironically, this feature of his myth, celebrated with particular pride by nationalists, was to increase his vulnerability to ostracism in the split.

Parnell's antecedents and manner rendered him immune to the traditional modes of denigration of Irish politicians, most famously exemplified in the *Times* attack on Daniel O'Connell:

> Scum condensed of Irish bog,
> Ruffian-coward-demagogue.[8]

English commentators sought unconvincingly, and on occasion offensively, to dissolve a mystique by which they were at once fascinated and repelled. G. W. E. Russell wrote that the fact that Parnell 'should have seemed "majestic", "regal", "prince-like" and all the rest of it, to the rabble of shop-boys, booking-clerks, whisky-sellers, and gombeen men who formed his political following is not so remarkable; for at any rate he had the appearance, manners and bearing of an English gentleman'.[9]

Time and again, commentators at a loss to explain the phenomenon of Parnell invoked his supposed 'Englishness'. G. K. Chesterton later observed, eccentrically comparing G. B. Shaw to Parnell, 'with him also a bewildered England tried the desperate dodge of saying that he was not Irish at all'.[10] W. E. H. Lecky wrote that 'of all the men who have played a prominent part in Irish politics, Parnell was probably the least like an Irishman'. While O'Connell embodied the Celtic nature, and Henry Grattan represented 'with hardly less fidelity the better qualities of the Anglo-Irish gentry', Lecky quoted with approbation an observation of Lord Cowper as to the Englishness of Parnell's character.[11] For Lecky, no less than for Healy, Parnell was an intruder in the course of Irish history.

The *Economist*, in 1883, in words which are probably those of the young Asquith, stated that Parnell

> rules because his followers, with the quick instinct of a melancholy people, have discerned that his faults and capacities exactly supplement theirs, that he supplies precisely what they lack.[12]

J. L. Garvin wrote after attending Parnell's funeral:

> O'Connell was supreme in the possession of gifts which are characteristic of his countrymen. Parnell was supreme in the possession of gifts which were the direct antitheses to the characteristics of his countrymen. That, as I have heard many say in the streets of Dublin, is why Ireland may well never have another Parnell.[13]

If the contrast was conducted in terms of more or less fatuous nineteenth-century racial stereotypes, it touched on a central truth. The Parnell myth was both the embodiment of a nationalist myth, and its corrective. He was at once the leader of nationalism and its most intuitively prescient critic. His perceptions of the deficiencies of nationalism shaped his political course to a far greater degree than contemporaries appreciated. Parnell at once led Irish nationalism and held it in check. The Parnell myth was in important respects defined in opposition to that of the nation; put alternatively, Parnell deployed the myth to contain the excesses of the nation. In this central aspect, the myth was a rational construct. It defied not merely English but Irish expectations. Directed in the first instance against England it was in turn re-projected on the screen of Irish political life. This was the logic of the myth and its defining tension, providing the fragile *trompe-l'oeil* of Parnell's supposedly unassailable supremacy which the split so rudely disturbed.

Parnell in the split was compelled to embark on the necessarily hazardous endeavour of turning his myth to immediate electoral advantage, of converting 'greatness' into the coin of electoral support. The attempt to exploit his myth necessarily entailed its vulgarisation. Parnell's had been a high intuitive practice of politics, irreducible to programmatic form. In the split he found himself compelled to popularise and debase his political strategy, by transforming the tacit premises of his policy into crude nationalist axioms. This appeared inevitably as a lapse from the politics of his earlier career, and seemed to many contemporaries horribly parodic of his career at its height.

Parnell's followers had particular difficulty striking a plausible rhetorical note, and had recourse to extravagant professions of loyalty, a crude rhetoric of chieftaincy, and vituperative denunciations of the treachery of the anti-Parnellites — all of which exposed them to Healy's withering derision. The *Freeman's Journal* hailed 'The Only Possible Leader', and 'Our Infallible Leader', and declared of Parnell that 'he who embodies the great attributes of patriotism and independence in his personality is the idol of the Irish people', placing him in the line of Sarsfield, Grattan, Hugh O'Neill, Wolfe Tone, and — of greatest comic potential for Healy — Brian Boru.[14]

A deep inhibition within the myth rendered Parnell's apparent omnipotence largely illusory. Perhaps the feature which most recommended Parnell was that he had not himself encouraged the cult of his personality. Authority had been vested in him as if by natural accretion, in unsolicited tribute to his efficacy as a politician. He had borne his power lightly. Probably, wrote *United Ireland* in 1883 on the occasion of the Parnell testimonial, 'no leader has ever lived who was so little jealous of, or even conscious of, his power, and the less store he sets by it the more it grows and warms upon him'.[15] T. P. O'Connor wrote after Parnell's death:

> It was a peculiarity of this man — up to the last nine months of his life — that he shrank with lofty pride from doing anything on his own behalf. Everything that he obtained came to him as the free gift of others: it was the tribute to what Mr. William O'Brien has often called his divine right of genius to govern.[16]

Parnell's stature was heavily contingent on the appearance of regal disinterestedness. His prestige was elusively sublime, and deserted him once he condescended to fight to maintain it.

The split disclosed a further severe limitation on Parnell's power inherent in the myth. His repute was as the champion of Irish interests against English government. It owed much to Irish perceptions of Parnell in heroic pose confronting the 'hereditary enemy' across the floor of the House of Commons. Westminster had to this extent provided the plinth of the Parnell myth. Many tributes to Parnell bear witness. William O'Brien contrasted the ineffectual opposition preceding generations had offered to English rule with Parnellite opposition to W. E. Forster as Chief Secretary ('The poor Irish wood-kerne had no Mr. Parnell to move the adjournment of the House'), and wrote of Parnell in relation to Forster as 'that pale, passionless young man, who ever coldly thwarted him'.[17] John Redmond, in an extended evocation of his leader's studied impassivity as a parliamentarian, recalled the sight of Parnell, on Redmond's first arrival at Westminster as a member of parliament in 1881, in the heat of the debate on the coercion bill which ended in the suspension of thirty-seven Irish members, 'with pale cheeks and drawn face, his hands clenched behind his back facing without flinching a continuing roar of interruption'.[18]

An Irish exile wrote on the first anniversary of Parnell's death: 'We imagined him standing with folded arms like a marble man when the House raved and roared through all its benches and longed with a brute fury to be able to tear him limb from limb'.[19] An Irish street ballad composed in response to Forster's attack on Parnell after the Phoenix Park murders, went:

> Parnell's the man that stood the scorn
> Of the British lion and the unicorn.[20]

The physical intensity of the popular nationalist identification with Parnell as an embattled parliamentarian is conveyed in the haunting comment of a nationalist writer two years after Parnell's death, at the close of an otherwise stereotyped description of Parnell facing down a hostile House of Commons, that 'he was the leader of the Irish nation, for on that day the Irish nation peered through Parnell's eyes'.[21]

There was among nationalists an ironic savouring of Parnell's impassivity, of his retortion on England of what were considered to be English stratagems of social domination. Two later nationalist apologists of Parnell's, commending obstructionism in terms of a reciprocation in legislative interference, celebrated Parnell's early parliamentary style in significant terms: 'worst of all, the chief *saboteur* treated his victims with the cold contempt of a landlord receiving his tenants' rent. And when they lost their tempers and howled at him they were treated as a supercilious ringmaster might treat unruly animals'.[22] It was a reversal of roles peculiarly gratifying to nationalists. J. L. Garvin wrote that Parnell 'disorganised the House of Commons; reversed the traditional relations of the races by making Englishmen furious while he remained calm.'[23]

In a revealing text of the later Parnell myth, Sir William Butler declared that he liked to hear of Parnell, not from his friends or admirers, preferring 'to see him through the glasses of his enemies — through the abuse they heaped upon him, and the efforts they made to compass his destruction. Rebel, tyrant, murderer, robber, traitor. He treated it all with superb disdain'.[24] In the divorce crisis George Bernard Shaw unavailingly strove to defend Parnell's position from within the logic of the myth, observing that 'it was indeed precisely by his inflexible indifference to the unsympathetic and unintelligible clamours which rise every now and then from the nurseries of English prejudice that Mr. Parnell has struck the popular imagination and created the Parnell myth'.[25]

In this respect, some anti-nationalist critics had unwittingly aided Parnell's rise. One Irish unionist was sufficiently infuriated at the early stages of parliamentary obstructionism to protest:

> Shall the House of Commons, before whose rising sun Elizabeth bowed her lofty head, which triumphed over Stuart violence, and Hanoverian corruption, yield to a Parnell or a Biggar? The idea is really too absurd.[26]

Parnell's political image was heavily adversarial in character, defined and limited in terms of his opposition to English power, and incapable of being deployed to equal effect in domestic controversy in Ireland. His indispensability as the subjugator of English parties already appeared diminished by Gladstone's espousal of home rule, and as he turned in 1890 to confront his enemies in Ireland, he found himself shorn of much of what had been believed to be his strength.

Parnell in the split moreover compromised a central attribute of his political image, his aspect of placidity and cold command. An American observer, hearing Parnell speak in Buffalo, New York, in 1880, wrote 'he carried a superb reserve, and used no epithets'.[27] Parnell was described in the French press during his first visit of 1881 as 'le moins agité des agiteurs'.[28] The adjectives applied to Parnell on his death in a poem by a Liberal admirer were 'calm, silent, and restrained,/Passionless yet passionate'.[29] Through his composure, he had achieved the metamorphosis of perceived Irish 'otherness' — passion, irrationality and violence — into a rival modality of power.

Five years before the split, John O'Leary had commended Parnell for a taciturnity unwonted in an Irish nationalist leader: 'it is one of the greatest, perhaps the greatest, of Parnell's many merits, that he knows better, I think, than any Irishman who has ever appeared on the political stage, how and when to hold his tongue'.[30] 'Mr. Parnell', noted *United Ireland* in 1883, 'does not utter words which he cannot make good.'[31] The *Economist*, in 1882, referred to

> the almost ostentatious indifference to the conventional artifices of a popular leader with which he conceals his singular powers of conciliating rivalry and subduing insubordination.[32]

J. L. Garvin was to characterise Parnell as 'the lock-mouthed master of loose-lipped men . . . exempt from the passion for replies'.[33] Darrell Figgis later sensitively argued that Parnell's reticence dispelled the suspicion of condescension, and forged the bond of affinity between him and the people he led: 'He stood with them. Behind his reserve, even because of that reserve, they knew that instantly; and in his spare direct phraseology he touched them as they touch one another'.[34]

In the split Parnell's severe reticence was forfeit. Damagingly, he appeared to throw into reverse the evolution of his myth, and to manifest the vehemence which had marked his rhetoric at the inception of the struggle. Parnell's very early parliamentary style, as an apprentice obstructionist, had been decidedly shrill. H. W. Lucy in 1876 described him as 'always at a white heat of rage', almost *déclassé* in his wild earnestness and exaggeration: 'a man who unites in his own person all the childish unreasonableness, all the ill-regulated suspicion, and all the childish credulity of the Irish peasant, without any of the humour, the courtliness, or dash of the Irish gentleman'.[35] Commentators watched with fascination the evolution of a public man, as Parnell mastered the deficiencies of his early style. A French observer wrote on his death: 'Sa victoire dans le parlement etait, d'abord et surtout, une victoire sur lui-même'.[36] Henry Harrison, a perceptive and sympathetic observer, not old enough to have known the young Parnell, surmised that the anecdotes of Parnell's 'self-possession, glacial calm, frozen hauteur and austere manner and the like' could be explained on the basis that Parnell had, in reaction against the excesses of his earlier parliamentary style and the hostility it excited, 'remade the surface of his manner so that nothing could shake his calm imperturbability — nothing could gall him, no compliments could shake him'.[37]

There was a recrudescence of his early vehemence in the fierce parliamentary struggles of the early 1880s, which were however almost unrecognisably more assured and rhetorically formidable, even terrible. T. P. O'Connor described one of the rare outbursts of 'that raging fire of fierce and devastating passion that burned within':

> It had a hoarse, sullen sound, the mouth became almost cruel, and the right arm was held forth in denunciation. I have seen the House of Commons literally quail before one of those outbursts of savage, though apparently cold, rage, and the remark was once made by a colleague that he looked almost like an Invincible in one of those accesses of passion.[38]

The impression of passion fiercely suppressed became part of Parnell's early mystique as a parliamentarian. The caricaturist E. T. Reed left an arresting description of Parnell's speech to the most hostile House of Commons he ever faced, after the Phoenix Park murders: 'It was a painful sight, this lonely man, feared and disliked by so many, almost rigid with combined fury and resentment, biting out his bitter words with not a movement of his body — pausing every now and then, with that nervous trick of his of gnawing at his slight fair moustache (always with him, a sign of strain and tension, and a fear of losing control)'.[39]

From 1882 onwards, Parnell having asserted his mastery in Ireland addressed himself to the construction of a parliamentary majority for home rule, and increasingly eschewed the intermittent vehemence of his early style. At Parnell's zenith, two years prior to the split, H. W. Lucy was prompted to write: 'he began parliamentary life in an ungovernable passion. He promises to end it in an atmosphere of icy calm'.[40] The Parnell of the split defied Lucy's prediction and general expectations. Public opinion in both countries, habituated to the Parnell of the middle phase, was unprepared for the abrupt reversion to fury in Parnell's rhetoric in the initial stages of the split. As the *Tablet* observed on his death, 'through every crisis, down to the last, he passed silent and a little saturnine'.[41] Justin McCarthy in February 1891 sought to justify the opposition to Parnell in terms of his forfeiture of his mythic attributes:

> The truth is that, from whatever cause, under whatever pressure of feeling, Mr. Parnell appeared suddenly to have changed his whole nature and his very ways of speech. We knew him before as a man of superb self-restraint — cool, calculating, never carried from the moorings of his keen intellect by any waves of passion around him — man with an eye and the foresight of a born commander-in-chief. We had now in our midst a man seemingly quite incapable of self-control; a man ready at any moment and on the smallest provocation to break into a very tempest and whirlwind of passion; a man of the most reckless and self-contradictory statements; a man who could condescend to the most trivial and vulgar personalities, who could encourage and even indulge in the most ignoble and humiliating brawls.[42]

Healy deftly exploited the advantage afforded by Parnell's loss of his habitual reserve at the outset of the split. The *National Press* wondered: 'will Ireland ever forget the amazement with which the revelation came upon it of the real character of the "cold", "self-contained", and "prudent" Parnell, when he ranted from platform to platform, loading the air with personalities?'[43]

Parnell's perceived composure was an aspect of the almost ascetic cast of his political image, as if his restraint in the face of provocation reflected a continence beyond that of ordinary men. His hieratic placidity, his celibate state, his gaunt features, together with his ill-health and reclusiveness, combined to suggest to his apologists and to the public at large a severe virtuousness, which was to render him peculiarly vulnerable to the disclosures of the divorce court. The asceticism had two aspects, of revolutionary severity and of self-abnegation.

T. P. O'Connor quoted an unidentified poet as observing that with such a face and air, Parnell was foredoomed to the scaffold. He noted Parnell's severity of purpose, what he described as 'the flint-like hardness, the terrible resoluteness of his face'.[44] George Howard, afterwards Lord Carlisle, applied to Parnell a quotation from Thackeray's *The Newcomers*: 'the figure of this *garcon* is not agreeable. Of pale, he has become livid'.[45] The French politician Henri Rochefort, who feted Parnell in Paris in 1881, discerned the austerity of disciplined ambition and resolve: 'The idol of the Irish people is a tall young man, extremely fair, whose leanness would have elicited from Caesar the remark he made about Cassius. His steel eye is severe; his almost ascetic features bear the impress of that calmness peculiar to men who have made up their minds'.[46]

A writer in *The World* in November 1880 contemplated with fascination and reserve 'this tall slender man of thirty-four years, with the iron face of a livid hue': 'Mr. Parnell is a man of singularly mild and gracious manners in private life, but one's eyes are constantly directed enquiringly to the cold and bloodless face in the endeavour to reconcile the frigid exterior with the courtesy of the lips'.[47]

In this as in other respects the Parnell myth was curiously symmetrical. That severity and impassivity which to the Irish attested to his patriotic resolve was to his enemies an aspect of a sinister criminality. G. W. E. Russell opined that perhaps the most marked feature of Parnell's character was 'that form of cruelty which consists in a callous indifference to suffering . . . Murder, torture, and their long-drawn anguish of expectant fear he regarded with unpitying eye'.[48] The myth encompassed a dichotomy between saint and cynic.

Parnell was resolutely unclubbable. This characteristic, which irrespective of political considerations, rendered him an object of suspicion to many of his English parliamentary compeers, shaped his myth. 'Incorruptible, sitting apart, jealous, solitary, with great intensity of purpose and very narrow sympathies', the *Spectator* wrote nervously in 1880, 'his mind reminds us of some of those which were most potent in the making of the great French Revolution . . .'[49] To most men, in the opinion of Lord Rendel, 'there was something disagreeably cold and even sinister about Parnell'.[50] In Curzon's account of him as a parliamentarian, Parnell's aspect of isolation ('remote, unfriended, melancholy, slow') was inextricably linked to his 'sudden and sombre prominence'.[51]

Quite apart from his politically motivated reserve at Westminster, Parnell responded to gregarious male ritual with evident distaste. Richard Adams, junior counsel in the state trials of 1881–2, noted that Parnell was not liked by the barristers acting for him and his associates: 'his manner was freezing. He was polite, but it was a glassy and chilly politeness. A wintry smile was the only tribute he paid to stories which had sent the library table in a roar'.[52] Parnell had committed the cardinal offence of failing to laugh at a barrister's joke.

Shortly after Parnell's death, Lord Ribblesdale recalled that in 1887 he had shared a railway compartment with Parnell from Euston to Holyhead. Parnell conversed agreeably on political subjects, until as the train pulled out from Rugby he 'proposed in a very serious voice our both trying to sleep'. At Holyhead, Ribblesdale did not encounter Parnell on the boat:

'We met and parted strangers. I never saw him to speak to again; even had we met again he would not have recognised me, for during the whole of that journey he never so much as looked at me'.[53] Parnell's aloofness can only have exacerbated the hostility of convivial cynics such as Healy's cronies, Henry Labouchere, and Harold Frederic of the *New York Times.*

More ominous was the imputation to Parnell of superhuman moral continence, of a monk-like chastity deemed to reflect a patriotism of almost religious intensity. Almost poignantly, the priest who introduced Parnell to the electors of Meath at the outset of his political career, perhaps at a loss for anything else to say, had commended him as 'one to whose lineage they could look with pride, whose honesty and goodness shone from his very face'.[54]

To his more perfervid apologists, Parnell's celibacy testified to the selflessness of his dedication to the Irish cause. An Irish journalist, in a sympathetic portrait of Parnell at his height for an English newspaper, wrote extravagantly:

> The Irish people . . . know that under that cold face beats a heart which throbs with love for Ireland. They know that handsome pale face, regal as Parian marble, wears a delicate look because of years of incessant toil and harassing thought on behalf of Ireland. He is, indeed, the 'Uncrowned King of Ireland', loved with a love and followed with a fidelity which no leader has commanded since the days of Hugh Roe O'Donnell. There is a kind of shadowy tradition that in his early manhood 'Charlie Parnell' was crossed in love. He certainly has not been crossed in love since he 'took off his coat' to fight the battle of Ireland. Like Hugh Roe, just mentioned, she has been his queen, his mistress, the only love of his heart, his Dark Rosaleen.[55]

The awful irony of this passage suggests just how susceptible the Parnell myth was, quite independently of Healy's excoriating rhetoric, to subversion by the disclosure of his relations with Katharine O'Shea. W. H. Duignan, the Walsall solicitor and correspondent of Chamberlain, wrote publicly in 1886 that when asked by him why he did not marry, Parnell had replied, 'I am married – to my country, and can best serve as I am'. If Parnell made such a reply, which may be doubted, he did so as a rebuff of chilling banality to the intrusive enquiry. Undeterred, Duignan enthused: 'Ireland may say to him as Hamlet said to Horatio: "Give me the man that is *not passion's slave*, and I will wear him in my heart's core – ay, in my heart of hearts, as I do thee"'.[56]

Fervent nationalists were not alone in pretending to discern in Parnell a saintly severity. Observing Parnell at the Special Commission, Gladstone's daughter Mary confided to her diary: 'Parnell's coolness wonderful. He really exhibited all the fruits of the Spirit, love, peace, patience, gentleness, forbearance, long-suffering, meekness . . . so done he sometimes seemed almost fainting'. She wrote to a friend: 'Loved Parnell's spiritual face, only one's heart ached over his awful delicate frame and look'. Of Parnell at Hawarden she wrote that 'he looks more ill than any other I ever saw off a death-bed'. A member of her circle, Margaret Cowell-Stepney, met Parnell at dinner and described him as 'having a beautiful face like a saint in a painted window, intensely quiet and reserved and utterly unselfconscious'. Margot Asquith, who never met Parnell, would later bizarrely comment on his 'almost Christ-like countenance'.[57]

This aspect of Parnell's myth owed something to the contrast between his fierce strength of purpose and his vulnerable appearance. A contemporary parliamentary sketch-writer thus described his appearance: 'Above the middle height, with fairly broad shoulders and a frame not at all attenuated, his physique, nevertheless, conveys the idea of weakness, if not of suffering'. A French journalist who saw Parnell in Paris in 1881, noting that Parnell hunted in what he inaccurately described as 'son immense domaine d'Avondale', slyly asserted the superior robustness of the French gentry: 'C'est l'aspect général d'un jeune *gentleman* de bonne famille, qui serait un peu fatigué par les nuits froides passées a chasser sur les lacs'.[58]

By the time of the pronouncement of the divorce decree nisi, as the *Spectator* shrewdly observed, 'a myth had accreted round the Irish leader's character, through which he was seen as a lofty patriot of the Deak type, cold, retiring, and secretive, but determined and pure, devoted to his country beyond all things, and ambitious only for her sake'.[59] The evidence of the divorce court blasted Parnell's perceived asceticism: the Irish leader had failed to conform to the requirement of the myth. Healy's most dangerous onslaughts in the split were directed at Parnell's 'belauded Spartan integrity'.[60]

Parnell's quasi-mythic stature itself rendered him vulnerable. His eminence became in the savage pantomime of Healy's rhetoric an estrangling attribute. Parnell's career had been freighted with excessive promise, all too readily archaicised as the stuff of a redundant mythology. He had seemed to break the pattern of Irish defeat: 'Ireland has had many heroes', wrote H. W. Lucy in 1875, 'but they have all been illustrious in misfortune'.[61] As early as 1880 the *Spectator* had written apprehensively that 'Mr. Parnell's figure is but too likely to become historical'.[62] A devotee enthused eight years after Parnell's death that while still a young man 'Parnell had entered into the glory of the Elysium of National Heroes'.[63] The course of the split demonstrated that this premature accession to the pantheon of patriotic heroes was not wholly advantageous. Parnell in the split was afflicted by the sclerosis of his own myth. His image had generated an artificial canon of expectations which severely restricted his flexibility of response.

Events and rhetoric conspired to render Parnell's 'kingship' faintly ridiculous. Defeat itself was the greatest solvent of the Parnell myth. Shorn of the mystique of his invincibility, Parnell was derided by Healy as a pathetic mountebank, and the cloak of 'chieftancy' ridiculed as a charlatan's prop. Healy discounted the significance of the crowds which Parnell continued to draw after his Kilkenny defeat:

> The fact is this: Mr. Parnell has not been to Ireland for a great many years. He is therefore, to many people, a great natural curiosity (*laughter*), and just as Sequah, the Indian medicine-man, by drumming round and advertising his wonderful cures, was always able to secure a crowd in any town in Ireland, so it would be very surprising indeed if Mr. Parnell, especially after his recent performance, did not succeed in attracting village attention (*laughter*). But one thing he has not succeeded in attracting, and that is votes (*loud cheers*).[64]

The Parnell of the split was thus reducible to a 'great natural curiosity': through the transformation of the divorce court the statesman had become a freak, and Parnellism 'a bedraggled harlequinade'.[65]

At Newry in March, Healy mocked: 'He draws crowds in some places it is said. Well, maybe he does, because there is a great natural curiosity to see him, but if he wants a meeting crowd as large as this, he will want to bring over a lady with him (*laughter and cheers*)'.[66] Myth had dissolved into spectacle. Healy asserted that the little that remained of Parnell's mystique accounted for the remnants of his support: his supporters in Dublin were 'misled by the attractions of past services and the glamour of a once-famed name'.[67]

In the split, panegyric turned abruptly to vituperation. The Parnell myth was rudely metamorphosed. Healy's political counter-myth of Parnell had three aspects: landlord, dictator, and Fenian pretender. In his personal character, Parnell was denounced as a libertine, a liar, and a cold and selfish cynic. Parnell became in Healy's rhetoric a nationalist Dorian Gray, whose handsome countenance masked an inner depravity.

The *National Press* defined the issue of the split as 'whether the country will permit its unity to be destroyed by the insane pretensions of a deposed and degraded man, who has shown himself resolved to sacrifice her sacred cause – first to his guilty passion, and then to selfish ambition'.[68] Parnell was denounced as a traitor and a schismatic who had subverted national unity on the eve of home rule. Healy assailed him in the course of a single speech as 'a disrupter and a dissentionist', an 'archfactionist' and the 'chief traitor'.[69] In dividing the country Parnell had shown himself 'the most deadly and dangerous enemy of Irish nationality', a theme Healy developed by comparing Parnell to the reviled informer James Carey:

> I say that no man has proved falser to Ireland than Charles Stewart Parnell. The treachery of the informer involves but a limited number of his circle. The treachery of James Carey did not ruin more than a score or two of human lives. The treachery of Charles Stewart Parnell has split asunder the Irish race.[70]

Parnell's treason could not prevail against the manifest destiny of the Irish nation:

> The cause of Ireland has survived the sword of Cromwell and the persecutions of William, and the informers of '98 and '48; the cause of Ireland survived James Carey; the cause of Ireland will survive Charles Stewart Parnell (*cheers*).[71]

The cause of Ireland endured. 'It does not lie in the power of any man to destroy the Irish cause (*cheers*). Our trust is not in Parnell; we trust in God above (*cheers*).'[72]

It was inevitable that Parnell should have been compared with 'the archetypal traitor of Irish popular historical convention', Dermot McMurrough, the twelfth-century king of Leinster whose claim to notoriety in the nationalist tradition lay in having abducted the wife of a neighbouring prince and invited the assistance of Henry II of England to retrieve his political position, thereby providing the immediate pretext for the Norman invasion. The *National Press* denounced 'Mr. MacMurrough Parnell', while Vesey Knox declared that Parnell 'had taken his place with MacMurrough and with Carey'. Disunion had been the curse of Ireland, declared William Martin Murphy, 'and Diarmuid MacMurchad, the original Parnell had run away with another man's wife'.[73]

The *National Press* condemned the 'disastrous heresy of Parnellism'. Healy compared the Parnell split to the schisms of the early church:

> It is a curious thing, if you read the history of the heresies in the 3rd and 4th centuries, the fellows who always started mischief-making were apostles like Parnell. They began as he did. They attacked certain principles they declared bad, which they said were forgetting the interests of the church, and you always find it announced the antipope or the heresiarch was the only possible leader.[74]

Healy denounced Parnell as a politician of limitless mendacity. He was 'honeycombed with deceit and falsehood', a 'living lie', who could not open his mouth without telling lies.[75] The *National Press* designated Parnell 'a disgraced and discredited trickster'. The name of Parnell had become 'a synonym for meanness, treachery and falsehood'.[76] T. D. Sullivan characteristically detected a dishonesty bred of the deceits of an illicit affair:

'Mr. Parnell has for years been carrying on a course of duplicity and falsehood and dishonour, and no man could have lived for years so without having his character tainted by it'.[77] Parnell's whole life, declared the anti-Parnellite John Pinkerton, 'had been a tissue of selfish intrigues'.[78]

So recently hailed as a politician of unrivalled disinterestedness, Parnell was suddenly depicted as a monster of selfishness. Towards the evicted tenants, wrote the *National Press*, he displayed 'that cool-hearted cynical indifference which is part of his character'.[79] Self-interest accounted for the contrast between his frenzied campaigning in the split and the preceding five years of inertia and neglect: 'His callous apathy while others suffered is changed to frantic activity when his own position is at stake'. The paper later added: 'the sufferings of the numberless victims of evictions and coercion could not strike one spark of pity from his cold heart, but the loss of his own position converted him into a flaming volcano'.[80]

Parnell practised the politics of egotism. Healy charged him with self-obsession, with neglecting the issue of Balfour's coercion in favour of 'the unapproachable theme of himself'. 'He has absolutely no policy', declared the *National Press*, 'except his fixed resolve to keep his own name before the public.' Of his speech at Newbridge in May the paper wrote 'self, self, self ran through every line of his speech'. On the eve of his death it declared: 'His policy is himself, his end is himself, his devotion is to himself'.[81]

What the *National Press* termed 'Mr. Parnell's evil ingenuity'[82] went beyond the issue of personal truthfulness. Parnell was presented as the practitioner of a form of politics no longer compatible with the high moral purpose of nationalism. With what was revealingly termed the 'conversion' of Gladstone to home rule, the need for a tough and sceptical politics was proclaimed to be over. Parnellism, now defined in terms of cynical ruthlessness, and equated with Parnell's adulterous subterfuges, was redundant.

Parnell's reckless monomania moreover verged on the lunatic. Healy declared that Parnell had 'gone politically raving mad'.[83] The *National Press* denounced Parnell's 'insane pretensions', and asserted that 'plain hints are thrown out that Mr. Parnell's mind is not well balanced and that this is the explanation of his conduct'. On his death, viciously suggesting that this madness was a moral visitation, the paper declared 'we shall not judge him by the deeds of the days of mad ambition, when for his sin God took away his understanding'.[84] The reversal of the Parnell myth was complete.

13

Myth and Mortality

He never wants it to be supposed that we are fighting over his body. It is a great principle he embodies.

T. M. Healy, 10 June 1891 [1]

Probably the cleverest and acutest of the whole lot was T. Healy; but it was impossible to imagine his equal in real brutality of conduct: what he delighted in most was to find a weak spot in his opponent and then to go on goading him there.

G. J. Goschen, January 1891 [2]

Who was it killed the Chief?
Says the Shan Van Vocht
Who was it cried 'Stop Thief'?
Says the Shan Van Vocht

'Twas Tim Healy's poisoned tongue,
Our chieftain dead that stung,
Better men than him were hung,
Says the Shan Van Vocht

Anon. [3]

Healy's polemics against Parnell comprise an astonishing corpus of rhetoric. In pressing nationalist imagery to its limits they achieve an extraordinary fecundity. Healy's language was marked by its intense physicality. In his exhaustive and troubling exploration of corporeal imagery, he attained a terrible and corrupted poetics of violence. His rhetoric of the flesh was a degenerate Catholic–nationalist baroque idiom which fused with the sacrificial language of nationalism Catholic themes of desire and retribution. Through a troubling rhetoric of salt and blood, he sought to achieve a violent and bitter catharsis. In the flensing violence of his rhetoric, Parnell became the nationalist Marsyas. Healy's rhetoric was both a pretended meditation on the human condition and the exemplary fable of a fallen class. The pursuit of Parnell was couched in an ostentatiously Catholic idiom of retribution: the mortification of the Protestant flesh. Sin, fate and caste co-mingle in a savage polemic of political decline and mortal decay. His discourse is defined by recurring antinomies, of desire and violence, of morality and malice, and finally of myth and mortality.

On Parnell's death, Healy was accused of having at the outset of the split vowed to drive Parnell to death or insanity. While dismissed by the *National Press* as *United Ireland*'s 'drive him into an-asylum-or-the-grave-yarns' this allegation entered Parnellite mythology.[4] That Healy made such a comment is improbable. No such remark appears in any newspaper report of Healy's speeches. V. B. Dillon did write to O'Brien on 22 December 1890 that home rule could be won at too dear a price if Parnell was to be sacrificed '"and the salt is to be rubbed well into him" until he dies or goes mad'. Harrington wrote to Dillon on 31 December alleging that Healy had declared he would 'rub the salt into Parnell until he drives him mad or makes him commit suicide'.[5] Harrington's allegation was probably misquoting a speech of Healy at Urlingford, County Kilkenny, in which he declared 'he would tell Mr. Parnell he would rub the salt well into him'.[6] A lesser possibility is that Harrington's was a garbled rendering of a comment privately attributed to Healy: it is noteworthy that Healy's friend and confidant Harold Frederic cabled a report to the *New York Times* of 4 January 1891 that the anti-Parnellites believed Parnell 'will never surrender while he lives and keeps out of a madhouse'.

If the Parnellite taunt against Healy of seeking to encompass Parnell's death is untenable, the ferocity of his physical rhetoric against Parnell is unrivalled in the annals of nationalist rhetoric. The coupling of Healy's personal antagonism towards Parnell and his political purpose here achieves its greatest intensity. The calculated violence of Healy's rhetoric towards Parnell had a dual purpose: directed at Parnell himself, it was addressed to the larger public.

Healy sought to shatter Parnell's composure and to break that concentration of will and intellect which was his strength. As if galled by the contrast with his own restless, fretful and inconstant ambition, Healy found the patrician calm of Parnell before the split (if not his unyielding demeanour in the split itself) deeply provoking, and repeatedly sought to discount Parnell's proud bearing as the callous and shallow egotism of the landlord class. He sought unceasingly to find a technique to pierce Parnell's pride and to penetrate the protective carapace of his myth. Yet it would be an error to underestimate the degree to which Healy's private animus was subordinated to his public purpose. The overriding purpose of his rhetoric was political, addressed to his nationalist audience rather than to Parnell. His was an iconoclastic violence, intended to complete the destruction of Parnell's political repute.

What was deemed Parnell's impenitence, the lingering after-grimace of the haughty mask, provided part of the rationale for the ferocity of the anti-Parnell attack. In this burned most fiercely the resentment of Parnell. Parnell's pride, the countenance of the unyielding aristocrat, was itself a moral affront, rendering inevitable homiletic comparison to Milton's Satan. 'With the fallen archangel', wrote the Bishop of Derry, 'he seems to think it is better to reign in h-ll [*sic*] rather than serve in heaven.'[7] For anti-Parnellite publicists, in Parnell's insouciance on the moral issue there seemed to endure still, like the fragment of an archaic smile from a shattered statue, the traces of his famous sang-froid. This perception was shared by English nonconformist moralists. W. T. Stead wrote that not merely had Parnell failed to manifest penitence, but 'he stands with head erect and with a smile of well-bred amazement on his features that anyone should dream of condemning his relations with Mrs. O'Shea'.[8]

Of Parnell's failure to resign on cue, the *Insuppressible* opined that he lacked 'the courage and the foresight to offer this satisfaction to the moral sense of the nation'.[9] Parnell's scandalous impenitence was an additional count to his sexual transgression in the anti-Parnellite moral indictment. Thus William Martin Murphy asserted:

> Mr. Parnell's offence was a gross offence, an offence against the highest social laws as well as against the religious laws, and if Mr. Parnell had recognised the fact and in any way had shown that he had the smallest particle of shame, no people in the world would have been more willing to forgive him. But Mr. Parnell brazened it out, and with the most indecent affrontry and he had had the indecency to tell them that in a short time he would hold his head higher than he had ever done before. That was his charge against Mr. Parnell in addition to the moral charge.[10]

Healy adroitly played on the theme of Parnell's impenitence:

> The Parnellites tell us King David was a sinner. Perhaps he was, but we would like to know whether we have heard Mr. Parnell's penitent psalms (*laughter*). He went down to Limerick and he spoke of my fault if it is

> a fault is not a fault against Ireland (*laughter*). He declared in Cork he was proud of himself. He declared what had occurred had purified and ennobled the Irish cause.[11]

The double-counting of Parnell's offences – of moral transgression and impenitence – was hardly fair. The 'impenitence' resided in his failure to withdraw from the leadership. He was morally assailed for his perseverance, for his refusal to submit to effacement. Healy's concern was with his political defiance rather than his moral transgression. The latter consideration however provided an invaluable rationale for the violence of his attacks on Parnell: morality provided a cover for the political flagellation of Parnell. The *National Press*, with provoking unctuousness, enquired: 'if at any time since the divorce decree the unhappy man had bowed his head and sought pardon, pity and oblivion, would there be one voice today uplifted against him? Is not the very essence of Christianity and Catholicity comprised in the words charity, sorrow and atonement?'[12] The virulent Canon Doyle condemned Parnell's failure to submit to a moral rustication: 'If he were not blindly selfish, ambitious, and utterly shameless, he would have retired from the public gaze long since, and hidden himself and his infamy in the woods and glens of Avondale'.[13]

Healy declared his intent to inflict on Parnell the anguish which guilt would have caused to a less morally callous man. The scourge of rhetoric would sting where the promptings of conscience had not. This was the most intimately vicious purpose of Healy's rhetoric. Parnell, declared T. D. Sullivan, was born 'destitute of every sense of shame'.[14] Of Parnell's assertion that his fault, if it were a fault, was not against Ireland, *Insuppressible* asked: 'Is it too much to say that the speaker of that sentence has lost all moral sense and is bereft of all moral judgement?'[15] Healy seized on this line of argument to subject Parnell to a virulently sectarian scheme of moral retribution. 'The man has really no moral sense', wrote the *National Press*, 'and, having no moral sense, cannot comprehend the mental attitude of a religious people towards his crime.'[16] Healy's rhetoric sought to contrive a public surrogate for the moral faculty which Parnell supposedly lacked. His lethal moralism was most concisely disclosed in a critical sentence in the 'Stop Thief' sequence of *National Press* leading articles: 'Human nature decays and gangrenes like any other corruptible matter once the salt of criticism – which in public now serves for the sting of conscience – is removed'.[17] This was the salt which Healy would 'rub well into' Parnell. It was not merely the enforcement of a Catholic moral code, but the application of a grotesque political simulation of the processes of the Catholic conscience. It became a personalised episode of Counter-Reformation, as if in horrid and exemplary illustration of the fate of a miscreant Protestant leader fallen among Catholic electors.

This assertion of the need for a public framework for the containment of moral deficiency likewise informed Healy's denunciation of the breach of the Irish party pledge by the Parnellite members in failing to abide by the majority verdict:

> Because, what foothold can you have in the human heart, what grappling iron can you cast to the human character to bind and anchor it, if when gentlemen and men of honour, pledge in writing to their constituents their sacred word that they will faithfully abide by that pledge, and then will break it on some wretched and frivolous pretence?[18]

Healy referred to 'the rack and thumbscrew of the pledge'[19] and rather more conventionally presented the campaign in the split in terms of a forcible education of Parnell in the principle of majority rule: 'We must make that principle a potion which Mr. Parnell must swallow if it was gall and wormwood to him'.[20] Healy varied his comparison in Committee Room 15 of the Parnell manifesto to a 'Nessus shirt' which would stick to him all his life, when he declared: 'the only way to deal with a man of that kind is to put a straight jacket on him. We will weave that jacket between now and the general election'.[21]

Healy's most disturbing trope was of probing a wound. He declared in January that 'he would put his hand on the spot and say what the whole cause was'.[22] Of Croke's speech which inspired the 'Stop Thief' sequence, Healy said they had to thank the Archbishop 'for having had the courage to put his finger on the sore spot and as far as I am concerned we will probe that same spot to the bottom'.[23] This imagery pervaded Healy's rhetoric. When the *Freeman's Journal* advocated the pursuit by Dillon and O'Brien of a conciliatory policy towards Parnell, the *National Press* retorted: 'There is other and nobler work for Mr. John Dillon than pouring balsam into the smarting wounds of his self-love'.[24]

Speaking in Drogheda in March, Parnell asked to have excluded from controversy personal matters, urging his opponents to refrain from 'striking below the belt'.[25] The phrase inevitably entered Healy's repertoire for the duration of the split. He replied with studied brutality the following week: 'Mr. Parnell complained of hitting below the belt, but all he could say was that he wished Parnell did not wear his belt so high up, because so far as he was concerned he would hit him wherever he would feel it most'.[26] Healy insisted that his rhetorical violence was merely retaliatory. He later asserted that Parnell and his lieutenants had themselves dropped the buttons from their foils, and that he was following the maxim *à corsair, corsair et demi.*[27]

Images of fighting or beating Parnell complemented the imagery of the hunt. The alias used by Parnell of 'Mr. Fox', as disclosed in the divorce court evidence, engendered the recurrent anti-Parnellite conceit of the landlord aristocrat himself hunted by nationalists.[28] Figures of lashing, of torture, humiliation and scourging, recurred through Healy's rhetoric, and marked the forensic violence of the 'Stop Thief' sequence in particular. The *National Press* looked to the position 'when we have scourged the Fund-grabber into confronting us before a jury', and in quoting *Othello* invoked the idiom of Shakespearian retribution: 'We will force him to face it, or amidst the contempt of his own supporters "lash the rascal naked through the world"'.[29]

Not for nothing did a gratified priest introduce Healy at a meeting in the Carlow by-election as 'Parnell's scourge'. The imagery of scourging, like that of the rubbing in of salt, is central to the scheme of retribution through which Healy expressed and sought to justify the virulence of his attacks on Parnell.

Through the exigencies of the Parnell myth, Healy argued, 'Mr. Parnell and Ireland became convertible terms'.[30] In the scheme of his rhetoric, Parnell's embodiment of the Irish nation had become a liability: it was now necessary to sever Parnell and Ireland, lest the nation be wounded through the excesses of the flesh of the man who had become the nation incarnate. Healy referred to Parnell as 'flecked and maculated . . . from the crown of his head to the sole of his foot, without a point at which he is not attackable'.[31] He shrewdly imputed the impulse to attack Parnell in the first instance to the Conservative party, 'the most unscrupulous party that ever a political organisation had to contend with':

> . . . do you suppose for one moment that unless we had a clean man to fight them that they would not dissect every piece of spotted flesh on his body (*cheers*) — that they would not be ready to flay him alive in order to hold on to their positions and keep their seats in parliament?

Nationalists could not in such circumstances allow themselves to be swayed by a sentimental allegiance to Parnell.[32] In a speech delivered in Dublin in September, Healy formulated perhaps the most electrifying image of the split:

> Just before Room Fifteen began we had to go through the London streets and had ribald songs about Brighton and Eltham and the fire-escape shouted in our ears. London music halls echoed to the music of the divorce court, and what I may call the governing classes of England have licked their wounds over the downfall of the leader of virtuous Erin. They have stopped now. They stopped with his deposition. Why? Because they no

> longer desire to injure their friend. We thrust that man aside because through his body the arrows of their satire would have pierced the heart of Ireland (*applause*).[33]

In this sculpted image of the physical union of Parnell and Ireland, a composite St. Sebastian, Healy asserted both the necessity to sever their association, and the ineluctable violence of the sundering.

It is significant that this image, startling in its anguished vehemence, was elicited by the contemplation of popular English ridicule and that of the governing classes of England. Healy sought to deploy the national sense of shame for his own purpose, and to invest it with a semblance of political rigour by presenting the repudiation of Parnell as a necessary act of purifying violence. With consummate subtlety he sought to rationalise and to assuage the sense of torn allegiance experienced by nationalists, and to validate his own rending rhetoric. Deftly acting out the split's dilemma, Healy sought to justify and contain its bitter acrimony by a redemptive logic of inescapable sacrificial violence. He thereby sought to invest his rhetoric with a meretricious severity of form, and to offer a resolution of illusory decisiveness, which belied the complexity of the dilemma with which nationalists were confronted. Citing the adage that a nation should be more jealous of its liberties than a woman of her honour, Healy asked rhetorically: had the majority adhered to Parnell in the split, 'would not we be the most unfaithful prostitutes ever entrusted with the life and honour and the patriotism of a nation?'[34] The violent repudiation of Parnell was posited as the only alternative to moral contamination.

Healy's argument asserted a complex retributive economy. The squalor of the divorce court could not be permitted to suffuse and taint nationalism but had to be turned back on Parnell. Parnell could not be allowed to succeed in his 'effort to inflict on the country the punishment due to his own infamies'.[35] The cleansing violence of the repudiation of Parnell was necessary to avert Conservative attack and purge nationalism of the acrid backwash of the divorce court.

Yet Healy's argument could not contain the morbidly exaggerated sensitivity to English sentiment, beyond the contingencies of parliamentary politics, which inspired it. It was predicated on a disquieting symmetry between the nationalist attack on Parnell and the apprehended Conservative assault on nationalism through the person of Parnell. To pre-empt the Tory attack, the anti-Parnellites had themselves to strike the first blows against Parnell. In seeking to argue from Conservative hostility and English ridicule, rather than from the narrower ground of opposition within the Liberal party to Parnell's continued leadership, Healy enlarged the issue from mere Liberal 'dictation' to one of broader significance. His exculpatory logic risked conceding the Parnellite contention that the split was enacted under external English promptings inconsistent with the independence of the Irish party, and presented the predicament of anti-Parnellism in peculiarly acute and troubling form.

Healy's rhetoric reached beyond stylised bodily violence to disturbing extremities of decay, disease, and putrefaction. The 'stench of the divorce court' suffused his rhetoric. The campaign against Parnell in its most sententious aspect was presented as a meditation on human mortality, a contemplation of the decay of the heroic flesh, of Parnell as the corrupted effigy: 'Long years of adulation have rotted the wholesome fibres of his nature and the practice of duplicity has petrified his heart'.[36] Parnell's campaign, opined the *National Press*, had merely 'exposed the barrenness of the common clay of which he is composed'.[37] Healy's disquietingly literal meditation on corruptibility was pressed to extremities of decay.

The imagery was less casual than might be imagined. Healy explained to Alfred Webb the Parnellite attitude after the split in the party thus: 'minds are attacked by disease like the body: the germs are there, the development is at first scarcely to be remarked — after a certain point it is difficult if not impossible to prevent destructive growth'.[38] Healy's assertion of the corruption wrought by power was artlessly confused with the frailties of the flesh in the Catholic homiletic sense, and both were submerged in his rhetoric of moral nausea. The Actonian premise was absorbed within a morbid imagery of putrefaction.

Healy adopted a rhetoric of scalpelled violence, directed to the extirpation of what he viewed as the disease of Parnellism. It was at the Galway by-election of 1886 that drastic action should have been taken:

> That was the time to have met the situation, but unfortunately the ulcer was allowed to grow until now it had eaten into the vitals of the Irish nation, and unless it was amputated the heart of this nation would be attacked, and all hope of national progress, so far as this generation was concerned was at an end.[39]

To this imagery Healy reverted shortly after Parnell's death, with some confusion of medical idiom:

> I believe no more wholesome and no more chastening step will be taken . . . than when Ireland, erect and in its strength, casts from the body politic the ulcer which these men endeavour to graft upon it (*loud applause*). We must purge Ireland of this corrupt humour with which they endeavoured to inoculate our blood (*applause*).[40]

Parnellism was in relation to the country 'the virus which has been sought to be injected into its veins', while 'the Parnell bacillus' provided a recurrent motif.[41] William Martin Murphy declared that the country had sloughed off 'the diseased epidermis of Parnellism'.[42] Healy sought to contain his descriptive rhetoric of disgust within a surgical idiom. The image of excising the poisoned flesh, of amputating the diseased organs of Parnellism, corresponds in the purifying simplicity of its violence with the allegorical transfixing of the effigy of Parnell, the sacrificial severing of Parnell and Ireland.

The motif of a fetid purulence, the conveying of moral nausea through images of physical decay, ran through Healy's rhetoric. He referred to the Parnell manifesto as 'springing like those foul fungi you would see in the fields, yellow with venom, proceeding from and rooted in the divorce court'.[43] He declared that 'Parnell in England and Ireland has been got rid of by a great national belch'.[44] As with all of Healy's images, this was more thoroughgoing and less readily explicable in terms of the robust conventions of Irish polemic than might at first appear. It was developed in disturbing directions. 'Who brought this squalid obscene incident across the pathway of the Irish nation to Liberty?', he asked. In an unpleasant development of the image, Healy paraphrased Gladstone's 'friendly letter' as stating that he could not carry home rule at the general election 'if Parnell, with the millstone of the Divorce Court, like a knapsack of foulness, persisted in clogging the wheels of his career of victory'.[45] In the 'knapsack of foulness', what Healy had referred to in Committee Room 15 as 'the stench of the divorce court'[46] was reified.

Healy propounded an excremental vision, declaring 'all the venom and all the sewage that has been emptied had all sprung and been generated by Charles Stewart Parnell himself'. He significantly depicted himself as the particular victim of the foul deluge of Parnellism. He asserted that 'the *cloaca maxima* of Parnellism was poured upon his head and shoulders', and that 'upon his head was poured all the sewage of Parnellism'.[47]

William O'Brien, noting that Healy 'affected a brutality of speech at which Rabelais or even Swift in his least dainty moment might have hesitated', recalled him concluding a speech with the declaration, 'I have nothing more to say to you: I have discharged my stomach'.[48] This image of rhetorical spewing suggests that Healy's sense of disgust in the split may have been heightened by an intimation of circularity: he found himself threatened by immersion in its foulness, a grotesque gargoyle at the split's polluted font.

The pretended anti-Parnellite autopsy of Parnellism in the split took a disquietingly literal rhetorical twist. The author of *Under Which Flag?* referred to 'Mr. Parnell's putrefying political corpse'.[49] In a speech in the

Carlow election, Healy fused the motifs of purulent decay and cleansing surgical violence in a unifying image of particular vileness:

> The other day Mr. Parnell's secretary got quite indignant that anyone should ever suggest that he had ever met Kitty O'Shea. If we have to refer to this subject we do it in the same way as a surgeon is obliged at times to cut up a corpse. If the corpse smells, it is not the doctor's fault; it is the fault of the corpse; and if the Parnell-O'Shea case had got a bad smell to it that is no fault of ours (*laughter*). The best thing for Parnell to do would be to lay her up in lavender a bit, because the introduction of this subject does, in my judgement, great harm.[50]

This affords perhaps the most vicious instance of Healy's political ordering of the natural shocks the flesh is heir to: the body of desire became that of decay, death, and of pathological incision.

Healy's images of wounding, excision and decay — his blood imagery of defilement and catharsis — form part of a sequence of anti-Parnellite motifs. It represents an extension of the more conventional conservative Catholic nationalist image of the stain.

Prior to leaving New York for Ireland at the outset of the split, T. D. Sullivan wrote in a characteristic effusion:

> Men may stain or ruin
> A record or a name,
> But Ireland's sacred banner
> Must never share the shame.[51]

Sullivan's most revealing use of the image of the stain was in conjunction with that of the wound:

> A wound is better than a stain.
> No guilty knight shall champion thee, motherland.[52]

The rending of the split was preferable to the moral blemish of Parnellism: the wound expunged the stain. These lines conformed to the premise of cathartic violence in Healy's rhetoric. The theme of defilement recurred through Sullivan's rhetoric. The Irish people had resisted Parnell's promptings 'to stain their cause with him, to put a blot on the history of the Irish cause'. With the opening of a home rule parliament, 'they would open a new and glorious chapter in their country's history. Across that page they would not have the word adulterer written'.[53] The sexual connotations of the imagery of 'staining' were rendered comically explicit in the declaration of Archbishop Logue in his Lenten pastoral: 'We shall never follow a banner which we are ashamed to unfurl, lest the nations should point to a dark stain on its folds'.[54] The image of the stain revealed the commingling of moral and religious sentiment with that deep self-consciousness which rendered conservative nationalists so morbidly sensitive to English ridicule. The stain was the rendering visible of the pervasive conservative nationalist sense of sin, mortification and impurity, reflecting the emergence and hardening of a Catholic nationalist moral sensibility defined by its sense of shame. The most exact and venomous use of the image of the stain came predictably in a pun in Healy's *National Press*. Referring to the Sussex village in which Parnell married Katharine O'Shea, the paper wrote (incorrectly): '"Steyning", the bridal village, is appropriately pronounced "staining"'.[55]

Healy's rhetoric suggests a curious, if not a flawed, sexual sensibility. The ugly undercurrent of sexual rancour in his rhetoric in the split recalls a passage in a curious, ostensibly humorous, story entitled 'Love's Young Dream', written by the twenty-year-old Healy for a nationalist periodical, which culminates in a bizarre nightmare sequence inspired by the narrator's sexual self-consciousness, and his obsession with a large pimple on the bridge of his nose:

> Monstrous cameras loomed upon my sight, from the mouth of which, as from some immense cannon, were belched forth all sorts of horrible portraits. Things with pimples placed in the strongest variety of positions glared at me; pimply abortions bounded through the room, like some huge potato possessed by a fiend; hideous objects, whose stunted legs ended in two huge stumpy pimples, like the pedal arrangements of the elephant, stamped heavily upon me, pounding with dull thuds upon my unfortunate body.[56]

Healy's sexual rhetoric in the split marks a critical intersection of his private animus and public rhetoric. Yet however repulsive or idiosyncratic Healy's sensibility may be considered, he fashioned from it a public idiom of Irish nationalism. His personal prejudices were mediated through recognisable nationalist and Catholic themes and motifs, and stamped indelibly the anti-Parnellite rhetoric of the split. That Healy's personal prejudices and peculiarities were insinuated so deeply into the rhetoric of anti-Parnellism, as well as demonstrating the alarming malleability of nationalist rhetoric, attested to the lost coherence of nationalism and the fracturing of the nationalist order with the fall of Parnell.

14

The 'Saxon Smile': Healy's Sexual Rhetoric Against Parnell

> He tells us to beware of the Saxon smile. Why does he not beware of it himself (*laughter and cheers*). He talks about English wolves. Ireland has known at any rate one English she-wolf (*laughter and cheers*) who has brought more misfortune on our country than all the coercion of Mr. Balfour.
>
> T. M. Healy, 30 September 1891[1]

> That bitch, that English whore, did for him, the shebeen proprietor commented. She put the first nail in his coffin.
>
> James Joyce, *Ulysses*[2]

Healy deployed to devastating effect in the split what Thomas Sexton had once euphemistically described as his 'Rabelaisian pungency'.[3] His bleak comedy of sexual allusion was a dominant feature of his rhetoric, reflecting his determination to thwart Parnell shifting his campaign from the disadvantageous terrain of the divorce court. Healy constructed a sustained *argumentum ad hominem*, an unnerving rhetoric which coupled lethal ridicule and selective logic. Proof against rational rejoinder by Parnell, it was devised to be unanswerable. The strategy of Healy's rhetoric corresponded perfectly with its substance. Compelling Parnell to run a gauntlet of ethnic humour, Healy's rhetoric enacted his ritual exclusion from the moral community of nationalism.

He derided Parnell as morosely self-absorbed and humourless. Humour, as the Dublin *Daily Express* noted after the Carlow rout, was not Parnell's strong point: 'Indeed it may be said that he owes his deposition to the fact that certain ridiculous allusions, quite irrelevant to politics, have been freely used against him'.[4] Healy cast his campaign as an excrescence of Irish jocularity which Parnell was dourly incapable of appreciating. Savagely assailing Parnell's personal life, he calmly proceeded to mock him for the humourlessness of his response.

Healy declared Parnell's speeches to have 'a very unsavoury theme, for from top to bottom he talks of nothing but himself'[5] and taunted Parnell that his speeches 'were as dull as ditchwater and all about himself';[6] the *National Press* asserted that Parnell's speeches 'have grown as monotonous as circulating decimals'.[7] Healy deftly coupled an attack on Parnell's inflated pretensions with a rare reference to his accent, when he told his audience at Newry that on leaving Dundalk the previous Sunday he had had the opportunity 'of hearing Mr. Parnell address three railway porters in his most polished English accent and he told them that the North is solid for the Chief'.[8] The Parnellites like Parnell were not merely morally incorrigible, but were not even amenable to reformation by ridicule. They were impervious to the comedy of their predicament: 'ridicule cannot touch them, or at least hold them back from any absurdity'.[9]

Healy proclaimed his determination, so long as Parnell was hailed as 'the only possible leader', not to shirk alluding to 'the only possible topic'.[10] He insisted that his references to the subject of Parnell's relations with Katharine O'Shea were not gratuitous, but were part of a scheme of retaliation which Parnell's persisting pretensions to ascendancy in Irish politics invited. He professed his refusal to engage in conventional political argument: his recourse to personal attack and ridicule was necessary to counter Parnell's strategy of evasion and diversion. Rarely have the premises of a rhetoric been so clearly or provokingly stated.

Healy's determination not to permit Parnell to shift from the quagmire of the divorce court to the high ground of resistance to Liberal dictation struck at the root of Parnell's strategy since the granting of the decree *nisi*. He went so far as to pay tribute to Parnell's skill in the pursuit of that course. Of Parnell's recovery of the poise he had temporarily forfeited in Kilkenny, Healy wrote in March: 'Mr. Parnell has resumed his native demeanour and soared home into the trackless altitudes of statescraft'.[11] Healy was not disposed to permit Parnell to take wing from the earthly realities of his relations with Katharine O'Shea. What anti-Parnellites condemned as Parnell's political audacity and moral effrontery was invoked to justify their endless reiteration of the circumstances of his relations with Katharine O'Shea. 'One might as well try to pull an eel out of a hole by catching it by the tail as to get Mr. Parnell to admit upon any consideration that he was in the wrong', complained T. D. Sullivan.[12]

Healy was determined to cheat Parnell of the political debate he craved, by defining and delimiting the issues of the split by ceaselessly harking back to the evidence of the divorce court. The split, the *National Press* asserted, had been created in 'the crucible of the divorce court'.[13] Healy rejected from the outset the proposition that those who were possessed of 'the most potent and terrible argument of all' were obliged to keep it 'lodged in their scabbards'.[14]

'As long as I live', he declared, 'whenever the question arises as to what is the cause of all this trouble, I shall answer in two words, "Charles Parnell and Mrs. O'Shea"'.[15] Healy refused to permit the controversy to digress from the issue of the divorce court and Parnell's relations with Katharine O'Shea which he designated, in a recurring phrase, the 'fons et origo malorum'.[16] The *National Press* in its first issue asserted that Parnell

> naturally enough wants the public to read the history in the middle of the sentence regardless of sense or sequence. He wants us to commence at the place where Mr. Gladstone's name comes in, and to ignore all that has gone before and compelled Mr. Gladstone to interpose.[17]

Healy sought to invest the campaign against Parnell with the inexorability of legal process. He had a forensic preference for the specific 'facts' of Parnell's relations with Katharine O'Shea over metaphysical or abstract political concepts. He thus marshalled the 'evidence' against Parnell at the Carlow convention:

> Evidence there is against Mr. Parnell, the evidence of a ruined home, of a degraded woman, of thousands of pounds spent we know not where, we know not what upon (*groans*). These are tangible, palpable, concrete facts. They stare you in the face. They look you in the eyes (*hear hear*).[18]

He proclaimed his refusal to submit either to discreet silence or to polite circumlocutions on the divorce issue. He declined to refer to the O'Shea divorce 'as a mathematician would designate an unknown quantity — call it "x" or "y"'. Healy responded to Joseph Kenny's remonstrances against his persisting attacks on Katharine O'Shea after Parnell's death:

> Dr. Kenny does not like my language (*laughter*). I do not veil my political prescriptions in Latin or Greek (*loud applause*) . . . I say this entire case which is involved in the divorce court is as much a part of the existing controversy as our souls are portions of our systems.[19]

The *National Press* dismissed Parnellite deprecations of Healy's references to Katharine O'Shea as exercises in spurious chivalry: 'in reality what hits them is the truth that lies behind'.[20] Mocking Parnell's hauteur, Healy insisted he would not be permitted to evade the issue of the divorce by raising extraneous issues, by taking refuge in his status as the improving landlord of Avondale or otherwise:

> You may discuss with Mr. Parnell iron mines, woodcutting, light railways, canals, logs, theosophy, geology, conchology (*laughter*), everything that comes within the purview of the human mind; but if you refer to the one sole subject which has brought disaster and disrepute upon this country, then, gentlemen, your scurrility puts you beyond the pale of public discussion.[21]

Healy took evident pleasure in goading the Parnellites with their inability to escape the repercussions of the divorce court. In his mockery of their diversionary stratagems, he showed himself an inventive and witty parodist of Parnell and Parnellism. Only Healy could have penned the elegantly derisive squib, published in the *Nation* in response to an attempt by T. C. Harrington to embark on a moral vindication of Parnell's relations with Katharine O'Shea, which included the lines:

> Better descant, as I've hinted before,
> On surgery, alchemy, magic, psychology
> Treat us to lots of legendary lore,
> But never go slap into moral theology.[22]

The *Insuppressible* taunted Parnell with his inability to find a suitable euphemism or diminutive to describe the decree of the divorce court, and ventured: '"The ickle ickle verdictums" would be too infantine. "The doty, nicy yumsy, divorce-kin" lacks vigour'.[23] Recourse to baiting gibberish was among the most provoking of Healy's rhetorical techniques. His refusal of rational political discourse led him to evolve a counter-language of ridicule and dismissive jocularity. He constructed a densely allusive anti-Parnellite idiom, spinning from the more risible disclosures of the divorce court and the extravagances of Parnellite rhetoric a clinging web of mockery.

In a coded discourse of proper names, ridiculous incidents, and rhetorical parody, Healy reduced Parnellism to a comic sequence of Victorian advertising slogans. By the skilful repetition of codewords and knowing references, he presented a selective fantasia of Parnellism, and promulgated a terse catechism of Parnellite cliché. The comprehensiveness of Healy's scheme of facetious epithets may be seen from the cartoon of the *Weekly*

National Press for 20 June 1891. Tim Harrington is caricatured as a somewhat menacing head waiter standing outside the National League headquarters — the restaurant of Parnell and Company — while a respectably attired peasant (wondering 'is there anything here now an honest Irish boy can ate?') surveys a bill of fare which strikes him as 'un-Irish entirely, entirely' :

> Gutter Sparrow, à la Kilkenny
> Grouse, from the Eltham Preserve
> Presbyterian Soup, à la Sligo
> Elbow de Balfour, with Parnell Sauce
> Campaign Tenants, done brown on Toast, à la Redmond
> Belfast Kidneys, with Orange Sauce
> Nicely Cooked Balance Sheet, à la Maitre d'Hotel
> Calf's head, à la Gray
> (Winter) Quarters of (Mr.) Fox, 'Matchless' flavour
> Roast Bishop à la Harrington.

In its ceaseless rehearsal of the circumstances of Parnell's relations with Katharine O'Shea as if exhausting the possible permutations of divorce court allusions, rhetoric maintained a calculatedly puerile taunting chant. Through the provoking idiocy of pun, joke and verse, he pursued a harlequin's revenge.

Healy refused to treat of the themes which Parnell introduced in the split other than in terms of personal abuse or ridicule. Thus, having tellingly mocked the attempted Parnellite justification of the refusal to abide by the view of the majority in Committee Room 15 ('Parnell plus Campbell is logically as forcible an arithmetic formula or fraction as Parnell plus twenty-six') Healy continued:

> Gentlemen who discuss this question as a matter of dialectics must face it as a question of logic . . . If gentlemen debate this as a matter of logic, I say, that by that means we reduce Mr. Parnell's position to an absurdity, and we reduce it to dishonour (*hear hear*). Therefore, astute a man as 'Mr. Fox' may be (*laughter*), I say that if you consider the position he assumes it is a position which we have riddled and torn by the grapeshot of logic (*hear hear*).[24]

'Logic' meant the selective rationality of Healy's ruthless casuistry. He insisted that the fact that the Parnellites had declined to abide by the decision of the majority placed them outside the pale of conventional political discourse.

The feeble Parnellite contention that Parnell had been irregularly deposed in that the majority had 'seceded' from Room 15 before a vote was taken excited Healy's mordant wit. He reduced the proposition to 'the contemptible ground that the majority is no longer a majority when it meets in another room':

> Exercising the jurisdiction always resident in any body of men, you dispense with that piece of furniture called a chairman and with that environment called a room, and meet somewhere else, then, forsooth, you suddenly lose all the power, virtue, and jurisdiction which belongs to you. The logic of that has been chopped long enough (*laughter*). I will chop no more of it. The chopper that is wanted now is a chopper of another kind.[25]

Healy sharply parodied what he asserted to be the bogus metaphysics of Parnellism, and reiterated his determination to meet Parnell with ridicule rather than rational argument:

> Now I would suggest to Mr. Parnell with reference to this cry of English dictation that he ought to get up a cry against Jewish dictation. There is such a thing as the ten commandments and I wonder he does not condemn that foreigner Moses (*laughter*) and declare that he the chieftain of the Wicklow hill will never allow himself to be dictated from a foreign mountain called Sinai. Gentlemen, I decline to argue with Mr. Parnell (*hear hear*). I will ridicule him, I will show up the man's absurdities (*hear hear*), but to treat him and his party as reasonable beings about this leadership craze — I would as soon argue with a cage of monkeys in a menagerie (*laughter*).[26]

Healy denied the possibility of a rational or bona fide adherence to Parnell. Whatever the allegiance of the ignorant, he declared it 'impossible for any educated or reasonable person having solely the interests of his country at heart, and being seized and possessed of the facts of the case, to support Mr. Parnell'.[27]

Somewhat contradictorily, he further justified his refusal to engage in conventional political argument by equating the split with controversies over questions of faith, to assert that the Parnellites were not amenable to rational persuasion:

> When men's passions and jealousies get entangled with their reasons you cannot argue with them. The Greek and Latin churches split on the question of a particle. Does anyone hope by arguments or controversy to convert the people of the Protestant religion? Do Protestants hope to convert Baptists? Do Baptists hope to convert Presbyterians? Or the Presbyterians the Methodists? No . . .[28]

Healy championed an idiom of brisk despatch, a confident assertion of the new political order: 'What happened to him whenever he appealed to the country? He has got only one answer, simply this – "get out of that"'.[29]

Healy's rhetorical technique, replete with dangers for the practice of democratic politics in Ireland, proved highly effective. Parnell had to await the release of Dillon and O'Brien before he was afforded the opportunity to engage in conventional argument. When Dillon injudiciously engaged in disputation with him, Parnell demonstrated his old mastery and expressed himself thankful for the opportunity. The *Weekly National Press* irritably observed that 'Mr. Parnell confirms our opinion of the folly of treating with him as an antagonist to chop logic with'.[30]

Healy dismissed the themes of Parnell's campaign as cynical ploys, meaningless and mischievous distractions from the precipitating issue of the split, the divorce case. Parnellism, he insisted, had no reality except as a cloak for Parnell's misfeasance. 'Mr. Parnell struck a match to make smoke to hide his own shame.'[31] Parnellism in the split was just a vehicle for Parnell's personal ascendancy, 'merely the spawn of the London Divorce Court'.[32] He derided 'catch-cries and flash phrases engendered in the Divorce Court . . . as hollow as a glugger egg'. He dismissed Parnellite attacks on clerical intervention as 'fungi which have subsequently sprouted out of the decayed roots of Parnellism'. Parnellite 'independent opposition' had a tainted pedigree: 'Independent opposition out of adultery – dam by fire-escape'. In January 1892 Healy mockingly serialised the litany of Parnellite catch-cries since the divorce court, dismissing each in turn.[33] Deriding Parnellism as the mumbo-jumbo of the credulous, the *National Press* wrote of the Parnellite espousal of the principle of 'independent opposition' that 'these poor creatures seem to be tied to phrases, like victims to the stake, and think they may be employed anyhow and anywhere as amulets, fetishes and charms'.[34] At Thurles, shortly before Parnell's death, Healy peremptorily dismissed Parnellism:

> My mind, my class of mind, refused to assimilate Parnellism. I can never digest moonshine (*cheers and laughter*). I oppose to the catch cries of Parnellism, one prolonged, eternal, everlasting fudge (*cheers*). I do not believe him, and when he says anything in the papers, I simply say I exclude from my mind the possibility of faith, or hope, or confidence in the man (*hear hear*).[35]

In the pincer movement of his rhetoric Healy sought to divest Parnell of his subjective mystique, while defeat eroded his objective political credibility. When Parnell at the National League convention of July 1891 sought to reconstitute his faltering cause through an ambitious programme of reform, the *National Press* in Healy's characteristic idiom derided the convention as yet another risible diversionary improvisation on Parnell's part, a desperate attempt to put the anti-Parnellite nation off the scent as the 'hunt' gathered pace:

> All the available forces of Parnellism were whipped into the Leinster Hall yesterday for a fresh start on a new trail. 'Mr. Fox' after his Carlow experience, is naturally anxious to draw public opinion off his own track before he is quite run to earth. Therefore, the old expedient of the red herring is tried. Therefore, the so-called National Convention devoted itself entirely to constitution-mongering, with not the most distant allusion to the cause and origin of the controversy by which the country has been so wantonly disturbed . . . But the country is now in full cry on Mr. Fox's track, and resolved to hunt him from public life, and it is merely peurile to draw a red herring across the trail. What the country wants is not to get a new National policy, but only to get rid of the degraded and treacherous leader who strove to ruin the old. The National cause was not disgraced in the Divorce Court. No shame has fallen upon it . . . It is idle to discuss the topics Mr. Parnell now raises and the new pledges he suggests. They are obviously foreign to the controversy.[36]

The passage illustrates the currency which Healy's rhetoric had attained: by this stage of the split it was possible to construct an entire argument in terms of its codewords, motifs and images.

The *National Press* relentlessly assailed the decadence of what it strikingly termed '*fin de siècle* Parnellism'. Parnellites and Parnellite dogma were alike reducible to the level of the divorce court. In Healy's rhetoric the Parnell myth became a pornographic conceit, the rhetoric of 'chieftaincy' a voyeuristic cult. Deriding 'Mr. Harrington and other grooms of the bedchamber of the National League', Healy observed that 'the whole of them in this business have been following the whip of Mrs. O'Shea'. The *National Press* denounced the 'besotted admirers of Elthamism'.[37]

Parnell's career and his technique of power itself were now reducible to the subterfuges and deceptions of an illicit relationship. His relationship with Katharine O'Shea provided the unifying thread of his career. The *arcana imperii* were those of the boudoir. The Parnell 'enigma' was now re-interpreted in terms of the furtiveness of an adulterous relationship.

His reclusiveness, his mysterious and prolonged absences, were, after all, readily explicable. To Parnell's pleas of ill-health, Healy retorted at Carlow:

> For ten years we did not know where Parnell lived. The Irish leader was living in caves and holes where nobody could find him. We are told that Mr. Parnell was all the time in bad health. He was and I will tell you what was the matter with him – he had *Kitty on the brain*.[38]

Healy went further. A decade of parliamentary nationalism was now re-assessed in terms of a *chronique scandaleuse* of Parnell's relations with Katharine O'Shea. The Kilmainham treaty became the object of Healy's crude and destructive revisionism:

> When Mr. Parnell was in jail in 1882 and when by staying in jail he could show what the strength of the country was, he signed the Kilmainham treaty to get out (*hisses*). He was only the instrument in her hand (*hisses*) and it is this man who for the sake of this base woman went behind the backs of his colleagues and left them behind him and out of Kilmainham.[39]

The *National Press* likewise sought to explain Parnell's initial refusal to sue the *Times* over the Piggot forgeries by reference to 'the fear that in a libel action the *Times* would expose the secrets of the alcoves at Eltham. The skeleton in the private closet thus barred the way to what was, in reality, a national vindication'.[40] In disregarding the considerations of political strategy which influenced two of the most important — and well-judged — *démarches* of Parnell's career, Healy recklessly and mischievously impugned not merely Parnell's statescraft, but the achievements of parliamentary nationalism under his leadership.

The tightness of rhetorical engagement in the split is well illustrated by a taunt and counter-taunt of Parnell and Healy respectively. Parnell in a speech in Cork asserted that during discussion of the draft of the home rule bill, 'a certain budding Lord Chancellor or Chief Justice' — by which Healy was intended — had enquired whether it provided for the appointment of a Lord Chancellor. Healy's riposte was swift and devastating, with a concoction 'as true' as Parnell's, in a speech at Carrickmacross:

> Now I will tell you what really occurred, and this story is as absolutely true as what I have read to you. When the Home Rule Bill was laid on the table Mr. Parnell asked me: 'Will it enable me to act like Henry VIII?' and I said no. Well, said he, can I set up a divorce court under it, and I said no. Well, he said, will I be able under this Bill as dictator to run off with other men's wives. And then Mr. Parnell put on his hat and said 'Good Evening'.[41]

Healy claimed that he had proposed, with a view to defusing attacks on the party, that the home rule bill should contain a provision precluding any member of the then Irish party from taking office under an Irish parliament:

> I never could get Parnell to make that suggestion to the British House of Commons. I suppose Kitty would not have allowed it (*laughter*). I

> suppose she thought she would cut a fine figure in the Viceregal lodge because I may tell you that one of the letters in the Divorce Court was to the effect that Captain O'Shea had the promise of being Under Secretary. He was to be made Sir William O'Shea by Parnell and O'Shea wrote a letter to Kitty. Although it was not read out it was one of the documents put in, describing to her the size of the Viceregal lodge, and O'Shea and his wife were to be in the Chief Secretary's lodge. It was a mighty convenient arrangement entirely (*laughter*). He would only have to step across the park (*more laughter*).[42]

Healy was not alone in the scabrousness of his sexual allusions. His parliamentary colleagues Matthew Kenny, Charles Tanner, John Deasy, T. J. Condon, and others were also vociferous contributors on the subject of the 'only possible topic',[43] as were large numbers of parish priests and local nationalist orators who took their lead from Healy. The most surprising venture into scurrility was that of Michael Davitt, who in the course of the Sligo by-election chose to mock Parnell's appeal to labour by a parody of the contemporary demand for a statutory eight-hour day:

> Eight hours work and eight hours play
> Eight hours in company of _________[44]

Evidently the missing reference was to 'Kitty O'Shea', coyly deleted by the *National Press* so as to provide its readership with an untaxing anti-Parnellite riddle. The phrase 'in company of' was itself an edited euphemism. Many years later, Healy regaled Lady Lavery with an unexpurgated version:

> Eight hours of work, eight hours of play,
> Eight hours in bed with Kitty O'Shea.[45]

T. P. O'Connor was the only anti-Parnellite publicly to dissociate himself from the personal attack on Parnell. In a speech in Liverpool in March O'Connor expressed himself at variance with Parnell's moral critics in England ('those ranting and calumniating pharisees'), and with some of his critics in Ireland. While Parnell was guilty of an act of immorality, he could not conclude that Parnell's offence was 'aggravated by the circumstances to one of peculiar and special heinousness', and he preferred to wait till Parnell's lips were unsealed.[46] It was a modest demur, but virtually unique among the anti-Parnellite members, and noteworthy in that it accepted the thrust of Parnell's own reply to the moral charge.

What gave Healy's rhetoric its particular incivility was his open exploitation of the fact that Parnell was constrained from offering any defence of his conduct until after the divorce decree was made absolute, by which stage the political damage to his reputation could not be undone. Healy knew Parnell was desperately anxious not to provoke the intervention of the Queen's Proctor. He wrote his wife during the contest in Committee Room 15: 'Parnell's determination to marry her is so great that he almost shudders at the name of the Queen's Proctor, or to any allusion of connivance on the part of O'Shea'.[47]

Parnell's concern was starkly revealed by an incident in Room 15, suppressed in the *Freeman's Journal* report evidently at his behest. Healy had at the time despatched a wire of protest to the paper which it did not publish. The *Insuppressible* later published an account of the incident. The Parnellite Joseph Nolan had taunted Justin McCarthy with his assertion at the Leinster Hall meeting that, had Lockwood been permitted to cross-examine O'Shea a different complexion, would have been put on the case. Parnell 'fiercely intervened' to say that McCarthy had no authority to have made such a statement, that he could not have done him a greater disservice, and requesting that the line of argument be not pursued. It was a 'practical admission of the adultery', Healy wrote his wife: 'His horror of the Queen's Proctor is greater than his fear of public opinion'. The *Insuppressible* went on to seek to impale Parnell on the horns of his dilemma by asking why he did not himself assert his innocence rather than leaving it to Tim Harrington: 'either Mr. Parnell is guilty in the O'Shea case or he is innocent'.[48] Healy pressed his advantage and repeatedly alluded to the Queen's Proctor, whose spectre he summoned up whenever a Parnellite apologist was incautious enough to suggest that Parnell had an answer to the moral charge.

Healy's incursion into Parnell's privacy was not confined to his attack on Katharine O'Shea. Parnell's sister Anna was moved to deny an allegation by Healy that she had not spoken to her brother since the 'Kilmainham treaty'.[49] But it was Katharine O'Shea who bore the brunt of Healy's onslaught. His epithets were predictably exhaustive. Appropriating a phrase from the conservative clubs, he described her as 'the Tory Joan of Arc'.[50] The *National Press* referred to her as 'Madame O'Shea'.[51] The references became most frequent during the Carlow by-election, following her marriage to Parnell. Healy referred to her variously as 'a degraded woman', and 'the base woman'.[52] At Bagenalstown after Parnell's marriage Healy elicited laughter and cheers with a reference to 'Kitty Parnell'.[53] In March he dubbed her 'the Brighton banshee'. At Thurles on the day of Parnell's death, Healy designated her 'the Brighton Shan Van Vocht',[54] rendering explicit the opposition between Katharine O'Shea and an allegorially feminised Hibernia. Reflecting a determination to lash the name as much as the vice, Healy reverted at every available opportunity to the subject of Parnell's relations with Katharine O'Shea. He gave Parnell cause to regret his unguarded invocation of the Irish adage concerning the Saxon smile at Limerick, to which he retorted at Carrick-on-Shannon:

> He [Parnell] told the Irish people to beware of the Saxon smile. Why did he not beware of it (*cheers*)? Beware of the Saxon smile on the lips of Mrs. O'Shea (*laughter and cheers*). He said that the air of Westminster was bad for them [the Irish members]. Was the air of Brighton good for him?[55]

An epigram in the *Irish Catholic* taunted that Parnell had succumbed to 'the guilty leers of Kitty'.[56]

Healy asserted that it was Parnell who was responsible for dishonouring the name of Katharine O'Shea: 'He tells us we should never have mentioned her name in public. It is hitting below the belt. Well, if he is so sensitive about her name and fame, why did Mr. Parnell drag her into the most shameful court in England and have it made a byword and a reproach'.[57] In a development of this theme, Healy sought to drive a wedge between Parnell's campaign and his professed desire to protect Katharine O'Shea from calumny. He argued that it was Parnell who, in persevering in his campaign, was subjecting his mistress to continuing public excoriation.[58]

Healy attacked Katharine O'Shea not merely as the adulterous wife of Captain O'Shea but as the ultimate arbiter of Parnellism. He imputed to her a preponderant influence in shaping the course of Parnell's politics both in the years of his ascendancy and in the split itself. She was the carnal embodiment of English dictation: 'in this business Parnell is only yielding to English dictation, and to the Saxon smile, and the person at the bottom of all this is Mrs. O'Shea'. She was in the words of the *Weekly National Press* 'the unfortunate woman, to whom he is as subservient as his followers are to him'. Of Parnell's speech at Westport the *National Press* commented: 'Mr. Parnell ground out the old tune about independent opposition, by which it is always to be understood he means unquestioning obedience to himself and the power behind his throne'.[59]

In Healy's rhetoric, Katharine O'Shea was in a double sense Parnell's mistress. He was a leader unmanned by desire, whose concupiscence had eroded his faculty of command. His infatuation subverted a masculine moral order and brought about an inversion of power. She was 'Queen Catherine of Arrogance', he 'the slave at Eltham'.[60] In the uncouth ribaldry of the split, Parnell's licentiousness became a partaking of the character of the partner, an assumption of effeminacy. That the mythically cold and masterful Parnell should have become the creature of his lover's whims was one of the most subtly destructive themes of Healy's rhetoric.

His depiction of Katharine O'Shea as Judith to Parnell's Holofernes was shrewdly calculated. It afforded a line of rationalisation for those who could more easily reconcile opposition to Parnell in the split with their former allegiance by the consideration that Parnell had been changed, as Healy declared, by 'one bad, base, immoral woman'.[61] In a heavily interrupted speech in the Kilkenny by-election he charged:

> When we declared against him we saw that the cause of Ireland was superior to the cause of Parnell, and I will never ruin Ireland for any man (*interruptions*). You can ruin Ireland if you like, and sacrifice the labourers (*interruptions*), and sacrifice the farmers, and the country (*interruptions*) by voting for the man who has broken up the Irish Party (*groans*), and who is determined for the sake of a woman. *A voice – Shut your mouth about the woman. Mr. Healy* — And a bad woman, too, who hates Ireland, who cares nothing for Ireland (*groans*), who has been spending the money of the Irish people, and ruined Parnell, and brought him to his present unhappy position (*groans*).[62]

Only Healy could have written a brutally whimsical piece of doggerel which appeared in the *National Press* suggesting that the split was being fought out at the insistence of Katharine O'Shea alone, and subtly investing the theme of domination with a hint of its sexual connotation. Entitled 'By the Only Possible [Leader]', it ran:

> She says I must fight for my station,
> Or forfeit her high admiration,
> To obey her will be
> Quite a pleasure for me
> So sweet is her English dictation.[63]

His attack drew part of its force from the prevalent perception of Katharine O'Shea among both Irish factions and among English observers as an extremely strong-willed woman capable of overbearing Parnell's own instincts. It is evident that Katharine O'Shea was a formidable and determined person. Even the gallant Henry Harrison was constrained to observe that 'she was reputed to be, and was, somewhat *difficile*', and that 'her allure, with her visible strength of type, suggested the empress rather than the nymph'.[64] Yet around her accreted an exaggerated myth — intensified after Parnell's death — by which she was held responsible both for the acquiescent strategy adopted by Parnell in the face of the O'Shea divorce petition, and for his political course in the split. In an obituary on her death in 1921, T. P. O'Connor detected her influence at work against compromise in the split in writing of 'an occult influence behind Parnell that dominated his will and obscured his own clear judgement'.[65] Dillon in conversation with W. S. Blunt in 1912 conveyed the prevalent view among nationalists of both camps in describing her as a force hostile to Parnell's patriotism, who brought to bear 'a disastrous influence' and procured the failure of the Boulogne negotiations.[66]

Even the usually astute and level-headed E. W. Hamilton discerned the vengeful influence of Katharine O'Shea at work from the outset of the split. On the publication of the Gladstone letter he wrote in his diary: 'One has to remember that Parnell is the most difficult and impossible of men to deal with, and that there is a woman behind him who (as George Lewis said to me yesterday) is a still more impossible and difficult person to deal with, and who will doubtless use all her powers to secure a revenge for herself and Parnell'. The Parnell manifesto 'displays such a spirit of revenge that it looks as if the woman (Mrs. O'Shea) must have had a hand in it'. Reflecting two days later on the 'awkward and momentous consequences' of the adultery, Hamilton wrote 'How Mrs. O'Shea must be chuckling with revengeful delight!'[67] Hamilton's comments show how, for an Englishman habituated to the Parnell of the high phase of the Liberal–nationalist alliance, the evil influence of Katharine O'Shea provided a compelling explanation for what was to them the bewildering ferocity of Parnell's response to the Gladstone letter.

There was also an element of male collusion in the attribution to Katharine O'Shea of a predominant responsibility for the catastrophe of the split. Lloyd George came in later years to see Parnell's relations with Katharine O'Shea as a precedent for his own with Frances Stevenson, who noted in 1936: 'D is very anti-Kitty O'Shea. But he is always inclined to blame the woman when it is a question of a man choosing between her and his career – he is always for the immolation of the woman'.[68]

For some observers, the fact that Katharine O'Shea was some eighteen months Parnell's senior, and that their relationship commenced when she was in her mid-thirties, itself raised an inference that hers was a dominating and manipulative character. Thus T. P. O'Connor, in his capacity as the facile and prolific novelist *manqué* of Parnell and Parnellism, wrote of her on her death in February 1921:

> Those who saw her at the time when Parnell first met her, unblinded by love, were unable to see the charms which proved to him so irresistible and devastating. She had already passed her first youth, and her influence was probably due as much to strength of will as to physical charm. Whether she had a right to do so or not, she certainly dominated Parnell.[69]

To William O'Brien, who guilelessly called on Katharine O'Shea during the Plan of Campaign with a view to ascertaining Parnell's whereabouts, she looked, according to O'Brien's wife, 'heavy and plain, older than my husband expected'.[70]

W. T. Stead, the eccentrically vehement publicist of the nonconformist conscience, denounced Katharine O'Shea as 'the Were-Wolf Woman of Irish politics'. Her influence was an incident in 'the story of the part played by women of late years in the great tragedy of contemporary history'. He cited also the example of the mistress of General Boulanger, over whose grave the French politician was to commit suicide a few days prior to Parnell's death. Stead's characterisation of Katharine O'Shea faithfully conveyed the conventional wisdom: she was 'a woman of great ambition, of free-and-easy manners, and of a suspicious temperament'.[71] *Vanity Fair* likewise referred to Katharine O'Shea as 'The Political Princess: O'Shea Who Must be Obeyed'.[72] Katharine O'Shea was also widely perceived as the sexual aggressor in her relations with Parnell. Of a passage in R. B. O'Brien's biography of Parnell concerning Parnell's nervous sleeping, Davitt sourly noted: 'Fear of being alone . . . this is a charitable plea for his response to Mrs. O'Shea's advances'.[73]

Long after the split, moralising nationalists continued to place the principal blame on Katharine O'Shea. A clerical historian writing of the Parnell of the split deplored 'that fatal witchery which had darkened his intellect and completely dominated his will'.[74] The most extreme inculpation of Katharine O'Shea occurred in an engagingly naive conspiracy theory propounded by Jasper Tully, an anti-Parnellite who sat for Leitrim South 1892–1906, in his maverick *Roscommon Herald* in 1926. Gladstone, breakfasting in Paris in the early 1880s complained to his host, 'the Jew Gambetta', of the difficulties created by Parnell's obstructionism. Gambetta helpfully ventured 'why don't you set a woman on him?' Thus it was, wrote Tully, that Katharine O'Shea, 'a lady of notorious reputation was engaged to trap Parnell, and she succeeded only too well'.[75]

Whether or not one accepts Katharine O'Shea's surely plausible insistence that the decision not to contest the divorce decree and to fight the leadership was Parnell's alone,[76] Healy's rhetoric damagingly exploited the pervasive belief that Parnell's fierce combativeness in the split owed much to her direct inspiration.

The deep suspicions which Katharine O'Shea excited were by no means confined to the anti-Parnellites. Parnell's parliamentary lieutenants condoned rather than sympathised with his relations with Katharine O'Shea, whom they regarded with feelings approaching horror. The romantic *élan* of Parnellite allegiance in the split, at least among his parliamentary supporters, derived from the excitement of fidelity to a heroically embattled Parnell, rather than from any approbation of Parnell's attachment to

Katharine O'Shea. However natural the tendency among many of Parnell's foremost parliamentary supporters privately to blame Katharine O'Shea for the calamity which had engulfed their cause, their proclivity to impute to her responsibility for Parnell's uncompromising politics in the split is suggestive. Such was the pervasive bewilderment and lack of understanding which Parnell's campaign elicited that her influence provided a convenient hypothesis to account for his intransigence in the split. Disturbingly, from Parnell's point of view, she became the supreme emblem of the widespread incomprehension of his political course in the split, even among his own supporters.

Healy cunningly devised his rhetoric to cheat Parnell even of the sympathy which heroic adversity might attract. In particular, he sought to deprive him of the romantic allure of the embattled lover. He charged that Parnell's relations with Katharine O'Shea were actuated by a combination of lust and venality. Parnell's purpose was to marry a woman who stood to inherit a substantial fortune from her aunt. Rather than the heroic paramour, Parnell was the grasping aristocrat, a testamentary opportunist on a par with Captain O'Shea, who along with other relatives had embarked on a challenge to the will of Katharine O'Shea's aunt. *Insuppressible* had announced at the outset that 'Mr. Parnell proposes to marry the legatee when the divorce is made absolute'.[77] When he did so, the *Weekly National Press* declared that he had 'secured the legal right to share the colossal fortune of the unhappy woman whose character he has ruined', putting the fortune at £200,000, and ascribing Parnell's expression of his happiness on his marriage to gratification at his enrichment.[78] Heckled in Derry in August by a Parnellite MP who stated Parnell could not be bought, Healy vituperated:

> I will tell you the price of him — the fortune of Mrs. O'Shea. They heard great talk about place-hunting, and great talk about selling their country, but the basest of all sales and barter was to sell the fortune, the faith and the rights of your country for the enjoyment of a loose woman.[79]

As Parnell's financial resources dried up, the *National Press* contended that 'nothing remains but the change of the interest in a possible legacy', rendering it impossible for the Parnellites to muster the sum of £40,000, the amount necessary to contest eighty seats at the general election. The paper later added, in a characteristic twisting of the barb, that if Parnell's supporters looked to a share in the spoils of Katharine O'Shea's inheritance, they were likely to be disappointed.

> For some time the 'Boys' expected that as soon as Mrs. O'Shea's legacies were realised there would be handsome subsidies for various charitable

> and patriotic purposes . . . but Captain O'Shea's wife is a prudent manager, and will not allow her money to be thrown away on a barren and useless fight.[80]

This line of argument reflected Healy's ineradicable conviction that Parnell's involvement with Katharine O'Shea owed much to her prospective inheritance. It was a variant of the Anglo-Irish theme of the pursuit of the heiress. He wrote his father that he would not be on the other side of the controversy 'for all Kitty's fortune'.[81]

Healy's rhetoric asserted a symmetry of duplicity and betrayal. Parnell's treachery to the Irish cause, and Katharine O'Shea's infidelity towards her husband, partook alike of a double game of treachery and divided allegiance. Parnellism in the split was defined as the politics of complaisance, an emanation of the diandrous proclivities of Katharine O'Shea. In the concept of 'the Parnell-O'Shea policy of Home Rule' Healy developed the political co-relative to the *ménage à trois* of Parnell and the O'Sheas:

> Yes, Captain O'Shea was a Parnellite before his time. He was a Parnellite before Parnell invented the 'hillside' doctrine (*laughter*), because he refused in 1886 the bill of Gladstone (*laughter*), and now Parnell is following O'Shea (*cheers and laughter*). Do you believe in the Parnell-O'Shea policy of Home Rule? Do you believe in masculine O'Shea on the Home Rule question or feminine O'Shea on the moral question? (*laughter and cheers*).[82]

Parnell thus shared the politics as well as the wife of Captain O'Shea, whom Healy mockingly referred to as 'that esteemed partner of Mr. Parnell's'.[83] 'The mere name "O'Shea"', declared the *National Press*, 'comprises a volume in this contest.'[84]

W. H. O'Shea's social and political antecedents afforded Healy a rhetorical opportunity he did not fail to exploit. Not merely was O'Shea politically a Whig, in the pejorative Irish sense of the term, but he was an almost parodic embodiment of the 'Castle Catholic'. An Irish-born, English-educated Catholic ex-army officer, O'Shea was in nationalist terms the archetype of the caddish, faintly disreputable, social opportunist.

He was in consequence particularly useful in Healy's gallery of Parnellite social types. In postulating a Parnell/O'Shea political axis, Healy constructed a polemical composite which assimilated Parnell as a landlord to the yet more reviled class of adventurer functionaries and imperial careerists, with non-existent or attenuated Irish connexions. Healy astutely used the social profile of W. H. O'Shea to downgrade by association Parnell's caste status. By this equation he subtly but damagingly eroded the perceived place of the Anglo-Irish landlord class in Irish history by implying its roots to be as shallow, its rapacity as transparent, as a later generation of imperial adventurers. The detraction from the aristocratic mystique of the Anglo-Irish in an epoch marked by the rise of a Catholic proprietorial middle class admirably conformed to Healy's larger purpose in the split. This consideration underlay Healy's attack on Parnell's choice of nationalist parliamentary candidates: 'Parnell would select some Irish whacker from Australia (*laughter*), some goldminer from Mashonoland, some ex-sub-Commissioner who had been planting rackrents upon you (*A voice: "Captain O'Shea"*) or some of his women's cast-off husbands'[85] This caricature of imagined Parnellite *arrivistes* corresponded closely to Healy's attack over the preceding decade on magistrates, and on the personnel appointed to administer the land acts.

The *Nation* of 17 January 1891 published a poem of five versus by Healy entitled 'Brighton Over All'. It was conceived as a retort to 'Bantry Over All', a balladic attack on the 'Bantry Gang' which Edward Harrington (himself from Bantry) had published in the Parnellite *Evening Telegraph*. McDonnell Bodkin, the editor of the *Insuppressible*, had declined to publish Healy's lines for fear of offending William O'Brien.[86] 'Brighton Over All' is a squib in the Gilbertian mode, bringing together the themes and motifs of Healy's sexual rhetoric against Parnell, and is here set out *in extenso.*

BRIGHTON OVER ALL

My fault, *if it has been a fault*, is not a fault against Ireland (*cheers*).

(Mr. Parnell at Limerick, 11 Jan. 1891)

Brighton over all, boys!
Brighton over all!
Eltham once so restful
Now begins to pall;
As a spot for hiding,
Safe from Country's call
Deaf to comrades chiding,
Brighton over all.

Should a gallant captain
Seek to gain our hall,
Fire escapes are handy
To save an ugly fall;
Nor plank bed here nor warder,
Nor gloomy prison wall,
Can cause the mind disorder,
Brighton over all.

Scribes may screech at Preston,
　　And Pharisees at Fox,
Scoffers make a jest on
　　Our noble steeds as 'crocks';
But 'President' and 'Dictator'
　　Champing in their stall,
Wax fat on Irish bounty,
　　In Brighton over all.

But hist! 'tis Henry Campbell,
　　(Hark, the bark of 'Grouse'!)
Success has crowned his ramble,
　　He's found another house!
There he'll rock the cradle
　　When the babies squall
Crooning: 'Though I'm paid ill,
　　Brighton over all!'

Now lusciously we languish,
　　By Brighton's pleasant shore,
And Ireland's cry of anguish
　　Can reach our ears no more;
Then 'stead of Erin's Sunburst
　　Quick hoist up Kitty's shawl!
On Clancy! Shout the slogan –
　　'Brighton over all!'

Edward Harrington (of Bantry)

Eltham was the location in Kent of Katharine O'Shea's former residence, adjacent to that of her aunt Mrs. Benjamin Wood, on whose death in May 1889 Parnell and Katherine O'Shea moved to Walsingham Terrace, Brighton. 'Preston' and 'Fox' were aliases used by Parnell in the negotiation of leases. 'President' and 'Dictator' were the names of Parnell's horses, and 'Grouse' that of his Irish setter, making up a bestiary of Anglo-Irish life and leisure.

The deceptively light cadences of the verses reflect Healy's lilting malignity. In their meticulous, even intimate, particularity, the lines achieve a calculated incursion into Parnell's privacy. The fantasia of future children is especially malign. For Healy, the conceit of Parnell's secretary Henry Campbell as a nursemaid rendered it irresistible. It obliquely subserved the values of nationalist moralists for whom Parnell's aspiration to a settled family life represented the domestication of an illicit relationship, which aggravated its heinousness.

The theme of Parnell's sybaritic exile is developed with destructive subtlety. The lines take effect through a brutal and politically charged voyeurism, a peep-show of voluptuousness perceived through the prison bars of oppression in Ireland, so as to heighten the contrast between the luxurious setting of Parnell's English venery, and the patriot's harsh abode ('languish'/'anguish'). The squire of Avondale had become the adulterer at Brighton. His domicile in the south of England was a study in the absenteeism of depravity: the landlord had found his natural habitat.

It is a sobering reflection that Healy's speeches and published journalism did not give full vent to the fecundity of his rhetorical imagination. Two of his collaborators on the *National Press* years later told John Muldoon MP, a partisan of John Dillon's, that Healy 'did a good deal of poetical work in the *National Press* days not all of which was published'.[87] The day after the publication of 'Brighton Over All', Healy at Edgeworthstown retorted in the same vein to Parnell's disingenuous enquiry at Limerick as to why Gladstone had not written him a letter earlier to convey his views:

> He would tell him why, because he didn't know Mr. Parnell's address (*laughter*). Would Mr. Parnell tell them where Mr. Gladstone was to write to. Was it to 'C. S. Parnell M.P. care of Kitty O'Shea'? They could make a rhyme out of it:
>
> C. S. Parnell MP
> Care of Kitty O'Shea
> Down at Brighton by the sea.[88]

Through the taunting puerilities of the nursery rhyme, Healy contrived to sharpen the goad of his refusal to engage in political argument with Parnell.

Healy's rhetoric underscored the fact that Parnell continued to reside in Brighton, and commuted to Ireland to campaign only at weekends, to assert that Parnell's geographically-divided allegiance was owed primarily to Katharine O'Shea. Parnell's frantic plying between the two islands afforded a marked contrast with his former prolonged absence from Irish platforms: 'And now, why he is over here every Sunday, and back again at Brighton every Monday, because, however great his duties to Ireland are, he is always most exact in having to go back every Monday morning to roll the perambulator'. Nor did he stop at Westminster en route to tend to Irish interests: 'the man's whole time and thought, his soul and body, is given up to himself and Mrs. O'Shea'.[89] Healy thereby cunningly contrived to ensure that any electoral benefit reaped by Parnell's weekly crossings was neutralised by the affirmation it afforded of his overriding commitment to Katharine O'Shea, rendering Parnell's campaign in Ireland a treadmill of futility.

Healy's attack on Parnell had elicited furious Parnellite reprisals. One in particular may have served to aggravate the virulence of Healy's attacks on Parnell and Katharine O'Shea. He wrote Maurice in January 'there is no end to the lying about us':

> My poor wife received a letter informing her that she had been Parnell's mistress before her marriage, and that this was the secret of my bitterness. Hooper tells me of a story that her child is illegitimate. It seems as if Parnell had taken off the lid of hell.[90]

One count was not added to Healy's indictment of Parnell's sexual mores, although it was considered. On 17 December 1890, Labouchere wrote to Herbert Gladstone that Healy and his co-adjutors were considering making public the allegation, deriving from the opening of the letter to Parnell at the meeting of the Land League executive in Paris in February 1881, that Parnell had an illegitimate child by a barmaid in Manchester. In the event Healy did not do so: the subject of Parnell's relations with Katharine O'Shea provided him with a more than adequate arsenal for his attack on Parnell. Labouchere's letter conveys the extent to which Healy's assessment of Parnell's relations with Katharine O'Shea was coloured by the belief that Parnell was cynically promiscuous, and the extremes to which Healy and his allies were willing to contemplate carrying the attack on Parnell. Labouchere's letter rather undermines Healy's self-congratulatory remark in his memoirs that Parnell's opponents in the split 'never revealed or made use of the incident, though ruthlessly attacked'.[91] Healy evidently consoled himself with the sanctimonious reflection that he had not abrogated *all* restraint in his attack on Parnell.

15

'Mr. Landlord Parnell': The Fall of a Protestant Patriot

. . . we are very certain that if Mr. Parnell had when a young man determined to follow in his father's steps, and led the life of a useful, active, and industrious resident gentleman and landlord of the county Wicklow, he would be an infinitely happier man today. Whether he thinks so himself or not we cannot tell. Politics, like gaming, are a passion . . . The Irish country gentleman often perhaps sighs to think that he has no part or share in the great game of public life, feeling that he has ideas, purposes, and talents which would be of service to the country if the country would recognise them. We have little doubt that he is a great deal better off where he is, and that an active and useful private life in times like these is the true life for every Irishman of honour and integrity.

Kilkenny Moderator, 6 June 1891

Parnell! What had this man done that all the people were so upset about him, one way or another? The mention of his name always gave rise to a boo or a cheer. The roman catholics who wouldn't let a word be said against him a while ago, now couldn't pick out words villainous enough to describe him; while protestants who were always ashamed of him, now found grace and dignity in the man the roman catholics had put beyond the pale.

Sean O'Casey, *Pictures in the Hallway*[1]

The aspect of the Parnell myth most dangerously susceptible to reversal, from adulation to denigration, was that of Parnell the patriot-aristocrat.

His myth drew heavily on his social origins: early nationalist encomia of Parnell tended to become hackneyed inventories of attributes considered aristocratic. For nationalists before the split, Parnell's social origins and bearing were a source of pride, prompting the *Spectator* to refer to 'the never-ending conflict in most Irish minds between aristocratic prepossessions and Jacobin ideas'.[2]

The *Freeman's Journal* hailed the young Parnell on the occasion of his first contested election in County Dublin in 1874: 'The Irish heart is untainted with socialistic venom. Irishmen pay position and ancient lineage a deference which is equally free from envy and servility. They welcome heartily into their ranks scions of the "good old stock"'.[3] References to the 'good old stock' had become notably less frequent in the intervening years. Healy in the split redefined allegiance to Parnell in terms of servility, and articulated a rhetoric of chauvinistic resentment against Parnell as an Anglo-Irish landlord. Those seigneurial attributes which formed so important a part of the myth were now turned remorselessly against Parnell, and repudiated as traces of an archaic deference.

Parnell's transcendence of the conventional politics of his class was now dismissed as a subterfuge. Healy's anti-modern and chauvinistic deconstruction of Parnell's persona and career — which openly impugned the possibility of achieving such a transcendence — was highly destructive of Parnell's political achievement, as well as damaging to the prospects for a sophisticated praxis of liberal democracy in Ireland.

Healy's relentless characterisation of Parnell as a landlord drew part of its force from a degree of psychological plausibility: like any effective caricature, it maintained a mangled fidelity to its subject. The suggestion that Parnell's formation as a landlord shaped his political technique — so suggestive of fierce intransigence in contractual engagement — as well as his political sensibility may not be altogether without insight. (T. P. O'Connor made the same point somewhat differently: 'He was born for making a bargain. In this respect he reminded me more of an Irish farmer than of an Irish squire'.[4])

This slight *aperçu* was however submerged in the vehemently chauvinistic reductionism of his attack which stripped Parnellism down to a stylised essence of 'landlordism'. Parnell's espousal of nationalism, rather than a historic transcending of provenance, became an endeavour, in the culminating cynicism of his caste, to embrace and divert for his own purposes the nationalist cause. Healy depicted Parnell as engaged in the ultimate act of despoliation, a bid for seisin not of an estate but of the entire Irish nation.

The organising concepts in Healy's attack on Parnell were those of landlord and 'chieftain', coupled in redundant grandiosity. Healy's relentless emphasis on Parnell's landlord provenance is less facile than might appear.

It is central to the split's dialectic that Healy apprehended with perfect lucidity Parnell's political strategy, and divined more clearly than any other contemporary nationalist leader the conflict between the direction of Parnell's policy and the aspirations of conservative Catholic nationalism. Healy rightly perceived in Parnell an enemy of a nation defined in terms of a predominant Catholic nationalist proprietorial order. To him Parnell was a traitor in the camp for reasons which went deeper than the immediate crisis of the split. In devastatingly caricaturing Parnell as the creature and exponent of 'landlordism', Healy was not merely attacking Parnell at what was in terms of domestic Irish politics his most vulnerable point. He was also subverting Parnell's most fragile endeavour, the shaping within the Irish polity of a framework to contain the excesses of Catholic nationalist power.

The attack on Parnell as a landlord had the considerable advantage that, in classifying him by reference to what was an economic function and a social role, it avoided an overtly sectarian attack on Parnell as a Protestant. Up to the split Parnell's Protestantism was an asset rather than a liability. It was an integral aspect of his achievement to have transfigured a potential impediment into a considerable advantage. Parnell's religious profession remained however a latent constraint on his leadership. It did not become an issue against him prior to the split in part because he was seen to be embedded within a matrix of Catholic power. The bulk of the party were Catholic, and the party enjoyed the staunch support of the Irish Catholic church. If Parnell's ascendancy eclipsed the collective stature of his party colleagues, they nevertheless performed a necessary mediating function. They interceded, and explained the ways of Parnell to men. Along with the clergy, they reassured nationalist voters who more readily identified with them socially. In this respect too the edifice of the myth was deceptively fragile, and was seriously destabilised by the loss in the split of the support of the majority of the Irish party and of the Catholic church. Parnell found himself stripped in the split of this defence against the sectarianism implicit in Healy's chauvinistic attack. Parnell's Protestantism was licensed and constrained. He was required to be a Protestant in such a way as not to offend Catholic susceptibilities. It was a condition of his hegemony with which he was unable to comply.

On the market place at Ballinakill in the Kilkenny election, Davitt countered an attack of Parnell: 'If he was miserable scum he had the honour of being a poor evicted peasant's child, and not the descendant of a common Cromwellian soldier'.[5] Healy likewise distinguished the majority, sons of the people, from the ascendancy figure of Parnell:

> They do not own broad acres, or as much land as would sod a lark (*laughter and cheers*). They are not the descendants of one of Cromwell's troopers

> (*applause*). There are no lords and ladies among our ancestors. We belong to the yellow clay, and the blood of the people is in our veins (*applause*). For the people we have lived and worked and fought, and will. Their sorrows are our sorrows, their hopes are our hopes, and their hopes are the hopes of Ireland.[6]

This mode of attack went beyond the conventional rhetoric of Irish elections, and was charged with a new ideological significance. It was a theme to which Healy reverted in later years, declaring in April 1894 'as for myself I am a peasant at heart. I am essentially and radically what you may call a common fellow'.[7] Nationalism was and remains a rhetoric of provenance.

The attack on Parnell's landlord origins, though subsequently most thoroughly developed by Healy, originated with Davitt. In an editorial in the *Labour World* written in a pseudo-socialist chauvinistic vein, Davitt assailed Parnell's landlord mystique:

> Mr. Parnell began his leadership of the Irish people in the Land League movement. He was one of the 'classes'. He was the only aristocrat in the organisation. He was lauded to the skies for having 'stepped down' from his 'social elevation' to head a movement against his own order. To do him justice he did not, at first, play the dictator. He did more than an ordinary man's share of the hard uphill work which the Land League had to go through in 1879 and 1880 . . . But it was not *the man* who was praised for his labour. It was the landlord, the 'superior' being, the member of the 'upper tier' who had espoused the cause of the people. To him all praise was given. Power followed praise, and in a short time Parnellism became a substitute for Nationalism, and the movement which began upon a principle and popular right became the political property of Charles Stewart Parnell . . . Parnellism or Personalism reigned supreme in Irish national politics down to the day when, in the proceedings of a filthy divorce case, the 'chief', the aristocrat, the man of 'social elevation', was shown to be a true member of his class and a leader who cared more for a 'Saxon smile' than for Irish independence.[8]

In denouncing the former Parnellite cult of personality, Davitt was implicitly criticising Healy and other anti-Parnellites for a practice which Davitt had always deprecated in the name of radical democracy, a consideration which rendered all the more striking their political collaboration in the split.

Healy sought to counter the instinct of allegiance to Parnell by inculcating an ideological revulsion. He ceaselessly insinuated a heightened Catholic nationalist self-consciousness. Allegiance to Parnell he derided as an archaic and demeaning act of deference to the Irish *ancien régime*: Parnellism was the perpetuation of Ascendancy by other means. He reduced Parnell's campaign in the split to an attempt to exploit social privilege, and to undermine the faith of the people in those who should be their natural leaders:

> One sad thing to me in the present situation is this – that some of our countrymen seem more inclined to believe the statements of a landlord, an aristocrat, and a Cromwellian, than they do those made by people of their own flesh and blood, of their own class, of their own thoughts and ways who were never false to them and with whom no fault could be found until they set aside an impossible politician. Yes, but we are told we are placehunters. We dwell amongst our own people. We don't live at Brighton or Eltham (*laughter and applause*). We live here in the city of Dublin, we look our friends and neighbours in the face, and we are not ashamed to look them in the face.[9]

In abusing him as 'a landlord, an aristocrat, and a Cromwellian', Healy stigmatised Parnell as an economic, social, and racial alien. He denounced the 'lack of democratic fibre' of Parnell's supporters, whose perverse allegiance he ascribed to their ineradicable obsequiousness:

> Because if they did not believe that this man was made of superior clay to themselves, that he was a 'gentleman', that he was a landlord, that he was a Protestant, would they for one moment have tolerated a dissentionist campaign. Would your fathers have tolerated it in a greater man than Daniel O'Connell?[10]

This was a repeated refrain of Healy's rhetoric. He denounced the suggestion that 'the masses of the Irish people could get no honest man to lead them or help them unless he had the blue blood of Cromwell's troopers in his veins': 'Black and bitter would be the day for Ireland when the landlords could infuse into the hearts of the Irish people this idea that, if they sent men of their own rank, stamp and condition of life into the House of Commons, they must necessarily be corrupted, and that they must only put their trust in landlords or the like of them'.[11] The anti-Parnellites repudiated what they identified as an anti-nationalist spirit of obeisance. William Martin Murphy later asserted that 'the rock on which we split in 1890 was in my opinion the fact that we were in the habit of looking up to this man as a sort of superior being whose will and views were not to be contested for one moment'.[12]

In the Carlow election, Healy sought to deflect the taunt of Whiggery by invoking against Parnell a Catholic nationalist solidarity of shared historical grievance:

> Upon what evidence is that charge made against us (*hear hear*), the sons of the people in whose heart flows the blood of the people, who have

> been cradled and crooned amongst popular traditions, who knew the wrongs of the people, whose sorrows are our sorrows, and whose anticipations and whose hopes are ours.
>
> If you are Irishmen I am Irish too (*hear hear*). If you are the sons of the people, my father was a poor man (*cheers*). If you have known oppression in your family so have I (*hear hear*). If your people have suffered wrongs from a British Government so have mine.[13]

In South Armagh in March Healy deepened the polarisation between Parnell 'with his blue blood', and the 'men like myself sprung from the people, who know what the grievances and the sorrows of the Irish people are . . . the humble men opposed to him'. He sharply differentiated the 'great Celtic race' from the Anglo-Irish, and assaulted Parnell as a patriotic *parvenu:*

> We who have been born amongst you, whose sorrows have been part of our lives, whose oppressions have fired our hearts, whose blood is in our veins, and belong to the great Celtic race that held this island before Cromwell or Parnell's ancestors ever came here, and who, please God, will hold it again before long (*cheers*), to tell us that we, the men of the people, are going to sell the people, to take place or pension from the British Government, I tell him that, from every platform on which I stand, I will cram that filthy lie down his throat (*cheers*) . . . I tell him and you that this cause was dear to us before ever the name of Parnell was dreamt of; I tell him we had not to go to school at Avondale to learn the miseries and sufferings of the Irish people; I tell him I am a man who cares less for the Saxon smile than he does.[14]

Healy visited upon Parnell the full weight of his own sense of grievance at the uprootedness of his childhood and the dispossession of his ancestors, which was invariably exacerbated – if it was not brought into existence – by the contemplation of Parnell's social origins and bearing. This vein of rhetoric not only conformed to Healy's political purpose, but fulfilled an emotional need to give form and coherence to his own fractured sense of identity.

The corollary of the casting out of Parnell was the celebration of the superior legitimacy of a leadership 'sprung from the people'. This marked the culmination of the rhetoric of the soil which Healy had devised in the preceding decade. The political nation was defined to comprise those who belonged, or were rhetorically assimilable, to the tenant class: those who were 'Irish of the Irish', who belonged to 'the great Celtic race'. In practical terms that meant Catholic nationalists. This contrived opposition between Parnell as the landlord-aristocrat and a cadre of political leaders 'sprung from the people' was central not merely to the legitimation of the anti-Parnellite political leadership, but to the consolidation of the conservative proprietorial order which the land movement was to bring about.

The line of argument was taken up by other anti-Parnellite apologists. The *Nation* declared, in what was a rare allusion to Parnell's accent as well as to his time at Magdalene College, that the voters of North Sligo would 'permit no ambitious aristocrat, listing the adjectives at Billingsgate in the accents of a Cambridge snob, to undo their trust in the honest, poor men, bone of their bone and flesh of their flesh who are toiling and slaving for Ireland while their abuser was dallying at Eltham'.[15]

Parnell was assailed as a political *arriviste* who had usurped a venerable tradition. In a characteristically fungous reworking of a Burkean image by the least Burkean of conservatives, the *National Press* declared in Healy's distinctive accents: 'the mushrooms of yesterday now vent their exhalations on the secular oaks of the forest. Mr. C. S. Parnell, who was first heard of in 1874, seems to imagine that Irish history began in that year'. The editorial proceeded to deride Parnell's appeals to '"the young men" who have not had the opportunity of studying Irish history, and who believe with Mr. Parnell that Irish nationality was cradled in Avondale'.[16]

The adaptability of this popular chauvinist idiom is well evidenced in Healy's response to Parnellite attacks on him as a barrister. To the charge of placehunting levelled against him by Parnell, Healy retorted by coupling a denunciation of Parnell as an alien aristocrat with a litany of patriotic barristers:

> It was the profession of Daniel O'Connell, of Isaac Butt, of Thomas Davis, of Philpot Curran, and I tell you this – if the people of Ireland believe the word of this landlord Cromwellian aristocrat, that they can get no son of the people, no son of God to act honestly and fairly by them, that they cannot trust such men in Parliament, I say the sooner you put yourselves under the neck of despotism the better.[17]

Healy thereby adroitly upheld his own status as a barrister in the natural governing stratum of nationalism. His ambitiousness and the rise of a Catholic nationalist proprietorial, professional and commercial class were inextricably bound up: his measuring himself up against Parnell itself represented a critical ideological moment.

It is one of the ironies of anti-Parnellism that Healy and others had recourse to what had been a standing unionist taunt against Parnell, that he was an oppressive landlord. That avid student of Parnellism, Richard Pigott, had in 1885 described Parnell as 'an evicting landlord', while an Irish unionist organisation attacked Parnell as 'a landlord and a landgrabber'.[18] The charges were false and unfair. Parnell's excesses as a landlord were rather of indulgence than severity.[19] Undeterred, Healy charged Parnell in January 1891 with having sought to eject a tenant at the previous

Wicklow quarter sessions (Parnell had in fact not instituted ejectment proceedings, but had commenced an action for arrears of rent against a substantial tenant farmer). In mock-parliamentary mode, Healy declared he would ask Balfour to provide a return of the number of ejectments brought by Parnell in Wicklow in the previous decade.[20]

Upon Parnell in the split were visited the sins of his caste. Nothing touching Parnell's landlord associations was overlooked. When Parnell suggested that he had applied the monies received by him for public purposes, the *National Press* responded by resurrecting an issue almost overlooked at the time: 'Probably the only public subscription anyone remembers from Mr. Parnell is the £1 from Kilmainham in 1881 to the Wicklow Hunt, when the country, to avenge the suspects, declared against foxhunting'.[21]

The public policy and private foibles of Parnell alike were ascribed to his social antecedents. Healy mocked 'Mr. Landlord Parnell'. The *National Press* denounced 'Mr. Parnell's aristocratic ambition', and inveighed against 'the inborn rascality of Mr. Charles Stewart Parnell'.[22] Patrick O'Donnell, Bishop of Raphoe, warned his flock against 'slippery lordlings of the pale'. Healy portrayed Parnell's treatment of the parliamentary majority in Committee Room 15 as paradigmatic of the relationship of landlord and tenant:

> He thought he was dealing with chessmen, with pawns, when he was dealing with eighty-five men of flesh and blood; he thought the birth of Parnell was Year One of Irish Nationality; he thought he had got a lease of all our souls and the Fee Simple of all Ireland, and that we, his serfs, should prefer his personality to the cause we had at heart.[23]

Of Parnell's dismissal of the majority of the party, Healy commented: 'well I suppose he can quarry a lot more men like us out of the quarries at Avondale'.[24]

Healy's taunt of arrogance against Parnell drew in part on what William O'Brien called 'the silliest of all the ignorant legends that have gathered round Parnell's name . . . that of his scornful masterfulness in dealing with his own lieutenants'. T. P. O'Connor wrote that Parnell was always 'intensely popular' with the party because he was always considerate. Healy himself in his memoirs exonerated Parnell from the charge of scornful discourtesy, writing that 'nothing in his personal dealings savoured of arrogance'.[25]

Parnell's pursuit in the split of a policy of constructive engagement with the Conservative ministry afforded Healy the opportunity to charge Parnell with reverting to type in adopting a policy true to his social origins. The allegation that Parnell was providing succour to an anti-nationalist administration, not alone by sundering the nationalist ranks and assailing Gladstone, but through an active sympathy with Conservative policy, gave Healy's taunt of 'landlordism' its cutting edge. Parnell he assailed as an ally of Balfour and of the Orange Order in Ireland. Healy declared of Parnell that 'having begun in a divorce court he would end up in an Orange Lodge'.[26] Parnell 'had simply become a Tory and Orange agent'.[27] 'Parnellism', declared the *National Press*, 'is copperfastened to Balfourism.'[28] The unifying thread of Parnell's attacks on the Liberals, and his heterodox land programme, was asserted to be an affinity with Toryism bred of caste: the *National Press* litanised 'Mr. Parnell the factionist, Mr. Parnell the "independent opponent" of the British Home Rulers, Mr. Parnell the panegyricist of Mr. Balfour's elbow, and Mr. Parnell the advocate of the land thieves' right to two thirds of Ireland'.[29]

Healy's polemical instinct was sure. The split revealed Parnell's vulnerability to crude reductionism. A naive rhetoric which lauded Parnell's selflessness and transcendence of social caste gave way to a restless querying of his motivation. The destruction of his former myth exposed him to an inquisition into his patriotism and reasons for entering public life which had previously been confined to unionist critics. The divorce crisis and the fall of Parnell prompted a stream of dubious attempts to identify the residues of caste or the roots of the psychological drive which might be supposed to have impelled him into Irish public life. This has survived in problematic efforts in modern historiography to deconstruct Parnell as a study in 'marginalised Irishness', or to comprehend his agrarian politics as moulded primarily by a determination to salvage the role of the southern Anglo-Irish class into which he was born.[30] Rarely has the vocation of a public man been subject to such persistent and unprofitable speculative enquiry.

In the anti-Parnellite canon the subjective intent and the objective effect of Parnellism alike were inimical to the interests of nationalism. Healy satirically alleged a 'Treaty of Brighton', one of whose articles was that, as a quid pro quo for Parnell bringing about the collapse of the Plan of Campaign, a Tory would not be run in Cork, so as not to split Parnell's vote in what had become for him a marginal seat.[31] At Newry Healy declared:

> You know that the Orangemen here are mad for Parnell. You feel it in the air. I expect that instead of the effigy of King William crossing the Boyne there will be a medal struck for the next Twelfth of July to be worn on every Orange breast: 'Parnell descending from the fire-escape'.[32]

Tory gratification afforded the measure of Parnell's treason. Healy insisted that 'the history of Parnellism will be written in the actions and expressions of the landlord and Tory party and their press, and . . . had we no other map to guide us that chart would be sufficient'.[33]

Healy's assault on Parnell as a landlord marks the culmination of his agrarian rhetoric of the preceding decade, and derives much of its force from its intimation of the waning of landlord power. His attack on Parnell was charged with the gathering strength and incipient triumphalism of the drive for proprietorship. Parnell's ten-year hegemony straddled a decisive shift in social power in Ireland. His fall became an allegory of the decline of the Anglo-Irish. The once acclaimed and supposedly omnipotent nationalist leader was derided as merely the most cunning representative of a weak and declining order. The split thus becomes an incident in the struggle for the land, and marks the explosive fusion of Healy's agrarian rhetoric in the 1880s with his increasingly ill-suppressed antagonism to Parnell. The fight against the landlords and British power had been a rehearsal for the ousting of Parnell: in a brutal revolutionary irony, Parnell became the victim of the struggle he had led, the Robespierre of the Irish land struggle.

Healy's rhetoric marked an intensification of the attack on the Anglo-Irish landlord class, a calculated aggravation in the contest for supremacy between landlord and tenant. The attack on Parnell became an essay in the heightening of the agrarian nationalist consciousness. Healy's rhetoric here reaches a pitch of intensity, reflecting the exactitude of the correspondence between his agrarian politics and his personal and political antipathy to Parnell, which gives his rhetoric its astonishing vigour. His anti-landlord rhetoric, which had been in the 1880s a stylised threat, crystallised in the anathematisation of the Anglo-Irish leader. Healy's language coupled sectarian levelling with proprietorial hankerings. His idiom reflected the *mauvaise foi* of his nationalism, the ugly contradictoriness of a politics which pursued a proprietorial solution to the land question through a virulent, pseudo-revolutionary chauvinism.

An abiding resentment of Anglo-Irish dispossession informed Healy's nationalism: 'Let us never forget that this is a small country, somewhat divided against itself by reason of the Plantation, cunningly devised two centuries ago, [which] has placed over a large space of our area a body of sturdy and intelligent men opposed to us in blood, in religion and I fear in patriotism.'[34] The key epithet is 'sturdy'. Healy dismissed any suggestion that the Anglo-Irish were vulnerable in the face of gathering nationalist triumph. Of Ulster unionist apprehensions regarding the second home rule bill, Healy was to declare in 1893:

> The way they speak of the Protestant religion you would think it was a piece of old crockery, a piece of small china, something so extremely delicate and fragile so that it would not bear the smallest handling. All the Protestants I have ever met in England have taken a pretty sturdy view of their religion.[35]

His peremptory dismissal of the threat to the intact survival of the unionist community in Ireland, and of the risk of sectarian predominance, was in marked contrast to the sense of the fragility of the Irish socio-economic equilibrium, and of the need to contain the preponderance of Catholic nationalist power, which informed Parnell's political course before and throughout the split. Healy looked openly to a *revanchiste* Catholic ascendancy.

Healy's rhetoric in the split marks a significant point in the transition from a rhetoric of nationalist revolt against English power to the politics of conservative nationalist resistance to the encroachment of centralised *nationalist* political authority. A systematic weakening of the authority of the nationalist leadership in relation to the emergent nationalist social order was implicit in Healy's argument.

Healy ceaselessly asserted the superior democratic credentials of the anti-Parnellite majority: 'Our offices are held from the constituencies. We are the representatives of the people'.[36] Their mandate derived from 'the common verdict of the common people'.[37] This democratic commitment contrasted with Parnell's attitude: 'After you have dug his political grave wider and deeper than even Sligo and Kilkenny did, he will go back and say "I don't care a snuff about Carlow" . . . Our position is very different from that of the Parnellites. We believe in the people'.[38] Healy championed an anti-Parnellite plebiscitary democracy. The *National Press* assessed the work facing the post-Parnellite Irish democracy, 'having scourged these creatures into obscurity':

> Conventions must be held. The country must learn to inform itself on the great issues that arise. No one man – no number of men – can make themselves absolute procurators or plenipotentiaries again. The mind of the country must be consulted by a veritable *referendum* on all great questions.[39]

Healy looked to mobilise Irish democracy for the next general election, urging his countrymen 'not to pause or stay until each man makes himself a centre of propaganda in his own community or district'.[40]

Healy declared of the party that 'my action in taking the stand I have done against its destruction is the greatest homage I could pay to the power of the people who created it'.[41] He proclaimed the Irish party 'the microcosm of the nation'. It was 'an instrument of wise, patient contrivance which took twelve long years to bring to perfection', and which Liberals and Conservatives had been compelled to respect. 'Organisation has been the main secret of Ireland's wonderful success in political warfare, for the last ten years.'[42] Healy's argument was that the political achievement of the previous decade was brought about by national unity rather than by the leadership of Parnell, who had at most provided its facilitating myth.

Healy's most ringing formulation of this proposition was at Belfast:

> The only safety then is in unity, and if Parnell embodies the courage of Brian Boru, the heroism of Sarsfield, and the self-sacrifice of Robert Emmet (*cheers*) – and takes his stand outside our party, and draws his sword against it, then we will draw ours against him (*loud and prolonged cheers*). For my part, I would rather be honestly wrong with the majority than factionally right with the minority. If it was only to vindicate this principle of the majority binding the minority I would fight Parnellism to the death.[43]

Healy's entire subsequent career violated this principle. After the death of Parnell Healy was almost invariably to proclaim himself 'factionally right with the minority'. What his later career revealed was that his predominant allegiance was to conservative Catholic proprietorial values rather than to the will of the majority of the Irish party. With the death of Parnell, the temporary conjuncture of parliamentary majority rule and conservative nationalism collapsed, and with it fractured the semblance of coherence of Healy's political creed in the split.

He systematically misrepresented the nomination system under Parnell's leadership, both as a crude device of Parnell's personal hegemony (the *National Press* proclaimed 'the *congé d'élire* from Eltham is a thing of the past'[44]), and as having an intrinsic aristocratic bias. At the Carlow convention, proclaiming that 'the days of nominees and dictators are past and gone', Healy enjoined the delegates to 'choose from amongst your ranks a man you know to be a man of rectitude, and honour, of good faith, be he the humblest man that walks, aye that sweeps the streets, and we ask no quality in him except the quality of fidelity to the Irish cause and ability to pursue it'. The way to select a member of parliament was 'to take an honest man with whom you have lived all your lives, against whose honour and probity no one can point the finger of scorn'.[45]

At the Maryborough convention, Healy, proclaiming the superiority of modest decency over aristocratic allure, denounced 'the humbug of old times that a Member of Parliament or a candidate was supposed to be a man with lackeys and attendants with gold lace round their hats'.[46] He anecdotally developed this spurious populism in a speech in April 1892. He claimed that Alexander Blaine, the member for South Armagh 1885–92, who was a Parnellite in the split, was the only man he had ever selected, having seen him up a ladder at the end of the hall at the convention. When he arrived in Dublin afterwards 'Mr. Parnell saluted me with "Healy, who the devil is this tailor you have brought in amongst us?" Well I was annoyed at Mr. Parnell for throwing a needless slur on a decent man because he worked a trade'.[47]

The essential attributes of a candidate in Healy's dispensation were representativeness and susceptibility to local influence. Criticising a number of Parnellite members as persons 'who have no root or foothold or grip in the Irish soil at all, who are not racy of it, who have not a trace of its honest earth upon them', he urged his audience at the Maryborough convention to 'get men who will be influencable by their neighbourhood and environment'.[48] This theme, presaging his later championship of constituency rights against the 'bossism' of the Irish party leadership, was to provide a central thread of continuity in Healy's career.

16

The Fenian Chieftain

If Home Rule comes in my day I shall have only one thing to ask of the new Parliament in Dublin. I shall propose that its first act be to purchase a large site on some sunny and picturesque slope of the Wicklow hills, and erect upon it a commodious asylum with a pleasant southern aspect, and build around that a high wall with spikes and broken glass on the top, and then put inside all the heroes and geniuses of Ireland. When this has been done, and I have seen the outer gate securely bolted, and can walk away with the key in my pocket, I shall for the first time have some faith in the future of my country.

A 'prominent Irishman' (T. M. Healy?) to Harold Frederic, during the Boulogne negotiations[1]

One man may go wrong. One man may get into the divorce court (*cheers*) . . . One man may go mad, one man may betray you . . . One man among the twelve apostles went wrong. The mass of men stood firm and we stand by the principle that only by the reliance and guidance of the great body of the people can the nation be brought right or the Home Rule achieved.

T. M. Healy, 22 March 1891[2]

. . . in Forum Foster I demosthrenated my folksfiendship, enmy pupuls felt my burk was no worse than their brite: Sapphrageta and Consciencia were undecidedly attached to me but the maugher machrees and the auntieparthenopes my schwalby words with litted spongelets set their soakye pokeys and botchbons afume: Fletcher-Flemmings,

> elisaboth, how interquackeringly they rogated me, their golden one, I unhesitant made replique: Mesdememdes to leursieuresponsor: and who in hillsaide, don't you let flyfire till you see their whites of the bunkers' eyes!
>
> James Joyce, *Finnegans Wake*[3]

Healy brilliantly derided the Parnellite cult of the leader in a parodic rhetoric of 'chieftaincy', a superb comic device which fused in mockery Parnell's own strength of will and the more preposterous accolades of his supporters. He devastatingly ridiculed Parnell's politics in the split as the anachronistic pseudo-Fenian posturing of an Anglo-Irish leader in an epoch of constitutional nationalism. He proclaimed the redundancy of the nationalist hero. He castigated what he asserted to be the Irish habit of exaggerated and uncritical allegiance to the leader. The *National Press* asserted that 'our fervid Celtic imagination leads us too easily into habits of deification and leader worship', and declared that 'Ireland has suffered enough in the past through infatuated loyalty'.[4]

The argument was in part prudential. Healy warned: 'Never again put all your eggs into one basket. Parnell was trusted as no man ever was trusted, and he suffered from a swelled head. Like Lucifer his pride became so great that he thought he was greater than all the rest of Ireland together'.[5] His most sustained and striking development of the theme was in a speech in Dublin in June in which he resoundingly proclaimed Parnell's dispensability:

> Now who was Gladstone and who was Parnell? Do you care a thraneen for any man, be he Parnell or Gladstone or Michelangelo? These men are but names to you. You see their pictures, it may be, on the wall, but what are they to you – the men who live by wages, the men who work with their hands? What you have to consider are not men, but principles (*hear hear*). Gladstone only embodied the idea of the democratic movement in England, Parnell only embodied a similar principle in Ireland; the two were working together, they had come into an alliance. Mr. Gladstone committed one undoubted crime. He did not believe in 'an only possible leader' (*laughter*). He conceived that the Irish people had sufficient pith and brawn in their land that among their 85 or 86 representatives or elsewhere they were not so bankrupt and poverty stricken that, on the eve of victory they could not get a single man out of the Irish race – a race which has produced so many generals and captains, commanders and statesmen – to take the place of a man who after all has only recently come upon the surface of Irish affairs (*applause*). Mr. Gladstone is fond of Homer and probably remembered that 'there were great men before Agamemnon', and thought there would be leaders after Mr. Parnell.[6]

Shortly after Parnell's death Healy declared Ireland to be greater than the sum of her heroes: 'I say O'Connell is gone; Emmet is gone; Fitzgerald is gone; Owen Roe is gone; Brian Boru is gone and the Irish cause lives on immortal and eternal'.[7] T. D. Sullivan likewise was affronted by the suggestion that Ireland, fecund genetrix of saints and statesmen, was now so barren as to have in Parnell its only begotten leader:

> No: it is the old land, the mother of statesmen, of orators, of heroes, of sages, and of saints – the mother of sons great in every domain in intellect and of action (*cheers*). This dear old motherland of ours has not come down to that wretched pitch that one man, and one man only, can lead us and save us (*applause*).[8]

The *National Press* asserted that 'no man is necessary to a nation', and Healy declined as he put it 'to sell my country for a mess of potage, or a cartload of Charles Stewart Parnells'.[9]

Healy savagely ridiculed the residual allegiance to Parnell, and reduced it to the instinct of deference, bred of a political culture debilitated by dispossession and degradation. In contrast to the robust shrewdness of the majority, the Parnellites remained abjectly gullible, sunk in the darkness of servitude. A piece of anti-Parnellite doggerel, the pithiness of which suggests Healy's authorship, went:

> No wonder that tyrants should rule them,
> And drill them, and drub them, and school them,
> When, up to their eyes,
> With the thinnest of lies,
> A shameless seducer can fool them.[10]

The shifts of the discredited leader in decline revealed and compounded the abasement of the Parnellites: 'is there no indignity that can stir them? Are they prepared to eat illimitable dirt in his service?' Theirs was an infinite gullibility: 'convict him of a lie and their faith is no wise disturbed – they wait wide-jawed for the next, with an avaricious swallow like a shark's'.[11]

On the eve of Parnell's death, the *National Press* denounced 'the scribblers who are now exhausting the dictionary of adulation towards him'.[12] The paper assailed not merely the Parnellite doctrine of 'chieftaincy', but its mode of dissemination, as revealingly archaic. Confident of its own strength and backed by the preponderance of the provincial press, the paper wrote mockingly that 'the latest method of Parnellite propaganda is the leaflet and the tract. We understand the merits of the "chief" are now being brought home to the recalcitrant masses by the means hitherto appropriated in this country to the diffusion of Mrs. Smyly's theology'.[13] The thrust was in part sectarian (the discerning nostrils of the *National Press* detected the 'odour of "soup"'). It also conveyed a suggestion of the obsolescence of Parnell's method of campaigning, over-reliant on his personal charisma and exertions, and taunted Parnell with his abiding failure to achieve a populist journalistic voice, or an organisation, to compare with that of the anti-Parnellites. A *Freeman's Journal* headline during the Carlow election which ran 'Dastardly Attack by Whigs'[14] was representative, and hardly likely to elicit the intended wave of national indignation. Like many Parnellite publicists, the sub-editors of the *Freeman's Journal* too often gave the impression of inhabiting an archaic era of patriotic gallantry and mannered prose. Having started on an unsustainably high note, the *Freeman's* aria became tiresomely shrill as Parnell's fortunes waned.

In one of the central conjunctures of his rhetoric, Healy coupled his attack on Parnell's imputed pretensions to dictatorship, with that on his 'appeal to the hillsides', to accuse him of abdicating his responsibilities as a constitutional politician. He asserted that Parnell, once the greatest champion of parliamentary nationalism, had become its most formidable adversary. His charge that Parnell had resiled from the principle of constitutional action raises a delicate issue of interpretation. In one of the great, and flawed, themes of his rhetoric, Healy restated the premises of constitutional action with unrivalled boldness and clarity. His forthright deprecation of the rhetoric of physical force was however marred by a deeply partisan purpose which involved a calculated travesty of Parnell's position.

Healy deliberately and systematically confused constitutional action with sustaining the Liberal alliance, as in his declaration: 'The cause of Ireland depended on our winning at the next election the support of the English people. You have no cannon, no arms, you have only votes'.[15] To the Parnellite contention that there existed a leadership of the Irish nation which remained vested in Parnell, quite apart from the disputed issue of the chairmanship of the Irish party, Healy responded with sharp and telling mockery:

> I saw Mr. Parnell claimed to have his commission from the Irish race. If he had he holds it. We sought only to depose him from the sessional chairmanship – but we had no authority to depose him from the leadership of the Irish race. That power is resident in the Irish race and if there exists, in nubibus or anywhere, such a post as leadership of the Irish race, it is in no way infringed or touched by the attempt of the Irish party to come to a decision. The decision left the hillside intact. Valley, field and mountain would still afford platforms to Mr. Parnell from which he could appeal against us to the Irish race.[16]

The last two sentences, dismissing Parnell's 'leadership of the Irish nation' as a quasi-Fenian conceit incompatible with parliamentary action, reflect Healy's peculiar genius as a rhetorician. He depicted Parnell as an extra-parliamentary outlaw on his keep, and reduced Parnellism to a mock-insurgency on the periphery of Irish politics.

In his attack on Parnell, Healy fused 'physical force' in the Fenian sense with what he condemned as the undercurrent of violence in Parnell's campaign to reconstitute his authority: 'One of the saddest changes that has come over the former leader of the Irish people is his absolute appeal everywhere to force, his unwillingness to allow these questions to be argued out before the people. So that everywhere that Parnellism goes like the march of the Ottoman army, there you have dislocation and devastation'.[17] In a shrewd but partial assessment of Parnell's political argument, Healy insisted that it was the Parnellites who had deliberately misstated the issue of the split:

> Observe the cunning of what has been done. The question at issue between the two parties is purely and simply a question of parliamentary procedure. It is not the question which split up the ranks of the Old Ireland and the Young Irelanders of 1848; it is not a question of physical force against moral force. Yet these men cunningly go about using the words of treason and rebellion and of the hillsider – masquerading as Robert Emmets and Lord Edwards (*laughter and applause*) and all the time they have no intention whatever as one of them declared in Edinburgh of bringing their heads within measurable distance of a policeman's baton (*laughter*); and I say that the most remarkable incident in the whole affair is that the spurious and bastard claptrap used by men who have no intention whatever of joining a secret society, or of heading a secret society, or of even becoming one of the drill sergeants of a hillside society, should be used on a purely parliamentary question.[18]

Healy's attack was at its most compelling when directed at what he decried as Parnell's subverting of his own achievement by forsaking constitutional principles. The *Insuppressible* charged that Parnell 'strives for his own purpose, to turn people back from the straight road which, as he taught, leads straight to national self-government, to turn them back once more from the very frontier of the promised land to bleak hopeless desert in which the nation had wandered for several centuries'.[19] Healy denounced what he asserted to be Parnell's abrogation of his responsibilities as a parliamentarian politician:

> I arraign that man as a traitor to his country, not because he makes and demands as a separatist the demands of Robert Emmet, Wolfe Tone, Lord Edward Fitzgerald, or Mitchel or Martin, but because – having waived

> these demands, having committed himself to a parliamentary policy, and knowing the length and breadth to which the policy can take us — he is now engaged in an endeavour to smash and ruin that policy and going back to these cries, which he knows are the merest clap-trap, to deceive the unfortunate people.[20]

In a forceful editorial in Healy's distinctive style, the *National Press* derided bombastic Parnellite invocations of Wolfe Tone and Robert Emmet, and proclaimed the redundancy of the 'great man' in the epoch of constitutional politics, of a native modality of power:

> It is worth living for to see the mind of Ireland liberated, to see here public men widely recognising that the age of traumaturgists and hierophants is gone . . . No man is necessary to a nation . . . We have not yet learned political perspective. The scaffold does not loom in the path of the patriot . . . we have fallen upon easier times than those of the Emmets and the Wolfe Tones, and it is the most silly and sickening histrionic frothing to talk (as Parnell and his merry men are talking) of sunbursts, and battle axes, and Brian Boru, and hillside operations, and readiness to face death and danger on the floor of the House of Commons or on the election hustings. We must get away from all that absurd talk and sanguinary declamation. We think Ireland is heartily sick of it.[21]

In a skilfully contrived juxtaposition of Parnell's pre-split and post-split positions, Healy charged Parnell with cynical opportunism:

> Parnell would have taken the very smallest measure he could have got. If he could have got a Vestry he would have called it a repeal of the Union. If he had a county council he would have called it Grattan's Parliament. That was the temper and tone of the man.

Yet this was the man who 'suddenly to the surprise of everybody blossomed forth as a hillside man. Nothing would do him now but the sword of Robert Emmet, the gibbet of Wolfe Tone, the arms of Owen Roe, and the trumpet call of "Ireland a Nation"'.[22]

The *Insuppressible* dismissed Fenianism as a phenomenon of the past, the creed of 'the gallant men and true, who, in the desperate old days, risked life and liberty for Ireland', which had no relevance for contemporary politics: 'It is quite safe now to express the utmost sympathy with physical force. A man may walk down O'Connell Street at noon and proclaim himself a Fenian to every policeman he meets, and yet provoke only a good-humoured smile'.[23] Healy damagingly mocked Parnell's high patriotic rhetoric as theatrical extravagance. He denounced 'these blood and thunder declarations which stage Irishmen and stage politicians have become famous for', and accused Parnell of distributing money and drink among the poor 'in the name of Wolfe Tone and Robert Emmet, and all of the other great patriots in the Irish lead role'.[24]

Healy maintained after Parnell's death his attack on what he charged to be the Fenianesque posturing of Parnellism. He warned of the perils of a facile Parnellite rhetoric which affected an extreme nationalism: 'What could be more easy for some nobody in the House of Commons than to get up and declare that this is not a Bill which Brian Boru would accept and then go back to his constituents in Ballyhooley?'[25] He would prefer 'to be a member of a party in which each individual is prepared to subordinate his own views, however intelligent he may be, however like Robert Emmet he may be, no matter how many pikes he may have buried in his barnyard'.[26] Of the Parnellites he mockingly declared: 'They may be the most honest men in the world, they may be all as they describe themselves – incorruptible patriotic unassailable compounds of Robert Emmet and Wolfe Tone with their blood composed of a kind of Bovril of all the ancient heroes of Ireland', but they had broken their parliamentary pledge. He taunted William Redmond with 'giving tips to Sarsfield'.[27]

The extravagance of Parnellite rhetoric prompted some of Healy's most inspired comic sallies. When it was proposed to summon a convention of nationalist literary societies, the *National Press* in Healy's distinctive accents wrote in brilliant mockery that what Parnellism needed was a 'Parnell Theosophical Society':

> We imagine it would catch on, and, at any rate, it would be highly in season just now . . . Perhaps Madame Blavatsky might revisit the glimpses of the moon . . . and preconise our Only Possible Leader. Failing her dear soul there is Mrs. Besant still in the flesh. She has no sour Nonconformist Conscience, and she might, at least, bring us a holograph message from Malachi of the Collar of Gold on Wicklow Mining, or from Art McMurrough, on the divorce case. Plainly then, Theosophy is the one thing remaining to galvanise Parnellism.[28]

The dissolving of the rhetoric of chieftaincy into the voguish mumbo-jumbo of theosophy in its Celtic variant (conceived in part as a jab at the young and still comparatively unknown W. B. Yeats who, in collaboration with John O'Leary, was organising in the Parnellite interest a convention of literary societies) reveals the astonishing alertness of Healy's rhetorical imagination.

Healy derided Parnell's 'appeal to the hillsides' as just one item in a speciously radical programme. He warned 'the extreme element to whom Mr. Parnell is sending round the fiery cross for support' of Parnell's insincerity in espousing 'the ignis fatuus of a republic today and some other cry tomorrow' to attract their support, 'because he figures as a universal provider — labourers, gasworkers, republicans, he has some will o' the wisp to lure them all'.[29]

He denounced the Parnellite corruption of the young: 'no more subtle poison was ever sought to be instilled into the young than that which now drops from the tongues of Parnellite missionaries'.[30] The anti-Parnellites drew on the conventional prudential argument against young men being lured into Fenian activity, unmindful of the risk posed by informers. Thus the *National Press* commented of Parnell: 'he has a number of people not old enough to remember Carey, whose minds cannot even go back to the betrayal which followed the Phoenix Park murders'.[31] Healy played on the spectre of the informer: 'Did Mr. Parnell pretend that he was going to lead the people to insurrection with some Major Le Caron behind, as Jack in the Box?'[32]

Healy posited a malign compact between Parnell and the Fenians, allied in a destructive purpose: 'Is it likely that Mr. Parnell would continue to be supported by the very men who have always been his enemies, who have been the bitterest antagonists of constitutional agitation, if it was not because he had now made himself the most potent leader to destroy the Parliamentary movement?' By asserting that Parnell's coquetting with Fenianism was entirely opportunistic, Healy could without contradiction enquire how, given the Fenian commitment to separatism, 'any self-respecting hillside man could throw in his support for Mr. Parnell upon any ground of principle'.[33]

Healy accused Parnell of cynical allusiveness, of a reckless trafficking in ambiguities. The *National Press* denounced 'Mr. Parnell's purposeless prattle about a Republic'.[34] 'Mr. Parnell has no policy except Mr. Parnell', it declared: 'he has vaguely indicated an insurrection and a Republic'.[35] Parnell's was the opportunism of desperation: 'He has no policy, he has no prospects. The wild talk of an appeal to physical force, such promises, for example as that he will make a republic of Royal Meath, are not madness in him but dishonesty'.[36] The *Insuppressible*, exaggerating and misrepresenting Parnell's 'appeal to the hillsides', professed to call his bluff:

> What does it all mean, this talk of the hillside men and the battlefield? Will Parnell speak out — or rather speak plainly — and tell us what are the ways and means on which he relies? Will he dress in a green uniform, make pikeheads out of the iron mines of Avondale, and lead the hillside men to the hills? If not, his vague incitements are a sham.[37]

The majority sought to expose Parnell's 'hollow imposture'[38] by contrasting his earlier deprecations of physical force. John Barry told his constituents that in former years Parnell 'never spoke of the Fenians except in terms of undisguised contempt'.[39] William Martin Murphy pointed to Parnell's disavowal of Fenianism at the Special Commission: 'Mr. Parnell was examined in the Commission Court in London and he swore till he was black in the face that he never made the "last link" speech, but he was going around the country making no end of last link speeches to boys who scarcely remember Carey'.[40] While Archbishop Croke archly referred to 'a featherbed hillsideman', by implication Parnell, the *National Press* questioned the combat credentials of the neurasthenic adulterer: 'of one thing, at least, we may be certain, he will never hurt those delicate hands of his by handling a pike, or endanger what is affectionately described as "his precious health" by being inside a prison'. 'He got into prison once by accident', wrote the *Weekly National Press*, 'and he stooped so low as to implore the intercession of Captain O'Shea for his release.'[41]

Healy charged that Parnell's campaign in the split was a brutal wrenching of the shallow roots of constitutional action in Irish politics. His rhetoric dangerously confounded Parnell's attack on Gladstone with a derogation from constitutional politics. It was simply false to assert, as did the *National Press* on Parnell's death, that, 'ere long he, the greatest Parliamentarian of his time, became the merest instrument of the bitterest opponents of the Parliamentary method'.[42] In travestying the issues of the split as a choice between constitutional politics as practised by the majority, and Parnellism as a movement tainted by physical force, Healy was embarking on an argument fraught with hazard for constitutional nationalism. In relentlessly imputing to Parnell an anti-parliamentary purpose, he succumbed all too readily to the dangerous temptation to seek to complete the marginalisation of Parnell in Irish constitutional politics. In thus claiming for the anti-Parnellite cause an exclusivity of democratic legitimacy, Healy compounded the damage wrought to the constitutional consensus by Parnell's rhetorical excesses in the split. Ostensibly at his most statesmanlike, Healy was at his most mischievously partisan. His sundering purpose extended beyond his personal goading of Parnell. Ironically his rhetoric in the split, which proclaimed Parnell the last leader, was to add the final touch of exaltation to Parnell's posthumous myth.

Healy was not merely deconstructing the cult of the leader; he was supplanting it with the myth of the proprietorial nation. He articulated a post-heroic nationalism, in which the people and the solitary hero were cast as opposites. His rhetoric in the split is the manifesto of a submerged Catholic nationalist tenurial order, emerging from a primitive dependency on heroic archetypes.

Healy's ruthless revisionism, while directed primarily against the Anglo-Irish tradition, did not altogether exempt the antecedent Gaelic order. His doctrine of 'chieftaincy' drew part of its force from its mockery of the cult of the hero in Irish folklore and popular belief, denying (even while it exemplified) what Francis Shaw discerned as a characteristic of the Gaelic tradition, 'the tendency to be at least mildly cynical about the heroic'.[43] Healy's conflating in his rhetoric of 'chieftaincy' of an Irish heroic tradition with the Parnellite cult of the leader represents a critical moment in the pseudo-modernising cultural process of nationalism. Nothing reveals so strikingly the conflict between the historic 'great Celtic race' which Healy professed to champion, and the conservative nationalist proprietorial order he espoused. Healy had a bitter sense of the political debility of the Gaelic order before the advent of Parnellite nationalism, and some of that unforgiving contempt suffuses his rhetoric of 'chieftaincy' and his furious resentment of Parnell.

Healy's was an aggressively militant imposition of the ideology and values of late-nineteenth-century conservative nationalism. The history of the antecedent 'native' Irish order was ruthlessly re-written in terms of the objectives of contemporary nationalism to provide the pre-history of proprietorship. It is a striking irony that in chauvinistic conservative nationalism a weakened Gaelic culture encountered a formidable enemy. The Anglo-Irish were not the sole victims of the relentlessly homogenising tendency of Healy's rhetoric.

Healy's attack on Parnell encompassed a subtle and oblique denigration of the eighteenth-century Protestant 'patriotic tradition'. The heroic tradition of political leadership in the preceding hundred years, the redundancy of which Healy proclaimed, was overwhelmingly Protestant. While Healy invoked the names of Tone and Emmet – figures in the revolutionary tradition – to make mock-heroic taunts against Parnell, his true target was the eighteenth-century parliamentary tradition of Henry Grattan (and more ambiguously of Sir John Parnell), who championed the rights of an Irish nation conceived primarily in terms of Irish Protestant interests, culminating in the achievement of legislative independence by the Irish parliament in 1782 and ending with the Act of Union in 1800, the era of what became known in nationalist tradition as 'Grattan's Parliament'. While Grattan's Parliament was still conventionally celebrated in nationalist rhetoric, its allure was fading in the face of the deepening nationalist suspicion of a patrician patriotism which was neither populist nor Catholic. Underlying Healy's rhetoric in the split was a fierce attack on Protestant aristocratic leadership in both its unionist and avowedly patriotic forms, a vehement Catholic nationalist retort to the eighteenth-century 'Ascendancy' nation whose attempts at the usurpation of the popular Catholic nation he believed Parnell's campaign to perpetuate. Healy was not alone in his resentment of the tradition which had provided the last Irish governmental caste. Davitt wrote grudgingly of the Anglo-Irish patriot tradition (in which he jumbled Grattan and Flood, Swift and Molyneux, Tone and Emmet) that 'it is only just to the Cromwellian settlers to say that all the constitutional leaders of this revolt against a grinding and debasing oppression, religious, social and political, were of English descent'.[44]

'Grattan's Parliament' was subversive of the pretensions of Catholic nationalist ideologues. Insofar as it could be considered to embody the pretensions of the Anglo-Irish leadership of the Irish nation in history, it represented for them a manifestation of Ascendancy in its purest form. It was not merely that 'Grattan's Parliament' was increasingly perceived as the legislature of an alien class: it challenged the simplifications of nationalist ideology, in which the history of Ireland was reducible to the unfolding of the destiny of an embattled Catholic native race, by suggesting a more complex and intractable historical reality. Healy was the most fecund of conservative nationalist revisionists, invoking a hidden Ireland of the submerged Catholic tenantry, emphasising sectarian dispossession and the infliction of civil disabilities through the penal laws. As Healy and other Catholic nationalists sought increasingly to appropriate the concept of the nation, they returned the exclusionary gesture of the 'Protestant nation' in propounding a Catholic nationalism to which the Protestant tradition was largely exogenous.

Healy discerned in the course of modern Irish history not merely a phenomenon of conquest, colonisation and dispossession, but the usurpation of the concept of the nation itself. He surveyed the Protestant patriot tradition with a resentful eye. One of Healy's bitterest historical intimations, which informed the ferociousness of his resentment of Parnell, was his belief that the 'native' Irish had been so cruelly treated by English and Anglo-Irish alike, as to have to postpone their patriotism to the quest for physical survival. Even in its most enlightened aspect, the Anglo-Irish tradition was irredeemably tainted by conquest and despoilation.

The plasticity of the concept of the Irish nation in history, which in the eighteenth century had permitted a class a few generations deep in the country to appropriate for itself the style and title of the Irish nation, represented to Healy and other nationalist ideologues a deep affront, an unacceptable reminder of the subjectivity and artificiality of their conception of the nation, which they asserted to be a transcendental entity, anterior to history and politics. Healy in a venture in polemical historiography pitted against the 'Protestant nation' an ideologically stylised immemorial Catholic nation, a Catholic proprietorial order sanctified by a rhetoric of conquest, sectarian dispossession, and persecution.

Healy's rhetoric in the split comprises a crucial chapter in the evolution of modern chauvinistic nationalism. Healy's attack on Parnell strikingly prefigured the writings of D. P. Moran, who is conventionally credited with the invention of chauvinistic nationalism in modern Ireland. That dubious honour belongs rather to Healy. Moran's *The Philosophy of Irish Ireland*, comprised of articles published 1898–1900, merely pressed to a further extreme the themes Healy enunciated in the split. In the achievement of legislative independence by 'Grattan's Parliament' in 1782, Moran discerned 'the finishing stroke' against 'Irish Ireland'. The movement of Grattan 'placed the Pale at the head of Ireland for the first time in history and ever since the Pale has retained that place. The '98 and '48 movements, the Fenians and the Parnellite agitation were Pale movements in their essence, even when they were most fiercely rebellious'.[45]

The violence with which Healy assailed the Irish *ancien régime*, even in its patriotic aspect, was destructive of conventions of continuity, and of the tradition of the Irish state, and inimical to any sophisticated conception of the Irish nation. It represented a succumbing to sectarian complacencies at a critical juncture in Irish history: a flinching from the severity of statehood, and a denial of the ironies of power which had informed Parnell's statecraft.

17

The Union of Hearts

Mr. Gladstone in 1871 told the late John Martin that he feared not to compete with him for the confidence of the Irish people. If success in this competition has encouraged him to try a similar contest now with their present leader, he may hope to issue triumphant from the lists if he achieves more rapidly and fully than Mr. Parnell the objects on which the Irish heart is set.

T. M. Healy, 1883[1]

If Achilles determines to withdraw from the fight, the one fact which concerns me, a poor ally of the Greeks, is that Achilles is withdrawing from the fight and that we must see whether we can get on without him or not.

Justin McCarthy of Gladstone, February 1891[2]

But lo, a great evil now befell them, for the heart of their great captain became puffed up with pride, and he waxed great, and thought that all men should follow him; and in the greatness of his conceit he minded not his ways, and followed evil courses, and fell into lasciviousness, and lo, he betrayed his friend's wife, and she who was minded to do evil concealed it from her husband, and helped her betrayer to escape from her chamber by a ladder which was fixed to a balcony . . . Let all men scorn him, and let him eat grass with the beasts of the field, for verily he is lower than they. Then will the cause of Ireland be taken up by the great leader who by common consent

> is called the Grand Old Man, and we shall have peace and prosperity within the borders of the kingdom.
>
> *The Fallen Idol*[3]

> Mr G . . . has long weened Parnell an hare and now finds him a hegge hogge with all his quills bristling.
>
> George Wyndham, December 1890[4]

Healy sought to prise apart the Parnell myth through the fissure opened by the difference between Parnell's references to the Liberal alliance before and after the Gladstone letter. He assailed the volte-face of the Parnell manifesto: 'I ask myself the question which Parnell am I to follow: the Parnell of 1890 or the Parnell of 1891?' Later urging his audience at Maryborough to be 'Parnellites before the Divorce Court', he affirmed his preference for the old Parnell over 'the Parnell of the fire-escape and the divorce court': 'I prefer to believe the word of Mr. Parnell up to 17th November 1890 to that of the wild and whirling words uttered now upon every platform'.[5] M. J. Kenny derided 'the two Mr. Parnells', while the *Irish Catholic* published in early 1891 a pamphlet entitled *The Parnell Handbook, Containing Handy Notes and Useful Extracts from the Speeches of Mr. C. S. Parnell M.P. before and after the Verdict of O'Shea versus O'Shea and Parnell.*[6]

In April, Healy denounced Parnell's inconstancy as a study in charlatanism:

> Mr. Chairman, if you belong to a creed you must be prepared to adopt its rosary (*hear hear*). If we support Mr. Parnell we must be prepared to mutter with him the incantations and recantations of his manifesto (*hear hear*); we must be prepared to subscribe to the doctrine of the Hawarden interview; we must be prepared to believe he was being befooled by Mr. Gladstone at Hawarden or was befooling us at Liverpool the same afternoon (*hear hear*) and which of these creeds does Parnell call on us to adopt? The Parnellism of 1891 calls upon you to believe that Gladstone was a 'Grand Old Spider', and the Parnellism of 1891 that Parnell was a 'GOM.' (*applause and laughter*). Are politics viewed from a kaleidoscope or by magic lantern? Before the vision of Ireland six months ago Mr. Parnell by his magic lantern calls up the ennobled, glorified, almost deified form of William Ewart Gladstone; and has the magician only to touch a spring of the limelight and the nimbus disappears, and where stood the glorious form of Gladstone, in its place presents itself some wrinkled and demonic representation (*applause*).[7]

Of Parnell's suddenly professed suspicion of the Liberals, Healy asked: 'Is it credible that the witchcraft of the Divorce Court has changed all these men, and that the ringing gold of their past declarations has been turned by the necromancy of the decree *nisi* in the Divorce Court into withered leaves and fairy grass?' The home rule bill 'like a child changed at birth was a fine healthy baby until the fairies looked at it'.[8] Parnell, complained the *National Press*, treated the Irish people 'as if they were fools, destitute of memory and common sense', and relied 'a great deal too much on the shortness of the public memory'.[9]

Central to Parnell's defeat was the pervasive belief in the imminence of home rule. Anti-Parnellite rhetoric was informed by an urgent sense of anticipation which reflected the degree to which the Liberal alliance had already revolutionised expectations in Ireland. Against this complacent reliance Parnell struggled in vain. 'At the moment when we were within sight of the harbour, when we could see the flash of the harbour lights', charged Healy, Parnell had split the Irish party by seeking to cling both to the leadership and to the wife of another man.[10] 'We were within a kick of the goal of Home Rule.'[11] Urging his countrymen to recommence the struggle at the point where he asserted the Parnellites had broken it off, Healy asked:

> My friends what was the situation two years ago? It was a situation in which every man of you believed that in the impending general election, but a twelve month off, victory would light upon the banners of Ireland, and suddenly, like an eclipse across the face of the moon, the dark shadow fell upon our work. Who was to blame for that? ('*Parnell*'). Were you to blame for it? Was I to blame for it? Were the English people to blame for it? Was Gladstone to blame for it? Was the Irish Party to blame for it? ('*No, no', and applause*). No; none of these men were to blame. The blame lay and rested on one man, and one man only.[12]

There was a vitiating inconsistency at the heart of anti-Parnellite rhetoric. A deep sense of insecurity underlay the anti-Parnellite dogma that the deliverance of Gladstonian home rule was assured if Parnell was put down by the nationalist partners in the home rule alliance. Gladstone's espousal of home rule was perceived as a break in the menacingly sombre clouds of nationalist history. Confident invocations of a providential destiny in nationalist rhetoric belied muted fears that history would once again cheat nationalist aspirations. The image of the cup of victory dashed from the lips of an allegorical Hibernia was deeply inscribed on the contemporary nationalist sensibility. A profound sense of suppressed unease informed the vehemence with which the anti-Parnellites sought to defend the Liberals against Parnellite attacks: the fierceness of the attack cannot be fully accounted for by the threat which Parnell was supposed to represent to the Liberal—nationalist alliance (given his minoritarian status, and the fact that, however damaging his attacks on the Liberals, he did not seek to repudiate the principle of an alliance).

Implicit in the anti-Parnellite argument was that the Liberal alliance provided a guaranteed means to the nationalist end. The anti-Parnellites could hardly profess a lesser position without conceding the Parnellite taunt of a feeble and supplicatory politics. Their rhetoric celebrated the Liberal alliance as the enabling achievement of the drive for home rule. Strategy hardened into rigidity. In the characteristically plain and forthright phrase of William Martin Murphy, 'they had a definite means of acquiring a definite end'.[13]

Healy's assertion that only the Liberals would concede home rule was beyond dispute. With the introduction of the home rule bill in 1886 the mould of English politics set hard around the Irish question, and the possibility of Conservative sponsorship of home rule in the ensuing quarter-century became academic. Yet, contrary to what Healy asserted and what a superficial interpretation of Parnell's campaign might seem to affirm, that was not the matter in dispute in the split. The issue was not that of the Liberal–nationalist alliance, but rather of the basis of the collaboration between its constituent parties. If the doctrine of independent opposition which Parnell so fiercely re-affirmed in the split was a strategic fiction, it embodied a necessary ethic of independence. One of the adverse consequences of the split was that the majority of the Irish party were forced into an overtly more dependent relationship with the Liberal party, with the effect of destabilising the alliance they sought to uphold.

The crude sentimentality of Healy's rhetoric itself disclosed what was in some degree the compromised integrity of the home rule alliance. A disconcerting contrast between the unconstrained mawkishness of Healy's lachrymose encomia of Gladstone, and his eviscerating attacks on Parnell, ran through his rhetoric. His rhetoric played on the contrasted greatness of Gladstone and Parnell, the radical incommensurability of their myths. There were no two leaders of late-nineteenth-century high politics whose political styles were more dissimilar. Gladstone's statecraft was swathed in often sententious moral purpose, while Parnell practised an astringent directness. The mode of Parnell's greatness was antithetical to, even deflationary of, Gladstone's. The tension gripped the public imagination, and provided the Liberal–nationalist alliance with some of its dynamism. It also, as shrewder unionist adversaries had realised from the outset, gave rise to its vulnerability. Healy for his own purposes in the split sought to widen the fissure, shamelessly lauding Gladstone's expansive moralism, and vilifying Parnell's leaner political technique.

Healy, in the early, less assured phase of his rhetoric in the split, asserted that 'the chief glory of Mr. Parnell's leadership, what had endeared him to the Irish race and induced them to rally round him closer and closer on every attack' was that he had brought about the Liberal alliance 'which at the next general election was to put an end to the sufferings of Ireland'.[14] This was precisely the spirit of sentimental gratitude which Parnellites condemned as destructive of the basic premise of nationalist parliamentary action.

Healy exploited the transformation of nationalist sentiment which the 'union of hearts' had wrought. His rhetoric asserted the redundancy as well as the amorality of Parnell's *Realpolitik*. The introduction of the home rule bill appeared part of an unfolding providential scheme, in which Gladstone attained a quasi-messianic stature.

Speaking in March 1891, Healy threw Gladstone's enormous moral authority in Ireland into the scales against Parnell.

> We stood to him as long as it was possible to stand to the man, but when the English people said we will have no adulterer, we will have no alliance with a man of this kind, and when they ask of us this simple demand, 'give us a clean man', can we refuse them? They said, if Gladstone with his eighty years upon him and his foot in the grave, is going to stain his grey hairs by consultation with such a man, we will get another leader and another party beside Gladstone's.[15]

Healy heavily stressed Gladstone's old age and venerability. Gladstone was 'that poor old man, in his eighty-first year, who had worked and slaved for Ireland as a lusty youth'.[16] He charged Parnell with opposing the statesman who conferred on Ireland the only benefits it had ever received, and with callously gambling on Gladstone's advanced age: 'that is the man whom Mr. Parnell is doing his best to drive broken-hearted into his grave, whom if he died in the morning, every Parnellite in Ireland would gloat over his death'.[17] He presented Parnell's attack on Gladstone as an unpardonable act of personal discourtesy: 'They could only win the general election by the aid of Mr. Gladstone and the Liberal party, but Mr. Parnell's policy was that they should go and say to Mr. Gladstone, "give us Home Rule or we will spit in your face"'.[18] This was a development of a line of argument which Healy had first used in Committee Room 15 in assailing Parnell's counterproposals to the Clancy amendment:

> Mr. Parnell describes 'this garrulous old man, this unrivalled sophist', to whom he asks us to go for terms. We are to insult him, to kick him, we are to call him nicknames . . . He is called a sophist and a garrulous old man, who never gave a straight answer, and yet we are to go hat in hand to this 'garrulous old man', who has given the latter years of his life to our cause (*applause*), and having trampled upon his grey hairs and bespattered them with mud, then you are to ask him for terms at the instance of the man who has maligned and insulted him. That is the position of Mr. Parnell.[19]

J. F. Taylor in 1896 applied to Healy a remark of Isaac Butt, who had admitted to 'an almost superstitious belief' in Gladstone.[20] Healy was by no means unique among nationalists in the extent of his sentimental allegiance to Gladstone. As the divorce crisis commenced, Archbishop Croke wrote to Gladstone of Parnell, as of a miscreant schoolboy, 'just to tell you how pained we all are here that Parnell has caused you so much trouble. He must abdicate or be deposed'.[21] T. P. O'Connor wrote to Mary Gladstone in July 1891 expressing the hope that her father's health had not been impaired by 'the sad and trying experience through which he has just passed', and added ingratiatingly 'I trust he was gratified by Carlow and that he and those who love him, know that it was an answer to calumnious attacks upon him by a once worthy Irish leader and a testimonial of Irish gratitude and confidence in him'.[22]

In the 1892 general election Healy vehemently repudiated the Parnellite charge that anti-Parnellites were excessively reliant on the Liberals. Intriguingly he became one of the first Irish political leaders to use the slogan 'Sinn Féin': 'Now they say against us that we put our hopes in the Liberal party and that we are bound hand and foot to the Liberal party. No. I give you the good old watchword of old Ireland – Shin Fain – ourselves alone . . .'[23]

The *Manchester Guardian*'s appellation of Healy on his death as 'a great Gladstonian',[24] if sentimentally valid, requires qualification in the light of Healy's attitude to Gladstone's last administration. Healy quickly became locked in dispute with Morley's Irish administration, and while he publicly supported the second home rule bill (and savagely assailed the Parnellites for failing to give it unqualified endorsement), he was bitterly critical of its provisions in the private councils of the party.[25]

Healy's truculent attitude did not inhibit him from despatching an extravagantly unctuous letter to Gladstone's wife from the National Liberal Club in praise of the Liberal leader the day after the second reading of the bill. He averred that 'the pride with which we listened to him last night was not that of mere partisanship, we gloried in the genius that set forth so worthily a cause for us so great, seizing on conceptions larger, bolder, fuller, than before, when it had seemed that everything had been said':

> It will not I hope be profane to add, that today with our poor people at home, to many must come the thoughts of those who gathered with locked doors, 'for fear of the Jews' in an upper room, upon whom the message of the Resurrection descended. They know who it is that from their country's grave has rolled away the stone.[26]

The letter had an intriguing sequel. Healy declined to permit the publication of the letter by Gladstone's daughter, writing her mother's biography in 1919. He explained that 'the disappointments of Ireland after the twenty-six years since enclosed was poured out, makes its publication inappropriate'. He continued: 'it was evidently a private and intimate letter written to a woman about her husband. If now printed it would give rise to the bitterest satire in Ireland, which would yield nothing but harm to the cause we have at heart. No one not living here can measure the resentment against those who trusted the promises of British Ministers for so long'.[27] The proposed publication of so ingratiating a letter was particularly unwelcome at a time when Healy was briskly moving to accommodate himself to the rise of Sinn Féin.

In his later career Healy broke openly with the doctrine of independent opposition, and asserted the redundancy of the parliamentary *Realpolitik* practised by Parnell. Of the constraints imposed by the Liberal alliance on the Irish party, he had written in 1887 that 'the Rapparee freedom of old times is gone'.[28] The immediate context of the remark was tactical; yet, as Healy's politics in the split and after made clear, its implications were strategic. In 1896 he used the same phrase. Attacking the Parnellites, he asserted that with the conversion of the Liberal party 'the Home Rule movement had passed beyond what he might call its casual or the Rapparee character . . . and whether they liked it or not Mr. Parnell [had] felt bound to acknowledge that that modified to a considerable extent his Parliamentary and political tactics'. Healy said that 'in his opinion the Parnell chapter, like the O'Connell chapter, or the Mitchel chapter, had closed and closed definitely'. In extolling Parnellism up to 1890, Healy put the closure of 'the Parnell chapter' at 1890–1. But on the logic of the speech it dated from 1886: the years 1886–93 became the downswing of an obsolescent policy.[29]

By 1896 Healy was not arguing, as he had in the split, for the primacy of the Liberal–nationalist alliance. He was on the contrary seeking to justify his own accommodation with the Conservative party, in the long era of its supremacy following Rosebery's defeat, 1895–1906. Having used his critique of 'independent opposition' to assail Parnellite strictures on Gladstone's second home rule administration, he imperturbably deployed the same critique against the opposition of the majority of the Irish party under Dillon's leadership to the Conservative government.

In January 1899 Healy declared he was 'no advocate of this so-called policy of independent opposition — I never held with it, I never will hold with it'. The Healyite *Nation* in 1897 differentiated the then prevailing political circumstances from those of 1880, 'the ideal epoch of agitation'. The theme was developed two years later by the *Daily Nation* as it sought to justify Healy's own dissent from the policy of the majority, and his espousal of a *rapprochement* with the Conservative government. In a passage which well reflects the lost coherence of Irish nationalist politics after

Parnell, the tenets of Parnell's statecraft were reduced to meaningless clichés, a gibberish of opportunistic catch-cries:

> . . . today we can no more reproduce the conditions of 1880 (recent as that date is) than restore the Mastadon. The National spirit is as sound as ever, and sound it will remain, but the channels in which it can be directed change with every year. Let us work, therefore, as hitherto, for the restoration of unity among our Parliamentary forces, while not forgetting that amidst the iron 'Unity' that prevailed from 1886 to 1890 Mr. Parnell himself was absolutely impotent, and that these were the years of the perpetual Coercion Act and the Pigott Commission. Our watchword for the situation, therefore, would be 'Unity plus Sanity'.[30]

In his most explicit repudiation of the principles of Parnellism, Healy declared in 1905, in defence of his pro-Conservative stance, 'personally I regard the so-called policy of independent opposition as exploded and would substitute for it independent friendliness to each party as it came into power, trying each in turn'.[31] Even this remarkable avowal did not convey the full extent of Healy's change of direction. He was in fact far more at ease with Conservative than with Liberal governments. Within a decade his position had become the diametrical opposite to that which he had taken in the split.

The two principles which Healy professed to uphold in his attack on Parnell and which he later insouciantly repudiated — majority rule and the maintenance of the Liberal alliance — were never more than instrumental. In the split they happened to coincide and to subserve his immediate political purpose. Healy's shifts of position, and his rebellions against the authority of successive leaders of the Irish party, owed much to his mercurial and fractious temperament. Yet in the recurrency of his revolt an ideological commitment to the entrenchment of a conservative Catholic nationalist social order can be discerned. This, as much as considerations of temperament, informed his hostility to secular nationalist political authority, and his antagonism to an Irish party leadership in confederacy with an increasingly progressive Liberal party. Healy's career cannot be understood merely as a study in vengeful caprice: he was the conservative anarch of modern Irish nationalism.

18

The Moral Question:
Nationality and Shame

> That question was, broadly speaking, whether or not the Irish had ceased to be religious? whether or not the Isle of Saints had become the isle of cynics? whether or not the Irish people, who stand in the very forefront of Christian civilisation for purity of life and the reverence paid to the sanctity of the domestic hearth, had abandoned its moral pre-eminence, and sunk to the moral level of the London clubs?
>
> W. T. Stead, on North Kilkenny[1]

> Let us not replace our flag, the Cross, and the Round Tower by the temple of Venus, and the massive and fearless wolf-dog by the pampered and puny lap-dog of a London courtesan.
>
> Canon Thomas Doyle[2]

> And the English Nonconformist conscience grafted on the Irish Catholic briar produces some of the most fantastic blooms in the garden of Christianity.
>
> Seamus O'Kelly[3]

> Affected Mob Follows in Religious Sullivence.
>
> James Joyce, *Finnegans Wake*[4]

To understand the significance of the moral rhetoric of anti-Parnellism for Irish nationalism, it is necessary to discard the conservative nationalist fiction of an immanent nationalist moral order, Parnell's infraction of which pre-ordained his fall. The idea of an innate Irish national morality in its modern form did not antedate, but was a product of the split itself, shaped by the altered configuration of social power in Ireland. In the split the deployment of the moral argument was intertwined with the ideological definition of a nationalist identity.

Set against the hackneyed rhetoric of the more old-fashioned nationalist rhetoricians such as T. D. Sullivan and William Martin Murphy, the innovativeness of Healy's rhetoric in the split can more readily be appreciated. With supple inventiveness he recast the clichés of nationalist rhetoric for his own purpose. He rooted Parnell's moral transgression in his landlord provenance, aware that he could achieve a more robust rhetorical bonding by that association than through the bland rhetorical coupling of Ireland and virtue. The moral issue was subsumed into a comprehensive ideological whole. Parnell was cast as the pariah of nationalism, an outcast whose ostracism itself served to define the contours of the society from which he was excluded. Healy linked the divorce and Parnell's social origins to charge the traditional limp association of nationalism and virtue with novel ideological force.

There was in the scabrous idiom of anti-Parnellite moral attacks on Parnell an ugly irony. Parnell, the Bishop of Derry declared, had emerged 'degraded and befouled from the Divorce Court': 'but it is a needless task to dilate upon his delinquencies or to hold him up to public odium, for hate cannot wish worse than guilt and shame have made him'. The Bishop of Down and Connor referred to Parnell as 'a man stained by a crime that should not be so much as named among Christians'.[5] While the foregoing might suggest that it was neither necessary nor desirable to particularise the circumstances of Parnell's guilt, this consideration did not inhibit anti-Parnellite publicists, lay or clerical. The *Freeman's Journal* denounced 'probably the most foul-mouthed rhetoric that has invaded modern politics', while *United Ireland* charged that Healy's speeches were 'turning Ireland into a cesspool'.[6]

Catholic anti-Parnellite apologists strove to justify the lewdly moralising rhetoric they directed at Parnell. The *Irish Catholic* referred to Parnell as 'a notorious, convicted, shameless, and unrepentant adulterer, whose conduct it would be criminal to publicly discuss were it not for the necessary public expression of its condemnation'. One clerical casuist declared, in the robust tradition of Irish homiletics: 'If ever unbecoming language was not only excusable but necessary it was during this crisis. Language was the expression of our ideas, and if one wanted to express the idea of a satyr he could not use language descriptive of a saint'.[7] The ferocious Dublin curate John Behan sought audaciously to gain the initiative by retorting on the Parnellites the taunt of obscenity: 'They were told that there was only one possible leader. That was disgusting language'.[8] The resolution of the dilemma which Healy achieved in his rhetoric lay in the use of a violence of language of such brutality as to crush any incidental voluptuousness in its subject-matter.

The Parnellite contention that morality and politics were severable was addressed at some length in two articles in the course of the split, the styles of which suggest Healy's authorship. The first, a leading article entitled 'Leave Morality out of the Question', in *Insuppressible* of 20 January 1891, was a dialectical exercise in constructing the case against Parnell in purely utilitarian terms, free from the reproach of bringing considerations of private morality to bear on public issues. For the purpose of the argument, the Parnellite premise was mockingly accepted:

> We will concede that every public man is built in watertight compartments, so that private vices and public virtues are in no danger of getting mixed. We will concede that a public man's character and conscience may be like a magpie's plumage, one part blue-black, the other part pure white. In fine, the story of Dr. Jekyll and Mr. Hyde shall no longer be a fable, and it will be possible in the same suit of clothes for two men to stand — the private man, selfish, sensual, and false; the public man pure, truthful, and self-devoted [*sic*].

The 'non-moral' case against Parnell was then put. It was prudential: Parnell should not have placed himself and the cause he championed in jeopardy.

> Whether the mode of life he led in Winter Quarters was moral or immoral is no affair of ours on the present terms of controversy. But, on the other hand, the Parnellites will concede that, rightly or wrongly, there was a strong public prejudice against it, and Mr. Parnell must have known that. He must have known that there was a great danger of detection, and that detection meant injury, if not ruin, to the sacred cause entrusted to his keeping.[9]

While judiciously vague, the reference to 'strong public prejudice' must be taken to refer primarily to English opinion. This then was the avowedly rational argument, deemed proof against Parnellite taunts of confounding morality and politics.

The *National Press* of 3 August returned to the theme to reject the Parnellite premise accepted for the purposes of argument in the *Insuppressible* article:

> . . . the argument is rotten to the core. A man is not built in water-tight compartments, that his private vices and public virtues cannot get mixed. A man's character is not in distinct spots, pure white and jet black. A liar cannot exist in the same personality with a truthful and honourable man. The hero of the Divorce Court cannot be trusted with the guardianship of a nation's destiny.[10]

While Healy asserted, so as to justify the coarseness of his moral rhetoric, that the matter of Parnell's private character was germane to the issue of the split, he insisted that his opposition to Parnell derived from political considerations, in particular what he presented as the objective reality of English public opinion. At Queenstown in March 1891, he argued the case against Parnell in terms of English, rather than Irish Catholic, moral sentiment, implicitly differentiating his position from that of overtly moralistic nationalists, lay and clerical:

> We hear we should not attack Mr. Parnell on the moral question. Well for my part I never attacked Mr. Parnell until he issued his lying manifesto. I would never be against him today but that he made himself impossible as a leader before the English people (*hear hear*) . . . and therefore when you hear it said that morals have nothing to do with politics I say it is a matter for the people to decide and in this business the people from whom we have to get Home Rule are the English voters, and if they say they won't give Home Rule to an adulterous Prime Minister for Ireland, I say 'this is a matter within their competence because they have the power to give it or refuse it'.[11]

Healy insisted that the case against Parnell was political rather than moral: whatever his moral conduct, he had revealed a want of elementary prudence, and shown himself recklessly indifferent to the inhibitions placed upon a politician in his position. Elsewhere, equating the constraints on Parnell to those on the clergy, Healy declared that 'he did not care as far as his private life was concerned whether Mr. Parnell was a moral or an immoral character, but when a man was entrusted with the great interests of this movement he should be as careful and as guarded as a bishop or a priest'.[12]

Healy at Belfast shortly before Parnell's death sought to turn against him the reference in his manifesto to 'the English wolves howling for my destruction':

> The blame lay and rested on one man only . . . if there were English wolves howling for his destruction, and he knew it, I make that fact the heaviest count in my indictment against him, because, I say, knowing these things, and with all these responsibilities upon your head as leader of the millions of the Irish race, why didn't you walk more warily?[13]

Healy resuscitated this prudential argument in a passage in the proofs of his memoirs which he deleted from the published version: 'No layman is entitled to criticise as a moralist, save to say that Parnell, as the leader of a nation, should have realised that he could not afford to take risks'.[14] This was more than a little disingenuous. Few politicians have made such relentless or effective recourse to attacks on the private life of another. What Healy sarcastically referred to as Parnell's 'high and stainless character'[15] remained very much an issue. However he could not be seen to rely on moral considerations *tout court*. The situation required a political argument. It was essential in terms of Irish and English politics alike that the anti-Parnellite position should be formally distinct from that of the Catholic church. Yet while Healy asserted his principal ground of opposition to be that Parnell had by his behaviour incapacitated himself from achieving home rule within the confines of the Liberal alliance, his rhetoric was shot through with moral considerations. What the *National Press* referred to as Parnell's 'private sin and public disgrace' were intimately connected in anti-Parnellite rhetoric.[16]

Healy was also reliant on the moral argument to invest the anti-Parnellite case with its aura of absolute right. His case in the split plied between the contingent and the transcendental. He deployed the argument on shifting and elusive planes, resistant to the kind of rational engagement which Parnell craved. The anti-Parnellite case was presented at once in pragmatic terms and as an issue of the deepest nationalist principle. While pretending to assail Parnell as a patriotic liability rather than a moral abomination, Healy drew heavily on a reservoir of morally absolute Catholic values: his rhetoric provided a secular grid through which Catholic nationalist doctrine and ecclesiastical influence could be diffused.

Healy's bleak comedy of sexual allusion permitted him to deploy the moral argument obliquely and to greatest effect, to invoke moral prejudice with forensic precision. Ridicule was a more efficacious solvent of Parnell's mystique than an overtly moral rhetoric which was open to the charge of sectarianism. Healy's invocations against Parnell of the moral argument in its pure form were consequently rare and perfunctory, as in the course of a speech at Carlow (and even then Healy associated Parnell in depravity with the forces of the crown):

> Above all, the fact of his having got married in a registry office is itself enough to bring demoralisation into the home of many an unfortunate family in Ireland (*hear, hear*). For how many soldiers and policemen will hold up to young girls the example of their ex-chief, Mr. Parnell? The misfortune which this man has caused is not only a political misfortune, but a religious misfortune as well (*hear, hear*).[17]

The anti-Parnellite moral argument was itself in reality highly political. Morality did not stand alone, but was an aspect of the supposed nationalist character, a pillar of the new Irish social order. The split itself constituted a crucial chapter in the definition of a concept of nationalist morality, and in the related emergence of the vein of moral conservatism which was to prove abidingly influential in the shaping of modern Irish nationalism. The perceptive *Daily News* correspondent noted during the Kilkenny by-election that 'the divorce argument has fallen somewhat flat upon the pious Catholic population of this Island of the Saints. Puritan England, and Scotland with her Deacons and her Kirk Elders, may well feel shocked at the Kilkennyite indifference to the moral aspect of the battle between Mr. Parnell and the Nationalists'.[18] To the modern eye, this observation is unexpected, and instructive. It relates to the early stages of the split, when the anti-Parnellite argument drew primarily on the imperatives of the Liberal alliance, rather than the later more formidable anti-Parnellite rhetoric which skilfully blended the political and the moral in positing a nationalist moral order defined in opposition to Parnell. The notion of an innate nationalist morality was a political construct which would revolutionise the nationalist sense of self-identity.

It also transfigured the external perception of nationalism. The stereotypes of English perception of the Irish did not at the outset of the split draw so heavily on the notion of the Irish as a race whose political faculties were numbed by a morose combination of moralism and piety, and paralysed in the grip of 'priestcraft'. The dominant image was rather of a pauperised peasantry, whose penchant for feckless violence had been given ruthless direction under Parnell's leadership, submissively abetted by a lamentably docile priesthood. In the course of the split the caricature was redrawn. Unionist publicists seized gratefully on the heightened religiosity of nationalist politics during and after the split as demonstrating just how 'Romish' home rule was likely to prove.

The scandalised moralists of anti-Parnellism were preoccupied to a perceptibly greater degree than was Healy by Parnell's 'moral offence'. Discountenancing conciliation towards the Parnellites, the *Nation* of 23 May 1891 declared:

> We are not now speaking of Mr. Parnell's moral guilt, scarlet and horrible as it must ever appear in the eyes of honest men and modest women. We recognise, as the whole country recognises, that to his offence against society and righteousness Mr. Parnell has added another — a political crime — which struck at the very heart of his country.[19]

Parnell, T. D. Sullivan pronounced, had been 'convicted in the Divorce Court of a disgraceful crime'.[20] Within the anti-Parnellite camp, there was a difference of emphasis, which reflected less a divergence of opinion than a division of labour. While Healy professed to emphasise the political case against Parnell, the conservative moralists of anti-Parnellism placed greater weight than Healy on the moral argument simpliciter.

The foremost exponents of the old-style conservative nationalist moral case were T. D. Sullivan and William Martin Murphy, and in the press the *Nation* and, most farouche of all, the *Irish Catholic* under the editorship of the morally excitable W. F. Dennehy. Together they made up the overtly moralistic and socially conservative wing of anti-Parnellism. They accepted, and in Dennehy's case celebrated, the tenets of supremacy of the Catholic church. The split was a providential opportunity for the ideologues, secular and ecclesiastical, of conservative nationalism. The implacable fervour with which they were to exploit the possibilities for polarisation inherent in the split served to deepen the alienation of independent-minded Catholics who favoured Parnell, and to increase the unease of sensitive anti-Parnellite Catholics.

Their explicitly moral and sectarian rhetoric was couched in terms of an archaically sentimental and naively moralistic Catholic nationalism. The insistence on moral purity as the predominant attribute of the Irish character became a tediously familiar theme in conservative nationalist rhetoric. In a passage which is representative, indeed almost parodic, of the thought processes of the moral wing of anti-Parnellism, the pseudonymous author of *Under Which Flag?* lauded the exquisiteness of the nationalist moral sensibility, confronted by the split's harsh choice, in a richly comical inventory of nationalist traits:

> Generosity and fidelity are prominent traits in the character of the Irish race . . . Noble and beautiful traits in the national character these undoubtedly are . . . But there is one other feature of the complex character of the Irish people, which, while it is still more noble and beautiful than either of these, is also more strongly marked. In fact it may be regarded and is regarded as the grand and distinguishing characteristic of the race. It is that to which Moore refers in the well-known lines:
>
> 'Though they love women and golden store,
> Yet they love honour and virtue more'.
>
> Yes, the great characteristic of the Irish race, which places them on an eminence of social purity far above any other people in the world, and elicits the admiration and astonishment even of their enemies, is their love of purity and their high sense of familiar honour and purity.
>
> Generosity, fidelity, chastity, then, are virtues, deeply-rooted in the Irish race, whether taken individually or collectively. What a conflict must arise

> in an Irishman's breast when these virtues impel him in opposite directions; when generosity and fidelity vehemently urge him in support of an old and valued friend, while chastity makes him recoil in horror from that same friend, on account of his filthy, stinking sensuality. Such precisely has been the struggle which the Irish nation has had to endure by reason of the noisome revelations made in the now, unhappily, too notorious divorce case of *O'Shea versus O'Shea and Parnell*.[21]

The issue of the split was thus presented as a crisis of ethnic choice in a dialectic of vacuous attributes. The clash of the defining nationalist virtues of morality and loyalty was resolved in favour of the former. The split forged a stern ordering of supposed attributes of the nationalist character which subserved the Catholic moral order.

The moral rhetoric of anti-Parnellism was predictably hackneyed. T. D. Sullivan proclaimed the vast majority of the Irish people 'true patriots — lovers of cleanliness and purity in every department of life'.[22] The hereditary sanctity and unique virtuousness of the Irish race were not to be compromised by external standards. Protesting against the *Freeman's Journal*'s argument that hypocritical English moral standards were uppermost in the opposition to Parnell, Sullivan asked: 'What was it to them if Lord Nelson or the Duke of Wellington were bad and evil men? They were not going to fix their standard of morality by that of any other people'.[23]

The Parnellite attack on 'clerical dictation' affirmed the deepest suspicion of anti-Parnellite moralists. Sullivan charged that Parnellism had eventuated in 'a crusade against religion'. He levelled against the Parnellites the historically evocative charge of 'priest-hunting', and morosely joked that the main fare at National League meetings was 'roast bishop'.[24]

The *Freeman's Journal* responded to the resolution of the general meeting of the bishops and archbishops of Ireland against Parnell by reiterating that 'we are not prepared to surrender our political judgement . . . We shall fight strenuously against any body of men, lay or cleric, who either wittingly or unwittingly favour the recrudescence of Whiggery and placehunting in this country'. The *National Press* retorted by denouncing the *Freeman*'s anti-Catholic policy, and declared: 'To most educated Catholics the overthrow of the spiritual authority of the Irish episcopacy would be a much more momentous evil than "the recrudescence of Whiggery"'.[25]

While in Healy's rhetoric the erasure of the dichotomies between politics and morals, church and state, was blurred and implicit, the conservative moralists overtly refused to entertain elementary liberal democratic distinctions. Theirs was a shrill insistence on the primacy of morality, which did not concede the existence of a discrete sphere of politics. The attack on Parnell's morality extended to an attack on the personal integrity of his adherents. Parnellite allegiance was incompatible with a personal sense of honour:

> Now, there can be nothing clearer than that the men who support Parnell thereby implicitly profess that there is some other consideration which weighs more with them than the honour of their wives, their mothers, and their sisters. They may theorise to their heart's content about the distinction, between the politician and the adulterer, but practically in supporting Parnell they support the adulterer, and no amount of protestations will convince any sane man that they hate the crime itself.[26]

The nation was defined as an aggregate of moral sentiment. This proposition, the central tenet of anti-Parnellist moralism, was succinctly stated by Davitt's collaborator Charles Diamond, later anti-Parnellite M.P. for Monaghan North, in an editorial in the *Labour World*: 'The politics of a nation are the morals of the people writ large'.[27]

It was an illiberal and sectarian politics which brooked no distinction between politics and the dictates of Catholic morality. Endeavouring to play on the more primitive fears of his Parnellite co-religionists, T. D. Sullivan warned that 'a terrible responsibility rested upon the souls and consciences of some of Mr. Parnell's followers'.[28] The menace of damnation was a theme more commonly encountered in the columns of the *Irish Catholic*.

The *National Press* appropriated an argument from the hardline conservative moralists to assert that, once the *Freeman's Journal* backed Parnell in terms which rendered it 'the declared foe of religion in Ireland', its fate was sealed: 'the answer is roughly embodied in the belief of the Irish peasant – the *Freeman's Journal* would doubtless call it superstition – that a blow struck against the Church would paralyse the arm that struck it'.[29] The *Nation* asserted that 'the best guarantee of the ultimate success of the struggle for Irish liberty is to be found in the maintenance of a healthy virtuous social life in Ireland'.[30] The argument in its more thoroughgoing form was that nationalism could not prevail while it maintained as its leader the morally tainted Parnell. A benign providence could not work through the contaminated conduit of Parnellism. The author of *Under Which Flag?* asserted that legislative independence, if it was achieved and to be of value, was a gift of God:

> Now had the Irish people persisted in maintaining as their leader a man publicly convicted of a most foul, and most revolting, a most open, and oft-repeated violation of one of the most sacred laws of God, could they have hoped that their cause would find favour with Him, or that He would bring it to a happy issue? Certainly not. Such hopes would have amounted to blasphemy . . . Had the Irish nation then persisted in retaining Parnell, they would have compelled God either to refuse them the boon, which was already almost within their grasp, or to make a convicted adulterer the channel through which His favour should be transmitted.[31]

A pious race was exhorted to spare the deity this grave dilemma.

For the purpose of the moralistic anti-Parnellite argument the split presented itself less as a tragic sundering than as a welcome opportunity to achieve a cleansing of the nationalist ranks. William Martin Murphy declared that 'he looked upon the whole thing as an interposition of divine providence'.[32] The divorce court afforded an epiphany of Parnell's true character. The *National Press* wrote: 'It is humiliating to think of ourselves as the fellow-countrymen of such a man, still more so that up to six months ago he was the Irish leader. But God has made him and his heart manifest in time'.[33]

The moralistic formulation of the case against Parnell bore the heavy impress of the pretensions to respectability of the emergent nationalist social order. William Martin Murphy observed that 'Parnell's offence was an offence against the highest social laws as well as against the religious laws', and condemned Parnell's 'social sin'. He warned that the retention of Parnell as the Irish leader would have entailed placing Katharine O'Shea 'at the pinnacle of Irish society': 'If the divorce case had been kept in the background and if it had only come about six months after the gaining of Home Rule, we would have had Mrs. O'Shea at the head of the social edifice, surrounded by Mr. Parnell's satellites'. It would have been 'an intolerable country to live in under such conditions', to which British government without home rule would have been preferable.[34] Healy warned of a future in which Katharine O'Shea would be queen of Ireland.[35] Matthew Kenny invoked the precedent of pagan decadence: 'if home rule were obtained under Mr. Parnell it would not be government of Ireland by Irishmen, but by Mr. Parnell and his satellites. They would have Parnell as King of Ireland, with the golden Crown of Caesar on his head, and Mrs. O'Shea sharing his throne in Dublin Castle'.[36] The *Nation* declared before the Carlow poll that to the men of the county fell 'the duty of declaring that Irishmen will not submit to the sway of a convicted libertine, or Irish society bend before the throne of a strumpet'.[37]

In anti-Parnellite rhetoric Parnell's relations with Katharine O'Shea were frequently presented in terms of a peasant allegory of improvidence. The complex of values invoked – and in some measure defined – in the attack on Parnell were less those of abstract morality than of the aspiration to respectability, good husbandry and commercial prudence, of tenurial shrewdness and frugality, and of masculine responsibility. The degree to which the case against Parnell was couched in terms of agrarian values of economy and continence was manifest in an ugly passage in a speech by Archbishop Croke in May 1891, in the course of his tour of his archdiocese:

> The strong point of the Parnellites is: 'is not our Chief as fit to be a leader today, as able and as energetic as he was at any time within the last fifteen years?' Why then should he be deposed and his place of guide and influence give to another? I am speaking to plain but intelligent people here today and I am desirous to cast my thoughts in plain and intelligible form.
>
> Let us suppose one of you goes to the fair of Cashel and purchases there a well-known and useful animal called a pig. He pays £4 for the pig. He brings the pig home, feeds it for a fortnight and at the end of the time finds it has got the measles (*laughter*). It is the same pig that he purchased a fortnight before, but is there no difference as far as he is concerned? (*hear hear*). The greatest, because if he had killed the pig the day he bought it they would have had wholesome food for himself and his family, whereas had he killed it later on though the pig was the same, the pork being measly was not fit for use. The moral of the illustration is not far to see (*cries of 'measly pork' and laughter*). Or again suppose one of the fine young men I see before me had proposed for a good looking well bred and well born Tipperary girl and that immediately after being accepted, Providence had visited her with a loathsome complaint such as leprosy, would he be bound to accept her as his wife in her present altered condition? Surely not as long as she continued except indeed that he was of a more romantic nature than youths in our days usually are. There are moral as well as physical leprosies and I need no further urge the illustration.[38]

The virtue of Irish women featured in the moral rhetoric of anti-Parnellism. Perfunctory references to the sustaining righteousness of the women of Ireland recur, generally in terms intended for male edification rather than directly addressed to the voteless sex. Women were hailed as buttresses of the nationalist moral order. Thus Healy in the Carlow by-election declared they were greatly reliant on women in the contest 'because their virtue is the corner stone of the family and the hinge of society itself'.[39] The steadfastly outraged Canon Doyle called upon 'the faithful fathers and loving husbands of Ireland, upon the virtuous and loving wives, upon our chaste young girls, and upon our chivalrous young men to put an immediate end to this infamy'.[40]

A curious manifesto was published in the course of the Kilkenny by-election, entitled an 'Address from the Women of Castlecomer to Charles Stewart Parnell, esq. MP'. The text however has all the ponderousness which marks the style of the split's male moralists. Parnell was apostrophised as '. . . you, who like another veiled prophet, stalked through the land polluting its sacred soil with your presence'. With a falsity of tone which deepens the suspicion of male authorship, the address extolled, writing of Ireland, female nationalist virtue:

> . . . one jewel shone out from its tear-gemmed crown with a quenchless lumination – the purity of its daughters, the sacredness of its domestic relations; and you are the man, the heartless despot, that would be the silencer of public opinion, the shameless destroyer of a home, unblushing betrayer of a friend, the false, the dishonourable – we ask are you that man to be our leader? No.[41]

The earnest male ritual of nationalist politics provided some of the split's more comical excesses. The *National Press* published a report of an attempted visit by Parnell in the company of the parish priest (one of a small minority of Parnellites among the clergy) to a convent in Bagenalstown in the course of the Carlow election, which it proclaimed 'will be read with a thrill of indignant astonishment through the length and breadth of Ireland'. The paper had been requested to state that Parnell had not penetrated within the convent walls. He had been admitted by the postern gate. 'The instant, however, the nuns learned who the personage was who had dared thus to intrude within the convent grounds, orders were given to exclude both Mr. Parnell and his reverend companion from the building itself. None of the sisters saw either of the visitors.'[42] Similar outrage was inspired by the presentation of a bouquet to Parnell by a deputation of Carlow ladies. T. A. Dickson, anti-Parnellite member for Stephen's Green and a Protestant businessman, described the incident as 'a disgrace to the name of womanhood', and curiously added that he would 'far rather have seen those women helping their fallen sisters'.[43]

The prominent involvement of a small coterie of Dublin Catholic women in the Parnellite cause, in what was perhaps the most striking independent intervention of women in nationalist politics since the Ladies Land League,[44] was for conservative nationalists a particularly hideous manifestation of the threat to moral order which they discerned in Parnellism. Of the Parnellite convention, the *National Press* observed 'it will be long before it is forgotten that a number of women were present to applaud the hero of the fire escape'.[45] When E. D. Gray of the *Freeman's Journal* wrote seeking the benediction of the pope, Archbishop Walsh wrote to Rome in opposition. In a surviving draft of the letter in the Walsh papers, he specifically pposed the request for a special blessing for the mother of E. D. Gray, in terms which convey the pervasive contemporary sense of affronted moralism.

> Her conduct has been a source of great trouble in Dublin. She is known to be one of the few Irishwomen who have so far forgotten themselves as to have openly associated themselves with this convicted adulterer. It is a subject of general conversation in Dublin, and the Archbishop believes it to be true, that on the occasion of one of Parnell's recent visits to the city, this lady walked with him publicly through several of the principal streets.[46]

There was an undercurrent of unease in male anti-Parnellite rhetoric. The same qualities which made women virtuous rendered them vulnerable. Fragile vessels of passion, they required anchorage in a masculine social order. The Bishop of Cork wrote aghast to Walsh of the 'extraordinary fact' that 'many women even devotees have gone mad in his favour, and I was horrified to find a convent of nuns infected with the fury which became known to the children', adding the observation that 'it may be that a liking for such people is a weakness of women's character'.[47] The exaggerated belief that women — at least those of the middle and upper classes — were susceptible to Parnell as an embattled romantic was not confined to the more vehement anti-Parnellites. Sophie O'Brien wrote, referring presumably to those of her own class, that women were the fiercest Parnellites. She asserted that many of those women had not been specially drawn to Parnell in the years of his ascendancy 'but when he lost his power for good in the Irish cause for a woman they all took arms for him'.[48]

The conservative male ethos of nationalism was at once protective — shielding women from the scandal of Parnellism — and defensive. It informed the popular rhetoric of anti-Parnellism, and partly accounts for the deployment of a brutal coarseness in defence of moral purity. The rhetoric was intended to enact an assured and knowing despatch of Parnell as a sexual predator. It was as if its calculated scabrousness was designed to signify that the stern virtue of nationalist manhood should not be attributed to any unmanly lack of awareness of licentious alternatives.

The most implacable and vituperative voice of anti-Parnellite moralism was that of W. F. Dennehy's *Irish Catholic*. The moralist rhetoric of anti-Parnellism attained one of its several climaxes in a leading article of 1 August 1891 entitled 'The Scandal of the Leinster Hall', which concerned 'the public honour paid to Mr. Charles Stewart Parnell' at the National League Convention. In a passage at once hysterical and contrived, Parnell's depravity was exhaustively reiterated like a motif in a contemporary sermon:

> On that day, on a public platform, before a large assembly, which included a number of women, stood a notorious, convicted, shameless, and unrepentant adulterer — a robber of another man's wife — a wrecker of another man's home — a deceiver — a liar — a wriggler in and out of another man's house by back doors, and side doors and windows, and balconies — a tripper down fire escapes from the scenes of his guilt — a skulker under false names — a man whose infamy has been the theme of the public press for many months — whose actions have furnished an unfailing source of mirth to society of the looser and baser sort — who is a standing jest of the music halls, the theme of unsavoury ballads, the

> subject of gross pictures – whose personal history for years is not fit to be known to Christian families – whose conduct would be criminal to publicly discuss were it not for the necessary expression of its public condemnation – a man against whose continuation in a position of popular trust and honour the venerated Catholic Hierarchy of Ireland have most earnestly and solemnly protested – this man, so standing before a large assembly of Irishmen, including some women, was hailed with loud applause, was complimented, praised, and cheered to the echo . . . The proceedings were one long continued act of homage to the adulterer . . . Where has this performance been matched since the worship of the 'goddess of Reason' by the Parisian revolutionists?[49]

The passage reflects a certain polemical aptitude in enacting the process of scandal in its movement, from the initial characterisation of Parnell as furtively sinful, to his exposure in the glare of Victorian and Catholic nationalist obloquy.

What is most significant about the editorial is its timing. It came after Parnell's third by-election defeat that the editorial policy of the *Irish Catholic* entered its most vehement phase. The seemingly perverse intensification of the attack on Parnell in defeat revealed the controlled provocativeness of the paper's mode of argument, and the gathering bitterness of the split's controversy even prior to Parnell's death. In part, the editorial line reflects the development of a tendency which antedated the split itself. The perceived imminence of home rule had precipitated a struggle for mastery within nationalism, manifested in the increased assertiveness of the *Irish Catholic*, and in the deepening unease with which it regarded the pretensions of secular nationalist politicians.

The second editorial in the same issue declared: 'We have to deal today not merely with an audacious attempt to place a convicted and unabashed adulterer in high places in a Christian land – we are face to face with a Satanic revolt against the dictates of religion and its authorised exponents, which demands from Catholics vigorous and determined action'. The call for 'vigorous and determined action' presaged a deepening intolerance. Of Parnellite attacks on the commingling of religion and politics, in particular a reference by T. C. Harrington to 'the attempt . . . to prostrate religion at the feet of Mr. Gladstone in Ireland' (words, it commented, which 'should have palsied the lips from which they fell and seared the hearts of those to whom they were addressed'), the paper enquired menacingly: 'Can it be possible, we ask in all frankness, that Catholic Ireland is in a mood to tolerate the formulation and publication of such accusations as those uttered by Mr. Harrington and printed and circulated with the utmost prominence in the columns of the *Freeman's Journal*?' Parnellism had progressed from the condonation of sin to an overt challenge to the Catholic faith: 'Parnellism now stands self-confessed in its own iniquity. Its aim is no longer merely the championship of individual immorality; it now seeks to establish the reign of irreligion and impiety, through the destruction of the influence of the Church'.[50]

The *Irish Catholic* returned to this theme the following week, asserting that Parnellism 'is not merely irreligious, it is infidel':

> We are face to face with what, despite its disguises, is undoubtedly a revolt against God, against the authority of the Church, against the teachings of morality, and against the first principles of divine and human legislation. Parnellism is an anti-Christian movement, having for its object the apotheosis of immorality.

The week after, the paper declared: 'Evil, evil inexpiable and unforgivable enshrouds Parnellism, and is of the very essence of the movement'. In a subsequent editorial it proclaimed the split 'a renewal of the ancient warfare between religion and irreligion, between morality and immorality, between the spiritual and the temporal, between Christ and Antichrist', and warned darkly of the infernal vista opening before Parnellite apologists: 'those who protest that politicians owe no allegiance to morality and ethics forget, or pretend to forget, that politicians have souls to be saved, and that heaven is as glorious and hell as terrible a fact in their case as that of other men'. The paper proclaimed its purpose of extirpation: 'we have stricken down Parnellism and mean to crush it underfoot'.[51] The following year it declared that the real character of the 'Satanic revolt' of Parnellism had become apparent, and that the split represented 'the most irreligious and anti-Catholic outbreak witnessed in this country since the time of the so-called Reformation'.[52]

This was the ruthlessly polarising technique of militant anti-Parnellism which James Joyce conveyed with superb accuracy in the Christmas dinner scene of *A Portrait of the Artist as a Young Man*. The Fenian Casey is goaded by the remorseless equating of anti-Parnellism with Catholicism into rhetorically rejecting both: the repudiation of the cruel deity of anti-Parnellism, a bitterly heroic affirmation for a Catholic in late-nineteenth-century Ireland.

It is difficult to attribute the remarkable vehemence of the *Irish Catholic* in the split's final phase to a defensive reaction to the perceived radicalisation of the Parnellite attack on clerical dictation. The attitude of the *Irish Catholic* is better understood in terms of relentless ideological opportunism, manifesting itself as a determination to seize the pretext of the split to promulgate a supremacist Catholic nationalism. This it did with an explicitness which can only have disconcerted the more subtle episcopal directors of ecclesiastical policy. Hence the dialectical intensification of its attacks on

Parnell as his campaign to reassert his leadership appeared to falter, as if the persistence of a defeated Parnellite faction as an enduring minority represented a yet greater affront to Catholic nationalist susceptibilities than Parnell's initial endeavour to regain his ascendancy.

The pursuit by the *Irish Catholic* of Catholic supremacy through the effacement of Parnell had awkward implications for anti-Parnellite nationalism generally. However preposterous its views, they were distinguishable from the predominant Healyite strain of anti-Parnellism only in point of vehemence, and were possessed of the superior lucidity of that vehemence. Complementing Healy's excesses in the secular domain, the *Irish Catholic* did not shrink from pressing its arguments to extremity. Healy had rendered anti-Parnellism disquietingly vulnerable to being over-reached by the zealotry of the *Irish Catholic*, which could all too plausibly represent itself to be the eschatological tendency of Healyite nationalism.

The editorial policy of the *Irish Catholic* culminated in a notorious editorial which treated Parnell's death as a mortally exact Catholic allegory. Emphasising the sequence of sin and death, it rejoiced in the affirmation of the severity of the moral order. Parnell's death called to mind 'the awful possibilities which lie beyond the tomb': 'Death has come upon him in a home of sin; he has died and his last glimpse of the world has been unhallowed by the consolation of religion; his memory is linked forever with that of her whose presence seems to forbid all thought of his repentance'. In all this, there was a world of sadness made 'all the more drear by the echo of a wailing whose sounds have not the cadence of prayer. The darkness is pierced indeed by the cry of sorrow, but the light of hope shines not, and there is naught but darkness drear and horrid. Charles Stewart Parnell is dead!'[53] While the editorial gave John Dillon the opportunity to dissociate himself from the more lunatic manifestations of Catholic nationalist moralism, it plunged the controversy to new depths of bitterness and intolerance. Its savage virtuous exaltation hardened the divisions of the split and completed the estrangement of many Parnellites, who would never forget the collusion between anti-Parnellism and the bleak divinity of a politicised Catholicism.[54] The second editorial in the *Evening Press* on Parnell's death paralleled the *Irish Catholic* article, but without its morbid eschatology. The *Evening Press* proclaimed that Parnell 'lay dead in the house of a woman who was his betrayer', and described his death as 'a terrible lesson to those who thought that the Irish nation should take his life as the lease of Ireland's safety. They almost pretended he was godlike and undying'.[55] The *pas de deux* between Healy's politics in the split and the shrill moralism of the *Irish Catholic* was maintained to the end.

Healy and his allies postulated a nation held together by a web of moral filaments, which provided a social paradigm radically different from the alien contrivances of power on the British model. Nationalist society was asserted to possess an immanent moral consensus: a contrast was sharply drawn between the supposedly natural nexus of the nationalist moral order and the alienating ordinances of British governance. Divorce became in anti-Parnellite rhetoric emblematic of the profanity of English power and government, and of its undermining of the moral code of Irish nationalism. The divorce issue itself brought into play a neglected strain in nationalist opposition to English power. Nationalism was not merely dedicated to challenging British power as external domination, but professed a specific objection to English liberal values of which divorce was a classic expression. Divorce was imperialism in its civil aspect. This informed the anti-Parnellite response to Parnell's marriage to Katharine O'Shea.

The *National Press* characterised Parnell's wife as 'the lady to whom the Registrar had contracted him'.[56] The introduction of the concept of contract in this context is instructive. Quite apart from the nationalist hostility to contract in land law (whereby the inviolability of contractual rights was regarded as an obscurantist dogma masking the inequality of bargaining strength between landlord and tenant), there was a broader anti-contractual strain in nationalism, rooted in an antipathy to what was perceived as an English ideology of contract which entailed an explicit recognition of the realities of human commerce, regarded by many nationalists as overtly cynical and vaguely profane. Divorce was not merely the product of English social depravity, but the culminating amoralism of liberal contractarian belief, and profoundly subversive of the ethical structure of nationalism.

Nationalist morality was pitted against the transition from status to contract. Neither divorce nor the contracting of a second marriage could divest Katharine O'Shea of her position as the wife of W. H. O'Shea. The *Weekly National Press*, headed its editorial on the subject 'Registered, Not Married'.[57] Parnell's unsanctified relationship with Katharine O'Shea could not transcend the condition of animal desire, a consideration which prompted the distasteful heading of the *Nation*'s report of the Parnell marriage: 'The Registrar Ties a Legal Knot – How the Guilty Pair were Tethered'.[58]

In the scheme of equivalence which Healy's rhetoric asserted, Parnell's violation of the principle of majority rule enacted of a wider violation of the nationalist moral order. Healy equated the parliamentary pledge with the marriage vow. At the inauguration of the National Federation he declared: 'For my part, I say this, that the pledge was the marriage tie of the Irish party, and it is not surprising that men who have no regard for the marriage tie should have no regard for the pledge'.[59] The sacraments of baptism and ordination were also called in aid to convey the multiple violation of nationalist values of which Parnell was guilty:

> The members of the Irish Party took a pledge to sit and vote with the Irish Party, and to work in the interests of Ireland in the same way that your godfathers and godmothers pledged you at your baptism that you would be true to your religion . . . Once let the people justify the breaking of pledges and you might as well expect sincerity in our Members of Parliament as you would expect chastity and morality in your priests if they were allowed to break their vows (*hear hear*). The most degraded thing in the eyes of an Irish Catholic is a priest who is false to his vows and who is suspended from his functions (*hear hear*) . . . Parnell broke his pledge to Ireland, Kitty broke her vow to her husband (*hear hear*), and how can we expect a man to be true and faithful to his country when he could not be faithful in regard to Captain O'Shea (*hear hear*), when in important matters like fidelity to his friend he brings upon him the greatest disgrace that one man can inflict upon another.[60]

The degree to which Healy's anathematisation of Parnell was political rather than moral is revealed in a significant passage in which, in a culminating irony, he invoked against Parnell the logic of the agrarian boycott:

> You protested against the conduct of a landgrabber. What about the conduct of a wifegrabber? And if you refuse to associate with the man who has anything to do with taking his neighbour's property, are bricks and mortar, sand and lime, more precious in your sight than all that is sacred in the human heart and family (*applause*)? And we are told forsooth that we should sacrifice Home Rule in order to maintain in his position the paramour of Mrs. O'Shea.[61]

The rhetoric of anti-Parnellism is an early essay in the politics of an assertively populist late-nineteenth-century Catholicism in Europe. Parnell was all too readily assimilable to the stock villain of late-nineteenth-century Catholicism — the liberal Protestant or freethinker opposed to incursions of Catholic power in politics. Anti-Parnellism rode the tide of social Catholicism, invoking Leo XIII's encyclical *Rerum Novarum*, published during the currency of the split, and hailed by Healy as 'the greatest pronouncement ever made on the cause of Labour'.[62]

Parnell's necessary self-defence against clerical attack was readily constructed by Healy as an attack on Catholicism itself. While Healy professed to eschew overtly sectarian or theocratic propositions, his rhetoric was suffused by religious and moral tinctures. His was a blatantly Catholic nationalist political idiom, reflecting an irruption of Catholic power within the nationalist tradition. It marked a critical infraction of the conventions of nationalist rhetoric, shattering the decades of compromise and reticence which had issued in a tenuous equilibrium within nationalism, and discarded the liberal ethic by which O'Connell sought to contain the championship of Catholic interests. Healy did not need to attack Parnell in explicitly sectarian terms, but could rely on second order sectarian considerations. He completed the ostracism of Parnell by appealing to the emotional depths of Catholic nationalism. It was a retreat into the realms of the Catholic nationalist psyche, a region in which Parnell could not pursue or engage him.

One of the most disquieting and enduring features of the nexus between the church and anti-Parnellite majority was the confounding of the rhetoric of church and nation. The intellectual flaccidity of nationalist rhetoric had rendered it susceptible in any event to the encroachment of ecclesiastical idiom. It was at the level of rhetoric that the concordat of the church and anti-Parnellite nationalism was sealed. An innate collusiveness of discourse permitted anti-Parnellite nationalists to assert, in disingenuously wounded accents, that theirs was a nationalism free from sectarian taint.

Healy's defence of the political role of the Irish church was subsumed in a larger theme, that of the necessity for a leadership of native stock. He proclaimed an alliance of clergy and peasantry rooted in shared social origins. The priesthood was celebrated as comprised of educated men sprung from the people, as the bulwark of the new social order.

> A roman collar is no disenfranchisement (*loud applause*). A man does not cease to be a nationalist when he enters Maynooth (*hear hear*). There is no disability in the sacrament of Holy Orders (*applause*). At least there is none when a decree of the divorce court creates no disability. And to say that when the Irish people have created a clergy – because they are of our making (*hear hear*); the colleges in which they were reared and educated were paid for and subscribed to by the common men of the country (*hear hear*); their organisation is sustained by the pennies of the poor; their education is drawn from the help of the masses of the Irish race (*hear hear*); and if you have picked out men whether they be MPs fulfilling their vocation in the House of Commons as your choicest representatives, or they be clerics fulfilling their vocation in another walk as the best and most educated of your fellow-countrymen, and I am told that suddenly because these men have adopted a career, which career gives them a certain spiritual influence, they are to cease to use the influence which education and their position would also confer on them (*loud applause*).[63]

Healy discounted Parnellite attacks on the political role of the clergy in the split as a diversionary tactic. He thus assailed the Parnellite candidate in the Carlow election:

Mr. Kettle has opened his address to you by telling you that the priests are good for nothing except to teach you to beg (*hisses and laughter*). I will tell you one thing your bishops teach you. They teach you to respect your women (*hear hear*); to respect your wives; to regard as false to principle, to duty, to humanity, one who inserts himself in the guise of friendship into your houses, and having eaten and drunk at your expense, inflicts upon you the greatest disgrace that one man can inflict upon another (*cheers*). When Mr. Kettle comes to tell you that your priests never taught you anything except to beg, tell him that they have taught you, at all events, to know the difference between the sacrament of matrimony and a performance in the registry office (*cheers*).[64]

More atavistically, Healy observed 'we hear a great deal about the priests. I hope we may have them by us when we are dying'.[65]

The opposition of the clergy and the hierarchy to Parnell was invoked as the verdict of a second jury to that of the party:

Now, which do you think is likely to be the madder man, the Archbishop of Cashel, say, or the Archbishop of Dublin, your Primate, or the hero of the Divorce Court? I put it to you, who know your priests. You have made them, you have educated them, and you have upheld the religion to which they are anointed pastors, and I put it to you as men of the world – leaving aside religious considerations and the sanctity of their cloth altogether to one side – is it likely that these men are all wrong, and Parnell and his little crowd all right (*cheers*).[66]

Conventional paeans to the patriotism of the priesthood now acquired an overtly political import. Banim's execrable 'Soggarth Aroon', commended by Stead to an English readership as an 'exquisite ballad', now acquired a direct political significance.[67] Proclaiming the innate harmony of church and people, predicated on a common provenance, Healy dismissed the idea of clerical dictation as a logical impossibility. 'It is absurd', proclaimed the *National Press*, 'to speak of ecclesiastical interference . . . the priests are powerful because they are of the people and with the people.'[68] The clerical-nationalist entente had co-equal status with the Liberal–nationalist alliance in anti-Parnellite rhetoric. The *National Press* eagerly defended the axis of the clergy and the peasantry against Parnellite attack: 'the divorce proceedings, in fact, are held to extend to divorce between the people and their clergy. Of the union between the Irish priests and their flocks we may say only that what God has joined together Mr. C. S. Parnell cannot pull asunder'.[69]

Disregarding the historical record of the Irish church in and after the Act of Union Healy hailed the political role of the clergy, whom he asserted to 'have been so long at the head of every public movement for the disenslavement of their countrymen'.[70] He proclaimed the clergy to be the patriotic profession *par excellence*: 'I say take any profession . . . and I say that a larger percentage of martyrs and confessors in the cause of Ireland in this present struggle has been furnished by the clergy than by any other'.[71]

He taunted Parnell with hypocrisy in attacking 'clerical dictation', having accepted the subscriptions of the priests and bishops to the 1883 Parnell testimonial: 'If Mr. Parnell tells you that, ask him will he kindly subtract from the £40,000 he received the five pound notes of the priests and the ten pound notes of the bishops before he begins to blackguard them'.[72]

Healy responded furiously to Parnell's taunts of sectarianism. The *National Press* denounced the revival of 'the old exploded absurdity that Home Rule means Rome Rule'.[73] Healy sought to reduce the Parnellite critique to the level of dubious anti-popish tracts, charging that 'the bogey of the Scarlet lady' had been exhumed by the Parnellites for the sole purpose of unsettling Protestant opinion in England, having failed to disrupt the Liberal alliance by other means.[74] The Parnellite critique was dismissed as a slander on the unimpeachable pluralism of the nationalist sensibility: 'Nothing but a malignant anxiety to represent the majority of the most tolerant people in the world as a tribe of terrorised ignorants living in the valley of darkness of sectarian hate could have begat such accusations . . . Such are the necessary pillars of Parnellism'.[75]

The *National Press*, attacking Parnell's speech at Irishtown, County Mayo, in April, declared: 'Mr. Parnell posed as the persecuted Protestant. The denunciation of the adulterer is twisted by him into a declaration that "Ireland is to be a nation of one religion only"'. To dispel the accusation of Catholic supremacism, the unwitting 'honest Irish Protestant' was called in aid. The issue was carefully put in terms of the condonation of adultery as distinct from the recognition of divorce:

> We have no hesitation in saying that there are some religions we hope will never be welcomed into the ranks of the Irish nation, and amongst others, the religion which puts among the disputed theses of its ethics the question of whether adultery is a fault. It must sicken honest Irish Protestants to witness the attempted identification of the cause of their liberties with the personal cause of this deplorable man.[76]

This favourite stock figure of nationalist rhetoric was also invoked by E. F. V. Knox M.P., himself a Protestant: 'there was not a decent Protestant in Ireland who would prefer Mr. Parnell's rule to that of the majority of the Irish party'.[77] Of Parnell's registry office marriage, Healy commented: 'there are ministers of religion of Mr. Parnell's own faith, the Protestant faith, and to their credit be it said that in all broad London he could not get a Protestant parson to marry them'.[78] Healy's reply to Parnell was hardly calculated to allay the fears of Irish Protestants. Rather it alarmingly demonstrated how readily any critique of nationalist sectarian proclivities could be reduced to an attack upon nationalism itself, and the extent to which, in conservative nationalist thinking, Protestant moral beliefs were to be on nationalist sufferance.

Quite apart from the question of maintaining faith with the Liberal alliance, and the legitimate fear of Conservative attacks on Parnell if he remained leader in English elections, there was a deep and confused nationalist sense of shame and mortification which percolated beyond the purely political logic of anti-Parnellism. The concept of shame, over-arching the categories of religion, morality and nationalist politics, is central to an understanding of the intensity of the opposition to Parnell in the split. In this sense of shame, Catholic moralism and wounded nationalist *amour propre* were blended. Shame suffused the anti-Parnellite argument, giving it its strange admixture of sentiment and brutality. Unamenable to rational rejoinder, it was to prove overwhelmingly damaging to Parnell.

The O'Shea divorce opened up a vista of modern moral depravity which excited the lurid apprehensions of nationalist moralists. It was represented as the shock of the first assault of contemporary English decadence on nationalist innocence: nationalist morality was pitted against modernity in its depraved English mode. Apart from the peculiar gravity with which divorce was regarded in Catholic moral thought, as sanctioning a recurrency of sin, divorce had in any case a particular historical resonance for Irish Catholics, considered as the pretext of the Henrician reformation, and as precipitating the sectarianisation of the antagonism between Ireland and England.

While Catholic nationalists proclaimed the sense of shame as a natural and unmediated emanation of an antique tradition of virtue and morality, it was an ideological construct, neither as absolute nor as endogenous to nationalism as it was asserted to be. In the first place, nationalist moral sentiment drew much of its inspiration from a reaction to what was considered to be the morally debased condition of English society. The paradigmatic contrast was with England, at once the historic and only enemy, a Protestant power, and the harbinger of a decadent industrial modernity. A virtuous Ireland was projected on the screen of English moral depravity.

To this was allied a profound and exaggerated sensitivity to English perceptions. England provided the external political theatre within which the split's moral drama was enacted. This contradictory phenomenon constitutes the split's heart of darkness, the deep and almost impenetrable region of the nationalist sensibility from which anti-Parnellite sentiment derived much of its intensity. It informs the complex and confused politico-moral scheme which underlay Healy's rhetoric, and gave it its intellectual impurity and its power. Healy's was an attempt to give political form and direction to a Catholic nationalist idiom of shame, remorse, retribution and decay. His repudiation of Parnell, while professedly in the interests of the Liberal alliance, drew much of its force from the smarting sense of shame at the divorce court disclosures, which had exposed nationalism to English ridicule on a moral issue, and from a resentment that the erstwhile 'uncrowned king', who had brought a new dignity to the Irish cause, should by his conduct have rendered that cause the object of prurient English derision.

What was common to both sides in the split was the sense that the Irish nation had bared its anguish to the world. The 'world' in nationalism was the outside. And the outside was England. Parnellites and anti-Parnellites alike decried the split as a squalid ritual of national abasement, conducted in the purview of, and subject to exploitation by, the English enemies of nationalism. For the Parnellites this arose from the Irish failure to stand by Parnell in the face of external pressure; for the anti-Parnellites it had its origins in the disgrace which the divorce court had brought upon the Irish cause. Each blamed the other for the destruction of the united Parnellite movement.

The imperative of beggary had manifested itself once again in Irish history. The divorce crisis had divested the nationalist cause of its recently acquired dignity. Healy accused Parnell of having 'made the Irish name once more a laughing stock among our enemies'.[79] 'How all Europe is on the broad grin at the pure morals of Catholic Ireland', wrote the eccentric and opportunistic F. H. O'Donnell to Davitt from Lausanne. He subsequently despatched a letter to the *National Press* opining that 'Ireland has often suffered, but she has never been menaced with laughter and contempt'.[80] The sense of humiliation in the face of Tory ridicule bit deeper than purely electoral considerations. Thus T. D. Sullivan graphically invoked the wounding ridicule to which nationalist Ireland would be exposed:

> He knew what the Tories at contested elections in England did, he knew what the Unionists did. They placed huge coloured posters on every dead wall, giving pictures of the misdeeds of the poor Irish people (*interruptions*) . . . But in addition to these posters and pictures he knew the sort of posters and pictures they should have on the dead walls at the next general election (*cries of 'Fire Escape'*). They would have pictures and presentations of Eltham and the rope ladder, and so on (*laughter*).[81]

W. T. Stead's exultant observation that 'there is no doubt that the spectacle of the conscience of England revolting against a convicted adulterer smote the conscience of Ireland',[82] while attesting to the complexity of interaction of English and Irish sentiment in the split, was misconceived. What was formative in cultural transmission was not as Stead believed the edifying example of English nonconformist morality, but the Irish recoil from English popular humour and anticipated Tory derision.

There existed within nationalism a fascinated disdain for English popular culture, as a reflection of modern depravity, and the popular English response to the divorce court disclosures excited a special thrill of distaste. Healy declared at Kilkenny: 'If one passed along any English city you heard abusive and obscene songs about Parnell and Mrs. O'Shea. The same matter was the chief topic for music hall songs and in the streets obscene pictures about the affair were thrust into one's hand'.[83]

It is to be doubted that the material to which he referred was actually obscene, or that this was why it was offensive to anti-Parnellite nationalists. The treatment of the O'Shea divorce in commercial popular culture in England appears to have been at worst mildly *risqué*, but of a flippancy peculiarly exasperating to sententious nationalists. Thus the concluding lines of a song to be sung at the London Pavilion on 1 December 1890 by one G. M. McDermott went:

> The fire-escape, the fire-escape,
> It was indeed a merry jape,
> When Charlie Parnell's naughty shape
> Went scooting down the fire-escape![84]

It is significant that the anti-Parnellite press used the language of English popular scandal to satirise Parnell and Parnellism. The *Nation* referred to 'the Parnell peep show',[85] while of Parnell's speeches the *National Press* wrote: '"Parnell's Sunday Shockers" would be a good headline for his weekly falsehoods'.[86] The *National Press* reported the accession of effigies of Parnell and Katharine O'Shea (together with a number of notable female criminals) to an English waxworks:

> To this has the Irish nation been reduced before the world by, the 'Only Possible Leader'. Does any thinking man suppose that English statesmen could ever discuss an Irish constitution with a personage whose escapades are the topics of ribald songs in every music-hall and who is thus pilloried in travelling waxworks?[87]

The frivolities of the music hall sat ill with the solemn pretensions of nationalism. Catholic nationalist moral indignation was set in a double frame, the inner of Catholic moral sentiment, the outer of Victorian scandal.

19

The Politics of Peasantry

What, then, is the nation we shall have in Ireland? It will be a nation of small farmers and of those dependent on small farmers — one vast, widespread, universal *petite bourgeoisie*. Well, Sir, we know perfectly well the main features of a *petite bourgeoisie* . . . We know the very features of the prosperous farmer's face. The cheek bone, the hard mouth, the sunken cheek, the keen and almost cunning eye. Go to the Royal Academy and look at the picture of him by a young painter of genius Mr. Aloysius O'Kelly, and you will be able to read the whole history of a farmer's life, with its good and its evil side. The farmer is frugal to avarice; his industry degenerates into drudgery, his wisdom into cunning; and, above all things, he has the hatred, the dread, and the despair of the revolutionary . . . Is a nation in which the farmers are the main, the dominant, almost the sole element, a nation likely to seek separation . . .?

T. P. O'Connor on the second reading
of the home rule bill, 3 June 1886[1]

Unique an individual as Mr. Healy is, he is so only by the possession in an abnormal degree of the Irish peasant's — that is to say our own — qualities and defects. He is a realist as only the peasant can be, but his realism, like the peasant's, has rifts of imaginative splendour.

C. P. Curran[2]

The split broke on a country at a critical moment of social transition. The solution of the land question by a substantial measure of land purchase establishing a peasant proprietary was by 1890-1 correctly believed to be inevitable. There was a widespread diffusion among tenants of heightened expectations, and the weight of proprietorial aspirations bore heavily on nationalist politics. The sacral primacy of the home rule objective over that of land purchase was never explicitly challenged or upset. Yet the land question swelled and pressed heavily against the fragile skein of the chrysalis of the home rule movement which enfolded it.

The thesis of the agrarian revolution betrayed — fostered contemporaneously by Michael Davitt, and in developed form by later radical historians — understates the inevitability of such a 'betrayal'. The tenurial landscape of Irish politics would always ensure that the spate of the agrarian 'revolution' would course in conservative channels. In reality, the choice lay, not as conventionally suggested between the agrarian radicals and the parliamentarians under Parnell, but between Parnell and Healy: their profound differences on the land issue simmered through the late 1880s, and flared into prominence in the split.

Through the preceding decade, Healy alone of Parnell's lieutenants grasped and did not shrink from the ideological direction the land struggle had taken. His opportunistic populist conservatism, reflected in his coupling of ferocious anti-landlord rhetoric with the unremitting pursuit of a solution by land purchase, set him apart from Davitt's wistfully obtuse radicalism, from O'Brien's exaggerated romanticism, and from Dillon's morosely ascetic patriotism. The consummate realist of the land question, he was unique in the acuity of his realisation of the full implications of proprietorship for Irish politics.

In the split Healy skilfully deployed agrarian themes in the attack on Parnell. His rhetoric skilfully blended the idioms of church, peasantry and nation. It was an exclusionary rhetoric, predicated on a nationalism defined in opposition to Parnell. The deepened chauvinism of his rhetoric against Parnell marks a watershed in the development of nationalist rhetoric, and its significance extends beyond its immediate purpose of procuring Parnell's defeat. While assailing Parnellism as a false ideology, Healy deftly substituted the opaque and intractable ideology of conservative Catholic nationalism. The nation in nationalist rhetoric had been defined as existing in opposition to the external reality of England. The line of differentiation now cleft nationalism internally, as Healy comprehensively anathematised Parnell and the Parnellites as anti-nationalist. The defining myth of nationalism was turned inward upon itself, its shibboleths rendered self-devouring. The split became an essay in lacerating self-definition.

In Healy's oratory and political writings there is a discernible chauvinistic contraction. What had been a romantic rhetoric of oppression acquired an ugly supremacist direction, as nationalist platitude was charged with conservative Catholic social power. It was a revolution within nationalist rhetorical convention which contrived to maintain a semblance of continuity. What had been the stuff of blandly extravagant patriotic declamation was invested with a novel ideological force. What had seemed the innocuous commonplaces of nationalist rhetoric were now directed within nationalism, to define the criteria of an exclusive nationalist authenticity.

Healy's was a sundering rhetoric. The consummate epigrammatist of nationalist chauvinism, he skilfully deployed aphoristic metaphors of race, religion and nation. In the simplifying violence of his rhetoric he sought to cut through the political complexity of the issue of the split, to posit with ruthless concision a stark patriotic choice between Parnell and Ireland. Of the dead Biggar, Healy asked 'would he be on the side of virtue and Erin, or Parnell and Mrs. O'Shea?' The *Weekly National Press* declared: 'It is for the Irish people to choose, hope or despair, Home Rule or coercion, Ireland or Parnell. Such is the choice facing them'.[3] The *National Press* cast the issue of the split in terms of the choice between Parnell and Gladstone and the associated consequences: 'The choice then placed before the Irish people was Gladstone and Home Rule, or Mr. Parnell, the Divorce Court, disgrace, and indefinite coercion'.[4] Healy in the split both canonically formulated a chauvinistic anti-Parnellite rhetoric, and was its *terrible simplificateur.* In the violence of its brevity, his rhetoric sharpened the isolation, and the alienation, of Parnellite opinion. His terse epithets belied the laxness of his political argument, and deepened the crisis of legitimacy and rationality within nationalism in the split.

Healy proclaimed the split a critical educative experience in the formation of Irish democracy. Parnell he accused of setting up 'doctrines which are as I believe, destitute of the very springs of constitutional action':

> My belief is this, that in the wisdom of Providence the period of trial through which we are passing has been appointed to bring us out pure through the fiery trial. I re-echo the sentiment that under Parnell Home Rule might have been a curse rather than a blessing (*cheers*). We are teaching them a lesson in self government.[5]

The casting out of Parnell was proclaimed to demonstrate a bracing vigour in the practice of democratic politics, manifesting that capacity to embrace harsh options in which the Irish were supposed to be lacking. The *National Press* declared that 'a nation given over to illusions and dreams, as many thought, has been forced to face root problems, and has shown keenness and intelligence in doing so'. The *Irish Catholic* proclaimed that 'under the pressure of hard trial the intelligence of our people has become analytical'.[6]

Healy skilfully argued that anti-Parnellism was the tough option, the hard choice, made against the tug of a sentimental allegiance. The split was presented as a strenuous pre-enactment of the harsh dilemmas which legislative independence would present: the rejection of Parnell became a constitutive act of nationhood, an ordeal of creation. The casting out of Parnell was necessarily rending. Any sense of remorse or doubt was attributable to the necessary cruelty of the decision, rather than to any residual allegiance to Parnell. The argument was redemptive of the violence of Healy's rhetoric, and provided its validating metaphysic of brutality.

Against the hard responsibilities embraced by the anti-Parnellites was set the irresponsibility of Parnell. Healy denounced the Parnellism of the split as bereft of political rigour. Vaunting the superior expertise and judgement of the anti-Parnellites in a passage which history has rendered ironic, Healy charged that Parnell's greatest offence lay in making facile promises which he knew to be unrealisable:

> The greatest crime that a man in authority or position can commit is to deceive the humble people whose fate and fortune are in his hands (*applause*). We enjoy special positions; we have had special means of knowledge; we have stood at the gateways of English power. We have stood at the hinges of the British Empire; and we understand in the House of Commons the way and the workings of British parties, and we know what will be and what cannot be. With this knowledge the man who deliberately deceives people was one of the greatest strangers and scoundrels that ever cursed his native land (*cheers*). I say it is the duty of men trusted with a representative position to speak in the face of the people the truth as they conceive it to be (*applause*). It is their duty to indulge in no flattery of the people, not to tell the people that they are the greatest nation under the sun, or that if they put their trust in them they will shortly be led into the promised land.[7]

Healy's own rhetoric could not be considered innocent of the charge which he levelled against Parnell of flattering the people. His campaign, with its flagrant playing on popular prejudice, and its chauvinistic championing of a native modality of power, was a sustained exercise in populist ingratiation. Healy thus seized on Parnell's charge of 'Whiggery' to deliver what was a far more devastating ideological retort.

The peculiar genius of Healy's rhetoric lay in its marriage of a time-hallowed nationalist idiom to a novel agrarian realism, so as to achieve a rhetoric which was at once immediately populist and ostensibly sanctified in tradition, beside which Parnell's rhetoric appeared stiltedly archaic and inauthentic. It was an ambitiously sustained and largely successful endeavour to strike the definitive idiom of modern nationalism. Healy's 'good and dear old Ireland'[8] and Murphy's 'the old land and the old cause'[9] were deceptively ideological concepts. The hackneyed perorations of conventional nationalist rhetoric, the maudlin passages of the crimson and the green, acquired a new function in validating the anti-Parnellite claim to exclusive political legitimacy, and in promulgating a narrowly exclusive conception of the Irish nation.

The cause of Ireland was, Healy proclaimed, older and greater than Parnell. Innocent of ideology, transcendental and eternal, it existed anterior to the history through which it was mediated, as timeless and enduring as the landscape:

> Irish patriotism did not begin and will not end with Mr. Parnell (*applause*). The people of Ireland imbibed the instincts of patriotism with their mother's milk. These instincts were imbibed from the history, the poetry and the traditions of their race. It came to them with the croon of the wind on the Irish hillsides, the lullaby of the Irish streams (*applause*) . . . they would carry out this fight until they plucked the crown of thorns from the nation's brow, and placed once more upon it the olive crown of victory (*long and prolonged cheers*).[10]

The casually blasphemous coupling of a Christian image of torture with a classical emblem of triumph illustrates the promiscuous fluidity of Healy's political imagery. 'Men have failed, passwords and shibboleths have passed away', he declared, 'but the aggregate of the sentiment of the nation lives on forever.' Nationalism was timeless, unbounded by epoch.

> We are not nineteenth century men. We are not twentieth century men. We are not persons of the epoch of 1880. We are Irishmen (*applause*). We are the descendants and successors of a long line of statesmen and kings. We may reflect but poorly the traditions they have handed down to us, but we can only do our best in our own time.[11]

The vindication of what Healy asserted to be the immemorial and immutable traditions of nationalism embraced its partialities as well as its principles: 'Our ideal is to maintain Irish nationality now as it has been in the beginning and please God ever shall be – to keep Ireland with its own traditions, with its feelings, if you like, with its prejudices'.[12] He enjoined nationalists to remain staunch to 'good and dear old Ireland' in the face of Parnell's pretensions:

> These are the times to try men's souls. These are the times for us to give proof of the faith that is in us – whether we love our native land, or whether we will see her cast down, humiliated, and in the dust at the

> feet of a callous and heartless dictator . . . A duty has been cast upon us from which we cannot subtract ourselves, a duty of standing to our native land.[13]

The disjuncture between the inventive ferocity of his attack on Parnell, and the blandness of his invocations of the spirit of the nation, runs through Healy's rhetoric. The violent alternation between the vehement and the sentimental gives his rhetoric much of its rhythm, and some of its force. Against the undying cause of nationalism was set the ephemerality of Parnellism, subject to the way of all flesh. 'The immortal principle of Irish Nationality', declared the *National Press*, 'is enthroned in the heart of the Irish people, who will not depose it to make room for the fetish worship of one guilty and treacherous man.'[14]

Healy deftly appropriated the rhetoric of Thomas Davis and of Young Ireland, the dominant vein of stock nineteenth-century nationalist eloquence. He brilliantly exploited this corpus of rhetoric by developing its cultural and moralistic conception of nationalism in a chauvinistic and illiberal direction, which subverted the avowedly pluralistic purpose of Davis. The utter lack of intellectual rigour in the rhetorical tradition rendered it peculiarly susceptible to exploitation, and it was now invested with an unanticipated ideological significance. There was in this a claim by the Healy–Sullivan connection to the rhetorical copyright of the Young Ireland tradition, mediated through the *Nation* newspaper, which A. M. Sullivan had taken over and which had been maintained by T. D. Sullivan: Maurice Healy's accusation that the Parnellites were contriving to have T. D. Sullivan's 'God Save Ireland' 'replaced by some factionist anthem of their own'[15] gave expression to their rhetorical possessiveness. Davis's famous lines

> Freedom comes from God's right hand,
> And Needs a godly train,
> And righteous men shall make our land
> A nation once again.

were predictably seized upon by anti-Parnellite moralists as prophetic of the issue of the split.[16]

Attacking the Young Ireland League promoted by John O'Leary and W. B. Yeats, the *National Press* in a striking essay in the new chauvinism, accused O'Leary of hostility to the Irish language, adding that 'the Parnellites who rallied round him are even more foreign-tasted than he'. Having invoked Davis in support of a broad and inclusive conception of nationality, and charged that the Young Ireland League was hostile to the legacy of Davis by virtue of its intolerance, the paper proceeded imperturbably to cite a passage of Davis as a prophetic excoriation of the Parnellites ('we want men who are not spendthrifts, drunkards, swindlers – we want honest men – men whom we would trust with our private money or with our families' honour . . .').[17] The *National Press* deployed against the Parnellites Gavan Duffy's lines

> Slaves and dastards, stand aside!
> Knaves and traitors, fag a' bealach![18]

The traditional stock of nationalist rhetoric was also plundered for sarcastic purposes. The *National Press* in bitter mockery applied to the prospect of a visit to Ireland by Katharine Parnell the lines of Thomas Moore:

> On she went, and her angel smile
> Lighted her safely round the green isle;
> And blest for ever was she who relied
> On Erin's honour and Erin's pride.[19]

Anti-Parnellite rhetoric gave a new ideological twist to what John O'Leary in another context called 'that spurious Irishism of Moore's songs, which associates Ireland with virtue and England with guilt'.[20] It was what perceptive Fenians had long feared: the fusion of a conservative nationalism with Catholic religious and moral values. The susceptibility of nationalist rhetoric to Healy's ideological purpose was itself disquieting: its flaccid sentimentality, its lack of a sense of governance or political form, rendered it too readily conformable to the emerging disposition of power in Ireland.

Healy's rhetoric appealed to the self-interest of 'the shrewd tenant farmers of Ireland'.[21] He set the pursuit of practical, palpable gains against what he derided as the mischievous abstruseness of Parnell's chieftaincy: 'A leader is but a means to an end. We cannot mistake the plough for the harvest. We were sent to Westminster not to bring back Mr. Parnell but to bring back a Parliament'.[22]

The *Spectator*'s astute observation in August 1891 that 'Mr. Parnell has tempted Irishmen to the commission of the great sin of quarrelling with their bread and butter' had been anticipated *ipsissimis verbis* by Healy in March:

> Do not suppose for a moment that this is a mere sentimental question of whether you will or will not wear a shamrock on St. Patrick's Day. This is a question of your bread and butter and it is of just as much importance to you to put down Mr. Parnell today as it was to put down the landlord and landgrabber yesterday.[23]

The *National Press* addressed 'the Irish farmer . . . in this supreme crisis of his fate'. In a homage to the acumen of the Irish tenant it declared:

> The Irish farmers are a shrewd race. Generous and self-sacrificing they have shown themselves when the occasion called. But, all the same, their shrewdness is unquestionable. They cannot be terrified nor cajoled to their own ruin. Their votes are not to be captured by the vague platitudes of Mr. Parnell, or by the organised violence of his partisans. They like plain facts and clear arguments.[24]

Healy espoused the pursuit of self-interest on the part of the tenantry as historically sanctioned and ideologically legitimate. The achievement of home rule and peasant proprietorship were inextricably associated: 'We have to win and gather the harvest of Home Rule. We want Home Rule and cheap lands'.[25] In the same speech Healy argued that every day of Parnell's campaign, in dividing the nationalist movement, drove up the price a tenant would have to pay for his farm. In an article published at the same time, Healy, in an exercise in the calculus of peasant proprietorship, asserted that the split had added three to five years' purchase to the price a landlord could expect to exact from a tenant for his holding.[26] 'When we had loosened the nails in the fabric of landlordism', Healy declared, 'Parnell has gone round and driven them home again.'[27] Buffeted by interruptions from a hostile crowd at Freshford in the Kilkenny election, he retorted in exasperation: 'you have a great deal to be proud of. When the rain is coming in through your roofs you will think of this'.[28]

The central parliamentary controversy of the split arose on the debate on Balfour's land purchase bill, originally introduced in the previous session, which Balfour brought forward again as the centrepiece of his Irish strategy.

From the outset Parnell switched his policy from constructive opposition to overt support, to present himself as the true champion of land purchase, and condemn the anti-Parnellites for opposing a bill which substantially benefited Irish farmers out of deference to the Liberal party. Parnell's policy was intended to demonstrate what might be achieved from a policy of independent opposition, or more specifically from the strategy of constructive engagement with the Conservative ministry on the land question which he espoused. Healy had little difficulty avoiding Parnell's crudely set trap. He denied the majority sought the defeat of the bill and professed himself anxious to see it pass in workable shape,[29] all the while trenchantly assailing the bill's defects and limitations and Parnell's collaboration with Balfour's administration.

The bill precipitated a bitter parliamentary confrontation between Healy and Parnell on 17 April. Healy denounced 'the new enthusiasm of the

Member for Cork and his colleagues for this measure'. Parnell had voted against a grant of further monies for land purchase under the provisions of the Ashbourne act and had opposed Balfour's bill the previous year 'not on a single ground, but firstly, secondly, thirdly, fourthly, fifthly, just like one of those "souping parsons" he is so fond of denouncing'. He cited Parnell's endorsement of land nationalisation as further evidence of his inconsistency. Parnell rose immediately to counter-attack, redirecting the taunt of inconsistency by charging Healy with not openly opposing the bill as he had opposed earlier bills, and instead combining with Liberals and radicals 'to do by stealth and by disguised methods what the honourable Member and his leader have not the courage to do openly'. Parnell declared that he did not 'sneak out of the House' on the second reading: 'I did not run away from the Second Reading like the hon. Member for Longford; I voted for the Second Reading because I believe that the Irish tenant farmers want this Bill to pass'. When Parnell asked what had happened to change Healy's mind in the interval, Healy sacrificed consistency to provocativeness to retort: 'Your misconduct'.[30] English members looked on fascinated at this rare parliamentary encounter between Parnell and Healy. Morley described the scene:

> Presently Healy spoke, rasping, biting, against Parnell, but not over-effectual. However it roused P. I have never seen such a sight of concentrated fury. He was not a foot off from Healy and Sexton. He glared into their very faces, hate and revenge in his eyes and in the harsh passionate, tones of voice. Chamberlain said to me, 'He's too clever for you'.[31]

Parnell's strenuous mastery did not however garner votes in Ireland.

The most controversial provision in the bill was its discrimination in favour of the smaller tenants in the allocation of land purchase monies. The bill as introduced excluded advances to finance the purchase of pastoral holdings. Healy responded swiftly to define nationalist anti-grazier sentiment as confined to opposition to large-scale Scotch graziers. These he explained were the men whom Isaac Butt intended to exclude from the land purchase provisions of the 1870 act:

> The idea of the grazier then was the exterminating land-grabber who destroyed the homes of the people, and with two or three collie dogs and Scots herdsmen managed miles of pasture in Galway and Mayo. Very different is the grazier in the eye of the law; the definition includes the small men who, when Ireland had run to waste and emigration had so thinned the population, that there were no labourers in harvest time, occupied his small farm as pasture land. On behalf of these – the men who farm the sweet pastures of Meath and Westmeath I protest against their exclusion from land purchase, and move the omission of the sub-section.[32]

Healy thus strove to confine the term 'graziers' to a narrow class of alien agricultural capitalists. He was thereby gelding the anti-grazier sentiments professed by radical nationalists so as to deprive them of much of their substance. Healy was here touching on one of the fundamental principles of conservative nationalism, the indivisibility of the tenants. This forbade any discrimination between tenants by reference to the size or type of their holdings.[33]

In response to a proposal put by Parnell, Balfour on 21 May introduced a different line of demarcation, which largely excluded tenants the rateable valuation of whose holdings exceeded £30 from the land purchase provisions. He put the proportion of tenants in the eligible category at 92 per cent. This was Balfour's most calculated political intervention in the politics of the split, pitched to embroil further the warring Irish factions, and to exacerbate tensions between nationalists and the Liberals, whose radical wing viewed land purchase measures with deep antipathy. It is difficult to believe that it was not also conceived in part to redress the balance of the Irish parties in Parnell's favour by presenting him as the arbiter of the act. The Balfour clause, emasculated under landlord pressure in the House of Lords, became law with the rateable valuation limit increased to £50.[34] In the event, the controversy was academic. The land purchase act, weighed down by complexities and limitations in a political environment where the tenants — and the landlords — were disposed to await a more favourable measure, was a conspicuous failure.[35]

The controversy over the land purchase bill extended beyond the parliamentary arena, and marks a critically important conjuncture between the issues of the split and the politics of land purchase. Parnell's championing of the bill in parliament and in Ireland proved a bad miscalculation, a contrived exercise in high politics almost parodic of his former parliamentary achievements. It showed him to be strangely out of touch in failing to appreciate the degree of confidence among the tenantry that an extensive measure of proprietorship would be forthcoming. His premise that the £30 million advanced under the act represented the limit of advances for the foreseeable future did not command widespread credence.

Most of all Parnell's position on land purchase exposed him to Healy's devastating counter-attack as pro-landlord and pro-Balfour. Healy remorselessly assailed Parnell's support of the bill as traitorous and divisive, the product of his landlord provenance and interests — the agrarian manifestation of his 'factionism'. After Balfour had signified his intention of introducing his controversial amendment, the *National Press* assailed what it variously described as 'the Parnell-Balfour plan', and Parnell's 'mad scheme'. Parnell was a landlord and an accessory to the Conservative purpose, sharing responsibility for the exclusionary proposal with 'his friend Mr. Balfour':

> The closer one considers Mr. Parnell's attempts to induce the Irish nation to abandon their old fight for the soil of Ireland, and surrender at the demand of an English party, the more insane does it appear. What he asks the Irish people to do is simply this: that they should limit the demand embodied in the cry 'Ireland for the Irish' to a claim to the ownership of one third of Ireland, and leave the garrison in undisputed and unquestioned possession of the other two-thirds.

The paper condemned 'the Balfour-Parnell exclusion trick' as 'a device intended to separate the smaller tenants from the larger men, with the object of weakening both and creating further dissension in the country'.[36]

Conversely Parnell's support for the proposal was consistent, 'intelligible from the point of view of the Orangeman, the Unionist, and the landlord'. In the first place, Ulster would get the lion's share of the advances under the scheme; and in the second 'the grip of the garrison would remain unrelaxed' and landlordism would endure.[37] Healy charged that Parnell's acceptance of the financial limit of £30 million aided Balfour:

> What is that but trying to puff up the price of land? My opinion is that we should make the land market a frost, to freeze the landlords so that you may get the land at something like a fair price, and not pay twice the value for it. Why does Parnell do this? Because he is a landlord himself and wants to sell his own estates.[38]

Of the scheme, the *National Press* commented 'its plain policy is to divide and plunder'.[39] Healy asserted that the unity of the tenants and their bargaining power would be broken: 'that is what Mr. Landlord Parnell wants to drive the tenants of Ireland into'. The tenants of over £30 valuation were 'to remain forever in a state of servitude with their rents "fined down" and with landlordism planted here as a perpetual inheritance amongst us'.[40]

In the Commons, Healy mocked Parnell's policy of constructive amelioration. He professed his disbelief in 'the Saxon smile' of Tory legislative bounty towards Ireland. Of the restrictiveness of Balfour's measure, he taunted 'I thought the Saxon smile on the face of the Tory would be at least as broad as the Saxon smile on the face of the Liberal'.[41] The *National Press* devastatingly reversed the taunt of submitting to English dictation by juxtaposing Parnell's vehement attacks on the Liberals with what was presented as his abject deference to Balfour:

> He can assume towards the Liberal Party and its leader, who declared their readiness to give Ireland the settlement of the land question in a native Parliament, a ferocious insolence, and assail them with unbounded license of epithet; but when Mr. Parnell has to deal with the Tory

> Government and Mr. Balfour, the Grand Sachem of the Hillsides roars you as gently as a sucking dove, and practically goes down upon his knees before the Lion and the Unicorn, telling the people that they have no option but to accept, in whatever shape a Tory Minister may mould it, the Landlord Relief Act that is now being passed through Parliament.

The anti-Parnellites could be trusted not to 'knuckle down to Mr. Balfour and Tory dictation in the cringing Parnellite style'.[42]

In the split Healy skilfully directed against Parnell the evicted tenants' issue, without ever himself assuming any direct responsibility for their plight. Sharing a platform with Dillon and O'Brien at Thurles on the day of Parnell's death, Healy depicted the Plan of Campaign as a pageant of affliction, a *tableau vivant* of the agrarian struggle. He counter-balanced his assertion that the upholding of the evicted tenants of the Plan of Campaign against the landlords 'concerns not only your hearts but your pockets' as follows:

> I heard it said that the movement of Dillon and O'Brien was folly . . . I say on the contrary, that even though men may have suffered, men may have been wounded, that through their sufferings Ireland bled (*cheers*). We can place our hands in the wounds, we see the streaming of their blood; but we would not see all over this land the smiling faces and homes which today would be wretched and miserable but for the men in Tipperary, in Youghal, in Woodford, and in Louth. Yes, men of Tipperary, we are fools, and Dillon and O'Brien, who have backed them are still more foolish. But by what rule, by what plumb, by what admeasurement is this folly sounded and plumbed? Is it the test of £-s-d that is to be applied? If it is, I answer, by the bankrupt coffers of the landlord syndicate, in the crumblement and breakdown of all efforts that Smith Barry could have made, Tipperary met him at the first onset (*cheers*). Where are his legions today? (*renewed cheers*). Fools! Yes, fools, who has suffered for his brethren is a fool. The whole set of men are fools – the men who devotedly sacrificed their lives on the battle plain; aye, and the men who devoted their days to religion are fools, because, as the resultant of their action, they have not a substantial balance at their bankers. That, forsooth, is the test of Parnellism.[43]

The ideological density of the rhetoric suggests how problematical it is to interpret the split as a contest between a moderate constitutional majority and an 'extreme' Parnell. Healy through the medium of blood linked a (casually blasphemous) Christian image with mock-Fenian parlance to contrive a metaphor of agrarian martyrdom. He readily deployed the extravagant rhetorical allusions to Tone and Emmet, for which he had relentlessly assailed Parnell. He drew a pointed contrast between what he derided as Parnell's patriotic posturings and selfish pretensions to 'chieftaincy', and the undemonstrative valour of the evicted tenants, evoking a humbler conception of nationalist virtue to supplant the archaic and vainglorious heroics of Parnellism. Deploying a sacrificial agrarian rhetoric, Healy was asserting the romantic purity of agrarian nationalism. In applying a pseudo-Fenian rhetoric to the Plan of Campaign, he was not merely parodying Parnell, but taunting old Fenians such as John O'Leary who had an engrained mistrust of agrarian nationalism in general and of the Plan of Campaign in particular. The passage, while stylised and almost parodic (and curiously anticipatory of Patrick Pearse's notorious apostrophe over the grave of O'Donovan Rossa), conveys how formidable was the ideology of chauvinistic agrarian nationalism, and how darkly fecund Healy's rhetoric of blood and soil. It was Healy rather than Parnell who was the innovatively vehement rhetorician in the split.

A consideration of the position of Michael Davitt, as the most left-wing of the nationalist leaders, throws into high relief the confused ideological configuration of the split. Davitt was the first prominent nationalist to attack Parnell after the divorce case, and he campaigned vigorously against him in the early phase of the split. His avowed overriding consideration was to uphold the Liberal alliance, which he described as 'a concordat of conciliation and justice'.[44] For Davitt it was an article of faith that the alliance would foster a radical democracy in both countries, and he misconstrued the union of hearts as an alliance of classes. All that remained of his radical aspirations depended by 1890–1 on the aroused democracy of England somehow pulling Ireland in its wake. He was increasingly reliant on the traction of the union of hearts to provide externally propelled radical change.

Doctrinally incapacitated from perceiving a conflict of interest between home rule nationalism and Gladstonian Liberalism, Davitt was alike unable to perceive the implications of the split for his own radical project. He not merely misperceived the split's ideological drift, but succumbed to the temptation to seek to express what professed to be an enlightened democratic analysis of the deficiencies of Parnellism in the crude idiom of chauvinistic nationalism.

There was a striking coincidence between the rhetoric of Davitt and that of Healy in the split. Both denounced Parnellism as anti-national, as socially regressive, and as pitting the principle of one-man power against the popular will. It was Davitt who at Kilkenny and in the columns of his *Labour World* pioneered the populist idiom of anti-Parnellism which

Healy would so exhaustively develop. Thus Davitt in the *Labour World* had written after Kilkenny 'the Parnell superstition has been fought, exposed and exorcised', that the country must learn 'the death of one-man power in Irish politics', and denounced 'the old craze of idol worship'.[45]

Davitt congratulated himself on being untainted by the former adulation of Parnell by the party. He complained on 12 December 1890 to a correspondent that the 'McCarthyite party' were lacking in courage: 'They have slobbered so much individually and collectively over Parnell that they seem inclined to embrace him again. I cannot help admiring the splendid audacity of the man! What a pity he is lost to a good cause'.[46]

To Davitt, the split appeared misleadingly as the culmination of the years of thwarted endeavour on his part which had followed the inception of the land struggle. At the inauguration of the National Federation, he decried the absence of a democratic nationalist organisation in the preceding years. He condemned the supplanting of nationalism by Parnellism: 'I think I can say I have striven for years to degrade this order of things and to bury forever the degrading and debasing idol worship and one-man power'.[47] He mistakenly assessed the split in terms of a vindication of his own critique of Parnellism in the preceding decade. In his tendency to assimilate the split to his forecast of an irresistible democratic tide, he was wistfully oblivious to the more complex eddies of the course of Irish nationalism. In regarding the anti-Parnellite victory in the split as in some way a belated endorsement of his own position in the 1880s he permitted his *amour propre* as a radical spurned to outweigh his political judgement. It was as if the suppressed passions of the years of restraint, during which he had at Parnell's behest censored his true political feelings, spilled over in the vehemence of his rhetoric in the split, marked as it was by a surprising degree of personal rancour towards Parnell.

Davitt's opposition to Parnell owed much to the naively schematic perception of Irish politics which had characterised his career subsequent to the initiation of the land struggle. In a lecture in 1887 on 'An Irish Parliament, its Parties and its Work', Davitt sought to predict ideological alignments under home rule. The nationalist majority he believed would divide into two parties. A party, which he designated 'Conservative Nationalist', with Parnell at its head, would be first to govern: 'Behind such a party there would be the great influence of the churches, Catholic and Protestant, the propertied and commercial classes, and, of course, the services, always disinterested, of the legal fraternity, which is adding so many Nationalist recruits every day to its already plethoric ranks', along with the larger farmers. It would be opposed by what he termed 'A Democratic or Radical Nationalist Party', comprising two wings, one holding advanced views on social questions and the other with separatist tendencies: in essence a reconstitution of the coalition which had underpinned the 'New Departure'.[48] Davitt's superimposition of a simplistic radical paradigm on nationalist politics led him to exaggerate the prospects for the emergence of a conventional left–right divide in Ireland. He neglected the stubborn intricacies of Irish politics, and in particular underestimated the impact of peasant proprietorship. He disregarded the risks of sectarian polarisation, and in lumping together in a 'Conservative Nationalist' party Parnell and Healy, that archetypal representative of the 'legal fraternity', obscured, or failed to perceive, their profound divergence of purpose.

Davitt dismissed Parnell's 'rather newly born' zeal for the labour cause as irreconcilable with his earlier career, in particular his opposition to Davitt's Irish Democratic Labour Federation.[49] He ridiculed Parnell as 'this whilom Conservative', whom he accused of plagiarising the *Labour World* for his social programme: 'Mr. Parnell has now succeeded in divesting me, politically speaking, of all my clothes, from my caubeen to my brogues. He has walked off with all my doctrines, and all my programme'. He wished from the bottom of his heart 'that Mr. Parnell had endorsed or enunciated a programme half as thorough as this even so late as six months ago'.[50]

Davitt had good reason to suspect the sincerity of Parnell's sudden conversion to the cause of labour. Yet, however opportunistic it may have appeared, Parnell's embrace of labour, taken in conjunction with the starkly conservative direction of the predominant Healyite strain of anti-Parnellism, should have alerted Davitt to the complexity of allegiance in the split, and induced him at the very least to stake out a distinctive position in the ranks of those opposed to Parnell's leadership.

In the split, Davitt threw into reverse the personal assessments he had formed over the previous decade. In referring publicly to 'my friend Tim Healy',[51] he suppressed his former mistrust of a politician to whom he had a long-standing antagonism as a ruthless lieutenant of Parnell and ally of the right-wing leadership of the National League in Britain, Barry and Biggar, who had strenuously opposed Davitt's radical designs on the Irish working class in England. In 1888, while hurt by Parnell's failure to show any appreciation for his preparatory work on the Special Commission, he had strikingly expressed his preference for the Irish leader over his lieutenants:

> Parnell is cold, and if you will, ungrateful. But what about his possible successors! Better from my point of view to stick to a sick lion though he has given you a paw now and then, than to have for masters a crowd of ambitious jackals who want to play the part of a lion, without possessing a single attribute of the nobler animal.[52]

Davitt's political enterprise was swallowed up within anti-Parnellite nationalism. His conception of progressive democracy and the Healyite proprietorial nation were ideologically incompatible. When Healy declared himself and his allies 'mere missionaries and exponents of the public will',[53] the public will was emphatically not that of Davitt's radical democracy.

Davitt's failure to translate his stature into influence within the anti-Parnellite party was apparent from the outset. He failed to induce the anti-Parnellites to run a labour candidate in the Kilkenny election, and was obliged instead to support the candidacy of James Pope Hennessy, 'that tricky politician',[54] a former protégé of Disraeli, whose first parliamentary vote after his election Davitt had occasion publicly to condemn. Davitt's course in the split enacted the fractured pattern of his career. Intervening strongly at the outset, his involvement thereafter waned. Rather than exploit the advantage his initial prominence had given him, he departed for America in May where he remained until after the death of Parnell.[55]

While he boasted of his percipience and consistency, Davitt's role in the opposition to Parnell deepened rather than resolved the contradictions of his career. The fall of Parnell precipitated his last significant intervention, and consumed his marginalisation, in Irish politics. To Richard McGhee he wrote in 1903: 'The Land League movement can of course in a sense be considered to have existed up to the Parnell split'.[56]

Ideologically burdened, and dogmatically aggrieved at the accommodations to Parnell's purpose that he had been compelled to make through the 1880s, Davitt was ill-equipped to comprehend the later Parnell. Reviewing the biography published by Davitt's admirer Francis Sheehy-Skeffington in 1908, T. M. Kettle observed with charity:

> It was not wise to set Davitt over in contrast to Parnell, and superior to Parnell, as Mr. Skeffington does. They are almost immeasurable. Parnell, combining the qualities of a mystic with those of a gambler, cannot be summed up in terms of a *ratio ratiocinans*, a reasoning reason such as Davitt essentially was.[57]

20

'Mobology': A Nation Divided

In the play of the split's lightning on the Irish political landscape, the configuration of power within nationalist Ireland was briefly and starkly illumined. The schism threatened the foundations of nationalism. It challenged the central political convention of nationalism whereby considerations of class and social conflict within nationalism were suppressed, notionally until after the attainment of home rule.

Conservative nationalist publicists of church and nation deprecated the ideologically fractious play of social interests, and evinced a conspicuous distaste for any elucidation of conflicting interests within nationalism. Economic determinism was regarded with particular aversion as a threat to the idealistic purity of nationalism. The positing of class divisions within nationalism was considered to be mischievous, if not profane: the application to Ireland of a distasteful paradigm derived from philosophical materialism, and more particularly from the sociology of English industrial capitalism. All invidious socio-economic differentiations within nationalism were subsumed in the dogma of the innate social harmony of the nationalist order. Parnell's infractions of the conventions of reticence, while guarded and fragmentary, were sufficient to threaten the obscurantist nationalist treatment of class and economic interest. Conservative nationalists discerned a cynical determination on Parnell's part to fight his way back to the leadership through the destabilisation of the nationalist polity, a mischievous turning back of the strategy of the land war upon *nationalist* society. At the same time both sides drew back from an unambiguous abrogation of the consensus. Parnell had no intention of abdicating his pretensions to the leadership of a unitary nationalism by provoking a purely sociological schism. It sufficed for his purpose to adumbrate a threat.

While the scale of the anti-Parnellite victories in the split's three by-elections and the general course of the split surpassed their most optimistic expectations, the apprehensions of anti-Parnellite publicists and ideologues were not stilled. The frenzied triumphalism of the anti-Parnellites disclosed an abiding insecurity. This can be attributed in part to an abiding fear of a Parnellite resurgence, a dread of Parnell's mastery asserting itself amidst the volatility of the shifting politics of home rule. Healy's correspondence disclosed his fears. He wrote to his father in March: 'It is a pity the Irish are such fools. I thought they had more acuteness'. In May he declared: 'I am a little out of conceit with the great Celtic race to think it comprises so many fools. However it is hasty to form any judgement on our poor countrymen as they have been deadly misled by those who knew better'.[1] Just before the 1892 general election, he complained: 'The English when they get roused are often a savage people. I always complained that we had not some of the — I will not say the vices — but some of the fierceness and determination of the English people. It is a fault of our Irish character that we are not bitter enough'.[2] This apprehension of the inconstancy of the Irish prompted his strategy of tightly marshalling political sentiment through a rhetoric of crisis, so as to resist the cauterising effect of victory on the rawness of the struggle.

The anti-Parnellites claimed they comprised the enlightened elements of the nationalist democracy, what Healy termed 'the organised intelligence' of the country. He contrasted Parnell's 'ignorant' supporters with his 'educated or reasonable' opponents.[3] He claimed that the anti-Parnellites commanded the support of 'the clergy and nine-tenths of the respectable laity',[4] and sought to emphasise the superior sagacity of the anti-Parnellite voter.

Thus he declared 'we seek not the verdict of the ignorant, the foolish, and the distempered. We ask for the calm, cool, considered, and collected judgement of the people'.[5] He discounted in similar vein the allure of Parnell for the younger generation of nationalists:

> It is natural that young people should be misled (*hear hear*). It is natural especially that those who do not understand the springs and movements of constitutional action in the House of Commons should be got to say: 'Here is a great man to fight our battles as he has done in the past'. These are catchcries. They are talking for those who do not read and study and who cannot appreciate the correlations of force in Irish life. It takes sensible men to be right in this business. It takes men of thought, not men of porter and whiskey.[6]

William Martin Murphy declared that 'whatever the noise and clamour may be on the other side I believe we have the solid men, the men who will influence the poll at the general election'.[7] Healy repeatedly asserted the social as well as the numerical supremacy of the opposition to Parnell. Predicting a Parnellite rout at the general election, he wrote: 'Mr. Parnell, of course, thinks or says otherwise, on the strength of galvanised meetings and torchlight processions carefully organised. It is not the froth on the waves that disturbs the pebbles on the shore, and the permanent forces of life in Ireland are arrayed against Mr. Parnell'.[8]

Putting conventional Irish election badinage to systematic purpose, Healy skilfully depicted Parnellism as a coalition of social extremes, bereft of support from the centre-ground of agrarian nationalism. This malign alliance embraced the landlords, the nationalist rabblement, and the 'Castle Catholics'.

> The ingredients which support Mr. Parnell down the country are very curious. I will say that while he has several honest men upon his side (*hear hear and nos*) it is a remarkable fact that every blackguard in Ireland is in his favour (*hear hear*). And certainly if the unpurchasable enthusiasm of the corner-boy could make Mr. Parnell leader, he is now the recognised leader of the Irish race standing at the bar (*laughter*). But I am far from saying that he has not a number of 'respectable' men with him (*'very few', and hear hear*). He has some of 'the most respectable men in the country', because he has every landlord in the country at his back (*hear hear*). And there is a kind of middle term — a kind of tertium quid — between these two — between the boy at the corners and the lord in his halls, the class who never joined in this movement in the past, and who were never worth a ha'porth for anything (*cheers*) . . . you will find that those who ape gentility, and who at the same time desire to be considered patriots are very glad of the opportunity of being at the same time terribly advanced Nationalists without offending the Tory Government of Mr. Balfour (*hear hear*).[9]

This was an elaboration of what he described in a letter to his father at the outset of the split as 'the horrid combination against us, Fenians, Factionists, landlords and grabbers, with a lining of honest fanatics'.[10] William O'Brien more temperately deplored 'the complete working understanding which this crisis has brought about between the Orange and Green extremities of the Irish body politic'.[11]

Among conservative nationalists there was a persisting fear of a destabilisation of the nationalist social order, which partly accounts for the paradox of escalating anti-Parnellite vehemence in victory. For them the split provided a foretaste of the bitter social conflict which they feared could emperil the stability of a home rule Ireland: their rhetoric reflects the sharpened apprehensions of a nascent order of government and property as to its grip on nationalist society at a critical moment of transition. It was this commingled fear of a Fenian resurgence and of social revolution — a compounding of agrarian unrest turned against the nationalist social order, and of revolutionary urban disaffection — which gave the rhetoric of anti-Parnellism its edge of nervous fury.

The sociological reality which underlay conservative nationalist fears was the existence of a vast deprived underclass. Beyond the urban and rural working class lay the desperately poor, those without agricultural land or fixed employment who existed outside the franchise, and beyond the political economy of nationalism. The fear and antipathy of conservative nationalists had their roots in a Malthusian intimation of overpopulation, for them the most ideologically powerful residue of the famine. The Irish land struggle had become, if it had not always been, a deeply conservative revolution, marked by a determination to generate a rhetoric and ideology not susceptible to radical elaboration. The significance of Healy's chauvinism of tenure was that it legitimated the status of the nationalist tenantry as against those above and below it in Irish society. The ideologically highly stylised conception of the Irish peasant was defined in opposition both to the landlord class and to the wretched of the nationalist earth.

In the rhetoric of conservative nationalism in the split, Fenianism was at once a specific political phenomenon and a convenient means of designating social forces potentially disruptive of the stability of nationalist society. The taunt levelled against Parnell of paltering to the Fenians was part of a wider charge of fomenting social disorder. The Bishop of Clogher condemned Parnell's appeal to 'the elements of disorder and revolution'.[12] In conflating a recrudescence of Fenian activity with social revolution, he was articulating a deep apprehension of conservative nationalists, lay and clerical, a bond of shared fear between farmer, cleric, and merchant.

The dourly clericalist *Irish News*, the northern sister paper to the *National Press*, treated Parnellism and Fenianism as virtually synonymous. Both were perceived to constitute a threat to constitutional nationalism, and to Catholic faith and morals. It alleged that 'as a last resort to hold up Parnellism in Ireland', attempts were being made to establish secret societies, and warned in terms at once grave and vague that 'there is no use blinking the fact that in some parts, at least of the country . . . there is being carried on an active propaganda of Fenianism, or some such form of antagonism to religious authority and to the constitutional movement in Ireland'.[13]

Conservative nationalists were constrained in their references to the underclass of nationalism. Yet in the vehemence of the split class rancour frequently broke through the sectarian and chauvinistic sentimentalities of their rhetoric. Archbishop Croke, in an incautious statement directed against Parnell's pretensions to the leadership of the Irish race, declared 'he would not be the leader of the Irish people, because three-fourths, at least, of the intelligence, nearly all the wealth, and an overwhelming share of Irish influence would be arrayed against him'.[14] In the face of Parnellite rejoinders, Croke struggled to limit the damage: 'I then believed, and still believe, that our farming, mercantile and professional, whether lay or ecclesiastical, forces, to say nothing of the artisans and labour elements, mostly all Home Rulers, represent in an overwhelming proportion, the wealth, intelligence and influence of our country'.[15]

Croke had merely given mild expression to the views he expressed privately to the Rector of the Irish College in Rome, to whom he had written that Parnell was 'stirring up everything that is dirty and discreditable in the lower stratum of Irish life'. He amplified this proposition in a further letter: 'Corner boys, blackguards of every hue, discontented labourers, lazy and drunken artisans, aspiring politicians, Fenians and in a word, all the irreligious and anti-clerical scoundrels in the country are at his back'.[16]

Croke's was the most striking expression of the dread of social anarchy. For clerical observers it was as if Parnell's depravity had summoned up a social coalition of the disreputable. The split exacerbated engrained ecclesiastical fears of a coupling of anti-clericalism and social revolution on the continental model: the lingering influence of continental seminaries deepened the lurid apprehensions of Irish churchmen. Social fear and revulsion underlay the conservative anti-Parnellite detestation of the components of Parnell's support. The *Irish Catholic* described in horrified tones the Parnellites assembled at Parnell's Cabinteely meeting and commented: 'Falstaff's ragged battalions were decent citizens in comparison with such personages, who will, nevertheless, appear in the columns of Monday's Freeman as "the sturdy yeomen of South Dublin"'.[17]

One of the considerations which underlay anti-Parnellite emphasis on the 'respectability' of their support, and the denunciations of Parnellite proletarianism, was the fact that Parnell's share of the vote was generally believed to understate his level of popular support. He was considered to be stronger among the unfranchised than among voters. The parliamentary electorate comprised 61 per cent of the adult male population in the counties, and only 45 per cent of the adult males in the boroughs.

Interrupted during the Carlow election by a Parnellite heckler whom another voice in the crowd declared did not have a vote, Healy taunted 'he will have a vote when Kitty is queen of Ireland (*much laughter*)'. Labouchere reflected the fears of his Irish sources in writing to Gladstone in November 1891 that 'matters are not quite so rosy in Ireland as they look. If there were manhood suffrage, the Parnellites would have a majority'. Yet Parnell did not argue for universal male suffrage, or seek to contend that the restricted franchise had cheated him of victory: the political nation remained limited by mutual consent. The Parnellite Edmund Leamy was provoked by Croke's outburst to mutter that 'he hoped the time would come when every man of full age would have a vote in the affairs of his country, and when that was so they would hear less about wealth and intelligence (*hear, hear*)'.[18]

The most extended anti-Parnellite sociology of the split is that of Healy's American friend and confidant Harold Frederic, whose writing on Ireland bore the heavy impress of Healy's influence. In a series of highly controversial articles published in the *Fortnightly Review* in 1893–4, he provided an extended analysis of what he had described on Parnell's death as the 'rude, ill-furnished, and vicious minds' which made up his support.[19]

Frederic's starting point was the assertion that the farmers and labourers whom he regarded as comprising the respectable rural classes made up a mere one-fifth of the population. In a *tour d'horizon* of Irish agrarian society, he wrote, 'the moment we quit the farm-land proper for the village, the evil and discouraging change begins', in the predominance of the aged, the mendicant, and the idle. Frederic asserted that in the preceding decade the number of 'idle, incompetent, and valueless males' had doubled, and that it was to this 'rapscallion class' that Parnell looked for his support. 'Since 1890', he wrote, 'every thoughtful Irishman has been contemplating with astonishment and dismay the numerical proportions of this vast army of urban riff-raff.' This then was the nationalist *canaille*, 'the permanently idle class, accepting just enough jobs to maintain a bare existence', the 'ever-swelling army of loafers and vagabonds', the 'infected human scum' which threatened the social order and economic viability of nationalist Ireland.[20] In Frederic's model of Irish society, the lineaments of the fearful sociology of conservative nationalism are discernible.

The existence of a large proletariat and a pauperised underclass in Dublin engendered a particular unease among conservative nationalists, lay and ecclesiastical. Dublin was perceived as a tinderbox of insurgency, the site of a combustible interaction of the socio-political instabilities of the nineteenth-century European city with advanced nationalism in its Parnellite or Fenian strains. Frederic accurately reflected conservative nationalist apprehensions in writing that Dublin 'contains a larger and more helpless class of permanently impoverished people, in proportion, than most of the other great cities of Europe'.[21] Conservative nationalists were unnerved by the contemplation of what the rabid anti-Parnellite priest John Behan categorised as 'this overgrown metropolis, filled with paupers'.[22] Behan's hysterical vision of Parnellite carnage had a specifically urban locus:

'he believed if Mr. Parnell had control of the armed forces of this country the blood of some of them would be running in the gutters, and some of their corpses would be decorating the pavement'.[23]

W. F. Dennehy, in impressing on Archbishop Walsh the need for organisation in Dublin, invoked the spectre of continental revolutionary anti-clericalism: 'It will be of little use to beat Mr. Parnell and his friends in Cork or Kilkenny, if they capture Dublin as similar men have seized Paris and Rome'.[24] The Parnellite capital could then contaminate the country: the Bishop of Dromore discerned a parallel with the French Revolution in which 'demagogues from Paris deluded the provinces with unholy teaching'.[25]

Dublin was the jewel the anti-Parnellite crown lacked. Its obdurate Parnellism contributed to the seemingly perverse fury in victory of anti-Parnellite ideologues. The adherence of the city's nationalist population to Parnell was a standing affront to anti-Parnellite pretensions: *Insuppressible* confessed that 'we are a little ashamed of Dublin in this crisis'.[26] The enduring Parnellism of Dublin thwarted Healy's avowed purpose of not merely defeating, but annihilating Parnell. The capital provided Parnellism with the electoral base which permitted it to hold out between the death of Parnell and the re-unification of the Irish party in 1900: four of the nine seats won by Parnellites at the general election of 1892 were in Dublin. Among the anti-Parnellite casualties were William Martin Murphy, who lost the St. Patrick's division of the city, and T. D. Sullivan who lost the College Green division. Anticipating Sullivan's defeat, Healy had earlier written to his brother 'the pity is that he has some sentimental fancy for sitting in College Green'.[27] Healy complained to his father as the election approached that the Dublin priests were 'Parnellites or tepid'.[28]

The existence of an overwhelming Parnellite majority in Dublin destroyed anti-Parnellite claims to a majority which was demographically representative as well as numerical. It attested to the awkward fact that Parnell commanded significant support in towns and cities throughout the country, albeit not sufficient in 1892 to return a Parnellite candidate in urban constituencies outside the cities of Dublin and Waterford. It permitted Parnell to assert that he had the support of the most progressive elements within nationalism, and that the rest of the country would follow Dublin's lead. Most importantly of all, it lent support to the Parnellite contention that the preponderant consensus against Parnell in most of rural Ireland was deceptive and artificial (if hardly the consequence merely of 'clerical dictation' as Parnellite apologists claimed).

Anti-Parnellite publicists sought to impugn the legitimacy of Dublin nationalism, asserting that the Parnellites of Dublin lacked that rootedness in the soil and historical experience of agrarian dispossession and hardship which could have permitted them to attain to the true nationalist vision: it was their unhappily *déraciné* condition which rendered them susceptible to the spurious and inflammatory politics of Parnellism.

Dublin was discounted as the centre of the historic Pale and the core of English power in Ireland. In a speech at Rostrevor (reported in the Derry *Irish News*, but tactfully suppressed in the Dublin *National Press*), Healy proclaimed that the bulk of the country was solidly anti-Parnellite, 'whereas Dublin of the Pale, Dublin of the wealthy aristocrats, and Dublin of the informers and sham squires, is the only place in which Parnellism has any quarter'.[29] Healy situated Dublin on an anti-patriotic urban periphery, its population cut off from the rhythms of rural life: 'I do not take the opinion of Ireland in the opinion of some Dublin corner boys. There is a little strip of inhabitants on this east coast of Ireland that know less of Leinster, Munster and Connaught than they know of the feelings and wishes and the interests of Switzerland'.[30] At the outset of the split, the anti-Parnellite Jasper Tully contrasted with 'the men of the South and West, who love their religion and country' with Dublin, 'the moral cesspool of Ireland'.[31] Provincial resentment of Dublin was felt most strongly in nationalist Ulster. E. F. V. Knox, anti-Parnellite M.P. for Cavan West, went so far as to question the siting of a home rule legislature in Dublin.[32]

To the theme that urban Parnellites were divorced from what he asserted to be the constitutive experiences of nationalism, Healy reverted in a speech in November 1892, after the general election had reduced Parnellism to a disproportionately urban minority:

> And they can always come together and boast, 'Sure we have Dublin at our back', or 'we have Waterford at our back' – cities that do not feel the agricultural or the agrarian question, that know nothing of the grievances of the labourers or the farmer in the field, men whom any kind of claptrap can catch, who know nothing of the grievances brought upon you by the corrupt grand juror, the corrupt ex officio guardian, the corrupt magistrate, the corrupt stipendiary, the evicting landlord, the grabber, the agent of the emergency man . . .[33]

After Redmond's failure to hold Parnell's Cork seat in November 1891, Healy spoke in terms of a besieged Parnellite capital:

> Their attempt to confine the national feeling of Ireland within the North Circular Road to make the bounds of Irish nationality dependent on the limits of the Grand and Royal canals has failed, and from outside Dublin, from that country where we all have come, have arisen the voices of Carlow, of Cork, of Sligo, of Kilkenny reverberating and thundering at the Gates of Dublin and reminding the men here that the fighting men

> of the Irish race all through our land and through the provinces are on the side of fidelity to the Irish cause and to its pledged party.[34]

The superb 'from that country where we all have come' epitomised the supremacy within nationalism of rural values which Healy's rhetoric proclaimed. Dublin in short was the Parnellite ghetto. In 1894 he compared Dublin Parnellism to a 'trout in a tank': 'They cannot escape beyond the confines of the North Circular Road. The moment they go outside, if ever they do, the environment of the free air of the countryside is poison to them'.[35]

Harold Frederic in 1893 memorably expressed the perception of Parnellism as a metropolitan phenomenon. Of the literary coterie of Dublin, and in particular of W. B. Yeats, Katharine Tynan, and Douglas Hyde, he wrote:

> It is characteristic of this lonely and forlorn little group of real geniuses that they should be vehement Parnellites – attracted from the romantic and etherealized standpoint, as the scourings of Dublin's gutters and whisky-soaked slums are drawn by lust for turbulence and affection for all forms of mutiny, towards that sad, strange shadowy figure, prophet, desperado, ruler, charlatan, madman, martyr all in one – the last commanding personality in hapless Ireland's history.[36]

Frederic's construction of Parnellism as an alliance of urban intellectuals and the underclass, though far-fetched, conveys something of the intensity of urban Parnellism, as well as a presentiment of the posthumous literary avenging of the Irish leader.

Healy condemned the recourse to violence which he asserted underlay Parnellism. He correctly characterised Parnell's strategy as intended to overwhelm public opinion at the outset of the split by means of organised demonstrations of support before the majority had established an organisation. Even after the reverse of the Kilkenny election, this strategy was echoed in the practice of the Parnellite press of treating Parnell's series of weekend meetings through Ireland as a triumphant plebiscitary progression: thus the *Freeman's Journal* of 2 February could proclaim, with a fatuousness which excited Healy's most lethal ridicule, that 'seven times within as many weeks has Ireland now pronounced for Parnell'.[37]

Healy denounced Parnell's vaunted 'appeal' to the country as an incitement to turbulence conceived in disregard of democratic principles: 'the country speaks through the ballot box by its members of parliament, the country is not the beery product of public houses shouting as a mob'.[38]

'Parnellism cannot be polled at railway stations or enumerated by the radiance of Roman candles', declared the *National Press.*[39] After Parnell's triumphal reception on his return to Dublin after Committee Room 15, Healy declared: 'He had just got a taste of a torchlight procession in Dublin. We hear of a torchlight procession marching down a man's throat, but I think this torchlight procession made its way into Mr. Parnell's brain'.[40]

Healy asserted, with considerable justification, that Parnellite bravado masked a flight from electoral realities, a flinching from the popular verdict.

> Watch our opponents' newspapers and you will see the test they have long proposed for themselves is this – whether a particular man is hooted or Roman-candled at a railway station (*laughter*). I say that is not the test (*hear hear*); and that the only way to test the opinion of the people is to test them in the ballot boxes, and to the ballot boxes they will not go.[41]

At Kilkenny he accused Parnell of a strategy of intimidation by mob violence:

> . . . he sought by organising hired mobs, many members of which were supplied with drink to impress outsiders by means of the *Freeman's Journal* with the idea that this clamouring crowd represented an educated public opinion in the district. Crowds at a railway station and voices hurling opprobrious epithets did not make public opinion. Were the leaders of the labouring, farming and shopkeeping classes amongst Mr. Parnell's supporters? . . . Looking back upon the past ten years, he regretted the bloody puddle in which they had arrived, and he felt inexpressibly sad and inexpressibly bitter.[42]

'You may work up public passions with the bellows of apostasy', he declared, but that was not intimidation, for the only form of intimidation recognised by the Parnellites was the supposed dictation of the clergy.[43]

Anti-Parnellites asserted the mob to be as integral a feature of Parnellite electioneering as the 'chief'. 'Without a mob to hoot down and terrify decent people he can get a reception nowhere', wrote Harold Frederic of Parnell at Sligo.[44] Healy in particular denounced what he asserted was a Parnellite penchant for violence. Following a brutal assault on him by the eccentric O'Brien Dalton in March 1891, Healy declared it was part of the Parnellites' policy 'to turn Ireland into a pandemonium'.[45] He denounced Parnellite 'mobology'.[46] The *Irish Catholic*, unnerved, discerned in Parnellism 'a tyranny which is in no way rendered legitimate or righteous because it is exercised through the rough-and-ready ways of the proletariat rather than by the swords of legionaries' and charged that Parnellism sought 'to coerce by the unholy and degrading tyranny of the mob the very conscience of the nation'.[47]

Parnellism as a drunken debauch was one of Healy's favoured themes. It was a commonplace of anti-Parnellite rhetoric that the Parnellites liberally distributed drink among the disaffected classes of nationalism. Healy charged that Parnell was 'scattering money and liquor among the poorer classes of our countrymen'.[48] The allegation evoked the bad old days of Irish elections, of violence and drunkenness, which the united Parnellite movement had eliminated and which its erstwhile leader was now accused of reviving. Parnell would find that 'there is a big difference between a ballot-box and a tierce of porter'. Healy's development of the theme culminated in a Swiftian metaphor. Of Parnellite blackguards, he declared 'for the work which Mr. Parnell needed, whether giving their throats for huzzahing or for porter, the class in question have been most useful to the party of Messrs. Harrington and Parnell'.[49] In this conceit of a Parnellite rictus, Healy evinced once more that mastery of the political idiom of the flesh which characterised his rhetoric in the split.

Healy's denunciations of Parnellite 'corner boys', if unexceptionable in Irish elections, brought into play in the split the age as well as the social standing of Parnell's supporters. He attacked the Parnellites for 'allowing the corner boy element to make organised opposition in the street', and declared, 'sure, if we talked nonsense we too could win the hurroos of corner boys'. He pronounced the majority of the Irish party a better judge of the political issues of the split than 'the cornerboys and youngsters of some of the towns in this country'.[50] Parnell, Healy declared, had 'the support of the boys, of the young men, as he calls them, all over the country — boys, who before they approach the ballot boxes will have in the words of David to his "envoys", to tarry at Jericho till their beards be grown'.[51] Healy's deriding of the voteless youthfulness of many of Parnell's sympathisers was unwise. It underwrote Parnell's claim to the allegiance of a rising generation of nationalists, and contributed to the reaping of the whirlwind of disillusionment in the years after Parnell's death.

17. T. M. Healy

18. John Dillon

19. William O'Brien

20. William Martin Murphy

21. John Redmond

HIGH TRAGEDY

Mr. William O'Brien as Mrs. Siddons

22. 'High Tragedy: Mr. William O'Brien as Mrs. Siddons' (*Punch,* 16 Mar. 1910)

23. Healy with two gentlemen circa 1910

A Reunited Party
E. T. Reed
John Redmond, T. M. Healy, John Dillon, William O'Brien.

24. 'A Reunited Party' (*Punch,* 5 Feb. 1908)

25. T. M. Healy in parliament (E. T. Reed, pencil sketch)

Two views of the Governor-General:

26. 'His Excellency the Dove' (Sir Bernard Partridge, *Punch,* 13 Dec. 1922)

27. 'Keeping Ireland Down': Irish republican handbill featuring the Governor-General. The cartoon also appeared in Sinn Féin (9 Aug. 1924)

28. The motorist: T. A. Finlay, S. J., is the intrepid front-seat passenger

29. The Governor-General receives members of the Irish hierarchy at the Viceregal Lodge (June 1923). His old friend and ally, the Cardinal Archbishop of Armagh, is seated on the left.

30. The Horse Show, the Royal Dublin Society (August 1926). From left to right: Lady Lavery, Kevin O'Higgins, T. M. Healy, the Maharajah of Alwar, John A. Costello, the Jam Sahib of Nawanagar (otherwise Ranji, a celebrated cricketer), and Mr. Justice W. E. Wylie.

31. The presentation of the Aga Khan trophy, the Horse Show (August 1926). The Governor-General salutes as the anthem is played. Lord Powerscourt holds the trophy. Mr Justice Wylie upstages the Maharajah.

32. T. M. Healy and W. T. Cosgrave at the funeral of Kevin O'Higgins (July 1927)

33. Healy and the Beaverbrooks, with Arnold Bennett behind, outside the Hotel Alfonso XII (Madrid, 1924)

34. The Governor-General at the Dublin wireless exhibition of November 1926, where he broadcast a brief address

35. T. M. Healy and W. T. Cosgrave

— Part III —

After the Fall: 1891–1931

21

After Parnell

I do not pretend to say that any of us are equal in skilled diplomacy, in reserve and power of silence, to Mr. Parnell. I think Mr. Parnell in that way was a national loss.

T. M. Healy, 26 April 1892[1]

When he thought of domestic affairs in the House of Commons, which had been so long a central preoccupation of his life, he recalled that he had seen the rise, the culmination and the decline of that marvellous Parliamentarian phenomenon, the Irish party under Mr. Parnell . . . He did not believe that in the whole history of our Parliament – he doubted whether in the history of any Parliament – there had been such a party for the sternness of its discipline and the extraordinary wealth of admirable speakers it contained, some of them great masters of elocution and admirable debaters, formidable from their knowledge of parliamentary methods and the use to which they put that knowledge – misuse as we Britons often thought it – but now he desired to speak impersonally, politics apart. In regard to the use those men put that knowledge he did not believe there had ever been so remarkable a party as that. He saw its rise and its small beginnings in the first Parliament of which he was a member, and he saw it when Parnell took the leadership, and he saw its culmination and its decline.

A. J. Balfour, 20 June 1922[2]

The Aftermath of Parnell's Death

With the death of Parnell, a terrible finality was achieved.

Alfred Webb wrote from Dublin three weeks after Parnell's death 'it is very unhappy here in many respects. Nearly all our close friends have gone Parnell worse than ever, and our circle is quite broken up. Walking the streets is like walking a city of the dead'. 'The sunderings of friends were terrible', recalled Katharine Tynan. T. P. Gill wrote that 'men who have passed through this crisis find themselves like revellers – some of them with very bad headaches – regarding the debris of a tragically interrupted love-feast in the cruel light of dawn'. Almost a half-century later Henry Harrison said that the year 1890–1 remained with him always: 'I did over two years as a junior officer in the front line in France, yet though I had many drastic experiences, none of that period lives with me as do the days of the Parnell tragedy'.[3]

News of Parnell's death reached Dublin the day after, 7 October. J. F. Taylor, the Dublin correspondent of the *Manchester Guardian* went to the offices of the *National Press*. The blinds were down. He came upon Healy just after he had heard the news: 'The sensation did not fail to have its effect on him as strong as upon anyone else, and in answer to a question as to what would be the probable outcome he had no answer to make except a melancholy shake of his head, as he moved away'.[4]

Healy had permitted himself to be carried along on the split's tide. He had submerged himself in the vehemence of his attack on Parnell, and given free rein to the suppressed thoughts and emotions of twelve years. He had abrogated all restraint and left nothing unsaid. He was now confronted by the disconsolate aftermath of the loss of all reticence. The need to counter the recriminations which he knew the death of Parnell would unleash was psychological as much as political. He had to renew the rhythm of the split. He sought to anticipate and re-direct the charge of responsibility for the death of Parnell. He is indisputably the author of the offensively moralising editorial in the *Evening Press* on the day after Parnell's death:

> Let us carry our minds back to the Parnell of the old day, the practical patriot, the cool, the fearless, the indomitable, before the cancer of a guilty passion forbidden by the laws of God and man ate into his heart . . . Characters it has been well said, are not cut in marble . . . Evil influences slowly eat out manhood and patriotism, truth and courage, from the heart of a man whom Ireland once regarded as her greatest. In this hour we cannot envy the feelings of those who are mainly responsible for blasting the dead man's career, blighting his reputation. Their servile flattery and encouragement it was that made his treason.[5]

The *National Press* editorials of the following day were in a similar vein. Parnell had been undone by the sycophancy of those who knew his course of action to be 'madness': 'No intellect, however great, can be proof against the assaults of floods of endless flattery'. Had Parnell accepted the offer conveyed by Sexton on behalf of the majority in Committee Room 15

> he would now be awaiting in not unremembered retirement that generous recall which those mindful of his past would gladly have spoken at the very earliest moment. Suspicion, however, at the sterner counsels of the upright grew rank in a mind accustomed only to parasitic incense.

A second article invited all patriots, excepting those Parnellites who 'knowing the right course, deliberately pursued the wrong', to 'shake hands over his open grave'. Preposterously entitled 'Let Dissension Cease', it was clearly intended to have the opposite effect.[6]

The charge of responsibility for the death of Parnell levelled at the anti-Parnellite leadership was most extravagantly formulated by *United Ireland*. It attributed to Healy during the Kilkenny election the threat that he would drive Parnell into the grave or a lunatic asylum, and cited his speech at Thurles on the day of Parnell's death.

> The grave now opens to receive him. Is Healy happy? Is the flush of success on his cheeks? Will the Federation burn tar barrels? 'Wipe him out we shall', said this man yesterday, 'for in this business I have neither ruth nor pity'. Nor had he. Nor had his lieutenants Dillon and O'Brien . . . Shall this fatal perfidy, this slow torture unto death, of our beloved leader go unavenged?

If Healy was unaffected by this absurd vituperation the same did not apply to his 'lieutenants'. O'Brien was outraged by his characterisation as 'dead Caesar's Brutus', while Dillon was deeply affronted to be denounced in the streets of Dublin as 'Parnell's murderer'.[7]

The strain on Healy now began to show, and there were signs that his self-control had completely fractured. When Katharine Parnell laid claim to a part of the Paris Funds, he declared that the funds had been frozen 'owing to the intervention of that lady whose name is such an offence to the Parnellites'. Within a month of Parnell's death he had twice denounced her as 'a proved British prostitute'. Only W. E. Gladstone's intervention restrained Healy from further attacks on Parnell's widow.[8]

Parliamentary nationalist politics rapidly divided into the hardline adversaries of the dead leader, grouped around Healy; the moderate anti-Parnellites who looked to O'Brien and Dillon; and those now led by John Redmond who had been loyal to Parnell. The fact that the division was tripartite ensured that the tendencies which might have brought about re-unification in a binary split were constantly thwarted by the vying for advantage among the three factions, envenomed by the proliferation of personal hatreds born of the split. Re-unification, when it came in 1900, was the product of exhausted recriminations, and the party was never to regain the *élan* and momentum it had possessed under Parnell's leadership.

Healy surveyed the future with the restive fury of a demobilised mercenary. In seeking to keep alive the animosities of the split, he was more concerned to maintain his control of the direction of anti-Parnellism than to vanquish the Parnellites. Healy's sense of embattlement was punctuated by a febrile ebullience. Before a meeting of the party in early February, he wrote to Maurice, fleetingly taking stock of the recent deaths of public figures: 'I wonder will anyone propose a resolution of regret at the death of Mr. Parnell, Cardinal Manning, the Duke of Clarence, Mr. W. H. Smith, or the Duke of Devonshire!!'[9]

While Healy sought to thwart any initiatives by Dillon and O'Brien to achieve an accommodation with the Parnellites, he was himself prepared to contemplate an arrangement with them which would strengthen his own hand against the moderate anti-Parnellite leaders. This opportunistic attitude had the additional merit from Healy's point of view of infuriating Dillon and O'Brien still further.

An abortive initiative of Healy's ally P. A. Chance in early 1892 starkly revealed the reciprocal suspicions of the nationalist factions. The Parnell loyalist Tim Harrington had told Chance that the anti-Parnellite to whom the Parnellites most objected was William O'Brien, by whom they felt betrayed, and that John Redmond favoured a compromise. Chance took this up in a manner that Harrington cannot have intended, and urged Healy to meet Redmond and Harrington over dinner. Healy's response was guarded. He confined himself to suggesting that if the Parnellites showed themselves more restrained at the next meeting of the National League, 'then perhaps we could get into a more reasonable temper'.

Reporting to Maurice, Healy professed his astonishment. Chance had 'recommended that, instead of thinking of amalgamation with anyone, we should make friends with the mule [Harrington]! I laughed, and said the idea was absurd . . .' Yet, aware of the 'frightful expenditure' which the Parnellites could cause them in contested elections, he was 'strongly disposed to favour any reasonable terms with the hostiles'. His attitude was however highly machiavellian. He added that:

> of course, if we agree to terms now, and they worked with us on a tacit understanding as to terms for their following at the General Election, they could not really enforce more than the constituencies would stand; and,

> having once come to an agreement with us, they could not well break up the Party a second time if the Convention rejected any of their candidates.

If Healy was prepared to consider tactical accommodations, his strategy continued to be based on the exploitation of hardline anti-Parnellite sentiment in Ireland. His cynical attitude made ominously plain that it would be virtually impossible to restore the political discipline which had been a defining characteristic of the Irish party in the 1880s.

For the Parnellites, the initiative of Chance, which they erroneously believed to have been taken at Healy's instigation, confirmed their suspicions of their dead leader's prime adversary. Redmond reported to T. P. Gill that Harrington had received a letter from Chance asking him to dine 'to meet and shake hands with wicked Tim'. Redmond construed this as an attempt to make terms behind Dillon's back to ensure control of the *Freeman's Journal*, and regarded the letter as an insult: 'It shows however the straits of the "antis" – what a happy family they are and what class of men Dillon took to his bosom and must rely upon'. He put the letter to the best use he could, showing it to Valentine Dillon in the knowledge that he in turn would communicate its contents to his cousin John.[10]

Healy at bay was an inconstant figure. William O'Brien wrote to John Dillon in late January:

> I had a long chat with Tim yesterday. The real secret of his soreness is the newspaper. He appears to be desperate as to the financial outlook of the N.P. He was as fitful as usual – at one moment denouncing me as an enemy of the N.P., at another pressing me to join the Board of the new paper. In one breath he announced that he would fight to the death any proposal to give away seats, and in the next said he would give them ten seats at the General Election, but not till then. He admitted that Chance is intriguing with Harrington.[11]

It was almost a matter of professional honour for Healy to show himself capable of engaging in private parleys with those whom he was savagely assailing in public; moreover the attractions of an outflanking manoeuvre against the moderate anti-Parnellites potentially outweighed any distaste he felt for a tactical alliance with the Parnellites. Years later, he wrote to his father of the death of the Parnellite J. L. Carew that just before the 1892 election at a dinner in Arnold Morley's attended by Gladstone and Spencer, 'I thought I had the "Split" settled with him, but Redmond held out'.[12]

The *Freeman's Journal*'s belated abandonment of Parnell two weeks before his death, and the support of Dillon and O'Brien, had arrested its decline. The promoters of the *National Press* were not prepared to commit the enormous resources required to maintain the circulation war, and reluctantly agreed to an amalgamation. The negotiations were exceptionally acrimonious, even by the standards of the split. Healy wrote to his brother of the negotiations with the Gray family who owned the *Freeman's Journal*: 'Sick as I was of them yesterday, I am vomiting against them today. They have neither heads nor hearts, and they go complaining to us like schoolboys to the Archbishop [of Dublin], who however acts very well and is very firmly on our side.' Healy was specially mistrustful of the young Edmund Dwyer Gray, whom he described as 'about as bad a type of youngster as I have met, thoroughly shifty, tricky, lying and unreliable. He will be as dangerous as a Malay for treachery and cold-bloodedness'. He complained that 'the way I have been worried and nagged over this business is worse than the Boulogne negotiations'.[13]

Healy sought to put the best face on the necessity to accept an amalgamation, writing to Maurice: 'The chief thing weighing with us of course is that, at the death of the *Independent*, the *Freeman* would once more become the Parnellite or criticising organ, whereas if we can capture it, and consolidate it with our own, we acquire control of two papers instead of one'.[14] In the event, the *Independent* was to survive (greatly to Healy's political benefit in the longer term), while the *Freeman's Journal* having absorbed the *National Press* would quickly revert to its former position as the scourge of Healyism.

The negotiations were successfully concluded. The last issue of the *National Press* appeared on 26 March 1892. The terms of the amalgamation left the former owners of the *National Press* with a majority on the board of directors. Healy had lost a newspaper, but acquired a second front. A protracted and bitter war for the control of the *Freeman* ensued. Of a fractious shareholders meeting in May 1892, Healy wrote to his brother 'you will see we finished our bastard Room Fifteen today'. He complained that 'Dillon's cold egotism surpasses belief, and he did and said meaner things, without Parnell's justification, than Parnell himself in Room Fifteen. I will never have the smallest regard for his character again, and I believe he is a thorough tyrant at heart . . .'[15]

Speaking in Dublin on 2 March 1892, Healy urged undiminished vigour in the prosecution of the struggle against the Parnellites. He quickly rediscovered the merits of the dead leader in attacking his successors. Condemning Redmond's temporising response to Balfour's local government bill, he declared that 'knowing what Parnell's character was, I could not help feeling contempt for the barren shallow men who hoped to wield the blow which he alone from that point of view at any rate was capable of wielding'. He provocatively adopted Parnell's argument in the split to reprove Parnellite familiarity with the leaders of the Liberal party:

> Now, if Mr. Parnell had lived, watchful shepherd of his flock that he was, nothing like that would be occurring. We would not see Mr. Redmond talking to Mr. John Morley in the lobby, nor Mr. Pierce Mahony talking to Sir William Harcourt, nor Mr. Henry Harrison talking to Sir William Harcourt's son, nor any of these curious combinations that mark the detritus of independence. You would not have the Local Government Bill denounced, but you would have a policy such as I have indicated in the sketch speech I have ventured to make on behalf of the deceased leader.

While doubting the ability of Dillon and O'Brien to reach an agreement with the Parnellites, he professed his willingness to suppress his misgivings if they did so. This ostensible concession afforded the pretext for a rallying-cry to the anti-Parnellite diehards:

> I hold, however, unflinchingly, that there is only one way to go about this business. I believed in nothing else since Room Fifteen, and if I am out-voted, I shall, at all events, remain an unrepentant sinner . . . I say let us go to the polls and let the people decide, and I regard any other doctrine as treason against constitutional practice . . . the general election is in the offing, and my view towards those gentlemen is the view of Little Bo Peep towards her missing quadrupeds,
>
> 'Leave them alone and they will come home
> Wagging their tails behind them.'[16]

Two weeks later Healy made a further onslaught on the Parnellites:

> Mr. Parnell was in no sense a small man. He was a very great man, and if those who pretend to be his followers would only let his memory alone until the miseries and misfortunes that crowded round the latest months of his career had been forgotten and tempered by time, I believe all Ireland would only be too happy to recognise the greatness of her son and that hour would come all the sooner if attempts were not made to hawk round his remains, so to speak, and to present him and his policy only in the aspects they assumed during the last fatal twelve months of his own life (*hear, hear*); but whoever lives or whoever dies, our cause must go on (*cheers*).[17]

With staggering infelicity, he returned to this theme just before the general election of July 1892:

> The past generation is behind us. It is dead. Its dead issues should have been allowed to slumber in Glasnevin. No good cause can benefit by their resurrection. The issues of Room Fifteen are as dead and decomposed as the bones of Julius Caesar. They have no relation to the coming time.[18]

The Liberals were deeply alarmed by the near-disintegration of the Irish party. Morley wrote to John Dillon in April 1892 that he would try to 'have a grave talk with Healy when he next appears on the scene. Unless he awakens to the necessity of an unbroken front, our work will be to no purpose'. Some days later Labouchere, engaged in a futile attempt to reconcile the anti-Parnellite factions, asked Morley if he wanted to dine with Healy, '*as Healy much wished it*'. This had all the hallmarks of a Labouchere ploy. Morley reported to Dillon on his meeting with an uncommunicative and defensive Healy.

> So last night I went. Nobody else there. To my surprise H. had really nothing to say. He studiously kept off the ground of the newspaper, and neither L. nor I could get him near it, though we tried. He defended his policy of no terms with the Parnellites, until after the election. The election, he said, would show the insignificant importance of that section, and then would be the time for such accommodation as might be desirable. I, on the other hand, pressed the point that if during the election there was a war of words in Ireland, and if after the election Redmond kept alive and published his distrust of the Liberals, and he eventually declared war against the H.R. Bill we should be infallibly dished, and H.R. dished with us for this time. I think I made some impression, but he then began to talk as if he were looking forward to some future election and a new movement. This however evidently was not serious. He spoke of himself as a Jonah, who was about to be thrown overboard – but when we asked him more precisely how or why, he would not say.[19]

As the general election approached, Morley wrote to Dillon that he was seeing Gladstone 'with a view to his influence being used for peace on a certain person'.[20] There is no record of any intervention by Gladstone nor was there any sign of Healy moderating his tone. He was in atrocious form. Furiously engaged in combat on a number of fronts with his adversaries, all of them nationalist, he indulged in bitter vituperation at party meetings. The wracking acrimony within the party was becoming unendurable. O'Brien wrote despondently to Dillon of a twelve-hour meeting of the party which failed to pass a resolution directing the board of the *Freeman's Journal* to accept him as a director.

> The Healy gang showed their teeth with the most brutal candour. All the applause on their side was done in the most insolent way by Chance in one corner, T.D. in another, Donal in another, and Murphy in another – it was one of the most shameful pieces of bulldozing ever attempted . . . Healy was so vilely offensive that he sickened everybody outside his own gang, but they cheered everything wildly . . . Tom Condon, who moved the vote of confidence, made a splendid speech opposed to

> adjournment. He was roused by a brutal cry from Healy during a speech of Sexton's, 'if you want a fight you will get it' . . .[21]

The general election of July 1892 was turbulent and bitter. Healy wrote to Maurice from Dublin:

> Blackguardism in the streets is pretty bad, in fact I never saw anything worse than the attack on myself on Thursday night. My life would not have been worth a moment's purchase if they could have got a few yards nearer to me, and the driver of the car was in league with them. One ruffian stopped the horse, and one of our men struck it, and the car rolled over the fellow.[22]

Against his personal inclinations, Healy contested North Louth 'lest the priests would tolerate Callan'. The priests were 'more or less apathetic and, as I suspected about Dundalk, its Parnellism is pro-Callanism'. It would be 'the nastiest fight in Ireland'. He won, though Callan attracted a substantial vote.[23]

Nationally, the anti-Parnellites triumphed. Healy had bet Dillon twenty pounds that the Parnellites would not take more than eight seats. In the event they won nine, against seventy-two for the anti-Parnellites. This left a Parnellite representation at Westminster which, though drastically diminished, was politically viable. Healy complained bitterly of Dillon, O'Brien and their allies to his brother that 'these men have acted frightfully and have not given us one morsel of real help, and have hindered and worried us in every way'.[24]

The first anniversary of Parnell's death prompted a final flourish from Healy in the *Freeman's Journal*, which remained in his control in the immediate aftermath of the amalgamation. A series of editorials written by him provided a virulent *reprise* of the journalism of the *National Press*.[25] With intentional crudity Healy sought to magnify – if not to invent – divisions within the Parnellite camp.

Some of the municipal leaders of Parnellism in Dublin favoured an address of welcome to the Liberal Lord Lieutenant, but had encountered opposition from *United Ireland* and from other Dublin Parnellites. Healy set to work:

> We know that Mr. Parnell himself in the House of Commons continually moved 'a humble address' to her Majesty, and that every member of his party has voted addresses to the Queen. But things in Dublin have reached such a pass that if journalists in quest of a fillip for faction or a subject for fulmination choose to discover in a meeting convened by the Lord Mayor-Elect some darkling treason to the person of Mr. John Redmond, forthwith half a hundred fuglemen will assemble in Ward meetings to pass resolutions in tumefied verbiage against the proscripts.

The proposers of the address had been 'pelted with every insulting epithet which a vocabulary enriched by long practise could supply'.[26]

On 6 October 1892, the first anniversary of Parnell's death, Healy in an editorial in the *Freeman's Journal* revisited some of his favourite topics:

> This day twelve months Mr. Parnell died. For Ireland's sake and for his fame's sake we would we could add that the dissension which he provoked died with him . . . It were, indeed, well that his last fatal year should be blotted from the memory of Ireland. The worst enemies of Mr. Parnell's memory are those who fix attention on his last year and set aside the teachings of the rest of his lifetime. The threatened disaster has been happily though not wholly averted. The National movement, though surely storm-tossed, escaped shipwreck, and the harbour again lies fair before it. Even the men who applauded Parnell during that wild year no longer dare to pursue the same policy . . . The Irish people are a grateful, a generous, a forgiving people. By the graveside of Mr. Parnell they would be willing to forget the evil he wrought, and to remember the good . . . But his abettors in that last wild year of his life will not have it so. Forgiveness for him implies censure for them. They strive to justify their own acts at whatever cost to the country's cause or their dead leader's reputation. It is not the Parnell of the brave old days they call upon the people to honour; not Parnell the preserver, but Parnell the destroyer of the work of his own hands. His reputation is the only asset in their bankrupt exchequer, the only bond by which honest but misguided men may be tied to faction. By the glamour of his reputation sober judgement may be perverted. They trade on his name for all it is worth, and strive to make his grave the central point and focus through which ill-will and dissension may be maintained through Ireland. This evil work has failed, and will fail.[27]

This was a small masterpiece of provocation. Healy was wielding the funeral thurible as a weapon of war. It was impossible to conceive a text better calculated to re-charge the animus of the split, once again transmuting the abiding sense of bereavement into the stuff of public contention. The effect was profoundly paradoxical. While the Parnellites' often hackneyed perorations could not bear the weight of Parnell's last achievement and promise, Healy's rhetoric provided perhaps the decisive twist in propelling the remembrance of Parnell to its classic posthumous plane. Pressing to the limit the dialectic of grief, Healy succeeded in furthering the myth of Parnell, even as he sought to exorcise it.

Healy used the Parnell commemoration to propound his thesis of an endemic tendency within Parnellism towards further fragmentation. He suggested that the choice of James O'Kelly to deliver the oration over the grave of Parnell represented the culmination of a division within the Parnellite ranks between 'what may be styled the non-kid-gloved section of the Factionist Party' and 'the snobbish element' represented by the party leader John Redmond. 'Henceforth . . . Mr. Redmond's dethronement may be regarded as accomplished'.[28] In O'Kelly's graveside oration, Healy professed to discern further evidence of this division, with O'Kelly representing 'the hillside section in the demonstration'.[29]

The Parnell commemoration itself Healy condemned as 'the exaltation of the last wild and reckless year' of Parnell's life:

> The ringleaders of the Redmondites or the O'Kellyites, or whatever else they please to call themselves, devour and destroy the reputation of Mr. Parnell, which is the sole means by which their political existence can be prolonged. . . . Faction cannot count a single man whom, on his own merits, the smallest section of his countrymen would follow and trust as leader. This is why they fasten like leeches on the reputation of Mr. Parnell, whose great name covers their littleness. This is why they would make his grave the camping ground of faction. The child's play with ivy leaves, borrowed from the British Primrosers, is part of the same policy of perpetuating dissension. But this game is played out.

Four days later he again ridiculed the wearing of ivy leaves in memory of Parnell by deriding the Parnellites as 'the Ivy-boys'.[30] Healy sought to maintain the momentum of his assault by proceeding to an attack on the Parnellite's position in relation to the Paris Funds, thereby contriving to resuscitate the wounding memory of the *National Press* 'Stop Thief' articles of June 1891.[31]

If Healy's writings and utterances on the Parnellites were exercises in pure provocation, his sallies were often irresistibly amusing. He devastatingly parodied the deficient rhetoric of the Parnellites. Of John Redmond's brother William he declared: 'The times are such that perhaps a certain economy of speech should be practised. We are not all Billy Redmonds (*laughter*). We cannot get up a fortnightly banquet of bosh for the delectation of fools.'[32]

This affords an example of one of Healy's most effective devices. With nonchalant audacity, he would begin an attack on an adversary with an observation which was more obviously applicable to himself, and then redirect the argument. There was in this a virtuoso extravagance: the implication that only he could dissect the premises of his own rhetoric was an adverse reflection on the abilities of his opponents.

Healy's goading editorials were a swan-song for the unremitting assault on Parnell and Parnellism in the *National Press* manner. Insensately provoking though they were, there was a certain wistfulness in his coat-trailing, the dallying recession of a thwarted but impenitent bully. He knew he could not hope to keep the antagonisms of the split at fever-pitch. Moreover the author of the *Freeman*'s editorials on the Parnell anniversary could not have retained serious pretensions to leadership. In the unrestrained provocativeness of his attacks, he was tacitly conceding the inevitability of his own marginalisation, which was to be consummated in the expulsions of November 1895.

Gladstone's Last Government

Regretting that Dillon and O'Brien had not acted more strongly against Healy, the Parnellite Tim Harrington in November 1892 played astutely on the susceptibility of T. P. ('Neutral') Gill.

> I saw Healy passing in Dublin yesterday and he does not look by any means happy. It seems to me that he always keeps his malignant purposes in his mind, for he passes through the streets with his head down, an angry frown on his face, and he altogether wears the look of a man who was nerving himself to do some desperate deed. I hope Dillon and O'Brien are going even now to be a little firm. I cannot get out of my mind the fact that they are extending a toleration to Healy which would have saved poor Parnell if they had given it to him.[33]

The anti-Parnellites were now hopelessly riven. The theatres of war were the party and its committee: the council of the National Federation; and the meetings of the directors and shareholders of the *Freeman's Journal*. As the Liberals took office, Healy lamented that 'it is a great misfortune that there is no-one in command of the Party, and that Dillon is such a dull man'. He characterised Justin McCarthy, the chairman of the anti-Parnellite party, as 'that weak creature'. Of the dispute over the control of the amalgamated *Freeman's Journal* he wrote, revealing at least a degree of self-knowledge:

> O'Brien pressed that both Dillon and I should retire from the Board for the sake of peace, and I was anxious to do this, but Murphy would not allow me. As however I cannot disguise my contempt for Dillon, I can quite see that it will ultimately come to the division of the Party into two camps.[34]

Correctly discerning that his position was threatened by Dillon and O'Brien ('that dithyrambic jackass'), Healy resolved to retaliate. He wrote to Maurice:

> I don't think there is such reason to be discoûraged at the situation as you suppose, but undoubtedly Dillon and O'Brien have made a permanent

> fissure in the Party, which ran sweetly and smoothly until they were released from jail . . .
>
> In consequence of this *Freeman* affair, and Sexton's attitude, coupled with the plain attempt to rig the Council of the Federation, and the certainty that there will be a bounder ticket for the committee of the Party, I think it has become absolutely necessary for us in self-preservation to take measures of precaution . . . I am convinced unless we can strengthen ourselves on the committee, we shall be completely crushed by a combination against us which is resolute and unscrupulous and relentless . . . Of course it is a dreadful thing to have this Open Sesame, but it is just as little use weeping over it as it is regarding Parnellism. They will knife us if we don't prevent them . . . They will dance a war-dance over my carcase at every opportunity. I am therefore going to take the field against them openly if necessary, and quietly in any case, to spare myself the alternative of being trampled upon . . . I greatly fear that the net result of the valuable assistance of Messrs. Dillon and O'Brien will be to create a third party in the country, unless the disease is immediately and vigorously taken in hand.[35]

When Gladstone returned to power after the 1892 election, Healy, behind a façade of harmony, became locked in conflict with his administration. In a bitter engagement with the hapless John Morley, Healy advocated executive action to subvert unionist power in Ireland in advance of home rule. As early as 1889, Healy had argued that the unionists in Ireland could be overborne by the executive *fiat* of a Liberal government: 'the moment the Liberals got into power, let them place the administration of this country in the hands of the national majority'. He looked then to the future Liberal government to reconstitute the grant juries, and to dismiss hostile sheriffs, magistrates and police.[36] Healy became infuriated by the refusal of the Gladstone government to adopt his prescription of executive action to break the spine of unionist power in Ireland, in advance of the introduction of home rule itself.[37]

He wrote to Maurice in October 1892 that 'there is a deadlock between us and the Executive on the magistrates question. Asquith when here frightened Morley and Walker. It seems that in the history of England only one man was appointed over the head of the County Lieutenant . . .'[38] Morley wrote to Healy from the Chief Secretary's Lodge on 13 September to remonstrate, having heard from a mutual friend that 'you think of treating this place and its tenant as if it were a scheduled area under a pleuro-pneumonia act'. Healy's reply, deprecating the failure to appoint Aberdeen as Lord Lieutenant, was not encouraging.[39]

Speaking in Dublin in September 1892 Healy warned that Morley was surrounded by hostile forces within the Irish administration.[40] The idea that Liberal Chief Secretaries in general, and Morley in particular, rapidly became prisoners of Dublin Castle became something of an obsession: in 1894 he discerned 'a constant tendency of officials to make proposals affecting Irish members which they would not dare to make when the Tories were in power'.[41] He was reluctant to accept an invitation from the Irish Lord Chancellor to dine with Morley: 'I cannot get over the feeling that they are the same "Castle" lot as of yore, and that we should have nothing to say to them. Morley means well, but I fear he may not do well, fettered as he is'. Healy's truculence towards Gladstone's Chief Secretary was out of all proportion to his grievance. Morley, bewildered, felt himself the subject of a boycott by Healy.[42]

From his residence in Mountjoy Square Healy reported to Maurice on 13 October:

> Only yesterday I refused to see Morley: but Asquith called here when I was not in. I wrote asking him to dine, whereupon Morley sent me a line asking might he call, to which of course I was obliged to say yes. I desire to hold aloof as much as possible from these people connected with the Irish Government, as one never could tell into what an intimacy might lead one.[43]

Healy's truculent attitude towards Morley's Chief Secretaryship owed much to his awareness that Morley was close to Dillon. In their dealings with the Irish party, the Liberals effectively recognised the troika of Dillon, Sexton and McCarthy who Gladstone met on at least three occasions in 1892, as the collective leadership of the anti-Parnellite party.[44] Likewise Healy did not participate in the consultations with Morley, initiated at Gladstone's prompting, on the provisions to be embodied in the second home rule bill.[45] Healy had increasingly shut himself out of the higher reaches of the alliance which he had so fiercely upheld in the travail of the split.

Gladstone's last strenuous undertaking, the second home rule bill of 1893 was the last great legislative set-piece of nineteenth-century British politics. The theatrical finale of the era of Victorian *haute politique*, it had from the outset an aura of unreality. Passed in the Commons, the bill went on to inevitable defeat in the House of Lords. When Gladstone entered the ommons to introduce the bill Healy ominously did not join the anti-Parnellite standing ovation which greeted him. He remained seated with, in the hostile testimony of T. P. O'Connor, 'the characteristic scowl on his face'.[46] The Parnellites lamented their lost leader, but voted with the anti-Parnellites in favour of the bill. Healy vociferously supported the bill in the Commons and attacked the Parnellites for failing to give it sufficiently unqualified and unstinted endorsement. He was out of sorts, highly critical in the private councils of the party committee of the financial provisions of a bill which he publicly hailed as a vindication of his opposition to Parnell in the split. In 1895, when his antipathy towards Healy was at its height, William O'Brien went so far as to charge that Healy had pronounced the bill a swindle and proposed that the Irish party leave the chamber in a body on its introduction.[47]

In the Commons, party tempers ran high. On 11 July William St. John Brodrick, later Earl of Midleton, and leader of the Southern unionists at the Irish convention of 1917–18, incautiously asserted in the Commons that the Irish members appeared to think that because they represented 'a garrulous and impecunious race', they had unlimited claims on the time and purse of the House of Commons. Sexton counter-attacked, and in the ensuing pandemonium was eventually removed from the House. Healy approached Brodrick as he passed through the lobby and said: 'Mr. Brodrick, if you think your conduct was gentleman-like tonight, I do not. If you want to fight, we are ready — and if you object to what I say, I will give you satisfaction in any way you wish'. Brodrick replied that had Healy been present when he had spoken the words, he would have known that they were quite innocent. Healy reiterated that 'they were ungenerous words to the Irish people and I am ready to give you satisfaction'. At Balfour's suggestion Brodrick mentioned this to Gladstone the next day, who jumped up and said 'A duel! Why, I haven't heard of such a thing in the House of Commons for fifty years'.[48]

This altercation was eclipsed by the scenes of mayhem on 27 July. When Chamberlain compared Gladstone to Herod, the chant of 'Judas! Judas!', initiated by T. P. O'Connor, rose from the Irish benches. As the Tories refused to let the House divide, a protracted brawl ensued. 'The House filled with uproar. In the gangway a tumultuous mass of men clutched at each other's throats. In the vortex of the maelstrom Mr. Tim Healy was seen struggling. Colonel Saunderson, his coat half torn off his back, struck out right and left.'[49] After the division on the second reading, as the cheering died away, the voice of William Redmond was heard from above the gangway forlornly calling for 'three cheers for Parnell'.[50]

For Gladstone and the Irish nationalists, the passage through the Commons of the second home rule bill was at least a solemn affirmation of the Liberal commitment to home rule. For most of the Liberals however, it was a parting homage to Gladstone, the close of a phase of policy which had commenced with the introduction of the first home rule bill of 1886, in which home rule was the chief preoccupation of the Liberal party. When Gladstone resigned the premiership in March 1894, his successor, Rosebery, accorded the home rule issue a lesser priority. This he made immediately plain by a speech in which he declared that before home rule could be granted 'England, as the predominant partner in the three kingdoms, will have to be convinced of its justice and equity'.[51]

Healy's attitude to the Liberal administration in Ireland remained critical after Gladstone's departure. He protested furiously at Morley's readiness to sanction the appointment of revising barristers – who were responsible for deciding questions arising in relation to the registration of voters – who were not necessarily sympathetic to the nationalists. He was particularly exercised over a rumour that the existing revising barrister for Derry, Wylie, would not be re-appointed, 'which means that the seat is lost to us'. He wrote a menacing letter to William O'Brien (whom he addressed as 'Mr. O'Brien'), warning that the ousting of Wylie would result not merely in the loss of the seat, but in 'what is far more important, the bitterest resentment in Ulster at Executive philo-Toryism . . . if it is consummated the existing discontents with the Executive will find open and determined expression'.[52] The premise of the letter – that O'Brien and his allies were responsible for the policy of the Liberal government in Ireland – revealed the extent of Healy's alienation and ill temper. He did however collaborate with John Morley both in relation to the select committee to consider amendments to the Irish land legislation, and the government's evicted tenants bill which was lost in the House of Lords.[53]

Anti-Parnellite Acrimony

Dillon and O'Brien were increasingly preoccupied with resisting the threat from what Dillon called 'the gang in Dublin', and one of his supporters called 'the Mountjoy Square lot' (Healy lived 1892–8 at No. 1 Mountjoy Square). Dublin was doubly-lost to the moderate anti-Parnellite leadership: while overwhelmingly Parnellite in allegiance, the Irish capital also harboured Healy, Murphy and their confederates. The thwarting of Healy was the principal subject of the voluminous correspondence of Dillon and O'Brien for much of the 1890s. O'Brien wrote in despair in late 1895:

> If the Parnellites had a spark of good sense, the country could be reunited in a week and Healy and his friends left out in the cold. But I am afraid the Parnell anniversary will only inflame them more and more to take advantage of our dissensions and widen the breach. Healy's silence as to my invitation shows that his single policy is one of lying low and getting the priests to stop the supplies.[54]

Healy complained in January 1894 that Dillon and O'Brien

> never go anywhere without some preachment about unity directed at us . . . They are a set of absolutely unscrupulous tyrants, who would just

give us the quarter of thugs. I would rather fall into the hands of Harrington and Redmond, and be at their mercy, rather than into those of Dillon and O'Brien.[55]

Even when outnumbered, Healy remained an unsettling adversary. A disconsolate O'Brien reported to Dillon of the havoc wreaked by one of Healy's terrible tantrums in March 1895:

The moment Healy heard of the requisition he went around like a raging beast, attacking and bullying everybody. He attacked Justin who replied admirably, and he brought tears to the unfortunate Alfred Webb's eyes. A lot of the miserable creatures allowed themselves to be intimidated into withdrawing their names . . . It was simply abject funk. Poor Alfred was inclined to throw the whole thing into the fire and to resign his seat.[56]

By the start of June 1895, as the general election approached, only the increasingly thin fiction of a common Parnellite adversary held the anti-Parnellite party back from open schism. By the chance of the ballot, J. F. Fox, a supporter of Healy, obtained a date for the second reading of a County Councils (Ireland) Bill. The committee of the Irish party provided no directions or assistance in the drafting of the bill, which was undertaken by Healy. Healy divined that Dillon and his allies were set on ensuring the bill's defeat, and had enlisted the support of Morley. Healy sarcastically described Morley's conduct as 'the most extraordinary performance of his great career'. Having told Healy that the government would oppose the bill, he was forced to back down when Healy threatened a retaliatory withdrawal of support from the government. The party met on the evening set for the second reading. While in the event the bill received an unopposed second reading the next day, the members of the party debated in Healy's absence a proposal to withdraw the bill. Healy's account to Maurice of what then transpired reveals the extent to which the anti-Parnellite party was by now irreparably riven.

I went back, and heard Blake make one of his most blackguard speeches I ever heard in my life, winding up with the declaration that the Bill was 'a gross attempt to pawn off a Bill which would have been rejected with indignation if proposed by Balfour'. I got up and tore the flesh off his bones, in a speech which frightened all the bounders . . . I left the room with the feeling that the malice and incompetence of these men rendered all co-operation with them impossible, and that the condition of the Party was hopeless. I never felt so disgusted in my life; but strangely enough, amidst this despondency, Arthur O'Connor came to me next day and said the occasion was the greatest triumph I ever had; and, as he is a man who never paid me a compliment before, I suppose I scored off the scoundrels.[57]

Healy was further angered by what he regarded as the covert opposition of Dillon and his allies to the Municipal Franchise (Ireland) Bill, which he had carried through the Commons.[58] Healy's temper at this time is conveyed in his reference to the inoffensive Justin McCarthy: 'The ferocity of the old ass is beyond conception'. Of Maurice's seat in Cork he wrote:

> With regard to yourself . . . the present time is such that I think you should cling on. You may be knifed by the plumpers and, if so, you will be well out of it. I feel quite sure the bounders will yield nothing. They have no care for the country, and the only thing that would induce them to yield in Cork would be the fear that the old jackass [J. F. X. O'Brien] would be beaten and not you.[59]

Healy wrote on 8 June:

> . . . I am satisfied that we can do no good, and that it will be best for us to get out. All the priests are thoroughly friendly everywhere, and we have all the intelligent men with us, but these fellows have all the place — expectants and that gang everywhere, and it is hopeless making headway against them. They have simply killed the movement. The priests won't subscribe, and the people, except their gang, are apathetic.[60]

The most furious encounter of the 1895 election took place at Omagh on 8 July. There a convention of delegates from the four Tyrone constituencies excepting North Tyrone assembled. The purpose of holding a single convention was to deprive the Healyite M. J. Kenny of the nomination for the Mid-Tyrone seat he held. Dillon went to Omagh to preside, and Healy determined to confront him. Healy caused an uproar by reading out a letter from Edward Blake on behalf of the leadership of the Irish party to the Liberal whip agreeing that the nationalists would refrain from contesting North Tyrone, effectively ceding four northern seats (including North and South Tyrone) to the Liberals. Healy reported with satisfaction to his brother: 'I read the Blake letter and gave Dillon the devil's scourging and he was livid with rage and hadn't a word to reply'. Coming in the wake of the controversy the previous year arising from the soliciting of subscriptions from leading Liberals to Irish party funds, the Omagh confrontation was extremely damaging to the anti-Parnellites. In the face of attacks by Dillon and his allies, Healy was defiant. He wrote to Maurice: 'Next to an exposure of the fraud on the Borough of Galway in 1886, when I stood alone with poor Biggar against Messrs. T. P. O'Connor & Co., I shall look back with satisfaction on my action in regard to Tyrone'.[61]

Healy persisted in regarding himself as the innocent victim of unprovoked persecution. Two weeks before the 1895 election, he wrote to Maurice that 'the attacks of the bounders on us these last few days I think completely exonerate us from any kind of restraint about them'. Healy was insensed by the declaration of William O'Brien at the Cork Convention — at which Maurice Healy was nominated — that he had triumphed over Redmondism, Toryism and Healyism in the city. He thought Maurice should publicly decline the nomination unless O'Brien apologised:

> You would give these fellows a mortal blow by such a letter. . . . As for the loss of the city, if O'Brien persists in attending and refuses to apologise, that is their affair. The country can't be made much worse now for having a few more Parnellites returned, especially when they are responsible men, such as the two selected for Cork . . . I would not hesitate about writing such a letter as I have indicated . . . Drive the dagger into these fellows' midriff now without hesitation.[62]

Healy again faced a bitter contest in North Louth, 'the most infernal seat in Ireland', where he was dependent on the protection of Cardinal Logue.

> Only for the hearty support of the priests which I am getting, the fight would be utterly hopeless . . . I had four hours with the Cardinal on Tuesday, who is getting all his priests to work tooth and nail for me. He told me he refused to respond to McCarthy's appeal for funds. Croke is also deadly bitter against the bounders, and I got a special invitation to his jubilee yesterday.

Healy in the event won handsomely, although elsewhere a number of his allies were ousted. His estrangement from the Liberals was evident in the equanimity with which he responded to the unionist victory in Britain:

> I can't say I am specially sorry, if the Liberals were to be beaten at all, that they got such a smashing; and Morley's defeat in Newcastle I regard as a Providential vengeance on him over the Christian Brothers question, which he refused to deal with, simply to save his seat, as he supposed.

Healy remained impenitent even in the face of his brother's remonstrances: 'I don't regret any act or word I have said or done which you condemn. On the contrary, I wish I had given the scoundrels less law'.[63]

In September, Healy supported William Martin Murphy's rogue candidacy for Kerry South in opposition to the party's nominee. Murphy's crushing defeat by a margin of almost three to one cleared the way for a concerted move against Healy. On 7 November he was removed from the Executive of the Irish National League of Great Britain. On 13 November he was expelled from the National Federation. The following day he was voted off the committee of the Irish party. As he wrote in his memoirs, 'I was now made an outlaw'.[64] Although not formally expelled until December 1900 (from the re-united party), he was no longer in communion with the anti-Parnellite party. Healy's exclusion from the party committee marks a decisive turning-point in his career. He had lost the war for ascendancy within the Irish party which the split had initiated. For most of the duration of his career at Westminster, which lasted until 1918, he stood outside the ranks of the Irish party.

While the coalition against Healy, which was made up chiefly of Dillon, O'Brien, McCarthy, Sexton and the *Freeman's Journal* had prevailed, he had exacted a terrible price and continued to do so. He still retained influential support within the country and within the party. In particular he enjoyed backing from the Catholic clergy: he had written to Maurice just before the general election that 'all the priests at Maynooth were against the bounders and all the bishops except two'.[65] He retained the status of an Irish nationalist, both in Ireland and at Westminster, where many parliamentarians and journalists (especially those opposed to home rule) regarded him in some ways as the archetypal Irish home rule member. However often expelled or proscribed, he remained, infuriatingly for the anti-Parnellite leadership, the enemy within.

He retained the ability to wreak havoc in Ireland and especially at Westminster, and did much to contribute to the slow-burning disillusionment with parliamentary politics which the fall of Parnell had ignited. To outside observers, the effective exclusion of so prominent a parliamentarian from the already divided ranks of an Irish party once celebrated for its cohesiveness and common purpose was bewildering. Writing in *Truth*, Labouchere sought to exploit that perception. He deplored the exclusion of 'unquestionably the ablest Parliamentarian of the Party', by what he with considerable audacity characterised as 'the vituperative triumvirate of Dillon, O'Brien and T. P. O'Connor'. There was in any event, he argued no longer any justification for the iron discipline they sought to impose: 'Parnell's leadership was a dictatorship, justified by the Irish people practically being *in statu belli*'.[66]

This last was an authentically Healyite proposition. Healy's behaviour, however erratic, served to advertise if not to validate his proposition that the Parnellite era was closed. No longer limited to the personality of Parnell, his attack now extended to the institutions he had created. Cheated of authority, or rather temperamentally incapable of its measured exercise, Healy was prepared to allow the remorseless logic of his anti-Parnellism to run its course.

Healy's ambiguous relationship to institutional nationalism was well adapted to his political genius, his ideological predispositions, and the attitudes of his larger constituency, in particular its ecclesiastical component which was abidingly suspicious of secular nationalist power. He contrived to maintain a foot on the terrain of the Irish party, and a foot in the no man's land beyond. It was not an elegant posture, but – with half-steps forward and back – it was to give him a longevity in Irish politics which outspanned that of his Irish parliamentary contemporaries.

Healy's expulsion from the party committee did not come as a particular shock to him. He had in any event already struck a compromise which permitted him to pursue a lucrative career at the bar, while maintaining a political career in which he could episodically intervene to promote his personal causes and to harry his enemies. His professional and commercial interests precluded continuously-sustained parliamentary attendance. At the time of his expulsion, he was momentarily diverted by the gold-mining speculation of his parliamentary allies, P. A. Chance and Florence O'Driscoll, in whose good fortune he hoped to share: 'It is simply dazzling to contemplate the prospects of the two gold-bugs'. Healy's wife vetoed a proposed visit to West Australia: 'Moreover I don't think it would have served me politically to have gone on the gold hunt'.[67]

Healy's exclusion from the inner councils of the Irish party followed close upon the return of a unionist government. He was thus simultaneously released from the necessity of subscribing to the views of the Irish party leadership and of supporting a Liberal administration. Although increasingly amenable to the idea of collaboration with the Conservatives, Healy bitingly assailed any such rapprochement on the part of the Parnellites. Four months before the 1895 general election, he denounced an amendment Redmond proposed to the address calling for a dissolution and the submission of a home rule question to a general election, which enjoyed Conservative support. He defended the Liberal alliance, but the thrust of his charge against Redmond was that he was allying himself with the Conservatives for no tangible gain. He charged Redmond with a reversion to 'the early course of altruism' of the Irish representation at Westminster: 'It may be Parnellism but I call it nonsense'. The least Redmond should have secured from the Conservatives was a promise of the release of the Irish political prisoners.[68]

Healy indulgently contemplated a long period of Conservative government. He told the *Daily Chronicle* in September 1895:

> What happened during the existence of the Liberal Government from 1892 to 1895 is a standing warning to Ireland on the Home Rule question . . . Home Rule for Ireland has been shown to be unobtainable under these circumstances, especially as the Liberals have shown that they are unable to get over the opposition of the House of Lords . . . I know I have been charged with ingratitude to the Liberal party. I deny that the charge is well-founded. I cannot feel anything else but gratitude to the Liberal Party, and I believe that their action was limited by their powers, but I cannot

> help seeing, on the other hand, that among the Tories there is no longer that acerbity which we formerly experienced. Even in Ireland, where the manifestations of high Toryism are always most bitter, I can detect a changed feeling.[69]

The Chief Secretaryship of Gerald Balfour (1895–1900) liberated Healy from his remaining inhibitions as a former Parnellite. His relations with Balfour as Chief Secretary were much better than with John Morley. In his memoirs he wrote of Balfour: 'In the retrospect of half a century I hold this Englishman to have been the ablest, most zealous, most unselfish, most painstaking, and best-equipped administrator that Ireland ever had under English rule.'[70] If the anti-Parnellite leaders had, or felt they had, an instinctive rapport with the Liberals, Healy was discovering the extent to which he was at ease with a Conservative ministry. It was an attitude which the Conservatives could not fail to encourage or to reward legislatively.

Healy strongly supported Balfour's Land Act of 1896 and his Local Government Act of 1898, both of which were regarded with purblind suspicion by John Dillon.[71] Of Healy's highly effective contribution to the committee stage of the land bill, H. W. Lucy observed: 'In several important respects Mr. Healy, impotent in the division lobby, invincible in debate, succeeded in compelling the Irish Secretary to concede amendments'.[72]

Healy was undismayed by the unravelling of Parnell's legacy. On the contrary he went so far as to argue complacently that the disintegration of the old Parnellite movement represented an advance:

> in the first place, whether we like it or whether we do not, the possession of great popular strength, of an unbroken party, of a compact organisation, is regarded by the minority of the Protestants or Conservatives of the country as more or less a threat to their existence. It is feared by the British Government, who, as we know, descended to the basest efforts, as we saw on the occasion of the *Times* Commission, to frighten the man or the men at the head of the popular strength; but we know that that movement has been more or less breached by time and by personal disputes, our opponents in the past are more inclined to look at it from the point of view of sanity and of reasonableness, and less from the position of personality. They have got over their stage fright at Home Rule.[73]

Reading such a speech, it is possible more readily to comprehend the almost speechless fury to which Healy's actions and utterances drove John Dillon. Healy pitted himself against the Parnellian conception of political action. His ebulliently refractory course starkly illumined the impasse of parliamentary nationalism after Parnell and Gladstone had quit the scene. In 1899 he dismissed independent opposition as 'a policy bottled up in a phrase'.[74] He missed no opportunity to proclaim that policy was superseded, if not misconceived from the start.

The election on 18 February 1896 of Dillon as leader of the anti-Parnellite party in succession to Justin McCarthy abrogated the remaining constraints on Healy's expressions of dissent. 'John wants the Chair' had become a Healyite chant. After what Healy called 'years of striving, Mr. Dillon's ambition was gratified'.[75]

Dillon was a politician of disconsolate integrity and unbending conviction. His political imagination had set in the early years of the Parnellite movement. While it was addressing its peculiar concerns, the *Leader* was not altogether incorrect in characterising Dillon in 1910 as 'a political fossil; he is a politician who has failed to grow up since thirty years ago'.[76] After the death of Parnell, he fought strenuously to replicate his achievement. The dour authoritativeness of his nationalism rendered him in some respects Parnell's most obvious successor. Devoid of Parnell's strategic insight and elegance in action, his promulgation of Parnellian tenets was depressingly mechanistic. Temperamentally intolerant of criticism, he believed that strict discipline and the unswerving maintenance of the Liberal alliance would ensure the belated realisation of Parnell's legacy.

With considerable justification, he regarded Healy's schismatic course as treasonable. Profound ideological disagreements fortified their mutual disesteem. Dillon was appalled by Healy's pandering to Catholic ecclesiastics, and his readiness to collaborate with the Conservatives. His stern belief in the primacy of home rule rendered him innately suspicious of land purchase, and he viewed Healy's championship of a socially conservative land-owning Catholic nationalist society with especial distaste.

While Dillon appreciated as Healy did not the necessity for disciplined political action, he was a poor tactician. He had a lofty disdain for Healy's cunning and his gifts as a parliamentarian. His preoccupation with Healy, amounting almost to a psychological dread, accentuated his own defects as a politician. In permitting himself to be driven to morbid fury by Healy's provocative conduct, he encouraged Healy further and rendered himself vulnerable to his irony. As Serjeant Sullivan observed, 'his sense of humour atrophied as the enemy became more witty'.[77]

Healy was incapable of regarding Dillon's championship of 'unity' as other than a naked exercise in self-aggrandisement. He despised what he considered to be Dillon's combination of righteous arrogance and political ineptitude, and revelled in Sexton's characterisation of Dillon as 'the melancholy humbug'.[78] Throughout his career he never ceased to regard himself as the innocent victim of Dillon's aggression, against which he felt free to retaliate with wounded fury.

Healy's thwarting of Dillon was consummate and thoroughgoing. Perfectly appreciating that a stalemate sufficed to achieve his ends, he readily embraced the fate that had twinned him and Dillon in reciprocal antagonism. He exploited the parallelism whereby his own excesses could appear to be merely the obverse of Dillon's. As a master of the black arts of negation in nationalist politics, Healy was without rival. In September 1896, Healy declared with cheerful cunning that the first thing to be done in Irish politics was to 'get rid of all those who have any pretensions to leadership. My name and Mr. Dillon's name are mere shibboleths of faction. We are both on that ground hopelessly disqualified from leadership. We are leaders of sides in what amounts to a civil war'.[79]

Earlier that year, the *Irish Catholic* had commenced publication of a series entitled 'The New Irish Leader'.[80] It was not hard to guess Healy's authorship of this extended account of Dillon's career in Irish politics, which depicted him as morosely ambitious, tactically inept, and temperamentally unsuited to political leadership. The articles were collated, slightly reworked, and published in 1898 under Healy's name as *Why Ireland is Not Free, A Study of Twenty Years in Irish Politics*. Healy's temper and technique as a polemical biographer are disclosed in his comments to his father as he neared the completion of the series. He wrote that it would be a relief to bring 'my account of Honest John to a close':

> Still, it was necessary to justify our attitude towards him. My conscience pricks me here and there, asking 'Am I doing this imbecile any injustice?' In retort, of course not, but while I shorten a phrase or two in final form, I can't see what he has to squall over. The records are his own speeches and acts, after all.[81]

The fleeting moment of self-scrutiny, quickly repressed, was characteristic.

Why Ireland is Not Free was an interim memoir, written in mid-career, an elaborate rationalisation of his opposition to Parnell as well as to Dillon. To his brother he wrote as he completed the reworking of the articles: 'I am inclined to begin a fresh revision of it, as I am clear I must put my name to it, and I have not exercised enough of my personal comments, or blended them sufficiently with the historic'. Significantly he was anxious that it should appear before R. Barry O'Brien's biography of Parnell, published later the same year.[82] An inspired propagandist, he sought to ensure that his polemic was the stuff of nationalist historiography. He sought not merely to influence contemporary opinion, but to sway the verdict of posterity. Outnumbered by Dillon's supporters, and possessed of the grim premonition that in relation to Parnell he was writing against the grain of history, he was doubly embattled.

Much of Healy's domestic strength derived from the backing he was able to command from the Irish episcopacy and clergy. His most influential and staunchest supporter was the Irish primate, Cardinal Logue, Archbishop of Armagh. His support among the clergy, while most highly concentrated in Ulster, was diffused across the country. His skilful championship of Catholic causes, the artful sectarianism of his rhetoric, and his instinctive hostility to progressive politics, brought him a degree of ecclesiastical protection even from those bishops and priests otherwise well disposed towards the anti-Parnellite leadership. He came to represent a check which could be applied to the pretensions of the Irish party to secular authority. Significantly Archbishop Walsh of Dublin, whose sympathies in the Parnell split and its immediate aftermath had lain strongly with Dillon and O'Brien, moved to repair his relations with Healy. Healy wrote to his brother in October 1896:

> I had a letter yesterday from the Archbishop of Limerick marked 'Confidential', suggesting that I should take the University question in hand, and that, if I made a couple of speeches upon in the Autumn, he felt sure I could drive the government to action! He also added that His Grace of Dublin was anxious that the old friendly relations between us should be restored, and he recommended me to make some approach to Dr. Walsh . . . He said he met Dr. Walsh recently, who spoke most kindly of me!! Evidently his Grace feels the want of some mouthpiece in the House, as Sexton is no longer there . . .[83]

Walsh shortly afterwards warned against any re-unification of the Irish party which did not include Healy.[84]

Conversely, Healy sought to extract the maximum electoral advantage from clerical suspicions of John Dillon:

> Today Mr. Dillon has got the upper hand with his policy. What do you see? You see in very many places throughout the country the clergy refusing to give him their support. What will be the result? In my opinion that inevitable result will be before long in many places the Parnellites will win back seats which they have lost.[85]

Driven from the high ground, Healy was no longer in a position to mount a direct challenge to Dillon's hegemony within the anti-Parnellite parliamentary party. He wrought around himself a diverse coalition of opposition to the anti-Parnellite leadership. Based primarily on family members and kinsmen, and close allies such as William Martin Murphy, it drew its support from propertied conservative nationalists and from the ranks of the Catholic clergy. While Healy did not command a broad popular constituency, the damage which his sympathisers inflicted on the Irish party was out of proportion to their numbers. They sustained refractory minorities in the constituencies, and starved the already depleted anti-Parnellite coffers of funds. Most significantly, Healy and his adherents successfully sabotaged the claim of the anti-Parnellite leadership to represent the united voice of nationalism outside the ranks of Redmond's Parnellite minority.

In November 1896 Healy received a cheque from a rural curate 'in support of those members of the Irish Parliamentary Party who work with Mr. Healy and act with him outside as well as inside the House of Commons'. Other donations to what became known as 'The People's Rights Fund' followed. The subscribers – of whom the largest group were Catholic priests – met in Dublin on 12 January 1897. The programme they adopted was classically Healyite. They proclaimed themselves in favour of the free choice of candidates by the constituencies. Opposed to the prevailing system for the payment of Irish members from the party funds, they demanded that where the payment of a nationalist member was necessary it should emanate from the constituencies or from a properly audited fund independent of the party. They declined to recognise the National Federation as then constituted and controlled as representative of the country. Lest there be any doubt as to their opposition to John Dillon's leadership of the anti-Parnellite party, a further resolution declared that 'we regard the attempt to stereotype a "permanent Chairman" or a "permanent majority" within the Irish party as mischievous to national interests'.[86]

The Committee of the Fund subsequently established the People's Rights Association, and provided the initiative for the establishment of a daily newspaper.[87] While it was not in any sense a popular organisation on the scale of the Irish National Federation, the People's Rights Association institutionalised Healy's challenge to Dillon, and diverted subscriptions away from the anti-Parnellite majority.

Healy badly needed the backing of a professionally run journalistic organ. From 1897, with some assistance from other supporters of Healy, William Martin Murphy took over the ailing *Nation* newspapers. From 12 June 1897 the *Nation* appeared as the *Weekly Nation*. It was joined from 1 October 1897 by the *Daily Nation* which survived until 29 August 1900 (after which it was merged with the formerly Parnellite *Independent* following its acquisition by Murphy). Over the three years of its existence the *Daily Nation* incurred heavy losses which Murphy funded. In William O'Brien's *Invincible*-laden image, 'Mr. Murphy bought the knives and Mr. Healy did the stabbing'.[88]

The reconstituted *Nation* newspapers, edited by W. F. Dennehy, were openly Healyite, and articulated a chauvinistic pro-clerical nationalism, explicitly celebrating a post-Parnellite social and political order. The *Weekly Nation* proclaimed itself the protector of 'this old Catholic nation'. Had the country acquiesced in the tyranny of the Irish party, 'we should have witnessed a degradation of the national conscience pregnant with possibilities of evil'. Condemning the Dillonite cry of 'unity' and the Parnellite tenet of 'independence' alike, the paper boasted 'we have helped to ring the tocsin which has roused the conscience and wisdom of Catholic and Celtic Ireland'.[89]

What was strikingly reactionary about the reconstituted *Nation* newspaper was its openly expressed desire to dismantle the political institutions of Parnellism, and its readiness to treat the axioms of Parnellite nationalism in the 1880s as the spent adages of an expired decade of social transformation. The *Daily Nation* referred to the divorce crisis as 'the great awakening of the national intelligence which took place in November 1890'. It condemned Dillon's 'system, of dictation and despotism in the selection of candidates, which could only have been tolerated in a period of social transition and revolution such as undoubtedly existed at the time when it was successfully enforced'.[90] Subject only to putting in place a final measure of land purchase, the Irish social revolution was over.

The *Daily* and *Weekly Nation* sought also to check the persisting mystique of Parnell. T. D. Sullivan complained of 'the creation of a sort of Parnell myth'. What particularly rankled with Healyite nationalists was the invocation of the image of Parnell to promote the activist nationalism they deplored. 'There were strong men before Agamemnon, and Irish Nationalists before Mr. Parnell', the *Weekly Nation* opined in 1898. The *Daily Nation* in 1899 complained that 'not the least of the mischiefs produced by the Split was the exaggerated ideas spread about the magic of Mr. Parnell's power in Parliament, and the "unity"-mongers take advantage of this by talking of wondrous things which could be effected by restoring the Party on its former bases'. The Parnellite axiom of independence had been likewise superseded:

> No Irish party by the so-called system of Independence can ever win Home Rule. The law of arithmetic is against it . . . This jargon about 'Independence' is, therefore, mere cant in the sense in which it is mouthed by Parnellite politicians.[91]

Healy's championship of the rights of nationalists in individual constituencies to their choice of nationalist parliamentary candidates fanned the flames of local discontent. He unceasingly, and often amusingly, poured scorn on the attempts of the Irish leadership to prevail on constituency organisations to accept its choice of nominee. Learning of 'the descent of a brace of "organisers" on North Louth' before the general election of 1900, he wrote to the *Dundalk Examiner*:

> Speeches are made loaded with adjectives specifying the virtues which the unknown and undiscovered new members should possess, and promises on their unborn behalf arise, as if the 'organisers' possessed a seer's divining rod. Why, then, are the besieged constituencies so rarely favoured with a hint of the hallowed names of the persons adorned by such noble qualifications? Platitudes are cheap today. It is not adjectives that are returned to Parliament but nouns! Anybody boasting the endowment of the beatitudes should surely possess a name and address.[92]

While Healy was quick to discern in British social legislation a design against Ireland, he was a tireless advocate of the expenditure of public monies on land purchase. This opportunistic dualism provided the thread of continuity which ran from his support of Gerald Balfour's Land Law (Ireland) Act of 1896, and of the Wyndham Irish Land Act of 1903 through to his vociferous objections to the Lloyd George budgets. For Healy the political economy of land purchase was that of hard cash. He had playfully made this clear in the debate on the Queen's Speech in 1892:

> These landlords may be very dull men on a great many points, but you come to where their heart is – the region of their pockets – no amount of rustle of paper will fetch them. They want the ring of the money; as we say in Ireland the *arragseesh* – the money down. You may praise your Land Stock as much as you please, you may flourish it into a Wagner harmony; but if the Irish landlords will not take it up, what is the good of it?[93]

The settled loathing between Dillon and Healy was eclipsed by the more operatic antagonism between O'Brien and Healy. Their relations had deteriorated in the aftermath of Parnell's death into open animosity, which expressed itself in absurd mutual vituperation.[94] O'Brien by this time held Healy almost single-handedly responsible for the disintegration of the Parnellite movement. He had been out of politics since his resignation of his Cork seat in 1895, but the launching of the neo-agrarian United Irish League at Westport on 16 January 1898 marked his re-entry. One of his chief purposes was to drive Healy out of Irish public life. The relative success of the League, given the prevailing political torpor, took contemporary observers by surprise.[95]

The quarrel between Healy and O'Brien, if it did little to enhance the repute of constitutional nationalist politics, at least provided some public entertainment in an interval of dismay. Healy savoured the rich comedy of O'Brien's speeches and editorials in his *Irish People* and became a droll connoisseur of his wilder excesses. His amusement was genuine. The *Weekly Nation* – in lines which only he could have written – seized upon a poem written by O'Brien to ridicule his exaggerated mode of patriotic declamation:

> 'Ababoo! Bannee-Hoo! Granua-Uaile!' We repeat the words, although we frankly confess to our shame we do not know their exact meaning, and only use them because they sound awful and tearful, and as we find them in a recent poetical contribution by Mr. William O'Brien to our esteemed contemporary, the *Weekly Freeman*.

Healy laughter rang through the columns of the *Weekly Nation* for some time thereafter. The paper celebrated the 'thrilling and heart-rending words of the refrain', 'the Balderdashical war-cry or love-cry — we do not know which it was meant to be — "Ababoo! Bannee-Hoo! Granua Uaile!"'. The predicament of Gerald Balfour, the Chief Secretary, was not to be envied: 'He may send his myrmidons to Westport . . . but Mr. William O'Brien, fearless and unmoved, hurls at him the proud defiance "Ababoo! Bannee-Hoo! Granua Uaile!"'. The paper concluded that 'Mr. O'Brien's name has become a synonym for the absurd'.[96]

T. D. Sullivan caricatured O'Brien fondly recalling his past glories as the most romantic of Parnell's lieutenants of the 1880s:

> Oh for the days of the 'Impariayl', and the two portmanteaus! — the days when pictures of the hayro, plain and coloured, used to be hawked through Munster villages and when in the by-streets and lanes of Cork ballad singers could be heard lilting the refrain:
>
> Hurrah for William O'Brien
> He is a son of Granuaile,
> And for the sake of Ireland
> He done three months in Jail![97]

22

Reunions and Estrangements, 1900–1909

> . . . Mr. Healy, in the classical sense of the word is an anarchist. He is one of the deniers and the defiers . . . But what an anarchist! There is hardly a more fascinating figure in Irish politics . . . Mr. Healy, the centre of storms of thunder, with this party and that party angry round him, denouncing him, belauding him, eager to make use of or to get rid of him, with clerics and dignitaries vehement for him or against him, with the Press cheering him on, or shouting him down, or laughing at him, stands a grey immovable cynical figure in the midst of it all, partyless and alone.
>
> Francis Cruise O'Brien, 1910[1]

> The cleverest man in the British Parliament is that witty Irishman Timothy Healy. He saves Parliament from tragedy.
>
> Otto von Bismarck in conversation with R. D. Blumenfeld[2]

The Reunion of the Irish Party

Early in 1899, the Parnellites under John Redmond took the first serious initiative to bring about the re-unification of the Irish party. Given the multiple schisms among the Irish nationalist parliamentarians, Healy's assessment of the prospect of creating a united political force was exceedingly bleak. He wrote to his brother:

> The truth is that we are divided on nearly every question that can separate the human mind except on the attainment of Home Rule. No patched-up union can effect any change amongst us. The Parnell party was possible largely because all the chief men were personal friends; now they are all bitter enemies, with a sufficient grudge each against the other to last a lifetime. The Party cannot be carried on without money, and the country will not subscribe to keep up the gang of fellows who are not worth, most of them, a pound a week in any trade or business, and who are useless in the House of Commons.[3]

After a protracted stand-off, the movement towards re-unification gathered pace in late 1899. Healy had regarded the cry for 'Unity' with suspicion, as a device to ensure Dillon's domination. He wrote to a correspondent in 1898 on the subject, referring to Dillon: 'Things are tending I think towards a solution of the original division amongst us, but the progress is slow, because of the determination of the apostle of unity not to permit it except at his price'.[4] He latterly suspended his misgivings, and played an active role in the negotiations for reunion, particularly with John Redmond.

Parnell's shattered party was reunited on 30 January 1900, and Redmond was elected its leader a week later. While Healy ebulliently jockeyed for advantage, Dillon's dread of his old adversary brought on a kind of paralysis. Unable to decide which of his twin fears — the entrenchment of a powerful Redmond-Healy axis or the hegemony of William O'Brien through the United Irish League — was greater, Dillon held aloof from the negotiations for reunion. He was only prevailed upon at the end, and then with the greatest difficulty, to vote for Redmond as leader. This left Healy with a considerable advantage, which he was rapidly to dissipate.[5]

At the outset, Redmond's grip on the reunited party was extremely tenuous. The antagonisms formed in the previous decade (most of them internal to the former factions) showed little sign of abating. A party so wracked by division provided Healy for a time with a congenial habitat. In the immediate aftermath of re-unification, his alliance with Redmond endured, while Dillon and his adherents kept their distance. The main outstanding issue was the relationship of the party to O'Brien's United Irish League. Determined to crush Healy, O'Brien sought to constitute the League as the national organisation of the Irish party. Dillon remained mistrustful, fearing that a convention to bring about that end would deliver the United Irish League into the control of a Redmond-Healy alliance.[6]

A letter from Healy to his brother in March 1900 charts the intricate geometry of antagonism within the reunited party.

> Redmond told me that Dillon hardly speaks to him and is undisguisedly sulky, and that T.P. is the same, and that both are equally sore with Blake,

> who is openly cut by T.P.!! Blake told Redmond that if they could they would break up the unity business, and were striving their best in that direction. Blake has been utterly disgusted with them for a long time, and told Redmond some stories about applications for funds which he said astonished him. O'Brien is willing to have a convention but wants it delayed . . . Redmond feels that, if he calls a convention without giving O'Brien some assurances, that he will set his Branches to work to denounce it, and that Dillon will fight the idea in the Party; and of course some 'mandate' from the Party to convene would be essential, as there is no other convening body in existence . . . Harrington is entirely opposed to O'Brien's game; but I could see Redmond does not want to give him too much of his confidence at present on some matters.[7]

Dillon's misconceived reserve made Redmond hesitant, and kept him in close relations with Healy. Redmond was also at this time desperately anxious to avail of Healy's good offices to persuade William Martin Murphy to purchase the insolvent *Irish Independent*. Healy had few illusions and sensed that O'Brien's influence would ultimately prevail against him. He wrote to Maurice on 29 April:

> As to Redmond, I confess I am very much discouraged. I regard him as having gone body and soul over to O'Brien, although of course to some extent unconsciously; but evidently he thinks it is on this side that his bread is buttered . . . I am beginning to fear that the original scheme which Dillon had for the Parnellite junction against us will be carried out by O'Brien through Redmond, although not vindictively or in the same way, but substantially as far as influence is concerned. Dillon is not friends with O'Brien at present, and I think views with dislike the rapprochement between the two . . . Redmond of course would protest the utmost friendship for us and contempt for O'Brien, but after his late speeches I am not inclined to place absolute confidence in his firmness.[8]

Healy's fears were well-founded, if not self-fulfilling. He stood fatalistically aloof from the convention of June 1900 at which the United Irish League became the national organisation of the united Irish party, with Redmond at its head.[9] This left Healy and his allies isolated and electorally vulnerable. His remaining leverage over Redmond lay in the influence he could bring to bear in the negotiations for the acquisition of the *Independent* by Murphy, whom he was advising. He sought, perhaps a little too transparently, to achieve a trade-off. He wrote to Maurice after a meeting with Redmond and Murphy in August:

> If Ireland is left at the mercy of a single paper (as it would before long unless our scheme goes through) the situation would be intolerable. I spoke to Redmond today, and he was in a more receptive frame of mind, and

> said there was no intention of opposing you in Cork, and that if it should be mooted, he would set his face against it. I told him I would insist on all our friends being returned if they desired, and that we could return them all. My reason for making representations was that contests would inflict a fine on us which we should not be asked to bear.[10]

Two days later, he wrote that 'Murphy will only buy the paper, I understand, if he controls it and its policy; but of course it would not be expedient to have this too plainly spoken'. As Redmond struggled to strengthen his still-fragile grip on the party, the shadow of William O'Brien loomed ever larger. Redmond told Healy that he disapproved of an approach which had been made to O'Brien to buy the *Independent*:

> I asked why, and he replied emphatically, 'Because I would rather the *Freeman* got the paper than O'Brien'. This does not show much love or confidence, whereas he treats us, who criticise him freely, as friends. Privately his attitude towards us all along has been confidential and trustful, yet he speaks in public with a constant fear of O'Brien before his eyes.
>
> Neither Dillon nor Davitt seems in line with O'Brien, while Redmond did not reject the idea I broached of having a Parliamentary Committee to arrange the election campaign. Harrington and Clancy separately spoke of resigning unless there was a peaceful understanding, and Harrington said he felt sure the protest he would make after his efforts to restore unity would have an effect on the country which O'Brien could not obliterate.[11]

Not the least irony was that, in seeking to ensure that the nomination of candidates would be under the control of a committee of the party – rather than of the United Irish League – Healy depended on the support of Harrington and Clancy, both of whom had been Parnellite in the split.

In August 1900 Murphy acquired the *Independent*, which he amalgamated with the *Daily Nation*. The first issue of the *Daily Independent and Nation* appeared on 1 September 1900.[12] While the paper did not achieve its full potential until its re-launch as the halfpenny *Irish Daily Independent* on 2 January 1905, there was now in existence a populist and properly funded rival to the *Freeman's Journal*, which was in effect the official organ of the Irish party. While relations between Healy and Murphy were often strained, and at times fractious, as a result of Murphy's refusal to impose an explicitly Healyite editorial policy on the paper, the *Independent* was ultimately to play a significant part in the downfall of the Irish party.

At the general election of October 1900, Healy and his allies, standing as independent nationalists, were everywhere confronted by a resurgent United Irish League. On 23 September William O'Brien descended on the town of Louth to rally the opposition to Healy. The confrontation between O'Brien and Healy which ensued quickly degenerated into farce. Healy and O'Brien addressed the crowd from the same brake. Healy resisted all attempts to shout him down or to eject him over three hours of turmoil and confusion. As the brake moved down the road Healy continued: 'This is O'Brien's circus (*laughter*); this is O'Brien's travelling gallows — he takes jury, judge, gallows and all, but will never be Lord High Executioner (*loud cheers*). I will fight to a finish (*renewed cheers*).'[13]

Healy was not worried about his own prospects ('all the priests have worked hard for me'), but William O'Brien's decision to stand in Cork put his brother's seat in jeopardy. Healy called in aid his experience of over twenty years of Irish elections, enumerating to Maurice the steps he should take to ensure his return:

> Your friends should at once meet as a convention, and you should get the men who formed the United League to go and organise meetings. My advice to you is to secure a mob and prevent O'Brien taking possession of the streets. I and Murphy will give you any money you require; and Murphy told me to tell you so. When he arrives at the station, there should be a mob there to groan him, and you should retain the bands of the city at any price, so that they will not come out for him. Work up the Parnellites and if possible try to get a Parnellite to stand with you . . . You should also see the Bishop, or have your friends see him, and get him to write a letter to you deprecating needless opposition when there was no political question at stake. If you could get a meeting of the Corporation called, protesting against the city being plunged into a contest, or the Board of Guardians, I think it would have a good effect. We shall have an article in the *Independent* on Monday condemning O'Brien's tactics as endangering unity . . . Don't be timorous, or despair in this matter, but act boldly, for you will be dealing with an unscrupulous set.[14]

It was all in vain. Even with the benefit of such expert advice, Maurice finished at the bottom of the poll, forfeiting the seat he had held since he was first elected, alongside Parnell, fifteen years previously. Tim Healy was inconsolable. When Maurice wrote that there was no hope, he responded with a highly emotional letter of commiseration, addressed to 'my darling boy'. 'My victory will do me no good now. I could not speak anywhere today since I heard the news. My eyes are full of tears . . . I am horribly cut up for you, my poor boy'.[15]

Nationally the result was a triumph for the United Irish League, and Redmond's position was for the first time rendered secure. Healy held North Louth by an adequate though not impressive margin. In addition to Maurice's defeat, William Martin Murphy's final attempt to return to parliament, for North Mayo, was heavily rebuffed. Arthur O'Connor was defeated in North Donegal. Unnerved by the strength of the United Irish League, and, ironically, the opposition of the Bishop of Raphoe, Patrick O'Donnell, T. D. Sullivan did not contest West Donegal, thereby bringing to an end his twenty-year parliamentary career.[16]

The 1900 election marked the end of Healyism, as it had existed in the 1890s, as an identifiable political force. Almost ten years to the month after the divorce crisis, Healy had been decisively vanquished in the struggle for ascendancy which had commenced with the deposition of Parnell, and had contrived to dissipate the great influence he had garnered in the split and its immediate aftermath. Yet he was more liberated than crushed by the defeat of his faction. The role of pariah was congenial to him. Alone at Westminster, he could still wreak havoc, and remained for the leaders of the Irish party an extremely dangerous adversary.

O'Brien, fearful of a convention sanctioning Healy's re-admission to the ranks of the Irish party, was implacable:

> The presence of Mr. Healy in the ranks of the Irish Party . . . would be like the presence of a poisoned bullet in the body of a man. The first remedy was to extract the bullet – that was to say to keep Mr. Healy outside the ranks of the party which he had made it his business to destroy. For his part he had not the slightest objection to Mr. Healy remaining in Parliament so long as he did not do so as a member of the Irish Party.[17]

At a convention in Dublin in December 1900, O'Brien proposed Healy's expulsion from the party. The resolution, opposed feebly by Redmond, and strenuously by Harrington, was overwhelmingly carried. Healy, who the previous month had privately characterised O'Brien as 'a crazy mountebank', cheerfully declared that 'I find so much fun in poor William O'Brien that I freely forgive him all his incantations'.[18]

Barrister and Parliamentarian

Healy can only have been relieved as the last decade of the nineteenth century came to a close. It had been for him a decade of violent vicissitudes of fortune, of the rending of old friendships, and of terrible vituperation. Time had diminished some of the split's asperities, if only through a process of exhaustion. Even though he had been swiftly excluded from the party, re-unification had benefited him in closing over some of the old rifts.

The early years of the new century were for Healy a period of comparative tranquillity. No longer encumbered by the leadership of a national faction, he contentedly awaited the breakdown of the united nationalist front from which he and his remaining confederates alone were excluded. Now in his middle forties, the embattled Victorian nationalist had emerged as a prosperous Edwardian.

The bar consumed an ever-increasing amount of Healy's time.[19] He was a natural barrister. He revelled in the unapologetic partisanship of forensic conflict. Francis Cruise O'Brien wrote with cutting perceptiveness: 'He has a mind, nay the soul, of a barrister. Special pleading is his religion'.[20] Martial's epigram on lawyers, *iras locant* (they hire out their anger), might have been invented for Healy.

His close relationship with his solicitor brother was professional as well as political and personal. He constantly belaboured the more frugal Maurice over the fees he was paid, and commented in 1920 of a case he sent him that it was 'the first soft job you ever gave me!'[21] His attitude to the barrister's craft is illumined in a shrewd letter to his brother suggesting that Maurice's son and namesake should become a barrister rather than a solicitor:

> I have no opportunity for forming any judgement of the boy's powers, but he is an agreeable, well-mannered, handsome and presentable boy, likely to make friends, and not wanting in push. He is better adapted I think for the Bar than for the more laborious business of a solicitor; and, while of excellent disposition and training, might think himself lost in a provincial town in the years to come, if buried in a solicitor's office while opportunities were being afforded to Catholics of distinction at the Bar.

He looked to 'the swamping of the Ascendancy Party, and to the probability that clever youngsters on our side will have better prospects at the Bar in the coming generation than could have been hoped for previously'.[22]

He was a formidable advocate. The reputation for aggression which preceded him was itself part of his forensic armoury. 'He often threw a witness completely off guard by his soothing mildness, eliciting all the case required, and nothing more'.[23] Healy's nephew Maurice wrote that he had 'one of the loveliest speaking voices I have ever heard, with great dramatic possibilities; and he well knew how to use it'. He had audacity, and luck. His nephew wrote: 'Whether he foresaw the extent of the success his tactics would attain I do not know; he was a mystic, and a sure instinct frequently led him to success along paths where others would plunge to disaster'.[24]

He was not without his critics. A hostile source, James O'Connor, wrote that he did not consider Healy a good advocate. 'I sometimes fancied he had rather a contempt for the science of law. But he has been known to get the truth out of a hostile witness by unscientific and sledge-hammer daring which no other advocate would attempt; though I am sure the same methods have often cost him the verdict'. (It was elsewhere suggested that he had lost a case over a joke.) O'Connor noted that he did not professionally flourish in London and continued malignly: 'In Ireland, the clients, rather than the attorneys, chose him; he said such good things that they thought all things which he said should be good. Ireland, too, is full of people who would rather lose a law case gaily – with the salt rubbed into the sore spots of an opponent's carcass – than win it soberly and sombrely'.[25] Such considerations evidently prompted Edward Martyn to brief Healy in 1906. He wrote to J. J. Horgan: 'I thought I told you that T. M. Healy M.P. was my counsel. I hope to pour plenty of boiling water into that nest of wasps in the Kildare St. Club. But I feel I have not much chance of winning'.[26]

Healy had rapidly built up a substantial practice. He had somewhat greater success than his great nationalist precursors at the Irish bar, Daniel O'Connell and Isaac Butt, in marshalling his earnings. His professional income was supplemented by what he derived from John Barry's substantial linoleum business, in which he was involved throughout his career, and from other investments. His wealth may also have been enhanced by the shrewd advice and generosity of Beaverbrook. A. G. Gardiner, who discerned in Healy 'a sort of cloistral quietude' was quick to add that 'in spite of his monkishness he is an uncommonly astute business man'.[27] Healy died a man of some substance.[28]

Healy's fierce antipathies were undimmed, but thenceforth were to be more skilfully deployed. He had learnt to avoid the wracking pitched battles to which he had committed himself in the previous decade. On occasions he displayed an unwonted restraint, and practised a certain economy of vehemence. He had attained to a limited self-knowledge, and showed some aptitude in negotiating his own defects of temperament. He was more inclined, at least privately, to take relativistic views.

In his war of attrition against Dillon and Redmond (this was the order in which he perceived them), he was unabashedly opportunistic. This he justified in part on the basis that, having excluded him from its ranks, the Irish party could hardly complain if he declined to observe the disciplines of collective action. Applying his considerable comic gifts in arch self-deprecation, he skilfully feigned a certain mellowing with the passage of the years. This was coupled with an indulgence towards Conservative ministers unique among nationalist parliamentarians. His mature parliamentary demeanour could even lead the unwary to believe they could discern an underlying benignity. The enduring ferocity of his attacks on the Irish party leadership and his private comments in his correspondence showed that his underlying attitudes were unaltered.

Healy's political isolation was counterbalanced by his high standing as a parliamentarian. In the Commons he often sat in the third corner seat below the gangway, a prominent position which Butt had at one time occupied, and which Parnell had habitually refrained from taking. H. W. Lucy noted that it had the additional attraction of enabling Healy to sit with his back conspicuously turned to Dillon.[29]

He was rated an exceedingly astute tactician, and a dangerous opponent. Above all, he was a speaker of arresting originality and verve. His wit was highly prized. He had an unrivalled knack of seizing the attention of the Commons with mock-ingenuousness, or coquettish understatement, and then moving abruptly on to the offensive. Alternately, sentimental and ferocious, after administering an anaesthetic of pleasurable drollness, he could strike with the speed and toxicity of a snakebite. The most talented member of the Irish party, Lord Curzon wrote in 1913, 'with an almost unsurpassed gift of corrosive humour and diabolical irony was, and is, Mr. Timothy Healy'.[30]

Hailed as a master of Irish sarcasm and pathos, he damagingly highlighted a certain stiffness of bearing on the part of the Irish party leaders. His rhetoric was more improvised and immediate than Redmond's, while his comic gifts made Dillon appear even more dourly humourless than he was by nature. (Margot Asquith later wrote that 'Sexton was copious, Dillon bored me, Healy was unexpected and full of wit'.)[31]

As a parliamentary figure, Healy acquired a considerable mystique: while in some respects derivative of Parnell's myth, it was its antithesis. The accolades which his performance attracted were never entirely innocent of partisan intent. Celebrated as a prodigy of Irish rhetorical fluency, he was the darling of parliamentary sketch-writers and commentators. He epitomised the desolate, almost poignant, ineffectuality of the Irish nationalist parliamentarian as perceived by the more sardonic adversaries of home rule at Westminster. He was, from the unionist vantage, a decidedly reassuring figure.

A perceptive sketch in the *Daily Telegraph* in February 1900 conveyed Healy's brilliance as a parliamentary speaker, and barrenness as a politician:

> There is something behind Mr. Healy's most outrageous diatribes which argues a reckless mental process that means nothing permanent, and this is why his most daring jests move the Government benches to transports of enjoyment rather than fury. . . . The strange exhibition, which had been like nothing so much as a satyr dancing upon a tombstone ended in a vein of melancholy and irreconcilable eloquence. The sheer cleverness of the member for Louth had left the House with a headache, and with that sense of utter futility and hopeless rancour of Irish politics which is never so depressingly conveyed as by the only intellect among the Nationalists that is touched with genius.[32]

Even for British politicians and commentators who were not unionist, the contemplation of Healy afforded if not a means of escape, at least a measure of relief, from addressing the tiresomely insistent realities of the Irish question. It permitted in some degree a consoling reversion to the Ireland of nineteenth-century literary fiction, the pastoral before Parnell. The sketch-writer of the *Manchester Guardian*, writing of the same speech, strove to portray Healy in a Gladstonian perspective. While written from opposing political standpoints, the two descriptions had much in common.

> All Mr. Healy's speeches since the failure of Home Rule had struck one note in various tones – a sort of melancholy, defiant resignation, an elegy of patient detachment, despairing for the moment, but nursing an unconquerable hope. His speeches have the bitter irony of a proud unhappy nation watching the success of another in which it has no share, but they have also the poetry of failure with all its unrealised ideas. His deepest feeling towards England is not hate but irony, and thus his speeches are masterpieces of Swift-like satire, mordant, remorseless, and yet every now and again lit up by soft lights of tender feeling and deep vistas of melancholy pathos. For nearly an hour this great performer – perhaps the most fascinating of all the speakers in the present House – performed to the British House of Commons this afternoon. At first the House slowly filled, and at the last there was the strange spectacle of rows of British members hanging intently on Mr. Healy's slightest word while yet with subtle irony and bitter sarcasm he held up the British Empire to the scorn of men. But none can help it. The House is compelled to listen while Mr. Healy speaks. He can command just that silence in which the voice can be dropped to the lightest whisper . . .[33]

A. G. Gardiner, the former editor of the *Daily News* and a staunch Liberal, wrote in 1925 a sympathetic and finely observed evocation of Healy as a parliamentarian. It strikingly complemented the *Daily Telegraph* and *Guardian* sketches of a quarter-century earlier:

> For a generation, he was *l'enfant terrible* of Parliament, the prince of guerrilla warriors, fighting for Ireland, but fighting still more his own inscrutable ends, flashing through the lists with a tongue that smote like a sword, solitary, defiant, whimsical, incalculable, sad and merry in the same breath, a strange, haunting figure of unrest and indignation, in which all the pathos and all the comedy and all the savageries of Ireland seemed to find expression . . . How often and with what expectation have we seen him rise from the corner seat below the gangway, his hands clasped behind his back, his quaint, pleasant figure swaying forward, his eyes gleaming through the glasses that sat so uneasily on his nose, gleaming with passion and mischief and malice and wit, all under the control of an incomparable serenity. And as he rose every door opening and the Chamber filling with a magical suddenness, as it only fills when the great artist is on the stage.

> And what an artist he was! Not an orator of the 'proud, full sail' of Redmond or the declamatory energy of Devlin. He spoke quietly, dreamily, as if communing with himself, with a touch of aloofness, a certain monkishness as of one who had come from a monastery bringing with him the atmosphere of strange and ghostly things. And of this reverie, in which the voice of the prophet and the cadence of the poet and dreamer were curiously mingled, there would leap some withering phrase that stabbed like death . . . He was the master of all moods. The soft, almost crooning accents, had the pathos of incommunicable things . . . His impudence was sublime, enveloped in a seriousness, a gravity, that made it gorgeous comedy.[34]

T. W. Russell described Healy's seated posture in the Commons: '. . . his hat well over his eyes, apparently unmoved by what is going on around. But once on his feet the Irish question is a reality'.[35] It was however, in terms of British politics, frequently a conveniently manageable reality.

Quite apart from epitomising a reassuringly familiar Ireland, he was not above shamelessly flattering his auditors, as in his widely-acclaimed speech on the second reading of George Wyndham's land bill of 1903. Adroitly sentimentalising the irony of the moment – that Arthur Balfour, who had fiercely opposed Gladstone's land bill of 1881, was now as prime minister promoting a bill which went very much further – Healy contrived to laud Gladstone and the Tories in the same breath. 'The landlords in a body would have taken Mr. Gladstone off to a lunatic asylum', had he proposed a solution by peasant proprietorship,

> and it is only by the long results of time and patience that the House of Commons has been educated under a different franchise. I have always said that this Conservative House of Commons is far more liberal, far kinder in its temper and spirit, than the Liberal House of Commons of that day. Therefore, it is absurd to throw any reproach upon the great name of Gladstone, whose memory will for ever live in fragrance in Ireland.

English parliamentarians and sketch-writers alike found themselves moved by Healy's closing peroration:

> I take my leave of this bill. I wish it a prosperous future, I have given it my humble support as I did the right hon. Gentleman's speech of last year . . . It has been introduced under the most favourable auspices . . . and I can only hope that these favourable auspices will continue, and that a measure like this, presented, as it is, a great measure of peace, will bring, as I hope it may, a new spirit, not merely into the heart of Ireland, but into the heart of England. I believe there is at this moment an attitude between the two countries favourable to peace, favourable to a general understanding.

> . . . You cannot deal with this question merely as decimals or percentages, or as £. s. d. It strikes hard a chord in the Irish character other than the sordid note of finance, it marks a reversal of a long period of dismal oppression and awful sorrow – of a breach of treaty faith committed, it is true, two centuries ago, but having to this day left a living effect. This Bill will change more than Ireland, it will change England too, and with that change I hope to see a brighter light in the eyes of dark Rosaleen.[36]

This speech was often to be cited as a classic example of Healy's power to move the Commons. The accolades which it attracted seem now perhaps a little excessive. H. W. Lucy, who was extremely well disposed to Healy, took the opportunity to laud Healy's contribution as one 'which revealed his stature towering head and shoulders above the ablest of his comrades in the Nationalist party' (who his speech was skilfully devised to exasperate and divide):

> Through nearly a quarter of a century he has whetted the razor of his wit on the strop of the House of Commons, and being of tempered steel he has got it now in fine workmanlike condition. It has come to pass that the *gamin* of early Eighties . . . has reached the position of commanding influence in the Mother of Parliaments. There are only two other members – and they speak with the authority of Cabinet Ministers – who can fill the House as does Tim Healy.[37]

Healy's parliamentary performances were uniquely vivid, arresting and often affecting, but in terms of the acclaim he could attract he enjoyed a number of further advantages. For Conservative commentators there was an obvious interest in lauding Healy at the expense of Redmond and Dillon. The socially complacent genre of sketch-writing was innately more favourable to Healy. He provided better copy than the Irish party leaders, earnestly engaged in pursuing home rule in alliance with the Liberals, at the head of a party whose composition had grown drably homogeneous. The contrast he was able to afford was an additional stimulus to Healy's virtuoso displays of individuality.

Healy was adept at obtruding Irish affairs into parliamentary debates at Westminster. Most famously, when forbidden by the Speaker from raising Irish matters in a debate on pending business (of which the Uganda Railway was part), Healy rose 'for the purpose of saying a few words upon the subject of the Uganda Railway (*laughter*) . . . Speaking as a native of Uganda, he wished to thank the Government for the great measure of advance they had made in Uganda, which he was sure would bring calm to Kerry and balm to Ballydehob'.[38] As he explained on another occasion, 'I have no Imperial soul. As I was born, so I will remain a parish politician'.[39] Yet this was somewhat disingenuous, as well as intentionally provocative. If he was suggesting that he was not favourably disposed to unnecessary imperialistic enterprises, he was still more concerned to dissociate himself from the radical anti-imperialism espoused by many Liberals and by John Dillon.

In the debate on the King's speech in February 1905, Healy made a memorable thrust at Lord Hugh Cecil, which delighted G. K. Chesterton:

> The noble Lord the Member for Greenwich professed not to know what nationality was. He would tell him. Nationality was something one was willing to die for. Even the noble Lord would not die for the meridian of Greenwich.[40]

In a celebrated sally, Healy attacked Walter Runciman. He suggested that the dapper President of the Board of Agriculture visit an Irish fair to assess the deleterious effects on Irish farmers of government policy on the eradication of foot and mouth disease: 'He may perhaps go disguised as an agriculturist'.[41]

As an orator, Healy was nothing if not resilient. In a debate on Morley's Evicted Tenants Bill in 1894, he became locked in an exchange with Joseph Chamberlain over an amendment on the subject of absentee landlords, Healy observed that the Duke of Devonshire rarely went to Ireland. Chamberlain responded that he was there last year. Oblivious to the peril, Healy persisted:

Mr. T. Healy:	Once in 10 years has he visited Ireland.
Mr. J. Chamberlain:	He had not been there since his brother was murdered.
Mr. T. M. Healy:	Has Lord Clanricarde lost a brother in Ireland? . . .

As Austen Chamberlain later wrote, the reference to the murder of Sir Frederick Cavendish would have finished most parliamentarians. 'Not so Healy. He shook himself like a spaniel coming out of water. In a few moments he was somehow back at the siege of Limerick, describing it with a burning passion that silenced the cheers and counter-cheers, and held the House breathless'.[42]

Supporters of the Irish party continued to regard Healy with mistrust and incomprehension. The mild and decent Alfred Webb, long an associate of the Sullivans, who at one time regarded Healy as 'my closest friend in politics' was driven to write of the 'Bantry gang' (primarily Tim and Maurice Healy, the Sullivans and W. M. Murphy) that 'extreme nationalists harboured a suspicion of them all along. This prejudice in later years, and since A.M.'s death has been justified, even to moderate nationalists. If Healy and Murphy had their way the National movement would have been brought to an end'.[43] The incomprehension was captured by Stephen Gwynn, a nationalist M.P. from 1906. While he acknowledged the eloquence and force of Healy's parliamentary speeches, 'I could never know what he was driving at'.[44]

Healy had from his youth an interest in the popular revival of the Irish language. As a young man he wrote in the *Nation* denouncing academic elitism, and championing the need for a phonetic notation of the language. He hoped that 'before long some real Irish scholar or seer, who not only honours a restricted past, but worships the possibility of an illimitable future, may appear to tear from our old tongue its Nessus garb . . .'[45]

The idea of Irish spelling reform, which had something in common with Healy's fascination with Isaac Pitman's system of shorthand writing, became a minor obsession for Healy, and more especially his brother. Maurice wrote a series of four letters to the *Freeman's Journal* on the subject in 1893, which were subsequently republished in pamphlet form, and contemplated writing a book on the subject.[46] Healy at least contrived to remain somewhat more humorous on the subject than his brother. T. O'Neill Russell brought Douglas Hyde to Healy's house in December 1893. Healy wrote:

> Of course he is entirely opposed to phonetic spelling, but he says he has so much respect for us he would not think of gainsaying anything we said!! And then he laid his head on the table and laughed boisterously and at his ease over your representation for the Our Father in Irish spelling. He thinks that since Shakespeare this is the greatest thing ever done!![47]

In the Commons the previous year, Healy defended the Irish language, urging that if children in Irish-speaking areas were to be educated compulsorily it should be in their own language, rather than have them 'compelled to learn a language as foreign to them as Chinese'. (He added: 'We often hear the stupidity of the illiterate Irish peasant denounced; but if I had to spend my life on a desert island with either an Irish peasant or an Irish Chief Secretary, I should prefer to be with the peasant.'[48])

While many of those associated with cultural nationalism from the end of the nineteenth century regarded Healy with suspicion on account of his role in the split, D. P. Moran's *Leader* expressed a degree of ambivalence. However much it disagreed with Healy, 'there is no intelligent Irishman who does not, after all, feel proud of his brilliant intellect, his virility, and above all his intellect. He is Irish from the top of his head to the sole of his foot, with many of the great virtues, and many of the characteristic faults, of his nation.' He had however failed to conform to the canons of cultural nationalism: 'He thinks he is an Irish Nationalist, when he is only little more than a mere modern Irish politician. As an Irish Nationalist, he is a sham, but he cannot see it. He, therefore, occupies some very curious positions. He is a sham who hates shams'.[49]

The Rapprochement with William O'Brien

Healy bore his parliamentary solitude with equanimity. When the Chief Secretary George Wyndham commented in the Commons that the League had created a united Irish party, Healy memorably responded that 'as a matter of fact it has deposited two parties, of which I am one'.[50] The Attorney General for Ireland referred to Healy in the Commons as 'a well-known and prominent leader of the Irish party; I might also call him a general of division'.[51]

Healy wrote with muted astonishment to his brother in March 1901: 'On the whole the Party are behaving well. They cheer my speeches as if nothing had happened'.[52] He could not discern any hostility to himself among the new party. 'If O'Brien is kept away, everything would come all right. Dillon has little influence among them; and Redmond will daily strengthen his hold'.[53] He wrote to Maurice on 26 July 1902: 'I must say they have all been very civil to me, and I have nothing to complain of in their attitude, except when they don't cheer!! They laugh, however. I suppose they can't always help this'.[54]

His isolation nonetheless took its toll. While he was favourably impressed by Redmond, he considered the new intake mediocre, and badly missed Maurice. He wrote to his father.

> I hate the wretched House now. Nor am I consoled by the bosh that 'justice will triumph and truth will prevail'. They never do, in this world, and never will. Happily, the Boers, being Protestant and God-fearing and -invoking, may gain their intercessions in this world. That would be an exception, and no clue to the general rule.[55]

He was later moved to write to his father that 'the loss of friends is even worse than shattered ideals'. To Maurice he wrote wearily in 1904: 'The House is dull and I am returning home in sheer ennui. Our wretched Party gives me the creeps'.[56]

The acrimony between Healy and O'Brien persisted. Healy's annoyance was tempered by his genuine amusement at O'Brien's eccentricities. He reported to Maurice in February 1901 that 'O'Brien's get-up is the most grotesque thing you ever saw. He is a regular Mad Mullah!' With a characteristic twist, he wrote the following year that 'I think it must have been the Dillon gang spread the rumour that William's mind was failing'.[57] Healy never loathed O'Brien as he did Dillon. He informed his father in mid-1901 that 'I wish him no harm personally, though he has hurt Ireland nearly as much as Parnell'.[58] O'Brien continued to fulminate against Healy. In February 1903 Healy wrote to his brother that 'T.D. brought me William O'Brien's paper yesterday, and he has five columns abusing me!! So much so that I am told by William Murphy that Kettle has a letter in today's *Freeman* telling William not to mind "Tim". I think really poor O'Brien is not right in his head'.[59]

Healy reported to Maurice in July 1903 'a great triumph over that scoundrel O'Brien', in the debate on Wyndham's land bill. When Healy moved to amend an amendment put down by the Irish party, O'Brien 'got up in his rattlesnake style of sibilance, and said "However sorry he was to differ with the most minute minority of his country" etc. etc.' Healy prevailed. Unsated, 'a few minutes later, I took it well out of William . . .'[60] This however was to prove virtually their last passage of arms. The Irish land act of 1903 set in train a realignment of nationalist politics which within five years was to unite Healy and O'Brien in their opposition to the Irish party leadership.

In 1902 the Irish Land Conference, made up of nationalist parliamentarians and influential landlords, reached agreement on a set of proposals for the resolution of the land question by a substantial extension of land purchase. Its report provided the basis for George Wyndham's Irish land bill. Healy extravagantly hailed the Land Conference report as the most remarkable occurrence in his political life save for Gladstone's espousal of home rule.[61] He was however at first dismissive of Wyndham's bill:

> I am very much disgusted with the Land Bill, and I think it is a very bad one for the tenants; but of course, if I were to say so, it would kill its chances. Indeed a mere puff would do so, and throw Wyndham and the Government out of office. He is so nervous himself that he has been wanting to see me all this week, but I have a touch of influenza, and after much negotiation I am crossing to London on Tuesday night to spend an evening with a friend where he will be . . . I expect there is a pretty complete understanding with the Redmondites, and fancy Wyndham wants to restore harmony in the Irish Party !! !! !! It is a funny world . . . Dillon, Davitt, Sexton, and the Archbishop of Dublin are all hostile to O'Brien's performance; and if I were to join them the Land Bill would be killed, and William and John would be dished; but I could not be guilty of such a piece of faction as to oppose this Bill when I hope it may be considerably modified.[62]

Healy's initial hostility turned into active collaboration with the Irish Secretary. He discussed the bill's provisions with Wyndham in private, and vigorously supported its passage.[63] Healy's attacks helped define

Conservative perceptions, particularly of Dillon, whom Wyndham characterised as 'a pure Agrarian sore-head', complementing Davitt, 'a pure Revolutionary Socialist', with whom he had joined forces to thwart conciliation.[64]

The Irish party and the national directory of the United Irish League endorsed the proposals of the Land Conference, but the appearance of unity was deceptive. The deep divisions were kept in check during the passage of Wyndham's bill. Thereafter, as William O'Brien waxed ever more enthusiastic, the opposition of Dillon, Davitt, Sexton (and the *Freeman's Journal*) to the collaboration between nationalists, landlords and a Conservative government on land purchase intensified. The party's precarious consensus was shattered by John Dillon, who in a speech to his constituents at Swinford, County Mayo, in August 1903, gave vent to his hostility to the land act and its underlying premise of the possibility of reconciliation between antagonistic classes and conflicting parties.

O'Brien not merely supported the report of the Land Conference, but came to acquire an almost mystical belief in the notion of conciliation, and the medium of conferences, which he believed could transcend the stale acrimony between nationalism and unionism in Ireland (whence the title of his highly polemical memoir *An Olive Branch in Ireland and its History*, published in 1910). O'Brien never forgave Dillon the 'Swinford revolt'. That speech marked the end of the close and affectionate collaboration between O'Brien and Dillon which dated back to the Plan of Campaign in 1886 and had enabled them together to wrest control of the anti-Parnellite party from Healy after Parnell's death. O'Brien's rupture with Dillon, and Redmond, whom he blamed for failing to stand up to Dillon, was consummated by his resignation from parliament and unopposed re-election in August 1904.[65]

As the party leadership divided in response to the Wyndham bill, Healy wrote to his father:

> There is practically a split, certainly a coolness, between Dillon and O'Brien. Wm O', except for John Redmond, is alone among the Tritons – on the other side being Davitt, Sexton, T. P. O'C and Dillon. Poor Blake is merely unhappy generally and wants a quiet life. If I live long enough I shall see them all at each other's throats. Their 'unity' was simply against me, which was the only thing they could agree on! The Party generally are mere 'rotters' . . . If O'Brien was out of the way, the majority would down Redmond and elect Dillon. Connaught bosses the Party, but there are fearful jealousies amongst the microbes.[66]

Always a close student of O'Brien's erratic political course, Healy observed with interest O'Brien's espousal of an evangelically moderate agrarian policy at odds with that of the Irish party leadership:

> T. D. Sullivan tells me that W. O'B. has dropped the pike and gun from between his paragraphs and substituted shamrocks!! And that he has an article this week entitled 'A Heart's Hug for All'!! Nothing like going the whole hog.[67]

Events were driving Healy and O'Brien closer together. At the United Irish League convention of April 1904 the breach between O'Brien and the Irish party leadership became irreparable. Healy's ironic gratification was pardonable: 'I hope this will give him a true "Healyite spirit". Certainly a dreadful nemesis has overtaken the fellow. Talk of the revolution devouring its children! He has guillotined himself!'[68]

Dillon rather than Healy now became the prime target of O'Brien's extravagant invective. Healy wrote: 'I must say O'Brien is gorgeous. I don't think Parnell after the Split showed more self-sufficiency or arrogance . . . His drive at Dillon yesterday, and the veiled allusion to the eternal fact that "John wants the Chair" was bitterer than anything I could at any time have attempted!!'[69] Healy's own fire was concentrated on what he called 'the Dillon-Sexton articulation', to which he claimed Redmond was captive.[70]

He remained guarded in his attitude towards O'Brien but came increasingly to appreciate the possibilities of an alliance with him, and to acquiesce in the drift of events in that direction. His allies remained bitterly resentful of O'Brien's role in their political exclusion. Healy however knew that while O'Brien had put his brother out of parliament, he could also put him back in. Skilfully dissembled fraternal solicitude played its part in his calculations. Writing to Maurice in December 1904, Healy artfully conveyed a hint of penitence on O'Brien's part: 'He denounces the idea of a "pledge-bound" Party, and will refuse to join it. I gather that he wishes to lay on Dillon the blame for the treatment of ourselves!'[71] The following year he gently sought to coax Maurice towards a realignment of their allegiances: 'Unpleasant as O'Brien's character is, and unscrupulous as has been his conduct, I think he is sound in his view of politics'.[72] His assessment that 'Redmond is a poor creature; Dillon an ass, and Sexton no Nationalist', left no possible ally other than O'Brien.[73]

The *rapprochement* between Healy and O'Brien was gradual and drawn-out. Healy's public references to O'Brien grew notably more polite. While he took issue with some matters in O'Brien's *Recollections*, which appeared in December 1905, he made plain his readiness to overlook their former disagreements.[74] O'Brien asked Healy to lunch. Healy was also retained to defend John O'Donnell, one of O'Brien's parliamentary followers, in a prosecution brought against him.[75]

Still isolated on the eve of the general election of January 1906 Healy managed an ironic flourish: 'The "Pledge" has now attained such dazzling popularity that the effort to turn it against its author recalls the story that the composer of the *Marseillaise* was guillotined to the music of his own song'.[76] In the event, episcopal protection spared Healy a contest in North Louth. Cardinal Logue publicly intervened on his behalf. More alarmingly for the party, when Healy's local adversaries incautiously proclaimed that their cause was that of the bishops and priests of Ireland, Archbishop Walsh wrote a public letter in the stated capacity of Healy's bishop to declare 'it certainly is not mine'. This permitted Healy to publish an appropriately unctuous letter of thanks: 'My re-election by an increased majority is certain, but sweeter to me than such a victory is the public manifestation of confidence in my integrity, not only by my most eminent constituent, the Cardinal, but by your Grace as my Bishop and friend'.[77]

At Dundalk Healy proclaimed himself a member of the Irish party 'whether they liked it or not'. Redmond was the hostage of his chief lieutenants:

> Poor Mr. Redmond has two bulldogs sitting beside him (*laughter*) – Mr. John Dillon sitting at his head, and Mr. Joseph Devlin sitting at his legs (*laughter*) – or perhaps sitting on his chest (*laughter*), and he was as much a free agent as a man heavily laden with Guinness who was being conducted to the Bridewell by two policemen (*laughter*).[78]

The 1906 election resulted in a Liberal landslide. Henry Campbell-Bannerman's government had a majority so large as to render it independent of the Irish party. The return of a Liberal government offered Healy the prospect of political advantage in his war of attrition against the Irish party leadership. He could boast that he, unlike the Irish party, was not beholden to the Liberals, or implicated in their secular, progressive programme. The concluding peroration of Healy's defence of Catholic education in opposition to the government's Education (England and Wales) Bill of 1906 created a considerable parliamentary éclat and deepened the admiration in which he was held by many priests and bishops in Ireland:

> I care very little for your education. I cannot spell myself. I cannot parse an English sentence. I cannot do the rule of three. I am supposed to know a little law, but I think that is a mistake. But if there is one thing which I and mine have got a grip of, it is the belief in the Infinite Christ to come . . .

The final sentence was to provide Healy's epitaph.[79]

The drift towards alliance with O'Brien continued. To his father he wrote in July 1906 that 'oddly enough, dear delightful William O'Brien now hails me in the lobby as if we were born cloudless chums'. (This was to be Healy's last letter to his father, who died on 24 October 1906.) He wrote to his brother in August 'you will be pleased to hear that I am in almost daily consultation with the entrancing O'Brien . . . He and his friends are more ferocious against the party than ever we were'.[80]

In March 1907 Healy appeared for O'Brien in a libel action against the *Freeman's Journal* which was exceptionally acrimonious even by the standards of Irish political litigation. In his closing address to the jury, Healy declared of the defendant newspaper that 'the Journal of the Sham Squire was started to blackguard Irish patriots and its descendants showed themselves worthy of its carrion ancestry'. Healy derided the patriotic fustian of the attacks on William O'Brien's support for the Wyndham act by an adroitly contrived analogy:

> When he was young, Nationalists used to be asked whether they were in favour of physical or moral courage. They might as well contrast it with the binomial theorem. 'I am in favour', one would say, 'of having Ireland great, glorious and free', forgetting that if the British Government put a battleship in Galway Bay, and another in Dublin, the cannon balls would meet in the centre of this little island. But what heroes these men were who said they favoured physical force.[81]

The jury showed outstanding good sense in awarding O'Brien a farthing for each of six libellous observations. Healy wrote with his usual air of affronted innocence to his brother: 'The Party are very bitter over it, and Billy Redmond today cut me for the first time! Even during the Split we occasionally spoke. He will come round'.[82]

In May 1907 the government introduced its Irish Council Bill. A scheme of administrative devolution, it was conceived as a placatory gesture towards the Irish party. Redmond miscalculated. He did not immediately repudiate the bill, and only came out against it at a nationalist convention in Dublin after the delegates had already expressed their overwhelming opposition.[83]

Healy did not equivocate. He declared that 'if we have spent twenty-seven years working for this we have been wasting our time'.[84] Returning to Dublin, he derided the bill in an interview of biting sarcasm in Murphy's *Irish Independent*. He explained that his main anxiety concerned to the fate of the ducks in the pond in St. Stephen's Green: 'It is clear that the control of the Phoenix Park, which is under the Board of Works, will not vest in the Irish authority, and I await with apprehension a decision as to the care of the poultry in Stephen's green'. To the 'half a loaf' argument Healy responded tartly: 'Half a loaf is half a loaf of bread — a wholesome nourishment — but this Bill, in my judgement, is a whole dose of poison . . .' He concluded with a withering denunciation of the response of the leadership of the Irish party to the bill:

> To have allowed it to be brought in was a disaster; to proceed with it would be a crime against the Irish nation. Its introduction was the worst

> day's work done for Ireland in my time, and, even if dropped, the memory of it will continue to have evil effects on future policy, and on the relations between Irish members and Ireland with the English Parties. To summon a Convention to deal with this wretched business is an abdication by those claiming to be National leaders of the exercise of ordinary judgement and foresight, and an attempt to throw responsibility on others less acquainted with the play of political forces in England and its Parliament.[85]

Healy later said of the bill, which was quickly dropped, that 'the moment it saw the light of day it shrivelled to bits like some skeleton that had lain in the earth for a thousand years, and the moment daylight got at it, crumbled into ashes and dust'.[86] It was the first bad stumble in the alliance between the Irish party and the Liberal government. Nationalist public opinion was at the time eager to overlook the Council Bill débâcle, but it augured ill for the future.

The bitter rift between O'Brien and Dillon became caught up in the exegetics of Irish party pledge. No longer the fierce Parnellite zealot of twenty years previously, Healy now took a minimalist view of the pledge. In a counterfactual repudiation of one of the primary tenets of Parnellism, Healy asserted that the pledge was limited to action within parliament, and was an agreement between the member and his constituents rather than with the Irish party. He complained in May 1907 that the pledge 'is now being treated as a penal law, when, in fact, it is a charter of freedom for the individual member'. He placed much of the blame for the opposition to the Wyndham land act on Thomas Sexton 'whom Mr. O'Brien placed in the chair of the *Freeman's Journal*, and whom he cannot now dislodge, and who will remain a thorn forever in his side'.[87]

While Healy declined an invitation to speak with O'Brien in Tralee in October 1907, explaining to him that 'I am no longer confident of the future of this generation politically', he declared publicly that 'of late the readiness of William O'Brien to face unpopularity and calumny for the sake of principle has revived my old feelings of personal regard'.[88] By late 1907, there was a groundswell once more for the re-unification of the Irish party, and negotiations between O'Brien and Redmond ensued. Healy was sceptical, and believed that Redmond would only act under pressure, as he explained to O'Brien:

> Unless funds are short, I do not believe R. will make terms. He did not do so in 1900 until the last sixpence in the locker of the *Independent* was exhausted, and there were no further means of raising the wind.[89]

O'Brien insisted that any re-unification of the party would have to include Healy, who wrote to his brother:

> Of course I don't specially want to go back amongst this gang, and I told O'Brien I thought it would be very unpleasant for both of us, and that our views would be obstructed and our efforts thwarted by the gang for a very long time, and I don't see how I could feel any cordiality towards them. In fact I feel far more divided today from the 'Party' than I did from the Parnellites when the reunion was accomplished.

William Martin Murphy was absolutely opposed to an arrangement of the kind envisaged, due as much to his perennial hostility to O'Brien as to his opposition to the Irish party. 'He distrusts O'Brien completely, and says that if he ever gets power again he will be as bad as ever. I don't think he will or that he will ever get such power again'.[90]

Healy's suspicions were as ever directed chiefly at Dillon, whom he correctly considered to be the most implacable opponent of his own re-admission. He wrote to O'Brien:

> Dillon is, always was, and ever will be, a trouble to his country. This perfectly honest ass has done more harm to Ireland than all the traitors that have been deliberately hurting her during the period of his existence.[91]

A week later he reported to O'Brien that his kinsman D. B. Sullivan KC had delivered 'a cutting analysis of Dillon's posture in politics as a "National Killjoy" trying to hinder poor peasants from acquiring their land, out of a mistaken political diagnosis of the result'.[92]

Just as O'Brien made clear that he was determined to ensure that Healy was re-admitted along with him to the party, and patiently solicited Healy's views, so Healy subordinated his own interpretation of the party pledge to O'Brien's desire for re-unification.[93] He wrote to Maurice justifying his acquiescence in O'Brien's course of action:

> I must say I was a little touched by O'Brien's anxiety to include me in the pact, and the way he again and again insisted . . . that unless I was included in the pact nothing could be done . . . Of course he has a personal glorification to secure, or at least a political vindication to register; but in the main I feel his objects are patriotic.[94]

O'Brien and Healy duly rejoined the Irish Parliamentary Party in January 1908.[95] In the Commons two months later Healy made clear that he had not thereby committed himself to unquestioning support of a Liberal-nationalist alliance:

> Since the days I gave in my allegiance to Mr. Gladstone's policy twenty-two years ago, I have never believed in the tactics merely of independent opposition for Ireland. I believe in a policy of independent friendship,

> and that our party should be ready as long as it is fairly met, to co-operate with either section in this House. We are not partisans of one party or the other; we are the ambassadors of a nation.[96]

The return of O'Brien and Healy to the Irish party fold was to prove short-lived. 'Unity' had lost its euphoria, and the authority once exercised by Parnell could not be reconstituted. It was clear almost immediately that nothing had changed. His scepticism vindicated, Healy wrote to his brother in April 1908:

> O'Brien is furious with the party generally, and does not attend the meetings! . . . his rage against the entire procedure and policy of the boys is especially bitter against Redmond's Home Rule motion etc. etc. I don't remind him that everything was to be all right as soon as we were admitted to the Party.[97]

In April 1908 H. H. Asquith (whom Healy had privately characterised in 1905 as 'a cold-blooded Yorkshireman, thoroughly selfish and without a generous trait')[98] succeeded Campbell-Bannerman as leader of the Liberal party and Prime Minister.

A convention of the United Irish League was convened at the Mansion House in Dublin on 9 February 1909 to consider a land bill proposed by the government which cut back on the land purchase arrangements under the Wyndham act. O'Brien, implacably opposed to the Liberal proposals, was shouted down. Healy hastened across the city from the Four Courts in vain. Outwardly O'Brien charged, with some justification, that the 'Baton Convention' had been rigged by the party leadership, acting through the agency of the northern nationalist leader, Joe Devlin, and the Ancient Order of Hibernians. The O'Brienites of Munster considered that, defenceless and outnumbered, they had been set upon by a ruthless northern nationalist machine.[99]

While Healy and O'Brien nominally remained members of the Irish party, the breach was final and irreparable. O'Brien was now more furiously opposed to the Irish party leadership than even Healy. An inveterate conspiracy theorist, he divined that the Irish party was in thrall to the Ancient Order of Hibernians (pejoratively designated the 'Molly Maguires'), whose influence he everywhere detected. He later came to believe that what he regarded as a sinister confederacy to establish 'a pseudo-Catholic Hibernian ascendancy'[100] was responsible for the partition of Ireland by its failure to make at the outset the limited concessions which he fatuously believed could have placated northern unionist opposition to home rule.

O'Brien announced the establishment of a new political organisation.

However he was unable to enlist the support of those such as the Earl of Dunraven who had been his allies in championing the Wyndham land act. Ill and disillusioned, O'Brien (for the third time in his career) resigned his seat and departed for Tuscany with his wife. Healy wrote to Maurice that O'Brien's 'astonishing conduct is *épatant*. He never consulted me about starting his League, nor apparently anyone else, no more than he did when resigning'. Unless it was a cleverly conceived trap for Redmond's party, 'no-one could rely on such an unstable character or go tiger-hunting with him again'.[101]

Healy's irritation was short-lived, not least because O'Brien's resignation opened the way for his brother's return to parliament. When Maurice's candidacy was mooted, Healy favoured his standing if only to expunge the bitter memory of his 1900 defeat: 'My mind goes back to the miserable evening in October 1900 when I got your letter on the day of my own victory, telling me you would be beaten by O'Brien'.[102] Maurice Healy, returned by a comfortable margin over Redmond's nominee, was denied admission to the Irish party. Healy denounced the exclusion, and commented 'I don't see where they are to get money from. The "Trade" are disgusted with their conduct over the Budget. I think they are on the brink of collapse for want of funds'. He wrote later that 'the downfall of the Irish parliamentary movement had begun'.[103]

23

The All-for-Ireland League

> Tonight there will be the million globes of London to look at, gleaming through the fog like monstrous and sinister oranges in some garden of life and death. Tomorrow afternoon we shall be in the House of Commons supping full of old calumnies and hatreds. But when is Ireland going to have her chance? When will voyagers, leaning on the deck-rail, catch the first purple glimpse of Wicklow with eyes innocent of political passion?
>
> T. M. Kettle, 'Crossing the Irish Sea', 1909[1]

The Spectre of Parnell

In Irish politics Yeats' 'unquiet wanderer' remained a troubling revenant. On 1 October 1911, flanked incongruously by 'Boss' Croker, John Redmond unveiled the monument of Parnell by Augustus St. Gaudens on O'Connell Street, in front of the Rotunda where Parnell had rallied his supporters on his return to Dublin after the break-up of the party twenty years before.[2]

Redmond's speech was an emotional tribute to Parnell as 'a man of heart'. Celebrating the dead Parnell as an emblem of unity, and reining in the fierce pathos of the split, he only permitted himself: 'We see how time brings its revenge to the great and noble (*hear, hear*). Where are the belittlers of Parnell's greatness now?' He proceeded to gamble heavily by linking an invocation of Parnell's memory with a declaration of the imminence of home rule.

> We have got back, at long last, to the point to which Parnell had led us (*hear, hear*), before he and our cause were submerged in that catastrophe of twenty years ago . . . It was certain as a human thing can be that there would be an Irish parliament assembled in this metropolis within four and twenty months (*cheers*) . . . Yes the promised land is before our eyes, and we are all about to enter it and as the spirit of Parnell watches over us, let us think of him.[3]

Redmond's moving homage conveyed his sense of relief that the Irish party would, as he believed, shortly be able at last to lay Parnell's insistent ghost.

Arthur Griffith looked on sceptically, eager to wrest possession of the Parnell myth from Redmond. While he wrote that 'twenty years is not so long a period as Mr. Redmond seems to believe', he was himself anxious to consign Parnell to a vanished epoch: 'Parnell has passed into the reign of history and his place is determined . . . Twenty years after Parnell is laid in Glasnevin the men who failed him appear in the white sheet in the centre of Dublin city. Let us leave it at that'. There remained many in Ireland who did not believe Parnell dead: 'I heard a group of men at ten o'clock on Sunday night at the base of his memorial reiterating their belief that he was not dead and that he would come back again'.[4]

Parnell remained coldly challenging in death as in life. The Dublin weekly *Leader* had in 1907 published a curious text of the Parnell myth, a fantasy of the leader's return by William Dawson. It was written as a satire on the *Freeman's Journal*'s support of John Dillon's obdurate fealty to the Liberals. The (unidentified) paper reports the circulation through Cork of 'an extraordinary *canard* . . . to the effect that the late Mr. Parnell landed at Queenstown this morning and proceeded to the house of a friend in Cork'. The rumour proves to be true: Parnell had returned from America where he had supposedly withdrawn in 1891. The parodic *Freeman's Journal* is aghast: ' . . . the return of Mr. Parnell at this juncture could in no way benefit the National Cause . . . The Irish people are not unmindful of the services rendered by Mr. Parnell in former years, but these give him no claim to interfere now with the United Irish League and the National Directory'. There follows the 'defection' of Redmond and a contingent of Irish members to Parnell, leaving Dillon forlorn. The fantasy loses its sharpness in its facile resolution: Parnell unleashes a nationwide agitation, and the Liberal government prepares to introduce a home rule bill.[5] Dawson's piece expressed the pervasive belief that constitutional nationalism since Parnell regressed rather than advanced. In its political aspect, his myth endured increasingly as an adverse, and often unfair, reflection on his successors.

Parnell re-entered public consciousness again in 1914 with the publication of his widow's two-volume *Charles Stewart Parnell: His Love Story and Political Life*. The book, which incorporated many of Parnell's letters to her, was heralded by a letter to the *Times* in September 1913 by her son Gerard O'Shea, who shared many of his father's less engaging characteristics, in which he took exception to a reference of William O'Brien to Parnell as 'rather a victim than a destroyer of a happy home'.[6] Healy — the inclement and ever-watchful deconstructionist of the Parnell myth — was intrigued, and wrote to his brother:

> As to young O'Shea's letter: I cannot imagine your view, as to the son being brought up in ignorance, can be the correct explanation. You have evidently forgotten his letter published in the divorce case in 1890 about 'that awful brute, Parnell' addressed to his papa. So he must be now over forty years of age, and no chicken. I think on the contrary that, like myself, he and the mother have seized on O'Brien's communication to boom a proposed volume!! She might have made thousands of pounds of it any time these twenty years back, but I suppose the consciousness of her shame withheld her.
>
> Probably the youngster was working on such a book, but could not persuade his mother to part with the letters, and that he used O'Brien's letter as a lever. The conception of Parnell as an arrant liar never seems to have occurred to O'Brien. He would rather disbelieve the Four Evangelists!! He wants 'the first touch of steel'!![7]

In a later letter, following the formal announcement of her memoirs, Healy wrote sarcastically of Katharine and her son: 'I have read with complete satisfaction the announcement of Kitty's great work. Master Gerard, who used to write of "that awful scoundrel Parnell" to his father before the divorce will also I hope have since discovered his greatness'.[8]

Reaction to the publication of her book in May 1914 was mixed. Ascetic nationalists were affronted. Even twenty-five years later P. S. O'Hegarty thought the letters from Parnell published by Katharine 'so maudlin and unreal that they give you nausea even yet'.[9] The effect of her book, which privileged the tragic lover over the impassive statesman, was to soften Parnell's severe mystique. It quickened the refiguring of the Parnell myth, its shift away from the domain of conventional politics. The phenomenon discerned by Conor Cruise O'Brien, whereby 'the Parnell of the split deviated from politics into literature',[10] owed much to its publication.

The views of the diehard opponents of Parnell in the split did not mellow with the years. Healy wrote in 1910 of John Barry:

> I should think he is in despair about Irish politics. He blames Parnell for everything, and cannot talk calmly about events of twenty years ago. He always urges me to chuck it as it is as a hopeless game, and he is certainly not a supporter of the Party or the League.[11]

The shadow of Parnell still fell between Healy and O'Brien. The publication of O'Brien's *An Olive Branch in Ireland* in 1910 raked the ashes of their old controversies. Healy wrote to his brother:

> I agree with what you say about O'Brien's book, except that I feel more pity for the poor man's deceptions . . . He wrestles heroically with the temptation to be himself!! where we are concerned, but all through it is patent that he rejoices over your defeat and sorrows over my election [in 1900]. Still having regard to what I wrote about Boulogne in my pamphlet [*Why Ireland is Not Free*], I can't blame him. I read what I wrote of him after reading his criticisms, and I think he was entitled to try to justify himself; but I am satisfied there never was a Pope since Peter who conceived himself as [so] infallible and impeccable.
>
> My own construction of the position is that he is conscious of using us, just as we are conscious of using him, and that he will never forgive anyone who opposed him in the split, except for expediency's sake. He is a very remarkable man, and I think a much more remarkable man than Parnell. Lizzie says his book is 'most fascinating', but the forty pages of it I read seem to me quite untrue in perspective. He wrote me a little apologetic note that he was sending me a book and that I would not half like some of the criticisms; but his hand-writing is so bad and I care so little what he says in his works that my sympathy for the man quite submerges any resentment I feel in wonderment at his want of perception or information. We must hang together or hang separately!![12]

The All-for-Ireland League

The general election of January 1910 saw the return of a substantial complement of seven O'Brienites, and Healy. In Louth, while the bulk of the priests had supported him, Healy had to contend with what he described as 'a bitter canvass against me by the local Administrator and his two curates'. While he still enjoyed the support of Logue, and more discreetly Walsh, he held the seat by only ninety-nine votes. To Healy's dismay, Maurice narrowly lost the Cork seat he had won less than a year previously. He was subsequently returned as O'Brien's nominee for Cork North-East, when O'Brien opted to sit for Cork City.[13] The result, the high-water mark of the O'Brienites, was counterweighed by the fact that the Liberals had lost their overall majority. Redmond's Irish party held the balance of power. The re-attainment, twenty-five years after the 1885 election, of the Parnellian equilibrium, placed intense pressure on Redmond to fulfil Parnell's legacy.

On 1 January 1910 the first issue of O'Brien's *Cork Accent* appeared. The title was a reference to the suggestion that the Belfast Hibernians had been directed to attack anyone with a Cork accent at the 'Baton Convention', and the paper was dedicated to saving Ireland from the 'degrading thraldom of an incompetent clique'. Six months later the *Cork Accent* was succeeded by the *Cork Free Press.*[14] As late as mid-February 1910 O'Brien remained opposed to the formation of a distinct party, on which Healy agreed with him.[15] However, emboldened by the election results, and inflamed by his animosity towards the Irish party, he established the All-for-Ireland League on 31 March 1910.[16]

The League was to be O'Brien's political vehicle until 1916, when it became moribund. It was completely dominated by O'Brien who defined its idiosyncratic programme. Dedicated to upholding the principles, deriving from the Land Conference and the Wyndham land act, of 'Conference Conciliation and Consent', it espoused an untaxing nationalism defined in opposition to that of Redmond's Irish party. Its membership card was endorsed with the lines of T. D. Sullivan:

> All for Ireland here are we,
> All for Ireland's liberty.[17]

The League was implacably opposed to the official Irish party and profoundly suspicious of the Liberals, both in relation to Ireland and to their general ideological direction. The League's policy, such as it was, was reducible to the proposition that the consensus on land purchase achieved in 1902–3 could readily be recreated on the issue of home rule, and extended to embrace northern as well as southern unionists. The public language of the League drew heavily on an absurd but gratifying equation of the position of the dissentient O'Brienite nationalists with the unionist opponents of home rule, victims alike of the dictatorial pretensions of the Irish party. O'Brien's resentment of the Irish party and its political machine (directed by Joseph Devlin) could thereby be articulated in sententiously anti-sectarian terms.

The All-for-Ireland League drew its support from the followers of William O'Brien, who were heavily concentrated in Cork city and county, some of Healy's political following, and a tiny coterie of unionist landowners who had been prominent in the movement which led to the land act of 1903.[18]

O'Brien had hopes of a strategic alliance with Sinn Féin. Healy along with Captain John Shawe-Taylor, O'Brien's emissary, met James Brady, a Dublin solicitor who was seeking to dissuade Sinn Féin from its policy of abstentionism, to urge a course of common action. What was envisaged was that O'Brien would provide funds to support Sinn Féin candidates in some Dublin constituencies while Sinn Féin would support O'Brien's candidates in the constituencies they contested in Munster. A National Council in Dublin was to decide when the Irish representatives were to attend, and to control their actions at Westminster. Sinn Féin did not reject the proposal out of hand: in particular Arthur Griffith wanted to explore the possibilities for an accommodation with O'Brien. P. S. O'Hegarty revealed the proposal in the *Irish Nation* and issued a thinly veiled warning to Griffith against any compromise. The project for a common front foundered on Sinn Féin's reiterated insistence on a strict policy of parliamentary abstentionism.[19]

O'Brien's hopes of a broad opposition to the Irish party were thus thwarted, and he felt unable to proceed with the holding of the inaugural meeting in Dublin. Its transfer to Cork, as he later complained 'gave the All-for-Ireland movement a certain sectional and provincial aspect which the implacable foes of "the Cork accent" were not slow to exploit'. Speaking in Kanturk, County Cork, in January 1912 he was reduced to referring to 'this dauntless little republic of our own we have established here in Cork'.[20]

While Healy was billed in the *Cork Accent* to speak at the inaugural meeting of the All-for-Ireland League, he was conspicuous by his absence. Maurice Healy spoke alongside William O'Brien.[21] O'Brien was regarded with antipathy by numerous conservative nationalists sympathetic to Healy. William Martin Murphy's mistrust of O'Brien was unassuagable. Moreover there was considerable hostility to O'Brien among many Catholic churchmen, who long regarded him as at heart an unreconstructed Parnellite, and latently anti-clerical. Cardinal Logue had warned Healy against the foundation by O'Brien of a new organisation.[22] Clerical suspicions of O'Brien posed a persisting difficulty for Healy; he wrote apprehensively to Maurice on 4 September that the last issue of the *Cork Free Press* was too anti-clerical: 'I mention this as it might lead to a misunderstanding among friendly priests outside who don't know how provokingly some of their brethren have acted'.[23]

Healy's holding back from identification with the All-for-Ireland League was only in part out of deference to Logue. He still retained some hopes of coming to an accommodation with the Irish party leadership in the aftermath of the January election. With the collapse of Healy and O'Brien's negotiations with Lloyd George over the budget in March, and the acrimony which ensued, that ceased to be a realistic prospect. In June Healy forwarded to O'Brien £500 received from an American sympathiser through the exertions of Moreton Frewen. In the letter endorsing the draft he wrote 'it will always be a pleasure to me to recall that in spite of past differences of policy, I preferred to side you in obloquy, when I deemed it right, than seek peace and praise with the Bungler's Brigade'. The *Cork Accent* in its characteristic style acclaimed 'A Princely Gift and a Still Princelier Letter'.[24]

Healy unconvincingly sought to place the blame for the division in the nationalist ranks on Redmond and his allies. 'At the beginning of the session, Mr. Redmond, who claims to have sole carriage of the National movement, excluded from invitation to the meetings of the Irish party every man likely to oppose barren peurilities selected for gallery purposes.' Redmond preferred a 'troupe of employees . . . whose views could be melted into a common stock'.[25]

This was the ground on which he sought to rely when in November 1910 he abandoned any pretence of distance from the All-for-Ireland League by speaking at a meeting to inaugurate a branch in Dublin. He asserted that while he was not in favour of two nationalist parties and organisations in Ireland, the establishment of a nationalist opposition to the Irish party had been rendered necessary by the exclusion of ten nationalist members after the election by the Irish party leadership. Heckled, he was characteristically defiant. It was not a time to shrink from unpopularity. 'For himself, he loved being unpopular (*laughter*). The shrieks and groans of the foolish were music in his ears (*renewed laughter*).'[26]

The formation of an organisation in opposition to that of the Irish party at a time when the party held the balance of power at Westminster attracted considerable ill will. The *Leader* quoted the observation of the *Irish Times* ('*the anti-Irish Times*') that the inauguration of the All-for-Ireland League was the beginning of the end for the Irish party, and opined that 'Poor William has simply gone over to the enemy, but he is too enthusiastic to see it'.[27] The coalescence of Healyism and O'Brienism seemed at the outset inherently unstable. The *Leader* declared towards the end of the year that 'there is a chasm between screeching William and the Healys that cannot be permanently nor for any length of time abridged'.[28] That the alliance in fact endured was due to the coincidence of their opposition to the Irish party, the looseness and indefiniteness of the policy of the All-for-Ireland League, and the fact that both men had exhausted the possibilities of forging alternative combinations in Irish politics.

The future for nationalist critics of the Irish party in 1910 appeared singularly unpromising. Yet in the longer term there were ample prospects for feeding off disillusionment with the Irish party. In September 1911 Healy told an All-for-Ireland League meeting that he feared that the coming home rule bill 'will only be the ghost of the measure which Ireland anticipates'. Asquith promised an Irish parliament, but the question was what were its powers to be: 'Is it going to be limited to making bye-laws about pig styes, or poultry, and potato patches, or is it to give us the control of what is the key to liberty in every constitution, £-s-d.?'[29]

The People's Budget

The relatively high vote for O'Brienite candidates at the election of January 1910 was attributable in part to opposition in Ireland to Lloyd George's 'People's Budget' of 1909. To fund social reform and naval re-armament it proposed a range of tax increases. What was most controversial in Ireland was the proposal to tax spirits which was perceived as threatening the business of the Irish distillers. On the faith of assurances of concessions Redmond believed he had extracted from Lloyd George, the Irish party suppressed its reservations. The concessions were not forthcoming. The budget was opposed by Healy and O'Brien, and, in the first display of its power, the *Irish Independent*.[30] With the rejection of the budget by the House of Lords on 22 November, its actual provisions were eclipsed by the greater issue of the veto of the Lords. The election of January 1910 followed.

After the election, Redmond and the Irish party supported Lloyd George's re-introduced finance bill, while Healy and O'Brien maintained their opposition. The division became envenomed. Healy wrote to his brother that he believed 'there is far more bitterness than there was during the split'.[31] The division on the Irish side did not present an edifying spectacle. Austen Chamberlain wrote on 23 February: 'No one knows even now whether Redmond means business or not. O'Brien took his speech as a surrender today and lashed out fiercely at him, loudly cheered by Healy'.[32] Healy believed that his and O'Brien's stance had succeeded in stiffening the Irish party's position on the budget question: 'Of course, if the Redmondites had been allowed to maunder along, they would have got the budget passed; and thanks to our attitude we shall have either Asquith's resignation or the certainty of scalps off the Lords!!'[33] They remained in an awkward predicament. Seeking to reassure O'Brien, Healy wrote 'we have seen harder times'.[34]

The Chancellor of the Exchequer was not slow to seek to exploit the fact that Redmond could not claim to speak on behalf of a united Irish nationalist representation at Westminster. He was eager to break down the nationalist opposition to the budget, and the cabinet had already vetoed his initial attempt to exclude Ireland from the operation of the proposed tax on whiskey. In the second week of March Lloyd George met Healy and O'Brien at the house of Sir Hudson Kearley. He held out the prospect of concessions on the budget, and indicated he would press for an enhancement of the land purchase arrangements under the 1903 act: however this was conditional on the concessions being requested by the Irish nationalist representation as a whole.[35]

The curious form that Lloyd George's negotiations took, owed as much to the position of Healy and O'Brien as to his own requirements. The initiative had come from Healy. His thinking was not entirely cynical. He evidently felt the necessity, given the altered parliamentary arithmetic, to restore some basis of common action between the two nationalist groupings. Part of his difficulty was that O'Brien, still furious after the abortive re-union of 1908, was reluctant to become involved. O'Brien wrote somewhat grudgingly, as if trying to silence his own reservations, referring to the Master of Elibank, the Liberal Chief Whip, that 'if (as seems likely) the M[aster] and his friends stand true to their offers to you and me, whatever the upshot, we are bound to come out on top'. Healy had considered writing to Redmond in the hope of breaking the impasse. While O'Brien professed not to object to Healy writing such a letter, he made clear he would under no circumstances do so himself:

> I understood the basis of your very effectual proposal to Lloyd George and the Master was that if R. should approach us, and that they should insist upon that as a condition of an agreement. If he does so, there could be no difficulty on our part, so far as common action upon the Budget and Land Purchase are concerned. But any suggestion that it is we who should go to Canossa would completely mystify the country as to what happened and cover us with well-merited contempt, without disarming a single opponent.[36]

Redmond complained to Dillon with understandable bitterness of Lloyd George's conference with Healy and O'Brien which he described as 'a very strange development':

> They made a definite proposal to him to the effect that, if he would make certain concessions on the budget, considerably less than we think necessary, and if he would give some sort of promise to do something in the future about Land Purchase, they declared that they were willing to support the Budget and to support the Government. This is Lloyd George's statement. Of course he may consider that the fear of the government making a concession to Healy and O'Brien may have the effect of weakening our position, and that may be his reason for negotiating with them at all . . . I take it for granted that O'Brien and Healy's game, if they got these concessions granted specifically to them, would be to denounce us as defeating a friendly government and restoring the Tories

> to power, in the event of our defeating the Budget. Certainly Irish politics are a dirty game. Think of O'Brien going to Lloyd George on the very day that the *Times* contained an abusive letter about me because he saw me speaking to Birrell in the House of Commons.[37]

Dillon discerned a further hazard created by Healy and O'Brien's intervention: 'George and many others have got it into their heads that all that is necessary is to square O'Brien and Healy, and that our attitude was entirely due to the fear of hostile criticism from O'Brien and Healy. This is a very dangerous mistake and may lead to serious complications in a situation almost desperate'.[38]

By the time Lloyd George met Healy and O'Brien again on 24 March, his stratagem had foundered in the face of the implacable opposition of Redmond and Dillon.[39] There was a squalid public sequel. O'Brien asserted that he had extracted concessions from Lloyd George which Redmond had failed to achieve.[40] Provoked by Redmond's accusation that he had abandoned home rule, O'Brien made an unbridled attack on the leader of the Irish party ('this little ex-House of Commons clerk was growing fat in the pay of England in the days when I was running the risk of penal servitude every day of my life for a considerably more uncompromising measure of National Independence than Gladstonian Home Rule').[41] Finding that his move had backfired, Lloyd George alleged against O'Brien 'a disgraceful breach of confidence'. Healy defended O'Brien in a public letter, and in the Commons on 18 April. Austen Chamberlain commented that Healy 'made a brilliant speech in his best form. He has done nothing as good for many years. His attack on Redmond was extraordinarily bitter'.[42]

The vehemence of their public posturing notwithstanding, the effect of O'Brien and Healy's actions was to undercut Redmond's negotiating position. Charles Hobhouse, the Financial Secretary to the Treasury was not alone in forming the impression from the negotiations that 'Healy was more buyable or complacent than Redmond'.[43] The Master of Elibank was similarly struck by Healy and O'Brien's amenability: '. . . dire necessity compelled me to keep my eye on the big battalions, although I confess I was sadly tempted at one time to finance twenty or thirty candidates in Ireland to assist Healy and O'Brien, and would certainly have done so if the Redmondites had failed us on the Budget and the Veto'.[44]

Redmond's primary concern was with the larger issue raised by the budget controversy, the bringing to an end the legislative veto of the House of Lords, which presented a standing obstacle to home rule. The government accepted the principle of the removal of the veto of the House of Lords in resolutions carried in the Commons, which laid the ground for the Parliament Act of the following year. The budget passed the

Commons with the support of the Irish party on 27 April.[45]

Redmond's role in the ending of the veto was at a price. The display of high Parnellian resolve did not have the hoped-for effect of restoring the *élan* and momentum of the old 'union of hearts'. Some in the Liberal cabinet never forgave Redmond's insistent stance. Their resentment was kept alive by relentless unionist taunting that Asquith, to stay in office, had compromised the constitutional integrity of the United Kingdom through a treasonable compact with the Irish leader.[46]

O'Brien and Healy's stance remained markedly opportunistic. They continued to berate Redmond for his failure to procure the defeat of what Healy called 'the abominable budget of 1910'.[47] While they had derided Redmond for his pusillanimousness in his dealings with Asquith, after the government had acceded to the demand of the Irish party on the veto question, Healy switched the direction of his attack, and damagingly criticised Redmond in the Commons on the grounds that he had failed to demonstrate Parnell's tact and suavity.

> I must say that I have never known, not merely an Irish leader, but an Irish Member, cut a sorrier figure than the Member for Waterford did. My complaint is that there is no bargain between him and the Prime Minister. I make the further complaint that he has gone up and down the country for the last three months, ever since the General Election; he has gone into every cross-road, and on to every platform — almost every beer-barrel which was available for him to stand on — to try and make it impossible for the Government to give him the slightest concession. I remember very well what Mr. Parnell did in 1885, when for the first time the Irish Members got the balance of power in this House. He did not go about gloating over it all down the length and breadth of Britain. He did not go blathering about it in the Irish newspapers. He kept his counsel. He made his bargain. Almost the only one of his letters which I have kept is a letter telling me to get some of those fools who in Ireland were talking about coercing the Tory party, to hold their idiotic tongues.[48]

Healy and O'Brien indulged in their lack of responsibility to the fullest extent. They did not have to define a coherent alternative course to that adopted by the Irish party. There was a whimsical complacency in their conviction that the constraints on the Irish party could readily be overcome by a marriage of O'Brien's patriotic ardour with Healy's parliamentary skills. He wrote to O'Brien in May 1910: 'I never felt so strongly that, with even a molecule of common sense, we could get a settlement of the Irish question, but alas, the bacillus of folly seems completely to eat up the bodies and souls of our alleged leaders'.[49] This was admittedly to some extent an exercise in flattery. Healy was at the same time writing to his brother that O'Brien was 'now full of some cracked project of getting a Conference . . .'[50] The controversy over the social policies of the Liberal government was kept alive in Ireland by Lloyd George's National Insurance bill, which was not enacted until the following year. Again Healy and O'Brien were vociferous in their opposition: Healy went so far as to urge O'Brien that 'we should preach Passive Resistance' to the legislation.[51] O'Brien also seized on the introduction of the payment of members of parliament in 1911 as evidence of a Liberal design to corrupt and enfeeble Irish parliamentary nationalism.[52]

In Ireland, the acrimonious controversy over the Lloyd George budget fed an inchoate disillusionment with parliamentary politics, albeit held in check by the expectation of home rule. The attacks on the support of the Irish party for what O'Brien designated 'this Radical-Socialist government'[53] deepened the suspicions of Catholic ecclesiastics and of conservative nationalists of the Irish arty's acquiescence in Liberal social radicalism, quite apart from the fury of the Irish licensed trade.

What was most disconcerting was the virulence of O'Brienite rhetoric against the budget. In a single editorial, headed 'Treachery!' in February 1910, the *Cork Accent* condemned 'the blackest treason perpetrated against Ireland since the Act of Union', went on to denounce Dillon's 'odious tyranny', and declared that 'the Irish Liberal Party', were it to support the budget, 'would be execrated from end to end of the land as the greatest pack of imbeciles and traitors that ever cursed any country'.[54] In the Commons, O'Brien described Redmond's support of the budget as 'something very little short of an act of national apostasy'.[55] If absurd hyperbole of this kind diminished O'Brien's credibility, it also damaged the idea of parliamentarianism. Even to many in Ireland who regarded O'Brien and Healy as disputatious mavericks, the ferocity of the conflict threatened to deprive constitutional politics of the aspect of rationality which most commended it.

William O'Brien attracted the attention of J. L. Garvin, the editor of the *Observer*. Garvin was an imperialist and a federalist, a staunch opponent of the Liberals and of home rule. Of Irish extraction, he had come to hero-worship Joseph Chamberlain as he had once revered Parnell. His call, following the death of Edward VII on 6 May, for a 'truce of God' presaged the attempt to resolve the political impasse by a conference of parties. In October 1910 Garvin pressed the idea further, advocating a conference to further a resolution of the Irish questions on federal lines in opposition to Gladstonian home rule.

Seizing the opportunity to demonstrate the merits of his policy of conference and conciliation, O'Brien responded with exuberant enthusiasm.

In a lengthy missive to the *Observer* he asserted that the end of landlordism, and what he deemed the tacit acceptance by both English parties on the inevitability of an Irish parliament, had quickened the dissolution of the old political order in Ireland,

> the dreaded Irish conspiracy is resolving into two wholesome elements – Radical and Progressively-Conservative – into which an Irish Parliament would perforce divide itself in order to do the country's works. The materials of these two Parties – which would neither be pro-English nor anti-Irish, much less Protestant or Catholic, but simply in Sir Samuel Ferguson's happy words, 'Kindly Irish of the Irish', are already crystallising . . .[56]

Whatever sympathy Garvin may have had with O'Brien's grandiose maunderings, he was alert to the possibilities of using what he described variously as the fifth party, or the 'Irish Centre Party', to break the Liberal government and the Irish party. He went so far as to raise money for O'Brien at the election of December 1910. He had to negotiate O'Brien's opposition to accepting monies from Conservative sources. Garvin reported to Lord Northcliffe on 21 November that he had the previous day got another £5,000 for O'Brien to be paid in notes 'from a genuine devolutionist source, but the splendid old O'Quixote is still considering whether he can conscientiously take even that. Last week he simply spurned ten thousand pounds of Tory money'.[57] Some monies were also raised by Moreton Frewen from American sources, although nothing like the sum of £25,000 which he boasted was available.[58] O'Brien's fastidiousness in declining funds from overtly Tory sources hardly overcame the basic problem of an avowedly nationalist party accepting secret contributions from sources hostile to Irish nationalism in general and to Redmond's Irish party in particular. The receipt of these monies did not temper the virulence of Healy and O'Brien's attacks on the funding of the Irish party.

Healy registered no dissent from O'Brien's involvement with Garvin. Maurice Healy pointedly confessed to a 'kind of *gradh* for Glastonian Home Rule', and observed that at least one knew what the home rule to which the Liberals were committed was.[59] Remarkably, Tim Healy, whose scepticism appeared to be reserved exclusively for the Irish party and the Liberals, had some hopes for reaching an understanding with Edward Carson. While he had written to O'Brien in October that 'I pay no attention to Carson beyond amazement', he wrote to Maurice two months later that he had received a very important message from Carson through Moreton Frewen 'saying that, if our friends carried Ireland in the next few years, they would accept Home Rule from us'.[60]

This arose from Frewen's endeavours to reach an agreement with Carson under which unionists and O'Brienites would not oppose each other in selected constituencies. Carson was unenthusiastic. Frewen continued to badger him, and wrote to Lord Grey: 'He grudges federation of course, but he came out very frankly at last and said if O'Brien and Healy can clean up the situation in Ireland, we would take from *them*, but never from the scoundrels who cheered the Mahdi and Methuen's capture'. When Carson learnt that Healy and his friends were claiming him as an ally on the strength of this conversation, he wrote making plain his refusal to countenance either federalism or collaboration with the O'Brienites.[61]

Defeat in North Louth

After the narrow result in North Louth in January 1910, Healy was aware that his chances of re-election were slim. He knew that were he to lose the seat he could only be returned to parliament for one of the Cork seats controlled by O'Brien. This was a prospect to which he began to reconcile himself, if not very eagerly, within a month of his return:

> I can't say that I regard with complacency the idea of accepting an O'Brienite seat. Hitherto I have been independent and have held my own in my own way . . . I can't therefore say I am in the least enthusiastic about returning under his auspices. I can never accept the views of another man because they are 'pontificated'. I am afraid therefore, if I return under O'Brien's patronage, I shall never be happy. As long as *one* of us was independent, the other had carriage of his affairs. If we both are reliant on O'Brien, neither of us will be free. No doubt he has changed and improved, but I greatly dread the prospect of variance of opinion with a man who is absolutely unable to take a lawyer's view of any question, or to conceive that differences may be no evidence of *mala fides*.[62]

At the election of December 1910, Healy no longer had the active support of Cardinal Logue or of the priests in the constituency, which he attributed to his alliance with O'Brien.[63] Facing a desperate struggle to hold his seat, Healy was not too proud to play, so far as he could, the Parnell card. At Dundalk in September 1910 he declared that the deplorable contemporary state of Irish politics had been brought about 'by the exclusion of all the men who were the foremost counsellors in the time of triumph of Charles Stewart Parnell (*loud cheers*)', and went on to exaggerate shamelessly his own role:

> Up to the time of the unhappy split, Mr. Parnell never took a step in his career of any importance without consulting him. On the night of the introduction of the Home Rule Bill, Parnell and himself sat up all night

> in a room in the House of Commons conning its provisions and seeing to what extent it could be made acceptable to the Irish people.[64]

While Healy remained optimistic throughout a bitterly fought campaign in North Louth[65] he lost the seat to Richard Hazleton, the youthful Irish party aspirant. Healy went on to campaign for his nephew, the son and namesake of his brother, who was running as an O'Brienite in West Waterford. He lost heavily, but against the trend his father regained the Cork City seat he had lost the previous January. The result of the second election of 1910 strengthened the position of Redmond's party. The electoral threat presented by the O'Brien–Healy axis, always geographically confined, was now receding. As a result of the outbreak of the Great War, there was not to be another general election for eight years.

For those of Healy's associates who disiked O'Brien, the outcome was not displeasing. Healy wrote to Maurice that his wife had met William Martin Murphy in a tram, 'and he was jubilant over O'Brien's defeat and over the disasters which have befallen us generally. She says he was in the height of good spirits at the way O'Brien's side had been crushed, and therefore the articles which appeared yesterday and today in his paper are written at his instructions'. Murphy had not forgiven O'Brien for his defeats in South Kerry in 1895, and North Mayo in 1900: 'it is not therefore I suppose altogether to be wondered at that a quiet Red Indian like Murphy should eat his vengeance cold and refuse to subordinate it to higher considerations'.[66]

Healy challenged the North Louth result. As he wrote to Maurice 'when we are fighting a powerful party and powerful organisation, we must teach them that the law equalises matters for the weaker side in the conduct of an election'.[67] Healy's petition was successful, and Richard Hazleton was unseated.[68] To avoid a further defeat, Healy resolved not to contest the fresh election in North Louth. Healy wrote to Maurice that 'the Cardinal's injunctions to his priests that they are not to do anything directly or indirectly connected with the election, and making it suspension *ipso facto* if they interfere, has greatly influenced my mind as to standing'. He had consulted a number of his old constituents 'and they practically agree with me that, after the Cardinal's letter, the absence of the priests will make a contest hopeless'.[69] In public, Healy expressed his grounds for not contesting the seat rather differently. His declared reasons were the likelihood of violence to his supporters, and 'the exclusion of the clergy from the contest and the loss of their moral influence in protecting humble voters'.[70]

On Healy's urging, Moreton Frewen had been nominated as an O'Brienite candidate for the North East Cork seat for which Maurice Healy had briefly sat, and been elected. Anglo-Irish with American interests, Frewen was married to Clare Jerome, the sister of Winston Churchill's mother. A right-wing federalist, he was not on any definition a nationalist. Healy was in the awkward position of having instigated Frewen's candidacy and professed himself reluctant to have Frewen prevailed on to resign in his favour. Frewen's opposition to the Parliament Bill to remove the legislative veto of the House of Lords, which threatened to embarrass the O'Brienites at forthcoming municipal elections, sealed his fate. Healy wrote abashedly to his brother: 'Poor Frewen is perfectly loyal and willing to resign whenever O'Brien requires. He hopes to make a speech on currency and Japanese or Chinese exchange!!' He later charitably observed of Frewen to O'Brien that 'the spread of his mind is too vast for our closer-knit parochial concerns'. Following Frewen's resignation, Healy was returned unopposed on 15 July 1911 for Cork North-East, the seat which he was to hold until his resignation in October 1918.[71]

Law and History

Healy had been called to the English bar in 1903 but had not carried on any significant practice. He was granted a patent of precedence as a King's Counsel in November 1910, and elected a Bencher of Grays Inn.[72]

Healy felt his Irish practice to be under attack by a boycott organised by adherents of the Irish party, in addition to the 'natural competition of younger men'.[73] He embarked on what was to be a relatively short-lived attempt to build up an English practice. F. E. Smith was 'very civil, and said I was certain to get business'.[74] Early the following year, he wrote to Maurice that 'Carson acted splendidly towards me; and spread my praises everywhere'.[75] Carson's helpfulness perhaps served to increase Healy's tendency to confuse professional collegiality with political common ground. He reported to Maurice from London in late 1913:

> I have been doing fairly well here this term. London juries are extremely stupid and prejudiced; and counsel here are quite up to every trick of the trade as we know it at home, but of course there is less personal friction in court.[76]

Healy did not develop a self-sustaining practice in London, although he continued to appear episodically in the English courts. He later complained 'my own idea of the English is that they will not have an Irishman if he is a Catholic or a Nationalist in big business unless they are compelled'.[77]

The Four Courts in Dublin remained overwhelmingly his main professional arena. His legal practice continued to consume most of his time. As he explained to O'Brien:

> Once the law term arrives, I must try and do business, if I can get it, here. I may as well say that the stories of my wealth are all piffle. I spend every penny I make, and have no savings, so I try not to fall back, once the courts open.[78]

Healy broadened his constituency in a somewhat unexpected direction with a number of appearances for the defence in prosecutions brought against advocates of women's suffrage. He was not a fervent advocate of votes for women, and rather was unable to see any good reason why they should not have the vote. In 1899 he declared that he always supported the extension to women of all civil and political rights although 'he had never done so with enthusiasm, but had acted in the belief that it was only right to do so upon the ground of abstract justice'.[79]

Healy's defence of suffragists offered him the opportunity of attacking the complacency of the Liberal establishment from an unexpected angle. A mischievous connoisseur of the foibles and follies of reforming Liberalism, his speeches in court were turned into onslaughts on Asquith and his government, and represented a slight but distinctive contribution on his part to Liberal England's strange death.

In August 1909 he appeared for eight members of the Women's Freedom League, including the redoubtable Madame Despard, who had been arrested in Downing Street where they had gone to present a petition to the Prime Minister on the charge of obstructing the police in the execution of their duty. He cited the Liberals' introduction of the Trade Disputes Act of 1906 to assail Asquith: 'it is he, who though he will allow men to beset your house, objects to gentle ladies standing in front of his own official residence, which he is paid large sums to occupy, for the purpose of humbly presenting a petition that they may get the vote which every policeman enjoys'.[80]

He wrote to Maurice in March 1912: 'I think you might as well attend and vote for Woman's Suffrage on Friday. It can't do us any harm — and I think it is worthwhile, as we have been always on their side. I think the extreme women must really have some Tory backing to behave as they are doing. Between the coal strike and the women, the Government are having a hot bath'.[81] He appeared in May for Mrs. Pethick Lawrence at the conspiracy trial at the Old Bailey in which she was prosecuted along with Mrs. Pankhurst and others. 'Suddenly, by means of a political transformation, the good, quiet, and useful life of this lady is turned into a conspiracy of this vague and varied class . . . I almost hesitate to treat this as a legal inquiry. I regard it as a vindictive political act'.[82]

In July 1912 Healy was asked to appear for English suffragists who had resorted to violence in protest against Asquith on his visit to Dublin. He wrote to Maurice:

> By the way, I have an offer of a hundred guineas to defend the Suffragettes in Dublin about the 2nd August. Should I take it? Please wire me your opinion on this point. They will be tried before Madden at Green Street, and I confess I don't like the job . . . Gerald Byrne tells me that the women don't care what sentence they get or what becomes of them!! It is a fine spirit which Penal Servitude would probably change.[83]

Healy in the event appeared for Gladys Evans, charged with attempting to burn down the Theatre Royal, the venue for Asquith's Dublin speech. Mrs. Leigh (against whom the charges of having thrown a hatchet at Asquith as he passed in a carriage, which missed the Prime Minister but grazed John Redmond's cheek, were not proceeded with) was tried separately on the same charges. Both women were convicted and sentenced to five years penal servitude. The *Freeman's Journal* reported with satisfaction that Healy, as he left Green Street courthouse after the sentencing, was booed by the crowd outside.[84]

Healy fell out with his kinsman Sergeant Sullivan, sixteen years his junior. Up to 1900 Sullivan had been a supporter of Healy. After the rout of the 1900 election, however, in the words of Healy (and Sullivan's) nephew Maurice, 'to the surprise of his relatives, A. M. Sullivan suddenly joined a branch of the United Irish League, giving as his reason a desire to keep a vigilant watch over the purity of Irish administration'.[85] Healy found Sullivan arrogant and impossible to deal with ('His snorts of triumph over opponents are intolerable. He has no manners'). He observed that if Sullivan heard his laugh as others heard it, he would never laugh again.[86] Sullivan appeared for Healy in the North Louth petition in 1911, but Healy came to feel let down by him.[87] When Sullivan later complained of Dillon's opposition to his preferment, Healy had little sympathy: 'He has eaten dirt enough when he crawled to Dillon's house to tell him he was no connection of ours, and was shown the door'.[88]

The antagonism between the two men came to a head when Sullivan in 1919 made a complaint to the Bar Council arising out of Healy's attacks on him in the course of a speech in a recent case. The Bar Council agreed that Healy had exceeded his privilege as an advocate, found him guilty of unprofessional conduct and directed that a notice with a copy of the resolution be screened in the Law Library till the end of the Michaelmas term.[89] The following month he wrote that 'Alex made another of his extraordinary speeches in the treason case on Thursday without the remotest provocation. I think his brain is not normal'. He did protest later in the year that 'although I am supposed to regard Alex like Dillon, this is not so'.[90]

Healy appeared unsuccessfully on behalf of the fishermen of Lough

Neagh in proceedings relating to the ownership of fishing rights on Lough Neagh and the river Bann, the subject of a disputed grant to Sir Arthur Chichester, Lord Deputy of Ireland 1604–15, and the chief architect of the Ulster plantation. Infuriated by the eventual outcome of the case, which went to the House of Lords and to which he had given 'the entire fortune of my time and thought',[91] he was drawn ever deeper into its pre-history.

He wrote to William O'Brien in October 1910: 'I began a story of Lough Neagh three months ago, but the more I read the more ignorant I find myself. Yet it is as interesting at least as the Crippen murder'. His hostility was not exclusively reserved for the founding figures of the great northern unionist dynasties: 'I see that at the Plantation, a John Dillon came from Stafford to grab O'Neill's territory in Armagh, and every Dillon in history was a bitter persecutor and official on the anti-Irish side in those days'.[92]

Over the ensuing two years Healy expended a prodigious amount of time in historical research, working after court and in the vacations in the Public Record Office in the Four Courts. That he should have done so, given his commitments as a busy King's Counsel and as a parliamentarian, attests to the extent to which the case touched his own deepest instincts as a nationalist. Every line was instinct with a sense of the affinity in dispossession between his own forbears (to whom he did not refer) and the fishermen of Lough Neagh.

Healy's *Stolen Waters: A Page in the Conquest of Ulster*, a narrative of despoliation and fraud which ran to 485 pages, appeared in 1913. Its concluding paragraph ran:

> The fishermen of the North are but a friendless company. Still, the tale of their undoing has a prelude which pierces to the marrow of Irish history. It also has a living import. For their sake it is that one whose eyes have never looked upon Lough Neagh, has 'written these lines and taken these pains'.[93]

The *Great Fraud of Ulster* which Healy published in 1917 was a revised and somewhat racier abbreviation of the argument of *Stolen Waters*. His preface proclaimed a more immediately contemporary purpose. His retelling of the story of Lough Neagh was undertaken in the hope 'that acquaintance with it may quicken and heighten the spirit of resistance to the statecraft of Partition':

> A stubborn fight for a great stake has been waged in the disputed area for three hundred years, and the struggle to clutch the prize exhibits more starkly than any other single theme the felonious continuity of the Anglo-Ulster administration.[94]

24

The Third Home Rule Bill

The Government of Ireland Bill

O'Brien and Healy, at the head of a small recalcitrant nationalist minority at a time when the Liberal–nationalist alliance was at its zenith, were politically isolated. Healy had returned to parliament at a critical juncture as Asquith prepared to face down the House of Lords. The Prime Minister intimated that the government would procure the enactment of the parliament bill in the form in which it had left the Commons, if necessary by means of the exercise of the royal prerogative of creating new peers.

O'Brien was determined to abstain on the vote on the parliament bill. Healy sought to reason with him:

> The King agrees to create Peers to carry a bill, or defeat an amendment. Could you, or I, afford to have it pretexted that we refused to support a thing, which the Crown was prepared to make peers to carry. . . . I agree with you that such a message from the throne will only embitter 'Ulster & Co.' against Home Rule, but our farsight will not be shared, and cannot be communicated to the mass of our supporters.[1]

To his brother he wrote that having talked the question over with O'Brien for an hour or two 'I made no impression on his mind; and like the good Mohamet he remained fixed in his opinion.[2]

Possessed by the delusions of 'conciliation', O'Brien complained that

Redmond had used his leverage 'as a catspaw to a small group of Radicals', rather than as 'a peacemaker to bring together the Liberal and Unionist parties in friendly agreement'.[3] Those radicals, his paper complained, 'have been the bane of this country'.[4]

In late July 1911 Healy sent O'Brien an account of a meeting with an unidentified English leader, probably Asquith. The meeting left Healy entranced, as private audiences with high political personages frequently did. Confusing personal affability with political amenability, he deplored the Irish party leaders' want of diplomatic finesse in dealing with English politicians and searingly denounced Dillon's cosmopolitan radicalism:

> I was most cordially received, altho' I began by saying that my heart was with Rebellion. He said he knew this! When I quoted *vir pietate gravis*, he laughed as heartily as yourself! The internal cancer amongst them, we cannot estimate. He said it was a privilege to learn our views. Never was I persuaded of the ease with which England might be won over to Ireland, if only our dismal colleagues had a trace of good sense. Fancy in a thrice afterwards I was listening to Dillon denouncing the Ex-Shah of Persia, bucking I know not what in Morocco, Egypt, Zanzibar, and the Cannibal Islands. As to what occurred today, I know, now that the latent heat of the stream of insult has been condensed, you will apprize oral froth as its corpse-worth. Don't be goaded by the picadors of the latrines.[5]

Healy was seeking to assuage O'Brien, who was smarting from the unprompted accusation that day by Thomas Lundon, a member of the Irish party, that he was descended from the informer Pierce Nagle. This led to an ugly scene in the Commons which ended with O'Brien calling Lundon 'an infamous liar and scoundrel'. Healy wrote to his brother of O'Brien:

> I am sorry to say he felt it keenly and was inclined to physically assault Lundon, which I don't believe would do any good. He also turned round on Dillon, and said he was the real author of the charge, and this I don't think Dillon capable of. I attribute the whole thing to Devlin, who is of the corner-boy type, but I agree that Redmond should have resented the outrage.[6]

Healy's remonstrances helped ensure that O'Brien at least did not vote against the parliament bill which finally was passed by the House of Lords in August 1911.

Healy struggled to hold O'Brien to moderate courses. On the subject of their relations with the Irish party, Healy counselled O'Brien from Glengariff in September 1911 that, while reunion with Redmond was not practical,

> my training as a barrister compels me to work with my worst enemies . . . The fact that we think Dillon an ass, or T.P. a knave, should not prevent our consorting with them, in a political Board Room, any more than we should refuse to council with Whigs or Tories, if it became expedient. I never could adopt the view, which I think you may incline towards, that a party is like a *conseil de famille* . . . I take no vow against confabulation with humbugs . . . The sense of personal insult quits me after a night's sleep.

Redmond's ascendancy had deepened O'Brien's sense of exasperation, and Healy endeavoured to impress upon him the necessity of forbearance:

> We should compel the Government to unroll their scrolls, before setting up counterpolicies. I absolutely agree with the wisdom of what you write, but what is the use of being wise, amidst regiments of fools? Jettison wisdom, for the residuum of 1911, and let us await 1912 before reassuming our considering-caps! . . . Redmondism holds the field, and commands both Press and Pulpit . . . Why should we try, as would be alleged, to cut athwart the hawse of Redmond's vessel. His cargo is of Asquith's loading. Let us see the manifest. You argue that we should avert fiasco, by counterproposals. I differ. If they would be adopted, well and good, but we know the contrary, and that mere paternity would damn them.

Besides, he continued, 'I have so often talked kindred plans over with Moore, Campbell et al. that I know their position is hopeless. Their voters want fight, right or wrong, and hate compromise, which they treat as selling the pass'. The Orangemen he explained, lacked the quickness of perception of trained politicians: 'Most of their voters are yokels, stirred by bands playing "Boyne War" who want war like the Die-Hards at any price'.

Healy dissented from O'Brien's advocacy of the pursuit of consensus through conferences. He forcefully argued that any analogy between the contemporary prospects for home rule and the situation which pertained when the local government act of 1898 and the land act of 1903 were enacted was hopelessly misplaced:

> You were able to offer the landlords a Bonus, and good terms of sale in 1903. In 1898, the Grand Juror class escaped ½ poor rate, for consenting to Local Government. Today where is our *quid pro quo*? Echo answers, where? Politics are only a translation of Self-Interest, whereas we have merely Abstractions, and high phrases, to offer an entrenched garrison, to induce surrender . . .
>
> Until therefore, some naked startling and unlikely proposal of Asquith arouses the Tories, it is in my judgement useless to talk Compromise or Conference. It would be rejected by the government, because the specific bears your Crest and Brand, while the Orangemen would dis-heed it, as involving a trap or a surrender.[7]

O'Brien was deaf to Healy's warnings against setting up counter-policies in advance of the government's home rule bill. On 4 November he submitted a memorandum to Asquith. It advocated in the first instance the largest measure of self-government on the Canadian model, or if this was impractical a 'general Federal scheme' for the United Kingdom and 'Experimental Home Rule, open to revision, say, in five years' in Ireland. During this period the Ulster unionists would have a suspensory veto on legislation of a home rule parliament, unless that legislation was approved by the imperial parliament. The minority were to have enhanced representation in the Dublin parliament. Nothing came of the proposal which, while lacking any prospect of success, could hardly have been more unhelpful to the position of the Irish party.[8]

On 11 April 1912, the government introduced its Government of Ireland Bill. A quarter-century after the defeat of the first home rule bill, the Liberals seemed poised to fulfil Gladstone's promise. Healy (unlike O'Brien) responded with opportunistic equanimity. While it did not diminish the asperity of his attacks on Redmond and Dillon, he anticipated like them a successful resolution of the long struggle for home rule. In time, as the prospects for satisfactory constitutional settlement which satisfied nationalist expectations gradually unravelled, he would without any great psychological strain work himself back up to his former pitch of fury against the Irish party leadership.

Healy told the *Daily News* that, as the home rule bill was the most moderate proposal that could be conceived, there was no reason why the Tories should not accept it to dispose of the Irish question.[9] However, he was unable to resist the temptation to cause at least some mischief. The phrasing of a leading article in the *Cork Free Press* leaves little doubt as to its authorship:

> It is passing strange that that austere patriot, Mr. John Dillon, should be grovelling in ecstasy over the Government of Ireland Bill. We genuinely thought that this last relic of early Victorian rectitude would take nothing less than a Grattan's Parliament or an Irish Republic. It is not so long since 'Boer Home Rule as a minimum' was his attitude . . . Now this ambitious patriot has accepted with fulsome glee a measure far less pretentious than those schemes which he once denounced as 'devolution dementia'.

Dillon's pride in the term 'parliament' was compared to the old lady revelling in 'that blessed word Mesopotamia'. In its conclusion the editorial swerved abruptly back to a grudging patriotic orthodoxy. They were not living in the days of Tone or Parnell. 'If, however, that is all we can get, we might as well take it'.[10]

The prospects for home rule were however by no means as favourable as they first appeared. While the bill made no special provision for the north-eastern counties, the government had made clear to Redmond that it reserved its right to do so. This was to prove an extremely ill-advised mode of proceeding, paradoxically more for its adverse effect on southern nationalist than northern unionist opinion. The unionists, now under the leadership of Andrew Bonar Law in Britain and of Edward Carson in Ireland, struck an immediate note of defiance with mass meetings in Balmoral, outside Belfast, and at Blenheim. Opposition in Ulster to home rule was pressed to the fore, not as a demand for partition, but as the strongest argument against home rule for any part of Ireland. In this first phase, unionists no less than nationalists declined to countenance partition.[11] This was to be productive of much wishful misunderstanding on the nationalist side.

O'Brien remained for Healy an exasperating collaborator. When he declined to vote on what he called 'small divisions', Healy reminded him that there were no such divisions where a defeat would precipitate the resignation of the government. Healy reported to Maurice

> . . . but he would listen to no argument – or rather he listened and got annoyed. He said there was a profound difference of principle between us, as to which I agreed, and he talked of retiring or of my retiring. I said I was quite willing to retire; and he said that would be the end of everything! We were quite friendly; and, although serious phrases were exchanged, there was nothing unpleasant.[12]

On 8 July Healy wrote to his brother that 'Home Rule apparently has sunk into the infinite azure of the future. We shall not hear about it again before October, I believe'.[13] Some days later he wrote defending O'Brien in the aftermath of Asquith's triumphal visit to Dublin:

> I can't say I am quite satisfied with our situation in the House of Commons, but I feel there has been great provocation for the line O'Brien wishes to pursue. We have been ignored in the most brutal manner, which to a man of his temperament must be very galling, and our friends in Cork are ill-treated . . . Birrell and his Executive are the merest tools of the Party . . . No doubt after Asquith's reception here yesterday, he will be still more at their beck and call . . . Such an event as the visit of Asquith, and the manner of his reception, must undoubtedly affect politics in future. He will not care to disappoint the hopes his visit will have roused; and besides it will hearten up his Party.[14]

William Martin Murphy: The Irish Independent, and the Dublin Lock-Out

Following its acquisition and amalgamation with the *Daily Nation* in 1900, the *Irish Independent* had been a financial burden on William Martin Murphy. By 1904 he had learnt, as he later explained, that 'newspapers as a "Side Show" to politics were never known to result in anything but a loss'. Exasperated, he found a likely purchaser. The experts commissioned by the prospective purchaser advised that the paper should become a half-penny paper, and the undertaking conducted as a commercial concern. Murphy appropriated the advice, and kept the paper. In January 1905 the *Irish Independent* was effectively re-launched as a half-penny morning paper. On 2 January 1909 Murphy proudly announced that 'the commercial success of Independent newspapers, as a profit-earning company, is now absolutely secured'. By 1914 it was making a substantial return.[15] By late 1915 it had a daily circulation of 100,000 and was making £15,000 a year, prompting Healy to observe: 'Nothing like capital allied to courage'. By 1918 it was making £40,000 a year.[16]

The *Irish Independent* was to prove a highly influential source of opposition to the Irish party. While many in the Irish party considered the paper to be a Healyite organ, the policy and coverage of the *Independent* was a standing grievance to Healy and O'Brien. The paper refrained from aligning its position with Healy, and was antagonistic to his alliance with O'Brien. The *Leader* shrewdly discerned 'a struggle between Murphy the haberdasher and Murphy of the Healy bias'.[17] At the hearing of the North Louth election petition in 1911, Healy protested that he had never been in the office of the *Irish Independent* in his life, and that 'he knew nothing about it except that it was hostile to himself'.[18] This was a gross misrepresentation, but there was nevertheless considerable tension between Healy and Murphy in relation to the *Irish Independent*.

Murphy held back from exercising direct control over the editorial policy of the *Independent*, which was delegated to its editor T. R. Harrington. In response to Healy's abrasive remonstrances, Murphy did intervene somewhat diffidently in October 1910. He wrote to Harrington that he did not accept William O'Brien's suggestion that the Irish party despised the *Independent*. 'They can no longer afford to do so, but I am quite sure they hate both me and the paper. The paper owes them nothing but ill-will and we are in a position to take a less timid attitude than has perhaps hitherto been available'. He had no personal concern for O'Brien 'but the Healys have always been my friends, and without identifying the paper with their party they should at least get the fullest consideration in the matter of reporting'.[19]

Healy's relations with Murphy remained close, but were never easy. He found him infuriatingly obtuse, and never ceased protesting at the paper's stance and coverage. He wrote to O'Brien in December 1910:

> I am afraid I have broken with William Murphy by letters commenting on his organ, and today and yesterday show that he has given his editor free rein. Funny to think the only sort of Home Rule we shall be offered, is one to enable Sexton to boss his Railways. Yet he rejoices at our mishaps.[20]

The following year, noting that the Irish party leaders 'in a boghole over finance' in the home rule bill, he reported that Murphy was 'deep in [Erskine] Childers' book [*The Framework of Home Rule*] and his paper will determinedly hammer at the Finance of Home Rule. Wm. now realises the power and danger of the Mollies!'[21]

Murphy continued impassively to endure Healy's onslaughts. In March 1912 Healy wrote to his brother after dining with Murphy: 'He renewed his dislike of the Molly Maguires . . . and I told him he had a large responsibility for their uprise, at which he winced but said nothing'.[22] On the threat of partition, he reported in January 1914 to Maurice that 'I have got Murphy to order his editor to stand fast against concessions; and he began today, very much against his grain'.[23] Dining with Murphy the following month, Healy 'spoke very strongly about his paper, which I told him was clogging the pores of truth all over the country. He says nothing now when I attack him'.[24] He complained to O'Brien in December 1914 that Murphy was 'quite hopeless – not for want of sympathy but from a total inability to appreciate journalism, or to keep in touch with his own paper'.[25] The old antipathy between William O'Brien and Murphy did not abate. O'Brien's *Cork Free Press* denounced the *Irish Independent*, 'Mr. Murphy's kept journal', as 'the most insidious because the most hypocritically "impartial" enemy of the All-for-Ireland League'.[26]

From 1914, Murphy asserted himself to a greater extent. The following year Healy wrote that Murphy was 'quite keen to attack the Party, but his editor is no good; and poor Murphy takes a week to write a paragraph. Only for Harrington we should have the whole country on our side. It is not Murphy's fault, as he can't control him, and does not understand politics'.[27] While Murphy's interventions were uncharacteristically tentative, they exasperated the editor of the *Independent* who was uninhibited by any sense of deference towards him. In June 1915 Harrington sought from Murphy a free hand on political questions and an assurance 'that you will not persist in forcing your unpopular political views on me with a view to getting them into the editorial columns of the *Independent*, especially when I tell you, as I often have done, that I believe such opinions would, if published in the paper in the form in which you want them, inflict untold injury on it'. As he had already 'rather heatedly' pointed out, 'there is a limit to human endurance and I am sick and tired of acting the "buffer" between you and your property . . .'[28]

Healy and O'Brien not merely deplored the absence of openly partisan editorials as of old. Inured to the verbatim reporting of their speeches in the 1880s, they were never reconciled to the severe abridgement of their speeches as published. Healy's disagreement with Murphy came to a head when he took furious exception to the misuse of inverted commas by a sub-editor in May 1916. He wrote to Murphy denouncing 'the blackguard Harrington': 'I often said that if your paper had allowed our speeches to be printed in your paper, the country would never have gone as it did'. Murphy's response was to the point:

> I entirely disagree with your opinion that the printing of your party's speeches would have prevented the country going as it did. If the new *Independent* was edited as you think it ought to be, and as Dennehy edited the old *Independent* in which money was poured as into a bottomless pit, you would not have any daily paper existing today that would print even 'snippets' from your speeches.[29]

It would however be a mistake to take too seriously Healy's irate protests. Alternating between abrasiveness and emollience, he was mediating as best he could what was a fraught triadic relationship. Healy, O'Brien and Murphy, whatever their personal differences, were the most formidable adversaries of the Irish party from within constitutional nationalism. Long before Sinn Féin came into its own, they had done much to subvert the authority of the Irish party.

William Martin Murphy became the most prominent opponent of the construction of a gallery in Dublin to house the paintings of Sir Hugh Lane. His populist philistinism elicited W. B. Yeats' patrician rebuke of December 1912, 'To a Wealthy Man who Promised a Second Subscription to the Dublin Municipal Gallery if it were proved the People wanted Pictures'.

> And Guidobaldo, when he made
> That grammar school of courtesies
> Where wit and beauty learned their trade
> Upon Urbino's windy hill,
> Had sent no runners to and fro
> That he might learn the shepherds' will.

Murphy in turn attacked 'the handful of dilettanti' who were promoting a project 'for which there is no popular demand and one which will never be of the smallest use to the common people of this city'.[30]

The controversy over the gallery was swiftly eclipsed by the Dublin lock-out of 1913. In August, Murphy's Dublin United Tramways Company refused to retain in its employment those who were members of the Irish Transport and General Workers Union. Murphy thus deliberately pitted himself against the charismatic and tempestuous Liverpool-Irish Labour leader Jim Larkin. The confrontation spread across Dublin as other employees felt constrained to follow Murphy's lead.

Murphy was determined to defeat Larkin. The archetype of the Catholic nationalist capitalist, he resolved to resist the spread of trade unionism, and the incorporation of Ireland on the periphery of a grid of British trade union power which he believed would further retard Irish industrial development. He knew that the employers had, as the workers did not, the economic resources to hold out over a protracted period of time. The bleak severity of an Irish Catholic entrepreneur presented something of a novelty in contemporary industrial relations. G. K. Chesterton distinguished Murphy from contemporary English capitalists: 'He was more like some morbid prince of the fifteenth century, full of cold anger, not without perverted piety'.[31]

In the lock-out the city was torn apart. The conservative nationalist dread of the threat to the existing social order posed by Larkin (a 'vituperative Socialist') was expressed in unusually explicit terms by the *Irish Catholic*, recalling some of its wilder utterances in the Parnell split. Following the riots which took place in the course of the lock-out, it wrote:

> Into these thoroughfares there have poured nightly all the foul reserves of the slums, human beings who life in the most darksome depths of a great city has deprived of most of the characteristics of civilisation. In the majority of instances they are beings whose career is generally a prolonged debauch, seldom broken by the call of labour . . . People of their type are to be found in every great centre of the human race – wrecks which litter the floor of life as many a foul and pest-haunted hulk lies midst the rocks and weeds at the bottom of the ocean . . .
>
> The unfortunate creatures to whom we refer are not in any way connected with the artisans or labourers of our metropolis; the aristocracy of toil regard them with a pitiful contempt, deserving neither their championship nor friendship.[32]

Larkin's attacks on the clergy demonstrated that 'Socialism is essentially Satanic in its nature, origin, and purposes'.[33] The paper subsequently wrote that Larkin's movement had 'fallen in like a crazy tenement house', a curiously gross observation given that seven people had died in the collapse during the lock-out of two tenement houses in Church Street.[34]

The government was increasingly concerned. Healy reported to Maurice in late September that Birrell, the Chief Secretary, had twice sent for Murphy: 'I think it is a very impudent proceeding, unasked by anyone, but evidently suggested by local busybodies'.[35] The following day it was announced that the Board of Trade would hold an official inquiry, presided over by Sir George Askwith, with the intention of bringing a settlement of the dispute.[36] Healy wrote 'the strike will continue until the men are exhausted'.[37]

There were in the lock-out distant echoes of the Parnell split. Healy had written to his brother that at the Parnell commemoration of 1911 'Larkin's labourers' had made up one-third of the crowd.[38] For Sean O'Casey, Larkin was Parnell's messianic successor.[39] The *Irish Independent* had been anxious to deny Larkin any claim to Parnell's mantle. On the occasion of the unveiling of the Parnell monument, it had reported that Larkin had been present, but that 'contrary to expectation that gentleman did not attempt to present himself on the platform where, if he did, it was rumoured that he would have been prevented getting on it'.[40]

The appearance of Healy (denounced by George Russell as 'the bitterest tongue that ever wagged in this island')[41] for the employers at the commission of inquiry, deepened the historical resonance. Murphy was 'very reluctantly' driven by the other employers to appear at the inquiry.[42] There Larkin confronted him. Under an intriguing misapprehension, Larkin charged him with using words ascribed to Healy in the demonology of Parnellism

> Mr. Larkin: 'Did you say that you would drive the late Mr. Parnell to his grave or into a lunatic asylum?'
>
> Mr. Murphy: 'I did not. That is an infamous lie . . .'
>
> Mr. Larkin: 'Are you responsible for the paper that published it?'
>
> Mr. Murphy: 'It was never published in any paper. It was a canard started by a man whose name I will not mention. It was attributed to another man and not to me. There was no truth at all in it . . .'
>
> Mr. Larkin: ' . . . Would this thing about Parnell be attributed to any of your family (cries of '*Oh, Oh*') . . .'
>
> Mr. Murphy: 'It was never used by any person that I know of, or by myself.'[43]

Addressing the commission, Healy referred to Murphy as the 'one man in the city who would not deal with Larkin and with whom Larkin could not deal', who in seizing the initiative against Larkin 'had taken time by the forelock'.[44]

Defending himself against his brother's criticisms, Healy claimed that an arrangement had been brokered by English labour leaders under which nothing was to be said after Healy's address. The parties were to retire and come to a private accommodation. Larkin was 'not only false to his promise but abused the employers personally and falsely. This is what led to the fact that no settlement was made. Had Larkin kept faith, then instead of men in Cork abusing me, as you state, they would have been throwing up their hats at the settlement I had made secure'.[45]

While Healy's views were somewhat more ambivalent than they appeared, he agreed with Murphy on the need to put down Larkin's challenge. He wrote to his brother that 'I fear the strike can only be settled as the Port of London strike was, by the surrender of the men'. However he could not see 'what the Dublin Masters can do about Larkin except fight'.[46] In the draft of his memoirs he wrote of Murphy: 'Despite the fool-patriots of the day, he defeated Larkin's hold-up of Dublin, and brigaded its merchants in self-defence'.[47]

Healy's reservations were political. However right-wing his socio-economic views, he was loath to diminish the challenge Larkin posed from the left to the hegemony of the Irish party in Dublin:

> I told Murphy he was fighting Redmond's battle, and he was well aware of it. Personally I should prefer Larkin to Devlin, and I told Murphy so. It is deplorable that his overthrow will mean the victory of the Mollies, and that we should be fighting their corner![48]

The *Cork Free Press* on the other hand looked gleefully to the 'approaching collapse of the whole gang, who have at least been found out in Dublin'.[49] Healy wrote to his brother:

> I am sorry to hear that Cork opinion is in the state you describe as to my acting against Larkin. I thought he was utterly discredited in Cork above every other place; and the condition to which he reduced the farmers of Dublin was such that I didn't suppose any sane man could sympathise with his divine mission to create discontent. I had hoped that Murphy could be got to utilise him, and I strongly urged this view upon him, as of course the fellow is absolutely corrupt and has been squared by other employers . . .
>
> I am afraid I have not been following the Dublin papers, as to the mischief Larkin has done, or the expressions he used. I agree that he has been useful in destroying the Mollies, and that is why I was keen to come to an understanding with him, especially as I believe he could prevent Lloyd George coming here next December!! He is however utterly impracticable, and I think a little astray in the head.[50]

Healy did not believe Larkin vanquished by the collapse of the lock-out. He wrote of Murphy in January 1914 that 'he thinks he is up against a strike, while I think he is up against a theory which however erroneous will render Larkin immune from unpopularity in his defeat. The Nationalists of yore cared nothing for defeat . . . This is the same position in my judgement . . .' Due to what he considered to be the pusillanimousness of the Catholic church in the face of Larkin's challenge, he believed that 'Dublin has ceased to be the capital for Redmondism'.[51] His antipathy towards Larkin remained finely counterbalanced by his hatred for the Irish party.

Beaverbrook

Max Aitken (who in 1916 was to be created Lord Beaverbrook), aged thirty-one and already a multi-millionaire, was returned for Ashton-under-Lyne at the second election of 1910. Healy and he rapidly became fast friends. Both were ebulliently opportunistic, with a sentimental streak, and in some degree outsiders. Beaverbrook revelled in Healy's company, esteemed him as a great parliamentary figure (if already almost of a bygone era), and valued his counsel. He served as Beaverbrook's parliamentary mentor: 'I was fortunate enough to make a friend of him, and sensible enough to realise my good luck. I sat at his feet and studied his methods with close attention'. He wrote in 1962 that 'Tim was my very dear friend. He was my teacher too'.[52]

Beaverbrook in turn appealed to Healy's taste for the company of raffish cynics who stopped just short of scoundrelism. Beaverbrook succeeded Henry Labouchere and Harold Frederic in his affections. The most politically significant aspect of their relationship for Healy was that Beaverbrook gave him a social access to leading Conservative politicians not enjoyed by any other nationalist parliamentarian. In particular Beaverbrook was close to Andrew Bonar Law, a fellow Canadian and Presbyterian, who on 13 November 1911 succeeded Balfour as the leader of the Unionist party. Healy's name appeared, along with those of Bonar Law and Rudyard Kipling, on the first page of the visitors book for 13–14 July 1912, at Beaverbrook's country house, Cherkely Court, outside Leatherhead in Surrey.[53] There they frequently passed weekends when parliament was in session, trading political confidences, conspiring against mutual adversaries, and convivially vying from their conflicting political standpoints for advantage. Healy benefited from Beaverbrook's habit of seeking to generate profits for his friends by investing his own money on their behalf. (Beaverbrook wrote shortly after the outbreak of the war that 'in the last year or 18 months I have tried again and again to invest some money for you but I have always been driven out of the market as quickly as I ventured in'.[54])

In addition to tutoring Beaverbrook on parliamentary matters, he advised on his literary style. Lamenting the influence of Edgar Allan Poe he discerned in Beaverbrook's writing, he commended a spare prose: 'Style is eternity . . . you want to furrow deep tracks into the soil of men's minds'. He was not above compromising his pedagogical role by gross flattery, writing to Beaverbrook in 1919 that 'your work possesses a permanent historic and literary value, which ensures for you lasting fame'.[55]

It was not only Healy's relations with Beaverbrook, and through him with Bonar Law which set him apart from the Irish party leadership. In February 1910 Sir Edward Carson was elected leader of the Irish Unionist parliamentary party. Healy's relations with his old adversary were friendly, though not close.[56] Sean O'Casey in his crudely polemical memoirs discerned an affinity between the two Irish barristers at Westminster:

> How dissimilar, yet how alike, was this man of the Nassau orange and blue, who had never been an orange-man, to his comrade King's Counsel, Timothy Healy . . . both men of a loud mouth, both using parties for their own ends; both wrapping themselves in the power of their several religions; both loyal to a king because it was expedient and profitable to be so; both determined to take no risk that would dim the polish on the knockers of their trim hall-doors.[57]

The Ulster Impasse

On 11 September 1913 the *Times* carried a letter from Lord Loreburn, Asquith's first Lord Chancellor, urging a conference of party leaders to explore the prospect of 'cooperation for the good of Ireland'.[58] This proposal, fraught with peril for the Irish party, was embraced by O'Brien with his habitual excess of zeal.

For Healy, O'Brien's favourable response to the Loreburn letter, and his general advocacy of changes to the home rule bill in the expectation of diminishing unionist opposition, were strategically misconceived. He wrote to Maurice that 'Lord Loreburn's letter, although it momentarily helps O'Brien, cannot I think lead to very much'.[59] While he had serious reservations about O'Brien's course, he was powerless to restrain him. He judged correctly that 'any compromise must be in the direction of whittling down the Bill. That is the reason I think O'Brien has done enough. If the concessions he outlines were only granted, it would be all right and an improvement, but that is not the way History is written'.[60]

Healy had some time before warned O'Brien that his equation of the home rule crisis with the prelude to the Wyndham land act of 1903 was unsustainable.[61] He pointed out to Maurice the immediate peril created by O'Brien's belligerent pursuit of 'conciliation': 'the Redmondites will throw the blame on him and on Loreburn if they are sold by the Cabinet, and I think they will be sold'.[62]

Healy's correspondence affords a striking insight into the attitude of an exceptionally well-informed parliamentary nationalist to the home rule crisis. While he dissociated himself with his habitual aptitude for ferocity from the policy of the Irish party leadership, and was to clamber to safety with unexpected agility from the shipwreck of parliamentary nationalism, his thinking differed remarkably little from that of Redmond and Dillon.

There is little trace of Healy's normal sceptical alertness in the assessments of unionist thinking he despatched to his brother. Searingly critical of the Irish party and the Liberals, he was disconcertingly credulous in his dealings with unionists. He appeared blithely unmindful of the purposes to which they could put their encounters with him, in using him as a sounding board, in the eliciting of information, and in seeking to accentuate the division in the nationalist parliamentary ranks. There was in this a certain symmetry. Just as John Dillon throughout his later career undeviatingly sustained the Liberals, and dogmatically opposed all policies emanating from the Conservatives in office, Healy's suspiciousness was reserved chiefly for the Liberals. Their divergent attitudes attested to the fractured coherence of parliamentary nationalism after Parnell.

The charitable conclusion is that Healy had succumbed to the classic fallacy of the avowed political 'realist': that one could engage more profitably with the party of the right than with its progressive rival. There was something more. In his despatches to his brother there was a note of muted pride. In his dealings with Conservative politicians Healy had gone where no nationalist contemporary had preceded him. In holding familiar social relations with unionists there was the exhilaration of what was, in Parnellite terms, a double transgression.

At Westminster Healy was preoccupied by the drama of the moment, receptive to rumours of accommodation, and much exercised by the possibilities for enlightened intrigue. To Healy, Ulster unionist opposition to home rule seemed to dissolve in this fluid medium. His exposure was to Conservative high politics rather than to popular unionist resistance to home rule in the north of Ireland. He was led to discount Ulster unionism, and to regard it as a cypher of the Tory leadership. It is a considerable irony that Healy's underestimation of the political strength of unionist opposition to home rule in Ulster owed perhaps as much to the high metropolitan altitude of Conservative politics at Westminster as to any vulgar predispositions as a nationalist.

On the question of Ulster, Healy's thinking was deeply contradictory. In this he was representative. It was not merely that the idea of partition was anathema. It did not feature in nationalist thinking at all until 1912, and was not for a considerable period thereafter considered a serious prospect. Nationalists tended to respond to partition with individual evasions which would later be aggregated into a disconsolate national legend of betrayal.

The temptation to travesty the nationalist failure to appreciate the amplitude of the problem of the north-east in terms of the morose (and passive) irredentism of a later phase of Irish politics is however to be resisted. Constitutional nationalist expectations had crystallised around Gladstone's two home rule bills. It is unremarkable that the nationalist accommodation to the abrupt emergence of Ulster unionist resistance as the stumbling block to a unitary home rule measure should have been imperfect. Moreover the lack of foresight was by no means confined to nationalists. Unionist politicians for long refused to countenance partition. They too were committed to the heroic adversity, ordained by political convention, between unionism and nationalism. At the outset, Ulster unionism was the bulwark of resistance to home rule for Ireland as a whole, rather than a secessionist phenomenon.

Healy closely observed the flux within Asquith's government. When Winston Churchill at Dundee in October 1913 intimated a willingness to consider the exclusion of Ulster, Healy complacently believed that he had 'merely thrown out a feeler, which he knows the Tories won't accept', thereby allaying the qualms of the King by a show of moderation. He added a more percipient caveat: 'Of course this is a very dangerous game, because he has inflamed Ulster feeling by acknowledging their grievance while leaving it unremedied, while he chilled the Nationalists. If I were in Redmond's place, I would charge the mischief that may arise upon our party!!' He saw both nationalists and unionists as 'engaged in a struggle for the body of the King'.[63]

Even as late as the autumn of 1913, Healy's views remained remarkably sanguine. He still believed that unionist objections to Ulster could be contained within the framework of home rule. He expected that Redmond would meet governmental pressure for compromise by conceding an Ulster Council with a veto on legislation in the province, and some administrative powers: 'Unless Redmond holds out, which is unlikely, it therefore appears as if in the end the Home Rule Bill will be passed as a consent measure!!'[64]

After spending the weekend with Beaverbrook, where he twice saw Bonar Law, Healy's assessment was more sombre. He added that E. F. V. Knox 'takes a very serious view of the feelings in the North, and says that pride will never let them submit to a Catholic Parliament after all that has happened, and if there is bloodshed there will be bitter feelings no matter who wins. He says they will never settle down the way we calculate'. From another source Healy knew that a strong section of the cabinet, comprising Grey, Lloyd George and Churchill, favoured a compromise over Ulster,

> and don't care how it is to be accomplished so long as there is no row and it is accepted by the Tories. Asquith has not declared himself because, if he quarrelled too soon with Redmond, he would lose his majority forthwith. But my informant treats as impossible the idea that they will pass Home Rule pure and simple with Ulster included in the crude way Redmond has been prophesying.

Healy remained clear that there was nothing to be gained from the idea relentlessly advocated by O'Brien of a conference, 'which can only end in Ulster being in some way excluded, either administratively or otherwise'. His demand for a conference 'should be slacked down, as tending only to the gain of the Orangemen; but of course it is impossible to teach O'Brien this'.[65] He wrote to O'Brien a week later:

> The word is now with Carson & Co. to seal the bargain. The King has been acting as a clearing house between the two sides, and passes on to each the views of the other. My impression is that Carson is in so tight a corner, that ultimately he will call off his 'civil war', on this basis, and if he yields, so will his Party. F. E. Smith favours a compromise on these lines . . . but so far, his views have not prevailed, and he is believed to be too much 'in' with Churchill. These two would like a coalition government, and thus defy Redmond, but that is a hopeless scheme . . .
>
> The Belfast gang would I hear accept peace on the mere exclusion of Down and Antrim, and care nothing for the 'scattered Protestants' elsewhere.

The seeming fecklessness of Healy's conclusion ('So whatever bill Redmond gets, he won't have much to be proud of'[66]) has to be understood by reference to his purpose of dissuading O'Brien from intemperate intervention.

In mid-December 1913 O'Brien requested Healy to arrange a meeting with Bonar Law. Healy thought this unwise, but made the necessary arrangements.[67] In January 1914 O'Brien without warning resigned his seat to seek re-election, in protest against the defeat suffered in local elections by most of the All-for-Ireland candidates and a number of Protestant home rulers.[68] After O'Brien's resignation was announced Healy observed to Maurice that 'the only thing is that he has resigned so often that it has a tinge of the old instability in the minds of the people'. His assessment of O'Brien was as shrewd as his dismissal of Ulster loyalism was facile:

> You and I are entirely in agreement as to the Tory game about Home Rule. They would be parting with their electoral bread and butter to consent to any compromise. They are split up over Tariff Reform and have only the Ulster business to unite them; but O'Brien is such an intense Irishman that he will not see this, and thinks the Tories should have a round-table – which would only be successful from his point of view

> by dishing themselves. He is still of the mid-Victorian opinion that Ireland occupies the same place that it did in English minds. The mass of the English regard it as practically settled . . . Ireland is 'hands off' with the politicians here, unless they can use it mechanically as Carson is doing by threatening civil war. The fact that he has to make such a threat to arouse interest is the best proof that the English would not otherwise care a damn . . . I have not the least doubt that Carson's influence has acted as a safety valve for the Orangeman of recent months, and that otherwise they would have got up sporadic riots, if left to themselves! The whole situation depends on whether Asquith has the nerve to meet them without flinching.[69]

Healy passed a weekend in late January 1914 at Beaverbrook's, where he met James Campbell, a leading Irish unionist and a fellow member of the Irish bar, together with the nephew of an unidentified English peer. The last mentioned prophesied civil war in England as well as in Ireland 'and that Willoughby de Broke and his men would ride up to London and attack Asquith, and that the soldiers would not resist'. If this was absurd aristocratic swashbuckling, Healy was taken aback at its ferocity. 'I never heard such lurid prophecies and dire threats as he made':

> While of course I don't swallow all this, I was astonished at their vehemence and their belief that Asquith would be funked. Campbell said they would instantly form a Provisional Government on the day the Bill became law, and that the Belfast Protestants would never allow themselves to be ruled from Dublin. I asked did they think the Government would allow them to seize the Custom House in Belfast, and he said their men would advance and take it, and get shot down, and that the moment Protestant blood was shed in Ulster, Asquith's life would not be worth very much. They are evidently relying on funking the Ministers, but whether they will succeed is the question; but with Birrell in charge anything is possible. Anyhow it is quite evident that there will be a hornet's nest in Down and Antrim, which is to be stirred up for the sake of influencing English opinion and inflaming opinion on the Tory side.
>
> They hope to get the King to veto the Bill, though this was not the wish of the more responsible of them; but as the time draws near I fancy it is the extremists' view which will prevail . . .[70]

Healy later added that Beaverbrook rather differed from Campbell's prediction of civil war 'in a way which I believe represents the English Tory view'.[71]

Healy remained disconcerted by O'Brien's advocacy of concessions to unionist opinion, adding: 'Besides every offer of the kind should be prefaced by the statement that it has been made necessary by the establishing of the Molly Maguires and the alarm they have caused in the minds of

Protestants'.[72] The rider was frankly cynical: Healy did not share O'Brien's conviction that Irish unionist opposition to home rule was attributable to the nationalist failure to espouse in time a federal solution, or to the influence of the Ancient Order of Hibernians.

Healy wrote to his brother of O'Brien's resignation that 'his courage certainly is beyond human computation or any previous exemplar. He would have made a formidable soldier on a big stage. He is almost wasted on Ireland'. This extravagant accolade was a by-product of Healy's struggle to contain his dissent from O'Brien's political course. He feared that O'Brien would refuse to support the home rule bill if the government did not meet his views, and was unable to see the logic of O'Brien's advocacy of a referendum in Britain and Ireland:

> O'Brien feels possibly embarrassed by his previous declarations that the Bill could not become law as it stands this year, and wants to prove a true prophet. This is forcing him into a position quite distinct from that which seeks to avert bloodshed in Ulster by concessions.
>
> I think the arrangement will give trouble, and that Redmond will have very little to congratulate himself upon when the Bill becomes law, owing to his rejection of conciliatory tactics: but my feeling is that we should do all we can to make the Bill law as it stands without any responsibility for the future. I am therefore somewhat nervous as to the shaping of our policy for the Session; still the courage and sincerity of O'Brien incline me to be less critical as to the points he put forward without consulting us. He is careful about consultations during the Session; and of course we are so scattered now that we can scarcely be reckoned with.[73]

While Healy privately reacted with irritation and unease to O'Brien's tendency to act on his own initiative throughout the home rule crisis, and was deeply sceptical of O'Brien's course of action, he remained steadfast in his public support of O'Brien. His reservations were tempered by the strange awe which O'Brien's reckless intrepidity inspired in him. Writing to his brother at the end of January 1914 he reiterated his criticism of O'Brien's pursuit of concessions to Ulster unionists at a political juncture of such delicacy. As if still conceptually unable to accept its full implications, he situated the difficulty created by Ulster unionist disaffection in an ill-defined post-home rule interregnum:

> It is true that he has gone further in his campaign for a conference than I ever supposed he would, and I didn't realise that it was such an obsession with him, or that he believed it so vehemently. His plucky and dauntless nature have undoubtedly had their effect, and I believe will redound to his credit should there be after-consequences in bloodshed and Ulster in case no compromise is reached. But in politics it is just as

> bad to be too far in front as to be too far behind, and those who have been used to the cry of 'Wolf!' from the North don't realise that this is the last occasion on which the shout can be raised; it may now be seriously made. I believe it is serious, and I think the Government know it also. Certainly the King knows it, and the worst of the situation is that it will be handled, like the Larkin strike manifestations, by stranger fools instead of by native resolutes. Dublin Castle created Larkin; and if Home Rule passes, its dispositions in Ulster will be still more idiotic, and of course the soldiers will have no heart whatever in the business, and the heads of the police still less.

Healy retained over-sanguine hopes of exploiting the divergence of interests between southern and northern unionists in Ireland. He reported an encounter with James Campbell:

> Campbell spoke luridly of Southern Protestants being engaged in barricading their houses and getting ready for defence, through fear of reprisals for what may happen in Belfast. They have raised the devil, and I believe cannot lay him . . .
>
> Of course Campbell's interest is quite distinct from Carson's personally, and he spoke of himself to me as having the special guardianship of the Southern Unionists – assigned to him I suppose in their secret conferences! I therefore counselled him to bring about a situation in which the Lords would be able to make changes in the Bill, so that it would pass as it were over Carson's head, and take away the main pretext for resistance.[74]

Healy continued to assert that Ulster unionist opposition was an exercise in bluff, albeit on a scale which would leave a bitter aftertaste, and very likely lead to bloodshed:

> All the unionist talk is of battle, but, although they may be weak enough when they find their stuff doesn't frighten Asquith, it seems to me that they have churned up such buttermilk in the North that it will be very sour drinking for everyone. I doubt that they can restrain their rowdies, and expect a massacre of Catholics at some stage.[75]

William Martin Murphy was much more hard headed than O'Brien, and discerned that no arrangement with the Ulster unionists could be achieved whereby they could be induced voluntarily to recognise a Dublin parliament if the bill were passed. Healy reported to Maurice:

> He was very ferocious and quite sincere. As Redmond will have a terrible handful of such men when the Bill becomes law, I think O'Brien may well let them take their course without let or hindrance, pointing out that they deliberately brought the country to this pass, first by their policy

> of the exclusion of the Cork members, then by spreading the Mollies, and then by giving no consideration whatever to the Protestants and treating their protests as those of men with dummy guns. I believe there will be a *baptême du feu* for the measure unless the Government provide that it is not to become operative until after a General Election, and this may be the way out.[76]

The concluding analysis was a gesture of obeisance to O'Brien rather than a reflection of Healy's personal views. He was seeking to coach Maurice in Cork in an argument to dissuade William O'Brien from outright opposition to the home rule bill.

As unease grew within the Irish party as to the likely extent of government concessions on Ulster, Healy noticed an unwonted friendliness towards him on the part of some of its members. He wrote to Maurice on 10 February that 'any members of the party who meet me privately are very civil' (three days later he reported that one of them had 'insisted on shaking my hand in the lavatory when there was no one present!'). Of the party he wrote:

> They are in a desperate hole or rather would be if the Opposition had any skill. In spite of Asquith's speech clearly pointing to the exclusion of Ulster, their speakers, instead of receiving this as a triumph, thundered at them as usual in the dullest way, thus saving the face of the Party in Ireland and before the public.

Healy went on to relate the circumstances of an unexpected encounter with the Prime Minister

> So obtuse are Englishmen that a speech I made last night, intended to be satirical, has been made the subject of praise by several Liberals, and (as a result I suppose) Asquith himself came up and shook hands with me as I was sitting by the fire in the library at 7.30, quite unaware of his presence until he touched me!! I asked him were they going to exclude Ulster, and he said not, but I don't believe him. The Party received him without cheers when he rose, and in silence when he sat down. They were in utter collapse, having evidently been told by Redmond at their meeting previously what had been communicated to him in Downing Street last week.

Healy discerned in Asquith's fluid approach a surfeit of urbanity: 'I believe his habits make him take a free and easy view of the world's affairs!!'

Leaving the cloakroom of the House of Commons, Healy had encountered Carson, who was unwell. Healy remonstrated over the line he was taking. Carson was 'quite reasonable over it, and good-natured'. When he warned Carson that Irish America would retaliate against imports of linen and the like from Belfast, 'he felt sure Ulster would come in later on, if now excluded, and I think the poor chap is only trying to get the best terms he can for the general body of the "loyalists" of Ireland'. While Carson was unhappy at the direction of events, Healy was overstating the extent of his misgivings.

Returning to this theme the following day Healy conveyed his impression that 'the bill is dead':

> This of course will be a complete justification for O'Brien, and he should be content with it. Whether we should make trouble for Redmond, and force him to out the Government over amputation, if that proves inevitable, is a matter for later consideration . . . I have been passing the word through F. E. Smith to the Tories to be moderate, but Austen Chamberlain was most humiliating tonight to the Irish as to the result of the exclusion of Ulster, saying it would be a statutory declaration of recognition that there was no Irish nation. Nevertheless the Party sat absolutely silent, although Redmond smiled feebly. They are routed, as far as I can see tonight, but of course things change continually, and it may be that in the end some other composition will be accepted.
>
> I don't think it is the occasion for mere sectional moralising, and that we should not drive Redmond, if the event happens, into absolute rejection of the Bill and the defeat of the Government. O'Brien has been so badly treated that he may take a more personal aspect of the case.[77]

Healy went on to confess that 'unless Redmond and his Party would go over to the Tories and obtain some Conservative settlement of the question, my mind has been recently influenced by Knox into the view presented by Carson that, if the stage-fright stage had been overcome, the North might afterwards join us voluntarily, but otherwise would never do so'.[78] This marked a significant stage in the uneven process by which Healy reconciled himself to a partitionist solution. Such consoling hopes he held as to the future amenability of northern unionists were not very great, and served to ease his transition rather than to determine his thinking. As a consummate politician (even when writing to his brother), Healy had already moved further than the shift of position he articulated. It was an intelligent politician's personal accommodation to what he as a nationalist experienced as a bitter disappointment.

Healy's private realism admittedly did little to moderate the ferocity with which he charged the Irish party leadership with the responsibility for partition. His thinking nonetheless diverged sharply from O'Brien's, to whose sentimental illusions he was unable to subscribe. O'Brien continued to insist that Ulster Protestants would have acquiesced in home rule were it not for what he considered to be the sectarian self-aggrandisement of the Irish party leadership and its political machine. He thereby characteristically contrived to advance an explanation of the failure of nationalism in relation to the north-east of Ireland which left intact its fundamental premises.

On 11 February Healy wrote to his brother from the National Liberal Club that his impression was that the exclusion of Ulster would be proposed by the government and accepted by Redmond. He believed that this had been arranged behind the scenes through the King. He had nevertheless held back: 'I could have struck in and destroyed Redmond, who carefully left the door open for the surrender of Ulster, while pretending to oppose it'.[79]

Healy watched closely as the Irish party, obliged (as he was not) to address immediate political realities, grappled with the onset of partition. In mid-February 1914 he contemplated with palpable satisfaction the predicament of John Dillon:

> Dillon is going about talking to the Liberals freely in favour of the exclusion of Ulster!! They all know that but for Devlin, it would be arranged. Dillon has been saying now the very contrary to his blather all along up to this. He says: How can we coerce Ulster with our own record against coercion? and that we cannot face civil war as a beginning to Home Rule!! They are in a state of most complete collapse . . . Devlin on account of Belfast cannot give in; but I see Dillon arguing with him earnestly . . .[80]

If Healy's personal gratification was in some degree understandable, the truth was that his political judgement of the situation differed little from that of his old adversary. He was fully sensible to the narrowing of nationalist options.

Healy wanted O'Brien to hold back until the bill reached the House of Lords: 'I look forward to that period as being the most probable time for compromise, as then we shall have in black and white the real Tory mind on the measure, and their minimum of acceptance'. He had not lost all hope of a satisfactory resolution:

> None of the Orangemen really want exclusion except for the purpose of annoying us or keeping their 'covenant', and that is the hopeful side of a hopelessly complicated position. When I say 'none of them', chaps like John Gordon or the Craigs or possibly William Moore might like it, but not Carson or Campbell or any Southern-minded Tory like the Guinnesses.[81]

For many southern Irish unionists, home rule with partition did represent the worst of the three possible outcomes. The preponderant influence of 'Southern-minded' Irish unionists was however fast becoming a nationalist delusion.

O'Brien's pontifical aloofness remained a source of irritation to Healy:

> I have before now realised that it is useless giving O'Brien information which does not tally with his own inspirations. Nevertheless the fact remains that, only for Devlin and his pals, the exclusion of Ulster would have been agreed to, and it is now a question of making the alternative of 'home rule within Home Rule' so unpalatable that even Devlin may be forced to acquiesce in exclusion. I have therefore made a suggestion quite apart from either method which I will unfold to you when you arrive, but of course it will be as dross for those who have their superior plans. Besides I don't think it will be accepted.
>
> The present bill seems to be like a Bill for Women's Suffrage, which everyone is anxious to see killed after having sworn to promote it!![82]

Healy was referring to a proposal he had conveyed to Asquith. It envisaged the passage by consensus of the Government of Ireland Bill together with a further bill, whose short title was to be the Temporary Powers (Ireland) Act, to provide for an Irish cabinet of fifteen members: seven nationalists, seven unionists, and one government nominee to be named in the bill. This Irish cabinet was to exercise most of the powers conferred by the Government of Ireland Act for three years. During that period, it was to submit proposals for the better government of Ireland (either by way of modification of, or as an alternative to, the Government of Ireland Act). If those proposals were approved they would be given legislative force by Order in Council, in which event the Government of Ireland Act would be deemed to have been repealed. Otherwise the Government of Ireland Act would come into force on St Patrick's Day, 1917. The memorandum was endorsed by Healy 'the above suggestions made to avoid the exclusion of Ulster counties, or severed interests of any kind'.[83]

Healy's proposals were intended to afford a respite from the immediate crisis, and to provide a mechanism whereby unionists would be compelled to agree the terms of a home rule settlement, during a fixed interval in which he evidently believed that unionist hostility to home would be softened by participation in a precursor administration to a fully fledged home rule government. Healy's ingenuity was wasted. While the more he thought of his scheme, 'the better it appears to me as compared with the alternative proposals so far adumbrated', this was authorial vanity. As was entirely predictable, his proposals did not impinge on the course of events – either in February when they were first advanced to Asquith, or in August when he forwarded them to Carson ('I heard that he said it would not do').[84]

O'Brien was meanwhile embarked upon a completely different trajectory. He succeeded in persuading himself that he and the King were proceeding along similar lines, as no doubt to some extent they were, but with quite different ends in view. 'Did Mr. O'Brien write the King's Speech?', unctuously enquired the *Cork Free Press*.[85]

On 9 March 1914, Asquith, moving for the third time the second reading of the home rule bill, abruptly announced his government's solution to the Ulster difficulty. This was to permit each of the counties in the province of Ulster, together with the county boroughs of Belfast and Derry, to decide by referendum whether to be excluded from the operation of the Government of Ireland Act for a period of six years. Redmond refrained from opposing a proposal he described as going 'to the extreme limit of concession'. Carson famously dismissed Asquith's compromise with the assertion that Ulster did not want a sentence of death with a stay of execution for six years.

Healy in the Commons scathingly voiced the opposition of nationalist Ireland to partition: 'if this proposal is accepted, *finis Hiberniae*'. He assailed Redmond (the Prime Minister's 'obedient acolyte behind me') and Joseph Devlin for abandoning their commitment never to acquiesce in partition. He warned that the exclusion of the unionist counties (the number of which he put at four) would not be limited to six years:

> We now come to this 'very slight concession' for which the Member for Trinity College [Edward Carson] asked. Would any sane Britisher go to civil war for the difference between six years and 666 years? Is there any sanc man amongst you would let loose the fires of civil war for such a mere form? Why cannot the Member for Waterford give that up, as he has given up everything else. The remains of his principles ornament every step of this Gangway. Accordingly, I take it, it is absolutely certain that exclusion will be made permanent.[86]

Redmond's characterisation of the government's proposals as going to 'the extreme limit of concession' was valiantly understated. For nationalists, the government's concession of partition, even on an avowedly temporary basis, was felt as a sickening heave in the motion of the nationalist barque, which was supposed to be embarked on the final stage of its triumphal voyage. Asquith's announcement portended an ignominious reversal of nationalist fortune, the slipping away of the historical initiative that nationalists believed they had held since the time of Parnell. Unprepared for the derogation of the north-eastern counties from home rule, even for a finite period, nationalist opinion in Ireland divided between those who remained loyal to Redmond, and those who insisted that the temporary exclusion in which he had acquiesced could not but lead to the permanent partition of Ireland.

In the opposition to Redmond, the *Irish Independent* came to the fore. Condemning 'this mutilation of Ireland', it described Asquith's formula as 'tantamount to permanent exclusion'.[87] William Martin Murphy had finally been roused from his semi-passive proprietorial role. He told Healy that nothing had interested him in politics so much as Asquith's speech and Redmond's acquiescence:

> He said he had never lost a night's sleep during the tram strike; but was awake all night from humiliation after these pronouncements. He went into his office every night, for four nights afterwards (a thing he never did before), to keep the paper straight.[88]

The sense of humiliation which Murphy expressed had been anticipated by Healy two months previously. As the elaborate game of double-bluff between Ulster unionists and Irish nationalists was played out at Westminster, Healy had written of his fear that Carson would be prevailed upon to acquiesce reluctantly in the exclusion of the north-eastern counties, 'and once the amputation is made the shame is consummated for generations'.[89] In this linkage of the concepts of severance and shame there is a brief recrudescence of the intensity of Healy's idiom in the Parnell split. The imagistic wound was perhaps as much to nationalist self-regard as to the integrity of the island-nation of nationalist ideology.

For William O'Brien, the fact that the Irish party 'should ever have listened without horror to the first suggestion of Partition will remain one of the ghastly riddles of Irish history'. The alternative he posited was facile and unconvincing. 'Parnell's response, there cannot be a shadow of a doubt, would have been ruthlessly to throw out the Government at the first whisper of such a treason, to force a General Election and negotiate a settlement by consent with the incoming Unionist majority, already more than half-converted'.[90] It was the second stage of course of action which O'Brien hypothetically imputed to Parnell that was the more problematical. Opposition to home rule, at least in the north-east of Ireland, ran far deeper than O'Brien could bring himself to acknowledge. Moreover as Healy commented at the time of the strategy advocated by O'Brien, 'the Ulstermen say they will fight no matter how many dissolutions condemn them to Dublin rule. A Dissolution therefore would not avert civil war from their point of view'.[91] Healy's private assessment of the situation remained much closer to that of the Irish party leadership than to O'Brien's, and he still did not altogether despair of the prospects for a satisfactory settlement.

In March Asquith's government responded in ominously supine fashion to the mutiny of cavalry officers stationed at the Curragh, who had declared that they would not move against Ulster if ordered to do so. Healy was however heartened by the response of the left wing of the Liberal party, and of the Labour party. He experienced a short-lived but intense re-awaking of the ardent affinity he had felt with the Liberals in the latter half of the 1880s. He wrote to Maurice on 26 March:

> As no one now believes the Irish papers on either side, I let you know my opinion of the upshot of the debate tonight. It is that the Government have emerged from it with the loss of a few tail feathers, but substantially uninjured, and that the Home Rule Bill will become law. Of course the Tories may organise a further mutiny in the Army, and it may be that the Irish officers will persist now in resigning, but nothing struck me more than the extraordinary and historical determination of the Radicals to face the Army crisis at all hazards, although it might have brought down the government. This sprang chiefly from the Labour Members in the first place, but soon the entire Government caught fire. No doubt the Ministry are lying, but they lie principally to save their faces with the court, and not that they disagreed with the rank and file. They have not told a tithe of the truth; but if it should be dragged from them it will not discredit them, because it is clear that their supporters are far in advance of themselves. They lie to placate Ulster and the Front Opposition Bench and the King; but the mass of the Liberals want war against these three elements and would welcome it. The Ministry in fact lags behind its supporters and cannot do anything extreme enough for them. We who lived through the Gladstonian epoch are Troglodytes with the Liberals of today. They would rejoice at a crisis with the army or with the King or with the Ulstermen, and they think the Government have gone much too far in concession and moderation.
>
> True I was thanked by several of the older men and some of the Government for the speech I made on Tuesday deprecating things being pushed too far, but it is idle not to recognise that the Liberals now are homogeneous in a way they never were before . . .
>
> In Parliament there is no one to tell these things to but O'Brien, and he would be furious at hearing the truth. True, too, another blunder by the Government (who seem capable of any folly) may throw the game again into the hands of the Opposition, but, as Birrell said, when they thought their grave was dug the Opposition filled up the cavity. They are not out of the wood of course, and may be unconscious of their own strength, but they may have showed high strategic Parliamentary qualities this week in face of the utmost peril, and I cannot doubt that the constituencies, where the classes are not in the majority, will support them.[92]

Healy was fearful that O'Brien would abrogate all restraint in the vehemence of his opposition to Asquith's proposals. He wrote to O'Brien urging support of the bill itself as providing for home rule. However 'the moment Redmond's blasphemy and abomination are engrafted on it we shall oppose the measure, believing that once vivisection takes place a permanent wound has been inflicted on Ireland'.[93]

When on 25 May the Government of Ireland Bill received its third reading, the members of the All-for-Ireland League abstained.[94] O'Brien sought to fix Redmond with the responsibility for partition:

> The game was lost for Ireland the day when the honourable member for Waterford and his friends consented to the Partition of Ireland (*interruptions*) . . . we regard this Bill as no longer a Home Rule Bill, but as a Bill for the murder of Home Rule such as we have understood it all our lives and we can have no hand, act or part in the operation.[95]

Healy's private realism did not inhibit recourse to the conventional pieties of nationalist politics, as in a speech in County Cork at the end of May 1914:

> And now for the first time in seven centuries when the cup of hope was being passed to the lips of Ireland, we are told that the country of St Patrick, the country of Owen Roe O'Neill, the country of Hugh Roe O'Donnell, the country where Irish blood besprinkled Irish grass and darkened it there more than anywhere else in Ireland, that that country must be handed over to the Planters and their descendants (*cries of 'Never'*) . . . Are you going to part with St Patrick for the sake of John Redmond? Are you going to part with the most sacred and historic spots in our country to convenience the Liberal Party?[96]

In July 1914, Healy's assessment of the prospects for a satisfactory measure of home rule in July 1914 was nevertheless more sanguine than that of many of the Irish party. He wrote to Maurice in mid-July that

> my conception of the whole business is that the Royal Assent will be given to the Home Rule Bill, that the Amending Bill will be dropped, and that there will be a Dissolution announced as soon as the Royal Assent is given. Carson cannot rebel with the prospect of his Party coming into office and repealing the Bill thus open to him.[97]

25

The Great War

We are now perilously close to the end of all things.

Cork Free Press, 4 Aug. 1914.

The Outbreak of War

As of 4 August 1914 Europe was at war. The outbreak of the First World War was to have incalculable consequences for the prospects for home rule, and for parliamentary nationalism in Ireland. Few if any nationalist parliamentarians at Westminster anticipated the repercussions, expecting instead a rapid victory by the powers of the triple entente, Great Britain, France and Russia. Healy was no exception. He approved of the government's action: 'I don't think the government have any option save to support France. I quite agree with Grey that, if Germany were victorious, and they remained neutral now, they would be in a pretty pickle at the end of the war'. He likewise agreed with Redmond's support of the government in parliament the previous day.[1]

Influenced in part by the favourable impression Redmond's speech had created, his initial assessment of the war's implications for home rule was sanguine. 'If, in the wake of allied victories, Asquith was to confirm that the home rule bill would be enacted forthwith, I don't see what Carson could do, as it would be intolerable to English feeling that he should show himself irreconcilable just now. There has never been such a chapter of political accidents as have occurred this session'.[2] The next day, en route to London, he observed that 'as Redmond lunched with Asquith yesterday, it would seem a treasonable repast unless he secures the Royal Assent to the bill in this month. The Party are to meet tomorrow, and there is great dissension amongst them . . .'[3]

Healy quickly realised that the ramifications of war were more complex, and less favourable, to home rule than he had initially imagined. It was a period, as he wrote in his memoirs, of 'racking anxiety'. He feared that the government intended to propose, and to prevail on Redmond to accept, the exclusion of at least five counties from home rule for the duration of the war, with the assurance that after the war the issue would be reconsidered. Of Redmond's predicament he wrote to his brother:

> I sounded O'Brien as to whether, if Redmond made any overture with a view to peace, he would respond; and he said nothing would induce him to rejoin Redmond's Party but he was willing to 'co-operate' with them. I don't think Redmond will agree to make any concession as to the exclusion unless he knows that O'Brien and his friends will not accept them, and I don't see how we can refrain from attacking them unless the Party was re-united.

He had seen Carson after speaking to O'Brien:

> I tried to make Carson see the importance for England of conferring Home Rule just now, but he thinks he can't desert his Covenanters who, he says, cannot realise how small they loom in the present situation. He doesn't want to be handed down as the Lundy who betrayed Ulster!! There is not, I believe any chance of his making a concession to ease the situation, but the question is whether Redmond will accept the formula for the omission of North East Ulster pending the war. I don't believe he can do so.[4]

The impact of the war on the prospects for home rule was in fact wholly adverse. The outbreak of hostilities brought about an immediate realignment between government and opposition at Westminster. Even though a coalition government was not formed until May 1915, the freedom of action of Asquith's Liberal administration on Irish matters was drastically curtailed. The Irish party's hold on the balance of power disappeared. The prosecution of the war took precedence over the resolution of the Irish question. The increased political role of the military, signalled in the appointment of the obtusely anti-nationalist Kitchener as Secretary of State for War, was to have disastrous consequences for constitutional nationalism. Contrary to Healy's initial assessment, it was Redmond rather than Carson who was hostage to the fortunes of war.

By 22 August, Healy was fully alive to the threat the war posed to home rule. An extended postponement of the bill's coming into effect would be opposed by the Irish party and unionists alike. From the government's point of view the politically compelling alternative was partition. He wrote to Maurice:

> Accordingly my impression is that the Government will seek the easier solution of omitting five counties altogether. Redmond could vote against it if the Opposition agreed to support the Government, as they now do; and Asquith could accompany the Bill with a declaration that it was only a temporary expedient during the war, and that he would try to devise a better solution meanwhile!! My forecast has the advantage of relieving the King of a painful duty under the Parliament Act . . . Redmond's power is gone, and so is that of the Welshmen and the Labour men once we have reached practically a Coalition basis, and of course the Tories don't want now to come into Office, and they are now treated by the Cabinet, so far as official information goes, as if they were members of it. The German success in Belgium cannot be ignored . . . We shall have been three weeks at war by Tuesday and, unless some victory then arrives, the Government will I think be in a very subdued mood, and will tell Redmond that they can't do more for him than what the Opposition agree to, namely the passage of the Bill by the Lords with the exclusion of the disputed counties.[5]

O'Brien circulated a memorandum to Asquith among others proposing that Ulster be given a direct suspensory veto on any bill of the Irish parliament, as well as increased representation in an Irish parliament.[6] On 18 September the home rule bill was enacted along with an amending act suspending its operation to a date to be determined 'not being later than the end of the present war'. The government was further pledged to giving parliament the opportunity in the interval of passing amending legislation to make special provision for Ulster.[7] A rift was thereby opened between Redmond's support of the war effort and the enactment of a home rule measure acceptable to Irish opinion within which national disillusion would fester throughout the long duration of the war.

In the Commons, Redmond had committed the Irish Volunteers, he hoped in conjunction with the Ulster Volunteers, to the defence of Ireland against Germany. Healy was squarely behind Redmond's stance: 'If the Irish make the blunder of not acting on Redmond's advice as to the Volunteers, and show themselves kickers, it will be simply playing into Carson's hands. Our friends should lend no countenance to any such manifestations'.[8]

Far from dissenting from Redmond's backing of the government, Healy and O'Brien sought if anything to surpass the Irish party in ardour. Healy was concerned to neutralise the effect of Irish unionist support for the war; O'Brien believed that solidarity in arms could dissolve Irish unionist resistance to home rule. 'Finding him so eager to help in the war', Healy proposed to O'Brien that they should declare their willingness to sign a joint address with Dillon and Redmond to Irish exiles abroad explaining the motives for their action.

> He said this was a good idea, but how to approach Redmond? I said 'leave that to me', and I went straight to Asquith, who had just been holding a Cabinet meeting, and strange to say my visit to Downing Street was missed by all the papers today. He was engaged with Simon, and received me very cordially, and when I told him the short purpose of my visit he was quite moved. 'This', he said, 'is most important, and I will never forget it', and his eyes moistened. He said he wanted some encouragement just now. So I left. I believe today that the reason of his speech today was the refusal of Redmond and Dillon to agree to our proposal.
>
> There was an ugly scene in the House today, which would have developed but Asquith pleaded, when Dillon rose, that there should be no further discussion. The Party grew very restive, and evidently considered themselves sold.[9]

On 2 September 1914, at a meeting in Cork City Hall, O'Brien passionately endorsed the war effort. He argued that 'we must be either open friends or open enemies of England'. Referring to the nationalist adage that England's difficulty was Ireland's opportunity, he declared that in supporting the war they had 'a priceless opportunity to give a new and magnanimous meaning to that ancient maxim'.[10] Frank Gallagher, the London correspondent and later editor of O'Brien's *Cork Free Press* (as much later of the *Irish Press*), was dismayed. An astute supporter of Sinn Féin, he regarded O'Brien as 'the nearest of the National leaders to Sinn Féin', who had 'kept much of the Fenian spirit'. He had vainly sought to dissuade O'Brien from making his Cork speech, arguing that while the All-for-Ireland League could become an important force in the emergent new nationalism, support for the war would destroy his influence. Gallagher's warning was to prove correct. The circulation of the *Cork Free Press* went into a decline, and support for the All-for-Ireland League began to fall away.[11]

O'Brien's fervour anticipated John Redmond's at Woodenbridge on 20 September. The Irish leader urged his audience of Volunteers 'to account yourselves as men, not only in Ireland itself but wherever the firing-line extends, in defence of right, of freedom, and of religion in this war'. This speech split the Volunteers into a majority of National Volunteers loyal to Redmond and the dissentient remnant of the Irish Volunteers.[12]

If Healy's public expressions of his views were somewhat more guarded, his attitude did not differ from Redmond's or O'Brien's. He went so far as to comment fecklessly to Maurice on 24 September that 'if Redmond had any sense he would allow a Conscription Bill to be carried for Ireland during the war, so as to put an end to all Orange outcry or competition of loyalty, and then he would have a trained army to cope with them after the war was over'.[13] As late as April 1916, the *Freeman's Journal* felt able to refer, if provocatively, to Healy and O'Brien as 'valiant supporters of the war and recruiting'.[14] Likewise William Martin Murphy did what he could to promote recruitment. He wrote in November 1915 to a conference of Dublin employers convened by the Lord Lieutenant stating that Wimborne's views would be conveyed to the employees of any venture with which he was associated, and agreeing to facilitate enlistment 'by undertaking to keep the men's positions open, and by some monetary encouragement as well'.[15]

The strange alliance between Healy and O'Brien endured and even strengthened. Healy wrote to Maurice on 10 December 'I had a nice letter from O'Brien today, addressed, for the first time since the Split, "My dear Tim . . ."' Healy's assessment of the political prospect was sombre:

> I am beginning to fear that Redmond has not gained anything by the placing of Home Rule on the Statute Book under the Parliament Act, beyond the moral effect of a verbal resolution in favour of Home Rule. I think the Ministry will have become completely stale, or so immersed in larger problems owing to the war, that they will patch up any compromise with Carson. Certainly the effect of the Ulstermen's enlistments over-topping those of all the other three Provinces will not be ignored. Redmond's hold of the balance of power has now disappeared; and he will be I fear treated accordingly. The feeling of gratitude towards him which was rife before the war effaced it, on account of his services to the Liberals, will by now have vanished, and the whole Irish situation will be viewed in a new light. There will be no one left inside the Government to make a fight for Ireland, and there is no one in the Liberal party capable or desirous of doing so.

This was Healy at his most lucid. The war had shifted the parliamentary arithmetic adversely to home rule. While the leadership of the Irish party could hardly be held responsible, it was clear that Healy would not be able for long to withstand the temptation to attack Redmond. He continued:

> It is now the artificial split created by Redmond tells most against the interests of the cause . . . According to my chauffeur Pat, everyone is

> opposed to his recruiting campaign. While the people are not pro-German they think the price too high for the kind of Home Rule that has been granted. Apparently O'Brien is not blamed for his attitude at all by those who take this view!![16]

Redmond's predicament was deepened by the refusal of the War Office, which had agreed to the establishment of an Ulster Division based on the Ulster Volunteer Force, to accede to Redmond's request for an Irish Division drawn mainly from the ranks of the National Volunteers. Healy wrote to O'Brien of the Irish party on Christmas Eve 1914:

> This brace of poltroons have I believe been 'rattled' by the anti-recruiters, and are limp enough. I don't think there is much pro-Germanism, but the farmers don't want their sons to leave their work, and perhaps return cripples, or not at all. The young priests hate the French anticlericals and talk of Austria's Catholicity. Our stalwarts (even in Cooley) are so persecuted by the Redmondites, that they think we should have left Johnnie to 'fry in his own fat', and blame us for coming to his rescue.
>
> I am against anything save newspaper pellets for the Bridgeguards, at present. I entirely concur in what you write (and I 'average' two words out of three mostly) and we must prepare the way by newspaper shrapnel first. I will try Murphy again.[17]

In this instance, Healy was seeking to hold O'Brien back, admittedly for reasons which had as much to do with the maintenance of their joint political credibility as with any eagerness to assist Redmond.

He had however a much sharper appreciation than O'Brien of the political constraints under which Redmond was operating, which reduced the frequency if not the ferocity of his attacks on the Irish party leadership. He also had a stronger commitment than O'Brien to Britain and its allies in the war. His eldest son Joe, a barrister, for whom he obtained a commission from Winston Churchill, enlisted.[18]

Healy oscillated phlegmatically. While generally a restraining influence on O'Brien, he yielded readily to the opportunities of the moment, and the urge to revenge himself upon the Irish party leadership. His position in his last four years as a parliamentarian was one of extreme flexibility as he responded to the dissolution of the Irish parliamentary *ancien régime*. Uncoupled from any rigid posture, he permitted himself to be borne by the tide of events, floating free as the old order crumbled around him.

Healy wrote to Maurice in late May 1915 of his attempts to dissuade O'Brien from precipitate action. He identified the two constraints on their communications: the illegibility of O'Brien's handwriting, and his well-justified fear that O'Brien would one day seek to publish his letters:

> This plunge redhot into things is one of his characteristics, and I will not be a party to it, as I believe I understand Parliamentary tactics at least as well as he does. Most of his three letters I am quite unable to decipher!!
>
> Of course I can't write him everything I know that has passed, because I could not be sure that some day or other my letters would not be published in a Diary or otherwise!![19]

Healy was instinctively more hostile to Sinn Féin than was O'Brien. He wrote to his brother in April 1915 that 'it is plain the Sinn Fein party here have no German money, because they could not raise a fee to brief me on their bail motion, and of course I would not do it for nothing in such a case, as I have no sympathy for them'.[20] While the rising the following year was to force Healy to revise his cost-benefit analysis of dealing with Sinn Féin, he remained for long sceptical. He realised that over-reaction on the part of the authorities was furthering the advance of Sinn Féin and the resurgence of republicanism. In 1915 he advocated to O'Brien opposing Birrell's retention as Chief Secretary on the grounds that he was part of 'the game which has gone on here for years, through Dillon's getting nominations for jobs — which is, the housebreaker is allowed entrance by the watchdog to whom he throws drugged meat'. Sir Matthew Nathan, the Under-Secretary, should go also: 'He is responsible for all these petty prosecutions of the Sinn Fein asses'.[21]

Part of Healy's hostility was attributable to his realisation that Sinn Féin would never make common cause with O'Brien and himself. Noting the failing popularity of the party by December 1915, he wrote irritably: 'At the same time the Sinn Fein gang never come into our bay, and run a rig of their own. They are a silly lot'. He was nevertheless a little intrigued, advising his brother that 'there is a cleverly-written Sinn Féin paper called *Nationality* published weekly, which is worthy of study sometimes'.[22]

The war was considerably less popular in Ireland than among the Irish political class at Westminster. In a characteristic exercise in sectarian realism, Healy in 1915 discerned a fleeting moment of conjuncture in Ulster politics: 'All Ulster, including the Orangemen, is I think pro-German. Outside the towns none of the Protestants have enlisted, nor will they do so. They say the Kaiser is a good Protestant!! The priests, on account of Austria, are in the same boat'.[23]

The war did not suspend Healy's capacity for intrigue. With the formation of the coalition government, it was envisaged that the Irish unionist James Campbell would replace Sir Ignatius O'Brien as Lord Chancellor of Ireland. Healy worked hard to ensure that the appointment of Campbell went through, seeing it as a serious blow to the Irish party 'as it cuts them off from the magistrates'. On 28 May he prematurely reported victory to Maurice: 'I have had my revenge upon Ignatius. Yesterday he was firmly in the saddle under the contract with Redmond that the Irish offices are to be left intact. Today, thanks to my efforts, James Campbell is Chancellor'. The Irish party, however, succeeded in thwarting Campbell's appointment: 'They threatened, I hear, to raise Ireland against the Government, and throw the country into turmoil. I expect it is all Dillon's work'.[24] Campbell had to wait. He was appointed Attorney General for Ireland in April 1916, and Lord Chief Justice of Ireland later that year. In June 1918 he was at last appointed Lord Chancellor, a position he relinquished just before the setting up of the Irish state, and was raised to the peerage as Lord Glenavy. Making his peace with the new *régime*, he was appointed Cathaoirleach of the Senate.[25]

Healy's analysis of the state of the Irish question alternated between astute parliamentary realism and a somewhat flippant dismissal of the position of northern Irish unionists. He wrote to O'Brien in mid-1915

> As to the negotiations, I prefer Court Martials.
>
> If Asquith thought they would eventuate fruitfully, he would hardly have remitted them to Lloyd George, to give him Kudos . . .
>
> To say 'partition' is ruled out is to say everything is ruled out, as the Ulstermen would have any other settlement save Ulster's exclusion, and loathe that. I therefore conclude that nothing will result, but I do know that the Orangemen are in terror of Redmond accepting Home Rule for three provinces and if that were agreed to in the secrecy of negotiation they would then commence counterproposals for an All-Ireland scheme. It is a game of bluff, this demand for exclusion. They hate it as much as we do and are relying on our hatred of it to accomplish their design of obstructing all reform. The moment anyone has the pluck to say 'yes, out with them', the next day they will turn round and try to fabricate an alternate scheme.
>
> I am therefore of opinion that to resist exclusion up to the eleven-thirtieth hour is good business, but that to break off on it is not, as when or if we yield (in private negotiation) their trouble begins.[26]

While Healy was admittedly seeking, as he habitually did, to restrain O'Brien, it is revealing that this whimsical analysis was written by a man whom many regarded as the most alert, astute and cynical Irish nationalist parliamentarian. His privileged access to unionist politicians at Westminster had led him to draw the erroneous conclusion that the Ulster-centred opposition to home rule was a feint.

In May 1915 Asquith had been obliged to reconstitute his government as a coalition. While Healy condemned the Irish party as a satellite of the Liberals, he was himself increasingly drawn into the orbit of the Conservatives. To a degree unique among nationalist parliamentarians, he was privy to Conservative disaffection within Asquith's administration. He wrote to Maurice on 1 September 1915 that he had met Bonar Law 'who merely said things were very bad, and that if he had known what he now knows, he would not have joined with the Liberals. I think this is very reasonable, and that the Tories were taken in and had not the least idea of the true state of affairs'.[27]

Healy's exposure to Tory table-talk served to deepen his already exaggerated belief that fundamental conflicts could be mediated by the kind of initiatives of which he believed Redmond and Dillon incapable of undertaking. Thus on the subject of partition, he wrote to Maurice outlining a proposal of remarkable *naïveté*:

> Recruiting has been slackened because they believe there will be compulsion. I think some moderate compulsion will be applied: that is, the compulsion of men in tweed, but not of men in corduroys. They would willingly leave Ireland out; but the Irish should make a bargain for Home Rule being brought into immediate operation in return for a promise to raise a quota. That is a matter which O'Brien should also consider whether he would not take the initiative upon. It need not mean the existing Home Rule Act, but some immediate form of self-government, which should be quickly and unanimously passed, giving a Council executive power, and further power of framing a scheme afterwards. I suggested this to F. E. Smith, and he said he would mention it to Lloyd George.
>
> Dillon made a very good speech the other night against Conscription, but was careful in both his speeches not to pledge himself absolutely against it in all circumstances. Only that I was quite alone, I was disposed to rise and express my agreement with him, but that might have offended O'Brien. I therefore held my tongue, and left the House early last night . . . I don't think they can win the war without conscription.[28]

The war was going badly. Healy was influenced by Beaverbrook's bleak assessment of the capacity of the allied command: 'the way Max criticises the generals at the front would make your hair curl'.[29] While in the absence of adequate intelligence he thought the war 'a prize-fight in which no-one can predict the result on our present state of information', he was dismayed in late August by the prevalent gloom in London: 'I have heard England's defeat prophesied as a certainty unless we change our managements and our commanders within the next month'.[30] Beaverbrook told Healy that he had made all his business arrangements on the basis that they were beaten, or that it would be a stalemate.[31] He wrote to Maurice in mid-October:

> I lunched today with Max, F.E., and Guest. They are all strong about the way the War is being 'messed', and I don't think it will be long before there is an explosion of protest.
>
> On the other hand, if they shunt Asquith or change Kitchener, it will

> disturb confidence in England, which has been opiated into somnolence, and would probably cause division where unity is essential.
>
> The present Ministry will not hold together. This would be important in its effect on the Irish situation if O'Brien would only attend here to take advantage of whatever is being organised.[32]

On 19 October Carson resigned as Attorney General in protest at the mishandling of the war. Healy wrote to Maurice on 3 November that Carson's speech the day before 'had made a bad impression on me, and I don't think the intrigue to shunt Asquith can now succeed'. That evening German bombs fell on Gray's Inn where Healy was dining.[33] He had other cause for concern. He and his wife had visited their son Joe, a barrister, at Blandford Camp before he embarked for Gallipoli. In December, when Joe was on the island of Lemnos, near Gallipoli, Healy wrote to Maurice: 'This Dardanelles business is the worst thing in British annals, and if Churchill is wise he will get himself killed, for it will not be forgiven him'.[34]

Healy observed closely and with satisfaction the mounting despondency of the Irish party in late 1915. He reported to Maurice in October that 'All the Redmond party are here, and looking disconsolate. Dillon is wearing a violet-hued coat, very badly fitting, and looks odd'.[35] By now there were deep differences between Redmond and Dillon, as the latter grew more infuriated at the government's treatment of nationalist Ireland, and the protraction of a war about which he had never ceased to have the gravest reservations.[36] Healy wrote in November: 'Redmond's speech yesterday was good in parts. . . . Dillon, to show his aloofness, stood at the Bar jingling money in his pockets'.[37]

O'Brien had increasingly withdrawn from the parliamentary fray, and his relations with Healy grew somewhat testy. Healy in turn was irritated by O'Brien's disdain for Westminster politics. He had 'small Parliamentary aptitude'. Conveying to Maurice comments at Westminster, he added 'of course this is what O'Brien calls "gossip"'. He complained that O'Brien 'thinks he understands Parliamentary opinion, and is further away from it than his cook'.[38]

Healy's strictures were not confined to the Irish side. He wrote to his brother that the British parties 'really are no less small-minded than the Parnellites and ourselves at the time of the Split. The abuse on each side is just the same sort of stuff. The articles in the English papers are contemptible sometimes'.[39] He had attained, if not quite sagacity, at least a degree of enlightened weariness of splits.

The 1916 Rising

Beaverbrook telephoned Tim Healy in Dublin, asking on Bonar Law's behalf, for news of the Easter Rebellion:

'Is there a rebellion?'
'There is!' said Tim.
'When did it break out?'
'When Strongbow invaded Ireland!'
'When will it end'
'When Cromwell gets out of Hell!'
Beaverbrook, *The Decline and Fall of Lloyd George*[40]

Irish politics were transformed by the rising of Easter 1916, or rather by the execution by firing party of the leaders which followed. The dismissal by constitutional nationalists of the rebellion as a futile gesture which recklessly jeopardised the lives of its participants and compromised the Irish position in a United Kingdom at war, yielded to a disconcerted realisation that the futility of the gesture was central to the surreal logic of its instigators. Healy was taken unawares as much as anyone else. Five weeks before he had witnessed five hundred members of the Irish Volunteers march past the General Post Office on St. Patrick's Day. 'They were quiet and orderly, but their port was not impressive.'[41]

O'Brien in London despatched an editorial to the *Cork Free Press* deploring the 'heart-breaking folly' of the rebellion. It was a sign of the times that this was met with a mutiny of the staff, all of whom were Sinn Féin supporters, and O'Brien was forced to agree a compromise policy which treaded a careful line between embracing Sinn Féin (thereby inviting suppression) and attacking it.[42]

On 30 April, the first day that travel was permitted after the rising, Healy hastened to London, concerned to prevent further executions and reprisals.[43] He spoke in the Commons on 11 May. While he was not overlooking the fact of the rebellion, or that it 'broke out at a moment when it was evidently done in concert with Germany', he attacked the response of the authorities in Dublin as 'foolish, and in some respects I might say insane'. It was moreover disproportionate: the rising was 'grossly exaggerated'.

> And for the sake of a revolt of 1,500 men, which I, old as I am, would have put down with the police, what did you do? For forty-eight hours you rained shells upon the poor old city, sometimes at the rate of fifteen to twenty shells a minute, sounding like the thuds of the clods on a father's coffin to those who love that city.

It was a shrewdly pitched speech which revealed Healy's determination to use the rising to strike at the Irish party. He denounced Redmond and Dillon 'with regard to the policy they have pursued for the last five or six years', and called for 'no more secret government from North Great George's Street' (where John Dillon lived).[44]

With a perversity which recalled its late editor William F. Dennehy, the *Irish Independent*, after the rising had been put down, worked itself into a frenzy on the necessity for stern measures. At a time when the main leaders of the rebellion, with the exception of the socialist James Connolly, had been executed, the paper warned against leniency towards the surviving leaders to meet 'an indiscriminate demand for clemency'. The fact that these editorials directly preceded, and coincided with, Connolly's execution gave rise to the charge that Murphy had used his newspaper to settle a score with his old adversary from the lock-out of 1913, whom the *Independent* had then described as 'a much abler and more plausible person than Mr. Larkin'. The charge would haunt Murphy for the short remainder of his life. The *Leader* missed no opportunity to deride the *Independent* as 'the champion of Dark Rosaleen and the advocate of James Connolly's execution'. With curious symmetry, Murphy became in popular demonology in relation to Connolly what Healy had long been in relation to Parnell, his enemy's assassin.[45]

Murphy had not in fact been responsible for the controversial editorials,[46] and in due course, like many of his nationalist countrymen, underwent a process of at least partial conversion. The effects of this were described by Healy to his brother in October 1916.

> . . . he is very blooded against Redmond, but it is pathetic how unable he is to grasp the means of using the power of his paper. It is like seeing water-power unharnessed. He spoke very feelingly when I told him to deal with amnesty, and to bring out Redmond's and Mooney's acquiescence in the sentences, as compared to the blame showered on him when he was not responsible and did not know of the articles recommending 'vigour', and that they were written by Harrington, and, until his attention was called to them, he had not even read them. He was evidently greatly affected by the thought that he had been accused of advising the shooting of Connolly, owing to the antagonism the man showed him. He said of course at first he felt bitter against the insurgents but, finding all the Tories gloating over the executions and imprisonments, he said every drop of Irish blood in his veins surged up, and he began, like others, to sympathise with them. He was quite moved; and his face flushed. I told O'Brien, and it pleased and surprised him.[47]

The suppression of the rebellion transformed the prospects for Sinn Féin. Disaffection was contagious. Healy wrote to his brother in late May that 'the arrests made in Ireland by the military have aroused dreadful bitterness, which I am beginning to feel myself'.[48] Writing again the following month, he mused on the political and moral ironies of the rebellion:

> The London Government now admits that Maxwell's ferocity was a mistake, but they can't get rid of him, and they can't release their victims for fear of their becoming further centres of 'infection'. They are like men who forged bills of exchange, and must forge more to keep themselves afloat. The doses of the drug must be increased . . .
>
> I don't know if the Dublin feeling has spread to Cork, but amongst moderate Catholics who are intensely loyal I find nothing but Sinn Fein sentiment. I don't care to mention names, as letters are opened, but I heard of one man, whose son was burned alive at Suvla Bay, who said he would now rather the Germans won. The looting of the soldiers – downright robbery and ruffianism against innocent people – the shocking ill-treatment of the prisoners, the insolence of the military in the streets, the foul language used to women, and the incompetence shown, all have aroused contempt and hatred for which there is no parallel in Irish history in our days. The small boys are singing: 'Who fears to speak of Easter week, who blushes at the name'!!
>
> Now the military have changed their tone, and the wind that blew north nearly three weeks ago is blowing south today. All to no purpose. They have lost the heart of this people beyond all hope of retrieving their mistakes. The clerics have discovered that 'a probable hope of success' in rebellion does not necessarily mean military success, and that Pearse achieved his object. Anyhow he builded better than he knew. I think Maxwell would now give a good deal to have him back safe and sound in jail.[49]

Healy continued to reflect upon, and to tease his brother with, the paradox of the insurrection: 'As one of the essentials to justify rebellion, in addition to a just cause, is the probable hope of success, this has been one of the most successful rebellions in the world from the standpoint of its authors. It has revolutionised Irish feeling, and I suppose that was what Pearse aimed at'.[50] This standing on its head of the Catholic moral law was an aspect of a larger transformation. Aside from its immediate political effect, the rising was to have profound ideological consequences in the longer term. Modern Irish nationalism was in time to be 'changed utterly' by the rising's appropriation of a Catholic idiom of sacrifice. This was not an accretion of later legend: with morbid deliberation Pearse had pre-inscribed a myth which the rising would activate. The premeditated cult of 1916 seemed to invest the posthumous myth of Parnell by contrast with an elegiac innocence.

After the Rising

While Healy condemned – if in somewhat formulaic fashion – the party's failure to resist partition, he was unable to proffer a politically coherent alternative. William O'Brien retained a messianic conviction that he could interpose to avert the exclusion of all or part of Ulster. Healy wrote to his brother on 22 May 1916:

> I had a long talk with Bonar Law, and I have arranged for him to meet O'Brien tomorrow night. He says there is no chance of a settlement unless on the basis of the exclusion of Ulster, and I fear this is true. The exclusion he spoke of was for five or six years. I don't think O'Brien will yield an inch. There is no doubt the others have agreed, I believe . . . The Redmondites are utterly crushed and broken-looking.[51]

As Healy had anticipated, O'Brien's encounter with Bonar Law foundered on the question of Ulster. Healy at O'Brien's request arranged a meeting with Lloyd George two days later. On 30 May O'Brien met Lloyd George and Carson together. The only consequence of their meeting was to deepen O'Brien's conviction that a settlement could be achieved by appealing to the sentiment of Irish nationality which he devoutly believed dwelt in the stoutest Ulster unionist breast.[52]

O'Brien's last venture in high politics was a memorandum to Lloyd George the day after their meeting. A characteristic essay in wishful thinking, it was expansively conciliatory to all, with the single exception of the Irish party. O'Brien advocated 'an "agreed" debate' in the Commons – a concept which he alone could have conceived – to be initiated by a message from the King. He conceded that the difficulties would be immense, but 'slight compared with those of setting up a Provisional Government while the present fever lasts'. He proposed a resolution seeking by conciliation and conference a solution to the problem of Irish self-government which would be acceptable in all quarters of the country. He was confident that Redmond and Devlin would subscribe to this, and that Dillon 'who had lost all weight with moderate opinion and will never succeed in disarming the Sinn Feiners' resentment at his venomous attacks on them up to the eve of the rising, would either accept the situation or make a miserable end to his political career'. He was persuaded that Carson would acquiesce in 'a new Federal arrangement which would secure to the Ulstermen substantially the same rights of imperial citizenship as Englishmen, Scotsmen or Welshmen'. Still more remarkably, he added that 'it can hardly be doubted that Mr. Bonar Law, Mr. Walter Long, and other men who carry weight in Ulster would co-operate with all their might'. He received no reply from Lloyd George.[53]

O'Brien's purpose was transparent. He was gripped by the fear of a swift concession of home rule in the wake of the rising. Ostensibly the reason for his concern was that this would inflame unionist opinion and copper-fasten partition; it also owed something to the dread of the concession of an Irish parliament which the Irish party would be in a position in dominate. From the point of view of Lloyd George, this could only be construed as a message that O'Brien and his allies were prepared to support any initiative to thwart the Irish party leadership that did not expressly countenance partition. Moreover, that O'Brien should advance such an unrealistic proposal suggested that his already tenuous relationship to political reality had finally snapped: the strain of reconciling the intractable divisions on the Irish question had proved too much for him. Thereafter he turned his attention increasingly away from Westminster. With inane self-regard he protested in September 1916: 'Without any pretension to the perfection of turning the other cheek to the smiter, I have on eight separate occasions exposed myself to humiliation by offers of co-operation in the country's interest, and have never received an answering word of kindness'.[54]

Healy was instinctively a politician in a way that those about him were not. As O'Brien withdrew from the fray, he was left to address the parliamentary unfolding of a solution to the Irish question. His brother was by now far more a Cork solicitor than a Westminster parliamentarian, and was implacably hostile to the Irish party and Sinn Féin alike. William Martin Murphy had at last asserted himself, but lacked political sophistication. With the naïve obduracy of an entrepreneur and newspaper proprietor in politics, he exaggerated his capacity to influence events, and in particular to achieve his *idée fixe*, the averting of partition.

In the wake of the rising, the government had sought again to find a way forward on the Irish question. Lloyd George was entrusted with the negotiation of a solution. He proposed the immediate grant of home rule with the exclusion of the six north-east counties. The difficulty was that the unionists and nationalists, with whom he conducted separate bilateral negotiations, were given conflicting versions of his proposals. The nationalists were given to understand that partition would be limited to the duration of the war only, while the unionists were presented with partition as a final exclusion of Ulster as a quid pro quo for the concession of home rule to the rest of Ireland. Carson on this basis was prevailed on to convince a recalcitrant Ulster Unionist Council in Belfast that home rule could not be resisted for the rest of Ireland, and of the wisdom of accepting the exclusion of six of the nine Ulster counties. Redmond acceded to the exclusion of the six counties on what was, he allowed himself to be persuaded, a temporary basis.[55]

Healy believed a partitionist settlement, of an avowedly temporary nature, to be imminent. 'If the Party hacks are indication, it is all cut and dried.' However, alarmed by the shift of events in Ireland in the direction of armed strife, he was not prepared to dismiss this out of hand. He wrote to his brother that he would need persuading 'before I offer absolute resistance *à outrance* to any proposal which may bring about temporary peace. Of course I hate the scheme, but that is a different question from the question of expedience'.[56]

Healy was far more pragmatic than his unyielding public demeanour suggested. He remained surprisingly sanguine, in part because of his conviction that Irish unionists did not ultimately wish for a partitionist outcome, and in part because he was caught up in the drama at Westminster:

> The Orange gang and the Soupers are evidently in terror lest some Bill should pass, and I confess their hatred of it makes me think something should be done. It will be easy for the Tories to repeal the Home Rule Act, but it would not be easy to upset such an Act as George contemplates, and it must I think lead to something better. I have not expressed this opinion to anyone but you and a little to O'Brien. To everyone else I said *Non Possumus.* I don't however suppose anything will be attempted now, as the Redmondites will be too cowed to connive as they intended at George's plans.
>
> Carson practically told the Belfast conference that a Bill would be passed willy nilly, and the fellows in the six counties were delighted and those in the three howled!! If he gets the six counties delegates to declare they are bound by the three counties mens' covenant, he will wear an air of sweet reasonableness although declaring himself absolutely powerless. It is hard to see where Carson's political cleverness lies except in results!! He has absolutely beaten the entire Irish Party and the Liberals together. Of course he had only numbskulldom opposed to him as far as the Irish were concerned, and the public don't know that.[57]

While Healy held back, the *Irish Independent*, as he put it, 'slaughtered' the Irish party: 'Lloyd George and Samuel both complained to Murphy about it'.[58] William Martin Murphy was more truly diehard than Healy. He went to London to see Lloyd George at the start of June and wrote two weeks later to warn of the disastrous consequences of partition. 'During my lifetime there were three Rebellions in Ireland – in '48, '68 and 1916, all arising from the same cause, viz. the falling away of Independence of the Irish Parliamentarians and their failure to assert themselves at Westminster. I want the recent rebellion to be the last'. Lloyd George, instinctively thinking in terms of a bloc he could mobilise against the Irish party, replied expressing the hope that he would have a further opportunity before any course was settled upon of meeting Murphy, O'Brien and Healy. Murphy cannot have been pleased to have been thus linked with O'Brien.[59]

On 15 June Healy embarked upon what he described as 'a hard experiment', meeting Lloyd George to propose a scheme of his own. He proposed that Lloyd George introduce the bill he intended excluding the six counties, but with a plebiscite under which the voters would be given the choice of accepting the bill or accepting home rule for all Ireland with an elaborate voting system he had devised. The electoral registers were to be divided between those holding property above a rateable valuation of £100, and all other voters. Each group would return one member to an Irish parliament, and elect equal numbers of members of local authorities. This arrangement would give northern Protestants the incentive of underwriting the position of their southern brethren. Healy summarised for his brother what he considered to be the wider merits of the scheme: 'My system would leaven local bodies with a respectable element, and would kill the power of the Mollies. I believe it would give the Protestants half the representation in many cases, and I can't see what harm this would do — once the National question was settled'. He hoped that if the scheme found favour, it might prove possible to avoid the proposed plebiscite altogether. If the scheme was well regarded by the Irish unionists when debated in the Commons 'then, when the Bill reached the Lords, let them knock out of it the part creating a separate enclave, and simply pass it for all Ireland as a joint Local Government Reform and Parliament Act'.[60]

Healy's highly contrived scheme had little to commend it. Apart from its democratically regressive nature, it was predicated on the belief that Ulster unionists would be prepared to submit to a scheme of home rule in which the rights of property were politically entrenched, in solidarity with their co-religionists elsewhere in Ireland. This sentimental premise of nationalist thinking at Westminster was already untenable. While acknowledging an element of 'paternal prejudice', Healy was for the while very pleased with his scheme. He reported to Maurice that 'the wizard liked my plan'. At the suggestion of the Lord Chief Justice he conveyed the proposal to Carson, who 'seemed a man entirely in the hands of his friends, and not to initiate anything'. He also saw Asquith, who 'was very nice, and said I "was always helpful"'.[61]

Even as Redmond's fortunes seemed to sink by the day, O'Brien's prestige suffered a blow from which it would never recover. On 23 June a meeting to protest against the Irish party's acquiescence in partition took place under the auspices of the All-for-Ireland League at Cork City Hall. Not a word of the old orator's declamation could be heard. The galleries were packed by Sinn Féin sympathisers, who sang songs of the rebellion throughout: 'great choruses, rollicking melodies, rapid humorous songs, and when they were not singing they were cheering the names of the 1916 men'. O'Brien carried on with his memorised text, which not even those sitting at the press table below him could hear, 'with all the gestures and all the apparent nonchalance he would normally have shown'.[62] For O'Brien to be unable to command a hearing at meeting in Cork was unprecedented. The mime to which his speech was reduced aptly symbolised his vanished influence.

O'Brien had not invited Healy to the meeting. He was not sorry 'although I took a ticket from Euston to Cork on the chance that he would do so'. The barracking of O'Brien was

> one of the most ungrateful and disgusting incidents I have ever known. It shows what utterly feather-headed creatures these are, and how foolish and impossible their ideas must be. They won't interrupt Redmond or embarrass him in any way, nor his supporters, but attack the only men who tried to do something sound for the country and who have protested against the humbug they declaim against.
>
> Of course it was a pity O'Brien could not have had information, or foreseen this kind of thing, for undoubtedly it injures him very much, and us too.[63]

Deeply demoralised, O'Brien was increasingly disposed to give way to Sinn Féin, and to doubt the possibility of playing an effective role at Westminster. In London a month later, O'Brien did not ask Healy to call. 'Moreton Frewen says he is now in a very gloomy frame of mind, and thinks nothing can be done. With this I entirely differ.'[64]

Redmond had succeeded in carrying the Belfast conference of Ulster nationalists in support of Lloyd George's proposals to bring the home rule act into immediate operation, but with the exclusion of the six north-eastern counties for the duration of the war. Healy privately approved

> Putridly as Redmond has managed our affairs, I must say I think, in the mess he was in, he was right politically to try to force his views on the Belfast convention. Of course he never should have allowed himself to be manoeuvred into such a hopeless situation but, granted that it existed, it would never have done for him to allow it to be said that Carson had carried his crowd, and that he could not carry the Nationalists. I therefore think he showed good political wisdom in forcing the decision he secured yesterday.
>
> I don't suppose such a Bill will ever pass, or that the Orangemen want exclusion, but, it having been proposed, he has now placed the Government and the Southern Unionists in a tight place, and it will be for them to search for some alternative; and this I am sure is what the thing will result in.[65]

Healy thus continued to profess the hope that Redmond's acceptance of partition would call the bluff of the Irish unionists, and open the way for a scheme of moderate home rule of the kind envisaged by O'Brien and himself, offering entrenched guarantees to the unionists. He asserted that the radical drift of British politics could make at least the southern Irish unionists more favourably disposed to a home rule state: 'All the southern Tories regard themselves as having been sold by the English, and would like to be free from British Budgets and Socialism, if they can be assured of a decent Government here'.[66]

The barracking of O'Brien in Cork was an early indication that Sinn Féin was was hardly less antagonistic to O'Brien and Healy than to Redmond and Dillon. Now expressing his belief that Lloyd George's proposals would go through, he wrote petulantly to Maurice on 6 July: 'As the Sinn Fein gang are as hostile to us as they are to Redmond, I confess I shall not kill myself to oppose the scheme. It is worthy of the spirit of Ireland – or rather of its good sense just now when men behave as the Cork crowd did'.[67]

Healy's attitude was profoundly ambivalent. While he joined in the vociferous attacks on the Irish party's acquiescence in partition, and continued privately to express the hope or conviction that the Irish unionists would pull back from the division of the country, he was increasingly persuaded that partition could not be averted:

> As for thinking that the North will ever join in, it is as improbable as that Rathmines [a unionist township of Dublin] would willingly join Dublin. We should be prepared to treat exclusion as permanent . . . Ronald McNeill told me yesterday he was satisfied with the arrangement, and, as he is one of the most determined of the lot, it is clear that exclusion is really desired by the Orange leaders. Certainly William Moore shows satisfaction at being cut off from southern Protestants, who he denounces vehemently as cowards. I have not seen the *Independent* since I came, but the groans of the *Irish Times* are sweet in my ears. The Ascendancy spirit thrives in Dublin quite as much as in Belfast, and it was there, and not in Belfast, that it was originally nurtured.[68]

This was a remarkable expression of Healy's thinking. He was consoling himself with the reflection that even with partition, home rule represented a historic defeat for the southern landlord and Dublin official classes against whom he had pitted himself at the outset of his career. He was summoning up the chauvinism of his nationalism to reconcile himself to the shrinkage of the prospective domain of a home rule state.

The result of the Lloyd George negotiations was a bill introduced on 25 July providing for the permanent exclusion of the six north-eastern counties of Ulster and the reduction of Irish representation in the imperial parliament after the establishment of a home rule parliament. Redmond repudiated the government's proposals, as he had to, but the partitionist lineaments of any Irish settlement were now clearly defined.[69]

As domestic opposition to the Irish party grew, Healy wrote to his brother in August 1916 that it was 'hard to see how Redmond can be rehabilitated', adding with a characteristic flash of candour and self-congratulation: 'we have been vindicated in the most unexpected manner'.[70] He wrote the following month: 'I think the Redmond party can never again command national support, and that the country will not be united on anything for another long spell. We have seen so much of sham unity, I don't suppose it matters'.[71] Avidly chronicling the party's fall from grace, he wrote the following month that 'from all I hear the people have turned with positive hatred from Redmond and his party, not because of the failure of Home Rule, but for their attitude about the Rebellion prisoners'.[72]

Healy remained a fluent and versatile propagandist. In August 1916 the *Cork Free Press* published a poem entitled 'Whistling Jigs to Milestones'. Written by Healy, it coupled an attack on the Irish party ('our well paid witlings writhe with shame, by parliament betrayed'), with a lament in the vein of T. D. Sullivan for the loss of Ulster: 'They've raised as Emmet's monument a broken shaft of shame'. The Irish party's acquiescence in partition was a violation of the axiom of national unity supposedly maintained through centuries of adversity: 'Midst rent and tattered treaties, we mourned no severed land'.[73]

Healy met H. E. Duke, who had just been appointed Chief Secretary, at Murphy's home in Dartry on 28 September 1916.

> I believe Duke is honestly striving to find some way of settling the Home Rule problem, and I don't think Partition will be revived, as far as he is concerned. He evidently met people who complained to him that England had swindled us, and I said: 'So she had'. Then said he: 'Are we a nation of thimble-riggers?', and, 'How can you complain of being swindled and denounce the project which was offered to you?' I said: 'The fact that the offer was only made to twenty-six counties, and that it was not carried out, added to the gravity of the bad faith shown; and we were entitled to say we were swindled even though the measure was unacceptable'. He is an honest man; and I should be sorry if O'Brien did anything to queer his pitch until he gets an opportunity to show his mettle.[74]

Healy was as well disposed to the unionist Duke, later Lord Merrivale, as he had been antipathetic to his Liberal predecessor Augustine Birrell.[75] In a conciliatory interview in the *Sunday Times* in December 1916, he emphasised the Irish yearning for a settlement, and advocated the release of republican prisoners. He looked to Sir Edward Carson and to James Craig as members of the government, both of whom 'may be regarded as men of moderate views among Irish unionists; both are patriots, both are earnest men who desire, I believe, the good of Ireland. But any improvement in the position of Ireland rests with them; they are the neck of the bottle'. He made flattering reference to Duke as the conscientious and well-intentioned occupant of a thankless office ('To be Irish Secretary is like walking about with peas in your boots').[76]

Lloyd George

On 5 December 1916 Asquith resigned as premier, and was succeeded by Lloyd George. The destinies of Healy and Lloyd George appeared inextricably linked. They had once been close. Shortly after Lloyd George was first returned to parliament, for Caernarvon Boroughs in April 1890, they had struck up a friendship, and were often nocturnal drinking companions at the National Liberal Club.[77] The ambitious Welsh radical was fascinated by what he regarded as the Celtic bravura of the mercurial Irish nationalist. He described Healy in a lecture in 1902 as 'the cleverest man in the House of Commons'. His early style bore the traces of his influence. The *Times* wrote in 1904 that 'Lloyd George . . . has added to the reputation for ability he had made in former years, though he shows a tendency to emperil it by an excessive production of epigrammatic and stinging jokes in the style of Mr. Timothy Healy'.[78] H. W. Lucy described the resemblance in more flattering terms: 'Early in his career he suffered from the indiscretion of an enthusiastic countryman who hailed him as "the Welsh Parnell" . . . But he has disclosed a perfect mastery of the subject, a readiness of force and resource in debate, much more nearly resembling the gifts of Mr. Tim Healy than the earlier stages of his career recalled the manner of Mr. Parnell'.[79] The comparison continued to suggest itself in unexpected quarters. John Dillon wrote to T. P. O'Connor in 1924: 'I wonder very much what you think of L.G.'s performance. He reminds me intensely of Healy – a very much bigger Healy'.[80]

Latterly, their relationship became increasingly adversarial, sharpened by an element of personal competitiveness rare between an Irish and a British parliamentarian, and by acute mutual comprehension. Healy had fiercely opposed the Lloyd George budgets of 1909–10, and the National Insurance Bill of 1911. Yet, even in the course of his attempts to block the latter measure, Healy had startled the Commons by observing of the Chancellor, with unexpectedly benign humour, that 'I regard him as my own boy'.[81]

In February 1913, Healy had renewed his onslaught on Lloyd George and the National Insurance Act. The act had limited the state contribution to doctors to a fixed proportion, but Lloyd George had agreed under pressure to an increase, for which he sought to make provision by means of a supplementary estimate. Realising that this was a breach of the requirement that the estimates should be confined to grants authorised by prior legislation, Healy went on to the offensive. On 10 February 1913 he went to the Speaker's home privately to advise him in relation to the point, and wrote to his brother 'I will make Lloyd George pretty sick before I have done with him'.[82] While Lloyd George sought to treat Healy's point with contempt, the government showed increasing discomfiture. At the request of Bonar Law Healy met with the Conservative front bench. Healy then raised the issue again in the Commons. The government was compelled to back down. Asquith announced that the government would introduce the necessary legislation to authorise the appropriation. Healy reported exultantly to his brother:

> I don't know if tomorrow's papers will convey that I have had the triumph of my life over Lloyd George. I don't think any Minister was ever so humiliated. He has funked coming to the House since, and Masterman's reply last night was as insolent as his own. Today I returned to the charge, and Asquith surrendered absolutely, and promised to bring in a Bill to legalise the Estimate!! The Opposition Front Bench thought so highly of the point yesterday that they called me into council, and made a very full house for my speech last night, which was greatly praised. Today when I returned to the attack, the Liberals were as mute as mice, and Asquith's surrender has completely justified everything I did, and completely thrown over George and Masterman. Seldom has there been so complete and dramatic a vindication after such a foul attack. I think the Treasury in future will be more careful in Estimates, and I am sure Asquith gave George, or will give him, a thorough wigging.[83]

When however the Chancellor's political survival was threatened two months later in the Marconi affair, Healy held back. He wrote to his brother that 'I am almost certain Lloyd George spoke to Lord Ashton to square me from attacking him over the Marconi contract', but asserted that the approach was unnecessary.

> O'Brien wanted me to attack him, but I refused. It has nothing to do with Ireland. . . . The Tories knew for the past four months of the Marconi investments, and Isaacs and Lloyd George knew since Christmas. English scandals don't concern us unless they affect the Irish Cause. Despite O'Brien's urgings, I told him I would not assail Lloyd George. Yet he said it was the occasion of a century. I still refused to join in the outcry.[84]

He spoke in the debate, but refrained from condemning Lloyd George 'although he deserves no mercy from us. I rather exculpated him'. He later asserted in his memoirs that he did so 'because Lloyd George, in spite of his gyrations, was mainly on Ireland's side'.[85] His attitude remained deeply ambivalent. He resisted, if a little resignedly, the inexorability of Lloyd George's rise. He wrote to his brother in July 1915:

> Lloyd George is continuing to give trouble, but I believe we have driven him out of thoughts of the Prime Ministership, and that he is now intriguing to be made head of the War Office. That would be fair enough, and I should not object to it. The blunders of the War Office over this war have been dreadful.[86]

He nevertheless had little difficulty accommodating himself to Lloyd George's displacement of Asquith, partly through an affinity of temperament, and partly because he knew that the equilibrium of what he regarded as the Liberal–nationalist cartel would be further destabilised under a Lloyd George premiership. As he observed the continuing decline of the Irish party, he dismissed Dillon as an unregenerate Asquithian, 'true to his old Liberal leanings'. The Irish party in the spring of 1917 was 'playing the Asquith game to down Lloyd George'.[87]

The Politics of Advocacy

From as early as 1915, Healy was appearing for republican prisoners. He defended some of those involved in the rising, including Seán MacEntee, at the court martials which ensued. At the enquiry which arose from the shooting in the course of the rising of the pacifist Francis Sheehy-Skeffington, Healy appeared for his widow.[88] According to an entry in the diary of Beatrice Webb, based on information from Alice Stopford Green, Healy declined to defend Roger Casement, for whom George Gavan Duffy, a solicitor of Sinn Féin sympathies, was acting.[89] Casement was instead defended by Gavan Duffy's brother-in-law Sergeant Sullivan in what was to prove an unhappy choice.[90] Healy visited Frongoch, where Irish prisoners were held, in August 1916.[91]

The fact that Healy spent most of his time in Dublin, plying between Chapelizod and the Law Library, rather than at Westminster, permitted him to monitor better than Redmond or Dillon the rhythm of disaffection in Ireland. He feared a wave of arrests of Sinn Féin sympathisers in early 1917 would lead to mischief: 'There is certain to be some attempt at reprisals, I fear, and I can't believe that Protestants like Darrell Figgis are engaged in the conspiracy which Duke alleges'. Bonar Law informed Healy that information had reached the government, from the same source that had warned in vain of the 1916 rebellion, that another rising was in the offing. A group of those detained however assured Gavan Duffy that they were innocent and did not know why they had been arrested.[92]

Healy felt that he had been put upon and on the train to Holyhead wrote an angry protest to Bonar Law:

> I had no chance to talk to Duke, or I would not pass over his head, to write even to you. I wish to say the information you gave me as warranting the deportations is utterly false.
>
> There is a gang in Ireland who funk the front, and use any excuse *pour se faire valoir.*
>
> I have had a number of the deported seen, and all, with one voice, say they are free from any intent to get up a rising. I have had other enquiries, which point to the capture of American letters advising mischief. If I urged you to betray the King, would that be a proof of your guilt, if my letter were found on you?
>
> It is strange that Redmond's manifesto today unconsciously repeats what I said at our chance *rencontre* viz. that if Bethmann Hollweg were at the helm, he could not better order matters for Germany.
>
> This is not Duke's fault, as he is universally respected. The accursed system, and the fool soldier cum the Khaki policeman, is responsible. You are brewing a black malt and we will have to drink it and our children after us.[93]

Healy's most dramatic court appearance at this time was in late 1917 at the inquest into the death of Thomas Ashe, who had been force-fed while on hunger strike, and whose funeral, reputedly larger than Parnell's, became in Dorothy Macardle's phrase 'a pageant of the nation'. Healy took full advantage of the relative licence of the Coroner's Court to turn the inquest into an arraignment of the government. Rapidly assimilating the idiom of the new nationalism, he characterised the death of Ashe as 'another blood stain on the Irish Calvary'. He waved aloft a letter to the Governor of Mountjoy Prison which he described as 'Ashe's death warrant'. The counsel for the authorities, who became so incensed that he temporarily withdrew in protest, fulminated in vain against Healy as 'a disgrace to the Bar', who 'disregarded every canon of decent advocacy', and engaged in 'conduct unparalleled in the history of the Irish bar'.[94]

Healy's populism as an advocate stood him in good stead. His forensic technique was astutely characterised by William Martin Murphy in relation to a purely commercial case, the determination of the compensation payable to the Dublin department store owned by Murphy for a strip of land compulsorily acquired. Murphy wrote gratefully: 'Tim Healy was counsel for Clery's and he turned it into a state trial'.[95] His court appearances did much to neutralise the hostility towards him and to permit his rehabilitation. Not since the late 1880s had Healy's political and legal roles so profitably complemented each other. These were Healy's first tentative steps in an uncertain transition.

The Irish Convention

In the attack on the Irish party, Murphy's *Irish Independent* had come to the fore. Healy wrote in July 1916: 'Murphy is now a bitterly unconscious "Healyite"!! The paper has been splendid'.[96] The carping quickly resumed, but directed chiefly at Murphy's editor: 'If the *Independent* could be relied on, everything would be hopeful, but Harrington is such a scoundrel, and Murphy is so incompetent to understand anything connected with the real bowels of editorialism, I am afraid his paper can never become a useful asset while Harrington is in control'. As long as Harrington remained, 'nothing can be done in the real smashing of the Party'.[97] Three days after the last comment, however, he described the *Independent* as 'going great guns'.[98]

As the stance of the *Independent* became more belligerently anti-party, Healy's chief criticism was of the belatedness of its conversion. Murphy was himself writing editorials against partition and in favour of full dominion home rule, of which Healy commented: 'They consist unconsciously of the speeches we used to make three or four years ago. It is as bad to be too soon as too late'.[99] He was still infuriated by Murphy's readiness to credit his editor with the success of the paper and its editorial policy. In August 1917 he wrote of Harrington, admittedly to console O'Brien whose attack on the Irish party, later published in pamphlet form, the *Independent* had refused to carry: 'He is the most determined party hack in Ireland, yet Murphy thinks the change is due to him instead of Pearse and de Valera'.[100]

He complained shortly afterwards: 'The weekly paper is full of Parnellism, and I am drawing Murphy's attention to it. One would think Mrs. O'Shea's book would shake this mawkishness'.[101] Healy's vigilance against his old chief never flagged. With Sinn Féin poised to oust the Irish party, a renewal of the cult of Parnell was certainly not in his interest.

Healy's complaints served their purpose in keeping pressure on Murphy and the *Independent*, and in holding together the disparate conservative nationalist coalition against the Irish Party. The positions of Healy and O'Brien, and Murphy and his newspaper, had for long been convergent, however periodically fractious their relations. When Murphy was confined with a cold for a week in September 1917, Healy confided to his brother that 'I am a bit anxious as to his health, for his life now is a matter of national concern owing to the control of the *Independent*'.[102]

The *Independent*'s role in the overthrow of the Irish party was widely acknowledged, and to some extent exaggerated. Healy wrote that the re-launch of Murphy's halfpenny *Independent* in 1905 'revolutionized the situation and ultimately destroyed both the parliamentary party and the *Freeman*'.[103] Even William O'Brien, no admirer of Murphy or the *Independent*, was driven to concede that the paper 'must be credited with a principal part in giving voice to the suppressed wrath of the country'.[104] T. P. O'Connor wrote that of the many agencies that finally broke the Irish party 'the *Daily Independent* and William Martin Murphy behind it must be regarded as the most potent . . . behind the more prominent and brilliant figure of Mr. Healy there always stood this silent, equable, mild, blue-eyed and thin man – the much more powerful personality of the two'.[105] He was also reflecting the views of John Dillon, who had felt deeply the breaking of the *Freeman's Journal*'s effective monopoly as a nationalist daily newspaper, to which he largely attributed the cataclysm which engulfed the Irish party at the 1918 election. Such an assumption of dependence on the *Freeman's Journal* suggests however an intrinsic vulnerability, as well as a confusion of cause and effect.

On 16 May 1917, Lloyd George wrote to Redmond, O'Brien and Carson, setting forth the government's proposals which included the establishment of a representative convention charged with reaching agreement on the future government of Ireland. Healy reported to Maurice:

> I have seen O'Brien tonight, after he had read Lloyd George's letter. He was very bitter, and said it was cunning and so forth . . .
>
> I think the second part of the paper containing the proposal for a 'convention' practically carries out O'Brien's famous policy. I told him this, and he said I was a very emotional man!! I said I did not pretend to be other than myself. He is utterly out of touch with Parliament and the House, which it is our trade to work in. It is like a great lawyer who never goes to court except once in a blue moon, and doesn't know the temper of the judges and the jurors.[106]

Healy conveyed to O'Brien the Chief Secretary's request for a meeting with him. O'Brien explained to Duke his suspicions of the government's intentions (particularly as to partition), and his criticisms of the proposed composition of the convention. While O'Brien in a memorandum to Bonar Law in March on the subject of a conference of representative Irishmen had not himself provided for the inclusion of Sinn Féin, their exclusion from the convention was one of his principal grounds of objection.[107]

Healy was sufficiently sceptical about the convention, and familiar with O'Brien's doggedness, not to exert himself to prevail on O'Brien to attend. Lloyd George wrote Healy an emollient letter asking him to urge O'Brien to reconsider. Healy replied that he would do so, 'but felt quite sure it would be useless'. While Healy did write to O'Brien as Lloyd George requested, he included in his letter, as he later informed his brother, criticism of the government's conduct towards Duke 'and that I thought it enough to make decent people refrain from attending'.[108]

William Martin Murphy participated in the convention, and also hoped to enlist Healy and O'Brien's participation. He wrote to his son: 'It is a pity that Tim is not with us. O'Brien is so bankrupt in policy and popularity I have an idea he may be counting on support from the Sinn Féiners at the next election. Tim however does not agree with this view'.[109] Murphy continued to blame them for standing apart. Healy wrote to O'Brien that 'his views and ours are leagues apart; and it is useless to try to argue with him'.[110] O'Brien's decision, abetted by Healy, to stay outside the convention was hard to fault. As Healy wrote in his memoirs, the convention was 'hopeless from the start, being framed on false and shallow lines', and 'finally dissolved into nothingness'.[111]

At the convention, William Martin Murphy proved the government's — and Redmond's — most determined adversary. He throughout refused to countenance partition, and opposed any scheme of home rule which did not concede adequate fiscal powers to the Irish legislature. The ailing Redmond, striving desperately for a solution, was the chief victim of the convention's failure. Healy wrote to his brother in January 1918 that Murphy was 'very strong about Redmond's jelly-fishness, and that he was habitually giving away one thing after another in turn, until in the end nothing was left. Certainly Murphy never gives away very much, whatever his statesmanship may be'.[112] The sting of the last comment reflected Healy's low estimate of Murphy's political skills. The following month he wrote to Maurice that 'Murphy, I fear, was bitten with the idea that he could succeed where others failed, and that, while originally he may have demanded Colonial Home Rule, knowing it would not be conceded, he gradually convinced himself that it would be granted if he remained adamant'.[113]

Healy reported on 1 March that Murphy's account of the convention was 'not cheerful'. Baulked by the chairman, he was determined to have a vote on colonial home rule. 'I asked him why, if he was being toyed with, he did not resign, and he said because he would not trust the Party men to remain firm for a day after he left. The Ulstermen favour every dodge to delay matters, yet Murphy sees no advantage in bringing things to a head by his resignation'.[114] By September he was referring to Murphy as 'now astonishingly Nationalist in an active way'.[115]

Murphy's participation in the Irish Convention was to be his last direct political role. He died on 26 June 1919.[116] The *Freeman's Journal* went into receivership shortly afterwards. Healy wrote: 'It is a pity Murphy did not live to see it down'. The paper lingered on until 1924, when the *Independent* acquired its assets.[117]

The Decline of the Irish Party

Healy's mordant hostility to his old colleagues did not abate. He wrote to Maurice in 1917 of T. P. O'Connor's appointment as film censor that the salary was a thousand a year: 'I am glad the wretch has got something'.[118]

He was predictably gratified by the inexorable decline of his old adversaries. He wrote to O'Brien in mid-1917: 'since we put the Liberals out in June 1885, I have not felt as flippant'.[119] His satisfaction verged on the indecent. Writing from London to O'Brien in October of the panic created by German air raids, he tastelessly commented that 'the roar of the guns at night will make pleasant music for the Commons when they meet and will serve as a "last volley" over the Redmondites (if they come they won't stay very long)'.[120]

Healy did not however drop his guard, and continued remorselessly to stalk the Irish party. His greatest fear was that it might somehow cheat its fate. He was particularly concerned to avert the danger of an early election on the old franchise, and to thwart what he believed to be the Irish party's attempt to ensure that the extension of the franchise was not applied to Ireland.[121] On this subject he asserted that 'I have croaked my warnings without arousing the faintest echo', and denounced 'the carrion recusants who prostitute the name of Irish representatives'.[122]

O'Brien continued to fulminate against the iniquities of the Irish party with a pamphlet entitled *The Party: Who They Are and What They Have Done.* He insisted that only the overthrow of the party could lead the Irish people back to constitutionalism, properly understood. Pronouncing that the Irish parliamentary situation immediately before the 1880 election 'closely resembled that on the eve of the Dublin rising of 1916', he did not shrink from describing it as 'Parnell's "Easter Week"'. Healy thought the pamphlet 'very good . . . and very Parnellite as usual'.[123]

There were occasional comic interludes. In December 1917 Healy wrote to O'Brien revelling in a display of animosity from members of the stricken Irish party aboard the *RMS Ulster*:

> This ship is full of the gang going over to try to wreck the Franchise Bill, by delay. As I came into the saloon to write this, I was saluted by tipsy cries of 'Leonard McNally'. Sorry to have chafed the poor darlings.[124]

Crushed by adversity, John Redmond died on 6 March 1918. The *Irish Independent* wrote, 'his last days very closely resembled those of O'Connell, Butt, and Parnell. Such has been the tragic fate of Irish leaders'.[125] His successor John Dillon favoured a more belligerent policy than that latterly pursued by Redmond, but it was far too late to change the direction of the party in the months that remained before the general election. Dillon moreover had been closely identified with Redmond. The veteran of countless controversies (chiefly with Healy) over the preceding forty years, he appeared at sixty-six an archetype of the old order.

Healy began to acquaint himself with the personalities of Sinn Féin. He reported to O'Brien in September 1917 of W. T. Cosgrave, who had been returned for Kilkenny City shortly before, the fourth Sinn Féin candidate to be returned at a by-election that year, that 'I had a nice letter from Cosgrave MP and gave him in return good advice most feelessly!' Later that month he urged a number of Sinn Féiners including Cosgrave to 'drop all programmes save "Turn the Rascals Out" . . . until after a General Election, and to give their reasons thereafter'.[126] Healy was seeking to wean Sinn Féin away from its policy of abstention, and thereby to open the way for a broad anti-Redmondite coalition at the general election. However, Healy's contacts with Sinn Féin were to remain limited and largely fortuitous, until late 1921. Initially his closest contact in Sinn Féin was Eamonn J. Duggan, a solicitor and future plenipotentiary in the treaty negotiations.

Kevin O'Higgins was to provide Healy's chief family link with Sinn Féin. As was common in the dense web of the Healy–Sullivan connexion, there was a double relationship: to Healy (O'Higgins was a great-grandson of Thomas Healy of Bantry, Healy's grandfather) and his wife (Erina Healy and O'Higgins' mother Annie were both daughters of T. D. Sullivan). Born the year after the death of Parnell, O'Higgins was a law student apprenticed — if somewhat nominally — to Maurice Healy. He was prosecuted in May 1918 after a speech in favour of Sinn Féin made in Kings Courts. Arrested in Dublin, he was taken from Mountjoy to Tullamore Jail, where his grandfather T. D. Sullivan had been lodged in 1886. Healy wrote to Maurice with mild sarcasm of the arrest of 'your brilliant apprentice'. Given the war service of his brother, 'I think his boyish eloquence might have been let pass . . . I suppose he will get three months'.[127] O'Higgins' influence — and the closeness of his relationship with Healy — lay in the future. Elected for Queen's County in the 1918 general election, he came to prominence during the treaty debates, and became in 1922, at the age of thirty, Minister for Home Affairs and Vice-President of the Executive Council of the Irish Free State.

In seeking to move towards an alignment with Sinn Féin, Healy had to negotiate the opposition of his brother. Seeking to bring Maurice round, he wrote that 'the Sinn Feiners may have blundered, but they are the only stick to beat the Party with, and on that account I wish them success'.[128] Closely watching the rise of Sinn Féin, Healy cast a backward glance at the political cycles of his lifetime. He wrote to his brother, on the mordant premise of 'your declared enthusiasm remaining unabated, and your belief in revolutions being so intense':

> As Black Jack Gallagher said in 1880, the country is gone to hell and the *Freeman* must go along with it!! The anti-unity party are now as ferocious and implacable against the unity men as the unity gang were against the most moderate dissidents. I suppose the O'Brienites could now take rank where Shaw and Colthurst nobly stood in 1880. We are disposed to forget the enormous number of innocent people who have been born meanwhile!! The Dillon gang had a great chance of reviving their influence by standing aside in Cavan; but, thank goodness, their folly stood to them, and will I hope spell obliteration, although we shall go with them.[129]

Healy thought Dillon's insistence on the Irish party contesting the East Cavan by-election against Arthur Griffith 'monstrous folly'.[130] He regarded Dillon as hopelessly trapped in an obsolete phase of policy, and unable to respond to the swiftly changing temper of Ireland. He contemplated Dillon's predicament with considerable satisfaction. He wrote that, confronted by the rise of Sinn Féin, 'Dillon's face is that of a sick cow. Doubtless the Sinn Feiners will make war on us in due time; but meanwhile I can enjoy myself'.[131] Dillon in turn kept an apprehensive eye on Healy, complaining to T. P. O'Connor that 'there can be no doubt L.G. has let loose *Hell* in Ireland'. The first effect of the threat of conscription had been necessarily to resurrect Sinn Féin. 'In a minor degree . . . it has revived O'Brien and Healy, who had been politically dead'.[132]

The Threat of Conscription

Even against the backdrop of a deteriorating Irish situation, Healy retained an emotional affinity with the allied cause. He did not share the deep political reservations in regard to the war held by John Dillon, of whom he wrote to Maurice in February 1917:

> The party is utterly discredited in the House and everybody thinks Redmond is done for. Dillon just now has made a furious speech against the Government on Salonika, loudly cheered by the pacifists and followed by Snowden. But it was perfectly loyal in tone; and he spoke of 'our troops' and 'our Army' just as if he were anxious only for the Allied success.[133]

Beaverbrook years later recalled an occasion on which Healy was denouncing the iniquitous effects of British rule in Ireland. Beaverbrook interrupted to repeat to him the words of a grim despatch from the British commander-in-chief in France: 'I looked at my companion, and suddenly there I saw the tears streaming down Healy's cheeks. In a passionate and vehement flow of words he dedicated himself, before God, to the service of the Allied cause – as though I was not even there as a spectator to his outburst'.[134] Beaverbrook was an unreliable memoirist, particularly after what was a considerable lapse of time, but the account rings true.

Yet a combination of fury at the course of British policy in Ireland and war-weariness took its toll. He wrote to Maurice in January 1918 that 'the idea is slowly fermenting in the English mind that the Germans cannot be beaten, and humanly speaking, I think this is correct'.[135] By May he was even prepared to espouse the *Realpolitik* of Sinn Féin: ' . . . I agree that events have altered my point of view, because I am certain we shall get no concession if victory inclines to the Allies. This is the sole reason which influences me'.[136] If this was hardly a reflection of Healy's settled convictions on the subject, it attested to the extent to which even moderate nationalist opinion had been alienated in the course of the war: it was inconceivable that Healy could have articulated such a dissociation between British and Irish interests in August 1914.

Healy's sense of the complexity of the interaction between the Irish and continental theatres of policy and war was movingly conveyed in a letter to Beaverbrook in February:

> How many Arks of the British Covenant will be splintered in this War? How many hoary mussel-bottomed Noah's Arks enshrining the Lion & the Unicorn in droves and menageries will make shipwreck? I don't suppose in any moment of the French Revolution was the loom of history warped with odder tapestry than what is now on the thrums. The color-scheme may not end to our liking, and it looks as if some of the Angels of Apocalypse were indeed donning their jackboots. Europe is a-child with fate. The outlying island whose people 'rode the ridge of war' for seven centuries unafraid, look on now from the coin of vantage – so they think. Still for you & me as I hope, comes savour of the days when the nightly order was 'Pea Soup and Rump steak' & we ate bread to the full.[137]

Healy vehemently opposed the application of conscription to Ireland in a *tour de force* in the Commons in April 1918, in which he warned that the government would be confronted by 'a strike *en masse* by the Irish people'. He began with a devastating critique of the military command at the front:

> For three years and eight months I have not criticised the conduct of the War or the conduct of the Government . . . Today for the first time you

> force us to examine your premises — you drive us to analytical criticism . . . I do not think that when a general — I am not referring to the Commander-in-Chief — has openly blundered and brought about most hideous losses, to put that man again in command of an Army is little better than manslaughter, if not assassination.

In one of Lloyd George's arguments Healy discerned 'the uneasy conscience of an ex-Home Ruler . . . Nobody of Celtic blood, as the Prime Minister is, and I would add of Celtic courage, nobody who knows the Welsh case but must understand the Irish'. This laid the ground for his onslaught on conscription:

> Let us consider it coldly. You have Ireland under Martial law. You got it, at the beginning of the War, a perfectly loyal country thoroughly with you. I have had three nephews killed in this War; I have plenty of other relatives serving. There is hardly a man who has not some member of his family either killed or wounded . . . Ireland . . . was the one bright spot. Poor John Redmond! You killed him, and you are using the election of his son in Waterford the other day practically to carry Conscription. Of course, had the election gone the other way you would never have dreamt of Conscription.[138]

This was Healy at his most dangerous. Deeply disconcerted by his menacingly restrained attack on the Allied military leadership, Lloyd George judged Healy the most formidable nationalist opponent of conscription.[139] William O'Brien's last speech in the House of Commons was likewise a condemnation of conscription.[140]

In seeking to impose conscription in Ireland, the British government succeeded in creating a united nationalist front against it. What became known as the Mansion House conference was convened in Dublin. Its membership included Griffith and de Valera, Dillon and Devlin, Healy and O'Brien, and Thomas Johnson and (the other) William O'Brien, representing the Labour party. An anti-conscription pledge drafted by de Valera was adopted, and Healy joined a deputation to the annual meeting of the Irish Catholic bishops which was taking place that evening in Maynooth. This fleeting moment of consensus among contending schools of nationalism was sanctified by the bishops' declaration against conscription.[141]

When the government used the pretext of the so-called 'German plot' to embark on the arrest of further Sinn Féin activists, including Griffith and de Valera, Healy's opposition stiffened further. He wrote to O'Brien that 'Lloyd George having found "no Popery" a damp squib in the *Times* turns to Pigott's tricks'.[142] Quite apart from his own increased tolerance of Sinn Féin, Healy regarded the arrest of its more politically adept leaders as an error of policy. He conveyed his assessment of some of them to Maurice in June 1918.

> I am sure Alderman Kelly shows much more sense than McNeill, who seems to me a poor creature. Valera was a fine fellow, and Griffith, though dour and glum, has brains but, as I remarked, it is easy to understand why the mass of Volunteers failed to rise in Easter Week with John McNeill in command. I believe however he is a learned man in old Irish history.[143]

Healy's favourable view of de Valera, to whom he looked as the most astute of the Sinn Féin leaders, was to last until the civil war. William O'Brien erred spectacularly in his estimation of de Valera. He wrote that 'de Valera is personally a charming man, but he is too good for this rough world, and will no doubt subside into a meek instrument of Dillon's'.[144]

At a session of the Mansion House Conference in May there occurred what a startled Healy described as 'the funniest incident of my life'. Dillon denounced de Valera's draft of a proposed address to the President of the United States. When Healy produced an alternative draft which sought to reconcile the positions of Sinn Féin and the Irish party, Dillon suspended his old animosity towards Healy to declare it 'a most magnificent State Paper . . . one of the best statements I ever heard'. When two of the Sinn Féin representatives took exception to parts of Healy's draft, he was able to point out that they originated in de Valera's manuscript.[145] Subsequently William Martin Murphy twice commended Healy's address, which he remarked was 'a great thing from so cold a man'.[146]

The Mansion House Conference was the curious coda to the relations between the two inveterate enemies of the old Irish party. The following month Healy reported to O'Brien: 'Late on Saturday night 15 June I got a letter beginning "My dear Healy" in a hand to me unknown . . . I turned to the signature and gasped. "Yours sincerely, John Dillon". No less!' The letter suggested modifications to Healy's draft address. While Dillon was desperately striving to contain the rise of Sinn Féin, there was perhaps a slight personal softening. If so, it was not reciprocated. Healy wrote inclemently to his brother that 'I expect Griffith's victory gives Dillon his death stroke, and that he knew it would take place when he twice addressed me as "My dear Mr. Healy"!!' To O'Brien he exclaimed: 'Yes they are down and out, nor in all the witlings' wild career was there ever a finale so foolish. Moralising I leave to sages'.[147]

Shortly before William O'Brien had published a letter seeking to coax Sinn Féin towards 'even an experimental toleration of Dominion Independence (which differs little except in name from Sovereign Independence)'. If Sinn Féin were to accept the idea, no substantial difference would remain between nationalists, and 'Dominion independence would become practical politics'. If rejected by Westminster, he surmised there would then be a nationalist consensus 'to press for the only remaining alternative – viz. representation for Ireland at the Peace Congress', and for 'breaking off all connection with the Westminster Parliament in the meantime'.[148] His efforts to achieve a conjuncture with Sinn Féin were unavailing.[149] Healy's own hopes of the possibility of a broad anti-Irish party alliance was more modest and lightly held than O'Brien's. When the fiercely Republican Hannah Sheehy-Skeffington told him that all the Irish in the United States were Sinn Féiners, he optimistically commented to Maurice that 'I suppose this means they are like ourselves – anti-Party'.[150]

Healy noted somewhat smugly that members of the Irish party were becoming discernibly more polite towards him. In August he wrote 'the Party men have shown me great civility, which is of course a proof of their powerless condition. Devlin spoke to me openly on the benches, and to-day Scanlan accosted me in Piccadilly!' He maintained a vigilant watch against any attempt by Dillon to retrieve the fortunes of the Irish party:

> I suppose the Mansion House Conference will be resumed soon, and we shall see or hear of the plans Dillon has been maturing for his convention to unite all Ireland!! It was I gave the tip to the *Independent* of his talk with T.P. and Bonar Law in the lobby. I shall be surprised if these gentlemen do not perform some dying wriggle before they are squelched.[151]

Healy, Dillon wrote glumly, was 'as mischievous and restless as ever. He is now busy making friends with the Sinn Feiners and the Transport Union'. At a recent meeting of the Mansion House Conference 'he calmly proposed that we should vote £1,000 in support of the Dublin Builders' Strike – a grotesque proposal – made of course simply for the purpose of having to spread amongst the working men that Healy proposed to give them £1,000. He is now cultivating Shortt & McMahon'.[152]

In London in August 1918 Healy asked Bonar Law to allow him to visit de Valera in jail, 'undertaking that I would not carry in or bring out any "hostile" communications'. Law referred him to the Home Secretary, who said he would have had to consult the Irish Office. Healy waited twenty-four hours in London for a reply, but none came. 'I construe this as a refusal and I am sorry, because I had hoped to secure from de Valera a message to his men favourable to peace'.[153] While Healy's hopes of eliciting such a message from de Valera were misplaced, he had embarked on what was to be a sustained endeavour to put his political connections to good use, and thereby to constitute himself an intermediary between Sinn Féin and the British government.

Fraternal Recriminations

In his letters to his brother, Healy provides a remorseless chronicle of the decline and fall of the Irish party and the rise of Sinn Féin by a major figure of the parliamentary nationalist *ancien régime*. Quite apart from disclosing his own process of accommodation as a politician to the new order, his correspondence affords a unique record of the response of an intelligent and well-informed middle-class nationalist of an older generation to Sinn Féin's sweeping triumph.

Lacking his brother's athletic adaptability, Maurice was unable to bring himself to take a sympathetic view of Sinn Féin. Healy struggled to convert him, equating the contemporary situation with the struggles of their youth, and insisting that the rise of Sinn Féin represented their own belated vindication in the unremitting war against the leadership of the Irish party which they had waged in their middle years. The spectral figures of the 1880s commingle in Healy's correspondence with the leaders of Sinn Féin in a nationalist *temps retrouvé*.

In May 1918 he strove to bring Maurice round to an imaginative affinity with the political culture of Sinn Féin:

> When I read Pearse's speech at the Rossa funeral, I thought it very extravagant and possibly insincere. He afterwards proved that at least he was not insincere, and fought and died for the opinions therein expressed. Surely that is as respectable a position as Hampden's or Cromwell's or Koskiuszko's?

Healy rebuked Maurice for his rigidity. Revolutions were uncertain affairs. Moreover he attacked his failure to comprehend visionary political fervour as an aspect of a broader mystical deficit, of which his indifference to the visions of the Catholic mystic Anne Catherine Emmerich was also symptomatic. Most of all, he claimed the victory of Sinn Féin as their own:

> Personally I take your view that the English have got Ireland in a tight cage and that she can't get out of it. Young people deny this, and the world lies with the young men in all struggles. They see visions, and contend that the British Empire is not eternal, and I am not sufficient of an inspired prophet to be able stoutly to gainsay this. As to what is the amount of justification requiring men to take up arms, I really don't believe it can be weighed by any system of *avoirdupois*. When the Czar was downed last year, it seemed a very hopeless business to start with. A little firmness on the part of James II or Louis Seize would have put down in the bud two bloody revolutions. You may be seer enough in your political observatory to decry the folly of all the youngsters. I say I don't know, and the matter does not easily lend itself to decision or solution.

> The fact that you cannot even interest yourself, apart from believing, in the visions of Catherine Emmerich stamps your mind, in my opinion, as one lacking a useful quality towards judgement. I believe substantially in the visions . . .
>
> On the other hand I lack your appreciation of Shakespeare and the musical glasses. Your mental arrogance increases with age, although age destroys all the sentimental considerations which affect the judgements of youth, who alone makes history. It doesn't matter a straw in the end which is right . . . Quite true, the country does not see our arguments against the Party and have hearkened to de Valera's or Thigue Barry's. What of that? In the end they have come round to our opinions, and I don't care by what road or reasoning. I rejoice that our enemies are in the dust . . .[154]

He wrote in September 1918 to Maurice who was considering coming to Dublin that 'you will find me quite harmless even if unconvinced by your mid-Victorian sentiments'.[155] He accused him of having forgotten the passion — and the amoral resolve — of their political youth:

> Your attitude towards the Sinn Feiners is merely a reproduction of your sneers at the Gaelic League — a sign of old age very common at our time of life. The new generation can do nothing good, and fate has debarred us from accomplishing all the fine things which we should have done much better only for something. One would think by your reference to outrages that the Land League was impeccable, and that spiking the meadows for a terrible purpose, and Mr. Hussey of the shears, had never been heard of. Nor do appeals to the Ten Commandments as a reproof to reprisals in the least affect me. Whatever the Sinn Feiners do has been provoked by the Government, and I will not sit in judgement on them, because I would not counsel or approve their actions in many cases.
>
> I don't think the British Government in Ireland is a bit more respectable than that of the Bolcheviks, which at least is free from hypocrisy and cant. Carson and the Orangemen are the root of the present trouble and it is idle to argue with me against the developments they have engineered. Quite true that for the moment the process of getting rid of the Party will cause much inconvenience in the checking of minor abuses and delaying Parliamentary corrections, but that is only a phase in the march of events; and it will be amended in due time with very little real loss to the public welfare at the finish. The punishing of the Irish Party and the striking them out of existence is a great reform. So was the downfall of the Czar though great evils followed afterwards. I thank God that I have lived to see the day when the country is about to spew these wretches out of her mouth. If you think otherwise, you should not be so active for the Franchise Bill.[156]

In February 1919, Healy indited his most exasperated retort to Maurice's re-iterated condemnation of Sinn Féin:

> Your argument is so powerful and close-knit that nothing is lacking to its pungency save the blotting out of the 750 years before 1919. This of course is a trifle, and I am glad to know on the advice of my solicitor that nothing counts previous to the present day in morals or casuistry. The English are here, as they are in London, as of course and as of right. Their title to make laws and repress crime is the same as in Middlesex . . . I seem however to remember that you were once a protesting member of the London Parliament, and that therein you and I frequently denied the authority and jurisdiction of that assembly . . . The most crack-brained twaddle of the Sinn Feiners seems to be preferable to your inconsequential platitudes.[157]

As he told Maurice later that year, 'the wheel has come full circle to avenge us'.[158] Apart from the gratification of revenging himself upon the Irish party of Redmond and Dillon, Healy grasped the opportunity to assert that through his fractured public life there ran a great and consistent patriotic argument. The comparison of the period 1918-21 with the Ireland of the Land League and of the rise of Parnell became a refrain in his correspondence. He wrote to Maurice in 1920 that 'I think that my comparison of your *état d'âme* with that of Whigs of 1881 is not imperfect!! I think the Sinns have won a great deal . . .'[159] If subjectively comprehensible, it was a crude historical argument. The course of events signified the final dissolution of the Parnellite consensus rather more than its renewal.

Thus driven to dwell upon the rise of the great Irish party of the 1880s, Healy did not engage in any revisionism in relation to its leader. On this subject his inclemency was enduring. He remained as much exercised by his disagreement with O'Brien over the character of Parnell as by any of their current differences. Opposition to Parnell remained a touchstone in his judgement of his contemporaries. Understandably at a loss to grasp how O'Brien had discerned in Morley's *Recollections* evidence of Morley's responsibility for Gladstone's repudiation of Parnell, Healy wrote to Maurice in 1918:

> On getting your letter I sent for the Morley volumes and examined them through the index for anything to explain William's article in the *Review*. I could not see anything to provoke him personally except total omission!! I think he is sincere in his post mortem appreciation of Parnell, which to my mind argues a littleness of spirit. The more I look back on Parnell, the less I think about him; and John Barry's arguments about Free Trade always seem to me to gain in soundness by reason of his contempt for Parnell!![160]

Healy's Resignation from Parliament

In February 1918 Healy met O'Brien at the Shelbourne Hotel in Dublin.

> Some kidney trouble, he said, brought him up; but like Talleyrand I asked what does he mean by it? I think he came to see the Sinn Feiners; and he mentioned that John [Eoin] MacNeill had been with him. He seemed in good spirits; but said in reply to my enquiry that he would not adopt the Sinn Fein platform, and would not again stand for Cork. I said that represented my own feelings and he amiably suggested there was a difference between our cases, and that, if I was not opposed, I should go forward. I fancy that is his own feeling too, in spite of his disclaimers. I don't think he would fight a Sinn Feiner, any more than I would; but I think if a Party candidate alone had to be faced he would not shrink from the ordeal! That is pretty much my own state of mind.[161]

O'Brien had already made his position plain in his pamphlet of the previous year in which he advocated giving Sinn Féin 'a lease of honest, self-respecting public confidence', free from electoral turmoil.[162] There was perhaps a hint of senescent coquettishness in O'Brien's stance: no doubt his resolve would have yielded to any softening of Sinn Féin's attitude. It was nonetheless a realistic and sensible accommodation to the course of events in Ireland. It permitted in the longer term a *rapprochement* with Sinn Féin: moreover withdrawal with a modicum of dignity would serve to highlight the ignominiousness of the rout of the Irish party.

Healy in contrast was markedly reluctant to forsake Westminster. As a pragmatist and an old parliamentary hand, he was instinctively opposed to the Sinn Féin doctrine of parliamentary abstentionism, especially as it would have the consequence of giving the Ulster unionists free rein at Westminster. Healy harboured the increasingly forlorn hope that Sinn Féin would prove tractable on the issue of absentionism, or would at least sanction the return of a residue of non-Irish party parliamentarians not bound by a policy of abstention. There was never any prospect of Sinn Féin agreeing to temper its abstentionism, which was its defining principle. Its leaders were moreover determined to achieve an electoral supremacy as decisive as possible. Sinn Féin had in any event less need than Healy to settle for the proposition that my enemy's enemy is my friend, while many in its ranks regarded Healy and O'Brien with scarcely less hostility than they did the Irish party.

As the election approached, it became increasingly plain that Sinn Féin would challenge any O'Brienites who stood. Healy still appeared to hope that its leaders might relent. When a prominent Sinn Féin figure, probably Eamonn Duggan, assured Healy that things would come right, he protested to O'Brien that 'they are so headless, folly is bound to come uppermost'. In reply, O'Brien repeated that he was resolved not to seek re-election: 'For good or ill, the Sinn Feiners are the only men of power for the immediate future. If they are going to win, the country will be wise to give them as overpowering a mandate as they gave to Parnell in 1880'. Again he politely distinguished Healy's situation. Healy's disappearance would be 'a national as well as (I am quite convinced) a personal misfortune and mistake'. He believed Healy could hold his seat.[163]

Healy still harboured the hope that he would be spared a contest, but feared that Maurice would be ousted, in which event 'I would not any further relish Parliamentary life under new conditions. I would far rather have opposition intimated, and retire with the rest of the group'. He was exasperated by the imprisonment of the main Sinn Féin leaders, whom he had hoped to convert at least to a limited derogation from the principle of abstention: 'The leaderless position of the Sinn Feiners of course makes it difficult for minor men to compromise on their high-flown principles, and it is of course monstrous that what will in future be the only real Nationalist party should have all its leaders in jail at a General Election'.[164] On the political prospect, Healy was profoundly pessimistic, and cynical as to the Prime Minister's motives. He wrote to O'Brien in October 1918 that the military had made arrangements to enforce conscription 'and Lloyd George wants to be able to tell the constituencies that he has played the strong man and he is utterly indifferent to any save the political side of the manoeuvre'.[165]

O'Brien restated his central argument: 'I feel every day more that we have no actual power of any kind, and that our most dignified course would be to stand aside and give Sinn Féin its chance (such as it is) to produce a state of things which would force England to make a really big bid'. He regretted that Sinn Féin had not the good sense to leave Healy 'a free hand', but (with considerable prescience in relation to Healy) pointed out that in a year or two, after the Irish party had been disposed of, fresh prospects would arise.[166]

Healy believed that Sinn Féin had requested of O'Brien that the independent nationalists should resign in a body before the dissolution, as a protest on behalf of the republican prisoners. He suggested somewhat desperately, writing to his brother, that if O'Brien were to accede to this request, 'it is a course which no doubt would give him a claim on them at the Dissolution; but they are so self-confident they might take the goods without paying the price'.[167] It was a forlorn hope, and merely marked a phase in the process whereby Healy accommodated himself to relinquishing his seat. The same day he wrote to O'Brien, his wistfulness a little forced:

> I agree with you that we should stand aside and let the Shins make their way at the elections unimpeded by us. What new developments may come

> with years will be for a younger brood to handle. We have got our *congé* and I move that a warm vote of thanks be inscribed on our tombstones.[168]

Healy still jibbed at the idea of standing down. He little realised that his fate was already sealed, and that he would be in the event the first of O'Brien's allies to resign. Indignant at a prison sentence imposed by a court martial on an actor 'who in some remote hamlet sang two Irish songs', he had written a letter to an amnesty meeting held under the auspices of Cumann na mBan in which he casually offered to resign his seat to permit such a victim of injustice to contest his seat.[169]

He was startled to receive a letter signed by the secretaries of Sinn Féin dated 12 October accepting his offer to resign. There followed an attempt to use his offer to procure the resignation of the other O'Brienites. Healy, who had conceived his offer as a rhetorical gesture, was infuriated at the prospect of being hustled out of parliament by men whom he regarded as political amateurs. While he had some reason to believe that Stephen O'Mara, a former nationalist M.P., and minor Sinn Féin potentate, had written the letter and appended the names of the secretaries, Sinn Féin did not repudiate the letter. He had no choice but to make good his offer.[170]

The *Irish Independent* of 30 October 1918, under the resonant heading 'Resignation of Mr. T. M. Healy, M.P. – Constitutional Party's Doom', carried a correspondence skilfully collated by Healy. In an exchange of letters with O'Brien he announced his resignation after thirty-seven years in Parliament:

> I simply want to give new methods a chance . . . I recant nothing; I renounce nothing; I regret nothing, and I have nothing but gratitude for those who undertake, in the new generation, to win for the country all that we have been unable to accomplish in the old.

The published correspondence included Healy's reply to a telegram from the committee on behalf of the Sinn Féin prisoners in Belfast. Healy explained that he could not intervene on behalf of the prisoners in the Commons because Sinn Féin had requested his resignation: 'I beg to acquaint you that I am debarred from further Parliamentary action on behalf of the Belfast prisoners, as I have sent my resignation to the Chancellor of the Exchequer'. Having thus suggested the folly of Sinn Féin's undiscriminating policy of abstention, he turned to deliver a parting shot at his old adversaries in the Irish party: 'I regret that the remnant of what is called the Irish Parliamentary Party is in effective connivance with Mr. Shortt in his attitude towards the prisoners'.[171]

In spite of Healy's fury, his resignation was to inure greatly to his benefit.

In his memoirs he recorded merely that 'the resignation of my seat in Parliament was tendered as a protest against the convictions for trivial causes by courts-martial'.[172] Part of Healy's resistance to O'Brien's resolve to quit the parliamentary arena was due to his fear of a resurgence by the Irish party, left unopposed at Westminster. Just as he had the previous year accused the party of seeking to undermine the franchise bill, he was vigilant against any possible initiative which might permit the party to survive as a force in Irish politics. Of the possibility of the imposition of an oath on local election candidates, Healy wrote to O'Brien 'I felt all along that Dillonism would not perish without a struggle'. His apprehensions endured to the last. When supporters of the Irish party in Cork appeared to moot the idea of an electoral pact in early November, Healy wrote to O'Brien that 'this sets my bald spot bristling. I hope it may at least lead you to delay the announcement of your withdrawal just yet, even though the Dissolution be proclaimed this week'.[173]

Healy was still far from reconciled to the course he had adopted, and doubted the acumen and capacity of the Sinn Féin leaders, or at least of those still at large. He wrote to O'Brien on 3 November:

> I gather that the Mansion House meeting is being pressed for by the youth amongst the Shins who find magic the plan of passing a resolution in favour of the blessed word self-determination. All the Field Marshals in that army are just beyond their teens and are full of the balmiest strategy. As Slavs and Czechs and Croats have gotten freedom, the fact has only to be communicated to John Bull, and he will at once sit up and take notice. If he does not they are quite ready to take the field once more.
>
> None of them were born when you published *When We Were Boys*. Their legal branch asked me to get the writ for North East Cork moved. I replied that after the *Gazette* notice of my appointment to the 'Chiltern Hundreds', this could be done, but not by me![174]

In a letter the following day – one of the longest he wrote to O'Brien – Healy explained what had occurred to provoke his irritation:

> . . . presuming you got the letter safely, I may now mention that it was provoked by the visit of two emissaries – one the Secretary on the run, I believe or guess, who demanded I should attend the Mansion House meeting – one of them said to proclaim self-determination and the other added 'a provisional government'. They said we should be backed by 80,000 men and blithered of the gorgeous precedents of the Yugo-Slavs and the Shugs Blabs and the Boobo Kalves.
>
> All perfectly sincere and self-sacrificing and piteous. This and O'Mara have convinced me that Shortt's jail-scythe has left only witlings in control of a great movement.

Healy believed that the approach arose from his refusal to attend the Mansion House conference save on the issue of conscription ('I did not see how I could in a non-representative capacity expose myself if I raised an objection on any point in a body where the *liberum veto* prevailed, to the taunt of "who do you represent?"'). He suspected a design against himself, Dillon, and Thomas Johnson at the conference, 'to get us all together and stampede us into some explosive resolution'.

> My two Sunday visitors, when I began saying that Dillon would dissent, fiercely said, 'we'll force him'. This I did not heed, but went on with arguments which sadly depressed them.
>
> I know I am prone to over-suspicion – 'all politicians are', wrote Gladstone . . .
>
> Now if they get us all together by varying expedients and pressures, what if my two visitors have in mind a little game to detail some of their 80,000 in front of the Mansion House at a given moment of our Conference?
>
> They are capable of any cracked attempt, and such a 'surprise party' might easily make history – tho' not in the mould of their hearts' desires.
>
> I told my visitors that the Government, for the first time, had this year got plenty of spies in their ranks. They hotly denied this, and said all Castle information about them was false. I never saw them before, and you may say perhaps they were police-agents themselves. Possibly, yet I know a hawk from a hand (or hern) saw. So I simmered over to you a little yesterday my impressions on field-marshals.

Healy angrily asserted that 'I conceive my obligation to them, which was less than slight, to be completely discharged'. While O'Brien had proceeded on the assumption that 'sensible statesmanship resided somewhere in their ranks outside prison', Healy concluded that those still at large were without constructive capacity: 'As scavengers of corruption, splendid, as builders and framers of policy, nowhere'.

> Like the wisdom *in gremio legis*, I conceived some closet conventicle of authority, well-guided, to which we might fairly attorn. There is nothing of the kind to give our allegiance to. You and I – meekly be it spoken – are as good as the brains of the whole hotchpot. . . . Of course the wild men may smooth down according to their daily draught of war news, but disappointment is eating at their hearts, and getting on their nerves. Forgive this long prose. Its tendency is to counsel that you should not evacuate the terrain too speedily, as in view of these facts I must own I have been led into doing.[175]

Healy had not previously met his republican visitors. From his letter to O'Brien, he made a shrewd guess as to the identity of one of them,

Harry Boland, one of the secretaries of Sinn Féin, who was on the run. He claimed not to have known or guessed until after the truce, when Boland told him, that the other was Michael Collins.

It was a remarkable, if somewhat comical, encounter between two generations of nationalist leaders. Collins was playing a more subtle game, and with a lighter touch, than Healy, still smarting from his enforced resignation, could bring himself to appreciate. His belligerent feint was at once a prank and an exercise to ascertain how far Healy could be drawn. Rather than presaging the kind of quasi-insurrectionary gesture of defiance feared by Healy, the Collins–Boland proposition was almost certainly conceived as a manoeuvre to compromise, or at least to outflank, the Irish party on the eve of the general election. Both sides later professed to treat the visit as a playful hoax, as to some degree it was. At Glenaulin after the truce Boland, according to Healy, flatteringly told him that they had known that they could not bluff him, but hoped to succeed with Dillon and the Lord Mayor.[176]

Displaying a fortitude in self-restraint for which there was little precedent in his earlier career, Healy mastered his anger at what he considered to be the fecklessness of Sinn Féin, which he instead poured out in his letter to O'Brien. He did not stand on his dignity. If this posture was somewhat self-abasing, he could console himself that it had much to recommend over the stiff hauteur with which Dillon was preparing to greet political oblivion. Healy was engaged in what became an ambitious political endeavour to reconstitute himself as the tutelary old parliamentary hand to the new movement, in a political extension to his professional role as a King's Counsel who defended Sinn Féin activists in government prosecutions. Conversely, the interview at Glenaulin served in Collins' jocular way as a kind of audition.

The dissolution followed swiftly on Healy's resignation. O'Brien's retirement address denounced the Irish party. Maurice Healy warned ambiguously of the dangers of 'turbulence, disorder and abortive rebellion'. O'Brien commended Maurice's address: it 'salts the party with fire and brimstone . . . Coming from so reserved and temperate a source it hits them harder than anything I ever said'.[177] Just before parliament was dissolved, Healy conveyed to O'Brien his belief that 'for those about to die there will be no hereafter'. He had an intimation of the strife to come. Glutted on animosity towards the Irish party, his troubled imagery was redolent of his rhetoric in the Parnell split:

> I doubt that Shindom will reign as long as Johndom, unless fresh gore replenishes its accumulators. Besides it is the editor of the *Independent* who will call the tune . . . Neither you nor I contributed to this welter. Nor can we frame specifications for the sewage tanks about to be laid down.[178]

The Irish party was electorally routed. Healy's old enemy John Dillon was crushed by de Valera in the East Mayo constituency for which he had sat since 1885. The only prominent survivors of the wreck of the old party were Joe Devlin, returned for Belfast (Falls), and T. P. O'Connor, who was re-elected for the Scotland division of Liverpool, a seat he had held continuously since he was first elected in 1885, when his decision to take the seat there had precipitated the Galway election all those years before.

Healy could not contain his exultation at the fall of the Irish party, and made no effort to do so. He wrote to O'Brien that he felt pitiless only towards two minor members of the party:

> Odd that one's dislikes should have shrunk to so small a compass.
> Dillon is so utterly busted that like the Kaiser, it hardly seems worthwhile drawing up an indictment. Yet in regard to Ireland his criminal folly is as vast as Wilhelm's in Germany.

Sending his greetings to O'Brien two days before the Christmas of 1918, he observed 'politically we shall never again enjoy such a festive season'.[179] Healy's seasonal cheer was reciprocated by O'Brien:

> Our friends are not merely satisfied. They are wild with joy. The cowardly bullies who made their lives miserable for the last fifteen years are put on a footstool under their feet. Our friends have the feeling, not altogether unjustly, that it is we, rather than Sinn Fein, that have triumphed.[180]

A full year later, Healy was still experiencing rushes of pleasurable glee. Though 'dog-tired, and letter-hating', he wrote in November 1919 acknowledging a note from O'Brien, which he described as

> flowing free as from a rill – while I writhe in constipation ink-puddled. Truly it is well with us in eld. Your preface [to O'Brien's re-issued *When We Were Boys*] I didn't half enough praise. There is one long sentence that I would have smashed to smithereens (or semi-colons) but save that breathless passage, needing a chopper, it is perfect. Lord, how you invest seriousness with the alembic of romance. How you preserve the freshness of the crusader in an age when instead of 'God wills it', there fumes at us from re-echoing craters a conjunct belch, that 'needs must when the devil drives'!! You will see ninety for you believe in existence . . . My own horoscope I will not cast, but I will own that my real pleasures date from my sixty-third birthday [18 May 1918]. Gobs, what fun we have had this blessed year of 1918–19, and go mbeimid beo an am seo arís . . . I feel like the *jongleur* in William's army at Hastings, coming most valiantly to his charge, crying Ha-Roo (see Freeman, not of Princes Street) which reminds me naturally of winding up. So if you are not at my funeral, I will be at yours. How jocund will we drive our hearse afield.[181]

26

The Anglo-Irish Treaty

When his followers, in panic, overthrew Parnell they destroyed Parliamentarism as a weapon of Irish National policy. An Englishman's threat had broken their will – it was obvious that in any future National crisis Irish Parliamentarism would bow to English menace and drag the fortunes of Ireland after it. It had to be got rid of if Ireland as a Nation was not to ignominiously perish. It has been got rid of and the soul of Ireland is freed and flaming.

Arthur Griffith, 1920[1]

The House of Commons will never again be the thrilling place it was when the Irish brigade sat as a solid phalanx, defiant and irreconcilable, below the gangway, a grim, resentful cloud, hanging over the Parliamentary sky, flashing with sudden lightnings, and reverberating with ceaseless thunders. What memorable figures there were in that phalanx – the 'Chief', pale, silent, secret, his hat over his eyes, his arms folded across his breast, a symbol of implacable revolt; John Redmond, spacious, generous, eloquent; the stately Dillon, the frenzied O'Brien, the odd, grotesque Biggar, the gay and chivalrous William Redmond, the trumpet-tongued Devlin, the brilliant Tom Kettle and many another. All have vanished, save the genial 'Tay-Pay' who, as Father of the House lingers on like a reminiscence of an epoch that has become 'one with Nineveh and Tyre'.

And in all that phalanx there was no more devastating presence than that of 'Tim' Healy . . .

A. G. Gardiner, 1925[2]

Interregnum

Alone of the survivors of the old parliamentary order in the south, Healy successfully adapted to the political revolution wrought by the election of December 1918, and contrived to play an active role in the turbulent interregnum of 1919–22. Those who looked to him in the first instance were the more enlightened figures within the divided British administration in Ireland, who were seeking to negotiate an exceedingly perilous hiatus. He maintained his British political connections, chiefly through the medium of Lord Beaverbrook. From Glenaulin and the Law Library of the Four Courts, with forays to London, he sought to exercise a restraining influence on British policy in Ireland, and latterly to promote a political settlement. In an uncharted and inhospitable landscape he stood out as a figure of reassuring familiarity and astuteness.[3]

His network of contacts only touched the edge of Sinn Féin. He could not purport to represent or to convey the views of the leaders of Sinn Féin, merely to offer a shrewd and imaginatively sympathetic assessment of their political intentions. At the start of 1919, Healy wrote to O'Brien in a feint of self-abnegation that 'the Captains of the new army need no counsel from those of the old, and the world starts new from 1919 for them'.[4] He wrote in April that 'the Shins have not approached me except on a legal point since'.[5]

On 21 January 1919 the first Dáil met in Dublin. By a baleful coincidence armed conflict commenced on the same day. Two policemen were shot dead in Soloheadbeg in Tipperary in the course of a republican seizure of a consignment of gelignite. It was to prove the first in the series of disparate engagements collectively designated the war of independence. Affected by the widespread hardening of opinion in favour of Sinn Féin, Healy wrote to O'Brien in April that 'at no time was there so much spirit of self-sacrifice and of pluck in Ireland. The Land League or the '67 men showed no such steely fibre *en masse*'.[6]

On 10 May 1919, returning from a lunch for an Irish-American delegation to the Paris Peace Conference, attended by de Valera, Griffith and Eoin MacNeill, Healy from a tramcar observed the massing of soldiers in Nassau Street. They were about to enter the Mansion House, where Sinn Féin's secessionist Dáil Eireann had its seat, in the vain hope of executing warrants for the arrest of Michael Collins and Robert Barton. Healy wrote to his brother: 'The stars in their courses fight in favour of the Sinn Feiners. Nothing that the wit of man could devise equalled the Mansion House raid of the military in folly. . . . Every damn fool seems to be in the employment of the British Government in Ireland'.[7]

Sinn Féin sought in vain to intervene at the Peace Conference in Paris.

Healy wrote to his brother in May that the Sinn Féin representatives were 'putting up a better shop-window-dressing in Paris than I expected. However futile it may be, it is respectable'. The American President 'threatens to become the pest of Europe . . . I hope to see Wilson hooted down Broadway'. He regarded Woodrow Wilson as the prisoner of his Ulster Presbyterian antecedents, and wrote later in the year that 'I think this dog Wilson is trying to fool the Irish in exactly the same way as the English have been doing with the Irish party'.[8]

In London in December 1919, Healy received a message that Lloyd George wanted him to make contact. He declined to do so, but said the Prime Minister could easily find him. Beaverbrook then asked Healy to stay over a weekend when Lloyd George was to come to lunch. Lloyd George subsequently sent word that the American ambassador was lunching with him, and asked Healy to join them. Healy reported, a little over-dramatically, to his brother: 'I did not go, stating that I would not break bread with him at his house'. He had been told that Lloyd George had said that if he could get agreement to leaving the six counties 'exactly as they are, he would be ready to concede to the rest of the country Dominion Home Rule free from Imperial taxation and with control of customs and excise'. Healy, disinclined to believe that Lloyd George had said any such thing, told his informant that 'this was a mere trap, as he would not be allowed to carry any such scheme, and that its proposal would only eventuate in some hotch-potch unacceptable to everyone'.[9] While he remained highly suspicious of Lloyd George's intentions, he no longer baulked at partition.

Healy remained unreconciled to the doctrine of abstentionism. In the vain hope of dissuading Sinn Féin from its uncompromising refusal to attend at Westminster, he had come up with an idea based on the precedent created by John Martin, the veteran nationalist who had represented Meath 1871–5 without taking the oath. As he wrote to O'Brien in 1926, he had sought to persuade Eamonn Duggan, then his closest contact in the Sinn Féin leadership, that the Sinn Féin candidates elected in 1918

> could without taking any oath, infest Parliament, its seats under the clock, its galleries and lobbies. Their roars of protest would have prevented the 1920 Act being brought in if they had made themselves 'generally useful' in 1919. Ministers are men first and the crashing protests that could have been made even in Lobbies and Dining Rooms by an organised force, acting as a unit — which no leader up to then truly commanded — could not have been ignored . . .
>
> The Shins were mostly ignorant of conditions at Westminster — tho' they had the precedent of John Martin to go by — and their absence gave Carson his chance . . .[10]

Healy had evidently racked his brains to find any alternative to, or variant of abstensionism, however far fetched.

After their resignation from parliament, Healy saw little of O'Brien but they maintained a considerable correspondence. Seeking to carry O'Brien with him, Healy provided him with political intelligence selected to that end. Exasperated by O'Brien's prolixity (which was aggravated by the illegibility of his script), he was alternately irritated and intrigued by his refusal to attorn to political realities. To Maurice he wrote in December 1919 that he was reading Erich Von Ludendorf's copious memoirs 'which remind me of a Prussian William O'Brien'.[11]

In late November 1919 William O'Brien published a remarkable introduction to a re-issue of his 1890 novel, *When We Were Boys*, a tale of Fenian youth, written during two separate terms of imprisonment in Galway jail. It was a belated riposte to those who had accused him of anti-clericalism in the creation of the character of Monsignor McGrudder. He claimed that his novel represented 'the first attempt of an Irish writer to analyse, except in terms of mawkish conventionality, the temperament and personality of the priests of Ireland which must always remain the master-key to the understanding of the deepest things in Irish life'. His chief purpose was to denounce the Irish party and to laud the new generation of nationalists. He identified the true acolytes of Mgr. McGrudder as the departed careerists of the Irish party, 'smelling, like their original, of the rancid unction of the Super-Catholic-politician'. O'Brien was evidently either insensible to Healy's overpowering ecclesiastical whiff, or found it a more fragrant scent.

He boasted of the book's prophetic accuracy, its tracking of the cycle of disillusionment with 'the Parliamentarian "putrefaction" (to use the awful word employed by Canon Sheehan) in which Fenianism had its origin, followed now as then by the same consecrated madness of revolt foretold with a prophetic inspiration in his *Graves at Kilnamorna*.' The novel's hero Ken Rohan was a precursor of Sinn Féin:

> No more startling testimony of the truth of the book's diagnosis of life in the Ireland of the 'Sixties need surely be adduced than the fact that the Ken Rohan of a generation ago might have sat for the portrait of almost any of the gallant men who only the other day faced the muzzles of the guns in something like an ecstasy in the execution-yard of Kilmainham Jail.[12]

The fervour with which O'Brien in old age embraced the new evangel, and his refusal to recognise any historical or ideological distinction between the 1916 rising and nineteenth-century Fenianism, were entirely in character, as was his frenzied restatement of his hatred of Redmond and Dillon's defeated Irish party to assert the coherence of the lurching course of his political career. Healy shamelessly flattered O'Brien in his comments on the preface. John Dillon wrote to T. P. O'Connor with much justification that it was 'horribly venomous, and really his egotism amounts to mania'.[13] Healy wrote to Maurice the following year that he was half-way through O'Brien's just published *Evening Memories*, which he described as 'very interesting, very egotistical, and in some places very false. Still, it will teach the Sinns that there were great men before Agamemnon, and I think that was his principal object'.[14]

As the tempo of violence in Ireland mounted, Healy renewed his debate with his brother, to whom he wrote with affectionate sarcasm in July 1920:

> Doesn't it look as if the 'misguided young men' would score again? Barristers and solicitors of nearly forty years standing, despite great expertness in advocacy and knowledge, seem not to prevail as quickly as the boys with bombs and revolvers . . . Of course Lloyd George is a liar from the beginning, and will wriggle and dodge for all he is worth, but in the result nothing less will be accepted than Colonial Home Rule with customs and excise . . .
>
> . . . All the old Tories now are practically converts to the idea of self-determination. It is painful to think that arson and felonies should be the chief argument for such a change of heart, but apparently Ireland is not an isolated example of this miracle.[15]

Healy followed closely the movement of events in London. The government was divided, and constrained by international opinion. He wrote to Maurice that 'of course if it was not for outside opinion, and the Irish in America, '98 tactics would be in full swing, but only a minority in the Cabinet now have faith in them'.[16] Lloyd George was under pressure from the Colonial Prime Ministers to produce an Irish settlement. Healy's contacts with the Sinn Féin leadership remained tenuous, but he conveyed, probably through E. J. Duggan, his belief that if Sinn Féin did not make a settlement in the autumn of 1920, before the American elections, they would miss the tide.[17]

Dr. Mannix, the Irish-born Archbishop of Melbourne, was arrested as his ship approached Cobh on 8 August, and taken on a destroyer to England. Healy wrote to Maurice that 'the folly of the Mannix hold-up is a great score for the Sinns'. At the same time he thought it an adverse reflection on abstentionism: he wrote of the government, 'the absence of criticism leads them into one idiocy after another'.[18]

He commented shortly afterwards that 'looking on the operations of both sides tactically and strategically, as if they were Poles and Russians, I must say that the British Government are very badly served, and that the Sinn Feiners outwit and out-general them daily'.[19] He remained nervous that the initiative would pass from Sinn Féin, and fearful of a military onslaught. In an article in Beaverbrook's *Sunday Express* he sought to goad the coalition into taking action to break the impasse:

> Its members wring their hands, asking: What are we to do? My belief is that, while their Government survives, nothing useful will be done for Ireland.
>
> Of course Mr. Lloyd George has declared his willingness to meet the leaders of any responsible section, but the leaders of no responsible section are willing to negotiate with him. To the naked vision of every observer Mr. Lloyd George is as powerless as the hall porter in Downing Street. Parley with him would lead nowhere. For, supposing that the Prime Minister, in spite of Sir Edward Carson, could cajole the House of Commons into considering some measure beyond the absurdity he has proffered, what would be the answer of the House of Lords?
>
> They make a majority, so the trapdoor of the House of Lords, with its murdering-hole for Irish legislation, does not beckon enticingly to those with whom Mr. Lloyd George desires to confer. Possibly, he might be ready to give them, for a consideration, his private I-O-U; but what would befall the attempt to discount such a scrap of paper? The Prime Minister's wish to meet them can only be gratified by a pilgrimage to Wormwood Scrubs.[20]

He gleefully reported to O'Brien that, espying John Dillon in the Visitors' Gallery, Lloyd George had said to Bonar Law, 'there's Dillon upstairs, as saturnine and melancholy as ever'.[21] The mercurial Healy was in his element in the flux which attended the demise of the Irish party. Writing to Maurice with cheerful cynicism in August 1920, his argument was coarsely parodic of Parnellian praxis:

> Let everything go into the mash-tub. The downfall of the Dillonites is now in remote perspective and does not weigh in my judgement. Something has been lost, no doubt, in the loss of an honest Irish representation, but it is balanced by gain. I confess I would have both the Rapparee organisations and the Parliamentary, to shake the nerves of the Cabinet; but the Sinns are young, and the stench of Mollydom is yet too great.[22]

Seeking to coax Maurice from his disapprobation of Sinn Féin, Healy proffered a belligerent epitaph of their parliamentary careers:

> Anyhow we fought and helped to smash a gang of fools who ruined the Parliamentary movement and did endless mischief for twenty years. Their successors may do no better, but they will last our time I fancy; and I was once greatly impressed by a remark by T.D. [Sullivan] when the Party were at their zenith – 'what a pity', said he, 'that A.M. and now yourself

> should seem always to have cut across the lines of the majority supporting the [illegible] party of the time'. Take this to heart now that we are old. Our enemies are in the dust; let us not needlessly make new ones when we can do no good nor affect a ripple on the stream.[23]

Returning from England in early August 1920, after a heated altercation with Bonar Law, Healy reported to Maurice that Churchill, Walter Long, and F.E. Smith were opposed to further concessions on Ireland,

> and that Bonar Law is prepared to support Lloyd George, and so is Balfour and the more reputable Tory Ministers. I met Bonar Law, who is very fierce; but I did not pretend that I knew this; but he seemed to outline that the new Bill would hang half a hundred of the Sinn Feiners. I hinted that if so he might look out for Downing Street. My opinion is that they are simply striking in the dark.[24]

He reported to O'Brien: 'Bonar has flitted from the pure Carsonites, but W. Long remains with them, abetted by Winston and F.E. L. Geo is the real obstacle. On partition he is a Siamese twin of Carson . . .'[25]

Healy sought to bring Beaverbrook, with whom he stayed while in England, to a more enlightened view of Irish affairs. In December 1919 he had angrily remonstrated over the treatment of Irish affairs by Beaverbrook's *Express* newspapers:

> When I spoke about my country to you, you truly said it does not interest you. Why then interest yourself against us? Can't you leave us alone? Our fallen and powerless land has been assailed and besmirched enough by the liars of the last 750 years, to supply England with all the provender she requires in that branch of industry. It only irritates, like the daily insults poured on our population by your soldiers – even on my son who served 4¾ years. Let us leave this to fishfags.[26]

As the end of 1920 approached, the war of independence entered its most violent phase. Convinced of the necessity to achieve a political settlement, Healy sought unceasingly to impress on Beaverbrook the sterility of British policy in Ireland, and the folly of ceding effective control of the country to the military. He wrote from the Law Library in November:

> The Shins have got thousands of recruits by the hanging of young Barry etc. Nobody has been frightened save those who have lost property and in no country do the propertied classes make or unmake revolutions. It is like when Clanrickarde said, 'they won't intimidate me by shooting my agents', and the young Shins own nothing and are reckless of their lives. . . . Of course like the man who tried to make his donkey do without food and would have succeeded only the brute died, your military geniuses

> are assuring Lloyd George that they are on the eve of success. Give them a few months more, a free hand and increased pay and allowances and the Irish will be wiped off the map . . . We shall have a very unpleasant winter, uglier things will be done, and then the damfools will be at the end of their resources and will be thrown over as branded failures. Hamar will then announce that he was against reprisals from the start.[27]

Beaverbrook told Healy he would pass the letter to Bonar Law.[28] Healy wrote again four days later from his home in Chapelizod. Infuriated by the pronouncements of Hamar Greenwood, the Chief Secretary, he warned of the impact of the Black and Tans on public opinion in Ireland.

> Every morning nothing but murders, every night nothing but lies and folly from Hamar. It's no use showing anything to Bonar but if the awful cost of the apparatus of slaughter as well as its futility could be brought home to the taxpayers, that might be useful. This morning on my way to Court, twenty huge motor lorries and two armoured cars swung by. Two loads of Black and Tans with rifles pointed at us, in our peaceful village, where every house sent one or two soldiers to the War, and where I saw two years ago the Shin Fein cavalcade hissed on its way to Wolfe Tone's grave.[29]

At the end of November he renewed his assault on the policy of the government in a further letter to Beaverbrook:

> The Ministers who made the unhappy boast that they would 'put down the murder gang' will soon be mocked at by their supporters, and for every lad they torture or hang, a dozen will come forward gaily to take their place. 'Mountjoy' is not ill-named.[30]

The following month Archbishop Clune of Perth went to Dublin with the acquiescence of Lloyd George to see Griffith and Collins. The Irish were prepared to agree to a truce, but the government required a surrender of arms. Infuriated by what he saw as a breach of faith, Healy despatched to Beaverbrook a searing indictment of the Prime Minister:

> No worse incident has occurred for a hundred years. The Irish have dozens of instances to cite of treachery and breach against the English. They have now been befooled into parley, through an Australian loyalist, selected not by them, but by L.G. Of course, they are woefully ignorant of England, and its cross-currents, just as the Gaelic Elizabethans were. They have no experience, or allowance for Cabinet difficulties, or necessary lying. They treat England as a single and simple Power, whereas we know that there is no such thing as 'England' as an abstraction, but only a hive of buzzers and swarmers, and damn fools, like ourselves.

> The point I gather, taken by the blessed Cabinet donkies was that the Shins should surrender arms before a truce. This is worthy of Gallipoli, Antwerp, Deniken, Wrangel and the cohort of cods. I am for doing business and making peace . . . Fail to accept the Clune compromise, and when you kill Collins, further amusements must spring up.[31]

The political impasse made Healy increasingly restive and revived his misgivings about abstentionism. He wrote to O'Brien in January 1921 'I don't think the *Shin* aloofness from Westminster an infallible specific. It has justification and merits. Existing horrors, and the 1920 Act swear out however against it'.[32] He wrote to Beaverbrook in March, responding to a comment of Bonar Law: 'Who sows and will reap in Ireland? The day of argument is past. Dynamic forces alone now count. These for the moment England wields, stript of all moral authority'.[33]

Healy continued to be bitterly dismissive of the obliquity of Lloyd George's soundings of Sinn Féin. He warned Beaverbrook in May 1921 that 'If L. Geo means peace he must table his proposals. He can't trap the Shins as he hopes. They know him and his dodges. Informal emissaries are employed and discredited. No hackle will disguise the hook'. The military admitted they could not win on their present tactics, and looked for more drastic methods. 'British statesmanship is bankrupt in Ireland and quite unteachable. All talk of peace is eye-wash, to tide over a difficulty'.[34] He wrote again later that month condemning the government's failure to accept the truce which Archbishop Clune had sought to broker: 'Those who rejected Clune's Xmas truce, in the belief that the Shins were busted, were poor 'prentice hands in the trade of State-craft, & of course felt that the English knew better than the natives'.[35]

Healy had lost all faith in the Chief Secretary, whom he characterised as 'a transient carpet-bagger':

> Greenwood's brag has had more disastrous consequences than even I had anticipated. Instead of cowing the Shins, he has nerved them to daring which I did not believe them capable of. He has not advanced an inch towards their suppression in the 6 months that have flown since Bishop Clune's 'Truce' was burned down by Bonar, F.E. & Winston. For all effective purposes British law is dead in Ireland outside armoured-car radius. . . . Out of Bedlam no such councillor of the King as Greenwood could have been selected. His lies alone would set the hearts of this people ablaze.[36]

In May 1921, on Beaverbrook's initiative, Healy approached de Valera to induce him to agree to meet James Craig, the Prime Minister of Northern Ireland. While barren of substantive results, the fact of their meeting had an intrinsic significance.[37] Healy had some success in persuading

Beaverbrook of the necessity for a political settlement with Sinn Féin. He wrote to Maurice on 6 June that 'strange to say, I had a note from Max yesterday, in which he said he was coming round to my views on Irish government'. Beaverbrook's conversion was impeccably timed. The support of the traditionally diehard unionist *Daily Express* was to counterweigh the opposition of more recalcitrant Conservatives, and ease the path to a treaty.[38]

As the pressure on the government to take the political initiative mounted, Healy wrote to his brother:

> . . . I have no expectation of a happy termination of the negotiations, simply because of my distrust for Lloyd George. He will try to manoeuvre the Sinns into such a position that they can be represented as abandoning the Republic, and then, having tried to discredit them, treat them as impossible to satisfy on more moderate lines.[39]

Healy observed the flux of coalition politics. On 21 June the Lord Chancellor, Birkenhead, made a theatrically grim speech in the Lords, ending with the declaration that 'if we should be forced to the melancholy conclusion that by force and force alone can this mischief be extirpated or prevented, however sorrowfully we accept it, we shall not hesitate logically and completely to act upon it'.[40] On 24 June the government resolved to invite de Valera, and Sir James Craig, to a conference in London to attempt to bring the conflict to an end. Healy wrote to O'Brien on 28 June that the cabinet had been

> nearly cleft asunder over Ireland, and at its second last meeting Lloyd George threw a chit across the table to Hamar which was thought to mean he must yield. Nevertheless a grudging decision was come to whereby F.E. was made the mouthpiece of the doctrine (against his will) that force was the sole remedy. The kick against the speech by both Peers and Commoners (many Peers abstained in the Division) led to the de Valera invitation. In this the colonial Premiers also counted for righteousness.
>
> Prior to this Lloyd George was determined to dissolve in the autumn, and arouse an anti-Irish and anti-Catholic issue.
>
> He only had a majority of one in the cabinet against a settlement with Ireland. *He* alone was the obstacle to a Truce in December, yet he told Archbishop Clune 'Tell Michael if he has difficulty with his colleagues, I have as great with mine'. This was false, and he brought in Field Marshal Wilson to defeat the Truce, by demanding surrender of arms, after 'Michael' had been prevailed on by the Archbishop to write a letter consenting to the Truce in terms stipulated by Lloyd George . . . Downing Street wiseacres were cocksure that 'Michael's' acquiescence meant that the I.R. army was bust.[41]

Healy was in receipt of excellent political intelligence, but did not pause to consider the tactical underpinning of Lloyd George's intransigence. Perhaps in part to play down the striking affinity of their political styles, Healy in a letter to O'Brien drew a brilliantly vivid caricature of the Prime Minister, a distillation of Catholic nationalist suspicions of a nonconformist radical:

> There is not an atom of sincerity in him. He hates Catholicity both in Ireland and Poland. Even French atheism he dislikes, because the Catholic death-bed looms in the offing.
>
> I don't like to treat his invitation to de Valera as a mere trap, but I know the truth is not in him. He is drunk with power. He is not a gentleman. Patagonia and Marconi tell his footsteps. I confess, in trying to establish the character of English ministers, I prefer Hatfield or Knowsley to Criccietth. The homely-pathetic Welsh grandfather (or step-uncle) I salute and reverence. Granted they were incorrupt in their Silurian isolation, where is David in the hotbed of Downing Street? All his generous ideas have wilted. He has shed everything that his class call 'principle' (i.e. opinion), often clottedly ignorant. He in my vision simply and starkly stands forth as an expert in thimble and pea. Will he diddle the Shins?[42]

Healy remained mistrustful of Lloyd George, whom he had condemned to Maurice in 1919 as 'a shallow unscrupulous incompetent man'.[43] Yet he wrote to O'Brien the following year 'if Lloyd George were not a bondsman to the Tories, he would make a Treaty with the Shins as with the Soviets'.[44] Healy's deeply ambivalent attitude to Lloyd George was tinged with certain sectarian animosity, and had an edge of personal rivalry. Healy on the one hand considered him cynical and personally hostile to Irish nationalism, in part due to his repression of his own ethnicity in the pursuit of ambition. On the other, he recognised in him an inspired and driven pragmatist, uniquely capable of overbearing the political resistance in Britain to an Irish settlement.

In one of its aspects Healy's antagonism to Lloyd George was the dread of an Irish nationalist coming to terms with what had become, if it had not always been, the inevitability of partition. His railing against the anti-Irish and anti-Catholic bias he imputed to Lloyd George owed much to the premonition that Lloyd George would achieve a partitionist Irish settlement which would leave Healy, realist though he was, with an unassuagable sense of personal defeat.

On 9 July a truce was declared. Healy wrote exultantly to Maurice from Glenaulin in the small hours:

> The 'misguided boys' have won!!
> 'Ain't the owners gay,
> 'Cos we fetched the Bolivar out across the bay'

The Cabinet has decided to grant full fiscal freedom and the control of all departments . . . There is to be no representation at Westminster, thank God . . .

Lloyd George will try to whittle down these concessions, but the majority of the Cabinet would break with him if he does. He wished to go to the country on an anti-Irish cry, but his rivals prefer the cry of 'Peace with Ireland' at the hustings . . . The Black and Tans may prove uncontrollable, and smash the truce, with the pretence that it was broken by the Sinns.[45]

The Treaty Negotiations

Healy still could not overcome his brother's scepticism towards Sinn Féin. Maurice's assessment of the situation was profoundly pessimistic. In particular he feared the consequences of republican violence. Healy responded to Maurice's expressions of concern (which were to prove in his own case well founded) with premature complacency:

With regard to the political situation, I cannot understand, when I explained matters to you, how you can speak of the undesirability of residence in Ireland next winter. The case as far as I know is settled, and victory achieved by the pluck and sacrifices of the men who risked their lives for their country. The names of those who have fallen will be held in general honour when ours are justly forgotten . . . I think the road is clear and safe to settlement.[46]

Healy justified his support for Sinn Féin partly in terms of its prospects of realising more than had been forthcoming under home rule: what he referred to as 'the full fiscal freedom of the country, and its administrative freedom'.[47]

On 29 July, he despatched an exasperated letter in response to Maurice's remonstrances, in which he adumbrated an historical argument of considerable lack of subtlety.

As to what you write politically, your frame of mind must be that of all the Tories in this Library, who deplore the victory of the Sinns . . . I am sure there will be pinpricks and bristles, but the main fact stares you in the face that the Sinns won in three years what we did not win in forty. You cannot make revolutions with rosewater, or omelettes without breaking eggs. If you read even the account of the judges' charges in the tithe war, the murders were as terrible as those lately committed, and for what a petty result. One of those orations was so like Serjeant Sullivan's late deliverance that the Tories in the Library repaid him with the charge of plagiarism, which I thought unjust . . . I dare say mistakes of detail will

> be made by inexperienced men and that the English Treasury will get the better of them on many points, but in broad outline they have got what was denied us by Gladstone, Asquith and Bannerman. Whether they have won it at the point of the revolver or by jaw-breaking oratory, the verdict of your future historian will matter little. The fact is that they have won.[48]

If Healy's argument for supporting the new order of Sinn Féin had become by 1921 compelling, the brusqueness with which he dismissed four decades of parliamentary nationalism approached the condition of a schism with his own past.

When Maurice complained about the actions of republicans in Cork, Healy indulgently retorted: 'The sins of ignorant youths without experience or training are I think to be judged very differently from those of an organised administration preaching law and order, and with hypocrisies about German atrocities on their lips. The Cork Sinns at any rate don't pretend to rob their victims for their good'.[49]

Healy wrote an article for Beaverbrook's *Sunday Express* on 21 August 1921, published under the title 'Who will break the Irish Truce?' A largely sagacious attempt to press forward an Irish settlement, it in some degree laid the ground for his own later intervention. The truce he believed would last.

> Meanwhile there is a long leeway of mistrust to be caught up on. To clear the slate will take time. The Archer-Shee angel and the de Valera devil are inevitable products of political romance. All that is happening behind the scenes is that quite amiable mortals on each shore of the Channel are trying to do the best they can for their countries.
>
> English statesmen can go a certain length to meet the Irish claim; but they are riding at an anchor moored by the state of public opinion as fixedly as Gibraltar. It is the same with their adversaries; and to a like bollard are the Orange leaders tied.

General Smuts, the South African Prime Minister, had sought in London and Dublin to use his good offices to promote a settlement. On 4 August before returning to South Africa, he had written a somewhat clumsy letter to de Valera urging acceptance of Lloyd George's proposals. The Prime Minister, without disclosing what they were, had published Smuts' letter. Healy's strictures on this proceeding conveyed that, even though out of parliament, he did not propose to let such prime-ministerial sleight of hand pass unremarked:

> To enlist the great Boer statesman to string the Government proposals into nursery-rhymes set to African lullabies for Irish ears was crudely inartistic. To publish this letter in advance of the text of the Cabinet

> offer, and thereby to give the world a false and unwarranted idea of its generosity, was sheer mischief.
>
> I yield Mr. Lloyd George full credit for the advance he has made; but it no more amounts to Dominion Home rule, as General Smuts alleged, than it proffers a republic. To say so, by such lips, might be reckoned by unrested minds as an attempt to deceive the people before they had an opportunity of knowing what the offer was. It injured the prospect of acceptance, as anything wearing an air of trickiness must. In a solemn affair prejudice and suspicion are a bad overture to business.
>
> I do not recall the incident by way of reproach to the Prime Minister (whose courage deserves bouquets rather than buffetings), but as some explanation of the attitude of Mr. De Valera and his friends.

Part of Healy's purpose was to allay the British public's mistrust of de Valera. His own erroneous assessment of de Valera as a patriot of ingenuous sanctity was compounded by his inability to resist a graceless cut at his old Irish party adversaries: 'The Irish leader I only met in 1918 for a few hours, and have not seen him since; but it was easy to discern that in his nature there is a strain of simplicity quite lacking in the Irish politicians with whom Mr. Lloyd George was familiar'. He went on to assert that 'no freak "Ulster" can have any save artificial life'.[50]

Healy continued to despatch reports of the government's divided councils. Writing to O'Brien he professed to believe in the possibility of a settlement that would avert partition by conceding to Belfast only a parliament with control of local affairs: 'L. Geo. of course has to be watched, but it is said that the Thanes will desert him if he jibs. He has bitter rivals in the Cabinet. This position will entirely justify the Truce and Settlement by the Shins'. Of the situation within the cabinet he wrote:

> Austen Chamberlain has behaved very well since Bonar resigned and in a cold way has taken our part. F. E. Smith, in spite of the speech Lloyd George forced him to make, is anxious for a settlement, and has become the 'desired' of the moderate Tories to replace Lloyd George . . . Only for Winston a cabinet transformation would have been wrought last May.[51]

On the delicate issue of how a settlement was to be ratified on the Irish side, William O'Brien had a surer intimation than Healy of what was to prove the sanguinary metaphysics of the Republic. At the time of de Valera's meetings with Lloyd George in London after the truce, Healy wrote to O'Brien that de Valera was 'very wisely going to submit any offer to the new Dail Erin [*sic*] leaving it to take the burden or acceptance of battle'. O'Brien thought that there should be a plebiscite to sanction the abandonment of the Republic. While Healy vaguely assented to this procedure for 'shedding the Republic', he was thinking in terms of a general election to follow the ratification of a treaty by the Dail rather than a referendum. Healy continued to repose an exaggerated trust in de Valera's resolve to carry a settlement in Ireland: 'I am not afraid of a reference to Dail Erin, when the fighting men are backing de Valera'.[52]

Healy wrote to O'Brien that 'de Valera and his men understand little of British cross-currents, and the embarrassment of their own difficulties may blind them to those on the English concessionist side'. He feared delay would shipwreck a settlement. 'Fortunately the English press is in a very different temper from 1886, while all the Irish unionists of influence north or south are old hands'. Healy was deeply affected by the threat of a renewed military onslaught in Ireland in the event of the negotiations breaking down: '. . . there would be immediately fifty executions, and all the Custom House prisoners would be tried and shot. Indeed the cabinet was engaged in the delicate discussion of substituting hangings for shootings when Smuts was got by the King to interfere'.

Healy credited Alfred Cope, the assistant Under-Secretary for Ireland, with much of the credit for wresting the initiative back from the military:

> The military here are humble enough now. Cope's conduct has surpassed that of Thomas Drummond.
>
> By the way Campbell was outed because he was going to reprieve Kevin Barry, and in hot haste French was sent back to Dublin to relieve him as Lord Justice.
>
> Had Greenwood been here instead of Cope these last ten days, the Military would have smashed all arrangements for a truce as the Shins having been sold last December when Archbishop Clune came from Lloyd George were highly and naturally suspicious of fresh trickery. Cope knowing the King was friendly, bearded Macready with high courage, while the old Castle gang wrung their hands over his temerity, and 'shameful surrender'.[53]

When the Dáil met on 16 August 1921, its members took an oath to the Republic.[54] This rhetorical reflex was to compound the difficulties involved in the ratification of a negotiated settlement. O'Brien wrote on 24 August that it was 'perhaps a misfortune' that he had been abroad when de Valera had called to see him at Mallow two weeks previously: 'It might have been possible to avert the convocation of the Dáil and the swearing in which made the lowering of the Republican flag all but impossible'. He had written to de Valera from France, but felt that it 'may now be too late to raise Partition as that which renders Lloyd George's terms unacceptable'. Healy sought to disabuse O'Brien of the idea of constituting himself a magus to Eamon de Valera: 'I return your memo but fear your visitor needs no sage counsellor of experience'.[55] O'Brien, as Healy reported to his brother, was greatly concerned about the oath taken by the Republicans: 'I am replying that they will find some formula to shuffle off that mortal coil, but that I dislike such circus-riding as much as himself'.[56]

Healy formed an early aversion to Erskine Childers. He wrote to O'Brien that 'the neo-extremists, forsooth, are led by Erskine Childers who has gone over to keep the I.R. flag flying at all costs, as a gallant Englishman'. When O'Brien concurred that 'it does seem a pity that de Valera should give Englishmen like Childers and Barton a look-in', Healy wrote to explain that his criticisms had not extended to Robert Barton: 'He is not English, but a Wicklow man of the Parnell type'.[57]

Healy's correction was intriguing. He realised it would not do, even in the coarse brushstrokes of chauvinistic nationalism, to equate Barton with Childers, the son of an English father and an Irish mother, who grew up in Wicklow, who had undergone a double conversion of escalating intensity, first to home rule and then to republicanism. The introduction of Parnell's name is suggestive. Healy's formulation avoided any necessity to designate either Wicklow Protestant as an Irishman *tout court*. He wrote around the same time to Maurice, that 'one of the intransigents forsooth, is Erskine Childers, a British officer who has only a drain of Irish blood in his veins!!'[58]

While the union of hearts was no more, one of the constraints Lloyd George was under was the necessity to attorn to American opinion: 'It is clear that Lloyd George cannot visit Washington unless he has settled with Ireland, and this is the only pull we have on him. Gladstonian generosity is buried in Westminster Abbey'.[59] Healy continued to mistrust Lloyd George, whom he suspected had been trying to lay 'a booby trap for the Sinns. Apparently his plan was to get them first to drop their extreme claims and then, having discredited them with their own extremists, to allow his "offer" to be whittled down in Parliament by hostile amendments'.[60]

In spite of his misgivings, Healy recognised that Lloyd George was central to any settlement. As he told Maurice, he had warned the Sinn Féin leaders 'of the instability of British politics, and that they should close while Lloyd George is in the saddle'. Casting round for a settlement, he was prepared to contemplate a more realistic approach to partition: 'if we could get the Catholic part of the Six Counties away from the Belfast jurisdiction, I should be disposed to recommend the acceptance of almost any reasonable compromise on other questions'.[61] The pursuit of such a policy was however seriously inhibited by the rhetorical and sentimental refusal of nationalists to countenance partition in principle (as well as by the related belief in the possibility of achieving a whittling down of the territory under the jurisdiction of the state of Northern Ireland which would deprive it of political viability).

The negotiations for a settlement commenced in London on 11 October. It was a considerable irony, and not without consequence, that Healy continued to have closer contacts with members of the British government, leading unionists, and senior figures in the administration in Ireland, than with Sinn Féin. Up to the time of the treaty negotiations, Healy's contacts with Sinn Féin were limited, and were chiefly through E. J. Duggan.[62] Healy seems to have intermittently encountered Michael Collins after Collins' and Boland's visit to Glenaulin in November 1918. According to Healy's daughter Collins while 'on the run' made several visits to Glenaulin, although her father's memoirs make no reference to them.[63] Healy later claimed to have warned Collins against going to London unless de Valera went, 'but he was too unselfish and unsuspecting to refuse'.[64] Healy's acquaintance with Arthur Griffith dated from the Mansion House conference. As a young man, Griffith had been an ardent Parnellite in the split, and had stood on the platform of Broadstone station as Parnell set off for his last meeting at Creggs.[65] While he showed himself impressively pragmatic, he cannot have regarded Healy with any personal warmth.

Healy had written to Maurice after the truce was declared in July that he had no relations whatever with Sinn Féin. He informed O'Brien that he was not 'in their councils and don't try to butt in'.[66] This was for want of an opening, and did not reflect any diffidence on Healy's part. The treaty negotiations were to provide his *entrée*. Healy sought to commend himself to Sinn Féin with an article which appeared in the *Irish Independent* of 19 October 1921 which commenced with the observation that 'the stumbling stone in the negotiations is whether the Ireland to which the Government had made tender is all Ireland or only a fraction thereof'. While the argument petered out in the conventional chronicle of betrayal, the 'Peace Conference Crux' of the the article's title was succinctly stated:

> In 1914, Mr. Redmond and Mr. Dillon at the Buckingham Palace Conference with Messrs. Carson and Craig, on the eve of war, refused to purchase Home Rule by any such surrender, yet seven years later, Sinn Feiners are expected to crawl down to a tamer position than that of the dethroned Parliamentarians and go forth to history as signatories to a pact in Downing Street which Mr. Redmond refused to make in a Royal Palace.
>
> Before they were invited 'to ascertain how the association of Ireland with that community of nations known as the British Empire may best be reconciled with Irish National aspirations', a *fait accompli* as to 'Ulster' was arranged and the most minute details as to partition received statutory vigour. They might, perhaps, be asked to hold aside the banner of the Republic in reverent repose, but how could any leader trail the flag of Ireland below the Redmond level?[67]

Healy's presentation of the treaty dilemma was intended to convey to Sinn Féin that he understood their position, and was capable of communicating some appreciation of it to the British side. His argument, which proceeded backwards from the problem of presenting and justifying a settlement on the Irish side, was crude and perfunctory. It was a far cry from the severe *haute politique* which Parnell had so masterfully practised.

Healy's renascence proceeded apace. The evening that his article appeared, the revenant of the old parliamentary order appeared to deliver the inaugural address at the annual conference of the Catholic Truth Society of Ireland in the Mansion House in Dublin. His address, on the subject of why the church was hated, was delivered to a formidable array of church dignitaries who entered in procession with Cardinal Logue at their head to loud applause from the assembled laity. The supposed hatred of the church Healy attributed to a reaction to the church's stern resistance to the theories on the origin of the species of 'so-called philosophers and scientists', whose thinking ('this bogey of the monkey and the microbe') led to 'loose thinking and loose living'.[68] It was an assured and amusing speech: he had lost neither his flair nor his bigoted anti-modernism. Ecclesiastically fortified, he was ready for his re-entry into the domain of secular politics.

Healy's involvement in the treaty negotiations was not public knowledge, and was considerably more extensive than the cryptic references in his memoirs suggested. No doubt he offered his counsel as a lawyer, and to place his constitutional and parliamentary expertise over almost four decades at the service of the Sinn Féin representatives, and sought thereafter to enlarge his role. While kept at a distance by the delegation, his access was enough to permit him to claim a certain standing in his discussions with British ministers. If it is unlikely that his role significantly affected the course of the negotiations or their outcome, it did much to achieve his rehabilitation with the Irish government that was to emerge from the treaty negotiations, and to pave the way for his appointment as Governor-General. To the extent that he enjoyed a degree of access to both sides, he was a uniquely privileged witness to the drama enacted in London between October and December 1921.

The counsel Healy gave Griffith, as rendered by Beaverbrook, reveals Healy's (and Beaverbrook's) approach to the negotiations. 'You can get a fresh deal for Ireland but you can only get as much as the Conservative Party can be persuaded to give you. The Premier himself is in chains to the Conservatives in this matter. Nevertheless, the great mass of sensible Conservative opinion will give you much if you handle the situation sensibly'.[69]

When the negotiations opened, Lloyd George sought preliminary assurances on the issues of allegiance to the crown, membership of the

British Empire, and on the British demand that the ports, harbours and inlets of Ireland be placed at the disposal of the Imperial Government for naval defence purposes, in peace or war. Healy saw the Irish delegates on Saturday 22 October and tendered his advice in relation to the Prime Minister's opening gambit.[70] His suggested line of response appears from a draft in his own hand, on the notepaper of The Vineyard, Fulham, Beaverbrook's London residence where he was staying:

> The Govt. is determined to wring a definite answer to the enquiry whether Ireland is ready to take her part in the British Empire or not. The Shins allege that the use of the word 'Ireland' is a trap and that the Govt. by the 1920 Partition Act split Ireland in twain and that by their legislation no such country now legally exists, & that two fictitious entities have been created known as Northern & Southern Ireland & that until the Govt. inform them what their intentions are as to perpetuating the division of the country no question can arise as to their allegiance to the Crown & Empire because the Partition destroyed the status of Irish subjects of His Majesty & they will never consent to be known as Southern Irishmen.[71]

Beaverbrook published two accounts of Healy's involvement at this juncture. According to Beaverbrook's 1925 account Healy asked him to advise as to the form the response should take, and he had assisted in drafting a response. He did not repeat this assertion in his 1963 version of events, in which he credited Healy with the formulation of the suggested reply. Beaverbrook immediately afterwards encountered Churchill, Bonar Law and Birkenhead at the home of Sir Edward Goulding. When Churchill offered to disclose the terms of the Prime Minister's most recent communication to the Sinn Féiners, Beaverbrook was able to boast that he knew not merely the terms of the Premier's letter but the Sinn Féin reply which had not yet been received. Beaverbrook claimed that he did not disclose his source, but those present were well aware of his close relations with Healy, whose credentials as an *interlocuteur valable* were thus established.[72]

Beaverbrook's account, an anecdote swollen in the ceaseless retelling, was wildly inaccurate so far as the course of the treaty negotiations were concerned. The measured and elliptical Irish reply to the British government of 27 October, further to the draft treaty proposals forwarded on 24 October, (although predicated on what was variously described as 'a free and undivided Ireland', and 'the unimpaired unity of Ireland'), did not incorporate the argument Healy had advanced. Moreover, the British demand, which was renewed in the initial response to the Irish draft treaty, was not quite the ultimatum suggested by Beaverbrook. Lloyd George, who professed to require an unequivocal response to enable him to overwhelm Conservative opponents of a settlement, arranged to meet Griffith to whom he complained that the Irish reply was 'so worded that he did not know where he stood'. Elucidating the reply, Griffith told him that 'he had sent us a document obviously couched for publication if the Conference failed. We had replied in similar terms'.[73]

Beaverbrook's account does make clear that Healy regarded himself as acting in concert with him, and had no compunction about disclosing political intelligence in relation to the thinking of the Irish delegation, and his estimate of their position.[74] Even though Healy's disclosures did not impinge on the outcome of the preliminary issue, the fact that Healy felt at liberty to convey to Beaverbrook what he had learnt of the Sinn Féin position was disquieting. Anything which detracted from the Irish delegation's aura of reticent aloofness took from the strength of their negotiating position. Healy's dealings with Beaverbrook revealed, apart from his compulsive indiscreetness, a disconcerting inability to recognise a clear line of demarcation between the interests of the Irish delegation and those of the British ministry. His commitment, no less than the government's, was to the conclusion of a treaty.

Beaverbrook was combining with considerable acumen his twin roles, as a politician and newspaper proprietor. The *Sunday Express* of 23 October ran as its lead story an account of the Prime Minister's sending 'by the hand of Michael Collins a virtual ultimatum to the Sinn Fein leaders in Dublin'. This was the demand that they state explicitly if they were not prepared to concede allegiance to the British Crown. Sinn Féin's reply, which the paper reported had already been decided on, would not be a direct refusal to accept the allegiance test, but 'simply a renewal of the hair-splitting' which characterised the correspondence preliminary to the negotiations. The Prime Minister would be left with no alternative but to dissolve, hoping to sweep the country on an anti-Sinn Féin cry:

> On the other hand, it is the determination of the Irish leaders, if they can control their own following, not to play into Mr. Lloyd George's hands by restarting the rebellion the moment the conference is declared off. *They will observe the Truce so long as the election lasts, on the ground that a new Government might be returned not pledged to Mr. George's decision.*

The true cause of the impending breakdown however lay in the resolve of unionists to resist any threat to the territorial integrity of Northern Ireland: 'Once again Ulster bars the way to peace with Southern Ireland'. This, rather than nationalist intransigence, as expressed in the recent letter of de Valera to the pope, was the root of the difficulty: ' . . . the British people ought to know the truth – that the breakdown of the conference is not due to letters between Kings and Popes and soi-disant Presidents, but to the conflicting desire of Catholics and Protestants to possess a few villages and acres in Fermanagh and Tyrone'.[75]

The article was evidently by diverse hands and based on disparate sources of which Healy was only one, and was not altogether consistent. Amid the italics and bold print, the direction of Beaverbrook's policy was discernible. He championed a settlement with nationalist Ireland: while the position of northern unionists had to be defended, it could not be permitted to ruin the prospects for a separate settlement with southern Ireland. If the *Sunday Express* line was intended to promote a settlement and avert the collapse of the negotiations, its brinkmanship risked bringing about the reverse. In exaggerating the degree to which Lloyd George's opening gambit constituted an 'ultimatum', it was in danger of creating a self-fulfilling prophesy. It was on Beaverbrook's part a characteristically perilous combination of exhilarating journalism and incautious statecraft.

The lead report in the *Daily Express* of 25 October was yet more accurate, referring to the three questions on which the British government had sought assurances. 'The gist of the Sinn Féin answer appears to be based on a celebrated Biblical precedent on the subject of rendering tribute unto Caesar. One set of questions is answered by another. What is Ireland? Until that question is answered the question of allegiance cannot be answered either . . . In a word, behind all this advance guard of dialectics lies the solid body of the Ulster problem'. The paper implicitly advocated the negotiation of 'a new religious and political frontier', based either on a plebiscite or on the census of 1919.[76] The leaks caused discord on both sides. Lloyd George accused Churchill of leaking information which appeared in the *Daily Express* of 25 October. The Irish representatives complained of leaks in general, and especially of those in the same edition of the *Daily Express*.[77]

Beaverbrook's position papers owed much to his hostility to Lloyd George, from whom he had been estranged for the previous eighteen months, and to a mistrust — largely inspired by Healy — of his intentions towards Ireland. Within days all this had changed. At Birkenhead's on 27 October, Beaverbrook and Lloyd George were reconciled, and reached an understanding in relation to Ireland. Beaverbrook was enlisted in support of what his host characterised as the troika of Lloyd George, Churchill and himself, who were resolved to face down the Tory diehards to force through a settlement with southern Ireland.[78] The *Express* newspapers continued thereafter to press for a treaty, and to assail hardline unionist opposition to a settlement in Northern Ireland and at Westminster.[79]

On 23 October, Healy had again met the Irish delegates at Hans Place, and then Lloyd George at Downing Street, apparently returning afterwards to Hans Place. The chronologically compressed entry in Childers' diary records:

> Healy here most of day. He saw Lloyd George and reported interview – black outlook. *Faux pas* was nearly committed of letting him have a memorandum for L.G. typed up here. J.C. [John Chartres, second secretary to the Irish delegation] and I protested and it was scrapped. Wonderful idea about setting up a Parliament in Ireland by Order of Council!![80]

Childers' scepticism was well-founded. A memorandum in Healy's hand in the papers of Michael Collins outlines Healy's scheme. Undated, it refers in its preamble to the negotiations which had taken place since 11 July between the British and Irish representatives. The document was a draft declaration by the British government and the Irish representatives. Under its terms, the British government undertook to ask for the assent of Parliament, as the first business of the following session, 'to the convocation in Ireland of a Constituent Assembly and to submit thereto in draft the terms of a Perpetual Treaty of Peace between the people of Ireland and the people of Great Britain and the British Empire'. The treaty would provide for the implementation of terms to be contained in a letter of the Prime Minister (what those terms were is not stated) 'and shall likewise define the safeguards required in Northern Ireland'. If the treaty was ratified with or without amendment by the Irish Constituent Assembly, it would be transmitted to the Imperial Parliament to be incorporated in a statute which could not be repealed or affected save by conjoint acts of the Irish parliament and the imperial parliament. With a view to the fuller and better representation of minorities the Irish representatives were 'prepared to assent to the invitation in manner to be prescribed by the Lord Lieutenant of representatives of such Protestant or other denominations as may desire to assist in debate on such a Treaty of Peace'.[81]

Healy's draft was predicated on the very optimistic assumption that the British government would permit the terms of a settlement to be largely determined by an Irish constituent assembly which would have a nationalist majority. The procedure prescribed was conceived not to allay the opposition of northern unionists, but to afford a political cover for a British government prepared tacitly to compel unionist participation in an all-Ireland state.

Quite apart from its dismissive attitude towards northern unionism (regarded, as was conventional in nationalist thinking, as a parasitic growth upon the trunk of British policy), the draft suggested a gross underestimation of the determination of the Conservative party to defend the position of northern unionists. That determination was shared by Lloyd George, either from personal conviction or out of the necessities of his position as a coalition Prime Minister. It had become abundantly clear that this was the minimum price for Conservative support for a settlement with Sinn Féin. Healy, as a confidant of Beaverbrook, had reason to know this better than most. His proposal was a rehearsal of the wistfully ingenious scheme he had long nurtured for an Irish settlement: it was essentially a *reprise* of what he had proposed to Asquith in February 1912, with the substitution of a constituent assembly for the bipartisan Irish cabinet.

Healy proceeded from Hans Place to Downing Street where at 5.00 p.m. he met Lloyd George, who was accompanied by the Attorney-General. A minute of the meeting of the British representatives the following day records Lloyd George's account of his meeting with Healy:

> Mr. Healy, after calling attention in bitter language to incidents which his family had endured at the hands of British officers in Ireland, had outlined certain proposals which it was understood he was suggesting to the Irish delegates, by whom he had been summoned to London. He proposed that there should be an Act of Parliament which should set up immediately for the whole of Ireland a legislature with Channel Island powers, and this legislature should negotiate a Treaty with this country. The Government of Ireland Act would not be repealed in the meantime, nor would the Ulster Bill be touched, but the legislature would be elected on a proportionate basis for the whole of Ireland. . . . The act of Union would be abolished, but allegiance to the Crown, inclusion in the Empire, and naval defence, would be admitted.
>
> There was some discussion as to the full effect of these proposals if they were adopted both by the British and Irish sides, and it was generally agreed that, apart from the difficulty involved by the abolition of the Act of Union and the position of Ulster, no steps could be taken by the British government to grant Channel Island powers to any Irish Government, unless beforehand the Irish representatives had agreed to definite proposals. The Prime Minister expressed the view that the Irish delegates would not agree to yield on the question of allegiance, independence, partition, and the navy, without reference back to Ireland. It would, therefore, be necessary to give them written terms so as to clear up ambiguity, and to invite them to submit those terms to the judgement of the Irish people.[82]

Healy's intervention was unhelpful. His scheme was unrealistic, and risked cutting athwart the Irish draft treaty which was received by the British cabinet immediately after the meeting at which Healy's proposal was considered.[83] He had however contrived to interpose himself in the negotiations, and proudly reported to Maurice the next day:

> I was in London yesterday, and by request saw the Prime Minister, after I had been discoursing with the Sinns at their suggestion. Both sides were very kind and gracious to me. . . . My impression is that things will come right . . . The Prime Minister sent for the Attorney-General to consider a proposal I made. He asked me to stay to advise the Sinns! I did not

> tell this to the Sinns, as, unless invited, I have my own business to look after. The worst that can be said of my visit is that I have kept things going. I should add that Griffith and Collins were very kind to me.[84]

Writing the same day to O'Brien, Healy again shamelessly exaggerated his own role:

> I think I should advise you that yesterday I saw both sides at the request of each, in London.
>
> I averted a break-off at least, and hope to have cluttered up a continuance. Word to this effect reached me tonight by telephone.[85]

Healy was back in London at the end of the following week. On his return he wrote to O'Brien from the Law Library:

> The situation is said to be a 'little easier' today in London, after an unhappy tangle on Sunday over the reply delivered on Saturday on 'allegiance' etc. by the Shins. All preparations were made to proclaim martial law in the twenty-six counties and the Military were jubilant. Then F.E. and Lloyd George met Arthur Griffith and Michael Collins secretly on Sunday night to talk over the trouble, but I am less confident of good results than I was.
>
> The Shins think the Empire is bust and that it is better to fight for two or three years. If it comes to that, 100,000 will be interned in ex-German camps as Lord French proposed last year and only those who take the oath of allegiance will be left at home. The ports and railways will be closed, and newspapers, telegrams and letters stopped, while all Courts will cease.
>
> The country will be ruined and the people starved, to save the faces of those who as you well said, took the impossible step at the Inauguration of the Dail lately. However all is not lost that's in danger.[86]

Healy's unveiling of this vista of devastation revealed the extent to which his thinking was coloured by the fear of the British administration in Ireland coming completely under military control, and the dread of economic collapse. The breakdown of the negotiations he feared did not occur. He wrote again to O'Brien on 14 November from Glenaulin:

> The present position may be translated so:— Lloyd George has been convinced of the sincerity and faithworthiness of the Shins, and that they will keep whatever promises they give. He has assured them he will put the settlement thro' if they don't let him down by Truce-Breach etc.
>
> The Shins now believe in Lloyd George's avowals, and that unless Thursday's Liverpool [Conservative Party] Conference would generate a thundercloud, the Ulsterites will be forced to yield.
>
> Fitzalan [the Lord Lieutenant] has been lobbying like a Trojan on the Irish side.

> Beaverbrook's promises to me have spiked B.Law's hostility, and tho' Max quarrelled with Lloyd George you will notice the Northcliffe sneer today at the 'violently pro-government attitude of the *Express*'.[87]

On Friday 25 November, Healy received a wire from Beaverbrook to cross to London at once.[88] The following day, he telegraphed O'Brien from Chapelizod: 'Strongly urge you to visit 22 Hans Place, London. Am going myself. Immediate outlook deplorable unless intervention improves prospects'. O'Brien was taken back at Healy's suggestion that he call on the Sinn Féin delegates in London. Two months previously he had asked Griffith if it would assist if he were to see Lloyd George. Griffith had then 'in the friendliest terms intimated that for the present any communication with Downing Street except through official channels might lead to an impression that Sinn Féin was weakening'. O'Brien telegraphed to Healy that he would go to London if invited.[89]

Healy's reply made clear that not merely was he himself uninvited, but that he was prepared to disregard any rebuff to intervene:

> I have your reply wire. I am no more invited than you but some touch on the tiller is needed. I thought as you knew Arthur Griffith it might do good. I called on him at the Mansion House yesterday, sent in a note, and he didn't even come out to see me. Still, where the country needs service, these slights are mere pinpricks. We are not questing for Stars and Garters. Whatever mi-aw [mí-ádh (bad luck)] is over the island, things are mistwisted today. Locked horns between Shindom and Belfast. 'You swear fealty and I'll talk about United Parliament'. 'You grant unity, and I'll consider Fealty'. Six of one or half a dozen of the other.

The ebulliently cynical tenor of Healy's letter can only have confirmed O'Brien's misgivings. Healy went on to disparage the stance adopted by the Sinn Féin delegates on the oath of allegiance in the negotiations two days previously:

> They undertook that the head of the Irish State should proclaim his allegiance of the King of the Empire, and that a Civil List to His Majesty should be voted, but the MPs were to take no oath! Hence no pressure could be put on Craig, who has gone home rejoicing. It is like saying you refuse to recognise your landlord, but you will pay the rent. The Moplahs, the Bedooin, the Fellahs, the Yankees, the French, the Germans, the Bolshies, are prayed in aid. 'The eyes of the fool are on the ends of the earth.'

Seeking to overcome O'Brien's reservations, Healy argued that 'Belfast now has a vocal organ by statute . . . Until 1918 only one Dillon plagued us. Hereafter, there will be a dozen Johns both in "Northern" and

"Southern" Ireland. The abstention policy has wrought this'. Healy's letter made clear to O'Brien that he was crossing to London at Beaverbrook's prompting:

> The English cabinet meet on Monday, I hear, so lest any hasty publication should be decided on, I sent a wire urging delay, but I don't see how things can be carried over next week . . . I got a wire from London yesterday to come over, from an English friend, who had been standing to us, but felt that unless you came I could be of small good. Still, altho' in view of your reply, I won't go tonight or tomorrow, I will at latest unshackle myself from the Four Courts on Tuesday, and go that night. I may go on Monday if asked to do so. I loathe all this Vermicelli.[90]

O'Brien's attitude was unaltered, and he later acerbically commented: 'upon what precise commission he acted in undertaking the mission to London I was never informed. Indeed, he rather rallied me on my ceremoniousness waiting for any invitation at all to butt in'.[91]

Writing the same day to Maurice, Healy knew the negotiations were moving to their crisis:

> I don't consider the Sinns well advised, and I hear Gavan Duffy blamed for their attitude . . . He believes, I fear, that between the Americans, the French, the Germans, the Russians, the Indians, and the Egyptians, England can be bluffed. Anyhow things are in a muddled state, and I shall certainly go on Tuesday night, in the hope that matters will not be finally smashed up when I arrive. I don't see how the conference can extend beyond next week.[92]

Healy crossed to London over the weekend. On Monday 28 November, Lloyd George asked Tom Jones, the assistant secretary to the cabinet, to arrange to bring Griffith and Collins to Chequers. On learning that Healy was about, the Prime Minister told Jones to bring him as well. Jones made contact with E. J. Duggan, who was with Griffith and Healy. Jones spoke to Griffith and Duggan: 'I offered them beds at Chequers but they were plainly eager to avoid accepting hospitality, nor did they wish to be mixed up with Tim Healy'. Alfred Cope made contact with Healy to get him to go, but Healy, belatedly taking the hint, was by then unwilling. Griffith and Duggan went down alone in the late evening.[93] If the delegates, or some of them, were prepared to entertain Healy's suggestions, they were determined to avoid any public association with him, and prudently refrained from reposing excessive trust in his discretion.

Sequestered in the Vineyard, Beaverbrook's Fulham residence, Healy wrote to O'Brien that evening:

> 'Allegiance' is the crux. They presented their solution at Downing Street today, and are going tonight to Chequers to discuss it, but I learnt it is

> unfavourably regarded by the government. They thought highly of it however themselves. I am to lunch with them tomorrow. I would have seen Lloyd George today, but do not like to butt in.
>
> Bonar Law is recovered and is hostile. Carson will throw up his job if Bonar Law makes a stand, but if the Allegiance crux was settled, a Dissolution would smother Ulsterics. I gather the recent Shin 'Cabinets' have tied the Delegates and that they do not regard themselves any longer as Plenipotentiaries. Besides they fear if they gave up the Republic, the government proposals would be whittled down in Parliament.
>
> This is the risk which confronts all Irish conferences.
>
> Lloyd George wants to start for Washington and this must hasten decision one way or another. They speak highly of Austen's and F.E.'s sincere desire to make a settlement and realise Lloyd George's difficulties in meeting their ideals, but seem no nearer a solution than at the time of the Gairloch correspondence.

William O'Brien's 'Secret History'

Healy once again sought to involve O'Brien. 'I don't believe they would resent any advice from you. They stood my plain talking very well and don't regard us as interlopers'. Beaverbrook had promised Healy 'he would break with Bonar to effect a settlement'.[94] William O'Brien had to go to Paris, where his mother-in-law was dying. He only received Healy's letter on his and his wife's arrival at their hotel on their way through London. It stiffened his determination not to intermeddle. In his unpublished 'Secret History' written five years later, he sought to put an orthodox republican gloss on his attitude. It was clear, he wrote, that Healy had gone to London at the request not of Sinn Féin, but of 'powerful British Ministers'. The Irish hierarchy also reposed trust in Healy, 'whom they had never since the Parnell split of 1890 ceased to regard more truly than any other Catholic layman as their champion'. The only commission Healy lacked was from 'the young soldiers of the Republican Army'. O'Brien absurdly claimed that it was because of the latter's sympathy for 'the doctrine I never conceded by the most conciliatory enterprises that Irish Nationalism consisted neither in "constitutional" methods nor in "unconstitutional" methods, but in a masterly combination of the two as opportunity afforded', that Healy had sought to enlist his support.[95]

Healy's chief reason for pressing O'Brien to intervene was probably to neutralise Griffith's reservations in regard to himself. He later explained to his brother:

> I am not, I hope, a very thrustful person, but I thought, as he had been always a friend of Griffith, that he might have come along, if only to say

> an encouraging word. It is true the Sinns sufficed for themselves, but I always thought they were glad of a word of encouragement. Their councils evidently were divided both in London and Dublin; and of course envy and jealousy are the cardinal human frailties.[96]

Healy's attempt to reactivate his old collaboration with O'Brien in the midst of the treaty negotiations was in any event seriously misconceived. The Irish delegates were hardly likely to have responded favourably to a duo of sexagenarian ex-parliamentarians seeking to press their counsel upon them. Moreover, O'Brien could not have been counted on to share Healy's view as to the imperative necessity of concluding a treaty.

On the morning of O'Brien's arrival in London, 30 November, Healy called on him at his hotel, with what O'Brien later described as 'news of extraordinary gravity'. What follows is O'Brien's later account of their conversation. Healy told him that the relations between the Sinn Féin delegates and the government had broken down,

> but that he had been urgently pressed (by whom he did not specify) to re-establish communications between them, and had to a great extent succeeded, and he entreated me to exercise my influence with the Delegates at Hans Place to smooth matters over. He described the poor fellows as in a state of pitiable helplessness, surrounded by busybodies of all sorts, addling them with polyglot advice.

O'Brien replied that any intervention on his part would only serve to increase the confusion. Healy confided that the delegates had been 'substantially offered Canadian Home Rule and that the crux was about the oath of allegiance, the veto of the Governor-General and so forth'. O'Brien said these were trivial matters in comparison with the issue of partition which was his besetting concern. Healy told him the Articles of Agreement would place the six northern counties in the first instance under the jurisdiction of the Dublin parliament, but with the option of seceding,

> and he intimated that the Sinn Fein delegates did not seem so intransigent on that point as upon the oath of allegiance, mentioning that they had lost a good deal of time discussing the transfer of this or that county or barony from one side of the border to the other.

O'Brien reiterated his opposition to partition.

> He then made a communication to me which he said ought completely to allay my anxiety on the subject of partition. The previous night he had been dining with Mr. Lloyd George and Mr. Winston Churchill, whether in Downing Street, or at Lord Beaverbrook's house at Leatherhead, I cannot distinctly recall. I carried away an impression that

> Sir F. E. Smith (afterwards Lord Birkenhead) was also of the party, but in this particular again, my recollection is less sure than upon the more vital matter which swallowed up all other interests. After dinner, a discussion arose concerning the new conditions in which the interrupted negotiations with Hans Place might be taken up and brought to a head. Mr. Healy emphasised the right of secession of the six counties as the point of all others likely to be intolerable to Irish national sentiment and to justify the Sinn Fein delegates in summarily putting an end to the mission. Mr. Churchill remarked that he need not worry himself on that point – the right would be little more than a nominal one, as a matter of practical politics. 'What', Mr. Healy asked, 'is the meaning of that rather cryptic oracle?' Mr. Churchill's reply was that the Government were ready to appoint a Boundary Commission so constituted as to ensure the transfer to the Free State of the counties of Tyrone, and Fermanagh, South Armagh, and (if I remember rightly) South Down, together with the towns of Londonderry, Enniskillen and Newry, and the inevitable result being that Sir James Craig, with the three counties left to him, would be compelled ('compelled' or 'forced' was quite certainly the word used) to follow the example. 'That', said Mr. Healy, 'is a statement of supreme importance. Do you mind repeating it, so as to enable me to transmit it to those men. I cannot imagine anything better calculated to silence their objections'. It was so done and Mr. Healy took the words down in shorthand as they came from Mr. Churchill's lips. 'Am I to understand', he asked, 'that that assurance is endorsed by the Prime Minister?' 'It certainly is', was Mr. Lloyd George's reply. These two statements were now read out to me from the note jotted down in his own neat Pitman characters.

O'Brien said that while this would meet his objection, he was unsure that the undertaking could be relied on. He wondered whether it was a trick on Sinn Féin, and whether the government could give effect to a commitment entered into behind the back of the Northern Ireland Government. 'He said they were quite ready to defy Craig, who was most unpopular in England: they had sent him back to England with a flea in his ear'. O'Brien expressed the concern that the effect of such a stratagem would be to make Craig fight, and to excite English sympathy on his side:

> He asked what else was there for those poor boys in Hans Place to do? The government had said their last word. They had all their arrangements made to shut up the whole population in two concentration camps – one for the loyalists and one for the Republicans, and to let the Black and Tans loose again upon the country to dispose of any resistance.

O'Brien agreed that the dangers were appalling, but did not think it wise for Healy or himself to assume responsibility for taking out of the hands of Sinn Féin the power they might never have again for making a better bargain. He believed more could be achieved, and advocated an effort to re-open the negotiations in some other form, to be subject to an all-Ireland plebiscite.

Healy, according to O'Brien's account, listened in a state of deep depression, and again implored O'Brien to go to Hans Place to submit the considerations he was urging to the delegates. O'Brien had to leave by the first train for Paris, but said that if the Sinn Féin delegates wished he would see them on his return. 'He said solemnly it would be too late.' O'Brien told Healy he would convey his assessment of the situation to the Sinn Féin delegates.[97]

Temperamental considerations reinforced O'Brien's well-founded reserve. Encumbered with a grandiose personal myth, he was reluctant to proffer unsolicited advice. He recoiled from the brazenness of Healy's intervention, and was to become increasingly critical of the ambiguity of his role. Healy irritably equated O'Brien's attitude with its reverse, that of his brother, to whom he wrote:

> As far as I could gather William's opinions, he was against everything, short of perfection certified by Archangels! Not being a perfect being, I fail to comply with the requisite conditions which might have assured him that everything had been perfectly well done. Whatever is accomplished, you will have no more complete critic as to the result. In fact I could not assemble, were it in my power, two souls more completely at one as yours and O'Brien's.[98]

There is no reason to doubt the substantial accuracy of O'Brien's account of what Healy told him, even if, in the absence of the 'shorthand note', the precise terms of the assurance given to Healy cannot be determined. Healy, along with Tom Jones, the assistant secretary to the cabinet, was made the conduit for informal and oblique indications from the British side in the treaty negotiations that the Boundary Commission would leave to Northern Ireland only three or four counties, and that the drastically diminished Northern Irish state would in consequence find itself compelled to accede to its inclusion in the Irish Free State.[99]

What is to be discounted is the weight which O'Brien attached to what he was told by Healy in determining the outcome of the treaty negotiations. The prospect held out by Lloyd George and Churchill was hardly capable of constituting a definite commitment, depending as it did, not merely on an anticipation of the outcome of the Boundary Commission, but on the surmise that a ceding of large areas to the jurisdiction of the Irish state would render the position of the Northern Ireland state unsustainable. Healy was too seasoned a politician to regard any private assurance from Lloyd George or Churchill as graven in stone, although he was excited at the possibilities of what might be achieved through the appointment of a chairman sympathetic to the nationalist position. From Healy's point of view, what he was told had the aspect of a collateral statement, not itself a term of a settlement which might or might not prove of ultimate worth, seized upon by a barrister to urge upon his principals the acceptance of an accommodation which he had already adjudged to be the best achievable.

The Sinn Féin delegates looked in any event to a favourable outcome to the work of the Boundary Commission, given its terms and purpose. Their hopes long antedated Healy's meeting with Lloyd George and Churchill. Griffith had in early November written to de Valera expressing the view that the appointment of a boundary commission would result in the assignment of most of Tyrone and Fermanagh, and part of Armagh and Down, to the Irish state.[100]

There was also a belief that a drastic delimitation of the extent of the Northern Ireland state would deprive it of viability. This hope was widely, if somewhat weakly, professed, a staging post on the long falling back from irredentist ambitions. It was hardly surprising that the British negotiators should seek to play on such sanguine anticipations. There is however little to sustain the premise of O'Brien's narrative of British duplicity and Irish innocence that any settled expectations as to the outcome of the Boundary Commission induced the Sinn Féin emissaries to sign the articles of agreement, or that Healy's voluble incursion broke the terrible solitude of their deliberation.

The Dáil debates on the treaty did not turn on the question of Northern Ireland or the Boundary Commission. According to P. S. O'Hegarty, Collins, in a private conversation during the treaty negotiations, confirmed the existence of what was described as 'a personal undertaking from Smith and Churchill that if Ulster opted out they would get only four counties and that *they* would make a four-county government impossible'. It remains highly improbable that this, as distinct from the terms of the treaty itself, had any decisive influence on Collins' thinking.[101]

O'Brien became obsessed by what Healy had told him, which he regarded as proof positive that the signature of the articles of agreement had been procured by British perfidy. In his unpublished 'Irish Free State: Secret History of its Foundation', written 1926–8, it provided the revelation which the title promised:

> The secret is that it was the mediation of Mr. Healy which secured, and could alone have secured, the signing of that agreement. At a moment when the parties had separated without much chance of resuming relations it was Mr. Healy's intervention which determined the Prime Minister and Mr. Winston Churchill to make a last bid for an accommodation with

> Sinn Fein and which determined Arthur Griffith and Michael Collins to close with it.[102]

It was Healy's shorthand note 'which decided and which alone could have decided' Collins and Griffith to sign the articles of agreement. 'That tremendous bribe' was the 'last desperate throw' of the British government.[103] With considerable polemical aptitude, O'Brien obscured the fact that this 'last desperate throw' preceded by more than a week the signing of the articles of agreement by the Irish delegates.[104]

O'Brien was to make veiled public reference to Winston Churchill giving assurances to the Irish delegates with the authority of Lloyd George on the boundary question, but not in such detail as to compromise Healy.[105] The full disclosure was reserved for the 'Secret History', intended for posthumous publication. His silence, he wrote, had often 'weighed heavily on my conscience'. His decision to set down his account avowedly coincided with the agreement whereby the existing border was affirmed, signed on 3 December 1925 and subsequently ratified by both parliaments, which he characterised polemically as 'the second London agreement'.[106]

Healy was generally reticent about his role in the treaty negotiations. In his memoirs, published in 1928, he referred merely to making two or three visits to London while the negotiations were in progress, during the first of which he met independently Lloyd George and the Sinn Féin delegates.[107] In an interview on leaving office as Governor General however, he bragged that he had been 'many times in Hans Place, during the deliberations on the treaty', and had seen Collins and the other plenipotentiaries on a number of occasions.[108]

Healy never provided an account of the meeting with Lloyd George and Churchill of which he spoke to O'Brien. He did repeatedly assert privately that he had made an arrangement for the appointment of a sympathetic chairman of the Boundary Commission, without ever setting forth the circumstances in which he had done so. Immediately after the signing of the treaty, he pressed in vain for the early appointment of the Boundary Commission. He reacted with mounting irritability to O'Brien's arguments on the subject of the treaty and the responsibility for partition. In response, he simultaneously reverted to a polemical pre-history of partition (condemning the acquiescence of the Irish party, subsequently compounded by Sinn Féin's abstentionism), and cast forward the blame for the delay in the appointment of the Boundary Commission on to de Valera's opposition to the treaty, and the civil war.

Healy's comments in his annotations of the proofs of O'Brien's *Irish Revolution*, published in 1923, convey his oblique response to O'Brien's charges. He did not take issue with O'Brien's statement that Churchill with the authority of Lloyd George had conveyed an assurance to the Irish delegates that the Boundary Commission would delimit the size of Northern Ireland so drastically as to compel its merger in the Irish Free State. However, where O'Brien asserted that the first violation of the treaty, at least in spirit, was to be charged against England, he wrote: 'I think this deplorable and quite untrue. The delay is solely due to de Valera's blackguardism. But for his rascalities partition would now be dead'. Where O'Brien wrote that the Boundary Commission was 'foredoomed to failure' and unable to give effect to Churchill's undertaking, Healy wrote: 'This is very bad. I had arranged in December 1921 a friendly British Commission and this the Archbishop of Dublin told de Valera'.[109]

Healy's contention that the delay in the appointment of the Boundary Commission was attributable to the civil war was incorrect. Churchill resisted pressure from Collins to expedite the post-treaty procedures by insisting that the month afforded the Northern Ireland government to elect whether or not it wished to be part of the Irish Free State should run only from Westminster's ratification of the Free State constitution. This in turn was deferred until after the Irish general election and did not take place until December 1922, by which time Lloyd George was out of office. Healy's argument was only correct in terms of chronological sequence. The Irish government did not formally propose the establishment of the Boundary Commission until July 1923, after the end of the civil war in May. It was only in November 1924 that a duly-appointed Commission actually set to work.[110]

The Treaty

Articles of agreement for a treaty between Great Britain and Ireland were signed on 6 December 1921. Of the delegates, Griffith, Collins and Eamonn Duggan favoured acceptance. When Robert Barton waveringly acquiesced, George Gavan Duffy likewise agreed to waive his objections.[111] Healy wrote with misplaced complacency to his brother: 'The peace terms will vex Belfast very much . . . it is a great victory for the Sinns; and their extremists won't, I think, give trouble':

> I must say I think the Cabinet have acted very well. I know I don't possess the patience Lloyd George always displayed. I found Gavan Duffy's meticulous requirements very trying. Collins, Griffith and Duggan showed a wise spirit. Barton held with Duffy!! I don't think however there will be very much friction amongst them as an aftermath.[112]

The *Irish Independent* carried Healy's telegraph to Arthur Griffith:

> A line to congratulate you and your colleagues on the signing of peace. I know nothing of the terms and don't want to know because I am satisfied that they are the best that pains, zeal and patriotism could make attainable for Ireland now. You and your friends have achieved a noble end in a dangerous task.[113]

O'Brien in Paris learnt of the signing of the articles of agreement from the French papers. He suppressed his initial impulse to send a telegram of congratulation to de Valera, but wrote in late December a letter to the *Irish Independent* calling for united action by the Dáil.[114] Thereafter his assessment of the treaty grew steadily more sombre and he came increasingly to align himself with its opponents.

As the existence of a large recusant minority in the Dáil bitterly opposed to the treaty became apparent, nationalist Ireland was confronted with its second great schism in just over thirty years. Driving to court on 12 December, Healy came upon Collins and Gearóid O'Sullivan. Their car had broken down, and he gave them a lift.

> They told me John McKeown was with them, and I knew Mulcahy was. In fact all the fighting men of the IRA and IRB. It is the pedants and pedagogues who are making trouble, such as Erskine Childers and his like. Ninety per cent of the population would support a settlement, but the pundits will take care that the utmost prejudice to the country will be done first.
>
> I think the Bishops today were wise not to pronounce, as they would not influence a man amongst the Dáil . . . I am afraid there is some mi-aw [mí-ádh (bad luck)] over this island if such leaders can plunge her afresh into the maelstrom. Of course anyone could bring down the house by asking 'Was it for this Kevin Barry or MacSweeney died?' They forget that no one would die for the difference between a dominion and a republic . . . If there is a split the Sinns of the extreme sort will be reduced to the position of the theosophists – beautiful balmy theories with no results. I don't know if any harm would be done by De Valera and his extremists standing aside and shouting their shibboleths at stated intervals; but, if they enter upon a campaign of the Parnellite sort, a minority of stalwarts could make a new Government impossible.[115]

Healy wrote in late December to S. W. Alexander, who acted as Beaverbrook's financial secretary, to whom he wrote because he feared that if he wrote directly to Beaverbrook at St. Moritz his letter could be intercepted. His purpose was to provide material which could assist the *Express* newspapers to allay concern in England at the course of the debates on the treaty. To that end he presented a grossly over-sanguine assessment of the pro-treaty position. He explained that if the debates extended over Christmas,

> this is done with the idea of the friends of peace bringing the pressure of public opinion on the doubtfuls. Tactically it has been remarked that there are a dozen fellows who would vote against it, but who will vote for it if they believe it is liable to be defeated. The constituencies moreover are now getting alive to the risk that is being run, and already the Clare County Council has been addressing de Valera, who sits for Clare. This will not of course move him, but like action will move weaker men. With this view delay is deemed desirable. 98% of the people favour acceptance of the Treaty and it may be essential to have a General Election to clear out the cranks from the representation before the business is settled.
>
> Nowhere I believe could an opponent of the Treaty be elected in any part of Ireland. The present Assembly was chosen because of the extremeness of the men, and especially the women, but it no longer reflects public opinion.

Healy added that, as well as forwarding this information to Beaverbrook, 'you can read this over to Blum also'. (R. D. Blumenfeld was the editor of the *Daily Express*.)[116]

While the debates on the treaty were still in progress, Healy sought to expedite the appointment of the Boundary Commission. He reported to O'Brien on 29 December:

> After the Treaty appeared I went over re Boundary Commission, as a fair Umpire is key to situation. Were Tyrone and Fermanagh alone given away, the Belfasters are burst. A Catholic cut of Armagh, Down and Derry would equally hit them.
>
> Craig sent a threatening letter to Lloyd George who replied so stiffly that Craig did not dare print it. Craig forsooth announced they would name no Arbitrator.
>
> I think an Impartial Colonial Statesman as Umpire would command the approval of Parliament and would not be coughed at by Carson. The coming over of Bonar Law after Craig's boasting of his support doubled the government's majority in both houses.
>
> Ireland owes a good deal to a friend whom you can guess and who will probably be consulted as to Umpire.

The last was a reference to Beaverbrook. Healy added angrily that 'only for De Valera the evacuation would now be proceeding under a Provisional Government of his own choosing'.[117]

William O'Brien in reply made plain his belief that the plenipotentiaries in London should have held out, and emphasised he was only prepared to support the Treaty as a *fait accompli* and the lesser of two evils. The Boundary Commission would 'only make Partition more odious than ever', by the trading of Catholic and Protestant districts through Ulster in such a way as further to heighten sectarian antagonisms. He pointedly added, in a veiled reference to their conversation in London: 'You have a confidence (which, I confess, I do not share) in Lloyd George's design to use the Boundary Commission to bring in the six counties'. He thought it more likely that Lloyd George would pick a quarrel with the Dáil, 'if once he gets it into his head that he has smashed the united power of the young men of Ireland and restored the political supremacy of the Bishops': this last observation was a somewhat bizarre recrudescence of the Fenianism of O'Brien's youth. If he believed that the plenipotentiaries should not have yielded to Lloyd George's threats, he was equally critical of de Valera and his allies who neglected partition, 'that great issue, on which they could have carried the sympathies of the country and of the world, and go on blowing their childish soap bubbles about the Republic, the Oath, the powers of the Governor-Generalship, etc., to which nobody outside a circle of perfectly honest *illuminati* attach an atom of importance'. He believed that 'a Provisional Government of the right kind may even yet save the situation'.[118]

Healy had hastened back to Dublin from London in late December 1921 in the hope of persuading de Valera to desist from his opposition to the treaty, on the strength of an assurance that a well-disposed chairman would be appointed to the Boundary Commission. Collins asked Healy to see the Archbishop of Dublin. Healy bitterly expostulated to O'Brien four years later:

> That week a Boundary Chairman favourable to us would have been nominated only for his internal misconduct. I hurried to Dublin, saw the Archbishop, and begged him to convey this news to de Valera. 'Ah', said he sadly, 'I have seen him already and cannot even understand the dialect he speaks, but I will try to see him again'. Vain hope. That great Statesman had all his plans laid for a *coup d'état* . . .[119]

Healy's project for the appointment of a sympathetic chairman to the Boundary Commission was freighted with a wistful vanity, and marked his last attempt at the kind of political coup to which he was compulsively drawn as a politician. A characteristic combination of sentimentality and guile led him to place an exaggerated belief in the possibility of prevailing by intrigue over entrenched political realities.

As time passed, Healy's hopes waned. On 20 March 1922 he wrote to his brother that he had met Bonar Law at Cherkley the previous day, 'and thanked him over his silence. I could see however that he is bitter against any change in the boundaries; and if Lloyd George resigns, he will be Prime Minister, and will not appoint a friendly umpire.'[120] If there was ever a realistic prospect for the appointment of a nationalist-leaning Boundary

Commission, the defeat of the Lloyd George coalition, and the return of a Conservative government under Bonar Law's premiership in October 1922 put an end to it. Healy still could not quite bring himself to abandon all hope for his cherished project. He wrote his brother on 23 October: 'As far as I can judge, Ireland will not suffer from the change of Government. Of course the Boundary question is a ticklish one; but I think even here Max will remain a useful factor'.[121]

In his memoirs Healy rehearsed one last time his argument that the opposition to the treaty, particularly on the part of de Valera, had thwarted the appointment of a sympathetic Boundary Commission. That opposition, he claimed, for three years deferred what he revealingly referred to as 'the attempt to enforce the Boundary Clause . . . When strife ended, the Coalition Government had disappeared, and three Prime Ministers in succession had succeeded Mr. Lloyd George, all unpledged to his commitments'. The reference to Lloyd George's 'commitments' stands as an affirmation of O'Brien's account of what Healy had told him in London.[122]

Civil War

In late December, James MacMahon, the under-secretary to the Lord Lieutenant, Viscount Fitzalan, suggested Healy's appointment as Attorney General for Ireland in succession to T. W. Brown K.C. Fitzalan saw the merits of having as a member of the government someone who was *persona grata* with Sinn Féin. The Chief Secretary Hamar Greenwood was more sensible: 'I'm all for making the best use of Healy and his great powers and influence with S.F., but I cannot believe that he would accept a post in the Imperial Government. His influence with many S.F.ers would be gone'. Moreover the post would cease to exist as soon as the Provisional Government was established. 'I hope the S.F.ers will make him their Attorney-General. He is qualified for any position.'[123] Healy would not have countenanced such an offer, but the fact such a proposal was even canvassed on the government's side reflected a remarkable misunderstanding of Healy's position, to which he had himself done much to contribute.

Healy wrote to his brother on 6 January 1922 while the treaty debates were in progress, referring first to de Valera:

> I suppose I should not conclude with an explosion [?] against the 'President'. Poor man, I think he has done his country more harm even than Parnell, with the very best intentions . . . I hear this morning that Barton's vote is even in doubt, and there is no end to the mischief which he and Duffy have done. Assuming their position that they signed under threat

> of consequences, surely they might consider that, if this threat had reality for them, it should be equally potent for the other members of the Dáil, or the rest of the inhabitants of Ireland . . . If the treaty is rejected, we shall see the converse of the Parnellite Split. There will be a broken movement, an Orange triumph, the withdrawal of the best elements of the fighting men, a dissatisfied population, and a gradual wearing down of the despairing minority by brute force and court martials, should the Government recognise the war.[124]

The divisions in the Dáil on the treaty taxed Healy's patience and revived his reservations about Sinn Féin. He posited a continuum of folly between Dillon and Sinn Féin: 'My summation of the position is, that the effort to build up a Castle of Cods, on a false bottom, has failed and that their progeny has been remitted to another generation'. Partition in 1920 had its birth in the withdrawal from Parliament. But for abstentionism, 'never could Catholic areas have been ceded to Belfast'.

> The Shin Fein vacuum bred this form of partition, and without six counties no viable birth of a Partition area could have taken place. Whether it will 'gang aglee' will depend on the abstention of the Catholics, and the economic boycott.

If this was still wishful thinking on the subject of partition, and not without its own contradictions, Healy had come close to accepting that by 1918 what was in issue was the geographical ambit of the area which fell under the authority of the government of Northern Ireland. He feared an escalation into civil war in Northern Ireland:

> I discern nothing but clouded horizons for the poor country, and take the view that when the Shins rejected from their armoury the Parliamentary weapon, they threw away their artillery.
>
> As Parnell said of poor Billy Redmond, 'you cannot put old heads on young shoulders'.

He believed that the political remnants of southern unionism harboured the hope that 'however maimed the Belfast abortion may be, it will serve to prevent the parturition of a man-child in Dublin'.[125]

Healy was dismissive of the semantics of statehood, in either language. O'Brien, distinguishing the 'Irish Free State' and the 'Free State of Ireland' had complained of the 'false Gaelic translation of *Saorstát Eireann*'. Healy replied parodying George Gavan Duffy's use of the Irish version of his name, Seórsa Gabháin Uí Dhubhtaigh: 'Would you spell Duffy Fol-the-didderol? And pronounce the effort a bright distilment from the alembic of truth and right?'[126]

On the eve of the Dáil vote, Healy wrote to Maurice: 'Before this reaches you the result I suppose will be determined. Only that I think prayer has had, and will have, its effects, the thin "high-piping Pehlevi" of de Valera would justify the worst hopes of Ireland's enemies'.[127] On 7 January 1922, the Dáil approved the treaty by sixty-four votes to fifty-seven. Healy was still prepared to make allowances for de Valera. 'Beset with wild women and wild men he resents too touchily the supposed slur on his position. It seems to me like something out of dreamland, when we remember old times.' He believed that de Valera's intransigence was attributable to the influence of doctrinaire republicans such as Cathal Brugha, Mary MacSweeney ('all the women of course are on the extreme side'), and Erskine Childers.[128]

Healy was especially critical of Childers. Revealingly, he coupled in chauvinistic denunciation Childers and Thomas Johnson, the scrupulously moderate leader of the Irish Labour party:

> There is a very infamous circular or proclamation from the Labour Party, which must be written by that Englishman Johnson, full of Bolshevism, and threatening reprisals . . . Fellows like Childers and Johnson should be deported to their own country. Johnson has no religion, but I don't know what Childers is, but their minds are quite un-Irish and unfitted for this latitude.[129]

In the same vein, Healy declared it extraordinary that 'men, who would not in a pious sense claim any high religious character, can trot out their "scruples" about the Oath and their consciences in the nude fashion we have been treated to'.[130] This sectarian chauvinism, of which Healy was so practised an exponent, was to disfigure the domestic politics of the Irish state. The illiberal moral and religious ethos of nationalism had crystallised in the casting-out of Parnell in 1890–1: in this respect at least, Healy's influence on the new state was as formative as Sinn Féin's.

Healy was still reluctant to believe that the opponents of the treaty would carry their opposition to the ultimate extreme of revolt against the authority of the new state. On 14 June he wrote: 'It looks as if de Valera did not mean to obstruct Griffith. Public sentiment towards him has changed to respectful pity'.[131] He wrote to O'Brien on 25 January, arguing that the opposition to the Treaty had facilitated the entrenchment of the Northern Ireland state:

> The Orangeers showed great skill in silently submitting to Carson's plan. They will never in our time melt in with the rest of Ireland. Vested interests will be created to prevent that. Already the North Eastern bar are drawing lots for the spoils and no litigant can from the six counties sue in Dublin, or *vice versa* . . .

> Nor do I hold things to be as hopeful as they looked before de Valera's outbursts. I believe he may have compassed the missing of the tide for Ireland. There is always some righteous purist to make our Isle a slavedom once again. . . . Had de Valera 'stood pat', the late session of Parliament would have enacted the treaty. Now who can guarantee what a new Parliament will do – with maybe a Carson-led House of Lords?[132]

Healy did what he could to allay British unease, writing to Beaverbrook on 15 February:

> There is no doubt in my mind that if patience is shown in London, things will right themselves here.
>
> De Valera's huge meeting on Sunday was what railway people call 'novelty traffic'. There was great curiosity and no enthusiasm . . . I dined last night where twenty priests, secular and regular were also guests. All were against de Valera tho' they feel sympathy as I do over a fallen man.[133]

The Sinn Féin Ard Fheis of 22-3 February endorsed an agreement between de Valera and Griffith to defer the holding of a general election until after the constitution of the Free State had been drafted. This, as Healy informed his brother, created an adverse impression in England:

> . . . the talk of compromise has undoubtedly alarmed the London Government. Macready [Commander in Chief of the Forces in Ireland] has been going about London preaching that the evacuation should be completely suspended, and so far has been successful. He tells the Government that there is a secret pact between Collins and de Valera as soon as the soldiers have left, to proclaim a republic. I contradicted this to a high personage yesterday, knowing the hatred between the factions, and I am to see Michael today. You will see that even the *Express*, which has been most friendly, fell into despair through a misunderstanding of the situation. Griffith had a majority of several hundred at the Ard Fheis, but I think it was a most natural thing that they should wish to postpone the election to give time for excitement to cool down.[134]

In one area where Healy might have been expected to have had a considerable influence, he left no mark. He was sent the drafts for the constitution of the Irish Free State. Too much a seasoned practitioner of the common law, he had evident difficulty taking the idea of a written constitution seriously. He despatched a whimsical and dismissive critique of the drafts to E. J. Duggan on 21 March. Its argument, which contradictorily advocated a text which would be at once dryly formalistic and studiedly vague, is difficult to comprehend and did nothing to inform the drafting of the constitution.[135]

He wrote again to his brother on 3 April 1922:

> How can you expect that the tangle of seven centuries will be settled without turmoil? The settlement approaches at a time when the mind of everyone has been upset by the Great War, and by its by-products . . .
>
> You persist in looking at the debit side of the ledger, making no allowances for credit.[136]

He watched the drift to civil war with mounting anger. When anti-treaty forces tried to seize the initiative in Limerick, Healy wrote to O'Brien: 'Limerick may well earn "Remember" before it. The poor fellows are justifying some of the oldest slanders against the race. However we are better yet than South America or Mexico'. He wrote bitterly in May: 'The welter now churned up makes our past very past. How accurately the English managed to bring about the fulfilment of their own prophesies of evil consequences when they departed. First partition; then evacuation before a replacing force could be substituted'. He retained a profound dread of economic devastation 'if the clash comes'. The ports would be shut. 'What will be left in the island will go to the "armies", and when enough skeletons are underground "peace" will be dolorously enthroned'.[137]

In advance of the convention of the anti-treaty section of the Irish Republican Army held on 26 March, Healy met de Valera in the hope of persuading him to disavow the convention which the Free State government had proclaimed. De Valera was 'very courteous and pleasant, but inexorable and infallible', although Healy was nevertheless persuaded that he had affected de Valera's attitude. Reminding him that he was 'an expert in "splits"', at which de Valera smiled, Healy warned against a recourse to rebellion. He wrote to his brother that 'they will become like the Parnellite faction thirty years ago'.[138] Four years later Healy bitterly recalled de Valera's intransigence at what was to be their final encounter:

> As a last resort I called on him myself before the Four Courts was seized and his Army Chiefs met on 25 March 1922. 'Twas like whistling jugs to milestones, and he is more responsible for the sufferings of Northern Catholics than any man alive. Ingredients of blame belong it is true elsewhere, but his guilt is blackest. Yet he now makes a stock topic out of the desertion of Northern Nationalists . . .

In consoling himself with the belief that de Valera's 'influence for evil here is at an end', Healy underestimated both de Valera's acumen and the resilience and durability of the Free State democracy.[139] His approach was not exclusively conciliatory. He unavailingly urged the government to enforce its proclamation of the convention, and to arrest at least de Valera, Brugha, Stack and O'Connor.[140]

While their difference on the subject of the treaty was increasingly marked, Healy sought to avert a falling-out with O'Brien, to whom he wrote in May 1922 thanking him for a letter 'which I hope I have made out':

> Whatever our dissatisfactions may be with the Treaty – and I have not seen any of the Signatories since last year, save Collins and Duggan and these very rarely – I will uphold their action, in the improbable event of my poor voice being needed to sustain them.[141]

On 15 May 1922 William O'Brien published a letter calling for an electoral pact which did not have as a precondition the acceptance of the treaty on its opponents. He argued that the election of a pro-treaty majority would deprive the British government of any opportunity to assert that the truce had been repudiated, while the return of a strong republican minority would strengthen the hand of the Irish government. Flattering 'the young soldiers of Ireland', he concluded 'I can see no power anywhere capable of saving the country unless the Dáil and the Army promptly re-form ranks and resolutely resume command of the situation'. Michael Collins sent an emissary to O'Brien to persuade him to modify the views he had expressed so as to state that the preliminary acceptance of the treaty by the Republicans might without humiliation be recommended as a condition of an agreed election. O'Brien was not prepared to accede to this, as he considered it would preclude the conclusion of an electoral pact. Moved however by 'the longing of a gallant soldier for re-union', O'Brien returned what he later described as 'a sympathetic verbal message'. Looking forward to the assembly returned at the election whose purpose was 'to frame a constitution in which a revision of the Articles of Agreement will be inevitable', it was at once unhelpful and hopelessly unrealistic.

O'Brien calculated that his message reached Collins on 18 May. On 20 May Collins and de Valera signed an electoral pact under which pro- and anti-treaty candidates would contest the general election in proportion to their representation in the outgoing Dáil. O'Brien's conviction that his intervention had a significant role in the formation of the pact was far-fetched. He came to believe that it was the additional provision to share out cabinet places after the election between pro- and anti-treaty members which sealed the fate of the pact. He later regretted that he had not gone at once to Dublin to see Collins. His widow 'often grieved that Michael Collins and William O'Brien never met. Somehow I fancy they would have understood one another. Michael Collins recalled to my husband his elder brother, whom he portrayed as Ken Rohan in *When We Were Boys*'. O'Brien's arrogant sentimentality endured to the last.[142]

On 22 June Field Marshal Sir Henry Wilson was shot dead in London. Winston Churchill responded with a bellicose speech in the Commons demanding that the Irish government take action against the Republicans who had occupied the Four Courts, and warning that the failure to do so would be regarded as a violation of the treaty which would restore to the British government full freedom of action to protect its interests.[143] From the point of view of the new Irish government, it was a speech of staggering indelicacy, and enabled its republican opponents to assert that the subsequent bombardment of the Four Courts was carried out on British orders. Healy's letter to his brother the next day strikingly conveyed the depth of anger among supporters of the treaty at Churchill's reckless compromising of the position of the Irish government:

> Churchill's speech yesterday was worthy of the designer of the Gallipoli campaign. Up to that I would have approved any course against the Four Courts gentry; but now I would certainly not obey his dictation. Griffith, I suppose, is too patriotic to resign; but if he did it would be a suitable answer for Churchill.[144]

The Irish capital in less than a decade had endured the successive shocks of the lock-out, the rising, and the war of independence. It was now pummelled in the first engagement of the civil war. On 30 June the besieged Four Courts caught fire, detonating a store of explosives. Many soldiers of the Free State lost their lives in the explosion, the force of which shook Healy's house at Chapelizod three miles upstream.[145] Gandon's ruined buildings became the emblem of the destruction wrought by the civil war. Healy wrote to his brother the following year:

> The loss of the Record Office is of course saddening, and the big mansions and their treasures cannot be replaced, yet I never pass the ruins in the Four Courts without feeling that it is better to have them so than in the hands of the gang who seized them. It is quite evident their purpose was a *coup d'état* and that they meant to seize the members of the Provisional Government.[146]

Absurdly if inevitably, Healy equated the civil war with the Parnell split: 'It is the Parnellite split without its justification of provocation'.[147] On 13 July, he wrote to his brother: 'The element of the comic sometimes transcends the tragic, as it is all so schoolboy-like. I hear the republicans would rather have the English back than the Free State!'[148]

The assassins of Sir Henry Wilson, Reginald Dunne and Joseph O'Sullivan, were sentenced to death. Both had served in the British army in the war. O'Sullivan had lost a leg at Ypres. Deeply exercised over their fate, Collins spoke to Healy. All Healy could do was to try to get Beaverbrook to intercede. The assassination had provoked a public outcry in England, which diehard opponents of an Irish settlement had sought to exploit. Writing to Beaverbrook on 29 July, he decided that the only slight hope was for a reprieve of O'Sullivan alone:

> I know they [the government] could not face the outcry that would arise if execution did not follow the Wilson murder, but it occurs to me that altho' both men are jointly responsible, a distinction could without offending public sentiment, be made in favour of the prisoner who lost his leg in the War. A life for a life would still be taken in law, and it would redound greatly to Imperial magnanimity if it were announced that England would not send hobbling to the scaffold a man who lost a limb in Flanders in her service, when the life of a second culprit was being held forfeit. I don't know whether Lady Wilson or any distinguished person could be got to make a plea for reprieve on that ground, nor am I a good judge of public temper in England just now, but it will greatly add to the horror if both men are hanged and add also to the risk of reprisal following the executions. Punishment in political cases is seldom a deterrent and this case must be looked at from every angle.
>
> The Orangemen in the Six Counties take life so easily that my feelings may be blunted . . . It is therefore impossible for me to judge the feelings of Englishmen who are kept ignorant of all the slaughter for which Sir H. Wilson is held responsible here.
>
> I make the suggestion that the lame man's life should be spared more in the interest of Britain than in his own, and feel sure that my motives will not be misconstrued by anyone to whom you may think it wise to convey my views.[149]

Even for so practised an advocate it was an exceptionally difficult plea to make. Beaverbrook in reply expressed himself personally sympathetic, but understood that friends of Lady Wilson were foremost in predicting that her husband's assassins would not be hanged: 'I expect that the Government's difficulties are so great that clemency is extremely difficult'.[150] Reginald Dunne and Joseph O'Sullivan were hanged at Wandsworth on 10 August.

On 5 August, de Valera had called on O'Brien at Mallow. O'Brien noticed the dark circles around his visitor's eyes. After their meeting de Valera departed cheerfully, but 'leaving me with a pathetic impression, as he stepped into his motor car, that he did not quite know where to bid his chauffeur to drive next'.[151] Healy later commented suspiciously to Maurice that 'I had a letter from O'Brien and he does not say anything about the alleged visit from de Valera, so that I should assume he has taken over the mantle of T. P. Gill in 1890'.[152]

Healy's disapprobation of the republican opponents of the treaty had a theological edge. He wrote to a clerical correspondent: 'It makes one see that both secular and religious teaching can be jettisoned to glut political passions. The demand from Mountjoy for Absolution via Hunger Strike reveals a phase of mind which treats the Sacrament as a superstition or mechanical spell wrought by the Priest irrespective of the state of the penitent's conscience'.[153]

Death stalked the birth of the Irish state. On 12 August, Arthur Griffith died. Ten days later Michael Collins was killed at Béal na mBláth in County Cork. Healy wrote in the *Daily Express* that having gone to London for the treaty negotiations at de Valera's insistence 'he had perished in the breach which that fatal leader foresaw would open before one or the other of them'. He wrote in tribute:

> His achievements and popularity left him unspoilt and as boyish as he was before his fame. Each of his men could freely approach him, and despite the narrowness of the stage, he displayed in warfare a genius which would have delighted the great Corsican . . . He towered among his friends in private as a king of laughter . . . Would that the Bandon ambushers could have known their victim![154]

27

Governor-General

You were to me in my youth something like a historical character, figuring in what I already held to be a heroic revolution; and this makes your name something more than your title . . .

G. K. Chesterton to T. M. Healy, 1924[1]

He has more than a sneaking affection for the English, and is not afraid to laugh at his countrymen. 'How did the English conquer and enslave us?', he said not long ago. 'By a very simple plan. They gave it out that we were a very clever people and that they were a stupid people. Now, we ar-r-ent and they are'.

A. G. Gardiner on T. M. Healy, 1925[2]

The Governor-Generalship

Healy continued to practise as a barrister. His political role was limited to occasional interventions in London on behalf of the Provisional Government. His name was occasionally mentioned as a possible Governor-General, but his prospects were not greatly favoured. As the appointment of the king's representative in Ireland was in the gift of the British rather than of the Irish government, it was generally expected that it would go to a British or Commonwealth nobleman or diplomat, or at best to a well-disposed Irish unionist peer.

While Healy's relations with the provisional government were friendly, they were not at this time close. Arthur Griffith, according to Oliver St. John Gogarty, had been opposed to Healy's appointment on the grounds that he 'betrayed Parnell'.[3] Griffith's death removed at least that impediment. In public perception, Healy remained closely identified with Irish parliamentarianism rather than Sinn Féin. Towards the end of 1922 he was being urged by his ecclesiastical allies, notably Cardinal Logue, to return to Westminster by standing as a nationalist in Tyrone.[4]

The office of the Governor-Generalship was a political embarrassment for the Irish government. At Collins' direction, the draft constitution furnished to the British government, which rejected it, had omitted the treaty clauses relating to the Governor-General, while providing that what was re-styled as the 'Commissioner of the British Commonwealth' was to be appointed with the prior assent of the Executive Council.[5]

The initiative for Healy's appointment came from Kevin O'Higgins (whose cabinet colleague Patrick McGilligan reported that he had 'simply said one day that he was going to propose his uncle'). O'Higgins was supported by W. T. Cosgrave, who had become Chairman of the Provisional Government on the death of Collins. Together they discussed the proposal with Healy at Glenaulin.[6] It was a shrewdly-conceived move to take the office of Governor-Generalship outside the arena of controversy so far as that could be achieved under the treaty. The plain fact was that Healy was the only Irish nationalist whom there was any prospect of prevailing on the British government to appoint.

On 20 October, Healy went to London at the urging of stock exchange and banking interests in Dublin to intervene against proposals to abolish the Bank of Ireland stock register of British funds. En route, he reported to Maurice the decision of the Provisional Government to request his nomination:

> The President made today formally the proposal about which I told you, and it was accepted. He said he thought the proposal would astonish the republicans and greatly shake them. I don't suppose Bonar would budge any more than Lloyd George. My journey however has nothing to do with this.[7]

The reference to Lloyd George, who had resigned the premiership the previous day, indicates that the proposal to appoint Healy had already been informally and unsuccessfully mooted. Birkenhead later wrote elliptically that had the Lloyd George coalition not fallen, he was 'not certain whether we should have had the courage to nominate Tim Healy'.[8]

Healy wrote again from London three days later:

I spent the weekend at Cherkley, and told Max what was proposed about myself, and he was perfectly satisfied it would be ratified. Yesterday Bonar called and I told him, and he was satisfied also. I had a word with him myself on another matter, and he used my Christian name!! I don't write very explicitly lest this should be opened or go astray . . .

Last night Cosgrave, whom I saw before starting, sent word that he would like to see Bonar, who agreed to see him late today; but before the appointment could be fixed he, Cosgrave, cancelled the idea of coming, whereas now Bonar may be nettled if they don't arrive. A wire to this effect is going to Cosgrave and, though I intend returning tonight, I may have to stay until tomorrow if he decides to come. I saw Cope today; and he tells me he was told officially to put up my name to them. I said he could see Max at three o'clock today if he had any special message to convey . . .[9]

Healy seriously misconstrued Bonar Law's response. Law, who can hardly have failed to be irritated to be placed by Healy in such an invidious position on the day before his appointment as Prime Minister, was doing no more than acknowledging that Healy's name was to be put forward by the Irish government. On his return from London, he wrote to his brother from Chapelizod:

As it may be dangerous to write, I will only say that the news I brought from London greatly pleased the chief men here, who said today that, if the proposal in my own case is carried through, it will greatly strengthen them and discourage their opponents. The new Secretary to the Colonies told the head of his Department that it was a very proper thing to do, and that he would recommend it to the Cabinet. Barring accidents, the thing seems settled, but of course if any news got about it would be opposed here.[10]

His conviction that his appointment enjoyed the approval of the British government was dangerously premature.

Kevin O'Higgins wrote on 27 October 1922 to Lady Lavery urging Healy's appointment. His letter, written with skilfully-feigned truculence, was intended for a wider political readership. It was duly passed to the Colonial Secretary, the Duke of Devonshire, who in turn forwarded it to the Prime Minister. O'Higgins wrote:

I know you will realise that I am pleading for my country – and not in any sense for my kinsman. You cannot measure the effect it would have here if they agreed to appoint him. It would be worth more than a completely smashing military victory. If they are *statesmen* they will do it – if they are merely politicians they probably won't, and a wonderful opportunity will have been lost.[11]

Healy's candidacy enjoyed the support of the triad of enlightened senior civil servants in Dublin and London engaged in the management of the transition, made up of Tom Jones, the assistant secretary to the cabinet secretariat; Lionel Curtis, the adviser to the Colonial Office on Irish Affairs; and Alfred Cope, the assistant Under Secretary for Ireland.[12]

Devonshire, the Colonial Secretary, needed little persuading. He responded with equanimity when the proposal was put to him, and declared his regard for Healy, who 'puts flowers once a year on the grave of Lord Frederick Cavendish', on the anniversary of his death. (Devonshire was the nephew of Cavendish.)[13]

The problem lay with the new Prime Minister. Tom Jones described the effort to win him over:

> Curtis and I strongly hoped that the Government would swallow Tim Healy as Governor-General. It was useless having a Viceroy like Fitzalan who did nothing, and no Lord from the South would do. B.L. had two objections to T.H. He was impulsive and drank too much whisky at night. I said there were precedents for the latter defect and that now he was old and less impulsive and his appointment would have a great effect on moderate opinion in Ireland . . . he thought it ought to be possible to find someone in the Diplomatic Service for the post, someone with no political past.[14]

Evidently, the impression Healy had made on Bonar Law at Cherkley over the previous decade was not quite what he imagined.

On 25 November W. T. Cosgrave wrote formally to the Prime Minister stating that he had the unanimous consent of his cabinet colleagues in proposing the appointment of Healy, which would be 'one of the best and surest means of winning general support for the new State and would be hailed here as an act of statesmanship the healing power of which it would be difficult to estimate'. Bonar Law responded on 28 November that the suggestion would be considered immediately by the cabinet.

The Prime Minister was confronted with the declared preference of the Irish government, the recommendation of his best advisers on Irish affairs, and the urgings of Beaverbrook to whom he owed a considerable political debt. While he chose not to stand on his objection to Healy, the government was only prepared to sanction the appointment on terms. The following day the cabinet decided that before Healy was formally offered the appointment, the Colonial Secretary was to seek a written undertaking from him in relation to the carrying out of his functions. The requirement the government conveyed to Healy was in the following terms:

> That you will keep a watchful eye on Bills & amendments & proposed amendments to Bills which may in any way conflict with the Treaty or

> may be such as might affect the relations of His Majesty with foreign States or relations with other parts of the Empire. And that you will immediately communicate with the Secretary of State in the case of any Bill or amendment which appears to you to fall within any of the above categories in order that, if thought desirable, representations may be made to the Irish Free State Government & if necessary Instructions as to the reservation of the Bill may be sent to you in pursuance of clause I of the Letters Patent. You will recognize that such questions are most conveniently discussed before the Bill reaches its final stage.

The British government sought thereby to create an early warning system in relation to any constitutionally significant legislation which the Irish legislature proposed to enact, and to commit Healy to an undertaking designed to preclude any juncture between the Governor-General and the Irish government against the British government.

Healy made his last appearance as an advocate in the Irish courts, and went unaccompanied to London. At the Colonial Office, the Duke of Devonshire showed him the patent of his appointment of Governor-General. Healy declined a Privy Councillorship. He wrote later that day a letter in the following terms:

> In thanking you for the great courtesy shown to me today, I think it right to give certain assurances which I think your Government might fairly look for. While I do not believe there is anyone of the existing Irish Executive who would be a party to any breach of the Treaty, or who even in thought contemplates a departure from it, still, as Ministries and Ministers change, it is my purpose to keep a watchful eye on Bills and Amendments or proposed amendments to Bills which may in any way conflict with the Treaty, or may be such as may affect the relations of His Majesty with foreign States or other parts of the Empire. My plan would be immediately to apprise the Secretary of State of any such Bill or Amendment, so that, if thought desirable, representations might be made to the Free State Government, or that instructions should be sent me for the reservation of any Bill falling within the above categories in pursuance of clauses in the Patent of the Governor-General, which your Grace was good enough to show me today.
>
> My hope and belief is that nothing will arise to call for such intervention. To borrow the Prime Minster's words, I shall strive to make the Treaty observed in 'letter and spirit'.

Healy was here acting on his own, without reference to the Provisional Government. While he was conveying his assent to the conditions which the British government attached to his nomination, he was careful to formulate his letter in terms which would allow him to argue, if the necessity arose, that they were proffered spontaneously rather than in response to a demand of the British government. The government thus secured an undertaking from Healy which went somewhat further than the Instructions agreed with the Irish government: the Governor-General would consult the Colonial Secretary in advance, and the ambit of his role in the reserving of bills was to extend beyond infractions of the treaty *simpliciter* to include any significant innovation which might affect the position of the Irish Free State within the British Empire.

Healy did not hesitate to compromise himself by this private accord with the British government. He realised that if he did not on his own initiative enter the engagement sought by the Colonial Secretary, he would embroil the provisional government in a further dispute with London, not the least consequence of which would have been to cause the British government to revise its view as to his own suitability to occupy the office of Governor-General. He no doubt convinced himself, with his habitual forensic aptitude, that the British government was perfectly within its rights in requiring such an undertaking, and that in its terms it did no more than reflect his own interpretation of the constitutional function of the office. The man of the new order remained his old self. Healy walked with Devonshire to Downing Street, where Bonar Law was the first to greet him as 'Your Excellency'. The Prime Minister wrote to Cosgrave confirming the agreement of his government to Healy's appointment, expressing himself very glad that 'in this instance', the British government had been able to meet his wishes.

Healy the same day sought to change the wording of the Instructions to the Governor-General agreed between both governments. He considered that the words authorising the grant of a pardon to an informer would be regarded in Ireland as 'a special device in view of the present disturbances' by those unaware that it was a provision common to all similar instructions to Dominion Governors. More importantly, he wanted to extend the power of pardon to include all sentences including those of the military courts. The British government was prepared to agree to Healy's request, but Cosgrave refused to agree to any amendment of the agreed terms. He was not prepared to countenance any dilution of the authority of the Irish executive, nor to acquiesce in any initiative independently embarked upon by Healy.[15]

Returning from London, Healy was met at Holyhead by Cosgrave and other members of the Irish government.[16] Notwithstanding Healy's undisclosed personal engagement, his nomination as Governor-General was a modest but important coup for the Irish government. The crown was to be represented in Ireland by a nationalist, albeit of the old dispensation. Even though republican critics were predictably unimpressed by what Sean O'Casey dismissed as 'Cosgrave's great conjuring trick to astonish Ireland',[17] it helped to diminish the affront to nationalist susceptibilities which the existence of the office represented. Moreover, in achieving the appointment of its own preferred candidate, the Irish government had established a significant precedent.

On 6 December 1922 Healy was sworn in as the first Governor-General of the Irish Free State at his home at Chapelizod. It was a brief ceremony for which no hour had been fixed 'as the city was in a dangerous condition, and the sound of firearms in the streets was constant'. Healy handed to the Chief Justice the letters patent from the King constituting his office, and the commission appointing him Governor-General, which the Chief Justice read aloud. The Chief Justice administered the oath of allegiance, which Healy had so often taken in the House of Commons at the opening of parliament, and the oath of office. Healy in turn administered the oath of allegiance to the Speaker of the Dáil, and he authorised him to administer to the members of the Dáil.[18]

Taking Office

The designated official residence for the Governor-General was the Viceregal Lodge in the Phoenix Park, recently vacated by Viscount Fitzalan, the last Lord Lieutenant. The government required Healy to move from his home to the Lodge as soon as possible, 'as being more defensible than Glenaulin'. Late in the night of 8 December, Healy took up residence in the Viceregal Lodge, whence he wrote to Maurice at midnight.[19]

He proclaimed his appointment a vindication of his career: 'What I do feel is that my appointment has been signalised by such general approval as to amount to a national testimonial, despite the slanders poured on me by the Dillon lot'. He did not fail to note that 'I have had telegrams from no Liberal', while

> many of the old Tory party have written to me. I was splendidly treated by the Ulster fellows in London recognising my authority on the cattle question. I got Craig to visit . . . the Colonial Office on the cattle question, and then led him into promising the release of some extremists who had been accused of infraction on the Ulster border, with dire consequences to themselves. Of course I am not such a fool as to think I can coddle or kiddle Northern or Southern Ireland into contentment.

He had 'received the greatest kindness from the Irish Government, and hope I may continue to retain their confidence while standing between them and the Colonial Office'. Healy's triumphalism was unwontedly perfunctory. He was played out, too grateful for his political renewal and too shrewd not to recognise its fortuitousness, to indulge in a sustained exercise in self-congratulation.

On the civil war, he observed that 'I cannot see what the Republicans have to grumble about, if they would only take their part in the constitutional government . . . On the other hand, I am obliged to declare that English Ministers have been absolutely straight towards Ireland'. Of the four Republican leaders who had been executed the previous day as a reprisal for the shooting of Sean Hales, a pro-treaty member of the Dáil, he wrote:

> It must have been a dreadful surprise for Rory O'Connor and his dupes to have been taken seriously, after six months. Evidently these men know nothing about the resources and determination of Governments, and considered themselves as play-actors. I am sorry for them, but their reprieve was entirely outside the terms of my Patent.[20]

William O'Brien had not been privy to Healy's appointment before it was announced. His unease had not yet hardened into the open opposition to the treaty and the new Irish government he later professed. If he had misgivings about Healy's acceptance of the Governor-Generalship of the state which emerged out of the treaty, he did not declare them at the time. His observation that when Healy arrived at the Vice-Regal Lodge 'it was to find two terrorisms, the official and the anti-official raging around him'[21] reflected his later more dogmatic antagonism to the new *régime.*

On 9 December O'Brien wrote to Healy urging him to use his office to promote national reconciliation. 'If the battle cries of "no quarter" and "no surrender" are to go on much longer', he argued, 'the country will perish miserably in blood and shame'. He proposed that the existing ministry resign; that the Dáil and Senate should delegate their powers until a general election to a National Peace Commission of notables presided over by Healy; that government ministers should retain until the election purely departmental functions; that political prisoners should be detained until the general election but shown every leniency, and that the jurisdiction of the military courts should be confined to matters of military discipline. O'Brien spoke only for himself, but said he found it hard to imagine that on such terms de Valera would be found irreconcilable.[22] Even by his own standards, O'Brien's proposals were wildly unrealistic.

O'Brien could not entrust his letter to the post, and it was taken to Dublin by Canon Madden, the Parish Priest of Charleville, County Cork, who had been prominent in the All-for-Ireland League. On reaching Glenaulin, he found Healy, who was to go to London the following day, engaged with his tailor. Reading the letter, Healy went back and forth to see callers, and wrote his reply in bursts. That evening Healy had an appointment to take formal charge at the Viceregal Lodge from the departing British administration. He pressed Madden to accompany him in his armoured car. When they arrived at the Lodge, Healy, according to the account Madden later gave O'Brien, was extremely amusing on the subject of the remaining ceremonial retainers. Insisting that he stay for dinner, Healy took Madden on a tour: 'He showed them through the State Rooms which were very fine, the English flunkies turning on the lights to let them see the portraits of the Georges and the Viceroys looking down from the walls upon their queer visitors . . .'[23] In his reply to O'Brien Healy wrote:

> Everyone wants peace, but who are to be negotiated with? De Valera is down and out. His own men won't obey him. L. Lynch who three times broke his parole (altho' an ex-British Private) is in effective command. Most of his men or rather children-in-arms are out for loot and will never again tackle honest work. I cannot discern the least bitterness against them amongst the Ministers or Officers who see me. I find nothing but the same wish for peace that you display. What pleasure is it to me, with a sick wife, to have my house turned into a barrack, and no other mode of motion than an armoured car? You don't think I want a continuation of horror. We are dealing with reckless lads who know or care nothing for History or the reputation of their country. Statesmanship is as foreign to their thoughts as Theology. . . .
>
> I am bound to act on advice of others, and they not on mine. The proffer to you as to the Senatorship was awkwardly made, but were you chosen (and Cosgrave would have nominated you for the asking), you would have had a platform to advance your views, and to learn those of others.

This infuriated O'Brien, who later complained Healy was under the 'grotesque impression' that he had refused to take a seat in the new Senate because the offer of appointment had been awkwardly conveyed, rather than on grounds of political principle. Healy's reference to a platform from which to learn the views of others was perhaps more cutting than he intended, and reflected his weary exasperation with his role as O'Brien's main conduit to conventional political reality. He concluded:

> I shall silently watch, until they slay me, the stricken field with evergrowing sadness. I cannot heal wounds not of my making. More I cannot add, as I reply in great stress to your note, save to say, that I know the Insurgents can have peace any day they like on terms involving no humiliation to any decent Irishman.[24]

As O'Brien wrote some five years later, there was no more to be said. He was then still irate at Healy's observation to Madden that partition was unlikely to be undone in their time:

> But it was never safe to take Healy too literally in his unguarded comments or to assume that he would have any difficulty in changing his

> opinions. Once when I rallied him upon having within two or three hours having changed his advice as to our position on a critical division against Partition, his reply was: 'Why not? What are we here for except to change?' But he came back to the right advice all the same. It is pretty Fanny's way.

Their personal relations 'continued to be of the friendliest character, within such narrow non-committal limits as they could be carried on at all'.[25]

Healy reported to Maurice that Madden had called as O'Brien's emissary 'with a letter in the 1890-91 vein. It is a pity that he should be cut off from communication save the press, which is mostly exaggerated or false'. On the death of Madden some months later he wrote: 'I presume you met William at the funeral, and that he was fuming like Vesuvius!! He sent the poor Canon here last January with some very imperious peace proposals'.[26] As O'Brien's reluctance to align himself with the government of the new state became increasingly clear, Healy's mind was carried back to the early stages of the Parnell split: 'I gathered . . . that William is an uncertain quantity. Of course, like Boulogne, he would have peace and was vexed with those who would not surrender everything to insure it. Cosgrave is of tougher fibre than Justin McCarthy!!'[27]

On 12 December 1922 Healy read a message from the King to a joint sitting of the Dáil and Senate.[28] He crossed to London to meet the King, who recalled sailing up Bantry Bay when he was in the navy. That evening Beaverbrook gave a dinner in his honour. Birkenhead proposed Healy's health and was followed by Walter Long. The next day,

> Lavery the painter asked me to lunch, and afterwards unexpectedly proceeded to paint me!! He is a very pleasant unassuming man, and his wife, who is an American, is intensely on our side. She entertained Collins, Griffith, Hogan, Cosgrave, and all the rest.[29]

In Dublin the same day, the Leicestershire Regiment handed over the Viceregal Lodge to soldiers of the Irish army. A puckish message from Healy was read to the departing troops:

> The Governor-General regrets that his unavoidable absence in England prevents him personally taking leave of the officers and men of the Leicester Regiment who have been on guard at the Viceregal Lodge. His Excellency desires them to be informed that it would have given him great pleasure to raise his hat to them on their departure from the Lodge.[30]

Reactions to Healy's appointment were decidedly mixed. After meeting Healy in London Lord Oranmore noted 'I am sure he will do his best, though it is curious to think of a man whom Parnell described as a "guttersnipe" representing the King'.[31] Writing to T. P. O'Connor, John Dillon responded with surprising equanimity, in large part because he considered the Governor-Generalship a poisoned chalice:

> What do you think of Tim's appointment? I imagine he must have some grounds for thinking he can make peace between the contending factions: if he had not, I hardly think he would have accepted. He has the advantage of having cultivated intimate relations with the leaders of both sides. But as you know, he has never been distinguished for sound judgement and I have doubts whether, in the existing temper here, peace is possible. If there is no peace – the executions will go on – and Tim's position will not be enviable.[32]

The disdain of republicans and left-wing critics of the new *régime* for the Governor-Generalship was not assuaged by the appointment of a King's Counsel and ex-parliamentarian of clericalist leanings who had been Parnell's chief adversary in the split. Sean O'Casey's polemical *Inishfallen Fare Thee Well* of 1949 conveys the radical hostility to Healy, 'the hound that brought down the noble stag, Parnell'. Of his appointment, O'Casey wrote: 'Now this Tim Healy has become an Excellency, and the red-robed and the purple-robed were all around him, meeting him in the doorway of their churches, providing him with a special *prie-dieu*, tucking him up in his car . . .' It prompted a last elegy for Parnell: ' . . . who will turn aside from his way to seek the place where Healy lies; or weave a wreath of laurel for its honour; or cast a sprig of ivy on the grave?'[33]

The Civil War's End

A pall of violence still hung over the new state. Writing to Beaverbrook in early January, Healy sought to allay concern in London at the protraction of the civil war: 'The position here is simplifying itself. De Valera is snuffed out by his own lot and they do not look to him any longer except as a figurehead. Their operators now act under the compulsion of a few desperate leaders'.[34] As the war entered its final phase, the Irish government stood firm. Healy wrote to Maurice: 'Our ministers take the view that the forces on the other side are utterly contemptible . . . Anyhow I have never seen, for men in such responsible positions, so much complete confidence.'[35] The Viceregal Lodge came under heavy fire on 18 January.[36] At the end of the month he reported that 'there was more firing here on Saturday night, when I had some members of the Bar to dinner; but the shots did not even hit the Lodge'.[37]

Healy had maintained a degree of respect for de Valera for longer than most on the pro-Treaty side, but the continuation of the civil war had exhausted his tolerance. To Maurice he wrote in January 1923 that 'so far as moral responsibility goes, I should rather be the Kaiser than de Valera. Jealousy, envy, vanity alone account for his performances. To these ingredients, loot must be added in the case of some of his underlings'. The following month he asserted that 'the civil war has become merely a vendetta by a half-breed Spaniard against his late colleagues'.[38]

On 7 February 1923, Healy exasperatedly wrote from the Viceregal Lodge of what had by then become a demonstrably futile Republican war of attrition against the new state:

> One day passes here the same as another. Every day brings some offer of 'peace' from the unhappy fools who are blowing up mansions and wrecking railways. Each one of them has for its first condition that the gang at the head of the sabotage shall be restored to their old army rank!! There is no patriotism in the business. It is simply a struggle for jobs even more sordid than that we were accustomed to under the Dillon regime. The Dillonites only wasted notepaper, but the present lot are prepared to slaughter their countrymen and destroy their habitations, in the vain hope that the Government will surrender to their solicitations. No spark of principle that I can discern seems to animate them.[39]

On 11 February 1923, Kevin O'Higgins attended a family party at the Viceregal Lodge, where he sang Irish songs 'in his fine baritone'. Returning to Government Buildings, he learnt of the murder by Irregulars of his father, Thomas Higgins, at Stradbally. Healy, writing late at night to Maurice, broke down: 'At this point comes the dreadful news of the murder of poor old Dr. Higgins. I can't write any more'. A few days later he wrote: 'When you reflect that an illiterate boy, hardly out of his teens, could inflict such woe on a large circle of people, it requires grace to be resigned'.[40]

Healy discountenanced concessions to the opponents of the treaty:

> Of course what the de Valera lot aim at is to inflict economic defeat on their opponents by their campaign of destruction, in the hope that sabotage will compel terms to be granted. But every crime they commit renders compromise with them more impossible. They are continually making peace overtures on the basis of army employment. Lynch wants to be on the staff, and originally they demanded a majority of the headquarters staff!! De Valera sent Swayne K.C. recently to Cosgrave, who would have nothing to do with the negotiations. Cosgrave's terms all along have been No Surrender, and he has acted in the pluckiest manner, and impressed Downing Street very much by his resolution and courage. Scotland Yard

showed him last week a lot of letters to America written by de Valera which they intercepted, but would not say how they were obtained, or allow them to be published. I can't believe the fellow as cracked as your informants seem to think. He may of course be browbeaten and bullied by Lynch, but that is a different thing.[41]

On the theology of the Republic, Healy was characteristically mordant:

I think their strength is waning fast. Still they are making desperate efforts to show the contrary, so as to drive us into giving them terms. I saw one of their priests on Monday, and his great point was about the oath. I said none of them need take it, as not one of them would be returned at an election!! I also suggested that they could easily get one of their casuists to hold that an oath taken under duress was not binding and was worthless, and that people who could commit crimes in defiance of the bishops' decision should not have such tender consciences as regards a verbal formula. They are evidently very sorry for themselves, but can get no one else to pity them.[42]

Healy continued to be especially mistrustful of the women on the republican side: 'these women seem to lose all sense'.[43]

The civil war, and the execution of republicans, continued. Healy wrote to Maurice on 23 March:

I had a visit from O'Hegarty suggesting that, as the Cork combatants were meeting this week to discuss peace, all executions should be stopped. I was not aware of any intended executions, but referred him to President Cosgrave. My own idea is that a patched-up peace will only lead to further violence later on, as murders of prominent men on either side would break the truce if one were made. Still it looks as if well-meaning ecclesiastics intend to invoke the angelic part of our nature!![44]

The concluding reference was to the arrival in Ireland of Monsignor Luzio, a special papal envoy, in response to republican requests to the Pope to intervene to bring about peace. Healy endorsed the rebuffing of Luzio by the Irish government, and went so far as to prepare text on the subject for the *Daily Express*.[45]

It was part of Healy's role to affirm the survival amid strife of civil society in the Free State. He wrote to Beaverbrook in April that he was going to the Punchestown races, 'as "mourning" has been ordered by the Irregulars. I was never there yet and I hardly know a Clydesdale from a Steeplechaser'. He afterwards reported to Maurice of the Republicans: 'They are a lot of mere boys and girls. I drove on both days to Punchestown with only one man and went out amongst the crowds to see the jumps'.[46]

As the republican challenge to the government disintegrated, Healy wrote to his brother:

> Why Stack should have preserved his note-brook containing the draft surrender, while de Valera was issuing an address to the 'republican forces' is more than I can understand . . . His statesmanship – or mentality – possibly led him to think it useful to pretend that he was forced to yield by the 'army council' at the very moment when he, loyal soul, was urging forward the republican army!! I have come to regard him as a weak, unstable and shuffling man, over-stocked with professorial fudge.
>
> . . . Stack's surrender without a fight amazes me as much as his preservation of the notebook containing the proposed message of surrender. They must have known that their only hope was intimidation and sabotage; and that, when this did not shake us, keeping up a fight was hopeless. It is better to have let them destroy twenty millions worth of property than make terms with them.
>
> The destruction of houses is a cruel business, but they don't affect the minds of men like Kevin and Hogan, who spent yesterday here. Their fear is that a patched-up peace would be concocted. Cosgrave however is as resolute as ever. The soldiers here seem to me as good as the British, in spite of their short training. The failure to capture De Valera is probably due to his residence in some monastery in the garb of a monk, and never going out . . .
>
> Poor Michael Collins did not buy enough of the irregular captains with promises of jobs. He could not see, as we now do, that it would have been cheaper to make berths from them. They thought it would be better to reign in hell than serve in heaven.[47]

A republican ceasefire was declared with effect from 30 April. Three days later the last two executions took place in Ennis, bringing the total number executed in the period since November 1922 to seventy-seven.[48]

Healy wrote to Maurice at the end of the month, once again denouncing de Valera, and affirming his faith in the future of the new state:

> There is no news here save the de Valera collapse, which I suppose spells some sort of peace . . . He seems an unscrupulous man, prepared to sanction any mischief to gain his ends. The murder of Dr. Higgins, and the destruction of mansions like Esmonde's and Plunkett's, as well as the attacks on roads, bridges, harbours and railways, make it I think impossible for him to hope to take part again in the public life of the country. Besides I am sure the Collins family could never forgive the death of poor Michael, so that, if de Valera is well advised, he should, as he himself said, try 'a simple quit' and leave the country.
>
> He offers no apology for his futile wickedness, and indeed compliments his gang on their supposed achievements. Besides the deaths, I suppose he has wasted fifty millions of money on his campaign. I am very sorry for his wife and family. His wife is an innocent and saintly woman, while his children bear a name that will be always hated by the majority of the people. His impudence is colossal.

> I can't however accept your view that we are witnessing the dissolution of civilisation. On the contrary, I think that in a year or two things will become as normal as under the British. There is a strong background of good sense in the Irish nature, despite the sentimental foolishness of a few and the predatory spirit lately shown by a minority.[49]

Healy was increasingly close to Kevin O'Higgins, Minister for Home Affairs and Vice-President of the Executive Council. Determined to give no quarter to those whom he regarded as the implacable foes of the new state, and of social order, O'Higgins was the member of the government most identified with the severity of the government's response in the latter stages of the civil war. Healy subscribed to O'Higgins' hawkish opinion that Richard Mulcahy, the Minister for Defence, was lacking in the requisite degree of sternness. He reported to Maurice in mid-March that there was a view in relation to the civil war that 'Mulcahy could by sheer vigour have ended the job'. There were not many contemporaries who considered Mulcahy deficient in vigour. Healy wrote the following month that he was coming to agree with his friend Senator John MacLoughlin's assessment of Mulcahy 'that he is a weak poetic man filled with fancies, and quite unacquainted with the resoluteness of the English to hold Ireland within the Empire and to sustain Ulster'.[50]

Healy was impressed by the calibre and resolve of the new government, perhaps a little clannishly giving pride of place to O'Higgins: 'Kevin has many bouts with Mulcahy to tune him up. Cosgrave is a fine, determined man. Hogan is a first-rate chap, and Duggan is zealous and whole-hearted'. He referred to Patrick Hogan, the Minister for Agriculture, as 'a very able and honest fellow. He is Kevin's great stand-by'.[51]

He told the *Daily Express* in early July: 'The Free State is established definitely, despite the internal assaults which have been made upon it'.[52] The ending of the civil war transposed to the electoral plane what had been a military confrontation. In the severity of the policies it had adopted to establish the new state and to meet the republican challenge to the treaty, the government had already been pushed somewhat adrift of the political centre. This gave rise to some premonitory unease among its members, who sought to console themselves with the delusive belief that de Valera, in permitting himself to be carried along in a military campaign against the new state, had ensured his permanent political marginalisation. Healy reported to Maurice on a discussion in the Viceregal Lodge in July 1923:

> I had three of the Ministers here last night, and they were of the opinion that, bad as the civil war had been, it was better than having de Valera tied about the country's neck for evermore, as he would have been

> had he accepted the Treaty. The violent parturition may therefore have been for the best.[53]

Healy treated de Valera's personal responsibility for the civil war as axiomatic, and observed his course of accommodation to the new state with a mordant eye. Writing to Maurice three days later, he referred to him as 'a conscious humbug, and to have very little respect for the intelligence of his opponents. I don't believe he will return half a dozen supporters . . . He seems to be the most disastrous person who has ever meddled in Irish affairs'.[54]

The only institution of the new state about which Healy had reservations was its electoral system. An old adept of the straight vote, which would have assured the government party, Cumann na nGaedhael, of a more decisive ascendancy over Sinn Féin than it achieved in the general election of 1923, Healy mistrusted proportional representation. On the eve of the poll he commented that 'P.R. certainly favours the Republicans'. On the day of the poll, 27 August, he wrote that 'it seems to me that P.R. is the very worst method of voting invented!! It entirely helps the active gang by its confusions, and keeps up the excitement for a week after the election'.[55] In the event the result fell far short of the government's expectations. Cumann na nGaedhael won 63 seats and Sinn Féin 44, against the background of a shrinking Labour vote.[56]

The Boundary Commission

As Governor-General, Healy continued to make frequent visits to London. The *Irish Times* wrote on his death that 'at times Mr. Healy had become a kind of Free State ambassador to London as well as the representative of the King in Dublin'.[57] Healy in this respect succeeded in enlarging his role beyond the narrow ambit of his office. On this ambiguous terrain, the political and social spheres were not rigidly demarcated. Healy put his English connections to the best use he could. He apprised Beaverbrook in February 1923 that Cosgrave was going to London to see Bonar Law: 'You should meet him. He is a shy man but jolly altho' he does not eat or drink to my knowledge'.[58] He defended Cosgrave against criticism in the *Daily Mail*, referring to his physical health: 'No doubt he is not a strong man, but he is sticking on very pluckily and showing great adroitness in the Dáil'.[59]

In March, dining with Lady Lavery, Healy met G. B. Shaw, whom he found 'a very unassuming fellow, with no side whatever'. Lady Lavery took him to see the Marquess of Londonderry, then the Northern Ireland Minister for Education, who 'spoke very moderately'.[60] Two months later, Healy was again at Lady Lavery's, where Churchill, Austen Chamberlain,

Cope, and Reginald McKenna were also present. He reported to Maurice from the Vineyard that evening, renewing their old debate: 'There is an odd impression here that the Irish Government have shown great courage!! There is a Gaelic proverb which I quoted for the Prime Minister: "Praise the young thing and it will flourish"'.[61]

On 19 January 1923 Healy in one of his first official acts wrote to the Duke of Devonshire to advise him that, acting in accordance with Article 12 of the treaty, the Irish Free State had appointed Eoin MacNeill as its representative on the Boundary Commission. There followed a series of delays, attributable in the first instance to the holding of preliminary tripartite discussions, proposed by the British government as a temporising measure. When the Irish Free State on 26 April 1924 forced the issue by formally requesting the British government to take steps to constitute the Boundary Commission, further delay was occasioned by the refusal of the government of Northern Ireland to appoint a representative. This necessitated the enactment into law in Britain and the Irish Free State of an agreement supplemental to the treaty to permit the British government to nominate the Northern Ireland representative. The Commission eventually sat for the first time on 5 November 1924.[62]

Healy wrote to his brother in April 1923 that he was going to London 'merely to have a chat with Max and others. Bonar's health is said to be poor, and the Boundary question is of such importance that much may turn on his resigning or remaining'[63] He stayed with Beaverbrook and met Bonar Law.[64] Bonar Law resigned on 20 May. Healy lunched with the stricken former Prime Minster at Moreton Frewen's in July, and four months later represented the Irish government at his funeral in Westminster Abbey.[65]

On Bonar Law's death, Healy wrote Beaverbrook a letter of condolence in which he claimed that 'I kept back the Boundary Commission to spare him trouble, and fear now it will be pressed on'.[66] While Healy was grossly overstating his own influence, and quite possibly in some degree misrepresenting his own position to ingratiate himself with Beaverbrook, the attitude he evinced was nevertheless remarkable. It was apparent that in a striking departure from his position a year previously, Healy was less eager in pressing for the immediate constitution of the Boundary Commission. He could no longer claim the personal influence with the British government which he naively believed himself to possess at the time of the signing of the treaty. He was moreover aware of how deeply entrenched partition had become. He knew that the appointment of a Boundary Commission could well serve to inflame nationalist opinion in the Irish Free State and in Northern Ireland, embarrass the Irish government, and damage Anglo-Irish relations. While some Irish ministers may have had like misgivings, it was not open to the Irish government to hold back from pressing for the establishment of the Commission.

Whatever his reservations, Healy threw discretion to the winds in an interview he gave to the *Daily Express* in early July 1923. He evidently felt that, with the civil war finally concluded, the Irish government was in a position to take a more assertive stance on partition, and that there was nothing to inhibit him as Governor-General from taking this upon himself. He expressed himself satisfied with the compliance by the British government with its obligations under the treaty, but attacked the government of Northern Ireland. He deplored the detention of individuals sympathetic to the Free State, and condemned the abolition of proportional representation in local government, coupled with gerrymandering. 'These indignities, apart from any other reasons, made it inevitable that the Boundary Commission should be appointed as rapidly as possible'. He opined that strictly speaking there was no 'Ulster' or 'Ulster problem', given that nearly half of the population of the six counties would vote themselves into the Free State if they were given the opportunity to do so. He referred to the 'unnatural arrangement of the population on the border', which it was the business of the Boundary Commission to rectify. Given that the Northern Ireland government had not nominated a representative and was not likely to do so, he asserted that the Commission should proceed, even if only on the basis that it was a matter for the Commission to determine whether or not it had jurisdiction to proceed.[67] Healy's comments were immediately condemned by Sir James Craig, the Prime Minister of Northern Ireland.[68]

In late 1923 Healy saw Devonshire again at his request on the boundary question. Of the proposed preliminary conference, he reported to his brother 'although I have not very much to hope from this expedient, I don't see that it can do any harm'.[69] He proffered advice (from Biarritz) in relation to the treatment by the Boundary Commission of Derry and the Inishowen peninsula. He was also credited with what Prof. Geoffrey Hand refers to as the 'euphonious gibe', in relation to the South African chairman of the Boundary Commission, of 'Feetham-cheat 'em!'[70]

While the Boundary Commission was deliberating in late 1924, Healy expressed himself with whimsical fatalism on the subject of partition in a letter to Beaverbrook. He continued to profess the hope that the British would compel the 'so-called loyalists (drunk, they curse England)' to join a central Irish government, 'to combat our museum of Old Maids and young cods, who know as much about a Republic as I do of the Sahara's buried cities'. England could by economic measures impose a central government in Ireland, 'but the ghosts of John Knox, Cranmer, Cromwell with other light and airy theologians forbid the Banns'.[71]

The Boundary Commission determined on an adjustment of the border involving an inter-transfer of territory which it was politically impossible for the Irish government to countenance. A political resolution was achieved by a tripartite agreement signed in London on 3 December 1925. The existing border was confirmed, and the Irish state relieved of some of the financial obligations imposed by the treaty.[72] William O'Brien was predictably outraged by the 'new London agreement', which he publicly condemned as 'perhaps the most disgraceful in our history' and suspected that Healy had played a part in bringing it about. This was surmise ('I recoil from the pain of too curiously investigating'), based on the fact that Healy was in London at the time of the negotiations, and that the speech made shortly after his return represented 'the first serious error of his Governor-Generalship'.[73] The observation to which O'Brien was referring was certainly remarkable, at least in its ineptitude. Speaking at a dinner in Dublin in March 1926 he declared that they owed the recent boundary settlement almost entirely 'to the simple kindness of heart and patriotism of Mr. Baldwin'.[74] Without subscribing to O'Brien's furious conspiracy theory, it can hardly be doubted that Healy used such limited influence as he possessed to promote the London agreement.

The Sage of Mallow

During the civil war, William O'Brien devoted himself to the writing of his polemical *The Irish Revolution and How It Came About*, which was published in 1923. The proofs were sent to Healy, not by O'Brien but by a third party. O'Brien wrote politely that he would not have dreamt of imposing on Healy by sending them to him, and was evidently apprehensive as to his reaction.[75] Healy was in fact impressed by the proofs on first reading them, although O'Brien may not have been pleased to find them returned with extensive annotations to his account of contemporary events. Healy wrote to Maurice:

> I congratulated O'Brien upon it, and received a nice and grateful response, but he made it clear that he was one of those crying 'A plague on both your houses!' He begged me not to show anything in the nature of taking sides with this government, as, if anything was certain, it was that it would disappear at the next election. I replied simply that I did not agree with his forecast.[76]

After what O'Brien described as his 'first over-indulgent assessment of the book', Healy had second thoughts. He wrote to O'Brien what he described as a 'respectful remonstrance', commenting to his brother that 'the last few pages of William are so ''neutral'' that it reminded me of his Boulogne attitude'. O'Brien responded that it was too late to make changes and continued:

> There is no reason why we should not frankly recognise that since the date of the truce of 1921 there has been a profound difference of opinion between you and me as to what happened in the negotiations of the treaty at the end of that year, both on the Irish and British sides, and ever since on the means by which (*selon moi*) and by which alone, peace among Irishmen might have been preserved or restored.

He observed somewhat self-importantly that 'any controversy between you and me, however courteously conducted, would not improve the temper of either of us, and be, I am sure, little short of a fresh disaster for the country'. He did not consider that the book's publication would stir especial public controversy, nor that it need disturb the friendship between them 'which in spite of many jolts and jars in this perverse world, has subsisted between us for more than an average lifetime'.[77]

O'Brien was understandably anxious to avoid the ridiculous spectacle of the two Parnellite *enfants terribles* in old age once again taking up the cudgels against each other. They had exhausted their quota of fractious controversy, and neither could afford to revive the memory of their mutual recriminations on the break in Louth in 1900. Their political survival into the era of the Free State had been narrowly and fortuitously achieved, and their reputations could scarcely have withstood a further outbreak of hostilities between them.

Healy was not immediately troubled by the reference to his own role: while O'Brien referred to the Lloyd George-Churchill 'assurance', he did not identify Healy as the individual whom he now described as 'Mr. Michael Collins' intermediary'.[78] Apart from his disagreement with O'Brien's criticisms of the treaty and of the Irish government, his main reservation related to O'Brien's disclosure of private conversations with contemporary politicians. He did not sanction the use of his own correspondence. (O'Brien lamented in the text 'had I his leave to publish them, Mr. Healy's letters, teeming with diamondiferous wit, and laden with piquant items of secret information, would make a valuable addition to the inner history of the time'.)[79] Healy reported to Maurice that in writing to O'Brien, while 'according unmeasured praise upon his great performances', he had suggested that he

> should take neutral opinion upon his disclosures of private conversations, and expressing the view that such publication will greatly hamper relations (otherwise than by megaphone broadcasting) between Ulster and ourselves, not to speak of England and Ireland. While in some sense he

justly attributes to war pressure the pliancy of Lloyd George, yet it is not fair, I told him, either to Joffre or Lloyd George that he should publish at the present time such conversations. I am afraid he will treat my appreciation of his great work as submerged by this criticism. I can't help it. Of course the piquancy of his volume will be greatly enhanced by his disclosures of talks with Carson, Lloyd George and Bonar Law; yet I think such disclosures not permissible at the present time, whatever may be said after the death of the principal actors. The habit of writing down the ephemeral notions of the moment, and then recording them in judgement against those who differ from his, harnessed to the faculty of the novelist or romancer, places him at a great advantage. I often said to you that, if Jim Gilhooly kept a diary on the Parnell Split, and no one else did, he would be known to future ages as 'the judicious Gilhooly'!!

Personal blemishes should not prevent you from reading O'Brien's proofs, for he has written stuff that will last, and must be an anchorage of history. When Sir Jonah Barrington is remembered as to the Union narrative, O'Brien will certainly live as to the disunion.[80]

The letter reveals Healy's acute sensitivity to the process by which popular historical judgements were shaped. Yet his prediction, so far as O'Brien's *Irish Revolution* was concerned, was not borne out. Its impact was negligible in comparison with his three earlier books of reminiscence. When it appeared, John Dillon described it to T. P. O'Connor as 'a more lying and disgusting treatment of the history of the last twenty years than any of his previous volumes'.[81]

The elaborate mutual politeness between Healy and O'Brien disclosed an underlying strain. Healy deplored what he considered to be O'Brien's lack of political realism, while O'Brien appeared to regard his old friend and the Governor-General as two distinct personae. William O'Brien forwarded a letter he received from Healy to his wife, saying it would amuse her: 'His language is appalling. If he used it in public, it would never be forgiven – so foul and disgusting, worthy of the worst of the Parnell split days'. He told her to keep the letter and his reply carefully: 'The day will come when these things will have their interest'.[82]

After the *Irish Revolution* O'Brien published his more measured *Edmund Burke as an Irishman* in 1924. In 1926 he published *The Parnell of Real Life*, largely a collation of his earlier accounts of Parnell. Writing to T. P. O'Connor, Dillon lamented that it was

a tragedy that the Old Party should go down in history in the lying books of F. H. O'Donnell, William O'Brien, Tim Healy and co. Have you read William O'Brien's latest – his book on Parnell? It makes a fair bid to outdo all his previous performances in lying, and misrepresentation, and frantic egotism, and the suppressions and insinuations are frequent and particularly vile . . .[83]

O'Brien's posthumous influence was chiefly as a memorialist of Parnell: Healy characterised him shortly after his death as 'the greatest champion of "the Chief"'.[84]

For the last two years of his life William O'Brien was engaged in writing his splenetic chronicle of contemporary events from the time of the treaty, 'The Irish Free State: Secret History of its Foundation'.[85] Had Healy had sight of the manuscript, as he had of the proofs of *The Irish Revolution*, he would have been aghast. O'Brien had elaborated Healy's account of the undertaking or assurance given by Churchill with the sanction of Lloyd George on the Boundary Commission, into an intricate and malign conspiracy theory of the origins of the Irish Free State. Though interlarded with unctuous references to him, O'Brien knew that much of the polemical force of his account derived from tainting the Free State by association with Healy.

O'Brien's was a polemical account of Irish hope betrayed. The narrative conformed to the specifications of his habitual mode of political argument. By directing his attack against English duplicity, he could at one level profess not to impugn the good faith of those in Ireland who had upheld the treaty. Just as he had latterly become persuaded that John Morley was responsible for precipitating the Parnell split, he now characterised Lloyd George and Winston Churchill as the authors of what he described as 'An Irish Civil War Made in England'.[86]

If O'Brien was thus spared the necessity of impugning the good faith of Collins and Griffith, he did extend the same indulgence to their successors. In particular he violently assailed W. T. Cosgrave and Kevin O'Higgins, who he blamed for the pursuit of a hardline strategy against the treaty's opponents which he argued was the diametrical opposite to that adopted by Collins and Griffith. The grand old man assailed the *arrivistes* of the new regime with the virulence of a prophet spurned. He complained that 'the infant state was committed to the guardianship of an inexperienced law student and an unknown spirit-grocer experienced only in the affairs of Dublin Corporation', and shamefully added that they both owed their lives 'to the unacquaintance of the general public with their persons and with their part in recent affairs'.[87]

O'Brien knew that the publication of his account would have led to a storm of recriminations, and embroiled him directly in controversy with Healy. He wrote that he was constrained by his 'fast personal friendship and affection' for Healy. Referring to the London agreement of 3 December 1925 which affirmed the existing border, he wrote that 'it was the secret bond of confidence between us which alone restrained me from exhausting my last energies in public resistance to the second London Treaty'.[88] Even in 1933, five years after O'Brien's death and two years after Healy's, by which time de Valera was in power, the publishers to whom the manuscript was sent replied that they were 'strongly advised that this was not the psychological time to bring it out'.[89]

From 1926 O'Brien was openly aligned with de Valera, who the following year established the Fianna Fáil party. In February 1926 de Valera in the course of a by-election read a letter from O'Brien condemning the London agreement of December 1925.[90] O'Brien declined an invitation to stand in Cork, but endorsed Fianna Fáil in the June election of 1927, designating the treaty 'An Act of Disunion between the two Irish States and between Ireland and England'.[91]

Just before the election, O'Brien wrote to Healy that he wanted to see him. Healy responded somewhat nervously that if the matter was 'concerned with political fluctuations, I must in advance disclaim capacity'. O'Brien wrote back to Healy with a set of proposals for the revision of the treaty and of the London agreement of 1925, sanguinely stating that he could not believe that Baldwin, or Amery, the Colonial Secretary, would block the way. Presuming that 'you would not care to interfere personally as a mediator', he wanted Healy to communicate his proposals to Cosgrave, observing that it should not be difficult to convey them to de Valera. Healy responded that he would prefer if O'Brien communicated directly with Cosgrave, and reminded him of the constitutional limitations on his role, for which he must for once have felt grateful.[92]

Their debate on the responsibility for partition continued, an obsessional revisiting of the events of the ten years 1912–22. While their views were deeply felt, particularly in O'Brien's case, they were both prone to engaging in recriminations against those of whom they disapproved on the nationalist side, at the expense of giving any sustained consideration to the strength of unionist resistance, both in Ulster itself, and in the context of contemporary British politics.

On 27 December 1927 Healy wrote what was to be his last letter to O'Brien. He commended his essay on happiness, included in his just-published *Irish Fireside Hours*. It was 'as good as a sermon in Bossuet'.[93] O'Brien died on a visit to London on 25 February 1928. He remained to the end preoccupied with the division of the country. In conversation with Michael McDonagh a couple of days before his death, he had proclaimed that 'every hero or saint whose name ever made Irish blood thrill cries out from the grave against partition'.[94] At the time of O'Brien's death, Healy was in Egypt, where he had gone on the expiration of his term as Governor-General. Thence he wrote to his daughter.

> I hope he will have a big cortège, for he deserved it and plenty [of the] blossoms of the Spring. O'Brien was a great chap. Devotion to Parnell

> blurred his historic vision for tho' Parnell jettisoned him in 1887 over the Plan of Campaign he always treated him as an unselfish patriot like himself. Paragraphs were O'Brien's pay. Parnell's was metallic.[95]

Healy's implacable harking back to the issue of the split reflected an awareness that his own career would be weighed chiefly in its relation to Parnell. He had conceived his juncture with O'Brien as much as a historical coupling as a political alliance, as if he did not wish to stand alone before the assize of posterity. He was always mindful of what he referred to in his last published piece as 'that ghostly doomster, "the future historian"'.[96]

Bereavements

In the civil war, Maurice Healy in Cork was more exposed than his brother in Dublin to the ravages of the civil war. He was put on a steamer out of Cork by Irregulars at the point of a revolver, in reprisal for having advised the merchants of Cork that the payment of republican levies could not discharge their income tax liabilities to the Irish state. He had stayed away for two months. Thereafter there had been an attempt to burn down his house.[97]

Healy's relations with his younger brother remained adamantly boyish. Visiting him shortly after his appointment as Governor-General, as they went into breakfast, Healy 'snatched off the black silk cap Maurice had worn since his illness, told him to have done with that sort of thing, and hurled it up into the air. The maid retrieved it and handed it to her master who told her that she had much better manners than His Excellency'.[98]

Maurice died at his home, Temple Hill, Ballintemple, on 9 November 1923, at the age of sixty-six. Tim Healy was inconsolable. He had lost as well as a brother, his closest confidant. His memoirs, dedicated to the memory of the '*drahareen og machree*' closed with Maurice's death. 'Had I preserved my brother's letters, as he did mine, these pages would not have lacked lustre'.[99]

At Christmas 1921, Healy's wife Erina had suffered a stroke which left her partially paralysed and with impaired speech.[100] She was incapacitated throughout Healy's Governor-Generalship until her death on 8 July 1927. On the day before her funeral, Healy in the grounds of the Viceregal Lodge received the news that Kevin O'Higgins, her nephew, had been shot. When he learned that O'Higgins lingered still, he had to be restrained 'almost by force' from setting out across the city to Booterstown, 'as there were fears of a general assassination plot'.[101]

The assassination of Kevin O'Higgins at the age of thirty-five removed the most pertinacious member of the Healy—Sullivan connection in Irish politics. His fierce resolve to uphold the institutions of the new state itself bore the impress of the trauma of the civil war, of which he was the last and belated casualty. W. B. Yeats in 'The Municipal Gallery Revisited', strove to capture his enigma:

> Kevin O'Higgin's countenance that wears
> A gentle questioning look that cannot hide
> A soul incapable of remorse or rest.

This second terrible blow, following almost immediately on the first, was political, as well as personal and familial. Healy wrote to Beaverbrook, 'you interpret rightly my feelings when you say I would willingly have taken his place'.[102] The following month Healy attended the annual Griffith-Collins anniversary commemoration on Leinster Lawn, a rallying of the Free State establishment in the aftermath of O'Higgins' assassination.[103]

Even Unto Heliotropolis

The Viceregal Lodge had suffered the depredations of successive Lord Lieutenants, each of whom had been permitted to take with him on leaving office a piece of furniture of his choosing. Two chimneypieces had been removed and replaced by what Maev Sullivan described as 'twin monstrosities in mottle-grey marble'. Believing his appointment to be for life, Healy at his own expense installed two Georgian chimneypieces from a house in Mountjoy Square. He also purchased at some expense vines for the hothouses. He was amused and pleased by the observation of the official of the Board of Works who had charge of the Lodge that 'these are the real gentry; the others were only the professional ones'.[104]

The expenses of the office borne by the state were very substantial, and embarrassing for the government: a republican handbill in 1924 proclaimed 'Tim Healy costs the Irish people £104 a day'.[105] Healy discountenanced Cosgrave's request that he move to the Chief Secretary's Lodge, reiterating his preference to reside in Glenaulin, which he knew to be unacceptable.[106]

Healy's office gave him a ceremonial social eminence. On his appointment, *Irish Life* enunciated a dismaying social credo: 'naturally, the outlook of the new Governor-General will be broader than that of the Lords-Lieutenant; but nothing is so beneficial as a social ladder, and we trust that ours will not be lost altogether'.[107] Healy contributed to the maintenance of an element of social continuity. The *Irish Times* wrote on his death that by his equanimity 'and by the tact and suavity of his social manner, he, perhaps, more than any other man, helped to allay the fears of the ex-Unionist minority'.[108] He also, in the culminating irony of his career, became the embodiment of such nexus as existed between the new state and the other *ancien régime*, that of the Irish party. Sir Dunbar Plunket Barton thought that towards the end of his life Healy 'mellowed almost beyond recognition'.[109]

Healy held occasional garden parties at the Viceregal Lodge, and attended a diverse range of social events. He continued resolutely to appear at Irish race meetings. He was regularly to be seen, and photographed, at the Spring Show and Horse Show of the Royal Dublin Society. There he was frequently accompanied by Kevin O'Higgins, and Lady Lavery. Much of the social glamour of his Governor-Generalship was lent by Hazel Lavery, whom Oliver St. John Gogarty in his impressionistic rendition of a dinner at the Viceregal Lodge had 'acting as Vice-Reine'.[110]

Healy spoke at a dinner on the occasion of the Tailteann games in August 1924, at which the heterogeneous attendance included W. B. Yeats, G. K. Chesterton, and John Devoy. Healy was at his most disarming and beguiling, prefacing his remarks by the observation that 'now that questions of politics and religion were excluded, he would like to say a word on sport, though he could not even play marbles'. He joined in Yeats' welcome to Devoy, 'from whose heart not even the great continent of America could wipe out the memory of this little spot of earth'.[111]

Healy's Governor-Generalship, in its social aspect, excited the contempt of republicans. Lady Gregory was struck by a poem which appeared in *An Phoblacht* in August 1925, inspired by Healy's attendance in the company of the Laverys, at a concert given by John McCormack. It had, notwithstanding its crude polemicism, a certain pathos.

In The Royal Box
(To the Man in the Royal Box at the McCormack
Concert, August 9 1925)

An old grey-bearded man, bowed to
the grave.
Radiant and fair
Women about him, and one imperially
gowned
Of an imperious beauty.
Roses lie dying there
Before them – and around
The hot bright air
Passionately pulses to the glamorous
sound
Of a god-moulded throat.

Dim in the shadows there,
Silken and sleek of coat
They pass behind him and they move
around
His Ministers, His Colonel,
And yes — I swear!
Stands darkly in the darkness, silence-
bound
A man whose eyes with all the woe of Hell
Burn on the other in a lidless stare.
Parnell!

J.[112]

Healy determinedly courted Senator W. B. Yeats, by whose (early) poetry he was enchanted. When Yeats wrote to Healy on the subject of the Lane pictures, Healy responded with an invitation to visit him whenever he wished in '"the bee-loud glade"'.[113] He urged Gogarty to bring 'your friend Yeats, the Sally gardener' to his box at the Spring Show.[114] Reining in the fascination Healy had for him, Yeats continued to maintain a certain reserve in relation to his Governor-Generalship.

Lady Gregory enlisted Healy's support in the matter of Sir Hugh Lane's paintings. Having bequeathed his collection of modern art to the National Gallery in London, Lane subsequently changed his mind, and in an unwitnessed codicil to his will left the paintings to the City of Dublin, before he perished on the *Lusitania*. Healy wrote to Beaverbrook early in 1923 that Lady Gregory, Lane's aunt, had sent W. B. Yeats ('the famous poet') to see him, 'on a special mission to try to persuade you to get the Prime Minister interested in the matter'. He asked Beaverbrook, 'with deep confidence in your wizardry', to use his influence with Bonar Law and with Curzon (who was opposed to a private bill validating the Lane codicil).[115] Nothing came of his initiative. Healy continued to seek to influence the British government, although not entirely to the satisfaction of Augusta Gregory, who complained of what she regarded as his and Cosgrave's 'lukewarmness'.[116]

Healy continued to cross frequently to London, where Barbara Cartland met him in the mid-twenties. She set off with Beaverbrook and Healy for a party held by the Canadian Sir James Dunn on the lawn of Templeton, near Richmond. The strains of the Russian quartet had long died away before they left.

> Max Beaverbrook, Tim Healy and I motored home as dawn was breaking. The old Irishman had done himself well and at the top of his voice and in the broadest brogue he sang hymns which I can only describe as 'the chapel type'. There was a lot about 'being washed in the blood of

> the Lamb', and many lines expressing the sorrow of a prodigal son. And every so often the Governor [*sic*] of the Irish Free State would turn to us and demand angrily – 'And why don't ye join in, ye heathen!'[117]

On the continent, his tastes were diverse. He had written to Beaverbrook in 1918 that 'grisly papist though I be, I was never in Rome', an omission he repaired by visiting Rome for the canonisation of St. Thérèse of Lisieux, on 17 May 1925, his seventieth birthday. Some days later he had an audience with Pius XI.[118] The spring of the previous year had found him with Beaverbrook and Arnold Bennett in Spain. Writing on their return to Beaverbrook, Bennett regretted only that he had 'not rivalled Healy in the vast business of putting champagne out of sight'.[119]

Last Hurrah

Healy had been for too long his own man to be an altogether submissive Governor-General. On two occasions he queried bills presented for his signature. He warned Cosgrave he was uneasy about signing the Public Safety (Emergency Powers) (No. 2) Bill, 1923, on the grounds that it suspended an article of the constitution. O'Higgins forcefully impressed upon him that he had no option but to signify the King's assent. He also took exception to the Intoxicating Liquor Bill of 1923 on the grounds that the Dáil had been dissolved. Confronted by an opinion of the Attorney-General and a decision of the Executive Council, he relented.[120]

The interview Healy gave to the *Daily Express* in July 1923 on the boundary question[121] was the first of a series of injudicious utterances as Governor-General. The estimate for the Governor-General's establishment was debated in the Dáil later that month. Thomas Johnson, the Labour leader, pointed out that the estimates were excessive, 'and with three aides-de-camp, conveyed the idea of the kind of duties devolving upon a Viceroy – social duties and duties appertaining to a King . . . They had been led to believe they were to be relieved of that sort of thing . . .' Referring to Healy's recent utterances, Johnson's colleague Cathal O'Shannon, who took care to say he did not suggest that Healy was acting as a mouthpiece for the government, commented that it would be well that the Governor-General should be reminded that 'even if he did express the majority opinion, he should not express that opinion if it touched upon what was pure politics'.[122] Healy irately complained to his brother: 'You will see the allegation of Johnson and O'Shannon that I make political speeches; and Johnson even complained of my interview on the Boundary question. Duffy too has joined in harassing the Government in spite of his being one of the Treaty signatories. I cannot understand him'.[123]

At a dinner given by the Irish Club in London on 6 July 1925, Healy made a highly impolitic reference to the powers of the King and to his own role:

> It is modern jargon to say that the King must be advised by his ministers. But I have had the audacity to tell my ministers that they had better take the advice of an old man. The idea that the sovereign has not the power of initiative, the power of remonstrance, or the insistence on reconsideration, is in my opinion, as great an error as the notion that mere feudal tyranny can be tolerated any longer.

In the Dáil the following day, Kevin O'Higgins skilfully deflected a parliamentary question from Thomas Johnson on the subject of Healy's remarks.[124]

Healy's speech at the Dublin Chamber of Commerce on 7 November 1926 was his most controversial. Ostensibly regretting the lack of an effective opposition, he spoke of 'a number of persons whom we never heard of before, except in connection with explosions and assassinations':

> To those gentlemen who say that they will not enter into the legislature of their country because their principle forbids them to take the oath of his Majesty, I would say, in the words of Gilbert and Sullivan: 'You are curious optimists; you never would be missed'. They are quite welcome to stay out, and the further out they stay the better some of us will be pleased.[125]

The display of open partisanship was at odds with the delicate equilibrium of the new state, and cut athwart the re-integration of the opponents of the treaty into a system of constitutional politics. On this occasion O'Higgins was absent at the Imperial Conference. Cosgrave, while he did not like 'letting the old man down', regarded the matter gravely. He approached Thomas Johnson to ensure that it was addressed in the least damaging manner that could be achieved. When Johnson raised the issue in the Dáil, referring to Healy's speech as that of a political partisan, Cosgrave responded that while the speech was not made on the advice of the Executive Council, he regretted that an occasion had arisen which necessitated reference in the Dáil to a speech of the Governor-General.[126]

On 10 November the Irish government decided that the term of office of the Governor-General should be five years, and that accordingly Healy's term 'should expire as soon after 6 December 1927 as could conveniently be arranged'. There is nothing to suggest that this decision was prompted by dissatisfaction with Healy personally: it was rather intended to build on the gains of the Imperial Conference of 1926 to emphasise the ascendancy of the elected government, and to render the office as conformable to modern democratic practice as was possible. Healy's political conduct, the erratic guttering of an old firebrand, nonetheless served to affirm the desirability of limiting his term of office. Healy was taken aback and angered by the decision of the government. He protested that he held office for life in the same manner as the King. In the end however he went quietly, and on 17 December consented in writing to the bringing of his term of office to a close on 31 January 1928.[127]

A banquet was given by the government on 7 January 1928 to mark the approach of the end of his term. In his speech he declared they had heard much talk about a 'foreign King'. That King was a gentleman and they knew his pedigree. He wished they knew as much about those who talked about his Majesty's interference in Irish affairs.[128] The members of the Executive Council present can only have reflected with relief on the fact that this was to be Healy's last speech in office, and congratulated themselves on the wisdom of their decision to deem his term to be at an end.

The injudicious outbursts which marred the latter part of his term of office suggest that Healy was increasingly losing touch with public opinion. They do not reflect failing powers: his memoirs, which he was writing at this time, do not suggest any decline in his faculties. It is however noteworthy that some of his unhappily colourful utterances were delivered at dinners, and distinctly possible that these almost wistful rehearsals of his old powers as a provocative rhetorician owed something to the consumption of alcohol.[129] Even without such stimulus, it is unlikely that the old pugilist would have been able to restrain himself from a few compulsive jabs as he neared the end of the last round.

Robert Bruce-Lockhart recorded seeing Healy fairly often in his last years, 'always at Max's and generally drunk'. The last occasion was in October 1930 at the Imperial Conference, when Healy was out of office, and six months before his death:

> He is getting infirm and rather feeble on his feet, but he was in great form, did full justice to the liquor, had been to the dinner at Buckingham Palace to the Imperial Delegates, and was full of the glories of British loyalty and of the British Empire. He told stories until far into the night. Tim says Irish delegation, who are raising question of their status at the Imperial Conference, are not really interested in the question at all and are not in the least desirous of leaving the British Empire. Whole business is a question of internal politics and is intended to do de Valera down.[130]

God, Parnell and Eamon de Valera

In a lengthy interview with a correspondent of Beaverbrook's *Daily Express* shortly after he relinquished office, Healy once again denounced Eamon de Valera:

> 'Jealousy, not patriotism, is the root of his position!' he exclaimed, showing the first trace of bitterness which he had manifested throughout our long conversation.
>
> 'He is a vain, shallow man without a shred of ability. Born in New York of a foreign father, he has insisted on splitting the Irish race by a pretended intransigence. His reign of terror in the name of an Irish Republic has brought us nothing but bloodshed and ill-will. He is nothing but a barren impostor . . .'[131]

At a dinner given by the Pilgrims in his honour on 17 May 1928, replying to Birkenhead, Healy declared that all he had done to deserve the applause was 'to sit quietly in a charming park, comfortably situated with beautiful surroundings, and sign Acts of Parliament in the name of His Majesty the King'.[132] Healy served as Treasurer of Gray's Inn for 1929. After a Grand Night in January attended by G. K. Chesterton and J. L. Garvin, Healy wrote to his daughter 'certainly they have not made me feel the "curse of Swift"'.[133]

From 1926, Healy was occupied in the writing of his memoirs. He had in Beaverbrook a uniquely formidable literary agent. With uncharacteristic punctiliousness, Beaverbrook expressed the view that the publication of the memoirs while still in office would constitute a breach of convention. This was of great concern to Healy, who at the time believed that he held office for life. He seized on the announcement by Jonathan Cape of a biography of him by the novelist and short-storywriter Liam O'Flaherty. Healy thought the biography, which was unlikely to be sympathetic, might perhaps afford a justification for the publication of his own memoirs while he was still in office. He wrote to Beaverbrook in April 1927 enclosing an advertisement for O'Flaherty's book: 'I am cheered to think the fools believe that anyone would give 12/6 for a book about me, by a man I had never heard of, but from enquiries I have made, it may entitle me to place myself in a posture of defence by a genuine narration'. He suggested that if O'Flaherty's book proved 'sufficiently malodorous', it could warrant a departure from any convention which might apply. 'As my narration excludes all reference to my four-and-a-half years in office, it can't be, I hope, condemned as a breach of official privacy'.[134]

An eccentric *Life of Tim Healy* was duly published under O'Flaherty's name, although it was in fact written by M. J. McManus, the friend and 'fellow-worker' of the declared author to whom it was dedicated. It was not well received. A reviewer in the *Observer* suggested that Healy's public response to the announced biography ('let him remember I can write his life') had cramped the author's style: 'The sooner Mr. O'Flaherty gets back to the literature of invention the better for all of us'.[135] Healy's *Letters and Leaders of My Day* appeared in November 1928.[136]

With the deaths of Maurice, and of William O'Brien, Beaverbrook was Healy's surviving political confidant. The themes of Healy's letters to Beaverbrook in the twilight of his life were as much religious (and mildly hypochondriacal) as political. Healy's readiness to proffer sanctimonious advice had for long been a comical aspect of their correspondence. He wrote to Beaverbrook in 1920: 'when in vexation you ejaculate "Christ", add thereto "be with us", or "have mercy on us", or "look upon us", so as to turn an imprecation into a blessing'.[137]

Jocular theological banter masked mild proselytising zeal. Healy had urged Beaverbrook to go to Rome 'where you will loaf in a mild winter, muse on the catacombs, and toy with predestination'.[138] When Beaverbrook did so, he was, as Healy reported to Maurice, greatly impressed by the Pope: 'They knelt for his blessing; and Max told me it was plain to him that the Pope must have some divine assistance or grace. This is astonishing for such a determined Presbyterian'.[139] Healy gently ribbed Beaverbrook ('stark Presbyterian that you are'), while characterising himself as 'the ruthless old Papist'.[140] He wrote to Beaverbrook that 'I must offend if I hold that your stiff-necked Presbyterianism is not a virtue but a vice', and urged him to prayer. He enjoyed Beaverbrook to 'abandon the mulish John Knox assishness'.[141] Somewhat in the manner of a latter-day Bouvard and Pécuchet, they sentimentally rejoiced in the complementarity of their respectively Catholic and Presbyterian upbringings.

Healy furiously reproved Beaverbrook for the serialisation in the *Daily Express* in 1928 of Emil Ludwig's *Son of Man*. The paper duly carried two articles by Healy taking issue with Ludwig, whom he described to Beaverbrook as 'the Jewish liar'. Of Beaverbrook's contributors on such topics, he wrote: 'If you care for an Irish circulation, pay a Catholic Censor to read atheistic articles like "After Death, What?"' He added limply that 'Catholics are not killjoys, witness the Archbishop of Cashel last Sunday throwing in the ball to start play between the Munster hurling teams'.[142] Healy objected to an essay on Christ by Beaverbrook as doctrinally unsound, and Beaverbrook put it aside until long after Healy's death. When it eventually appeared in 1962, unblushingly entitled *The Divine Propagandist*, Beaverbrook in his preface quoted Healy's remonstrance: 'Our old monks kept a separate pen to write the name of God and always did so on their knees'.[143]

Beaverbrook in late 1929 launched his 'Empire Crusade' for imperial protectionism which Baldwin was skilfully, but not without some difficulty, to thwart. Healy's extravagant enthusiasm for Beaverbrook's campaign, in its repudiation of free trade, marked the severance of his last links with the values of Gladstonian Liberalism. Beaverbrook initially attracted much public support in Britain, and Healy wrote in March 1930 that 'your triumph exceeds that of 1885-6, when Gladstone attorned to Parnell'. Later that year he wrote, 'you have revolutionised British politics with your single sword'.[144]

Healy was keeping a close watch on mortalities among his professional colleagues. He wrote to his brother's pious widow in October 1925 'so many legal deaths this year gives one pause. [Stephen] Ronan [KC] had a priest after sixty years, so had D.[enis] Henry [KC]'.[145] The shade of Parnell returned to haunt the survivors of the split in old age. John Muldoon found T. P. O'Connor, writing his *Memoirs of an Old Parliamentarian* (published in 1929), 'obsessed with the human side of Parnell's fall, saying the great misfortune was the attempt to throw him out of public life'.[146] The ranks of those who, in O'Connor's phrase, 'moved in the dazzling orbit of Parnell's extraordinary genius'[147] were thinning. John Dillon died in August 1927. On O'Brien's death in February 1928, Healy wrote to his daughter that 'the only residuum of 1880 now are T. P. O'Connor, Sexton and myself. Next please!'[148]

T. M. Healy died at the age of seventy-five on 26 March 1931. T. A. Finlay S.J., his close friend of many years, wrote to Healy's daughter: '. . . as I knelt by the body, and looked upon his face which seemed to bear the impress of the eternal peace on which he had entered, I thought of the storms of that life now ended in great calm'.[149] His funeral took place in the pro-Cathedral in Dublin. He was buried in Glasnevin where Parnell was laid forty years before.[150] Beaverbrook went up to London for a solemn requiem sung for Healy in Westminster Cathedral. The catafalque was covered with a gold-embroidered black velvet pall, over which was placed the flag of the Irish Free State. He thought the ceremony finer than any opera he had ever seen.[151]

The *Irish Times* observed of the passing of Healy and of Lord Glenavy, who had died four days before him, that 'here in Ireland, if we have lost something of the old genius, we have lost much of the old violence, the old prejudices, and the old suspicions'.[152] Healy was given one monument. The reconstructed mountain road once known as the Kerry Pass, which cut across the Glengariff peninsula to link the counties of Cork and Kerry was on his death named the Healy Pass.[153]

Notes and References

1: CHILDHOOD AND EXILE

1 T. D. Sullivan, *Bantry, Berehaven and the O'Sullivan Sept* (Dublin, 1908), appendix.
2 *Letters and Leaders*, pp. 15–18; Liam O'Flaherty, *The Life of Tim Healy* (London, 1927), p. 15; Maev Sullivan, 'Tim Healy', pp. 2, 184; Maev Sullivan, *No Man's Man*, p. 41.
3 Maev Sullivan, 'Tim Healy', pp. 2–3; *Letters and Leaders*, i. pp. 15, 18. It was absurdly alleged in the North Louth election of December 1910 that his father's appointment in Lismore was an exercise in jobbery procured by Healy. In his evidence in the election petition which followed, Healy referred to his father as having been postmaster in Bantry and thereafter in Lismore (*C.F.P.*, 11 Dec. 1911).
4 *F.J.*, 5 May 1886, NL.
5 *Letters and Leaders*, i. p. 17; Maev Sullivan, *No Man's Land*, p. 3. For a more considered treatment see John T. Collins 'The Healys of Donoughmore' in *The Journal of the Cork Historical and Archaeological Society*, vol. 48 (1943), pp. 124–32; see also *Cork Examiner*, 3 July 1937. (Both are in the Healy-Sullivan Papers, UCD P6/F/6.); T. D. Sullivan, *Bantry Berehaven and the O'Sullivan Sept*, pp. 42–3 and passim.
6 Maev Sullivan, 'Tim Healy'; Maev Sullivan, *No Man's Man*, p. 3.
7 T. M. Healy, *Why there is an Irish Land Question and an Irish Land League* (Dublin, 1881), p. 1. Conversely, as Healy re-iterated in 1887, 'the struggle in Ireland today is a continuance of the old warfare of the clansmen for a foothold on the soil of their fathers' (Healy, 'Jubilee Time in Ireland', *Contemporary Review*, vol. 57, p. 130, Jan. 1887).
8 T. M. Healy, *Stolen Waters* (London, 1913), pp. 484–5; *The Great Fraud of Ulster* (Dublin, 1917); T. M. Healy, '"The Sack of Baltimore"', *The Shamrock and Irish Emerald* (29 Mar. 1919), pp. 12–13; see also T. M. Healy, *The Planter's Progress* (Dublin, 1921); and Healy's attack on the Duke of Devonshire's rights to the Blackwater (*Hansard*, vol. 285, cols. 796–8, 6 Mar. 1884). Healy on one occasion made fleeting

reference to having been sent to Cork jail half a dozen times 'and so had his wife and sister, who were prosecuted for a "trespass" which consisted in going for a cup of spring water to a well on their own land' (*F.J.*, 12 Oct. 1885, Parnell's-cross, Wexford).

9 T. M. Healy, 'Jubilee Time in Ireland', in *Contemporary Review*, vol. 57, p. 126 (Jan. 1887).

10 *Letters and Leaders*, i. pp. 16-17; O'Flaherty, *Tim Healy*, p. 29; O'Connor, *Parnell Movement*, p. 375. The following year Bantry relented, and Healy and his brother paid for the erection of a limestone cross: Healy to Maurice, Healy Papers, 27 Aug. 1887, *Letters and Leaders*, i. p. 276; Healy to Maurice Healy snr., 3 June 1887, Healy-Sullivan Papers UCD P6/A/9; T. D. Sullivan, *Recollections*, p. 5.

11 *F.J.*, 24 June 1889, Wexford.

12 Foster, *Parnell*, pp. 3, 32; Lyons, *Parnell*, pp. 15-16, 20.

13 O'Connor, *Parnell*, p. 22.

14 *Nation*, 2 April 1887 (obituary to Daniel Sullivan); *Nation*, 12 May 1888; *S.C.P.*, vol. 8, cols. 216-17 (23 May 1889); Special Commission Brief, T. D. Sullivan Proofs; A. M. Sullivan, *Speeches and Addresses* (2nd ed., Dublin, 1882); T. D. Sullivan, *Recollections*, passim; *F.J.*, 14 May 1880, T. D. Sullivan as ed. d. 13 May; T. D. Sullivan, *A. M. Sullivan, A Memoir* (Dublin, 1885), passim.

15 Sullivan, *Recollections,* passim.; James Coleman, *Bibliography of the Brothers Sullivan, read to the Bibliographical Society of Ireland 23 Feb. 1926* (Wexford, 1926); *Irish Society*, 26 July 1890.

16 *U.I.*, 28 Nov. 1885; *F.J.*, 27 June 1919; *I.I.*, 27 June 1919; family notes by William Lombard Murphy, Murphy Papers. Supporting T. D. Sullivan at the 1885 election, Murphy said he was discharging a debt of gratitude 'for it was at the knees of members of that family he had learned his political creed' (*F.J.*, 23 Nov. 1885).

17 Callanan, *Parnell Split*, pp. 236-7.

18 *Letters and Leaders*, i. p. 169; T. M. Healy to Maurice Healy snr., n.d., fragment, Healy-Sullivan Papers, UCD, P6/A/48; Mrs. William O'Brien, *My Irish Friends* (Dublin and London 1937), p. 69. *Dod's Parliamentary Companion* 1890-1. Erina was a patriotic name which T. D. Sullivan devised for his daughter, which never quite caught on outside the family. Maev Sullivan once asked her mother what Healy was like in his youth. She smiled and after reflection replied that 'he was *farouche*' (Maev Sullivan, 'Tim Healy').

19 J. J. Horgan, *Parnell to Pearse* (Dublin, 1948), p. 25.

20 Birkenhead, *Contemporary Personalities* (London, 1924), p. 213; O'Connor, *Parnell Movement*, p. 376; *N.Y.T.*, 7 Aug. 1887. Years later Healy wrote a fairy story for Beaverbrook's third son, Peter, about a talking football called Leatherhead, the name of the town in Surrey close to Beaverbrook's country residence, Cherkley Court (Healy to Peter Aitken, 19 Mar. 1919, Beaverbrook Papers, c/161, House of Lords Record Office).

21 *Letters and Leaders*, i. pp. 18-19, 23.

22 *Letters and Leaders*, i. p. 23; Healy to Maurice Healy snr., 19 June 1876; Healy-Sullivan Papers, UCD P6/A/3.

23 *Letters and Leaders*, i. p. 23; O'Connor, *Parnell Movement*, p. 377; John Denvir, *The Irish in Britain* (2nd ed., London, 1894), pp. 264-5; *W.N.P.*, 19 Sept. 1891, 'John Barry', by Daniel Crilly; T. W. Moody, *Davitt*, pp. 68, 133-4.

24 John Denvir, *The Irish in Britain*, p. 275; O'Connor, *Parnell Movement*, p. 376; *Nation*, 1 Nov. 1873, 3 Feb. 1877; *United Irishman*, 13 Jan. 1877. Charting Healy's involvement, particularly in the columns of the *United Irishman*, is problematic because of the tendency to refer to a 'T. Healy' at a period when Healy's brother

Thomas was also involved in *émigré* politics in Newcastle. T. M. Healy was however very much more active than Thomas.

25 *Letters and Leaders*, i. pp. 32-6; Thornley, *Butt*, pp. 195-202, 230-4.

26 Fergus D'Arcy, 'The Irish in Nineteenth Century Britain: Reflections on their role and experience', *Irish History Workshop*, i. (1981), p. 10.

27 *United Irishman*, 25 Nov. 1875, 'T. Healy', Newcastle-upon-Tyne, to ed., d. 20 Nov.

28 *Nation*, 6 Feb. 1876, 'T.M.H.', Newcastle-upon-Tyne, to ed. d. 1 Feb.

29 *F.J.*, 1 July 1891; Callanan, *Parnell Split*, p. 233.

30 F. H. O'Donnell, *The Irish Party*, ii. pp. 240-1. I am indebted to the late Sean MacBride for imparting to me an elaborate conspiracy theory in which Healy features not merely as a Fenian, but as an accomplice to murder, the informer on the Invincibles, and thereafter a perennial government spy. MacBride's allegation is of interest as exemplifying the abiding mistrust of Healy within the republican movement, a mistrust which, had it not already existed, it would have been necessary to invent on his appointment as Governor-General of the Irish Free State. Maud Gonne MacBride also, at the time of the publication of the O'Flaherty biography of Healy, characterised him as 'a British spy'. (Author's memorandum of conversation with Sean MacBride at the Law Library, Dublin, 10 Nov. 1981.) MacBride's allegations are canvassed and discussed in T. P. Coogan, *Michael Collins* (London, 1990), pp. 389-91.

31 Fergus D'Arcy, 'The Irish in Nineteenth-Century Britain', p. 10. The most prominent nationalist in Newcastle-upon-Tyne, Bernard MacAnulty, from County Down, a successful merchant from County Down who had started life as a packman, supported both the Fenian and home rule movements; see John Denvir, *Life Story of an Old Rebel* (Dublin, 1910), pp. 56-7; W.N.P., 4 July 1891, profile of MacAnulty by Daniel Crilly.

32 *Letters and Leaders*, i p. 117; *Nation*, 17 Feb. 1877. The *Times* extracted this reference in preparing its case for the Special Commission (Special Commission, 'Extracts', NLI).

33 *Newcastle Weekly Chronicle*, 22 Dec. 1877; M. O'Hanlon to ed.; see also 1, 15 Dec. 1877.

34 Healy to Maurice Healy snr., 22 Feb. 1878, *Letters and Leaders* Proofs.

35 *Letters and Leaders*, i. p. 55; O'Connor, *Parnell Movement*, p. 375; *N.Y.T.*, 7 Aug. 1887; entry for T. M. Healy by Joseph Hone, *Dictionary of National Biography* 1931-40, p. 413; Maev Sullivan, 'Tim Healy', pp. 207-8, 223. Passing the head of the stone stairs in the Viceregal Lodge that led to the basement, from which sounds of servants' revelry were audible, Healy with a smile said to Chesterton, 'the isle is full of noises'. Healy's linguistic precocity afforded Maurice an opportunity for a wry joke, recorded by Maev Sullivan: 'Once when they were holidaying in Norway, T. M. H. stopped a Norwegian gentleman in the street and tried some recently acquired few words of Norse on him to ask his way. He found he was not understood, and he was making more eloquent and idiomatic attempts to explain himself when Maurice gently interposed "It is evident, Tim", he said, 'that this gentleman does not understand Norse"' (Maev Sullivan, 'Tim Healy').

36 *Letters and Leaders*, i. p. 76; ii, pp. 365, 402-4; Callanan, *Parnell Split*, p. 308.

37 *Letters and Leaders*, i. p. 55; *Newcastle Daily Chronicle*, 10 Mar. 1882.

38 Maev Sullivan, *No Man's Man*, pp. 11-12.

39 Healy to Maurice Healy, n.d. *Letters and Leaders* Proofs, Twenty-One; see also Healy to Maurice Healy, 5 Jan. 1877, *Letters and Leaders* Proofs, Twenty. Healy in his memoirs errs in the date of the meeting and in suggesting that Biggar attended: *Letters and Leaders*, i. p. 55, *Newcastle Daily Chronicle*, 10 Sept. 1877.

40 Healy to Maurice Healy, 28 May 1877, *Letters and Leaders* Proofs, Twenty; *Nation*, 28 Sept. 1877.

41 Healy to Maurice Healy, 23 Nov. 1877, *Letters and Leaders* Proofs, Seventeen.
42 *U.I.*, 29 Aug. 1885, T. M. Healy, 'A Last Look-Round'.
43 Healy to Maurice Healy snr., 20, 22 Feb. 1878, *Letters and Leaders* Proofs, Twenty-One; O'Connor, *Parnell Movement*, p. 377.
44 O'Connor, *Parnell Movement*, p. 376.
45 'The Pilgrims: Speeches at a Dinner to T. M. Healy K.C.' (London, 1928); *Times*, 18 May 1928.
46 *Nation*, 23 March 1878, meeting at Irish Literary Society, Newcastle, 13 March 1878.
47 *F.J.*, 17 Nov. 1893, Mercantile Branch NF. 21

2: JOURNALISM AND POLITICS

1 O'Connor, *Parnell*, p. 72.
2 Michael McDonagh, *Reporters Gallery*, (London, 1913), pp. 412-17.
3 Healy to Maurice Healy, 10 May 1878, *Letters and Leaders* Proofs, Twenty-Four.
4 Healy to Maurice Healy, 14 Apr. 1878, *Letters and Leaders*, i. p. 61. Healy later applied for a ticket to the reading room of the British Museum giving his profession as that of a law student. W. E. Lysaght Finegan signed the attached recommendation (application dated 21 June 1880, BM Add. MS. 48341 f. 248).
5 O'Connor, *Parnell Movement*, p. 378. Healy's early literary taste can be gleaned from his letter to the *Freeman's Journal* republished (along with those of Parnell, Lecky, Croke, John O'Leary, William O'Brien and Samuel Ferguson among others) in the highly instructive *The Best Hundred Irish Books* by 'Historicus'. Healy was glad to learn that William Dillon (John Dillon's brother, whose two-volume *Life of John Mitchel* was published in 1888) was assembling Mitchel's fugitive writings: 'No more pious task was ever undertaken by a Nationalist, and no patriot's memory ever better deserved than solicitude' (ibid., p. 42). Years later Healy, having taken charge of Max Aitken's literary education, included Mitchel's writings among half a dozen he sent him for a sea voyage. He explained: 'Tho' John Mitchel's are anti-English, it is nervous English and often high-styled' (Healy to Beaverbrook, 28 May 1913, Beaverbrook Papers c/161, House of Lords Records Office).
6 Richard Bagwell, 'Erin stops the way', *Dublin University Magazine*, xc (Sept. 1877), pp. 365-6. Bagwell wrote that there was reason to fear that Parnell's supremacy among the obstructives was now unassailable, while adding the vain hope 'even Meath may weary of her Aristides' (ibid., pp. 368, 376).
7 Healy to Maurice Healy, 31 Aug. 1877, *Letters and Leaders*, i. p. 55.
8 Healy to Maurice Healy, 10 May 1878, *Letters and Leaders* Proofs, Twenty-Five.
9 Healy to Maurice Healy, 1 Aug. 1878, *Letters and Leaders* Proofs, Twenty-Six.
10 *Nation*, 22 June, 6 July, 20 July 1878.
11 *Nation*, 17 Aug., 12 Oct. 1878.
12 *Nation*, 10 Aug. 1878.
13 Thornley, *Butt*, pp. 372-4.
14 *Nation*, 7 Dec. 1878.
15 *Nation*, 7, 14 Dec. 1878; *F.J.*, 7 Dec. 1878; O'Connor Power to *F.J.* d. 6 Dec.; Thornley, *Butt*, p. 374.
16 *Nation*, 14 Dec. 1878.
17 *Nation*, 22 Feb. 1879.
18 *Nation*, 10 May 1879. Butt's biographer quotes from and accepts the general thrust of Healy's assessment: Thornley, *Butt*, p. 378.
19 *U.I.*, 20 Aug. 1885.
20 With unblushing audacity, Healy later made the fierceness of Dillon's attack on

Butt a count in his indictment of Dillon: Healy, *Why Ireland is not Free*, pp. 2-4; *Letters and Leaders*, i. p. 66.

21 *Nation*, 4 May 1878. This did not appear in Healy's London Letter, but in a letter sent by him to the paper signed 'T' dated 29 Apr. 1878, for the authorship of which see Healy to Maurice Healy, 10 May 1878, *Letters and Leaders* Proofs, Twenty-Four. Healy was the author of other letters to the *Nation* which did not appear under his name. He wrote to Maurice in 1881 'I regret now, when fellows speak to me as if I only studied politics yesterday, that I did not sign the many letters I contributed to the *Nation* during the "obstruction controversy" – partly through shyness and partly that the *Nation* might get the benefit of the supposition that it had a number of correspondents' (Healy to Maurice Healy, Apr. 1881, *Letters and Leaders* Proofs, B8).

22 *Nation*, 27 Apr. 1878.

23 *Nation*, 16 Nov. 1878.

24 *Nation*, 26 Aug. 1876, annual convention of the Home Rule Confederation, 21 Aug., Dublin, attended by 'T. Healy'.

25 *Nation*, 28 Sept., 26 Oct. 1878.

26 *Nation*, 12 Apr., 16 Aug., 28 June 1879; *Letters and Leaders*, i. p. 39.

27 *Nation*, 17 Nov. 1877, 'T' to ed., d. 10 Nov.; Nation 2 Aug. 1879.

28 Healy to Maurice Healy snr., 17 July 1879, *Letters and Leaders* Proofs, Thirty.

29 *Nation*, 31 Aug. 1878; see also *Nation*, 7 June 1879.

30 *Nation*, 7 Sept., 26 Oct. 1878.

31 *Nation*, 8 Mar. 1879; see also *Nation*, 20 Mar. 1878.

32 *Nation*, 12 July 1879.

33 *Nation*, 24 Aug. 1878.

34 *Nation*, 7 June 1879; see also 19 Apr. 1879. Of the Afghan war the previous year he wrote: 'As providence sides with the best artillery I hope there is a good stock of Krupps at the wrong end of the Khyber' (*Nation*, 5 Oct. 1878).

35 *Nation*, 28 June 1879.

36 *Nation*, 29 Mar. 1879; see also 15 Mar. 1879.

37 *Nation*, 14 June 1879.

38 *Nation*, 5 July 1879.

39 *Nation*, 22 Mar. 1879.

40 *Nation*, 24 May 1879, 11 May 1878.

41 *Nation*, 22 June 1878.

42 *Nation*, 24 May 1879.

43 *Nation*, 21 June 1879.

44 *Nation*, 22 Feb. 1879.

45 *Nation*, 14 Sept. 1878.

46 *Letters and Leaders*, i. p. 64.

47 Healy to Maurice Healy, 18 July 1880, *Letters and Leaders* Proofs, Forty-Five.

48 O'Brien, *Recollections*, p. 247 n. Healy wrote in *United Ireland* in July 1884 that 'Crank Hugh's latest trick is to expropriate from the old James Stephens vocabulary a number of choice denunciations of "parliamentarianism"' (*U.I.*, 26 July 1884).

49 *Hansard*, vol. 284, cols. 1478-82 (20 Feb. 1884); *N.P.*, 8 July 1891.

50 Healy to Maurice Healy, 28 May 1877, *Letters and Leaders* Proofs, Twenty.

51 Healy to Maurice Healy, 10 May 1878, *Letters and Leaders* Proofs, Twenty-Four.

52 Healy to Maurice Healy, 5 July 1878, *Letters and Leaders* Proofs, Twenty-Six.

53 Healy to Maurice Healy, 1 Feb. 1879, *Letters and Leaders* Proofs, Twenty-Seven.

54 Healy to Maurice Healy, 5 Apr. 1879, *Letters and Leaders* Proofs, Twenty-Eight.

55 Healy to Maurice Healy, 24 Nov. 1879, *Letters and Leaders* Proofs, Thirty-Five.

56 *Nation*, 5 June 1880; see also *Nation*, 5 Oct. 1878.
57 *Nation*, 19 July 1879, Parnell to Michael Considine, secretary of the Ennis Congregated Trades, d. 12 July.
58 Healy to Maurice Healy snr., 17 July 1879, *Letters and Leaders*, i. pp. 68-9; T. D. Sullivan to Healy, 17 July 1879, *Letters and Leaders* Proofs, Twenty-Nine.
59 Healy to Maurice Healy snr., 17 July 1879, *Letters and Leaders* Proofs, Twenty-Nine, published with slight editing, *Letters and Leaders*, i. pp. 68-9; T. M. Healy, application to British Museum for reader's ticket, 21 June 1880, BM Add. MS. 48341 f. 248.
60 Healy to Maurice Healy, Aug. 1879, *Letters and Leaders* Proofs, Thirty-One.
61 *U.I.*, 5 Aug. 1885, 'A Last Look-Round'; Healy to Maurice Healy, 7 Aug. 1879, *Letters and Leaders* Proofs, Thirty-One; Callanan, *Parnell Split*, p. 235; *U.I.*, 8 Dec. 1883.
62 *Nation*, 2 Aug. 1879.
63 *F.J.*, 1 Aug. 1879.
64 Maurice Healy, 7 Aug. 1879, *Letters and Leaders* Proofs, Thirty-Two; see also W. O'Brien, *Recollections*, pp. 222-3; R. B. O'Brien, *Parnell*, p. 192.
65 T. D. Sullivan to Healy, 3 Aug. 1879, *Letters and Leaders*, i. p. 71; Donal Sullivan to Healy, 20 July 1879, *Letters and Leaders* Proofs, Twenty-Nine.
66 Healy to Maurice Healy, 7 Aug. 1879, *Letters and Leaders* Proofs, Thirty-Two; see generally Lyons, *Parnell*, pp. 93-5.
67 *Nation*, 9 Aug. 1879.
68 Healy, *Letters and Leaders*, i. p. 72.
69 Justin McCarthy, 'Charles Stewart Parnell', *Contemporary Review*, vol. LX (Nov. 1891), p. 631.
70 O'Connor, *Parnell*, pp. 110-11.
71 *Nation*, 21 Sept., 26 Oct. 1878.
72 Healy to Maurice Healy, 1 Aug., Oct. 1878, *Letters and Leaders*, i. pp. 64-5.
73 Healy to Maurice Healy, 11 Apr., 22 Oct. 1879, *Letters and Leaders*, ii. pp. 68, 76.
74 *Nation*, 30 Nov. 1878.
75 Healy to Maurice Healy, 1 Feb. 1879, *Letters and Leaders* Proofs, Twenty-Seven.
76 Healy to Maurice Healy, 11 Sept. 1879, *Letters and Leaders* Proofs, Thirty-Four.
77 Healy to Maurice Healy, 9 Nov. 1879, *Letters and Leaders*, i. pp. 76-7.
78 Healy to Maurice Healy, 24 Nov. 1879, *Letters and Leaders* Proofs, Thirty-Five; quoted in part *Letters and Leaders*, ii. pp. 77-8.
79 Healy to Maurice Healy, 4 Dec. 1879, *Letters and Leaders*, i. p. 78. For a fine assessment of Healy's early criticisms of Parnell, in which he is compared with one of Balzac's *jeunes ambitieux*, see C. C. O'Brien, 'Timothy Healy', pp. 167-8.
80 *U.I.*, 29 Aug. 1885, 'A Last Look-Round'.
81 Justin McCarthy, 'Charles Stewart Parnell', *Contemporary Review*, vol. LX (Nov. 1891), pp. 626-7.
82 Healy was not alone in levelling the charge of political plagiarism against Parnell. F. H. O'Donnell later claimed that 'in the years 1877, '78 and '79, I had taught him all that he was ever able to understand of the Active Policy'. Dismissing 'the Parnell legend', he cheerfully asserted that 'Parnell never knew anything and never did anything' (O'Donnell, *The Lost Hat*, pp. 7, 18).
83 *Letters and Leaders*, i. pp. 73-8; *F.J.*, 20 Mar. 1880; for an angry indictment of her brother's failure to bring out with him a secretary, see Fanny Parnell to T. D. Sullivan, 5 May (1880), Sullivan Papers, NLI MS. 8327(4). Patrick Egan in an interview in 1916 claimed that Parnell had not asked for Healy, but had simply asked Egan to 'send a secretary by the next steamer' (*Boston American*, 23 July 1916).
84 Healy to Maurice Healy, 20 Mar. 1880 (written over successive days), *Letters and*

Leaders, i. p. 85; *Nation*, 27 Mar. 1880, Boston Pilot report. One such 'interview' in the *New York Herald* of 27 Mar. 1880 was entirely Healy's work.

85 Alexander Sullivan, *North American Review*, June 1887, pp. 612-13; there is a copy in the Davitt Papers, TCD MS. 9380.

86 Healy, *Letters and Leaders*, i. p. 81; *Letters and Leaders* Proofs, Forty.

87 *Cork Daily Herald*, 15 Apr. 1880; *Nation*, 1 May 1880, Parnell to *F.J.* d. 22 Apr.

88 Healy to Maurice Healy, 20 Mar. 1880, *Letters and Leaders* Proofs, Forty. This is deleted from the text of the letter published in *Letters and Leaders*, i. p. 86. While what was involved were expenses, Healy was anxious to avoid the suggestion that he was in any way beholden to Parnell: *Letters and Leaders*, i. p. 112.

89 *Letters and Leaders*, i. pp. 81-2; Devoy, *Post Bag*, i. pp. 382-3; *Nation*, 20 Mar. 1880, Parnell to Patrick Egan d. 1 Mar. 1880. The letter to Egan however failed to provide for the designation of monies for specifically electoral purposes, and vested the control of the monies collected for political purposes in the Land League.

90 Healy to Maurice Healy, 20 Mar. 1880, *Letters and Leaders* Proofs, Forty.

91 Healy to Maurice Healy, 20 Mar. 1880, *Letters and Leaders* Proofs, Forty; R. B. O'Brien, *Parnell*, i. p. 205; *Letters and Leaders*, i. p. 83.

92 Healy to Maurice Healy, 20 Mar. 1880, *Letters and Leaders* Proofs, Forty-One; R. B. O'Brien, *Parnell*, pp. 205-6.

93 Healy, *Letters and Leaders*, i. p. 83. William Carroll in a letter to John Devoy of 29 Apr. 1880 referred sarcastically to 'the distinguished Mr. Healy who had hailed the Second O'Connell as "The Uncrowned King of Ireland"' (Devoy, *Post Bag*, i. p. 520). When Parnell failed to attend the dinners Katharine O'Shea gave to further her husband's career, and she was told that he notoriously ignored even the most important political hostesses in London, 'I then became determined that I would get Parnell to come', and said, amid laughter and applause: 'The uncrowned King of Ireland shall sit in that chair at the next dinner I give' (O'Shea, *Parnell*, i. p. 135).

94 Healy to Maurice Healy, 20 Mar. 1880, *Letters and Leaders* Proofs, Forty-One.

95 *U.I.*, 29 Aug. 1885, Healy, 'A Last Look-Round'.

96 Healy to Maurice Healy, 20 Mar. 1880, *Letters and Leaders* Proofs, Forty-One.

97 R. B. O'Brien, *Parnell*, i. p. 206; *Letters and Leaders*, i. p. 85.

98 *Letters and Leaders*, i. p. 89; *F.J.*, 22 Mar. 1880; *Cork Examiner*, 22 Mar. 1880. Healy's reservations did not prevent him publicly sustaining the mythic image, if somewhat perfunctorily, as circumstances required. Thus in 1883 he told his former constituents with extravagant implausibility that he had seen Parnell 'with tears in his eyes going from city to city in America pleading for the people who were dying of hunger' (*F.J.*, 10 Oct. 1883, Wexford).

99 Healy to Maurice Healy, 20 Mar. 1880, *Letters and Leaders* Proofs, Forty.

100 *Daily Telegraph*, 10 Mar. 1924, 'Parnell's Secretary'; O'Connor, *Memoirs*, i. p. 103; *Letters and Leaders*, i. p. 112.

101 Byrne, *Parnell*, p. 23; Davitt, *Fall of Feudalism*, pp. 207-9.

102 C. C. O'Brien, 'Timothy Michael Healy', pp. 168-9; *Letters and Leaders*, i. p. 85.

103 P.M.G., 8 Dec. 1890. Healy's characterisation of Fanny Parnell in his memoirs was less emotional: *Letters and Leaders* i., p. 81.

104 *Nation*, 25 Dec. 1880, Fanny Parnell, 'John Dillon', first published in the *Boston Pilot*.

105 *U.I.*, 29 Aug. 1885, 'A Last Look-Round'; Healy to Maurice Healy, 27 Mar. 1880, *Letters and Leaders* Proofs, Forty-Two.

106 *F.J.*, 20 Apr. 1880, Quinn to *F.J.*; 21 Apr., Healy to *F.J.* d. 20 Apr.; *Nation*, 24 Apr. 1880.

107 *Nation*, 24 Apr. 1880, Healy to *Cork Examiner*, d. 14 Apr.

108 *Cork Daily Herald*, 12 Apr. 1880; *F.J.*, 9 Apr. 1880.

109 *Cork Daily Herald*, 15 Apr. 1880.
110 Healy to Maurice Healy, 18 July 1880; *Letters and Leaders* Proofs, Forty-Five; *Letters and Leaders*, i. p. 90; *U.I.*, 29 Aug. 1885, 'A Last Look-Round; R. B. O'Brien, *Parnell*, i. pp. 214–19.
111 *Spectator*, 17 July 1880.
112 R. B. O'Brien, *Parnell*, i. p. 296.
113 *The World*, 29 Dec. 1880.

3: PARLIAMENT

1 *F.J.*, 5 May 1880, *Nation*, 8 May 1880. The meeting was enlivened by the speech of the Rev. H. Behan lamenting the loss to Meath of 'their darling Parnell': 'He was now going to sit for the rotten borough of Cork. All the salt in the sea would not purify the dirty, rotten, Whig carcass of Cork city' (*F.J.*, 5 May 1880). The *Nation* subsequently asserted that Parnell had not suggested the proviso, and taken exception to the use of the word 'follower' in the original draft of the resolution (*Nation*, 15 May 1880).
2 *Nation*, 1 Aug. 1896, Terence O'Brien to ed.; H.R.N. (pseud. John J. Dunne) *Here and There Memories* (London, 1896), p. 260; A. M. Sullivan, *Speeches and Addresses* (Dublin, 1882), pp. 32–3. In his speech in defence of Parnell and others in the conspiracy trial of 1880–1, Sullivan hyperbolically referred to Parnell as 'the grandson of an illustrious Irish Protestant Patriot, a youth bearing honours from the halls of an English university', a not altogether accurate description of the circumstances of Parnell's departure from Cambridge (ibid., p. 213; see Foster, *Parnell*, pp. 107–10).
3 *Nation*, 7 Apr., 15 June, 28 July 1877.
4 Healy to Maurice Healy, 8 May 1877, *Letters and Leaders*, i. pp. 52–3. The article in question is likely to be that which appeared in *The World* for 11 Apr. 1877, part-quoted in Kee, *The Laurel and the Ivy*, p. 136.
5 Healy to Maurice Healy, 17 Mar. 1878, *Letters and Leaders* Proofs, Twenty-Two.
6 *Nation*, pp. 8, 15, 22 May 1880; *F.J.*, 5, 18 May 1880; T. D. Sullivan, *A. M. Sullivan, A Memoir* (Dublin, 1885), pp. 135–7 where Sullivan erroneously asserts that Healy withdrew his candidature. Healy's challenge to Sullivan had curious parallels with the circumstances of Parnell's original election for the seat in 1875. Sir Charles Gavan Duffy had been offered the nomination by a conference of the clergy of Navan. He received a telegram from William Dillon asking if he would accept Isaac Butt's theory of home rule. When Duffy replied that he would stand as a repealer if he stood at all, the Home Rule Association resolved that it would not be desirable to run a non-home rule candidate, 'and a deputation was sent to Meath to canvass for Parnell', as Gavan Duffy complained bitterly to T. D. Sullivan almost ten years later (Gavan Duffy to T. D. Sullivan, 28 Nov., 8 Dec. 1884 (NLI MS 82317[2]).
7 O'Connor, *Parnell*, pp. 79–80; *F.J.*, 18 May 1880.
8 *Nation*, 29 May 1880; Healy to Maurice Healy, 18 July 1880; *Letters and Leaders* Proofs, Forty-Five.
9 Healy to Maurice Healy, 18 July 1880, *Letters and Leaders* Proofs, Thirty-Five; *Letters and Leaders*, i. pp. 95, 100, 112.
10 *Nation*, 29 May 1880.
11 *Nation*, 5 June 1880; see also *Nation*, 14 Aug. 1880, for Healy's defence of Parnell against the criticism of not bringing forward a home rule resolution.
12 *Nation*, 26 June, 5 June 1880.
13 *Nation*, 26 Aug., 14 Aug. 1880; Healy to Maurice Healy snr., 5 Aug. 1880, *Letters and Leaders*, i. p. 99.

14 *Nation*, 5, 26 June 1880.
15 *Nation*, 24 July 1880.
16 *Nation*, 12 June 1880.
17 *Letters and Leaders*, i. pp. 95, 98.
18 *Nation*, 29 May, 26 June 1880.
19 *Nation*, 17 July, 28 Aug. 1880.
20 *U.I.*, 27 Aug. 1881, 'Among the Saxons'.
21 *Nation*, 26 June 1880.
22 *Nation*, 12 June 1880; see *Nation*, 31 Aug. 1878, for an early reference to Chamberlain.
23 See generally Lyons, *Parnell*, pp. 132-5.
24 *Letters and Leaders*, i. pp. 99-101.
25 *Cork Examiner*, 3, 28, 25 Oct. 1880.
26 *Letters and Leaders*, i. pp. 191-3; O'Connor, *Parnell Movement*, pp. 381-2; *F.J.*, 16 Dec. 1880.
27 *F.J.*, 12 Oct. 1885.
28 *Hansard*, vol. 181, col. 668 (20 Aug. 1907).
29 *Letters and Leaders*, i. pp. 102-3; W. S. Blunt, *The Land War in Ireland* (London, 1912), entry for 21 May 1886; *Nation*, 30 Oct., 13 Nov. 1880; *F.J.*, 25 Nov., 16 Dec. 1880. Parnell did not attend Healy's trial, in spite of a note from Healy urging him to do so (Parnell to Katharine O'Shea, 13 Dec. 1880, O'Shea, *Parnell*, i. pp. 164-5).
30 W. O'Brien, *Recollections*, p. 249. The remarks quoted do not appear in *Hansard*, which still at this time practised a form of bowdlerisation of remarks considered unparliamentary (*Hansard*, vol. 257, cols. 540-47, 11 Jan. 1881).
31 Quoted *Nation*, 15 Jan. 1881; O'Connor, *Parnell Movement*, p. 378.
32 Quoted *Nation*, 29 Jan. 1881.
33 O'Connor, *Parnell Movement*, pp. 388-417; T. P. O'Connor, *Gladstone's House of Commons*, pp. 109-23; McDonagh, *Home Rule Movement*, pp. 145-59. Healy's widely disseminated pamphlet *A Word for Ireland* was based on a short history of the Irish question which he wrote to provide part of the brief of the lawyers appearing for the traversers, which went through a number of editions in Ireland and the United States, and was translated into French as *Le cri d'Irlande*: see T. M. Healy, *A Word for Ireland* (Dublin, 1886); T. M. Healy, review of John E. Pomfret, 'The Struggle for Land in Ireland', *Studies*, vol. 19 (Dec. 1930), p. 694.
34 O'Connor, *Parnell Movement*, pp. 413-17; C. C. O'Brien, *Parnell and his Party*, pp. 56-65; Lyons, *Parnell*, pp. 147-9.
35 *F.J.*, 15 Feb. 1881, PA telegram of 14 Feb., *F.J.*, 19 Feb. 1881; Kettle, *Material for Victory*, p. 43; O'Shea, *Parnell*, i. pp. 135-58; Kee, *The Laurel and the Ivy*, pp. 335-9.
36 *Letters and Leaders*, i. pp. 107-8; Kee, *The Laurel and the Ivy*, pp. 335-6.
37 Kettle, *Material for Victory*, p. 432; *Letters and Leaders*, i. p. 107.
38 *Letters and Leaders*, i. pp. 107-9.
39 T. M. Healy, *A Record of Coercion* (Dublin, Oct. 1881), iv. *The Freeman's Journal* reported that an 'ingenious test' had confirmed reliable information that, on the orders of the government, letters from Land Leaguers were being read during their transit through the post office (*F.J.*, 15 Feb. 1881).
40 *Letters and Leaders*, i. pp. 107-9. Healy's account of Parnell's arrival does not square with that of Andrew Kettle, which implies that he arrived in the same carriage as Parnell (Kettle, *Material for Victory*, pp. 43-5).
41 C. C. O'Brien, *Parnell and his Party*, pp. 65-5; *F.J.*, 9 Feb. 1881; Andrew Kettle, *Material for Victory*, pp. 44-5.
42 *F.J.*, 17 Feb. 1881, Parnell to the Central Branch of the Land League, d. 13 Feb. 1881; quoted in part and considered, Davitt, *Fall of Feudalism*, pp. 306-8.

43 This idiom recurs in Healy's speech at Gateshead shortly after his return (*F.J.*, 21 Feb. 1881). Curiously Kettle later wrote that when Parnell read a statement of his position to the executive in Paris, Dillon attributed its authorship to Katharine O'Shea (Kettle, *Materials for Victory*, p. 45).
44 *Letters and Leaders*, i. pp. 109–12.
45 *D.T.*, 10 Mar. 1924, 'Parnell's Secretary'; see also O'Connor, *Memoirs*, i. pp. 104–5. In the proofs of his memoirs Healy repudiated O'Connor's account in the same article of the termination of his own secretaryship to Parnell (*Letters and Leaders* Proofs, B3–4).
46 *F.J.*, 15 Feb. 1881.
47 *F.J.*, 17 Feb. 1881, *L'Intransigeant*, 16, 19, Feb. 1881.
48 *F.J.*, 17 Feb. 1881.
49 *L'Intransigeant*, 16 Feb. 1881; *F.J.*, 17 Feb. 1881.
50 *L'Intransigeant*, 18 Feb. 1881.
51 *L'Intransigeant*, 18 Feb. 1881; L. Nemours Godré, *Parnell, Sa Vie et Sa Fin* (Paris, 1892), pp. 64–5. In relation to *L'Intransigeant*, see J. P. T. Bury, *Gambetta's Final Years* (London and New York, 1982), p. 222.
52 *L'Instransigeant*, 27 Feb. Parnell to Hugo, Paris, d. 24 Feb.; *F.J.*, 26 Feb. The French was not Parnell's but presumably that of O'Kelly, who had acted as his interpreter in Paris: *Le Gaulois* noted in its correspondent's interview with Parnell that 'on all embarrassing questions he referred to Mr. Parnell which gives an idea of the discipline of parties in the English parliament' (*F.J.*, 18 Feb. 1881).
53 *Parnell, Sa Vie et Sa Fin*, pp. 61–2. Nemours Godré who later met Parnell wrote of him: 'Ce que la gravure ne pouvait rendre, c'était cet air de force et de resolution qui se dégageait du personnage, quand sa voix nette et grave l'animait un peu, quand son oeil qui, en repos, semblait toujours rever d'une lointaine vision, dardait tout à coup sur vous un rapide et fauve éclair. Celui-là était veritablement un chef, un meneur d'hommes. C'était Samson avant Dalila'. While he felt the force of Parnell's 'charme étrange' he expressed his preference for O'Connell, of whom he had also written a life (ibid., pp. 63–4).
54 *L'Intransigeant*, 2, 3 Mar. 1881.
55 *F.J.*, 17 Feb. 1881, quoting *Daily News*; *F.J.*, 21 Feb. 1991, interview with *F.J.* correspondent. Stephens restated his political philosophy in an interview in Paris two years later. He held to the opinion 'that nothing would save Ireland but utter separation, and that could be won neither by poetry nor rhetoric, nor yet by the craft of the lobbies keeping a close eye [*sic*] on the division bells, or heroic wakefulness on the well-stuffed cushions of St. Stephen's' (*F.J.*, 13 Mar. 1883, interview with the Paris correspondent of the *Standard*). Parnell was not to meet Stephens until over ten years later, a week before his own death, when the old Fenian had returned from exile (Callanan, *Parnell Split*, p. 252).
56 Lomasney to John Devoy, 18 Feb. 1881, Devoy, *Post Bag*, ii. pp. 39–40; Lyons, *Parnell*, p. 154.
57 *Letters and Leaders*, ii. p. 112 (in his memoirs T. P. O'Connor recalls Healy's phrase but misremembers the context [O'Connor, *Memoirs*, i. pp. 174–5]); *F.J.*, 25 Feb. 1881, Parnell's interview with *Triboulet*; *F.J.*, 28 Feb. 1881; Kee, *The Laurel and the Ivy*, p. 349.
58 C. C. O'Brien, *Parnell and his Party*, p. 64.
59 C. C. O'Brien, *Parnell and his Party*, p. 64; *Nation*, 26 Feb. 1881; *F.J.*, 21, 25 Feb. 1881, A. M. Sullivan to Bellingham d. 17 Feb.; Bellingham to *F.J.* d. 18 Feb.; *Times* 16 Feb. 1881, Bellingham to *Times*.
60 *Letters and Leaders*, i. pp. 90–1; *F.J.*, 1 July 1880; *Nation*, 3 July 1880.

61 *Letters and Leaders*, i. pp. 98–9. An entry in W. S. Blunt's diary for 8 Mar. 1912 records a conversation with John Dillon: 'Parnell, he said, as a young man had been no paragon of virtue, but his loves had not before been with married women, nor had they been serious' (W. S. Blunt, *My Diaries*, [London, 1919], 1932, ed. p. 795).

62 *Letters and Leaders* Proofs, Forty-Four; *Letters and Leaders*, i. p. 93.

63 *Nation*, 24 Apr., 1 May 1880.

64 *Letters and Leaders*, i. p. 110.

65 Labouchere to Herbert Gladstone, 17 Dec. 1890, Viscount Gladstone Papers, BM Add. MS 46016 f. 146.

66 O'Connor, *Parnell*, p. 133.

67 *I.W.I.*, 5 Oct. 1895, J. J. O'Kelly, 'A Dark Chapter: The Story of the Great Betrayal'.

68 Lyons, *Parnell*, pp. 149–50; *Letters and Leaders*, i. p. 108; K. O'Shea, *Parnell*, i. pp. 145–6, 152–4, 156, 163, 169–71.

69 Lyons, *Parnell*, pp. 149–50. James Dillon was in error in recalling that Healy's account of what transpired in Paris first appeared in Beaverbrook's memoirs (ibid.). What so provoked his father was Birkenhead's character-sketch of Healy which appeared in the *Sunday Times* in August 1924 and was republished in his *Contemporary Personalities* of the same year. Birkenhead faithfully conveyed Healy's account of the Paris meeting: 'Parnell's intrigue with Mrs. O'Shea had commenced, but was then unknown to his colleagues. Healy however was in possession of a still more anxious, sinister, and analogous, secret connected with his chief; and brought to Paris a number of letters to Parnell, unopened, which made that secret plain'. The letter which Healy delivered up was 'charged with vital consequence; and betrayed a secret at once destructive and discreditable . . . Later on Parnell unjustly blamed Dillon for tampering with his private letters' (*Contemporary Personalities*, pp. 209–10). John Dillon's fury at Healy's disclosure of the matter is itself very much more consistent with the letter having been written by a woman other than Katharine O'Shea (memorandum of the author's conversation with James Dillon, 26 Sept. 1978, corrected in Dillon's hand).

70 Healy, *Why there is an Irish Land Question*, p. 5.

71 *Hansard*, vol. 261, col. 1469 (27 May 1881); vol. 262, cols. 805–6 (17 June 1881); vol. 263, col. 1160 (18 July 1881); vol. 209, cols. 229–304 (5 May 1882).

72 *Letters and Leaders*, i. p. 120; Healy to Maurice Healy, Apr. 1881, July 1881, *Letters and Leaders* Proofs, B8, 14.

73 Healy to Maurice Healy, 25 May 1881, *Letters and Leaders* Proofs, B11.

74 Healy to Maurice Healy, 12 July 1881, *Letters and Leaders*, i. p. 127.

75 *D.E.*, 29 July 1881.

76 *F.J.*, 8 Dec. 1883, 'The Making of the Irish Parliamentary Party – V' (T. P. O'Connor himself is the friend in question); O'Connor, *Memoirs*, i. p. 179. Healy himself referred to the clause as 'slipped in quietly and nicely' (*F.J.*, 6 Sept. 1881, Newtownstewart). For the parliamentary proceedings, see *Hansard*, vol. 263, cols. 1980–2 (27 July 1881).

77 *Adams v Dunseath* (1882) 10 LR Ir 109. For Healy's critique of the judgement, see T. M. Healy, *The Land Law (Ireland) Act 1881, . . . being a Practical Exposition of the Act . . .* (Dublin, 1882), pp. xv–xix. For the later jurisprudence, see Richard R. Cherry, *The Irish Land Law and Land Purchase Acts 1881, 1885, and 1887* (Dublin, 1888), pp. 45–8.

78 Healy to Maurice Healy, June 1881, *Letters and Leaders* Proofs, B13; *Letters and Leaders*, i. p. 125; *F.J.*, 6 Sept. 1881, Newtownmountstewart; see also *Ulster Guardian*, 11 Aug. 1906, T. W. Russell, 'Mr. Timothy Healy'.

79 O'Brien, *Recollections*, pp. 309-11; *F.J.*, 4 Dec. 1904; Healy to *F.J.*, 3 Dec. 1904.
80 Irish Party Minutes, 5, 19 May 1881; *F.J.*, 6, 20 May 1881.
81 Healy to Maurice Healy, 22 May 1881, *Letters and Leaders* Proofs, B11.
82 *Letters and Leaders*, i. pp. 123-5; Healy to Maurice Healy, July 1881, *Letters and Leaders* Proofs, B14; Healy, *Why Ireland is not Free*, p. 8.
83 *Hansard*, vol. 262, col. 814 (17 June 1881).
84 Healy to Labouchere, n.d., quoted in Labouchere to Chamberlain, 12 Nov. 1885, in Thorold, *Labouchere*, p. 241.
85 Healy to Maurice Healy, 22 May 1881, *Letters and Leaders* Proofs, B11.
86 W. O'Brien, *Recollections*, pp. 336-44; *Letters and Leaders*, i. p. 134; *Irish World*, 26 Nov. 1881, speech of Healy on 17 Nov.
87 *Evening Standard*, 14 Oct. 1881.
88 T. M. Healy, *Tenant's Key to the Land Law Act 1881* (Dublin, 1881). This went through several editions, and was succeeded by his *Land Law (Ireland) Act 1881 with the statutes incorporated therewith* (Dublin, 1882); see also *U.I.*, 17 Sept. 1881, T. M. Healy, 'The Land Act Analysed'; *U.I.*, 24 Sept. 1881, 'Among the Saxons'.
89 Healy to Maurice Healy, 22 Dec. 1881, *Letters and Leaders*, i. p. 144
90 Florence Arnold Forster, *Irish Journal*, ed. Moody and Hawkins (Oxford, 1988), p. 248; see on the other hand Richard Pigott's deliberately obtuse assessment of Healy's position in 'The Irish Question', *Macmillan's Magazine* (Dec. 1881), at p. 168.
91 Healy to Maurice Healy, 20 Mar. 1880, *Letters and Leaders* Proofs, Forty-One.
92 Sir James O'Connor, *History of Ireland*, 1798-1924 (London, 1925), i. p. 283.
93 W. O'Brien, *Recollections*, p. 303; *Letters and Leaders*, i. p. 159.
94 John Denvir, *Life Story of an Old Rebel* (Dublin, 1919), p. 246; see James O'Connor, *Recollections of Richard Pigott* (Dublin, 1889), pp. 13-15.
95 Pigott to Egan, 16 May 1881, *S.C.P.*, vol. 5, paras. 52, 971-53, 072 (22 Feb. 1889); *U.I.* 17 Dec. 1881; Egan to *F.J.*, d. 7 Dec.
96 *U.I.*, 17 Dec. 1881, Egan to *F.J.*, d. 7 Dec.; Special Commission Brief, O'Brien Proofs, p. 8.
97 W. O'Brien, *Recollections*, p. 301; Special Commission Brief, O'Brien Proofs, pp. 9-10; *S.C.P.* vol. 7, paras. 60, 467-60, 492 (Parnell, 3 May 1889), vol. 8, paras. 70, 7826-70, 798 (O'Brien, 21 May 1889).
98 T. D. Sullivan memorandum, NLI 8237 (14); T. D. Sullivan to Egan (copy), 14 July 1881, Sullivan to Kenny 16 July 1881, Sullivan Papers NLI 8237(5); *Nation* 8 Aug. 1896, 'Occasional Notes' by T. D. Sullivan; *S.C.P.*, vol. 7, para. 60, 497.
99 Healy to Maurice Healy, 21 July 1881, *Letters and Leaders* Proofs, B14.
100 Pigott to Forster, 11 Aug. 1881, *S.C.P.*, vol. 5, pp. 559-60 (22 Feb. 1889).
101 *S.C.P.*, vol. 7, paras. 60, 643, 60, 474 (3 May 1889).
102 Healy's parliamentary letter in *United Ireland* was initially entitled 'Among the Saxons', by 'A Good Looker On', and thereafter appeared simply as from an unnamed parliamentary correspondent. O'Brien, *Recollections*, pp. 357, 435-6, 474. Writing to Maurice on 24 Nov. 1882 Healy referred to 'my London letter' (*Letters and Leaders* Proofs, B40).
103 Hammond, *Gladstone*, pp. 248-50; Lyons, *Parnell*, pp. 166-8; *F.J.*, 10 Oct. 1881; *Letters and Leaders*, i. pp. 135-6.
104 Tighe Hopkins, *Kilmainham Memories* (London, 1896), p. 24.
105 Lyons, *Parnell*, pp. 164-9; Callanan, *Parnell Split*, p. 222.
106 *U.I.*, 15 Oct. 1881.
107 *Letters and Leaders*, i. pp. 137-9.
108 Harcourt to his wife, 13 Oct. 1881, in A. G. Gardiner, *Life of Sir William Harcourt* (London, 1923).

109 *Evening Standard*, 18 Oct. 1881.
110 Healy to Maurice Healy, 14 Oct. 1881, *Letters and Leaders* Proofs, B20.
111 *Letters and Leaders*, i. pp. 139-52; *Irish World*, 19, 26 Nov. 1881, *U.I.*, 18 Feb. 1882; Healy to Maurice Healy snr., 8 Jan. 1882, *Letters and Leaders*, i. p. 148; *Newcastle Daily Chronicle*, 10 Mar. 1882.
112 *U.I.*, 24 Dec. 1881 (Boston), 17 Dec. 1881 (Providence); see also the interview with Healy in Boston, *New York Herald*, 12 Feb. 1882.
113 *Hansard*, vol. 271, col. 279 (23 June 1882); *Letters and Leaders*, i. p. 141; *S.C.P.*, vol. 9, paras. 80, 576-713. For Healy's response see *Hansard*, vol. 271, cols. 295-9 (23 June 1882); vol. 39, cols. 387-8 (24 July 1888).
114 *Newcastle Daily Chronicle*, 9-16 Mar. 1882, 'The Irish and the Land League in America'.
115 *Hansard*, vol. 271, col. 299 (23 June 1882).
116 Healy to Maurice Healy, 25 Feb. 1882, *Letters and Leaders* Proofs, B29.
117 *Republic*, 24 June, 23 Dec. 1882. In his *Republic* letter, Healy made plain his ideological affiliations. In the debate on the second reading of the home rule bill in 1886 he openly proclaimed his opposition to Patrick Ford and the *Irish World*, cited by the enemies of the Irish party 'because for years the *Irish World* has never ceased to attack us — has been our enemy'. His remarks were condemned by Davitt (*Hansard*, vol. 306, pp. 109-11 [24 May 1886]. Davitt's attack on Healy in the *Freeman's Journal* is set forth in a unionist leaflet: ILPU Leaflet No. 9, quoting Davitt to *F.J.*, d. 27 May 1886). The quotations which follow from Healy's letters to the Boston *Republic* are taken from George A. Colburn's doctoral thesis. 'T. M. Healy and the Home Rule Movement', Michigan State University, 1971.
118 *Republic*, 25 Nov. 1882.
119 Healy to Maurice Healy, 25 Feb. 1882, *Letters and Leaders* Proofs, B28-9.
120 *S.C.P.*, vol. 7, 58, 736-42 (30 Apr. 1889); Maurice Healy in his evidence stated there were only two interviews, a long interview preparatory to the draft, after which he called again to settle the draft with Parnell (*S.C.P.*, vol. 8, 74,971-85, 28 May 1889).
121 Callanan, *Parnell Split*, p. 230; Alfred Robbins to the *Times*, d. 10 Nov. 1923; *Letters and Leaders*, i. p. 156; *Belfast Weekly Examiner*, 26 Sept. 1885.
122 Healy to Maurice Healy, 18 Sept., 24 Nov. 1882, *Letters and Leader* Proofs, B38, 40.
123 Healy to Maurice Healy, 23 Apr. 1883, *Letters and Leaders* Proofs, B47.
124 *S.C.P.*, vol. 8, p. 357 (28 May 1889).
125 Healy to Maurice Healy, 16 Mar. 1882, n.d., 24 Nov. 1882, *Letters and Leaders* Proofs, B29-40. Healy had written to Maurice from Kentucky in December 1881 looking to the defeat of the government on a Conservative resolution in favour of land purchase: 'Of course the Tories may not care to put themselves in the position of having to carry out an immense scheme of Purchase, if they were returned to power. Yet the difficulty is more imaginary than substantial' (Healy to Maurice Healy, 22 Dec. 1881, *Letters and Leaders* Proofs, B23-4).
126 Healy to Maurice Healy, 1 Apr. 1882, *Letters and Leaders* Proofs, B30. On Dillon's health, see F. S. L. Lyons, *Dillon* (London, 1968), pp. 61-4.
127 *Hansard*, vol. 268, col. 193 (28 Mar. 1882).
128 *Hansard*, vol. 268, cols. 727-8 (17 Apr. 1882). Healy's resentment of the Land League did not relate exclusively to its social radicalism. The League was also infuriatingly oligarchic. Even the left-leaning Dillon had complained publicly in late 1880 that 'they knew that the greatest power in this country was a power that told the people that parliamentary representation was a sham. They all knew that if they wanted to decide on a land bill they must go up to Sackville Street, and ask the Land League before they could decide on a plan of action' (*F.J.*, 28 Dec. 1880).
129 Chamberlain, *Political Memoir*, pp. 36-7, 51-2.

130 *Letters and Leaders*, i. pp. 153–5, ii. 408–11; Chamberlain, *Political Memoir*, pp. 36–43, 51–5. The circumstances in which the meeting took place were illumined in an altercation between Healy and Chamberlain over ten years later. In the Commons on 27 July 1894 Chamberlain referred to Healy having 'been a suppliant for favours'. This prompted an exchange of notes. Chamberlain advised that 'he was thinking of the time when you asked for an interview through Captain O'Shea'. When Healy denied this Chamberlain replied 'I can only say that I was told that you had asked for the interview'. Chamberlain made a statement in the Commons to the effect that no imputation of dishonour was intended: 'I will only add that, although the hon. and learned Member and myself have been bitterly opposed to each other, I never thought of attributing to him anything of a dishonourable character'. *Letters and Leaders*, ii. pp. 408–11; Healy to Chamberlain, three notes dated 27 July 1894, Chamberlain Papers, University of Birmingham MS JC 8/6/3j(1–3); *Hansard*, 4th ser., vol. 27, cols. 1152, 1165 (27 July 1894).

131 Lyons, *Parnell*, pp. 189–201.

132 Healy to Maurice Healy, 16 Mar. 1882, *Letters and Leaders* Proofs, B29.

133 The text is set forth in Lyons, *Parnell*, pp. 200–1.

134 *Letters and Leaders*, i. p. 156; Chamberlain Special Commission Brief, McCarthy Proof, p. 65; Chamberlain to Morley, 16 Aug. 1888, Chamberlain, *Political Memoir*, pp. 59–60. Gladstone surprisingly wrote to Morley: '. . . I never knew that Chamberlain desired to succeed Forster . . . Had I known Chamberlain's wish, I should not have set it aside without consideration and counsel'. Gladstone to Morley (copy), 11 Aug. 1888, Gladstone Papers, Add. MS 44255 f. 256. It is exceedingly difficult to accept this assertion at face value.

135 O'Shea to Gladstone, n.d. (8 May 1882), Gladstone Papers BM Add. MS 56446 f. 74.

136 *F.J.*, 19 Jan. 1891; Callanan, *Parnell Split*, p. 234.

137 Davitt notes on R. B. O'Brien's *Parnell*; Davitt Papers TCD MS 9377; R. B. O'Brien, *Parnell*, i. p. 350; see generally Davitt, *Fall of Feudalism*, pp. 363–4. In his memoirs Healy asserted that 'the Kilmainham business was a device of Parnell, chiefly moved by his wish to get back to Mrs. O'Shea at once' (*Letters and Leaders*, ii. p. 410).

138 A. M. Sullivan to Davitt, n.d. (late May 1882), Davitt Papers, TCD MS 9332.

139 *The Dynamiter* (1925 ed.), foreword, p. v.

140 Lyons, *Parnell*, pp. 209–14; *Letters and Leaders*, i. pp. 157–61; Chamberlain, *Political Memoir*, pp. 62–3. McCarthy's account of what Parnell said is taken from his proof of evidence for the Special Commission (Special Commission Brief, McCarthy Proof, p. 64) which amplifies the account published in McCarthy and Praed, *Book of Memories*, p. 96.

141 *D.E.*, 8 May 1882.

142 *U.I.*, 13 May 1882, quoted W. O'Brien, *Recollections*, pp. 435–6. Healy later wrote: 'The year 1882 was the most difficult and anxious of his career. The debates of the "Kilmainham Treaty" and his release from prison gave Extremists a handle for sneers and taunts of Whiggery' (Healy, 'A Great Man's Fancies').

143 *Republic*, 17 June 1882.

144 Florence Arnold Forster, *Irish Journal*, entry for 8 May 1882, p. 489; see also *Letters and Leaders*, i. p. 160; John Redmond, *Historical and Political Addresses* (Dublin and London, 1898), pp. 12–13.

145 Lyons, *Parnell*, pp. 212–13; Katharine O'Shea to W. E. Gladstone, 30 Jan. 1886, Gladstone Papers BM Add. MS 44269 f. 284. In the folder in the National Library which contains some of O'Shea's Papers there are, curiously, two transcriptions of Parnell's letter to O'Shea of 28 Apr. 1882, one with and one without the controversial passage (NLI MS 5752 ff. 107,115). In the Commons in 1905, Healy

observed of the reading of that part of Parnell's letter where he promised to cooperate cordially with the Liberal party in advancing Liberal principles, 'it would be remembered what a shudder and gasp, almost of consternation, it created in Irish Nationalist circles' (*Hansard*, vol. 140, col. 810 [21 Feb. 1905]).

146 Davitt notes on R. B. O'Brien's *Parnell*, Davitt Papers, TCD MS 9377.

147 *Hansard*, vol. 269, cols. 500-13 (11 May 1882).

148 W. H. O'Shea to Gladstone, 12, 13 May 1882, BM Add. MS 44269 ff. 46, 48; Healy, *Letters and Leaders*, i. p. 161.

149 O'Shea to Chamberlain, 15 June 1882, Chamberlain Papers, University of Birmingham, JC 8/8/1/9.

150 W. H. O'Shea to Parnell, 23 June 1882, draft, NLI MS 5752 f. 144.

151 Thorold, *Labouchere*, pp. 161-70. The published texts correspond with the letters in the Chamberlain Papers, save for the deletion of the opening of Labouchere's letter of 17 May: 'I have explained the situation to Healy. He says that the Prime Minister paid him a compliment in the House, and evidently since that date he has become his ardent admirer'. (Chamberlain Papers, University of Birmingham, JC/5/50/4.) The published letters do not include the undated letter marked 'Thur.' from Labouchere to Chamberlain in the Gladstone Papers (BM Add. MS 44125, f. 150).

152 Labouchere to Chamberlain, n.d. marked 'Thurs.', Gladstone Papers BM Add. MS 44125 f. 150. While Parnell may well have referred to the risk of assassination – he appears to have made a similar remark to Chamberlain at their meeting of 7 May – he can hardly have anticipated the gusto with which this was propagated by Labouchere. Nor could he have foretold the particular 'spin' which Labouchere would later put on it in his correspondence with Herbert Gladstone where he relentlessly advanced the idea that Parnell was a coward, physically and politically. (Thorold, *Labouchere*, pp. 163, 165; Chamberlain, *Political Memoir*, pp. 62-3.

153 Chamberlain to Gladstone, 7 June 1882, Gladstone Papers BM Add. MS 44125, f. 145.

154 Hamilton, *Diary*, i. p. 278.

155 *Hansard*, vol. 271, cols. 1127-30 (20 June—1 July 1882); *Letters and Leaders*, i. pp. 163-4; O'Connor, *Parnell Movement*, pp. 462-7; Lyons, *Parnell*, p. 225.

156 Davitt to Dillon, 'Thurs.' (24 Aug. 1882), Dillon Papers, TCD MS 6728.

157 *Republic*, 15 July 1882; see also 20 May, 17 June 1882; *Letters and Leaders*, i. p. 157; Devoy, *Post Bag*, p. 127.

158 *U.I.*, 12 Aug. 1882; see generally Lyons, *Parnell*, pp. 227-8.

159 Special Commission Brief, Davitt Proof, p. 79.

160 Healy to Maurice Healy, 5 Oct. 1882, *Letters and Leaders* Proofs, B38.

161 *Letters and Leaders*, i. p. 169; R. B. O'Brien, *Parnell*, ii. pp. 367-9; Healy, 'a Great Man's Fancies'. Of the account published by R. B. O'Brien, Davitt noted 'story of N.L. not told. Healy's part very much exaggerated' (Davitt, notes on R. B. O'Brien's *Parnell*, i. Davitt Papers, TCD MS 9377).

162 *F.J.*, 16, 18 Oct. 1882; C. C. O'Brien, *Parnell and his Party*, pp. 127-8.

4: PARNELL ASCENDANT

1 McCarthy, *Reminiscences* (London, 1899, 2 vols.), ii. pp. 101-2.

2 *Hansard*, vol. 257, col. 541 (11 Jan. 1881).

3 *Hansard*, vol. 258, col. 1910 (28 Feb. 1881).

4 *F.J.*, 12 Dec. 1883.

5 T. M. Healy, 'The Irish Parliamentary Party', *Fortnightly Review*, vol. 32, p. 625 at p. 627 (1 Nov. 1882).

6 *F.J.*, 5 Dec. 1883, banquet at the Mansion House, Dublin.
7 *F.j.*, 10 Oct. 1881, Wexford, banquet.
8 Callanan, *Parnell Split*, p. 236.
9 *F.J.*, 20 June 1883.
10 T. P. O'Connor, *Parnell Movement*, pp. 375-9; *Daily Express*, 25 July 1881. The portrait of Healy in T. P. O'Connor's *Parnell Movement* is taken from an article he published under his pseudonym of 'Scrutator' in the *Freeman's Journal* of 1 Jan. 1884, which was conceived in part as a challenge to the hostile portrayal of Healy in the British press.
11 Florence Arnold Forster, *Irish Journal*, eds. T. W. Moody and R. A. J. Hawkins (Oxford, 1988), p. 312 (entry for 15 Nov. 1881).
12 H.W. Lucy, *A Diary of Two Parliaments* (London, 1886, 2 vols.), ii. p. 184 (15 July 1881), p. 318 (3 Mar. 1882).
13 *I.T.*, 12 Aug. 1889; *Harsard*, vol. 264, cols. 1559-83 (11 Aug. 1881).
14 *Times*, 22 Aug. 1881.
15 Healy to Herbert Gladstone, 22 Aug. 1881, Viscount Gladstone Papers, BM Add. MS 46049, f. 7; see also Gladstone's draft reply, f. 13.
16 A. M. Sullivan to H. Gladstone, 4 Feb. 1882, Viscount Gladstone Papers, BM Add. MS 46049, f. 136.
17 *F.J.*, 25 Sept., 9 Oct., 27 Nov. 1883. Healy had to overcome the problems created by the *Freeman's Journal* coverage of his speeches: 'In my speech at Clare I mentioned most of the flaws in the Land Act; but Dunlop, the *Freeman* reporter, left out everything worth inserting. There will be a meeting at Wexford on Sunday, and I have got Dunlop hindered from going over there' (Healy to Maurice Healy, 5 Oct 1882, *Letters and Leaders* Proofs, B38).
18 *F.J.*, 4 Dec. 1882; *Letters and Leaders*, i. p. 172.
19 *F.J.*, 4 Dec. 1882, 29, 25 Jan. 1883. Ironically the chief casualty of the prosecution was the Attorney-General, William Moore Johnson Q.C. When Healy entered the court of Queen's Bench, Johnson shook hands with him. This exercise in urbanity proved costly. Pilloried in the English press, he was compelled to relinquish the Attorney-Generalship and to accept a judicial appointment (*F.J.*, 6 Dec. 1882; *Letters and Leaders*, i. pp. 172-3; M. Healy, *Munster Circuit*, pp. 32-3).
20 *F.J.*, 25 Jan. 1883.
21 *F.J.*, 26 Jan., 8 Feb. 1882; *Times*, 8 Feb. 1882; Lyons, *Dillon*, pp. 85- 6.
22 *F.J.*, 9 Feb. 1883.
23 Davitt to Richard McGhee, 2 Mar. 1883, Davitt Papers, TCD, *Letters and Leaders*, i. pp. 172-8, 183-6; Healy to Maurice Healy, 24 Mar. 1883, *Letters and Leaders* Proofs, B46; Healy to Cahir Davitt, 19 July 1924, Davitt Papers, TCD.
24 *Letters and Leaders*, i. pp. 178, 185; Healy to Maurice Healy, 5 Apr. 1883, *Letters and Leaders* Proofs, B46.
25 Healy to Maurice Healy, 5 Apr. 1883, *Letters and Leaders* Proofs, B49.
26 *F.J.*, 5, 6 June 1883; *U.I*, 16 June 1883. For Spencer's careful justification of the releases of the Queen, see Spencer to Victoria R., 4 June 1883, in *The Red Earl, the Papers of the Fifth Earl of Spencer*, ed. Peter Gordon (Northampton, 1982, 2 vols.), i. p. 249.
27 *F.J.*, 16 June 1883.
28 *Letters and Leaders*, i. p. 190; *F.J.*, 14 June 1883; *U.I.*, 16 June 1883.
29 *F.J.*, 20 June 1883; *F.J.*, 20 June 1883, Clones.
30 Healy, 'A Great Man's Fancies'; *Letters and Leaders*, i. p. 190; see also *Weekly Sun*, 7 June 1896 (T. P. O'Connor).
31 *S.C.P.*, vol. 8, paras. 71, 639-44 (O'Brien evidence, 22 May 1880).

32 O'Brien, *Recollections*, pp. 474-8.
33 Healy to O'Brien, 7 Jan. 1914, NLI MS 8556.
34 *Times*, 17, 18, 20 Aug. 1883; *F.J.*, 20 Aug. 1883; T. P. O'Connor, *Memoirs*, i. p. 106; see also T. P. O'Connor, *Parnell Movement*, p. 381. In a later Commons attack on Clifford Lloyd, an openly biased and exceedingly unpopular magistrate, Healy denounced the character of the women with whom he associated (*Hansard*, vol. 290, col. 16712 [18 July 1884]). Lloyd was a particular target of Healy's: see Clifford Lloyd, *Ireland Under the Land League* (Edinburgh and London, 1892), passim.
35 *Hansard*, vol. 283, cols. 967-8 (17 Aug. 1883); vol. 58, col. 31 (10 May 1898); D.E., 18 Aug. 1883.
36 *Hansard*, vol. 283, cols. 1132-57 (18 Aug. 1883); *D.E.*, 19 Aug. 1883.
37 *F.J.*, 20 Aug. 1883; *U.I.*, 25 Aug. 1883. Corry Connellan was a senior Dublin Castle official, originally Private Secretary to the Viceroy, and subsequently Cornwall's predecessor as Secretary of the Post Office, who was implicated in a homosexual scandal. He figured in Thackeray's comic ballad, 'The Shannon Shore' (Healy, *Letters and Leaders*, i. p. 195; O'Brien, *Evening Memories*, pp. 17-18).
38 O'Brien, *Evening Memories*, pp. 17-22.
39 *Young Ireland*, 26 June 1920.
40 *Hansard*, vol. 289, col. 705 (17 June 1884).
41 O'Brien, *Evening Memories*, pp. 17-32; *U.I.*, 12 July 1884; *Weekly News*, 25 Feb., 5 Mar. 1887, Thomas Sherlock, 'William O'Brien'.
42 O'Brien, *Evening Memories*, pp. 24-5, 33-6; *Hansard*, vol. 289, col. 710 (17 June 1884); *U.I.*, 14 June, 1, 5 Aug. 1884; *Weekly News*, 5 Mar. 1887.
43 O'Brien, *Evening Memories*, p. 33; Special Commission Brief, O'Brien Proof, p. 20.
44 *F.J.*, 16, 19 Feb. 1900, O'Brien to ed. d. 14 Feb., Healy to ed. d. 16 Feb.
45 *N.Y.T.*, 7 Aug. 1887.
46 *Dictionary of National Biography*, 1931-40, entry for T. M. Healy, p. 414; *F.J.*, 9 Mar. 1883; O'Connor, *Memoirs*, ii. p. 106.
47 Healy, *Letters and Leaders*, i. p. 195.
48 Healy had been treated by Sir William Wilde, presumably on account of the deafness in one of his ears. In his memoirs he wrote that, after the jury had disagreed in the first trial of Oscar Wilde, he had urged Sir Frank Lockwood, the Liberal Solicitor-General, not to have Wilde tried a second time. Lockwood said he would not do so save for 'the abominable rumours against ______' (*Letters and Leaders*, ii. p. 416). The occluded reference is evidently to Rosebery, whose name is actually inserted in the text of the letter quoted in Richard Ellmann, *Oscar Wilde* (London, 1987, p. 437; see also pp. 402-4; see also Hamilton, *Diary*, iii. p. 298). Edward Marjoribanks in his life of Carson claims that as Carson, who had appeared for the Marquess of Queensbury, entered the lobby at Westminster very shortly after Wilde's arrest, 'bitter political opponents like Tim Healy and Swift MacNeill, his countrymen and Wilde's, patted him on the back. "Well done", they said. Carson shrugged his shoulders. It had been a filthy business: he was tired and exhausted. Whatever else it was certainly no cause for congratulation' (Edward Marjoribanks, *The Life of Lord Carson* [London, 1932], i. p. 228). The innuendo at least is doubtful: if Healy congratulated Carson it is likely to have been intended as a forensic compliment to a fellow-barrister rather than as a display of exultation at Wilde's ruin (even if that would not divest the acclamation of Carson in such circumstances of its tastelessness).
49 *F.J.*, 8 Apr. 1885, NL.
50 *F.J.*, 1 Oct. 1884 NL; *Letters and Leaders*, i. pp. 187-89.
51 *U.I.*, 30 Aug. 1884. For an anthology of the attacks see the pamphlet *'United Ireland'*

on Spencer, Trevelyan and Gladstone (London and Dublin, 1888), published by the Irish Loyal and Patriotic Union.

52 *S.C.P.*, vol. 8, paras. 71,924-6 (23 May 1880); see also Special Commission Brief, O'Brien proof, p. 19.

53 *F.J.*, 16 Feb. 1900, O'Brien to ed. d. 14 Feb.; 17 Feb. 1900, Healy to ed. d. 16 Feb. O'Brien wildly charged that while he as editor was enduring condemnation for the attacks, 'Mr. Healy was breakfasting at Lord Spencer's and having a country visit to Sir George Trevelyan'.

54 O'Brien, *Evening Memories*, pp. 13, 35. O'Brien's remorse to some degree even extended back to the ferocity of the attacks upon W. E. Forster by nationalist parliamentarians: he wrote semi-apologetically in September 1888 that 'it is too often forgotten that in these contests speech is the only Irish weapon left unproclaimed' (W. O'Brien, 'The Forster Tragedy in Ireland', *Westminster Review*, vol. 130 [September 1888], p. 355).

55 *Hansard*, vol. 257, col. 1699 (28 Jan. 1881).

56 Healy to W. E. Gladstone, 1 Aug. 1881, Gladstone papers, BM Add. MS 44471 f. 3.

57 Labouchere to Chamberlain, 17 May 1882, Joseph Chamberlain papers, University of Birmingham, JC 5/50/4.

58 Mary Gladstone, *Diaries and Letters*, ed. Lucy Masterman (London, 1930) (entry for 28 Nov. 1882), p. 274.

59 Victoria to Gladstone, 24 June 1882; Gladstone to Victoria, 25 June 1882, Philip Guedella, *The Queen and Mr. Gladstone* (London, 1933, 2 vols.), ii. pp. 200-1; *Hansard*, vol. 271, col. 295 (23 June 1882); see also Victoria to Gladstone, 26 Mar. 1882, ibid., ii. pp. 182-3; Hamilton, *Diary*, i. pp. 241-3. The lines quoted by Healy were:

> Wha' the De'il ha' ye gotten for a King,
> But a wee wee German lairdie.

60 Healy to Gladstone, 14 Feb. 1883, Gladstone Papers BM Add. MS 44479, f. 225; memorandum endorsed by Herbert Gladstone, BM Add. MS 44485, f. 206.

61 Trevelyan to Spencer, 23, 24 Feb. 1884, quoted Alan O'Day, *The English Face of Irish Nationalism* (Dublin, 1977), p. 64.

62 *F.J.*, 15 Apr. 1884, Kildare.

63 *F.J.*, 4 Sept. 1884; see *The World*, 10 Sept. 1884.

64 *F.J.*, 18 Oct. 1882; 13 Oct. 1885, Longford.

65 T. M. Healy, *A Record of Coercion* (Dublin, 1881), p. iv; Irish Party Minutes, 31 Mar. 1882.

66 Healy to Maurice Healy, 23 Apr. 1883, *Letters and Leaders* Proofs, B47.

67 *Hansard*, vol. 284, cols. 1465-82 (20 Feb. 1884). *United Ireland* had in 1882 condemned the inconstancy of O'Connor Power: 'What he did was to be a Nationalist and not a Nationalist; a Land Leaguer and not a Land Leaguer; an obstructionist and not an obstructionist; a Parnellite and an insidious enemy of Mr. Parnell; an insulter of the clergy and their secret flatterer; a runner with the hare and a hunter with the hounds'. The cadences are those of Healy rather than O'Brien (*U.I.*, 16 Apr. 1882).

68 *Letters and Leaders*, i. p. 124.

69 *U.I.*, 6, 12 Jan. 1884.

70 *F.J.*, 18-27 Mar. 1884; *U.I.*, 29 Mar. 1884. Healy had been appointed co-secretary of the National League with Harrington, but had never acted in that capacity, as he told the Commons in 1887. He explained, somewhat disingenuously, that he had not always agreed with Harrington 'in what I thought were his stringent methods against the branches of the League . . . But I now see my hon. friend was right and I was wrong. I now see that the course he took was the right and proper one; but I see that instead of getting any thanks for it he is taunted by hon. Gentlemen opposite' (Hansard, vol. 320, col. 142 [26 Aug. 1887]).

71 *F.J.*, 29 Mar. 1884.

72 Healy to Maurice Healy, 23 Apr. 1883, Healy (in Richmond Jail) to Maurice Healy, *Letters and Leaders* Proofs, B47.

73 W. O'Brien, *Evening Memories*, p. 66; T. M. Healy, 'The Irish Parliamentary Party', *Fortnightly Review*, vol. 32 (1 Nov. 1882), p. 633; *F.J.*, 15 June 1883, Cork; *U.I.*, 13 Jan. 1883.

74 *U.I.*, 10, 17 June, 1, 15, 23 July 1882, 17 May 1884; *F.J.*, 27 Mar. 1884; see C. C. O'Brien, *Parnell and his Party*, pp. 265-71.

75 *U.I.*, 27 June 1885, Knocklong 22 June; see also his speech at Herbertstown, 23 June.

76 *U.I.*, 11 July 1885; see also *U.I.*, 10 Jan., 18 July 1885; *F.J.*, 3 Jan. 1885.

77 *U.I.*, 18 July 1885.

78 *F.J.*, 12 Nov. 1883, Limerick.

79 *P.M.G.*, 28 Dec. 1883, T. M. Healy, 'The Secret of Mr. Parnell's Power'. The article was carried in the *Freeman's Journal* of 29 Dec.

80 Davitt to Richard McGhee, copy, n.d., 'Sun', Davitt Papers, TCD MS 9328.

81 *F.J.*, 15 Apr. 1884, Kildare; 31 Aug. 1884, Dungarvan.

82 *F.J.*, 29 Mar. 1884; *Letters and Leaders*, i. p. 205; *F.J.*, 21 Aug. 1884; see C. C. O'Brien, *Parnell and his Party*, pp. 140-3. In 1905, when a rebel against the Irish party under the leadership of John Redmond, Healy claimed that a series of articles in *United Ireland* written by him had brought Parnell to a reluctant acceptance of the necessity for a parliamentary pledge. Parnell he asserted 'doubtless realised that it operated as a check on his authority by interposing the Party vote as a buffer against the sole authority of the Chairman' (*I.I.*, 3 July 1905). Healy was re-writing history, seeking to justify his repudiation of the disciplines of collective action on the spurious grounds that the purpose of the party pledge was to protect the position of the individual member. His own view at the time of its first adoption was the diametrical opposite.

83 *U.I.*, 31 Oct. 1885.

84 *F.J.*, 13 Oct. 1885, Longford.

85 Roy Jenkins, *Sir Charles Dilke* (London, 1958), p. 186; C. C. O'Brien, *Parnell and his Party*, pp. 86-8; B. Walker, 'The Irish Electorate 1868-1915', *Irish Historical Studies*, xviii. no. 71 (Mar. 1973), pp. 359-406.

86 E. W. Hamilton to W. E. Gladstone, 17 Jan. 1884, BM Add. MS 44190, f. 6.

87 Gwynn and Tuckwell, *The Life of the Rt. Hon. Sir Charles W. Dilke* (2 vols., London, 1917), ii. pp. 5, 124.

88 *F.J.*, 25 Jan., 15 Apr. 1885.

89 *F.J.*, 24 Sept. 1885.

90 *F.J.*, 2 Sept. 1885.

91 *Vanity Fair*, 3 Apr. 1886, 'Jehu Junior', profile of Healy.

92 *Nation*, 27 Oct. 1883, 10 Jan. 1885. Healy brought through the Commons the Coroners (Ireland) Act 1881 which increased the remuneration of Irish coroners. The grateful beneficiaries offered to discharge Healy's bar fees, which he declined. He accepted the gift of a law library (*Letters and Leaders*, i. p. 126; Healy to Maurice Healy, July 1881, *Letters and Leaders* Proofs, B14; *Times*, 2 May 1883).

93 *Letters and Leaders*, i. pp. 95, 218; records of Gray's Inn; Memorial of T. M. Healy to be admitted to Degree of Barrister at Law, dated 18 October 1884, King's Inns Dublin; *Irish Law Times*, vol. xviii. no. 929 (15 Nov. 1884).

94 For his early cases, see *Sunday Independent*, 29 Mar., 5 Apr. 1931.

95 Notes on Salaries of Irish M.P.s (1888); Healy to Maurice Healy snr., 24 Dec. 1888, Healy-Sullivan papers, UCD P6/A/12.

96 O'Connor, *Parnell*, pp. 72-3.

97 *Weekly Sun*, 2 Aug. 1896.
98 W. O'Brien, *Recollections*, p. 250; O'Connor, *Memoirs*, i. pp. 103–4.
99 Healy to Maurice Healy, 20 Mar. 1884, *Letters and Leaders* Proofs, B56.
100 *The World*, 10 Sept. 1884.
101 Parnell to T. C. Harrington, 18 Aug. 1884, Rathdrum, Harrington Papers (2).
102 O'Connor, *Memoirs*, ii. pp. 15–19.
103 *Letters and Leaders*, i. pp. 230–1.
104 O'Connor, *Memoirs*, i. pp. 103–4; ii. p. 5.
105 Chamberlain to Gladstone, 26 Oct. 1885, Chamberlain, *Political Memoir*, p. 163. W. H. O'Shea in a letter to the *Freeman's Journal* after the Galway election referred darkly to Healy's conduct on the eve of the Fermanagh election (*F.J.*, 18 May 1886, W. H. O'Shea to ed. d. 15 May). In Katharine O'Shea's memoirs, a letter from Parnell of 23 October 1885 is quoted: 'H. behaved very badly about Fermanagh, threatening and striking "O'K" on Monday evening to intimidate him from going forward, but the latter squared up to him like a man and cowed him'. A note identifies 'O'K' as James O'Kelly, who is referred to in a separate context earlier in the same letter. It is likely that the letter was mistranscribed and that the second reference was to Campbell rather than to O'Kelly. From the date of the letter, it is evident that the incident did not take place at the convention and presumably occurred at a meeting of the organising committee in Morrison's Hotel: Healy was not present at the South Fermanagh convention at which Campbell was nominated (which was attended and addressed by O'Kelly) (*F.J.*, 24 Oct. 1885). Campbell was returned on 4 December.
106 O'Connor, *Memoirs*, i. p. 105, ii. pp. 14–15.
107 *F.J.*, 16 Feb. 1900, O'Brien to ed. d. 14 Feb.; 17 Feb. 1900, Healy to ed. d. 16 Feb.
108 *F.J.*, 5 Oct. 1885; Healy to Maurice Healy, 21 Nov. 1885, 22 Nov. 1885, *Letters and Leaders* Proofs, B75.
109 M. J. F. McCarthy, *The Irish Revolution* (Edinburgh and London, 1912), p. 452.
110 Callanan, *Parnell Split*, pp. 229–30; *F.J.*, 16 Sept. 1900, Healy to ed., *Dundalk Examiner* d. 7 Sept. 1900. A letter to John Redmond reveals the extent of Healy's role in the nomination of candidates. Healy explained regarding the North Wexford seat, that, as between J. E. Redmond and J. F. Small, 'personally I am in a fix between you, considering how you retired for me in '80 and again Small was largely brought in on my suggestion in '83. . . . I feel sure all will be arranged satisfactorily, if we have a little meeting of the Party at which you and Small are both present' (Healy to J. E. Redmond, 1 Oct. 1885, Redmond Papers NLI MS 15, 196). The seat went to Redmond.
111 *F.J.*, 22 June 1883, Carrickmacross.
112 W. E. H. Lecky, *The Leaders of Public Opinion in Ireland* (London, 1871), p. 232.
113 F.J., 2 June 1884, Mullingar. To have coupled in attack, and pitted against each other, two minorities was a virtuoso performance on Healy's part.
114 *U.I.*, 23 Sept. 1881.
115 *U.I.*, 24 Sept. 1881, 'A Good Looker-on'.
116 *F.J.*, 1 Jan. 1885, interview with Glasgow evening paper. Supporting Parnell's land nationalisation at Drogheda in April 1884, *United Ireland* denounced Henry George, Davitt's inspiration and collaborator, as an 'Anglo-Californian adventurer' (*U.I.*, 19 Apr. 1884).
117 *U.I.*, 15 Aug. 1885.
118 *U.I.*, 7 Feb. 1885, see also 20 June 1885; T. M. Healy, 'The Irish and the Government', *Fortnightly Review*, vol. 36, p. 649 (Nov. 1884).
119 For a representative statement of O'Brien's position see his lecture 'The Lost

Opportunities of the Irish Gentry', delivered 8 Sept. 1887, in William O'Brien, *Irish Ideas* (London, 1893), pp. 13-29.

120 *F.J.*, 5 May 1886, NL.

121 *U.I.*, 5 Sept. 1885, Derry 28 Aug.

122 *F.J.*, 10 Dec. 1885, Central News interview.

123 *F.J.*, 5 May 1886, NL.

124 T. M. Healy, 'Ireland and the Tory Party', in the *Fortnightly Review*, vol. 34, p. 734 (1 Nov. 1883).

125 17 Oct. 1883, Roslea, Co. Fermanagh.

126 *F.J.*, 11 Oct. 1883, NL; *Hansard*, vol. 32, col. 171 (21 Jan. 1886).

127 T. M. Healy, *Loyalty Plus Murder* (Dublin, 1884); see also *P.M.G.*, 18 Jan. 1884, T. M. Healy, 'An Even Keel'.

128 T. M. Healy, 'Ulster and Ireland', *Contemporary Review*, vol. 48, pp. 723-31 (Nov. 1885); for his response to the election result, see *Derry Journal*, 7 Dec. 1885, *U.I.*, 12 Dec. 1885 (speech of 5 Dec.).

129 Healy to Labouchere, 15 Oct. 1885, copy, Viscount Gladstone Papers, BM Add. MS 46015, f. 41.

130 T. M. Healy, *A Word for Ireland* (Dublin, 1886), p. 153.

131 Labouchere to Herbert Gladstone, 19 Dec. 1885, Viscount Gladstone Papers, BM Add. MS 46015, f. 85. 3

5: NATIONALISTS AND RADICALS

1 Joseph Chamberlain Papers, University of Birmingham, JC/5/24/547.

2 T. M. Healy, 'Ireland and the Tory Party', *Fortnightly Review*, vol. 34 (1 Nov. 1883), pp. 728-36 at p. 731.

3 *F.J.*, 10 Aug. 1885, Liverpool.

4 *U.I.*, 18 Feb. 1882, editorial entitled 'War on the Radicals'.

5 C. C. O'Brien, *Parnell and his Party*, pp. 115-17.

6 *Young Ireland*, 23 June 1876, T. M. Healy 'Bonfire Night: A Story of St. John's Eve'.

7 *Nation,* 5 Oct. 1878, 19 Apr., 7 June 1879.

8 *Nation,* 18 Sept. 1880.

9 *Nation,* 7 Sept. 1878.

10 *Nation,* 31 Aug. 1878.

11 *Nation,* 26 June 1880; see also *Nation,* 29 May 1880.

12 *Nation,* 29 May, 3 July, 10 July 1880; Arnstein, *Bradlaugh*, pp. 177, 207; see also Healy to Maurice Healy, 18 July 1880, *Letters and Leaders* Proofs, Forty-Five.

13 *Hansard*, vol. 260, cols. 2052-3 (6 May 1881); Lyons, *Dillon*, pp. 50-1.

14 Arnstein, *Bradlaugh*, p. 214; *National Reformer*, 12 Mar., 2 Apr. 1882; Healy to Maurice Healy, 4 May 1882, *Letters and Leaders* Proofs, B32.

15 *F.J.*, 28 Jan. 1884; on the position of the Irish party, see Arnstein, *Bradlaugh*, pp. 201-25; Fergus D'Arcy, 'Charles Bradlaugh and the Irish Question' in *Studies in Irish History Presented to Robin Dudley Edwards* (Dublin, 1979), pp. 228-56.

16 See in particular *Hansard*, vol. 284, cols. 469-71 (11 Feb. 1884); Arnstein, *Bradlaugh*, pp. 276-9.

17 *F.J.*, 6, 7 July 1885; Arnstein, *Bradlaugh*, pp. 298, 209-11.

18 *Nation,* 9 Nov. 1878.

19 *F.J.*, 14 Sept. 1883, Newcastle-on-Tyne.

20 Heyck, *Radicalism*, pp. 90-100; T. M. Healy, 'The Irish and the Government', *Fortnightly Review*, vol. 36, pp. 649-56.

21 Lyons, *Parnell*, pp. 268-74.

22 *F.J.*, 8 Feb. 1883 (speech of Healy at NL); *F.J.*, 12 Mar. 1883 (text of bill); see also *F.J.*, 13 Oct. 1886 (speech of Healy at NL); T. M. Healy, 'The Advance towards Home Rule', *Contemporary Review*, vol. 48, p. 435 (Sept. 1885); Hammond, *Gladstone*, p. 341.

23 Healy to W. H. Duignan, 11 Jan. 1885, Joseph Chamberlain Papers, University of Birmingham, JC/8/3/2/2; Chamberlain to Duignan, 7 Feb. 1885, Joseph Chamberlain Papers, University of Birmingham, JC/8/3/1/28; see Heyck, *Radicalism*, pp. 101–2.

24 W. O'Brien, *Evening Memories*, pp. 3–4.

25 *U.I.*, 30 May, 6, 13, 20, 27 June, 4 July 1885. *United Ireland* was not alone. The future Catholic Archbishop of Dublin, William Walsh, received in Rome a letter from Dilke seeking letters of introduction for their Irish tour. *En route* to Genazzano, he bought at the station in Rome a copy of the *Daily News* which carried a report of a speech of Chamberlain attacking Carnarvon for granting an inquiry into the Maamtrasna murders and other cases. 'When we reached a telegraphic station – probably Segni – I telegraphed to Dilke: "Regret, Colleague's Hackney speech makes compliance with your request impossible"'. He considered his telegraph 'had a good deal to do with the breaking up of their project' (Walsh to Davitt, 7 Feb. 1893, Davitt Papers, TCD MS 9332, f. 283).

26 Chamberlain to Dilke, 30 June 1884, copy, Joseph Chamberlain Papers, University of Birmingham, JC 5/24/423; Labouchere to Chamberlain, 17 July (1885), Joseph Chamberlain Papers, University of Birmingham, JC 5/50/25; see also W. H. O'Shea's furious letter to his wife in O'Shea, *Parnell*, ii. p. 212. According to Michael Lynch, O'Shea's rival in Galway, O'Shea quoted Parnell as saying of Chamberlain and Dilke's proposed visit 'that they must be very smart fellows if they could make out what the Irish people really want – that he had been trying to make it out for the last seven years but failed to do so' (*F.J.*, 31 May 1886, Lynch to *F.J.*, d. 29 May).

27 Special Commission Brief, O'Brien Proofs, pp. 20–1.

28 O'Shea wrote to Chamberlain that Parnell rarely interfered with *United Ireland* and that the person responsible for the attacks was Healy. Healy was the author in particular of *United Ireland*'s condemnation of on an article written on Chamberlain's authority by Sir George Fottrell, whom Healy despised (O'Shea to Chamberlain, 13 July 1885, Chamberlain, *Political Memoir*, pp. 154–5; 'Local Government and Ireland', *Fortnightly Review*, n.s., vol. 38 [July 1885] pp. 1–16; *U.I.*, 4 July 1885). O'Brien asked Healy to temper the attack on Fottrell's article in deference to Parnell's wishes. Healy declined, leaving it to O'Brien as editor to make such alterations as he saw fit (Healy, *Letters and Leaders*, i. p. 250).

29 Robbins, *Parnell*, pp. 29–30; Callanan, *Parnell Split*, pp. 234–5; *I.I.*, 23 June 1892; W. O'Brien, *Evening Memoirs*, p. 117.

30 *Hansard*, vol. 299, cols. 1140–9, 1090 (17 July 1885).

31 T. M. Healy, 'The Advance towards Home Rule', *Contemporary Review*, vol. 48 (Sept. 1885), pp. 433–8 at p. 438.

32 Healy, *Letters and Leaders*, i. pp. 209–10.

33 Lyons, *Parnell*, pp. 283–8; Justin McCarthy, 'Charles Stewart Parnell', *Contemporary Review*, vol. LX (Nov. 1891), p. 630.

34 W. S. Blunt, *The Land War in Ireland* (London, 1912), p. 32 (diary entry for 23 Feb. 1886), quoted Alan O'Day, *The English Face of Irish Nationalism* (Dublin, 1977), p. 105; Lyons, *Parnell*, p. 279; Hamilton diary, entry for 12 May 1889, BM, Add. MS 48650.

35 *N.Y.T.*, 7 Aug. 1887; see also Frederic's 'What do Irishmen want? By an American in London', *P.M.G.*, 16 Dec. 1885, enclosed in Frederic to W. E. Gladstone, 17 Dec. 1885 (BM, Add. MS 56446, f. 186).

36 H. W. Lucy, *Sixty Years in the Wilderness* (3 vols., London, 1916), iii. [*Nearing Jordan*], pp. 10–11.

37 Frederic perhaps over-exactly dated the change from the occasion when the Conservatives joined the Irish to defeat a government proposal to apply the cloture, so as to secure the Irish vote against the government's Egyptian policy (*N.Y.T.*, 7 Aug. 1887).

38 On Labouchere generally see Thorold, *Labouchere*; Hesketh Pearson, *Labby* (London, 1936); Hind, *Labouchere; Dictionary of National Biography*, 1912–21; for indulgent Irish assessments, see W. O'Brien, *Evening Memories*, pp. 6–8; O'Connor, *Memoirs*, ii. pp. 74–7. For Labouchere's unhappy responsibility for section II of the Criminal Law Amendment Act of 1885 (under which Oscar Wilde and many others were to be convicted), a Foucauldian black comedy, see F. B. Smith 'Labouchere's Amendment to the Criminal Law Amendment Bill', *Historical Studies*, vol. 17 (Oct. 1976), pp. 165–73.

39 *Dictionary of National Biography*, 1912–21.

40 *U.I.*, 2 Dec. 1882.

41 Labouchere to Rosebery, n.d. ('Sat.'), Rosebery Papers, NLS 11041 f. 42.

42 Jenkins, *Gladstone*, p. 526; Lyons, *Parnell*, p. 291.

43 Chamberlain to O'Shea, 15 July 1885, NLI MS 5752, f. 216. 'G.O.M.' stood of course for 'the Grand Old Man', the *soubriquet* for W. E. Gladstone minted by Labouchere which entered general currency (Jenkins, *Gladstone,* p. 460).

44 Thorold, *Labouchere*, p. 235 et passim; Healy, *Letters and Leaders*, i. p. 236; Viscount Gladstone, *After Forty Years* (London, 1928), p. 287. A little of the correspondence is also cited in Sir Charles Mallet, *Herbert Gladstone, A Memoir* (London, 1932).

45 Cooke and Vincent, *Governing Passion*, pp. 316–17. Labouchere's role first received modern scholarly consideration in R. J. Hine's fine *Henry Labouchere and the Empire* (London, 1972), although without reference to the extraordinary position in which Healy was placing himself. Aspects of the Herbert Gladstone-Labouchere correspondence were also addressed in Alan O'Day, *Parnell and the First Home Rule Episode* (Dublin, 1986).

46 On the unsuccessful quest for Labouchere's papers see Hind, *Labouchere*, pp. 253–4. The general accuracy, but heavy truncation, of correspondence concerning Healy in Thorold's *Labouchere* is confirmed by a consideration of the published version of Labouchere's important letter to Chamberlain of 22 July 1885 (see *Labouchere*, pp. 230–2, and the full published text in Chamberlain, *Political Memoir*, Appendix B, pp. 330–1). The two originals of letters from Healy to Labouchere which are extant (22 Nov. 1885, Joseph Chamberlain Papers, University of Birmingham, JC 5/50/36; 22 July 1886, Viscount Gladstone Papers, BM, Add. MS 46016, f. 106) are of little significance. Labouchere's rendition of Healy's letter of 10 November 1885 in writing to Chamberlain is largely accurate (Healy to Labouchere, 10 Nov. 1885, Rosebery Papers, NLS MS 11041, f. 9; Labouchere to Chamberlain, 12 Nov. 1885, Thorold, *Labouchere*, p. 241).

47 Labouchere to Herbert Gladstone, 14 Dec. 1885, Viscount Gladstone papers, BM,. Add. MS 46015, f. 74.

48 Labouchere to Chamberlain, 17 Dec. (1880), Gladstone Papers, BM, Add. MS 44125, ff. 53–6.

49 *Truth*, 3 Nov. 1881.

50 Labouchere to H. Gladstone, 2 Mar. (1885), BM, Add. MS 46015, f. 24.

51 Labouchere to Chamberlain, 17 July 1885, Joseph Chamberlain Papers, University of Birmingham, JC 5/50/25; Chamberlain to Labouchere, 18 July 1885, quoted

in part in Thorold, *Labouchere*, pp. 228-9. Hesketh Pearson observed that 'it was unfortunate for Labby's schemes that he had to deal with three such humourless egotists as Gladstone, Parnell and Chamberlain . . .' (Hesketh Pearson, *Labby*, p. 199).

52 Labouchere to Chamberlain, 18 Oct. 1885, Thorold, *Labouchere*, pp. 237-8.

53 Healy to Labouchere, 22 July 1885, quoted in extenso, Chamberlain, *Political Memoir*, pp. 311-3. The version published in Thorold, *Labouchere*, at pp. 230-2 is heavily truncated. The reference to Parnell's ill-treatment at the hands of an Irish mob relates to a turbulent election meeting at Enniscorthy on 28 March 1880: Lyons, *Parnell*, pp. 119-21. (Healy was not present at the meeting, and his description of Parnell as 'like a man of bronze' relates to the following day [O'Connor, *Parnell*, p. 78].)

54 Herbert Gladstone diary, entry for 4 Aug. 1885 (Glynne-Gladstone Papers, St. Deiniol's Library, Hawarden, MS 1867). Herbert Gladstone was not so much hostile to the Irish leader as smarting from the fact that Parnell had invoked a speech of his at Leeds the previous month in favour of a vaguely-conceived Irish parliament to insist on home rule, rather than a 'central board' scheme of the type favoured by Chamberlain. Cooke and Vincent's cryptic reduction of this passage to 'Healy's claim that Parnell did not want home rule' is hardly warranted (*Governing Passion*, p. xiii).

55 Healy to Labouchere, 7 Oct. 1885, copy taken by H. Gladstone on Hawarden notepaper, Viscount Gladstone Papers, BM, Add. MS 46015; for Parnell's Arklow speech, see Lyons, *Parnell*, p. 296.

56 Labouchere to H. Gladstone, n.d. enclosing Healy to Labouchere, 7 Oct. 1885, Viscount Gladstone Papers, BM, Add. MS 46015, f. 30.

57 H. Gladstone to Labouchere, 12 Oct. 1885, copy, Viscount Gladstone Papers, BM, Add. MS 46015, f. 33.

58 Healy to Labouchere, 15 Oct. 1885, copy (part quoted, Thorold, *Labouchere* at pp. 235-9); Labouchere to H. Gladstone, 15 Oct. 1885; H. Gladstone to Labouchere, 18 Oct. 1885, copy; Labouchere to H. Gladstone, 20 Oct. 1885; Viscount Gladstone Papers, BM, Add. MS 46015 ff. 41-6.

59 Labouchere to Rosebery, 12 Nov. (1885), Healy to Labouchere, 10 Nov. 1885, Rosebery Papers, NLS MS 11041, ff. 7, 9; Labouchere to Chamberlain, 12 Nov. 1885, Thorold, *Labouchere*, pp. 241-2.

60 Labouchere to Chamberlain marked 'private', n.d., endorsed 10 Nov. 1885, Joseph Chamberlain Papers, University of Birmingham, JC 5/50./32. No copy of such a letter from Herbert Gladstone exists in his papers.

61 H. Gladstone to Labouchere, 16 Nov. 1885, Viscount Gladstone Papers, BM, Add. MS 46015, ff. 51-2.

62 Labouchere to H. Gladstone, 17 Nov. 1885, enclosing T. P. O'Connor to Labouchere, 16 Nov., Viscount Gladstone Papers, BM, Add. MS 46015, ff. 53-4. Labouchere was obsessed with the notion that O'Connor was corrupt: see Labouchere to H. Gladstone, 9, 10, 12 Dec. 1885, Viscount Gladstone Papers, BM, Add. MS 46015, ff. 64, 71, 74; Labouchere to Rosebery, 23 Nov. (1885), Rosebery Papers, NLS MS 11041, f. 16.

63 Labouchere to Rosebery, 19 Nov. (1885), Rosebery Papers, NLS MS 11041, ff. 10-13.

64 *F.J.*, 22 Nov. 1885; *Letters and Leaders*, i. p. 231; see generally Lyons, *Parnell*, pp. 302-4.

65 Healy to Labouchere, 22 Nov. 1885, Joseph Chamberlain Papers, University of Birmingham, JC 5/50/36.

66 Labouchere to Rosebery, 25 Nov. (1885), Rosebery Papers, NLS MS 11041, f. 18. The fastidiously elliptical qualification in the last sentence came close to conceding the flawed premise of Labouchere's entire venture.

67 Labouchere to H. Gladstone, 3 Dec. 1885, Viscount Gladstone Papers, BM, Add. MS 46015, f. 55.

68 H. Gladstone to Labouchere, 7 Dec. 1885, Viscount Gladstone Papers, BM, Add. MS 46015, ff. 60, 63.

69 Labouchere to H. Gladstone, 8 Dec. (1885); Herbert Gladstone to Labouchere, 9 Dec. 1885, Viscount Gladstone Papers, BM, Add. MS 46015, ff. 60, 63.

70 Labouchere to H. Gladstone, 9 Dec. 1885; Healy to Labouchere, 7 Dec. 1885, Labouchere to H. Gladstone, Viscount Gladstone Papers, BM, Add. MS 46015, ff. 64–7; Thorold, *Labouchere*, pp. 247–8.

71 H. Gladstone to Labouchere, 10 Dec. 1885; Labouchere to H. Gladstone, 10 Dec. 1885, Viscount Gladstone Papers, BM, Add. MS 46015, ff. 69, 71; Healy to Labouchere, 10 Dec. 1885; Thorold, *Labouchere*, pp. 249–50.

72 Labouchere to McCarthy, Dec. 1885 [reply to letter of 11 Dec.], McCarthy and Praed, *Book of Memories*, Draft. He explained that Randolph Churchill favoured resigning but that Salisbury, the Prime Minister, did not: 'The old Woman is furious at the idea and doing Her best to prevent it'.

73 Herbert Gladstone to Rosebery, 10 Dec. 1885, with enclosures, Rosebery papers, NLS MS 11041, ff. 20–7.

74 Labouchere to H. Gladstone, 14 Dec. 1885, Viscount Gladstone Papers, BM, 46015, f. 74; see Justin McCarthy, *Reminiscences* (2 vols., London, 1899), ii. 113. When, as he inevitably did, Labouchere relayed to Churchill what McCarthy had told him, Churchill called Carnarvon 'a damned traitor' (Labouchere to Rosebery, 22 Dec. [1885], Rosebery Papers, NLS MS 11041, f. 38).

75 Labouchere to Rosebery, 14 Dec. (1885), Rosebery Papers, NLS MS 11041, f. 28.

76 Labouchere to Rosebery, 16 Dec. (1885), Rosebery Papers, NLS MS 11041, f. 30. Writing to Rosebery on 10 Dec. 1885, Herbert Gladstone had added as a postscript: 'Labouchere will know that you have seen the enclosed letters from him' (Gladstone to Rosebery, 10 Dec. 1885, Rosebery Papers, NLS MS 11041, f. 20).

77 Wemyss Reid to H. Gladstone, 13 Dec. 1885, Viscount Gladstone Papers, BM, Add. MS 46041, f. 65.

78 Herbert Gladstone, *After Thirty Years*, pp. 306–14.

79 H. Gladstone to Wemyss Reid, 14 Dec. 1885, copy, Viscount Gladstone papers, BM, Add. MS 46041.

80 Herbert Gladstone diary, 14–17 Dec. 1885, Glynne-Gladstone, MS 1867, St. Deiniol's Library, Hawarden; Herbert Gladstone, *After Thirty Years*, pp. 306–14; Hammond, *Gladstone,* pp. 438–50; Jenkins, *Gladstone,* pp. 526–30). Lord Jenkins' comment that there was no evidence that W. E. Gladstone had substantially discussed Reid's letter or Herbert's expedition to London is put in doubt by the *ex cathedra* tenor of the response to Reid's letter.

81 Labouchere to H. Gladstone, 19 Dec. 1885, Viscount Gladstone Papers, BM, Add. MS 46015, ff. 85–95; Labouchere to Rosebery, n.d. ('Sat'), Rosebery Papers, NLS MS 11041, f. 42; Labouchere's letter to Chamberlain of 19 December (in Thorold, *Labouchere*, at pp. 250–2) is a summary of the letter to Herbert Gladstone.

82 Labouchere to Rosebery, 18 Dec. (1885), Rosebery Papers, NLS MS 11041, f. 34.

83 Labouchere to H. Gladstone, 'Sun' (20 Dec. 1885); see also Labouchere to Chamberlain 'Sun', in Thorold, *Labouchere*, p. 252; W. E. Gladstone to H. Gladstone, 21 Dec. 1885; H. Gladstone to Labouchere, 21 Dec. 1885, draft: Viscount Gladstone Papers, BM, Add. MS 46015, ff. 95, 98, 99.

84 Labouchere to Rosebery, 22 Dec. (1885), Rosebery Papers, NLS MS 11041, f. 38. He went on to make a characteristically fatuous observation concerning Chamberlain: 'Joe socially has never got beyond the mayor of Birmingham, and he does like being written to by Mr. G. One of his grievances was that he had not had a letter from him for a long time'.

85 Labouchere to H. Gladstone, 27 Dec. 1885, Viscount Gladstone Papers, BM, Add. MS 46015, f. 121; see also Labouchere to Rosebery, 26 Dec. 1885, Rosebery Papers, NLS MS 11041, f. 46.
86 H. Gladstone to Labouchere, 28 Dec. 1885, Viscount Gladstone Papers, BM, Add. MS 46015, ff. 131-3.
87 Labouchere to H. Gladstone, 29 Dec. (1885), Viscount Gladstone Papers, BM, Add. MS 46015, f. 134.
88 *Times*, 28 Dec. 1885, quoted in part, Thorold, *Labouchere*, pp. 264-70; Labouchere to H. Gladstone, 27 Dec. (1885), Viscount Gladstone Papers, 46015, f. 121. The *Times* letter and related correspondence, including further letters from Labouchere, are reprinted in *Home Rule: A Reprint from the Times of recent articles and letters* (London, 1886). Labouchere's letter emphasised the conservative tendencies of the Irish nationalists: 'I am inclined to think that had they a Parliament of their own they would surprise us by their Conservative legislation'.
89 Labouchere to Rosebery, 26 Dec. (1885), Rosebery Papers, NLS MS 11041, f. 46. Asked in an interview with the Central News on 15 December whether the Irish had formulated a home rule scheme, Healy responded: 'That is a rather large question, and cannot be safely answered in the context of any interview' (*F.J.*, 16 Dec. 1885). Healy had told Labouchere that he and others had been charged to prepare a report on federations generally. It is possible that Parnell may have made some use of their endeavours in preparing the 'proposed constitution for Ireland' forwarded by Katharine O'Shea to W. E. Gladstone on 30 October (Thorold, *Labouchere*, p. 237; Lyons, *Parnell*, p. 299; Hammond, *Gladstone,* pp. 421-5).
90 Grosvenor to Gladstone, 5, 6 Jan. 1886, Gladstone Papers, BM, Add. MS 44316, ff. 160, 162.
91 Grosvenor to W. E. Gladstone, 5, 6, 7 Jan. 1886, Gladstone Papers, BM, Add. MS 44316, ff. 160, 162, 170.
92 W. E. Gladstone to Grosvenor, 7 Jan. 1886, copy, Gladstone Papers, BM, Add. MS 56447, f. 3; a second copy exists in Gladstone Papers, BM, Add. 44316, f. 165. Grosvenor's allegations thus provide the basis for what Cooke and Vincent refer to as 'what Gladstone mysteriously called "the Randolph-Healy concordat"' (*The Governing Passion*, p. 316).
93 *F.J.*, 10 Aug. 1885, Liverpool; *F.J.*, 1 Dec. 1886, Brian Boru branch, NL. Years later Healy lauded the early advocacy of land purchase by 'the late lamented Lord Randolph Churchill, whose dash of Irish blood gave him more insight into our problems than any of his predecessors' (11, 19 Feb. 1903, Healy to ed., *Morning Post*).
94 *Hansard*, vol. 302, col. 174 (21 Jan. 1886). Following his speech on the Maamtrasna murders in July 1885, Randolph Churchill approached Healy and made the highly unusual request that Healy address a meeting in Kerry, where a virtual agrarian uprising was feared. Healy did address a meeting in Killarney, with William O'Brien, the following October, if hardly in deference to Churchill's request. (*Letters and Leaders*, i. pp. 212-13, 227; on the state of Kerry see H. Spencer Wilkinson, *The Eve of Home Rule* [London, 1886], pp. 83-115.) At a meeting of the Conservative cabinet on 3 August 1885 Churchill had openly referred to his contacts with the Irish, prompting Lord Cranbrook to write to the Prime Minister to protest against Churchill's 'evident relations with Parnell and Healy . . . I dread his secret action and believe it to be wrong and dangerous' (Cooke and Vincent, *Governing Passion*, p. 283; Alan O'Day, *The English Face of Irish Nationalism* [Dublin, 1977], p. 104).
95 For Churchill's dealings with nationalists, and what is more important, the impression they created, see R. F. Foster, *Lord Randolph Churchill* (Oxford, 1981),

pp. 224-34; Alan O'Day, *The English Face of Irish Nationalism* (Dublin, 1977); Lucy, *Salisbury Parliament*, p. 143. When Parnell in 1890-1 pursued a limited *rapprochement* with the Conservatives, Herbert Gladstone recalled 'the somewhat analogous position of 1885': 'Some time before the downfall of the Liberal government, on numberless occasions leading members of the Parnellites, notably Mr. Healy and Mr. Sexton, were to be seen in close intercourse with leading Tories, and notably Lord Randolph Churchill' (draft of speech, Viscount Gladstone Papers, BM, Add. MS 36116, f. 83).

96 Labouchere to Gladstone, 16 Jan. 1886, Viscount Gladstone Papers, BM, Add. MS 46015, f. 151. Healy's letter, enclosed by Labouchere, is not in the Viscount Gladstone papers, and only survives in its published version: Healy to Labouchere, 15 Jan. 1886, Thorold, *Labouchere*, pp. 285-6.

97 Healy to Labouchere, 17 Jan. 1886, in Thorold, *Labouchere*, p. 286. The text forwarded by Labouchere to Gladstone is similar but not identical to Thorold's (Healy to Labouchere, copy in Labouchere's hand, Viscount Gladstone Papers, BM, Add. MS 46015, f. 155).

98 Labouchere to H. Gladstone, 20 Jan. 1886, Viscount Gladstone Papers, BM, Add. MS 46015, f. 159.

99 Labouchere to McCarthy, three letters, n.d., in McCarthy and Praed, *Book of Memories* Draft.

100 Chamberlain to Labouchere, 23 Oct. 1885, Joseph Chamberlain Papers, University of Birmingham, JC 5/50/29 (deleted, Thorold, *Labouchere*, p. 241). Labouchere parroted the image, equating Gladstone's determination to return to power to 'the erotic passion of an old man for a girl': Labouchere to Chamberlain, 'Sun' (Dec. 1885), Joseph Chamberlain Papers, University of Birmingham, JC 5/50/47.

101 K. O'Shea to Gladstone, 30 Oct. 1885, Gladstone Papers, BM, Add. MS 44269, f. 232; Lyons, *Parnell*, pp. 299, 308.

102 K. O'Shea to Gladstone, 29 Dec. 1885, 7 Jan. 1886, BM, Add. MS 44269, ff. 270, 275.

103 Labouchere to Chamberlain, 22 Jan. 1886, Thorold, *Labouchere*, pp. 286-8; Labouchere to H. Gladstone (2), 22 Jan. 1886 (2), Viscount Gladstone Papers, BM, Add. MS 46015, ff. 161-2; Cooke and Vincent, *The Governing Passion*, p. 332; J. L. Garvin and L. S. Amery, *The Life of Joseph Chamberlain* (London, 1935-51, 4 vols.), ii. pp. 166-8.

104 K. O'Shea to W. E. Gladstone, 23 Jan. (1886), Gladstone Papers, BM, Add. MS 44269, f. 280; W. E. Gladstone to K. O'Shea, 26 Jan. 1886 (copy), Gladstone Papers, BM, Add. MS 56447, f. 88.

105 K. O'Shea to Gladstone, 23, 30 Jan. 1886, Gladstone Papers, BM, Add. MS 46015, f. 280, 284; Grosvenor to K. O'Shea, 30 Jan. 1886 (copy), Gladstone Papers, BM, Add. MS 44316, f. 178; see Labouchere's very different account, Labouchere to H. Gladstone, 27 Jan. 1886, Viscount Gladstone Papers, BM, Add. MS 46015, f. 172.

106 Labouchere to H. Gladstone, 2, 11 Feb. 1886, Viscount Gladstone Papers, BM, Add. MS 46016, ff. 1, 4.

107 Labouchere to H. Gladstone, 17 Feb. (1886), Viscount Gladstone Papers, BM, Add. MS 46016, f. 10.

108 W. E. Gladstone to Hartington, 30 May 1885, cited Hammond, *Gladstone,* p. 373.

109 Healy in his memoirs erroneously relates this to the formation of Gladstone's first home rule administration. Labouchere's celebrated exclusion from office came not in 1886, but in 1892 when he had serious expectations of office: *Letters and Leaders*, i. p. 310; Thorold, *Labouchere*, pp. 373-8.

110 Hamilton diary, entry for 30 Dec. 1885, Hamilton Papers, BM, Add. MS 48642,

pp. 65-6; Harcourt to Gladstone, 4 Jan., 23 Mar. 1886, Gladstone Papers, quoted in Hind, *Labouchere*, p. 141.

111 *Letters and Leaders*, i. p. 254; see also O'Connor, *Memoirs*, ii. p. 28; R. B. O'Brien, *Parnell*, ii. p. 45.

112 Harcourt diary, entry for 2 Jan. 1886, Harcourt MSS, Bodleian Library, Oxford. Cooke and Vincent are therefore wrong in their statement, based on the same entry, that Healy and Chamberlain dined together.

113 *Referee*, 25 Nov. 1928, Robbins, *Parnell*, pp. 155-6; Davitt to Healy, 12 Nov. 1903, Healy-Sullivan Papers, UCD P6/B/45; Healy, *Letters and Leaders*, i. p. 254.

114 Tynan, *Memories*, p. 15; *Twenty-Five Years*, p. 90.

6: THE FIRST HOME RULE BILL

1 W. H. O'Shea to Parnell, n.d., NLI MS 5752, f. 7; see also W. H. O'Shea to K. O'Shea, 19 Nov. 1885, O'Shea, *Parnell*, ii. pp. 101-2.

2 Chamberlain to Mulqueeny, 6 Oct. 1885, copy NLI MS 5752. This was a reply to Mulqueeny's letter of 29 September.

3 Parnell to K. O'Shea, 23 Oct. 1885, O'Shea, *Parnell*, ii. pp. 85-6; O'Connor, *Memoirs*, ii. p. 6.

4 O'Shea to Parnell, 2 Nov. 1885, copy/draft NLI MS 5752, f. 246. O'Shea's letter to his wife of the same date shows a similar temper (O'Shea, *Parnell*, ii. pp. 90-1).

5 Chamberlain to W. H. O'Shea, 3 Nov. 1885, NLI MS 5752, f. 250. O'Shea complained of his mistreatment at Parnell's hands to politicians of all parties save the nationalist: W. H. O'Shea to K. O'Shea, n.d., 'Wed', O'Shea, *Parnell*, ii. p. 213.

6 Labouchere to W. H. O'Shea, 16 Nov. (1885), NLI MS 5752, f. 256; *Nation*, 31 July 1880. In his memoirs T. P. O'Connor claimed that Healy was responsible for thwarting the mid-Armagh project (*Memoirs*, ii. p. 6), but Healy was not alone in his opposition. O'Shea wrote to James O'Kelly after the defeat of the home rule bill referring to a conversation with Parnell and O'Kelly at Morrison's Hotel in the autumn of 1885 'in the course of which you expressed a strong opinion on the ingratitude with which I was being treated by certain members of your party' (O'Shea to James O'Kelly, copy/draft 12 Aug. 1886, NLI MS 5752, f. 318).

7 Chamberlain to W. H. O'Shea, 20, 22 Nov. 1885, NLI MS 5752, ff. 264, 272.

8 Lyons, *Parnell*, pp. 306-7. Parnell wrote to his election agent that it would not be possible for him to be present on any day of the election in his Cork constituency 'as my presence is much required in Liverpool and Lancashire' (Parnell to John Horgan, 22 Nov. 1885, NLI MS 18,286).

9 *F.J.*, 26 Nov. 1885; T. P. O'Connor, *Memoirs*, ii. pp. 10-11.

10 Labouchere to Chamberlain, n.d. (endorsed 10 Nov. 1885), Joseph Chamberlain Papers, University of Birmingham, JC 5/50/32.

11 Lyons, *Parnell*, pp. 218-9, 455.

12 Labouchere to Rosebery, 23 Nov. (1885), Rosebery Papers, NLS MS 11041, f. 18. For Manning's involvement on other occasions, see Lyons, *Parnell*, pp. 313, 456; Kee, *Laurel and the Ivy*, pp. 535-6; O'Shea, *Parnell*, ii. p. 221.

13 Labouchere to H. Gladstone, 19 Dec. 1885, Viscount Gladstone Papers, BM Add. MS 46015, f. 85; see also Labouchere to Chamberlain, 19 Dec. 1885, Joseph Chamberlain Papers, University of Birmingham, JC 5/50/46. Labouchere sent a similar account to Rosebery, commenting of Parnell's relationship with Katharine O'Shea: 'That intrigue is however off now, and they hear that he has retired to warm salt water baths with some new Egeria, they do not know exactly where'

(Labouchere to Rosebery, 18 Dec. [1885], Rosebery Papers, NLS MS 11041, f. 34; quoted Crewe, *Lord Rosebery* [London, 1931, 2. vols.], i. p. 253).

14 Healy in the split made an assertion which he never repeated elsewhere: 'Mr. Biggar had stood for fifteen years by his [Parnell's] side, and I know that so far back as 1881 – ten years ago – he sat down and wrote a remonstrance to Parnell beging him to give up Mrs. O'Shea as a connection ruinous to Ireland. That was ten years ago; so Parnell cannot say he was not well warned' (*N.P.*, 16 Mar 1891, Newry).

15 Parnell to Healy, 17 Dec. 1885, Healy-Sullivan Papers, UCD P6/B/18; Healy, *Letters and Leaders*, i. p. 237.

16 Chamberlain to O'Brien, 9 Dec. 1885, NLI MS 5752, f. 284; *Letters and Leaders*, i. pp. 239–40; the full text of Healy's letter to the *Freeman's Journal* appears in *Letters and Leaders* Proofs, B77–8; T. P. O'Connor, *Parnell*, pp. 164–7; T. P. O'Connor, *Memoirs*, ii. pp. 94–6. The publication in R. B. O'Brien's *Parnell* (i., pp. 121–3) of what was essentially Healy's version of events elicited a libel writ from T. P. O'Connor. Denouncing 'that cur Barry O'Brien', to John Dillon, O'Connor complained that the account published was 'a deliberate piece of personal revenge'. He confessed that he had lost his temper and sued. If Carson, his leading counsel, advised he had no case, he would withdraw 'however humiliating it may be' (O'Connor to Dillon, 18 Nov. 1898, Dillon Papers, TCD MS 6740, f. 52). O'Connor subsequently discontinued the proceedings in what the contemporary Healyite organ aptly characterised as 'an abject skedaddle' (*Daily Nation*, 25 Nov. 1898).

17 *Letters and Leaders*, i. pp. 243–4; Biggar to Gray, 6 Feb. 1886, Healy to Gray, 6 Feb. 1886, in T. W. Moody, 'Parnell and the Galway Election', *Irish Historical Studies*, ix. no. 35 (Mar. 1955), pp. 319–38 (hereinafter cited as Moody, 'Galway Election').

18 Healy to Nolan, 7 Feb. 1886, *Letters and Leaders* Proofs, B79.

19 *P.M.G.*, 8 Dec. 1890; T. P. O'Connor, *Memoirs*, pp. 103–5; *Weekly Sun*, 5 July 1896; *W.N.P.*., 23 May 1891.

20 Moody, 'Galway Election', pp. 324–6; C. C. O'Brien, *Parnell and his Party*, pp. 324–6.

21 *F.J.*, 8 Feb. 1886; Moody, 'Galway Election', pp. 325–6.

22 *F.J.*, 9 Feb. 1886.

23 *Letters and Leaders* Proofs, B80; only the last, and (in part) the penultimate telegrams are set forth in the published memoirs (*Letters and Leaders*, i. p. 241). The account of an unidentified journalist present at Galway for the *Weekly National Press* during the split claimed the widespread refusal to attach credence to the rumours about Parnell and Katharine O'Shea was shaken only by 'the fact that Mr. Parnell was openly in communication with Mrs. O'Shea by telegraph during the context, not under any assumed name'. Even though the return of O'Shea was only declared at midnight, 'it was not too late for Mr. Parnell to wire the news to Eltham. The brief despatch on that occasion cost the modest sum of seven shillings' (*W.N.P.*., 23 May 1891; see also *Letters and Leaders*, i. p. 242). At the Galway post office telegrams were evidently not so much transmitted as broadcast.

24 My note for this reference is Gill Papers, NLI 14,506 (14). I have been unable to re-locate the document at this reference, and must conclude that the reference is incorrect or that the document has been mislaid.

25 *F.J.*, 10 Feb. 1886; O'Connor, *Parnell*, p. 170; O'Connor, *Memoirs*, ii. p. 98; *Weekly Sun*, 5 July 1895, T. P. O'Connor, 'Mr. Biggar'; see also *I.I.*, 16 Nov. 1900 (speech of T. C. Harrington, North Dock Ward, NL). Katharine Parnell recalled Parnell saying of his political activities that 'it was only the "beginnings" he hated, and that he was all right when he was "once started"' (O'Shea, *Parnell*, ii. p. 241).

26 O'Connor, *Parnell*, pp. 173-4; O'Connor, *Memoirs*, ii. pp. 99-102; *Weekly Sun*, 12 July 1896, T. P. O'Connor, 'Parnell's Back to the Wall'; *F.J.*, 10 Feb. 1886; *D.E.*, 10 Feb. 1886.

27 O'Connor, *Parnell*, p. 175; *Weekly Sun*, 12 July 1896; C. C. O'Brien, *Parnell and his Party*, pp. 182; O'Brien, *Evening Memories*, p. 104.

28 James O'Kelly to W. H. O'Shea, 8 June 1886, W. H. O'Shea to James O'Kelly, 12 Aug. 1886, copy/draft, NLI MS 5752, ff. 312, 318.

29 *F.J.*, 9, 10, 12 Feb. 1886; *Nation*, 13 Feb. 1886. For the reaction to Sullivan's article and his defence by Anna Parnell, see T. D. Sullivan, *Recollections*, pp. 195-6; *W.N.*, 23 Oct. 1897. Davitt considered it 'the utmost poetic justice that Healy and Biggar should stand accused of plotting against Parnell' (Davitt to Richard McGhee, 17 Feb. 1886, Davitt Papers, TCD MS P328).

30 Biggar to T. D. Sullivan, 11 Feb. 1886, Healy-Sullivan Papers, UCD P6/B/10.

31 Handbill entitled 'Lord Mayor Sullivan's Dinner: To the Patriotic Artizans and Citizens of Dublin', endorsed by T. D. Sullivan, on the basis of information provided by Patrick O'Brien MP, as the work of J. J. Clancy (Sullivan Papers, NLI MS 8237[1]); *F.J.*, 17 Feb. 1886; Nation, 20 Feb. 1886.

32 McCarthy to Campbell Praed, n.d., McCarthy and Praed, *Book of Memories* Draft.

33 Labouchere to Gladstone, 10 Feb. (1886), Viscount Gladstone Papers, BM, Add. MS 46016 f.4.

34 Labouchere to Rosebery, 13 Feb. (1886), Rosebery Papers, NLS MS 11041, f. 54.

35 *Times*, 10 Feb. 1886; *Saturday Review*, 13 Feb. 1886; *Galway Express*, 13. Feb. 1886; see also *St. James Gazette*, 9, 10 Feb. 1886.

36 Quoted in W. H. Hurlbert, *Ireland under Coercion* (Edinburgh, 1888, 2 vols.), i. p. 32.

37 *U.I.*, 13 Feb. 1886.

38 *F.J.*, 13, 18, 25, 31 May 1886; Times, 19 May 1886; *Nation*, 22 May 1886; O'Brien to O'Shea, telegram 18 May 1886, NLI MS 5752 ff. 308-10.

39 Hamilton diary, 24 Feb., 4 Apr. 1886, BM, Add. MS 48643; Morley, *Gladstone*, iii. pp. 304-5. The strict Gladstonian position continued to be that there had been no negotiations. Even after the 1886 election, Herbert Gladstone could assert: 'Of one thing I am really glad – to think that we have had no negotiations of any kind with the Parnellites. In regard to the practical question negotiations could not have improved our position, and in regard to the party they would have been fatal' (H. Gladstone to Labouchere, 17 Nov. 1886, copy, Viscount Gladstone Papers, BM, Add. MS 46016, f. 123).

40 K. O'Shea to Gladstone, 25 Mar. 1886, 'secret', Gladstone Papers BM, Add. MS 56447, f. 92.

41 W. H. O'Shea to K. O'Shea, 25 Mar. 1886, copy, NLI MS 5752, f. 296, with accompanying note by O'Shea; K. O'Shea to W. E. Gladstone, 26 Mar. 1886, W. H. O'Shea to 'dearest' (K. O'Shea), n.d. 'Thurs morning', Gladstone Papers, BM, Add. MS 56447, ff. 96, 104. The extravagant conjecture of A. B. Cooke and John Vincent that O'Shea forged the letter in his wife's name 'in order to compromise Gladstone by an ill-judged furtive meeting with Parnell, which would find its way into the papers just as the home rule bill was announced' (*Governing Passion*, pp. 389-90) is unwarranted.

42 Labouchere to H. Gladstone, 26 Mar. 1886, Viscount Gladstone Papers, BM, Add. MS 46016, f. 18.

43 Hamilton diary, 31 Mar., 2, 6 Apr. 1886, BM, Add. MS 48643; Hamilton, *Diary*, iii. pp. 32-3; Morley, *Gladstone*, iii. pp. 305-6; W. O'Brien, *Evening Memories*, pp. 107-10; Cooke and Vincent, *Governing Passion*, pp. 399-402. Labouchere's chattering off-stage continued: 'I don't know whether the Irish are to have Customs

and Excise, but I am sure that Parnell, in view of the difficulties of carrying Home Rule, would yield on this point – particularly if the Irish Government could have patronage, and be able to put the cousins of ardent patriots into little places in Customs and Excise' (Labouchere to H. Gladstone, 5 Apr. [1886], BM, Add. MS 46016, f. 20).

44 Irish Party Minutes, 7 Apr. 1886; Robbins, *Parnell*, pp. 26-7.

45 *Letters and Leaders*, i. pp. 251, 254; Irish Party Minutes, 8 Apr. 1886; O'Connor, *Parnell*, p. 183; O'Connor, *Memoirs*, ii. p. 31; *Weekly Sun*, 2 Aug. 1889; C. C. O'Brien, *Parnell and his Party*, p. 186.

46 *Hansard*, vol. 304, cols. 1207-44 (9 Apr. 1886); W. O'Brien, *Evening Memories*, p. 117; Frederic, 'The Ireland of Tomorrow', p. 17.

47 Labouchere to H. Gladstone, 10 Apr. (1886), BM, Add. MS 4601, f. 26.

48 *Hansard*, vol. 306, cols. 106-26 (25 May 1886); W. O'Brien, *Evening Memories*, p. 130.

49 Lyons, *Parnell*, p. 346; Labouchere to H. Gladstone, 11 May 1886 (2), BM, Add. MS 46016, ff. 66, 68, setting forth Parnell's scheme (incomplete).

50 Labouchere to H. Gladstone (12 May 1886), BM, Add. MS 46016, f. 86; Thorold, *Labouchere*, pp. 289-323.

51 *Hansard*, vol. 306, col. 678 (1 June 1886). Later the same day Chamberlain took his revenge in responding somewhat cruelly to Healy's unguarded characterisation of himself and others some days previously: 'It is all very well for the hon. and learned Member, with his magnificent physique, to stigmatise as "puny whipsters" men not gifted by Providence with his great personal gifts' (*Hansard*, vol. 306, cols. 117 [25 May 1886], 696 [1 June 1886]).

52 Lyons, *Parnell*, pp. 286-7; *Letters and Leaders*, i. pp. 255-7; *F.J.*, 24 June 1892 (speech at Mercantile Branch, NF).

53 Hamilton diary, entry for 6 May 1886, BM, Add. MS 48643.

54 *Hansard*, vol. 306, col. 1245 (8 June 1886).

55 Healy to Labouchere, 22 July 1886, enclosed with Labouchere to H. Gladstone, 23 July 1886, Viscount Gladstone Papers, BM, Add. MS 46016, f. 104.

56 Labouchere to H. Gladstone, 3 Aug. 1886, enclosing McCarthy to Labouchere, 1 Aug. 1886, BM, Add. MS 46016, ff. 112, 4.

57 Labouchere to H. Gladstone, 7 Aug. 1886, Viscount Gladstone Papers, BM, Add. MS 46016, f. 115. Labouchere enclosed Healy's reply to his letter which has not survived in the papers. Healy's article 'Jubilee-Time in Ireland' in the *Contemporary Review* for January 1887 (vol. 57, pp. 120- 30) may be the article which Labouchere was anticipating.

58 Labouchere to H. Gladstone, 7, 21 Aug. 1886; T. P. O'Connor to Labouchere, 21 Aug. 1886; BM, Add. MS 46016, ff. 115, 117, 121.

59 H. Gladstone to Labouchere, copy, 7 Nov. 1886, copy, BM, Add. MS 46016, f. 123.

60 *Hansard*, vol. 308, cols. 394 (24 Aug. 1886), 629 (26 Aug. 1886).

61 Maurice Healy to Healy, 26 Aug. 1886 (misdated 6 Aug.), *Letters and Leaders* Proofs, B88, deleted *Letters and Leaders*, i. p. 259.

62 Irish Party Minutes, 4 Aug. 1886, 27 Jan. 1887; *Nation*, 7 Aug. 1886.

63 Parnell to Healy, 17 Jan. 1887, Healy-Sullivan Papers, UCD P6/B/19.

64 *Nation*, 29 Jan. 1887.

65 Labouchere to McCarthy, 31 July 1886; Labouchere to McCarthy, 5 Aug. 1886, enclosing text of H. Gladstone to Labouchere, 1 Aug. 1886; McCarthy and Praed, *Book of Memories* Draft. Labouchere analysed the split in the Liberal ranks partly in terms of the rupture between Chamberlain and Morley, both radicals of old. Chamberlain 'has been fool enough to ruin himself and his prospects, mainly from pique against Morley. The latter is not a good fighter of a long game. He whimpers

and loses courage. He has written me several letters recently. The burthen of them is that "Joe" is so wicked and so unkind, and that never, never will he submit to "Joe's" dictatorship' (Labouchere to McCarthy, 4 Aug. 1886).

66 Memorandum dated 18 August 1886, McCarthy and Praed, *Book of Memories*, p. 48.

67 McCarthy to Campbell Praed, 20 June 1888, McCarthy and Praed, *Book of Memories*, p. 154.

68 Morley to Gladstone, 7 Dec. 1886, Gladstone Papers, BM, Add. MS 44255, f. 134.

69 Gladstone to Morley, 8 Dec. 1886, copy, Gladstone Papers, BM, Add. MS 44255, f. 139, deleted Morley, *Gladstone*, iii. p. 371; Morley to Gladstone, 9 Dec. 1886, Gladstone Papers, BM, Add. MS 44255, f. 141.

70 Morley to Gladstone, 12 Dec. 1886, Gladstone Papers, BM, Add. MS 44255, f. 143.

71 Morley to Gladstone, 2 Jan. 1887, Gladstone Papers, BM, Add. MS 44255, f. 173.

72 Morley, *Gladstone*, ii. pp. 354–8; see generally Michael Hurst, *Joseph Chamberlain and Liberal Reunion* (London, 1967).

73 Morley to Gladstone, 14 Sept. 1887, Gladstone Papers, BM, Add. MS 44255, f. 219.

74 Labouchere to H. Gladstone, 31 July 1886, Viscount Gladstone Papers, BM, Add. MS 46016, f. 109.

75 *Hansard*, vol. 308, cols. 1220–4, 1224–6 (3 Sept. 1886). For an anticipation of Parnell's emphasis on the spontaneous nature of contemporary land agitation, in contrast to 'the Land League movement of 1879', see *Hansard*, vol. 302, cols. 154–8 (21 Jan. 1886).

76 Morley to Gladstone, 4 Sept. 1886, Gladstone Papers, BM, Add. MS 44255, f. 155.

77 *F.J.*, 9 Sept. 1886; Morley, *Gladstone*, iii. p 369.

78 Morley to Gladstone, 10 Sept. 1886 (2), Gladstone Papers, BM, Add. MS 44255, ff. 118, 1222; *F.J.*, 14, 21 Sept. 1886; see generally Lyons, *Parnell*, pp. 359–60.

79 *U.I.*, 23 Oct. 1886. Further articles appeared on 6, 20 Nov. 1886.

80 *F.J.*, 10 Nov. 1886, *U.I.*, 13 Nov. 1886, NL.

81 *Letters and Leaders*, i. p. 266.

82 *F.J.*, 16 June 1883, Cork; *U.I.*, 5 Sept. 1885, Killarney, 30 Aug; *F.J.*, 5 Oct. 1885, Errigal Truagh; see also *U.I.*, 21 Feb. 1885.

83 *U.I.*, 15 Aug. 1885; see also *U.I.*, 22 Aug, 19 Sept. 1885.

84 W. O'Brien, *Evening Memories*, pp. 156–7; Labouchere to Gladstone, 16 Jan. (1887), Gladstone Papers, BM, Add. MS 56449, f. 202; *Letters and Leaders*, i. p. 266; see generally C. C. O'Brien, *Parnell and His Party*, pp. 262–3.

85 Morley to Gladstone, 7 Dec. 1886, Gladstone Papers, BM, Add. MS 44255, f. 134; see also Morley's diary entry for 7 Dec. 1886, in Morley, *Gladstone*, iii. p. 370.

86 O'Brien Proofs, Special Commission Brief, p. 21; W. O'Brien, *Evening Memories*, pp. 177–83; see generally C. C. O'Brien, *Parnell and his Party*, pp. 205–6.

87 W. O'Brien, *Evening Memories*, pp. 183, 351. By 1920 O'Brien was implacably opposed to John Dillon and determined to accentuate Parnell's suspicions of him.

88 Morley to Gladstone, 12 Dec. 1886, Gladstone Papers, BM, Add. MS 44255, f. 143; see also Morley, *Gladstone*, iii. p. 370.

89 Healy to Labouchere, n.d., in Thorold, *Labouchere*, p. 329; referred to and part quoted in Morley to Gladstone, 7 Dec. 1886, Gladstone Papers, BM, Add. MS 44255, ff. 128, 132. In his 1898 polemic against Dillon Healy presented the inception of the Plan as an act of insubordination: 'In the teeth of Mr. Parnell's authority, and without even the cooperation of Mr. Davitt, Messrs. Dillon and O'Brien revived the agrarian movement and started the Plan of Campaign' (Healy, *Why Ireland is Not Free*, p. 18).

90 *F.J.*, 1 Dec. 1886, Mountjoy Ward NL; see also *F.J.*, 27 Oct. 1886, Central Branch NL.

91 Morley to Gladstone, 7 Dec. 1886, Gladstone Papers, BM, Add. MS 44255, f. 134; see also W. O'Brien, *Evening Memories*, p. 183; *F.J.*, 8 Dec. 1886.
92 *F.J.*, 22 Dec. 1886, NL.
93 *F.J.*, 19 Jan. 1887, NL.
94 O'Brien to Healy, 24 Dec. 1886, *Letters and Leaders*, i. p. 267. The original does not survive in the Healy-Sullivan Papers.
95 Morley to Gladstone, 30 Nov. 1887, Gladstone Papers, BM, Add. MS 44255, f. 230.
96 *F.J.*, 9 May 1888; C. C. O'Brien, *Parnell and his Party*, pp. 218–9.
97 C. C. O'Brien, *Parnell and his Party*, p. 220; Lyons, *Parnell*, p. 95; proof of article telegraphed by O'Brien to *United Ireland*, Dillon Papers, NLI MS 6736, f. 13.
98 O'Brien to Dillon, n.d. 'Fri' (July 1888), Dillon Papers, TCD MS 6736, f. 15.
99 O'Brien to Dillon, 14 July 1888, Dillon Papers, TCD MS 6736, f. 17.
100 O'Brien to Dillon, n.d. 'Wed', Dillon Papers, TCD MS 6736, f. 18.
101 Morley to Gladstone, 7 Dec. 1886, Gladstone Papers, BM, Add. MS 44255, f. 134.
102 E. W. Hamilton to W. E. Gladstone, 19 Dec. 1886, Gladstone Papers, BM, Add. MS 44191.
103 Labouchere to Gladstone, 16 Jan. (1887), Gladstone Papers, BM, Add. MS 56449, f. 202.
104 Labouchere to H. Gladstone, 21 June 1887, Viscount Gladstone Papers, BM, Add. MS 46016.
105 Morley to Gladstone, 5 Oct. 1887, BM, Add. MS 44255, f. 222.
106 Macarthy and Praed, *Book of Memories*, pp. 108, 110, 115–6; see also p. 151. McCarthy himself was tired and unwell, and wanted to resign. Parnell prevailed on him to stay on, on the grounds that English public opinion would conclude that he was renouncing the party for reasons he would not state, that Gladstone would be taken aback, and that 'if at this crisis I were at once to resign, the party would be sure to elect as vice-chairman some extreme man' (*ibid.*, p. 115).
107 *Punch*, 18 June 1887.
108 R. B. O'Brien, *Parnell*, ii. pp. 179, 181.
109 *Nation*, 5, 18 Mar. 1887.
110 Morley, *Gladstone*, iii. pp. 376–7.
111 *Nation*, 5 Mar. 1887.
112 *Nation*, 16 Apr. 1887.
113 Irish Party Minutes, 5 May 1887; C. C. O'Brien, *Parnell and his Party*, pp. 243–4, n.5.
114 Morley to Gladstone, 30 May 1887, Gladstone Papers, BM, Add. MS 44255, f. 203.
115 C. C. O'Brien, *Parnell and his Party*, pp. 242–3; *Nation*, 21 May, 11 June 1887.
116 Healy to Maurice Healy, Zurich, 3 July 1887, *Letters and Leaders* Proofs, B97–8. In the published memoirs Healy conflates three separate letters, Cologne (22 July 1887), Constance (30 June 1887), and Zurich (3 July 1887) into a single letter from Cologne (*Letters and Leaders*, i. pp. 274– 5).
117 Healy to Maurice Healy, 5 July 1887, *Letters and Leaders* Proofs, B98.
118 McCarthy to Campbell Praed, n.d., *Book of Memories* Draft; *Book of Memories*, pp. 122–2; *Hansard*, vol. 318, cols. 440–6 (28 July 1887).
119 Healy to Maurice Healy, 27 Aug. 1887, *Letters and Leaders* Proofs, B99.
120 Healy, *Why Ireland is not Free*, p. 18; see also *Nation*, 23 July 1887.

7: THE SPECIAL COMMISSION

1 *Hansard*, vol. 313, cols. 1089–91, 1123–8 (15 Apr. 1887); *Nation*, 23 Apr. 1887.
2 *Letters and Leaders*, i. p. 271; *Nation*, 23 Apr. 1887. Labouchere told Lady Gregory that when asked whether Parnell had written the letters, Healy had retorted 'the

cur – he never had the pluck' (Lady Gregory to W. S. Blunt, 23 Nov. 1888, Lady Gregory, *Seventy Years*, ed. Colin Smythe [Gerrard's Cross, 1974], p. 233). This is likely to owe more to Labouchere's compulsive liberality in the attribution of his own views to others than to anything Healy actually said.

3 Lyons, *Parnell*, pp. 376-7. Over ten years later Healy, in opposing the provision in the Criminal Law Amendment Bill which permitted defendants in criminal trials to give evidence in their own defence, impressionistically recalled Parnell's lame denial of authorship of the letter: 'Anybody who heard Mr. Parnell making that statement, trying to exculpate himself, would admit that such a laboured statement was never made, and that the reasons given to prove that he could not have written the letters were the most ridiculous on record. I remember groaning when I heard him assure the House that he could not have written the Pigott letters, because he did not turn his L's upward. The *Times* produced scores of genuine letters where he did turn his L's upward. The Attorney General assures the House of the great weight which will be attached to the statement of a burglar at the Old Bailey, who has to account for the possession of a jemmy, when this House, by an enormous majority, refused to listen to the statement of one of the greatest statesmen who has appeared in this assembly during the last century'. (*Hansard*, vol. 56, cols. 1022-3 [25 Apr. 1898].) Ironically as Governor-General, Healy on 1 August 1924 signified the King's assent to the Criminal Justice (Evidence) Bill which made equivalent provision in Irish law (Claire Jackson, 'Irish political opposition to the passage of criminal evidence reform at Westminster 1883-98' in *The Common Law Tradition*, ed. John McEldowney [Dublin, 1989], pp. 185-201).

4 *Nation*, 30 Apr., 16 July 1887.

5 Lyons, *Parnell*, pp. 388-9; F. H. O'Donnell, *The Irish Party*, ii. pp. 224-52.

6 *Times*, 9, 10 July 1888; O'Donnell, *The Irish Party*, ii. pp. 239-44; *Hansard*, vol. 328, cols. 575-82 (6 July 1888); *B.D.P.*, 6 July 1888. Herbert Gladstone furnished to Biale correspondence from O'Donnell and a memorandum of an interview in April-May 1882 (Biale to Gladstone, 25 May 1882, n.d., 30 May 1882, Viscount Gladstone Papers, BM, Add. MS 46053, ff. 32, 38, 40). Other nationalists such as Biggar and Davitt also provided assistance to O'Donnell (Special Commission Brief, Quinn Proof, p. 37).

7 *Times*, 6 July 1888.

8 Hamilton diary, 5 July 1888, BM, Add. MS 48649, pp. 23-4.

9 *Times*, 9 July 1888. In the divorce crisis, O'Donnell wrote triumphantly to Herbert Gladstone from Lausanne: 'Two years ago I forced the Parnellites to meet the accusations of the *Times*. Today all the world has about the same opinion of Mr. Parnell that I have all along entertained. Egoist, profligate, liar, treacherous friend, systematic dissembler – this is he, and your father has at length found him out'. He complained that Gladstone's letter to Morley was too mild: 'The debaucher of his friend's wife knew that poor O'Shea, *being a Catholic*, could never remarry again even after divorce. He lied to escape facing O'Shea's pistol. It was out of the £40,000 contributed by the Irish people that he hired the houses . . .' The only sensible observation in this farrago was its conclusion: 'if your father spares him, he will not spare your father' (F. H. O'Donnell to H. Gladstone, 30 Nov. 1890, Viscount Gladstone Papers, BM Add. MS 46053, f. 149). It might be thought that the authorship of a letter of such purblind pomposity did much to acquit O'Donnell of the suspicion of witting complicity with the *Times*.

10 *Letters and Leaders*, i. p. 279; *Times*, 9 July 1888, Davitt at Glasgow Green; *Times*, 24 Aug. 1888; *F.J.*, 29 Sept. 1888.

11 *B.D.P.*, 6 July 1888; Robbins, *Parnell*, pp. 52, 70-1.

12 Labouchere to H. Gladstone, 30 Oct. (1888), Viscount Gladstone Papers, BM, Add. MS 46016, f. 135; Labouchere to W. E. Gladstone, Gladstone Papers, 30 Oct. (1888), BM, Add. MS 56449, f. 214. At the Special Commission Sir Charles Russell cross-examined W. H. O'Shea about a meeting with E. C. Houston, the secretary of the Irish Loyal and Patriotic Union. Houston, O'Shea said, had made reference to rumours linking O'Shea and others – possibly Pigott, although he could not be sure – with the procuring of the letters from Parnell. Asked whether Houston had mentioned any other names, O'Shea added, 'Mr. Philip Callan whom I have not spoken to for years' (*S.C.P.*, vol. 1, paras. 451-94 [31 Oct. 1888]; Robbins, *Parnell*, p. 70).

13 *Letters and Leaders*, i. p. 124. Mitchel Henry, an anti-obstructionist home rule leader who sat for Galway 1871-85 wrote to the *Times* recalling Frank Byrne, the secretary of the National Land League who was complicit in the Phoenix Park murders, as an impecunious reporter in whom Butt had taken a benevolent interest. He surmised sanctimoniously that Byrne was then innocent of involvement in political crime: 'No doubt he fell into an abyss of infamy through the terrible incitements to outrage and crime which I so often denounced in the House of Commons, in the presence of Mr. Parnell and his party' (*Times*, 10 July 1888, Mitchel Henry to ed., 9 July 1888).

14 Special Commission Brief, Proof of Thomas Quinn. When Quinn missed an important division and was reported to have dozed off in the smoking room of the House of Commons, Healy lilted 'Sing, oh hurrah, let England quake,/Tom Quinn's awake, Tom Quinn's awake' (*Letters and Leaders*, i. p. 273).

15 Lyons, *Parnell*, pp. 189, 430; McDonald, *Daily News Dairy*, p. 11, 187-9; *I.C.*, 30 Aug. 1890 (Byrne's composition with his creditors).

16 *Times*, 4 July 1888.

17 Special Commission Brief, Proof of Thomas Quinn. Little is known of the later career of Lysaght Finegan. It appears that not long after his re-election for the Ennis seat he had won in 1879 his health gave way. Healy wrote in November 1882 that 'poor Lysaght Finegan has resigned his seat' (*U.I.*, 4 Nov. 1882).

18 Hamilton diary, 5, 7 July 1888, BM, Add. MS 48649.

19 Morley, *Gladstone*, iii. pp. 396-7.

20 Labouchere to W. E. Gladstone, 27 Oct. (1888), Gladstone Papers, BM, Add. MS 56449, f. 208.

21 *Hansard*, vol. 329, cols. 384-5 (24 July 1888).

22 *Hansard*, vol. 329, cols. 380-94 (24 July 1888).

23 *Hansard*, vol. 329, cols. 1156-60 (31 July 1888); cols. 1172-82 (1 Aug. 1888); col. 1342 (2 Aug. 1888).

24 *Hansard*, vol. 329, col. 1139 (31 July 1888); cols. 1351-3 (2 Aug. 1888).

25 *D.E.*, 2 Aug. 1888.

26 Morley to Gladstone, 9, 10 Aug. 1888, Gladstone Papers, BM, Add. MS 44255, ff. 250, 252.

27 Morley, *Gladstone*, ii. pp. 398-9; Gladstone to Morley, 11 Aug. 1888, copy, Morley to Gladstone, 11 Aug. 1888, Gladstone Papers BM, Add. MS 44255, ff. 256, 260.

28 Morley to Gladstone, 24 Aug. 1888, Gladstone Papers, BM, Add. MS 44255, f. 264; Hamilton diary, 21 Sept. 1888, BM, Add. MS 48650, p. 60.

29 Esher to Stead, 22 Feb. 1889, *Journals and Letters of Reginald Viscount Esher* (2 vols., London, 1934), ed. Maurice V. Brett, i. p. 139; see also Morley to Gladstone, 14 Apr. 1889, Gladstone Papers, BM, Add. MS 44256, f. 7.

30 *Letters and Leaders*, i. pp. 287-90.

31 Harrington to Healy, 18 Oct. 1888, Healy-Sullivan Papers, UCD P6/B/27, set forth

in *Letters and Leaders* Proofs, B109-10 but deleted in the published text; Healy to Maurice Healy, 21 Oct. 1888, in *Letters and Leaders*, i. p. 292. Healy's comment to his father is in his letter of 23 Oct. 1888 (Healy-Sullivan Papers, UCD P6/A/11, deleted from the published text of his memoirs [*Letters and Leaders*], i. p. 294]).

32 Biggar to Healy, 22 Oct. 1888, Healy-Sullivan Papers, UCD P6/B/28, *Letters and Leaders*, i. p. 293; Barry to Healy, 22 Oct. 1888, *Letters and Leaders* Proofs, B111 (original not in Healy-Sullivan Papers).

33 Healy to Maurice Healy snr., 23 Oct. 1888, Healy-Sullivan Papers, UCD P6/A/11, deleted from published text, *Letters and Leaders*, i. p. 294.

34 Labouchere to W. E. Gladstone, 30 Oct. (1888), Gladstone Papers, BM, Add. MS 56449, f. 214.

35 Healy to Maurice Healy snr., 23 Oct. 1888, Healy-Sullivan Papers, UCD P6/A/11, deleted from text published in *Letters and Leaders*, i. p. 294; Healy to Maurice Healy, 23 Oct. 1888, *Letters and Leaders*, i. p. 293.

36 Sophie O'Brien, 'Recollections', p. 201. The same remark is cited and considered by T. P. O'Connor in his *Memoirs*, i. p. 108.

37 *S.C.P.*, vol. 1, pp. 399-411 (1 Nov. 1888); Referee, 25 Nov. 1928.

38 *B.D.P.*, 8 Oct. 1891.

39 Harrington to Healy, 18 Oct. 1888, Healy-Sullivan Papers, UCD P6/B/27; Hamilton diary, 14 May 1889, BM, Add. MS 48650, p. 128. In an interview in 1893, Lewis characterised Parnell as 'a man of the most secretive, suspicious, and distrustful disposition' (Harry How, 'Illustrated Interviews IX – Sir George Lewis', *Strand Magazine* [1893], p. 646).

40 Davitt, *Fall of Feudalism*, p. 535; *Weekly Sun*, 2 Aug. 1896, 'Parnell and Mr. Gladstone' by T. P. O'Connor; *Truth*, 15 Oct. 1891. Parnell told McCarthy he thought Pigott's disappearance a great misfortune as it would prevent them having the whole case out (McCarthy and Praed, *Book of Memories*, p. 175).

41 *S.C.P.*, vol. 1, paras. 383, 425.

42 Chamberlain to W. H. O'Shea, 31 Dec. 1888, NLI MS 5752, f. 377.

43 O'Shea, *Parnell*, ii. pp. 200-1, 214-15; Kee, *Laurel and the Ivy*, pp. 487-9, 493-4, 500. For a prime specimen of O'Shea's humbug, see W. H. O'Shea to W. A. Nally, 4 Feb. 1887, NLI MS 22826.

44 McDonald, *Daily News Diary*, pp. 9-12.

45 Labouchere to W. E. Gladstone, 27 Oct. 1888, Gladstone Papers, BM, Add. MS 56449, f. 208.

46 *D.C.*, 23 Oct. 1888.

47 *D.C.*, 24 Oct. 1888.

48 *S.C.P.*, vol. 1, pp. 297, 301 (30 Oct., 1 Nov. 1888); Healy to Maurice Healy, 30 Oct. 1888, *Letters and Leaders*, i. p. 295.

49 *D.C.*, 31 Oct. 1888.

50 *S.C.P.* vol. 1, pp. 355, 370 (31 Oct. 1888); *D.C.*, 1 Nov. 1888. Of O'Shea's intervention in the controversy between Parnell and Chamberlain in the course of the debates on the Special Commission Bill, the Dublin unionist *Daily Express* had archly enquired: 'What fatal temptation, what appalling indiscretion, led Mr. Parnell to make an enemy of Captain O'Shea?' (*D.E.*, 3 Aug. 1888; see generally Lyons, *Parnell*, pp. 395-402).

51 W. H. O'Shea to K. O'Shea, 2 Nov. 1885, O'Shea, *Parnell*, ii. p. 90; quoted Kee, *Laurel and the Ivy*, pp. 491, 638.

52 *D.C.,* 1 Nov. 1888; Healy to Erina Healy, 31 Oct. 1888, *Letters and Leaders*, i. p. 300; *S.C.P.* pp., vol. 1. pp. 382-3 (31 Oct. 1888).

53 McDonald, *Daily News Diary*, pp. 161, 165.

54 Labouchere to H. Gladstone, 3 Nov. (1888), Viscount Gladstone Papers, BM, Add. MS 46016, f. 136; see also Hesketh Pearson, Labby (London, 1936), pp. 209-10. O'Shea had told the Special Commission that he had destroyed his memoranda relating to the Kilmainham treaty following a hint from Sir William Harcourt that he should do so in anticipation of a parliamentary inquiry into it (MacDonald, *Daily News Diary*, p. 11).

55 James O'Connor, *Recollections of Richard Pigott* (Dublin, 1889), pp. 24-5.

56 *D.T.*, 4 Mar. 1889; McDonald, *Daily News Diary*, pp. 161-9, 349; Lyons, *Parnell*, pp. 417-22. Healy in his memoirs professed his doubts that Pigott had committed suicide, on the unconvincingly lawyerly ground that there was no extradition treaty between Spain and Great Britain (*Letters and Leaders*, i. p. 303).

57 *D.C.*, 27 Feb. 1889; McDonald, *Daily News Diary*, p. 162.

58 *D.T.*, 2 Mar. 1889; MacDonald, *Daily News Diary*, p. 171.

59 Davitt, *Fall of Feudalism*, pp. 586-7; J. Comyns Carr, *Some Eminent Victorians* (London, 1908), p. 187.

60 MacDonald, *Daily News Diary*, p. 165.

61 MacDonald, *Daily News Diary*, p. 169.

62 McCarthy and Praed, *Book of Memories*, p. 175.

63 Sir Edward Clarke, *The Story of my Life* (London, 1918), pp. 275-6; Lyons, *Parnell*, pp. 425-6.

64 *Truth*, 21 Mar. 1889.

65 Harcourt to Gladstone, 9 Mar. 1889, Gladstone Papers, BM, Add. MS 44201, f. 216.

66 *D.T.*, 2 Mar. 1889.

67 *D.T.*, 2 Mar. 1889.

68 *Letters and Leaders*, i. p. 305; W. O'Brien, *Evening Memories*, pp. 409-10; Hamilton diary, 4 Dec. 1889, 16 Jan. 1890, BM, Add. MS 48650, 48652. On Russell's approach, see also The Earl of Oxford and Asquith, *Memories and Reflections* (2 vols., London, 1928), i. pp. 77-8. The overconfidence of the counsel involved may have owed something to the curious fact that the views of Hannen and the Attorney-General frequently found their way to George Lewis. Hamilton cited his table talk: 'He was saying it was extraordinary how everything came round to him. Ladies and especially Irish ladies were the best tell-tales: neither Judge Hannen nor the Attorney General could ventilate any opinion, however quietly given, without it being reported to him somehow' (Hamilton diary, 14 May 1889, BM, Add. MS 48650). Nothing impairs the judgement of a barrister quite so much as the possession of information he is not meant to have.

69 *S.C.P.*, vol. 6, pp. 409-63 (2-12 Apr. 1889); *Letters and Leaders*, i. p. 305; Robbins, *Parnell*, p. 108.

70 *S.C.P.*, vol. 7, p. 244 (3 May 1889); Morley to Gladstone, 4 May 1880, Gladstone Papers, BM, Add. MS 44256, f. 9; Mary Gladstone, *Letters and Diaries*, ed. Lucy Masterman (London, 1930), pp. 408-9; Lyons, *Parnell*, pp. 427-9. This admission prompted Algernon Charles Swinburne to compose 'The Ballade of Truthful Charles' whose first stanza ran:

> Charles Stewart, the crownless king whose hand
> Sways Erin's sceptre – so they sing,
> The bards of holy Liarland –
> Can give his tongue such scope and sting,
> That all who fear its touch must dread it:
> But now we hear it witnessing –
> 'I meant to cheat you when I said it'.

The poem asserted an equivalence in mendacity between Parnell and Pigott, 'splashed black with mud they fling'. Swinburne wisely chose not to publish this undistinguished but instructive 'ballad' which appeared posthumously (Algernon Charles Swinburne, *Posthumous Poems*, ed. Edmund Gosse and Thomas James Wise [London, 1917], pp. 151-2).

71 MacDonald, *Daily News Diary*, pp. 296-9; Hamilton diary, 13 July 1889, BM, Add. MS 48651, p. 41.

72 See especially Margaret O'Callaghan, *British High Politics and a Nationalist Ireland* (Cork, 1994), pp. 104-21; Lyons, *Parnell*, pp. 429-32.

73 *Parnell v Walter & Anor*, 24 QBD [1890] 441-53.

74 *B.D.P.*, 4 Feb. 1890; Hamilton diary, 3 Feb. 1890, BM, Add. MS 48653. Moreover the settlement of the action in advance of the report of the Special Commission proved well advised.

75 *Hansard*, vol. 341, cols. 51-119 (11 Feb. 1890); Hamilton diary, 12 Feb. 1890, BM, Add. MS 48652; *B.D.P.*, 14 Feb. 1890.

76 *B.D.P*, 14, 19 Feb., 24 Mar. 1890.

77 Morley to Gladstone, 18 Feb. 1890, Gladstone Papers, BM, Add. MS 44256, f. 14.

78 *B.D.P.*, 24 Mar. 1890.

79 *F.J.*, 23 Apr. 1889.

80 Davitt, *Fall of Feudalism*, p. 601; *S.C.P.*, vols. 8, 9, *passim*.

81 *F.J.*, 17 July 1889. *The Irish Catholic* expressed a similar view (*I.C.*, 20 July 1889).

8: BEFORE THE SPLIT

1 R. B. O'Brien, *Parnell*, ii, p. 334. The 'old Fenian' is almost certainly John O'Leary: see Birkenhead, *Contemporary Personalities* (London, 1924), p. 212.

2 *N.Y.T.*, 7 Aug. 1887. Of Healy's brother Maurice, Frederic wrote: 'He is above middle height, slender, and with stooping shoulders, and has a thin shrewd face, fringed with a thin brownish beard that has never been shaved'.

3 O'Connor, *Memoirs*, i. p. 110; Tynan, *Twenty-Five Years*, p. 147.

4 *N.Y.T.*, 7 Aug. 1887. Over two decades later, Frank Cruise O'Brien was to write: 'Mr. Healy is eminent for his tongue. He makes it a scorpion sting, a scourge of venom, a rod of bitter steel' (*Leader*, 9 Apr. 1910).

5 H. W. Lucy, 'Orators in the House, and Others', *Universal Review*, Jan. 1889, pp. 45-6; Lucy, *Salisbury Parliament*, pp. 142-3 (31 Dec. 1888).

6 O'Connor, *Memoirs*, i. p. 107.

7 *N.Y.T.*, 7 Aug. 1887.

8 R. B. O'Brien, 'Federal Union with Ireland', *Nineteenth Century* (Jan. 1886), p. 35; Katharine Tynan, 'William O'Brien M.P.', *Catholic World*, vol. 48, p. 157 (Nov. 1888).

9 T. M. Healy, 'Jubilee Time in Ireland', *Contemporary Review*, vol. 57, p. 129 (Jan. 1887).

10 *F.J.*, 26 Sept. 1888, NL; *F.J.*, 29 Apr. 1889, Grandard.

11 *F.J.*, 30 June 1886.

12 *F.J.*, 10 Oct. 1887; see also Healy's superbly comic description of the emaciated grand juries of Munster, *F.J.*, 3 Apr. 1888 (Mitchelstown); see also *F.J.*, 27 Sept. 1887, Tullow. Healy likewise expressed the hope of seeing the mortgagee of Lord Granard 'squeezing him out as you would squeeze out a lemon or an orange, and when they throw away the skin I hope to see you give it a kick and send it to its proper place' (*Times*, 8 Nov. 1887, quoted Mark Bence Jones, *Twilight of the Ascendancy* [London, 1987], p. 69).

13 *F.J.*, 27 Sept. 1887, Tullow.

14 *F.J.*, 17 Feb. 1886.

15 *F.J.*, 17 July 1889, NL.
16 *F.J.*, 27 Sept. 1887, Tullow.
17 *F.J.*, 10 Oct. 1887, 17 July 1889.
18 *F.J.*, 7 Oct. 1890, meeting of the Irish party, Dublin.
19 *F.J.*, 26 Sept. 1888.
20 *Nation*, 27 Aug. 1887; see also 12 Mar., 11 June 1887. W. F. Dennehy wrote two polemics against Balfour which attested to the Chief Secretary's effectiveness in needling nationalist commentators: *Nation*, 6 Apr. 1887, 'W.F.D.' to ed., 'Viva Coercion'; 3 Dec. 1887, W. F. Dennedy to ed., d. 28 Nov., 'Mr. Balfour – A Psychological Study'. For a very shrewd assessment of Balfour's provoking indifference to the barbs of Healy and others, see M. J. McCarthy, *Mr. Balfour's Rule in Ireland* (Dublin and London, 1891). William O'Brien referred to 'the soubriquet of "Buckshot", by which Mr. Forster became known, and which seems to have wounded him as the nickname "Bloody" is said to tickle Mr. Balfour highly' (William O'Brien, 'The Forster Tragedy in Ireland', *Westminster Review*, vol. 130, p. 351 [Sept. 1888]).
21 *Hansard*, vol. 331, col. 97 (3 Dec. 1888). In an onslaught on Balfour's predecessor Healy had declared: 'He is thinking not of the Irish people, but of the effect of his language on the English constituencies, and of what will benefit his miserable Party. He is thinking "Will a little bloodshed in Ireland cement the Liberal alliance?" (*Cries of 'Shame' and 'Order!'*)'. Under pressure from the chair Healy made a highly tentative expression of regret (*Hansard*, vol. 311, col. 1195 [3 Mar. 1887]).
22 *F.J.*, 13 Feb. 1889, NL. He devised the verb to 'Cromwellise' in attacking Balfour. Not to be outdone, William Martin Murphy referred to a magistrate as 'out-Heroding Herod' at the same meeting.
23 Gray's Inn's Admissions and Calls; 'Memorial of T. M. Healy, 18 October 1884, certified by D. B. Sullivan BL and Sergeant Hemphill, King's Inns, Dublin; *Irish Law Times*, vol. 18, p. 578 (15 Nov. 1884); T. M. Healy, 'Some Recollections of Gray's Inn', *Graya*, IV, p. 10 (Easter 1929); *Letters and Leaders*, i. pp. 95-6, 218.
24 See in particular *In re John Sullivan*, 22 *L.R.I.*, 98; *Nation*, 11 Feb. 1888; *In re Thomas Heaphy & Ors*, 22 *L.R.I.*, 510; see generally *Nation*, 23 June 1888; *The Star*, 23 June 1888; V. T. H. Delaney, Christopher Palles (Dublin, 1960), pp. 97-106; for a rare but illuminating attack by Healy on Palles, see *F.J.*, 19 Jan. 1887. One pseudonymous writer commented that the Exchequer had 'of late years become a sort of permanent court of jail delivery' (Rhadamanthus, *Our Judges* [Dublin, 1890], p. 23). At least in the higher courts, judges and barristers surveyed with ironic equanimity the shifting balance of political power. When an adjournment to the following Friday was being discussed, Baron Dowse interposed that 'Mr. Healy may be Solicitor General before next Friday'. Stephen Ronan K.C. for the crown replied, 'then we will change sides, My Lord' (*Nation*, 30 June 1888).
25 *F.J.*, 17 July 1880, NL.
26 *F.J.*, 19 Sept. 1887, Newtown, Co. Waterford.
27 *F.J.*, 19 Sept. 1887; M. McDonnell Bodkin, *Recollections of an Irish Judge* (London, 1914), p. 161.
28 *F.J.*, 23 Jan. 1889; W. O'Brien, *Evening Memories*, pp. 367-72.
29 *Nation*, 23 Feb. 1889; *U.I.*, 23 Feb. 1889.
30 *F.J.*, 18 Oct.–1 Nov. 1889; *N.P.*, 8, 9 July 1891; *F.J.*, 8, 9 July 1891.
31 *F.J.*, 31 Oct. 1889.
32 M. J. Kenny to John J. Dunne, 16 Nov. 1889, NLI MS 19046 (7).
33 *F.J.*, 20 Nov. 1889. Peter ('The Packer') O'Brien, who appeared for the prosecution pointed out in his memoirs that McFadden was the principal victim of the Maryborough pleas: 'Although he escaped sentence, he received ample punishment.

His parishioners resented that he, for whom the crime had been committed, should go free while others suffered. A feeling of hostility sprang up amongst his flock and eventually he had to leave the parish' (*Reminiscences of the Rt. Hon. Lord O'Brien (of Kilfenora)*, ed. Georgina O'Brien [London, 1916], p. 96). M. J. Kenny wrote that the outcome had destroyed the authority of McFadden as a parish priest (M. J. Kenny to John J. Dunne, 16 Nov. 1889, NLI MS 19046 [7]). For a general account, see Proinsias O'Gallchobhair, *History of Landlordism in Donegal* (Donegal, 1962, re-issued 1975).

34 *N.P.*, 9 July 1891; *Letters and Leaders*, ii. p. 375; *N.P.*, 10 Mar. 1892; *N.P.*, 8 Aug. 1891 (Arran Quay NL). The issue of damages, on which the jury had disagreed, had gone to arbitration. By way of comparison, in David Sheehy's action against the *Freeman* where a lodgement of £100 was narrowly beaten, the Lord Chief Justice commented: 'The £100 paid into Court seems enormous. I have long experience at the Bar, and I never experienced anything like it paid into court in a libel case' (*N.P.*, 29 Jan. 1892).

35 Parnell to K. O'Shea, 6 Jan. 1886, enclosed with K. O'Shea to Gladstone, 7 Jan. 1886, Gladstone Papers, BM, Add. MS 44269, ff. 275, 277. Gladstone replied that the proposal contained in the enclosure was 'indeed a large and important one', but that he was not in a position to engage in negotiations (Gladstone to K. O'Shea, 9 Jan. 1886, Gladstone Papers, BM, Add. MS 56447, f. 84).

36 *Hansard*, vol. 302, cols. 158-60 (21 Jan. 1886).

37 *F.J.*, 11 May 1891.

38 Healy to Maurice Healy, 22 June 1887, *Letters and Leaders* Proofs, B97.

39 *Hansard*, vol. 331, cols. 165-7, 173-4 (26 Nov. 1888).

40 Hamilton diary, entries for 16, 20, 25 Feb., 15 Apr. 1890, Hamilton Papers, BM, Add. MS 48652.

41 *Hansard*, vol. 343, col. 1654 (29 Apr. 1890).

42 Morley to Gladstone, 14 Apr. 1890, Gladstone Papers, BM, Add. MS 44256; see also *B.D.P.*, 15 Apr. 1890.

43 Morley, *Recollections*, i. p. 245.

44 *Hansard*, vol. 343, cols. 980-95 (21 Apr. 1890).

45 *Hansard*, vol. 343, cols. 1288-303; Morley, *Recollections*, i. p. 245; *B.D.P.*, 23, 25, 26 Apr. 1890.

46 *B.D.P.*, 23, 28 Apr. 1890.

47 Hamilton diary, entry for 23 Apr. 1890; see also his entry for 25 Feb. 1890, Hamilton Papers, BM, Add. MS 48652 pp. 125, 70.

48 *Hansard*, vol. 343, col. 1365 (24 Apr. 1890); see also col. 1557 (28 Apr. 1890). Robbins in the *Birmingham Daily* Post quoted one of the Irish leaders (probably Healy) as denying any division in the party: 'This, as far as it is based upon the fact that the Nationalists did not greatly cheer Mr. Parnell last night, he ridicules, and asks whether it is usual to applaud purely arithmetical statements any more than syllogisms in logic or demonstrations in Euclid' (*B.D.P.*, 23 Apr. 1890).

49 *Hansard*, vol. 343, cols. 1553-75 (28 Apr. 1890).

50 Lucy, *Salisbury Parliament*, pp. 270-1.

51 *Hansard*, vol. 346, cols. 1516-23 (11 July 1890).

52 *B.D.P.*, 14 July 1890.

53 *B.D.P.*, 15 July 1890.

54 *B.D.P.*, 15 July 1890.

55 Morley, *Recollections*, i. pp. 251-6; Morley to Gladstone, 13 Nov. 1890, Gladstone Papers, BM, Add. MS 44256, ff. 63-7.

56 *F.J.*, 26 Mar. 1890, NL.

57 *N.Y.T.*, 13 July 1890, quoted but wrongly dated in Lyons, *Parnell*, pp. 438–9. Healy knew Frederic from 1884, and visited Maamtrasna with him that year (*N.Y.T.*, 7 Aug. 1884; *Letters and Leaders*, i. p. 187). He exempted Frederic from his strictures on press correspondents on the Irish question (T. M. Healy, 'The Prospect for Ireland', *Catholic World*, vol. 42, p. 45 [Dec. 1885]). In October 1890, Healy wrote Gladstone soliciting a favourable notice of a historical novel by Frederic, whom he described as a friend he valued highly, and 'staunchly friendly to the Irish cause' (Healy to W. E. Gladstone, 12 Oct. 1890, Gladstone Papers, BM, Add. MS 44511, f. 81). Born the year after Healy in Utica, New York, Frederic became a novelist of some distinction. He died in London in 1898 at the age of forty-two (*N.Y.T.*, 20 Oct. 1898; Healy to Maurice Healy, 30 Oct. 1898, Healy typescripts).

58 *I.C.*, 20 Sept. 1890, Healy to Philadelphia Times, d. 2 Sept. 1890; *I.C.* 2 Aug. 1890; *N.Y.T.*, 3 Aug. 1890; Callanan, *Parnell Split*, p. 283. There is nothing to corroborate the assertion of M. J. Kenny, that Parnell 'knowing the writer and his relations with Healy' had written to Frederic seeking the authority for his remarks, and that this had led to a visit by Frederic to Healy in Dublin 'for a Council of War in Great Charles Street at which the men of Bantry assembled in their thousands and bound themselves like Kataline and his confederation in wine and blood to contest the supreme rule of Parnell and his friends. It is going to develop a little further and I am inclined to think a little unfavourably for the clansmen of Iveragh' (M. J. Kenny to J. J. Dunne, 24 July 1890, NLI MS 19046 [7], quoted and considered in Lyons, *Parnell*, p. 438). Thwarted ambition drove Kenny to the wider reaches of crudity, as in his profession of ennui: 'Dublin is as dull as hell. It is but the image reflected in a shit pond of a real capital, the classes in this city are utterly base' (M. J. Kenny to J. J. Dunne, 24 Jan. 1890, NLI MS 10946 [7]).

59 *U.I.*, 26 May 1888.

60 Healy to Maurice Healy, 3 July 1887, *Letters and Leaders* Proofs, B98.

61 *F.J.*, 23 May 1888, NL; see also *F.J.*, 28 May 1888, Waterford.

62 *F.J.*, 28 May 1888, Waterford.

63 *F.J.*, 23 May 1888.

64 Lyons, *Dillon*, p. 94.

65 *F.J.*, 11 Sept. 1889.

66 *F.J.*, 25 Sept. 1889, NL, Healy's laical temerity was duly reproved, though in friendly terms, by the *Irish Catholic* (*I.C.*, 28 Sept. 1889); see also *F.J.*, 1 Oct. 1889, *I.C.*, 5 Oct. 1889.

67 *Hansard*, vol. 348, cols. 554–69 (11 Aug. 1890).

68 Lloyd George to Margaret Lloyd George, 12 Aug. 1890, *Lloyd George Family Letters*, ed. Kenneth Morgan (Cardiff and London, 1973), p. 34.

69 *Weekly News*, 28 Apr. 1888, *I.C.*, 5 May 1888.

70 *Nation*, 19, 26 Apr. 1890.

71 *I.C.*, 5 May 1888.

72 *I.C.*, 2 Mar. 1918; Cornelius Dennehy, *Letters on the Banking Systems and Industrial Resources of Ireland, Taxation of Ireland etc.* (Dublin, 1870); *Nation*, 13 Sept. 1890.

73 *I.C.*, 21 June 1889; *F.J.*, 3 Oct. 1893, Healy to *F.J.*, d. 2 Oct.

74 *I.C.*, 2 Mar. 1918; Walsh to Dillon, 6 Apr. 1894, Dillon Papers, TCD MS 6765, f. 62; see also Dillon to O'Brien, 21 Jan. 1895, Dillon Papers, TCD MS 6738.

75 *I.C.*, 12 Apr. 1890.

76 *I.C.*, 7 Sept. 1889.

77 *I.C.*, 18 Aug.–1 Sept. 1888, 28 June 1890.

78 *I.C.*, 15 Sept.–1 Dec. 1888.

79 *I.C.*, 5 Apr. 1890; see also *I.C.*, 3, 10, 17 May 1891.

80 *I.C.*, 24 May 1890, article by 'WFD'.
81 Minutes of the Irish Party, 11 Feb. 1890.
82 *F.J.*, 20 Feb. 1890; *B.D.P.* 20 Feb. 1890.
83 McCarthy to Campbell Praed, Feb. 1890, McCarthy and Praed, *Book of Memories*, p. 219.
84 *U.I.*, 22 Feb. 1890; Healy to Maurice Healy snr., 28 Feb. 1890, Healy-Sullivan Papers, UCD P6/A/13, quoted in part *Letters and Leaders*, i. p. 313.
85 Healy to Maurice Healy snr., 19 Nov. 1900, Healy-Sullivan Papers, UCD P6/A/35, modified *Letters and Leaders*, i. p. 452.
86 Healy was infuriated by Parnell's later invocations of Biggar's memory, as in Parnell's reference in the speech at which he was re-elected leader of the Irish party on 23 November 1890 to 'the fight he and his dead friend, Joseph Biggar, commenced'. In his memoirs Healy reproached Parnell for his failure to attend Biggar's requiem, without alluding to what he elsewhere referred to as Parnell's 'irrepressible horror' of funerals. He was intrigued by Parnell's statement to J. M. Tuohy of the *Freeman's Journal* on the eve of the break-up of the party that Biggar had appeared to him (*Letters and Leaders*, i. pp. 313, 323, 335; Healy, 'A Great Man's Fancies').
87 Hamilton diary, entry for 6 July 1889, Hamilton Papers, BM, Add. MS 48651, pp. 33-4; see also entry for 25 July 1889, p. 51.
88 McCarthy and Praed, *Book of Memories*, pp. 186-7. The *National Press* after Parnell's death alleged that the Irish party's support of Gladstone on the royal grants was procured by Parnell against the wishes of the majority. It claimed that Parnell, having been absent for some days prior to the vote, 'glided' to his place minutes before the division, and told a colleague that in the absence of a decision of the party, he himself proposed to vote in favour of the grants. His colleagues followed for the sake of unity (*N.P.*, 8 Jan. 1892). McCarthy's memoirs however make clear that he and other Irish members were aware of 'the combined opinion of Gladstone and Parnell'. It was in Parnell's obvious interest to avoid a party decision: even if he could have commanded a majority, it would hardly have been prudent for the party to take an official position in favour of the royal grants.
89 Hamilton diary, entry for 14 May 1889, Hamilton Papers, BM, Add. MS 48650.
90 *Hansard*, vol. 283, cols. 970-1 (17 Aug. 1883); vol. 58, col. 31 (18 May 1898).
91 *Hansard*, vol. 336, cols. 1749-50 (3 June 1889).
92 Irish Party Minutes, 9 Aug. 1889; *Hansard*, vol. 339, col. 1697 (19 Aug. 1889); Robbins, *Parnell*, pp. 174-5; *F.J.*, 17 Jan. 18901, Tralee.
93 *Hansard*, vol. 348, cols. 1080 et seq. (14 Aug. 1890); *B.D.P.*, 16 Aug. 1890.
94 *F.J.*, 30 Aug. 1890, NL; *F.J.*, 23 Aug. 1890; Healy to *F.J.*, d. 18 Aug.; see also Murphy to *F.J.*, d. 18 Aug.
95 *F.J.*, 27 Aug., 25 Sept. 1890.
96 *Nation*, 15 Sept. 1888, Knockaroo, Queen's County, 8 Sept.
97 *Hansard*, vol. 304, col. 1216 (9 Apr. 1886).
98 *F.J.*, 5 May, 16 June 1886; 12 Oct. 1887; see also *Nation*, 20, 27 Aug. 1887.
99 *F.J.*, 29 Dec. 1886, Glasgow.
100 *F.J.*, 7 Feb. 1887, Tullow.
101 *F.J.*, 1 Dec. 1886, Mountjoy Ward, NL.
102 *Nation*, 23, 30 Apr. 1887. T. D. Sullivan subsequently embarked on a somewhat comical revisionist project, the re-writing of his 'God Save Ireland': 'It was written at a time when the relations between the two countries was very strained, and I would gladly see it superseded by another version of the anthem which I have written, but somehow or other the people will not take to it, and the new version remains at the present time almost unknown' (*P.M.G.*, 27 May 1889).

103 Morley to Dillon, 10 Oct. 1888, Dillon Papers, TCD, MS 6798.
104 Healy to W. E. Gladstone, 13 Aug. 1888, BM Add. MS 44487, f. 161. W. E. Gladstone to Healy, 14 Aug. 1888, Healy-Sullivan Papers, UCD P6/A/20.
105 McCarthy to Campbell Praed, 2 Dec. 1888, McCarthy and Praed, *Book of Memories*, p. 204.
106 Lyons, Parnell, pp. 450–1; Gladstone memorandum, 23 Dec. 1889, Gladstone Papers, BM, Add. MS 44,773, ff. 170–1.
107 Healy to Maurice Healy snr., 24 Dec. 1888, Healy-Sullivan Papers, UCD P6/A/12.
108 Hamilton diary, entry for 17 June 1890, Hamilton Papers, BM, Add. MS 48653, p. 41; for Healy's speech see *Hansard,* vol. 345, cols. 1196-201 (17 June 1890). Healy's forcible civilisation involved submitting to a fatuous discourse by Gladstone on Walter Scott, and in particular on *The Bride of Lammermoor and Kenilworth*, which Gladstone regarded as his *chefs-d'oeuvre:* 'Aeschylus was the only man who could have written the first, and Shakespeare the second'. This is presumably the dinner which Healy in his memoirs refers to as having taken place in 1893 (*Letters and Leaders*, ii. pp. 369-7). Healy was not the only Irish member to dine with Gladstone. William O'Brien wrote in November 1888 to Herbert Gladstone that he was 'much annoyed to find that the newspapers had got hold of the fact that I had the privilege of dining with your father last night', and denied any responsibility for the disclosure (O'Brien to H. Gladstone, 21 Nov. 1888, Viscount Gladstone Papers, BM, Add. MS 46053, f. 98).
109 *F.J.*, 23 Mar. 1891, W. A. McDonald to ed.
110 Edward Byrne to Theophilus McWeeney, 26 Nov. 1889, McWeeney Papers, NLI MS 21936.
111 Byrne, *Parnell*, pp. 12–17; *F.J.*, 18, 19 Dec. 1889.
112 *B.D.P.*, 7 May, 24 June 1890.
113 Irish Party Minutes, 11 Mar, 12 July 1887; 14, 21 June 1888, 12 Aug. 1889; *U.I.*, 8 Feb. 1890; *Hansard*, vol. 224, col. 146, quoted in Claire Jackson 'Irish political opposition to the passage of criminal evidence reform at Westminster, 1883-98' in the *Common Law Tradition*, ed. John McEldowney (Dublin, 1989), p. 195; see also Parnell to Joseph Kenny, 19 Jan. 1888, in R. B. O'Brien, *Parnell*, ii. p. 181. Among Parnell's lesser known functions was keeping the peace among his lieutenants. A letter to Peter McDonald, the member for Sligo North, to resolve a dispute with Mr. Joseph Kenny, who then sat for Cork South, reveals Parnell's social tact, and his almost eighteenth-century manner.

> 'My Dear Sir,
> 'I had a conversation with Dr. Kenny when he was last in London, with reference to the unhappy dispute which has so unfortunately arisen between you and him.
> 'Dr. Kenny then assured me that he was quite willing to withdraw any expression towards yourself which you might consider of an injurious character, if I thought he ought to do so.
> 'I am therefore of opinion that you may regard these expressions as having been withdrawn by Dr. Kenny, and that you need not give yourself any further concern about the matter.
> 'I am my dear Sir,
> 'Yours very truly
> 'Chas. S. Parnell'

(Parnell to Peter McDonald, 1 Mar. 1888. I am grateful to Fiona Reddington for drawing this letter, which is in private hands, to my attention.)
114 *F.J.*, 14, 17 June 1890; Robbins, *Parnell*, pp. 30–2. See Callanan, *Parnell Split*, p. 262. Conservative politicians exaggerated the possibility of exploiting what was

as much an institutional contest as a personal rivalry between the ecclesiastic and the politician. Randolph Churchill according to Labouchere characterised Walsh as 'a very ambitious man. He will never permanently submit to the ascendancy of Parnell'. (Labouchere to H. Gladstone, 22 Dec. 1885, Gladstone Papers, BM, Add. MS 46016, f. 103).

115 *F.J.*, 20 June 1890; *Nation*, 28 June 1890; Lyons, *Parnell*, pp. 468–9.
116 *Nation*, 27 July 1889, Edinburgh, 20 July.
117 Healy, *Why Ireland is Not Free*, p. 27; *Letters and Leaders*, i. p. 318.
118 Healy to Mrs. W. H. Lucy, 26 May 1900, H. W. Lucy, *Diary of a Journalist* (3 vols., London, 1922), ii. p. 153.
119 Thorold, *Labouchere*, p. 329; Healy to Maurice Healy, 2 Sept. 1887, *Letters and Leaders* Proofs, B100.
120 Lucy, *Salisbury Parliament*, p. 23 (9 Feb. 1888), p. 33 (23 Feb. 1888); see also, for a later period, Lucy, *Unionist Parliament*, pp. 107–8, 357.
121 *D.E.*, 15 Aug. 1890.
122 Lyons, *Parnell*, pp. 432–3; O'Brien to Dillon, 4 Aug. 1889, Dillon Papers, TCD MS 6736, f. 28.
123 J. J. Clancy to 'Dr.' (Joseph Kenny), 3 Sept. 1889, Gill Papers, NLI 13500 (7).
124 O'Brien to T. P. Gill, n.d., Gill Papers, NLI MS 13492 (11); Lyons, *Parnell*, pp. 432–6; W. O'Brien, *Evening Memories*, pp. 428–9.
125 O'Brien to Dillon, 8 Mar. 1890, Dillon Papers, TCD MS 6736.
126 *F.J.*, 17 July, 16 Sept. 1889.
127 Healy to Maurice Healy, 27 Aug. 1887, *Letters and Leaders* Proofs, B99.
128 O'Brien to T. P. Gill, 14 Aug. 1890, Gill Papers, NLI MS 13478 (8).
129 Morley to Gladstone, 13 Nov. 1890, Gladstone Papers, BM, Add. MS 44256, ff. 63–7; Morley, *Recollections*, i. p. 251.
130 Lyons, *Dillon*, p. 111; O'Connor, *Memoirs*, ii. p. 293; Sophie O'Brien, 'Recollections', p. 158.

9: DIVORCE

1 Edward Clarke, *The Story of My Life* (London, 1918), p. 293. James Joyce likewise observed: 'They did not throw him to the English wolves. They tore him to pieces themselves' (James Joyce, *The Critical Writings of James Joyce*, ed. Ellsworth Mason and Richard Ellmann [London, 1959], pp. 223). The quotation is from Joyce's 'L'Ombra di Parnell', published in *Il Piccolo della Sera*, 16 May 1912.
2 *F.J.*, 30 Dec. 1889; *D.E.*, 31 Dec. 1889.
3 *F.J.*, 31 Dec. 1889.
4 *F.J.*, 4 Jan. 1890; B.D.P., 4 Feb. 1890.
5 Hamilton diary, entry for 1 Jan. 1890, Hamilton Papers, BM, Add. MS 48652; *Times*, 3 Feb. 1927.
6 *P.M.G.*, 30 Dec. 1890; M. J. Kenny to John J. Dunne, 16 Nov. 1889, NLI MS 10946 (7).
7 Tynan, *Memories*, pp. 15–16.
8 *F.J.*, 31 Dec. 1889; O'Brien to Dillon, 7 Jan. 1890, Dillon Papers, TCD MS 6736, f. 31; see also O'Brien to Gill, 30 Dec. 1889, Gill Papers, NLI MS 13506 (2).
9 Parnell to O'Brien, 14 Jan. 1890, in W. O'Brien, *Evening Memories* at p. 366; referred to also in W. O'Brien, *Olive Branch in Ireland*, p. 2; O'Brien to Gill, 'Sat' (late Jan. 1890), Gill Papers, NLI MS 13478 (5).
10 Davitt, *Fall of Feudalism*, p. 637; W. T. Stead, 'The Story of an Incident in the Home Rule Cause', *Review of Reviews*, ii. (Dec. 1890), p. 600; Lyons, *Parnell*, pp. 463, 465–7.

11 *F.J.*, 30 Dec. 1889; *U.I.*, 4 Jan. 1890.

12 *U.I.*, 10 Jan. 1890; see also Gill to Tuohy, 3 Jan. 1890, NLI MS 3882 (13). A letter from Parnell to the clerk of the Ennis Union to the effect that the allegations contained in the petition 'insofar as it concerns public bodies, may be more advantageously met with the deadly weapon of silent contempt', published in the unionist Dublin *Daily Express*, was branded a forgery by *United Ireland* (*B.D.P.*, 9 Jan. 1890; *U.I.*, 11 Jan. 1890).

13 McCarthy to Campbell Praed, Jan. 1890, McCarthy and Praed, *Book of Memories*, p. 213.

14 McCarthy to Campbell Praed, Jan. 1890, McCarthy and Praed, *Book of Memories*, p. 214.

15 Hamilton diary, entry for 3 Feb. 1890, Hamilton Papers, BM, Add. MS 48653; Morley to Harcourt, 3 Feb. 1890, A. G. Gardiner, *Life of Sir William Harcourt* (2 vols., London, 1923), ii. p. 81.

16 Hamilton diary, entry for 21 Mar. 1890, Hamilton Papers, BM, Add. MS 48653; Hamilton, *Diary*, iii. p. 112.

17 Sophie O'Brien, *Recollections*, pp. 120-7; T. P. Gill, 'William O'Brien, Some Aspects', *Studies*, vol. 17, p. 605 (Dec. 1928); W. S. Blunt, *The Land War in Ireland* (London, 1912), pp. 447-8, quoted W. O'Brien *Evening Memories*, p. 472, n. 1; W. O'Brien, *Olive Branch in Ireland*, p. 2, n. 1.

18 *F.J.*, 28 June 1890; *Nation*, 5 July 1890; W. O'Brien, *Olive Branch in Ireland*, p. 2.

19 Morley to Gladstone, 14, 23 Sept. 1890, Gladstone Papers, BM, Add. MS 44256, f. 55; *F.J.*, 7 Oct. 1890; Nation, 11 Oct. 1890; *U.I.*, 11 Oct. 1890; Irish Party Minutes, 6 Oct. 1890; McCarthy to Campbell Praed, 5 Oct. 1890, McCarthy and Praed, *Book of Memories*, p. 252.

20 Morley to Gladstone, 3, 13 Nov. 1890, Gladstone Papers, BM, Add. MS 44256, ff. 60, 63-7; Morley memorandum, in Morley, *Recollections*, i. pp. 251-6.

21 Harrison, *Parnell Vindicated*, pp. 128-9, 171; O'Shea, *Parnell*, ii. pp. 157-61 *et passim*. F. S. L. Lyons, like Harrison, accepts in the substance her account (Lyons, *Parnell*, p. 461). In an interview to promote her book, she characterised Parnell in terms redolent of Madame Bovary: 'Parnell the lover was ever a "most parfait gentil knight", always most gentle, tender and considerate; but even here was sternly compelling, fiercely jealous, uncompromising and passionate, brooking nothing that stood between us, giving all and exacting all' (*Daily Sketch*, 18 May 1914).

22 *D.T.*, 9 Feb. 1921.

23 Harrison, *Parnell Vindicated*, p. 108.

24 *Journals and Letters of Reginald Viscount Esher*, ed. M. V. Brett (London, 1934), i. p. 142.

25 *D.T.*, 9 Feb. 1921.

26 Harrison, *Parnell Vindicated*, p. 151. George Henry Lewis (1833-1911) was knighted in 1893. The friend and solicitor of the Prince of Wales, he was painted by Sargent, and caricatured by Beerbohm, and in *Vanity Fair* by 'Spy'. The Lewises had been early friends and patrons of Oscar Wilde, although he did not retain Lewis in his calamitous joust with the Marquess of Queensbury. Wilde said of him: 'George Lewis? Brilliant. Formidable. Concerned in every great cause in England. Oh – he knows all about us, and he forgives us all' (quoted John Juxon, *Lewis and Lewis* [London, 1983], p. 15).

27 Morley to Gladstone, 3 Nov. 1890, BM, Add. MS 44256, f. 60.

28 Harrison, *Parnell Vindicated*, pp. 146-7; Lyons, *Parnell*, pp. 458-63.

29 *Times*, 14, 17 Nov. 1890. From the *Times* report it appears that Edward Clarke is incorrect in suggesting in his memoires that Katharine O'Shea's defence was initially a simple denial which was later amended to extend to the additional grounds

(Edward Clarke, *The Story of My Life*, p. 289), but it is clear that the first allusion to Anna Steele was in the further particulars of 25 July.

30 Harrison, *Parnell Vindicated*, pp. 128-9; Edward Clarke, *The Story of My Life*, p. 289; Lyons, *Parnell*, p. 462. For public rumours of a settlement, see *B.D.P.*, 22 Apr. 1890. *Pace* Lyons, Clarke did not believe that his client would not appear in court; this is rather a view which Clarke attributed to the solicitors for the other side.

31 Morley to Gladstone, 3 Nov. 1890, BM, Add. MS 44256, f. 60.

32 *Times*, 14 Nov. 1890; *P.M.G.*, 14 Nov. 1890.

33 Edward Clarke, *The Story of My Life*, p. 289; A. E. Pease, *Elections and Recollections* (London, 1932), p. 276. Pease's account is based on a contemporaneous note. Labouchere attributed to Parnell a comment similar to that quoted by Lockwood: Parnell was quoted as saying during the course of the divorce proceedings of the newspaper reports 'my people will never believe all this' (*Truth*, 15 Oct. 1891).

34 O'Shea, *Parnell*, ii. pp. 157-61. William O'Brien in his letter to the *Cork Free Press* in 1913 had asserted that Lockwood had dissuaded Parnell from giving evidence that would have established that he was 'rather the victim than the destroyer of a happy home'. Lockwood Katharine O'Shea described as 'terribly distressed about us and his inability to "save Parnell for his country"' (*ibid.*, i. vii-xiii, ii. p. 161). A writer in the St. Stephen's Review claimed shortly after Parnell's death that he had been told by Lewis that Parnell had left him fully instructed and ready to fight the case, but that on the evening of the day before the hearing had received a telegram from Parnell countermanding the instructions and insisting on the passive strategy (*St. Stephen's Review*, 17 Oct. 1891). The account – erroneous in many particulars, not least in that George Lewis was not then acting – is of some interest as evidence of contemporary rumours, consistent with Katharine O'Shea's account, of last-minute instructions from Parnell to adopt a passive strategy.

35 G. R. A. Askwith, *Lord James of Hereford* (London, 1930), p. 220; Harrison, *Parnell Vindicated*, pp. 153-4. A curious and confused letter signed 'B.B.' in the Observer of 16 Nov. 1930 contains a thoroughly unreliable hearsay account of the dispute between Parnell and Lockwood.

36 *Cork Free Press*, 6 Sept. 1913; W. O'Brien, *Olive Branch in Ireland*, p. 26; W. O'Brien, *Evening Memories*, p. 466; W. O'Brien, *Parnell*, pp. 146-7. In the tense interval between the publication of the Gladstone letter and the reconvened meeting of the Irish party, J. M. Tuohy reported in the *Freeman's Journal* that Parnell had a lengthy interview with Lockwood on the evening of 27 November (*F.J.*, 28 Nov. 1890). The purpose of the disclosure was of course to signal that Parnell had been legally constrained from putting his side of the case.

37 Healy to Maurice Healy, 13 Sept. 1913, *Letters and Leaders*, ii. p. 528 (see also i. p. 318); Healy to Maurice Healy, 11 Sept. 1913, *Letters and Leaders* Proofs, 229.

38 Edward Clarke, *The Story of My Life* (London, 1918), pp. 289-90; *Times, F.J.*, 17, 18 Nov. 1890.

39 For narratives of the split, see Lyons, *Fall*; Callanan, *Parnell Split*.

10: HEALY'S RHETORICAL STRATEGY IN THE SPLIT

1 James Joyce, *Finnegans Wake*, p. 581.

2 *I.N.*, 1 Oct. 1891, Belfast.

3 *W.N.P.*, 27 June 1891, Carlow Convention, 23 June.

11: T. M. HEALY: ARTIFICER AND REVISIONIST

1 *I.N.*, 1 Oct. 1891.

2 Quoted *N.P.*, 8 Oct. 1891. The editorial is remarkably entitled 'Peace to his Memory'. The quotation, from George Eliot, was a favourite of Healy's, and one

he had already used in the split (Callanan, *Parnell Split*, p. 118). He wrote years later in a letter to William O'Brien, that 'character is not cut in marble, but sudden dry rot is unusual' (Healy to O'Brien, 16 Oct. 1911, NLI MS 8556).

3 *N.P.*, 23 Apr. 1891, Central Branch NF.
4 *N.Y.T.*, 7 Aug. 1887
5 Katharine Tynan, 'The Irish Leader', *Catholic World*, Feb. 1889, p. 661.
6 J. L. Garvin, 'Parnell and His Power', *Fortnightly Review*, 1 Dec. 1898, p. 871.
7 W. E. H. Lecky, *The Leaders of Public Opinion in Ireland* (London, 1871), p. 226.
8 *Spectator*, 19 Nov. 1898; for ascription to Lecky, see *A Memoir of the Rt. Hon W. E. H. Lecky, by his Wife* (2nd ed., London, 1910), p. 321.
9 *P.M.G.*, 28 Dec. 1883.
10 *F.J.*, 13 June 1883, North City Ward; *F.J.*, 16 June 1883, Bandon.
11 *Letters and Leaders*, i. p. 234. Healy thus presciently seized on the most absurd line from Davis's flaccid poem, which became after Parnell's death a prophetic Parnellite text: see W. B. Yeats, *Tribute to Thomas Davis* (Cork, 1965) (speech delivered 20 Nov. 1914), at p. 13.
12 *Nation*, 15 Aug. 1885 speech at Liverpool, 11 Aug.
13 *F.J.*, 13 June 1883, North City Ward.
14 1883, quoted *N.P.*, 17 June 1891.
15 *F.J.*, 13 June 1883, Bandon.
16 See generally Lyons, *Parnell*, pp. 244–7.
17 Richard Pigott, 'The Parnellite Programme', in *Fortnightly Review*, vol. 37 (June 1885), p. 861. Pigott had earlier written that while Parnell had 'solid claims to be considered a gentleman', what was 'not so notorious – in England at least – is that he is utterly ignorant of his own country, and that his property is heavily encumbered' (Richard Pigott, *Personal Recollections of an Irish Nationalist Journalist* 2nd ed. [Dublin, 1883]). By this intriguing coupling of historical ignorance with indebtedness, Pigott contrived to suggest that Parnell lacked deep roots in the loam of Irish life.
18 *Hansard*, vol. 286, cols. 1735–6, 4 Apr. 1884.
19 *F.J.*, 17 Jan. 1885.
20 *F.J.*, 3 Feb. 1888, Dublin, meeting awaiting the arrival of John Morley and Lord Ripon.
21 *F.J.*, 12 Jan. 1891, Nenagh.
22 *N.P.*, 18 May 1891, Carrickmacross
23 *N.P.*, 13 Aug. 1891, Central Branch, NF.
24 *F.J.*, 3 June 1892, Bray.
25 *N.P.*, 11 June 1891, North Dock Ward, NF.
26 *N.P.*, 30 Dec. 1891, Glasgow.
27 *F.J.*, 27 Apr. 1892, North Dock Ward NF. For Healy's Leinster Hall speech, see Callanan, *Parnell Split*, pp. 10–13.
28 Healy to Maurice Healy snr., 10 May 1891, UCD Healy-Sullivan Papers, P6/A/18: *Letters and Leaders*, i. p. 361. The published version is incorrectly dated and substitutes 'poor man' for 'poor devil'.
29 Healy to Maurice Healy snr., 17 Dec. 1890, Healy-Sullivan Papers, UCD P6/A/16; *Letters and Leaders*, i. p. 344.
30 *Sunday Sun*, 12, 19 July 1891; *N.P.*, 30 June 1891; *Nation*, 13 June 1891.
31 Healy, 'Rise and Fall', p. 203.
32 Frederic, 'The Rhetoricians of Ireland', p. 720; Healy, *Why Ireland is not Free*, pp. 30–53.
33 *P.M.G.*, 8 Dec. 1890: for a commentary see C. C. O'Brien, *Parnell and his Party*, p. 351.

34 Healy to Erina Healy, 2 Dec. 1890, *Letters and Leaders*, i. p. 333; *N.P.*, 18 Mar. 1891, Carrickmacross.
35 *N.P.*, 8 Oct. 1891.
36 *Westminster Gazette*, 2, 3 Nov. 1893. For an alternative assessment of Parnell's superstitiousness, see Callanan, *Parnell Split*, pp. 166-7.
37 *Sunday Sun*, 11 Oct. 1891.
38 *N.Y.T.*, 11 Oct. 1891.
39 Healy to Maev Sullivan, 23 Apr. 1929, Healy-Sullivan Papers, UCD P6/E/2.
40 Birkenhead, *The Life of F. E. Smith* (London, 1959), p. 70.
41 *The Diaries of Sir Robert Bruce Lockhart*, ed. K. Younger (2 vols., London, 1973), i. p. 274 (entry for 13 Sept. 1933). Lady Lavery was able to entertain Lockhart by reporting the 'eight hours work, eight hours play, eight hours in bed with Kitty O'Shea!' line, which was in fact of Davitt's minting. Lockhart's entry continues: 'Kitty was "pure as snow!" – "I know that now", says Tim, – "hoar-frost"'.
42 *The Irish Statesman*, 23 Feb. 1929.

12: THE HEROIC PREDICAMENT

1 *Sunday Sun*, 11 Oct. 1891. Seeking to account for the posthumous cult of Disraeli, O'Connor wrote: 'Above all, Lord Beaconsfield has the same advantage which, according to M. Ranke, Gambetta had over all other competitors for French favour – he has a legend'. (T.P. O'Connor, *Lord Beaconsfield A Biography* (8th ed. [London, 1905], p. xiii.)
2 *Spectator*, 29 Nov. 1890.
3 James Joyce, *Ulysses*, pp. 530-2.
4 Oscar Wilde, *De Profundis*, 3rd ed. (London, 1905), p. 133.
5 *Spectator*, 10 Oct. 1891.
6 *Parnellism Unmasked, Its Finance Exposed* by 'an Irish Nationalist' (Dublin, 1885); P. H. D. Bagenal, *Parnellism Unveiled* (London, 1880).
7 *F.J.*, 9 Oct. 1891.
8 *Times*, 28 Nov. 1835, quoted Oliver MacDonagh, *The Emancipist, Daniel O'Connell 1830-47* (London, 1989).
9 G. W. E. Russell, *Portraits of the Seventies* (London, n.d.) p. 212.
10 G. K. Chesterton, *George Bernard Shaw* (London and New York, 1910), pp. 40-1.
11 *Spectator*, 19 Nov. 1898.
12 *Economist*, 15 Dec. 1883, quoted Ruth Dudley Edwards, *The Pursuit of Reason, The Economist 1843-1993* (London, 1993), p. 363.
13 *Newcastle Daily Chronicle*, 12 Oct. 1891.
14 *W.F.J.*, 27 Dec. 1890.
15 *U.I.*, 15 Dec. 1883.
16 T. P. O'Connor, *Parnell*, pp. 79-80.
17 William O'Brien, 'The Forster Tragedy in Ireland' in the *Westminster Review*, Sept. 1888, vol. 30, pp. 350, 355-6.
18 Redmond's lecture '15 Years in the House of Commons', delivered in New York on 29 Nov. 1896, is reprinted in J. E. Redmond, *Historical and Political Addresses* (Dublin and London, 1898) at pp. 1-30. It depicts Parnell heroically at four critical moments: the debate on the coercion act in February 1881; condemning the Phoenix Park murders; rising to address the House of Commons on the evening of Gladstone's introduction of the home rule bill; and receiving impassively the ovation of Gladstone and the Liberal party after the breaking of Pigott.
19 *U.I.*, 9 Oct. 1892, 'What he was to an Irish Exile'. The writer credited Parnell with transforming the standing of Irish exiles in England from 1885: '. . . Parnell was

to us, above all, the Vindicator'.

20 Quoted in Richard Pigott, 'The Political Poetry and Street Ballads of Ireland', *Gentleman's Magazine*, June 1885, vol. 258, p. 592.

21 *U.I.*, 14 Oct. 1893, 'Parnell the Irishman'.

22 Sean Ó hEigeartaigh and Ruaridhe Mac Aodha, *Parnell*, Paimphléidi Reatha No. 2 (Dublin, n.d.), p. 9. Elizabeth Bowen more elegantly wrote that Parnell took on and adapted the methods of Biggar, 'an impious Ulsterman, without regard for the sanctities of the House', which he raised 'from the plane of an exhibition to a fine-strung exasperation of English nerves'. (Elizabeth Bowen, *Bowen's Court* [London, 1952], p. 261.)

23 J. L. Garvin, 'Parnell and his Power', *Fortnightly Review*, vol. 64 (1 Dec. 1898), p. 875.

24 Sir William Butler, *The Light of the West* (Dublin, 1909), p. 78.

25 G. B. Shaw to the *Star*, 27 Nov. 1890, quoted in G. B. Shaw, *The Matter with Ireland* ed. D. H. Greene and D. H. Laurence (London, 1962), p. 28.

26 Richard Bagwell, 'Erin Stops the Way', *Dublin University Magazine*, vol. XC (Sept. 1877), p. 366.

27 Elbert Hubbard, 'Parnell and Kitty O'Shea', in *Little Journeys to Homes of Great Lovers*, vol. XVIII, no. 5 (May 1906), pp. 114–15. This essay is considerably more perceptive than the bizarre title of the periodical might suggest.

28 *F.J.*, 18 Feb. 1881.

29 Poem on Parnell's death by John Stuart, quoted T. C. Luby, R. F. Walsh and J. C. Curtin, *The Story of Ireland's Struggle for Self-Government* (New York, 1893), p. 743.

30 *U.I.*, 29 Aug. 1885, Kickham anniversary speech at Mullinahone, 27 Aug. Dismissing his greatness ('his later career has shown conclusively that he did not possess the elements of higher statemanship') the parliamentary correspondent of the *Leeds Mercury* wrote on Parnell's death: 'He owed much to his faculty of holding his tongue, and this again was due as much to constitutional dislike of speaking as to deliberate policy' (*Leeds Mercury*, 8 Oct. 1891). It is tempting to speculate on the possibility that Parnell's fabled reticence may have been in part a reaction to the theatrical excesses of his mother's patriotic manner. On Parnell's arrest in 1881 she spoke at a meeting attended by T.P. O'Connor in the Steinway Hall in New York, declaring: 'I started out as a Fenian, and have never retraced my footsteps. I hope again to visit Ireland, and then, if it be the fate of woman to be gibbetted in Ireland, I will die with "God Save Ireland" on my lips'. This avowal was greeted with deafening applause. (*Evening Standard*, 18 Oct. 1881.)

31 *U.I.*, 15 Dec. 1883.

32 *Economist*, 10 June 1882, quoted in Ruth Dudley Edwards, *The Pursuit of Reason, The Economist 1843-1993*.

33 J. L. Garvin, 'Parnell and his Power', *Fortnightly Review*, vol. 64 (1 Dec. 1898), p. 880.

34 Darrell Figgis, *Bye-Ways of Study* (Dublin and London, 1918), p. 10 (first published as a review of Katharine Parnell's memoirs, *Nineteenth Century*, 1 July 1914).

35 *The World*, 29 Mar. 1876; see also *D.T.*, 8 Oct. 1891, 'The Uncrowned King', by 'An Intimate Friend' (T. P. O'Connor).

36 *L'Illustration*, 17 Oct. 1891 (Augustin Filon).

37 Harry Harrison, 'Memories of an Irish Hero', *Listener*, vol. 45 (22 Mar. 1951), pp. 455–6. Harrison went on to posit a sequence of tragic romance, of Parnell's necessary aloofness conducing to loneliness, which in turn led to romance, calamity and death.

38 *Sunday Sun*, 11 Oct. 1891, 'Recollections of Mr. Parnell' by 'T.P.' (O'Connor).

39 *Edward Tennyson Reed 1860-1933*, incomplete autobiography, ed. Shane Leslie (London, 1957), p. 39.

40 H. W. Lucy, 'Orators in the House, and others', *Universal Review* (Jan. 1889), p. 46.

41 *Tablet*, 10 Oct. 1891.

42 Justin McCarthy, 'The Deposition of Mr. Parnell', *North American Review*, vol. 152 (Feb. 1891), p. 242. This article, of which I was not aware at the time of writing the *Parnell Split*, is an important account of McCarthy's understanding of, and reaction to, Gladstone's two interventions in the wake of the divorce crisis.

At the same time the split, in giving a new aspect to Parnell's solitude, brought something of a softening in the severity of his old mystique. In 1936, Lloyd George spoke to Frances Stevenson of Parnell: 'D told me he saw him come into the House after his disgrace, erect and defiant, amidst a dead silence, with everyone shunning him. And how Jacob Bright, the Quaker, stainless of character, and ultra responsible, got up from his seat behind the Government benches, and went over and sat down by Parnell, shook hands with him and chatted with him. D said that one day when William Parry was in the Gallery, he (D) asked Parnell if he could introduce him to a Welshman who was an admirer of his. "Ah!", said Parnell, "I did not know I had any admirers left in Wales"' (Frances Stevenson, *Lloyd George, A Diary*, ed. A. J. P. Taylor [London, 1971], p. 322 [27 Apr. 1936]).

43 *N.P.*, 8 Apr. 1891.

44 *D.T.*, 8 Oct. 1891, 'The Uncrowned King'; T. P. O'Connor, *Parnell and Home Rule* (London, n.d.), p. 31.

45 Quoted G. W. E. Russell, *Portraits of the Seventies* (London, n.d.) p. 204.

46 *L'Intransigeant*, 18 Feb. 1881. The excellent translation appears in the *Freeman's Journal*, 17 Feb. 1881.

47 *The World*, 24 Nov. 1880, 'Mr. Parnell at Avondale House'.

48 G. W. E. Russell, *Portraits of the Seventies* (London, n.d.), p. 206.

49 *Spectator*, 17 July 1880. Justin McCarthy advanced an alternative explanation for Parnell's social reserve: 'He went very little into the social life of London, partly because he had a strong impression that English people in general disliked him, and that even where his host and hostess were thoroughly friendly, some of their guests might be reluctant to meet him. "The truth is", he said to me more than once, "I am nervous about being disliked; I hate to be hated".' (Justin McCarthy, *Reminiscences* [2 vols., London, 1899], ii. pp. 103-4.)

50 *The Personal Papers of Lord Rendell*, ed. F. E. Hamer (London, 1931), pp. 29-30.

51 Curzon, *Modern Parliamentary Eloquence* (London, 1913), p. 50.

52 *Irish Packet*, 12 Mar. 1904, Richard Adams, 'Men I have Met: Parnell'. Parnell's demeanour at least assisted him to resist unwelcome requests that he exercise his influence in the matter of appointments and the like. He wrote to a former acquaintance who sought his intercession: 'Any service in my power to render you would be a very great pleasure to me, but it is most unfortunate that the request you make is quite impossible for me to comply with. I have never, since I have been in public life, yet used my influence on behalf of the interests of any individual. To do so would be to lessen my already too small power for effecting public good, to materially damage my position with the government and to diminish my opportunities for working to the advantage of the great National interest so much under my care. I should be at any time most pleased to talk over this matter as well as old times with you whenever you happen to be in London' (Parnell to Thomas H. Howe, 12 Nov. 1883, NLI MS 15, 735).

53 Ribblesdale, 'A Railway Journey with Mr. Parnell' in *Nineteenth Century* (Dec. 1891), pp. 969-74.

54 *Irishman*, 17 Apr. 1875, Navan, 12 Apr.

55 J. Connellan, 'Life of Charles Stewart Parnell, esq., M.P.' (London, 1888), reprinted from *The Leader*.

56 *Nation*, 2 Jan. 1886; quoted Bew, *Parnell*, p. 42.

57 Mary Gladstone, *Diaries and Letters*, ed. Lucy Masterman (London, 1930), pp. 408-11; Margot Oxford, *More Memories* (London, 1933). Mary Gladstone deleted from the published version of the *Diaries and Letters* a passage in her diary entry for 18 Dec. 1889 relating to Parnell's visit to Hawarden in which she described her friend Kathleen Clive 'finding herself counting the moments till he will look at her again' (BM MS 46262; see published version, p. 411). Kathleen Clive may also have been the 'Englishwoman of Liberal sympathies' who met Parnell at dinner in 1889 and wrote: 'I cannot exaggerate the impression he made on me. I never before felt such power and magnetic force, in any man. As for his eyes, if he looks at you, you can't look away, and if he doesn't you are wondering how soon he will look at you again. I am afraid that I have very little trust in his goodness; I should think it's a very minus quality; but I believe absolutely in his strength and his power of influence. I should be sorry if he were my enemy; I think he would stop at nothing' (quoted G. W. E. Russell, *Portraits of the Seventies* (London n.d.), p. 214).

Katharine Tynan, admittedly a fervent Parnellite, publicly described him, even before the romantic exaltation of the split, as 'the most distinguished man I have ever seen in looks' (Katharine Tynan, 'The Irish Leader', *Catholic World* [Feb. 1889], p. 661; see also R. B. O'Brien, *Parnell*, ii. p. 297). Labouchere, characteristically, demurred. While conceding that Parnell was 'certainly a very handsome man, with well-cut features, and a good figure', he commented that Parnell's much-noticed eyes were 'as a matter of fact . . . so shifty, and so what is termed "fishy", that they marred his face' (*Truth*, 15 Oct. 1891).

Political menace served to heighten erotic appeal. In one Parnell myth, indeed the sole literary text of the Parnell myth in England, Virginia Woolf's *The Years*, first published in 1937, Parnell is the subject of politically inspired erotic reverie (Virago ed., London, 1977, pp. 20, 66 et passim). In Kate O'Brien's *The Ante-Room* (1934), the heroine Agnes dissents from the hackneyed observation that Parnell resembled a demigod. On being asked what he did look like, she replies 'Well – a god perhaps. One of the fierce ones'. (Virago ed., London, 1989, p. 210.)

58 David Anderson, *'Scenes' in the Commons* (London, 1884), p. 203; *Le Figaro*, 19 Feb. 1881.

59 *Spectator*, 29 Nov. 1890.

60 *F.J.* 10 Oct. 1892, editorial. The context was an attack on James O'Kelly's speech over Parnell's grave on the first anniversary of his death.

61 *Spectator*, 14 Aug. 1875, 'The O'Connell Centenary'.

62 *Spectator*, 17 July 1880.

63 *I.W.I.*, 8 Oct. 1898.

64 *Insuppressible*, 24 Jan. 1891, Leinster Hall; see also *N.P.*, 31 Aug. 1891.

65 *N.P.*, 5 June 1891.

66 *N.P.*, 16 Mar. 1891.

67 *N.P.*, 11 June 1891, North Dock Ward.

68 *N.P.*, 24 July 1891.

69 *N.P.*, 23 Mar. 1891, Queenstown.

70 *N.P.*, 25 July 1891; *N.P.*, 24 June 1891, Carlow Convention; see also Healy's speech at Tynock, *N.P.*, 6 July 1891, 4 July.

71 *N.P.*, 9 Mar. 1891, Lislea, Co. Armagh.

72 *N.P.*, 16 Mar. 1891, Newry.

73 Maire and Conor Cruise O'Brien, *A Concise History of Ireland* (3rd ed., London, 1985); *N.P.*, 23 June 1891; *N.P.*, 7 July 1891, speech of Murphy at Bagenalstown; see also 'MacMurchad' by 'Jack Dawe', *Nation*, 10 Jan. 1891.

74 *N.P.*, 29 June 1891; *N.P.*, 11 June 1891, North Dock Ward, NF.
75 *N.P.*, 23 Apr. 1891, Central Branch, NF; *N.P.*, 27 Aug. 1891, Central Branch, NF.
76 *N.P.*, 26 June 1891; *N.P.*, 19 June 1891.
77 *N.P.*, 29 May 1891, Blackrock. Sullivan's fellow moralist, the virulently anti-Parnellite curate John Behan, proclaimed Parnell 'the champion liar of the nineteenth century' (*N.P.*, 19 May 1891, Saggart).
78 W.*N.P.*, 22 Aug. 1891, Loughgiel, Co. Antrim, 22 Aug.
79 *N.P.*, 9 May 1891.
80 *N.P.*, 6 July 1891.
81 *F.J.*, 24 Jan. 1891; *N.P.*, 7 Mar, 4 May, 5 Oct. 1891; see also *The Parnell Handbook* (Dublin, n.d.), p. 26.
82 *N.P.*, 7 Sept. 1891.
83 *N.P.*, 29 June 1891, Tullow.
84 *N.P.*, 24 July 1891, 7 June 1891, 8 Oct. 1891.

13: MYTH AND MORTALITY

1 *N.P.*, 11 June 1891, North Dock Ward NF.
2 Quoted Hamilton diary, entry for 9 Jan. 1891, BM Add MS 48654, p. 129.
3 Quoted Jules Abels, *The Parnell Tragedy* (London, 1966), p. 369.
4 *N.P.*, 13 Oct. 1891; *Letters and Leaders*, ii. p. 367; see also *N.P.*, 8 Oct. 1891; for a variation of the remark alleged see O'Connor, *Memoirs*, ii. p. 299.
5 V. B. Dillon to O'Brien, 22 Dec. 1890, Gill Papers, NLI MS 13506 (II), Harrington to Dillon, 31 Dec. 1890, Dillon Papers, TCD MS 6732A.
6 *D.E.*, 19 Dec. 1891
7 *N.P.*, 29 May 1891, J. F. O'Doherty to P. Donnelly, dated 27 May 1891; see also *F.J.*, 16 Nov. 1892.
8 W. T. Stead, *The Discrowned King of Ireland* (Office of the Review of Reviews, London, 1891), NLI IR 92, p. 17.
9 *Insuppressible*, 17 Jan. 1891.
10 *N.P.*, 22 Apr. 1891, Rathfarnham.
11 *N.P.*, 23 Mar. 1891, Queenstown.
12 *N.P.*, 18 May 1891.
13 W. T. Stead, *Discrowned King of Ireland*.
14 *Nation*, 24 Jan. 1891, Belfast 21 Jan.
15 *Insuppressible*, 17 Jan. 1891.
16 *N.P.*, 27 June 1891.
17 *N.P.*, 6 June 1891.
18 *N.P.*, 24 June, Carlow Convention.
19 *F.J.*, 27 Apr. 1891, North Dock Ward NF.
20 *N.P.*, 11 Mar. 1891, Inaugural Meeting NF
21 *N.P.*, 9 Mar. 1891, Lislea, Co. Armagh.
22 *F.J.*, 12 Jan. 1891, Nenagh.
23 *N.P.*, 11 June 1891, North Dock Ward, NF.
24 *N.P.*, 30 July 1891.
25 *F.J.*, 3 Mar. 1891.
26 *F.J.*, 10 Mar. 1891.
27 *I.T.*, 1 Apr. 1931, Dunbar Plunket Barton, 'Timothy Healy, IV'. Plunket Barton's *Timothy Healy, Memories and Anecdotes* (Dublin and Cork, 1933) was a revised and expanded version of his articles in the *Irish Times* shortly after Healy's death (*I.T.*, 28 Mar.-1 Apr. 1931). The original article makes clear, as the book (at p. 36) does not, that the remark was Healy's own.

28 See in particular *W.N.P.*, 11 July 1891, whose cartoon depicts Parnell as a fox in sly flight from Carlow to Brighton, a kettle tied to his tail. Healy at Queenstown declared a determination to force Parnell to 'break covert' (*W.F.J.*, 13 June, Queenstown, 23 Mar.). The *Insuppressible* spoke of chasing Parnell from Ireland 'like a mad dog' (*Insuppressible*, 13 Jan. 1891).
29 *N.P.*, 2 June 1891. Healy also quoted from *Othello* in a speech at the National Federation; *N.P.*, 27 Aug. 1891. For the 'Stop Thief' articles, see Callanan, *Parnell Split*, pp. 121–4.
30 Healy, *Rise and Fall*, p. 196.
31 *N.P.*, 8 Apr. 1891, Central Branch NF.
32 *N.P.*, 1 Oct. 1891, Belfast.
33 *N.P.*, 23 Sept. 1891, Trinity Ward, NF
34 *N.P.*, 1 Oct. 1891, Belfast
35 *N.P.*, 7 Sept. 1891
36 *Insuppressible*, 2 Jan. 1891.
37 *N.P.*, 13 Apr. 1891.
38 Alfred Webb to John Dillon, 7 Feb. 1897, Dillon Papers, TCD MS 6760.
39 *F.J.*, 13 Dec. 1890, Kilkenny.
40 *N.P.*, 16 Oct. 1891, Cavan.
41 *N.P.*, 22 June 1891; *N.P.*, 12 Mar. 1891; *Insuppressible*, 27 Dec. 1891; see also Healy's speech at the National Federation, *N.P.*, 8 Apr. 1891. These references owed much to the contemporary work of the German bacteriologist Robert Koch (1843–1910) whose name was occasionally invoked in anti-Parnellite rhetoric. Koch's techniques enabled him to identify the bacteria responsible for diseases such as anthrax, cholera and tuberculosis.
42 *N.P.*, 30 July 1891, Central Branch NF.
43 *I.N.*, 1 Oct. 1891, Belfast.
44 *N.P.*, 8 Mar. 1891, Lislea, S. Armagh; see also *N.P.*, 10 Aug. 1891.
45 *N.P.*, 20 Aug. 1891, Derry; *N.P.*, 9 Mar. 1891, Lislea.
46 Callanan, *Parnell Split*, p. 46.
47 *N.P.*, 7 Aug. 1891, Arran Quay, Dublin; *F.J.*, 12 Jan. 1891, Nenagh, Jan. 10, 11. For nauseous nationalist excremental imagery, see the correspondence of the bitter and foul-mouthed barrister and anti-Parnellite MP Matthew J. Kenny with John J. Dunne (NLI MS 10946[7]).
48 W. O'Brien, *Recollections*, p. 250.
49 *Under Which Flag*, p. 4.
50 *N.P.*, 29 June 1891, Carlow. It may be that this outburst was prompted in part by an observation of Frank Lockwood Q.C. who had acted for Katharine O'Shea, recorded in Healy's memoirs: Lockwood 'noted how she held her fan before her face to shield him from her offensive breath', *Letters and Leaders*, i. p. 318.
51 *Nation*, 3 Jan. 1891, Queenstown. The lines are quoted from a poem of Sullivan's, 'Ireland Over All'.
52 *P.M.G.*, 26 Jan. 1891; *I.C.*, 31 Jan. 1891, 'My Motherland'.
53 *N.P.*, 1 June 1891, Liverpool.
54 *F.J.*, 9 Feb. 1891.
55 *N.P.*, 27 June 1891.
56 *Young Ireland*, 4 Mar. 1876, pp. 116–17.

14: THE 'SAXON SMILE'

1 *I.N.*, 1 Oct. 1891, Belfast.

2 James Joyce, *Ulysses*, p. 531.
3 *F.J.*, 25 June 1883.
4 *D.E.*, 14 July 1891.
5 *Insuppressible*, 24 Jan. 1891, Leinster Hall.
6 *N.P.*, 16 Mar. 1891, Newry.
7 *N.P.*, 25 Mar. 1891
8 *N.P.*, 16 Mar. 1891, Newry.
9 *N.P.*, 11 July 1891.
10 *N.P.*, 20 Aug. 1890, Derry.
11 Healy, 'Rise and Fall'.
12 *N.P.*, 20 Aug. 1891, North Dock Ward, NF.
13 *N.P.*, 9 Apr. 1891.
14 *N.P.*, 12 Jan. 1891, Nenagh.
15 *N.P.*, 21 May 1891, Central Branch NF.
16 *F.J.*, 12 Jan. 1891, Nenagh; *N.P.*, 7 Mar. 1891.
17 *N.P.*, 7 Mar. 1891.
18 *N.P.*, 24 June 1891.
19 *N.P.*, 20 Aug. 1891, Derry, 5 Nov. 1891, Central Branch, NF.
20 *N.P.*, 8 Apr. 1891.
21 *N.P.*, 8 Apr. 1891, Central Branch, NF.
22 *Nation*, 31 Jan. 1891, 'Twitterings, by a Gutter Sparrow'.
23 *Insuppressible*, 30 Dec. 1890.
24 *Insuppressible*, 27 Dec. 1890, General Meeting, 25 Dec.
25 *N.P.*, 27 Aug 1891, Central Branch NF.
26 *N.P.*, 27 Aug. 1891.
27 *N.P.*, 8 Apr. 1891
28 *N.P.*, 13 Aug. 1891, Central Branch, NF.
29 *N.P.*, 11 June 1891, North Dock Ward.
30 *W.N.P.*, 22 Aug. 1891; see also Healy, *Why Ireland is Not Free*, p. 47.
31 *N.P.*, 6 July 1891, Tynock.
32 *N.P.*, 7 Aug. 1891, Arran Quay NF.
33 *N.P.*, 3 July 1891, Maryborough, 27 Aug., 1891, Central Branch NF, 22 Jan. 1892, Mullingar.
34 *N.P.*, 9 Sept. 1891.
35 *N.P.*, 2 Oct. 1891, Thurles.
36 *N.P.*, 24 July 1891.
37 *N.P.*, 27 Mar. 1891, 21 May 1891, speech of Healy at Central Branch NF, 19 June 1891.
38 *N.P.*, 6 July 1891.
39 *N.P.*, 6 July 1891, Tynock; see also his speech at Nenagh (*F.J.*, 12 Jan. 1891) and his reference to a 'Treaty of Brighton' (*F.J.*, 23 Apr. 1891, Central Branch, NF).
40 *N.P.*, 6 June 1891.
41 *N.P.*, 18 Mar. 1891.
42 *N.P.*, 6 July 1891, Carlow.
43 See Callanan, *Parnell Split*, p. 66. Tanner was certainly the most aggressively eccentric member of the Irish party. Healy wrote of him to his brother in August 1894: 'Tanner's conduct yesterday was that of a drunken cornerboy towards Clarickarde, which is almost calculated to gain sympathy for Clarickarde. He is a low ruffian, and I believe the shaving of his head must have been done in the French jail into which he got during his sympathetic attendance at the Carnot funeral. He will some day utterly disgrace us' (Healy to Maurice Healy, 15 Aug. 1894, Healy typescripts).

44 *N.P.*, 1 Apr. 1891, Sligo; Callanan, *Parnell Split*, p. 295.
45 *The Diaries of Sir Robert Bruce Lockhart*, ed. K. Younger (2 vols., London, 1973), entry for 13 Sept. 1933, p. 274; see also Healy, *Why Ireland is Not Free*, p. 45; Callanan, *Parnell Split*, p. 295.
46 *N.P.*, 26 Mar. 1891.
47 Healy to Erina Healy, 3 Dec. 1890, *Letters and Leaders*, i. p. 333.
48 *Insuppressible*, 31 Dec. 1890; Healy to Erina Healy, 5 Dec. 1890, *Letters and Leaders* Proofs, B137, deleted *Letters and Leaders*, i. p. 335. The account of Parnell's intervention in Healy's letter corresponds to that in the *Insuppressible*.
49 *N.P.*, 23 Mar. 1891, Healy speech at Queenstown; 30 Mar. 1891, Anna Parnell to *N.P.*, d. 27 Mar. 1891. The allegation was first published in the *P.M.G.* of 13 Jan. 1891.
50 *F.J.*, 13 Dec. 1890, Kilkenny.
51 *N.P.*, 1 June 1891.
52 *N.P.*, 24 June 1891, Carlow, 4 July 1891, Tynock.
53 *N.P.*, 30 June 1891. *The Oxford English Dictionary* (2nd ed.) gives an obsolete Scottish usage of 'Kitty' to mean a young girl or woman, and occasionally to designate a loose woman. It is not clear that the term in Ireland had, as has been suggested, popular connotations of prostitution or wantonness. The invariable practice in anti-Parnellite rhetoric of referring to 'Kitty' O'Shea was a gesture of calculated disrespect, of mocking familiarity. Parnell in fact never addressed Katharine as 'Kitty' (O'Shea, *Parnell*, i. p. 183).
54 *N.P.*, 23 Mar. 1891, Queenstown, 7 Oct. 1891, Thurles.
55 *F.J.*, 24 Feb. 1891.
56 *I.C.*, 24 Jan. 1891.
57 *N.P.*, 18 Mar. 1891, Carrickmacross.
58 *N.P.*, 7 Mar. 1891.
59 *N.P.*, 6 July 1891, Tynock; W.*N.P.*, 4 Jul. 1891; *N.P.*, 7 Sept. 1891.
60 *N.P.*, 4 July 1891.
61 *N.P.*, 6 July 1891, Tynock, Co. Carlow.
62 *F.J.*, 13 Dec. 1890, Freshford.
63 *N.P.*, 20 June 1891. For a variation on the argument, see the speech of E. F. V. Knox, *W.N.P.*, 12 Sept. 1891.
64 Harrison, *Parnell Vindicated*, pp. 28, 254.
65 *D.T.*, 9 Feb. 1921.
66 W. S. Blunt, *My Diaries* (London, 1919, 1932 ed.), p. 795 (entry for 8 Mar. 1912).
67 Hamilton diary, entries for 26, 29 Nov., 1 Dec. 1890, Hamilton Papers, BM, Add. MS 48654.
68 Frances Stevenson, *Lloyd George, A Diary*, ed. A. J. P. Taylor (London, 1971), p. 322. Lloyd George was not unrepresentative of the political class in his view.
69 *D.T.*, 9 Feb. 1921.
70 Sophie O'Brien, 'Recollections', p. 167.
71 W. T. Stead, 'An Incident in the Home Rule Cause', *Review of Reviews*, Dec. 1890, p. 598.
72 *Vanity Fair*, 22 Nov. 1890, quoted R. F. Foster, *Paddy and Mr. Punch* (London, 1993), p. 136.
73 Notes on R. B. O'Brien, *Parnell*, Davitt Papers, TCD MS 9377. The embittered and eccentric F. H. O'Donnell suggested that Katharine O'Shea's attachment to Parnell 'possibly began in her being a Sister of Mercy to the depressed and helpless invalid', and that this in turn facilitated the deception of her husband, 'a genial and warmhearted officer and gentleman' (F. H. O'Donnell, *The Lost Hat*, pp. 18-21).

74 E. A. D'Alton, *History of Ireland*, vi. p. 382.
75 *Roscommon Herald*, 6 Mar. 1926.
76 O'Shea, *Parnell*, ii. pp. 157–63.
77 *Insuppressible*, 31 Dec. 1890.
78 *W.N.P.*, 18 July 1891.
79 *N.P.*, 20 Aug. 1891.
80 *N.P.*, 29 May 1891, 19 Sept. 1891.
81 See A. P. W. Malcolmson, *The Pursuit of the Heiress, Aristocratic Marriage in Ireland 1750-1820* (Ulster Historical Foundation, 1982); Healy to Maurice Healy, snr., June 1891, *Letters and Leaders*, ii. p. 361.
82 *N.P.*, 24 June 1891, Carlow Convention.
83 *Insuppressible*, 27 Jan. 1891.
84 *N.P.*, 8 Apr. 1891.
85 *N.P.*, 3 July 1891.
86 Healy to Maurice Healy, 14 Jan. 1891, *Letters and Leaders*, Proofs, B138.
87 Healy was always delighted by odd names. When a member called Vicary Gibbs was speaking in the Commons, Healy scribbled on a scrap of paper the lines:

Hicary Vicary Gibbs
A mouse ran up his ribs,
His ribs were bare
And he got a great scare
Hicary Vicary Gibbs.

(M. McDonnell Bodkin, *Recollections of an Irish Judge* [London, 1914], p. 239.) Healy is also the likely author of the lines on T. P. Gill, whom he derided as 'Neutral' Gill in the split, published in the *Freeman's Journal* in late 1892:

And Neutral Gill
Say what you will,
Is neutral still.

(*F.J.* 14 Oct. 1892.)
88 *F.J.*, 19 Jan. 1891, Edgeworthstown. Captain O'Shea pronounced his name as if it were 'O'Shee', although the name in its Irish pronunciation was 'O'Shay': see Joyce Marlow, *The Uncrowned Queen of Ireland* (London, 1975) at p. 301.
89 *N.P.*, 16 Mar. 1891, Newry; *N.P.*, 18 March 1891, Carrickmacross.
90 Healy to Maurice Healy, 9 Jan. 1891, *Letters and Leaders* Proofs, B146.
91 *Letters and Leaders*, i. p. 100.

15: 'MR LANDLORD PARNELL'

1 *Pictures in the Hallway* (1942), republished in Seán O'Casey, *Autobiographies* 1, p. 181.
2 *Spectator*, 6 Dec. 1891.
3 *F.J.*, 10 Mar. 1874, quoted Foster, *Parnell*, p. 131.
4 *Sunday Sun*, 2 Aug. 1896. G. K. Chesterton referred to 'the great Parnell, a squire who had so many of the qualities of a peasant (qualities the English so wildly misunderstood as to think them English, when they were really very Irish)'. (G. K. Chesterton, *Irish Impressions* [London, 1919], p. 42.)
5 *F.J.*, 17 Dec. 1890.
6 *N.P.*, 18 Mar. 1891, Carrickmacross.
7 *F.J.*, 9 Apr. 1894, Nenagh.

8 *Labour World*, 31 Jan. 1891; editorial pencilled 'MD' in the file of the paper in the Davitt Papers, TCD MS 9632.
9 *N.P.*, 11 June 1891, North Dock Ward NF.
10 *N.P.*, 27 June 1891, Carlow Convention, 23 June.
11 *Nation*, 28 Feb. 1891, Carrick-on-Shannon, 22 Feb.
12 *F.J.*, 21 June 1892.
13 *N.P.*, 24 June 1891, Carlow Convention; *N.P.*, 30 June 1891, Bagenalstown. Taking this cue from Healy, William Martin Murphy avowed in 1895: 'He belonged to the people . . . He felt himself belonging to the common clay of Ireland. It was in his nature and bones and he felt he could not put it out of them'. (*F.J.*, 23 May 1895, St. Patrick's Branch, NF.)
14 *N.P.*, 9 Mar. 1891, Lislea.
15 *Nation*, 11 Apr. 1891.
16 *N.P.*, 17 June 1891. Making a different if related point, the absurdly pretentious F. H. O'Donnell later referred to Parnell as 'a man of historic family, though of modern and exotic origin' (F. H. O'Donnell, *The Lost Hat*, p. 19).
17 *N.P.*, 23 Mar. 1891, Queenstown.
18 Richard Pigott, 'The Parnellite Programme', *Fortnightly Review*, XXXVI, June 1885, p. 861; ILPU Leaflet No. 1, 'Mr. Parnell as a Landlord and a Landgrabber' (Dublin, n.d.). During the split, allegations against Parnell were resurrected from as far back as 1873: see *N.P.*, 3, 6 July 1891.
19 See generally Foster, *Parnell*, pp. 166–84.
20 *F.J.*, 19 Jan. 1891; *Insuppressible*, 19 Jan. 1891; see *F.J.*, 20 Jan. 1891, Kerr to *F.J.*, d. 19 Jan., Stephen Brown to *F.J.*, d. 19 Jan.
21 *N.P.*, 8 June 1891.
22 *N.P.*, 21 May 1891, Central Branch NF; *N.P.*, 27 Apr. 1891; *N.P.*, 17 Aug. 1891.
23 *N.P.*, 23 Sept. 1891, Trinity Ward Branch NF; the *National Press* likewise observed: 'Really, one would think that the interests of Ireland were a mere political warehouse of which Mr. Parnell was the sole proprietor' (*N.P.*, 9 May 1891).
24 *N.P.*, 21 Apr. 1891, Central Branch NF.
25 W. O'Brien, *Parnell*, p. 59; *Weekly Sun*, 11 Oct. 1891; *Letters and Leaders*, i. p. 367. Justin McCarthy later wrote: 'I have lately read a great deal about his chilling manners, about his haughty superciliousness, about his positive rudeness to strangers . . . I can only say that, if the man thus described was Parnell, then I never knew Parnell at all, could never even have seen him' (*Reminiscenses* [2 vols., London, 1899], ii. p. 91).
26 *Insuppressible*, 19 Jan. 1891; *F.J.*, 19 Jan. 1891, Edgeworthstown.
27 *N.P.*, 16 Mar. 1891, Newry.
28 *N.P.*, 30 Mar. 1891.
29 *N.P.*, 5 Oct. 1891.
30 R. F. Foster, *Paddy and Mr. Punch* (London, 1993), p. 42; Bew, *Parnell*, pp. 15, 28.
31 *N.P.*, 23 Apr. 1891, Central Branch NF.
32 *N.P.*, 16 Mar. 1891.
33 *N.P.*, 3 July 1891, Maryborough.
34 *F.J.*, 27 Apr. 1892, North Dock Ward NF.
35 *F.J.*, 20 Apr. 1893, Fulham.
36 *N.P.*, 11 Mar. 1891, Inaugural Meeting NF.
37 *N.P.*, 24 July 1891, Holborn.
38 *N.P.*, 29 June 1891, Carlow.
39 *N.P.*, 26 Sept. 1891.
40 *N.P.*, 8 Apr. 1891, Central Branch NF.

41 *N.P.*, 3 July 1891, Maryborough.
42 *N.P.*, 23 July 1891, Holborn; 3 July 1891, Maryborough; *N.P.*, 7 Mar. 1891.
43 *I.N.*, 1 Oct. 1891.
44 *N.P.*, 22 Apr. 1891.
45 *N.P.*, 24 June 1891.
46 *N.P.*, 3 July 1891, Maryborough.
47 *F.J.*, 27 Apr. 1892, South Dock Ward NF; see also *Letters and Leaders*, i, pp. 230–4. The suggestion that Blaine was the only candidate whose nomination Healy had procured was demonstrably false, while the casual mode of nomination itself ran counter to the allegation that Parnell had systematically controlled the nomination of members of the party. The account of the exchange in the first draft of Healy's memoirs suggests that Parnell's comment was directed to Healy's role in the nomination of parliamentary candidates (Healy, Letters and Leaders, draft, p. 337, Beaverbrook Papers, House of Lords Record Office).
48 *N.P.*, 3 July 1891, Maryborough.

16: THE FENIAN CHIEFTAIN

1 'The Rhetoricians of Ireland', Frederic, p. 713.
2 *N.P.*, 23 Mar. 1891, Queenstown.
3 James Joyce, *Finnegans Wake*, p. 542.
4 *N.P.*, 14 Apr., 9 May, 1891.
5 *I.N.*, 1 Oct. 1891.
6 *N.P.*, 11 June 1891, North Dock Ward NF.
7 *N.P.*, 2 Nov. 1891, Longford.
8 *N.P.*, 11 Mar. 1891, Inaugural Meeting NF.
9 *N.P.*, 26 Sept. 1891; *W.N.P.*, 27 June 1891, Carlow, 23 June.
10 *W.N.P.*, 27 June 1891, 'Reflections (After Reading the Report of the Ballina Meeting)'.
11 *N.P.*, 29 June; 7 Sept. 1891; see also *N.P.*, 13 Apr. 1891.
12 *N.P.*, 5 Oct. 1891.
13 *N.P.*, 26 May 1891.
14 *F.J.*, 6 July 1891.
15 *N.P.*, 9 Mar. 1891, Lislea, Co. Armagh.
16 *N.P.*, 11 Mar. 1891, Inaugural Meeting NF.
17 *N.P.*, 8 Apr. 1891, Central Branch NF.
18 *N.P.*, 13 Aug. 1891, NF.
19 *Insuppressible*, 22 Jan. 1891.
20 *N.P.*, 13 Aug. 1891, Central Branch NF.
21 *N.P.*, 26 Sept. 1891.
22 *N.P.*, 20 Aug. 1891, Derry.
23 *Insuppressible*, 16, 22 Jan. 1891.
24 *N.P.*, 27 Aug. 1891, Central Branch NF.
25 *N.P.*, 16 Mar. 1892.
26 *F.J.*, 28 July 1892, NF.
27 *F.J.*, 21 Oct. 1892, Queens County Convention; *F.J.*, 16 Nov. 1892, National Convention NF.
28 *N.P.*, 4 Sept. 1891. For a further anti-Parnellite exegesis of the excesses of Parnellite rhetoric, specifically the execrable Parnellite verses of the American Robert Stevens Pettet, see *Nation*, 7 Mar. 1891.
29 *N.P.*, 8 Apr. 1891, Central Branch NF.
30 *N.P.*, 11 June 1891, North Dock Ward NF.

31 *N.P.*, 11 June 1891; see also *N.P.*, 22 Apr. 1891, William Murphy, Rathfarnham.
32 *F.J.*, 12 Jan. 1891. Henri Le Caron was the alias of Thomas Miller Beach, a British agent who infiltrated the American Fenian movement and who testified to the Special Commission: see J. A. Cole, *Prince of Spies* (London, 1984).
33 *N.P.*, 8 Apr. 1891, Central Branch NF.
34 *N.P.*, 28 Mar. 1891.
35 *N.P.*, 14 Mar. 1891.
36 *W.N.P.*, 15 May 1891; for Parnell's statement see Callanan, *Parnell Split*, p. 215.
37 *Insuppressible*, 22 Jan. 1891.
38 *N.P.*, 18 Mar.
39 *N.P.*, 24 Mar. 1891, Taghmon, Co. Wexford.
40 *N.P.*, 22 Apr. 1891, Rathfarnham.
41 *W.N.P.*, 23 May 1891, speech at Drangan, 17 May; *N.P.*, 18 June 1891; *W.N.P.*, 16 May 1891.
42 *N.P.*, 8 Oct. 1891.
43 Francis Shaw SJ, 'The Canon of Irish History - A Challenge', *Studies*, vol. LXI (Summer 1972), p. 134.
44 Davitt, *Fall of Feudalism*, p. 26. For the role of Sir John Parnell, see Foster, *Parnell and his Family*, pp. 4–10.
45 D. P. Moran, *The Philosophy of Irish Ireland*, 2nd ed. (Dublin, n.d.), pp. 32, 38. For Moran, see Margaret O'Callaghan, 'D. P. Moran and the Irish Colonial Condition, 1891-1921' in *Political Thought in Ireland since the Seventeenth Century*, ed. George Boyce, Robert Eccleshall and Vincent Geoghegan (London, 1994); Patrick Maume, *D. P. Moran* (Dundalk, 1995).

17: THE UNION OF HEARTS

1 T. M. Healy, 'The Secret of Mr. Parnell's Power', *P.M.G.*, 28 Dec. 1883.
2 Justin McCarthy, 'The Deposition of Mr. Parnell', *North American Review*, vol. 152, p. 239 (Feb. 1891).
3 *The Fallen Idol; or, the Fate of the Uncrowned King* (Manchester, n.d.) (BM 12314 k.50), pp. 7-8. This quotation is ascribed to 'the Ancient Book of Uncrowned Kings', a Gladstonian Liberal squib published after the divorce case.
4 Wyndham to his mother, 20 Dec. 1890, J. W. Mackail and Guy Wyndham, *Life and Letters of George Wyndham* (2 vols., London, n.d.), i. p. 258. Wyndham was admiringly parodying Wynknyn de Worde's 'Treatise of Fysshynge wyth an Angle', which he was at the time reading.
5 *N.P.*, 16 Mar. 1891, Newry; 3 July 1891, Maryborough.
6 *N.P.*, 27 May 1891; *The Parnell Handbook* (Dublin, n.d.). On the day of the first commemoration of Parnell's death, the *Freeman's Journal* under Healy's direction published as a riposte to the Parnellite *Words of the Dead Chief* a compilation of quotations from Parnell before the split under the heading 'Mr. Parnell's Principles — "Words of the Dead Chief" — Important Declarations' (*F.J.*, 8 Oct. 1892).
7 *N.P.*, 8 Apr. 1891, NF.
8 *N.P.*, 3 July 1891, Maryborough; *N.P.*, 27 Aug. 1891, NF; see also *N.P.*, 6 July 1891, Tynock; *I.N.*, 1 Oct 1891, Belfast.
9 *N.P.*, 7 Sept. 1891, 16 Mar. 1891.
10 *N.P.*, 6 July 1891, Tynock, 4 July.
11 *F.J.*, 13 Dec. 1890, Freshford, Co. Kilkenny.
12 *I.N.*, 1 Oct. 1891, Belfast.
13 *N.P.*, 30 July 1891, NF.

14 *F.J.*, 24 Jan. 1891, National Committee.
15 *N.P.*, 9 Mar. 1891, Lislea.
16 *F.J.*, 13 Dec. 1890, Kilkenny, 12 Dec.; see also W.*N.P.*, 27 June 1891, Carlow.
17 *N.P.*, 29 June 1891, Tullow.
18 *F.J.*, 17 Jan. 1891, Edgeworthstown.
19 *F.J.*, 5 Dec. 1890. For the Clancy amendment, see Callanan, *Parnell Split*, pp. 42–7.
20 *Nation*, 19 Sept. 1896, quoted from the *Manchester Guardian*.
21 Croke to Gladstone, 30 Nov. 1890, Gladstone Papers, BM Add. MS 45511.
22 T. P. O'Connor to Mary Drew, July 1891, Gladstone Papers, BM Add. MS 46251, f. 274. O'Connor added the simpering postscript that 'it is a pity there was not more about Gladstone's mother. We Celts think that his mother contributed much to his greatness'.
23 *F.J.*, 14 June 1892, Letterkenny.
24 Quoted *I.I.* 28 Mar. 1931.
25 *F.J.*, 4 Sept. 1895, Killorglin; Healy, *Why Ireland is not Free*, p. 143; for Healy's reply see I.C., 7 Dec. 1896, speech of 4 Dec.
26 Healy to Catherine Gladstone, 22 Apr. 1893, Gladstone Papers, BM MS 46253, f. 154.
27 Healy to Mary Drew, 4 July 1919, Gladstone Papers BM Add. MS 46253, f. 152; see Mary Drew, *Catherine Gladstone* (London, 1919). For Healy's panegyric on Gladstone's retirement see *F.J.*, 19 Mar. 1894. On Gladstone's death Healy despatched a telegram to Herbert Gladstone advising that he and Maurice would visit Hawarden Church and recite the words of the requiem: Healy to Herbert Gladstone n.d. (evidently late May 1898), Viscount Gladstone Papers, BM Add. MS 46057, f. 41. In a speech in the Commons in 1910, Healy referred to 'poor old Gladstone – for whose memory I pray every day of my life' (*Hansard*, vol. 20, col. 153 [18 Nov. 1910]).
28 *Nation*, 21 May 1887.
29 *F.J.*, 28 Feb. 1896, Mercantile Branch NF.
30 *Nation*, 27 Feb. 1897; *D. Nat.*, 18 Sept. 1899.
31 *I.I.*, 17 July 1905.

18: THE MORAL QUESTION

1 W. T. Stead, 'North Kilkenny and its Moral', in *The Paternoster Review* vol. 1, no. 4 (Jan. 1891), p. 334.
2 *Wicklow People*, 10 Oct. 1891, Thomas Canon Doyle to the editor, d. 7 Oct. The letter was written the day after Parnell had in Doyle's phrase 'gone to his awful account'.
3 Seamus O'Kelly, *The Parnellite, A Play in Three Acts* (Naas, n.d.), p. 60.
4 James Joyce, *Finnegans Wake*, p. 602.
5 *N.P.*, 29 May 1891, J. K. O'Doherty to P. Donnell, d. 27 May; *F.J.*, 29 Jan. 1891, Patrick McAlister to J. O'Connor, d. 28 Jan.
6 Quoted *N.P.*, 2 July 1891; *U.I.*, 11 July 1891.
7 *I.C.*, 1 Aug. 1891; *N.P.*, 11 Sept. 1891; Fr. D. Ryan, Arran Quay Ward NF.
8 *N.P.*, 19 May 1891, Saggart.
9 *Insuppressible*, 20 Jan. 1891.
10 *N.P.*, 3 Aug, 1891.
11 *N.P.*, 23 Mar. 1891, Queenstown.
12 *F.J.*, 19 Jan. 1891, Edgeworthstown.
13 *I.N.*, 1 Oct. 1891, Belfast.
14 *Letters and Leaders*, Proofs, B150.

15 *N.P.*, 24 June 1891, Carlow Convention.
16 *N.P.*, 21 Sept. 1891.
17 *Nation*, 4 July 1891, Carlow, 28 June.
18 *D.N.*, 23 Dec. 1890.
19 *Nation*, 23 May 1891.
20 *N.P.*, 13 Mar. 1891, Arran Quay Ward NF. It was commonplace among anti-Parnellite rhetoricians to assert that Parnell's relations with Katharine O'Shea constituted a crime. Adulterous conversation with the wife of another man was an actionable tort at the husband's suit (by the confusingly entitled action for criminal conversation), as well as a ground of divorce at his suit, but was not a crime.
21 *Under Which Flag?*, pp. 3–4. The pseudonymous pamphlet was published by J. J. Lalor of Middle Abbey Street, the printer of the *Insuppressible*, the *Nation*, and the *Irish Catholic*. Authorship of the article has been frequently ascribed to Healy (see St. John Ervine, *Parnell* [2nd ed., London, n.d.] at p. 288). While Healy probably used the pseudonym 'A Gutter Sparrow' in a polemical piece of verse, entitled 'Twitterings', of which he is the likely author (*Nation*, 31 Jan. 1891), considerations of style and content alike preclude his authorship of *Under Which Flag?*, for which W. F. Dennehy or an unknown cleric must be the principal suspect.
22 *N.P.*, 8 Apr. 1891, North Dock Ward NF; see also Sullivan's speech at Taghmon, Co. Wexford, *N.P.*, 24 Mar. 1891.
23 *Insuppressible*, 30 Dec. 1890.
24 *N.P.*, 13 Mar. 1891, Arran Quay Ward NF; *N.P.*, 13 Apr. 1891, Rathvilly.
25 *F.J.*, 27 July 1891; *N.P.*, 28 July 1891.
26 *Under Which Flag?*, p. 11.
27 *Labour World*, 20 Dec. 1890. The copy of the issue in the *Labour World* file in the Davitt Papers is marked 'Diamond': TCD MS 9632.
28 *N.P.*, 8 Apr. 1891, North Dock Ward NF. Infernal menace was to provide a recurrent theme in the moral rhetoric of Irish nationalism. Of members of the Dáil ready to defy Catholic moral law by voting for the 1974 Contraceptives Bill Deputy O. J. Flanagan commented: 'They may be in this house for five, ten or twenty years more, but, believe me, it is only on the approach of the midnight of life that one realises how one has abused one's responsibilities'. *Dáil Éireann Debates*, vol. 173, col. 297 (11 July 1974) (Control of Importation, Sale and Manufacture of Contraceptives Bill 1974).
29 *N.P.*, 4 July 1891.
30 Nation, 17 Jan. 1891.
31 *Under Which Flag?*, pp. 6–7.
32 *N.P.*, 17 Mar. 1891, Boharnabreena.
33 *N.P.*, 5 June 1891.
34 *N.P.*, 27 Apr. 1891, Rathfarnham; *N.P.*, 2 May 1891, Wood Quay Ward NF.
35 *F.J.*, 6 July 1891, Carlow.
36 *N.P.*, 15 June 1891, Lucan; see also *N.P.*, 29 June 1891, Tullow.
37 *Nation*, 4 July 1891.
38 *N.P.*, 22 May. 1891, New Inn, Co. Tipperary. For an attack on Croke's idiom, see Harrington's speech at the National League: 'Did it contribute to the advancement of morality among our people to use language of the character of 'the measly pig', or 'the leprous girl', whatever idea that conveyed to the Irish child who awaited the sacrament of confirmation at the hands of his Grace, should be used? (*F.J.*, 3 June 1891).
39 *Nation*, 4 July 1891, Tullow, June 28.
40 *F.J.*, 29 Nov. 1890, Canon Doyle to *F.J.*, d. 24 Nov.

41 *Labour World*, 21 Dec. 1891.
42 *N.P.*, 6, 7 July 1891; see also *Nationalist*, 11 July 1891.
43 *N.P.*, 2 July 1891, Rathmines; for the presentation see *F.J.*, 30 June 1891; *N.P.*, 4 July 1891, 'A Bagenalstown Lady' to *N.P.*, d. 30 June.
44 On 2 October 1886, as part of an Irish deputation to Hawarden, Kate Sullivan, the wife of T. D. Sullivan and Lady Mayoress of Dublin, read to Gladstone an address from 500,000 Irish women, who wished 'to see an ending to that political strife which imposes so many sacrifices on our husbands and sons'. Healy's wife Erina was among those present (*Nation*, 9 Oct. 1886; *Graphic*, 16 Oct. 1886; T. D. Sullivan to W. E. Gladstone, 12 Aug. 1886, BM Add. MS 46052, f. 185).
45 *N.P.*, 25 July 1891.
46 Undated draft in reply to E. D. Gray letter to the pope of 27 Apr. 1891, Walsh Papers, DDA. For Mrs. Gray's promenade with Parnell see *Nation*, 7 Feb. 1891; Edward Byrne to William O'Brien, 8 Feb. 1891, O'Brien Papers, NLI MS 13507 (4).
47 O'Callaghan to Walsh, 20 Dec. 1890, Walsh Papers DDA. T. P. O'Connor in an obituary to Katharine Parnell published thirty years later, having observed that 'the fidelity, loyalty, and courage he had shown in his defence of a woman gained many women to his side', made the improbable assertion that 'it was one of the many ironies of this tragic conflict, in which many people regarded the fight as one for the purity of the home, that Parnell had on his side most of the occupants of convents in Ireland — those retreats of prayer and self-sacrifice and purity unstained by such weaknesses of the flesh' (D.T., 9 Feb. 1921, T. P. O'Connor, 'Mrs. Parnell').
48 Sophie O'Brien, 'Recollections', p. 199. For a gracious gesture of apolitical sympathy towards Parnell from young women outside the middle class in the Carlow election, see Callanan, *Parnell Split*, pp. 131-2.
49 *I.C.*, 1 Aug. 1891.
50 *I.C.*, 1 Aug. 1891, editorial entitled 'Parnellism and the Priesthood — A Plain Duty'.
51 *I.C.*, 8, 15, 22 Aug. 1891.
52 *I.C.*, 9, 23 July 1892.
53 *I.C.*, 10 Oct. 1891.
54 *F.J.*, 19 Oct. 1891. Katherine Tynan denounced the editor of the *Irish Catholic*: '. . . this man doth smite/The dead man lying in the rain at night/And having smitten the sad body/Spares not to smite the trembling soul . . .' (*U.I.*, 24 Oct. 1891).
55 *Evening Press*, 7 Oct. 1891. No copies of the *Evening Press* which was published from 26 Sept. 1891 to 16 Mar. 1892 are extant in any public collection. The article is quoted elsewhere: *I.N.*, 8 Oct. 1891, D.E., 8 Oct. 1891. The Parnellites of the National Club condemned the 'cold-blooded cry of exultation and utterly atrocious libel on Parnell' of the *Evening Press* (*N.P.*, 8 Oct. 1891); see also *U.I.*, 24 Oct. 1891.
56 *N.P.*, 29 June 1891.
57 *W.N.P.*, 4 July 1891.
58 *Nation*, 4 July 1891.
59 *N.P.*, 11 Mar. 1891.
60 *N.P.*, 6 July 1891, Tynock, 4 July.
61 *N.P.*, 18 Mar. 1891, Carrickmacross.
62 *N.P.*, 2 July 1891, Leighlinbridge; see also *N.P.*, 4 May, 4, 10, 11 Sept. 1891. Norman Stone perceptively categorises Parnell as the Irish victim of the rise across Europe of a lower middle class 'social Catholicism' pitted against liberalism and socialism: Norman Stone, *Europe Transformed* (London, 1988 ed.), p. 57.
63 *N.P.*, 11 Mar. 1891; see also Healy's speech at Arran Quay, *N.P.*, 11 Aug. 1891; see generally Frank Callanan, '"Clerical Dictation": Reflections on the Catholic

Church and the Parnell Split', *Archivium Hibernicum*, xlv (1990), pp. 64-75.
64 *N.P.*, 6 July 1891, Tynock, Co. Carlow, 4 Jul.
65 *N.P.*, 29 June 1891, Tullow.
66 *N.P.*, 9 Mar. 1891, Lislea, Co. Armagh.
67 W. T. Stead, 'North Kilkenny and its Moral', in *The Paternoster Review*, vol. 1, no. 4 (Jan. 1891), p. 340.
68 *N.P.*, 27 May 1891.
69 *N.P.*, 24 June 1891.
70 *N.P.*, 7 Aug. 1891, Arran Quay NF.
71 *N.P.*, 27 Aug. 1891, Central Branch NF.
72 *N.P.*, 24 June 1891, Carlow Convention.
73 *N.P.*, 3 Apr. 1891.
74 *N.P.*, 27 Aug. 1891, Central Branch NF.
75 *N.P.*, 14 Apr. 1891.
76 *N.P.*, 20 Apr. 1891.
77 *F.J.*, 17 Mar. 1891.
78 *N.P.*, 29 June 1891, Carlow; see also *N.P.*, 14 July 1891; *N.P.*, 10 Aug. 1891, Walsh to *N.P.*, d. 9 Aug.; *I.C.*, 8 Aug. 1891, Walsh to *I.C.*, d. 5 Aug.; Callanan, *Parnell Split*, p. 137, n. 63.
79 *N.P.*, 24 June 1891, Carlow Convention.
80 F. H. O'Donnell to Davitt, n.d. Davitt Papers, TCD MS 9380 f. 115 (from Davitt's endorsements the letter was received by him during the Kilkenny election); *N.P.*, 10 May 1891. The letter to the *National Press* was sent at the time of the launching of the paper but was withheld by Healy until the irascible O'Donnell, as Healy had anticipated, changed sides and backed Parnell. O'Donnell in his memoirs insouciantly reversed his contemporaneously published perceptions: 'From Vienna to Paris, and further, the ladies were Parnellite . . . Everybody was hugely amused at Mr. Gladstone's morality' (F. H. O'Donnell, *The Irish Party*, ii. p. 302).
81 *Nation*, 24 Jan. 1891, Belfast 21 Jan.
82 W. T. Stead, 'An Incident in the Home Rule Cause', *Review of Reviews*, Dec. 1890, p. 606.
83 *Insuppressible*, 15 Dec. 1890, Kilkenny, 12 Dec.
84 *St. Stephen's Review*, 29 Nov. 1890.
85 *Nation*, 30 May 1891.
86 *N.P.*, 14 Sept. 1891.
87 *N.P.*, 12 Mar. 1891; see also *N.P.*, 18 May 1891.

19: THE POLITICS OF PEASANTRY

1 *Hansard*, vol. 306, cols. 853-4.
2 C. P. Curran, 'The Reminiscences of Mr. Healy', *The Irish Statesman*, 23 Feb. 1929, p. 495.
3 *F.J.*, 13 Dec. 1891, Kilkenny; *W.N.P.*, 16 May 1891; see also *N.P.*, 3 Aug. 1891.
4 *N.P.*, 3 Oct. 1891.
5 *N.P.*, 24 June 1891, Carlow Convention.
6 *N.P.*, 27 May 1891; *I.C.*, 23 Apr. 1891.
7 *N.P.*, 7 Aug. 1891, Arran Quay Ward NF.
8 *I.N.*, 1 Oct. 1891, Belfast.
9 *N.P.*, 7 July 1891, Bagenalstown.
10 *N.P.*, 20 Aug. 1891, Derry; see also Healy at Nenagh; *F.J.*, 12 Jan. 1891.

11 *N.P.*, 23 July 1891, Holborn Restaurant, banquet for John Hammond, the victor of the Carlow by-election.
12 *N.P.*, 23 Sept. 1891, Trinity Ward NF.
13 *I.N.*, 1 Oct. 1891, Belfast.
14 *N.P.*, 30 Sept. 1891.
15 *F.J.*, 19 Oct. 1891, Douglas, Cork.
16 Quoted *Labour World*, 21 Dec. 1890, Address from the Women of Castlecomer to Charles Stewart Parnell, esq., M.P.; *N.P.*, 18 Sept. 1891, Rev. J. McGrath, Drumcondra NF.
17 *N.P.*, 18 Sept. 1891.
18 *N.P.*, 31 July, 10 Aug. 1891; see Leon O'Broin, *Charles Gavan Duffy* (Dublin, 1967), pp. 10-11.
19 *N.P.*, 19 Aug. 1891.
20 John O'Leary, *Recollections of Fenians and Fenianism* (2 vols, London, 1896), i. p. 30. O'Leary, who had disdained the agrarian agitation, mused of Parnell in the split: 'Good God in heaven, when he was ruining the morals of the country they were all with him. Now that it is only a question of his own morals they are all against him': Tynan, *Twenty-Five Years*, p. 344.
21 *N.P.*, 22 May 1891.
22 *N.P.*, 30 Dec. 1891, Glasgow; see also *N.P.*, 30 June 1891, Bagenalstown.
23 *N.P.*, 18 Mar. 1891, Carrickmacross. Healy varied the image in a speech after the general election: 'It is for you a bread and butter question. It is no question of Room 15. It is no question of Eltham or Brighton or the fire escape (*laughter*) or anything of that kind' (*F.J.*, 7 Nov. 1892, Clonard).
24 *N.P.*, 6 Apr. 1891, *N.P.*, 31 Mar. 1891.
25 *N.P.*, 30 June 1891, Bagenalstown; see also *Insuppressible*, 12 Jan. 1891, Nenagh.
26 Healy, 'Rise and Fall', p. 203.
27 *N.P.*, 6 July 1891, Tynock, 4 July.
28 *F.J.*, 13 Dec. 1890.
29 *Hansard*, vol. 352, col. 1050 (21 Apr. 1891); col. 1836 (30 Apr. 1891).
30 *Hansard*, vol. 352, cols. 835-43 (17 Apr. 1891).
31 Morley, *Recollections*, i. p. 266, diary entry for 17 Apr. 1891.
32 *Hansard*, vol. 353, cols. 325-28 (7 May 1891).
33 On the graziers' issue see David S. Jones, 'The Cleavage between Graziers and Peasants in the Land Struggle, 1890-1910' in Samuel Clark and James S. Donnelly, *Irish Peasants* (Manchester, 1983), pp. 374-413.
34 Purchase of Land (Ireland) Act 1891, 54 & 55 Vict. c. 48, s. 11.
35 Elizabeth R. Hooker, *Readjustments of Land Tenure in Ireland* (North Carolina, 1938), pp. 69-70; Callanan, *Parnell Split*, pp. 280-7. Healy had predicted that the 'rotten' Balfour proposal would 'have the effect of choking and killing all form of effective land purchase' (*N.P.*, 21 May 1891, Central Branch NF).
36 *N.P.*, 13 May 1891; *W.N.P.*, 16 May 1891.
37 *N.P.*, 13 May 1891; *W.N.P.*, 16 May 1891.
38 *N.P.*, 30 June 1891, Bagenalstown.
39 *N.P.*, 20 May 1891.
40 *N.P.*, 21 May 1891, Central Branch NF.
41 *Hansard*, vol. 353, cols. 92, 226 (4, 6 May, 1891).
42 *W.N.P.*, 16 May 1891; *N.P.*, 13 May 1891.
43 *N.P.*, 7 Oct. 1891. Healy in similar vein in the House of Commons described the evicted tenants as 'these pioneers in a movement of self-sacrifice . . . Whether they made mistakes or not is not for me to discuss. They are men of Irish blood, of

our own race . . .' (*Hansard*, vol. 353, col. 930 [22 May 1891]; vol. 355, col. 1800 [20 July 1891]).

44 *Labour World*, 3 Jan. 1891. The file copy in the Davitt Papers is initialled 'M.D.': Davitt Papers, TCD MS 9632. The position of John Ferguson, the Belfast-born Presbyterian radical, closely matched Davitt's in the split: see *I.N.*, 3 Oct. 1891, Ferguson to *I.N.*, 1 Oct.; see also *F.J.*, 11 May 1890, John Ferguson to *F.J.*, d. 4 May.

45 *Labour World*, 3, 31 Jan. 1891. The articles are initialled 'M.D.' in the file in the Davitt Papers: TCD MS 9632.

46 Davitt to Richard McGhee, 12 Dec. 1890, Davitt Papers, TCD MS 9328.

47 *N.P.*, 11 Mar. 1891; for commentary see *F.J.*, 17 Mar. 1891.

48 *F.J.*, 17 Nov. 1887, Limerick.

49 *N.P.*, 11 Mar. 1891, Inaugural Meeting NF.

50 *N.P.*, 16 Mar. 1891, Newry; Davitt wrote in 1902 that Parnell had enjoyed popular support when he fought Davitt's advocacy of land nationalisation in 1883–4; and that while 'singularly enough, he came round almost completely to my views after the unhappy split of 1890' (a misrepresentation of Parnell's position), the country had remained faithful to the idea of peasant proprietary: Michael Davitt, *Some Suggestions for a Final Settlement of the Land Question* (Dublin, 1902), p. 6.

51 *N.P.*, 16 Mar. 1891.

52 Davitt to Richard McGhee, 8 Oct. 1888, Davitt Papers, TCD MS 9328.

53 *N.P.*, 23 Mar. 1891, Queenstown. The split moreover had wrecked Davitt's political work in England. Keir Hardie wrote that, prior to the split, Davitt's *Labour World* seemed assured of success: 'Davitt threw himself bitterly, and, as I thought at the time, mistakenly, into the anti-Parnellite campaign . . . his anti-Parnellism killed the *Labour World*'. (J. Keir Hardie, 'Michael Davitt', *The Socialist Review*, vol. 1 no. 8 [Aug. 1909], p. 413.)

54 Davitt to Richard McGhee, 12 Dec. 1890, Davitt Papers, TCD MS 9328.

55 *N.P.*, 15 May 1891.

56 Davitt to Richard McGhee, 7 Aug. 1903, Davitt Papers, TCD MS 9328.

57 *The Socialist Review*, vol. 1, no. 8 (Aug. 1908), p. 442.

20: 'MOBOLOGY'

1 Healy to Maurice Healy snr., 12 Mar. 1891, Healy-Sullivan Papers, UCD MS P6/A/17 (bowdlerised into a reflection on the human condition in *Letters and Leaders*, ii. at p. 358); Healy to Maurice Healy snr., 10 May 1891, Healy-Sullivan Papers, UCD MS P6/A/18.

2 *F.J.*, 9 June 1892, John Mitchel Branch, NF.

3 *N.P.*, 23 Mar. 1891, Queenstown; *N.P.*, 8 Apr. 1891, Central Branch NF.

4 Healy, 'Rise and Fall', p. 199.

5 *N.P.*, 7 Oct. 1891, Thurles.

6 *N.P.*, 11 June 1891, North Dock Ward NF.

7 *N.P.*, 2 May 1891, Wood Quay Branch NF.

8 Healy, 'Rise and Fall', p. 202; see also *N.P.*, 5 Aug. 1891.

9 *Insuppressible*, 24 Jan. 1891, T. M. Healy, Leinster Hall meeting to establish NF.

10 Healy to Maurice Healy snr., 17 Dec. 1890, Healy-Sullivan Papers, UCD MS P6/A/13; the epithet 'horrid' is deleted in the version published in *Letters and Leaders*, i. p. 344.

11 *Speaker*, 29 Aug. 1891, 'Among the Clouds in Ireland'. It might be unkindly

suggested that this was the most aptly entitled of all O'Brien's effusions on Irish nationalism.

12 *F.J.*, 9 Feb. 1891, Donnelly to diocesan clergy, d. 5 Feb.
13 *I.N.*, 21, 29 Sept. 1891.
14 *F.J.*, 3 Mar. 1891, Croke to ed. *F.J.*, d. 2 Mar.
15 *F.J.*, 4 Mar. 1891, Croke to ed. *F.J.*, d. 3 Mar.
16 Croke to Kirby, 21, 29 Jan. 1891, quoted Larkin, *Fall*, pp. 248-9. Croke was perhaps being deliberately simplistic to coach the plodding rector in an argument calculated to allay papal mistrust of the involvement of the Irish bishops in nationalist politics, but the views expressed are not unrepresentative of episcopal perceptions of the sociology of Parnellism: see Brownrigg to Walsh, 13 Dec. 1890, Walsh Papers, DDA, quoted Lyons, *Parnell*, p. 343.
17 *I.C.*, 19 Sept. 1891.
18 B. M. Walker, 'The Irish Electorate 1868-1915', in *Irish Historical Studies*, vol. xviii. p. 359; *N.P.*, 29 June 1891, speech of Healy at Tullow, Co. Carlow; Labouchere to W. E. Gladstone, 18 Nov. 1891, Gladstone Papers, BM Add. MS 56449 f. 238; *F.J.*, 9 May 1891, speech of Leamy at the National League.
19 *N.Y.T.*, 11 Oct. 1891; Frederic, 'The Ireland of Today', 'The Rhetoricians of Ireland', 'The Ireland of Tomorrow'. The articles were published by Frederic pseudonymously as 'X'. Contemporary speculation on the authorship of the articles is revealing. Davitt wrote to Dillon: 'Your suspicion about the Healy gang being connected with the "X" articles in the *Fortnightly* may not be far astray. There is a decidedly Catholic touch about the first article . . . I am half inclined to think that Finlay the Jesuit had a hand in these articles. These men don't believe in Home Rule. What they want is Catholic ascendancy and in this game they have the cussedness of Healyism to help them' (Davitt to Dillon, 4 Dec. 1894, Dillon Papers, TCD MS 6728, f. 32).

John Hooper was more astute and, detecting Healy's inspiration rather than authorship, correctly identified Frederic as the writer: 'There are some opinions and expressions in it that bring it very close to our friend, but I doubt if he himself is the writer. Would the writer be Harold Frederic? He I believe acted as a conduit pipe on a couple of occasions before for the same poison' (Hooper to Dillon, 'Mon', n.d., Dillon Papers, TCD MS 6839 f. 59). The impeccably well-informed E. H. Ennis wrote from Dublin Castle to T. P. Gill: 'What do you think of the articles by "X"? J. F. Taylor is not the author, and you may place your bottom dollar upon Harold Frederic. So I am assured' (E. H. E[nnis] to T. P. Gill, 12 Dec. 1893, Gill Papers, NLI MS 13,479 [5]). For the attribution to Frederic, see Thomas F. O'Donnell and Hoyt C. Franchere, *Harold Frederic* (New York, 1961); The *Wellesley Index to Victorian Periodicals* (5 vols., Toronto, 1989), ii. p. 1176, v. p. 279; see also Horace Plunkett, *Ireland in the New Century* (London, 1905), p. 162. For contemporary public responses to the article see: Horace Plunkett, 'Ireland Today and Ireland Tomorrow', *Fortnightly Review*, no. 327 (1 Mar 1894), pp. 287-93; Michael Davitt, 'The Rhetoricians', *The Speaker*, 9 Dec. 1893, pp. 634-6.

20 Frederic, 'The Ireland of Today', pp. 686-706.
21 Frederic, 'The Ireland of Tomorrow', p. 6.
22 *N.P.*, 2 May 1891, Usher's Quay Ward NF.
23 *N.P.*, 8 Apr. 1891, North Dock Ward NF.
24 W. F. Dennehy to Walsh, 25 Dec. 1890, Walsh Papers DDA.
25 *N.P.*, 16 Mar. 1891, Thomas McGivern to Fr. McPolin.
26 *Insuppressible*, 24 Dec. 1890.
27 Healy to Maurice Healy, 22 Jun. 1892, *Letters and Leaders* Proofs, p. 162, deleted *Letters and Leaders*, ii. p. 378.

28 Healy to Maurice Healy snr., 25 June 1892, Healy-Sullivan Papers, UCD P6/A/23, deleted *Letters and Leaders*, ii. p. 379.
29 *Irish News*, 27 Aug. 1891.
30 *N.P.*, 13 Aug. 1891, Central Branch NF.
31 *Roscommon Herald*, 20 Dec. 1890, quoted Bew, *Parnell*, p. 123.
32 *N.P.*, 10 Sept. 1891, Central Branch NF.
33 *F.J.*, 7 Nov. 1892, Clonard.
34 *N.P.*, 20 Nov. 1891, Inn's Quay and Rotunda Ward NF.
35 *F.J.*, 18 Oct. 1894, St. Patrick's Division, NF.
36 Frederic, 'The Ireland of Today', p. 705.
37 *F.J.*, 2 Feb. 1891.
38 *N.P.*, 11 June 1891, North Dock Ward NF.
39 *N.P.*, 10 Aug. 1891.
40 *Insuppressible*, 27 Dec. 1890, National Committee, 24 Dec.
41 *N.P.*, 13 Aug. 1891, Central Branch NF.
42 *F.J.*, 13 Dec. 1890.
43 *N.P.*, 7 Aug. 1891, Arran Quay.
44 *N.Y.T.*, 22 Mar. 1891.
45 *N.P.*, 26 Mar. 1891; for the assault on Healy, see Callanan, *Parnell Split*, pp. 112-13.
46 *N.P.*, 30 Mar. 1891.
47 I.C., 22 Aug. 1891, 23 July 1891.
48 *N.P.*, 27 Aug. 1891; see also *N.P.*, 11 Mar. 1891, speech of T. D. Sullivan; *N.Y.T.*, 26 Apr. 1891.
49 *Insuppressible*, 24 Jan. 1891.
50 *N.P.*, 26 Mar. 1891, interview; N.P, 3 July 1891, Maryborough; *N.P.*, 9 Mar. 1891, Lislea.
51 *N.P.*, 8 Apr. 1891, Central Branch NF.

21: AFTER PARNELL

1 *F.J.*, 27 Apr. 1892, Arran Quay, NF.
2 *Times*, 21 June 1922, speech at City of London Conservative and Unionist Association, Grocers' Hall.
3 Alfred Webb to J. F. X. O'Brien, 26 Oct. 1891, NLI MS 13, 431. Katharine Tynan, *Twenty Five Years* (London, 1913), p. 330, T. P. Gill, MS draft of article, Gill Papers, NLI MS 13,520 (4); Henry Harrison to Margaret Leamy, 30 Aug. 1934, quoted Margaret Leamy, *Parnell's Faithful Few* (New York, 1936), p. 144.
4 *M.G.*, 8 Oct. 1891.
5 *E.P.*, 7 Oct. 1891, quoted *N.P.*, 8 Oct. 1891. There is however no reason to believe that Healy was the author of the more virulent editorial (quoted *I.N.*, 8 Oct. 1891) considered earlier.
6 *N.P.*, 8 Oct. 1891.
7 *U.I.*, 10 Oct. 1891; *N.P.*, 16 Oct. 1891, O'Brien to ed. d. 15 Oct.; Healy, *Why Ireland is Not Free*, p. 50; W. O'Brien, *Olive Branch in Ireland*, pp. 64-5. For Healy's speech at Thurles see Callanan, *Parnell Split*, p. 178.
8 *F.J.*, 17 Oct. 1892, S. Wexford; Callanan, *Parnell Split*, pp. 187-91.
9 Healy to Maurice Healy, 31 Jan. 1892, Healy typescripts.
10 Healy to Maurice Healy, 12 Jan. 1892, Healy typescripts; Redmond to Gill, 14 Jan. 189(2),Gill Papers, NLI MS 13492 (12); see also T. P. Gill to Dillon, 27 Jan. 1892; Dillon Papers, TCD MS 6754, f. 530.
11 O'Brien to Dillon, 24 Jan. 1892, Dillon Papers, TCD, MS 6736, f. 125.

12 Healy to Maurice Healy snr. 31 Aug. 1903, Healy-Sullivan Papers, UCD P6/A/40.
13 Healy to Maurice Healy, 21, 31 Mar. 1892, Healy typescripts; *N.P.*, 24, 26 Mar. 1892; *F.J.*, 26 Mar. 1892. Healy's estimate of Gray was shared by Dillon, who referred to him as 'a miserable wretch' (Dillon to O'Brien, 4 Apr. 1892, Dillon Papers, TCD MS 6736, f. 146).
14 Healy to Maurice Healy, 6 Mar. 1892, Healy typescripts.
15 Healy to Maurice Healy, 20 May 1892, Healy typescripts; see also W. M. Murphy, *The Story of a Newspaper* (Dublin, 1912), reprinted from *I.I.*, 2 Jan. 1909, pp. 4–5. An exhaustive account of the infighting between the partisans of Dillon and of Healy is contained in the Parnellite pamphlet *The Prize Fighters of Dublin,* published by the *Evening Herald*. Healy was driven off the board of the *Freeman's Journal* in March 1894 (*Letters and Leaders*, ii. p. 423).
16 *N.P.*, 3 Mar. 1892, Central Branch NF.
17 *N.P.*, 16 Mar. 1892, Manchester.
18 *F.J.*, 21 June 1891, Dublin, INF convention.
19 Morley to Dillon, 4, 17 Apr. 1892, Dillon Papers, TCD MS 6798, f. 16, 17; J. J. Clancy to Redmond, 24 May 1802, Dillon Papers, TCD MS 6747, f. 2; Lyons, *Irish Parliamentary Party*, pp. 35–6.
20 Morley to Dillon, 1, 4 June 1892, Dillon Papers, TCD MS 6798, ff. 22, 23.
21 O'Brien to Dillon, 11 Apr. 1892, Dillon Papers, TCD MS 6736, f. 161 (see also 8 Apr., f. 156); Healy, *Why Ireland is Not Free*, pp. 63–4.
22 Healy to Maurice Healy, 28 June 1892, Healy typescripts.
23 Healy to Maurice Healy, 19 May, 28 June 1892, Healy typescripts.
24 Lyons, *Irish Parliamentary Party*, p. 37; Healy to Maurice Healy, 10 May, 28 June 1892, Healy typescripts.
25 For Healy's authorship of the editorials, and comments thereon, see O'Brien to Dillon, n.d. (13 Sept. 1892), 15 Oct. 1892, Dillon Papers, TCD MS 6736, ff. 167, 228.
26 *F.J.*, 26 Sept., 13 Oct. 1892.
27 *F.J.*, 6 Oct. 1892.
28 *F.J.*, 8 Oct. 1892.
29 *F.J.*, 10 Oct. 1892 (see also 11 Oct.).
30 *F.J.*, 10, 14 Oct. 1892.
31 *F.J.*, 13, 14, 15 Oct. 1892; see Callanan, *Parnell Split*, pp. 121–4. Healy's temper was not improved by a brief experiment in abstinence from alcohol. His wife wrote to Maurice that 'Tim and I are giving up drink!! I feel all right, but Tim looks ghastly, and we are both very cranky'. Healy added a note: 'I am bound to add that of all forms of human error that I ever tried, teetotalism is the most melancholy. My wife gives me no encouragement in it, and I believe that I shall ultimately fill a drunkard's grave' (Erina Healy to Maurice Healy, 13 Oct. 1892, Healy typescripts).
32 *F.J.*, 22 Sept. 1892, NF. Elsewhere he wrote that William Redmond's 'flatulent periods are daily a source of bitterness to critics on his own side' (*F.J.*, 8 Oct. 1892).
33 Harrington to T. P. Gill, 17 Nov. 1892, Gill Papers, NLI.
34 Healy to Maurice Healy, 13 Oct. 1892, Healy typescripts.
35 Healy to Maurice Healy, 13, 20 Jan. 1893, Healy typescripts.
36 *F.J.*, 25 Sept. 1889.
37 *F.J.*, 15 Nov. 1895 (Healy interview), 28 Nov. 1895 (Healy speech), 3 Dec. 1895 (O'Brien speech); Healy to Maurice Healy, 13 Oct. 1892, Healy typescripts.
38 Healy to Maurice Healy, 1 Oct. 1892, Healy typescripts.
39 Healy, *Letters and Leaders*, ii. pp. 382–4.
40 *F.J.*, 22 Sept. 1892, NL.

41 *Hansard*, vol. 22, col. 134, 12 Mar. 1894.

42 Healy to Maurice Healy, 20 Oct. 1892, Healy typescripts, slightly altered *Letters and Leaders*, ii. p. 386; Morley to Healy, 13, 18 Sept. 1892, Healy-Sullivan Papers, UCD P6/B/36, 37. Years later Healy heard that at a dinner held by Dillon a story was told that on being asked how Morley should be treated, Healy had replied: 'Like an ass at a fair; let him alone until he goes astray, and then fire stones at him'. Healy was unamused by this joke, the thrust of which was unerringly accurate, and complained bitterly to Maurice: 'Wasn't that pretty? I suppose they told Morley this lie' (Healy to Maurice Healy, July 1903, *Letters and Leaders*, ii. p. 463).

43 Healy to Maurice Healy, 13 Oct. 1892, Healy typescripts.

44 Healy to Maurice Healy, 13 Oct. 1892, Healy typescripts; Lyons, *Dillon*, pp. 155–6. In the lexicon of anti-Parnellism and of Gladstonian Liberalism when strictly applied, the anti-Parnellite party were 'Nationalists', a term which excluded the Parnellites; see e.g. W. E. Gladstone to Morley, copy 28 Dec. 1892, BM, Add. MS 44257.

45 Lyons, *Dillon*, pp. 157–8. In a letter marked 'secret' Gladstone had written to Morley that it would be very desirable to 'feel the pulse of the Nationalist leaders in a preliminary way on your own behalf' (Gladstone to Morley, 15 Nov. 1892, copy, BM, Add. MS 44257, f. 39). A number of meetings ensued, with Dillon, Sexton and Edward Blake, in which Justin McCarthy presumably had some role. On 7 December Morley wrote to Gladstone enclosing a copy of 'our friends' ', scheme for a Senate (Morley to Gladstone, 7 Dec. 1892, BM, Add MS 44257, f. 48). He wrote in February 1893 that Dillon wanted to see the draft bill along with Sexton and Blake secretly before it went to press: 'There would be no communication to the party. They only want to safeguard against any slips . . .' (Morley to Gladstone, 16 Feb. 1893, BM, Add. MS 44257). Morley recalled of the conferences which took place with 'three or four of the Irish leaders' that 'the secret consultations oddly enough were carried on at the not very secret Shelbourne hotel, for, as I was told, the etiquette of the moment strictly forbade an Irish member to cross the threshold of either Castle or Lodge' (Morley, *Recollections*, i. p. 358).

46 O'Connor, *Memoirs*, i. p. 109.

47 *Letters and Leaders*, i. p. 393; Healy to Maurice Healy, 5, 27 Jan. 1893, Healy typescripts; Lucy, *Home Rule Parliament*, pp. 10, 15, 409; *F.J.*, 3 Dec. 1895.

48 Note in the Midleton Papers, PRO (London) 30/67/2; Midleton, *Records and Reactions 1856-1937* (London, 1939), pp. 222–3; *Hansard*, vol. 14, col. 1537 (11 July 1893); R. B. McDowell, *The Irish Convention 1917-18* (London, 1970), p. 88.

49 Lucy, *Home Rule Parliament*, pp. 197–208; Healy, *Letters and Leaders*, ii. p. 397.

50 Lucy, *Home Rule Parliament*, p. 114. Lucy commented: 'Mr. Parnell, however had his ovation four years ago, when the Liberals, led by Mr. Gladstone, leaped to their feet, welcoming the Irish chief as he entered the House on the day of Pigott's flight. Now Mr. Parnell is dead and buried, forgotten by all but the grotesque yet faithful Irishman who has planted himself out among the flower of the British aristocracy above the gangway on the Conservative side.'

51 Lyons, *Dillon*, p. 161; *Letters and Leaders*, ii. p. 413.

52 Healy to O'Brien, 19 June 1894, NLI MS 8556. As the Liberal government left office in 1886 Healy had urged on Labouchere the appointment of 'good revising barristers in certain Ulster places'. Labouchere spoke to Morley and wrote to Herbert Gladstone that 'it might be as well to waken him up, as Healy says there is yet time' (Labouchere to H. Gladstone, 19 June [1886] BM, Add. MS 46016, f. 86).

53 *Letters and Leaders*, ii. pp. 412–13; Healy to Maurice Healy, 4, 9, 12 Aug. 1894, Healy typescripts.

54 Dillon to O'Brien, 12 Oct. 1893, copy, Dillon papers, TCD MS 6737, f. 349; J. Hooper to Dillon, 11 June 1894, Dillon Papers, TCD MS 6839, f. 96; Healy to Maurice Healy, 31 Jan. 1892, Healy typescripts; O'Brien to Dillon, 20 Sept. 1895 (see also 26 Sept. 1895), Dillon Papers, TCD MS 6738, ff. 658, 665. O'Brien wrote to Dillon that it was remarkable how Healy's progress followed Parnell's, 'even to the fact that Dublin alone is with him' (O'Brien to Dillon, Dillon Papers, 'Fri', n.d. [1893], TCD MS 6737, f. 383). Within Dublin, Dillon regarded the Law Library of the Four Courts as a centre of hostile intrigue, not altogether without justification. At the time of the re-unification negotiations, John Muldoon wrote to Dillon: 'Healy and Clancy have been in consultation all day at the Library. I dare say they will perfectly understand one another at the conference'. He complained three years later that 'Healy's ascendancy continues at the Four Courts' (John Muldoon to Dillon, 20 Nov. 1899, 14 Nov. 1902, Dillon Papers, TCD MS 6734, ff. 50, 66).

55 Healy to Maurice Healy, 26 Jan. 1894, Healy typescripts.

56 O'Brien to Dillon, 29 Mar. 1895, Dillon Papers, TCD MS 6737, f. 291.

57 Healy, *Why Ireland is Not Free*, pp. 11204; *Hansard*, 4th ser., vol. 34, passim; Healy to Maurice Healy, 2 June 1895, Healy typescripts. The text published in *Letters and Leaders*, ii. pp. 41506 is diluted.

58 Healy, *Letters and Leaders*, ii. pp. 414–19; *Why Ireland is Not Free*, pp. 114–15; *Hansard*, vol. 34, passim.

59 Healy to Maurice Healy, 3 June 1895, Healy typescripts.

60 Healy to Maurice Healy, 8 June 1895, Healy typescripts.

61 Healy to Maurice Healy, 7, 8 July, misdated 7, 8 June 1895, Healy typescripts; Healy, *Why Ireland is Not Free*, pp. 106, 123–6; Healy, *Letters and Leaders*, ii. pp. 420–2; Lyons, *Irish Parliamentary Party*, pp. 51–2; see generally Margaret A. Banks, *Edward Blake, Irish Nationalist, A Canadian in Irish Politics* (Toronto, 1957), pp. 86–108, 112–37.

62 Healy to Maurice Healy, 7 July 1895, Healy typescripts.

63 *Letters and Leaders*, ii. p. 418; Healy to Maurice Healy, 19 July 1895, Healy typescripts.

64 Lyons, *Irish Parliamentary Party*, pp. 53–7; Healy, *Why Ireland is Not Free*, pp. 132–3; *Letters and Leaders*, ii. p. 324. The published version differs subtly from the proofs: 'I now became an outlaw' (*Letters and Leaders* Proofs, 187).

65 Healy to Maurice Healy, 3 June 1895, Healy typescripts.

66 *Truth*, 23 Nov. 1895, quoted *I.C.*, 30 Nov 1895.

67 Healy to Maurice Healy, 3 June, 30 Sept., 4 Oct. 1895.

68 *Hansard*, vol. 30, cols. 495–502 (11 Feb. 1895).

69 *Nation*, 5 Sept. 1896, *Daily Chronicle* interview.

70 *Letters and Leaders*, ii. p. 426. Long after, Healy told Arthur Balfour that his brother was 'the best Chief Secretary that Ireland ever had' (A. J. Balfour to T. M. Healy, 29 Dec. 1922, quoted Andrew Gailey, *Ireland and the Death of Kindness* [Cork, 1987], p. 131). Lady Fingal recalled that Healy had 'almost an adoration' for Gerald Balfour (Lady Fingal, *Seventy Years Young* [London, 1937, repr. Dublin 1991], p. 232). In the Commons in 1905, Healy defended his support for Balfour, and declaring that he 'certainly had been most anxious for many years to see whether they could not bring some measure of detachment to bear on their relations to English parties', surveyed the history of those relations (*Hansard*, vol. 140, cols. 808-17 [21 Feb. 1905]).

71 *Nation*, 22 Aug. 1896; Healy, 'The New Irish Land Act: What it does for the Tenant', *Saturday Review*, 15 Aug. 1896; D.N., 22 Feb. 1898.

72 Lucy, *Unionist Parliament*, p. 97 (26 July 1896).

73 *D.Nat.*, 19 Nov. 1897, Dundrum.

74 *D.Nat.*, 27 Jan. 1899.

75 Lyons, *Irish Parliamentary Party*, pp. 56–62; Lyons, *Dillon*, pp. 170–1; Healy, *Why Ireland is Not Free*, p. 147.

76 *Leader*, 17 Sept. 1910. The remark, made in the narrow context of Dillon's refusal to accommodate himself to the Irish–Ireland movement may have been inspired by Maurice Healy's reference to Dillon shortly before as 'the fossil toad of Irish politics' (*C.F.P.*, 29 Aug. 1910).

77 Harold Frederic wrote perceptively of Dillon in 1887 that:

> he always impresses me as feeling that he is the visible connecting link between the poetic and chivalrous uprising of 1848 and the severely practical and hard-fisted bargaining of 1886. And the imaginative Irish people seem to thus regard him, too, for everywhere in Ireland he is held in the deepest love, and his name is mentioned with a deferential tenderness that differs equally from the awe and impersonal devotion which Mr. Parnell inspires, and from the turbulent affection in which Healy, Davitt, William O'Brien, and the Redmonds are held.

Of the impression of almost morose severity which Dillon frequently created, Frederic wrote: 'He may not be either a gloomy or self-enwrapped man, but he gives the stranger as chilling a sense of being both as if he were a materialized portrait of Philip II stepping out of his framed entombment in the Escurial' (*N.Y.T.*, 7 Aug. 1887).

77 A. M. Sullivan, *Old Ireland, Reminiscences of an Irish K.C.* (London, 1927), p. 135.

78 A. M. Sullivan, ibid.

79 *Nation*, 5 Sept. 1896, *Daily Chronicle* interview.

80 The first article appeared in *I.C.*, 7 Mar. 1896, the last in the *Nation*, 3 Apr. 1897.

81 Healy to Maurice Healy snr., 11 Feb. 1897, Healy-Sullivan Papers, UCD P6/A/32. In the preface to the text, which relied extensively on newspaper quotations *in extenso*, Healy wrote: 'Those who may question the conclusions of this narrative, can confine themselves solely to the extracts — taken from sources which are indisputable — and base a judgement upon them alone'.

82 Healy to Maurice Healy, 30 Oct. 1898, Healy typescripts.

83 Healy to Maurice Healy, 25 Oct. 1896, Healy typescripts.

84 *Nation*, 23 Jan. 1897; Healy, *Why Ireland is Not Free*, pp. 176–7.

85 *F.J.*, 2 Dec. 1896, Wexford.

86 *Nation*, 16 Jan. 1897; Lyons, *Irish Parliamentary Party*, pp. 63–4. As if to celebrate ecclesiastical support for the Healy-Sullivan connection, T. D. Sullivan in January 1897 published some excruciating and fawning verses entitled 'Fair Halls of Maynooth', to be sung to the air of 'Believe me if all those endearing young charms' (*Nation*, 9 Jan. 1897).

87 *Nation*, 23, 30 Jan., 13, 20 Feb. 1897.

88 *Nation*, 6 Feb. 1897; *W.N.*, 12 June 1897; *D.Nat.*, 1 Oct. 1897, 28 May 1900; *The Liffey at Ebb Tide*, pp. 35–6.

89 *W.N.*, 4 June 1898; *D.Nat.*, 16 Mar. 1899. The paper's editorial prejudices were predictable. It was for example robustly anti-Dreyfusard, endorsing the Rennes judgement which upheld the conviction of 'the wretched traitor'. In this it was not unrepresentative. The *Daily Nation* in turn deplored the publication by the *Freeman's Journal* of a cartoon 'amidst the delirium of the expulsion policy depicting Mr. Healy as "Dreyfus degraded by Erin"' (*D.Nat.*, 11 Sept. 1900, 13 Jan. 1900). The *Daily Nation* referred distastefully to William O'Brien's *Irish People* as 'the expensive periodical which, either at his own expense or that of his Hebrew

connections, the creator of Mgr. McGrudder issues once a week' (*D.Nat.*, 2 Feb. 1900). O'Brien's wife Sophie was of a wealthy French Jewish family; Monsignor McGrudder was the fictional Irish priest unflatteringly portrayed by O'Brien, for whose creation he was never forgiven by many Irish clergymen.

90 *D.Nat.*, 24 Mar., 8 Feb. 1899.

91 *W.N.*, 8 Oct. 1898; *D.Nat.*, 7 Apr. 1899.

92 *I.I.*, 8 Sept. 1900, Healy to ed. *Dundalk Examiner*, 7 Sept.; *I.I.*, *F.J.*, 10 Sept. 1900.

93 *Hansard*, 4 ser., vol. 1, col. 546 (15 Feb. 1892). *'Arragaseesh'* was *Hansard*'s brave attempt at *'airgead síos'*.

94 Their reciprocal recriminations were collated by members of the Young Irish League and published by the United Ireland Branch in 1910, by which time Healy and O'Brien were once again steadfast allies, in a highly entertaining pamphlet, *'The Liffey at Ebb Tide': Mr. William O'Brien's Opinion of Mr. T. M. Healy M.P.; and Mr. T. M. Healy's Opinion of Mr. William O'Brien M.P.* The title was taken from an attack on O'Brien by the *Daily Nation*: 'Mr. O'Brien glories in the language of the virago and the drab, and he is never so happy as when he is pouring out adjectives which inevitably remind the reader of the Liffey when the tide is on the ebb' (*D.Nat.*, 2 Nov. 1899). Healy in December 1895 sent Maurice 'what I conceived to be a funny article' about William O'Brien for the *Irish Catholic* which he had stayed up till four o'clock in the morning to write. He wanted Maurice's opinion. 'I confess however to having smacked my chops over it' (Healy to Maurice Healy, 4 Dec. 1895, Healy typescripts).

95 Lyons, *Irish Parliamentary Party*, p. 70.

96 *W.N.*, 19 Mar., 2, 16 Apr., 1898; *The Liffey at the Tide*, pp. 24–5.

97 *D.Nat.*, 3 May 1900. The 'Impariayl', was the Imperial Hotel in Sackville Street where O'Brien used to stay when in Dublin.

22: REUNIONS AND ESTRANGEMENTS

1 *The Leader*, 9 Apr. 1910.

2 Ralph D. Blumenfeld, *R.D.B.'s Procession* (London, 1935), p. 245.

3 Healy to Maurice Healy, 2 Apr. 1899; see Lyons, *Irish Parliamentary Party*, pp. 78–9.

4 *D. Nat.*, 22 Nov. 1899, 31 Jan. 1900; Healy to Walker Leonard Cole, 12 Oct. 1898, Cole papers in the possession of Dorothy Walker.

5 *Letters and Leaders*, ii. pp. 434–5, 443–4; Lyons, *Irish Parliamentary Party*, pp. 78–89; J. V. O'Brien, *William O'Brien*, pp. 122–7.

6 Lyons, *Irish Parliamentary Party*, pp. 90–7.

7 Healy to Maurice Healy, 1 Mar. 1900, Healy typescripts.

8 Healy to Maurice Healy, 29 Apr. 1990, Healy typescripts.

9 Lyons, *Irish Parliamentary Party*, pp. 95–7.

10 Healy to Maurice Healy, 3 Aug. 1900, *Letters and Leaders* Proofs, B200.

11 Healy to Maurice Healy, 9 Aug. 1900, *Letters and Leaders* Proofs, B201; see Harrington to Redmond, 30 Mar. 1900, Redmond Papers, NLI MS 15194.

12 *Letters and Leaders*, ii. pp. 449–50, 613; *Souvenir of Presentation by Staff of Independent Newspapers Ltd. to Dr. William Lombard Murphy, 20 June 1914* (Murphy papers); W. M. Murphy, *The Story of a Newspaper* (Dublin 1909), reprinted from *I.I.*, 2 Jan. 1900, pp. 5–7.

13 *I.I.*, 24 Sept. 1900, Louth, Co. Louth; Healy, *Letters and Leaders*, ii. p. 452; *The Liffey at Ebb Tide*, pp. 12–14; W. O'Brien, *An Olive Branch in Ireland*, pp. 128–9, n.1. A few weeks later Healy appeared for the defendant in a breach of promise action. When he embarked on a vigorous cross-examination of the plaintiff on

the subject of her previous love-life, her counsel, who enjoyed some repute as a drinker, interposed 'please remember, Mr. Healy, that you are not on a brake at Dundalk'. This was unwise. Healy retorted 'I would rather be on a brake in Dundalk than on a bend in Rathmines' (M. Healy, *Munster Circuit*, p. 241; John J. Horgan, *Parnell to Pearse* [Dublin, 1948], p. 55).

14 Healy to Maurice Healy, 22 Sept. 1900, Healy typescripts. For Healy's account of O'Brien's recent actions, intended to assist Maurice in his campaign, see Healy to Maurice Healy, 27 Sept. 1900, Healy typescripts.

15 Healy to Maurice Healy, 3 Oct. 1900, Healy typescripts.

16 Healy to Maurice Healy, 3 Oct. 1900, Healy typescripts; T. D. Sullivan, *Troubled Times in Irish Politics* (preface). Of the North Mayo contest, Healy had written: 'All the priests and the Bishop are for Murphy, and so are the Ballina Parnellites' (Healy to Maurice Healy, 22 Sept. 1900, Healy typescripts). For the Parnellites of Ballina, see Callanan, *Parnell Split*, p. 114.

17 *I.I.*, 9 Nov. 1900, Westport. It was a measure of Healy's isolation that one of the few voices raised in his defence was that of the perennial maverick F. H. O'Donnell, in an entertaining letter extolling Healy's virtues and condemning 'the Cabal of Lilliputians' by whom he was outlawed (*I.I.*, 22 Dec. 1900, F. H. O'Donnell to ed.).

18 *I.I.*, 12, 13 Dec. 1900; Healy to Maurice Healy snr., 19 Nov. 1900, Healy-Sullivan Papers, UCD P6/A/35; *Letters and Leaders*, ii. pp. 453-4; Lyons, *Irish Parliamentary Party*, p. 98; J. V. O'Brien, *William O'Brien*, p. 127.

19 Lucy, *Unionist Parliament*, pp. 107-8, 357.

20 *Leader*, 9 Apr. 1910.

21 Maev Sullivan, 'Tim Healy'; Healy to Maurice Healy, 30 Apr. 1920, Healy typescripts.

22 Healy to Maurice Healy, 31 Jan. 1906, Healy typescripts. In an earlier letter, while acknowledging that Maurice would have a ready-made practice as a solicitor, Healy had written: 'If he got into practice as a barrister, I think it is a nicer way of living than a solicitor's, but he might wait long before he made money enough to keep himself at the Bar. I having remarked to John Hynes the other day in the Library that the Four Courts was a doomed institution, he replied that he heard Fleming say so twenty years ago!' (Healy to Maurice Healy, typescripts 15 Oct. 1905, Healy typescripts). In the event, Maurice Healy went to the bar. He practised 1910-14 on the Munster Circuit, and thereafter on the English Midland Circuit. He was made a King's Counsel in 1931, and later a bencher of the Inner Temple. He is the author of *The Old Munster Circuit* (London, 1939), and of *Stay Me with Flagons* (London 1940; republished with annotations by Ian Maxwell Campbell and a memoir by Sir Norman Birkett [London, 1949]).

T. M. Healy, for all his demotic verve, was sensitive to the need to conserve the barrister's mystique. He told George O'Brien in the Law Library not to smoke a cigarette while wearing his wig and gown, explaining that barristers robed and wigged so as not to appear like ordinary men, and that the cigarette ruined the effect. I am grateful to Charles Edward Lysaght for this information.

23 *I.I.*, 31 March 1931, J. B. Hall, 'Mr. T. M. Healy as an Advocate'; J. B. Hall, *Random Records of a Reporter* (London and Dublin, n.d.), pp. 106-7.

24 M. Healy, *Munster Circuit*, pp. 216, 240.

25 James O'Connor, *History of Ireland*, pp. 79-80. Mrs. William O'Brien, *My Irish Friends* (Dublin and London, 1937), p. 69. Stephen Gwynn likewise wrote on Healy's death that it was often said 'litigants insisted on having Healy because, even if they did not get the verdict, they got satisfaction through his handling of the adversary'

(*Observer* 29 Mar. 1931). According to his daughter, Healy had declined James O'Connor's request to intervene in support of O'Connor's pursuit of judicial office. Healy had reportedly responded: 'It's like the case of a bee with its sting. If I were to use my power even once, it would be the end of me' (Maev Sullivan, 'Tim Healy').

26 Edward Martyn to J. J. Horgan, 29 Jan. 1906, Horgan MSS NLI P4645.

27 *D.N.*, 19 Dec. 1925, A.G.G., 'Mr. "Tim" Healy'.

28 Healy left an estate of £28,523-10s-10d (Will and Grant of Probate to the Estate of T. M. Healy, 1931, No. 568, Public Record Office Dublin).

29 H. W. Lucy, *Unionist Parliament*, p. 13 (31 Aug. 1895), p. 329 (9 Feb. 1900).

30 Curzon, *Modern Parliamentary Eloquence* (London, 1913), p. 51.

31 Lady Oxford, *More Memories*, p. 55.

32 Quoted *D.Nat.*, 10 Feb. 1900.

33 *M.G.*, quoted *D. Nat.*, 9 Feb. 1900.

34 *D.N.*, 19 Dec. 1925, A.G.G., 'Mr. "Tim" Healy'.

35 T. W. Russell, 'Mr. Timothy Healy', *Ulster Guardian*, 11 Aug. 1906.

36 *Hansard*, vol. 121, cols. 52-6 (7 May 1903).

37 H. W. Lucy, *Balfourian Parliament*, pp. 256-9.

38 *Hansard*, vol. 113, cols. 29, 41, 57-8 (18 Oct. 1902); Healy, *Letters and Leaders*, ii. pp. 460-1.

39 *Hansard*, vol. 78, col. 858 (7 Feb. 1900).

40 *Hansard*, vol. 140, col. 813 (21 Feb. 1905); *Letters and Leaders*, ii. p. 472.

41 *Hansard*, vol. 42, col. 1660 (18 Oct. 1912); *Letters and Leaders*, ii. p. 508.

42 *Hansard*, vol. 27, cols. 1212-14 (27 July 1894); Austen Chamberlain, *Down the Years* (London, 1935), p. 84.

43 Alfred Webb, 'Memoirs', concluded Mar. 1905, pp. 410, 505, Library of the Society of Friends.

44 *Observer*, 2 Dec. 1928.

45 *Nation*, 1 Dec. 1877, 'T.M.H.' to ed.

46 *F.J.*, 19-23 Oct. 1893; Maurice Healy, *A Plea for Irish Spelling Reform* (Dublin, 1893); Healy to Maurice Healy, 13 Dec. 1893, Healy typescripts. Eoin MacNeill objected that to remodel the literary language 'on the basis of purely colloquial Irish would be disastrous to the interests of the language' (*F.J.*, 24 Oct. 1893).

A quarter of a century later, Healy waspishly accused his brother of pedantry in his opposition to Sinn Féin: 'I believe you should have published your Gaelic primer twenty years ago. I believe you should have taken an interest in the amendment of the law of joint tenants in common!!' (Healy to Maurice Healy, 21 May 1918, Healy typescripts).

47 Healy to Maurice Healy, 13 Dec. 1893, see also 24 Jan. 1894, Healy typescripts. Healy described Hyde as 'a nice modest fellow, a student without any dogmatism, and quite unlike what I expected'. Hyde's views had evidently mellowed somewhat in the two years since February 1892, when he recorded in his diary having a cigar and a glass of punch with a friend, 'in the company of the scoundrel Tim Healy, but without speaking to him' (Dominic Daly, *The Young Douglas Hyde*, p. 150). Such a comically limited form of dissociation suggested that even then Hyde's disapprobation was fighting a losing battle with curiosity.

48 *Hansard*, vol. 5, cols. 271-8 (30 May 1892).

49 *Leader*, 10 Aug. 1901.

50 *Hansard*, vol. 89, col. 964 (22 Feb. 1901).

51 *Hansard*, 4th ser., vol. 79, cols. 754-5 (21 Feb. 1900); Lucy, *Unionist Parliament*, p. 343.

52 Healy to Maurice Healy, 14 Mar. 1901, *Letters and Leaders* Proofs 203.

53 Healy to Maurice Healy, 21 Mar. 1901, Healy typescripts.

54 Healy to Maurice Healy, 26 July 1902, Healy typescripts.

55 Healy to Maurice Healy, 24 July 1901, *Letters and Leaders* Proofs; Healy to Maurice Healy snr., 2 June 1901, Healy-Sullivan Papers, UCD P6/A/37.

56 Healy to Maurice Healy snr., 31 Aug. 1903, Healy-Sullivan Papers, UCD P6/A/40; Healy to Maurice Healy, 9 Mar. 1904, *Letters and Leaders* Proofs, B210.

57 Healy to Maurice Healy, 15 Feb. 1901, 24 Jan. 1902, Healy typescripts.

58 Healy to Maurice Healy snr., 2 June 1901, Healy-Sullivan Papers, UCD P6/A/37.

59 Healy to Maurice Healy, 7 Feb. 1903, Healy typescripts.

60 Healy to Maurice Healy, 22 July 1903, Healy typescripts.

61 *I.I.*, 19 Feb. 1903, Healy in the *Morning Post.*

62 Healy to Maurice Healy, 3 Mar. 1903, Healy typescripts; *Letters and Leaders*, ii. p. 462.

63 *Letters and Leaders*, ii. pp. 460-5. Both Healy and O'Brien were susceptible to the appeal of Wyndham. O'Brien's biographer Michael McDonagh wrote that 'Wyndham, the handsomest and most sensitive man in the House of Commons of his day, used to remind me after his fall of the description of Shelley — "a rare but ineffectual angel, beating in the void his luminous wings in vain"' (McDonagh, *William O'Brien*, p. 184).

64 George Wyndham to his father, 21 Nov. 1903, in J. W. Mackail and Guy Wyndham, *Life and Letters of George Wyndham* (London, 2 vols. n.d.), ii. p. 474.

65 W. O'Brien, *An Olive Branch in Ireland*, pp. 168-291; Lyons, *Irish Parliamentary Party*, pp. 99-109. Concluding his assessment of Dillon in the *Dictionary of National Biography*, Stephen Gwynn wrote: 'He had great gifts in counsel, but his long foresight was ever tempered by an excessive pessimism. The breach between him and O'Brien, who counterbalanced this defect, was a great misfortune for Ireland' (*D.N.B.* 1922-30, p. 266). John O'Leary on the other hand considered O'Brien 'a historic lunatic', an assessment in which Davitt concurred (Davitt to John O'Leary, 12 May 1906, Davitt Papers TCD MS 9377).

The acrimonious stasis of Cork politics after O'Brien's breach with Redmond and Dillon is finely evoked in Frank O'Connor's short story of 1942 'The Cornet-Player who Betrayed Ireland' (republished in *The Cornet-Player who Betrayed Ireland* [Dublin, 1981]). At the story's end the bandmaster says: 'The curse of God on the day we ever heard of Remond or O'Brien! We were happy men before it'. The cornet-player is based on O'Connor's father who, although a supporter of O'Brien, was a drummer in an Irish party band: 'It was a superb band, and Father liked music so well that he preferred it to politics. For the sake of the music he even endured the indignity of playing for Johnny Redmond. Naturally, whenever he attended a demonstration at which William O' was criticised, he withdrew, like a good Catholic from a heretical service'. He subsequently joined an O'Brienite band (Frank O'Connor, *An Only Child*, p. 7).

66 Healy to Maurice Healy snr., 31 Aug. 1903, Healy-Sullivan Papers, UCD P6/A/40.

67 Healy to Maurice Healy, 2 Nov. 1903, Healy typescripts.

68 Healy to Maurice Healy, 22 Apr. 1904.

69 Healy to Maurice Healy, 13 Aug. 1904, Healy typescripts.

70 *I.I.*, 19 Oct. 1904, interview with *Pall Mall Gazette.*

71 Healy to Maurice Healy, 10 Dec. 1904, *Letters and Leaders* Proofs, B211.

72 Healy to Maurice Healy, 9 Oct. 1905, Healy typescripts.

73 Healy to Maurice Healy, 15 Oct. 1905, Healy typescripts.

74 *I.I.*, 4 Dec. 1905, Healy to ed. 3 Dec.; see also *I.I.*, 17 July 1905, Healy interview.

75 Healy to Maurice Healy, 3 Dec. 1905, Healy typescripts; *Letters and Leaders*, ii. p. 474.

76 *I.I.*, 1 Jan. 1906, Healy to Rev. B. Connellan, d. 31 Dec. 1905.

77 *I.I.*, 8, 9 Jan. 1906.
78 *I.I.*, 5 Jan. 1906, Dundalk.
79 *Hansard*, vol. 156, col. 1533 (10 May 1906); *Letters and Leaders*, ii. pp. 475–8; Maev Sullivan, 'Tim Healy'.
80 Healy to Maurice Healy snr., 28 July 1906, Healy-Sullivan Papers, UCD P6/A/47; Healy to Maurice Healy, 18 Aug. 1906, Healy transcripts. For the death of Healy's father see Maev Sullivan, 'Tim Healy', and *Letters and Leaders*, ii. p. 480.
81 *I.I.*, 15 Mar. 1907.
82 *Letters and Leaders*, ii. p. 480; *I.I.*, 9–16 Mar. 1907.
83 Lyons, *Irish Parliamentary Party*, pp. 115–16; Lyons, *Dillon*, pp. 293–8.
84 *I.I.*, 10 May 1907, *Standard* (interview).
85 *I.I.*, 14 May 1907.
86 *C.F.P.*, 11 Sept. 1911.
87 *I.I.*, 14 May 1907, interview with *Cork Examiner*. Sexton conducted the affairs of the *Freeman's Journal* 1892-1912. Two years earlier Healy had advanced a similar interpretation of the pledge, and asserted that he had published a series of articles in *United Ireland* which converted a reluctant Parnell to the idea of a pledge. Healy absurdly argued that Parnell had implicitly recognised that the pledge represented a check on his authority (*I.I.*, 3 July 1905).
88 Healy to O'Brien, 10 Oct. 1907, NLI MS 8556; *I.I.*, 21 Oct. 1907.
89 Healy to O'Brien, 30 Oct. 1907 (see also 16 Nov. 1907), NLI MS 8556.
90 Healy to Maurice Healy, 22 Nov. 1907, Healy typescripts.
91 Healy to O'Brien, 10 Nov. 1907, NLI MS 8556.
92 Healy to O'Brien, 16 Nov. 1907, NLI MS 8556. This was a standard count in the Healyite indictment of Dillon. Healy told a meeting in Dungarvan three years later that Dillon 'did not believe you would be nationalists unless you were kept beggars' (*C.F.P.*, 19 Sept. 1910).
93 *I.D.I.*, 23 Nov., 24 Dec. 1907, 18 Jan. 1908; Healy to O'Brien, 20 Dec. 1907, NLI MS 8556; O'Brien to Redmond, 14, 19 Dec. 1907, Redmond Papers, NLI MS 15212 (12).
94 Healy to Maurice Healy, 13 Dec. 1907, Healy typescripts.
95 *F.J.*, 18 Jan. 1908; Lyons, *Irish Parliamentary Party*, p. 122.
96 *Hansard*, 5 ser., vol. 187, col. 230 (30 Mar. 1908).
97 Healy to Maurice Healy, 2 Apr. 1908, Healy typescripts.
98 Healy to Maurice Healy snr., 12 Dec. 1905, UCD P6/A/45; *Letters and Leaders*, ii. p. 475.
99 Lyons, *Irish Parliamentary Party*, pp. 124–5; O'Brien, *Olive Branch in Ireland*, pp. 441–56; McDonagh, *William O'Brien*, pp. 179–84; J. V. O'Brien, *William O'Brien*, pp. 186–8.
100 O'Brien, *Irish Revolution*, p. 5.
101 Healy to Maurice Healy, 20 Mar. 1909; see also 1, 2 Apr. 1909, Healy typescripts; McDonagh, *William O'Brien*, pp. 184–5; Joseph O'Brien, *William O'Brien*, pp. 188–90.
102 Healy to Maurice Healy, 15, 28 Apr. 1909, Healy typescripts; *Letters and Leaders*, ii. p. 485.
103 Healy to Maurice Healy, 28 May 1909, Healy typescripts; Healy, *Letters and Leaders*, ii. pp. 485–6. For an assessment of the significance of the Cork election of 1909 in the longer term see J. J. Horgan, *Parnell to Pearse* (Dublin, 1948), pp. 174–7.

23: THE ALL-FOR-IRELAND LEAGUE

1 T. M. Kettle, 'Crossing the Irish Sea' (1909), in *The Day's Burden* (Dublin, 1937), p. 21.

2 *I.I.*, 2 Oct. 1911; *F.J.*, 20 Oct. 1911. The statue of St. Gaudens was the subject of lively controversy. The *Irish Independent* condemned its replication of 'the face of the Parnell of the weekly cartoon and the old-fashioned sugar bowl' (see generally Timothy J. O'Keefe, 'The Art and Politics of the Parnell Monument', *Eire-Ireland*, Spring 1984, pp. 6-23). The sculptor said that his greatest assistance came from hostile caricatures of Parnell. One, by Harry Furniss, representing Parnell as a dog, the body crouched on the ground with the forepaws extended, 'the suggestion being that the subject was desirous of springing at the throat of England', had particularly inspired him (*F.J.*, 30 Sept. 1911). Even before Joyce's *Ulysses*, the solemn statuary of Dublin elicited civic ribaldry. F. H. O'Donnell, in his introduction of his polemical pamphlet *The Lost Hat*, addressed to Archbishop Walsh of Dublin, began with the announcement that 'in the most conspicuous street of your Archdiocese the semi-Pagan inspiration of a great American sculptor has erected a Phallic Pillar as the completion and culmination of his conception of a congenial statute to the late Mr. Charles Stewart Parnell' (F. H. O'Donnell, *The Lost Hat*, p. 5). On passing the Parnell monument, a seminarian friend of Austin Clarke recounted an anecdote of a young labourer from the Gloucester Street tenements, attending confession in the pro-Cathedral, referring to a young girl holding what he demurely described as 'me parnell, Father'. His friend went on to expound his theory that 'in the poorer districts some obscure instinctive memory of ancient priapic cults might have been stirred by that obelisk . . .' (Austin Clarke, *Twice Round the Black Church* [London, 1962, repr. Dublin, 1990], p. 125).

3 *I.I.*, 2 Oct. 1911.

4 *Sinn Féin*, 7 Oct. 1911.

5 *Leader*, 16 Feb. 1907; Patrick Maume, *D. P. Moran* (Dundalk, 1995), p. 16.

6 K. O'Shea, *Parnell*, i. pp xii–xiii.

7 Healy to Maurice Healy, 13 Sept. 1913, Healy typescripts. The text published in *Letters and Leaders*, ii. p. 528, is heavily edited.

8 Healy to Maurice Healy, 26 Apr. 1914, Healy typescripts.

9 P. S. O'Hegarty, review of Henry Harrison, *Parnell, Joseph Chamberlain & Mr. Garvin*, in *The Dublin Magazine*, vol. 14 [Jan. 1939], p. 74). On the response generally see 'Love, Politics and Textual Corruption: Mrs. O'Shea's Parnell' in R. F. Foster, *Paddy and Mr. Punch* (London, 1993), pp. 123–38; and see F. H. O'Donnell, *The Lost Hat*. Roger Casement observed to W. S. Blunt that if Katharine O'Shea's revelations had been made two years previously there would have been no statue to Parnell (W. S. Blunt, *My Diaries* [London, 1919, 1932 ed.], p. 839 [later recollection of conversation of 14 May 1914]).

Lloyd George used Katharine O'Shea's two volumes to good purpose, presenting them to his secretary Frances Stevenson, who was within four weeks to become his mistress. The Parnell precedent was never far from his mind. Frances Stevenson wrote in her diary in January 1916: 'He says though that he could face disgrace with me now, and still be happy. "I can understand Parnell for the first time", he said to me' (Frances Lloyd George, *The Days that are Past* [London, 1967]; Ruth Longford, *Frances, Countess Lloyd George: More than a Mistress* [London, 1996], p. 11; *Sunday Times*, 24 May 1996, review by Anthony Howard; Frances Stevenson, *Lloyd George, A Diary*, ed. A. J. P. Taylor [London, 1971], pp. 91–2).

10 C. C. O'Brien, *Parnell and his Party*, p. 356.

11 Healy to O'Brien, 4 Aug. 1910, NLI MS 8556.
12 Healy to Maurice Healy, 29 Oct. 1910, Healy typescripts.
13 Lyons, *Irish Parliamentary Party*, p. 127; O'Brien, *Olive Branch in Ireland*, pp. 463–70; Healy to Maurice Healy, 19 Jan. 1910, Healy typescripts; *Letters and Leaders*, ii. pp. 491–2; see also T. P. O'Connor to Dillon, 1 Jan. 1910, Dillon Papers, TCD MS 6740, f. 162.
14 *C.F.P.*, 11 June 1910. The first leading article was written by Canon P. A. Sheehan (*C.F.P.*, 7, 8 Oct. 1913).
15 Healy to Maurice Healy, 14 Feb. 1910, Healy typescripts.
16 *I.I.*, 1 Apr. 1910; O'Brien, *Irish Revolution*, p. 55.
17 O'Brien, *Irish Revolution*, p. 64; O'Brien, 'Secret History', introduction by Sophie O'Brien.
18 O'Brien, *Olive Branch in Ireland*, pp. 470–3; *Irish Revolution*, pp. 62–73. The byzantine sociology of Cork urban politics continued to bear the impress of the Parnell split. One commentator wrote of the election of December 1910 that while the 'respectable' voters tended to favour the Irish party, the working classes were O'Brienite: 'In many quarters the issue was fought on the old Parnellite and anti-Parnellite lines. Among many of the lower classes in Cork there is a very strong prejudice against the name of Redmond' (*Leader*, 31 Dec. 1910, *Corcaigheach*, 'Reflections on Political Cork'). Sympathy was forthcoming from unexpected quarters. The once clear-headed Parnellite Katharine Tynan Hinkson, now an expatriate, commended 'the little band of Independent Nationalists which will save Ireland from being the Liberal tail' (*C.A.*, 2 Feb. 1910).
19 Sean O'Luing, *Art O'Griofa* (Dublin, 1953), pp. 199–205; J. V. O'Brien, *William O'Brien*, pp. 19–23; O'Brien, *Irish Revolution*, pp. 66–8; see also O'Brien, *Olive Branch in Ireland*, p. 473. O'Brien's *Cork Free Press* in 1913 published a series of articles by Griffith on a subject on which their shared opposition to the Irish party permitted them to agree, 'Place-Hunting in Irish Politics' (*C.F.P.*, 26 Apr.–5 July 1913). Relations between Griffith and O'Brien had started on a low note. In the Mayo South by-election of February 1900, O'Brien had denounced Major John McBride, who stood as an independent nationalist supported by Griffith, as a Healyite (George A. Lyons, *Some Recollections of Griffith & his Times* [Dublin, 1923], pp. 37–9).
20 O'Brien, *Irish Revolution*, p. 68; *C.F.P.*, 15 Jan. 1912.
21 *C.A.*, 26 Mar., 1 Apr. 1910.
22 Healy to Maurice Healy, 20 Mar., 5 May 1910, Healy typescripts.
23 Healy to Maurice Healy, 4 Sept. 1910, Healy typescripts.
24 *C.A.*, 9 June 1910, Healy to O'Brien, d. 7 June; The *Leader* had earlier referred derisively to the prospect of an 'All-for-William League' (27 Mar. 1909). *William O'Brien*, p. 259.
25 *C.A.*, 26 Apr. 1910, Healy to the Town Clerk of Kilkenny, d. 23 Apr. *Letters and Leaders*, ii. pp. 492–4.
26 *C.F.P.*, 4 Nov. 1910; Healy to Maurice Healy, 29 Oct. 1910, Healy typescripts.
27 *Leader*, 9 Apr. 1910; see also 16, 30 Apr. 1910.
28 *Leader*, 26 Nov. 1910; see also 19 Mar. 1910.
29 *C.F.P.*, 11 Sept. 1911.
30 Gwynn, *Redmond*, pp. 161–6.
31 Healy to Maurice Healy, 6 Feb. 1910, Healy typescripts; Roy Jenkins, *Mr. Balfour's Poodle* (London, 1954), p. 134; see also *C.A.*, 17 May 1910, speech of Maurice Healy.
32 Austen Chamberlain, *Politics from Inside* (London, 1936), p. 203.
33 Healy to Maurice Healy, 14 Feb. 1910, Healy typescripts.
34 Healy to O'Brien, 21 July 1911, NLI MS 8556.

35 Peter Rowland, *The Last Liberal Governments* (2 vols., New York, 1969), i. p. 294; *Hansard*, vol. 15, cols. 1739-78 (18 Apr. 1910); *Letters and Leaders*, ii. p. 495; Healy to Maurice Healy, 30 Mar. 1910, Healy typescripts.
36 Healy to O'Brien, 19 Mar. 1910, NLI MS 8556.
37 Redmond to Dillon, 14 Mar. 1910, Dillon Papers, MS 6748 ff. 448 TCD.
38 Dillon to C. P. Scott, 19 Mar. 1910, Dillon Papers, TCD MS 6843, f. 7; see also T. P. O'Connor to John Dillon, 9, 10, 15 Mar. 1910, Dillon Papers, TCD MS 6740, ff. 176, 176A, 178.
39 Rowland, *The Last Liberal Governments, op. cit.*, i. p. 294.
40 Roy Jenkins, *Mr. Balfour's Poodle* (London, 1954), pp. 131-2; *I.I.*, 4, 11, 12 Apr.; *C.A.*, 14 Apr. 1910.
41 *I.I.*, 11 Apr. 1910.
42 *C.A.*, 14 Apr. 1910, Healy to ed. d. 13 Apr.; *C.A.*, 19 Apr. 1910; *Hansard*, vol. 15, cols. 1739-78 (18 Apr. 1910); Austen Chamberlain, *Politics from Inside* (London, 1936), p. 254.
43 Charles Hobhouse, *Inside Asquith's Cabinet: From the Diaries of Charles Hobhouse*, ed. Edward David (London, 1977), p. 88 (entry for 10 Mar. 1910); J. V. O'Brien, *William O'Brien*, pp. 195-6.
44 Memorandum quoted in Arthur C. Murray, *Master and Brother: Murrays of Elibank* (London, 1945), p. 48. Murray was told by O'Brien that Redmond was terrified of his 'mother-in-law', John Dillon.
45 Mansergh, *Unresolved Question*, p. 37.
46 Ronan Fanning, 'The Irish Policy of Asquith's Government and the Cabinet Crisis of 1910', in Art Cosgrove and Donal McCartney, ed., *Studies in Irish History* (Dublin, 1979), pp. 301-3.
47 *C.A.*, 26 Apr. 1910, Healy to town clerk of Kilkenny; *C.A.*, 9 June 1910.
48 *Hansard*, vol. 16, cols. 1776-82 (18 Apr. 1910). The reference is to Parnell's letter to Healy of 17 Nov. 1885 enjoining him to impress upon the newly elected nationalist members the necessity of avoiding 'violent, boastful and extreme' language (Parnell to Healy, 17 Nov. 1885, Healy-Sullivan Papers, UCD P6/B/18). Healy had earlier criticised Redmond's stance in a letter to his brother: 'Redmond's speech last night wound up with a demand that there should be an immediate Dissolution, and that the Prime Minister should see the King beforehand and demand assurances, and if he was refused dissolve, practically with the cry of "Down with the King"; the most absurd yet delivered. In fact these men have no solvent for the situation, and no policy worthy of the name' (Healy to Maurice Healy, 30 Mar. 1910, Healy typescripts). For a selection of O'Brien's attacks on Redmond, delivered mainly on the premise that the pursuit of the removal of the Lords veto was chimerical, see the United Irish League broadsheet, *Mr. William O'Brien as a Prophet: What he said on the Veto Question* (undated, but evidently 1912).
49 Healy to O'Brien, 14 May 1910, NLI MS 8556.
50 Healy to Maurice Healy, 5 May 1910, Healy typescripts.
51 Healy to O'Brien, 23 Dec. 1911, NLI MS 8556.
52 O'Brien later wrote that the Liberals had had the daring 'to convert the entire Nationalist party into pensioners of the British Treasury'. This, added to the patronage which the Irish party was able to exercise under the National Insurance Act, resulted in a corruption of Irish life 'compared with which the debauchment of a few score of peers and bankrupt country gentlemen for the carrying of the Union was a transaction of mean dimensions' (W. O'Brien, 'Is there a way out of the chaos in Ireland?', *Nineteenth Century*, vol. 80 [Sept. 1916], p. 491).
53 *C.F.P.*, 4 Oct. 1910, O'Brien article in London *Standard.*

54 *C.A.*, 5 Feb. 1910.

55 *Hansard*, vol. 17, cols. 68-74 (25 Apr. 1910); see also vol. 18, col. 1883 (30 June 1910).

56 *Observer*, 23 Oct. 1910, *C.F.P.*, 23 Oct. 1910. O'Brien somewhat pathetically asserted that 'a conference of a dozen British editors I could name might have a more permanent influence on the relations between the two islands than the politicians' conference of eight'.

57 Gollin, *The Observer & J. L. Garvin* (London, 1960), pp. 168-80; Ayerst, *Garvin of the Observer* (Kent, 1985), pp. 100-2. According to Frewen, Garvin had observed of O'Brien that 'that man is as some old prophet in Israel' (*C.F.P.*, 12 Dec. 1910). The Quixote image was perhaps the more apt.

58 Alan J. Ward, 'Frewen's Anglo-American campaign for Federalism, 1910-21', *I.H.S.*, vol. 15, p. 260, 274; J. V. O'Brien, *William O'Brien*, pp. 201-2.

59 *C.F.P.*, 24 Oct. 1910; see also 15 Aug. 1910.

60 Healy to O'Brien, 1 Oct. 1910, NLI MS 8556; Healy to Maurice Healy, 22 Nov. 1910, Healy typescripts.

61 Frewen to Grey, n.d., quoted in Alan J. Ward, 'Frewen's Anglo-American Campaign for Federalism', *op. cit.*, pp. 268-9.

62 Healy to Maurice Healy, 1 Feb. 1910, Healy typescripts.

63 Healy to Maurice Healy, 24 Nov. 1910, Healy typescripts. He had written in mid-1910 to O'Brien that the cardinal was 'simply pestered with typewritten letters of abuse for having taken my side at the last election' (Healy to O'Brien, 5 May 1910, NLI MS 8556).

64 *I.I.*, 9 Sept. 1910, Dundalk.

65 Healy to Maurice Healy, 1, 6 Dec. 1910, Healy typescripts.

66 Healy to Maurice Healy, 17 Dec. 1910, Healy typescripts. Healy had described Murphy in the dark days after the 1900 election as behaving 'like an Indian at the stake. He never blenches or complains . . .' (Healy to Maurice Healy, 19 Nov. 1900, *Letters and Leaders*, ii. p. 453).

67 Healy to Maurice Healy, 18 Dec. 1910, Healy typescripts.

68 *C.F.P.*, 9-24 Feb. 1911. Healy pursued the hapless Hazleton for the costs of the action, which he believed the Irish party should have met. Hazelton sought to shed himself of the liability to pay Healy's costs by the device of resigning the North Galway seat for which he was elected in December 1910, submitting to bankruptcy, and re-contesting the seat immediately after this discharge as a bankrupt. This Healy successfully thwarted. Healy maintained his pursuit of the costs of the petition, but desisted at the request of Hazleton's counsel when Hazleton lost his seat at the 1918 election. For this sorry saga, see *Letters and Leaders*, ii. pp. 554-5, 557.

69 Healy to Maurice Healy, 27 Feb., 1, 8, Mar. 1911.

70 *C.F.P.*, 15 Mar. 1911.

71 Healy to Maurice Healy, 17, 18 Dec. 1910, 4, 5, 10, 15, 18, 20, 24, 29 (2) Mar., 10, 11 (2) May, 3, 4, 5, July 1911, Healy typescripts; Healy to O'Brien, 29 July 1911, NLI MS 8556; *C.F.P.*, 7, 10 Apr. 1911.

To Bonar Law, Frewen subsequently claimed that he resigned 'for the reason that the passing of the Parliament Act would make Ulster irreconcilable and Home Rule impossible' (Frewen to Bonar Law, 26 Feb. 1914, Bonar Law Papers, 31/3/43 House of Lords Record Office). Frewen continued undeterred to promote a federalist solution. He believed that through Dunraven, Healy and O'Brien could be brought to a situation where they would oppose home rule in favour of a federal solution in which minority rights would be protected by a strong second chamber at Westminster. Healy in turn sought to use Frewen (see Frewen to Bonar Law, 24 Aug. 1912, 27 Oct. 1913, Bonar Law Papers, House of Lords Records Office, 27/2/11,

30/3/54). Frewen went so far as to sign the Ulster Covenant in the belief that he could thereby convert Carson to support of a federalist solution to the Irish question (Shane Leslie, *Studies in Sublime Failure*, pp. 286-7). He was bitterly critical of Redmond and Dillon for failing to seize what he considered the compelling opportunity of conciliating Ulster unionism by espousing a federalist policy. By July 1914 home rule as a concept had become for him 'vile and aborted' (Frewen to Bonar Law, n.d. 22 [July 1914], Bonar Law Papers, House of Lords Record Office, 33/1/43).

For the astonishing Frewen, see Anita Leslie, *A Victorian Adventurer* (London, 1966); Shane Leslie, *Studies in Sublime Failure* (London, 1932), pp. 179-246; Alan J. Ward, 'Frewen's Anglo-American Campaign for Federalism', op. cit.

72 Grays Inn, *Book of Orders*, vols. xx, xxii.

73 Healy to Maurice Healy, 29 Oct. 1910, Healy typescripts.

74 Healy to Maurice Healy, 17 Nov. 1910, Healy typescripts.

75 Healy to Maurice Healy, 14 Feb. 1911, Healy typescripts.

76 Healy to Maurice Healy, 18 Dec. 1913, Healy typescripts.

77 Healy to Maurice Healy, 14 Oct. 1920, Healy typescripts.

78 Healy to O'Brien, 14 Sept. 1911, NLI MS 8556.

79 *D. Nat.* 8 Nov. 1900, inaugural meeting of the Solicitors' Apprentices Debating Society of Ireland.

80 T. M. Healy, KC, M.P., *Votes for Women: Defence at Bow Street* (published by the Women's Freedom League).

81 Healy to Maurice Healy, 11 Mar. 1912, Healy typescripts.

82 *Suffrage Speeches from the Dock made at the Conspiracy Trial, Old Bailey,* May 15th-22nd, 1912 (published by the Woman's Press).

83 Healy to Maurice Healy, 23 July 1912. The sense of the letter is radically altered in the published text: *Letters and Leaders*, ii. p. 507.

84 *F.J.*, 7, 8 Aug. 1912; *Irish Citizen*, 10 Aug. 1912; Gwynn, *Redmond*, p. 210; Roy Jenkins, *Asquith* (London, 1964), p. 246. Healy had been briefed to appear for the defence in the trial of Irish suffragists the previous month, and 'much disappointment was occasioned' by his inability, at the last moment, to leave London (*Irish Citizen*, 12 July 1912). In 1917, repeating the view that women 'could not make a worse job of human government than we have done', Healy expressed the belief that an extension of the franchise in England 'will have a useful result in forcing German opinion towards woman suffrage', which would assist in the preservation of peace after the war (Healy to Maurice Healy, 17 May 1917, Healy typescripts).

85 M. Healy, *Munster Circuit*, p. 175.

86 Healy to Maurice Healy, 1 Feb. 1910, 11 Feb. 1911, Healy typescripts; A. M. Sullivan, *Old Ireland* (London, 1927), p. 98.

87 Healy to Maurice Healy, 11 Feb. 1911, 10 Dec. 1914, Healy typescripts.

88 Healy to Maurice Healy, 19 July 1912, Healy typescripts. Dillon and his adherents in turn were mistrustful of Sullivan, whom John Muldoon described as 'a public ruffian worse than Tim Healy and Maurice Healy put together and combined' (Muldoon to Dillon, 19 Sept. 1911, Dillon papers, TCD MS 6734, f. 144).

89 Minutes of the Bar Council, 4 July 1919-15 Jan. 1920. Healy wrote to his brother (Sullivan's brother-in-law) of the resolution: 'I have not read it, and only that it would advertise Master Alex I would apply for an injunction to remove it. The brave fellows who passed it did not append their names, and I was told that it was done by a Bar Quorum of the great Council in the absence of every responsible barrister. Several men asked me to demand a meeting of the Bar, as the Library was almost universally in my favour, but I would not enter into a wrangle with this creature' (Healy to Maurice Healy, 11 Dec. 1919).

90 Healy to Maurice Healy, 14 Oct. 1920, Healy typescripts.
91 Healy to Maurice Healy, 16 July 1910, Healy typescripts.
92 Healy to O'Brien, 22 Oct. 1910, NLI MS 8556.
93 Healy, *Stolen Waters* (London, 1913), *Letters and Leaders*, ii. pp. 524-5; Maev Sullivan, 'Tim Healy', p. 485. The preface is dated 21 Jan. 1913. The reviews of *Stolen Waters* were for the most part favourable. To some degree they followed party lines. The *Irish Catholic* opined that 'in France it would be crowned by the Academy', while the *Birmingham Post* commented that 'if he will forgive us for saying so, he cannot write a book'. The *Times* predictably complained that 'no mere list of mistakes could correct the false impressions conveyed by innuendo, assumption, and special pleading. It is simpler to regard the whole book as one vast *erratum*' (quoted in Healy, *The Great Fraud of Ulster*). The *Times* did not carry Healy's reply (Healy to Maurice Healy, 11, 13, 18 Sept. 1913, Healy typescripts; *Letters and Leaders*, ii. p. 529). Healy wrote to Maurice: 'The *Irish Times* notice was very hostile. Probably written by [Richard] Bagwell' (Healy to Maurice Healy, 28 Mar. 1913, Healy typescripts).
94 Healy to Maurice Healy, 1 Mar., 22 July, 7 Aug. 1917, Healy typescripts; Healy, *The Great Fraud of Ulster* (Dublin, 1917). A modern re-issue (Kerry, 1971) contains a foreword by Dennis Kennedy which addresses the subsequent history of the controversy, which again flared into prominence with the rise of the Northern Ireland Civil Rights Association: in 1969 there were clashes on the Lough between fishermen and the bailiffs of the Toome Eel Fisheries company (*ibid.*, pp. 5-12).

On 22 December 1918, Healy delivered a lecture at a meeting of the National Literary Society entitled 'The Pale Blackguards' (typescript, Healy-Sullivan Papers, UCD P6/F/2). He published and re-entitled the lecture as *The Planters Progress*, adding an additional essay on 'The Victims of 1615' (Dublin, 1921). He had previously delivered in Gray's Inn a lecture on 'Great Documentary Frauds' to the Solicitor's Managing Clerks' Association (Healy-Sullivan Papers, UCD P6/F/5).

24: THE THIRD HOME RULE BILL

1 Healy to O'Brien, 21 July 1911, NLI MS 8556.
2 Healy to Maurice Healy, 21 July 1911, typescripts.
3 *C.F.P.*, 18 Dec. 1911.
4 *C.F.P.*, 1 Jan. 1912.
5 Healy to O'Brien, 27 July 1911, NLI MS 8556.
6 *Hansard*, vol. 23, cols. 1804-5 (27 July 1911); *Letters and Leaders*, ii. p. 504; Healy to Maurice Healy, 27 July 1911, Healy typescripts. Healy later referred to the Lundon allegation as 'the acme of Satanic and cold-blooded infamy' (Healy to O'Brien, 11 Sept. 1911, NLI MS 8556).
7 Healy to O'Brien, 1 Sept. 1911, NLI MS 8556; J. V. O'Brien, *William O'Brien*, p. 204. Healy headed this unusually extended meditation from 'Glengariff (alleged) Castle'.
8 O'Brien, *Irish Revolution*, pp. 146-8; *C.F.P.*, 28 Jan. 1913; J. V. O'Brien, *William O'Brien*, p. 205; Denis Gwynn, *A History of Partition*, pp. 70-5.
9 *C.F.P.*, 15 Apr. 1912.
10 *C.F.P.*, 23 May 1912.
11 See Nicholas Mansergh's masterly analysis in his *Unresolved Question*, pp. 43-58.
12 Healy to Maurice Healy, 2 July 1912, Healy typescripts.
13 Healy to Maurice Healy, 8 July 1912, Healy typescripts.
14 Healy to Maurice Healy, 19 July 1912, Healy typescripts.

15 W. M. Murphy, *The Story of a Newspaper* (Dublin, 1909), reprinted from the *Irish Independent* of 2 Jan. 1909 (NLI IR 941 P36, pp. 6-7); *Souvenir of Presentation by Staff of Independent Newspapers Ltd. to Dr. William Lombard Murphy*, 29 June 1941, pp. 20-4 (Murphy Papers). Healy, *Letters and Leaders*, ii. pp. 488-51, 613; W. M. Murphy to T. R. Harrington, 30 June 1915, Murphy Papers; Healy to O'Brien, 14 May, 4 Aug., 14 Dec. 1910, NLI MS 8556.
16 Healy to Maurice Healy, 27 Nov. 1915, 17 Aug., 1918, Healy typescripts.
17 *Leader*, 23 Apr. 1910.
18 *C.F.P.*, 11 Feb. 1911.
19 W. M. Murphy to T. R. Harrington, 23 Oct. 1910, Murphy Papers.
20 Healy to William O'Brien, 17 Dec. 1910, NLI MS 8556.
21 Healy to O'Brien, 25 Dec. 1911, NLI MS 8556. Healy in his memoirs observed that Murphy's 'bible was Erskine Childers' *Finance* [sic] *of Home Rule*' (*Letters and Leaders*, ii. p. 589).
22 Healy to Maurice Healy, 11 Mar. 1912, Healy typescripts.
23 Healy to Maurice Healy, 5 Jan. 1914, Healy typescripts.
24 Healy to Maurice Healy, 19 Feb. 1914, Healy typescripts.
25 Healy to O'Brien, 15 Dec. 1914, NLI MS 8556.
26 *C.F.P.*, 13, 18 Nov. 1913.
27 Healy to Maurice Healy, 14 June 1915, Healy typescripts. In a brief respite in August 1915 he ventured that Murphy 'has I think at last dominated Harrington'. The complaints however were quickly resumed (Healy to Maurice Healy, 29 Aug., 5 Dec. 1915, Healy typescripts).
28 T. R. Harrington to W. M. Murphy, 26, 28 June 1915, W. M. Murphy to T. R. Harrington, 30 June 1915, Murphy Papers.
29 Healy to W. M. Murphy, 22 May 1916, W. M. Murphy to Healy, 24 May 1916, Murphy Papers. Healy and O'Brien were imperfectly reconciled to the altered conditions of twentieth-century politics. In the nineteenth century the speeches of leading politicians were faithfully transcribed in the major dailies. J. A. Spender, editor of the *Eastern Morning News* in Hull in the 1880s, wrote: 'It never occurred to us possible that speeches by Gladstone, Salisbury, Joseph Chamberlain, or Harcourt should receive less than the full honours of a verbatim report' (quoted John P. Mackintosh, *The British Cabinet* [2nd ed., London, 1968], p. 225, n. 1). The same applies to the speeches of the leading Irish politicians in the Irish newspapers of the period.
30 *I.I.*, 22 Jan. 1913. Impervious to Yeats' biting satire, *The Irish Catholic* wrote that 'it seems to follow that what our citizens are now called upon to do is to pledge themselves to raise £22,000 or £23,000 in order to provide housing accommodation for £70,000 worth of canvasses. The expenditure seems to us as disproportionate as would be that of a man who spent a similar sum on a box to hold seventy thousand sovereigns' (*I.C.*, 5 Dec. 1912).
31 G. K. Chesterton, *Irish Impressions*, (London, 1919), p. 75. Healy's friend P. A. Chance commented that Murphy went through life with the Companies Act in one hand and the *Imitation of Christ* in the other (Healy, *Letters and Leaders* Proofs, 259).
32 *I.C.*, 6 Sept. 1913.
33 *I.C.*, 27 Sept. 1918.
34 *I.C.*, 14 Feb. 1914, Larkin, *James Larkin*, p. 126; Mary E. Daly, *Dublin The Deposed Capital* (Cork, 1985), p. 311.
35 Healy to Maurice Healy, 25 Sept. 1913, Healy typescripts.
36 Larkin, *James Larkin*, p. 131.
37 Healy to Maurice Healy, 27 Sept. 1913, Healy typescripts.

38 Healy to Maurice Healy, 4 Oct. 1911, Healy typescripts.
39 Sean O'Casey, *Autobiographies*, 2. p. 572.
40 *I.I.*, 2 Oct. 1911.
41 Larkin, *James Larkin*, p. 136.
42 Healy to Maurice Healy, 29 Sept. 1913, Healy typescripts.
43 I.I., 4 Oct. 1913.
44 *Dublin Strikes 1913, Facts Concerning the Labour Disputes Contained in Speech of Mr. T. M. Healy KC MP at Court of Enquiry held in Dublin Castle on Wednesday 1 Oct. 1913* (Dublin, 1913).
45 Healy to Maurice Healy, 14 Oct. 1913, Healy typescripts.
46 Healy to Maurice Healy, 20 Sept., 10 Oct. 1913, Healy typescripts.
47 Healy, *Letters and Leaders* Proofs, 259.
48 Healy to Maurice Healy, 10 Oct. 1913, Healy typescripts. For the attitude of the Irish party, and in particular Dillon, to Larkin, see Lyons, *Dillon*, pp. 334–6. Dillon wrote to T. P. O'Connor: 'Dublin is Hell! And I don't see the way out. Murphy is a desperate character, Larkin as bad. It would be a blessing if they exterminated each other' (Dillon to T. P. O'Connor, 1 Oct. 1913, Dillon Papers, TCD MS 6740, f. 195).
49 *C.F.P.*, 6 Nov., see also 21 Nov. 1913.
50 Healy to Maurice Healy, 11 Oct. 1913, Healy typescripts.
51 Healy to Maurice Healy, 12 Jan. 1914, see also 19 Jan., Healy typescripts.
52 *Sunday Express*, 22 May 1927; see also Beaverbrook, *Men and Power*, pp. 294–9; Beaverbrook, *Divine Propagandist*, vii–ix; Taylor, *Beaverbrook*, pp. 315–16; Beaverbrook to Maev Sullivan, 2 Sept. (1931), Healy-Sullivan Papers, UCD P6/7/15.
53 Tom Driberg, *Beaverbrook, A Study in Power and Frustration* (London, 1956), p. 10; Beaverbrook, *Divine Propagandist*, ix. Bonar Law remained commendably resistant to Beaverbrook and Healy's mythology of politics. Fond of crime and mystery stories, on becoming the Conservative leader he was presented by Beaverbrook with a collection of histories and biographies selected by Healy. He responded that if he was obliged to read them to constitute himself a competent leader he would prefer to resign (Beaverbrook, *Decline and Fall of Lloyd George*, pp. 209–10).
54 Beaverbrook to Healy, 11 Aug. 1914, Beaverbrook Papers c/161, House of Lords Records Office. Healy had sought Beaverbrook's advice for the benefit of his secretary: 'Miss Little the writer of the enclosed wants to invest £300 (all she has in the world) which she saved as a School Teacher in 40 years' (Healy to Beaverbrook, 6 Aug. 1914).
55 Healy to Beaverbrook, 26 Nov. 1915, 11 Oct. 1919, Beaverbrook Papers, House of Lords Record Office C/161, 162. Among Beaverbrook's friends, Healy was not alone in the extravagance of his accolades: see Adam Sisman, *A. J. P. Taylor, A Biography* (London, 1994, repr. 1995), pp. 282, 314, 359.
56 Edward Marjoribanks, *The Life of Lord Carson*, i. (London, 1932), pp. 42–4.
57 O'Casey, *Autobiographies*, 2. p. 316.
58 Mansergh, *Unresolved Question*, pp. 70–2; O'Brien, *Irish Revolution*, pp. 195–208.
59 Healy to Maurice Healy, 13 Aug. 1913, Healy typescripts.
60 Healy to Maurice Healy, 18 Sept. 1913, Healy typescripts.
61 Healy to O'Brien, 1 Sept. 1911, NLI MS 8556.
62 Healy to Maurice Healy, 23 Sept. 1913, Healy typescripts.
63 Healy to Maurice Healy, 10, 11 Oct. 1913, Healy typescripts; Gwynn, Redmond, pp. 230–1.
64 Healy to Maurice Healy, 16 Oct. 1913, Healy typescripts, modified in *Letters and Leaders*, ii. p. 531.

65 Healy to Maurice Healy, 20 Oct. 1913, Healy typescripts. E. F. Vesey Knox was a barrister, and former nationalist. An ally of Healy's, he had sat for Cavan West 1890–5, and Derry City 1895–9. He had become involved in an embarrassing fracas in 1908. The Attorney General made a representation to the Treasurer in Gray's Inn, 'to the effect that on a recent occasion blows were exchanged in open court between Mr. V. Knox, K.C., a member of this bench, and of the Middle Temple, and Mr. Roskill K.C. a member of the Inner Temple'. He was severely reprimanded by the benchers of Gray's Inn with a direction 'that this order be screened in Hall and communicated to the other Inns of Court'. He resigned his membership of the committees of the Bench of Gray's Inn (Gray's Inn, Book of Orders, vol. xxii). It is a sobering reflection that at least one of Healy's erstwhile confederates surpassed him in partisan ardour.

66 Healy to O'Brien, 26 Oct. 1913; see also 9, 12 Dec. 1913, NLI MS.

67 Healy to Maurice Healy, 15 Dec. 1913, Healy typescripts; Healy to Beaverbrook, 11 Dec. 1913, Beaverbrook Papers c/161, House of Lords Record Office.

68 *I.I.*, 19 Jan. 1914.

69 Healy to Maurice Healy, 19 Jan. 1914, Healy typescripts.

70 Healy to Maurice Healy, 26 Jan. 1914, Healy typescripts. Lord Willoughby de Broke was a flamboyantly diehard opponent of the home rule bill, described by the biographer of Edward Carson as 'that gay and gallant Englishman', who founded in 1913 the British League for the Support of Ulster and the Union (Ian Colvin, *Carson The Statesman* [New York, 1935], p. 186).

71 Healy to Maurice Healy, 31 Jan. 1914, Healy typescripts.

72 Healy to Maurice Healy, 28 Jan. 1914, Healy typescripts.

73 Healy to Maurice Healy, 30 Jan. 1914, Healy typescripts.

74 Healy to Maurice Healy, 31 Jan. 1914, Healy typescripts.

75 Healy to Maurice Healy, 6 Feb. 1914, Healy typescripts.

76 Healy to Maurice Healy, 9 Feb. 1914, Healy typescripts.

77 Healy to Maurice Healy, 10, 13 Feb. 1914, Healy typescripts.

78 Healy to Maurice Healy, 10, 13 Feb. 1914, Healy typescripts. For the political background, see Mansergh, *Unresolved Question*, p. 70; Roy Jenkins, *Asquith* (London, 1964), p. 302.

79 Healy to Maurice Healy, 11 Feb. 1914, Healy typescripts.

80 Healy to Maurice Healy, 13 Feb. 1914, Healy typescripts.

81 Healy to Maurice Healy, 14 Feb. 1914, Healy typescripts. Healy also quoted the over-subtle view of A. G. Gardiner, the editor of the Liberal *Daily News* that 'Asquith was playing a very deep game, and that there would be no exclusion'.

82 Healy to Maurice Healy, 18 Feb. 1914; see also 14 Feb., Healy typescripts.

83 Memorandum in Healy's handwriting, 16 Feb. 1914, Asquith Papers, Bodleian Library.

84 Healy to Maurice Healy, 19 Feb., 12 Aug. 1914, Healy typescripts.

85 *C.F.P.*, 12 Feb. 1914; see also O'Brien's speech in Cork, *C.F.P.*, 10 Feb. 1914.

86 *Hansard*, vol. 59, cols. 941–5 (9 Mar. 1914); Healy to Maurice Healy, 5 Mar. 1914, Healy typescripts; Mansergh, *Unresolved Question*, pp. 72–3. In his speech Healy predicted, if not threatened, a boycott of the excluded counties by nationalist Ireland and the United States.

87 *I.I.*, 10, 17 Mar. 1914.

88 Healy to O'Brien, 17 Mar. 1914, NLI MS 8556.

89 Healy to O'Brien, 2 Jan. 1914, NLI MS 8556.

90 W. O'Brien, *The Downfall of Parliamentarianism* (Dublin and London, 1918), p. 29; see also pp. 55–6.

91 Healy to Maurice Healy, 19 Feb. 1914, Healy typescripts.
92 Healy to Maurice Healy, 26 Mar. 1914. For Healy's assessment of the mutiny itself, and his information in relation to it, see Healy to Maurice Healy, 25 Mar. 1914, enclosing the text of a letter of the same date to his wife (Healy typescripts).
93 Healy to O'Brien, 5 Apr. 1914, NLI MS 8556.
94 Mansergh, *Unresolved Question*, pp. 72–3; O'Brien, *Irish Revolution*, p. 205; J. V. O'Brien, *William O'Brien*, p. 211.
95 O'Brien, *Irish Revolution*, pp. 203–4; O'Brien, *The Responsibility for Partition* (Dublin and London, 1921), pp. 29–33.
96 *I.I.*, 1 June 1914, Glanworth, Co. Cork.
97 Healy to Maurice Healy, 16 July 1914, Healy typescripts; see also Healy to Maurice Healy, 13, 14 July 1914, *Letters and Leaders* Proofs, 236.

25: THE GREAT WAR

1 Healy to Maurice Healy, 4 Aug. 1914, Healy typescripts; Gwynn, *Redmond*, pp. 356–7.
2 Healy to Maurice Healy, 8 Aug. 1914, Healy typescripts.
3 Healy to Maurice Healy, 9 Aug. 1914, Healy typescripts.
4 *Letters and Leaders*, ii. p. 549; Healy to Maurice Healy, 12 Aug. 1914, Healy typescripts.
5 Healy to Maurice Healy, 22 Aug. 1914, Healy typescripts; see also 15 Sept. 1914.
6 J. V. O'Brien, *William O'Brien*, p. 214.
7 Mansergh, *Unresolved Question*, p. 85.
8 Gwynn, *Redmond*, pp. 356–7; Healy to Maurice Healy, 12 Aug. 1914, Healy typescripts.
9 Healy to Maurice Healy, 1 Sept. 1914, Healy typescripts.
10 *C.F.P.*, 3 Sept. 1914; J. V. O'Brien, *William O'Brien*, pp. 212–13.
11 David Hogan (pseud. Frank Gallagher), *The Four Glorious Years* (Dublin, 1958), pp. 222–4. Gallagher erroneously has O'Brien's speech postdating Redmond's speech at Woodenbridge.
12 Gwynn, *Redmond*, pp. 391–2; Macardle, *Irish Republic*, pp. 118–19.
13 Healy to Maurice Healy, 24 Sept. 1914, Healy typescripts.
14 Quoted *Leader*, 15 Apr. 1916. The *Freeman*'s attack was on the basis that Healy and O'Brien were objecting to the budget, whose purpose was to raise money to finance a war which they supported.
15 *I.I.*, 24 Nov. 1915.
16 Healy to Maurice Healy, 10 Dec. 1914. Healy was indulgent towards O'Brien's somewhat rambling editorials in the *Cork Free Press*: 'O'Brien's sentences are of wondrous length, running sometimes to 150 words, but his stuff is very good'.
17 Healy to O'Brien, 24 Dec. 1914, NLI MS 8556. 'Bridgeguards' was a derisive reference to the National Volunteers, a body of whom had been entrusted with the guarding of bridges in Cork (O'Brien, *Irish Revolution*, p. 23). Healy elsewhere refers to them as 'Bridgeteers' (Healy to O'Brien, 20 Jan. 1915, NLI MS 8556).
18 *Letters and Leaders*, ii. p. 554; Healy to Maurice Healy, 10 Dec. 1914, Healy typescripts.
19 Healy to Maurice Healy, 31 May 1915, Healy typescripts.
20 Healy to Maurice Healy, 23 Apr. 1915, Healy typescripts.
21 Healy to O'Brien, 21 May 1915, NLI MS 8556. Healy subsequently prevailed on Murphy to denounce Nathan in the *Irish Independent* (Healy to Maurice Healy, 27 Nov. 1915, Healy typescripts).
22 Healy to Maurice Healy, 5 Dec. 1915, Healy typescripts.

23 Healy to Maurice Healy, 27 Nov. 1915, Healy typescripts.

24 Healy to Maurice Healy, 28, 31 May, 10 June 1915, Healy typescripts. Healy, *Letters and Leaders*, ii. pp. 552-3; Gwynn, *Redmond*, pp. 427-33; Lyons, *Dillon*, pp. 365, 367, 375-6.

25 It was of James Campbell that Healy uttered one of his most celebrates *bons mots.* When Campbell, an astute and hard-bitten advocate, wept in opening a divorce case to the jury, Healy for the defence referred to it as 'the greatest miracle since Moses struck the rock' (M. Healy, *Munster Circuit*, p. 240; Plunket Barton, *Timothy Healy*, pp. 93-4).

26 Healy to O'Brien, 1 June 1915, NLI MS 8556.

27 Healy to Maurice Healy, 1 Sept. 1915, Healy typescripts.

28 Healy to Maurice Healy, 17 Sept. 1915, Healy typescript. Healy had written to Maurice earlier that year: 'I would welcome conscription for this country, as it would put our people on an equality with Carson's Orangemen in point of drill and discipline' (Healy to Maurice Healy, 15 May 1915, Healy typescripts).

29 Healy to Maurice Healy, 13 July 1915, see also 31 May 1915, Healy typescripts.

30 Healy to Maurice Healy, 29, 30 Aug. 1915.

31 Healy to Maurice Healy, 1 Sept. 1915, Healy typescripts.

32 Healy to Maurice Healy, 15 Oct. 1915, Healy typescripts.

33 Healy to Maurice Healy, 3 Nov. 1915, see also 8 Nov., Healy typescripts; *Letters and Leaders*, ii. pp. 554-5.

34 Healy to Maurice Healy, 5 Dec. 1915, Healy typescripts; *Letters and Leaders*, ii. pp. 554-6.

35 Healy to Maurice Healy, 14 Oct. 1915, Healy typescripts.

36 Gwynn, *Redmond*, p. 142; Lyons, *Dillon*, pp. 355-6.

37 Healy to Maurice Healy, 3 Nov. 1915, Healy typescripts.

38 Healy to Maurice Healy, 15 Oct., 5 Nov., 14 Dec. 1915, Healy typescripts.

39 Healy to Maurice Healy, 5 Dec. 1915, Healy typescripts, *Letters and Leaders* Proofs, p. 243.

40 Beaverbrook, *Decline and Fall of Lloyd George*, p. 96. Beaverbrook's chapter on the Treaty negotiations is entitled 'When Cromwell got out of Hell'.

41 *Letters and Leaders*, ii. p. 559. Healy had at least a fleeting professional acquaintance with Patrick Pearse. Healy *in absentia* led Pearse in McBride's case (I.R. [1906] 2, p. 181) in an appeal against the conviction of a cart-owner who, being legally obliged to display his name on his cart, had his name painted in the Irish language and in Irish characters. It was Pearse's only case as a barrister (Ruth Dudley Edwards, *Patrick Pearse, The Triumph of Failure* [London, 1977], pp. 79-81; Arthur Clery, 'Patrick Pearse's Only Case', in Louis J. Walsh, *Old Friends* [Dundalk, 1934], pp. 113-15).

42 David Hogan, *The Four Glorious Years* (Dublin, 1953), pp. 225-6. Frank Gallagher later assisted Desmond FitzGerald, Dáil Eireann's director of publicity, in the production of the *Irish Bulletin*, of which he co-wrote large sections with Erskine Childers (Macardle, *Irish Republic*, p. 310, n. 444). Healy wrote to his brother in January 1922 that he was told that de Valera's manifesto 'was written for him throughout by the editor of the *Cork Free Press*, Gallagher, who troubled poor William O'Brien!! It is fair to say that Gallagher was a wanted man during the terror. He had an article in the first number of the *Republic* which I thought clever' (Healy to Maurice Healy, 10 Jan. 1922, Healy typescripts). Gallagher subsequently edited the *Irish Press.*

43 Maev Sullivan, 'Tim Healy'; *Letters and Leaders*, ii. pp. 561-6.

44 *Hansard*, 5th ser., vol. 83, cols. 960-66 (11 May 1916). William O'Brien wrote in September 1916 that 'the hapless Mr. Birrell gave the key of his conscience to his Irish spiritual directors, and their advice has left him, in his own pathetic words,

amidst the ruins of his political career as well as of Dublin' (W. O'Brien, 'Is there a way out of the chaos in Ireland?', *Nineteenth Century*, vol. 80 [Sept. 1916], p. 491).

45 *I.I.*, 20 Sept. 1913, 10, 11, 12 May 1916; *Leader*, 7 Oct. 1916. An Irish Party handbill in the 1918 election, entitled 'The *Independent* and the Treatment of the Sinn Feiners', made skilful use of the relevant passages from the editorials.

46 Murphy's chief preoccupation in the immediate aftermath of the rising was as the head of the Dublin Fire and Property Losses Association, pressing the government to ensure that adequate compensation was forthcoming to compensate those whose premises had been damaged (*I.I.*, 20 May 1915).

47 Healy to Maurice Healy, 4 Oct. 1916, Healy typescripts; see also *Letters and Leaders*, ii. pp. 561-2.

48 Healy to Maurice Healy, 22 May 1916, Healy typescripts.

49 Healy to Maurice Healy, 10 June 1916, Healy typescripts.

50 Healy to Maurice Healy, 18 June 1916, Healy typescripts.

51 Healy to Maurice Healy, 22 May 1916, Healy typescripts.

52 O'Brien, *Irish Revolution*, pp. 256-80.

53 O'Brien to Lloyd George, 31 May 1916 enclosing memorandum, Lloyd George Papers, House of Lords Record Office D/14/44; W. O'Brien, 'Is there a way out of the chaos in Ireland?', *Nineteenth Century*, vol. 80 (Sept. 1916), pp. 499-501; J. V. O'Brien, *William O'Brien*, pp. 224-5.

54 W. O'Brien, 'Is there a way out of the chaos in Ireland?', *Nineteenth Century*, vol. 80 (Sept. 1916), p. 498.

55 Mansergh, *Unresolved Question*, pp. 90-100.

56 Healy to Maurice Healy, 7 June 1916, Healy typescripts. Healy even fleetingly reconsidered the attitude he had taken to the Irish Council Bill of 1907: 'O'Brien was of opinion we should have swallowed Anthony MacDonnell's Bill to which we were very much opposed; and in the events which have happened, he may have been right, although it seemed otherwise at the time'.

57 Healy to Maurice Healy, 10 June 1916, Healy typescripts.

58 Healy to Maurice Healy, 10 June 1916, Healy typescripts. The pre-eminence of the *Irish Independent* at this time was revealed by the fact that, as Healy complained to Maurice, it was invariably stolen out of the National Liberal Club (Healy to Maurice Healy, 18 June 1916, Healy typescripts).

59 W. M. Murphy to Lloyd George, 14, 20 June 1916; Lloyd George to Murphy, copy 17 June 1916, Lloyd George Papers, House of Lords Records Office, D14/2/10, 19, 38; *Letters and Leaders*, ii. p. 567.

60 Healy to Maurice Healy, 15 June 1916, Healy typescripts; *Letters and Leaders*, ii. pp. 569-77.

61 Healy to Maurice Healy, 16, 18, 23 June 1916.

62 Sophie O'Brien, introduction to William O'Brien, 'Secret History'; David Hogan, *The Four Glorious Years*, pp. 226-7. Gallagher gives an intriguing account of how O'Brien prepared his speeches for his set-piece declamations at All-for-Ireland League meetings. He spoke his speech to his wife, who took it down in shorthand and then transcribed it. O'Brien then read over the script in front of a mirror. It remained fixed in his mind so that he could deliver the exact text without notes. On this occasion Gallagher had to hasten from the meeting back to the offices of the *Cork Free Press* to amend the heroic account of the speech he had already written, in which he interpellated O'Brien's script with the conventional enthusiastic cheers, hand-clapping, and foot-stamping.

63 Healy to Maurice Healy, 23, 24 June 1916, Healy typescripts.

64 Healy to Maurice Healy, 28 July 1916, Healy typescripts.

65 Healy to Maurice Healy, 24 June 1916; for the Ulster nationalist conference, see Gwynn, *Redmond*, pp. 505-12; Mansergh, *Unresolved Question*, pp. 97-8.

66 Healy to Maurice Healy, 24 June 1916; for the Ulster nationalist conference, see Gwynn, *Redmond*, pp. 505-12; Mansergh, *Unresolved Question*, pp. 97-8.

67 Healy to Maurice Healy, 6 July 1916, Healy typescripts.

68 Healy to Maurice Healy, 7 July 1916, Healy typescripts.

69 Mansergh, *Unresolved Question*, pp. 99-100.

70 Healy to Maurice Healy, 28 Aug. 1916, Healy typescripts; *Letters and Leaders*, ii. p. 575.

71 Healy to Maurice Healy, 6 Sept. 1916, Healy typescripts.

72 Healy to Maurice Healy, 19 Sept. 1916, Healy typescripts.

73 *C.F.P.*, 12 Aug. 1916. For Healy's authorship of the verses, published over the letter 'H', see Healy to Maurice Healy, 6 Aug. 1916, Healy typescripts.

74 Healy to Maurice Healy, 29 Sept. 1916, Healy typescripts. The letter refers to the others present as Arthur Chance, L. A. Waldron, and T. A. Finlay S.J. In the published text Erskine Childers is also listed as a guest. An exchange between them cannot have endeared Healy to Childers: Healy asked 'how he came to write a book on home rule finance, being an Englishman, and he laughed, saying he was hardly that' (*Letters and Leaders*, ii. pp. 576-7). News of the dinner with Duke leaked out to the *Freeman's Journal* and to the *Leader*. An open letter to Murphy by a correspondent in the *Leader* declared: 'Not only did you dine at his official residence, but he graced your rebel home at Dartry. The fact that the world-renowned statesman, Mr. Tim Healy, M.P., was present no doubt contributed to a level-headed and impersonal discussion of public affairs'. The writer accused Murphy of ensuring that his papers carried no criticism of the Chief Secretary (*Leader*, 7 Oct. 1916, 'Dublin Nationalist', open letter). Healy concluded: 'It is plain the informant was someone on Duke's side. He will have plenty of Tory enemies in the Castle' (Healy to Maurice Healy, 6 Oct. 1916, Healy typescripts). The *Freeman's Journal* mischievously carried a report that those present at the 'Dartry Dinner' resolved on an immediate campaign to promote voluntary recruitment: 'Their influence with their countrymen is so well known that Mr. Duke is said to entertain no doubt as to their success' (*F.J.*, 9 Nov. 1915).

75 The following year he wrote of Duke: 'He is dead against Partition, and convinced me that the English don't want it and regard it as no settlement whatever'. He wrote later that 'Duke was forced out because he was honest about Home Rule' (Healy to Maurice Healy, 2 June 1917, 21 May 1918, Healy typescripts; *Letters and Leaders*, ii. pp. 582, 599).

76 *Sunday Times*, 23 Dec. 1916.

77 Lloyd George, *Family Letters 1885-1936*, ed. Kenneth O. Morgan (Cardiff and London, 1973), pp. 34, 44, 53, 100-1; P. Whitwell Wilson, 'Tiger Tim', *Pearson's Magazine*, vol. 33 (1912), pp. 284-6.

78 *North Wales Observer*, 4 Apr. 1902; *Times*, 15 Aug. 1904. Cuttings of both are in the Lloyd George papers.

79 H. W. Lucy, *Diary of the Unionist Parliament*, quoted John Grigg, *The Young Lloyd George* (London, 1973), pp. 207-8.

80 Dillon to O'Connor, 17 June 1924, Dillon Papers, TCD MS 5744, f. 95.

81 P. Whitwell Wilson, 'Tiger Tim', *Pearson's Magazine*, vol. 33 (1912), pp. 384-5.

82 Healy to Maurice Healy, 10 Feb. 1913, Healy typescripts. Amusingly, this sentence in the published text in Healy's memoirs is rendered: 'Lloyd George will be sorry for including Ireland in the Bill' (*Letters and Leaders*, ii. p. 513).

83 Healy to Maurice Healy, 12 Feb. 1913, Healy typescripts; *Letters and Leaders*, ii. pp. 506-23.

84 Healy to Maurice Healy, 3 Apr. 1913, Healy typescripts; *Letters and Leaders* Proofs, B228.

85 *Letters and Leaders*, ii. p. 525.

86 Healy to Maurice Healy, 13, 30 July 1915, Healy typescripts. The 'we' refers to Healy, Beaverbrook, and Beaverbrook's friends. He reported a fortnight later 'I think the Lloyd George intrigue completely squelched'

87 Healy to Maurice Healy, 8, 20 Mar. 1917, Healy typescripts. He wrote the following year: 'I regard the Asquith cycle as over; and I feel sure Devlin is secretly with Lloyd George and can be fooled by him. There is no love lost, I believe, between Dillon and George' (Healy to Maurice Healy, 11 May 1918, Healy typescripts).

88 Batt O'Connor, *With Michael Collins in the Fight for Irish Independence* (London, 1929), pp. 28-30; *I.I.*, 7, 10 June 1916.

89 Beatrice Webb, *Diaries 1912-17*, ed. Margaret Cole (London, 1952), entry for 21 May 1916. Healy's own reference to the Casement trial in his memoirs is entirely incidental: *Letters and Leaders*, ii. p. 570; for his assessment of E. D. Morel as a German spy, see pp. 548-9.

90 Brian Inglis, *Roger Casement* (London, 1973), pp. 329-49.

91 *Letters and Leaders*, ii. p. 574; Maev Sullivan, 'Tim Healy'. He wrote to Maurice a week later 'I applied for a permit to visit Reading Prison today, but the Jew did not reply' (Healy to Maurice Healy, 18 Aug. 1916, Healy typescripts). 'The Jew' refers to Herbert Samuel, the home secretary in Asquith's government. Such prejudices provided a ready key to international politics: 'If Korniloff is not going to restore the Czar, I prefer him to Kerensky, who is a Jew' (Healy to Maurice Healy, 12 Sept. 1917, Healy typescripts). He later observed of Hamar Greenwood, 'it is strange that Greenwood's name figures in the *Jewish Who's Who*' (Healy to Maurice Healy, 22 Aug. 1920, Healy typescripts). It remains preferable to classify Healy as a reactionary Catholic in his social views rather than as anti-semitic. Thus, writing to Beaverbrook in November 1924 on the subject of the future of American politics, he deplored contraception: '. . . it is plain that the breeding races must ultimately govern. They are Jews, Germans, Italians, Poles and Irish. Is Lord Dawson so anti-English that he advocates the spermatic destruction of the descendants of Agincourt? The fool saith in his heart there is no God' (Healy to Beaverbrook, 17 Nov. 1924, NLI MS 23273).

92 Healy to Maurice Healy, 27 Feb., 11 Mar. 1917, Healy typescripts; Macardle, *Irish Republic*, p. 242.

93 Healy to Bonar Law, 9 Mar 1917, Bonar Law Papers, 81/4/9, House of Lords Record Office. In terms of their personal relations, Healy's dealings with Bonar Law as Colonial Secretary on the subject of the release of the Irish prisoners were of some significance. Healy subsequently gave Birkenhead an account of his urging upon Bonar Law the release of the 1916 prisoners, on which Birkenhead relied in his 1925 character-sketch of Healy. In Birkenhead's rendering, Healy had found Bonar Law 'embedded in clouds of smoke' in his room behind the Speaker's chair. He assured Law that the prisoners' enduring penal servitude suffered so terribly 'that for their own sakes, and the sakes of their families, they would not again be likely to enter upon violent courses'. Healy, Birkenhead explained, did not personally know any of the prisoners, and his advice had been 'based upon the experience of an earlier generation, and went back to the arrests and trials in 1865 and 1867'.

Birkenhead did not attribute to Healy any particular responsibility for the government's decision to release the 1916 prisoners, announced by Bonar Law on 15 June 1917 (Macardle, *Irish Republic*, p. 221). The context of his remarks was rather Bonar Law's sanctioning as Prime Minister of Healy's appointment as Governor-General in 1922, when he 'might easily have reproached him with a mistake in judgement on Irish affairs, because he had urged upon him the release of de Valera and his accomplices in the 1916 rebellion'.

The elaborate apologia for Healy's actions bear traces of remorse on Healy's part, in the aftermath of the civil war, at having played a part (which he characteristically exaggerated) in procuring the release of de Valera and others, as well as gratitude to Bonar Law for not holding this against him. When Birkenhead wrote that 'it is certainly arguable that if de Valera and his abettors had endured a while longer the sentence which justice awarded, the course of Irish affairs would have flowed in different channels' (Birkenhead, *Contemporary Personalities* [London, 1925], pp. 206–8), he was almost certainly conveying Healy's own retrospective view.

94 Macardle, *Irish Republic*, pp. 227–9; *I.I.*, 10–17 Oct., 2 Nov. 1917.

95 W. M. Murphy to William Lombard Murphy, 17 Feb. 1918, Murphy Papers.

96 Healy to Maurice Healy, 25 July 1916, Healy typescripts.

97 Healy to Maurice Healy, 6, 26 Sept. 1916, Healy typescripts.

98 Healy to Maurice Healy, 29 Sept., 4 1916, Healy typescripts. For critiques of the opportunistic editorial positions of the *Irish Independent* from 1914, and particularly its swift *volte-face* after the 1916 rising, see *Leader*, 30 Sept., 7 Oct. 1916; *F.J.*, 7 Oct. 1916.

99 Healy to Maurice Healy, 13 Mar. 1917, Healy typescripts.

100 O'Brien to Healy, 5, 15 Aug. 1917; Healy to O'Brien, 19 Aug. 1917, NLI MS 8556; see also Healy to Maurice Healy, 20 Aug. 1917, Healy typescripts.

101 Healy to Maurice Healy, 20 Aug. 1917, Healy typescripts.

102 Healy to Maurice Healy, 6 Sept. 1917, Healy typescripts.

103 *Letters and Leaders*, ii. p. 470. In a passage deleted from the published text, he wrote admiringly: 'Anchored on realities, Murphy could not be flustered or driven from his purpose. He had spent £80,000 on a halfpenny paper to compete with the *Freeman* before a farthing of profit reached his till, and would have spent as much more had need been' (*Letters and Leaders* Proofs, B259, 269).

104 William O'Brien, *'The Party': who they are and what they have done* (Dublin and London, 1917), p. 31.

105 O'Connor, *Memoirs*, ii. p. 58.

106 Healy to Maurice Healy, 16 May 1917, Healy typescripts; see generally Lyons, *Dillon*, p. 416; Gwynn, *Redmond*, pp. 550–61.

107 O'Brien, *Irish Revolution*, pp. 316–21; J. V. O'Brien, *William O'Brien*, pp. 230–1.

108 *Letters and Leaders*, ii. pp. 583–4; Lloyd George to Healy, 20 July 1917, typescript copy, Lloyd George Papers, F27/2/2; Healy to Maurice Healy, 22 July 1917, Healy typescripts.

109 W. M. Murphy to W. L. Murphy, 20 June, 5 Aug. 1917, Murphy Papers.

110 Healy to O'Brien, 4 Jan., 23 Feb. 1918, NLI MS 8556. O'Brien later wanted to take part in a committee which the convention proposed to establish to draw up a scheme for the completion of land purchase. Murphy, according to Healy, had little sympathy with O'Brien, 'because he is the author of the predicament in which he is placed by his own refusal to attend contrary to Murphy's advice' (Healy to Maurice Healy, 24 Sept. 1917, Healy typescripts).

111 *Letters and Leaders*, ii. pp. 587–8, 594. Healy's scepticism was no doubt confirmed by his low estimate of its chairman Horace Plunkett, in reference to whom he had written in February 1914 during the debates on the home rule bill that he disliked 'all these milk-and-water persons so much that I cannot attribute interest or importance to their declarations' (Healy to Maurice Healy, 14 Feb. 1914, Healy typescripts).

112 Healy to Maurice Healy, 16 Jan. 1918, Healy typescripts. Murphy cleaved to the views already expressed in his pamphlet *The Home Rule Act Exposed* (Dublin, May 1917).

113 Healy to Maurice Healy, 17 Feb. 1918, Healy typescripts.

114 Healy to Maurice Healy, 1 Mar. 1918, Healy typescripts.

115 Healy to Maurice Healy, 6 Sept. 1918, Healy typescripts.

116 *I.I.*, 27 June 1919. According to information from his family, Murphy had declined first a knighthood and then a baronetcy (memorandum of author's conversation with Thomas V. Murphy, 7 July 1982). Healy wrote that Northcliffe during the war had told Murphy he would have a dukedom if he could resolve the Irish question, prompting Healy to observe semi-ironically: 'A kink in Murphy's fibre was that he did not want to be a duke' (*Letters and Leaders* Proofs, 250).

117 Healy to Maurice Healy, Healy typescripts, 1919, n.d. (4 Sept. 1919); *Letters and Leaders*, ii. p. 613). Healy's abiding animus against the *Freeman* is reflected in a deleted passage in the proofs of his memoirs: in the 1916 rising, 'British guns set fire to the *Freeman* premises. When the first shell fell on it the insurgents in the G.P.O. cheered' (*Letters and Leaders* Proofs, 269).

118 Healy to Maurice Healy, 15 Jan. 1917, Healy typescripts. Healy had written to O'Brien years before of O'Connor's estranged American wife: 'Bessy bombards the cabinet with letters against T.P. . . . She vows she will drive him into resignation' (Healy to O'Brien, 26 June 1911, NLI MS 8556).

119 Healy to O'Brien, 13 July 1917, NLI MS 8556.

120 Healy to O'Brien, 3 Oct. 1917, NLI MS 8556.

121 Healy to Maurice Healy, 13, 19 Oct. 1917, Healy typescripts; *Letters and Leaders*, ii. pp. 581, 586–7.

122 11, 16 Oct. 1917, Healy to Fr. Jas. E. McKenna, P.P., Dromore, Co. Tyrone.

123 W. O'Brien, *'The Party': Who they are and what they have done* (Dublin & London, 1917), pp. 5, 6; Healy to Maurice Healy, 14 Sept. 1917, Healy typescripts. O'Brien dismissed the myth that all the benefits of the preceding four decades could be attributed to 'The Party' as 'as fanciful as the belief in "the good people", and has been very much more harmful to the country' (ibid., p. 3). The comparison between contemporary public opinion and that prevailing at the Parnellite dawn of 1880 became a recurrent theme. Healy wrote to O'Brien: 'As for the Sinn Feiners, the country is in a high fever; and in 1918 reminds me very much of 1880' (Healy to O'Brien, 22 Feb. 1918, NLI MS 8556).

124 Healy to O'Brien, 3 Dec. 1917, NLI MS 8556.

125 *I.I.*, 7 Mar. 1918. William O'Brien's obituary of Redmond was tiresomely predictable: had Redmond not felt compelled to betray the policy of conciliation deriving from Wyndham's land act of 1903, the home rule impasse would have been averted (*National News*, 10 Mar 1919). He had more pithily formulated his characterisation of Redmond in 1910: 'Mr. Redmond is an opportunist, who always misses his opportunities; a politician whose judgement is nearly always right and whose action is almost as invariably wrong (*Observer*, 23 Oct. 1910).

126 Healy to O'Brien, 2, 15 Sept. 1917, O'Brien Papers, NLI MS 8556.

127 Terence de Vere White, *Kevin O'Higgins* (London, 1948, rep. 1966), pp. 1, 22–4; Healy, *Letters and Leaders*, ii. pp. 586, 597; Maev Sullivan, 'Tim Healy', pp. 193, 195; Healy to Maurice Healy, 11 May 1918, Healy typescripts; *Nation*, 15 Oct. 1887 (reporting the marriage of Annie Sullivan, third daughter of T. D. Sullivan, to Thomas Higgins, surgeon and the coroner for Queen's County). O'Higgins was ultimately, Minister for Home Affairs, called to the Irish bar (*W.I.T.*, 24 Jan. 1925).

128 Healy to Maurice Healy, 10 Feb. 1918, Healy typescripts.

129 Healy to Maurice Healy, 7 May 1918, Healy typescripts. 'Black Jack' Gallagher was the editor of the *Freeman's Journal* at the time of Parnell's rise (Healy, *Letters and Leaders*, i. pp. 76, 93). It is perhaps apt that it is by no means clear what Healy meant by the 'anti-unity party' and the 'unity gang': he appears to have been referring respectively to the O'Brienites, reinforced by Sinn Féin, and to Dillon's Irish party.

130 Healy to Maurice Healy, 11 May 1918.

131 Healy to Maurice Healy, 21 May 1918, Healy typescripts.

132 Dillon to O'Connor, 23 Apr. 1918, Dillon Papers, TCD MS 6742, f. 23.

133 Healy to Maurice Healy, 20 Feb. 1917, Healy typescripts. The sense of the letter is completely lost in the text published in *Letters and Leaders*, ii. p. 579. As to Dillon's attitude to the war, the graceless provocation afforded by his reference to the fallen T. M. Kettle in the House of Commons is revealing: 'Kettle went to France though he was a bitter Nationalist and was brought up in the hatred of England. He died gallantly fighting in your war (*Hon. Members: 'Our War!'*). It is not. It is a French war and a Russian war' (*Hansard*, vol. 86, col. 686 [18 Oct. 1916]).

134 Beaverbrook, *Politicians and the War* (London, 1960), pp. 34–5.

135 Healy to Maurice Healy, 18 Jan. 1918, Healy typescripts.

136 Healy to Maurice Healy, 23 May 1918, Healy typescripts.

137 Healy to Beaverbrook, 13 Feb. 1918, NLI MS 23265. This was the concluding paragraph of a letter of congratulation to Beaverbrook on his appointment as Minister for Information: 'Now you are a Cabinet Minister, plus a Bank, a newspaper, and half a hundred other things'. Healy hoped Beaverbrook might in due course be given a post 'other than a War job': 'The Colonial Office needs a Hercules, and I should like to see a Canadian boot indenting the posterior of beaurocracy [*sic*]'. When Beaverbrook resigned in October 1918, Healy wrote 'I wish we had a Commercial Foreign Office and you were chief thereof' (Healy to Beaverbrook, 14 Nov. 1918, NLI MS 23, 265).

138 *Hansard*, vol. 104, cols. 1432–43 (9 Apr. 1918).

139 Jones, *Whitehall Diary*, pp. 56–7.

140 J. V. O'Brien, *William O'Brien*, p. 233.

141 Macardle, *Irish Republic*, pp. 249–52; Healy, *Letters and Leaders*, ii. pp. 595–6; O'Brien, *Irish Revolution*, pp. 361–3; J. Anthony Gaughan, *Thomas Johnson, 1872-1963, First Leader of the Labour Party in Dáil Eireann* (Dublin, 1980), pp. 86–122.

142 Healy to O'Brien, 18 May 1918, NLI MS 8556; Macardle, *Irish Republic*, pp. 253–4.

143 Healy to Maurice Healy, 15 June 1918, Healy typescripts.

144 O'Brien to Healy, 2 May 1918, NLI MS 8556.

145 Healy to Maurice Healy, 24 May 1918, Healy typescripts, modified in Healy, *Letters and Leaders*, ii. pp. 599–601.

146 Healy to Maurice Healy, 15 June 1918, Healy typescripts.

147 Healy to Maurice Healy, 21 June 1918, Healy typescripts; Healy to O'Brien, 23 June 1918, NLI MS 8556. Healy's implacability towards Dillon was very occasionally punctuated by unaccountable ebullitions of tenderness. On one occasion during the war, Dillon and Healy found themselves on the same boat to Holyhead, on a rough crossing. Healy approached Dillon and, saying that he had a cabin but would be comfortable elsewhere, thrust the key into Dillon's hand. Sir James McMahon, who was with Healy at Torquay when he learnt of the death of John Dillon, told Dillon's son that tears streamed down Healy's cheeks, and that turning away, he said 'God rest his noble soul'. As James Dillon noted 'Healy was a very demonstrative man much given to polemics or sentiment' (author's

memorandum of conversation with James Dillon, 26 Sept. 1979, corrected in Dillon's hand; Maev Sullivan, 'Tim Healy').

148 *I.I.*, 8 June 1918, O'Brien to ed., 7 June.
149 Healy to Maurice Healy, 15 June 1918.
150 Healy to Maurice Healy, 6 Sept. 1918, *Letters and Leaders* Proofs, 265.
151 Healy to Maurice Healy, 21 June, 9, 17 Aug. 1918, Healy typescripts.
152 Dillon to O'Connor, 23 Aug. 1918, 6742, f. 518.
153 Healy to Maurice Healy, 9 Aug. 1918, Healy typescripts. All reference to this is deleted in the published text of the letter (*Letters and Leaders*, i. pp. 604–5).
154 Healy to Maurice Healy, 21 May 1918, Healy typescripts. Anne Catherine Emmerich (1774–1824) was a nun of the Augustinian order at the convent of Agnetenberg at Dulmen, Westphalia. Her visions were recorded by Clemens Brentano, chiefly in *The Dolorous Passion of Our Lord Jesus Christ according to the visions of the devout Anne Catherine Emmerich*. Healy had contemplated in 1914 undertaking its translation from the German (Healy to Maurice Healy, 10 Dec. 1914, Healy typescripts).
155 Healy to Maurice Healy, 8 Sept. 1918, Healy typescripts.
156 Healy to Maurice Healy, 10 Sept. 1918, Healy typescripts; reproduced in part in edited form, *Letters and Leaders*, ii. p. 606.
157 Healy to Maurice Healy, 15 Feb. 1919, Healy typescripts.
158 Healy to Maurice Healy, n.d., Healy typescripts, p. 11 (4 Sept. 1919).
159 Healy to Maurice Healy, 19 Aug. 1920, Healy typescripts.
160 For O'Brien's thesis of Morley's responsibility for the split, see W. O'Brien, *The Downfall of Parliamentarianism, A Retrospect for the Accounting Day* (Dublin and London, 1918), pp. 5–7; W. O'Brien, *Irish Revolution*, p. 96; W. O'Brien, 'A Missing Page of Irish History', *Catholic Bulletin*, xiii. no. 12 (Oct. 1923), pp. 690–706; W. O'Brien, 'Secret History', ii. p. 3; W. O'Brien, *Parnell*, pp. 150–79.
161 Healy to Maurice Healy, 17 Feb. 1918, Healy typescripts.
162 W. O'Brien, *'The Party' : Who they are and what they have done* (Dublin and London, 1917), p. 38.
163 Healy to O'Brien, 3 Sept. 1918; O'Brien to Healy, 18 Sept. 1918, NLI MS 8556.
164 Healy to Maurice Healy, 6 Sept. 1918, Healy typescripts.
165 Healy to O'Brien, 6 Oct. 1918, NLI MS 8556.
166 O'Brien to Healy, 10 Oct. 1918, NLI MS 8556.
167 Healy to Maurice Healy, 12 Oct. 1918, Healy typescripts.
168 Healy to O'Brien, 12 Oct. 1918, NLI MS 8556.
169 Healy to Maurice Healy, 6 Sept. 1918, Healy typescripts; Healy to O'Brien, 28, 30 Oct. 1918, NLI MS 8556; Maev Sullivan, 'Tim Healy', p. 35.
170 Healy to Maurice Healy, 12, 13, 30 Oct. 1918, Healy typescripts; Maev Sullivan, 'Tim Healy'.
171 *I.I.*, 30 Oct. 1918.
172 *Letters and Leaders*, ii. p. 607.
173 Healy to O'Brien, 6, Oct., 11 Nov. 1918, NLI MS 8556.
174 Healy to O'Brien, 3 Nov. 1918, O'Brien Papers, NLI MS 8556; see also Healy to Maurice Healy, 2 Nov. 1918, Healy typescripts.
175 Healy to O'Brien, 4 Nov. 1918, NLI MS 8556; see also Healy to Maurice Healy, 7 Nov. 1918, Healy typescripts; Healy, *Letters and Leaders*, ii. pp. 608, 651.
176 Healy, *Letters and Leaders*, ii. p. 650.
177 *I.I.*, 18, 25 Nov. 1918; O'Brien to Healy, 23 Nov. 1918, copy, O'Brien Papers, NLI MS 8556. O'Brien's pamphlet of October 1918, *The Downfall of Parliamentarianism, A Retrospect for the Accounting Day* (Dublin and London, 1918) was in

effect a historical apologia for Sinn Féin conducted in terms of a polemic against the Irish party leadership after Parnell. Its final section was ingratiatingly headed 'Ave Juventus' (ibid., p. 61; J. V. O'Brien, *William O'Brien*, p. 236).

178 Healy to O'Brien, 20 Nov. 1918, NLI MS 8556.

179 Healy to O'Brien, 30 Nov., 23 Dec., 1918, copies, O'Brien Papers, NLI MS.

180 O'Brien to Healy, 2 Jan. 1919, NLI MS 8556.

181 Healy to O'Brien, 21 Nov. 1919, NLI MS 8556. The reference is to the historian Edward Augustus Freeman. The previous month, he had written of the invitation made to O'Brien to tender for the failing *Freeman's Journal*: 'Oh my, why was I left out?' He prefaced some observations on the reversal of fortune of Thomas Lundon, who had cast aspersions on the patriotism of O'Brien's ancestry with the statement: 'Sweet however as recent revenges have been, I now propose to fill up your gluttonous chalice with a few drops of extra dry Monopole' (Healy to O'Brien, 9 Oct. 1918, NLI MS 8556).

26: THE ANGLO-IRISH TREATY

1 *Young Ireland*, 23 June 1920.

2 *D.N.*, 19 Dec. 1925, A.G.G., 'Mr. "Tim" Healy'.

3 Healy was to create at Glenaulin something approaching an ambassadorial court. William O'Brien's description was based on their correspondence:

> During the whole course of the Black and Tan wars, his services as a sort of informal liaison officer between Sinn Féin and friendly Englishmen had been of priceless value. His house at Glenaulin was a favourite place of pilgrimage for British Ministers and Ex-Ministers of all parties visiting the country and for Dublin Castle officials of the new school whom Sir Andrew Cope, the Assistant Under-Secretary, had arrayed against the Andersons and the Macreadys . . . Lord Dunraven and the Archbishop of Dublin and Sinn Féiners 'on the run' made an occasional call, and Mr. Eamonn Duggan a close personal friend kept the owner of Glenaulin discreetly familiar with the inner councils of the Sinn Féin leaders.
>
> (O'Brien 'Secret History', iv. p. 13.)

4 Healy to O'Brien, 3 Jan. 1919, NLI MS 8556.

5 Healy to O'Brien, 7 Apr. 1919, Healy typescripts.

6 Healy to O'Brien, 7 Apr. 1919, NLI MS 8556.

7 Healy to Maurice Healy, 11 May 1919, Healy typescripts; *Letters and Leaders*, ii. p. 611; Macardle, *Irish Republic*, p. 295.

8 Healy to Maurice Healy, 24 May, 8 Sept. 1919; see also Healy to O'Brien, 23 Nov., 23 Dec. 1918, NLI MS 8556.

8 Healy to Maurice Healy, 11 Dec. 1919, Healy typescripts; *Letters and Leaders*, ii. p. 166; Healy to O'Brien, 10 Dec. 1919, NLI MS 8556.

10 Healy to O'Brien, 2 Mar 1926, NLI MS 8556; *Letters and Leaders*, ii. p. 644.

11 Healy to Maurice Healy, 11 Dec. 1919, Healy typescripts.

12 William O'Brien, *When We Were Boys* (Dublin and London, 1919), introduction to the re-issue, pp. iii–xvii.

13 Healy to O'Brien, 9 Oct., 16, 21 Nov. 1919, NLI MS 8556; Dillon to T. P. O'Connor, 27 Nov. 1919, TCD MS 6743, f. 712. In his letter of 16 Nov. Healy said he would like to re-read the novel 'but my palate is gone. I could not take up even *Stolen Waters* to larrup my own nigger!' The phrase comes from Fonblanque, *England Under Seven Administrations:* 'Is this a land of liberty where a man can't larrop his own nigger?' (quoted, *O.E.D.*, 2nd ed., vol. xiii).

14 Healy to Maurice Healy, 8 July 1920, Healy typescripts.

15 Healy to Maurice Healy, 2 July 1920, Healy typescripts.
16 Healy to Maurice Healy, 27 July 1920, Healy typescripts.
17 Healy, *Letters and Leaders*, ii. pp. 617–8.
18 Healy to Maurice Healy, 10 Aug. 1920, Healy typescripts; *Letters and Leaders*, ii. p. 624; Macardle, *Irish Republic*, p. 379.
19 Healy to Maurice Healy, 23 Aug. 1920, Healy typescripts.
20 *Sunday Express*, 8 Aug. 1920.
21 Healy to O'Brien, 16 Aug. 1920, O'Brien Papers, NLI MS 8556; Healy to Maurice Healy, 16 Aug. 1920, Healy typescripts; *Letters and Leaders*, ii. p. 625.
22 Healy to Maurice Healy, 19 Aug. 1920, Healy typescripts.
23 Healy to Maurice Healy, 10 Aug. 1920, Healy typescripts; modified *Letters and Leaders*, ii. p. 264.
24 Healy to Maurice Healy, 4 Aug., see also 27 July 1920, Healy typescripts. The modifications to the letter in its published version for once conveys more than the original: 'I hinted that, if so, he should ward Downing Street until he caught them. We parted "unfriends"' (*Letters and Leaders*, ii. p. 624; for Healy's discussions with Bonar Law generally, see p. 573).
25 Healy to O'Brien, 16 Aug. 1920, see also 26 July 1920, NLI MS 8556.
26 Healy to Beaverbrook, 13 Dec. 1919, Beaverbrook Papers, c/162, House of Lords Record Office.
27 Healy to Beaverbrook, 15 Nov. 1920, NLI MS 23266.
28 Beaverbrook Papers, c/162, House of Lords Records.
29 Healy to Beaverbrook, 19 Nov. 1920, NLI MS 23267.
30 Healy to Beaverbrook, 30 Nov. 1920, NLI MS 23266.
31 Healy to Beaverbrook, 23 Dec. 1920, NLI MS 23268; for the Clune mission, see Macardle, *Irish Republic*, pp. 412–16; Dangerfield, *Damnable Question*, p. 322.
32 Healy to O'Brien, 21 Jan. 1921, O'Brien Papers, NLI MS 8556.
33 Healy to Beaverbrook, 16 Mar. 1921, NLI MS 23268.
34 Healy to Beaverbrook, 9 May 1921, see also 4 May 1921, NLI MS 23269.
35 Healy to Beaverbrook, 24 May 1921, NLI MS 23269. With this letter, Healy enclosed as he did from time to time what he called 'Shin-lets', copies of the *Irish Bulletin*, a mimeographed sheet published initially by the Sinn Féin Department of Publicity, and later by Dáil Eireann (Macardle, *Irish Republic*, pp. 318–19).
36 Healy to Beaverbrook, 27 Apr. 1921, NLI MS 23268; 28 May 1921, Beaverbrook Papers c/163, House of Lords Record Office.
37 Taylor, *Beaverbrook*, p. 253; Healy, *Letters and Leaders*, ii. p. 637. Healy wrote to Beaverbrook that 'the Belfast Orangemen knew that Craig's statement about being invited by De Valera to meet, is false & that the truth is he invited De V. by request of the Govt., and took nothing thereby. Craig will never be forgiven the deception & has injured himself very deeply. If he had told the facts, everyone wd. have applauded him except a few extremists in Belfast' (Healy to Beaverbrook, 9 May 1921, NLI MS 23269; Beaverbook Papers, c/163, House of Lords Record Office).
38 Healy to Maurice Healy, 6 June 1921, Healy typescripts; Beaverbrook, *Politicians and the Press* (London n.d.), pp. 34–44; A. J. P. Taylor, *Beaverbrook*, pp. 253–4; Chisholm and Davie, *Beaverbrook*, pp. 176–81.
39 Healy to Maurice Healy, 6 June 1921, Healy typescripts.
40 Birkenhead, *Frederick Edwin, Earl of Birkenhead, The Last Phase* (London, 1935), pp. 145–7; John Campbell, *F. E. Smith, First Earl of Birkenhead* (London, 1983), pp. 554–5.
41 Healy to O'Brien, 28 June 1921, NLI MS 8556. T. P. O'Connor likewise regarded Lloyd George as 'thoroughly hardened about Ireland', while Birkenhead in spite

of his aggressive speech on Ireland in the House of Lords was for conciliation (T. P. O'Connor to John Dillon, 24 June 1921, Dillon Papers, TCD MS 5744, f. 847). For a magisterial assessment, quite close to Healy's, of Lloyd George's position see Mansergh, *Unresolved Question*, pp. 148, 154-63.

42 Healy to O'Brien, 28 June 1921, NLI MS 8556. Healy's attack stands as an Irish nationalist counterpart to John Maynard Keyne's celebrated polemic against Lloyd George, in which he referred to him as at once 'this syren, this goat-footed bard, this half-human visitor to our age from the hag-ridden magic and enchanted woods of Celtic antiquity', and 'rooted in nothing' (J. M. Keynes, *Essays in Biography* [1933, repr. New York, 1963], pp. 35-6).

43 Healy to Maurice Healy, 24 May 1919, Healy typescripts.

44 Healy to O'Brien, 25 June 1920, NLI MS 8556.

45 Healy to Maurice Healy, 9 July 1921, Healy typescripts; *Letters and Leaders*, ii. p. 639.

46 Healy to Maurice Healy, 27 July 1921, Healy typescript.

47 Healy to Maurice Healy, 9, 29 July 1921; *Letters and Leaders*, ii. pp. 639-40.

48 Healy to Maurice Healy, 29 July 1921, Healy typescripts. Healy wrote in the *Sunday Express* in August: 'We had no such self-sacrificing, death-defying lads as the IRA in the Land League struggle. Farmers then were fighting for material advantage, and while willing to risk eviction and the loss of land and home, they would not readily have faced death' (*Sunday Express*, 21 Aug. 1921).

49 Healy to Maurice Healy, 21 Sept. 1921, Healy typescripts.

50 *Sunday Express*, 21 Aug. 1921 (the paper's editorial pointedly dissociated it from Healy's views on Ulster); Macardle, *Irish Republic*, pp. 488-9; David Hogan, *The Four Glorious Years* (Dublin, 1953), pp. 31-41. This is the article quoted in Packenham, *Peace by Ordeal* (London, 1935, 1992 ed.), p. 76. Colonel Archer Shee was a backbench Tory strenuously opposed to all concessions to Irish nationalism.

51 Healy to O'Brien, 9, 13 July 1931, NLI MS 8556.

52 Healy to O'Brien, 13, 15 July 1921; O'Brien to Healy, 14 July 1921, NLI MS 8556.

53 Healy to O'Brien, 13 July 1921, NLI MS 8556.

54 Macardle, *Irish Republic*, p. 496.

55 O'Brien to Healy, 24 Aug. 1921; Healy to O'Brien, 26 Aug. 1921, NLI MS 8556. When a beleaguered de Valera called on O'Brien a year later, in the course of the civil war, O'Brien suggested that original error was to have compelled the taking of the oath at the first meeting of the Dáil. De Valera's reply was that he had been away, and that Griffith was presiding when the oath was taken (O'Brien, 'Secret History', x, pp. 9-20).

56 Healy to Maurice Healy, 26 Aug. 1921, Healy typescripts.

57 Healy to O'Brien, 13, 21 July; O'Brien to Healy, 14 July 1921, NLI MS 8556.

58 Healy to Maurice Healy, 19 Aug. 1921, Healy typescripts; *Letters and Leaders*, ii. p. 640.

59 Healy to Maurice Healy, 19 Aug. 1921, Healy typescripts.

60 Healy to Maurice Healy, 21 Sept. 1921, Healy typescripts.

61 Healy to Maurice Healy, 26 Sept. 1921, Healy typescripts.

62 Healy to Maurice Healy, 9 July 1921, Healy typescripts; *Letters and Leaders*, ii. p. 636. Duggan was almost certainly the Sinn Féiner whom he described to Beaverbrook as 'a solicitor, the only chap I could count on to be inwardly friendly to myself', whom Healy visited in prison in November 1920 to promote a truce (Healy to Beaverbrook, 30 Nov. 1920, NLI MS 23267).

63 Maev Sullivan 'Tim Healy'. She further claimed that Healy had pressed Collins to stay at Glenaulin any time he needed shelter. She complained that Sir John Lavery's portrait of Collins did not give a true impression, making him resemble

a blacksmith: 'When I met Collins at Glenaulin, he looked like a statue. He was very pale – perhaps from confinement – with a shock of dark hair, a high forehead, and massive, clear-cut features, rather like a tall and very Irish version of Napoleon. However, fortunately for himself as it probably helped his many escapes, he seems to have impressed everybody in a different way. His manners were pleasant, and almost boyish, although one suspected reserves of strength' (ibid.). The suggestion of marmoreal pallor evokes descriptions of Parnell: even for so inveterate an anti-Parnellite as Healy's daughter, his attributes had been incorporated in the canon of Irish heroism.

64 *Letters and Leaders*, ii. p. 644; *D.E.*, 23 Aug. 1922.

65 Callanan, *Parnell Split*, p. 179.

66 Healy to Maurice Healy, 9 July 1921, *Letters and Leaders* Proofs 279; Healy to O'Brien, 15 July 1921, NLI MS 8556.

67 *I.I.*, 19 Oct. 1921, 'Peace Conference Crux'. Dillon wholly misconstrued Healy's stance: 'Tim's article is a deadly stab at the Conference and at Sinn Fein. I hear there has been a rift between him and his Sinn Fein friends' (Dillon to T. P. O'Connor, 19 Oct. 1921, TCD MS 6744, f. 862).

68 *I.I.*, 20 Oct. 1921.

69 Beaverbrook, *Decline and Fall of Lloyd George*, p. 97.

70 The diary of Erskine Childers, one of the secretaries of the delegation, contains the entry: 'Healy came. Consulted on Ulster' (R. E. Childers, diary entry for 22 Oct. 1922, TCD MS 7814).

71 Undated memorandum, NLI MS 23270; quoted Taylor, *Beaverbrook*, p. 254; Beaverbrook, *Decline and Fall of Lloyd George* (1963), pp. 97–9; Jones, *Whitehall Diary*, pp. 132-41. While the nature of the memorandum remains unclear, it is evidently in the nature of a briefing document (presumably to advise Beaverbrook of the argument he was advancing and which he believed Sinn Féin would adopt).

72 Beaverbrook, *Politicians and the Press* (London, 1925), pp. 41-2; Beaverbrook, *Decline and Fall of Lloyd George*, pp. 97-100.

73 Memorandum of the Irish delegates, 27 Oct. 1922, Griffith to de Valera, 31 Oct. 1922: Mulcahy Papers, UCD P7/A/72; Longford, *Peace by Ordeal*, pp. 157–9.

74 A pencilled note in a hand other than Healy's survives in the Healy folders in the Beaverbrook papers. It first recites the three matters on which Lloyd George insisted on a response from the Irish on 21 October and which were embodied in an *aide-mémoire* to the Irish. The document is likely to be a note of what was in effect a briefing by Healy. The Sinn Féin delegation is stated to be 'prepared to take Oath if they get Settlement'. The note continues: 'Mich. is moderate. Not stupid. Charming manners. George likes him. They think George is anti-Catholic and is using the Pope'. The note goes on to refer to Greenwood ('Sinn Fein softens to him') and to the leading Irish civil servants. The statement after the recital of the three matters on which Lloyd George required a response – 'not a word on these points until Friday' – suggests that the immediate purpose may have been to convey information for the use of the *Daily Express* (Beaverbrook Papers, c/163).

75 *Sunday Express*, 23 Oct. 1922. The emphasis is the newspaper's. The 'few villages and acres in Fermanagh and Tyrone' anticipated Churchill's celebrated weary reference to the 'dreary steeples' of the same counties (in *The Aftermath, being a Sequel to the World Crisis* (London, 1941)): even if those villages and acres with their undreaming spires were to envenom the relations between the two Irish states, they should not be permitted to disturb the high ambience of the treaty negotiations.

76 *D.E.*, 25 Oct. 1921. The article's concluding enquiry was: 'Will the Government publish the political and religious map of this area drawn up by the Irish Local

Government Board for the Buckingham Palace Conference in 1914?'

77 Jones, *Whitehall Diary*, p. 147; Cab 43/1 PRO London (NLI microfilm P6432).

78 Beaverbrook, *Decline and Fall of Lloyd George*, pp. 101–10; Beaverbrook, *Politicians and the Press*, op. cit., pp. 4–5.

79 See in particular *D.E.*, 2, 9, 10, 15–18, 30 Nov., 5, 7, 9 Dec. 1921. On 28 November the 'Wreckers' were the Tory diehards; by 9 December the 'Wrecker' was Eamon de Valera. The shift reflected progress of a sort.

80 R. E. Childers diary entry for 23 Oct. 1921, TCD MS 7814.

81 National Archives, DE 2/354.

82 7th Meeting of British representatives, 12.20, 24 Oct., Downing St., Cab 43/4, pp. 43/4, POR London; microfilm NLI P6433.

83 Jones, *Whitehall Diary*, p. 141.

84 Healy to Maurice Healy, 24 Oct. 1921, Healy typescripts. The published text suppresses the statement that his meeting with Lloyd George was at the latter's request (*Letters and Leaders*, ii. p. 645).

85 Healy, Glenaulin, to O'Brien, 24 Oct. 1921, NLI MS 8556.

86 Healy to O'Brien, 1 Nov. 1921, NLI MS 8556; see Jones, *Whitehall Diary*, pp. 150–1.

87 Healy to O'Brien, 14 Nov. 1921, NLI MS 8556.

88 Healy to Maurice Healy, 26 Nov. 1921, Healy typescripts.

89 O'Brien, 'Secret History', iv. pp. 1–2.

90 Healy to O'Brien (Friday) 26 Nov. 1921, O'Brien Papers, NLI MS 8556; Jones, *Whitehall Diary*, pp. 174–5.

91 O'Brien, 'Secret History', iv. p. 2.

92 Healy to Maurice Healy, 26 Nov. 1921, Healy typescripts.

93 Jones, *Whitehall Diary*, p. 176.

94 Healy to O'Brien, 28 Nov. 1921, NLI 8556.

95 O'Brien, 'Secret History', iv. pp. 9–17. O'Brien professed what he described as his lifelong faith that 'wisdom in Irish politics does not consist in being "constitutional" or in being "extreme", but in knowing how to be either one or the other at the right time' (ibid., xvi. p. 21).

96 Healy to Maurice Healy, 28 Dec. 1921, Healy typescripts. Reviewing O'Brien's *Evening Memories*, Griffith had written 'it is not necessary to agree in all of Mr. O'Brien's judgements to be convinced of the fine sincerity of the writer in his devotion to his country' (*Young Ireland*, 26 June 1920).

97 O'Brien, 'Secret History', iv. pp. 1–29; introduction (by Sophie O'Brien), pp. 6–8; Healy to Maurice Healy, 1 Dec. 1921, Healy typescripts.

98 Healy to Maurice Healy, 1 Dec. 1921, Healy typescripts.

99 Joseph M. Curran, *Irish Free State*, p. 133; see also O'Brien, *Irish Revolution*, pp. 440–2; P. S. O'Hegarty, *A History of Ireland under the Union* (London, 1952), p. 754; Jones, *Whitehall Diary*, p. 181.

100 Mansergh, *Unresolved Question*, p. 187; Laffan, *Partition*, p. 83.

101 O'Hegarty, *Ireland under the Union*, p. 754; Laffan, *Partition*, p. 93. T. Ryle Dwyer in a 1982 article discussed the effect of the assurances given to Healy as to the Boundary Commission. It is based on a series of articles published in 1938 detailing O'Brien's account, rather than on the 'Secret History' itself. As in the O'Hegarty account, Birkenhead becomes one of the protagonists. Mr Ryle Dwyer points out that, as O'Brien's account puts the Lloyd George dinner at 29 November, the assurances could not have suddenly altered Collins' thinking between 3 November, when he expressed dissatisfaction at the provisions of the draft treaty in relation to the north-east, and his signing of the treaty. Ryle Dwyer sensibly concludes: 'It seemed that Collins really based his whole case on what he thought was the

only logical interpretation of clause 12 of the Treaty – that the Boundary Commission would have to hand over the contiguous nationalist areas of Northern Ireland . . .' (T. Ryle Dwyer, 'Key to ending partition that Michael Collins couldn't turn', *Sunday Independent*, 22 Aug. 1982).

102 O'Brien, 'Secret History', i. pp. 14–15.

103 O'Brien, 'Secret History', v. pp. 304, xix. p. 2.

104 The fact that Healy had had some involvement in the final stage of the treaty negotiations was known to republican critics, but only in very general terms. A handbill published in March 1928 attacked Healy, who was then in Egypt, 'who succeeded, when England's cabinet ministers had failed, in persuading Ireland's unfortunate representatives to betray their country on the night of December 6th 1921, and who has acted as the agent of the King of England for the last five years' ('After Ireland – Egypt', handbill published by the Independence Centre, issue 18 Mar. 1928, NLI ILB 300, p. 12). Starved of definite and precise information, there was not a great deal more the treaty's republican opponents could make out of Healy's involvement.

105 O'Brien, *Irish Revolution*, pp. 440–3; O'Brien, 'Secret History', i. pp. 21–4, xv. pp. 28–33.

106 O'Brien, 'Secret History', i. pp. 18–19, 28; Mansergh, *Unresolved Question*, pp. 237–9.

107 *Letters and Leaders*, ii. pp. 645, 650.

108 *D.E.*, 7 Feb. 1928.

109 O'Brien, *Irish Revolution*, pp. 441–3, 454; Proofs of 'Irish Revolution' annotated by Healy, NLI MS 8558; *Letters and Leaders*, ii. p. 647.

110 Laffan, *Partition*, pp. 94–100.

111 Packenham, *Peace by Ordeal*, pp. 243–4.

112 Healy to Maurice Healy, 6 Dec. 1922, Healy typescripts. The published text (*Letters and Leaders*, i. p. 645) is subtly modified.

113 *I.I.*, 8 Dec. 1921, Healy to Griffith, telegraph d. 6 Dec.

114 O'Brien, 'Secret History', Sophie O'Brien introduction, pp. 8–9; Healy, *Letters and Leaders*, ii. p. 648.

115 Healy to Maurice Healy, 13 Dec. 1921, Healy typescripts; *Letters and Leaders* Proofs 283; *Letters and Leaders*, ii. pp. 645–6. When the Bishops did pronounce, Healy wrote to Maurice: 'The Bishops' manifesto was modified to meet the request of the supporters of the Treaty. It would not have influenced any of the votes, despite its weight with the public' (Healy to Maurice Healy, 15 Dec. 1921, Healy typescripts).

Collins showed considerable courage in accepting a lift from Healy who was a notably erratic motorist. (His nephew charitably characterised his method of driving as 'unorthodox and invariably ad hoc'.) Not the least merit of Healy's appointment as Governor-General was that it put an end to his furious passages through the Phoenix Park on his way to the Four Courts (Maurice Healy, *Munster Circuit*, p. 29; Healy to Maurice Healy, 2, 17 Apr. 1920 et passim.).

116 Healy to S. W. Alexander, n.d., typescript, Beaverbrook Papers, c/163, House of Lords Records Office; for Alexander, see Taylor, *Beaverbrook*, p. 857.

117 Healy to O'Brien, 29 December 1921, NLI MS 8556.

118 O'Brien to Healy, 30 Dec. 1921, O'Brien Papers, NLI MS 8556. A legible transcription of this letter can be found in O'Brien, 'Secret History', v, p. 28.

119 *Letters and Leaders*, ii. p. 647; Healy to O'Brien, 2 Mar. 1926, O'Brien Papers, NLI, MS 8556. Punning on the Archbishop's comment, Healy in his memoirs referred to de Valera as 'The Dialectician' (ibid.).

120 Healy to Maurice Healy, 20 Mar. 1922, Healy typescripts.

121 Healy to Maurice Healy, 23 Oct. 1922, Healy typescripts.

122 *Letters and Leaders*, ii. pp. 639, 647.
123 Fitzalan to Lloyd George, 27 Dec. 1921; Greenwood to Lloyd George, 29 Dec. 1921, Lloyd George Papers, House of Lords Record Office.
124 Healy to Maurice Healy, 6 Jan. 1922, Healy typescripts.
125 Healy to O'Brien, 4 Jan. 1922, O'Brien Papers, NLI MS 9556. O'Brien vehemently disputed Healy's placing of the blame on abstention: it was a fault of the 'Hibernian Parliamentary Party', who consented to partition in 1916 (O'Brien, 'Secret History', v. p. 42). Healy wrote to his brother in March: 'The creation of the Six County Parliament is the greatest condemnation of the policy of Abstention from the House of Commons' (Healy to Maurice Healy, 27 Mar. 1922, Maev Sullivan, 'Tim Healy'; this letter does not appear in the Healy typescripts).
126 Healy to O'Brien to Healy 30 Dec. 1921; Healy to O'Brien, 4 Jan. 1922, NLI MS 8556.
127 Healy to Maurice Healy, 6 Jan. 1922, Healy typescripts. The quotation is from Edward Fitzgerald ('In divine high piping Pehlevi . . . the Nightingale cries to the Rose').
128 Healy to Maurice Healy, 10 Jan. 1922, *Letters and Leaders*, ii. p. 648–9. The observation in parentheses is contained in Healy's letter to his brother of 15 Dec. 1921 (Healy typescripts); the 'of course' is deleted in the published version (*Letters and Leaders*, ii. p. 646).
129 Healy to Maurice Healy, 12 Jan. 1922, Healy typescripts.
130 Healy to Maurice Healy, 11 Jan. 1922, *Letters and Leaders*, ii. p. 649.
131 Healy to Maurice Healy, 3 Apr. 1922, Healy typescripts.
132 Healy to O'Brien, 25 Jan. 1922 (misdated 1921), O'Brien Papers, NLI MS 8556.
133 Healy to Beaverbrook, 15 Feb. 1922, NLI MS 23271. Healy wrote that Sinéad de Valera's closest friend in Greystones where she was living had warned her against the horrors of another split, and that 'both deV and his wife are scrupulous Catholics – whatever their camp followers may be'.
134 Healy to Maurice Healy, Healy typescripts. The reference to 'Michael' recalls Healy's references to 'Charles' over forty years previously (Healy to Maurice Healy, 20 Mar. 1880, *Letters and Leaders*, ii. pp. 85–8). Healy also referred to 'Michael' in his letter to his brother of 23 Jan. 1922, revised to 'Collins' in the published text (Healy typescripts; *Letters and Leaders*, ii. p. 650).
135 Brian Farrell, 'The Drafting of the Irish Free State Constitution: IV', *Irish Jurist*, n.s. vi. (1971); T. M. Healy to E. J. Duggan, 21 Mar. 1922, NLI MS 3906.
136 Healy to Maurice Healy, 3 Apr. 1922, *Letters and Leaders* Proofs B287.
137 Healy to O'Brien, 10 Mar., 3 May 1922, O'Brien Papers, NLI MS 8556.
138 Macardle, *Irish Republic*, pp. 677–9; Healy to O'Brien, 3 May 1922, O'Brien Papers, NLI MS 8556; Healy to Maurice Healy, 25, 27 Mar. 1922, Healy typescripts; *Letters and Leaders*, ii. p. 653. In the published version of the letter of 25 March Healy considered it prudent to add to the comparison of the anti-Treatyites to the Parnellites the qualification 'only worse'.
139 Healy to O'Brien, 2 Mar. 1926, O'Brien Papers, NLI MS 8556.
140 *Letters and Leaders*, ii. p. 654; Healy to Maurice Healy, 15 Apr. 1923, Healy typescripts.
141 Healy to O'Brien, 19 May 1922, O'Brien Papers, NLI MS 8556.
142 O'Brien, 'Secret History', Ch. VI, 18–32; Sophie O'Brien, introduction, pp. 11–13; Mansergh, *Unresolved Question*, pp. 211–12.
143 Macardle, *Irish Republic*, pp. 740–2.
144 Healy to Maurice Healy, 27 June 1922, Healy typescripts.
145 Macardle, *Irish Republic*, p. 751; Healy to Maurice Healy, 7 July 1922, Healy typescripts.

146 Healy to Maurice Healy, 15 Apr. 1923, Healy typescripts.
147 Healy to Maurice Healy, 6 Mar. 1922, Healy typescripts.
148 Healy to Maurice Healy, 13 July 1922, Healy typescripts.
149 Meda Ryan, *The Day Michael Collins was Shot* (Dublin, 1989), p. 18; Healy to Beaverbrook, 29 July, 1922, NLI MS 23271.
150 Beaverbrook to Healy, 1 Aug. 1922, typescript copy, Beaverbrook Papers, c/163, House of Lords Record Office.
151 O'Brien, 'Secret History', x. pp. 9-20. O'Brien's account recalls his description of de Valera on first meeting him at the Mansion House Conference in 1918, with its ludicrous misreading of de Valera's character: 'His transparent sincerity, his gentleness and equability captured the hearts of us all. His gaunt frame and sad eyes deeply buried in their sockets had much of the Dantesque suggestion of "the man who had been in hell"' (W. O'Brien, *Irish Revolution*, pp. 361-2).
152 Healy to Maurice Healy, 12 Oct. 1922, Healy typescripts. Healy had derided the attempts of T. P. ('Neutral') Gill throughout the split for his attempts to broker a reconciliation between the Parnellites and anti-Parnellites.
153 Healy to Rev. Thomas Dawson, O.M., 20 Aug. 1922, NLI MS 18516.
154 *D.E.*, 24 Aug. 1922; see also *D.E.*, 27 Feb. 1928.

27: GOVERNOR-GENERAL

1 G. K. Chesterton to Healy, 14 Aug. 1924, Healy-Sullivan Papers, UCD P6/C/29.
2 *D.N.*, 19 Dec. 1925, A.G.G., 'Mr. "Tim" Healy'.
3 Gogarty, *As I Was Going Down Sackville Street* (London, 1937), p. 97; Sean O'Luing, *Art O'Griofa* (Dublin, 1953), p. 399.
4 Healy to Maurice Healy, 29 Nov. 1922, Healy typescripts; *Letters and Leaders*, ii. p. 660.
5 Mansergh, *Unresolved Question*, pp. 210-12; Sexton, *Governor-Generalship*, pp. 55-63.
6 Sexton, *Governor-Generalship*, pp. 76-7; *D.E.*, 6 Feb. 1928.
7 Healy to Maurice Healy, 20 Oct. 1922, Healy typescripts. In relation to the banking matter on which Healy subsequently spoke to Bonar Law, see Healy to Maurice Healy, 24, 29 Nov. 1922, Healy typescripts.
8 Birkenhead, *Contemporary Personalities* (London, 1924), p. 206.
9 Healy to Maurice Healy, 23 Oct. 1922, Healy typescripts. The alterations in the published text (*Letters and Leaders*, ii. pp. 659-60) are instructive.
10 Healy to Maurice Healy, 26 Oct. 1922, Healy typescripts.
11 E. Marsh, Colonial Office to Waterhouse, 30 Oct. 1922 enclosing Kevin O'Higgins to Lady Lavery, 27 Oct. 1922, Bonar Law Papers, 114/1/20, House of Lords Record Office. March observed, perhaps archly, that Lady Lavery 'as I dare say you know is a great friend of many of the Provisional Government'. A hostile account of Healy's Governor-Generalship by Criostóir MacAonghusa appeared in the *Irish Press* of 8 March 1966, based on information from an evidently disaffected member of the Provisional Government at the time of his appointment, exaggerated the role of Lady Lavery. When the idea of Healy's appointment was accepted, 'we wrote to Lady Lavery and requested her to get in touch with the members of the British Government to ascertain if they would be satisfied with Healy'. Donough O'Malley, then Minister for Health, forwarded a translation of the article to the Taoiseach, Seán Lemass, whom he was sure would find it of considerable interest (N.A., MS s8539).
12 Jones, *Whitehall Diary*, pp. 25, 217-18. Healy had previously conveyed his view that Cope, who 'had risked his life in Ireland & rendered service which no other could

have done', should be provided for by a senior position in another ministry rather than be 'stranded by political changes' (unaddressed letter from Healy, 18 Mar. 1922, written from Cherkley, Beaverbrook Papers, c/163, House of Lords Records Office).

13 Jones, *Whitehall Diary*, p. 217. The respect was reciprocated. Healy reported to Maurice in June 1923: 'One of the Colonial Office officials described the Cavendishes to me as people who have not had a cad in their family for 300 years!! He has certainly proved this as regards his treatment of Ireland and its people' (Healy to Maurice Healy, 30 June 1923, Healy typescripts). The town of Lismore, where the Dukes of Devonshire had a castle, and where Healy spent five years as a child, created a further bond between Healy and the Devonshires (Plunkett Barton, *Timothy Healy*, pp. 11-12; *Letters and Leaders*, i. p. 16).

14 Jones, *Whitehall Diary*, p. 218 (16 Nov. 1922).

15 The foregoing account draws heavily on Brendan Sexton's admirable *Ireland and the Crown, 1922-36: The Governor-Generalship of the Irish Free State* (pp. 81-6). See also *D.E.*, 6 Feb. 1928; *I.T.*, 6 Dec. 1922; Healy to W. T. Cosgrave, 14 Dec. 1922, N.A. MS s8539. Bonar Law later gave Birkenhead an account of why he sanctioned Healy's appointment. He claimed to have been struck by Healy's meticulous grasp of the issues involved in the proposed abolition of the Bank of Ireland stock register. Bonar Law's unconvincing response was hardly candid, and reflects a shrewd mistrust of Birkenhead's relations with Healy and Beaverbrook, and of his sense of discretion (Birkenhead, *Contemporary Personalities* [London, 1924], pp. 206-7).

16 *I.T.*, 6 Dec. 1922; *D.E.*, 6 Feb. 1928.

17 O'Casey, *Autobiographies*, 2. p. 127.

18 Sexton, *Governor-Generalship*, pp. 88-9; *D.E.*, 6 Feb. 1928; *Iris Oifigúil*, 30 Dec. 1922; N.A. MS s8529

19 Healy to Maurice Healy, 8 Dec. 1922, Healy typescripts; Sexton, *Governor Generalship*, pp. 98-9. Two weeks later his wife and his daughter Erina moved across, followed the next day by Healy's collection of silver and glass which had been kept under guard (Healy to Maurice Healy, 23 Dec. 1922, Healy typescripts). Healy had expressed to Cosgrave a preference to remain at Glenaulin, pointing out that 'Lord Fitzallin's [*sic*] account of the waste and extravagance at the Viceregal Lodge would alarm a millionaire' (Healy to W. T. Cosgrave, 3 Dec. 1922, N.A. MS s/8539). For Healy's description of the Viceregal Lodge, see *Letters and Leaders*, ii. pp. 662-3; T. M. Healy, 'Memories of the Viceregal Lodge', in *The Voice of Ireland*, ed. W. G. FitzGerald (Dublin and London), pp. 426-8.

20 Healy to Maurice Healy, 8 Dec. 1922, Healy typescripts.

21 O'Brien, 'Secret History', xi. pp. 5-7.

22 O'Brien to Healy, 9 Dec. 1922. The semi-illegible original in O'Brien's hand is in NLI MS 8556 (28) along with a transcript; the text is also set forth in W. O'Brien, 'Secret History', xi, pp. 21-3.

23 O'Brien, 'Secret History', xi, pp. 10-26.

24 Healy to O'Brien, 11 Dec. 1922, NLI MS 8556; O'Brien, 'A Secret History', xi. pp. 1-28. For O'Brien's refusal of a seat in the senate, see J. V. O'Brien, *William O'Brien*, p. 241.

25 W. O'Brien, 'Secret History', xi. pp. 26-9.

26 Healy to Maurice Healy, 14 Dec. 1922, 18 July 1923, Healy typescripts.

27 Healy to Maurice Healy, 23 Jan. 1923, Healy typescripts.

28 Sexton, *Governor-Generalship*, pp. 88, 91; Healy to Maurice Healy, 8 Dec. 1922, Healy typescripts.

29 Healy to Maurice Healy, 14 Dec. 1922, Healy typescripts; *D.E.*, 6 Feb. 1928; Taylor,

Beaverbrook, pp. 273–4. William Orpen had some years previously painted Healy, who left the portrait in his will to his daughter Maev (*D.E.*, 3 Feb. 1928; grant of probate to the estate of T. M. Healy). Healy was painted by Lavery on a further occasion in 1925, in the Viceregal Lodge: 'Sir John started to paint the interior of the drawing room here which, with Liz and myself in the foreground, ended up very much better than I expected and is very clever' (Healy to Annie Healy, 11 Aug. 1925, Healy-Sullivan Papers, UCD P6/A/131). Lord Devonport commissioned a portrait of Healy by the fashionable Philip de Lazlo, which he later donated to Gray's Inn. Healy commented to the artist, 'the only fault I find is that it is too angelic. Put a touch of devilry in' (Healy to Maev Sullivan, 10, 20 Feb. 1928, Healy-Sullivan Papers, UCD P6/A/76, 77; Gray's Inn Catalogue of Portraits). There is a bust of Healy by Joseph Davidson in the King's Inns, Dublin for which see Wanda Ryan-Smolin, *King's Inns Portraits* (Dublin, 1992), p. 79).

30 *I.T.*, 15 Dec. 1922.

31 'Lord Oranmore's Journal, 1913–27', ed. John Butler, *I.H.S.*, Nov. 1995, vol. 11 (Nov. 1995), p. 553 *et seq.* (diary entry for 14 Dec. 1922).

32 Dillon to O'Connor, 4 Dec. 1922, Dillon Papers, TCD MS 6744, f. 904.

33 Sean O'Casey, *Autobiographies*, 2, pp. 127–8. O'Casey elsewhere referred to Healy as 'a clever bearded oul' suct whose skin stretched tight over a portly bag of rowdy venom' (*Autobiographies*, 1, p. 493). Healy admired *Juno and the Paycock*, and wrote to Maurice's widow: 'Ernest Blythe told me he knew O'Casey very well, and that he was at times Protestant, using his Rosary beads; a Catholic and a profound theosophist; a Fenian with Orange sympathies, and all the rest of the Aeolian Harp!' (Healy to Annie Healy, 3 Feb. 1928, Healy-Sullivan Papers, UCD P6/A/142). This was perhaps a sharper, and certainly more subtle characterisation, than O'Casey's of Healy.

For an instance of republican criticism of Healy before his appointment, see Healy to Maurice Healy, 7 Oct. 1922, Healy typescripts. Republican antipathy to Healy intensified with the appearance of his memoirs: see the review by Frank Gallagher, *The Dublin Magazine*, iv. (Apr. 1929), pp. 59–60.

34 Healy to Beaverbrook, 9 Jan. 1923, NLI MS 23272.

35 Healy to Maurice Healy, 19 Jan. 1923, Healy typescripts; see also 23 Jan. 1923.

36 Sexton, *Governor-Generalship*, p. 99.

37 Healy to Maurice Healy, 30 Jan. 1923, Healy typescripts.

38 Healy to Maurice Healy, 23 Jan., 11 Feb. 1923, Healy typescripts.

39 Healy to Maurice Healy, 7 Feb. 1923, Healy typescripts.

40 Terence de Vere White, *Kevin O'Higgins* (London, 1948, repr. 1966), pp. 146–7; Maev Sullivan, 'Tim Healy', p. 217; Healy to Maurice Healy, 11, 16 Feb. 1923, Healy typescripts. Higgins' widow and children stayed with Healy at the Viceregal Lodge until mid-April (Healy to Maurice Healy, 18 Apr. 1923, Healy typescripts).

41 Healy to Maurice Healy, 16 Feb. 1923; see also 19 Feb., Healy typescripts. Healy added four days later: 'Every "peace" proposal contains a condition about their army ranks, as if anyone would ever trust them in the Army, after their conduct' (Healy to Maurice Healy, 20 Feb. 1923, Healy typescripts). Liam Lynch was the Chief of Staff of the Republican army, who was fatally wounded shortly after.

42 Healy to Maurice Healy, 20 Feb. 1923, Healy typescripts; see also 19 Feb. 1923.

43 Healy to Maurice Healy, 26 Feb. 1923. He complained particularly of Hannah Sheehy-Skeffington, for whom he had appeared at the inquest into the murder of her husband in 1916. She had 'published appalling lies about me in the *Irish World* to the effect that I offered her a bribe from Asquith and threatened to deprive her of her own son if she did not consent!! . . . She used to visit Glenaulin and bring her son [Owen Sheehy-Skeffington] there for many years after my alleged

attempt to corrupt her. Until now she professed the greatest gratitude and friendship for my services, which cost her nothing' (Healy to Maurice Healy, 13 Mar. 1923, Healy typescripts). He reported to Maurice in February: 'The two Amazons who were on strike in Mountjoy have given in, which is another sign of the expected break-down. One of them, Miss Comerford, used to go around with a revolver, and rob post-offices etc.' (Healy to Maurice Healy, 2 Feb. 1923, Healy typescripts).

44 Healy to Maurice, 20 Mar. 1923, Healy typescripts. Healy was presumably referring to Diarmuid O'Hegarty, the secretary of the provisional government who had been appointed Commandant-General.

45 'A Roman Candle', typescript draft article heavily amended in Healy's hand, Beaverbrook Papers, c/163, House of Lords Record Office; see generally Macardle, *Irish Republic*, pp. 840-2.

46 Healy to Beaverbrook, 7 Apr. 1923, NLI MS 23272; Healy to Maurice Healy, 25 Apr. 1923, Healy typescripts.

47 Healy to Maurice Healy, 15 Apr. 1923, Healy typescripts.

48 Macardle, *Irish Republic*, p. 849.

49 Healy to Maurice Healy, 29 May 1923, Healy typescripts.

50 Healy to Maurice Healy, 13 Mar., 15 April 1923, Healy typescripts. For the division between O'Higgins and Mulcahy, which precipitated Mulcahy's departure from the government after the army mutiny in March 1924, see Lee, *Modern Ireland*, pp. 96-105.

51 Healy to Maurice Healy, 18 Apr., 14 July 1923, Healy typescripts.

52 *D.E.*, 5 July 1923; *I.I.*, 6 July 1923.

53 Healy to Maurice Healy, 18 July 1923, Healy typescripts.

54 Healy to Maurice Healy, 21, 23 July 1923, Healy typescripts.

55 Healy to Maurice Healy, 26, 27 Aug. 1923; see also 31 Aug. 1923, Healy typescripts. He had written three years earlier to Maurice of meeting the priest who had organised the Sinn Féin victory in local government elections in Tyrone, 'a very rustic sober little man with a wizened face, thoroughly acquainted with the mysteries of proportional representation' (Healy to Maurice Healy, 8 July 1920, Healy typescripts; *Letters and Leaders*, ii. p. 618).

56 Lee, *Ireland*, pp. 82-6, 94-6.

57 *I.T.*, 27 May 1931.

58 Healy to Beaverbrook, 8 Feb. 1923, NLI MS 23272.

59 Healy to Beaverbrook, 28 Mar. 1923, NLI MS 23273.

60 Healy to Maurice Healy, 13 Mar. 1923, Healy typescripts.

61 Healy to Maurice Healy, 30 June 1923, Healy typescripts.

62 Mansergh, *Unresolved Question*, pp. 231-5.

63 Healy to Maurice Healy, 18 Apr. 1923, Healy typescripts.

64 Healy to Maurice Healy, 18, 25 Apr. 1923, Healy typescripts.

65 Healy to Maurice Healy, 14 July, 2 Nov. 1923, Healy typescripts; *Times*, 6 Nov. 1923.

66 Healy to Beaverbrook, 23 May 1923, NLI MS 23273.

67 *D.E.*, 5 July 1923; *I.I.*, 6 July 1923.

68 *D.E.*, 6 July 1923; *I.I.*, 7 July 1923. Craig's stentorian response reflected the extent to which the government of Northern Ireland considered itself already immutably entrenched: 'Ulster has now reached a stage of peace and prosperity, and woe betide any man, no matter what his position, who directly or indirectly, or by calling to mind old disputes, stirs up any trouble or creates once more a state of chaos in that part of the British Empire which desires to remain under the King's

constitution in which its people were bred and born'. Healy's personal relations with Craig continued to be friendly: St. John Ervine, *Craigavon, Ulsterman* (London, 1949), pp. 488-9, 571. In addition to Craig's response, there was a detailed rejoinder to Healy's interview by a 'high official of the Ulster government' somewhat chillingly inviting those who owed allegiance to the Free State to leave Northern Ireland to make way for Protestants on the Irish side of the border. The 'high official' further stated: 'Mr. Healy has expressed astonishment that the arrangement of the six counties of Ulster should have come into being, but surely he has forgotten that the arrangement is simply the result of what Mr. Healy has fought for since the days of Parnell' (*D.E.*, 6 July 1923).

69 Healy to Maurice Healy, 2 Nov. 1923, Healy typescripts. Healy had met Devonshire at the Colonial Office in June (*Irish Life*, July 1923).

70 Geoffrey J. Hand, 'MacNeill and the Boundary Commission', in *The Scholar Revolutionary: Eoin MacNeill, 1867-1945, and the Making of the New Ireland*, ed. F. X. Martin and F. J. Byrne (Shannon, 1973), pp. 221-44. Arthur Clery claimed credit for a similar pun (Patrick Maume, *D. P. Moran* [Dundalk, 1995], p. 44).

71 Healy to Beaverbrook, 17 Nov. 1924, NLI MS 23273.

72 Mansergh, *Unresolved Question*, pp. 237-9; Laffan, *Partition*, pp. 101-5.

73 O'Brien, 'Secret History', xv. pp. 5-6; *I.I.*, 8 Feb. 1926. O'Brien wrote with characteristic exaggeration: 'He need not have threatened his resignation of the Governor-Generalship to intimate that it was an occasion for asking to be relieved by Messrs. Churchill and Lloyd George from the dread secret of which he was the principal of the excessively few living confidants, a mere hint on the subject would have sufficed to open new avenues for the revision of Article 12 [of the treaty]'.

74 Sexton, *Governor-Generalship*, p. 105.

75 Healy to Maurice Healy, 2 Feb. 1923, Healy typescripts; O'Brien to Healy, 3 Mar. 1923, NLI MS 8556.

76 Healy to Maurice Healy, 2 Feb. 1923; see also 20 Feb. 1923, Healy typescripts; Healy to O'Brien, 26 Feb. 1923, O'Brien Papers, NLI MS 8556.

77 O'Brien to Healy, 3 Mar 1923, NLI MS 8556; Healy to Maurice Healy, 8 Mar. 1923 (misdated 1922), Healy typescripts. Healy's 'remonstrance' has not survived in the Healy-O'Brien correspondence in the National Library of Ireland.

78 W. O'Brien, *Irish Revolution*, pp. 440-2.

79 W. O'Brien, *Irish Revolution*, p. 339 n.1.

80 Healy to Maurice Healy, 24 Feb. 1923 (Viceregal Lodge, 2 a.m.), Healy typescripts. Healy's letter, to which O'Brien's of 3 Mar. is a reply, does not survive in the Healy-O'Brien correspondence in the National Library (NLI MS 8556). James Gilhooly, who sat for Cork West 1885-1916, was latterly a staunch and stolid O'Brienite.

81 Dillon to T. P. O'Connor, 12 May 1923, Dillon Papers, TCD MS 6762, f. 931.

82 William O'Brien to Sophie O'Brien, n.d., encl. William O'Brien to Healy, 17 Apr. 1923. Ironically Healy's letter is missing from the Healy–O'Brien correspondence in the National Library (NLI MS 8556).

83 O'Brien, *The Parnell of Real Life* (London, 1926). Dillon to T. P. O'Connor, 11 Mar. 1926, Dillon Papers, TCD MS 6744, f. 989.

84 T. M. Healy, review of John E. Pomfret, *The Struggle for Land in Ireland, Studies*, vol. 19 (Dec. 1930), p. 696. In the same article Healy dismissed St. John Ervine's *Parnell* of 1925 as 'the vapid sketch of Parnell by the Belfast journalist Mr. St. John Irvine'.

85 O'Brien's health was breaking down and his progress was uneven. At the time

of his death in February 1928 the text was complete but required revision. His widow was 'not sure he had not intended to rewrite a good deal' (O'Brien, 'Secret History', Sophie O'Brien introduction, p. 14).

86 W. O'Brien, 'Secret History', title of xviii.

87 O'Brien, 'Secret History', ix. pp. 10–18, x. pp. 4–8. In entering the agreement of 1925 to abide by the existing border, Cosgrave and O'Higgins had, according to O'Brien, enabled Lloyd George (who was not then in office) and Churchill to 'tear up the Secret Pact altogether'. O'Brien surmised that O'Higgins, as a relative of Healy's, was aware of the Lloyd George-Churchill undertaking (ibid., x. p. 4). Of O'Higgins he wrote: 'The timber of a fanatic he never was, but from his mother, a daughter of the famed old bard T. D. Sullivan (of whom another and nobler daughter was the wife of Mr. Healy) derived his Irish nationality from a pure source' (ibid., ix. p. 6).

O'Brien was exaggerating and distorting the unquestionable fact that in the immediate aftermath of the death of Collins, the policy of the Provisional Government operated on a single plane, the prosecution of the civil war to a successful conclusion: 'Collin's death removed the main conciliating influence in the cabinet and inevitably hardened the resolve of the survivors' (Lee, *Modern Ireland*, p. 66). O'Brien's premise that Collins could have ended the civil war by other than military means was integral to the later myth of Collins in one of its aspects.

88 O'Brien, 'Secret History', i. p. 27.

89 W. G. Lyon (Talbot Press) to Sophie O'Brien, 10 Nov. 1933; W. G. Lyon to Michael McDonagh, 15 Nov. 1933. Both letters are pasted into the front of the manuscript of the 'Secret History'.

90 *I.I.*, 8 Feb. 1926.

91 McDonagh, *William O'Brien*, pp. 254–5; J. V. O'Brien, *William O'Brien*, pp. 242–3.

92 O'Brien to Healy, 16, 18 June 1927; Healy to O'Brien 17, 20 June 1927, NLI MS 8556. The proposals enclosed with O'Brien's letter of 18 June are not extant, and it is only possible to glean his thinking in very general terms from his conversation with his biographer a couple of days before his death (McDonagh, *William O'Brien*, pp. 257–9).

93 Healy to O'Brien, 27 Dec. 1927, NLI MS 8556; W. O'Brien, *Irish Fireside Hours* (Dublin, 1927), pp. 1–27.

94 McDonagh, *William O'Brien*, p. 258; see also McDonagh's obituary of O'Brien, *Catholic Bulletin*, vol. xviii. (Mar. 1928), pp. 267–79.

95 Healy to Maev Sullivan, 27 Feb. 1928, Healy-Sullivan Papers, UCD P6/A/78. Writing some days later from the Semiramis Hotel, Healy commented 'the political atmosphere in Cairo resembles Dublin in 1921–2' (Healy to Maev Sullivan, 1 Mar. 1928, Healy-Sullivan Papers, UCD P6/A/79). The same thought had occurred to left-wing Irish republicans who, in a handbill headed 'After Ireland-Egypt-Timothy Healy', suspiciously enquired: 'What is he doing there? . . . Egypt is in the throes of a struggle to overthrow British domination, so is India, Iraq and China. When England fails by force of arms to hold her dominions, she employs her Smuts, Tim Healys and Simons to fool National Leaders' (handbill, issued 18 Mar. 1928 by the Independence Centre, NLI ILB 300 P12).

96 T. M. Healy, review of John E. Pomfret, *The Struggle for Land in Ireland, Studies*, vol. 19 (Dec. 1930), p. 696.

97 Maev Sullivan, 'Tim Healy'.

98 Maev Sullivan, 'Tim Healy'.

99 *Cork Examiner*, 10, 12 Nov. 1923; *I.I.*, 10, 12 Nov. 1923; *Irish Life*, Nov. 1923; Maev Sullivan, 'Tim Healy'; *Letters and Leaders*, ii. pp. 657, 663; Annie Healy to Rev.

Thomas Dawson, 23 Jan. 1924, NLI MS 18516. James O'Connor wrote with snideness, but not impercipiently, having disparaged Tim Healy's attributes as a lawyer, 'Maurice Healy was a solicitor with a genuine lawyerlike brain. Cold, emotionless, analytical, logical, unimaginative . . . One is sometimes led to reflect — what a perfect genius would have resulted from the combination of the mental qualities of Tim Healy and Maurice Healy' (Sir James O'Connor, *History of Ireland* [2 vols., London, 1925], ii. p. 82).

100 Healy to O'Brien, 4 Jan. 1922, 22 Jan. 1927, NLI MS 8556; Elizabeth Healy to Rev. Thomas Dawson, 3 Sept. 1923, NLI MS 18516. Maev Sullivan recalled her mother being wheeled out to watch some units of the Irish army march through the Phoenix Park. '"They're our own", she managed to say, and burst into tears' (Maev Sullivan, 'Tim Healy', p. 219).

101 Maev Sullivan, 'Tim Healy', p. 222; *W.I.T.*, 16 July 1927.

102 Healy to Beaverbrook, 18 July 1927, NLI MS 23276.

103 *W.I.T.*, 27 Aug. 1927.

104 Maev Sullivan, 'Tim Healy'; Oliver St John Gogarty, *As I Was Going Down Sackville Street* (London, 1937), pp. 95–6. In the same vein, Lady Fingal commented of the fireplaces: 'all the Lord Lieutenants had put up with those others, but Tim Healy could not bear to look at anything so ugly' (Lady Fingal, *Seventy Years Young* [London, 1937, repr. Dublin 1991], p. 404).

105 Undated handbill referring to the 1924 estimates, NLI ILB 300, p. 8 (item 9).

106 Sexton, *Governor-Generalship*, p. 109; *W.I.T.*, 19 June 1926.

107 *Irish Life*, Dec. 1922.

108 *I.T.*, 27 Mar 1931. The London *Times* conceded with some asperity that 'to the general surprise and satisfaction', he had enhanced the dignity of his office (*Times*, 29 Mar. 1931).

109 *I.T.*, 1 Apr. 1931; Plunket Barton, *Timothy Healy*, p. 116.

110 Sexton, *Governor-Generalship*, pp. 79–100; *W.I.T.*, 20 June 1927; Oliver St. John Gogarty, op. cit., pp. 117, 119. Healy's social calendar was chronicled in *Irish Life*: see for example *Irish Life*, Sept. 1923, Sept. 1925.

111 *W.I.T.*, 9 Aug. 1924; *Irish Life*, Sept. 1924; Oliver St. John Gogarty, op. cit., pp. 117–18. Healy described Devoy as 'a most interesting old chap but very deaf and nearly blind'. While he had previously deprecated Devoy earlier to de Valera, he did now register a dissent from Devoy's characterisation of de Valera as 'a Jewish bastard' (Healy to Annie Healy, 19 Aug. 1924, Healy-Sullivan Papers, UCD P6/A/103; Healy to Maurice Healy, 10, 16 July 1920, Healy typescripts).

112 *An Phoblacht*, 21 Aug. 1925; Lady Gregory, *Diaries*, ii. p. 440 (1 June 1929); Healy to Annie Healy, 11 Aug. 1925, Healy-Sullivan Papers, UCD P6/A/131. The poem stands perhaps as an anti-Treatyite 'Ivy Day in the Committee Room'. Lady Gregory professed a snobbish disdain for the Governor-Generalship. She wrote in January 1922 that Augustine Birrell, with whom she had lunched was opposed to the appointment of a Governor-General, 'knowing, as I do, how much vulgarity could crowd around' (*Lady Gregory's Journals*, i. ed. Daniel J. Murphy [Gerrard's Cross, 1978], p. 327 [22 Jan. 1922]).

113 *Lady Gregory's Journals*, i. op. cit., p. 461 (4 June 1923).

114 Oliver St. John Gogarty, op. cit., p. 95.

115 Healy to Beaverbrook, 9 Jan. 1923, Beaverbrook to Healy, 10 Jan. 1923, typescript copies, Beaverbrook Papers, sc/163, House of Lords Record Office; *Lady Gregory's Journals*, op. cit., p. 427.

116 *Lady Gregory's Journals*, op. cit., p. 523 (17 April 1924) et passim.

117 Barbara Cartland, *The Isthmus Years* (London, 1943), pp. 33–5.

118 Healy to Beaverbrook, 14 Nov. 1918, NLI MS 23265; Maev Sullivan, 'Tim Healy', p. 205. Healy to Annie Healy, 18, 24 May 1925, Healy-Sullivan Papers, UCD P6/A/124-5.

119 Chisholm and Davie, *Beaverbrook*, p. 241. As Beaverbrook was wont to observe 'how I loved my Arnold and how he loved my champagne' (Taylor, *Beaverbrook*, p. 316), Bennett's joke may have somewhat miscarried. For the constitutional dilemma posed by Healy's absences, see Sexton, *Governor-Generalship*, pp. 106-7.

120 Sexton, *Governor-Generalship*, pp. 920-4; Gerard Torsney, 'The Monarchy and the Irish Free State, 1922–23', UCD M.A. thesis, p. 87; Note on 'The King's assent to Bills', 1924, N.A. MS S3241. In the interview he gave on his return from London after the announcement of his appointment, Healy appeared to have an exaggerated idea of his responsibilities (*I.T.*, 6 Dec. 1922; Sexton, *Governor-Generalship*, pp. 86-7).

121 *D.E.*, 5, 6 July 1923.

122 *I.T.*, 20 July 1923.

123 Healy to Maurice Healy, 21 July 1923, Healy typescripts.

124 Sexton, *Governor-Generalship*, pp. 102-12; Torsney, op. cit., pp. 87-8.

125 *I.T.*, 8 Nov. 1926; Torsney, op. cit., p. 89.

126 Sexton, *Governor-Generalship*, pp. 102-4; Torsney, op. cit., p. 90.

127 Sexton, *Governor-Generalship*, pp. 110-11; Torsney, op. cit., pp. 91-2. On one issue, Healy for a time held out. On his retirement he wrote to the government claiming the income tax deducted from his salary on the grounds that he had been 'in the same position, before the law, as the King of England'. His daughter eventually prevailed on him to withdraw this claim (Torsney, op. cit., pp. 92-3; see also Sexton, *Governor-Generalship*, pp. 107-8).

128 Sexton, *Governor-Generalship*, p. 105.

129 A co-relation between alcoholic conviviality and Healy's more demonstrative ebullitions to the crown also arises in relation to an account (admittedly at second-hand) of a Viceregal dinner party in 1924 in Lady Gregory's journals: 'the Governor-General suddenly stood up when they were in the middle of dessert – raspberries and cream – and proposed "The King!". However all stood up, including John McCormack who had said before he would not do so'. *Lady Gregory's Journals*, op. cit., p. 603 (9 Aug. 1924).

When the Colonial Secretary L. S. Amery visited Ireland for the Horse Show of August 1925, Healy observed greater punctilio. In the account in his memoirs, which resembled the report of an inspector of schools on a remote and somewhat wayward establishment, Amery noted approvingly that Healy 'every night himself drank the King's health in the most dignified fashion at the end of dinner' (L. S. Amery, *My Political Life*, ii. [1914-29], pp. 371-2. Healy was likewise prone to swift declensions into informality. Eileen Gormanston recalled that at a charity Horse Show ball, Healy, having at the outset addressed her as 'Lady Gormanston' switched as the meal progressed to 'Mee dear gurl' (Eileen Gormanston, *A Little Kept* [London and New York, 1954], p. 89).

On the occasion of the Colonial Secretary's visit, Cosgrave complained to Healy of Amery's travelling in an open car, 'but I said he would do nothing else. Whereupon he remarked, "he must be in a state of grace"' (Healy to Annie Healy, 11 Aug. 1925, Healy-Sullivan Papers, UCD P6/A/131).

130 *The Diaries of Sir Robert Bruce Lockhart*, ed. Kenneth Young (entries for 5 Oct. 1930, 23 Mar. 1931), i. pp. 128, 159. Of the same occasion Lockhart recalled: 'At Cherkley Tim had a bad leg, so he came down to dinner in a dinner-jacket on top of ordinary trousers (grey). He drank and talked a great deal, and I helped him to bed and took off his elastic-sided boots for him (ibid., p. 159).

131 *D.E.*, 3 Feb. 1928. The interviews published in the *Daily Express* of 3–7 February 1928 were with C. J. Ketchum.

132 *The Pilgrims: Speeches at a Dinner to T. M. Healy KC*, copy in Healy-Sullivan Papers, UCD P6/F/6; *Times*, 18 May 1928.

133 Records of Gray's Inn. Healy's reminiscences of Gray's Inn were published in *Graya*, iv. pp. 10-14 (Easter 1929); see also Francis Cowper, 'Timothy Healy KC', *Graya* xxxii., pp. 125-34 (Michaelmas, 1950). After Healy left office as Governor-General a dinner was given in his honour on 15 Feb. 1928, at which Birkenhead, whose toasts to Healy had by then become set-pieces, declared that Healy while a very obscure member of Gray's Inn 'on equal terms could take part in debate with the verbose Gladstone and could even defeat the reticent Parnell' (*Graya*, ii. pp. 15-17 [Easter, 1928]).

134 Healy to Beaverbrook, 19 Apr. 1927, NLI MS 23, 275.

135 *Observer*, 12 June 1927. I am indebted to Proinsias MacAonghusa for the information in relation to the authorship of the *Life of Tim Healy* (Jonathan Cape, 1927) which comes from Brendan O'hEithir. The account of McManus's authorship is borne out by the whimsical dedication, the archness of the preface, and the inferiority of the text.

136 Healy had the satisfaction of beating T. P. O'Connor into print. O'Connor's *Memoirs of an Old Parliamentarian* were published in 1929. Healy dined in January at Gray's Inn with Birkenhead and William Harrison, a friend of Birkenhead who had acquired the *Daily Chronicle* and reportedly paid T. P. O'Connor £6,000 for his memoirs: 'He could not get his paper to publish extracts as the Editor said it was rehashed piffle. It only dates down to 1892'. It is difficult to dissent from the editor's view, or to fail to admire O'Connor's acumen in securing a very substantial advance for memoirs consisting largely of the anecdotes and impressions he had been liberally re-cycling from the early 1880s onwards. Having skimmed O'Connor's two volumes when they appeared, Healy wrote to his daughter: 'his snigs against me are not envenomed – principally that I have the "gift of tears", and that Parnell told him before the Split I was selfish and always trying to knife him. This I shall survive' (Healy to Maev Sullivan, 30 Jan., 15 Apr. 1929, Healy-Sullivan Papers, UCD P6/A/86, 88; Stephen Koss, *The Rise and Fall of the Political Press in Britain* [London, 1981, repr. Fontana 1990], p. 885).

Healy had continued to fit tiny pieces into the scrambled jigsaw of Parnell's life. He wrote to his brother's widow in 1925: 'By the way, according to Mrs. O'Shea's book, Henniker Heaton must have been wrong in saying that he saw her with Parnell at the Gare du Nord in 1882. She had just had her baby, and I fancy the lady he saw Parnell with was her sister' (Healy to Annie Healy, 21 Apr. 1925, Healy-Sullivan Papers, UCD P6/A/120).

137 Healy to Beaverbrook, 23 Dec. 1920, typescript copy, Beaverbrook Papers, House of Lords Record Office, c/162.

138 Healy to Beaverbrook, 14 Nov. 1918, NLI MS 23265.

139 Healy to Maurice Healy, 23 Oct. 1922, Healy typescripts. The Pope complained to Beaverbrook about what he considered Lloyd George's betrayal of commitments given in relation to the holy places of Palestine, and Healy commented: 'It seems an astonishing thing that Lloyd George should behave in such a way, and shows he was completely in the hands of the Zionists. When Max told him of the Pope's complaint, he made no reply'.

Beaverbrook's trip was less bizarre than Lloyd George's own trip years before, at least as reported to A. J. Sylvester, his private secretary, in 1928. He had gone to Rome in 1897 with a letter of introduction from Healy to the Rector of the

Irish College. He claimed that just before his private audience ended, the Pope produced a number of coloured sweets which he blessed. 'He handed them to me and said I must share them with Tim Healy, John Dillon and myself. We were to eat the sweets which, having been blessed by the Pope, would serve to heal the feud between the two men and enable a settlement of the long-standing problem of Ireland to be reached'. Lloyd George forgot all about the sweets, which someone else devoured. 'Poor Tim Healy and Dillon never got their sweets, and the Irish problem dragged on' (A. J. Sylvester, *The Real Lloyd George* [London, 1947], pp. 63–4; John Grigg, *The Young Lloyd George* [London, 1973], p. 246). This comical anecdote is evidently highly embellished, if not entirely invented, by Lloyd George in puckish vein.

140 Healy to Beaverbrook, 28 Mar., 29 Apr. 1929, NLI MS 23273.

141 Healy to Beaverbrook, 19 Jan. 1928, NLI MS 23276.

142 Healy to Beaverbrook, 17 July 1928, NLI MS 23277; *D.E.*, 18, 19 June 1928; for Healy's 'Impressions of Jerusalem', see *D.E.*, 20 June 1928.

143 A. J. P. Taylor, *Beaverbrook*, p. 829; Beaverbrook, *The Divine Propagandist* (London, 1962), pp. vii–ix.

144 Taylor, *Beaverbrook*, pp. 359–403; Healy to Beaverbrook, 11 Mar., 11 Nov. 1930, NLI MS 23281, 23283. Beaverbrook continued to be a benefactor of Healy. When Healy ceased to be Governor-General Beaverbrook wrote to Maurice Healy, Healy's barrister nephew, 'invent some work for Tim'. He subsequently paid Healy £1,000 a year to act as legal adviser to the *Daily Express* (Taylor, *Beaverbrook*, p. 315; see also Healy to Maev Sullivan, 7 Dec. 1928, Healy-Sullivan Papers, UCD P6/A/82).

145 Healy to Annie Healy, 8 Oct. 1925, Healy-Sullivan Papers, UCD P6/A/137.

146 Muldoon to Dillon, 2 July 1927, Dillon Papers, TCD MS 6734, f. 201.

147 *D.T.*, 10 Mar. 1924.

148 Healy to Maev Sullivan, 27 Feb. 1928, Healy-Sullivan Papers, UCD P6/A/78. T. P. O'Connor, six years Healy's senior, predeceased him on 18 November 1929. The last survivor of Parnell's circle of close advisers was Thomas Sexton. For long a complete recluse, he died in Dublin on 1 November 1932. Of those who had been prominent in the 1880s, it was perhaps symbolically apt that Edward Carson, created Lord Carson of Duncairn, born the year before Healy, lived on until 22 November 1935.

149 T. A. Finlay to Sister Bernard, 29 Mar. 1931, Healy-Sullivan Papers, UCD, P6/E/35. Healy was survived by the six children of his marriage, three daughters and three sons in succession. The daughters were Elizabeth (Liz), Maev, and Erina. Liz resided with Healy at the Viceregal Lodge. She cared for her stricken mother, helped Healy in carrying out the social functions of his office, and typed up from the shorthand originals letters to Maurice on which Healy based *Letters and Leaders of my Day*. Maev Sullivan, the steadfast defender of her father's memory, married Timothy Sullivan, the son of T. D. Sullivan and thus her uncle, who became President of the High Court and subsequently Chief Justice. Erina became a member of the Ursuline order, taking the name Sister Bernard. Of Healy's three sons, Joseph (Joe) became a barrister, Paul a Jesuit, and Timothy become the Master of the Coombe Hospital in Dublin. Joe lived at Glenaulin until 1953.

150 *I.I.*, 30 Mar. 1931. Healy's death taxed to breaking point the charity of his adversaries of old. David Sheehy had been a longstanding member of the Irish party, a moderate anti-Parnellite closely allied to Dillon. When he learnt that a mass he was attending was for the repose of Healy's soul, he walked out (Conor Cruise O'Brien, *States of Ireland* [London, 1972], p. 107).

151 *The Diaries of Sir Robert Bruce Lockhart*, ed. Kenneth Young (London, 2 vols.), i.

p. 163) (entry for 16 Apr. 1931); *I.T.*, 17 Apr. 1931; *Times*, 9, 17 Apr. 1931. The requiem masses for John Dillon and William O'Brien, both of whom had died in London, had taken place in Westminster Cathedral (McDonagh, *William O'Brien*, p. 261).

152 *I.T.*, 27 Mar. 1931. Frank Cruise O'Brien had written of Healy in April 1910: 'In an Ireland which could afford him, Mr. Healy would be amusing. But our Ireland cannot afford him' (*Leader*, 9 Apr. 1910). His son came independently to the same conclusion a half-century later: 'The Greek Church, I believe, had a word for the practice of a charitable, and often silent, tolerance: it called this practice Economy. In that sense, as perhaps in others, economy is not one of our virtues and Healy was one of the supreme examples of the uneconomic Irishman. We could not afford many more like him' (C. C. O'Brien, 'Timothy Michael Healy' in C. C. O'Brien, ed. *The Shaping of Modern Ireland* [London, 1970]). T. M. Kettle had likewise characterised Healy as 'a brilliant calamity'.

153 Maev Sullivan, 'Tim Healy'; see also Plunket Barton, *Timothy Healy*, p. 117.

Index